H.H. ARNASON
HISTORY OF MODERN ART

PAINTING SCULPTURE ARCHITECTURE PHOTOGRAPHY
FIFTH EDITION

193-218

PETER KALB
REVISING AUTHOR, FIFTH EDITION

236-66
400-434

PEARSON
Prentice Hall

Prentice Hall, Inc.

Published 2003 by Prentice Hall, Inc.
A Division of Pearson Education
Upper Saddle River, New Jersey 07458

10 9 8 7 6 5 4 3 2 1

ISBN 0-13-184069-X

Front cover and spine: Piet Mondrian, *Broadway Boogie-Woogie*, 1942–43. Oil on canvas, 50 x 50" (127 x 127 cm). The Museum of Modern Art, New York (anonymous gift, © 2003 Mondrian/Holtzman Trust, c/o HCR International). Digital image © The Museum of Modern Art/Scala, Florence.

Back cover: Robert Delaunay, *Simultaneous Contrasts: Sun and Moon*, 1913 (dated 1912 on painting). Oil on canvas, diameter 53" (134.6 cm). The Museuem of Modern Art, New York (Mrs Simon Guggenheim Fund). Digital image © The Museum of Modern Art/Scala, Florence.

This book was designed and produced by Laurence King Publishing Ltd, London
www.laurenceking.co.uk

For Prentice Hall, Inc.:
Vice President and Editorial Director: Charlyce Jones-Owen
Executive Editor: Sarah Touborg
Editorial Assistant: Sasha Anderson
Media Editor: Anita Castro
Director of Production and Manufacturing: Barbara Kittle
Prepress and Manufacturing Manager: Nick Sklitsis
Prepress and Manufactuing Buyer: Sherry Lewis
Senior Marketing Manager: Chris Ruel
Marketing Assistant: Kimberly Daum

For Laurence King Publishing:
Editor: Jessica Spencer
Development Editor: Kara Hattersley-Smith
Designer: Ian Hunt
Cover designer: Keith Lovegrove
Picture Researcher: Emma Brown

Printed in Singapore

Table of Contents

Preface to fifth edition

At the start of the twenty-first century, the term "modern art" already has something of a venerable ring to it. It has joined other capacious art historical categories, such as "Renaissance" or "Romanticism," which, though they may usefully serve to give shape to broad contours of art history, become less clear in meaning and more open to dispute the closer you get to detailed discussion of specific works of art. The only difference between these and "modern art" is that modern art as a temporal category is still open-ended: it is, by one definition, simply the art of the present day. But it also includes the early paintings of Matisse and Malevich, Braque's Cubist collages, and the first building designs by Frank Lloyd Wright—products of a world that now feels very distant indeed, separated from us by two world wars, the atomic bomb, and the Internet. The words "modern art" have soaked up so much history that they can never again mean what they once meant (or at least, not with the same heady conviction): shockingly new, bewilderingly progressive, utterly of the present moment, unprecedented—though they still encompass that.

A Short History of *History of Modern Art*

Just as "modern" is a many-layered term, this book, now in its fifth edition, has a history of its own. As the term "modern art" has broadened and been reinterpreted over time, successive scholars, editors, and specialist contributors have amended and added to Harvey H. Arnason's original text, which Arnason himself fully revised some years after the book was first published in 1969. This has been a process not only of fine-tuning and updating information but also of revisiting much of Arnason's material in the context of a scholarly and educational environment that has changed significantly from the one in which he wrote. There are parallels to this process in other cultural arenas, for example in the reorganization and reinterpretation of museum and gallery displays. The core of the collection remains the same, the objects have the same indelible presence and fascination, but, juxtaposed with new acquisitions and displayed under different lighting conditions, they lead viewers to look at them in different (sometimes very different) ways.

In this sense, while this new edition of *History of Modern Art* contains much added material, it is still essentially Arnason's creation. This Preface offers a brief investigation into the marathon staying-power of his original endeavor, even through successive revisions have seen the book evolve over the years to take account of new directions in art and art history. After more than three decades and four new editions, Arnason's vision remains the core of this standard work of art historical reference.

The Art of Looking

Arnason was Professor and Chairman of the University of Minnesota's art department from 1947 to 1961, and he had a long association with New York's Solomon R. Guggenheim Museum as its Vice President for Art Administration. He embarked on *History of Modern Art* relatively late in life. The project was conceived and intended as a long-term landmark—the first book of its kind—and it drew on the experience of his distinguished career as an art historian. Two deep-rooted convictions underpin Arnason's *History*: first, that understanding art is a matter of fundamental importance; second, that the way to learn about art is to look for yourself. His Preface unequivocally emphasized his belief in the importance of the individual's face-to-face experience of art—a belief that, as he saw it, gave the book its rationale and its structure:

> The thesis of this book, insofar as it has a thesis, is that in the study of art the only primary evidence is the work of art itself. Everything that has been said about it, even by the artist himself, may be important, but it remains secondary evidence. Everything that we can learn about the environment that produced it historically, socially, culturally is

important, but again is only secondary or tertiary evidence. It is for this reason that an effort has been made to reproduce most of the works discussed. For the same reason a large part of the text is concerned with a close analysis of these works of art and with detailed descriptions of them as well. This has been done in the conviction that simple description has an effect in forcing the attention of the spectator on the painting, sculpture, or building itself. If, after studying the object, he disagrees with the commentator, all the better. In the process he has learned something about visual perception.

Encouraging his readers to look at art was Arnason's first objective. But he had a further, more challenging aim in view, which was to get people thinking about what it means to go beyond the realm of words—facts, opinions, descriptions, books (no matter how inspiring or enlightening these may be)—and experience art as a purely visual phenomenon. "The principal emphasis of this book," he wrote,

> revolves around [the] problem of seeing modern art. It is recognized that this involves two not necessarily compatible elements: the visual and the verbal. Any work of art history and/or criticism is inevitably an attempt to translate a visual into a verbal experience. Since the mind is involved in both experiences, there are some points of contact between them. Nevertheless, the two experiences are essentially different and it must always be recognized that the words of the interpreter are at best only an approximation of the visual work of art.

Why does Arnason consider looking at modern art such an important art to master? The valuation that society places on art, and the reasons for that valuation, change with time, and here again, since *History of Modern Art* first appeared, shifts have occurred in our perception of why art matters.

Experience and Interpretation

The distant roots of Arnason's belief that looking at art is in itself a profoundly worthwhile activity can be traced to the liberal, secular educational ideals of the nineteenth century. These ideals presumed that exposure to the "highest" kind of cultural experiences could make people, whatever their social or ethnic background, better citizens and happier individuals.

More recent generations of scholars and writers have fiercely questioned the foundations of this outlook, but its monuments remain at the center of Western cultural life. The conviction that simply looking at paintings and sculptures, or entering a grandly beautiful building, were necessarily uplifting and "ennobling" experiences was an important factor in the nineteenth-century enthusiasm in Europe and North America for establishing public art collections and opening great private collections to the public. As a scholar working in the orbit of major American collections, Arnason was a direct heir to the tradition of promoting contact with art for the general good. These collections, and later ones founded on their model, still provide the public with their most important point of access to art.

His belief in the power of art to work its own magic in our lives marks Arnason as a man very much of his time and background. Today art has lost none of its cultural glamour, but the role of interpretation is now regarded as not merely helpful for the viewer's own experience but in certain ways essential for it. The idea of art history as a unitary field of knowledge has been replaced by the recognition of diverse art histories, each shaped by a particular interpretative approach. Likewise, the old notion of the canon—a roll-call of indisputable masterpieces that set the standard for all artistic achievement—has given way to a far more inclusive view of what constitute legitimate objects of art historical attention.

These changes have affected the ways in which art is made, viewed, presented, and taught. Textbooks locate art within contemporaneous social, historical, political, and philosophical themes. Museums, too, which at one time were regarded as palaces or temples for the display of self-evidently significant cultural treasures, now see the interpretation of these treasures as an equally important activity, recognizing that any work of art may well mean quite different things to different viewers. To take one obvious example, it is now comfortably accepted, as it would not have been in art history pre-Feminism, that Western art's long preoccupation with the naked female body, in particular the centrality the nude has enjoyed in histories of Western art, does not carry the same messages for women as for men. It is not that we look any more carefully or subtly at art than earlier generations did, only that the range of information regarded as relevant to an understanding (or understandings) of art has been vastly extended.

This new edition, as one would expect, acknowledges interpretative standpoints more openly and, inevitably, more self-consciously that did Arnason's original text. This will be especially evident to the reader in the substantially revised and expanded chapters dealing with art after around 1970, a period during which critical theory and the awareness of multiple interpretations came to inform much art practice.

How Arnason would have interpreted the art of the final quarter of the twentieth century can only be guessed, but he would no doubt have applauded the emphasis on the need for art education to work on a broad front. "[It] is recognized," he wrote, "that a work of art or architecture cannot exist in a vacuum. It is the product of a total environment—a social and cultural system—with parallels in literature, music, and the other arts, and relations to the philosophy and science of the period." But when he wrote *History of Modern Art*, you quickly gather, following up these parallels was not his primary concern. The two world wars, the Russian Revolution, the rise of Nazism and the

Depression era of the thirties stalk Arnason's narrative of the first half of the twentieth century, but they are largely felt as distant thunder, heard in the background while artists got on with the business of making art.

Charting a Path through Time and Space

In *History of Modern Art*, Arnason built on the liberal educational tradition in two particular areas. First, he sought to present modern art as essentially the latest phase of a tradition in Western art reaching back to the Renaissance. He acknowledged, but at the same time tended to play down, the dramatic, contentious "shock of the new"—the image of modern artists setting out not only to find new ways of doing things but, as part of this process, loudly and violently rejecting the art of the past. In Arnason's account, modern approaches to making art are more the result of a conversation than an adversarial contest; his model is evolutionary rather than revolutionary.

Second, he addressed "the problem of seeing modern art" as a problem that concerns not only students of art but links to our ability to orient ourselves within the world as we find it. The "problem" could be stated like this: why is it that, a century and more after these works were produced, the Lumière brothers' early motion pictures of Parisian street scenes look quaint, antique, yet familiar, while Picasso's Demoiselles d'Avignon can still excite and affront us with its strangeness? "There is no question," asserted Arnason, "that the efforts of the pioneers of modern art changed modern artist's way of seeing, and in some degree, modern man's." What is more questionable is whether the modern person's way of seeing has yet caught up with the work of those pioneers. In a sense, the old reverence for "realistic" appearances still rules: audiences accustomed to the presentational modes of photography, television, and commercial movies may have no more of an advantage here than did the followers of tired, overblown academic painting in the 1890s.

This problematic situation reveals another reason why, for Arnason, modern art matters so much: it is a grand project of exploration, a journey into space. There are no limits to artists' capacity to explore space or to take a willing and well-informed audience with them. Arnason's reflections on space in art illustrate his critical method, and are worth quoting at some length. His Preface begins:

> The arts of painting, sculpture, and architecture are arts of space. For this reason it is essential to approach these arts in the twentieth century, or in any other period, through an analysis of the artist's attitude toward spatial organization. Since space is normally defined as extension in all directions, this attitude can be seen relatively easily in architecture and sculpture, which traditionally are three-dimensional masses or volumes surrounded by space, and, in the case of architecture, enclosing space.

Painting, however, offers an altogether more complex universe:

> It is probably more difficult for the spectator to comprehend the element of space in painting than in either architecture or sculpture. A painting is physically a two-dimensional surface to which pigments, usually without appreciable bulk, have been applied. Except insofar as the painter may have applied his paint thickly, in impasto, the painting traditionally has no projecting mass, and any suggestion of depth on the surface of the canvas is an illusion created through various technical means. The instant a painter draws a line on the blank surface he introduces an illusion of the third dimension. This illusion of depth may be furthered by overlapping or spacing of color shapes, by the different visual impacts of colors—red, yellow, blue, black, or white, by different intensities or values, and by many other devices known throughout history. The most important of these, before the twentieth century, were linear and atmospheric perspective.

Arnason then noted, with a decisive stroke, the shift that first made modern painting modern:

> Perspective, although known in antiquity, became for the Renaissance a means for creating paintings that were imitations of nature—visual illusions that made the spectator think he was looking at a man, a still life, or a landscape rather than at a canvas covered with paint. Perhaps the greatest revolution of early modern art lay in the abandonment of this attitude and the perspective technique that made it possible. As a consequence, the painting ... became a reality in itself, not an imitation of anything else; it had its own laws and its own reason for existence.

The idea that "laws" might be deduced for modern art would have led an art historian of a more theoretical temper to attempt to formulate them. Arnason preferred an empirical approach: "As will be seen," he continued, "after the initial experiments carried out by the Impressionists, Post-Impressionists, Fauves, and Cubists, there has been no logical progression." Art is not like science or technology, in that experiments and discoveries do not lead to work that is progressively better or more effective, but they do expand (to use a spatial term) the range of possibilities. With *History of Modern Art* as our guide, Arnason seemed to be saying, we can proceed with confidence, but on a case-by-case basis.

The Primacy of Experience

Arnason's views on art were in keeping with the critical stance of his influential contemporary, the American art writer Clement Greenberg, who in his 1961 book *Art and Culture* asserted: "Art is a matter strictly of experience, not of principles, and what counts first and last in art is quality; all other things are secondary." Greenberg was banging the drum for abstract art here, taking on its critics who clung to the persuasion that representational art was somehow "superior" to non-representational. Judging art, he was saying, is not a matter of laws or principles, as academic artists and critics believed—there is no automatic right or wrong about it. Instead, art should be judged by "Experience, and experience alone"—in other words, the aesthetic effect it has on the viewer.

Though Arnason's approach can clearly be aligned with Greenberg's formalism and his advocacy of American Abstract Expressionist art, he was far less tendentious. Rather, his great virtue as a writer and educator is that he was prepared to share his insights without insisting that readers share his ideology. It is this inherent generosity that has, in fact, made it possible for later writers of different critical persuasions to revise and augment his original project without subverting its vision.

In practice, of course, our experience of art includes the recognition that an object can be classed as "art," and it is therefore always an activity of some cultural complexity. In Arnason's view, the process of "[learning] something about visual perception" involves a preparedness to countenance conflicting arguments rather than rush to judgment. This caution applies particularly to assessments of aesthetic value based on non-aesthetic criteria. Who, after all, can sit in final judgment on the relative virtues of those great contemporaries Matisse and Picasso? Produced during the Nazi occupation of France, Matisse's work of the early forties makes no obvious reference to the events of the time, whereas Picasso's *Guernica* delivers a high-voltage indictment of fascist brutality. Matisse's political leanings during this murky period in French political life have been thought suspect, but not even the more politically outspoken Picasso could touch him in his command of color.

This example recalls a passage in Greenberg's *Art and Culture* that has considerable bearing on Arnason's critical method: "That a picture gives things to identify, as well as a complex of shapes and colors to behold, does not mean necessarily that it gives us more as *art* ... The explicit comment on historical events offered in Picasso's *Guernica* does not make it necessarily a better or richer work than an utterly 'nonobjective' painting by Mondrian." In general, Arnason left it to others to open up the question of exactly how and on what levels art is wired to the world outside. For his part, he found plenty of drama in what takes shape in the studio.

How Modern is Modern?

One question that was never directly addressed in *History of Modern Art*'s early editions was the meaning of the term "modern," the limitations and slippages of which have already been outlined. In one sense, of course, its use is purely chronological, referring to art produced at any time after the modern era in art was held to have begun (in Arnason's account, as in numerous others, this was around the mid-nineteenth century in France). Modern art, as chapter 1 explains, rejected the moribund academicism of Salon artists, the conventions of illusionistic space organized according to the rules of linear perspective. But beyond this, the term was hardly more closely defined. In particular, there was no definition of the label "modernist," which, together with the later coinage "Post-modernist," is now generally seen as part of the basic toolkit for any discussion of twentieth-century culture.

Whereas the term "modern" is a historical catch-all, "modernist" usefully refers to a much more specific vision of what art is for and the form it ought to take—in other words, it carries both moral and aesthetic imperatives. Reinforced concrete is a modern building material, but not all architects who adopted it were modernists: of the two most famous early proponents of ferroconcrete construction, Auguste Perret was a staunch defender of French classical tradition, while Le Corbusier was the archetypal modernist, dedicated to art's mission to speak to the concerns of the modern world through an international formal vocabulary that was at once both austerely beautiful and determinedly functional.

Post-modernism, a term originally applied to architecture, emerged as a self-conscious counter-current to modernism during the decade after *History of Modern Art*'s first edition. By this time modernism, despite its early twentieth-century affiliation with utopian socialism, was identified by many with the values of a social and cultural elite. Modernism, it was argued, was just one of any number of stylistic vocabularies; it had no more claim to be seen as essentially progressive than, say, the ubiquitous classicism of the eighteenth and nineteenth centuries, with its Greco-Roman litany of columns, cornices, and pediments. Post-modernism stepped aside from the single-minded trajectory of modernism and asked why art and architecture should not be allusive, eclectic, ornamental, easy-going in their stylistic loyalties, and even ironic or humorous (modernism tended to take itself very seriously). Where modernism is frequently absolute and prescriptive (as in its aversion to ornament and "frivolous" decoration), Post-modernism is relativistic and pluralistic, and skeptical of attempts to correlate form and meaning in any systematic way. Throughout the twentieth century, there had always been artists who challenged prevailing orthodoxies, including modernism. In the Post-modern world-view, the very notion of orthodoxy was discarded.

Both modernism and Post-modernism are terms that reach beyond art to connect with broader cultural and historical trends. This fifth edition of *History of Modern Art* touches more often on non-artistic contemporary events than did Arnason's early editions. At the same time, it respects Arnason's original approach, in which the reader is enjoined first of all to look, to enjoy art as visual sensation before plunging into the intellectual discourse that surrounds it.

A Book That Moves with the Times

Arnason died shortly before the third edition of this book was published. Because of his failing health, the project of revising the third edition was undertaken by Daniel Wheeler, who extended the book's historical scope up to the mid-eighties. By this time, modernism's role as a once-dominant artistic ideology that contemporary art of the seventies and eighties was reacting against necessitated a fresh look at Arnason's account of the progress of modern art up until that point. As Wheeler wrote:

> Since so much of the new art produced during the 1970s and thereafter represents some form of reaction against the whole modernist tradition that went before … the earlier chapters have received almost as much fresh attention as the new chapters addressed to the various forms of Conceptual Art, to Photorealism, Pattern, Decoration, and the New Imagery, to Neo-Expressionism and, finally, a resurgent, albeit radically altered, abstraction.

The third edition incorporated new research and, in particular, took the chronological narrative deep into Post-modernist (or in Wheeler's preferred term Post-Minimalist) territory, pointing up the nature of late-twentieth-century artists' and architects' reactions to the modernist legacy.

Another new element was the introduction of photography, which had presented itself as a modern art form almost from its first development in the mid-nineteenth century, although it had taken much longer for it to be accepted as such in the academic view of what qualified as art. Photography, said Wheeler, was now included,

> not only to acknowledge the aesthetic importance of the work realized in the medium of photography, but also to provide a background for photography's current ubiquitous presence among the mix of media increasingly favored, by all manner of artists, for their endless capacity to yield new figurative, formal, and expressive effects.

In other ways, Wheeler followed Arnason's lead in placing the direct, face-to-face experience of art at the heart of the book. He sounded a more tentative note about this approach, however, since by the eighties it could no longer be presented as entirely ideologically neutral:

> I have attempted not so much to present new material as to discover it, as the curious viewer/reader himself might in the act of following contemporary art through its present and ongoing processes of unforeseeable, yet ultimately logical, development. … Moreover, in discovering, studying, or revealing works of art and architecture, I have carefully avoided the role of critic, as well as that of theorist. Rather than engage in speculative value judgments, or some narrowly defined ideological approach, I invariably find it more rewarding and instructive … to remain open to the distinctive qualities of each work or trend, to learn its special language, and to allow the particular truth this conveys to unfold.

Wheeler maintained that art is like poetry, in that it "almost always seeks a deeper, less obvious reality." No longer a confident, imperative exploration of space, art was presented here as the doorway to inner, subjective reality. In terms that evoke, but do not entirely assent to, the distinctively Post-modern fracturing of meaning, "criticality" was seen not as a search for truth but as a balancing of competing interests and interpretations. "The challenge of that reality," Wheeler continued,

> can be further enriched by the findings of those who have interviewed the artist, observed his work at length, and commented upon its possibilities in a knowing, constructive manner. Once the art has been experienced from these several perspectives, criticality emerges, as problems are posed, resolved, and assessed, like a cat's cradle of checks and balances, woven by the competing interests of time, place, personal circumstance, and sociocultural context. Thus, what I have wanted to offer is a balanced view of recent events in the visual arts—a view balanced, that is, between the subjective vision of the artist himself, an objective, informed consideration of what that vision produced, and my own keen sense of identification with both.

History of Modern Art, it will by now be clear, is itself a monument to a line of art historical and educational thinking that relies on the primacy of experience, guiding but not prescribing, and welcoming the new on equal terms with the old. At the same time, the pressure to look again, to reconsider and update, has continued. Twelve years after Wheeler's revision, Marla F. Prather prepared a fourth edition, bringing subsequent scholarship in a number of fields to bear on the task while attempting "to cut or shrink the old text in order to permit the inclusion of another fifteen years of art, in addition to the history of photography, without making the book an object that only a weight-lifter could handle." Prather rewrote the chapter on Cubism, and added coverage of work in newer art media, such as video and performance art, and by women artists.

The Fifth Edition—Fresh Perspectives

For the fifth edition, the entire text—made up of Arnason's original, Wheeler's and Prather's contributions, and specialist material supplied by numerous other scholars—has again been overhauled from start to finish. Peter Kalb thoroughly recast chapters 24 to 27, taking the story of modern art up to the year 2000 with in-depth coverage of artists and art movements of the last twenty years. He also contributed to the revision of earlier chapters, with Michael Bird who revised chapters 1 to 24, restructuring and subdividing much of this compendious material into a more manageable sequence as a reference source.

Parts of the narrative have been realigned so that, for example, where the fourth edition included a number of important women artists in its survey of the "pluralistic seventies," the new chapter 24 has a section on Feminism, explaining how this wider social and cultural movement interacted with existing trends in art such as installation and performance. Throughout, the new text incorporates the work of women artists as important and integral to the history of modern art. The design of the text has also been greatly enhanced by the use of color throughout the book. Art historians are today much more at home with the concept of the collaborative making of art than in earlier days when the notion of the lone genius prevailed. In its evolution through successive editions, this book has become a richly collaborative project. But it would also be true to say that it holds to its original aim, concisely stated by Arnason in his Preface:

> This book is intended for the general reader and the student of modern art ... Aside from being a broad, analytical survey of modern art and architecture, the book is conceived as a dictionary in which much factual information is included. This is particularly true of the latter part [which is] intended to suggest the main directions of contemporary art and architecture rather than to pretend completeness.

If we take a mid-nineteenth-century start date, "modern" art is now entering its third century. Sometime, someone will draw the line. But it is a fair bet that serious students of the modern era in art will continue, whatever their critical perspectives or cultural allegiances, to reach for this book on the shelves.

Michael Bird
May 2003

Acknowledgments

First and second editions
Charles Rufus Morey (1875–1955), Robert Goldwater, Anna Golfinopoulos, Susan Earl, Joan Hall, Robert Mates, Paul Katz, Darrie Hammer, Ward Jackson, Milton S. Fox, Sam Cauman, Barbara Lyons, Mary Lea Bandy, Dorothy Anderson, Francis Naumann, Edith M. Pavese, and Margaret L. Kaplan.

H. H. A.

Third edition
Colin Eisler, Robert Goldwater, Jim Jordan, Theodore Reff, Robert Rosenblum, William Rubin, Gert Schiff, Ruth Kaufmann, Charles Stuckey, Anthony F. Janson, Marian Burleigh Motley, Ursula Meyer, Sidney Geist, Sabine Rewald, Madeleine Fidell Beaufort, Peter Galassi, Sam Wagstaff, John Waddell, Pierre Apraxine, Monika Schmela, Christine Faltermeier, Maria Morris Hambourg, Beth Gates-Warren, Gerd Sander, Margaret Kaplan, Barbara Lyons, Pamela Phillips, Pamela Bass, Alexis Gregory.

D.W.

Fourth edition
Eve Sinaiko, Anna Hammond, Katherine Rangoon Doyle, Catherine Ruello, Julia Moore, Monica Mehta, Anne F. Collins, Christine Liotta, Anne F. Collins, Saundra Goldman, Anna Hammond, Gloria Kury, Roxana Marcoci, Frank Kelly, Nancy Anderson, Jeffrey Weiss, Mark Rosenthal, Nan Rosenthal, David Sylvester, Angelica Zander Rudenstine, Peter Galassi, Beatrice Kernan, Lynn Matheny.

M.P.

Fifth edition
Thank you to our academic reviewers, whose comments helped greatly in developing this new edition: Edward Gleeman, Normandale Community College; Keith Hollingworth, Westfield State College; Kerr Houston, Lyon College; Matthew Rohn, St. Olaf College; Lisa Stokes, Seminole Community College; Christopher Williams, University of Nevada, Reno. Thanks are also due to the editorial and design team at Laurence King Publishing, London, who prepared this edition for publication—especially the project editor, Jessica Spencer, who was responsible for managing the project's many strands.

M.B.

1
The Sources of Modern Painting

Various dates have been proposed for the birth of modern art. The most commonly chosen, perhaps, is 1863, the year of the Salon des Refusés in Paris, where Édouard Manet first showed his scandalous painting *Déjeuner sur l'herbe* (see fig. 2.19). But other and even earlier dates may be considered: 1855, the year of the first Paris Exposition Universelle (a kind of world's fair), in which **Gustave Courbet** (1819–77) built a separate pavilion to show *The Painter's Studio* (fig. **1.1**); 1824, when the English landscapists John Constable and Richard Parkes Bonington exhibited their brilliant, direct-color studies from nature at the Paris Salon (an annual exhibition of contemporary art juried by members of the French Academy);

or even 1784, when **Jacques-Louis David** (1748–1825) finished his *Oath of the Horatii* (fig. **1.2**) and the Neoclassical movement had assumed a position of dominance in Europe and the United States.

Each of these dates has significance for the development of modern art, but none categorically marks a completely new beginning. For what happened was not that a new outlook suddenly appeared; rather, a gradual metamorphosis took place in the course of a hundred years. It embodied a number of separate developments: shifts in patterns of patronage; in the role of the French Academy; in the system of art instruction; in the artist's position in society. The period under discussion was one of profound social

1.1 Gustave Courbet, *The Painter's Studio (Atelier)*, 1854–55. Oil on canvas, 11'10" × 19'7" (3.6 × 6 m). Musée d'Orsay, Paris.

1.2 Jacques-Louis David, *The Oath of the Horatii*, 1784. Oil on canvas, 10'10" × 14' (3.4 × 4.3 m). Musée du Louvre, Paris.

and political upheaval, with bloody revolutions in the United States and France and industrial revolution in England. Artists are, like everyone else, affected by changes in society—sometimes, as in the case of David or Courbet, quite directly. Social changes lead inevitably to changes in attitudes toward artistic means and issues—toward subject matter and expression, toward the use of color and line, and toward the nature and purpose of a work of art and the role it plays vis-à-vis its diverse audience.

This book charts the development of modern art through examining a great diversity of works in different media—primarily painting, sculpture, and architecture, but also printmaking, photography, installation, and other art forms. It includes artists whose achievements have, with the passing of time, come to be recognized as preeminent or particularly significant, but it also looks at those whose names occur less frequently or prominently in standard histories of modern art. For example, while American artists before World War II in many ways took their cue from development in western Europe, this history covers the work of American artists throughout the whole course of modern art from the mid-nineteenth century to the early twenty-first. Likewise, although it was not until the later decades of the twentieth century that the achievements of women artists received adequate recognition, this book places the work of women artists in earlier periods in the context of their times.

This chapter provides a brief overview of premodern art from the fifteenth century onward, setting the scene for

the emergence of art forms, and approaches to painting in particular, that can be thought of as "modern." The meaning of this term, which is also used in histories of political, economic, and social change, of literature and music, as well as in the simple, relative sense of new or recent, is not easy to define precisely. In art it is bound up with the emergence of capitalism, industrialism, and democracy, as well as the long series of reactions against forms of artistic expression that were felt to have outlived their usefulness or vigor, and the corresponding search for new modes of expression that continued unabated throughout the twentieth century.

Changing Perspectives: From Renaissance to Baroque

A major aspect of modern art is the challenge it posed to traditional methods of representing three-dimensional space. Perspective space was a method of representing depth that had governed European art for four hundred years. Its basis was single-point perspective, perfected by Italian artists in early fifteenth-century Florence and the logical outcome of the naturalism of fourteenth-century art. It assumed a single viewpoint, with all lines at right angles to the visual plane being made to converge toward a single point on the horizon, the vanishing point. These mathematical–optical principles were discovered by the architect Filippo Brunelleschi before 1420, first applied by the painter Masaccio in 1425, and then written down by

1.3 Piero della Francesca, *Flagellation of Christ*, c. 1450. Tempera on panel, 23¼ × 32" (59.1 × 81.3 cm). Galleria Nazionale delle Marche, Palazzo Ducale, Urbino, Italy.

the artist and theorist Leon Battista Alberti in about 1435. Fifteenth-century artists produced the illusion of organized depth in their paintings by using the converging lines of roof beams and checkered floors to establish a scale for the size of figures in architectural space, and to give objects a diminishing size as they recede from the eye.

Nowhere in the Early Renaissance did this science receive a more lucid or poetic expression than in the painting of **Piero della Francesca** (c. 1406–92). Mystically convinced that a divine order underlay the surface irregularities of natural phenomena, this mathematician–artist endowed his forms with ovoid, cylindrical, or cubic perfection, fixed their relationships in exact proportions, and further clarified all these geometries with a suffusion of cool, silvery light (fig. **1.3**). Such is the sense of wonder produced by this conceptual, abstract approach to perceptual reality that it would continue to fascinate modern artists, from David to Pablo Picasso, even as they explored other approaches.

Piero and his fifteenth-century peers in Italy elaborated the one-point perspective system by shifting the viewpoint to right or left along the horizon line, or above or below it. Atmospheric perspective, another fifteenth-century technique, was developed in Flanders rather than Italy. It added to the illusion of depth by progressively diminishing color and value contrasts relative to the presumed distance from the viewer. Thus, a distant background landscape might be painted with less saturated colors, especially blues and greens, and soft contours, in contrast to strongly colored and sharply defined foreground figures (fig. **1.4**). With these as their means, Renaissance painters attained control over naturalistic representation of the human figure and environment.

Early in the sixteenth century, the Renaissance conception of space reached a second major climax with **Raphael Sanzio** (1483–1520), in such works as *The School of Athens* (fig. **1.5**), where the nobility of the theme is established by

the grandeur of the architectural space. For this supreme masterpiece of the High Renaissance, Raphael employed both linear and atmospheric perspective not only as devices for unifying a vast and complex pictorial space but also as a metaphor of the longing for harmonious unification. The converging lines of Raphael harmonized the divergent philosophies of Plato and Aristotle, the human and the divine, the ancient and the modern, and, perhaps most of all, the searing divisions that afflicted Christendom on the eve of the Protestant Reformation.

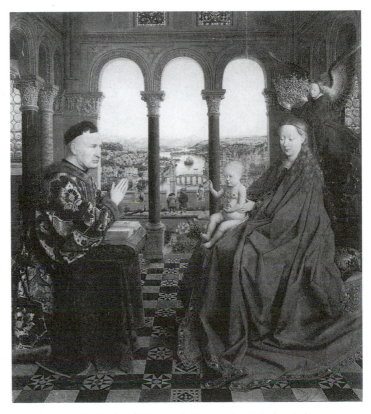

1.4 Jan van Eyck, *Madonna with Chancellor Nicolas Rolin*, c. 1435. Oil on panel, 26 × 24⅜" (66 × 61.9 cm). Musée du Louvre, Paris.

1.5 Raphael Sanzio, *The School of Athens*, 1510–11. Fresco. Stanza della Segnatura, Vatican Palace, Rome.

So exquisite was the balance struck by Raphael and his contemporaries, among them Leonardo da Vinci, Michelangelo, and Titian, that the succeeding generation of painters gave up studying nature in favor of basing their art on that of the High Renaissance, an art that had already conquered and refined nature. Thus, where the older masters had looked to nature and found their grand harmonious style, the new artists discovered what the sixteenth century called *maniera* (a manner), which in the early twentieth century was defined as Mannerism. This stylistic designation describes the work of certain artists after the High Renaissance and includes the late work of Michelangelo. Mannerist paintings may include figural grace exaggerated into extreme attenuation and twisting, choreographic poses, jammed, irrational spaces or distorted perspectives, shrill colors, scattered compositions, cropped images, polished surfaces, and an atmosphere of glacial coolness, even in scenes of high, often erotic, emotion or violence. All of these qualities apply to the work of one of the finest Italian Mannerists, **Agnolo Bronzino** (1502–72), whose supreme technical skills created compositions of sensuous beauty and dazzling complexity (fig. **1.6**). In their preference for allowing the ideal to prevail over the real, the Mannerists can be seen as forerunners of the tendency toward abstraction that would become a dominant trend in modernist art, whether pursued for

1.7 Matthias Grünewald, *Crucifixion*, center panel of the *Isenheim Altarpiece* (closed), 1512–15. Oil on panel, 9'9½" × 10'9" (3 × 3.3 m). Musée d'Unterlinden, Colmar, France.

reasons of objective formal analysis or to express some inner emotional or spiritual state.

Emotional or spiritual necessity lay at the core of the *Isenheim Altarpiece,* painted by Raphael's German contemporary **Matthias Grünewald** (d. 1528), the creator of a harrowing and moving Crucifixion (fig. **1.7**). In this dreadful scene, set against a darkening wilderness and floodlit with a harsh, glaring light, the tortured body of Christ hangs so heavy on the rude cross that the arms seem all but wrenched from their sockets, while the hands strain upward like claws frozen in rigor mortis. Under the fearsome diadem of brambles, the head slumps, with eyes closed and the mouth twisted in agony. Supporting the lacerated body are the feet, crushed together by a heavy spike. As the ghostly pale Virgin Mary swoons in the arms of Saint John, Mary Magdalene falls to the ground wringing her hands in grief, while John the Baptist points to the martyred Christ with a stabbing gesture, as if to re-enact the violence wreaked upon him. Here the unity of the human and the divine has been sought not in harmonious perfection of outward form, such as that realized by Raphael, but rather in an appalling image of spiritual and physical suffering. Placed upon the high altar of a hospital chapel in the monastery of Saint Anthony at Isenheim in Alsace, Grünewald's *Crucifixion* was part of an elaborate polyptych designed to offer example and solace to the sick and the dying. With its contorted forms, dissonant colors, passionate content, and spiritual purpose, the *Isenheim Altarpiece* stands near the apex of a long tradition that later resurfaced in the Expressionist art of twentieth-century Europe and even more explicitly in the art of the contemporary American painter Jasper Johns (see fig. 21.14).

1.6 Agnolo Bronzino, *Allegory of Time and Love*, c. 1546. Oil on panel, 61 × 56¼" (154.9 × 143 cm). The National Gallery, London.

In the seventeenth century, along with the religious Counter-Reformation, came an aesthetic reform designed to cleanse art of Mannerism's excesses and reinvigorate it with something of the broad, dramatically communicative naturalism realized in the High Renaissance. It began with one of the most revolutionary and influential painters in all of history, the Italian Michelangelo Merisi, known as **Caravaggio** (1572–1610). Singlehandedly, and while still in his twenties, Caravaggio introduced a blunt, warts-and-all kind of naturalism that sought to make the greatest mysteries of the Christian faith seem present and palpable (fig. **1.8**). Once enhanced by the artist's sense of authentic gesture and his bold light–dark contrasts, full-bodied illusionistic painting assumed an optical and emotive power never before seen in European art. Its impact was felt with stunning force among countless Italian followers, in the Spain of Diego Velázquez, the Netherlands of Rembrandt van Rijn, and the France of Georges de la Tour.

The innovations of Caravaggio ushered in the age of the Baroque, which gave rise during the eighteenth century to such decorative artists as Giovanni Battista Tiepolo

(1696–1770), in whose hands perspective painting became an expressive instrument to be merged with architecture and sculpture in the creation of gigantic symphonies of space, a dynamic world of illusion alive with sweeping, rhythmic movement. Tiepolo resorted to every *trompe l'oeil* trick of perspective and foreshortening learned in two centuries of experimentation in order to create the illusion of seemingly infinite space. Only with the advent of Neoclassicism at the end of the eighteenth century was there a halt in representing the expansion of space—and indeed, a desire to limit it severely.

Making Sense of a Turbulent World: Neoclassicism and Romanticism

Neoclassicism, which dominated the arts in Europe and America in the second half of the eighteenth century, has at times been called an eclectic and derivative style that perpetuated the classicism of Renaissance and Baroque art, a classicism that might otherwise have expired. Yet in Neoclassical art a fundamental Renaissance visual tradition was seriously opposed for the first time—the use of perspective recession to govern the organization of pictorial space. Indeed, it may be argued that David's work was crucial in shaping the attitudes that led, ultimately, to twentieth-century abstract art. David and his followers did not actually abandon the tradition of a pictorial structure based on linear and atmospheric perspective. They were fully wedded to the idea that a painting was an adaptation of classical relief sculpture (fig. **1.9**): they subordinated atmospheric effects; emphasized linear contours; arranged their figures as a frieze across the picture plane and accentuated that plane by closing off pictorial depth through the use of such devices as a solid wall, a back area of neutral color, or an impenetrable shadow. The result, as seen in *The Oath of the Horatii*, is an effect of figures composed along a narrow stage behind a proscenium, figures that exist in space more by the illusion of sculptural modeling than by their location within a pictorial space that has been

1.8 Caravaggio, *The Entombment of Christ*, 1602–4. Oil on canvas, 9'10¼" × 6'8" (3 × 2 m). Pinacoteca Vaticana, Rome.

1.9 Detail of the *Ara Pacis*, scene of an imperial procession, 13–9 B.C.E., marble frieze. Rome.

constructed according to the principles of linear and atmospheric perspective (see fig. 1.2).

David's followers in the first half of the nineteenth century were increasingly concerned with placing an emphasis on an art of ideal subject matter. Both Neoclassicism and Romanticism (see below) could be seen as flights from the immediate world to a reality evoked from impressions of the Orient, Africa, or the South Seas; or to a fictional world derived from the art and literature of classical antiquity, the Middle Ages, and the Renaissance. The differences between the two approaches lay partly in the particular subjects selected, the Neoclassicists obviously leaning to antiquity and the Romantics to the Middle Ages or what they considered exotic, the East. Even this distinction was blurred as the century wore on, since Ingres (see below), the classicist, made rather a speciality of Oriental odalisques, and Eugène Delacroix, the Romantic, at various times turned to Greek mythology.

The clearest formal distinction between Neoclassical and Romantic painting in the nineteenth century may be seen in the approaches to plastic form and techniques of applying paint. The Neoclassicists continued the Renaissance tradition of glaze painting to attain a uniform surface unmarred by the evidence of active brushwork, whereas the Romantics revived the textured surface of Peter Paul Rubens, Rembrandt, and the rococo period. Neoclassicism in painting established the principle of balanced frontality to a degree that transcended even the High Renaissance or the classical Baroque of **Nicolas Poussin** (1594–1665) (fig. **1.10**). Romantic painters relied on diagonal recession in depth and indefinite atmospheric–coloristic effects more appropriate to the expression of the inner imagination than the clear light of reason. During the Romantic era there developed an increasingly high regard for artists' sketches, which were thought to capture the individual touch of the artist, thereby communicating authentic emotion. Such attitudes were later crucial for much abstract painting in America and France following World War II (see chapters 19 and 20).

Figure Painting

In analyzing classical, Romantic, and Realist painting in the first part of the nineteenth century, a number of factors other than attitudes toward technique or spatial organization must be kept in mind. The Neoclassicism of David and his followers involved moralistic subject matter related to the philosophic ideals of the French Revolution and based on the presumed stoic and republican virtues of early Rome. Yet painters were hampered in their pursuits of a truly classical art by the lack of adequate prototypes in ancient painting. There was, however, a profusion of ancient sculpture. Thus, it is not surprising that Neoclassical paintings such as *The Oath of the Horatii* (see fig. 1.2) should emulate sculptured figures in high relief within a restricted stage, as in the ancient Roman *Ara Pacis* (Altar of Peace) (see fig.1.9), which David saw in Rome, where he painted *The Oath*. The "moralizing" attitudes of his figures make the stage analogy particularly apt, for David's radically distilled composition results from his attitude toward the subject—a deliberate attempt to replace the elaborate art of the eighteenth-century royal court with republican simplicity and austerity. Though commissioned for Louis XVI, whom David, as a Deputy, later voted to send to the guillotine, this rigorous composition of

1.10 Nicolas Poussin, *Mars and Venus*, c. 1630. Oil on canvas, 5'1" × 7' (1.55 × 2.1 m). Museum of Fine Arts, Boston.

brothers heroically swearing allegiance to Rome came to be seen as a manifesto of revolutionary sentiment.

One of David's greatest paintings, *The Death of Marat* (fig. **1.11**), contains all the elements referred to—spatial compression, sculptural figuration, highly dramatized subject. But it also reminds us of David's power of realistic presentation, a power brought to bear not on a scene from classical antiquity but, significantly, on a contemporary event. Murdered by a counterrevolutionary in his bath (where he sought relief from a painful skin disease), the revolutionist Marat becomes in David's hands a secular martyr, and a means to highly effective political propaganda. By virtue of its convincing verisimilitude, this painting forms a link between the French portraitists of the eighteenth century and the nineteenth-century Realist tradition of Courbet and his followers.

Like David, the American painter **Benjamin West** (1738–1820) turned to the *Ara Pacis* when composing his scene from antiquity (fig. **1.12**). West and his contemporary John Singleton Copley, a portraitist best known for his painting *Paul Revere*, were the first artists from colonial America to achieve international distinction. Pennsylvanian by birth, West studied in Rome and settled permanently in London, where he was a founding member and eventually president of the Royal Academy, and painter to King George III, a unique distinction for an American artist. West's art was securely rooted in a European tradition that elevated history painting, depictions in the grand manner of historical or religious subjects, above all other genres. He translated his Roman sketches of the *Ara Pacis* into a sober funerary procession, the quintessence of classical dignity and repose.

1.11 Jacques-Louis David, *The Death of Marat*, 1793. Oil on canvas, 63¾ × 50⅜" (161.9 × 127.9 cm). Musées Royaux des Beaux-Arts de Belgique, Brussels.

1.12 Benjamin West, *Agrippina Landing at Brundisium with the Ashes of Germanicus*, 1768. Oil on canvas, 5'4½" × 7'10½" (1.64 × 2.4 m). Yale University Art Gallery, New Haven.

Another classicist of paramount importance to the development of modern painting was **Jean-Auguste-Dominique Ingres** (1780–1867), a pupil of David who during his long life remained the exponent and defender of the Davidian classical tradition. Ingres's style was essentially formed by 1800 and cannot be said to have changed radically in works painted at the end of his life. Although he was a vociferous opponent of most of the new doctrines of Romanticism and Realism, he did introduce certain factors that affected the younger artists who opposed in spirit everything he stood for. Ingres represented to an even greater degree than did David the influence of Renaissance classicism, particularly that of Raphael. Although David was a superb colorist, he tended to subordinate his color to the classical ideal except when he was carried away by the pageantry of the Napoleonic style. Ingres, on the contrary, used a palette both brilliant and delicate, combining classical clarity with Romantic sensuousness, often in liberated, even atonal harmonies of startling boldness (fig. **1.13**).

The sovereign quality that Ingres brought to the classical tradition was that of drawing, and it was his drawing, his expression of line as an abstract entity—coiling and uncoiling in self-perpetuating complications that seem as much autonomous as descriptive—which provided the link between his art and that of Edgar Degas and Picasso.

One of the major figures of eighteenth- and nineteenth-century art, who had a demonstrable influence on what

occurred subsequently, was the Spaniard **Francisco de Goya** (1746–1828). In a long career Goya carried his art through many stages, from penetrating portraits of the Spanish royal family to a particular concern in his middle and late periods with the human propensity for barbarity. The artist expressed this bleak vision in monstrous, even fantastic images that were the result of penetrating observation. His brilliant cycle of prints, *The Disasters of War* (fig. **1.14**), depicts the devastating results of Spain's popular uprisings against Napoléon's armies during the Peninsular War. In one of the most searing indictments of war in the history of art, Goya described atrocities committed on both sides of the conflict with reportorial vividness and personal outrage. While sympathetic to the modern ideas espoused by the great thinkers of the Enlightenment, or the Age of Reason, Goya was deeply cynical about the irrational side of human nature and its capacity for the most grotesque cruelty. Because of their inflammatory and ambivalent message, his etchings were not published until 1863, well after his death. During his lifetime Goya was not very well known outside Spain, despite the final years he spent in voluntary exile in the French city of Bordeaux, but once his work had been rediscovered by Édouard Manet in the mid-nineteenth century it made a strong impact on the mainstream of modern painting.

Among Goya's late works is a stunning and eerie self-portrait that, as vehicle for the investigation of a personal

1.13 Jean-Auguste-Dominique Ingres, *Odalisque with Slave*, 1842. Oil on canvas, 30 × 41½" (76.2 × 105.4 cm). The Walters Art Museum, Baltimore.

1.14 Francisco de Goya, Plate 30 from *The Disasters of War*, 1810–11. Etching, 1863 edition, image 5 × 6⅛" (12.8 × 15.5 cm). Hispanic Society of America, New York.

psyche, rather than a means to create a heroic message for public consumption, anticipates countless images of modern alienation in twentieth-century art.

The French Romantic movement really came into its own with **Eugène Delacroix** (1798–1863)—through his exploration of exotic themes, his accent on violent movement and intense emotion, and, above all, through his reassertion of Baroque color and emancipated brushwork (fig. **1.15**). The intensive study that Delacroix made of the nature and capabilities of full color derived not only from the Baroque but also from his contact with English color painters such as John Constable, Richard Bonington, and Joseph Mallord William Turner (see below). His greatest originality, however, may lie less in the freedom and breadth of his touch than in the way he juxtaposed colors in blocks of mutually intensifying complementaries, such as vermilion and blue-green or violet and gold, arranged in large sonorous chords or, sometimes, in small, independent, "divided" strokes. These techniques and their effects had a profound influence on the Impressionists and Post-Impressionists, particularly Vincent van Gogh (who made several copies after Delacroix) and Paul Cézanne.

Landscape Painting

Although the main lines of twentieth-century painting are traditionally traced to French Neoclassical, Romantic, and Realist art, Romanticism found its most characteristic manifestation in Germany rather than in France. Indeed, there were critical contemporary developments in Germany, England, Scandinavia, and the Low Countries throughout much of the nineteenth century. One may, in fact, trace an almost unbroken Romantic tradition in Germany and Scandinavia—a legacy that extends

1.15 Eugène Delacroix, *The Lion Hunt*, 1861. Oil on canvas, 30⅛ × 38¾" (76.5 × 98.4 cm). The Art Institute of Chicago.

from the late eighteenth century through the entire nineteenth century to Edvard Munch, the Norwegian forerunner of Expressionism, and the later German artists who admired him.

A number of Romantic painters were active in these countries at the beginning of the nineteenth century: the Germans Caspar David Friedrich and Philipp Otto Runge, the Danish–German Asmus Jacob Carstens, and two Englishmen, William Blake and Joseph Mallord William Turner. These artists developed very individualized styles but based their common visionary expression on the vastness and mystery of nature rather than on the religious sources traditional to much art from the Medieval through the Baroque periods. Comparable attitudes are manifest in the work of European and American landscapists, from Constable or Thomas Cole to the early landscapes of Piet Mondrian. Implicit in this Romantic vision is a sense that the natural world can communicate spiritual and cultural values, at times formally religious, at times broadly pantheistic.

With **Caspar David Friedrich** (1774–1840), the leading German painter of Romantic landscape, the image of nature was by definition a statement of the sublime, of the infinite and the immeasurable. His landscapes are filled with mysterious light and vast distances, and human beings, when they appear, occupy a subordinate or largely contemplative place (fig. **1.16**). In his ghostly procession of monks into the ruined apse of a Gothic church, Friedrich clearly draws formal parallels between the towering forms of the apse and the framing "architecture" of nature.

Although landscape painting in France during the early nineteenth century was a relatively minor genre, by midcentury certain close connections with the English landscapists of the period began to have crucial effects. The painter Richard Parkes Bonington (1802–28), known chiefly for his watercolors, lived most of his brief life in France, where, for a short time, he shared a studio with his friend Delacroix. Bonington's direct studies from nature exerted considerable influence on several artists of the Romantic school, including Delacroix, as well as Camille Corot and his fellow Barbizon painters (see below). Although he painted cityscapes as well as genre and historical subjects, it was the spectacular effects of Bonington's luminous marine landscapes that directly affected artists like Johan Barthold Jongkind and Eugène Boudin, both important precursors of Impressionism (see fig. 2.26). Indeed, many of the English landscapists visited France frequently and exhibited in the Paris Salons, while Delacroix spent time in England and learned from the direct nature studies of the English artists. Foremost among these were **John Constable** (1776–1837) and **Joseph Mallord William Turner** (1775–1851). Constable spent a lifetime recording in paint those locales in the English countryside with which he was intimately familiar (fig. 1.17). Though his paintings and the sketches he made from nature were the product of intensely felt emotion, Constable never favored the dramatic historical landscapes, with their sublime vision of nature, for which Turner was justifiably famous in his own day. Ambitious, prolific, and equipped

1.16 Caspar David Friedrich, *Cloister Graveyard in the Snow*, 1819. Oil on canvas, 48 × 67" (121.9 × 170.2 cm). Formerly Nationalgalerie, Berlin (destroyed in World War II).

1.17 John Constable, *The Hay Wain*, 1819–21. Oil on canvas, 51¼" × 6'1" (130.2 cm × 1.9 m). The National Gallery, London.

1.18 Joseph Mallord William Turner, *The Burning of the Houses of Parliament*, 1834–35. Oil on canvas, 36½ × 48½" (92.7 × 123.2 cm). The Cleveland Museum of Art.

with virtuoso technical skills, Turner was determined to make landscapes in the grand tradition of Claude Lorrain and Poussin. His first trip to Italy in 1819 was an experience with profound consequences for his art. In his watercolors and oils Turner explored his fascination with the forces of nature, often destructive ones, and the ever-changing conditions of light and atmosphere in the landscape. His dazzling light effects could include the delicate reflections of twilight on the Venetian canals or a dramatic view across the Thames of the Houses of Parliament in flames (fig. **1.18**). Turner's painterly style could sometimes verge on the abstract, and his paintings are especially relevant to developments in twentieth-century art.

The principal French movement in Romantic landscape is known as the Barbizon School, a loose group named for a village in the heart of the forest of Fontainebleau, southeast of Paris. The painters who went there to work drew more directly on the seventeenth-century Dutch landscape tradition than on that of England. In this, the emphasis continued to be on unified, tonal painting rather than on free and direct color. It was the interior of the forest of Fontainebleau, rather than the brilliant sunlight of the seashore, that appealed to them. This in itself could be considered a Romantic interpretation of nature, as the expression of intangibles through effects of atmosphere. The Romantic landscape of the Barbizon School merged into a kind of Romantic Realism in the paintings of **Jean-François Millet** (1814–75), who paralleled Courbet in his passion for the subject of peasants at work but whose interpretation, with primary emphasis on the simplicity and nobility of agrarian experience, was entirely different in manner (fig. **1.19**). As if to redeem the grinding poverty of unpropertied farm life, he shaped his field laborers with the monumentality of Michelangelo and integrated them into

1.19 Jean-François Millet, *The Gleaners*, 1857. Oil on canvas, 33 × 44" (83.8 × 111.8 cm). Musée d'Orsay, Paris.

landscape compositions of Poussinesque grandeur and calm. Because of this reverence for peasant subjects Millet exerted great influence on Van Gogh (see chapter 3).

Another painter who worked outdoors in the Fontainebleau forest was **Rosa Bonheur** (1822–99), who is best known for her skillful and sympathetic depictions of animals in the landscape. To prepare her most celebrated picture, *The Horse Fair* (fig. **1.20**), she visited the horse market dressed as a man (for her skirts would have been a "great hindrance") and studied the animals' anatomy and movement. As was often the case with popular works of art in the nineteenth century, this painting was reproduced as a lithograph and circulated widely in Europe and the United States.

An influential French landscapist of the nineteenth century before Impressionism was **Camille Corot** (1796–1875). Only peripherally associated with the Barbizon School's, Corot's work cannot easily be categorized. His studies of Roman scenes have a classical purity of organization comparable to that of Poussin and a clarity of light and color similar to that of the English watercolorists. Like his English contemporaries, Corot spent a good deal of his time drawing and painting directly from nature. Beginning in 1825, he spent three years in Italy making open-air studies that in their delicate tonalities capture the special character of southern light. One of his best-known works from this Italian sojourn, *Island and Bridge of San Bartolomeo* (fig. **1.21**), possesses a classical balance and clarity while demonstrating Corot's striking approach to form. His structures are tightly interlocking horizontals and verticals, all harmoniously defined within a narrow range of ochers and browns. The strong sense of architectural geometry, of contrasting masses and planes, emerges not by way of conventional modeling, but through a regard for form as a series of nearly abstract volumes. These small landscapes exerted a great influence on the development of the Impressionism and Post-Impressionism of Claude Monet and Cézanne. From the landscapes of his Roman period, Corot turned to a more Romantic mode in delicate woodland scenes in tones of silvery gray, Arcadian landscapes sometimes populated by diminutive figures of nymphs and satyrs (see fig. 2.25). His late portraits and figure studies, on the contrary, are solidly realized and beautifully composed, works that are closely related to the studio scenes and figures of Post-Impressionist, Fauve, and Cubist tradition.

1.20 Rosa Bonheur, *The Horse Fair*, 1853; retouched 1855. Oil on canvas, 8'¼" × 16'7" (2.4 × 5.1 m). The Metropolitan Museum of Art, New York.

1.21 Camille Corot, *Island and Bridge of San Bartolomeo*, 1826–28. Oil on paper mounted on canvas, 10⅝ × 16⅞" (27 × 16.9 cm). Private collection.

Academic Art and the Salon

Since a large part of this book is concerned with revolts by experimental artists against the academic system, a brief summary of the official academy of art, particularly as it existed in mid-nineteenth-century France, is in order.

The term "academy," in the sense of a school of arts, letters, philosophy, or science, may be traced back to Plato and Athens in the fourth century B.C.E. It was revived in the later fifteenth century C.E. with the renewal of interest in Platonism in Italy. During the Middle Ages and much of the Renaissance and Baroque periods, guilds were organized chiefly to protect artists' rights as craftspeople rather than as creative artists. The origin of the modern academy of art is associated with Leonardo da Vinci at the end of the fifteenth century, after which the idea gained strength in Italy during the sixteenth century as painters and sculptors sought to elevate their position from the practical to the liberal arts. The academy in its modern sense really began in the seventeenth century, when academies of arts and letters and of science were established in many countries of Europe. They aimed to promote a rational, logical approach to these fields of human endeavor. In the case of the arts, they helped to bring about a new understanding of the term "art," which had previously been used to mean technical skill or accomplishment, but which gradually acquired "higher" associations of intellectual seriousness.

The academies that were established throughout Europe in the seventeenth and eighteenth centuries sought both to regulate and advance the professional practice of art, and to act as training institutions for young artists. Academic practice and theory were based on the study of officially approved models (students were required to spend many hours copying plaster casts of classical sculpture) and the belief that art was governed by rules akin to the laws of nature or grammatical structures. These precepts were challenged by the Romantic notion of individual genius, which cast the true artist as a rebel who necessarily rejected rules and conventions. In reality, the divide was sometimes less clear-cut than this: for example, Turner, the British artist who revolutionized landscape painting and was acknowledged as an important influence by many later avant-garde artists, remained a passionately loyal member of London's Royal Academy.

The French Académie des Beaux-Arts (Academy of Fine Arts) was founded in 1648 and, in one form or another, dominated the production of French art until the 1880s. An artist's survival could depend on his or her acceptance in the annual Salons, large public exhibitions that were open only to Academy members and held for many years in the Louvre. In 1791, during the French Revolution, the jury that judged the Salon entries was disbanded and the exhibition was opened to all artists. The results proved so disastrous that the jury was reinstated. Similar exhibitions were staged in London by the Royal Academy, founded in 1768. In the eighteenth century it is difficult to find a painter or sculptor who is well recognized today who was not an academician and did not exhibit in the Salons, though revisionist histories of the period have carefully searched out the developments that took place outside this mainstream.

Until 1790, membership to women in the French Academy was limited to four at any given time. In fact, two of David's contemporaries, Elisabeth Vigée-Lebrun and Adélaïde Labille-Guiard, served there with distinction, virtually dominating the genre of portraiture in the years before the Revolution. It was thanks to the efforts of Labille-Guiard that after the Revolution the Academy ceased to impose limits on female enrollment, and by 1835 the number of women exhibiting at the Salon exceeded twenty percent. Women, however, were not admitted to the prestigious École des Beaux-Arts until the late nineteenth century, nor were they allowed to compete for the most coveted of academic honors, the Prix de Rome, an award that funded the winner's classical education in Rome.

During the nineteenth century, the Salons occupied an even more influential place. In contrast to previous centuries, they now became vast public affairs in which thousands of paintings were hung and thousands rejected, for the revolutionary attempt to "democratize" the academic Salon resulted in a very eclectic mélange that contrasted sharply with the relatively small invitational exhibitions of the eighteenth century. Although the new Salons were selected by juries, presumably competent and occasionally distinguished, they reflected the tastes of the new middle-class buyers of art, which differed markedly from those of the aristocratic or ecclesiastical patrons of art of earlier centuries. At the same time, the authority of the academic tradition persisted, and the reputation, and even the livelihood, of artists continued to be dependent upon acceptance in these official exhibitions.

Typical Salon paintings ranged from pseudoclassical compositions, whose scale tended to attention-gaining vastness, to the nearly photographic history paintings of Jean-Louis-Ernest Meissonier. Among the many other genres on which the largely second- and third-rate artists of the Salon depended, particularly popular were works of extreme sentimentality combined with extreme realism and superficially classical erotic compositions like those by William-Adolphe Bouguereau.

Although the revolution of modern art was in large degree the revolt against this cumbersome academic Salon system, it must be remembered that the leading artists of the nineteenth century participated gladly in the Salons—indeed, they could rarely afford not to. The famous Salon of 1855 devoted a room each to Delacroix and Ingres, and both were awarded grand medals of honor. Courbet may have built a separate pavilion to show *The Painter's Studio* (see fig. 1.1), which had been rejected, but he also showed other works in the official Salon. Not only did many of the Romantics, Realists, and Impressionists whom we now regard as pioneers of modern art exhibit regularly or occasionally in the Salon, but there were certainly a number of "Salon painters" of distinction, among them Henri Fantin-Latour and Pierre Puvis de Chavannes (see fig. 3.13). It is also true that Édouard Manet, Odilon Redon, and Edgar Degas, and many other artists highly regarded today for their stylistic innovations, were, to one degree or another, successful Salon painters.

2
Realism, Impressionism, and Early Photography

In the industrial expansion of the nineteenth century, the new and prosperous middle class assumed a larger and larger part in every arena of European and American life. Although governmental patronage of the arts persisted, official commissions and state purchases were a feasible income source for only a limited number of artists, and by 1880 the French state relinquished its control over the ever-popular Salon exhibitions (see chapter 1). The new patrons were predominantly the newly rich bourgeoisie. Fundamentally materialistic in its values, this increasingly dominant segment of society had less interest in the fantasy of Romantic art than in a kind of pictorial verisimilitude that could convey meticulous visual facts verifiable in the external world of here and now. Such developments in the market and in the attitudes of the public consumers of art helped bring about the eventual demise of history painting. Private collectors did not covet large, cumbersome scenes from antiquity, but preferred the genres of portraiture, landscape, and scenes from daily life.

New Ways of Seeing: Photography and its Influence

The public taste for visual fact served as an all-important stimulant to the research that finally brought about the invention of the first practical photographic processes. In August 1839, **Louis-Jacques-Mandé Daguerre** (1789–1851) publicly demonstrated a new mechanical technology for permanently fixing upon a flat surface and in minute detail an exact tonal, if not full-color, image of the three-dimensional world. From that time, Western painters would hardly be able to create new imagery without some consciousness of the special conditions introduced by the medium of photography (literally "drawing with light"). Nor, it should be added, would photographers ever feel altogether free to work without some awareness of the rival aesthetic standards, qualities, and prestige imposed by the age-old, handwrought image-making processes of painting and drawing.

Long before anyone had ever seen a daguerreotype, painters had already anticipated many of the salient characteristics of photographic form: a snapshotlike cropping of figures by the framing edges (see fig. 2.34); motion arrested or frozen in full flight or midstep in a way seldom perceptible to the naked eye; a related "stop-action" informality of human pose and gesture; ghostly residual or afterimages left in the wake of speeding objects; imagery defined purely in terms of tone, free of contour lines; wide-angle views and exaggerated foreshortening; and, perhaps most of all, a generalized flatness of image even where there is depth illusion, an effect produced in normal photography by the camera's relative consistency of focus throughout the field and its one-eyed (monocular) view of things.

None of these characteristics, however, became a commonplace of painting style until the mass proliferation of photographic imagery made them a ubiquitous and unavoidable feature of modern life, and photographic conventions became synonymous with the "modern" way of looking at life. The most immediate and obvious impact on painting can be seen in the work of artists eager to achieve a special kind of optical veracity unknown until the advent of photography, a trend often thought to have culminated in the "instantaneity" of Impressionism, and resurgent in the Photorealism of the 1970s (see chapter 24).

Other artists, however, or even the same ones, took the scrupulous fidelity of the photographic image as good reason to work imaginatively or conceptually and thus liberate their art from the requirement of pictorial verisimilitude. Some saw the aberrations and irregularities peculiar to photography as a source of fresh ideas for creating a whole new language of form. And among painters of the period were some accomplished photographers, such as Edgar Degas and Thomas Eakins. Photography could also serve painters as a shortcut substitute for closely observed preparatory drawings and as a vastly expanded repertoire of reliable imagery, drawn from whatever remote, exotic corner of the globe into which adventurous photographers had been able to lug their cumbersome nineteenth-century equipment.

2.1 Louis-Jacques-Mandé Daguerre, *An early daguerreotype, taken in the artist's studio*, 1837. Société Française de Photographie, Paris.

Meanwhile, early photographers found their work relating closely to painting, just as painters were bound up with photography. Buoyed by pride in their technical superiority, photographers even felt compelled to match painting in its artistic achievements. For painters enjoyed the freedom to select, synthesize, and emphasize at will and thus attain not only the poetry and expression thought to be essential to art but also a higher order of visual, if not optical, truth. In one of the earliest known photographs, Daguerre, who was already famous for his immense, sensationally illusionistic painted dioramas, had sought to emulate art as much as nature. The reality he chose to record was that of a still life arranged in a manner conventional to painting since at least the seventeenth century

(fig. **2.1**). This was a daguerreotype, a metal plate coated with a light-sensitive silver solution, which, once developed in a chemical bath, resulted in a unique likeness that could not be replicated, but that recorded the desired image with astonishing clarity.

Simultaneously in England, the photographic process became considerably more versatile when **William Henry Fox Talbot** (1800–77) discovered a way of fixing a light-reflected image on the silver-treated surface of paper, producing what its creator called a calotype. Talbot invented a technique that converted a negative image into a positive one, a procedure that remains fundamental to photography. Because the negative made it possible for the image to be replicated an infinite number of times, unlike the daguerreotype, painting-conscious photographers such as **Oscar G. Rejlander** (1813–75) could assemble elaborate, multifigure compositions in stagelike settings. They pieced the total image together from a variety of negatives and then orchestrated them, rather in the way history painters prepared their grand narrative scenes for the Salon (fig. **2.2**). Indeed, Rejlander emulated not only the artistic methods and ambitions of academic masters, but also their pretensions to high moral purpose. British photographer **Henry Peach Robinson** (1830–1901) used sketches (fig. **2.3**) to prepare his elaborate exhibition photographs, which he compiled from multiple negatives (fig. **2.4**).

But just as the Realist spirit inspired some progressive painters to seek truth in a more direct and simplifying approach to subject and medium, many enlightened photographers sought to purge their work of the artificial, academic devices employed by Rejlander and concentrate on what photography then did best—report the world and

2.2 Oscar G. Rejlander, *The Two Ways of Life*, 1857. Combination albumen print. Royal Photographic Society, England.

2.3 Henry Peach Robinson, Sketch for *Carrolling*, 1886–87. Pencil on paper, 13 × 25" (33 × 65.5 cm). Royal Photographic Society, England.

2.4 Henry Peach Robinson, *Carrolling*, 1887. Combination albumen print. Royal Photographic Society, England.

its life candidly. The practitioners of this kind of documentary photography achieved art and expression through the choice of subject, view, framing, light, and the constantly improving means for controlling the latter—lenses, shutter speeds, plates, and processing chemicals. Even the work of Daguerre and Talbot (figs. **2.5**, **2.6**) shows this taste for creating a straightforward record of the everyday world, devoid of theatrics or sentiment. Their first street scenes already have the oblique angles and random cropping of snapshots, if not the bustling life, which moved in and out of range too rapidly to be caught by the slow photosensitive materials of the 1830s and 1840s. Contemporaries called Daguerre's Paris a "city of the dead," since the only human presence it registered was that of a man who stood still long enough for his shoes to be shined and, coincidentally, his picture to be taken.

Among the first great successes in photography were the portraitists, foremost among them France's **Nadar** (Gaspard-Félix Tournachon; 1820–1910) and England's

Julia Margaret Cameron (1815–79), whose powerful personalities gave them access to many of the most illustrious people of the age and the vision necessary to render these with unforgettable forthrightness and penetration (fig. **2.7**). A prolific writer, as well as caricaturist, hot-air balloon photographer, and dynamic man about Paris, Nadar wrote in 1856:

> Photography is a marvellous discovery, a science that has attracted the greatest intellects, an art that excites the most astute minds—and one that can be practiced by any imbecile. … Photographic theory can be taught in an hour, the basic technique in a day. But what cannot be taught is the feeling for light. … It is how light lies on the face that you as artist must capture. Nor can one be taught how to grasp the personality of the sitter. To produce an intimate likeness rather than a banal portrait, the result of mere chance, you must put yourself at once in communion with the sitter, size up his thoughts and his very character.

2.5 Louis-Jacques-Mandé Daguerre, *Boulevard du Temple, Paris*, c. 1838. Daguerreotype. Bayerisches Nationalmuseum, Munich.

2.6 William Henry Fox Talbot, *Trafalgar Square, London, During the Erection of the Nelson Column*, London, England. 1843. Salt print from a paper negative, 6¾ × 8⅜" (17.1 × 21.3 cm). The Museum of Modern Art, New York.

2.7 Nadar (Gaspard-Félix Tournachon), *Sarah Bernhardt*, 1864. Photograph, 9⅜ × 9⅜" (23.8 × 24.5 cm). Bibliothèque Nationale de France, Paris.

Cameron liked to dress up her friends and family and reenact scenes from the Bible and Tennyson's *Idylls of the King* (a series of poems based on the legends of King Arthur) as photographed costume dramas, styled in the manner of Pre-Raphaelite painting (fig. **2.8**). She also approached portraiture with an intensity that swept away all staginess but the drama of character and accentuated chiaroscuro (fig. **2.9**). Throughout her work, however, she maintained, like the good Victorian she was, only the loftiest aims. In answer to the complaint that her pictures always appeared to be out of focus, Cameron stated:

> What is focus—who has a right to say what focus is the legitimate focus—My aspirations are to ennoble Photography and to secure for it the character and uses of High Art by combining the real & ideal & sacrificing nothing of Truth by all possible devotion to Poetry & Beauty.

In America the daguerreotype experienced wild popularity from the moment the first instruction manuals and equipment arrived on the East Coast. The many commercial photographic studios that sprang up, especially in New York and Philadelphia, gave rise to hundreds of amateur photographers. They provided inexpensive portrait services to sitters who could never have afforded a commissioned painted portrait. An American propensity for visual fact guaranteed the particular success of the daguerreotype, at least on an economic if not on an aesthetic level. From the countless efforts of anonymous photographers emerge forthright records of ordinary citizens and valuable likenesses of extraordinary personalities, such as a portrait of the eminent abolitionist writer and orator Frederick

2.8 William Holman Hunt, *The Hireling Shepherd*, 1851. Oil on canvas, 30⅛ × 43⅛" (76.4 × 109.5 cm). Manchester City Art Galleries, England.

Douglass (fig. **2.10**). An escaped slave, Douglass informed his eloquent public protests against slavery with firsthand experience. He was an adviser to President Abraham Lincoln during the Civil War and afterward became the first African-American to hold high office in the United States government. The photograph of Douglass as a

2.9 Julia Margaret Cameron, *Mrs. Herbert Duckworth as Julia Jackson*, c. 1867. Albumen print, 13⅜ × 9⅝" (34 × 24.4 cm). International Museum of Photography at George Eastman House, Rochester, New York.

2.10 Unknown photographer, *Frederick Douglass*, 1847. Daguerreotype, 3¼ × 2¾" (8.3 × 7 cm). Collection William Rubel.

young man was taken at the end of a lecture tour he had given in Great Britain and Ireland in order to avoid recapture in America. Like the best daguerreotypes, it possesses tremendous appeal by virtue of its unaffected, straightforward presentation of the sitter.

Documentary pursuits were well served by photography's representational integrity. When the French photographer **Charles Nègre** (1820–79) dragged his heavy paraphernalia high up among the gargoyles of Paris's Notre Dame Cathedral (fig. **2.11**), he created an image of extraordinary visual juxtapositions and architectural

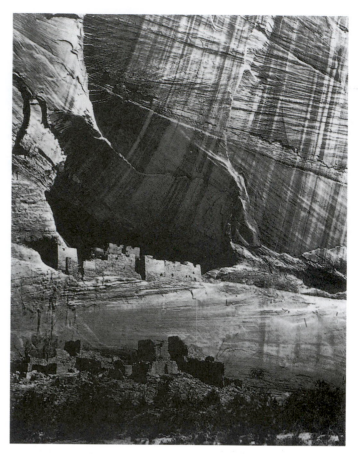

2.11 Charles Nègre, *The Gargoyle of Notre Dame*, Original negative 1840s or 1850s, reprinted 1960. Calotype, 13⅛ × 9¼" (33.3 × 23.5 cm). The Metropolitan Museum of Art, New York.

2.12 Timothy O'Sullivan, *Ancient Ruins in the Cañon de Chelle*, 1873. Collodion print, 10⅞ × 8" (27.6 × 20.3 cm). National Archives, Washington, D.C.

interest. Documentary photographers could provide eager audiences with images of the relatively unknown western American landscape (fig. **2.12**), the wonders of ancient Egypt, or the exotic backstreets of old China.

When it came to war, photography robbed armed conflict of the operatic glamour often given it by traditional painting. This first became evident in the photographs taken by Roger Fenton during the Crimean War of 1853–56, but it had even more shattering effect in the work of **Mathew Brady** (1823–96) and such associates as Alexander Gardner, who bore cameras onto the body-strewn fields in the wake of battle during the American Civil War (fig. **2.13**). (Because the required length of exposure was still several seconds, the battles themselves could not be photographed.) Now that beautifully particularized, mutely objective—or indifferent—pictures disclosed all too clearly the harrowing calm brought by violence, or the almost indistinguishable likeness of the dead on either side of the conflict, questions of war and peace took on a whole new meaning. When Brady's photograph is compared to a contemporary Civil War scene by one of the greatest American painters of the era, Winslow Homer (see fig. 2.48), it becomes clear that photography brought home the graphic reality of war in a way no painter could.

2.13 Mathew Brady, *Dead Soldier, Civil War*, c. 1863. Gelatin-silver print. Library of Congress, Washington, D.C.

A Chastened Vision: Realism in Art

As a medium of communication, as well as expression, photography was both the product and the agent of the powerful social changes that had been taking place in Western civilization since the political revolutions of the late eighteenth century. Along with photography, and its popularization of pictorial imagery, came the immense expansion of journalism, as newspapers and periodicals were in some measure liberated from government censorship. A new kind of journalism and a new kind of critical writing were everywhere evident. Many of the leading authors and critics of France and England wrote regularly for the new popular reviews.

These changes in attitude are perhaps best seen in the emergence of the caricature—the satirical comment on life and politics, which became a standard feature of journals and newspapers. Although visual attacks on individuals or corrupt economic or political systems have always existed, and artists such as Goya have been motivated by a spirit of passionate invective, drawings that ranged from gentle amusement to biting satire to vicious attack now became a commonplace in every part of Europe and America. These images could be cheaply disseminated through the popular medium of lithography. Just as the rise of Realism in art and the seemingly opposed expansion of the inflated Salon picture were closely allied to the emergence of large-scale bourgeois patronage, so were the expansion of the newspaper and journal and the popularity of the daily or weekly caricatures of the problems—and sometimes the tragedies—of everyday life.

France

The greatest of the satirical artists to emerge in this new environment was **Honoré Daumier** (1808–79), who, although best known for some four thousand lithographic drawings he contributed to French journals such as *La Caricature* and *Le Charivari*, was also an important painter and sculptor. But while Daumier was concerned with all the details of everyday life in Paris, and his satire is thus rooted in realistic observation, he cannot be called only a Realist. His paintings dealing with themes from the writings of Cervantes and Molière place him partly in the Romantic camp, not only for his use of literary subjects but also for the dramatic chiaroscuro he employed to obtain his effects. This drama of light and shade transforms even mundane subjects, such as *The Third-Class Carriage* (fig. **2.14**), from simple illustration to a scene of pathos. The painting is a crucial example of French Realist art in its sympathetic depiction of contemporary working-class life.

Daumier's studies of the theater, of the art world, and of politics and the law courts range from simple commentary to perceptive observation to bitter satire. His political caricatures were at times so biting in their attacks on the establishment that they were censored. For a caricature he did of King Louis Philippe, the artist was imprisoned for six months. The profundity of Daumier's horror at injustice and brutality is perhaps best illustrated in the famous lithograph *Rue Transnonain* (fig. **2.15**), which shows the dead bodies of a family of innocent workers who were murdered by the civil guard during the republican revolt of 1834. With journalistic bluntness, the title refers to the street where the killings occurred. In its powerful exploitation of a black-and-white medium, as well as the graphic description of its gruesome subject, this is a work comparable to Goya's *Disasters of War* (see fig. 1.14).

Like Daumier, **Gustave Courbet** (1819–77) inherited certain traits from his Romantic predecessors. Throughout his life, he produced both erotic subjects that border on academicism and Romantic interpretations of the artist's world in many self-portraits. But most important, he created unsentimental records of contemporary life that secure his place as the leading exponent of modern Realism in painting. These works possess a compelling physicality

2.14 Honoré Daumier, *The Third-Class Carriage*, c. 1863–65. Oil on canvas, 25¼ × 35½" (64.1 × 90.2 cm). The Metropolitan Museum of Art, New York.

2.15 Honoré Daumier, *Rue Transnonain, April 15, 1834*, Published in *L'Association Mensuelle*, July 1834. Lithograph, 11½ × 17½" (29.2 × 44.5 cm). Graphische Sammlung Albertina, Vienna.

and an authenticity of vision that the artist derived from the observed world. Most notably, Courbet insisted upon the very material with which a painting is constructed: oil paint. He understood that a painting is in itself a reality—a two-dimensional world of stretched canvas defined by the nature and textural consistency of paint—and that the artist's function is to define this world.

A Burial at Ornans (fig. **2.16**) is significant in the history of modern painting for its denial of illusionistic depth, its apparent lack of a formal composition, and an approach to subject matter so radical that it was seen as an insult to everything for which the venerable French Academy stood. In his assertion of paint texture, the artist drew on and amplified the intervening experiments of the Romantics, although with a different end in view. Whereas the Romantics used broken paint surfaces to emphasize the intangible elements of the spirit or sublime natural phenomena (see fig. 1.18), Courbet employed them as a means to make the ordinary world more tangible. The *Burial* documents a commonplace event in Courbet's small provincial hometown in eastern France, but its ambitious size conforms to the dimensions of history painting, a category reserved for the noblest events from the past. Courbet's casual, friezelike arrangement of village inhabitants, made up mostly of his friends and relatives, is an accurate depiction of local funerary customs (men and women are segregated, for example), but it carries no particular narrative message. It was not only this lack of compositional hierarchy and pictorial rhetoric that outraged French critics. Courbet's representation of ordinary residents of the countryside did not coincide with established Parisian norms for the depiction of rural folk. These are not the ennobled peasants of Millet (see fig. 1.19) or the pretty, happy maids of traditional academic painting.

Rather, they are highly individualized, mostly unattractive, and aggressively real.

Combined with his unorthodox approach to formal matters, Courbet's Realism in his unpolished treatment of working-class subjects was associated with left-wing dissidence. Any art-historical consideration of Realism is inextricably tied to the tumultuous political and social history during this period in France, the country where Realism developed most coherently. Following the devastating defeat of France's imperial government by the Germans in the Franco–Prussian War in 1871, Courbet took part in the popular uprising that resulted in the short-lived, radically republican Paris Commune. As head of the Federation of Artists, he proposed the peaceful dismantling of a Napoleonic monument in Paris, the Vendôme column. After the column was actually toppled and destroyed by the Communards, the conservative regime that brutally suppressed the Commune imprisoned Courbet and held him financially responsible for the damage. To avoid confiscation of his work, the artist eventually fled to Switzerland.

In a group of landscapes of the 1850s and 1860s, *The Source of the Loue* among them (fig. **2.17**), Courbet had experimented with a form of extreme close-up of rocks abruptly cut off at the edges of the painting. A view from the artist's native province of Franche-Comté, *The Source* may owe something to the emerging art of photography, both in its fragmentary impression and in its subdued, almost monochromatic color. Courbet's landscape, however, combined a sense of observed reality with an even greater sense of the elements and materials with which the artist was working: the rectangle of the picture plane and the emphatic texture of the oil paint, which asserted its own nature at the same time that it was simulating the rough-hewn, sculptural appearance of exposed rocks.

2.16 Gustave Courbet, *A Burial at Ornans*, 1849–50. Oil on canvas, 10'3½" × 21'9" (3.1 × 6.6 m). Musée d'Orsay, Paris.

2.17 Gustave Courbet, *The Source of the Loue*, 1864, Oil on canvas, 39¼ × 56" (99.7 × 142.2 cm). The Metropolitan Museum of Art, New York.

In his later career, Courbet experimented with many different approaches to the subjects of landscape, portrait, still life, and the figure. His ability to combine precise observation of nature with the aggressive, expressive statement of the pictorial means culminated in a group of seascapes of the late 1860s. In such works as *The Waves* he translated an unrelieved expanse of open sea into a primarily two-dimensional organization in which the third dimension is realized as the relief texture of the projecting oil paint. Like *A Burial at Ornans,* this seascape is not structured around a central pictorial focus. Indeed, it is devoid of all human presence and concentrates, to a degree previously achieved only by Turner, on sea and sky, all tangibly evoked with vigorous strokes from Courbet's palette knife.

England

The paintings of the English colorists Constable, Turner (see fig. 1.18), and Bonington had a profound influence on the French Romantics, particularly on the Barbizon School of landscapists and, eventually, the Impressionists. Constable's textural statement of brush gesture was well adapted to Romantic narrative and landscape, out of which Courbet's painting emerged. The radiant color used by the Englishman was a revelation. When *The Hay Wain* (see fig. 1.17) was shown at the 1824 Salon in Paris it caused a sensation, even sending Delacroix back to his studio to rework one of his paintings. Its sun-filled naturalism, however, was premature for the French Realists and Romantics. With the exception of Delacroix, they continued to prefer the more subdued color harmonies and the less vivid light of the studio when painting the out-of-doors. From early in his career, Constable dedicated himself to the close observation of the life and landscape around his father's property in Suffolk. Yet his bucolic visions of the English countryside rarely make reference to the harsher realities of agricultural life during a period of economic strife and civil unrest among agrarian workers.

That task would be left to later English painters such as Ford Madox Brown (see fig. 2.18). Constable could produce accurate, unaffected nature studies composed entirely in the open air (a half-century before the Impressionists), while remaining committed to the study of the landscapes of the seventeenth-century French classical painter Claude Lorrain. The paint texture of his *Hay Wain* is direct and unconcealed to a degree rarely observed in painting before his time, but his landscapes are still seen with the eyes of the Renaissance–Baroque tradition. Space opens up into depth, and paint is converted into fluffy, distant clouds, richly leaved trees, and reflecting pools of water.

During the early decades of Queen Victoria's long reign (1837–1901), the social and artistic revolution that fueled the Realist movement in France assumed virtually religious zeal, as a group of young painters rebelled against what they considered the decadence of current English art. They called for renewal modeled on the piously direct, "primitive" naturalism practiced in Florence and Flanders prior to the late work of Raphael and the High Renaissance, which they saw as the beginning of what had become a stultifying academic tradition. **William Holman Hunt** (1827–1910), John Everett Millais (1829–96), and Dante Gabriel Rossetti (1828–82) joined with several other sympathetic spirits to form a secret, reform-minded artistic society, which they called the Pre-Raphaelite Brotherhood. The ardent, if not monkish, Pre-Raphaelites determined to eschew all inherited Mannerist and Baroque artifice and to search for truth in worthwhile, often Christian, subject matter presented with naive, literal fidelity to the exact textures, colors, light, and, above all, the outlines of nature.

For *The Hireling Shepherd* (see fig. 2.8) Hunt pursued "truth to nature" in the countryside of Surrey, where he spent the summer and fall of 1851 working en plein air, or out-of-doors, to set down the dazzling effect of morning sunlight. Reviving the techniques of the fifteenth-century Flemish masters, Hunt laid—over a white wet ground—glaze after glaze of jewellike, translucent color and used the finest brushes to detail every wildflower blossom and blade of grass. Late in life, he asserted that his "first object was to portray a real Shepherd and Shepherdess … sheep and absolute fields and trees and sky and clouds instead of the painted dolls with pattern backgrounds called by such names in the pictures of the period." But it seems that he was also motivated to create a private allegory of the need for mid-Victorian spiritual leaders to cease their sectarian disputes and become true shepherds tending their distracted flocks. Thus, while the shepherd, ruddy-faced from beer in his hip keg, pays court to the shepherdess, the lamb on her lap makes a deadly meal of green apples, just as the sheep in the background succumb from being allowed to feed on corn. Gone are the smooth chiaroscuro elisions, rhythmic sweep, and gestural grace of earlier art, replaced by a fresh-eyed naturalism.

Although he never became an official member of the Pre-Raphaelites, **Ford Madox Brown** (1821–93) was introduced to the group by the precocious young poet and painter Rossetti. The large canvas *Work* (fig. **2.18**), which preoccupied him for several years, is Brown's monumental testament to the edifying and redemptive power of hard toil. Like Hunt, he relies on a microscopic accuracy of detail to deliver his moralizing message. At the center of the sun-drenched composition are the muscular laborers who dig trenches for new waterworks in the London suburb of Hampstead. A proliferation of genre vignettes circle around this central action of the painting; these reinforce Brown's theme with emblems of the various social strata that made up contemporary Victorian society. At the far left, for example, is a ragged flower seller followed by two women distributing temperance tracts. In the shade of a tree at the right, an indigent couple tends to their infant while in the background an elegantly dressed couple rides horseback. The two men at the far right are portraits: the philosopher Thomas Carlyle and a leading Christian Socialist, Frederick Denison Maurice, "brainworkers" whose relatively conservative ideas about social reform dovetailed with Brown's own genuine attempts to correct social injustice. His painting is the most complete illustration of the familiar Victorian ethic that promoted work as the foundation of material advancement, national progress, and spiritual salvation.

Seizing the Moment: Impressionism and the Avant-Garde

The various scandals surrounding Courbet's life and work had introduced the public to the idea of a radical, often shocking, alternative to academic Salon art that was more or less closely identified with left-wing politics. From this time onward the idea of an artistic avant-garde, or vanguard, became firmly established. Each new wave of avant-garde art was greeted with outrage by conservative public opinion—an outrage that frequently turned to acceptance, and even admiration, with the passing of time and the arrival of newer, yet more shocking, developments in art.

Manet and Whistler

Although he probably would have been sympathetic to Brown's left-wing politics, **Édouard Manet** (1832–83) was a realist with an artistic temperament far from the Englishman's accumulation of exacting detail. Despite his commitment to depict subjects of modern life in a modern

2.18 Ford Madox Brown, *Work*, 1852, 1855–63. Oil on canvas, 4'5" × 6'5 ¹¹/₁₆" (1.35 × 2 m). Manchester City Art Galleries, England.

2.19 Édouard Manet, *Déjeuner sur l'herbe (Luncheon on the Grass)*, 1863. Oil on canvas, 6'9⅛" × 8'10¼" (2.1 × 2.7 m). Musée d'Orsay, Paris.

style, Manet sought recognition through the Salon. He never exhibited with his fellow Impressionists in the eight independent exhibitions they organized between 1874 and 1886. Manet's *Déjeuner sur l'herbe* (fig. **2.19**), rejected by the Salon of 1863, created a major scandal when it was shown in the Salon des Refusés, the exhibition mounted by the state that year to house the large number of works barred by jurors from the main Salon. Although the subject was based on Renaissance academic precedents—Giorgione's *Pastoral Concert* (1510) and an engraving by Marcantonio Raimondi of *The Judgment of Paris* (c. 1520), after a lost cartoon by Raphael—popular indignation arose because the classical, pastoral subject had been translated into contemporary terms. Raphael's goddesses and Giorgione's nymphs had become models, or even prostitutes, one naked, one partially disrobed, relaxing in the woods with two men whom Salon visitors would have recognized by their dress as artists or students. The woman in the foreground is Victorine Meurent, the same model who posed for *Olympia* (see fig. 2.20) the men are Manet's relations. Manet clearly abided by the convictions of his

supporter Charles Baudelaire, the great poet and art critic who exhorted artists to paint scenes of modern life and to invent contemporary contexts for old subjects such as the nude. But in his ironic quotations from Renaissance sources, Manet created what seemed to be a conscious affront to tradition, and by failing to encode his contemporary scene as idealized allegory, he seemed deliberately to flout accepted social convention.

Manet ostensibly adopted the structure of Raphael's original composition, with the bending woman in the middle distance forming the apex of the classical receding triangle of which the three foreground figures serve as the base and sides. However, his broad, abrupt handling of paint and his treatment of the figures as silhouettes rather than carefully modeled volumes tend to collapse space, flatten forms, and assert the nature of the canvas as a two-dimensional surface. Manet's subject, as well as the sketchiness of technique, infuriated the professional critics, as though they sensed in this work the prophecy of a revolution that was to destroy the comfortable world of secure values of which they felt themselves to be the guardians.

2.20 Édouard Manet, *Olympia*, 1863. Oil on canvas, 4'3" × 6'2¾" (1.3 × 1.9 m). Musée d'Orsay, Paris.

Manet's *Olympia* (fig. **2.20**), painted in 1863 and exhibited in the Salon of 1865, created an even greater furor than the *Déjeuner*. Here, again, the artist's source was exemplary: Titian's *Venus of Urbino*, which Manet had copied as a young man visiting Florence. *Olympia*, however, was a slap in the face to all the complacent academic painters who regularly presented their exercises in scarcely disguised eroticism as virtuous homage to the gods and goddesses of classical antiquity. Venus reclining has become an unidealized, modern woman who, by details such as her ribbon and slippers, as well as her name, would have been recognized as a prostitute. She stares out at the spectator with an impassive boldness that bridges the gap between the real and the painted world in a startling manner, and effectively shatters any illusion of sentimental idealism in the presentation of the nude figure. *Olympia* is a brilliant design in black and white, with the nude figure silhouetted against a dark wall enriched by red underpainting that creates a Rembrandtesque glow of color in shadow. The black maidservant brings flowers offered by a client; the cat clearly reacts to her. The volume of the figure is created entirely through its contours—again, the light-and-dark pattern and the strong linear emphasis annoyed the critics as much as the shocking subject matter. Even Courbet found *Olympia* so unsettling in the playing-card flatness of its forms, all pressed hard against the frontal plane, that he likened the picture to "a Queen of Spades getting out of a bath."

Portrait of Émile Zola (fig. **2.21**), an informal portrait, continues the Realists' critique of the academic concept of the grand and noble subject, carrying the attack several steps further in its emphasis on the plastic means of painting itself. Zola, the great Realist novelist and proponent of social reform, was Manet's friend and supporter. Manet included in the work certain details that are perhaps more revealing of his own credos than of those of the writer who had so brilliantly defended him against his detractors. On the desk, for example, is the pamphlet Zola wrote on Manet. The bulletin board at the right holds a small print of *Olympia*, behind which is a reproduction of *Bacchus* by the seventeenth-century Spanish master Velázquez. Beside *Olympia* is a Japanese print, and behind Zola's figure is seen part of a Japanese screen. The Japanese print and screen are symptomatic of the growing enthusiasm for Asian and specifically Japanese art then spreading among the artists of France and throughout Europe. In the art of Asia avant-garde French painters found some of the formal qualities they were seeking in their own work. Manet's conscious "appropriation" of the work of older artists, sometimes for the sake of homage as well as irony, has become a major strategy of Postmodern artists (see fig. 26.2).

After photography, the most pervasive influence on the nineteenth-century advance of modernist form came from Asian art, especially the color woodcut prints that began their way west shortly after the American naval officer Matthew Perry had forced open the ports of Japan in 1853 after two centuries of closure to Western vessels. With their steep and sharply angled views, their bold, snapshotlike croppings or near–far juxtapositions, and their flat-pattern design of brilliant, solid colors set off by the purest contour drawing, the works of such masters as Kitagawa Utamaro, Katsushika Hokusai, and **Andō Hiroshige** (1797–1858; fig. **2.22**) struck European eyes as amazingly new and fresh. These prints reinforced the growing belief in the West that pictorial truth lay not in illusion but in the intrinsic qualities of the artist's means and the opaque planarity of the picture surface.

The attraction of this art for Manet is evident in every aspect of the *Portrait of Zola*. The critic Henri Fouquier denounced the picture in the newspaper *Le National*, declaring: "The accessories are not in perspective, and the trousers are not made of cloth." The criticism contained an obvious but remarkable truth: the trousers were not made of cloth; they were made of paint.

By the mid-1870s Manet had turned his attention to plein-air painting in which he sought to apply his brush-sketch technique to large figure compositions and to render these in full color that caught all the lightness and brilliance of natural sunlight. Although he did not show in their exhibitions, he had been in close contact with

2.22 Andō Hiroshige, *Moon Pine at Ueno* from *One Hundred Views of Famous Places in Edo*, 1857. Color woodcut, 13¾ × 8⅝" (34.9 × 21.9 cm). The Brooklyn Museum, New York.

the Impressionists Claude Monet, Edgar Degas, Auguste Renoir, and Camille Pissarro (see below). Like Degas, Manet was predominantly a painter of the human figure, not a landscapist like his friend Monet. But in the 1870s he moved gradually away from his modernizations of past art to contemporary genre scenes, which he composed in the heightened palette and loose brushwork of the Impressionists.

Closely allied to his friend Manet in the search for a new pictorial reality suitable for "a painter of modern life" was the American expatriate artist **James Abbott McNeill Whistler** (1834–1903). Whistler, who trained in Paris and resided in London, exhibited a painting at the 1863 Salon des Refusés that caused a critical scandal rivaling the one incited by Manet's *Déjeuner sur l'herbe*. Much more than Manet, however, Whistler transformed Japanese sources into an emphatic aestheticism, in which Japanese-inspired style *(japonisme)* became the means to express a lyrical, atmospheric sensibility. Even so, in an authentic Realist manner, he consistently painted what he had observed. Whistler's approach was evident in the early 1860s, when he made pictures like *Symphony in White No. II: The Little White Girl* (fig. **2.23**), where *japonisme* makes its presence felt not only in the obvious décor of an Asian blue-and-white porcelain vase, painted fan, and azalea blossoms, but also in the more subtle, and more important, flattening effects of the nuanced, white-on-white rendering of the model's dress and the rectilinear, screenlike divisions of the architectural framework. Further reinforcing the sense of

2.21 Édouard Manet, *Portrait of Émile Zola*, 1868. Oil on canvas, 57⅛ × 44⅞" (145.1 × 114 cm). Musée d'Orsay, Paris.

2.23 James Abbott McNeill Whistler, *Symphony in White No. II: The Little White Girl*, 1864. Oil on canvas, 30⅛ × 20⅛" (76.5 × 51.1 cm). Tate Gallery, London.

2.24 James Abbott McNeill Whistler, *Nocturne in Black and Gold: The Falling Rocket*, 1875. Oil on oak panel, 23¾ × 18⅜" (60.3 × 46.7 cm). The Detroit Institute of Arts.

an overriding formalism is the off-center composition, with its resulting crop of the figure along two edges of the canvas. To emphasize his commitment to the principle of art for art's sake, an art committed to purely formal values, Whistler gave his pictures musical titles—arrangements, symphonies, and nocturnes—thereby drawing analogies with a more immaterial, evocative, and nondescriptive medium. Such analogies were very much in the spirit of late nineteenth-century Aestheticism, summed up in 1873 in the English critic Walter Pater's dictum, "All art constantly aspires towards the condition of music." This approach emphasized the formal qualities of art as being more important than subject matter, and indeed Whistler's aim was to create not a duplicate of nature, but rather what he called "an arrangement of line, form, and color first." By the mid-1870s, when the artist had settled permanently in London, his painting *Nocturne in Black and Gold: The Falling Rocket* (fig. **2.24**) seemed so purely abstract that it prompted the art critic John Ruskin to accuse Whistler openly of "flinging a pot of paint in the public's face." Whistler brought a libel suit against the critic and won a token judgment, for indeed he had worked from an observed subject, the fiery bursts and glittering sparks of a nocturnal fireworks display sprayed over a midnight sky.

Impressionism and its Antecedents

A great part of the struggle of nineteenth-century experimental painters was an attempt to recapture the color, light, and changeability of nature that had been submerged

in the rigid stasis and studio gloom of academic tonal formulas. The color of the Neoclassicists had been defined in local areas but modified with large passages of neutral shadows to create effects of sculptural modeling. The color of Delacroix and the Romantics flashed forth passages of brilliant blues or vermilions from an atmospheric ground. As Corot and the Barbizon School of landscape painters sought to approximate more closely the effects of the phenomenal world with its natural light, they were almost inevitably bent in the direction of the subdued light of the interior of the forest, of dawn, and of twilight. Color, in their hands, thus became more naturalistic, although they did choose to work with those effects of nature most closely approximating the tradition of studio light. However, the increasingly delicate and abstract, almost monochromatic tonality of the post-1850, proto-Impressionist landscapes painted indoors by Corot (fig. **2.25**), so different from the clear colors and structural firmness of his earlier Italian work (see fig. 1.21), may well have been an attempt to imitate the seamless, line-free value range of contemporary photography, a medium that greatly interested him. In their smoky tissues of feathery leaves and branches, the moody, autumnal, parklike scenes painted by

2.25 Camille Corot, *Ville d'Avray*, 1871–74. Oil on canvas, 21⅝ × 31½" (54.9 × 80 cm). The Metropolitan Museum of Art, New York.

the aging Corot seem to be painterly counterparts of the blurred landscape photographs of the period.

One of the few French landscapists of the mid-nineteenth century determined to work away from the forest in full sunlight was **Eugène Boudin** (1824–98), who painted the fashionable vacationers at seaside resorts around Le Havre, Normandy, with a direct, on-the-spot brilliance that fascinated both Courbet and Baudelaire (fig. **2.26**). It inspired Claude Monet, Boudin's student and friend, and, through Monet, the movement of Impressionism.

Artists had always sketched in the open air and, as we have seen, some such as Corot and the Barbizon painters made compositions entirely en plein air, though even these artists usually completed paintings in the studio. The Impressionists were the most consistently devoted to plein-air painting, even for some of their most ambitious works, and to capturing on canvas as faithfully as possible the optical realities of the natural world. However, the more the Realist artists of the mid-nineteenth century attempted to reproduce the world as they saw it, the more they understood that reality rested not so much in the simple

2.26 Eugène Boudin, *On the Beach at Trouville*, 1863. Oil on panel, 10 × 18" (25.4 × 45.7 cm). The Metropolitan Museum of Art, New York.

objective world of natural phenomena as in the eye of the spectator. Landscape in actuality could never be static and fixed. It was a continuously changing panorama of light and shadow, of moving clouds and reflections on the water. The same scene, observed in the morning, at noon, and at twilight, was actually three different realities. Further, as painters moved out of doors from the studio they came to realize that nature, even in its dark shadows, was not composed of black or muddy browns. The colors of nature were the full spectrum—blues, greens, yellows, and whites, accented with notes of red and orange, and often characterized by an absence of black.

In the sense that the artists were attempting to represent specific aspects of the observed world more precisely than any before them, Impressionism offered a specialized view of the world, based on intense observation as well as new discoveries in the science of optics. But Impressionism was much more than this. Behind the landscapes of Monet and the figure studies of Renoir lay not only the social realism of Courbet and the romantic realism of the Barbizon painters but also the significant sense of abstract structure that had appeared with David and Ingres and developed into a new aesthetic with Courbet and Manet.

Louis Leroy, the satirical critic for *Le Charivari*, was the first to speak of a school of "Impressionists," a term he derisively based on the title of a painting by **Claude Monet** (1840–1926) (fig. **2.27**) that was included in the first Impressionist exhibition at the studio of the photographer Nadar in 1874. The show marked a significant historical occasion, for it was organized by a group of artists outside the official apparatus of the Salon and its juries, the first of many independent, secessionist group exhibitions that punctuate the history of avant-garde art in the modern period.

Monet's painting offers a harmony of sky and water, an example of the type of atmospheric dissolution later explored by Whistler in his Nocturnes (see fig. 2.24). It is a thin veil of light gray-blue shot through with the rose-pink of the rising sun. Reflections on the water are suggested by short, broken brushstrokes, and the ghostly forms of boats and smokestacks are described with loose patches of color, rather than gradations of light and dark tones. *Impression: Sunrise,* for Monet, was an attempt to capture the ephemeral aspects of a changing moment, more so, perhaps, than any of his paintings until the late Venetian scenes or *Waterlilies* of 1905. *The Bridge at Argenteuil* (fig. **2.28**) might be considered a more classic version of developed Impressionism. It represents a popular sailing spot in the Parisian suburb of Argenteuil, where Monet settled in 1871. Scenes of contemporary leisure were a mainstay of Impressionist subject matter. The painting glistens and vibrates, giving the effect of brilliant, hot sunlight shimmering on the water in a scene of contemplative stillness. Monet employed no uniform pattern

2.27 Claude Monet, *Impression: Sunrise*, 1872. Oil on canvas, 17¾ × 21¾" (45.1 × 55.2 cm). Musée Marmottan, Paris.

2.28 Claude Monet, *The Bridge at Argenteuil*, 1874. Oil on canvas, 23⅝ × 31½" (60 × 80 cm). Musée d'Orsay, Paris.

of brushstroke to define the surface: the trees are treated as a relatively homogeneous mass; the foreground blue of the water and the blue of the sky are painted quite smoothly and evenly, while the reflections of the tollhouse in the water are conveyed by dabs of thick yellow impasto; the boats and the bridge are drawn in with firm, linear architectural strokes. The complete avoidance of blacks and dark browns and the assertion of modulated hues in every part of the picture introduce a new world of light-and-color sensation. And even though distinctions are made among the textures of various elements of the landscape—sky, water, trees, architecture—all elements are united in their common statement as paint. The overt declaration of the actual physical texture of the paint itself, heavily brushed or laid on with a palette knife, derives from the broken paint of the Romantics, the heavily modeled impasto of Courbet, and the brush gestures of Manet. But now it has become an overriding concern with this group of young Impressionists. The point has been reached at which the painting ceases to be solely or even primarily an imitation of the elements of nature.

In this work, then, Impressionism can be seen not simply as the persistent surface appearance of natural objects but as a never-ending metamorphosis of sunlight and shadow, reflections on water, and patterns of clouds moving across the sky. This is the world as we actually see it: not a fixed, absolute perspective illusion in the eye of a frozen spectator within the limited frame of the picture window, but a thousand different glimpses of a constantly changing scene caught by a constantly moving eye.

Monet's intuitive grasp of the reality of visual experience becomes particularly evident when a work like *Boulevard des Capucines, Paris* (fig. **2.29**)—painted from an upstairs window in Nadar's former studio—is compared with contemporary photographs of a similar scene (fig. **2.30**; see fig. 2.5). Whereas both camera-made images show "cities of the dead," the one because its slow emulsion could record virtually no sign of life and the other because its speed froze every horse, wheel, and human in midmovement, Monet used his rapidly executed color spotting to express the dynamism of the bustling crowd and the flickering, light- and mist-suffused atmosphere of a wintry day, the whole perceived within an instant of time. Still, far from allowing his broken brushwork to dissolve all form, he so deliberated his strokes that simultaneously every patch of relatively pure hue represents a ray of light, a moment of perception, a molecule of atmosphere or form in space, and a tile within the mosaic structure of a surface design. With its decorative clustering of color touches, its firm orthogonals, and its oblique Japanese-style or photographic view, the picture is a statement of the artist's sovereign strength as a pictorial architect. Monet's is a view of modern Paris, for throughout the Second Empire Louis-Napoléon, through his Prefect of the Seine, Baron Georges-Eugène Haussmann, undertook a major program of urban renewal that called for the construction of wide boulevards and new

2.29 Claude Monet, *Boulevard des Capucines, Paris (Les Grands Boulevards)*, 1873–74. Oil on canvas, 31¼ × 23¼" (79.4 × 59.1 cm). The Nelson-Atkins Museum of Art, Kansas City, Missouri.

2.30 Edward Anthony, *A Rainy Day on Broadway, New York*, from the series *Anthony's Instantaneous Views*, 1859. One-half of a stereograph. International Museum of Photography at George Eastman House, Rochester, New York.

sewers, parks, and bridges. While the renovations generally improved circumstances for commerce, traffic, and tourism, they destroyed many of the narrow streets and small houses of old Paris. Life in these bustling new *grands boulevards,* and in the cafés and theaters that lined them, provided fertile subjects for the painters of modern life.

The artists associated with the Impressionist movement were a group of diverse individuals, all united by a common interest, but each intent on the exploration of his or her own separate path. **Auguste Renoir** (1841–1919) was essentially a figure painter who applied the principles of Impressionism in the creation of a lovely dream world that he then transported to the Paris of the late nineteenth century. *Moulin de la Galette* (fig. **2.31**), painted in 1876, epitomizes his most Impressionist moment, but it is an ethereal fairyland in contemporary dress. This scene of a commonplace afternoon Sunday dance in the picturesque Montmartre district of Paris is transformed into a color- and light-filled reverie of fair women and gallant men, who, in actuality, were the painters and writers of Renoir's acquaintance and the working-class women with whom they chatted and danced. The lights flicker and sway over the color shapes of the figures—blue, rose, and yellow— and details are blurred in a romantic haze of velvety brush- work that softens their forms and enhances their beauty. This painting and his many other comparable paintings of the period are so saturated with the sheer joy of a carefree life that it is difficult to recall the financial problems that Renoir, like Monet, was suffering during these years.

The art of the Impressionists was largely urban. Even the landscapes of Monet had the character of a Sunday in the country or a brief summer vacation. But this urban art commemorated a pattern of life in which the qualities of insouciance, charm, and good living were extolled in a manner equaled only by certain aspects of the eighteenth century. Now, however, the portrayal of the good life no longer involved the pastimes of the aristocracy but reflected the pleasures available even to poverty-stricken artists. But the moments of relaxation were relatively rare and spaced by long intervals of hard work and privation for those artists who, unlike Cézanne or Degas, were not blessed with a private income.

Though born into a family belonging to the *grande bourgeoisie,* **Edgar Degas** (1834–1917) was in fact far from financially secure, especially after the death of his father in 1874. He thought of himself as a draftsman in the tradition of Ingres, yet he seems to have had little inter- est in exhibiting at the Salon after the 1860s or in selling his works. On the contrary, he took an active part in the Impressionist exhibitions between 1874 and 1886, in which he showed his paintings regularly. But while associated with the Impressionists, Degas did not share their enthusi- asm for the world of the out-of-doors. Even his racehorse scenes of the late 1860s and early 1870s, which were open- air subjects, were painted in his studio. Though he pro- duced extraordinary landscapes in his color monotypes,

2.31 Auguste Renoir, *Moulin de la Galette*, 1876. Oil on canvas, 51½ × 69" (130.8 × 175.3 cm). Musée d'Orsay, Paris.

drawing horses and people remained Degas's primary interest, and his draftsmanship continued to be more precise than that of Manet's comparable racetrack subjects. This was particularly true in later works, where Degas became one of the first artists to exploit the new knowledge of animal movement recorded in the 1870s and 1880s by **Eadweard Muybridge** (1830–1904) and others in a series of stop-action photographs (figs. **2.32**, **2.33**). These images made forever obsolete the "rocking-horse"

pose—legs stretched forward and backward—long conventional in paintings of running beasts.

When Degas became really interested in light and color–light organization, an interest that arose from his enthusiasm for the world of the theater, the concert hall, and the ballet, he expressed it in terms of dramatic indoor effects. Theater and ballet gave him unequaled opportunities for the exercise of his brilliant skill as a draftsman, for the exploration of artificial light, and for creating an

2.32 Edgar Degas, *The Jockey*, 1889. Pastel on paper, 12½ × 19¼" (31.8 × 48.9 cm). Philadelphia Museum of Art.

2.33 Eadweard Muybridge, *Horse in Motion*, 1878. Wet-plate photographs.

essentially abstract organization from the costumes and motions of ballet dancers. Degas was a student and avid collector of Japanese prints and was strongly influenced by their patterns. He was also an accomplished photographer, and earlier than almost any other painter, he discovered how to use photography as a means for developing a fresh, original, even oblique vision of the world. The pastel *Ballerina and Lady with a Fan* (fig. **2.34**), for instance, could be a photographic fragment vividly translated into color, but what appears casually conceived is in fact precisely constructed. This dance scene, like many others

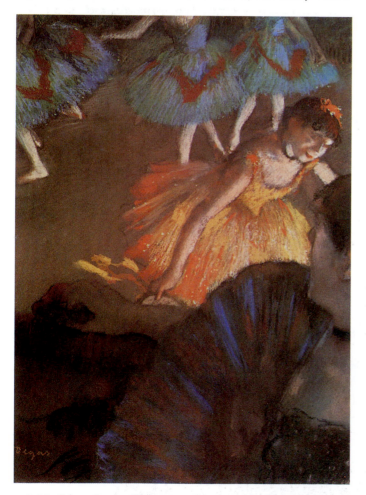

2.34 Edgar Degas, *Ballerina and Lady with a Fan*, 1885. Pastel on paper, 25⅛ × 19¼" (63.8 × 48.9 cm). Philadelphia Museum of Art.

created by Degas during the 1880s and 1890s, is presented from above, with the woman in the loge acting as the observer who, when our vantage point as viewers is taken into account, also becomes part of what is observed. The performers in blue in the background are abruptly decapitated and the bowing ballerina in the foreground is truncated from the knees down. The rhymes created between forms—the fan and the tutus, for example—and the juxtaposition of forms, such as the faces of the spectator and the foreground dancer, which are actually separated by considerable distance, are typical of the ingenious visual puns Degas made in these works to reinforce the essentially two-dimensional nature of the image. By concentrating on the members of the audience as well as the performers in many of his ballet pictures, Degas could exploit the social and psychological nuances of theater life, where seeing was as important as being seen.

In addition to being a skilled draftsman, painter, and photographer, Degas was also an accomplished printmaker and sculptor (see fig. 6.2). Increasingly, during the 1880s and 1890s, he employed these media to explore commonplace subjects: milliners in their shops; exhausted laundresses; women occupied with the everyday details of their toilet: bathing, combing their hair, dressing, or drying themselves after the bath. In a work like *The Tub* (fig. **2.35**) Degas goes beyond any of his predecessors in presenting the nude figure as part of an environment in which she fits with unconscious ease. Here the figure is beautiful in the easy, compact sculptural organization, but the routine character of her pose takes away any element of the erotic, while the bird's-eye view and the cutoff edges translate the photographic fragment into an abstract arrangement reminiscent of Japanese prints. When Degas exhibited this work among a group of similar pastels in the last Impressionist exhibition in 1886, many critics responded to them with descriptions, such as comparisons to animals, that betrayed a virulent but commonplace misogyny. In his unflattering, naturalistic depictions of women, Degas had failed to create the eroticized objects of desire that inhabited academic paintings of the nude and that were, as feminist art historians have pointed out, designed for consumption by a predominantly male audience. While

2.35 Edgar Degas, *The Tub*, 1886. Pastel on cardboard, 23⅝ × 32⅝" (60 × 82.9 cm). Musée d'Orsay, Paris.

Degas's pastels were destined for the same viewers, they transgress accepted norms of "femininity" and, in their monumental simplicity, are among the most moving treatments of the nude in modern art.

Two painters who showed regularly with the Impressionists and who identified strongly with the Manet–Degas orbit were the Frenchwoman **Berthe Morisot** (1841–95) and the American **Mary Cassatt** (1845–1926). Unlike her brother-in-law Manet, Morisot exhibited in all but one of the eight exhibitions organized by the Impressionists. Despite considerable success in her lifetime, the first retrospective of her work in the twentieth century did not take place until 1987. Morisot's subject of choice, like that of Cassatt, was modern domestic life, one arena of Parisian life to which these upper-class women could gain unrestricted access at a time when women were subject to severe limitations on their involvement in public life. They brought to their subjects an unsentimental detachment that male artists reserved for the street or the café. Morisot frequently employed her family members as models, as in *Hide and Seek* (fig. **2.36**), which portrays her sister Edma during a stroll in the country with her daughter. Morisot joined Monet and Renoir in banishing black from her palette and developed a unique style of sketchy, deftly applied strokes to realize scenes and figures as materializations of light and color. The Philadelphia-born Cassatt, who arrived in Paris with her wealthy family in 1866, had an almost Japanese love of line, but often used it with the painterly freedom of Manet and the high-keyed color of the plein-air Impressionists. In her skewed perspectives, intimate views, and photographic cropping, however, she was at one with Degas, her closest artistic associate (fig. **2.37**). Like Degas, she was a keen observer of the theatrical world, and she possessed a strong graphic sensibility which made her a highly successful printmaker. Like Morisot, Cassatt generally kept to mother-and-child subjects, but the sensuous immediacy and directness with which she treated them betrayed the daring modernity of her whole approach to art. Cassatt's elite social status

2.36 Berthe Morisot, *Hide and Seek*, 1873. Oil on canvas, 17¾ × 21¾" (45.1 × 55.2 cm). Collection Mrs. John Hay Whitney.

2.37 Mary Cassatt, *Little Girl in a Blue Armchair*, 1878. Oil on canvas, 35 × 51" (88.9 × 129.5 cm). National Gallery of Art, Washington, D.C.

permitted her to play the all-important role of taste-maker to American millionaires, whose acquisitions of Impressionist masterpieces helped to elevate standards of art appreciation in the United States, as well as establishing the foundations of the great collections of modern art now accessible in American museums.

By the mid-1880s, the Impressionists were undergoing a period of self-evaluation, which prompted Monet and his circle to move in various directions to renew their art once again, some by reconsidering aspects of traditional drawing and composition, others by enlarging or refining the premises on which they had been working. Foremost among the latter stood Monet, who remained true to direct visual experience, but with such intensity, concentration, and selection as to push his art toward antinaturalistic subject-

ivity and pure decorative abstraction. In series after series he withdrew from the urban and industrial world, once so excitingly consistent with the nine-teenth century's materialist concept of progress, and looked to unspoiled nature, as if to record its scenes quickly before science and technology could destroy them forever. Monet magnified his sensations of the individual detail perceived in an instant of time so that, instead of fragmenting large, complex views like that in *Boulevard des Capucines, Paris* (see fig. 2.29), he broke up simple, unified subjects—poplars, haystacks, the façade of Rouen Cathedral—into rep-resentations of successive moments of experience. Each, by its very nature, assumed a uniform tonality and texture that tended to reverse objective analysis into its opposite: subjective synthesis. In a long, final series, painted at his home at Giverny, in the French coun-tryside, Monet retired to an environment of his own cre-ation, a water garden, where he found a piece of the real world—a sheet of clear liquid afloat with lily pads and flow-ers, and reflections from the sky above—perfectly at one with his conception of the canvas as a flat, mirrorlike surface shimmering with an image of the world as a dynamic mate-rialization of light and atmosphere (fig. **2.38**). In these late, deeply pondered masterpieces, Monet's empirical interest in luminary phenomena had become a near-mystical obses-sion, its lyrical poetry often expressed in almost mono-chrome blue and mauve. As single, all-over, indivisible images, they also looked forward, from 1926, when the long-lived Monet died, to the late forties and fifties, the time of the New York Abstract Expressionists, who would produce a similarly "holistic" kind of painting, environmen-tal in its scale but now entirely abstract in its freedom from direct reference to the world outside (see fig. 19.10).

2.38 Claude Monet, *Les Nuages (Clouds)*, 1916–26. Oil on canvas, left panel of three, each panel 6'6¾" × 13'11⅜" (2 × 4.3 m). Musée de l'Orangerie, Paris.

Nineteenth-Century Art in the United States

At the opening of the twentieth century, American painting and sculpture, like their counterparts in Great Britain, lagged considerably behind the most progressive developments in continental Europe. American artists historically lacked the critical support systems of established art academies (therefore many studied abroad) and a tradition of government patronage. Despite the shortcomings of its art apparatus, American culture had sporadically generated major figures, such as Benjamin West (see fig. 1.12) and John Singleton Copley in colonial times, and the late nineteenth-century expatriates Whistler, Cassatt, and John Singer Sargent (see fig. 2.46), capable of holding their own in the European art capitals. After the Civil War Americans had proved vigorously original in architecture and through this medium (see chapter 4) had made a decisive contribution to the visual arts. But that promising start was brought to a halt by the same academic bias that had held so many painters and sculptors in thrall to outmoded aesthetics inherited from the classical and Romantic past. While the more self-assured and talented European artists grew strong through resistance to the tyrannical academy, Americans generally felt the need to master tradition rather than innovate against it. While the absence of such a tradition could lead artists into the pitfalls of provincialism, it also provided opportunities for greater freedom of expression. American artists were aware that, to progress in their art, it would be necessary to achieve their own artistic identity, assimilating influences from the generative centers in Europe until these had been transformed by authentic native sensibility into something independent and distinctive.

Early American Artists and the Hudson River School

Many American artists of the nineteenth century saw art as a means to define the American national character as a distinct quality. American history and culture seemed at this time to be curiously polarized between the material and the mystical. In the colonial period, and for some time after, Americans most consistently expressed their artistic personality in some form of Realism.

George Catlin (1796–1872) was particularly concerned with national identity, but in a manner quite apart from the landscapists of the Hudson River School (see below). He abandoned a successful practice as a portraitist for wealthy white patrons in Philadelphia to paint the individuals and culture of America's indigenous populations. For six years Catlin traveled west of the Mississippi, executing portraits and scenes of daily life among more than fifty Native American peoples. Then thought to be on the verge of extinction (due to aggressive government policies to "remove" them from United States territories), Native Americans were a source of tremendous curiosity for European Americans. Catlin presented his paintings,

together with actual costumes and artifacts, in a famous "Indian Gallery" that toured the United States and Europe, bringing images of an exotic world to audiences who felt nostalgia for the disappearance of America's native inhabitants while for the most part sanctioning their obliteration. Among Catlin's many paintings of tribal leaders is a striking portrait of the chief of the Blackfoot tribe, *Buffalo Bull's Back Fat* (fig. 2.39), which was shown in the Paris Salon of 1846 and admired by the poet and critic Charles Baudelaire. While Catlin's paintings stand as important ethnographic sources because of their accurate depictions of Native American dress and custom, they are also powerful examples of the art of portraiture.

The American taste for realism occasionally grew so obsessive in its concern for the integrity of palpable things that reality, once scientifically measured, delineated, or actually dissolved, entered the realm of the ideal, thereupon becoming a vehicle of feeling, intuition, or metaphysical meaning. This tendency is evident in the rivetingly precise portraiture of John Singleton Copley and in the almost magical illusionism of *Rubens Peale with a Geranium* (fig. 2.40), painted by **Rembrandt Peale** (1778–1860). Peale was the son of Charles Willson Peale, an enlightened man of many talents, chiefly interested in natural history and painting. Charles helped to found the Pennsylvania Academy of the Fine Arts in Philadelphia and headed an extraordinary family dynasty of artists. Like his father, Rembrandt (most of the seventeen children were

2.39 George Catlin, *Buffalo Bull's Back Fat, Head Chief, Blood Tribe*, 1832. Oil on canvas, 29 × 24" (73.7 × 61 cm). National Museum of American Art, Smithsonian Institution, Washington, D.C.

2.40 Rembrandt Peale, *Rubens Peale with a Geranium*, 1801. Oil on canvas, 28¼ × 24" (71.7 × 61 cm). National Gallery of Art, Washington, D.C.

2.41 William M. Harnett, *The Old Violin*, 1886. Oil on canvas, 38 × 24" (96.5 × 61 cm). National Gallery of Art, Washington, D.C.

2.42 Thomas Cole, *The Oxbow (The Connecticut River near Northampton)*, 1836. Oil on canvas, 4'3" × 6'4" (1.3 × 1.9 m). The Metropolitan Museum of Art, New York.

named after old-master painters or famous scientists) excelled at portraiture, though he also tried his hand at history painting. His touching and meticulous portrayal of his farsighted younger brother, a botanist who posed with what was purportedly the first geranium specimen to enter the country, is his greatest work. The two interests of the Peale family—science and art—are brought together in this freshly conceived composition, just as the two genres of still life and portraiture are seamlessly merged.

An obsessive concern with exactitude in American art, as a means of revealing the true nature of things, emerges dramatically in the *trompe-l'oeil* painters of the late nineteenth century, most notably John Frederick Peto (1854–1907) and **William Michael Harnett** (1848–92).

The latter's *The Old Violin* (fig. **2.41**) is a *tour de force* of verisimilitude, visual deception, and classical simplicity. While Harnett's still lifes delighted the public, nineteenth-century critics often condemned the work as old-fashioned illusionism bereft of elevating moral content. It was not until the thirties that Harnett's reputation was resurrected, when a taste for Surrealism and abstraction revised attitudes about his technical wizardry and highly structured formal organization. Harnett's examination of the nature of visual perception reemerged in the later twentieth century in the Superrealist art of Richard Estes and Duane Hanson (see Figs. 24.71, 24.76).

America's greatest artistic achievements in the mid-nineteenth century came in the development of a kind of landscape painting that merged elements of scientific Realism with idealized, even religious interpretations of nature that owed much to European Romanticism, notably the work of Turner (see fig. 1.18). This occurred particularly in the works of the so-called Hudson River School, a diverse group of artists (not a literal school or association) who worked in New England and upstate New York. For the most part, their landscapes presented the young American republic as a land of pristine wilderness which, by virtue of its majestic scale and untouched beauty, seemed suffused with divine presence. Artists thus invested landscape painting with moral meaning and used it as a vehicle for defining America's national identity as a new "Promised Land." *The Oxbow (The Connecticut River near Northampton)* (fig. **2.42**), an icon of American art that established a virtual formula for landscapes of the Hudson River School, was painted by its founder, **Thomas Cole** (1801–48). *The Oxbow* offers a vast panoramic view of a famous bend in the Connecticut River from a stormy promontory where, amid the rocks and tree trunks, Cole has depicted himself at his easel. Symbolically, the storm clouds at left have passed over the fertile, cultivated fields on the banks of the river, signs of a benign human presence in nature where dwell, according to Cole, "freedom's offspring—peace, security, and happiness." More than the artists who followed him, Cole expressed through his paintings serious doubts about the country's expansionist tendencies, which resulted in the destruction of wilderness as new frontiers were settled.

Cole's greatest protégé was **Frederic Edwin Church** (1826–1900), who reinforced his fine-art education by traveling extensively, mostly in North and South America, and by studying the theories of Alexander von Humboldt, a famous German naturalist who called for a "heroic landscape painting" that would bring scientific accuracy to the depiction of nature's grandest scenes. Church was a master of virtuoso, highly theatrical interpretations of those grand scenes, from volcanos in the Ecuadorian Andes to icebergs in the Arctic north. In *Twilight in the Wilderness* (fig. **2.43**), he translated a blazing sunset into a sublime vision of biblical proportions, implying, as had Cole, a spiritual, pantheistic view of nature. It has also been suggested,

2.43 Frederic E. Church, *Twilight in the Wilderness*, 1860. Oil on canvas, 40 × 64" (101.6 × 162.6 cm). The Cleveland Museum of Art.

however, that the fiery skies of the painting could portend the imminent conflagration of the Civil War. Though it is difficult to imagine in today's art world, *Twilight* caused a sensation when it, like Church's other masterpieces, was exhibited by itself in a New York gallery, where visitors paid an entrance fee to see the artist's newest creation.

Robert Scott Duncanson (1821–72), Church's contemporary, was from Cincinnati, where a thriving landscape tradition in the Hudson River School style had developed. Born into a poor family of free African-American tradespeople, Duncanson was a serious advocate of the abolitionist movement, frequently donating his work in support of antislavery causes. In the art of painting he was self-taught, though in nineteenth-century America this

was often the case with white artists as well (Cole, for example). Like his fellow painters in the East, Duncanson took the valleys and rivers of his own region as the subjects for his landscapes (fig. **2.44**). The tranquillity of mood in *Blue Hole, Flood Waters, Little Miami River* and the symmetrical organization of its composition suggest a classical vision of landscape in the manner of the seventeenth-century French artist Claude Lorrain.

By the end of the nineteenth century, the tight, descriptive style of the Hudson River School had been transformed in the hands of artists like **George Inness** (1825–94) into something more subjective and less dependent on the phenomena of the natural world (fig. **2.45**). An admirer of the French Barbizon painters, Inness painted unpretentious subjects in a highly poetic style far from the grandiose statements of Frederic Church. For him, nature is the domesticated landscape, rather than untamed wilderness, and it is filled with evocative atmosphere and soft harmonies of green and gold. The way in which formal concerns supersede the need for literal transcription in Inness's work has parallels with many American and European artists at the end of the nineteenth century, who were creating the foundation for twentieth-century abstraction.

New Styles and Techniques in Later Nineteenth-Century American Art

Whatever the developments in painting and sculpture back home, no artists had sensed the coming of the new more presciently than glamorous expatriates such as Whistler and Cassatt, whose histories belong within the context of their European contemporaries. Born to American parents living abroad, **John Singer Sargent** (1856–1925) also spent most of his career in Paris and London, though he received

2.44 Robert S. Duncanson, *Blue Hole, Flood Waters, Little Miami River*, 1851. Oil on canvas, 29¼ × 42¼" (74.3 × 107.3 cm). Cincinnati Art Museum.

2.45 George Inness, *Sundown*, 1894. Oil on fabric, 45 × 70" (114.3 × 177.8 cm). National Museum of American Art, Smithsonian Institution, Washington, D.C.

many portrait commissions from leading American families. His flashing, liquid stroke and flattering touch in portraiture made him one of the most famous and wealthy artists of his time. Moreover, in a major work like *Madame X* (fig. **2.46**) Sargent revealed himself almost mesmerized, like a latter-day Ingres (see fig. 1.13), by the abstract qualities of pure line and flat silhouette. At the same time, he so caught the explicit qualities of surface and inner character that the painting created a scandal when publicly shown at the Salon, for in addition to the figure's already décolleté dress, Sargent had placed the left-hand strap off her shoulder. To placate an offended public, he adjusted the strap as seen here after the Salon closed. The experience

prompted the artist to leave Paris eventually and establish his practice in London. In his most painterly works, meanwhile, Sargent carried gestural virtuosity, inspired by Frans Hals and Diego Velázquez, to levels of pictorial autonomy not exceeded before the advent of the Abstract Expressionists after World War II.

Americans who chose photography as their medium of expression stood out in the international Salons organized for exhibiting the new camera-made art, and indeed often won the major prizes and set the standards for both technical mastery and aesthetic vision. This will be seen in the images of Man Ray, Edward Steichen, Alfred Stieglitz, Paul Strand, and Edward Weston, reproduced in later chapters as examples of the best work of its kind. Meanwhile, Whistler, Cassatt, and Sargent also had their American peers in photography, principally **Gertrude Käsebier** (1852–1934) and Clarence H. White, both of whom worked in the Impressionist manner favored by many of the so-called Pictorialist photographers during the later nineteenth century (fig. **2.47**). Like Cassatt, Käsebier

2.46 John Singer Sargent, *Madame X (Mme Gautreau)*, 1884. Oil on canvas, 6'10⅛" × 3'7" (2.1 × 1.1 m). The Metropolitan Museum of Art, New York.

2.47 Gertrude Käsebier, *Blessed Art Thou Among Women*, c. 1900. Platinum print on Japanese tissue, 9⅜ × 5½" (23.8 × 13.9 cm). The Museum of Modern Art, New York.

2.48 Winslow Homer, *Prisoners from the Front*, 1866. Oil on canvas, 24 × 38" (61 × 96.5 cm). The Metropolitan Museum of Art, New York.

specialized in the mother-and-child theme, while White aligned himself with the elite social content of Sargent's portraiture and the Orientalizing aestheticism of Whistler's musical "arrangements." The camera offered an unparalleled capacity to render the reality so beloved by Americans, while it also could easily transform visual facts, as Käsebier and White did with their soft focus, and thus endow them with the special meaning characteristically sought by American artists.

More exclusively rooted in American experience than Whistler, Cassatt, and Sargent, and thus more representative of the point of departure for American art in the twentieth century, were **Winslow Homer** (1836–1910) and Thomas Eakins. As an illustrator for *Harper's Weekly* magazine in New York, Homer, a virtually self-taught artist, was assigned to the front during the Civil War. In his illustrations and in the oil paintings he began to make during the war, Homer tended to focus on the quiet moments of camp life rather than the high drama of battle. A landscape laid waste by those battles is the setting for the artist's greatest early work, *Prisoners from the Front* (fig. **2.48**). At the left, three Confederate soldiers—a disheveled youngster, an old man, and a defiant young officer—surrender to a Union officer at the right. Although Homer's painting represents a fairly unremarkable occurrence in the war, it achieves

the impact of history painting in the significance of its theme. His subtle characterization of the varying classes and types of the participants in the tragic conflict alludes to the tremendous difficulties to be faced during Reconstruction between these warring cultures.

In 1866 Homer traveled to Paris, where *Prisoners from the Front* was being exhibited. While he shared in the practice of plein-air painting and some of the subject matter of the Impressionists, Homer always insisted on the physical substance of things, rarely allowing paint to disintegrate form. Much of his mature work centered on the ocean, either breezy, sun-drenched watercolors made in the

2.49 Winslow Homer, *The Fox Hunt*, 1893. Oil on canvas, 38 × 68½" (96.5 × 174 cm). The Pennsylvania Academy of the Fine Arts, Philadelphia.

2.50 Thomas Eakins, *Max Schmitt in a Single Scull*, 1871. Oil on canvas, 32½ × 46¼" (82.6 × 117.5 cm). The Metropolitan Museum of Art, New York.

Caribbean or dramatic views of the human struggle with the high seas off the coast of Maine, where he settled in 1884. In *The Fox Hunt* (fig. **2.49**), the struggle between the forces of nature plays itself out in a haunting drama featuring a fox, weakened by the deprivations of winter, descended upon by hungry crows. The spareness of this striking composition, with its graceful silhouettes, cropped forms, and slanted perspectives, attests to Homer's sophisticated knowledge of *japonisme* as well as his ability to extract great emotional intensity from the simplest of scenes.

In his determination to fuse art and science for the sake of an uncompromising Realism in painting, the Philadelphia painter **Thomas Eakins** (1844–1916) all but revived the Renaissance tenets of Leonardo da Vinci. Not only did Eakins dissect cadavers right along with medical students (a traditional method of artistic training) and join Eadweard Muybridge in his studies of motion with stop-action photography (see fig. 2.33), especially those devoted to human movement, but he even had an assistant pose on a cross in full sunlight as the model for a Crucifixion scene and provided a nude male model for his female drawing students, a step that forced his resignation from the august Pennsylvania Academy of the Fine Arts. Eakins's extraordinary early painting *Max Schmitt in a Single Scull* (fig. **2.50**) was his first treatment of an outdoor subject. In the foreground the artist's friend, a celebrated oarsman, pauses

2.51 Thomas Eakins, *The Gross Clinic*, 1875. Oil on canvas, 8' × 6'6" (2.4 × 2 m). Jefferson Medical College of Thomas Jefferson University, Philadelphia.

momentarily while rowing on Philadelphia's Schuylkill River and looks toward the viewer; in the middle distance, Eakins has depicted himself midstroke, also looking at us. A crystalline light and carefully ordered composition lead us into this rational pictorial space, in which each detail is keenly observed and convincingly rendered. Eakins has here produced a Realism that transcends mere illusionism by way of a magical clarity, as if time were suspended in a single instant.

Eakins was arguably the greatest American portraitist of the nineteenth century, and his large painting *The Gross Clinic* (fig. **2.51**) is a masterpiece of the genre. The artist looked to the seventeenth-century precedent of Rembrandt's *Anatomy Lesson of Dr. Tulp* for his heroic portrayal of a distinguished surgeon performing an operation before his class. Like Max Schmitt, Dr. Gross looks up during a break in the action. In the midst of the dark, richly hued painting, light falls on his forehead, the intellectual focal point of the scene, and, even more dramatically, on

2.52 Henry Ossawa Tanner, *The Banjo Lesson*, 1893. Oil on canvas, 49 × 35½" (124.5 × 90.2 cm). Hampton University Museum, Hampton, Virginia.

the details of the surgery. The work is instructive for the ways in which artists can signify gender difference. The only female observer of the event, the mother of the patient, turns away in horror. Unlike the dispassionate male participants, she is overcome with emotion and reduced to a passive role, just as were the female members of the Horatii family in David's painting (see fig. 1.2).

Henry Ossawa Tanner (1859–1937) was an African-American artist who, by the end of the nineteenth century, had achieved significant international distinction. During the so-called Harlem Renaissance of the twenties, he was recognized as the most important black artist of his generation. Though he studied in Philadelphia with Eakins, whose portrait style profoundly influenced his own, Tanner found a more accepting atmosphere in his adopted city of Paris. He exhibited widely during his lifetime, including at the Paris Salon, and eventually befriended members of the avant-garde circle around Paul Gauguin in the rural artists' communities of Brittany. The French government awarded him the prestigious Légion d'honneur. Tanner's best-known work, *The Banjo Lesson* (fig. **2.52**), was probably made during a trip to Philadelphia, when he said he painted "mostly Negro subjects," a genre he felt had been stereotypically cast by white artists. With a loose weave of elongated strokes, Tanner softly defines the central pair of figures, bathing them in a light that imparts a spiritual stillness to the scene, a light not unlike that used in the many compositions of religious subjects that make up the bulk of Tanner's work. The painting overcomes the stereotypical treatment of banjo-playing, as entertainment for a white audience, and instead focuses on the passing on of a tradition.

In the art of **Albert Pinkham Ryder** (1847–1917) the sense of dream is utterly dominant, even in paintings so overloaded with the material substance of thick paint that, as the critic Lloyd Goodrich has written, "a tiny canvas weighs heavy in the hand." This was the product of years spent in a trial-and-error process of working and reworking a single picture, carried out by a painter who declared that "the artist should fear to become the slave of detail. He should strive to express his thought and not the surface of it. What avails a storm cloud accurate in form and color if the storm is not therein." The storm Ryder wanted was of the sort stirred up by the German composer Richard Wagner, whose sublimely Romantic music deeply touched the artist, as it did many of his contemporaries. Ryder, a solitary figure, was unfortunately a dangerously experimental technician, applying wet paint on wet paint and mixing his oils with what was probably bitumen, so that his pictures did not dry properly, but have gone on "ripening" until they have actually darkened and decayed, ironically destroying many of the exquisite nuances he had sought in endless modifications. What remains, however, tends to dramatize the extraordinary reductiveness of the final image (fig. **2.53**). With all detail refined away and the whole simplified to an arrangement of broad, dramatically contrasted shapes, a painting by Ryder often evokes the convoluted, emotional rhythms of Rubens and Delacroix as well as the Gothic, visionary world of German Expressionism. Little wonder that Ryder was featured in the famous 1913 Armory Show in New York as a progenitor of modernism, as well as the painter whom the young Jackson Pollock most admired among all his American pictorial forebears.

As for American sculpture during the later nineteenth century, it was nothing if not prolific, especially in public commissions. The expanding economy led to innumerable sculptural monuments and architectural decorations, though these mostly followed the academic traditions of Rome or Paris. **Augustus Saint-Gaudens** (1848–1907)

2.54 Augustus Saint-Gaudens, *Adams Memorial*, 1886–91. Bronze and granite, height 70" (177.8 cm). Rock Creek Cemetery, Washington, D.C.

2.53 Albert Pinkham Ryder, *Moonlight Marine*, c. 1890s. Oil on panel, 11⅜ × 12" (28.9 × 30.5 cm). The Metropolitan Museum of Art, New York.

received academic training in New York, Paris, and Rome, though, contrary to most nineteenth-century academic sculptors, European or American, he took fresh inspiration from sculptures of the Renaissance, notably those of Donatello. By infusing the classical tradition with his own brand of naturalism, Saint-Gaudens produced a number of first-rate portraits and could enliven the most banal of commemorative or allegorical sculptural monuments. But the request he received from the author Henry Adams to create a memorial to his late wife, who had committed suicide, presented challenges quite apart from the usual equestrian statue or portrait made from life (fig. **2.54**). The sculptor's inspired solution, stimulated by Adams's interest in Buddhism, was an austere, mysteriously draped figure that seems to personify a state of spiritual withdrawal from the physical world. With eyes downcast and a face shrouded in shadow, the sculpture constitutes an unforgettable image of eternal repose.

3
Post-Impressionism

So various and distinctive were the reactions against the largely sensory nature and supposed formlessness of Impressionism that the English critic Roger Fry, who was among the first to take a comprehensive look at these developments, could do no better than sum them up, in 1910, with the vague designation "Post-Impressionism." The inadequacy of the term is borne out by the fact that, unlike Impressionism, it did not become widely used until a quarter-century after the first appearance of the artistic phenomena it purported to describe. Among other things, it implies that Impressionism was itself a homogeneous style, when in fact it covered a highly diverse range of artistic sensibilities. In reality, the Post-Impressionists were schooled in Impressionism and many of them continued to respect its exponents and share much of their outlook. Cézanne, for example, who could not abide the paintings of Paul Gauguin, always admired the work of Monet. Gauguin, on the other hand, learned to paint in part from the Impressionist Pissarro and, like most of those in his circle, came to regard Cézanne as an almost legendary figure, even collecting his paintings. Yet both artists are considered key Post-Impressionists. Despite its shortcomings as a term, Post-Impressionism has become a convenient label for an innovative group of artists working in France in the late nineteenth and early twentieth centuries. And it does highlight the one element that Seurat, Cézanne, Gauguin, and Van Gogh all had in common—their determination to move beyond what they regarded as the relatively passive rendering of perceptual experience practiced by the Impressionists and to give expression to ideas and emotions.

By the 1880s numerous schisms and ideological differences had surfaced within the Impressionist ranks as the artists set about organizing their independent exhibitions. Renoir, Monet, and Degas, as we have seen, were all beginning to reconsider their painting in the light of their own altered consciousness. The Impressionists were far from mindless or uncritical portrayers of bourgeois ease and pastoral pleasures, as they have sometimes been called; these artists were all vibrantly in tune with their times and capable of highly subjective interpretations of their world. By the 1880s, that world had begun to change rapidly in ways that could only distress a Europe imbued with the nineteenth-century positivist belief in ever-accelerating progress driven by science and industry. Change was rapid indeed at this time, but not always progressive. As industrial waste combined with expanding commerce to destroy the unspoiled rivers and meadows so often painted by Monet, the master withdrew ever deeper into his "harem of flowers" at Giverny, a "natural" world of his own creation that was inextricably bound up with his late painting. As rising socioeconomic expectations throughout industrialized Europe met with conservative backlash, the clash of ideologies brought anarchist violence. As scientists broke down the theories of classical science, a new physics, chemistry, and psychology emerged. The radical philosopher Friedrich Nietzsche announced the death of God and sharply criticized the moral outlook associated with traditional religion. This in turn provoked new debates concerning the role of religion and religion-inspired morality. The most advanced artists of the period found little to satisfy their needs in the optimistic utilitarianism that had dominated Western civilization since the Enlightenment in the eighteenth century. Gradually, therefore, they abandoned the Realist tradition of Daumier, Courbet, and Manet (see chapter 2) that had opened such a rich vein of aesthetic exploration, culminating in the Impressionism of the 1870s. Instead, they sought to discover, or recover, a new and more complete reality, one that would encompass the inner world of mind and spirit as well as the outer world of physical substance and sensation.

Inevitably, this produced paintings that seemed even more shocking than Impressionism in their violation of both academic principles and the polished illusionism desired by eyes now thoroughly under the spell of photography. And so, just as Monet and Renoir were beginning to enjoy a measure of critical and financial success, the emerging painters who inspired the term Post-Impressionist reopened the gap—wider now than ever before—that

3.1 Georges Seurat, *A Sunday Afternoon on the Island of La Grande Jatte*, 1884–86. Oil on canvas, 6'9½" × 10'1¼" (2.1 × 3.1 m). The Art Institute of Chicago.

separated the world of avant-garde art from that of society at large. Whatever their differences, the Post-Impressionists all brought heightened tension and excitement to art by reweighting their values in favor of the ideal or romantic over the real, of symbol over sight, of the conceptual over the perceptual. Less and less were perception and its translation into art seen as an end unto themselves; rather, they became a means toward the knowledge of form in the service of expressive content. In arriving at the antinaturalism that followed, artists depended upon and counterbalanced the dualities of mind and spirit, thought and emotion.

The Poetic Science of Color: Seurat and the Neo-Impressionists

Trained in the academic tradition of the Paris École des Beaux-Arts, **Georges Seurat** (1859–91) was a devotee of classical Greek sculpture and of such classical masters as Piero della Francesca (see fig. 1.3), Poussin, and Ingres (see fig. 1.13). He also studied the drawings of Hans Holbein, Rembrandt, and Millet, and learned principles of mural design from the academic Symbolist Pierre Puvis de Chavannes (see fig. 3.13). He early became fascinated by theories and principles of color organization, which he studied in the writings and paintings of Delacroix, the texts

of the critics Charles Blanc and David Sutter, and the scientific treatises of Michel-Eugène Chevreul, Ogden Rood, and Charles Henry. These researches in optics, aesthetics, and color theory studied, among other phenomena, the ways in which colors affect one another when placed side by side. According to Chevreul, for example, each color will impose its own complementary on its neighbor: if red is placed next to blue, the red will cast a green tint on the blue, altering it to a greenish blue, while the blue imposes a pale orange on the red. Although the rational, scientific basis for such theories appealed to Seurat, he was no cold, methodical theorist. His highly personal form of expression evolved through careful experiments with his craft. Working with his younger friend Paul Signac he sought to combine the color experiments of the Impressionists with the classical structure inherited from the Renaissance, employing the latest concepts of pictorial space, traditional illusionistic perspective depth, and recent scientific discoveries in the perception of color and light.

It is astonishing that Seurat produced such a body of masterpieces in so short a life (he died at thirty-one in a diphtheria epidemic). His greatest work, and one of the landmarks of modern art, is *A Sunday Afternoon on the Island of La Grande Jatte* (fig. **3.1**). Known as *La Grande Jatte*, it was the most notorious painting shown in the last of the eight Impressionist exhibitions, in 1886. Seurat worked for over a year on this monumental painting, preparing it with twenty-seven preliminary drawings (fig. **3.2**) and thirty color sketches. Seurat's hauntingly beautiful conté crayon drawings reveal his interest in masters of black and white from Rembrandt to Goya. He avoided lines to define contours and depended instead on shading to achieve soft, penumbral effects. In the preparatory works for *La Grande Jatte*, ranging from studies of individual figures to oils that laid in most of the final composition, Seurat analyzed, in meticulous detail, every color relationship and every aspect of pictorial space. His unique color system was based on the Impressionists' intuitive realization that all nature was color, not neutral tone. But the Impressionist painters had generally made no organized, scientific effort to achieve their remarkable optical effects. Their technique involved the placement of pure, unblended colors in close conjunction on the canvas, which are actually perceived by the eye as glowing, vibrating patterns of mixed color. This effect appears in many paintings by Monet, as anyone realizes who has stood close to one of his works, first experiencing it simply as a pattern of discrete color strokes, and then moving gradually away from it to observe all the elements of the scene come into focus.

Building on Impressionism and scientific studies of optical phenomena, Seurat constructed his canvases with an overall pattern of small, dotlike brushstrokes of generally

3.2 Georges Seurat, *The Couple*, study for *La Grande Jatte*, 1884. Conté crayon on paper; 12¼ × 9¼" (31.1 × 23.5 cm). The British Museum, London.

complementary colors—red and green, violet and yellow, blue and orange—and with white. Various names have been given to Seurat's method, including Divisionism (Seurat's own term), Pointillism, and Neo-Impressionism. Despite their apparent uniformity overall, on close inspection the "dots" vary greatly in size and shape and are laid down over areas where color has been brushed in more broadly. The intricate mosaic produced by Seurat's painstaking technique is analogous to the actual medium of mosaic; its glowing depth of luminosity gives an added dimension to color experience. Unfortunately, some of the pigments he used were unstable, and in less than a decade oranges had turned to brown and brilliant emerald green had dulled to olive, reducing somewhat the original chromatic impact of the painting.

In *La Grande Jatte* Seurat began with a simple contemporary scene of middle-class Parisians relaxing along the banks of the Seine River. What drew him most strongly to the particular scene, perhaps, was the manner in which the figures could be arranged in diminishing perspective along the banks of the river, although delightful inconsistencies in scale abound throughout the composition. At this point in the picture's evolution the artist was concerned as much with the recreation of a fifteenth-century exercise in linear perspective as with the creation of a unifying pattern of surface color dots. Broad contrasting areas of shadow and light, each built of a thousand minute strokes of juxtaposed color-dot complementaries, carry the eye from the foreground into the beautifully realized background. Certainly, Seurat was here attempting to reconcile the classical tradition of Renaissance perspective painting with a modern interest in light, color, and pattern. The immense size of the canvas gives it something of the impact of a Renaissance fresco, and is especially dramatic since it is composed of brushstrokes smaller than a pea. The painting's scale also shows avant-garde art asserting its status relative to the academic tradition (and thus, paradoxically, developing a new "grand tradition" of its own).

More important in the painting than depth or surface pattern is the magical atmosphere that the artist was able to create from the abstract patterns of the figures. The art historian Meyer Schapiro notes that Seurat depicts "a society at rest and, in accord with his own art, it is a society that enjoys the world in pure contemplation and calm." Seurat's figures are like those of a mural by Piero della Francesca in their quality of mystery and of isolation. By placing the figures in strict profile or frontal views, he flattens their forms and endows them with the immobility of stage flats, producing a static atmosphere critics have often described as "Egyptian." In the accumulation of commonplace details, which are filled with amusing vignettes of social caricature, there is an effect of poetry that makes of the whole a profoundly moving experience. Seurat's paintings anticipate not only the abstraction of Piet Mondrian but also the strange Surrealist stillness and space of Giorgio de Chirico and René Magritte (see fig. 15.31). The most

3.3 Georges Seurat, Study for *Le Chahut*, 1889. Oil on canvas, 21⅞ × 18⅜" (55.6 × 46.7 cm). Albright-Knox Art Gallery, Buffalo.

scientific and objective of all the painters of his time is, curiously, also one of the most poetic and mysterious.

In a preparatory oil for a later painting, such as the study for *Le Chahut* (fig. **3.3**), the color dots are so large that the figures and their spatial environment are dissolved in color patterns that cling to the surface of the picture. The painting depicts a provocative and acrobatic dance, then popular in Parisian cafés, which Seurat beautifully orchestrates into a series of decorative rhythms, giving form to a then-current theory that ascending lines induce feelings of gaiety in the viewer. For his imagery Seurat was clearly inspired by the colorful posters that were placed around Paris to advertise the dance halls. Around the study for *Le Chahut* he painted a border of multicolored strokes (as he had for *La*

Grande Jatte) and he probably painted the wooden frame around the work as well. Van Gogh and Gauguin also expressed interest in the way their works were framed, preferring solutions much simpler than the ornate, gilded frames usually placed on their paintings.

Seurat's chief colleague and disciple was **Paul Signac** (1863–1935), who strictly followed the precepts of Neo-Impressionism in his landscapes and portraits. Like his colleagues, Signac regarded his revolutionary artistic style as a form of expression parallel to his radical political anarchism. This movement was closely associated with other Neo-Impressionists in France and Belgium who believed that only through absolute creative freedom could art help to bring about social change. In his later, highly coloristic seascapes, Signac provided a transition between Neo-Impressionism and the Fauvism of Henri Matisse and his followers (see chapter 7). And through his book, *D'Eugène Delacroix au Néo-impressionisme,* he was also the chief propagandist and historian of the movement. His portrait of the critic Félix Fénéon (fig. **3.4**), who had been the first to use the term Neo-Impressionism, is a fascinating example of the decorative formalism that the artists around Seurat favored. The painting, with its spectacular spiral background inspired by patterns Signac had found in a Japanese print, contains private references to the critic's ideas and to those of the color theorist Charles Henry, with which Signac was very familiar.

In the hands of other painters, Seurat's Neo-Impressionist technique too often declined into a decorative formula for use in narrative exposition. This was also the fate of Impressionism; as it gradually became accepted and then, much later, immensely popular throughout the world, its color and light, quotidian subjects, radical

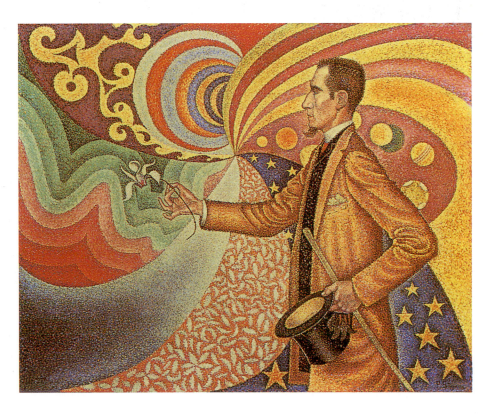

3.4 Paul Signac, *Opus 217. Against the Enamel of a Background Rhythmic with Beats and Angles, Tones and Tints, Portrait of M. Félix Fénéon in 1890,* 1890. Oil on canvas, 29⅛ × 36½" (73.5 × 92.5 cm). Private collection.

cropping, and photographic immediacy—initially so shocking—were all too quickly discovered to be charming, endearing, and capable of every kind of vulgarization. Seurat's Neo-Impressionism, on the other hand, affected not only Fauvism and certain aspects of Cubism in the early twentieth century, but also some Art Nouveau painters and designers.

Form and Nature: Paul Cézanne

Of all the nineteenth-century painters who might be considered prophets of twentieth-century experiment, the most significant was **Paul Cézanne** (1839–1906). Cézanne struggled throughout his life to express in paint his ideas about the nature of art, ideas that were among the most revolutionary in the history of art. Son of a well-to-do merchant turned banker in Aix-en-Provence in southern France, he had to resist parental disapproval to embark on his career, but once having won the battle, unlike Monet or Gauguin, he did not need to struggle for mere financial survival. As we view the splendid control and serenity of his mature paintings (two qualities that, in particular, became touchstones for modernist art), it is difficult to realize that he was an isolated, socially awkward man of a sometimes violent disposition. This aspect of his character is evident in some of his early mythological figure scenes, which were baroque in their movement and excitement. At the same time he was a serious student of the art of the past, who studied the masters in the Louvre, from Paolo Veronese to Poussin to Delacroix.

Early Career and Relation to Impressionism

Cézanne's unusual combination of logic and emotion, of reason and unreason, represented the synthesis that he sought in his paintings. Outside of Degas, the Impressionists in the 1870s largely abandoned traditional drawing in an effort to communicate a key visual phenomenon—that objects in nature are not seen as separated from one another by defined contours. In their desire to realize the observed world through color, with both the objects themselves and the spaces between them rendered in terms of color intervals, they tended to destroy objects as three-dimensional entities existing in three-dimensional space. Instead they recreated solids and voids as color shapes functioning within a limited depth. Because it did not make a clear distinction between three-dimensional mass (objects) and three-dimensional depth (spaces), Impressionism was criticized as formless and insubstantial. Even Renoir felt compelled to restudy the drawing of the Renaissance in order to recapture some of that "form" which Impressionism was said to have lost. And Seurat, Gauguin, and Van Gogh, each in his own way, consciously or unconsciously, was seeking a kind of expression based on, but different from, that of the Impressionists.

Certainly, Cézanne's conviction that Impressionism ignored qualities of Western painting that had been important since the Renaissance prompted his oft-quoted (and frequently misunderstood) remark that he wanted to "make of Impressionism something solid like the art of the museums." By this he clearly did not mean to imitate the old masters. He realized, quite correctly, that artists like Veronese or Poussin had created in their paintings a world that was similar to but quite distinct from the world in which they lived—that painting, resulting from the artist's various experience, created a separate reality in itself. It was this kind of reality, the reality of the painting that was neither a direct reflection of life, like a photograph, nor a completely separate entity, which Cézanne sought in his own work. And he felt progressively that his sources must be nature and the objects of the world in which he lived, rather than stories or myths from the past. For this reason he expressed his desire "to do Poussin over again from nature."

Cézanne arrived at his mature position only after long and painful thought, study, and struggle with his medium. Late in his life, the theoretical position that he tried to express in his idiosyncratic language was probably achieved more through the discoveries he made painting from nature than through his studies in museums. In the art of the museum he found corroboration of what he already instinctively knew. In fact, the art of his mature landscapes is in many ways anticipated by such an early work as *Uncle Dominic as a Monk*, which depicts his mother's brother in the white habit of the Dominican order. The sources in Manet and Courbet are evident, but the personality revealed by the portrait—the forceful temperament of the artist himself—is different from that in the work of either predecessor. Modeled out from the blue-gray ground in sculptured paint laid on in heavy strokes with the palette knife, the painting is not so much a specific portrait as a study of passion held in restraint. It exemplifies Cézanne's use of the matrix of paint to create a unified pictorial structure, a characteristic of all his work.

Throughout the 1860s, Cézanne exorcised his own inner conflict in scenes of murder and rape and, around 1870, he attempted his own *Déjeuner sur l'herbe* in a strange, heavy-handed variant on Manet's painting. After his exposure to the Impressionists, he returned to the violence of these essays in his *Battle of Love* (fig. **3.5**), a curious recasting of the classic theme of the bacchanal. Here he has moved away from the somber tonality and sculptural modeling of the 1860s into an approximation of the light blue, green, and white of the Impressionists. Nevertheless, this painting is remote from Impressionism in its subject and effect. The artist subdues his greens with grays and blacks, and expresses an obsession with the sexual ferocity he is portraying that is notably different from the stately bacchanals of Titian and even more intense than the comparable scenes of Rubens. At this stage he is still exploring the problem of integrating figures or objects and surrounding space. The figures are clearly outlined, and thus exist sculpturally in space. However, their broken contours,

3.5 Paul Cézanne, *Battle of Love*, c. 1880. Oil on canvas, 14⅞ × 18¼" (37.8 × 46.2 cm). National Gallery of Art, Washington, D.C.

sometimes seemingly independent of the cream-color area of their flesh, begin to dissolve solids and integrate figures with the shaped clouds that, in an advancing background, reiterate the carnal struggles of the bacchanal.

In the 1880s all of Cézanne's ideas of nature and painting came into focus in a magnificent series of landscapes, still lifes, and portraits. During most of this period he was living at Aix, largely isolated from the Parisian art world. *The Bay from L'Estaque* (fig. **3.6**) is today so familiar from countless reproductions that it is difficult to realize how revolutionary it was at the time. Viewed from the hills above the red-tiled houses of the village of L'Estaque and looking toward the Bay of Marseilles, the scene does not recede into a perspective of infinity in the Renaissance or Baroque manner. Buildings in the foreground are massed close to the spectator and presented as simplified cubes with the side elevation brightly lit. They assert their fluctuating identity, both as frontal color shapes parallel to the picture plane and as the walls of buildings at right angles to it. The buildings and intervening trees are composed in ocher, yellow, orange-red, and green, with little

differentiation as objects recede from the eye. Cézanne once explained to a friend that sunlight cannot be "reproduced," but that it must be "represented" by some other means. That means was color. He wished to recreate nature with color, feeling that drawing was a consequence of the correct use of color. In *The Bay from L'Estaque*, contours are the meeting of two areas of color. Since these colors vary substantially in value contrasts or in hue, their edges are perfectly defined. However, the nature of the definition tends to allow color planes to slide or "pass" into one another, thus to join and unify surface and depth, rather than to separate them in the manner of traditional outline drawing. The composition of this painting reveals Cézanne's intuitive realization that the eye takes in a scene both consecutively and simultaneously, with profound implications for construction of the painting and for the future of modern painting.

The middle distance of *The Bay from L'Estaque* is the bay itself, an intense area of dense but varied blue stretching from one side of the canvas to the other and built up of meticulously blended brushstrokes. Behind this is the

3.6 Paul Cézanne, *The Bay from L'Estaque*, c. 1885. Oil on canvas, 31½ × 39⅝" (80 × 100.6 cm). The Art Institute of Chicago.

curving horizontal range of the hills and, above these, the lighter, softer blue of the sky, with only the faintest touches of rose. The abrupt manner in which the artist cuts off his space at the sides of the painting has the effect of denying the illusion of recession in depth. The blue of the bay asserts itself even more strongly than the ochers and reds of the foreground, with the result that space becomes both ambiguous and homogeneous. The painting must be read simultaneously as a panorama in depth and as an arrangement of color shapes on the surface.

Even at the end of his life, Cézanne never had any desire to abandon nature entirely. When he spoke of "the cone, the cylinder, and the sphere" he was not thinking of these geometric shapes as the end result, the final abstraction into which he wanted to translate the landscape or the still life, as has sometimes been assumed. Abstraction for him was a method of stripping off the visual irrelevancies of nature in order to begin rebuilding the natural scene as an independent painting. Thus the end result was easily recognizable from the original motif, as photographs of Cézanne's sites have proved, but it is essentially different: the painting is a parallel but distinct and unique reality.

Later Career

Few artists in history have devoted themselves as intently as Cézanne to the separate themes of landscape, portrait,

and still life. It is important to understand that to him these subjects involved similar problems. In all of them he was concerned with the recreation, the realization, of the scene, the object, or the person. The fascination of the still life for Cézanne, as for generations of painters before him and after, lies in the fact that its subject is controllable as no landscape or portrait sitter can possibly be. In *Still Life with Basket of Apples* (fig. **3.7**), he carefully arranged the wine bottle and tilted basket of apples, scattered the other apples casually over the tablecloth, and placed the plate of biscuits at the back of the table, thus setting up the relationships between these elements on which the final painting would be based. The apple obsessed Cézanne as a three-dimensional form that was difficult to control as a distinct object and to assimilate into the larger unity of the canvas. To attain this goal and at the same time to preserve the nature of the individual object, he modulated the circular forms with small, flat brushstrokes, distorted the shapes, and loosened or broke the contours to set up spatial tensions among the objects and unify them as color areas. By tilting the wine bottle out of the vertical, flattening and distorting the perspective of the plate, or changing the direction of the table edge under the cloth, Cézanne was able, while maintaining the appearance of actual objects, to concentrate on the relations and tensions existing among them. As Roger Fry observed, the subtleties through which Cézanne

3.7 Paul Cézanne, *Still Life with Basket of Apples*, c. 1895. Oil on canvas, 24⅜ × 31" (61.9 × 78.7 cm). The Art Institute of Chicago.

gained his final result "still outrange our pictorial apprehension." However, we can comprehend that he was one of the great constructors and colorists in the history of painting, one of the most penetrating observers, and one of the most subtle minds.

Cézanne's figure studies, such as the various versions of *The Card Players* (fig. **3.8**), remind one in their massive, closed architecture of his paintings of quarries. The artist brings great solemnity to this genre subject by his grandly balanced composition, by the amplitude of the figures, who solidly occupy their space, and by discarding the usual narratives included in older paintings on this theme, such as the card-shark subjects of Caravaggio. Although the sitters were local farmhands with whom the artist was

probably long acquainted, there is little sense of particularized portraiture in *The Card Players*.

Cézanne usually relied on friends or family members as models, most frequently his patient wife, Hortense Fiquet, but for *Boy in a Red Waistcoat* (fig. **3.9**) he hired a young

3.9 Paul Cézanne, *Boy in a Red Waistcoat*, 1888–95. Oil on canvas, 35¼ × 28¾" (89.5 × 73 cm). National Gallery of Art, Washington, D.C.

3.8 Paul Cézanne, *The Card Players*, 1890–92. Oil on canvas, 25¾ × 32¼" (65.4 × 81.9 cm). The Metropolitan Museum of Art, New York.

Italian boy as a model. During a residence in Paris between 1888 and 1890, he painted four portraits of the seemingly melancholy boy in the same white shirt, blue cravat, and brilliant red waistcoat. Only in this composition, however, did the artist situate his subject frontally, to maximize the relaxed contrapposto of the boy's lanky torso. He is centered against a large swag of drapery so variegated by patches of color that its local hue is indeterminate. The painting is constructed as much by its network of broken lines as by the all-over tessellation of its flat, planar strokes. At the same time that the lines contour forms and endow them with an unmistakable fullness, they also intersect and continue from edge to edge, across figure and ground alike, thereby integrating the whole of the field into a kind of asymmetrical armature. A similar equilibrium of volume and plane occurs in the brushwork, where the squarish, "constructive" strokes build up forms while articulating the surface as a mosaic pattern of translucent, painterly slabs.

After 1890 Cézanne's brushstrokes became larger and more abstractly expressive, the contours more broken and dissolved, with color floating across the canvas, sustaining its own identity independent of the objects it defined. These tendencies were to lead to the wonderfully free paintings done at the very end of the artist's life, of which

Mont Sainte-Victoire Seen from Les Lauves of 1902–6 is one of the supreme examples (fig. **3.10**). Here the brushwork acts the part of the individual musician in a superbly integrated symphony orchestra. Each stroke exists fully in its own right, but each is nevertheless subordinated to the harmony of the whole. This is both a structured and a lyrical painting, one in which the artist has achieved the integration of structure and color, of nature and painting. It belongs to the great tradition of Renaissance and Baroque landscape, seen, however, as an infinite accumulation of individual perceptions. These are analyzed by the painter into their abstract components and then reconstructed into the new reality of the painting.

To the end of his life, Cézanne held fast to his dream of remaking Poussin after nature, continuously struggling with the problem of how to pose classically or heroically nude figures in an open landscape. For the largest canvas he ever worked, Cézanne painted as Poussin had done—that is, from his imagination—and relied on his years of plein-air experience to evoke Impressionist freshness. *The Large Bathers* (fig. **3.11**), in many ways the culmination of thirty years of experiment with the subject of female bathers in an outdoor setting, was painted the year of Cézanne's death and is unfinished. In it the artist subsumed the fierce

3.10 Paul Cézanne, *Mont Sainte-Victoire Seen from Les Lauves*, 1902–6. Oil on canvas, 25½ × 32" (64.8 × 81.3 cm). Collection Mrs. Louis C. Madeira, Gladwyne, Pennsylvania.

3.11 Paul Cézanne, *The Large Bathers*, 1906. Oil on canvas, 6'10" × 8'2" (2.1 × 2.5 m). Philadelphia Museum of Art.

emotions expressed in the earlier *Battle of Love* (see fig. 3.5) within the grandeur of his total conception. Thus, while the figures have been so formalized as to seem part of the overall pictorial architecture, their erotic potential now charges the scene. It can be sensed as much in the high-vaulted trees as in the sensuous, shimmering beauty of the brushwork, with its unifying touches of rosy flesh tones and earthy ochers scattered throughout the delicate blue-green haze of sky and foliage. *The Large Bathers,* in its miraculous integration of linear structure and painterly freedom, of form and color, of eye and idea, provided the touchstone model for Fauves and Cubists alike, as well as the immediate antecedent for such landmark, yet disparate paintings as Matisse's *Bonheur de vivre* (see fig. 7.6) and Picasso's *Les Demoiselles d'Avignon* (see fig. 10.6).

A Visual Language of the Heart and Soul: Symbolism

The formulation of modern art at the end of the nineteenth century involved not only a search for new forms but also a search for new content and new principles of picture-making. This search was meaningful in itself; it was not simply a continuation of outworn clichés taken from antiquity, French history, or mythology. It became, as we

shall see, a conscious program in Gauguin's paintings, first in the small artists' colony of Pont-Aven in Brittany and later in the South Seas. In both places the subjects he pursued were those of the Romantic tradition: the exotic, the otherworldly, the mystical. In this, Gauguin and the artists who were associated with him at Pont-Aven and later at Le Pouldu in Brittany, as well as very different painters like Odilon Redon and Gustave Moreau, were affected by the Symbolist spirit.

Symbolism in literature and the visual arts was a popular—if radical—movement of the late nineteenth century, a direct descendant of the Romanticism of the eighteenth and the early nineteenth centuries that stemmed from a reaction against Realism in art and against materialism in life. In literature, its founders were mainly poets: Charles Baudelaire and Gérard de Nerval; the leaders at the close of the century were Jean Moréas, Stéphane Mallarmé, and Paul Verlaine. In music, the German Richard Wagner was a great force and influence, as was Claude Debussy the outstanding French master. Baudelaire had defined Romanticism as "neither a choice of subjects nor exact truth, but a mode of feeling"—something found within rather than outside the individual—"intimacy, spirituality, color, aspiration toward the infinite." Symbolism arose from the intuitive ideas of the Romantics; it was an approach to an ultimate reality, a pure essence that transcended particular physical experience. The belief that the work of art should spring from the emotions, from the inner spirit of the artist rather than representing observed nature, dominated the attitudes of the Symbolist artists and was to recur continually in the philosophies of twentieth-century Expressionists, Dadaists, Surrealists, and even of Mondrian and other makers of abstract art.

For the Symbolists the reality of the inner idea, of the dream or symbol, was paramount, but could be expressed only obliquely, as a series of images or analogies out of which the final revelation might emerge. Symbolism led some poets and painters back to organized religion, some to mysticism and arcane religious cults, and others to aesthetic creeds that were essentially antireligious. During the 1880s, at the moment when artists were pursuing the idea of the dream, Sigmund Freud was beginning the studies that were to lead to his theories of the significance of dreams and the subconscious. In the visual arts Symbolism was manifested in a diverse range of styles. Paul Gauguin, one of the movement's leading exponents, sought in his paintings what he termed a "synthesis of form and color derived from the observation of the dominant element." He advised a fellow painter not to "copy nature too much. Art is an abstraction; derive this abstraction from nature while dreaming before it, but think more of creating than the actual result."

In these statements may be found many of the concepts of twentieth-century experimental painting, from the idea of color used arbitrarily rather than to describe an object visually, to the primacy of the creative act, to painting as abstraction. Gauguin's ideas, which he called "Synthetism," involved a synthesis of subject and idea with form and color, so that his paintings are given their mystery, their visionary quality, by their abstract color patterns.

Symbolism in painting—the search for new forms, anti-naturalistic if necessary, to express a new content based on emotion (rather than intellect or objective observation), intuition, and the idea beyond appearance—may be interpreted broadly to include most of the experimental artists who succeeded the Impressionists and opposed their artistic goals. The Symbolist movement, while centered in France, was international in scope and had adherents in America, Belgium, England, and elsewhere in Europe. These artists had a common concern with problems of personal expression and pictorial structure. They were anticipated, inspired, and abetted by two older academic masters—Gustave Moreau and Pierre Puvis de Chavannes—and also by Odilon Redon, an artist born into the generation of the Impressionists who attained his artistic maturity much later than his exact contemporaries.

Moreau and the Fin-de-Siècle

Gustave Moreau (1826–98) was appointed professor at the École des Beaux-Arts in 1892 and displayed remarkable talents as a teacher. His students included Henri

Matisse and Georges Rouault, as well as others who were to be dubbed the Fauves, or "wild beasts," of early modern painting. Inspired by Romantic painters such as Delacroix, Moreau's art exemplified the spirit of the *mal-du-siècle,* an end-of-the-century tendency toward profound melancholy or soul sickness, often expressed in art and literature through decadent and morbid subject matter. In several compositions around 1876, Moreau interpreted the biblical subject of Salomé, the young princess who danced for her stepfather Herod, demanding in return the execution of Saint John the Baptist. The bloody head of the saint appears in Moreau's painting as if called forth in a grotesque hallucination (fig. **3.12**). He conveys his subject with meticulous draftsmanship and an obsessive profusion of exotic detail combined with jewellike color and rich paint texture.

Moreau's spangled, languidly voluptuous art did much to glamorize decadence in the form of the *femme fatale*, or "fatal woman." The concept of woman as an erotic and destructive force was fostered by Baudelaire's great poems *Les Fleurs du Mal (The Flowers of Evil)* (1857) and the mid-century pessimistic philosophy of Arthur Schopenhauer. Among scores of male artists in the last decades of the nineteenth century, Salomé frequently served as the archetype of a castrating female who embodied all that is debased,

3.12 Gustave Moreau, *The Apparition,* c. 1876. Oil on canvas, 21¼ × 17½" (54 × 44.5 cm). Fogg Art Museum, Harvard University Art Museums, Cambridge, Massachusetts.

sexually predatory, and perverse. The *femme fatale* also played a central role in the work of such composers as Wagner and Richard Strauss, writers including Gustave Flaubert, Joris-Karl Huysmans (who admired Moreau's painting enormously), Stéphane Mallarmé, Oscar Wilde, and Marcel Proust, and a great number of artists, ranging from Rossetti and Moreau to such *fin-de-siècle* figures as Redon, Aubrey Beardsley, Edvard Munch, and Gustav Klimt. Moreover, the deadly temptress thrived well into the twentieth century, as she resurfaced in Picasso's *Les Demoiselles d'Avignon*, (see fig. 10.6), the paintings and drawings of Egon Schiele, and the *amour fou* ("mad love") art of the Surrealists (see chapter 15).

Although **Pierre Puvis de Chavannes** (1824–98), with his simple, naive spirit, bleached colors, and near-archaic handling, would seem to have stood at the opposite pole from the elaborate, hothouse art of Moreau, the two painters were alike in a certain academicism and in the curious attraction this held for the younger generation. In Puvis, the reasons for such an anomaly can be readily discerned in his mural painting *Summer* (fig. 3.13). The allegorical subject and its narrative treatment are highly traditional, but the organization in large, flat, subdued color areas, and the manner in which the plane of the wall is respected and even asserted, embodied a compelling truth in the minds of artists who were searching for a new idealism in painting. Although the abstract qualities of the mural are particularly apparent to us today, the classical withdrawal of the figures—as still and quiet as those in Piero della Francesca and Seurat—transforms them into emblems of that inner light which the Symbolists extolled.

Symbolism in painting found one of its earliest and most characteristic exponents in **Odilon Redon** (1840–1916), called the "prince of mysterious dreams" by the critic and novelist Huysmans. His artistic roots were in nineteenth-century Romanticism, while his progeny was the twentieth-century Surrealists. Redon felt Impressionism lacked the ambiguity that he sought in his art, and though he

frequently found his subjects in the study of nature, at times observed under the microscope, they were transformed in his hands into beautiful or monstrous fantasies.

Redon studied for a time in Paris with the painter Jean-Léon Gérôme, but he was not temperamentally suited to the rigors of academic training. He suffered from periodic depression—what he called his "habitual state of melancholy"—and much of his early work stems from memories of an unhappy childhood in and around Bordeaux, in southwest France. Like Seurat, Redon was a great colorist who also excelled at composing in black and white, and the first twenty years of his career were devoted almost exclusively to monochrome drawing, etching, and lithography, works he referred to as his "*noirs*," or works in black. His activity in printmaking contributed to the rise in popularity of etching in the 1860s, prompted in part by a new appreciation in France of Rembrandt's prints, which Redon especially admired for their expressive effects of light and shadow. Redon studied etching with Rodolphe Bresdin, a strange and solitary artist who created a graphic world of meticulously detailed fantasy based on the work of the northern European masters Dürer and Rembrandt. Redon later found a closer affinity with the graphics of Francisco Goya, the greatest printmaker of the early nineteenth century (see fig. 1.14). Redon himself became one of the modern masters of the medium of lithography, in which he invented a world of dreams and nightmares based not only on the examples of past artists but also on his close and scientific study of anatomy.

Redon's own predilection for fantasy and the macabre drew him naturally into the orbit of Delacroix, Baudelaire, and the Romantics. In his drawings and lithographs, where he pushed his rich, velvety blacks to extreme limits of expression, he developed and refined the fantasies of Bresdin in nightmare visions of monsters, or tragic-romantic themes taken from mythology or literature. Redon was close to the Symbolist poets and was almost the only artist who was successful in translating their words into visual equivalences. He dedicated a portfolio of his lithographs to Edgar Allan Poe, whose works had been translated by Baudelaire and Mallarmé, and he created three series of lithographs inspired by Gustave Flaubert's *Temptation of St. Anthony*, a novel that achieved cult status among Symbolist writers and artists in the 1880s. Huysmans reviewed Redon's exhibitions enthusiastically at the same time that he was himself moving away from Émile Zola's naturalism and into the Symbolist stream with his novel of artistic decadence *Against the Grain*, in which he discussed at length the art of Redon and of Gustave Moreau.

After 1890, Redon began to work seriously in color, almost immediately demonstrating a capacity for exquisite, original harmonies, in both oil and pastel, that changed the character of his art from the macabre and the somber to the joyous and brilliant. Gone are the nightmarish visions of previous decades, replaced by a new enthusiasm for religious and mythological subjects. Yet in *Roger and*

3.13 Pierre Puvis de Chavannes, *Summer*, 1891. Oil on canvas, 4'11" × 7'7½" (1.5 × 2.3 m). The Cleveland Museum of Art.

3.14 Odilon Redon, *Roger and Angelica*, c. 1910. Pastel on paper on canvas, 36½ × 28¾" (92.7 × 73 cm). The Museum of Modern Art, New York.

Angelica (fig. **3.14**), the subject—the rescue of Angelica by the hero Roger, based on a Renaissance poem—seems almost incidental. We can hardly decipher the two tiny figures, Roger on a winged horselike hippogriff, at left, and Angelica at right, naked and chained to a rock. They are lost amid clouds of brilliant, amorphous color, where nothing is fixed in space and everything is subsumed in an atmosphere of overpowering sensuality.

The Naive Art of Henri Rousseau

Although **Henri Rousseau** (1844–1910) was actually four years older than Paul Gauguin, his name tends to be linked with a younger generation of artists, including Picasso and Robert Delaunay, because of the remarkable artistic circles with which he associated, sometimes unwittingly, in Paris. Though Rousseau shared many formal concerns with his Post-Impressionist contemporaries, such as Gauguin and Seurat, he is often regarded as a phenomenon apart from them, for he worked in isolation, admired the academic painters they abhorred, and was "discovered" by several younger avant-garde artists. In its rejection of traditional illusionism and search for a poetic, highly personalized imagery, his work partakes of concerns held by many Symbolist artists at the end of the century. For younger artists, however, his work chimed with their

growing interest in "primitive" art—whether the prehistoric or folk art of Europe or the art of other cultures and peoples whose works were untouched by what they saw as the dead hand of Western academic tradition.

In 1893, Rousseau retired from a full-time position as an inspector at a municipal toll station in Paris. He is known as the "Douanier" because he was thought to have been a customs inspector, one of many myths about this self-taught painter. Once he turned his full energies to painting, Rousseau seems to have developed a native ability into a sophisticated technique and an artistic vision that, despite its ingenuousness, was not without aesthetic sincerity or self-awareness.

Rousseau was a fascinating mixture of naïvety, innocence, and wisdom. Seemingly humorless, he combined a strange imagination with a way of seeing that was magical, sharp, and direct. In 1886, he exhibited his first painting, *Carnival Evening* (fig. **3.15**), at the Salon des Indépendants. The black silhouettes of the trees and house are drawn in painstaking detail—the accretive approach typically used by self-taught painters. Color throughout is low-keyed, as befits a night scene, but the lighted bank of clouds beneath the dark sky creates a sense of clear, wintry moonlight, as do the two tiny figures in carnival costumes in the foreground, who glow with an inner light. Despite the laboriously worked surface and the naïvety of his drawing, the artist fills his painting with poetry and a sense of dreamy unreality.

By 1890 Rousseau had exhibited some twenty paintings at the Salon des Indépendants. His work had achieved a certain public notoriety, due to the constant mockery it endured in the press, but it also increasingly excited the interest of serious artists and such important writers as the poet and playwright Alfred Jarry and, somewhat later, Guillaume Apollinaire. Redon had already seen something unique in the art of Rousseau, and during the 1890s his admirers included Degas, Henri de Toulouse-Lautrec, and even Renoir. Despite such recognition, Rousseau never made a significant living from his painting and spent most of his post-retirement years in desperate poverty. His self-portrait, entitled *Myself: Portrait Landscape*, extols the great 1889 Exposition Universelle in Paris and shows the Eiffel Tower, a hot-air balloon, a flag-decked ship, and an iron bridge over the Seine, the Pont des Arts. In the foreground stands the bearded artist, dressed in black and with a black beret. He holds his brush and palette, inscribed with the names of his past and present wives. Rousseau, whose confidence in his own talent bordered on the delusional, unabashedly presents himself as a master of modern painting.

With painstaking care and deliberation, Rousseau continually painted and drew scenes of Paris, still lifes, portraits of his friends and neighbors, and details of plants, leaves, and animals. His romantic passion for jungles filled with strange terror and beauty recurred in several of his best-known canvases. While such subjects had precedents in Salon painting, Rousseau's tropical paintings are worlds away from the clichéd academic scenes of North Africa or other exotic locales. Yet to the end of his life Rousseau continued his uncritical admiration for the Salon painters, particularly for the technical finish of their works. *The Sleeping Gypsy* (fig. 3.16) is one of the most entrancing and magical paintings in modern art. By this time he could create mood through a few elements, broadly conceived but meticulously rendered. The composition has a curiously abstract quality (the mandolin and bottle foretell Cubist studio props; see figs. 10.17, 10.26), but the tone is overpoweringly strange and eerie—a vast and lonely landscape framing a mysterious scene. In this work, as in others, Rousseau expressed qualities of strangeness that were unvoiced, inexpressible rather than apparent, anticipating the standard vocabulary of the Surrealists. This painting was lost for years until it was rediscovered in 1923 in a coal dealer's shop by Louis Vauxcelles, the art critic who had created the term "Fauves." In fact, it has been suggested that the term, meaning "wild beast," occurred to Vauxcelles because one of Rousseau's jungle paintings was exhibited very near the works of Matisse and his colleagues at the notorious 1905 Salon d'Automne (see chapter 7).

3.15 Henri Rousseau, *Carnival Evening*, 1886. Oil on canvas, 46 × 35⅛" (116.8 × 89.2 cm). Philadelphia Museum of Art.

3.16 Henri Rousseau, *The Sleeping Gypsy*, 1897. Oil on canvas, 4'3" × 6'7" (1.3 × 2 m). The Museum of Modern Art, New York.

The last series painted by Rousseau, and the acme of his vision, also present scenes of the jungle. The animals and plants he observed in the Paris Zoo and Botanical Garden were transformed in his paintings into scenes of tropical mystery. The setting in each is a mass of broad-leaved jungle foliage, gorgeous orchids, exotic fruits, and curious animals peering out of the underbrush. The climax of such scenes is *The Dream* of 1910, Rousseau's last great work, painted not long before he died. In the midst of a wildly abundant jungle, with its wide-eyed lions, brilliant birds, pale moon, and dark-skinned flute player, a nude woman rests incongruously on a splendid Victorian sofa. Rousseau's charmingly simple explanation of this improbable creation was that the woman on the couch dreamed herself transported to the midst of the jungle.

During his later years, Rousseau became something of a celebrity for the new generation of artists and critics. He held regular musical soirées at his studio. In 1908 Picasso, discovering a portrait of a woman by Rousseau at a junk shop (though he no doubt knew Rousseau's work already), purchased it for five francs and gave a large party for him in his studio, a party that has gone down in the history of modern painting. It was half intended as a joke on the innocent old painter, who took himself so seriously as an artist, but more an affectionate tribute to a naive man recognized to be a genius. In 1910, the year of his death, Rousseau's first solo exhibition was held in New York at Alfred Stieglitz's Gallery 291, thanks to the efforts of the young American painter Max Weber (see fig. 18.12), who had befriended Rousseau in Paris.

Innocence and Experience: Gauguin and Van Gogh

Gauguin

Paul Gauguin (1848–1903) was unquestionably the most powerful and influential artist to be associated with the Symbolist movement. But while he became intimate with Symbolist poets, especially Mallarmé, and enjoyed their support, Gauguin deplored the literary content and traditional form of such artists as Moreau and Puvis. He also rejected the optical naturalism of the Impressionists, while initially retaining their rainbow palette and then vastly extending its potential for purely decorative effects. For Gauguin, art was an abstraction to be dreamed in the presence of nature, not an illustration but a synthesis of natural forms reinvented imaginatively. His purpose in creating such an anti-Realist art was to express invisible, subjective meanings and emotions. He attempted to free himself from the corrupting sophistication of the modern industrial world, and renew his spirit by contact with an innocence and sense of mystery that he sought in nonindustrial societies. He constantly described painting in terms of an analogy with music, of color harmonies, of color and lines as forms of abstract expression. In his search he was attracted, to a greater degree even than most of his generation, to so-called "primitive" art. In his art we find the origins of modern primitivism, the desire to discard the accumulation of Western culture and the results of industrialization and urbanization. Gauguin turned away from these corrupt forces to what were regarded as the elemental verities of "primitive" societies, whether the religious art of Breton peasants in northwest France or the traditions of the Maori peoples in Polynesia. By establishing contact with supposedly "uncivilized" cultures, so the myth went, the enlightened artist could be in touch with the primitive side of his or her own nature and express it through art. Of course, such notions were forged at a time when European countries were aggressively colonizing the very societies Western artists sought to emulate.

In searching for the life of a "savage," no French artist traveled farther from the reaches of Western urban life than Gauguin. He has become, sometimes to the detriment of a serious consideration of his art, a romantic symbol, the personification of the artist as rebel against society. After years of wandering, first in the merchant marine, then in the French navy, he settled down, in 1871, to a prosaic but successful life as a stockbroker in Paris, married a Danish woman, and had five children. For the next twelve years the only oddity in his respectable, bourgeois existence was the fact that he began painting, first as a hobby and then with increasing seriousness. He even managed to show a painting in the Salon of 1876 and to exhibit in four Impressionist exhibitions from 1879 to 1882. He lost his job, probably due to a stock-market crash, and by 1886, after several years of family conflict and attempts at new starts in Rouen and Copenhagen, he had largely severed his family ties, isolated himself, and become involved with the Impressionists.

Gauguin had spent the early years of his childhood in Peru, and he seems almost always to have had a nostalgia for far-off, exotic places. This feeling ultimately crystallized in the conviction that his salvation, and perhaps that of all contemporary artists, lay in abandoning modern civilization to return to some simpler, more elemental pattern of life. From 1886 to 1891 he moved between Paris and the Breton villages of Pont-Aven and Le Pouldu, with a seven-month interlude in Panama and Martinique in 1887 and a tempestuous but productive visit with Van Gogh in Arles the following year. In 1891 he sailed for Tahiti, returning to France for two years in 1893 before settling in the South Seas for good. His final trip, in the wake of years of illness and suffering, was to the island of Hivaoa in the Marquesas Islands, where he died in 1903.

The earliest picture in which Gauguin fully realized his revolutionary ideas is *Vision after the Sermon*, painted in 1888 in Pont-Aven (fig. 3.17). This is a startling and pivotal work, a pattern of red, blue, black, and white tied together by curving, sinuous lines and depicting a Breton peasant's biblical vision of Jacob wrestling with the Angel. The innovations used here were destined to affect the ideas

3.17 Paul Gauguin, *Vision after the Sermon*, 1888. Oil on canvas, 28¾ × 36¼" (73 × 92.1 cm). National Gallery of Scotland, Edinburgh.

of younger groups such as the Nabis and the Fauves. Perhaps the greatest single departure is the arbitrary use of color in the dominating red field within which the protagonists struggle, their forms borrowed from a Japanese print. Gauguin has here constricted his space to such an extent that the dominant red of the background visually thrusts itself forward beyond the closely viewed heads of the peasants in the foreground. Though the brilliant red hue may have been stimulated by his memory of a local religious celebration which included fireworks and bonfires in the fields, this painting was one of the first complete statements of color as an expressive end in itself.

From the beginning of his life as an artist, Gauguin did not restrict himself to painting. He carved sculptures in marble and wood and learned the rudiments of ceramics to become one of the most innovative ceramicists of the century. (It is a feature of modern art in general that artists, including Picasso, Matisse, and many others, have been less constrained by the boundaries between the academic disciplines of painting and sculpture, or between so-called fine-art and craft practice, than artists of earlier post-Renaissance generations.) By the late 1880s Gauguin had ventured into printmaking, another medium to which he brought all his experimental genius. One of his most enigmatic works, made in Brittany during an especially

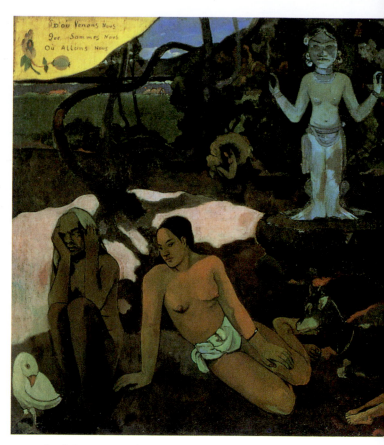

3.19 Paul Gauguin, *Where Do We Come From? What Are We? Where Are We Going?* 1897–98. Oil on canvas, 4'6¾" × 12'3" (1.4 × 3.7 m). Museum of Fine Arts, Boston.

3.18 Paul Gauguin, *Be in Love and You Will Be Happy,* 1889. Painted wood relief, 37½ × 28½" (95.3 × 72.4 cm). Museum of Fine Arts, Boston.

despondent period for the artist, is a wooden panel that he carved in low relief, painted, and titled with the cynical admonition *Be in Love and You Will Be Happy* (fig. **3.18**). Here a woman, "whom a demon takes by the hand," faces the forces of temptation, symbolized in part by a small fox. Such themes, the struggle between knowledge and innocence, good and evil, life and death, recur in Gauguin's Tahitian compositions. Among the faces in the relief, the one with its thumb in its mouth, at the upper right, is the artist himself.

Gauguin was disappointed, upon his arrival in Tahiti, to discover how extensively Western missionaries and colonials had encroached upon native life. The capital of Papeete was filled with French government officials, and the beautiful Tahitian women often covered themselves in ankle-length missionary dresses. Nor was the island filled with the indigenous carvings of ancient gods Gauguin had hoped for, so he set about making his own idols, based in part on Egyptian and Buddhist sculptures he knew from photographs. One such invention can be seen at the left in his grand, philosophical painting *Where Do We Come From? What Are We? Where Are We Going?* (fig. **3.19**). Over twelve feet (3.5 m) long, this is the most ambitious painting of Gauguin's career. It presents a summation of his Polynesian imagery, filled with Tahitians of all ages situated at ease within a terrestrial paradise devoid of any sign of European civilization. "It's not a canvas done like a Puvis de Chavannes," Gauguin said, "with studies from nature, then preliminary cartoons etc. It is all dashed off with the tip of the brush, on burlap full of knots and wrinkles, so that its appearance is terribly rough." The multiple forms and deep spaces of this complex composition are tied together by its overall tonalities in green and blue. It was this element—color—that the artist called "a mysterious language, a language of the dream."

Van Gogh

Whereas Gauguin was an iconoclast, caustic in speech, cynical, indifferent, and at times brutal to others, **Vincent van Gogh** (1853–90) was filled with a spirit of enthusiasm for his fellow artists and overwhelming love for humanity. This love had led him, after a short-lived experience as an art dealer and an attempt to follow theological studies, to become a lay preacher in a Belgian coal-mining area. There he first began to draw in 1880. After study in Brussels, the Hague, and Antwerp, he went to Paris in 1886, where he met Toulouse-Lautrec, Seurat, Signac, and Gauguin, as well as members of the original Impressionist group.

In his early drawings, Van Gogh revealed his roots in traditional Dutch landscape, portrait, and genre painting, using the same perspective structures, and depicting the broad fields and low-hanging skies that the seventeenth-century artists had loved. Van Gogh never abandoned perspective even in later years, when he developed a style with great emphasis on the linear movement of paint over the surface of the canvas. For him—and this is already apparent in his early drawings—landscape itself had an expressive, emotional significance.

After his exposure to the Impressionists in Paris, Van Gogh changed and lightened his palette. Indeed, he discovered his deepest single love in color—brilliant, unmodulated color—which in his hands took on a character radically different from the color of the Impressionists. Even when he used Impressionist techniques, the peculiar intensity of his vision gave the result a specific and individual quality that could never be mistaken.

The passion in Van Gogh's art arose from his intense, overpowering response to the world in which he lived and to the people whom he knew. His mental troubles are, though not well understood, a famous part of his larger-than-life reputation as it developed during the twentieth century. Such episodes as the incident in which he sliced off part of his ear during Gauguin's visit have overshadowed a reasoned understanding of his work. More than any other artist, Van Gogh has come to typify the figure of the lone artist-genius, spurned and misunderstood by society. This legend is only partly borne out by the more complex reality of his life and work. Van Gogh may have suffered from a neurological disorder, perhaps a severe form of epilepsy, that was no doubt exacerbated by physical ailments and excessive drinking. He was prone to depression and suffered acutely during seizures, but he painted during long periods of lucidity, bringing tremendous intelligence and imagination to his work. His letters to his brother Theo, an art dealer who tried in vain to find a market for Vincent's work, are among the most moving

3.20 Vincent van Gogh, *The Night Café*, 1888. Oil on canvas, 27½ × 35" (69.9 × 88.9 cm). Yale University Art Gallery, New Haven.

and informative narratives by an artist that we have. They reveal his wide knowledge of art and literature, and a highly sensitive perception that is fully equal to his emotional response. He was sharply aware of the extraordinary effects he was achieving through his expressive use of color. "Instead of trying to reproduce exactly what I have before my eyes, I use color more arbitrarily," he wrote, "in order to express myself forcibly." Echoing the Symbolist ideas of Gauguin, Van Gogh told Theo that he "was trying to exaggerate the essential and to leave the obvious vague."

Van Gogh could also present the darker side of existence. Thus, of *The Night Café* (fig. **3.20**) he says: "I have tried to express the terrible passions of humanity by means of red and green." *The Night Café* is a nightmare of deep-green ceiling, blood-red walls, and discordant greens of furniture. The perspective of the brilliant yellow floor is tilted so precipitously that the contents of the room threaten to slide toward the viewer. The result is a terrifying experience of claustrophobic compression that anticipates the Surrealist explorations of fantastic perspective, none of which has ever quite matched it in emotive force.

Vincent van Gogh carried on the great Netherlandish tradition of portraiture, from his first essays in drawing to his last self-portraits, painted a few months before his suicide in 1890. The intense *Self-Portrait* from 1888 was made in Arles and was dedicated to Gauguin (fig. **3.21**). It formed part of an exchange of self-portraits among Van Gogh's artist friends to support his notion of an ideal

3.21 Vincent van Gogh, *Self-Portrait*, 1888. Oil on canvas, 24½ × 20½" (62.2 × 52.1 cm). Fogg Art Museum, Harvard University Art Museums, Cambridge, Massachusetts.

brotherhood of painters. The beautifully sculptured head (which Van Gogh said resembled that of a Buddhist monk) and the solidly modeled torso are silhouetted against a vibrant field of linear rhythms painted, according to the artist, in "pale malachite." The coloristic and rhythmic integration of all parts, the careful progression of emphases, from head to torso to background, all demonstrate an artist in superb control of his plastic means. "In a picture," he wrote to Theo, "I want to say something comforting as music. I want to paint men and women with that something of the eternal which the halo used to symbolize, and which we seek to give by the actual radiance and vibration of our colorings."

The universe of Van Gogh is forever stated in *The Starry Night* (fig. **3.22**). This work was painted in June 1889 at the sanatorium of Saint-Rémy, in southern France, where he had been taken after his second breakdown. The color is predominantly blue and violet, pulsating with the scintillating yellow of the stars. *The Starry Night* is both an intimate and a vast landscape, seen from a high vantage point in the manner of the sixteenth-century landscapist Pieter Brueghel the Elder. In fact, the peaceful village, with its prominent church spire, is a remembrance of a Dutch rather than a French town. The great poplar tree in the foreground shudders before our eyes, while above whirl and explode all the stars and planets of the universe. Van Gogh was intrigued by the idea of painting a nocturnal landscape from his imagination. Scholars have tried to explain the content of the painting through literature, astronomy, and religion. Though their studies have shed light on Van Gogh's interests, none has tapped a definitive source that accounts for the astonishing impact of this painting, which today ranks among the most famous works of art ever made. When we think of expressionism in painting, we tend to associate with it a bravura brush gesture, arising from the spontaneous or intuitive act of expression and independent of rational processes of thought or precise technique. The anomaly of Van Gogh's paintings is that they are supernatural or at least extrasensory experiences evoked with a touch as meticulous as though the artist were painfully and exactly copying what he was observing before his eyes.

A New Generation of Prophets: The Nabis

Neo-Impressionism, the quasi-scientific handling of color created by Seurat and Signac, made its appearance in 1884, when a number of artists who were to be associated with the movement exhibited together at the Groupe des Artistes Indépendants in Paris. Later that year the Société des Artistes Indépendants was organized through the

3.22 Vincent van Gogh, *The Starry Night*, 1889. Oil on canvas, 29 × 36¼" (73.7 × 92.1 cm). The Museum of Modern Art, New York.

efforts of Seurat, Henri-Edmond Cross, Redon, and others, and was to become important to the advancement of early twentieth-century art as an exhibition forum. Also important were the exhibitions of Les XX (Les Vingt, or "The Twenty") in Brussels. Van Gogh, Gauguin, Toulouse-Lautrec, and Cézanne exhibited at both the Indépendants and Les XX. James Ensor, Henry van de Velde, and Jan Toorop exhibited regularly at Les XX and its successor, La Libre Esthétique, whose shows became increasingly dominated first by the attitudes of the Neo-Impressionists and then by the Nabis.

The Nabis, who took their name from the Hebrew word for "prophet," were a somewhat eclectic group of artists whose principal contributions—with some outstanding exceptions—lay in a synthesizing approach to masters of the earlier generation, not only to Seurat but also to Cézanne, Redon, and Gauguin, particularly the last, for his art theory as well as the direct example of his painting.

Gauguin had been affected by the ideas of his young friend Émile Bernard when the two were working together in Pont-Aven in the summer of 1888. He may well have derived important elements of his style from Bernard's notion of *cloisonnisme,* a style based on medieval enamel and stained-glass techniques, in which flat areas of color are bounded by dark, emphatic contours. Certainly, the arbitrary, nondescriptive color, the flat areas bounded by linear patterns, the denial of depth and sculptural modeling—all stated by Gauguin in *Vision after the Sermon* (see fig. 3.17)—were congenial to and influential for the Nabis as well as for Art Nouveau decoration (see chapter 5).

Paul Sérusier (1863–1927), one of the young artists under Gauguin's spell at Pont-Aven, experienced something of an epiphany when the older master undertook to demonstrate his method during a painting session in a picturesque wood known as the Bois d'Amour: "How do you see these trees?" Gauguin asked. "They are yellow. Well then, put down yellow. And that shadow is rather blue. Render it with pure ultramarine. Those red leaves? Use vermilion." This permitted the mesmerized Sérusier to paint a tiny work on a cigar-box lid (fig. **3.23**), which proved so daring in form, even verging on pure abstraction, that the artist and his friends thought it virtually alive with supernatural power. And so they entitled the painting *The Talisman* and dubbed themselves the "Nabis." The group

included Sérusier, Maurice Denis, Pierre Bonnard, Paul Ranson, and later Aristide Maillol, Édouard Vuillard, Félix Vallotton, Ker-Xavier Roussel, and Armand Séguin. The Nabis were artists of varying abilities, but included three outstanding talents: Bonnard, Vuillard, and Maillol.

The Nabis were symptomatic of the various interests and enthusiasms of the end of the century. Among these were literary tendencies toward organized theory and elaborate celebrations of mystical rituals. Denis and Sérusier wrote extensively on the theory of modern painting; and Denis was responsible for the formulation of the famous phrase, "a picture—before being a warhorse, a female nude, or some anecdote—is essentially a flat surface covered with colors assembled in a particular order." The Nabis sought a synthesis of all the arts through continual activity in architectural painting, the design of glass and decorative screens, book illustration, poster design, and stage design for the advanced theater of Ibsen, Maurice Maeterlinck, Strindberg, Wilde, and notably for Alfred Jarry's shocking satirical farce *Ubu Roi* (King Ubu).

La Revue Blanche, a magazine founded in 1891, became one of the chief organs of expression for Symbolist writers and painters, Nabis, and other artists of the avant-garde. Bonnard, Vuillard, Denis, Vallotton, and Toulouse-Lautrec (who was never officially a Nabi, although associated with

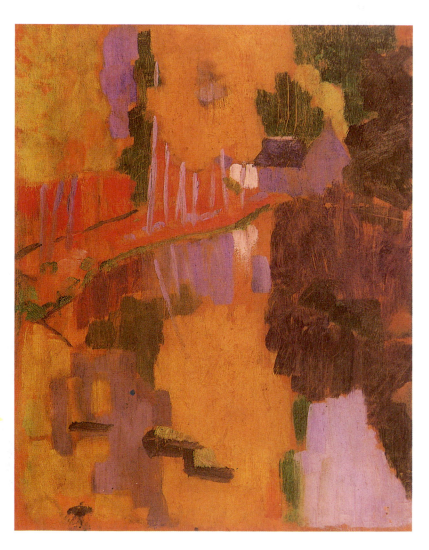

3.23 Paul Sérusier, *The Talisman (Landscape of the Bois d'Amour),* 1888. Oil on wood cigar-box cover, 10½ × 8⅜" (26.7 × 21.3 cm). Private collection.

the group) all made posters and illustrations for *La Revue Blanche*. The magazine was a meeting ground for experimental artists and writers from every part of Europe, including Van de Velde, Edvard Munch, Marcel Proust, André Gide, Ibsen, Strindberg, Wilde, Maxim Gorky, and Filippo Marinetti.

Vuillard and Bonnard

The Nabis produced two painters of genius, Édouard Vuillard (1868–1940) and Pierre Bonnard, whose long working lives linked the art of *fin-de-siècle* France to the mid-twentieth century. Both were much admired; their reputations, however, were for a long time private rather than public. Their world is an intimate one, consisting of corners of the studio, the living room, the familiar view from the window, and portraits of family and close friends. In his early works Vuillard used the broken paint and small brushstroke of Seurat or Signac, but without their rigorous scientific methods. In *Woman in Blue with Child* (fig. **3.24**) he portrayed the Parisian apartment of Thadée Natanson, cofounder of *La Revue Blanche*, and his famously beautiful and talented wife, Misia, who is depicted in the painting playing with her niece. As was often his practice, Vuillard probably used his own photograph of the apartment as an *aide-mémoire* while working up his composition. It is a typical turn-of-the-century interior, sumptuously decorated with flowered wallpaper, figured upholstery, and ornaments. In Vuillard's hands, the interior became a dazzling surface pattern of muted blues, reds, and yellows, comparable to a Persian painting in its harmonious richness. Space may be indicated by the tilted perspective of the chaise longue and the angled folds of the standing screen, but the forms of the woman and child are flattened so as to be virtually indistinguishable from the surrounding profusion of patterns. Such quiet scenes of Parisian middle-class domesticity have been called "*intimiste*"; in them, the flat jigsaw puzzle of conflicting patterns generates shimmering afterimages that seem to draw from everyday life an ineffable sense of strangeness and magic.

Of all the Nabis, **Pierre Bonnard** (1867–1947) was the closest to Vuillard, and the two men remained friends until the latter's death. Like Vuillard, Bonnard lived a quiet and unobtrusive life, but whereas Vuillard stayed a bachelor, Bonnard early became attached to a young woman whom he ultimately married in 1925. It is she who appears in so many of his paintings, as a nude bathing or combing her hair, or as a shadowy but ever-present figure seated at the breakfast table, appearing at the window, or boating on the Seine.

After receiving training both in the law and in the fine arts, Bonnard soon gained a reputation making lithographs, posters, and illustrated books. His most important early influences were the work of Gauguin and Japanese prints. The impact of the latter can be seen in his adaptation of the *japoniste* approach to the tilted spaces and

3.24 Édouard Vuillard, *Woman in Blue with Child*, c. 1899. Oil on cardboard, 19⅛ × 22¼"
(48.6 × 56.5 cm). Glasgow Art Gallery and Museum, Kelvingrove.

3.25 Pierre Bonnard, *Promenade of the Nursemaids, Frieze of Fiacres*, 1899. Color lithograph on four panels, each 54 × 18¾" (137.2 × 47.6 cm). The Museum of Modern Art, New York.

3.26 Pierre Bonnard, *Nu à contre jour (Nude against the Light)*, 1908. Oil on canvas, 49 × 42½" (124.5 × 108 cm). Musées Royaux des Beaux-Arts de Belgique, Brussels.

decorative linear rhythms of his paintings. But from the beginning Bonnard also evinced a love of paint texture. This led him from the relatively subdued palette of his early works to the full luminosity of high-keyed color rendered in fragmented brushstrokes, a development that may well owe something to both the late works of Monet and the Fauve paintings of Matisse.

The large folding screen *Promenade of the Nursemaids, Frieze of Fiacres* (fig. **3.25**) is made of four lithographs, based on a similarly painted screen. With its tilted perspectives and abbreviated, silhouetted forms, it shows Bonnard at his most *japoniste* and decorative. At the same time, the figures of mother and children, the three heavily caped nurses, and the marching line of fiacres, or carriages, reveal a touch of gentle satire that well characterizes the penetrating observation Bonnard could combine with a brilliant simplicity of design. Like his fellow Nabis, Bonnard believed in eliminating barriers between the realms of popular decorative arts and the high-art traditions of painting and sculpture. He envisioned an art of "everyday application" that could extend to fans, prints, furniture, or, in this case, color lithographs adapted to the format of a four-part Japanese screen.

In *Nude against the Light* (fig. **3.26**), Bonnard has moved from the public sphere of Parisian streets to the intimate world of the nude in a domestic interior, a subject he exploited throughout his career as a means to investigate light and color. Bonnard silhouetted the model, his ever-youthful wife, Marthe, against the sun-drenched surfaces of her boudoir. Light falls through the tall French windows, strongly illuminating the side of the woman turned from our view but visible in the mirror at left. This use of reflections to enlarge and enrich the pictorial space, to

stand as a picture within a picture, became a common strategy of Bonnard's as well as Matisse's interiors (see fig. 7.18). But in its quiet solemnity and complete absence of self-consciousness, Bonnard's nude is deeply indebted to the precedent of Degas's bathers, even to the detail of the round tub (see fig. 2.35). Like those of the older artist, Bonnard's composition is disciplined and complex, carefully structured to return the eye to the solid form of the nude, which he surrounds with a multitude of textures, shapes, and colors. But Bonnard creates an expressive mood all his own. As she douses herself with perfume, the model seems almost transfixed by the warm, radiant light that permeates the scene.

Bonnard's color became progressively brighter. By the time he painted *Dining Room on the Garden*, in 1934–35 (fig. **3.27**), he had long since recovered the entire spectrum of luminous color, and had learned from Cézanne that color could function constructively as well as sensually. In this ambitious canvas Bonnard tackled the difficult problem of depicting an interior scene with a view through the window to a garden beyond, setting the isolated, geometric forms of a tabletop still life against a lush exterior landscape. Now the model, his wife Marthe, is positioned to one side, an incidental and ghostly presence in this sumptuous display. By the mid-thirties, virtually all the great primary revolutions of twentieth-century painting had already occurred, including Fauvism, with its arbitrary, expressive color, and Cubism, with its reorganization of Renaissance pictorial space. Moreover, painting had found its way to pure abstraction in various forms. Perfectly aware of all this, Bonnard was nonetheless content to go his own way. In the work seen here, for instance, there is evidence that he had looked closely at Fauve and

3.27 Pierre Bonnard, *Dining Room on the Garden*, 1934–35. Oil on canvas, 50⅛ × 53½" (127.3 × 135.9 cm). Solomon R. Guggenheim Museum, New York.

Cubist paintings, particularly the works of Matisse—who was a devoted admirer of his—and had used what he wanted of the new approaches without at any time changing his basic attitudes.

Toulouse-Lautrec

Although **Henri de Toulouse-Lautrec** (1864–1901) may be seen as the heir of Daumier in the field of printmaking, he also served, along with his contemporaries Gauguin and Van Gogh, as one of the principal bridges between nineteenth-century avant-garde painting and the early twentieth-century experiments of Edvard Munch, Pablo Picasso, and Henri Matisse. Lautrec was interested in Goya and the line drawings of Ingres, but he was above all a passionate disciple of Degas, both in his admiration of Degas's draftsmanship and in the disengaged attitude and calculated formal strategies he brought to the depiction of his favorite subjects—the theaters, brothels, and bohemian cabarets of Paris.

Due to years of inbreeding in his old, aristocratic family, Lautrec was permanently disfigured from a congenital disease that weakened his bones. Against his family's wishes, he pursued art as a profession after receiving an education in the private Parisian studios of Léon Bonnat and Fernand Cormon, painters who provided students with a more open and tolerant atmosphere than that found in the École des Beaux-Arts. In Cormon's studio Lautrec met Bernard and Van Gogh, both of whom he rendered in early portraits.

Lautrec is best known for his color lithographs in the 1890s of performers in Montmartre dance halls, but in the previous decade he had proved himself to be a sensitive portraitist with paintings and drawings of a colorful cast of characters, including Carmen Gaudin, the woman portrayed in *"À Montrouge"—Rosa La Rouge* (fig. **3.28**). The artist was drawn to the simple clothes, unruly red hair, and tough look of this young working-class woman, who, arms dangling informally, averts her face as she is momentarily

3.28 Henri de Toulouse-Lautrec, *"À Montrouge"—Rosa La Rouge*, 1886–87. Oil on canvas, 28½ × 19¼" (72.4 × 48.9 cm). The Barnes Foundation, Merion, Pennsylvania.

3.29 Henri de Toulouse-Lautrec, *Moulin Rouge—La Goulue*, 1891. Color lithograph, 6'3¼" × 4' (1.9 × 1.2 m). Victoria and Albert Museum, London.

silhouetted against the lighted window. Lautrec creates this simplified composition out of his characteristically long strokes of color in warm, subdued tonalities. But the somber mood of the painting has also to do with its subject. Lautrec's painting was inspired by a gruesome song written by his bohemian friend, the famous cabaret singer Aristide Bruant, about a prostitute who conspires to kill her clients.

The naturalism of Lautrec's early portraits gave way in the 1890s to the brightly colored and stylized works that make his name synonymous with turn-of-the-century

Paris. His earliest lithographic poster, designed for the notorious dance hall called the Moulin Rouge (fig. **3.29**), features the scandalous talents of La Goulue ("the greedy one"), a dancer renowned for her gymnastic and erotic interpretations of the *chahut*, the dance that had attracted Seurat in 1889 (see fig. 3.3). Lautrec's superb graphic sensibility is apparent in the eye-catching shapes that, albeit abbreviated, were the result of long observation. Their snappy curves and crisp silhouettes were born of an Art Nouveau aesthetic (see chapter 5) that dominated the arts across Europe at the time.

4
The Origins of Modern Architecture and Design

In architecture, a pattern of stylistic revivals had predominated in Europe since the fifteenth century and in the Americas since the sixteenth century, when early settlers brought with them the architectural styles and traditions of different European regions. Throughout the nineteenth century, architects continued to expand this tendency. By the first decades of the nineteenth century, the Neoclassical movement was well established in both Europe and America as the dominant style. In America, this Neoclassical style, or classical revival, coincided with the aims of a young republic that regarded itself as the new Arcadia. The Neoclassical style in architecture, which consisted of endless recombinations of ancient Greek and Roman motifs, symbolized the ideal public virtues of democracy, liberty, and reason. During the later eighteenth century, particularly in England, an opposing trend, the Gothic Revival, had also gained considerable momentum and continued to make headway during the first half of the nineteenth; it was accompanied by revivals of Renaissance and Baroque classicism. All these movements, which were stylistically backward-looking, produced much of the monumental civic architecture of the late nineteenth century and the early twentieth. Modern styles and concepts, by contrast, took root more quickly in commercial, industrial, and residential architecture.

Palaces of Iron and Glass: The Influence of Industry

New ideas in architecture emerged during the nineteenth century in the context of engineering, with the spread of industrialization and the use of novel building materials, notably iron, glass, and hollow ceramic tile. The use of iron for structural elements became fairly common in English industrial building only after 1800, although there are sporadic instances during the eighteenth century. These new materials—developed or improved during the Industrial Revolution—permitted greater flexibility and experimentation in design, as well as larger scale since iron could be used to span far larger spaces than was possible in stone or wood construction. During the first half of the nineteenth century, a concealed iron-skeleton structure was used in buildings of all types, and exposed columns and decorative ironwork appeared, particularly in nontraditional structures and notably in the Royal Pavilion at Brighton (fig. **4.1**), designed by **John Nash** (1752–1835). Iron was also used extensively in the many new railway bridges built throughout Europe, as the railway system expanded (fig. **4.2**). **Gustave Eiffel** (1832–1923) built his famous 984-foot (300 m) tower for the Paris Exposition Universelle of 1889. It was the most dramatic demonstration of the possibilities of exposed-metal construction and used iron in a variety of ways. Roofs of iron and glass over commercial galleries or bazaars became popular and ambitious in design at this time, especially in Paris. In greenhouses, iron gradually replaced wood as a frame for glass panes, with a consequent enlargement of scale. The Jardin d'Hiver (Winter Garden) in Paris, designed by Hector Horeau in 1847 and since destroyed, measured 300 by 180 feet (91 by 55 m) in floor plan and rose to a height of 60 feet (18 m)—a quite remarkable size at the time. Works such as this gave rise to the concept of the monumental glass-and-metal structure, of which the Crystal Palace, created for the Great Exhibition in London in 1851 by **Sir Joseph Paxton** (1801–65), was the most famous example (fig. **4.3**). The Crystal Palace was erected through modern building methods that are today taken for granted—prefabricated modules that allow for easy assembly. Paxton developed the ridge-and-furrow roof construction while designing greenhouses. Yet the building, an airy barrel-vaulted gallery, also recalls the space and shape of a gigantic, secular cathedral. The Crystal Palace was dismantled and reassembled in Sydenham, in south London, where it remained until it was destroyed by fire in 1936.

The sheds of the new railway stations, precisely because they were structures without tradition, provided some of the most daring and experimental buildings in iron and glass. The Gare Saint-Lazare in Paris supplied the

4.1 John Nash, Royal Pavilion, Brighton, England. 1815–23, as remodeled.

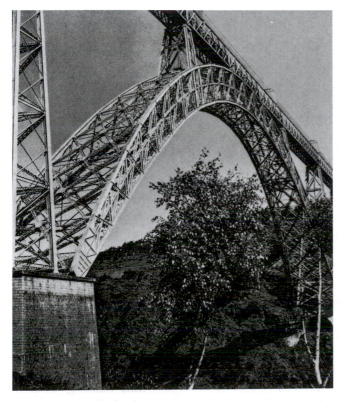

4.2 Gustave Eiffel, Truyère Bridge, Garabit, France. 1880–84.

4.3 Sir Joseph Paxton, Crystal Palace, London. 1851.

4.4 Henri Labrouste, Reading room, Bibliothèque Sainte-Geneviève, Paris. 1843–50.

painter Monet with a new experience in light, space, and movement, which he painted several times. Exposed iron columns supporting iron-and-glass arches were employed even in some traditional structures, such as the Bibliothèque Sainte-Geneviève (fig. **4.4**) by **Henri Labrouste** (1801–75). Stamped, cast-iron details were very popular, and a substantial industry in their prefabrication developed before 1850. For decades thereafter, however, the structural and decorative use of cast iron declined, largely because of the conservative tastes of revival-oriented theorists in architec-

ture. Only at the very end of the nineteenth century, with the new Art Nouveau style (see chapter 5), did metal emerge once more as the architectural element on which much of twentieth-century architecture was based.

In architecture, as in the decorative arts, the latter half of the nineteenth century was a highly eclectic period. The classical and Gothic revivals of the early century had been largely superseded by elaborate buildings in the Renaissance- and Baroque-revival styles. Of these the Paris Opera (fig. **4.5**), designed by **Charles Garnier** (1825–98), is perhaps the supreme example. These remained, far into the twentieth century, the official styles for public and monumental buildings. At the turn of the century, America, with its growing population, burgeoning cities, and expanding economy, was emerging as a world power. The expression of this in public buildings showed a heightened consciousness of historical revivalism, which could encompass Gothic, classical, or colonial styles, among others. More and more American architects received their training at the École des Beaux-Arts in Paris, the international heart of academicism in architecture. For American banks, civic monuments, libraries, capitols, and other public buildings coast to coast, the preferred mode was academic classicism on a grandiose scale. For example, the enormous central mall in Washington, D.C., which runs between the Capitol and the Lincoln Memorial, and which is lined with mostly classical façades, was a product of this period.

4.5 Charles Garnier, The Opera, Paris. 1861–74.

"A Return to Simplicity": The Arts and Crafts Movement and Experimental Architecture

The tremendous expansion of machine production during the nineteenth century led to the development of mass consumption of new, more cheaply manufactured products. This growing mass market put the emphasis on products' cheapness rather than their quality or beauty. Thus there arose early in the nineteenth century the profession of modern advertising, which followed the principle that the most ornate, unoriginal products sell best. By the time of the Great Exhibition of 1851, the vast array of manufactured objects exhibited in Paxton's daring glass-and-metal Crystal Palace represented and even flaunted the degeneration of quality brought about by the emergence of a machine economy.

To a Romantic, progressive nineteenth-century thinker and artist like William Morris, friend and collaborator of the Pre-Raphaelites (see chapter 2), the machine was destroying the values of individual craftsmanship on which the high level of past artistic achievement had rested. Poet, painter, designer, and social reformer, Morris fought against the rising tide of what he saw as commercial vulgarization, for he passionately believed that the industrial worker was alienated both from the customer and the craft itself and was held hostage to the dictates of fashion and profit. Morris founded an artists' cooperative, called the Firm, which made furniture, fabrics, and wallpapers (see fig. 5.1). He turned to the Middle Ages for design inspiration as well as for the medieval model of guild organization for skilled laborers. His friend, the artist and designer Walter Crane, summarized their common goals by calling for "a return to simplicity, to sincerity; to good materials and sound workmanship; to rich and suggestive surface decoration, and simple constructive forms." Morris's designs were intended to raise the dignity of craftsperson and owner alike and to enhance the beauty of ordinary homes. The Firm's progeny was the Arts and Crafts movement in the British Isles, which exerted tremendous influence in the United States, especially on the oak Mission Style furniture of Gustav Stickley.

Morris asked the architect **Philip Webb** (1831–1915) to design his own home, called the Red House, in Kent, in 1859 (fig. **4.6**). In accordance with Morris's desires, Red House was generally Gothic in design, but Webb interpreted his commission freely. Into a simplified, traditional, red-brick Tudor Gothic manor house, with a steeply pitched roof, he introduced exterior details of classic Queen Anne windows and oculi. The effect of the exterior is of harmony and compact unity, despite the disparate elements. The plan is an open L-shape with commodious, well-lit rooms arranged in an easy and efficient asymmetrical pattern. The interior, from the furniture and stained-glass windows down to the fire irons, was designed by Webb and Morris in collaboration with Morris's wife, Jane, and the Pre-Raphaelite artists Rossetti and Edward Burne-

4.6 Philip Webb and William Morris, Red House, Bexley Heath, Kent, England. 1859–60.

Jones. Aware of such English experiments, the influential American architect Henry Hobson Richardson (see below) developed his own style of domestic architecture, which fused American traditions with those of medieval Europe. The Stoughton House, in Cambridge, Massachusetts, is one of his most familiar structures in the shingle style (named for the wooden tiles or shingles used as wall cladding) then rising to prominence on the eastern seaboard. The main outlines are recall Romanesque- and Gothic-revival traditions, but these are architecturally less significant than the spacious, screened entry and the extensive windows, which suggest his concern with the livability of the interior. The shingled exterior wraps around the structure of the house to create a sense of simplicity and unity.

While the firm of **McKim, Mead & White** was in some degree responsible for the hold that academic classicism had on American public architecture for half a century, the firm's historicism was based less on generic Greek and Roman prototypes than on American eighteenth-century architecture. These prolific architects produced some of the most successful classical public buildings in America, including the Boston Public Library, New York's magnificent Pennsylvania Railroad Station (see fig. 12.7), sadly demolished in 1966, and the influential Rhode Island State Capitol in Providence, which established the model for many state capitols in the early years of the twentieth century. In their domestic architecture, McKim, Mead & White drew on the qualities of American colonial building and, like Webb and Morris, were able to select the historical or geographic style that best suited a particular site or commission. The William G. Low House of 1886–87 (fig. **4.7**), a superb example of the shingle style in Bristol, Rhode Island, is revolutionary when viewed in contrast to the enormous mansions in revivalist styles that were then fashionable in nearby, wealthy Newport. The shingle-covered structure, with its bay windows and extended side porch, is formed of a single triangular gable, and has a striking geometric integrity.

4.7 McKim, Mead & White, William G. Low House, Bristol, Rhode Island. 1886–87. Demolished 1960s.

Twentieth-century architecture is rooted in nineteenth-century technological advances and in the invention of new types of structures—railway stations, department stores, and exhibition halls, buildings without tradition that lent themselves to experimental design. However, many of modern architecture's most revolutionary concepts—attention to utility and comfort, the notion of beauty in undecorated forms, and of forms that follow function—were first conceived in modest individual houses and small industrial buildings. The pioneer efforts of Webb in England and of Richardson and McKim, Mead & White in the United States were followed by the important experimental housing of Charles F. Voysey, Arthur H. Mackmurdo, and Charles Rennie Mackintosh in the British Isles, and in the United States by the revolutionary house designs of Frank Lloyd Wright.

Charles F. Voysey (1857–1941), through his wallpapers and textiles, had an even more immediate influence on European Art Nouveau than did the Arts and Crafts movement of William Morris. The furniture he designed had a rectangular, medievalizing form with a simplicity of decoration and a lightness of proportion that some historians have claimed anticipated later Bauhaus furniture, though Voysey was perplexed by such assertions. Voysey's architecture was greatly influenced by Arthur H. Mackmurdo (1851–1942), who, in structures such as his own house and his Liverpool exhibition hall, went beyond Webb in the creation of a style that eliminated almost all reminiscences of English eighteenth-century architecture. A house by Voysey in Bedford Park, London, dated 1891 (fig. **4.8**), is astonishingly original in its rhythmic groups of windows and door openings against broad white areas of unadorned, starkly vertical walls. While Voysey was a product of the English Gothic Revival, he looked not to the great cathedrals for inspiration, but to the domestic architecture of rural cottages. In his later country houses he returned, perhaps at the insistence of clients, to suggestions of more traditional Tudor and Georgian forms. He continued to treat these, however, in a ruggedly simple manner

4.8 Charles F. Voysey, Forster House, Bedford Park, London. 1891.

in which plain wall masses were lightened and refined by articulated rows of windows.

Largely as a result of the work of **Charles Rennie Mackintosh** (1868–1928), Glasgow was one of the most remarkable centers of architectural experiment at the end of the nineteenth century. Mackintosh's most considerable work of architecture, created at the beginning of his career, is the Glasgow School of Art of 1898–99 and its library addition, built between 1907 and 1909 (fig. **4.9**). The essence of this building is simplicity, clarity, monumentality, and, above all, an organization of interior space that is not only functional but also highly expressive of its function. The huge, rectangular studio windows are imbedded in the massive stone façade, creating a balance of solids and voids. The rectangular heaviness of the walls, softened only by an occasional curved masonry element, is lightened by details of fantasy, particularly in the ironwork, that show a relationship to Art Nouveau, but derive in part from the curvilinear forms of medieval Scottish and Celtic art. The library addition is a large, high-ceilinged room with surrounding balconies. Rectangular beams and columns are used to create a series of views that become three-dimensional, geometric abstractions.

The same intricate play with interior vistas seen in this library is apparent in a series of four public tea rooms, also in Glasgow, commissioned by Catherine Cranston. For the last of these, the Willow Tea Rooms, Mackintosh was able to design the entire building. Most details of the interior design, furniture, and wall painting are the products of both Mackintosh and his wife, Margaret Macdonald. They shared with Morris and the followers of the Arts and Crafts movement the notion that all architectural elements, no matter how small, should be integrated into a total aesthetic experience. The stripped-down rectangular partitions and furniture, including Mackintosh's famous ladder-back chairs, and the curvilinear figure designs on the walls illustrate the contrasts that form the spirit of Art Nouveau. The decorations are close to those in paintings of Gustav Klimt and works of the Vienna Secession movement (see fig. 5.5), and in fact may have influenced them. Mackintosh exhibited with the Vienna Secession in 1900, and his architectural designs, furniture, glass, and enamels were received more favorably there than they had been in London. He died virtually penniless in 1928, and it was not until the sixties that his reputation was fully revived. Today his furniture and decorative arts are among the most coveted of the modern era.

After 1900, the architectural leadership that England had assumed, particularly through designs for houses and smaller public buildings by Webb, Voysey, and Mackintosh, declined rapidly. In the United States, Frank Lloyd Wright and a few followers carried on their spectacular experiments in detached domestic architecture. However, for many years even Wright himself was given almost no large-scale building commissions. The pioneer efforts of Louis Sullivan and the Chicago School of architects were challenged by the massive triumph of the Beaux-Arts tradition of academic eclecticism, which was to dominate American public building for the next thirty years.

"Form Follows Function": The Chicago School and the Origins of the Skyscraper

Modern architecture may be said to have emerged in the United States with the groundbreaking commercial buildings of **Henry Hobson Richardson** (1838–86), an architect who, though eclectic, did not turn to the conventional historicist styles of Gothic pastiche and classical revival. In his Marshall Field Wholesale Store in Chicago (fig. **4.10**), now destroyed, Richardson achieved an effect of monumental mass and stability through the use of graduated rough blocks of reddish Massachusetts sandstone and Missouri granite in a heavily rusticated structure inspired by Romanesque architecture and fifteenth-century Italian Renaissance palaces. The windows, arranged in diminishing arcaded rows that mirror the gradual narrowing of the masonry wall from ground to roof, are integrated with the interior space rather than being simply holes punched at

4.9 Charles Rennie Mackintosh, Library, Glasgow School of Art. 1907–9.

4.10 Henry Hobson Richardson, Marshall Field Wholesale Store, Chicago. 1885–87. Demolished 1931.

intervals into the exterior wall. The landmark Marshall Field building was constructed with traditional load-bearing walls, columns, and girders (rather than the steel frames of later skyscrapers), but its elemental design, free of picturesque ornament, influenced the later work of the Chicago School, specifically that of Louis Sullivan and, ultimately (though he would never acknowledge it), Frank Lloyd Wright.

Throughout the nineteenth century, continual expansion and improvement in the production of structural iron and steel permitted raising the height of commercial buildings, a necessity born of growing urban congestion and rising real-estate costs. At the same time, there were sporadic experiments in increasing the scale of windows beyond the dictates of Renaissance palace façades. A vast proportion of Chicago was destroyed in the great fire of 1871—an event that cleared the way for a new type of metropolis fully utilizing the new architectural and urban-planning techniques and materials developed in Europe and America over the previous hundred years.

The Home Insurance Building in Chicago (fig. **4.11**), designed and constructed between 1883 and 1885 by the architect **William Le Baron Jenney** (1832–1907), was only ten stories high, no higher than other proto-skyscrapers already built in New York (the illustration shown here includes the two stories that were added in 1890–91). Its importance rested in the fact that it embodied true skyscraper construction, in which the internal metal skeleton carried the weight of the external masonry shell. This innovation, which was not Jenney's alone, together with the development of the elevator, permitted buildings to rise to great heights and led to the creation of the modern urban landscape of skyscrapers. With metal-frame construction, architects could eliminate load-bearing walls and open up façades, so that a building became a glass box in which solid, supporting elements were reduced to a minimum. The concept of the twentieth-century skyscraper as a glass-encased shell framed in a metal grid was here stated for the first time.

Among the many architects attracted to Chicago from the East or from Europe by the opportunities engendered by the great fire was the Dane **Dankmar Adler** (1844–1900), an engineering specialist. He was joined in 1879 by a young Boston architect, **Louis Sullivan** (1856–1924), and in 1887 the firm of Adler and Sullivan hired a twenty-year-old draftsman, Frank Lloyd Wright. The 1889 dedication of the Adler and Sullivan Auditorium helped stimulate a resurgence of architecture in Chicago after the devastations of the fire. And, like Jenney's Home Insurance Building, it emerged under the influence of Richardson's Marshall Field store (see fig. 4.10). The Auditorium included offices, a hotel, and, most significantly, a spectacular new concert hall, then the largest in the country, with a highly successful acoustical system designed by Adler. Shallow concentric arches in the hall made for a majestic yet intimate space, and Sullivan's use of a sumptuous decoration of natural and geometric forms, richly colored mosaics, and painted panels proved that ornament was one of the architect's great strengths as a designer. By the late twenties, the Chicago Opera Company had moved to new quarters—fortunately, however, demolishing the Auditorium during the ensuing years of national depression proved too expensive to carry out.

Adler and Sullivan entered the field of skyscraper construction in 1890 with their Wainwright Building in St. Louis. Then, in the Guaranty Trust Building (now the Prudential Building) in Buffalo, New York, Sullivan designed the first masterpiece of the early skyscrapers (fig. **4.12**). Here, as in the Wainwright Building, the architect attacked the problem of skyscraper design by emphasizing verticality, with the result that the piers separating the windows of the top ten stories are uninterrupted through most of the building's height. At the same time, he seemed well aware of the peculiar design problem involved in the skyscraper, which is basically a tall building consisting of a large number of superimposed horizontal layers. Thus, Sullivan accentuated the individual layers with ornamented bands under the windows, as well as throughout the attic story, and crowned the building with a projecting cornice that brings the structure back to the horizontal. This tripartite division of the façade—base, piers, and attic—has frequently been compared to the form of a classical column.

4.11 William Le Baron Jenney, Home Insurance Building, Chicago. 1884–85. Demolished 1929.

When compared with the "stacked" effect of superimposed stories in Jenney's Home Insurance Building, however, the vertical emphasis of Sullivan's building has a fundamentally modern, antiacademic character. Meanwhile, the treatment of the columns on the ground floor emphasizes the openness of the interior space. Above them, the slender piers between the windows soar aloft and then join under the attic in graceful arches that tie the main façades together. The oval, recessed windows of the attic, being light and open, blend into the elegant curve of the summit cornice. Sullivan's famed ornament covers the upper part of the structure in a light, overall pattern, helping to unify the façade while also emphasizing the nature of the terracotta sheathing over the metal skeleton as a weightless, decorative surface, rather than a weight-bearing element. "It must be every inch a proud and soaring thing," said Sullivan of the tall office building, "rising in sheer exaltation that from bottom to top as a unit without a single dissenting line." In theory, Sullivan felt that a building's interior function should determine its exterior form, hence his famous phrase, "form follows function." But practical experience taught him that function and structure did not always generate the most appealing forms.

The progressive influence of Richardson's proto-American architecture and the Chicago School was counteracted after Richardson's death as more and more young American architects studied in Paris in the academic environment of the École des Beaux-Arts (where, in fact, Richardson had trained). The 1893 World's Columbian Exposition in Chicago, a vast and highly organized example of quasi-Roman city planning (fig. **4.13**), was a collaboration among many architects, including McKim,

4.13 Richard Morris Hunt; McKim, Mead & White; Burnham and Root; and other architects, World's Columbian Exposition, Chicago. 1893. Demolished.

Mead & White, the Chicago firm of **Burnham and Root**, and **Richard Morris Hunt** (1827–95), the doyen of American academic architecture. This world's fair celebrated the four-hundredth anniversary of Columbus's voyage. Though modeled on European precedents, the Columbian Exposition set out to assert American ascendancy in industry and particularly the visual arts. Ironically, while international expositions in London and Paris had unveiled such futuristic architectural marvels as the Crystal Palace and the Eiffel Tower, America looked to the classical European past for inspiration. This resulted, in part, from an anxiety that pragmatic Chicago-style architecture might give a provincial appearance to America's first world's fair. The gleaming white colonnades of the

4.14 John Augustus Roebling, Brooklyn Bridge, New York. 1869–83.

buildings, conceived on an awesome scale and arranged around an immense reflecting pool, formed a model for the future American dream city, one that affected a generation of architects and their clients. Thus, although the Chicago School of architecture maintained its vitality into the first decade of the twentieth century, neoacademic eclecticism remained firmly established, with New York architects leading the way.

The Gothic Revival style could be applied to structures other than buildings, such as the Brooklyn Bridge (1869–83), which, as one of the country's most spectacular suspension bridges, represented a triumph of American technology (fig. **4.14**). It was designed by **John Augustus Roebling** (1806–69), who barely lived to see work on the project begun (his son Washington completed the work with his wife, Emily). Before construction of the bridge, the East River was crossed by up to a thousand ferry trips a day. With its soaring Gothic towers and graceful steel suspension cables, the Brooklyn Bridge forms a dramatic gateway to New York City. No wonder numbers of American painters and photographers were drawn to its grandeur as a pictorial motif. By 1913 the Woolworth Building (fig. **4.15**), designed by **Cass Gilbert** (1859–1934), loomed 792 feet (241 m) above the streets of New York—fifty-two stories of Late Gothic-style stone sheathing serving mainly to add weight, disguise the metal-case construction frame, and create a sense of soaring verticality. Until 1931, the Woolworth Building was New York's tallest building, a Gothic cathedral of the modern age and a shining symbol of American capitalism. It has since been overshadowed by later and taller buildings, but remains one of the most distinguished structures on the New York skyline.

4.15 Cass Gilbert, Woolworth Building, New York. 1911–13.

5

Art Nouveau and the Beginnings of Expressionism

As seen in chapters 3 and 4, the *fin de siècle* was a period of synthesis in the arts, a time when artists sought new directions that in themselves constituted a reaction against the tide of "progress" represented by industrialization. At the same time, the architects discussed in the previous chapter recognized that new patterns of life in the industrial age called for new types of buildings—bridges, railroad stations, and skyscrapers. The great innovators, such as Richardson, Sullivan, or Mackintosh, were able to draw selectively upon older styles without resorting to academic pastiche, and to create from the past something new and authentic for the present. While these architects did not abandon tradition, their work constituted a powerful countercurrent to Beaux-Arts historicism. At the same time, the search of the Symbolist poets, painters, and musicians for spiritual values was part of this reaction. Gauguin used the term "synthetism" to characterize the liberating color and linear explorations that he pursued and transmitted to disciples. The phenomenal thing about this synthesizing spirit is that, in the last decades of the nineteenth century and the first of the twentieth, it became a great popular movement that affected the taste of every part of the population in both Europe and the United States. This was the movement called Art Nouveau, a French term meaning simply "new art." Art Nouveau was a definable style that emerged from the experiments of painters, architects, craftspeople, and designers and for a decade permeated not only painting, sculpture, and architecture, but also graphic design, magazine and book illustration, furniture, textiles, glass and ceramic wares, jewelry, and even clothing. As the name implies, Art Nouveau represented a rejection of historical revivalism and academic classicism and reflected a conscious search for new and genuine forms that were capable of expressing the modern age. Its emphasis on elaborate and intricate decorative motifs, however, meant that it was rapidly superseded in the first decade of the twentieth century by more radical forms of modern, machine-age art and architecture.

Natural Forms for the Machine Age: The Art Nouveau Aesthetic

Art Nouveau grew out of the English Arts and Crafts movement, whose chief exponent and propagandist was the artist and poet **William Morris** (1834–96) (see chapter 4). The Arts and Crafts movement evolved as a revolt against the new age of mechanization, a Romantic effort on the part of Morris and others to implement the philosophy of the influential critic John Ruskin, who stated that true art should be both beautiful and useful and should base its forms on those found in nature (fig. **5.1**). They saw the world of the artist–craftsperson in the process of destruction by mass production, and they fought for a return to some of the standards of simplicity, beauty, and craftsmanship that they associated with earlier centuries, notably the Middle Ages. Ironically for these social reformers, it was only the wealthy, in the end, who could afford their handcrafted goods. The ideas of the Arts and Crafts movement spread rapidly throughout Europe and found support in the comparable theories of French, German, Belgian, and Austrian artists and writers. A key characteristic of the movement was the concept of a synthesis of the arts based on an aesthetic of dynamic linear movement. Many names were given to this phenomenon in its various manifestations, but ultimately Art Nouveau became the most generally accepted, probably through its use by the Parisian shop and gallery called the Maison de l'Art Nouveau, which, with its exhibitions and extensive commissions to artists and artisans, was influential in propagating the style. In Germany the term "Jugendstil," or "youth style," after the periodical *Jugend*, became the name.

In 1890, it must be remembered, large quantities of mainstream painting, sculpture, and architecture were still being produced in accepted academic styles using traditional methods. In contrast to the Arts and Crafts movement, Art Nouveau made use of new materials and machine technologies both in buildings and in decoration. Moreover, although Art Nouveau artists could not avoid

5.1 William Morris, Detail of *Pimpernel* wallpaper, 1876. Victoria and Albert Museum, London.

the influence of past styles, they explored those that were less well known and out of fashion with the current academicians. They looked to medieval or Asian art forms or devices that were congenial to their search for an abstraction based on linear rhythms. Thus the linear qualities and decorative synthesis of eighteenth-century rococo; the wonderful linear interlace of Celtic and Saxon illumination and jewelry; the bold, flat patterns of Japanese paintings and prints (see fig. 2.22); the ornate motifs of Chinese and Japanese ceramics and jades were all used as sources for ideas. The Art Nouveau artists, while seeking a kind of abstraction, discovered most of the sources for their decoration in nature, especially in plant forms, often given a symbolic or sensuous overtone. They also drew on scientific discoveries, such as the forms of microorganisms that new explorations in botany and zoology were making familiar.

Painting and Graphic Art

In the later works of Seurat and his followers (see chapter 3), line took on an abstract, expressive function. The formal innovations of Gauguin and of the Nabis were rooted in linear as well as color pattern. Toulouse-Lautrec reflected (and influenced) the Art Nouveau spirit in his paintings and prints, particularly in his subtle use of descriptive, expressive line. Through his highly popular posters (see fig. 3.29), aspects of Art Nouveau graphic design were spread throughout the Western world. While

Art Nouveau in architecture was largely a phenomenon of continental Europe, there were many precursors of the movement in England, particularly in painting. The mystical visions of **William Blake** (1757–1827; fig. **5.2**), expressed in fantastic rhythms of line and color, were an obvious ancestor, as were the late, highly decorative paintings of the Pre-Raphaelite artist Dante Gabriel Rossetti.

The drawings of the young English artist **Aubrey Beardsley** (1872–98) were immensely elaborate in their black-and-white stylization and decorative richness (fig. **5.3**). Associated with the so-termed "aesthetic" or "decadent" literature of Oscar Wilde and other *fin-de-siècle* writers, they were admired for their beauty and condemned for their sexual content. They probably constitute the most significant contribution of the English to Art Nouveau graphic art. Beardsley, like Edgar Allan Poe and certain of the French Symbolists, was haunted by Romantic visions of evil, of the erotic, and the decadent. In watered-down imitations, his style in drawing appeared all over Europe and America in popularizations of Art Nouveau book illustrations and posters. Beardsley based one of his illustrations for Wilde's 1894 poem *Salome* on this drawing, in which the stepdaughter of Herod holds up the severed head of Saint John the Baptist in a gesture of grotesque eroticism.

One of the most influential figures in all the phases of Art Nouveau was the Belgian **Henry van de Velde** (1863–1957). Trained as a painter, he eventually produced abstract compositions in typical Art Nouveau formulas of color patterns and sinuous lines (fig. **5.4**). For a time he

5.2 William Blake, *The Great Red Dragon and the Woman Clothed with the Sun*, 1805–10. Watercolor, 16⅛ × 13⅛" (41 × 33.5 cm). National Gallery of Art, Washington, D.C.

tect and designer that he made his major contributions to Art Nouveau and the origins of twentieth-century art.

In Austria, the new ideas of Art Nouveau were given expression in the founding in 1897 of the Vienna Secession and, shortly thereafter, in its publication, *Ver Sacrum* ("Sacred Spring"). This diverse group was so named because it seceded from Vienna's conservative exhibiting society, the Künstlerhaus, and opposed the intolerance for new, antinaturalist styles at the Academy of Fine Arts. The major figure of the Secession was **Gustav Klimt** (1862–1918), in many ways the most talented exponent of pure Art Nouveau style in painting. Klimt was well established as a successful decorative painter and fashionable portraitist, noted for the brilliance of his draftsmanship, when he began in the 1890s to be drawn into the stream of new European experiments. He became conscious of Dutch Symbolists such as Jan Toorop, of the Swiss Symbolist Ferdinand Hodler, of the English Pre-Raphaelites and of Aubrey Beardsley (see fig. 2.8; see figs. 2.18, 5.3). His style was also formed on a study of Byzantine mosaics. A passion for erotic themes led him not only to the creation of innumerable drawings, sensitive and explicit, but also to the development of a painting style that integrated sensuous nude figures with brilliantly colored

5.3 Aubrey Beardsley, *Salome with the Head of John the Baptist*, 1893. India ink and watercolor, 10⅞ × 5¾" (27.6 × 14.6 cm). Aubrey Beardsley Collection, Manuscripts Division, Department of Rare Books and Special Collections, Princeton University Library, New Jersey.

5.4 Henry van de Velde, *Tropon*, c. 1899. Advertising poster, 47⅝ × 29⅛" (121 × 74 cm). Museum für Kunst und Gewerbe, Hamburg.

was interested in Impressionism and read widely in the scientific theory of color and perception. He soon abandoned this direction in favor of the Symbolism of Gauguin and his school and attempted to push his experiments in symbolic statement through abstract color expression further than had any of his contemporaries. Ultimately, Van de Velde came to believe that easel painting was a dead end and that the solution for contemporary society was to be found in the industrial arts. Though significantly influenced by Morris's theories, unlike the Englishman he regarded the machine as a potentially positive agent that could "one day bring forth beautiful products." It was finally as an archi-

5.5 Gustav Klimt, Detail of dining-room mural, Palais Stoclet, Brussels. c. 1905–8. Mosaic and enamel on marble.

decorative patterns of a richness rarely equaled in the history of modern art. He was increasingly drawn to mural painting; his murals for the University of Vienna involved elaborate and complicated symbolic statements composed of voluptuous figures floating through an amorphous, atmospheric limbo. Those he created for the Palais Stoclet, designed by Josef Hoffmann, in Brussels between 1905 and 1910 (fig. **5.5**, see also fig. **5.15**) are executed in glass, enamel, metal, and semiprecious stones. They combined figures conceived as flat patterns (except for modeled heads

and hands) with an overall pattern of abstract spirals—a glittering complex of volumetric forms embedded in a mosaic of jeweled and gilded pattern. Although essentially decorative in their total effect, the Stoclet murals mark the moment when modern painting was on the very edge of nonrepresentation. Through his relationship with the younger Austrian artist Egon Schiele, as well as through his own obsessive, somewhat morbid and febrile eroticism (fig. **5.6**), Klimt also occupies a central place in the story of Austrian Expressionism.

Architecture and Design

The Aesthetic Movement of the 1870s and 1880s, with its emphasis on beautiful but useful objects and a decorative style largely shaped by the reigning craze for *japonisme,* was an important forerunner of Art Nouveau. A masterpiece of the period is James Abbott McNeill Whistler's famous Peacock Room from 1876–77 (fig. **5.7**), made in collaboration with the architect Thomas Jeckyll (1827–81) for the London house of the shipping magnate Frederick Richards Leyland. Designed to showcase Leyland's Chinese porcelain collection, the Peacock Room was eclectic in style, as was typical of the Aesthetic Movement, but it is generally suffused with an exotic, Oriental flavor. Like his exact contemporary William Morris (and perhaps in response to him), Whistler, known for his paintings and prints (see figs. 2.23, 2.24), wished to prove his strength as a designer of an integrated decorative environment. The result is a shimmering interior of dark greenish-blue walls embellished with circular abstract patterns and golden peacock motifs,

5.6 Gustav Klimt, *Death and Life*, 1908–11. Oil on canvas, 70⅛" × 6'6" (178.1 cm × 2 m). Private collection.

5.7 James Abbott McNeill Whistler, *The Peacock Room*, 1876–77. Panels: oil color and gold on tooled leather and wood. Installed in the Freer Gallery of Art, Washington, D.C.

5.8 Louis Comfort Tiffany, Table Lamp, c. 1900. Bronze and Favrile glass, height 27" (68.6 cm), shade diameter 18" (45.7 cm). Lilian Nassau Ltd., New York.

which Whistler called *Harmony in Blue and Gold*. On the south wall of the room he depicted two fighting peacocks, one rich and one poor, which slyly alluded to a protracted quarrel between the artist and his patron. Leyland, who refused to pay Whistler for a great deal of work on the room that he had never commissioned, finally banned the irascible artist from the house after he invited the public and press to view his creation without Leyland's permission. The room was later acquired intact by an American collector and is now housed in the Freer Gallery of Art in Washington, D.C.

It is difficult to speak of a single, unified Art Nouveau style in architecture except in the realms of surface ornament and interior decoration. Despite this fact, certain aspects of architecture derive from Art Nouveau graphic art and decorative or applied arts, notably the use of the whiplash line in ornament and a generally curvilinear emphasis in decorative and even structural elements. The Art Nouveau spirit of imaginative invention, linear and spatial flow, and nontraditionalism fed the inspiration of a number of architects in continental Europe and the United States and enabled them to experiment more freely with ideas opened up to them by the use of metal, glass, and reinforced-concrete construction. Since the concept of Art Nouveau involved a high degree of specialized design and craftsmanship, it did not lend itself to the developing field of large-scale mass construction. However, it did contribute substantially to the outlook that was to lead to the rise of a new and experimental architecture in the early twentieth century.

The architectural ornament of Louis Sullivan in the Guaranty Trust Building (see fig. 4.12) or the Carson Pirie Scott store in Chicago was the principal American manifestation of the Art Nouveau spirit in architecture, and a comparable spirit permeated the early work of Sullivan's great disciple, Frank Lloyd Wright (see fig. 12.1). The outstanding American name in Art Nouveau was that of **Louis Comfort Tiffany** (1848–1933), but his expression lay in the fields of interior design and decorative arts, notably his table lamps, which combined the stylized natural forms so typical of Art Nouveau with his patented Favrile glass, which appeared handmade although it was industrially manufactured (fig. **5.8**). Tiffany was not only in close touch with the European movements but himself exercised a considerable influence on them.

In Spain, **Antoni Gaudí** (1852–1926) was influenced as a student by a Romantic and Symbolist concept of the Middle Ages as a Golden Age, which for him and other Spanish artists became a symbol for the rising nationalism of Catalonia. Also implicit in Gaudí's architecture was his early study of natural forms as a spiritual basis for architecture. He was drawn to the work of the influential French architect and theorist Eugène Emmanuel Viollet-le-Duc. The latter was a leading proponent of the Gothic Revival and a passionate restorer of medieval buildings who analyzed Gothic architectural structure in the light of modern technical advances. His writings on architecture, notably his *Entretiens* ("Discussions"), which appeared in French, English, and American editions in the 1860s and 1870s, were widely read by architects. His bold recommendations on the use of direct metal construction influenced not only Gaudí, but a host of other experimental architects at the end of the nineteenth century. While Gaudí's early architecture belonged in part to the main current of Gothic Revival, it involved a highly idiosyncratic use of materials, particularly in textural and coloristic arrangement, and an even more imaginative personal style in ornamental ironwork. His wrought-iron designs were arrived at independently and frequently in advance of the comparable experiments of mainstream Art Nouveau. Throughout his later career, from the late 1880s until his death in 1926, Gaudí followed his own direction, which at first was parallel to Art Nouveau and later was independent of anything that was being done in the world or would be done until the middle of the twentieth century, when his work was reassessed.

Gaudí's first major commission was to complete the Church of the Sagrada Familia in Barcelona (fig. **5.9**), already begun as a Gothic Revival structure by the architect Francisco de Villar. Gaudí worked intermittently on this

5.9 Antoni Gaudí, Church of the Sagrada Familia, Barcelona. 1883–1926.

church from 1883 until his death, leaving it far from complete even then. The main parts of the completed church, particularly the four great spires of one transept, are only remotely Gothic. Although influences of Moorish and other architectural styles may be traced, the principal effect is of a building without historic style—or rather one that expresses the imagination of the architect in the most personal and powerful sense. The decoration of the church contains a profusion of fantasy in biological ornament flowing into naturalistic figuration and abstract decoration. Brightly colored mosaic embellishes the finials of the spires. These forms were not arbitrary; they were tied to Gaudí's structural principles and his often hermetic language of symbolic form, informed by his spiritual beliefs. To complete the church according to the architect's plans, an enormous amount of construction has been undertaken since his death and continues today.

At the Güell Park in Barcelona (also unfinished), Gaudí produced a demonstration of sheer fantasy and engineering ingenuity, a Surrealist combination of landscaping and urban planning. This gigantic descendant of the Romantic, Gothic-style English gardens of the eighteenth century is a mélange of sinuously curving walls and benches, grottos, porticos, and arcades, all covered with brilliant mosaics of broken pottery and glass (fig. **5.10**). It exemplifies the strongly sculptural quality of Gaudí's architecture, a quality that differentiates it from most aspects of Art Nouveau. He composed in terms not of lines but of twisted masses of sculpturally conceived masonry. Even his ironwork has a sculptural heaviness that transcends the usually attenuated elegance of Art Nouveau line.

Gaudí designed the Casa Milá apartment house, a large structure around open courts, as a whole continuous movement of sculptural volumes. The façade, flowing around the two main elevations, is an alternation of void and sculptural mass. The undulating roof lines and the elaborately twisted chimney pots carry through the unified sculptural theme. Ironwork grows over the balconies like luscious exotic vegetation. The sense of organic growth continues in the floor plan, where one room or corridor flows without interruption into another. Walls are curved or angled throughout, to create a feeling of everlasting change, of space without end. In his concept of architecture as dynamic space joining the interior and external worlds and as living organism growing in a natural environment, in his daring engineering experiments, in his imaginative use of materials—from stone that looks like a natural rock formation to the most wildly abstract color organizations of ceramic mosaic—Gaudí was a visionary and a great pioneer.

If any architect might claim to be the founder of Art Nouveau architecture, however, it is the Belgian **Victor Horta** (1861–1947). Trained as an academician, he was inspired by Baroque and rococo concepts of linear movement in space, by his study of plant growth and of Viollet-le-Duc's structural theories, and by the engineer Gustave Eiffel (see fig. 4.2).

The first important commission carried out by Horta was the house of a Professor Tassel in Brussels, where he substantially advanced Viollet-le-Duc's structural theories. The stair hall (fig. **5.11**) is an integrated harmony of linear rhythms, established in the balustrades of ornamental iron, the whiplash curves atop the capitals, the arabesque designs

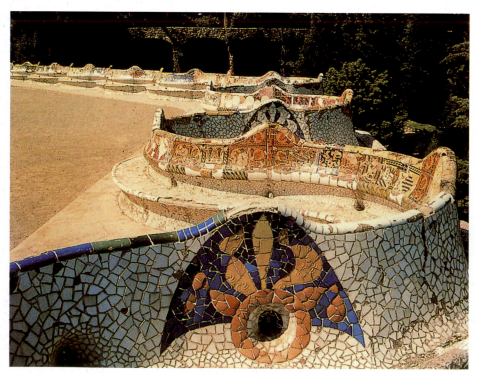

5.10 Antoni Gaudí, Detail of surrounding wall, Güell Park, Barcelona, 1900–14.

5.11 Victor Horta, Stairwell of interior, Tassel House, Brussels. 1892–93.

a form of building without traditions, and its functions lent themselves to an architecture that emphasized openness and spatial flow as well as ornate decorative backgrounds. The façade of Horta's department store in Brussels, À l'Innovation (fig. **5.12**), is a display piece of glass and curvilinear metal supports. Such department stores, like Sullivan's Carson Pirie Scott store (1899–1904), sprang up all over Europe and America at the beginning of the twentieth century. Their utilitarian purpose made them appropriate embodiments of the new discoveries in mass construction: exposed-metal and glass structure and decorative tracery. Horta's design was notable for its expression of the interior on the glass skin of the exterior, so that the three floors, with a tall central "nave" and flanking, four-story side aisles, are articulated in the façade.

Many distinguished architects were associated with Art Nouveau in one context or another, but few of their works can be identified with the style to the same degree as Horta's. The stations designed by **Hector Guimard** (1867–1925) for the Paris Métropolitain (subway) can be considered pure Art Nouveau, perhaps because they were less architectural structures than decorative signs or symbols. Guimard's Métro stations were constructed for the enormous Exposition Universelle in 1900 out of prefabricated parts of cast iron and glass. At odds with the prevailing

on the walls and floor, and the winding steps. Line triumphs over sculptured mass as a multitude of fanciful, tendrillike elements blend into an organic whole that boldly exposes the supporting metal structure. In Horta's Maison du Peuple, built in 1897–99 as the headquarters of the Belgian Socialist Party, and now destroyed, the architect worked for a clientele that departed from the usual upper-middle-class patrons of his houses. The façade was a curtain wall of glass supported on a minimum of metal structural frames and wrapped around the irregularly curving edge of an open plaza. The auditorium interior effectively became a glass enclosure in which the angled, exposed frame girders formed articulated supports for the double curve of the ceiling. The interior was given variety and interest by the combination of vertical glass walls, angled metal struts, and an open, curving ceiling, and in general achieved a harmonious unity between ornament and articulated structure.

Many of the chief examples of Art Nouveau architecture are to be found in the designs of department stores and similar commercial buildings. The large-scale department store was a characteristic development of the later nineteenth century, superseding the older type of small shop and enclosing the still older form of the bazaar. Thus it was

5.12 Victor Horta, À l'Innovation department store, Brussels. 1901. Destroyed by fire 1967.

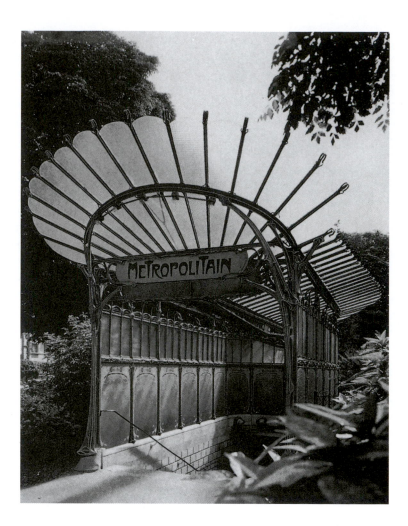

taste for classicism, they created a sensation in Paris, causing one critic to compare them to a dragonfly's wings. His entrance for the Porte Dauphine station (fig. **5.13**) is a rare example of an original Guimard canopy still intact.

Aside from the elaborate "sea horse" ornament on its façade, the Atelier Elvira by **August Endell** (1871–1925) in Munich (fig. **5.14**) is a relatively simple and austere structure. However, details of the interior, notably the stair hall, did continue the delicate undulations of Art Nouveau.

The Palais Stoclet in Brussels (fig. **5.15**) by the Austrian architect **Josef Hoffmann** (1870–1955), is a flat-walled, rectangular structure, although the dining-room murals by Klimt (see fig. 5.5) and the interior furnishings and decorations represent a typical Art Nouveau synthesis of decorative accessories. Hoffmann's starkly abstract language is closer to the elegant geometry of the Viennese Jugendstil school than the flourishes of the Belgian Art Nouveau, and really belongs in the context of works such as Otto

5.14 August Endell, Atelier Elvira, Munich. 1897.

5.15 Josef Hoffmann, Palais Stoclet, Brussels. 1905–11.

Wagner's Postal Savings Bank in Vienna and the architecture of Peter Behrens, Adolf Loos, Joseph Maria Olbrich, and van de Velde, all discussed in chapter 12 (see figs. 12.9, 12.10, 12.11, 12.12, 12.13).

Toward Expressionism: Late Nineteenth-Century Painting beyond France

In retrospect it is apparent that Jugendstil was as important for the new ideas it evoked in painters of the era as for the immediate impetus given architects and designers working directly in an Art Nouveau style. The Norwegian Edvard Munch, who had a sizable impact on German Expressionism; the Swiss Ferdinand Hodler; the Belgian James Ensor, a progenitor of Surrealism; and the Russian Vasily Kandinsky, one of the first abstract artists, all grew up in the environment of Jugendstil or Art Nouveau. Although some of the artists in this section formed their highly individual styles in response to advanced French art, they also drew extensively from their own local artistic traditions.

Scandinavia

By 1880, at the time **Edvard Munch** (1863–1944) began to study painting seriously, Oslo (then Kristiania), Norway, had a number of accomplished painters and a degree of patronage for their works. But the tradition was largely academic, rooted in the French Romantic Realism of the Barbizon School and in German lyrical naturalism, in part because Norwegian painters usually trained in Germany. In Kristiania, Munch was part of a radical group of bohemian writers and painters who worked in a naturalist mode.

Thanks to scholarships granted by the Norwegian government, Munch lived intermittently in Paris between 1889 and 1892, and he had already spent three weeks in the French capital in 1885. Though it is not clear what art he saw while in France, the Post-Impressionist works he must have encountered surely struck a sympathetic chord with his incipient Symbolist tendencies. In 1892 his reputation had grown to the point where he was invited to exhibit at the Verein Berliner Künstler (Society of Berlin Artists). His retrospective drew such a storm of criticism that the members of the Society voted to close it after less than a week. Sympathetic artists, led by Max Liebermann, left the Society and formed the Berlin Secession. This recognition—and controversy—encouraged Munch to settle in Germany, where he spent most of his time until 1908.

In evaluating Munch's place in European painting it could be argued that he was formed not so much by his Norwegian origins as by his exposure first to Paris during one of the most exciting periods in the history of French painting, and then to Germany at the moment when a new and dynamic art was emerging. The singular personal quality of his paintings and prints, however, is unquestionably a result of an intensely literary and even mystical approach that was peculiarly Scandinavian, intensified by his own tortured psyche. The painter moved in literary circles in Norway as well as in Paris and Berlin, was a friend of noted writers, among them the playwright August Strindberg, and in 1906 made stage designs for Ibsen's plays *Ghosts* and *Hedda Gabler.*

Although he lived to be eighty years old, the specters of sickness and death hovered over Munch through much of his life. His mother and sister died of tuberculosis while he was still young. His younger brother succumbed in 1895, five years after the death of their father, and Munch himself suffered from serious illnesses. Sickness and death began to appear early in his painting and recurred continually. The subject of *The Sick Child*, related to the illness and death of his sister (fig. 5.16), haunted him for years. He reworked the painting over and over, and made prints of the subject as well as two later versions of the painting.

Munch's mentor, the leading Norwegian naturalist painter **Christian Krohg** (1852–1925), had earlier explored a similar theme, common in the art and literature of the period, but he did so with an astonishingly direct and exacting style (fig. **5.17**). This sitter confronts the viewer head-on, her pale skin and white gown stark against the white pillow. Krohg, who had also watched his sister die of tuberculosis, avoided the usual sentimentality or latent eroticism that normally pervaded contemporary treatments of such subjects. While his version could not have predicted the melodrama or painterly handling of Munch's painting, the connection between the two canvases is obvious, though Munch, typically, denied the possibility of influence.

Munch was enormously prolific, and throughout his life experimented with many different themes, palettes, and styles of drawing. The works of the turn of the century, in

5.16 Edvard Munch, *The Sick Child*, 1885–86. Oil on canvas, 47 × 46⅝" (119.4 × 118.4 cm). Nasjonalgalleriet, Oslo.

5.17 Christian Krohg, *The Sick Girl*, 1880–81. Oil on wood, 40⅛ × 22⅞" (101.9 × 58.1 cm). Nasjonalgalleriet, Oslo.

destructive force seem at times to provide classic examples of the problems Freud was exploring. In many works, *The Dance of Life* among them (fig. **5.19**), Munch transformed the moon and its long reflection on the water into a phallic symbol. *The Dance of Life* belongs to a large series Munch called The Frieze of Life, which contained most of his major paintings (including *The Scream*), addressing the central themes of love, sexual anxiety, and death. The subject of this painting, based on Munch's troubled personal history of love and rejection, was in step with international trends in Symbolist art.

Munch was one of the major graphic artists of the twentieth century, and like Gauguin, he took a very experimental approach to printmaking and contributed to a revival of the woodcut medium. He began making etchings and lithographs in 1894 and for a time was principally interested in using the media to restudy subjects he had painted earlier. The prints, however, were never merely reproductions of the paintings. In each case he reworked the theme in terms of the new medium, sometimes executing the same subject in drypoint, woodcut, and lithography, and varying each of these as each was modified from the painting. For *Vampire* (fig. **5.20**), Munch used an ingenious method he had invented for bypassing the tedious printmaking process of color registration, which involves inking separate areas of the woodblock for each color and painstakingly aligning the sheet for every pass

which the symbolic content is most explicit, are characterized by the sinuous, constantly moving, curving line of Art Nouveau, combined with color dark in hue but brilliant in intensity. Influences from Gauguin and the Nabis are present in his work of this period. The anxieties that plagued Munch were frequently given a more general and ambiguous, though no less frightening, expression. *The Scream* (fig. **5.18**) is an agonized shriek translated into bands of color that echo like sound waves across the landscape and through the blood-red sky. The image has its source in Munch's experience. As he walked across a bridge with friends at sunset, he was seized with despair and "felt a great, infinite scream pass through nature." *The Scream*, the artist's best-known and most widely reproduced image, has become a familiar symbol of modern anxiety and alienation.

Munch was emerging as a painter at the moment when Sigmund Freud was developing his theories of psychoanalysis. His obsessions with sex, death, and woman as a

5.18 Edvard Munch, *The Scream*, 1893. Oil and tempera on board, 35¾ × 29" (90.8 × 73.7 cm). Nasjonalgalleriet, Oslo.

5.19 Edvard Munch, *The Dance of Life*, 1900. Oil on canvas, 4'1½" × 6'3½" (1.26 × 1.9 m). Nasjonalgalleriet, Oslo.

(one for each color) through the press. Munch simply sawed his block into sections, inked each section separately, and assembled them like a puzzle for a single printing. In *Vampire*, he actually combined this technique with lithography to make a "combination print." Through these innovative techniques, Munch gained rich graphic effects, such as subtly textured patterns (by exploiting the rough grain of the woodblock), and translucent passages of color. His imagery, already explored in several drawings and paintings made in Berlin, is typically ambiguous. While the redheaded woman could be embracing her lover, the ominous shadow that looms above them and the title of the work imply something far more sinister.

Northern and Central Europe

The Swiss artist **Ferdinand Hodler** (1853–1918) also knew the ravages of sickness and death, and, like Van Gogh, had undergone a moral crisis in the wake of deep religious commitment. In his paintings, he avoided the turbulent drama of earlier Romantic expressions and sought instead frozen stillness, spareness, and purity, the better to evoke some sense of the unity within the apparent confusion and complexity of the world of experience. This can be discerned in the famous *Night* (fig. **5.21**), where the surfaces and volumes of nature have been described in exacting detail, controlled by an equally intense concern for abstract pattern, a kind of rigorously balanced, friezelike

5.20 Edvard Munch, *Vampire*, 1902. Woodcut and lithograph, from an 1895 woodcut, 14⅞ × 21½" (38 × 54.6 cm). Munch-Museet, Oslo.

5.21 Ferdinand Hodler, *Night*, 1889–90. Oil on canvas, 3'9¾" × 9'9¾" (1.17 × 3 m). Kunstmuseum, Bern.

organization the artist called "parallelism." As in Munch's *The Scream*, the imagery in *Night* was an expression of Hodler's own obsessive fears. The central figure, who awakens to find a shrouded phantom crouched above him, is a self-portrait, as is the man at the upper right, while the women in the foreground are depictions of his mistress and ex-wife. The painting was banned from an exhibition in Geneva in 1891 as indecent, but encountered a better reception when it was later shown in Paris.

James Ensor (1860–1949), whose long life was almost exactly contemporary with Munch's, differed from the Norwegian in being the inheritor of one of the great traditions in European art—that of Flemish and Dutch painting. The consciousness of this heritage even compelled him to assume from time to time, though half satirically, the appearance of Rubens (fig. **5.22**), and it is difficult to believe that he could have conceived his pictorial fantasies without knowledge of the late-medieval works of Hieronymus Bosch (despite his denials) and Pieter Brueghel the Elder. Outside of a three-year period of study at the Royal Academy of Fine Arts in Brussels, Ensor spent his entire life in his native Ostend, on the coast of Belgium, where his Flemish mother and her relatives kept a souvenir shop filled with toys, seashells, model ships in bottles, crockery, and, above all, the grotesque masks popular at Flemish carnivals.

By 1881, Ensor could produce such accomplished traditional Realist–Romantic paintings that he was accepted in the Brussels Salon and by 1882 in the Paris Salon. His approach was already changing, however, with the introduction of brutal or mocking subject matter, harshly authentic pictures of miserable, drunken tramps and inexplicable meetings of masked figures. *Scandalized Masks,* for instance, shows a familiar setting, the corner of a room, with a masked figure sitting at a table. Another masked figure enters through the open door. The masked figures obviously derive from the Flemish carnivals of popular tradition, but here, isolated in their grim surroundings, they cease to be merely masked mummers. The mask becomes the reality, and we feel involved in some communion of monsters.

This troubling and fantastic picture reveals intensification of the artist's inner mood of disturbance. In any event, the new works did not please the judges of the Brussels Salon, and in 1884 all Ensor's entries were rejected.

Ensor's mature paintings still have the capacity to shock. He was something of an eccentric and much affected by

5.22 James Ensor, *Portrait of the Artist Surrounded by Masks*, 1899. Oil on canvas, 47 × 31½" (119.4 × 80 cm). Menard Art Museum, Aichi, Japan.

nineteenth-century Romanticism and Symbolism, evident in his passionate devotion to the tales of Poe and Balzac, the poems of Baudelaire, and the work of several contemporary Belgian writers. He searched the tradition of fantastic painting and graphic art for inspiration—from the tormented visions of Matthias Grünewald and Bosch to Goya. Ensor was further affected by Daumier and his social commentaries (see figs. 2.14, 2.15), the book illustrator Gustave Doré, Redon, and the decadent-erotic imagery of the Belgian artist Félicien Rops.

During the late 1880s Ensor turned to religious subjects, frequently the torments of Christ. They are not interpreted in a narrowly religious sense, but are rather a personal revulsion for a world of inhumanity that nauseated him. This feeling was given its fullest expression in the most important painting of his career, *The Entry of Christ into Brussels in 1889* (fig. **5.23**), a work from 1888–89 that depicts the Passion of Christ as the center of a contemporary Flemish kermis, or carnival, symptomatic of the indifference, stupidity, and venality of the modern world. Ensor describes this grotesque tumult of humanity with dissonant color, compressing the crowd into a vast yet claustrophobic space. Given the enormous size of *The Entry of Christ* (it is over twelve feet, or 3.5 m, wide), it has been suggested that Ensor painted it in response to Seurat's *La Grande Jatte* (see fig. 3.1), which had been much heralded at an exhibition in Brussels in 1887. While the French painting was a modern celebration of middle-class life, Ensor's was an indictment of it. The figure of

Christ, barely visible in the back of the crowd, was probably based on the artist's own likeness. This conceit—the artist as persecuted martyr—was being exploited by Gauguin in Brittany at virtually the same time. By extension, Ensor's hideous crowd refers to the ignorant citizens of Ostend, who greeted his work with incomprehension.

Even members of a more liberal exhibiting group of Brussels, called L'Essor, were somewhat uneasy about Ensor's new paintings. This led in 1884 to a withdrawal of some members, including Ensor, to form the progressive society Les XX (The Twenty). For many years the society was to support aspects of the new art in Brussels. Although it exhibited Manet, Seurat, Van Gogh, Gauguin, and Toulouse-Lautrec, and exerted an influence in the spread of Neo-Impressionism and Art Nouveau, hostility to Ensor's increasingly fantastic paintings grew even there. *The Entry of Christ* was refused admission and was never publicly exhibited before 1929. The artist himself was saved from expulsion from the group only by his own vote.

During the 1890s Ensor focused much of his talent for invective on the antagonists of his paintings, frequently with devastating results. Some of his most brilliant and harrowing works were produced at this time. The masks reappeared at regular intervals, occasionally becoming particularly personal, as in *Portrait of the Artist Surrounded by Masks* (see fig. 5.22), a painting in which he portrayed himself in the manner of Rubens's self-portraits—with debonair mustache and beard, plumed hat, and piercing glance directed at the spectator. The work is reminiscent of

5.23 James Ensor, *The Entry of Christ into Brussels in 1889*, 1888–89. Oil on canvas, 8'5" × 12'5" (2.6 × 3.8 m). J. Paul Getty Museum, Malibu.

5.24 Arnold Böcklin, *Island of the Dead*, 1880. Oil on wood, 29 × 48" (73.7 × 122 cm). The Metropolitan Museum of Art, New York.

an earlier 1883 self-portrait by Ensor and, in a curious way, of a painting by Hieronymus Bosch of Christ surrounded by his tormentors (here, Ensor's critics): the personification of Good, isolated by Evil but never overwhelmed.

The ancestors of twentieth-century Surrealism can also be found in a trio of artists who emerged in German-speaking Europe during the Symbolist era: Böcklin, Klinger, and Kubin. The eldest of these was **Arnold Böcklin** (1827–1901), born in Basel, educated in Düsseldorf and Geneva, and then resident in Italy until the end of his life. Like so many others within contemporary German culture, Böcklin fell prey to the classical dream, which prompted him to paint, with brutal, almost grotesque academic Realism, such mythical beings as centaurs and mermaids writhing in battle, or in some sexual contest between a hapless, depleted male and an exultant *femme fatale*. One of his most haunting images, especially for later painters like Giorgio de Chirico and the Surrealists, came to be called *Island of the Dead* (fig. **5.24**), a scene depicting no known reality but universally appealing to the late Romantic and Symbolist imagination. With its uncanny stillness, its ghostly white-cowled figure, and its

eerie moonlight illuminating rocks and the entrances to tombs against the deep, mysteriously resonant blues and greens of sky, water, and tall, melancholy cypresses, the picture provided inspiration not only for subsequent painters but also for numerous poets and composers.

The German artist Max Klinger (1857–1920) paid homage to Böcklin by making prints after several of his paintings, including *Island of the Dead*. Klinger is best known for a ten-part cycle of prints, entitled *A Glove*, whose sense of fantasy may owe something to the dark, sinister imaginings of Goya. The Czech artist and illustrator Alfred Kubin (1877–1959) proved capable of phantasms well in excess of those found in the art of either Böcklin or Klinger. Indeed, he may be compared with Redon, though his obsession with woman-as-destroyer themes places him alongside *fin-de-siècle* artists like Rops as well as anticipating the Freudian world of Surrealism. Kubin was to become a member of Kandinsky's Munich circle, and in 1911 he joined a set of brilliant and experimental artists in Germany called Der Blaue Reiter (the Blue Rider). Meanwhile, in 1909, he published his illustrated novel entitled *The Other Side,* often regarded as a progenitor of the hallucinatory fictions of Franz Kafka.

6
The Origins of Modern Sculpture

In the twentieth century, sculpture as an expressive and experimental art form enjoyed something of a renaissance. Its modern development has been even more remarkable than that of painting. The painting revolution was achieved against the background of an unbroken great tradition extending back to the fourteenth century. In the nineteenth century, despite the prevalence of lesser academicians, painting was the principal visual art, producing during the first seventy-five years such artists as Goya, Blake, Friedrich, David, Ingres, Géricault, Delacroix, Constable, Turner, Corot, Courbet, and Manet. The leading names in sculpture during this same period were Bertel Thorvaldsen, François Rude, Pierre-Jean David d'Angers, Antoine-Louis Barye, Jean-Baptiste Carpeaux, Jules Dalou, Alexandre Falguière, and Constantin Meunier, none of whom, despite their accomplishments, have the world reputations of the leading painters.

The eighteenth century also was an age of painting rather than sculpture. During that century, only the French Neoclassical sculptor Jean-Antoine Houdon and the Italian Antonio Canova may be compared with the most important painters. Thus, the seventeenth century was the last great age of sculpture before the twentieth century and then principally in the person of the Baroque sculptor Gianlorenzo Bernini. In the United States, with the exception of one or two artists of originality, such as Augustus Saint-Gaudens (see fig. 2.54), sculptors were secondary figures until well into the twentieth century.

When we consider the dominant place that sculpture has held in the history of art from ancient Egypt until the seventeenth century of our era, this decline appears all the more remarkable. It was not for want of patronage. Although the eighteenth century provided fewer large public commissions than the Renaissance or the Baroque periods, during the nineteenth century mountains of sculptural monuments crowded the parks and public squares, and adorned architecture. By this time, however, academic classicism had achieved such a rigid grip on the sculptural tradition that it was virtually impossible for a sculptor to gain a commission or even to survive without conforming. The experimental painter could usually find a small group of enlightened private patrons, but for the sculptor the very nature of the medium and the tradition of nineteenth-century sculpture as a monumental and public art made this difficult. After the eighteenth century, the center for sculpture in western Europe shifted from Italy to Paris, due in part to technological innovations and new sources for patronage, and the French Romantic period produced several sculptors of note, such as Carpeaux and Barye. (Paris was to remain Europe's major center of art from around 1720 to 1920, when other centers emerged in the more pluralistic adventures of modernism.) This geographical shift was accompanied by a tendency of artists to turn away from the preferred Neoclassical technique of carving marble to the practice of modeling plaster and wax. These materials could carry the inflection of the artist's hand and serve as a means to make the work reveal the process of its own creation. The models could then be cast in permanent form, in bronze.

The basic subject for sculpture from the beginning of time until the twentieth century had been the human figure. It is in terms of the figure, presented in isolation or in combination, in action or in repose, that sculptors have explored the elements of sculpture—space, mass, volume, line, texture, light, and movement. Among these elements, volume and space and their interaction have traditionally been a primary concern. Within the development of classical, medieval, or Renaissance and Baroque sculpture we may observe progressions from static frontality to later solutions in which the figure is stated as a complex mass revolving in surrounding space, and interpenetrated by it. The sense of activated space in Hellenistic, Late Gothic, and Baroque sculpture was often created through increased movement, expressed in a twisting pose, extended gesture, or by a broken, variegated surface texture whose light and shadow accentuated the feeling of transition or change. The Baroque propensity for space, movement, and spontaneity was part of the nineteenth-century sculptural tradition.

One of the most conclusive symptoms of the revival of sculpture at the turn of the century was the large number of important painters who practiced sculpture—Gauguin, Degas, Renoir, and Bonnard among them. These were followed a little later by Picasso, Matisse, Amadeo Modigliani, André Derain, Umberto Boccioni, and others.

The Painter–Sculptors: Daumier, Degas, and Gauguin

The pioneer painter–sculptor of the nineteenth century was Honoré Daumier (see chapter 2). His small caricatural busts were created between 1830 and 1832 to lampoon the eminent politicians of Louis Philippe's regime. Daumier could not resist mocking the apelike features of the Comte de Kératry (fig. 6.1), for he was not only a government official, but an art critic as well. These satirical sculptures anticipate the late works of Auguste Rodin in their expressive power and the directness of their deeply modeled surfaces. Daumier's *Ratapoil* ("hairy rat") of 1851 is not based on an actual person but is a personification of all the unscrupulous agents of Louis-Napoléon (later Napoléon III). Their arrogance and tawdry elegance are subtly communicated through the figure's twisting pose and the fluttering flow of clothing, counterpoised by the bony armature of the figure itself. Out of fear that it would be destroyed by the very forces it satirized, the clay figurine was kept hidden until after Daumier's death, when, like the earlier busts, it was cast in bronze.

The sculpture of Daumier, now much admired, was a private art, little known or appreciated until its relatively recent "discovery."

Like Daumier's, the sculpture of Edgar Degas (see chapter 2) was little known to the sculptors of the first modern generation, for most of it was never publicly exhibited during his lifetime. Degas was concerned primarily with the traditional formal problems of sculpture, such as the continual experiments in space and movement represented by his dancers and horses. His posthumous bronze casts retain the immediacy of his original modeling material, a pigmented wax, which he built up over an armature, layer by layer, to a richly articulated surface in which the touch of his hand is directly recorded. While most of his sculptures have the quality of sketches, *Little Dancer Fourteen Years Old* (fig. 6.2) was a fully realized work that was exhibited at the 1881 Impressionist exhibition, the only time the artist showed one of his sculptures. By combining an actual tutu, satin slippers, and real hair with more

6.2 Edgar Degas, *Little Dancer Fourteen Years Old*, 1878–81. Wax, hair, linen bodice, satin ribbon and shoes, muslin tutu, wood base, height 39" (99.1 cm) without base. Collection Mr. and Mrs. Paul Mellon, Upperville, Virginia.

6.1 Honoré Daumier, *Comte de Kératry (The Obsequious One)*, c. 1833. Bronze, 4⅞ × 5¼ × 3⅝" (12.4 × 13.3 × 8.9 cm). Hirshhorn Museum and Sculpture Garden, Smithsonian Institution, Washington, D.C.

traditional media, Degas created an astonishingly modern object that foreshadowed developments in twentieth-century sculpture (see fig. 24.76).

Like Degas, Paul Gauguin (see chapter 3) was a painter with an often unorthodox approach to materials. Throughout his career he worked in a diverse range of media. In addition to making paintings, drawings, woodcuts, etchings, and monotypes, he carved in marble and wood and was one of the most innovative ceramic artists of the nineteenth century. His largest work in this medium, *Oviri* (fig. **6.3**), was executed during a visit to Paris between two Tahitian sojourns. The title means "savage" in Tahitian, a term with which Gauguin personally identified, for he later inscribed "Oviri" on a self-portrait. The mysterious, bug-eyed woman crushes a wolf beneath her feet and clutches a wolf cub to her side. Whether she embraces the cub or suffocates it is unclear, though Gauguin did refer to her as a "murderess" and a "cruel enigma." The head was perhaps inspired by the mummified skulls of Marquesan chiefs, while the torso derives from the voluptuous figures, symbols of fecundity, on the ancient Javanese reliefs at Borobudur, in Southeast Asia, of which Gauguin owned photographs. In his turning to non-Western sources and his determination to create an image of raw, primitive power, Gauguin anticipated some of the abiding concerns of European and American artists in the twentieth century (the influence of African art on Matisse and his contemporaries is discussed in chapter 7). When it was exhibited in Paris after his death in 1906, *Oviri* made a significant impact on, among others, the young Pablo Picasso.

An Art Reborn: Auguste Rodin

It was the achievement of the French sculptor **Auguste Rodin** (1840–1917) to rechart the course of sculpture almost singlehandedly and to give the art an impetus that led to a major renaissance. There is no one painter who occupies quite the place in modern painting that Rodin can claim in modern sculpture. He introduced modern ideas into the tradition-bound form of figural public sculpture. Unlike avant-garde painters such as Gauguin or Van Gogh, however, Rodin became an admired and respected public figure, thus helping to draw modern art into the cultural mainstream.

Early Career and *The Gates of Hell*

Rodin began his revolution, as had Courbet in painting (see chapter 2), with a reaction against the sentimental idealism of the academicians. His *Man with the Broken Nose* (fig. **6.4**) was rejected by the official Salon as being offensively realistic on the one hand and, on the other, as an unfinished fragment, a head with its rear portion broken away. Rodin sought the likeness rather than the character of his model, a poor old man who frequented his neighborhood. This early work was already mature and accomplished, suggesting the intensity of the artist's approach to his subject as well as his uncanny ability to exploit simultaneously the malleable properties of the original clay and the light-saturated tensile strength of the final bronze material.

Rodin's examination of nature was coupled with a re-examination of the art of the Middle Ages and the Renaissance—most specifically, of Donatello and Michelangelo. Although much academic sculpture paid lip service to the High Renaissance, it was viewed through centuries of imitative accretions that tended to obscure the unique expression of the old masters. Rodin was in possession of the full range of historical sculptural forms and techniques by the time he returned in 1875 from a brief but formative visit to Italy, where he studied firsthand the work of Michelangelo, who, he said, "liberated me from academicism."

6.3 Paul Gauguin, *Oviri*, 1894. Partially glazed stoneware, 29½ × 7½ × 10⅜" (74.9 × 19.1 × 27 cm). Musée d'Orsay, Paris.

6.4 Auguste Rodin, *Man with the Broken Nose*, 1864. Bronze, 12¼ × 7½ × 6½" (31.1 × 19 × 16.5 cm). Hirshhorn Museum and Sculpture Garden, Smithsonian Institution, Washington, D.C.

The Age of Bronze (fig. **6.5**), Rodin's first major signed work, was accepted in the Salon of 1877, but its seeming scrupulous realism led to the suspicion that it might have been in part cast from the living model—which became a legitimate technique for making sculpture only in the sixties (see fig. 21.23). Although Rodin had unquestionably observed the model closely from all angles and was concerned with capturing and unifying the essential quality of the living form, he was also concerned with the expression of a tragic theme, inspired perhaps by his reaction to the Franco–Prussian War of 1870, so disastrous for the French. The figure, which once held a spear, was originally titled *Le Vaincu* (the vanquished one) and was based firmly on the *Dying Slave* of Michelangelo. By removing the spear, Rodin created a more ambivalent and ultimately more daring sculpture. The suggestion of action, frequently violent and varied, had been an essential part of the repertory of academic sculpture since the Late Renaissance, but its expression in nineteenth-century sculpture normally took the form of a sort of tableau of frozen movement. Rodin, however, studied his models in constant motion, in shifting positions and attitudes, so that every gesture and transitory change of pose became part of his vocabulary. As he passed from this concentrated study of nature to the later Expressionist works, even his most melodramatic subjects and most violently distorted poses were given credibility by their secure basis in observed nature.

In 1880 Rodin received a commission, the most important one of his career, for a portal to the proposed Museum of Decorative Arts in Paris. He conceived the idea of a free interpretation of scenes from Dante's *Inferno*, within a design scheme based on Lorenzo Ghiberti's great fifteenth-century gilded-bronze portals for the Florence Baptistry, popularly known as the Gates of Paradise. Out of his ideas emerged *The Gates of Hell* (fig. **6.6**), which remains one of the masterpieces of nineteenth- and twentieth-century

6.5 Auguste Rodin, *The Age of Bronze*, 1876. Bronze, 71 × 28" (180.3 × 71.1 cm). The Minneapolis Institute of Art.

6.6 Auguste Rodin, *The Gates of Hell*, 1880–1917. Bronze, 20'10" × 13'1" × 2'9"½ (6.4 m × 4 × 0.85 m). Musée Rodin, Paris.

sculpture. It is not clear whether the original plaster sculpture of *The Gates* that Rodin exhibited at the Exposition Universelle in 1900 was complete, though it is clear that the idea of academic "finish" was abhorrent to the artist. *The Gates* were never installed in the Museum of Decorative Arts, and the five bronze casts that exist today were all made posthumously. Basing his ideas loosely on individual themes from Dante but also utilizing ideas from the poems of Baudelaire, which he greatly admired, Rodin created isolated figures, groups, or episodes, experimenting with different configurations over more than thirty years.

The Gates contain a vast repertory of forms and images that the sculptor developed in this context and then adapted to other uses, and sometimes vice versa. For example, he executed the central figure of Dante, a brooding nude seated in the upper panel with his right elbow perched on his left knee, as an independent sculpture and exhibited it with the title *The Thinker; The Poet; Fragment of the Gate*. It became the artist's best-known work, in part because of the many casts that exist of it in several sizes. *The Gates* are crammed with a dizzying variety of forms on many different scales, above and across the lintel, throughout the architectural frieze and framework, and rising and falling restlessly within the turmoil of the main panels. To convey the turbulence of his subjects, Rodin depicted the human figure bent and twisted to the limits of endurance, although with remarkably little actual distortion of anatomy. Imprisoned within the drama of their agitated and anguished state, the teeming figures—coupled, clustered, or isolated—seem a vast and melancholy meditation on the tragedy of the human condition, on the plight of souls trapped in eternal longing, and on the torment of guilt and frustration. Like *The Thinker*, many of the figures made for *The Gates of Hell* are famous as individual sculptures, including *The Three Shades*, who stand hunched atop the gates. The tragedy and despair of the work are perhaps best summarized in *The Crouching Woman*, whose contorted figure, a compact, twisted mass, attains a beauty that is rooted in intense suffering.

The violent play on the human figure seen here was a forerunner of the Expressionist distortions of the figure developed in the twentieth century. An even more suggestive and modern phenomenon is to be found in the basic concept of the *Gates*—that of flux or metamorphosis, in which the figures emerge from or sink into the matrix of the bronze itself, are in the process of birth from, or death and decay into, a quagmire that both liberates and threatens to engulf them. Essential to the suggestion of change in the *Gates* and in most of the mature works of Rodin is the exploitation of light. A play of light and shadow moves over the peaks and crevasses of bronze or marble, becoming analogous to color in its evocation of movement, of growth and dissolution.

Although Rodin, in the sculptural tradition that had persisted since the Renaissance, was first of all a modeler, starting with clay and then casting the clay model in

6.7 Auguste Rodin, *Thought (Camille Claudel)*, 1886. Marble, 29½ × 17 × 18" (74.9 × 43.2 × 45.7 cm). Musée d'Orsay, Paris.

plaster and bronze, many of his most admired works are in marble. These also were normally based on clay and plaster originals, with much of the carving, as was customary, done by assistants. Rodin closely supervised the work and finished the marbles with his own hand. The marbles were handled with none of the expressive roughness of the bronzes (except in deliberately unfinished areas) and without deep undercutting. He paid close attention to the delicate, translucent, sensuous qualities of the marble, which in his later works he increasingly emphasized—inspired by unfinished works of Michelangelo—by contrasting highly polished flesh areas with masses of rough, unfinished stone. In his utilization of the raw material of stone for expressive ends, as in his use of the partial figure (the latter suggested no doubt by fragments of ancient sculptures), Rodin was initiating the movement away from the human figure as the prime medium of sculptural expression. The remarkable portrait of his lover and fellow sculptor, Camille Claudel (fig. **6.7**), does away with the torso altogether to personify meditation through the abrupt juxtaposition of a smoothly polished, disembodied head with a coarsely hewn block of marble.

The Burghers of Calais and Later Career

As a somewhat indirect memorial to French losses in the Franco–Prussian War, the city of Calais began formulating plans in 1884 for a public monument in memory of Eustache de Saint-Pierre, who in 1347, during the

Hundred Years' War, had offered himself, along with five other prominent citizens, as hostage to the English in the hope of raising the long siege of the city. The commission held particular appeal for Rodin. In the old account of the event, the medieval historian Froissart describes the hostages as delivered barefoot and clad in sackcloth, with ropes around their necks, bearing the keys to the city and fortress; this tale permitted the artist to be historically accurate and yet avoid the problem of period costumes without resorting to nudity. After winning the competition with a relatively conventional heroic design set on a tall base, Rodin created a group of greater psychological complexity, in which individual figures, bound together by common sacrifice, respond to it in varied ways (fig. **6.8**). So he studied each figure separately and then assembled them all on a low rectangular platform, a nonheroic arrangement that allows the viewer to approach the figures directly. It took some doing for Rodin to persuade Calais to accept the work, for rather than an image of a readily recognizable historical event, he presented six particularized variations on the theme of human courage, deeply moving in their emotional range and thus very much a private monument as well as a public one.

The debt of *The Burghers of Calais* to the fourteenth- and fifteenth-century sculptures of Claus Sluter and Claus de Werve is immediately apparent, but this influence has been combined with an assertion of the dignity of common humanity analogous to the nineteenth-century sculptures of the Belgian artist Constantin Meunier. The rough-hewn faces, powerful bodies, and the enormous hands and feet transform these burghers into laborers and peasants and at the same time enhance their physical presence, as do the outsize keys. Rodin's tendency to dramatic gesture is apparent here, and the theatrical element is emphasized by the unorthodox organization, with the figures scattered about the base like a group of stragglers wandering across a stage. The informal, open arrangement of the figures, none of whom touch, is one of the most daring and original aspects of the sculpture. It is a direct attack on the classical tradition of closed, balanced groupings for monumental sculpture. The detached placing of the masses gives the intervening spaces an importance that, for almost

6.8 Auguste Rodin, *The Burghers of Calais*, 1886. Six figures, bronze, 6'10½" × 7'11" × 6'6" at base (2.1 × 2.4 × 2 m). Hirshhorn Museum and Sculpture Garden, Smithsonian Institution, Washington, D.C.

the first time in modern sculpture, reverses the traditional roles of solid and void, of mass and space. Space not only surrounds the figures but interpenetrates the group, creating a dynamic, asymmetrical sense of balance. Rodin's wish that the work be placed not on a pedestal but at street level, situating it directly in the viewer's space, anticipated some of the most revolutionary innovations of twentieth-century sculpture.

Many of Rodin's later figures are characterized by extreme and highly sensual poses. In *Iris, Messenger of the Gods* (fig. **6.9**) the maimed, truncated form and contorted pose of the headless, one-armed torso, embodies tremendous vitality and displays a sexual boldness that far exceeds the thinly veiled, clichéd eroticism of academic sculptures of the female nude. Though the partial figure seems the sculptural equivalent of a sketch, it is a fragment that reaches an expressive completeness.

Rodin's *Monument to Balzac*, a work he called "the sum of my whole life," was commissioned in 1891 by the French Writers' Association, at the urging of the novelist Émile Zola. Here the artist plunged so deeply into the privacy of individual psychology—his own perhaps even more than the subject's—that he failed to gain acceptance by the patrons. What these and the public perceived was a tall, shapeless mass crowned by a shaggy head so full of Rodin's "lumps and hollows" that it seemed more a desecrating caricature than a tribute to the great novelist Honoré

de Balzac, who had died in 1850. Little were they prepared to appreciate what even the artist characterized as a symbolism of a kind "yet unknown." The work provoked a critical uproar, with some proclaiming it a masterpiece and others reviling it as a monstrosity, whereupon it was withdrawn from the Paris Salon in 1898.

Rodin struggled to realize a portrait that would transcend any mere likeness and be a sculptural equivalent of a famously volcanic creative force. He made many different studies over a period of seven years, some of an almost academic exactness, others more emblematic. In the end, Rodin cloaked Balzac in the voluminous "monk's robe" he had habitually worn during his all-night writing sessions. The anatomy has virtually disappeared beneath the draperies, which are gathered up as if to muster and concentrate the whole of some prodigious inspiration, all reflected like a tragic imprint on the deep-set features of the colossal head. The figure leans back dramatically beneath the robe, a nearly abstract icon of generative power.

This symbolism of a kind "yet unknown" may have had its greatest impact in the photographs that Rodin commissioned **Edward Steichen** (1879–1973) to make of the original plaster cast of *Balzac* (fig. **6.10**). With a typical sureness of aesthetic instinct, Rodin proposed that Steichen try working by moonlight. Not only did this technique

6.9 Auguste Rodin, *Iris, Messenger of the Gods*, 1890–91. Bronze, 32 × 36 × 24" (81.3 × 91.4 × 61 cm). Hirshhorn Museum and Sculpture Garden, Smithsonian Institution, Washington, D.C.

6.10 Edward Steichen, *Balzac—The Open Sky*, 1908. Photogravure from *Camera Work*, no. 34–35, 1911, 8 × 6⅛" (20.3 × 15.6 cm). The Museum of Modern Art, New York.

6.11 Auguste Rodin, *Study of Isadora Duncan*, Pencil and watercolor on paper, 12¼ × 9" (31.1 × 22.9 cm).

avoid the flattening effect that direct sunlight would have had on the white material, but the long exposure that the dim light required invested the pictures with a sense of timelessness totally unlike the stop-action instantaneity normally associated with the camera. Rodin detested such imagery as a treacherous distortion of reality. "It is the artist," he insisted, "who is truthful, and it is photography that lies, for in reality time does not stop, and if the artist succeeds in producing the impression of a movement which takes several moments for accomplishment, his work is certainly less conventional than the scientific image, where time is abruptly suspended." Rodin spent most of his creative life studying motion and improvising ways to express its drama and emotive effect in sculptural form. Often he did this in drawings made from a moving model, as in a famous series based on the dancer Isadora Duncan (fig. **6.11**), but always for the purpose of capturing in line the impression of a flowing, continuous process, not an arrested action.

Exploring New Possibilities: Claudel, Maillol, Bourdelle, and Rosso

Until the eighties, when long overdue retrospectives of her work were held, **Camille Claudel (1864–1943)** was known largely as Rodin's assistant and mistress. Tragically, she never recovered from her failed relationship with the

sculptor and was confined to mental hospitals for the last thirty years of her life. Claudel's work shares many formal characteristics with that of her mentor; nevertheless, hers was a highly original talent in a century that produced relatively few women sculptors of note, and at a time when it was still extremely difficult for women artists to have their work taken seriously. By the time she entered Rodin's studio at age twenty, she was already exhibiting at the Salon. Though she was an accomplished portraitist—she produced one of the most memorable images of Rodin— Claudel's particular strength lay with inventive solutions to multifigure compositions. An unusual and decidedly unheroic subject for sculpture, *Chatting Women* (fig. **6.12**) presents four seated figures, rapt in discussion, who form a tightly knit group in the corner of a room. An immediacy of expression and the quotidian nature of the subject seem at odds with the inexplicable nudity of the figures and the use of strongly veined and colored onyx, which serves to underscore the abstract nature of the representation.

French artists who chose to work in a more traditional mode—**Aristide Maillol (1861–1944)** and **Antoine Bourdelle (1861–1929)**—represent opposition to Rodin in their attempts to preserve but also modernize the classical ideal. Maillol focused his attention on this restatement of classicism, stripped of all the academic accretions of sentimental or erotic idealism. Concentrating almost exclusively

6.12 Camille Claudel, *Chatting Women*, 1897. Onyx and bronze, 17¾ × 16⅝ × 15⅜" (45 × 42.2 × 39 cm). Musée Rodin, Paris.

on the single nude female figure, standing, sitting, or reclining, and usually in repose, he repeatedly restated the fundamental nature of sculpture as integrated volume, as mass surrounded by tangible space.

Maillol began as a painter and tapestry designer; he was almost forty when the onset of a dangerous eye disease made the meticulous practice of weaving difficult, and he decided to change to sculpture. He began with wood carvings that had a definite relation to his paintings and to the Nabis and the Art Nouveau environment in which he had been working at the turn of the century (see chapters 3 and 5). However, he soon moved to clay modeling and developed a mature style that changed little throughout his life. That style is summarized in one of his very first sculptures, *The Mediterranean*, a massive, seated female nude, integrated as a set of curving volumes in space. He developed a personal brand of classicism that simplified the body into idealized, geometric forms and imparted a quality of psychological withdrawal and composed reserve. Maillol could also achieve an art of dynamic movement, as in *The River* (fig. **6.13**), a work that may have been affected by the late paintings and the sculptures of Renoir.

Antoine Bourdelle was a student and assistant of Rodin. Like Maillol, he sought to revitalize the classical tradition. His eclectic, somewhat archaeological approach drew on archaic and early fifth-century B.C.E. Greek sculpture, as well as the Gothic. *Hercules the Archer* (fig. **6.14**) discloses Bourdelle's indebtedness to Rodin; its scarred modeling is an echo of Rodin's *Thinker* translated into violent action. The figure, braced against the rocks in a pose of fantastic effort, is essentially a profile, two-dimensional alternation of large areas of solid and void, possibly inspired by the famous Roman sculpture of the *Discobolus,* itself based on a Greek original.

Medardo Rosso (1858–1928) was born in Turin, Italy, in 1858, and worked as a painter until 1880. After being dismissed from the Accademia di Brera in Milan in 1883, he lived in Paris for two years, worked in Dalou's atelier, and met Rodin. After 1889 Rosso spent most of his active career in Paris, until his death in 1928, and thus was associated more with French sculpture than with Italian. In a sense, he always remained a painter. Rosso extended the formal experiments of Rodin, deliberately dissolving sculptural forms until only an impression remained. His favorite

6.13 Aristide Maillol, *The River*, Begun 1938–39; completed 1943. Lead (cast 1948), 4'5¾" × 7'6" × 5'6" (1.37 × 2.3 × 1.68 m), on lead base designed by the artist, 9¾ × 67 × 27¾" (24.3 × 170.1 × 70.4 cm). The Museum of Modern Art, New York.

6.14 Antoine Bourdelle, *Hercules the Archer*, 1909. Bronze, 25 × 24 × 10¼" (63.5 × 61 × 26 cm). The Art Institute of Chicago.

6.15 Medardo Rosso, *The Concierge (La Portinaia)*, 1883. Wax over plaster, 14½ × 12⅝" (36.8 × 32 cm). The Museum of Modern Art, New York.

medium, wax, allowed the most imperceptible transitions, so that it becomes difficult to tell at exactly what point a face or figure emerges from an amorphous shape and many-textured surface. "Nothing is material in space," Rosso said. The primacy he gave to the play of light and shadow is evident in the soft *sfumato* that envelops the portrait of his old doorkeeper (fig. **6.15**), a work once owned by Émile Zola. This quality has sometimes led critics to call him an "Impressionist" sculptor. In his freshness of vision and his ability to catch and record the significant moment, Rosso added a new dimension to sculpture, in works that are invariably *intimiste*, small-scale, and antiheroic, and anticipated the search for immediacy that characterizes so much of the sculpture that followed.

7
Fauvism

*D*onatello *au milieu des fauves!* "Donatello among the wild beasts!" was the ready quip of Louis Vauxcelles, art critic for the review *Gil Blas,* when he entered Gallery VII at Paris's 1905 Salon d'Automne and found himself surrounded by blazingly colored, vehemently brushed canvases in the midst of which stood a small neo-Renaissance sculpture. With this witticism Vauxcelles gave the first French avant-garde style to emerge in the twentieth century its name, thereby provoking one of modernism's classic "scandals." It should be noted, however, that Vauxcelles was generally sympathetic to the work presented by the group of young painters, as were other liberal critics.

The starting point of Fauvism was later identified by Henri Matisse, the sober and rather professorial leader of the Fauves, as "the courage to return to the purity of means." Matisse and his fellow painters—André Derain, Maurice de Vlaminck, Georges Rouault, Raoul Dufy, and others—allowed their search for immediacy and clarity to show forth with bold, almost unbearable candor. While divesting themselves of Symbolist literary aesthetics, along with *fin-de-siècle* morbidity, the Fauves reclaimed Impressionism's direct, joyous embrace of nature and combined it with Post-Impressionism's heightened color contrasts and emotional, expressive depth. They emancipated color from its role of describing external reality and concentrated on the medium's ability to communicate directly the artist's experience of that reality by exploiting the pure chromatic intensity of paint. Fauvism burst on to the Parisian art scene at a time when the heady pace of change in the arts, as in society as a whole, was coming to be seen as part of the new, modern world order. Moreover, as artists from many different countries and backgrounds were drawn to Paris, seeking contact with the exciting new developments in art there, Fauve paintings made a deep impression on the new generation of avant-garde artists who were also coming to terms with the possibilities for painting opened up by Cézanne.

Inevitably, the Fauves' emphasis on achieving personal authenticity meant that they would never form a coherent movement or issue the kind of joint theoretical manifestos produced by many subsequent avant-garde movements. But before drifting apart as early as 1907, the Fauves made certain definite and unique contributions. Though none of them attempted complete abstraction, as did their contemporaries Vasily Kandinsky or Robert Delaunay, for example, they extended the boundaries of representation, based in part on their exposure to non-Western sources, such as African art. For subject matter they turned to portraiture, still life, and landscape. In the last, especially in the art of Matisse, they revisualized Impressionism's culture of leisure as a pagan ideal of *bonheur de vivre,* the joy of life. Most important of all, the Fauvist painters practiced an art in which the painting was conceived as an autonomous creation, delicately poised between expression derived from emotional, subjective experience and expression stimulated by pure optical sensation.

"Purity of Means" in Practice: Henri Matisse's Early Career

Henri Matisse (1869–1954) was born only two years after Bonnard (see chapter 3) and outlived him by seven years. These two contemporaries had much in common as artists. They were among the greatest colorists of the twentieth century, and each learned something from the other. Yet Matisse, one of the pioneers of twentieth-century experiment in painting, seems to belong to a later generation and to a different world. Like Bonnard, he at first studied law, but by 1891 he had enrolled in the Académie Julian, studying briefly with the academic painter Bouguereau, who came to represent everything he rejected in art. The following year he entered the École des Beaux-Arts and was fortunate enough to study with Gustave Moreau (see fig. 3.12), a dedicated teacher who encouraged his students to find their own directions through constant study in museums, as well as through individual experiment. In his class, Matisse met Georges Rouault, Albert Marquet, Henri-Charles Manguin, Charles Camoin,

7.1 Henri Matisse, *La Desserte (Dinner Table)*, 1896–97. Oil on canvas, 39¼ × 51½" (99.7 × 130.8 cm). Private collection.

and Charles Guérin, all of whom were later associated with the Fauves.

Matisse's work developed slowly from the dark tonalities and literal subjects he first explored. By the late 1890s he had discovered Neo-Impressionism and artists such as Toulouse-Lautrec and, most importantly, Cézanne. In about 1898 he began to experiment with figures and still lifes painted in bright, nondescriptive color. In 1900, Matisse entered the atelier of Eugène Carrière, a maker of dreamily romantic figure paintings. There he met André Derain, who introduced him to Vlaminck the following year, completing the principal Fauve trio. Around that time, Matisse also worked in the studio of Antoine Bourdelle (see fig. 6.14), making his first attempts at sculpture and demonstrating the abilities that were to make him one of the great painter–sculptors of the twentieth century.

Earliest Works

Among the paintings that Matisse copied in the Louvre during his student days under Moreau was a still life by the seventeenth-century Dutch painter Jan Davidsz. de Heem. Matisse's version was a free copy, considerably smaller than the original. In 1915, he was to make a Cubist variation of the work. At the Salon de la Société Nationale des Beaux-Arts (known as the Salon de la Nationale) of 1897, he exhibited his own composition of a still life, *Dinner Table* (fig. **7.1**), which was not favorably received by the conservatives. Though highly traditional on the face of it, this work was one of Matisse's most complicated and carefully constructed compositions to date, and it was his first truly modern work. While it still depended on locally descriptive color, this painting revealed in its luminosity an interest in the Impressionists. The abruptly tilted table that crowds and contracts the space of the picture anticipated the artist's subsequent move toward radical simplification in his later treatment of similar subjects (see fig. 7.11). *Male Model* of about 1900 (fig. **7.2**) carried this process of simplification and contraction several stages further, even

to the point of some distortion of perspective, to achieve a sense of delimited space. The modeling of the figure in abrupt facets of color was a direct response to the paintings of Cézanne, whose influence can also be seen in *Carmelina*, an arresting, frontalized arrangement in which the nude model projects sculpturally from the rectangular design of the background. With his own face reflected in

7.2 Henri Matisse, *Male Model (L'Homme Nu; "Le Serf" Academie bleue; Bevilacqua)*, Paris, 1900. Oil on canvas, 39⅛ × 28⅝" (99.3 × 72.7 cm). The Museum of Modern Art, New York.

7.3 Henri Matisse, *Luxe, calme et volupté*, 1904–5. Oil on canvas, 37 × 46" (94 × 116.8 cm). Musée d'Orsay, Paris.

the mirror behind the model, Matisse introduced two themes—the studio interior and the artist with his model—to which he often returned in the course of his life, as if to restate the modernist's abandonment of direct attachment to the outside world in favor of an ever-greater absorption in the world of art.

Between 1902 and 1905 Matisse exhibited at the Salon des Indépendants and at the galleries of Berthe Weill and Ambroise Vollard. The latter was rapidly becoming the principal dealer for the avant-garde artists of Paris. When the more liberal Salon d'Automne was established in 1903, Matisse showed there, along with Bonnard and Marquet. But most notorious was the Salon d'Automne of 1905, in which a room of paintings by Matisse, Vlaminck, Derain, and Rouault, among others, is supposed to have occasioned the remark that gave the group its permanent name.

The *Fauve* Period

The word *fauves* made particular reference to these artists' brilliant, arbitrary color, more intense than the "scientific" color of the Neo-Impressionists and the nondescriptive color of Gauguin and Van Gogh, and to the direct, vigorous brushwork with which Matisse and his friends had been experimenting the previous year at St. Tropez and Collioure on the Riviera in the south of France. The Fauves accomplished the liberation of color toward which, in their different ways, Cézanne, Gauguin, Van Gogh,

Seurat, and the Nabis had been experimenting. Using similar means, the Fauves were intent on different ends. They wished to use pure color squeezed directly from the tube, not to describe objects in nature, not simply to set up retinal vibrations, not to accentuate a romantic or mystical subject, but to build new pictorial values apart from all these. Thus, in a sense, they were using the color of Gauguin and Seurat, freely combined with their own linear rhythms, to reach effects similar to those which Cézanne constantly sought. It is no accident that of the artists of the previous generation, it was Cézanne whom Matisse revered the most.

Earlier in 1905, at the Salon des Indépendants, Matisse had already exhibited his large Neo-Impressionist composition *Luxe, calme et volupté* (fig. **7.3**), a title taken from a couplet in Baudelaire's poem *L'Invitation au voyage:*

> Là, tout n'est qu'ordre et beauté,
> Luxe, calme et volupté.

"There, all is only order and beauty/Richness, calm, sensuality."

In this important work, which went far along the path to abstraction, he combined the mosaic landscape manner of Signac (who bought the painting) with figure organization that recalls Cézanne's many compositions of bathers (see fig. 3.11), one of which Matisse owned. At the left of this St. Tropez beach scene, Matisse depicted his wife,

Amélie, beside a picnic spread. But this mundane activity is transported to a timeless, arcadian world populated by languid nudes relaxing along a beach that has been tinged with dazzling red. With *Luxe*, therefore, Matisse offered a radical reinterpretation of the grand pastoral tradition in landscape painting, best exemplified in France by Claude Lorrain and Poussin (see fig. 1.10). As in many of the paintings that postdate this work, his idyllic world is exclusively female. Matisse was wary of all theories in art, and though this bold painting could hardly be considered an orthodox example of Neo-Impressionism, his experimentation with the staccato strokes of that style gave way to other modes.

At the Salon d'Automne of 1905, Matisse also exhibited *The Open Window* (fig. 7.4) and a portrait of Madame Matisse called *Woman with the Hat*. *The Open Window* is perhaps the first fully developed example of a theme favored by Matisse throughout the rest of his life. It is simply a small fragment of the wall of a room, taken up principally with a large window whose casements are thrown wide to the outside world—a balcony with flowerpots and vines, and beyond that the sea, sky, and boats of the harbor at Collioure. It was at this Mediterranean port, during the summer of 1905, that Matisse and Derain produced the first Fauve paintings. In *The Open Window* the inside wall and the casements are composed of broad, vertical stripes of vivid green, blue, purple, and orange, while the outside world is a brilliant pattern of small brushstrokes, ranging from stippled dots of green to broader strokes of pink,

white, and blue in sea and sky. This diversity of paint handling, even in adjoining passages within the same picture, was typical of Matisse's early Fauve compositions. Between his painterly marks, Matisse left bare patches of canvas, reinforcing the impact of brushstrokes that have been freed from the traditional role of describing form in order to suggest an intense, vibrating light. By this date, the artist had already moved far beyond Bonnard or any of the Neo-Impressionists toward abstraction.

In Neo-Impressionism, as in Impressionism, the generalized, all-over distribution of color patches and texture had produced a sense of atmospheric depth, at the same time that it also asserted the physical presence and impenetrability of the painting surface. Matisse, however, structured an architectural framework of facets and planes that are even broader and flatter than those of Cézanne, suppressing all sense of atmosphere; internal illumination, the play of light within a painting that suggests physical depth, is replaced with a taut, resistant skin of pigment that reflects the light. Rather than allowing the viewer to enter pictorial space, this tough, vibrant membrane of color and pattern draws the eye over and across, but rarely beyond, the picture plane. And even in the view through the window, the handling is so vigorously self-assertive that the

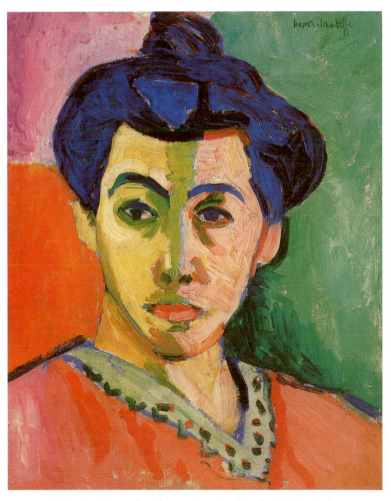

7.4 Henri Matisse, *The Open Window*, 1905. Oil on canvas, 21¾ × 18⅛" (55.2 × 46 cm). Collection Mrs. John Hay Whitney, New York.

7.5 Henri Matisse, *Portrait of Mme Matisse/The Green Line*, 1905. Oil and tempera on canvas, 15⅞ × 12⅞" (40.3 × 32.7 cm). Statens Museum for Kunst, Copenhagen.

scene appears to advance more than recede, as if to turn inside out the Renaissance conception of the painting as a simulacrum of a window open into the infinite depth of the real world. As presented by Matisse, the window and its sparkling view of a holiday marina become a picture within a picture. This is a theme the artist often pursued, transforming it into a metaphor of the modernist belief that the purpose of painting was not to represent the perceptual world but rather to use visual stimuli that would take the viewer beyond the perceptual reality—or the illusion of perceptual reality—that was the stock in trade of earlier Western art.

Matisse's *Woman with the Hat* caused an even greater furor than *The Open Window* because of the seemingly wild abandon with which the artist had applied paint over the surface, not only the background and hat but also in the face of the sitter, whose features are outlined in bold strokes of green and vermilion. Paradoxically, much of the shock value sprang from the actual verisimilitude of the painted image, its closeness to a recognizable subject providing an obvious measure of the degree of distortion imposed upon reality by the painter. At a later, more developed state of abstraction, modernist art was to become so independent of its sources in the material world as to seem less an attack on the familiar than an autonomous and thus a relatively less threatening, purely aesthetic, object. In 1905 Matisse could liberate his means mainly by choosing motifs that inspired such freedom—the luminous, relaxed, holiday world of the French Riviera, a flag-decked street, or one of the period's fantastic hats.

Shortly after exhibiting *Woman with the Hat*, Matisse painted another portrait of Madame Matisse that in a sense was even more audacious, precisely because it was less sketchlike, more tightly drawn and structured. In *Portrait of Mme Matisse/The Green Line* (fig. **7.5**), the sitter's face is dominated by a brilliant pea-green band of shadow dividing it from hairline to chin. At this point Matisse and his Fauve colleagues were building on the thesis put forward

7.6 Henri Matisse, *Le Bonheur de vivre (The Joy of Life)*, 1905–6. Oil on canvas, 5'8½" × 7'9¾" (1.74 × 2.4 m). The Barnes Foundation, Merion, Pennsylvania.

by Gauguin, the Symbolists, and the Nabis: that the artist is free to use color independently of natural appearance, building a structure of abstract color shapes and lines foreign to the figure, tree, or still life that remains the basis of the structure. Perhaps Matisse's version was more immediately shocking because his subject was so simple and familiar, unlike the exotic scenes of Gauguin or the mystical fantasies of Redon, in which such arbitrary colorism seemed more acceptable. With its heavy, emphatic strokes and striking use of complementary hues, the painting is actually closest to portraits by Van Gogh (see fig. 3.21).

The artist's experiments with arcadian figure compositions climaxed in the legendary *Le Bonheur de vivre* (fig. 7.6), a painting filled with diverse reminiscences of past art, from *The Feast of the Gods*, by Giovanni Bellini and Titian, to Persian painting, from prehistoric cave paintings to a composition by Ingres. In this large work (it is nearly eight feet, or 2.5 m, wide), the artist has blended all these influences into a masterful arrangement of figures and trees in sinuous, undulating lines reminiscent of contemporary Art Nouveau design (see chapter 5). *Le Bonheur de vivre* is filled with a mood of sensual languor; figures cavort with Dionysian abandon in a landscape that pulsates with rich, riotous color. Yet the figure groups are deployed as separate vignettes, isolated from one another spatially as well as by their differing colors and contradictory scales. As Matisse explained, *Le Bonheur de vivre* "was painted through the juxtaposition of things conceived independently but arranged together." He made several sketches for the work, basing his vision on an actual landscape at Collioure, which he painted in a lush sketch without figures that still contains some of the broken color patches of Neo-Impressionism. The circle of ecstatic dancers in the distance of *Le Bonheur de vivre*, apparently inspired by the sight of fishermen dancing in Collioure, became the central motif of Matisse's painting from 1909–10, *Dance (II)* (see fig. 7.19). *Le Bonheur de vivre* is an all-important, breakthrough picture; it made a considerable impression on Picasso, whose *Les Demoiselles d'Avignon* (see fig. 10.6), produced the following year, came about partly in response to it. Though radically different in spirit and style from Picasso's notorious picture, Matisse's painting was, like *Les Demoiselles*, intended as a major statement, a kind of manifesto of his current ideas about art. While Picasso's canvas was not exhibited publicly until 1937, *Le Bonheur de vivre* was bought immediately by the American collectors and writers Gertrude and Leo Stein, who introduced the two men to one another, and whose apartment was eventually filled with work by them and other avant-garde artists. In their collection, Picasso could study *Le Bonheur de vivre* at length.

The Influence of African Art

In 1906 Matisse, Derain, and Vlaminck began to collect art objects from Africa, which they had first seen in ethnographic museums, and to adapt those forms into their art.

Of all the non-Western artistic source material sought out by European modernists, none proved so radical or so far-reaching as the art of Africa. Modern artists appropriated the forms of African art in the hope of investing their work with a kind of primal truth and expressive energy, as well as a touch of the exotic, what they saw as the "primitive," or, in Gauguin's word, the "savage." Unlike the myriad other influences absorbed from outside contemporary European culture—Asian, Islamic, Oceanic, medieval, folk, and children's art—these African works were not only sculptural, as opposed to the predominantly pictorial art of Europe, but they also embodied values and conventions outside Western tradition and experience. Whereas even the most idealized European painting remained ultimately bound up with perceptual realities and the ongoing history of art itself, African figures did not observe classical proportions and contained no history or stories that Europeans understood. With their relatively large, masklike heads, distended torsos, prominent sexual features, and squat, abbreviated, or elongated limbs, they impressed Matisse and his comrades with the powerful plasticity of their forms (mostly unbound to the literal representation of nature), their expressive carving, and their iconic force.

When finally examined by such independent artists as Matisse and Picasso (first introduced to African art by Matisse), the figures seemed redolent of magic and mystery, the very qualities that European progressives, from Gauguin on, had been struggling to recover for new art. Obviously, such objects, once they reached Europe, had been stripped of their original contexts and functions, often as a result of European colonization of the very people who made them. The response on the part of progressive Western artists, who had virtually no understanding of the original conditions that shaped these works, was largely ethnocentric. They assimilated African forms into a prevailing aesthetic determined by their search for alternatives to naturalism and for a more stylized, abstract conception of the figure.

An early example of African influence in Matisse's art occurred most remarkably in *Blue Nude: Memory of Biskra* (fig. 7.7), which, as the subtitle implies, was produced following the artist's visit to Biskra, a lush oasis in the North African desert. The subject of the painting—a reclining female nude—is a dynamic variation of a classic Venus pose, with one arm bent over the head and the legs flexed forward. Matisse had made the reclining nude central to *Le Bonheur de vivre*, and such was the interest it held for him that he then restudied it in a clay sculpture (see fig. 9.3). Now, working from memory and his own sculpture, and evidently encouraged by the example of African sculpture, he abstracted his image further. These influences produced the bulbous exaggeration of breasts and buttocks; the extreme contrapposto that makes torso and hips seem viewed from different angles, or assembled from different bodies; the scarified modeling, or vigorously applied contouring in a brilliant, synthetic blue; and the masklike character of the face. But however much these traits reveal

7.7 Henri Matisse, *Blue Nude: Memory of Biskra*, 1907. Oil on canvas, 36¼ × 56⅛" (92.1 × 142.5 cm). The Baltimore Museum of Art.

the impact of African art, they have been translated from the plastic, freestanding, iconic sculpture of Africa into a pictorial expression by means of the Cézannism that Matisse had been cultivating all along. This can be seen in the dynamic character of the whole, in which rhyming curves and countercurves, images and afterimages, and interchanges of color and texture make figure and ground merge into one another.

In its theme, *Blue Nude* belongs to the tradition in nineteenth-century painting of the odalisque, or member of a North African harem (see fig. 1.13). This subject of the exotic, sexually available woman, exploited by Delacroix, Ingres, and countless lesser Salon artists, was destined for visual consumption by a predominantly male audience. But the level of abstraction Matisse imposes on his subject, as with Cézanne's bathers, moves the figure beyond the explicitly erotic. Responding to the charges of ugliness made against *Blue Nude,* Matisse said: "If I met such a woman in the street, I should run away in terror. Above all, I do not create a woman, *I make a picture.*" Inspired by the example of what he called the "invented planes and proportions" of African sculpture, Matisse did not restructure the human face and figure in the overt, aggressive manner of Picasso. Rather, he used these sources in his own subtle, reflective fashion, assimilating and synthesizing until they are scarcely discernible.

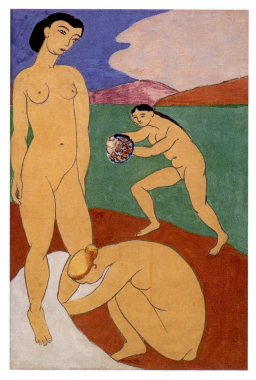

7.8 Henri Matisse, *Le Luxe II*, 1907–8. Casein on canvas, 6'10½" × 4'6" (2.1 × 1.38 m). Statens Museum for Kunst, Copenhagen.

With *Le Luxe II,* a work of 1907–8 (fig. **7.8**), Matisse signaled a move away from his Fauve production of the preceding years. It is a large painting, nearly seven feet (2.1 m) tall, that Matisse elaborately prepared with full-scale charcoal and oil sketches. The oil sketch *Le Luxe I* is much looser in execution, and closer to Fauvism than are the flat, unmodulated zones of color in the final version. Though *Le Luxe II* explores a theme similar to that of *Luxe, calme et volupté* and *Le Bonheur de vivre* (see figs. 7.3, 7.6), the figures are now life-size and dominate the landscape. Coloristically, *Le Luxe II* is far more subdued, relying on areas of localized color bound by crisp lines. Despite the artist's abandonment of perspective, except for the arbitrary diminution of one figure, and modeling in light and shadow, the painting is not merely surface decoration. The figures, modeled only by the contour lines, have substance; they exist and move in space, with the illusion of depth, light, and air created solely by flat color shapes that are, at the same time, synonymous spatially with the picture plane. The actual subject of the painting remains elusive. The crouching woman, a beautiful, compact shape, seems to be tending to her companion in some way (perhaps drying her feet?), while another rushes toward the pair, proffering a bouquet of flowers. Matisse may have implied a mythological theme, such as Venus's birth from the sea, but, typically, he only hints at such narratives.

"Wild Beasts" Tamed: Derain, Vlaminck, and Dufy

André Derain (1880–1954) met the older Matisse at Carrière's atelier in 1900, as already noted, and was encouraged by him to proceed with his career as a painter. He already knew Maurice de Vlaminck, whom Derain in turn had led from his various careers as violinist, novelist, and bicycle racer into the field of painting. Unlike Vlaminck, Derain was a serious student of the art of the museums who, despite his initial enthusiasm for the explosive color

of Fauvism, was constantly haunted by a more ordered and traditional concept of painting.

Although Derain's Fauve paintings embodied every kind of painterly variation, from large-scale Neo-Impressionism to free brushwork, most characteristic, perhaps, are works like *London Bridge* (fig. **7.9**). It was painted during a trip commissioned by the dealer Vollard, who wanted Derain to make paintings that would capture the special atmosphere of London (Claude Monet's many views of the city had just been successfully exhibited in Paris). To compare Derain's painting with the Impressionist's earlier work, *Bridge at Argenteuil* (see fig. 2.28) is to understand the transformations art had undergone in roughly thirty years, as well as the fundamental role Impressionism had played in those transformations. While in London, Derain visited the museums, studying especially the paintings of Turner, Claude, and Rembrandt, as well as African sculpture. Unlike Monet's view of the Seine, his painting of the Thames is a brilliantly synthetic color arrangement of harmonies and dissonances. The background sky is rose-pink; the buildings silhouetted against it are complementary green and blue. By reiterating large color areas in the foreground and background and tilting the perspective, Derain delimits the depth of his image. In the summer of 1906, several months after the trip to London, Derain spent time in L'Estaque, the famous site of paintings by Cézanne (see fig. 3.6). But his grand panorama of a bend in the road (fig. **7.10**) takes its cue from Gauguin (see figs. 3.17, 3.19) in its brilliant palette and the evocation of an idealized realm far from the urban bustle of London's waterways. With this work Derain travels to new extremes of intensity and antinaturalism in his color, a world in which the hues of a single tree can shift dramatically half a dozen times.

Derain was essentially an academic painter who happened to become involved in a revolutionary movement, participated in it effectively, but was never completely happy in the context. In 1906 he became a friend of

7.9 André Derain, *London Bridge*, 1906. Oil on canvas, 26 × 39" (66 × 99.1 cm). The Museum of Modern Art, New York.

7.10 André Derain, *Turning Road, L'Estaque*, 1906. Oil on canvas, 4'3" × 6'4¾" (1.3 × 1.9 m). The Museum of Fine Arts, Houston.

Picasso and was drawn into the vortex of proto-Cubism (see chapter 10). But throughout the years of World War I (1914–18), in which Derain fought, and later, when Picasso and Braque were expanding their discoveries in Synthetic Cubism and exploring alternative styles, Derain was moving back consistently from Cézanne to that artist's sources in Poussin and Chardin. His direction was away from the very experiments of the twentieth century he had helped to develop, back through the innovators of the late nineteenth century, to the Renaissance. Derain's return to optical realism formed part of a larger "call to order" around World War I, when a number of French artists and writers sought to renew their art through the more classical forms of Western art. Picasso's classicizing work from the second half of the 1910s and early twenties belongs to this phenomenon (see figs. 14.18, 14.20–23), as does, in the preceding chapter, the work of Maillol (see fig. 6.13). Perhaps most indicative of this gradual but thoroughgoing change in Derain's outlook is that in 1930 he sold several African sculptures from his collection to buy Renaissance and antique artworks. His new conservatism resulted in a very uneven output of landscapes, nudes, still lifes, and portraits and a serious decline after World War II in his reputation, which is now being reexamined.

The career of **Maurice de Vlaminck** (1876–1958) presents many parallels with Derain's, even though the artists were so different in personality and in their approach to the art of painting. Vlaminck was born in Paris of Flemish stock, a fact of considerable importance to him personally and one that may have contributed to the nature of his painting. Impulsive and exuberant, he was a

7.11 Maurice de Vlaminck, *Picnic in the Country*, 1905. Oil on canvas, 35 × 45⅝" (88.9 × 45.6 cm). Private collection.

self-taught artist with anarchist political leanings who liked to boast of his contempt for the art of museums. From the time he met Derain and turned to painting, he was enraptured with color. Thus the Van Gogh exhibition at the Bernheim-Jeune Gallery in Paris in 1901 was a revelation to him. At the Salon des Indépendants in the same year, Derain introduced him to Matisse, but it was not until 1905, after exposure to the work of both artists, that Vlaminck's work reached its full potential, despite his false claims to have been the leader of the Fauves. Van Gogh remained Vlaminck's great inspiration, and in his Fauve paintings Vlaminck characteristically used the short, choppy brushstrokes of the Dutchman to attain a comparable kind of coloristic dynamism, as in *Picnic in the Country* (fig. **7.11**). Two figures are isolated within a coil of swirling color patches; they are foreigners from the world of nature, picnicking in a forest of paint. His small but dramatic *Portrait of Derain* (fig. **7.12**) is one of several likenesses the Fauves made of one another. Vlaminck has here moved beyond the directional, multicolored daubs of *Picnic in the Country* to a boldly conceived image in which Derain's face is predominantly an intense, brilliant red with black contours, yellow highlights, and a few strokes of contrasting green shadow along the bridge of

7.13 Raoul Dufy, *Street Decked with Flags, Le Havre*, 1906. Oil on canvas, 31⅞ × 25⅞" (81 × 65.7 cm). Musée National d'Art Moderne, Paris.

the nose, recalling Matisse's *Portrait of Mme Matisse/The Green Line* (see fig. 7.5).

By 1908 Vlaminck too was beginning to be affected by the new view of Cézanne that resulted from the exhibitions after Cézanne's death in 1906. And although for a time he was in touch with the new explorations of Picasso and Braque leading toward Analytic Cubism, and even used various forms of simplification based on their ideas, in actuality he, like Derain, was gradually retreating into the world of representation by way of Cézanne. By 1915 Vlaminck had moved toward a kind of expressive realism that he continued to pursue for the rest of his life.

Raoul Dufy (1877–1953) was shocked out of his reverence for the Impressionists and Van Gogh by his discovery of Matisse's 1905 painting *Luxe, calme et volupté*, when, he said, "Impressionist realism lost all its charm." In a sense, he remained faithful to this vision and to Fauve color throughout his life. His *Street Decked with Flags, Le Havre* (fig. **7.13**) takes up a subject celebrated by the Impressionists, but the bold, close-up view of the flags imposes a highly abstracted geometric pattern on the scene.

Influenced by Georges Braque, his fellow painter from Le Havre, Dufy after 1908 experimented with a modified form of Cubism, but he was never really happy in this vein. Gradually he returned to his former loves—decorative color and elegant draftsmanship—and formulated a personal style based on his earlier Fauvism. His pleasurable

7.12 Maurice de Vlaminck, *Portrait of Derain*, 1906. Oil on cardboard, 10¾ × 8¾" (27.3 × 22.2 cm). The Metropolitan Museum of Art, New York.

subjects were the horse races and regattas of his native Le Havre and nearby Deauville, the nude model in the studio, and the view from a window to the sea beyond. He maintained a rainbow, calligraphic style until the end of his life, applying it to fabrics, theatrical sets, and book illustrations as well as paintings.

For Matisse, Fauvism was only a beginning from which he went on to a rich, productive career that spans the first half of the twentieth century. Derain and Vlaminck, however, did little subsequently that had the vitality of their Fauve works. It is interesting to speculate on why these young men should briefly have outdone themselves, but the single overriding explanation is probably the presence of Henri Matisse—older than the others, more mature and, ultimately, more gifted as an artist. But in addition to Matisse and Rouault (see below), there was also Georges Braque, who, after discovering his first brief and relatively late inspiration in Fauvism, went on to restudy Cézanne, with consequences for twentieth-century art so significant that they must await a subsequent chapter on Cubism.

Colors of the Spiritual Eye: Georges Rouault

The one Fauve who was almost exclusively concerned with a deliberately Expressionist subject matter is perhaps not to be considered a Fauve at all. This is **Georges Rouault** (1871–1958), who exhibited three works in the 1905 Salon d'Automne and thus is associated with the work of the group, although his paintings were not actually shown in the room with theirs. Throughout his long and productive career, Rouault remained deeply religious, deeply emotional, and profoundly moralistic. He came from a family of craftsmen, and he himself was first apprenticed to a stained-glass artisan. In the studio of Gustave Moreau he met Matisse and other future Fauves, and soon became Moreau's favorite pupil, for he followed most closely Moreau's own style and concepts.

By 1903 Rouault's art, like that of Matisse and others around him, was undergoing profound changes, reflecting a radical shift in his moral and religious outlook. Like his friend the Catholic writer and propagandist Léon Bloy, Rouault sought subjects to express his sense of indignation and disgust over the evils that, as it seemed to him, permeated bourgeois society. The prostitute became his symbol of this rotting society. He depicted her with a fierce loathing, rather than objectively, or with the cynical sympathy of Toulouse-Lautrec—who, it must be added, represented individuals rather than Rouault's general types. Rouault invited prostitutes to pose in his studio, painting them with attributes such as stockings or corsets to indicate their profession. In many of these studies, done in watercolor, the woman is set within a confined space, to focus attention on the figure (fig. **7.14**). Some of the poses and the predominantly blue hues of these watercolors stem in part from Rouault's admiration for Cézanne. The women's

yellow-white bodies, touched with light-blue shadows, are modeled sculpturally with heavy, freely brushed outlines. Here the masklike grimace of the face is reflected in the mirror, like a twisted paraphrase of the classical Venus, who contemplates her beauty in a looking glass. It was perhaps not until the twenties, with the work of the Berlin artist George Grosz, who bore witness through his art to the moral failings of postwar German society, that prostitutes were interpreted with comparable vehemence.

Rouault's moral indignation further manifested itself, like Daumier's, in vicious caricatures of judges and politicians. His counterpoint to the corrupt prostitute was the figure of the circus clown, sometimes the carefree nomad beating his drum, but more often a tragic, lacerated victim. As early as 1904 he had begun to depict subjects taken directly from the Gospels—the Crucifixion, Jesus and his disciples, and other scenes from the life of Christ. He represented the figure of Christ as a tragic mask of the Man of Sorrows deriving directly from a crucified Christ by Grünewald (see fig. 1.7) or a tormented Christ by Bosch. Rouault's religious and moral sentiments are perhaps most movingly conveyed in a series of fifty-eight prints, titled *Miserere*, that was commissioned by his dealer Vollard (whose heirs the artist later had to sue to retrieve the contents of his studio). For years, Rouault devoted himself to

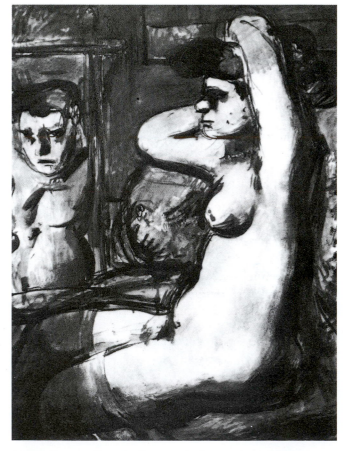

7.14 Georges Rouault, *Prostitute before a Mirror*, 1906. Watercolor on cardboard, 27⅝ × 20⅞" (70.2 × 53 cm). Musée National d'Art Moderne, Centre National d'Art et de Culture Georges Pompidou, Paris.

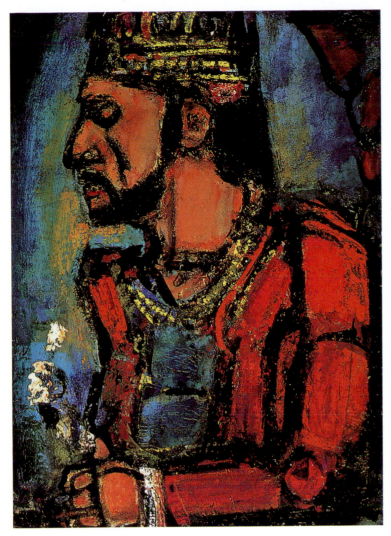

7.15 Georges Rouault, *The Old King*, 1916–36. Oil on canvas, 30¼ × 21¼" (76.8 × 54 cm). Carnegie Museum of Art, Pittsburgh.

Egyptian-style profile of the king's head and the square proportions of his torso. Paint is applied heavily with the underpainting glowing through, in the manner of Rembrandt. Rouault also captures some of the Dutch master's mood in this serene image of a world-weary ruler, who clutches a flower in his hand, one of the few traces of white in the entire painting. Although Rouault never entirely gave up the spirit of moral indignation expressed in the virulent satire that marked his early works, the sense of calm and the hope of salvation in the later paintings mark him as one of the few authentic religious painters of the modern world.

The Belle Époque on Camera: The Lumière Brothers and Lartigue

Developments in photography contemporary with the years of Fauvism include the first photographers to take up a color process, after one was finally made public in 1904 and commercially feasible in 1907 by **Auguste** and **Louis Lumière** (1862–1954; 1864–1948) of Lyons, France (fig. 7.16). By coating one side of a glass plate with a mixture of tiny, transparent starch particles, each dyed red, green, or blue (the three primary photographic colors), and the other side with a thin panchromatic emulsion, the Lumières created a light-sensitive plate that, once exposed, developed, and projected on a white ground, reproduced a full-color image of the subject photographed. The Autochromes—as the Lumières called the slides made by their patented process—rendered images in muted tonalities with the look of a fine-grained texture, an effect that simply heightened the inherent charm of the bright subject matter. This was especially true for a Fauve generation still entranced with Neo-Impressionism. Their invention was

the production of the etchings and aquatints of *Miserere*, which were printed between 1922 and 1927, but not published until 1948, when the artist was seventy-seven. Technically, the prints are masterpieces of graphic compression. The black tones, worked over and over again, have the depth and richness of his most vivid oil colors.

The characteristics of Rouault's later style are seen in *The Old King* (fig. 7.15). The design has become geometrically abstract in feeling, and colors are intensified to achieve the glow of stained glass. A heavy black outline is used to define the rather

7.16 Lumière brothers, *Young Lady with an Umbrella*, 1906–10. Autochrome photograph. Fondation Nationale de la Photographie, Lyons, France.

7.17 Jacques-Henri Lartigue, *In My Room: Collection of My Racing Cars*, 1905. Gelatin-silver print, 5⅜ × 7" (13.7 × 17.8 cm).

immediately taken up by professional photographers, especially the so-called Pictorialists, such as Edward Steichen, as well as amateurs around the world.

Dufy's privileged, Belle Époque world of regattas and racecourses was also celebrated by the French contemporary photographer **Jacques-Henri Lartigue** (1894–1986), once the fast-action handheld camera had been introduced in 1888 and then progressively improved. Such developments encouraged experimentation and enabled this affluent child artist (he began making photographs at age seven) to capture not only his family and friends at their pleasures, but also the gradual advent of such twentieth-century phenomena as auto races and aviation. At his death in 1986 Lartigue, who was a painter professionally, left behind a huge number of photographs and journals that document a charmed life of holidays, swimming holes, and elegantly clad ladies and gentlemen. He was eleven when he aimed his camera at the toy cars in his bedroom (fig. **7.17**), and his image adopts a child's angle on the world. The tiny cars, at eye level, take on strange dimensions, all of which is compounded by the mysteriously draped fireplace that looms above them. Owing to his view of photography as a pursuit carried on for private satisfaction and delight, Lartigue did not become generally known until a show at New York's Museum of Modern Art in 1963, when his work took an immediate place in the history of art as a direct ancestor of the "straight" but unmistakably distinctive vision of such photographers as Brassaï and Henri Cartier-Bresson.

Modernism on a Grand Scale: Matisse's Art after Fauvism

Fauvism was a short-lived but tremendously influential movement that had no definitive conclusion, though it had effectively drawn to a close by 1908. The direction of Matisse's art explored in *Le Luxe II* is carried still further in *Harmony in Red* (fig. **7.18**), a large painting destined for the Moscow dining room of Sergei Shchukin, Matisse's important early patron who, along with Ivan Morozov, is the reason Russian museums are today key repositories of Matisse's greatest work. This astonishing painting was begun early in 1908 as *Harmony in Blue* and then repainted in the fall, in a radically different color scheme. Here Matisse returned to the formula of *Dinner Table*, which he had painted in 1896–97 (see fig. 7.1). A comparison of the two canvases reveals dramatically the revolution that had occurred in this artist's works—and in fact in modern painting—during a ten-year period. Admittedly, the first *Dinner Table* was still an apprentice piece, a relatively conventional exploration of Impressionist light and color and contracted space, actually more traditional than paintings executed by the Impressionists twenty years earlier. Nevertheless, when submitted to the Salon de la Nationale it was severely criticized by the conservatives as being tainted with Impressionism. In *Harmony in Red* we have moved into a new world, less empirical and more abstract than anything ever envisioned by Gauguin, much less the Impressionists. The space of the interior is defined by a single unmodulated area of red, the flatness of which is reinforced by arabesques of plant forms that flow across the walls and table surface. These patterns were actually derived from a piece of decorative fabric that Matisse owned. Their meandering forms serve to confound any sense of volumetric space in the painting and to create pictorial ambiguities by playing off the repeated pattern of flower baskets against the "real" still lifes on the table. This ambiguity is extended to the view through the window of abstract tree and plant forms silhouetted against a green ground and blue sky. The red building in the extreme upper distance, which reiterates the color of the room, in some manner establishes the illusion of depth in the landscape, yet the entire scene, framed by what may be a window sill and cut off by the picture edge like other forms in the painting, could also itself be a painting on the wall. In essence Matisse has again—and in an even greater

degree than in *Le Luxe II*—created a new, tangible world of pictorial space through color and line.

In two huge paintings of the first importance, *Dance (II)* and *Music*, both of 1909–10 (figs. **7.19**, **7.20**), and both commissioned by Shchukin, Matisse boldly outlined large-scale figures and isolated them against a ground of intense color. The inspiration for *Dance* has been variously traced to Greek vase painting or peasant dances. Specifically, the motif was first used by Matisse, as we have seen, in the background group of *Le Bonheur de vivre*. In *Dance*, the colors have been limited to an intense green for the earth, an equally intense blue for the sky, and brick-red for the figures. The figures are sealed into the foreground by the color areas of sky and ground, and by their proximity to the framing edge and their great size within the canvas, but they nevertheless dance ecstatically in an airy space created by these contrasting juxtaposed hues and

7.18 Henri Matisse, *Harmony in Red (The Dessert)*, 1908. Oil on canvas, 5'10⅞" × 7'2⅝" (1.8 × 2.2 m). The Hermitage Museum, St. Petersburg.

7.19 Henri Matisse, *Dance (II)*, 1909–10. Oil on canvas, 8'5⅝" × 12'9½" (2.6 × 3.9 m). The Hermitage Museum, St. Petersburg.

7.20 Henri Matisse, *Music*, 1909–10. Oil on canvas, 8'5⅝" × 12'9¼" (2.6 × 3.9 m). The Hermitage Museum, St. Petersburg.

by their own modeled contours and sweeping movements. The depth and intensity of the colors change in different lights, at times setting up visual vibrations that make the entire surface dance. *Music* is a perfect foil for the kinetic energy of *Dance,* in the static, frontalized poses of the figures arranged like notes on a musical staff, each isolated from the others to create a mood of trancelike withdrawal. Matisse's explanation of Fauvism as "the courage to return to a 'purity of means' " still holds true here. In both paintings the arcadian worlds of earlier painters (see fig. 1.10) have been transformed into an elemental realm beyond the specificities of time and place. When they were exhibited in the 1910 Salon d'Automne, these two extraordinary paintings provoked little but negative and hostile criticism, and Shchukin at first withdrew his commission, though he soon changed his mind. These monumental works further show Matisse locating his art in relation to the grand classical tradition. Modernist in conception, they nevertheless aligned Matisse with the elite world of wealthy patronage that had previously sustained (and indeed still sustained) conventional academic art. Other modernist artists—notably Picasso—were to tread a comparable path,

simultaneously becoming respected public figures while retaining, at least to a degree, the avant-garde ability to disconcert conventionally minded viewers.

In *The Red Studio* (fig. **7.21**), Matisse returned to the principle of a single, unifying color that he had exploited in *Harmony in Red*. The studio interior is described by a uniform area of red, covering floor and walls. The space is given volumetric definition only by a single white line that indicates the intersection of the walls and floor, and by the paintings and furniture lined up along the rear wall. Furnishings—table, chair, cupboard, and sculpture stands—are dematerialized, ghostlike objects outlined in white lines. The tangible accents are the paintings of the artist, hanging on or stacked against the walls, and (in the foreground) ceramics, sculptures, vase, glass, and pencils. (*Le Luxe II* can be seen at the upper right.) By 1911, when this was painted, Picasso, Braque, and the other Cubists, as we shall see, had in their own ways been experimenting with the organization and contraction of pictorial space for some five years. Matisse was affected by their ideas, but sought his own solutions. Later works by Matisse are discussed in chapter 13.

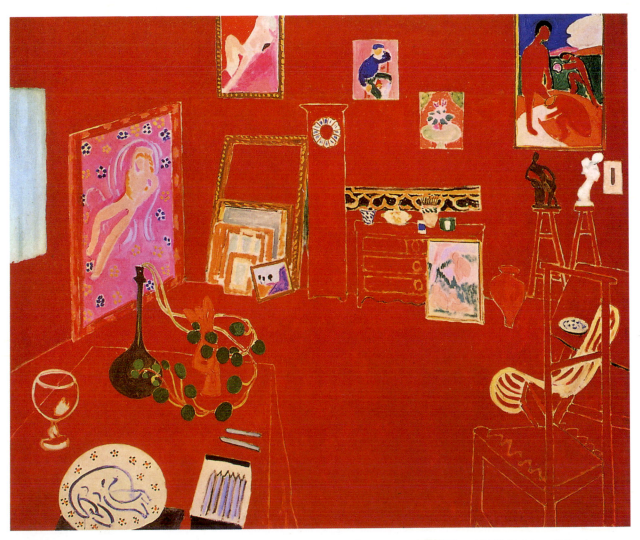

7.21 Henri Matisse, *The Red Studio*, Issy-les-Moulineaux, 1911. Oil on canvas, 5'11¼" × 7'2¼" (1.81 × 2.2 m). The Museum of Modern Art, New York.

8
Expressionism in Germany

In its most general sense, "expressionism" is a term that has been applied by art historians to tendencies recurring in the arts since antiquity. The aim of all art is, of course, to communicate, to express ideas or sentiments that evoke responses in the viewer. But in the early twentieth century, the term was applied to art that conveyed, through a wide range of styles and subject matter (or in the case of abstract art, no subject at all), the emotions and spiritual preoccupations of the artist—what Vasily Kandinsky called "inner necessity." Herwarth Walden, critic, poet, musician, and the founder in 1910 of the German avant-garde periodical *Der Sturm* (The Storm), drew the distinction between new, revolutionary tendencies after the turn of the century and Impressionism. Expressionist artists, including the Fauves (see chapter 7), built on the discoveries of the Post-Impressionists, who rejected Impressionist devotion to optical veracity and turned inward to the world of the spirit. They employed many languages to give visible form to their feelings, but generally they relied on simple, powerful forms that were realized in a manner of direct, sometimes crude expression, designed to heighten the emotional response of the viewer. The essence of their art was the expression of inner meaning through outer form.

Important forerunners of Expressionism included Van Gogh, Munch, Klimt, Hodler, Ensor, Böcklin, Klinger, and Kubin. However, the young Expressionists in Germany also drew inspiration from their own native traditions of medieval sculpture and folk or children's art, as well as the art of other cultures, especially Africa and Oceania. In contrast to the Fauves, whose stylistic affinities were never expressed through a formal artistic grouping, German Expressionism involved the formation of groups of artists in several cities, primarily Dresden, Munich, and Berlin. We will see that separate developments also took place in Vienna. The period of German Expressionism began in 1905 with the establishment of the new artists' alliance known as Die Brücke (The Bridge) in Dresden, and lasted until the end of World War I, when radical Dada artists (see chapter 13) in Germany rejected all forms of Expressionism in their turn. Many Expressionist artists welcomed World War I as a new dawn that would see the destruction of an old, moribund order. But as the horror in the trenches dragged on, the war took its toll on artists: some died in battle; others suffered psychological trauma and profound spiritual disillusionment.

Making it Personal: Modersohn-Becker and Nolde

Paula Modersohn-Becker (1876–1907) was born in Dresden and settled in the artists' colony at Worpswede near Bremen in 1897. Although she was not associated with any group outside of the provincial school of painters at Worpswede, Modersohn-Becker was in touch with new developments in art and literature through her friendship with the poet Rainer Maria Rilke (who had been Rodin's secretary), as well as through a number of visits to Paris. In these she discovered successively the French Barbizon painters, the Impressionists, and then, in 1905 and 1906, the works of Van Gogh, Gauguin, and Cézanne. Following this last trip, she embarked on a highly productive and innovative period, distilling and simplifying forms while heightening the expressiveness of color. In her extensive letters and diaries, the artist wrote of her desire for an art of direct emotion, of poetic expression, of simplicity and sensitivity to nature: "Personal feeling is the main thing. After I have clearly set it down in form and color, I must introduce those elements from nature that will make my picture look natural." She worried about the implications of marriage and motherhood for her professional life and, tragically, died prematurely following the birth of her only child, leaving us with only a suggestion of what she might have achieved. But in works such as *Self-Portrait with Camellia Branch* (fig. **8.1**) there is a clear grasp of the broad simplification of color areas she had seen in Gauguin as well as in the Egyptian and early classical art she had studied at the Louvre.

8.1 Paula Modersohn-Becker, *Self-Portrait with Camellia Branch*, 1907. Oil on paperboard, 27½ × 11¾" (62 × 30 cm). Museum Folkwang, Essen, Germany.

Emil Nolde (1867–1956) was the son of a farmer from northwestern Germany, near the Danish border. The reactionary, rural values of this area had a profound effect on his art and his attitude toward nature. Strong emotional ties to the landscape and yearning for a regeneration of the German spirit and its art characterized the popular *völkisch* or nationalist tradition. Early in his career, Nolde depicted the landscape and peasants of this region in paintings reminiscent of the French artist Millet (see fig. 1.19). As an adult, he even took as his surname Nolde, the name of his native village (he was born Emil Hansen), to underscore a strong identification with the land.

As a youth, Nolde studied woodcarving and worked for a time as a designer of furniture and decorative arts in Berlin. His first paintings, of mountains transformed into giants or hideous trolls, drew on qualities of traditional Germanic fantasy. The commercial success of some of these images enabled Nolde to return to school and to take up painting seriously in Munich, where he encountered the work of contemporary artists such as Adolph Menzel and Arnold Böcklin (see fig. 5.24), and then in Paris. While in Paris in 1899–1900, he, like so many art students, worked his way gradually from the study of Daumier and Delacroix to Manet and the Impressionists, and his color took on a new brilliance and violence as a result of his exposure to the latter. In 1906 he accepted an invitation to become a member of the Dresden group Die Brücke. Essentially a solitary person, Nolde left Die Brücke after a year and devoted himself increasingly to a personal form of Expressionist religious paintings and prints.

Among his first visionary religious paintings was *The Last Supper* of 1909 (fig. **8.2**). When compared with celebrated old master paintings of Jesus among his disciples, such as Rembrandt's *Christ at Emmaus* or even Leonardo da Vinci's *Last Supper*, Nolde's mood is markedly different from the quiet restraint of these earlier works. His figures are crammed into a practically nonexistent space, the red of their robes and the yellow-green of their faces flaring like torches out of the surrounding shadow. The faces

8.2 Emil Nolde, *The Last Supper*, 1909. Oil on canvas, 33⅞ × 42⅛" (86 × 107 cm). Statens Museum for Kunst, Copenhagen.

themselves are skull-like masks that derive from the carnival processions of Ensor (see fig. 5.23). Here, however, they are given intense personalities—no longer masked and inscrutable fantasies but individualized human beings passionately involved in a situation of extreme drama. The compression of the group packed within the frontal plane of the painting—again stemming from Ensor—heightens the sense of impending crisis.

Nolde believed in the ethnic superiority of Nordic people. In 1920 he became a member of the National Socialist or Nazi party. His art was for a time tolerated by Joseph Goebbels, Hitler's minister of propaganda, but by 1934 it was officially condemned by the Nazis as stylistically too experimental—"primitive" and "un-German." In 1936, like other Expressionist artists in Germany, he was banned from working. Over one thousand of Nolde's works were among the sixteen thousand sculptures, paintings, prints, and drawings by avant-garde artists that were confiscated from German museums by Nazi officials. In 1937 many of these were included in a massive exhibition called "Entartete Kunst," or "Degenerate Art" (see fig. 13.44). Designed to demonstrate the so-called decadent art that offended the Nazi government, which preferred watered-down classicist depictions of muscular Aryan workers, pretty nudes, or insipid genre scenes, the exhibition contained art in a tremendous range of styles and featured work by most of the artists discussed in this chapter. During four months in Munich, the exhibition was seen by two million visitors, a staggering attendance even by the standard of today's "blockbuster" exhibitions. Many of the works exhibited, including several by Nolde, were later destroyed by the Nazis, or lost during World War II.

Joining the Revolution: Die Brücke

In 1905 Ernst Ludwig Kirchner, Erich Heckel, Karl Schmidt-Rottluff, and Fritz Bleyl formed an association they called Die Brücke—the bridge linking "all the revolutionary and fermenting elements." These young architecture students, all of whom wanted to be painters, were drawn together by their opposition to the art that surrounded them, especially academic art and fashionable Impressionism, rather than by any preconceived program. Imbued with the spirit of Arts and Crafts and Jugendstil (see chapter 5), they rented an empty shop in a workers' district of Dresden, in eastern Germany, and began to paint, sculpt, and make woodcuts together. The influences on them were many and varied: the art of medieval Germany, of the French Fauves, of Edvard Munch, of non-Western sculpture. For them, Van Gogh was the clearest example of an artist driven by an "inner force" and "inner necessity"; his paintings presented an ecstatic identification or empathy of the artist with the subject he was interpreting. The graphic works of Munch were widely known in Germany by 1905, and the artist himself was spending most of his time there. His obsession with symbolic subjects struck a sympathetic chord in young German artists, and from his mastery of the graphic techniques they could learn much. Although they worked in many media, it was probably their intensive study of the possibilities of woodcut that did most to formulate their styles and to clarify their directions. Among historic styles, the most exciting discovery was art from Africa and the South Pacific, of which notable collections existed in the Dresden Ethnographic Museum.

In 1906 Nolde and Max Pechstein joined Die Brücke. In the same year Heckel, then working for an architect, persuaded a manufacturer for whom he had executed a showroom to permit the Brücke artists to exhibit there. This was the historic first Brücke exhibition, which marked the emergence of twentieth-century German Expressionism. Little information about the exhibition has survived, since no catalogue was issued, and it attracted virtually no attention.

During the next few years the Brücke painters exhibited together and produced publications designed by members and manifestos in which Kirchner's ideas were most evident. The human figure was studied assiduously in the way Rodin had studied the nude: not posed formally but simply existing in the environment. Despite developing differences in style among the artists, a hard, Gothic angularity permeated many of their works.

The Brücke painters were conscious of the revolution that the Fauves were creating in Paris and were affected by their use of color. However, their own paintings maintained a Germanic sense of expressive subject matter and a characteristically jagged, Gothic structure and form. By 1911 most of the Brücke group were in Berlin, where a new style appeared in their works, reflecting the increasing consciousness of French Cubism (see chapter 10) as well as Fauvism, given a Germanic excitement and narrative impact. By 1913 Die Brücke was dissolved as an association, and the artists proceeded individually.

Kirchner

The most creative member of Die Brücke was **Ernst Ludwig Kirchner** (1880–1938). In addition to his extraordinary output of painting and prints, Kirchner, like Erich Heckel, made large, roughly hewn and painted wooden sculptures. These works in a primitivist mode were a result of the artists' admiration for African and Oceanic art. Kirchner's early ambition to become an artist was reinforced by his discovery of the sixteenth-century woodcuts of Albrecht Dürer and his Late Gothic predecessors. Yet his own first woodcuts, done before 1900, were probably most influenced by Félix Vallotton and Edvard Munch. Between 1901 and 1903 Kirchner studied architecture in Dresden, and then, until 1904, painting in Munich. Here he was attracted to Art Nouveau designs and repelled by the retrograde paintings he saw in the exhibition of the Munich Secession. Like so many of the younger German artists of the time, he was particularly drawn to German

8.3 Ernst Ludwig Kirchner, *Street, Dresden*, 1908 (dated 1907 on painting). Oil on canvas, 4'11¼" × 6'6⅞" (1.51 × 2 m). The Museum of Modern Art, New York.

Gothic art. Of modern artists, the first revelation for him was the work of Seurat. Going beyond Seurat's researches, Kirchner undertook studies of nineteenth-century color theories that led him back to Johann Wolfgang von Goethe's essay *History of the Theory of Colors.*

Kirchner's painting style about 1904 showed influences from the Neo-Impressionists combined with a larger, more dynamic brushstroke related to that of Van Gogh, whose work he saw, along with paintings by Gauguin and Cézanne, in the exhibition of the Munich Artists' Association held that year. On his return to Dresden and architecture school in 1904 Kirchner became acquainted with Heckel, Schmidt-Rottluff, and Bleyl, and with them, as already noted, he founded the Brücke group.

For subject matter Kirchner looked to contemporary life—landscapes, portraits of friends, and nudes in natural settings—rejecting the artificial trappings of academic studios. In both Dresden and Berlin, where he moved in 1911, he recorded the streets and inhabitants of the city and the bohemian life of its nightclubs, cabarets, and circuses. *Street, Dresden* (fig. **8.3**) of 1908 is an assembly of curvilinear figures who undulate like wraiths, moving toward and away from the viewer without individual motive power, drifting in a world of dreams. Kirchner

probably had Munch's street painting *Evening on Karl Johan* in mind when he made this work, and, as was frequently his habit, he reworked it at a much later date. In Berlin he painted a series of street scenes in which the spaces are confined and precipitously tilted, and the figures are elongated into angular shards by long feathered strokes. Kirchner made rapid sketches of these street scenes, then worked up the image in more formal drawings in his studio before making the final paintings. These scenes' strong sense of movement may indicate his borrowing from Italian Futurist painting (see chapter 11), as well as the impact of Cubism, and his distorted Gothic forms express the condition of modern urban life, in which close physical proximity is coupled with extreme psychological distance.

If Kirchner's *Market Place with Red Tower* (fig. **8.4**) is compared with one of the French Cubist painter Robert Delaunay's Eiffel Tower studies, the difference between the German and the French vision becomes evident. Delaunay's *Eiffel Tower in Trees* of 1910 (see fig. 10.43) represents an expressive interpretation of Cubism in which the expression is achieved by the dynamism of abstract color shapes and lines. Kirchner's *Market Place* is expressive in a more explicit way. It reveals the artist's knowledge of

8.4 Ernst Ludwig Kirchner, *Market Place with Red Tower*, 1915. Oil on canvas, 47½ × 35⅞" (120.7 × 91.1 cm). Museum Folkwang, Essen, Germany.

8.5 Ernst Ludwig Kirchner, *Self-Portrait with Cat*, 1919–20. Oil on canvas, 47¼ × 33½" (120 × 85 cm). Busch-Reisinger Museum, Harvard University Art Museums, Cambridge, Massachusetts.

Cubist works, but uses Cubist geometry with caution, combining it with defined perspective space distorted in the manner of Van Gogh for the similar end of creating a claustrophobic effect of compression—what Kirchner called the "melancholy of big city streets."

When World War I broke out Kirchner enlisted in the field artillery, but he suffered a mental and physical breakdown and was discharged in 1915. He recuperated in Switzerland, where he continued to live and work near the town of Davos until his death by suicide in 1938. During this late period in his career Kirchner continued to renew his style, painting many of his older themes along with serene Alpine landscapes and sympathetic portrayals of Swiss peasant life. The Swiss landscape can be seen through the window in Kirchner's moving *Self-Portrait with Cat* (fig. **8.5**), in which the artist's weary countenance betrays his protracted struggle with illness and depression.

Heckel, Müller, Pechstein, and Schmidt-Rottluff

Erich Heckel (1883–1970) was a more restrained Expressionist whose early paintings at their best showed flashes of psychological insight and lyricism. After 1920 he turned increasingly to the production of colorful but essentially Romantic–Realist landscapes. A painting such as *Two Men at a Table* (fig. **8.6**) evokes a dramatic interplay in which not only the figures but the contracted, tilted space of the room is charged with emotion. This painting, dedicated "to Dostoyevsky," is almost a literal illustration from the Russian novelist's *Brothers Karamazov*. The painting of the tortured Christ, the suffering face of the man at the left, the menace of the other—all refer to Ivan's story, in the novel, of Christ and the Grand Inquisitor.

Using the most delicate and muted colors of all the Brücke painters, **Otto Müller** (1874–1930) created works that suggest an Oriental elegance in their organization. His nudes are attenuated, awkwardly graceful figures

8.6 Erich Heckel, *Two Men at a Table*, 1912. Oil on canvas, 38⅛ × 47¼" (96.8 × 120 cm). Kunsthalle, Hamburg.

whose softly outlined, yellow-ocher bodies blend imperceptibly and harmoniously into the green and yellow foliage of their setting (fig. **8.7**). He was impressed by ancient Egyptian wall paintings and developed techniques to emulate their muted tonalities. The unidealized, candid depiction of nudes in open nature was among the Brücke artists' favorite subjects. They saw the nude as a welcome release from nineteenth-century prudery and a liberating plunge into primal experience. As Nolde proclaimed, echoing the widely shared, if unwittingly patronizing, view of "primitive" peoples that was current at the time, "Primordial peoples live in their nature, are one with it and are a part of the entire universe." The relative gentleness of Müller's treatment of this theme found an echo in the contemporary photographs of the German-born photographer **Heinrich Kühn** (1866–1944), who, like early twentieth-century modernists in painting, sought to flatten space and create a more two-dimensional design—a Pictorial effect, as the photographers would have said—by viewing his subject or scene from above (fig. **8.8**).

8.8 Heinrich Kühn, *The Artist's Umbrella*, 1910. Photogravure on heavy woven paper, 9 × 11⅜" (23 × 28.9 cm). The Metropolitan Museum of Art, New York.

8.9 Max Pechstein, *Indian and Woman*, 1910. Oil on canvas, 32¼ × 26¼" (81.9 × 66.7 cm). The Saint Louis Art Museum.

Max Pechstein (1881–1953) had a considerable head start in art by the time he joined Die Brücke in 1906. He had studied for several years at the Dresden Academy, and in general enjoyed an earlier success than the other Brücke painters. In 1905 he had seen a collection of wood carvings from the Palau Islands in Dresden's ethnographic museum, and these had a formative influence on his work. In 1914 he traveled to these islands in the Pacific to study the art at first hand. Pechstein was the most eclectic of the Brücke group, capable of notable individual paintings that shift from one style to another. The early *Indian and Woman* (fig. **8.9**) shows him at his dramatic best in terms of the exotic subject, modeling of the figures, and Fauve-inspired color. Pechstein's drawing is sculptural and curvilinear in contrast to that of Müller or Heckel, and it was not tinged by the intense anxiety that informed so much of Kirchner's work.

In 1910 **Karl Schmidt-Rottluff** (1884–1976) portrayed himself as the very image of the arrogant young Expressionist—in a green turtleneck sweater, complete with beard and monocle, against a roughly painted background of a yellow doorway flanked by purplish-brown curtains (fig. **8.10**). Aside from Nolde, Schmidt-Rottluff was the boldest colorist of the group, given to vivid blues

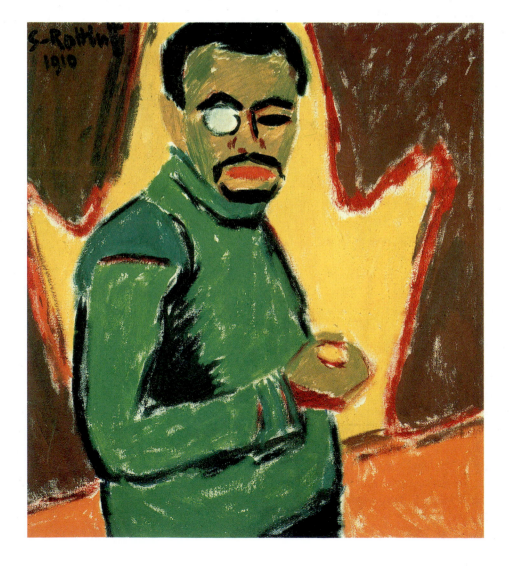

8.10 Karl Schmidt-Rottluff, *Self-Portrait with Monocle*, 1910. Oil on canvas, 33⅛ × 30" (84.1 × 76.2 cm). Staatliche Museen zu Berlin, Preussischer Kulturbesitz, Nationalgalerie.

and crimsons, yellows and greens, juxtaposed in jarring but effective dissonance. Although never a fully abstract painter, he was probably the member of Die Brücke who moved furthest and most convincingly in the direction of abstract structure. Schmidt-Rottluff had been traumatized by his service in Russia during World War I, and was later commissioned to redesign the imperial German eagle, casts of which were placed on buildings throughout Germany. Despite this service to his country, when the Nazis came to power he was dismissed from his position as professor of art in Berlin in 1933 and forbidden to work. His *Self-Portrait with Monocle* was seized from the museum that had acquired it in 1924 and included in the 1937 Degenerate Art show staged by the Nazis.

Graphic Impact: Expressionist Prints

One of the principal contributions of German Expressionism was the revival of printmaking as a major form of art. During the nineteenth century a large number of the experimental painters and sculptors had made prints, and toward the end of the century, in the hands of artists like Toulouse-Lautrec (see fig. 3.29), Gauguin, Redon, Klinger, and Ensor, printmaking assumed an importance as an independent art form beyond anything that had existed since the Renaissance. Several early twentieth-century artists outside Germany—Picasso, Munch, Rouault—were important printmakers as well as painters. In Germany, however, a country with a particularly rich tradition of printmaking, this art form occupied a special place, and its revival contributed to the character of painting and sculpture. Expressionist artists sought a direct engagement with their materials and adapted their technique to the exigencies of the medium in order to achieve maximum expressive power. It was especially the simplified forms of the woodcut, a form of printmaking with a long and distinguished history in German art, that they felt conveyed most authentically the desired emotion. The artists of Die Brücke brought about a veritable renaissance of this medium.

Considerably older than these artists, the painter and printmaker **Lovis Corinth** (1858–1925) formed a link between German Romanticism and later German Expressionist art. In his lengthy academic training in Germany and France he learned that a firm grounding in draftsmanship was fundamental to his art. Like his favorite artist, Rembrandt, one of Corinth's preferred subjects was his own face, which he explored in *Death and the Artist* (fig. **8.11**). This print belongs to his series *Dance of Death*, his interpretation of a medieval theme that reminds us of our own inevitable mortality. Although Corinth made woodcuts occasionally, he favored lithography, etching, and especially drypoint, a technique that produces a rich, velvety line.

Of the Brücke group, Nolde was already an accomplished etcher by the time he made his first woodcuts.

8.11 Lovis Corinth, *Death and the Artist,* from the *Totentanz (Dance of Death)* series, 1921. Soft-ground etching and drypoint on Japanese paper, plate 9½ × 7" (24 × 17.8 cm), sheet 11¾ × 9⅜" (30 × 24.7 cm). National Gallery of Art, Washington, D.C.

His *Prophet* of 1912 owes something to Late Gothic German woodcuts as well as the prints of Munch, with its intense black-and-white contrast and bold, jagged shapes that exploit the natural grain of the woodblock. His lithographs, which differ in expression from the rugged forms of this woodcut, include *Female Dancer* (fig. **8.12**), one of the greatest of all German Expressionist prints. Nolde appreciated the artistic freedom afforded him by the lithographic medium, which he used in experimental ways, brushing ink directly on the stone printing matrix to create thin, variable washes of color. He was interested in the body as an expressive vehicle, and had made sketches in the theaters and cabarets of Berlin, as had Kirchner. But the sense of frenzied emotion and wild abandon in *Female Dancer* evokes associations with some primal ritual rather than with urban dance halls. Nolde had studied the work of non-European cultures in museums such as the Berlin Ethnographic Museum, concluding that Oceanic and African art possessed a vitality that much Western art lacked. He argued for their study as objects of aesthetic as well as scientific interest and made drawings of objects that were then incorporated into his still-life paintings. In 1913, shortly after making this lithograph, Nolde joined an official ethnographic expedition to New Guinea, then a German colony in the South Pacific, and later traveled to East Asia. He made sketches of

8.12 Emil Nolde, *Female Dancer*, 1913. Color lithograph, 20⅞ × 27⅛" (53 × 69 cm). Nolde-Stiftung Seebüll, Germany.

the landscapes and local inhabitants on his journeys, from which he returned highly critical of European colonial practices.

Kirchner, in both black-and-white and color woodcuts, developed an intricate, linear style that looked back to the woodcuts of Dürer and Martin Schongauer. In a powerful portrait of the Belgian Art Nouveau architect Henry van de Velde, he used characteristic V-shaped gouges to create complex surface patterns. By contrast, Heckel's color woodcut *Standing Child* (fig. **8.13**) is a spare composition. Heckel's adolescent subject was a girl named Fränzi, who, with her sister Marcella, was a favorite model of the Brücke group. The artist reserved the color of the paper for the model's skin and employed three woodblocks—for black, green, and red inks—in the puzzle technique invented by Munch (see fig. 5.20), for the brilliant, abstracted landscape behind her. It is a gripping image for its forthright design and the frank, precocious sexuality of the sitter.

Like Nolde, Pechstein chose dance as his subject for a color woodcut of 1910 (fig. **8.14**), a work he may have been inspired to make after seeing a Somali dance group perform in Berlin that year. The dancers are portrayed against a colorful backdrop that resembles the kind of hangings with which the Brücke artists decorated their studios. Pechstein sought a deliberately crude execution here,

8.13 Erich Heckel, *Standing Child*, 1910. Color woodcut, 14¾ × 10¾" (37.5 × 27.5 cm). Los Angeles County Museum of Art.

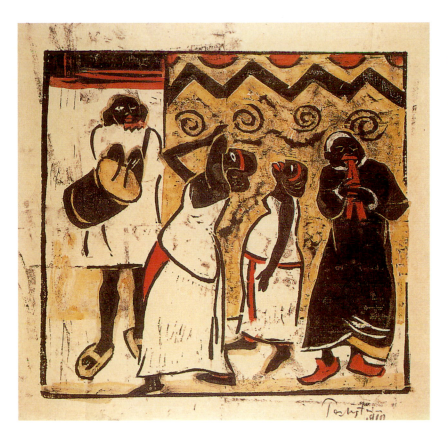

8.14 Max Pechstein, *Somali Dancers*, 1910. Hand-colored woodcut, 12½ × 14⅜" (31.8 × 36.5 cm). Brücke-Museum, Berlin.

with schematically hewn figures and a surface covered with irregular smudges of ink.

Käthe Kollwitz (1867–1945) devoted her life and her art, both printmaking and sculpture, to a form of protest or social criticism. She was the first of the German Social Realists who developed out of Expressionism during and after World War I. Essentially a Realist, and powerfully concerned with the problems and sufferings of the underprivileged, she stands somewhat aside from Die Brücke or other Expressionists, such as Kandinsky or Der Blaue Reiter. When she married a doctor, his patients, predominantly the industrial poor of Berlin, became her models.

As a woman, Kollwitz had been prevented from studying at the Academy, so she attended a Berlin art school for women. There she was introduced to the prints and writings of Max Klinger and decided to take up printmaking rather than painting. The graphic media appealed to Kollwitz for their ability to convey a message effectively and to reach a wide audience, because each image could be printed many times. Like Klinger, she produced elaborate print cycles on a central theme. Such is the case with *Death Seizing a Woman* (fig. **8.15**), which belongs to her last great series of lithographs. Kollwitz had first explored the theme of a mother cradling her dead child much earlier and had no doubt witnessed such loss among her husband's patients. But the death of her youngest son (who, poignantly, had served as an infant model in the earlier works) in World War I transformed the subject into one of personal tragedy.

8.15 Käthe Kollwitz, *Death Seizing a Woman* (1934) from the series *Death*, 1934–36. Lithograph, printed in black, composition: 20 × 14⅞" (50.8 × 36.7 cm). The Museum of Modern Art, New York.

8.16 Käthe Kollwitz, *Female Nude with Green Shawl Seen from Behind*, 1903. Color lithograph, sheet 23½ × 18½" (59.7 × 47 cm). Staatliche Kunstsammlungen, Dresden.

Although best known for her black-and-white prints and posters of political subjects, Kollwitz could be an exquisite colorist. Her lithograph of a nude woman (fig. **8.16**), with its luminous atmosphere and quiet mood, so unlike her declarative political prints, demonstrates her extraordinary skill and sensitivity as a printmaker.

The Spiritual Dimension: Der Blaue Reiter

The Brücke artists were the first manifestation of Expressionism in Germany but not necessarily the most significant. While they were active, first in Dresden and then in Berlin, a movement of more far-reaching implications was germinating in Munich around one of the great personalities of modern art, **Vasily Kandinsky** (1866–1944).

Kandinsky

Born in Moscow, Kandinsky studied law and economics at the University of Moscow. Visits to Paris and an exhibition of French painting in Moscow aroused his interest to the point that, at the age of thirty, he refused a professorship of law in order to study painting. He then went to Munich,

where he was soon caught up in the atmosphere of Art Nouveau and Jugendstil then permeating the city.

Since 1890, Munich had been one of the most active centers of experimental art in Europe. Kandinsky was soon taking a leading part in the Munich art world, even while undergoing the more traditional discipline of study at the Academy and with older artists. In 1901 he formed a new artists' association, Phalanx, and opened his own art school. In the same year he was exhibiting in the Berlin Secession, and by 1904 had shown works in the Paris Salon d'Automne and Exposition Nationale des Beaux-Arts. That year the Phalanx had shown the Neo-Impressionists, as well as Cézanne, Gauguin, and Van Gogh. By 1909 Kandinsky was leading a revolt against the established Munich art movements that resulted in the formation of the Neue Künstler Vereinigung (NKV, New Artists Association). In addition to Kandinsky, the NKV included Alexej von Jawlensky, Gabriele Münter, Alfred Kubin, and, later, Franz Marc. Its second exhibition, in 1910, showed the works not only of Germans but also of leading Parisian experimental painters: Picasso, Braque, Rouault, Derain, and Vlaminck.

During this period, Kandinsky was exploring revolutionary ideas about nonobjective or abstract painting, that is, painting without literal subject matter, that does not take its form from the observed world. He traced the beginnings of this interest to a moment of epiphany he had experienced in 1908. Entering his studio one day, he could not make out any subject in his painting, only shapes and colors: he then realized it was turned on its side. In 1911 a split in the NKV resulted in the secession of Kandinsky, accompanied by Marc and Münter, and the formation of the association Der Blaue Reiter (The Blue Rider), a name taken from a book published by Kandinsky and Marc, which had in turn taken its name from a painting by Kandinsky. The historic exhibition held at the Thannhauser Gallery in Munich in December 1911 included works by Kandinsky, Marc, August Macke, Heinrich Campendonck, Münter, the composer Arnold Schönberg, the Frenchmen Henri Rousseau and Robert Delaunay, and others. Paul Klee, already associated with the group, showed with them in a graphics exhibition in 1912. This was a much larger show. The entries were expanded to include artists of Die Brücke and additional French and Russian artists: Roger de La Fresnaye, Kazimir Malevich, and Jean Arp, an Alsatian.

In his book *Concerning the Spiritual in Art*, published in 1911, Kandinsky formulated the ideas that had obsessed him since his student days in Russia. Always a serious student, he had devoted much time to the question of the relations between art and music. He had first sensed the dematerialization of the object in the paintings of Monet, and this direction in art continued to intrigue him as, through exhibitions in Munich and his continual travels, he learned more about the revolutionary new discoveries of the Neo-Impressionists, the Symbolists, the Fauves, and the Cubists. Advances in the physical sciences had called into question the "reality" of the world of tangible objects, strengthening his conviction that art had to be concerned with the expression of the spiritual rather than the material. Despite his strong scientific and legal interests, Kandinsky was attracted to Theosophy, spiritism, and the occult. There was always a mystical core in his thinking—something he at times attributed to his Russian roots. This sense of an inner creative force, a product of the spirit rather than of external vision or manual skill, enabled him to arrive at an art entirely without representation other than colors and shapes. Deeply concerned with the expression of harmony in visual terms, he wrote, "The harmony of color and form must be based solely upon the principle of the proper contact with the human soul." And so, along with František Kupka, Delaunay, Piet Mondrian, and Malevich, Kandinsky was one of the first, if not—as traditionally thought—the very first, modern European artist to break through the representational barrier and carry painting into total abstraction. But while other pioneers of pictorial nonobjectivity worked in a Cubist-derived geometric mode, Kandinsky

worked in a painterly, improvisatory, Expressionist, biomorphic manner that has had many illustrious heirs, from the Surrealist art of André Masson, Joan Miró, and Matta to the environmentally scaled compositions of Jackson Pollock and beyond, to many contemporary practitioners of gestural painting.

As he was moving toward abstraction, the early paintings of Kandinsky went through various stages of Impressionism and Art Nouveau decoration, but all were characterized by a feeling for color. Many also had a fairy-tale quality of narrative, reminiscent of his early interest in Russian folktales and mythology. Kandinsky pursued this line of investigation in the rural setting of the Bavarian village of Murnau, where he lived for a time with Gabriele Münter. Münter took up *Hinterglasmalerei* (painting behind glass), a local form of folk art in which a painting is done on the underside of a sheet of glass, and Kandinsky followed her example. The archaism of the style and its spiritual purity forecast the more radical simplifications soon to come. Like his contemporaries in Germany and France, Kandinsky was interested in native Russian art forms and in 1889 had traveled on an ethnographic expedition to study the people of Vologda, a remote Russian province north of Moscow. He was moved by the interiors of the peasants' houses, which were filled with decorative painting and furniture. "I learned not to look at a picture from outside," he said, "but to move within the picture, to live in the picture."

Because of his wish to associate his work with an image-free art form that spoke directly to the senses in modernist fashion, Kandinsky began using titles derived from music, such as "Composition," "Improvisation," or "Impression." He made ten major paintings titled "Composition," which he considered to be his most complete artistic statements, expressive of what he called "inner necessity" or the artist's

8.17 Vasily Kandinsky, *Sketch for Composition II*, 1909–10. Oil on canvas, 38⅜ × 51¾" (97.5 × 131.5 cm). Solomon R. Guggenheim Museum, New York.

intuitive, emotional response to the world. A close examination of *Sketch for Composition II* (fig. **8.17**) reveals that the artist is still employing a pictorial vocabulary filled with standing figures, riders on horseback, and onion-domed churches, but they are now highly abstracted forms in the midst of a tumultuous, upheaving landscape of mountains and trees that Kandinsky painted in the high-keyed color of the Fauves. Although Kandinsky said this painting had no theme, it is clear that the composition is divided into two sections, with a scene of deluge and disturbance at the left and a garden of paradise at the right, where lovers recline as they had in Matisse's *Le Bonheur de vivre* (see fig. 7.6). Kandinsky balances these opposing forces to give his all-embracing view of the universe.

In general, Kandinsky's compositions revolve around themes of cosmic conflict and renewal, specifically the Deluge from the biblical book of Genesis and the Apocalypse from the book of Revelation. From such cataclysm would emerge, he believed, a rebirth, a new, spiritually cleansed world. In *Composition VII* (fig. **8.18**), an enormous canvas from 1913, colors, shapes, and lines collide across the pictorial field in a furiously explosive composition. Yet even in the midst of this symphonic arrangement of abstract forms, the characteristic motifs Kandinsky had distilled over the years can still be deciphered, such as the glyph of a boat with

three oars at the lower left, a sign of the biblical floods. He did not intend these hieroglyphic forms to be read literally, so he veiled them in washes of brilliant color. Though the artist carefully prepared this large work with many preliminary drawings and oil sketches, he preserved a sense of spontaneous, unpremeditated freedom in the final painting.

In 1914 the cataclysm of World War I forced Kandinsky to return to Russia, and, shortly thereafter, another phase of his career began (discussed in chapter 11), a pattern repeated in the careers of many artists at this time. In looking at the work of the other members of Der Blaue Reiter up to 1914, we should recall that the individuals involved were not held together by common stylistic principles but rather constituted a loose association of young artists, enthusiastic about new experiments and united in their oppositions. Aside from personal friendships, it was Kandinsky who gave the group cohesion and direction. The yearbook *Der Blaue Reiter*, edited by Kandinsky and Franz Marc, appeared in 1912 and served as a forum for the opinions of the group. The new experiments of Picasso and Matisse in Paris were discussed at length, and the aims and conflicts of the new German art associations were described. In the creation of the new culture and new approach to painting, much importance was attached to the influence of so-called primitive and naive art.

8.18 Vasily Kandinsky, *Composition VII*, 1913. Oil on canvas, 6'6¾" × 9'11⅛" (2 × 3 m). Tretyakov Gallery, Moscow.

8.19 Franz Marc, *The Large Blue Horses*, 1911. Oil on canvas, 41⅝ × 71⅝" (105.7 × 181.1 cm). Walker Art Center, Minneapolis.

Marc

Of the Blaue Reiter painters, **Franz Marc** (1880–1916) was the closest in spirit to the traditions of German Romanticism and lyrical naturalism. In Paris in 1907 he sought personal solutions in the paintings of Van Gogh, whom he called the most authentic of painters. From an early date he turned to the subject of animals as a source of spiritual harmony and purity in nature. This became for him a symbol of that more primitive and arcadian life sought by so many of the Expressionist painters. Through his friend the painter August Macke, Marc developed, in about 1910, enthusiasms for color whose richness and beauty were expressive also of the harmonies he was seeking. The great *Blue Horses* of 1911 is one of the masterpieces of Marc's mature style (fig. **8.19**). The three brilliant blue beasts are fleshed out sculpturally from the equally vivid reds, greens, and yellows of the landscape. The artist used a close-up view, with the bodies of the horses filling most of the canvas. The horizon line is high, so that the curves of the red hills repeat the lines of the horses' curving flanks. Although the modeling of the animals gives them the effect of sculptured relief projecting from a uniform background, there is no real spatial differentiation between creatures and environment, except that the sky is rendered more softly and less tangibly to create some illusion of distance. In fact, Marc used the two whitish tree trunks and the green of foliage in front of and behind the horses to tie foreground and background together. At this time Marc's color, like that of Kandinsky, had a specifically symbolic rather than descriptive function. Marc saw blue as a masculine principle, robust and spiritual; yellow as a feminine principle, gentle, serene, and sensual; red as matter, brutal and heavy. In the mixing of these colors to create greens and violets, and in their proportions one to the other on the canvas, the colors formed abstract shapes and took on spiritual or material significance independent of the subject.

During 1911–12 Marc was absorbing the ideas and forms of the Cubists and finding them applicable to his own concepts of the mystery and poetry of color. His approach to art was religious in a manner that could be described as pantheistic, although it is interesting that in his paintings only animals are assimilated harmoniously into nature—never humans. Marc, with Macke, visited Delaunay in Paris in 1912 and saw his experiments with color and form; in the same year Marc was impressed by an exhibition of Italian Futurists he saw in Munich. Out of the influences of Kandinsky, of Delaunay's color abstraction, and of the Futurists' use of Cubist structures, Marc evolved his later style—which, tragically, he was able to explore for only two or three more years until he was killed in the war in 1916.

In *Stables* (fig. **8.20**) he combined his earlier curvilinear patterns with a new rectangular geometry. The horses, massed in the frontal plane, are dismembered and recomposed as fractured shapes that are dispersed evenly across the surface of the canvas. The forms are composed parallel to the picture plane rather than tilted in depth. This treatment was in accordance with the experiments of Delaunay in his *Simultaneous Disk* series (see fig. 10.44). At this stage, however, Marc's paintings were still far less abstract than Delaunay's, and their sense of nervous energy made them akin to the work of the Futurists. Intense but light-filled blues and reds, greens, violets, and yellows flicker over the structurally and spatially unified surface to create a dazzling illusion. Marc's use of color at this stage owed much to Macke, who frequently used the theme of people reflected in shop windows as a means of distorting space and multiplying images.

8.20 Franz Marc, *Stables*, 1913–14. Oil on canvas, 29⅛ × 62¼" (74 × 158.1 cm). Solomon R. Guggenheim Museum, New York.

Unlike Kandinsky's, Marc's imagery was predominantly derived from the material world. But in a group of small compositions from 1914 and in notebook sketches, there was evidence of a move to abstraction. Some of his later works carry premonitions of the world conflict that ended his life. In a virtually abstract painting, *Fighting Forms* of 1914, Marc returned to curvilinear pattern in a violent battle of black and red color shapes, of light and darkness. The forms are given such vitality that they take on the characteristics of forces in an ultimate encounter.

Macke

Of the major figures in Der Blaue Reiter, **August Macke** (1887–1914), despite his close association with and influence on Franz Marc, created work that was as elegantly controlled as it was expressive. Macke, like Marc, was influenced by Kandinsky, Delaunay, and the Futurists, and perhaps more immediately by the color concepts of Gauguin and Matisse. Since he was killed in September 1914, one month after the beginning of World War I, his achievement must be gauged by the work of only four years.

8.21 August Macke, *Great Zoological Garden*, 1912. Oil on canvas, 4'3⅛ × 7'6¾" (1.3 × 2.3 m). Museum am Ostwall, Dortmund, Germany.

After some Fauve- and Cubist-motivated exercises in semiabstraction, Macke began to paint city scenes in high-keyed color, using diluted oil paint in effects close to that of watercolor. *Great Zoological Garden*, a triptych of 1912 (fig. **8.21**), is a loving transformation of a familiar scene into a fairyland of translucent color. Pictorial space is delimited by foliage and buildings that derive from the later watercolors of Cézanne. The artist moves easily from passages as abstract as the background architecture to passages as literally representational as the animals and the foreground figures. The work has a unity of mood that is light and charming, disarming because of the naive joy that permeates it.

Macke occasionally experimented with abstract organization, but his principal interest during the last two years of his life continued to be his cityscapes, which were decorative colored impressions of elegant ladies and gentlemen strolling in the park or studying the wares in brightly lit shop windows. In numerous versions of such themes, he shows his fascination with the mirrorlike effects of windows as a means of transforming the perspective space of the street into the fractured space of Cubism.

Jawlensky

Alexej von Jawlensky (1864–1941) was well established in his career as an officer of the Russian Imperial Guard before he decided to become a painter. After studies in Moscow he took classes in the same studio in Munich as Kandinsky. Although not officially a member of Der Blaue Reiter, Jawlensky was sympathetic to its aims and continued for years to be close to Kandinsky. After the war he formed the group called Die Blaue Vier (The Blue Four), along with Kandinsky, Klee, and Lyonel Feininger.

By 1905 Jawlensky was painting in a Fauve palette, and his drawings of nudes of the next few years are suggestive of Matisse. About 1910 he settled on his primary theme, the portrait head, which he explored thenceforward with mystical intensity. *Mme Turandot* is an early example (fig. **8.22**), painted in a manner that combines characteristics of Russian folk painting and Russo-Byzantine icons—sources that would dominate Jawlensky's work.

In 1914 Jawlensky embarked on a remarkable series of paintings of the human head that occupied him intermittently for over twenty years. Each of these "mystic heads" assumed a virtually identical format: a large head fills the frame, with features reduced to a grid of horizontal and vertical lines and planes of delicate color, more a schema for a face than an actual visage. In the twenties Jawlensky made a series, *Constructivist Heads* (fig. **8.23**), in which the eyes are closed, casting an introspective, meditative mood over these images, which, for the artist, were expressions of a universal spirituality. Like Kandinsky's compositions, they were variations on a theme, but in their restrictive, repetitive structure, they are closer in spirit to the neoplastic work of Piet Mondrian (see fig. 17.21). In the mid-thirties the geometry gradually

8.22 Alexej von Jawlensky, *Mme Turandot*, 1912. Oil on canvas, 23 × 20" (58.4 × 50.8 cm). Collection Andreas Jawlensky, Locarno, Switzerland.

8.23 Alexej von Jawlensky, *Love*, from the *Constructivist Heads* series, 1925. Oil on paper, 23¼ × 19⅝" (59 × 49.8 cm). Städtische Galerie im Lenbachhaus, Munich.

loosened, and Jawlensky dissolved the linear structure into dark, forcefully brushed abstractions that he called "Meditations."

Klee

Paul Klee (1879–1940) was one of the most varied, influential, and brilliant talents in the twentieth century. His stylistic development is difficult to trace even after 1914, since the artist, from this moment of maturity, continually reexamined his themes and forms to arrive at a reality beyond the visible world. He developed a visual language seemingly limitless in its invention and in the variety of its formal means. His complex language of personal signs and symbols evolved through private fantasy and a range of interests from plant and zoological life to astronomy and typography. Also interested in music, he wanted to create imagery infused with the rhythms and counterpoint of musical composition, saying that color could be played like a "chromatic keyboard."

Klee was born in Switzerland. The son of a musician, he was initially inclined toward music, but having decided on the career of painting, went to Munich to study in 1898. During the years 1903–6 he produced a number of etchings that in their precise, hard technique suggest the graphic tradition of the German Renaissance, in their mannered linearity Art Nouveau, and in their mad fantasy a personal vision reflecting the influence of the Expressionist printmaker Alfred Kubin. These were also among the first of Klee's works in which the title formed an integral part of

8.24 Paul Klee, *Hammamet with its Mosque*, 1914. Watercolor and pencil on paper, 8⅛ × 7½" (20.6 × 19.1 cm). The Metropolitan Museum of Art, New York.

his creative work. Klee brought tremendous verbal skill and wit to his paintings, drawings, and prints, using letters and words literally as formal devices in his compositions, which he then gave a literary dimension with poetic and often humorous titles.

Between 1901 and 1905 Klee traveled extensively in Italy and France and probably saw works by Matisse. Between 1908 and 1910 he became aware of Cézanne, Van Gogh, and the beginnings of the modern movement in painting. In 1911 he had a solo exhibition at the Thannhauser Gallery in Munich and in the same year met the Blaue Reiter painters Kandinsky, Marc, Macke, Jawlensky, and Münter. Over the next few years he participated in the Blaue Reiter exhibitions, wrote for *Der Sturm*, and, in Paris in 1912, met Delaunay and saw further paintings by Picasso, Braque, and Henri Rousseau.

He took a trip with Macke to Tunis and other parts of North Africa in 1914. Like Delacroix and other Romantics before him, he was affected by the brilliance of the region's light and the color and clarity of the atmosphere. To catch the quality of the scene Klee, like Macke, turned to watercolor and a form of semiabstract color pattern based on a Cubist grid, a structure he frequently used as a linear scaffolding for his compositions (fig. **8.24**). Although he made larger paintings, he tended to prefer small-scale works on paper. Klee had a long and fertile career, the later phases of which will be traced in chapter 17.

Feininger

Although **Lyonel Feininger** (1871–1956) was born an American of German-American parents, as a painter he belongs within the European orbit. The son of distinguished musicians, he was, like Klee, early destined for a musical career. But before he was ten he was drawing his impressions of buildings, boats, and elevated trains in New York City. He went to Germany in 1887 to study music, but soon turned to painting. In Berlin between 1893 and 1905 Feininger earned his living as an illustrator and caricaturist for German and American periodicals, developing a brittle, angular style of figure drawing related to aspects of Art Nouveau, but revealing a very distinctive personal sense of visual satire. The years 1906–8, in Paris, brought him in touch with the early pioneers of modern French painting. By 1912–13 he had arrived at his own version of Cubism, particularly the form of Cubism with which Marc was experimenting at the same time. Feininger was invited to exhibit with Der Blaue Reiter in 1913. Thus, not surprisingly, he and Marc shared the sources of Orphism and Futurism, which particularly appealed to the Romantic, expressive sensibilities of both. Whereas Marc translated his beloved animals into luminous Cubist planes, Feininger continued with his favorite themes of architecture, boats, and the sea. In *Harbor Mole* of 1913 (fig. **8.25**), he recomposed the scene into a scintillating interplay of color facets, geometric in outline but given a sense of rapid change by the transparent, delicately graded color

8.25 Lyonel Feininger, *Harbor Mole*, 1913. Oil on canvas, 31¾ × 39¾" (80.6 × 101 cm). Private collection.

areas. In this work Feininger stated in a most accomplished manner the approach he was to continue, with variations, throughout the rest of his long life: that of strong, straight-line structure played against sensuous and softly luminous color. The interplay between taut linear structure and Romantic color, with space constantly shifting between abstraction and representation, created a dynamic tension in his paintings.

In 1919 Feininger was invited to join the staff of the Bauhaus, the great experimental German school of architecture and design. He remained associated with the institution until it was closed by the Nazis in 1933, although he had stopped teaching full-time in the twenties because the schedule interfered with his own painting. Feininger's work steadily developed in the direction he had chosen, sometimes emerging in shattered architectural images, sometimes in serene and light-filled structures full of poetic suggestion. He returned to the United States in 1937 and settled in New York, a difficult move for an artist who had made his reputation in Europe. Once he was "spiritually acclimatized," as he said, to his new home, he moved in a new stylistic direction, one less restricted by the "straitjacket" of Cubism and characterized by a freer application of color.

In 1912 Herwarth Walden opened a gallery in Berlin for avant-garde art, the Sturm Galerie, where he exhibited Kandinsky and Der Blaue Reiter, Die Brücke and the Italian Futurists, and grouped as French Expressionists Braque, Derain, Vlaminck, Auguste Herbin, and others. Also shown were Ensor, Klee, and Delaunay. In 1913 came the climax of the Sturm Galerie's exhibitions, the First German Autumn Salon, including three hundred and sixty works. Henri Rousseau's room contained twenty paintings, and almost the entire international range of experimental painting and sculpture at that moment was shown. Although during and after the war the various activities of Der Sturm lost their impetus, Berlin between 1910 and 1914 remained a rallying point for most of the new European ideas and revolutionary movements, largely through the leadership of Walden.

Self-Examination: Expressionism in Austria

To understand the various directions in which Expressionism moved during and after World War I, we may look at two artists who were associated in some degree with Expressionism in Austria, where its practitioners were never formally organized into a particular group. Like Klee and Feininger, the Austrians Egon Schiele and Oskar Kokoschka each had his highly individualized interpretation of the style.

Schiele

Egon Schiele (1890–1918) lived a short and tragic life, dying in the worldwide influenza epidemic of 1918. He was a precocious draftsman and, despite opposition from his uncle (who was his guardian after his father died insane, an event that haunted him), studied at the Vienna Academy of Art. His principal encouragement came from Gustav Klimt (see chapter 5), at his height as a painter and leader of the avant-garde in Vienna when they met in 1907. The two artists remained close, but although Schiele was deeply influenced by Klimt, he did not fully share his inclination toward the decorative.

Schiele's many self-portraits rank among his supreme achievements. They range from self-revelatory documents of personal anguish to records of a highly self-conscious and youthful bravado. *Schiele, Drawing a Nude Model before a Mirror* (fig. **8.26**) demonstrates his extraordinary natural skill as a draftsman. The intense portrayal, with the artist's narrowed gaze and the elongated, angular figure of the model, differs from even the most direct and least embellished of Klimt's portraits. Here Schiele explores the familiar theme of the artist and model, but does so to create an atmosphere of psychological tension and explicit sexuality. Schiele's models included his sister Gerti, as well

8.26 Egon Schiele, *Schiele, Drawing a Nude Model before a Mirror*, 1910. Pencil on paper, 21¾ × 13⅞" (55.2 × 35.2 cm). Graphische Sammlung Albertina, Vienna.

8.27 Egon Schiele, *The Self Seer II (Death and the Man)*, 1911. Oil on canvas, 31⅝ × 31½" (80.3 × 80 cm). Private collection.

as friends, professional models, and prostitutes. But when, albeit innocently, in 1912 he sought out children for models in his small village, he was imprisoned for twenty-four days for "offenses against public morality."

A comparison of paintings by Klimt and Schiele is valuable in illustrating both the continuity and the change between nineteenth-century Symbolism and early twentieth-century Expressionism. Klimt's painting *Death and Life* (see fig. 5.6) is heavy with symbolism presented in terms of the richest and most colorful patterns. Schiele's *The Self Seer II* (fig. **8.27**), painted in 1911, is comparable in subject, but the approach could not be more different. The man (a self-portrait) is rigidly frontalized in the center of the painting and stares out at the spectator. His face is a horrible and bloody mask of fear. The figure of Death hovers behind, a ghostly presence folding the man in his arms in a grim embrace. The paint is built up in jagged brushstrokes on figures emerging from a background of harsh and dissonant tones of ocher, red, and green.

In Schiele's portraiture, other than the commissioned portraits he undertook occasionally to support himself, there persisted the same intensity of characterization. But in his later work the tense linear quality we have seen gave way to painterly surfaces built up with abundant, expressive brushwork. In one of his last works Schiele dramatically portrays his friend, the artist Paris von Gütersloh, with hands held aloft, fingers spread, as though the hands of the artist possessed some mysterious, supernatural power.

Kokoschka

Oskar Kokoschka (1886–1980), like Schiele, was a product of Vienna, but he soon left the city, which he found gloomy and oppressive, for Switzerland and Germany, embracing the larger world of modern art to become one of the international figures of twentieth-century Expressionism. Between 1905 and 1908 Kokoschka worked in the Viennese Art Nouveau style, showing the influence of Klimt and Aubrey Beardsley. Even before going to Berlin at the invitation of Herwarth Walden in 1910, he was instinctively an Expressionist. Particularly in his early "black portraits," he searched passionately to expose an inner sensibility—which may have belonged more to himself than to his sitters. Among his very first images is the 1909 portrait of his friend, the architect Adolf Loos (fig. **8.28**), who early on recognized Kokoschka's talents and provided him with moral as well as financial support. The figure projects from its dark background, and the tension in the contemplative face is echoed in Loos's nervously clasped hands. The Romantic basis of Kokoschka's early painting appears in *The Tempest* (fig. **8.29**), a double portrait of himself with his lover, Alma Mahler, in which the two figures, composed with flickering, light-saturated brushstrokes, are swept through a dream landscape of cold blue mountains and valleys lit only by the gleam of a shadowed moon. The painting was a great success when Kokoschka exhibited it in the 1914 New Munich Secession. The year before, he wrote to Alma about the work, then in progress:

8.28 Oskar Kokoschka, *Portrait of Adolf Loos*, 1909. Oil on canvas, 29⅛ × 35⅞" (74 × 91.1 cm). Staatliche Museen zu Berlin, Preussischer Kulturbesitz, Nationalgalerie.

8.29 Oskar Kokoschka, *The Tempest*, 1914. Oil on canvas, 5'11¼" × 7'2⅝" (1.81 × 2.2 m). Öffentliche Kunstsammlung Basel, Kunstmuseum.

I was able to express the mood I wanted by reliving it. … Despite all the turmoil in the world, to know that one person can put eternal trust in another, that two people can be committed to themselves and other people by an act of faith.

Seriously wounded in World War I, Kokoschka produced little for several years, but his ideas and style were undergoing constant change. In 1924 he abruptly set out on some seven years of travel, during which he explored the problem of landscape, combining free, arbitrary, and brilliant Impressionist or Fauve color with a

traditional perspective-space organization. Throughout his long life Kokoschka remained true to the spirit of Expressionism—to the power of emotion and the deeply felt sensitivity to the inner qualities of nature and the human soul. In 1933, in financial difficulties, the painter returned from his long travels. He went first to Vienna and then to Prague. During this period his works in public collections in Germany were confiscated by the Nazis as examples of "degenerate art." In 1938, as World War II approached, London became his home, and later Switzerland, although whenever possible he continued his restless traveling.

9
The Figurative Tradition in Early Twentieth-Century Sculpture

Auguste Rodin lived until 1917, his reputation increasing until, by the time of his death, it had become worldwide. Aristide Maillol did not die until 1944 and he continued to be a productive sculptor until his death. Antoine Bourdelle lived until 1929. The figurative tradition of these artists was, as we saw in chapter 6, reinforced by the growing recognition accorded the sculpture of older artists such as Edgar Degas and Paul Gauguin. While these men challenged some of the most time-honored sculptural traditions, they did so within the confines of the figurative mode. In his startling *Little Dancer Fourteen Years Old* (see fig. 6.2), Degas's introduction of actual materials heightened the psychological relationship between object and viewer. Subsequently, in major works such as *The Burghers of Calais* (see fig. 6.8), Rodin explored new spatial concepts to break down traditional barriers between sculpture and its audience. Gauguin, in his painted wood reliefs or ceramics such as *Oviri* (see figs. 3.18, 6.3), moved away from the notion of sculpture as a public art form toward one of hermetic, Symbolist content that drew on non-European sources. These tendencies proved critical to virtually all of the artists discussed in this chapter.

Despite revolutionary experiments being carried on by Cubist and abstract sculptors in the early twentieth century, the figurative tradition was central to the development of modernism, and it continued to dominate the scene in Europe and the United States. Unlike early twentieth-century experimentalists in construction and assemblage, who regarded sculptural form as a means of shaping space (see figs. 10.27, 10.31), the artists discussed in this chapter held to the notion of sculpture as mass or volumes in space. They used traditional methods of creating those volumes—modeling clay or carving marble and wood. In their hands, the figure is a source of seemingly inexhaustible expression, ranging from the relatively conservative efforts of Georg Kolbe to the radical innovations of Constantin Brancusi. While Kolbe still belongs within the classical tradition, others among his contemporaries, namely Derain, Matisse,

and Brancusi, deliberately turned to nonclassical sources, such as Oceanic or pre-Columbian art, for inspiration.

Among the twentieth-century painter–sculptors, Matisse depicted the human figure throughout his life, while Picasso began to desert naturalistic representation with a group of primitivist wood carvings, dated 1907, in which the influence of Iberian, archaic Greek, and African sculpture is even more explicit than in his paintings of that year. Also in 1907, André Derain carved *Crouching Man* (fig. **9.1**), transformed from a single block of stone—a startling example of proto-Cubist sculpture. David Smith, one of the outstanding American sculptors of the twentieth century (see figs. 19.39, 19.40), frequently contended that

9.1 André Derain, *Crouching Man*, 1907. Stone, 13 × 11" (33 × 27.9 cm). Galerie Louise Leiris, Paris.

modern sculpture was created by painters. Although this cannot be taken as literally true, given the achievements of Rodin, Brancusi, Raymond Duchamp-Villon, and Jacques Lipchitz, major contributions to sculpture were certainly made by such painters as Degas, Gauguin, Picasso, Amadeo Modigliani, and Matisse.

A Parallel Medium: The Sculpture of Henri Matisse

Matisse said he "sculpted like a painter," and that he took up sculpture "to put order into my feelings and to find a style to suit me. When I found it in sculpture, it helped me in my painting." Throughout his career, Matisse explored sculpture as a medium parallel to his painted oeuvre, often setting up a dialogue between the two. He studied for a time with Bourdelle (see fig. 6.14), and was strongly influenced by Rodin, then at the height of his reputation. Matisse's *The Serf* (fig. **9.2**) was begun in 1900, but not completed until 1904. Although sculpted after a well-known model, Bevilacqua, who had posed for Rodin and of whom Matisse also made a painting in a Cézannesque style (see fig. 7.2), it was adapted in attitude and concept (although on a reduced scale) from a Rodin sculpture called *Walking Man*. In *The Serf* Matisse carried the Expressionist modeling of the surface even further than Rodin, and halted the forward motion of the figure by adjusting the position of the legs into a solidly static pose and truncating the arms above the elbow.

9.3 Henri Matisse, *Reclining Nude, I (Nu couché, I; Aurore)*. Collioure, winter 1906–7. Bronze, 13½ × 19¾ × 11¼" (34.3 × 50.2 × 28.6 cm). The Museum of Modern Art, New York.

Aside from the great Fauvist figure compositions seen in chapter 7, Matisse in the years between 1905 and 1910 was studying the human figure in every conceivable pose and in every medium—drawing, painting, linoleum cut, and lithography, as well as sculpture. The sculpture entitled *Reclining Nude, I* (fig. **9.3**) is the most successful of the

9.2 Henri Matisse, *The Serf*, 1900–4. Bronze, 36 × 13⅞ × 12¼" at base (91.4 × 35.3 × 31.1 cm). Hirshhorn Museum and Sculpture Garden, Smithsonian Institution, Washington, D.C.

9.4 Henri Matisse, *Two Women*, 1907. Bronze, 18¼ × 10½ × 7⅞" (46.6 × 25.6 × 19.9 cm). Hirshhorn Museum and Sculpture Garden, Smithsonian Institution, Washington, D.C.

9.5 Henri Matisse, From left to right: *Back I*, 1909. Bronze relief, 74" × 44" × 6½" (188.9 × 113 × 16.5 cm). *Back II*, 1913. Bronze, 74" × 47" × 8" (188.6 × 119.4 × 20.3 cm). *Back III*, 1916–17. Bronze, 74" × 44¼" × 6" (188 × 112.4 × 15.2 cm). *Back IV*, c. 1930. Bronze, 74" × 45" × 7" (188 × 114.3 × 17.8 cm). Hirshhorn Museum and Sculpture Garden, Smithsonian Institution, Washington, D.C.

early attempts at a reclining figure integrated with surrounding space through its elaborate, twisting pose. Working under the influence of African sculpture, Matisse used this pose to dramatic effect in *The Blue Nude* (see fig. 7.7), painted at about the same time; it is interesting to compare his resolution of this spatial problem in the two media. Matisse was to experiment over the years with a number of sculpted variants of this reclining figure, generally more simplified and geometrized, and she frequently appeared in his later paintings.

Matisse also tried his hand at a very different kind of sculptural arrangement in the small *Two Women* (fig. **9.4**), which consists of two figures embracing, one front view, and the other back view. Although it may have some connection with Early Renaissance exercises in anatomy in which artists depicted athletic nudes in front and back views, its blocky, rectangular structure has a closer connection with some frontalized examples of African sculpture. This influence is not surprising, given that Matisse began to collect African sculpture shortly before he made *Two Women*, which is based on a photograph from an ethnographic magazine depicting two Tuareg women from North Africa.

Matisse's most ambitious excursion in sculpture was the creation of the four great *Backs*, executed between 1909 and 1931 (fig. **9.5**). While most of his sculptures are small-scale, these monumental reliefs are more than six feet high (1.8 m). They are a development of the theme stated in *Two Women*, now translated into a single figure in bas-relief, seen from the back. But Matisse has here resorted to

9.6 Henri Matisse, *Jeannette V* (Jean Vaderin, 5th state), Issy-les-Moulineaux, 1916. Bronze, height 22⅞ × 83⅜ × 10⅜" (58.1 × 21.3 × 27.1 cm). The Museum of Modern Art, New York.

an upright, vertical surface like that of a painting on which to sculpt his form. *Back I* is modeled in a relatively representational manner, freely expressing the modulations of a muscular back, and it reveals the feeling Matisse had for sculptural form rendered on a monumental scale. *Back II* is simplified in a manner reflecting the artist's interest in Cubism around 1913. *Back III* and *Back IV* are so reduced to their architectural components that they almost become abstract sculpture. The figure's long ponytail becomes a central spine that serves as a powerful axis through the center of the composition. Here, as in *The Blue Nude*, Matisse has synthesized African and Cézannesque elements, this time, however, in order to acknowledge, as well as resist, the formal discoveries made by the Cubists.

Matisse's other major effort in sculpture was a series of five heads of a woman, done between 1910 and 1916. *Jeannette I* and *Jeannette II* are direct portraits done from life in the freely expressive manner of late Rodin bronzes. But with *Jeannette III, Jeannette IV,* and *Jeannette V* (fig. 9.6), he worked from his imagination, progressively transforming the human head first into an Expressionist study, exaggerating all the features, and then into a geometric organization of shapes. Picasso had produced his Cubist *Woman's Head* in 1909 (see fig. 10.15), and this work may have prompted Matisse's experiments. In turn, Picasso probably had Matisse's examples in mind when making his so-called Bosgeloup heads in the early thirties. In Matisse's work, serial sculptures such as the *Backs* and the *Jeannettes* do not necessarily constitute a set of progressive steps toward the perfection of an idea. Rather, they are multiple but independent states, each version a definitive solution in and of itself.

Developments in Germany: Lehmbruck, Kolbe, Banlach, and Kollwitz

With the exception of such older masters as Maillol, the tradition of Realist or Realist–Expressionist sculpture flourished more energetically outside France than inside, after 1910. In Germany the major figure was **Wilhelm Lehmbruck** (1881–1919). After an academic training, Lehmbruck turned for inspiration first to the Belgian sculptor of miners and industrial workers, Constantin Meunier (1831–1905), and then to Rodin. During the four years he spent in Paris, between 1910 and 1914, Lehmbruck became acquainted with Matisse, Modigliani, Brancusi, and Aleksandr Archipenko. His *Standing Woman* of 1910 reveals the influence of Maillol, as well as classical Greek sculpture. The emotional power of Lehmbruck's work, however, comes not from his studies of the past but from his own sensitive and melancholy personality. His surviving works are few, for the entire oeuvre belongs to a ten-year period. In *Seated Youth* (fig. 9.7), his last monumental work, the artist utilized extreme elongation—possibly suggested by figures in Byzantine mosaics and Romanesque sculpture—to convey a sense of contemplation and withdrawal. This work represents a departure from Maillol and from a nineteenth-century tradition that emphasized volume and mass. Lehmbruck's figure, with its long, angular limbs, is penetrated by space, and exploits for

9.7 Wilhelm Lehmbruck, *Seated Youth*, 1917. Composite tinted plaster, 40⅝ × 30 × 45½" (103.2 × 76.2 × 115.5 cm). National Gallery of Art, Washington, D.C.

9.8 Georg Kolbe, *Young Woman*, 1926. Bronze, height 50⅝" (128.6 cm). Walker Art Center, Minneapolis.

expressive ends the abstract organization of solid and voids. With its mood of dejection and loss, *Seated Youth* expresses the trauma and sadness Lehmbruck experienced in Germany during World War I—suffering that finally, in 1919, led him to suicide.

The human figure was so thoroughly entrenched as the principal vehicle of expression for sculptors that it was even more difficult for them to depart from it than for painters to depart from landscape, figure, or still life. It was also difficult for sculptors to say anything new about the subject, or startlingly different from what had been said before.

Other leading German sculptors of the early twentieth century included **Georg Kolbe** (1877–1941), Ernst Barlach, and Käthe Kollwitz. Kolbe began as a painter but developed an interest in sculpture during a two-year stay in Rome. His later encounter with Rodin's work in Paris had considerable impact on his work. For his figures or portrait heads, Kolbe combined the formal aspects of Maillol's figures with the light-reflecting surfaces of Rodin's. After some essays in highly simplified figuration, Kolbe settled into a lyrical formula of rhythmic nudes (fig. **9.8**)—appealing, but essentially a Renaissance tradition with a Rodinesque broken surface. His depictions in the thirties of heroic, idealized, and specifically Nordic figures now seem uncomfortably compatible with the Nazis' glorification of a "master race."

In addition to making sculpture carved from wood or cast in bronze, **Ernst Barlach** (1870–1938) was an accomplished poet, playwright, and printmaker. Although, like Lehmbruck, he visited Paris, he was not as strongly influenced by French avant-garde developments. His early work took on the curving forms of Jugendstil and aspects of medieval German sculpture. In 1906 he traveled to Russia, where he was deeply impressed by the peasant population, and his later sculptures often depicted Russian beggars or laborers. Once he was targeted as a "degenerate artist" by Nazi authorities in the thirties, Barlach's public works, including monumental sculptures for cathedrals, were dismantled or destroyed. He was capable of works of sweeping power and the integration in a single image of humor and pathos and primitive tragedy, as in *The Avenger* (fig. **9.9**). His was a storytelling art, a kind of socially conscious Expressionism that used the outer forms of contemporary experiment for narrative purposes.

Käthe Kollwitz is best known for her graphics (see figs. 8.15, 8.16), but she was capable of an equally intense expression in sculpture, with which she was increasingly involved throughout her last years. Given the intrinsically sculptural technique of carving and gouging a block of wood to make a woodcut, it is not surprising that a printmaker might be drawn to sculpture, though Kollwitz never actually made sculpture in wood. Like Lehmbruck, she learned of Rodin's work on a trip to Paris and admired the sculpture of Constantin Meunier, whose subjects of workers struck a sympathetic chord. But perhaps the most significant influence on her work in three dimensions was that

9.9 Ernst Barlach, *The Avenger*, 1914. Bronze, 17¼ × 23 × 8¼" (43.8 × 58.4 × 21 cm). Hirshhorn Museum and Sculpture Garden, Smithsonian Institution, Washington, D.C.

9.10 Käthe Kollwitz, *Lamentation: In Memory of Ernst Barlach (Grief)*, 1938. Bronze, height 10¼" (26 cm). Hirshhorn Museum and Sculpture Garden, Smithsonian Institution, Washington, D.C.

of her friend Barlach. The highly emotional tenor of her work, whether made for a humanitarian cause, or in memory of her son killed in World War I, arose from a profoundly felt grief that transmitted itself to her sculpture and prints. *Lamentation: In Memory of Ernst Barlach (Grief)* (fig. **9.10**) is an example of Kollwitz's relief sculpture, a moving, close-up portrait of her own grieving.

Forms of the Essential: Constantin Brancusi

In France during the early years of the twentieth century, the most individual figure—and ultimately one of the most influential sculptors of the time—was **Constantin Brancusi (1876–1957).** Born in Romania, the son of peasants, he left home at the age of eleven. Between 1894 and 1898 he was apprenticed to a cabinetmaker and studied in the provincial city of Craiova, and then at the Bucharest Academy of Fine Arts. In 1902 he went to

Germany and Switzerland, arriving in Paris in 1904. After further studies at the École des Beaux-Arts under the sculptor Antonin Mercié, he began exhibiting, first at the Salon de la Nationale and then at the Salon d'Automne. Impressed by his contributions to the 1907 Salon d'Automne, Rodin invited him to become an assistant. Brancusi stayed only a short time. As he later declared, "Nothing grows under the shade of great trees."

The sculpture of Brancusi is in one sense isolated, in another universal. He worked with few themes, never really deserting the figure, but he touched, affected, and influenced most of the major strains of sculpture after him. From the tradition of Rodin's late studies came the figure *Sleep*, in which the realistic form of a shadowed face appears to sink into the matrix of the marble. The theme of the Sleeping Muse was to become an obsession with Brancusi, and he played variations on it for some twenty years. In the next version (fig. **9.11**), and later, the head was transformed into an egg shape, with the features lightly but

9.11 Constantin Brancusi, *Sleeping Muse 1*, 1909–10. Marble, 7 × 11½ × 8" (17.8 × 29.2 × 20.3 cm). Hirshhorn Museum and Sculpture Garden, Smithsonian Institution, Washington, D.C.

sharply cut from the mass. As became his custom with his basic themes, he presented this form in marble, bronze, and plaster, almost always with slight adjustments that turned each version into a unique work.

In a subsequent work, the theme was further simplified to a teardrop shape in which the features largely disappeared, with the exception of an indicated ear. To this 1911 piece he gave the name *Prometheus*. The form in turn led to *The Newborn*, in which the oval is cut obliquely to form the screaming mouth of the infant. He returned to the polished egg shape in the ultimate version, entitled *The Beginning of the World* (fig. **9.12**), closely related to a contemporary work called *Sculpture for the Blind*. In this, his ultimate statement about creation, Brancusi eliminated all reference to anatomical detail. A similar work, as well as *The Newborn*, can be seen at the bottom of Brancusi's photograph of his studio taken around 1927 (fig. **9.13**). The artist preferred that his work be discovered in the context of his own studio, amid tools, marble dust, and incomplete works. He was constantly rearranging his work, grouping the sculptures into a carefully staged environment. Brancusi left the entire content of his studio to the French state; a reconstruction of it is in the Georges Pompidou Center in Paris. The artist took photographs of his own works (a privilege he rarely allowed others) in order to disseminate their images beyond Paris and to depict his sculptures in varying, often dramatic light. His many pictures of corners of his studio convey the complex interplay of his sculptural shapes and the cumulative effect of his search for ideal form. "Why write [about my sculptures]?" he once said. "Why not just show the photographs?"

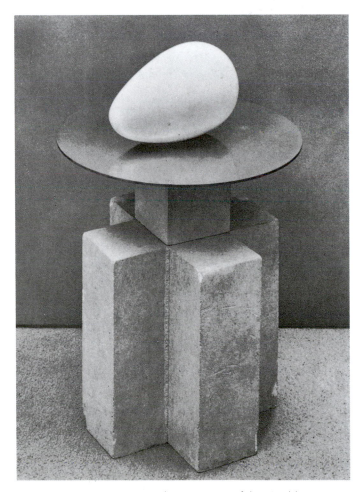

9.12 Constantin Brancusi, *The Beginning of the World*, c. 1920. Marble, metal, and stone, 29⅝ × 11⅜" (75.2 × 28.9 cm). Dallas Museum of Art.

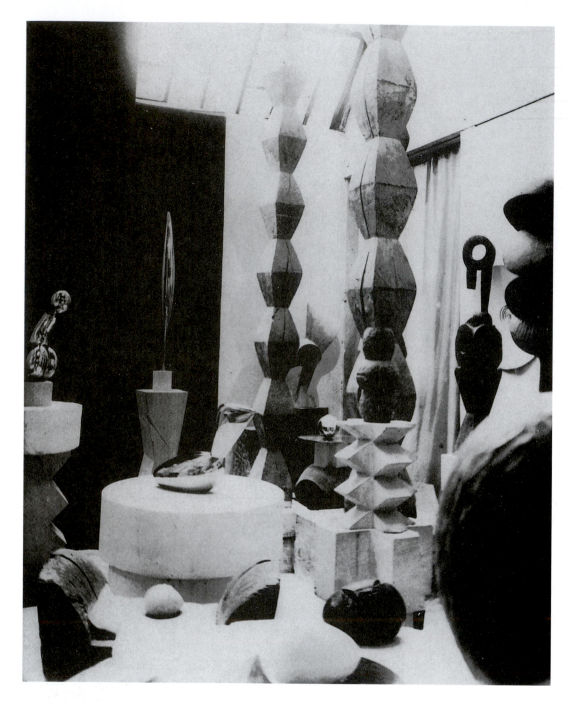

9.13 Constantin Brancusi, *The Studio*, c. 1927. Photograph, mounted on glass, 23¾ × 19¾" (60.3 × 50.2 cm). Pascal Sernet Fine Art, London.

This tale of the egg was only one of a number of related themes that Brancusi continued to follow, with a hypnotic concentration on creation, birth, life, and death. In 1912 he made his first marble portrait of a young Hungarian woman named Margit Pogany, who posed several times in his studio. He portrayed her with enormous oval eyes and hands held up to one side of her face. This form was developed further in a number of drawings and in later variations in marble and polished bronze, in which Brancusi refined and abstracted his original design, omitting the mouth altogether and reducing the eyes to an elegant, arching line of a brow that merges with the nose. *Torso of a Young Man* (fig. **9.14**) went as far as Brancusi ever did in the direction of geometric form. In this polished bronze

from 1924, he abstracted the softened, swelling lines of anatomy introduced in his earlier wood versions of the sculpture into an object of machinelike precision. Brancusi was clearly playing on a theme of androgyny here, for while the *Torso* is decidedly phallic, it could also constitute an interpretation of female anatomy.

An artist who shared Brancusi's quest for the essence of things and discovered it in images of remarkable purity and cool elegance was the American photographer **Edward Weston** (1886–1958). Indeed, Weston's picture of a pair of gleaming nautilus shells, set against a velvet-black ground (fig. **9.15**), seems to be nature's own organic version of Brancusi's formal concerns. Here the photographer truly achieved his goal of a subject revealed in its "deepest

9.14 Constantin Brancusi, *Torso of a Young Man*, 1924. Polished bronze, 18 × 11 × 7" (45.7 × 28 × 17.8 cm), stone and wood base, height 40⅜" (102.6 cm). Hirshhorn Museum and Sculpture Garden, Smithsonian Institution, Washington, D.C.

moment of perception." Weston rigorously controlled form through his selection of motif, exposure time, and use of the ground-glass focusing screen of a large-format camera. In this way he could previsualize his prints and eliminate the random effects of light, atmosphere, and moment. He created a timeless image, leaving behind the Pictorialism of earlier aesthetic photography and entering the mainstream of modern art.

The subjects of Brancusi were so elemental and his themes so basic that, although he had few direct followers, little that happened subsequently in sculpture seems foreign to him. *The Kiss*, 1916 (fig. **9.16**), depicts with the simplest of means an embracing couple, a subject Brancusi had first realized in stone in 1909. Although this had been the subject of one of Rodin's most famous marbles, in the squat, blockish forms of *The Kiss* Brancusi made his break with the Rodinesque tradition irrefutably clear. He was also aware of developments in Cubist sculpture, as well as works in a primitivist vein, such as the crudely carved wooden figures of the German Expressionists and especially Derain (see fig. 9.1).

The artist was particularly obsessed with birds and the idea of conveying the essence of flight. For over a decade he progressively streamlined the form of his 1912 sculpture *Maiastra* (or "master bird," from Romanian folklore), until he achieved the astonishingly simple, tapering form of

9.15 Edward Weston, *Shells*, 1927. Gelatin-silver print.

9.16 Constantin Brancusi, *The Kiss*, 1916. Limestone, 23 × 13 × 10" (58.4 × 33 × 25.4 cm). Philadelphia Museum of Art.

Bird in Space (fig. **9.17**). The image ultimately became less the representation of a bird's shape than that of a bird's trajectory through the air. Brancusi designed his own bases and considered them an integral part of his sculpture. In *Bird in Space*, the highly polished marble bird (he also made bronze versions) fits into a stone cylinder that sits atop a cruciform stone base. This, in turn, rests on a large X-shaped wooden pedestal. He made several variations on these forms, such as that designed for *Torso of a Young Man*.

These bases augment the sense of soaring verticality of the bird sculptures. In addition, they serve as transitions between the mundane physical world and the spiritual realm of the bird, for Brancusi sought a mystical fusion of the disembodied light-reflecting surfaces of polished marble or bronze and the solid, earthbound mass of wood. He said, "All my life I have sought the essence of flight. Don't look for mysteries. I give you pure joy. Look at the sculptures until you see them. Those nearest to God have seen them."

9.17 Constantin Brancusi, *Bird in Space*, 1925. Marble, stone, and wood, 71⅝ × 5⅜ × 6⅜" (181.9 × 13.7 × 16.2 cm), stone pedestal 17⅝ × 16⅜ × 16⅜" (44.8 × 41.6 × 41.6 cm), wood pedestal 7¾ × 16 × 13⅜" (19.7 × 40.6 × 34 cm). National Gallery of Art, Washington, D.C.

9.18 Constantin Brancusi, *King of Kings*, c. 1930. Oak, height 9'10" (3 m). Solomon R. Guggenheim Museum, New York.

In his wood sculptures, although he occasionally strove for the same degree of finish, Brancusi usually preferred a primitive, roughed-out totem. In *King of Kings* (fig. **9.18**), which he had previously titled *The Spirit of Buddha*, reflecting his interest in Eastern spirituality, the great, regal shape comprises superimposed forms that are reworkings of the artist's wooden pedestals. Brancusi intended this sculpture for a temple of his design in India, commissioned by the Maharajah of Indore, who owned three of the artist's *Birds in Space*. The temple was never built. In fact, Brancusi's only outdoor work on a vast scale was a sculptural ensemble installed in the late thirties in Tirjiu-Jiu, Romania, not far from his native village. This included the immense cast-iron *Endless Column* (fig. **9.19**), which recalls ancient obelisks but also draws upon forms in Romanian folk art. The rhomboid shapes of *Endless Column* also began as socle (pedestal) designs that were, beginning in 1918, developed as freestanding sculptures. Wood versions of the sculpture can be seen in Brancusi's photograph of his studio (see fig. 9.13). *Endless Column* was the most radically abstract of Brancusi's sculptures, and its reliance upon repeated modules became enormously important for Minimalist artists of the sixties.

9.19 Constantin Brancusi, *Endless Column*, 1937–38. Cast iron, height 98' (29.9 m). Tirjiu-Jui, Romania.

10
Cubism

The various modes of Cubism that Pablo Picasso developed jointly with Georges Braque in France between 1908 and 1914 offered a radically new way of looking at the world. Their shared vision had an inestimable impact on the avant-garde art that followed it. Although Cubism was never itself an abstract style, the many varieties of nonobjective art it helped usher in throughout Europe would have been unthinkable without it. From Italian Futurism to Dutch Neo-Plasticism to Russian Constructivism, the repercussions of the Cubist experiment were thoroughly international in scope. But the legacy of Cubism was not exhausted in the first quarter of the twentieth century, when these movements took place. Its lingering influence can be felt in much art after World War II, in works as diverse as the paintings of Willem de Kooning (see fig. 19.4), the sculpture of David Smith (see fig. 19.39), the multimedia constructions of Robert Rauschenberg (see fig. 21.11), the photographs of David Hockney (see fig. 21.7), and the architecture of Frank Gehry (see fig. 25.32).

Cubism altered forever the Renaissance conception of painting as a window into a world where three-dimensional space is projected onto the flat picture plane by way of illusionistic drawing and one-point perspective. The Cubists concluded that reality has many definitions, and that therefore objects in space—and indeed, space itself—have no fixed or absolute form. Together, Picasso and Braque translated those multiple readings of the external world into new pictorial vocabularies which had remarkable range and invention.

The English critic Roger Fry, one of their early supporters, said of the Cubists, "They do not seek to imitate form, but to create form, not to imitate life but to find an equivalent for life." By 1911 the Cubist search for new forms was gaining momentum well beyond the studios of Picasso and Braque, and eventually spawned a large school of Cubist painters in Paris. The work of these later practitioners of Cubism is discussed in the second half of this chapter.

The invention of Cubism was truly a collaborative affair, and the close, mutually beneficial relationship between Picasso and Braque was arguably the most significant of its kind in the history of art. According to Braque, it was "a union based on the independence of each." We have seen how much of the modern movement was the result of collective efforts between like-minded artists, as in Die Brücke or Der Blaue Reiter in Germany (see chapter 8) or the Fauves in France (see chapter 7). But there was no real precedent for the intense level of professional exchange that took place between Picasso and Braque, especially from 1908 to 1912, when they were in close, often daily contact. "We were like two mountain climbers roped together," Braque said. Picasso called him "pard," in humorous reference to the Western novels they loved to read (especially those about Buffalo Bill), or "Wilbur," likening their enterprise to that of the American aviation pioneers, Wilbur and Orville Wright. Braque was a Frenchman, Picasso a Spaniard, and their temperaments, both personal and artistic, were strikingly dissimilar. Whereas Picasso was impulsive, prolific, and anarchic, Braque was slow, methodical, and meditative. He had little of Picasso's personal magnetism or colossal egotism, and the tendency toward lyrical painterliness in his work stood in strong contrast to Picasso's expressionist sensibility. Their close working relationship was brought to an end by World War I. In August 1914 Braque was called up for active military duty; as a Spanish expatriate, Picasso was not called and remained behind, staying mostly in Paris and southern France during the war.

Taking Possession: Picasso's Early Career

Pablo Ruiz Picasso (1881–1973) achieved legendary status even within his lifetime. The critic John Berger went so far as to say that by the forties, if Picasso wanted to possess anything, all he had to do was draw it. His career dominated three-quarters of the century, during which he produced a staggering output of art in virtually every conceivable medium, from small-scale prints, drawings, and ceramics to mural-size paintings and monumental public sculpture. The catalogue raisonné of his paintings and drawings alone runs to thirty-three volumes. With a combination of virtuoso technical facility and a virtually unparalleled ability to invent new forms, Picasso could easily compose in several styles simultaneously. As a result, the single-minded focus of his Cubist years, when he collaborated with a fellow artist more closely than at any other time in his career, presents something of an anomaly.

Nearly as well known as Picasso's art are the stormy details of his personal life, which was littered with emotionally destructive relationships, whether with lovers, children, or friends. More than is so for his contemporaries (including Braque), knowledge of Picasso's life is essential to a thorough understanding of his art; as a quintessential modernist, autobiography infiltrates his imagery in overt and covert ways. As William Rubin, one of the leading Picasso specialists, has written, the biographical references in Picasso's art "often constitute a distinct and consistent substratum of meaning distinguishable from, but interwoven with, the manifest subject matter." No other twentieth-century artist discussed in this book has been studied in as much depth as Picasso. To justly serve the complex nature of his long and multifaceted career, his oeuvre, of which Cubism proper really only encompasses six years, is addressed in the course of several chapters.

Training and Move to Paris

Picasso was born in the small, provincial town of Málaga, on the southern coast of Spain. Though an Andalusian by birth (and a resident of France for most of his life), he always identified himself as a Catalan, from the more industrialized, sophisticated city of Barcelona, where the family moved when he was thirteen. Picasso's father was a painter and art teacher who, so the fable goes, was so impressed by his adolescent son's talents that he handed over his brushes to him and renounced painting forever. Many such self-aggrandizing legends originated with Picasso himself or his friends and were perpetuated by his biographers. Nevertheless, the artist is recorded as saying, "In art one must kill one's father," and he eventually did revolt against all that his father tried to teach him.

Though Picasso was no child prodigy, by the age of fourteen he was making highly accomplished portraits of his family. In the fall of 1895, when his father took a post at Barcelona's School of Fine Arts, the young Picasso was allowed to enroll directly in the advanced courses. The following year, he produced his first major figure composition, *The First Communion*, which was included in an important exhibition in Barcelona. At the urging of his father, Picasso spent eight or nine months in Madrid in 1897, where he enrolled at but rarely attended the Royal Academy of San Fernando, the most prestigious school in the country. In Madrid, Picasso studied Spain's old masters at the great Prado Museum, admiring especially Diego Velázquez, whose work he copied. Several decades later, Picasso made his own highly personal interpretations of the old masters he saw in the museums (see fig. 20.4).

Picasso suffered serious poverty in Madrid and chafed under the strictures of academic education, already setting his sights on Paris. First, however, he returned for a time to Barcelona, a city that provided a particularly stimulating

10.1 Pablo Picasso, *Le Moulin de la Galette*, 1900. Oil on canvas, 35½ × 46" (90.2 × 116.8 cm). Solomon R. Guggenheim Museum, New York.

environment for a young artist coming of age at the turn of the century. As the capital of Catalonia, a region fiercely proud of its own language and cultural traditions, Barcelona was undergoing a modern renaissance. Its citizens were vying to establish their city as the most prosperous, culturally enlightened urban center in Spain. At the same time, poverty, unemployment, and separatist sentiments gave rise to political unrest and strong anarchist tendencies among the Catalans. As in Madrid, the latest artistic trend in Barcelona was *modernista*, a provincial variation on Art Nouveau and Symbolism (see fig. 5.9) that was practiced by young progressive artists and that left its mark on Picasso's early work.

Upon his return to Barcelona, Picasso declined to resume his studies at the Academy or to submit to his father's tutelage. Essential to his development was Els Quatre Gats (The Four Cats), a tavern that provided a fertile meeting ground for Catalan artists and writers. Picasso illustrated menus for Els Quatre Gats in the curving, stylized forms of *modernista* and made portraits of the habitués that were exhibited on the tavern walls. These incisive character studies amply illustrate that he had arrived at a personal mode well beyond his previous academic exercises. A watercolor from 1898–99, *The End of the Road*, contains aspects of the *modernista* style in the undulating forms of paths along which stooped figures shuffle toward a gateway presided over by an enormous angel of death, while, to their left, the wealthy travel by carriage to the same destination. "At the end of the road death waits for everybody," the artist said, "even though the rich go in carriages and the poor on foot." Picasso's biographer John Richardson has observed that this image stems from the death in 1895 of his younger sister, Conchita. This early trauma was compounded by the family's inability to afford a suitable funeral. In more general terms, Picasso may have been responding to the poverty around him, including the ranks of mutilated veterans who had returned from Spain's colonial wars and were reduced to begging in the streets. But *The End of the Road* was also in step with the pessimistic mood that permeated international Symbolist art toward the end of the century. We have seen this melancholic soul sickness in the works of artists such as Aubrey Beardsley and Edvard Munch (see figs. 5.3, 5.18). Picasso's preoccupation with poverty and mortality was to surface more thoroughly in the work of his so-called Blue Period (see fig. 10.2).

In 1900 one of Picasso's paintings was selected to hang in the Spanish Pavilion of the Universal Exposition in Paris. At age nineteen he traveled to the French capital for the first time with his friend and fellow painter Carles Casagemas. Picasso, who spoke little French, took up with a community of Spanish (mostly Catalan) artists in Paris and soon found benefactors in two dealers, a fellow Catalan, Pedro Mañach, and a Frenchwoman, Berthe Weill, also an early collector of works by Matisse. She sold the first major painting Picasso made in Paris, *Le Moulin de la Galette* (fig. 10.1), a vivid study of closely packed figures in the famous dance hall in Montmartre. Although he no doubt knew Renoir's Impressionist rendition of the same subject (see fig. 2.31), Picasso rejected the sun-dappled congeniality of the Frenchman for a nocturnal and considerably more sinister view. This study of figures in artificial light relates to the dark, tenebrist scenes typical of much Spanish art at the time, but the seamy ambience recalls the work of Degas or Toulouse-Lautrec, both shrewd chroniclers of Parisian café life.

Blue and Rose Periods

Picasso's companion during this sojourn in Paris, Carles Casagemas, became completely despondent over a failed love affair after the artists arrived back in Spain. He eventually returned to Paris without Picasso and, in front of his friends, shot himself in a restaurant. Picasso experienced pangs of guilt for having abandoned Casagemas (though he soon had an affair with the very woman who had precipitated the suicide), and he later claimed that it was the death of his friend that prompted the gloomy paintings of his Blue Period. Between 1901 and 1904, in both Barcelona and Paris, Picasso used a predominantly blue palette in many works for the portrayal of figures and themes expressing human misery—frequently hunger and cold, the hardships he himself experienced as he was trying to establish himself. The thin, attenuated figures of Spain's sixteenth-century Mannerist painter, El Greco, found echoes in these works by Picasso, as did the whole history of Spanish religious painting, with its emphasis on mourning and physical torment.

One of the masterpieces of this period is the large allegorical composition Picasso made in Barcelona, *La Vie* (*Life*) (fig. 10.2), for which he prepared several sketches. For the gaunt couple at the left Picasso depicted Casagemas and his lover, though X-rays reveal that the male figure was originally a self-portrait. They receive a stern gaze from the woman holding a baby at the right, who emerged from studies of inmates Picasso had made in a Parisian women's prison (where he could avail himself of free models), many of them prostitutes suffering from venereal disease. By heavily draping the woman, he gives her the timeless appearance of a madonna, thus embodying in a single figure his famously ambivalent and polarized view of women as either madonnas or whores. In their resemblance to a shamed Adam and Eve, the lovers (like their equivalent in the painting on the wall behind them) also yield a religious reading. From events in his own life Picasso built a powerful modern interpretation of the universal themes of love, life, and death. The pervasive blue hue of *La Vie* turns flesh into a cold, stony substance while compounding the melancholy atmosphere generated by the figures. Many Symbolist painters, and Romantics before them, understood the richly expressive potential of the color blue, including Gauguin in his great canvas from 1897, *Where Do We Come From? What Are We? Where Are We Going?*

(see fig. 3.19), a painting that also confronts life's largest questions. Gauguin, whose work made a significant impression on the young Spaniard, died in the distant Marquesas Islands while Picasso was at work on *La Vie*.

In the spring of 1904 Picasso settled again in Paris; he was never to live in Barcelona again. He moved into a tenement on the Montmartre hill dubbed by his friends the Bateau Lavoir ("laundry boat," after the laundry barges docked in the Seine) that was ultimately made famous by his presence there. Until 1909 Picasso lived at the Bateau Lavoir in the midst of an ever-growing circle of friends:

painters, poets, actors, and critics, including the devoted Max Jacob, who was to die in a concentration camp during World War II, and the poet Guillaume Apollinaire, who was to become the literary apostle of Cubism. In 1921 Picasso paid tribute to both men in his two versions of *The Three Musicians*, discussed in chapter 14 (see fig. 14.25).

Among the first works Picasso made upon arriving in Paris in 1904 is a macabre pastel in which a woman with grotesquely elongated fingers and hunched shoulders kisses a raven. The subject evokes Edgar Allan Poe, a favorite writer among *fin-de-siècle* Parisian artists,

10.2 Pablo Picasso, *La Vie*, 1903. Oil on canvas, 6'5⅜" × 4'2⅝" (2 × 1.29 m). The Cleveland Museum of Art.

particularly Odilon Redon, whose own brilliant pastels may have been a source for Picasso's (see fig. 3.14). The model for *Woman with a Crow* was an acquaintance of Picasso who had trained her pet bird to scavenge crumbs from the floors of the Lapin Agile, a working-class cabaret in Montmartre frequented by the artist and his entourage. Her skeletal form is silhouetted against an intense blue, but the chilly hues and downcast mood of the Blue Period were giving way to the new themes and the warmer tonalities that characterize the next phase of Picasso's work, the Rose Period.

Between 1905 and 1906 Picasso was preoccupied with the subject of acrobatic performers who traveled from town to town, performing on makeshift stages. Called *saltimbanques*, these itinerant entertainers often dressed as Harlequin and Pierrot, the clownish characters from the Italian tradition of *commedia dell'arte* who compete for the amorous attentions of Columbine. These subjects were popular in France as well as Spain in nineteenth-century literature and painting, and Picasso certainly knew pictorial variations on the themes by artists such as Daumier and Cézanne. His own interest in circus subjects was stimulated by frequent visits to Paris's Cirque Médrano, located near his Montmartre studio.

Like his predecessor Daumier, Picasso chose not to depict the saltimbanque in the midst of boisterous acrobatics but during moments of rest or quiet contemplation. His masterpiece of this genre is *Family of Saltimbanques* (fig. **10.3**); at seven and one-half feet tall (2.3 m), it was the largest painting he had yet undertaken and stands as a measure of his enormous ambition and talent in the early years of his career. He made several preparatory studies for the work, and X-rays reveal that at least four variations on the final composition exist beneath the top paint layer. The painting began as a family scene, with women engaging in domestic chores and Harlequin (the figure seen here at the far left) watching a young female acrobat balance on a ball. But in the end Picasso settled upon an image virtually devoid of activity, in which the characters, despite their physical proximity, hardly take note of one another. Stripped of anecdotal details, the painting gains in poetry and mystery. The acrobats gather in a strangely barren landscape painted in warm brown tones that the artist loosely brushed over a layer of blue paint. An enigmatic stillness has replaced the heavy pathos of the Blue Period pictures, just as the predominant blues of the earlier work have shifted to a delicately muted palette of earth tones, rose, and orange. The identities of the individual saltimbanques have been ascribed to members of Picasso's circle, but the only identification experts agree upon is that of Picasso, who portrayed himself, as he often did, in the guise of Harlequin, easily identifiable by the diamond patterns of his motley costume. These homeless entertainers, who eked out a living through their creative talents, existing on the margins of society, have long been understood as modernist surrogates for the artist. Their marginal status, including their role as satirists of mainstream society, and the vulnerability that accompanies it, provide a very different image of that

10.3 Pablo Picasso, *Family of Saltimbanques*, 1905. Oil on canvas, 6'11¾" × 7'6⅜" (2.1 × 2.3 m). National Gallery of Art, Washington, D.C.

10.4 Pablo Picasso, *Gertrude Stein*, 1905–6. Oil on canvas, 39¼ × 32" (99.7 × 81.3 cm). The Metropolitan Museum of Art, New York.

artist than the isolated figure of the Romantic genius or the socially engaged Realist (see fig. 1.1).

Before completing this large canvas, Picasso exhibited over thirty works at a Paris gallery, including several saltimbanque subjects. Little is known about the sales, if any, that resulted from the show, but subsequently Picasso tended to refrain from exhibiting his work in Paris, except in small shows in private galleries (his favorite venue was his own studio). Although he was still seriously impoverished, his circumstances improved somewhat during these years as his circle of admirers—critics, dealers, and collectors—continued to grow.

One remarkable member of that circle was the American writer Gertrude Stein, who, with her brothers Leo and Michael, had lived in Paris since 1903 and was building one of the foremost collections of contemporary art in the city. She met Picasso in 1905 and introduced him the following year to Matisse, whose work the Steins were collecting. In their apartment Picasso had access to one of the great early Matisse collections, including the seminal *Bonheur de vivre* (see fig. 7.6). He was keenly aware of Matisse as a potential artistic rival, particularly following the uproar over the 1905 Salon d'Automne, in which the Fauves made their public debut. Gertrude Stein said she sat for Picasso ninety times while he painted her portrait (fig. 10.4). Her ample frame, characteristically draped in a heavy, loose-fitting dress, assumes an unconventional pose for a female sitter, one that clearly conveys the self-assured

nature of a woman who freely proclaimed her own artistic genius. She fills her corner of space like some powerful, massive work of sculpture. Picasso abandoned the portrait over the summer while he vacationed in Spain and repainted Stein's face from memory upon his return. Its masklike character, with eyes askew, anticipates the distortions of coming years.

By the end of 1905 Picasso's figures had taken on an aura of beauty and serenity that suggests a specific influence from ancient Greek white-ground vase paintings. This brief classical phase was prompted by several factors, including his contented (at least temporarily) relationship with a young woman named Fernande Olivier, his studies of antiquities in the Louvre, and the 1905 retrospective of the work of Ingres, the French Neoclassical painter who died in 1867 (see fig. 1.13). Picasso's subjects during this period were primarily nudes, either young, idealized women or adolescent boys, all portrayed in a restrained terracotta palette evoking the ancient Mediterranean. By the end of 1906, following a trip with Olivier to the remote Spanish village of Gósol, this classical ideal had evolved into the solid, thick-limbed anatomies of *Two Nudes* (fig. 10.5), a mysterious composition in which we confront a woman and what is nearly but not quite her mirror reflection. The

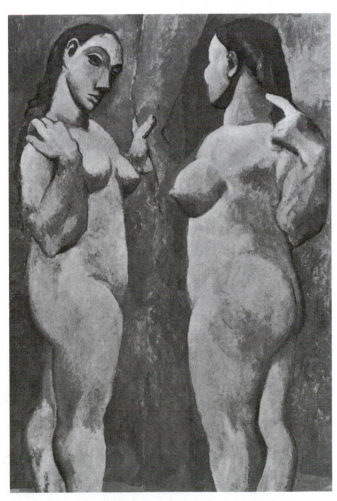

10.5 Pablo Picasso, *Two Nudes*, Paris, late 1906. Oil on canvas, 59⅝ × 36⅝" (151.5 × 93 cm). The Museum of Modern Art, New York.

image is drained of the sentimentalism that inhabited the artist's Blue and Rose Period pictures. Significantly, Picasso was making sculpture around this time and earlier in 1906 had seen a show at the Louvre of Iberian sculpture from the sixth and fifth centuries B.C.E. These works, produced by a people that inhabited the eastern and southeastern coastal region of Spain during the first millennium B.C.E., were of particular interest to him since they had been excavated fifty miles (80 km) from his hometown. In 1907 he actually purchased two ancient Iberian stone heads, which he returned in 1911, after discovering they had been stolen from the Louvre. In addition, the 1906 Salon d'Automne had featured a large retrospective of Gauguin's work, including the first important public presentation of his sculpture (see fig. 6.3). As an artist who plundered the art of non-Western and ancient cultures for his own work, Gauguin provided Picasso with a crucial model. Picasso's own preoccupation with sculptural form at this time, his encounter with the blocky contours of the ancient Iberian carvings, and the revelatory encounter with Gauguin's "primitivizing" examples left an indelible mark on paintings such as *Two Nudes*. It has even been proposed that the corpulence of Gertrude Stein influenced the hefty proportions of the models in this work. Certainly the nudes' simplified facial features, with their wide, almond-shaped eyes, recall the Stein portrait.

Les Demoiselles d'Avignon

Picasso's large canvas, *Les Demoiselles d'Avignon* (fig. 10.6), has been called the single most important painting of the twentieth century. It is an astonishing image that, in the iconoclastic spirit of modernism, virtually shattered every pictorial and iconographical convention that preceded it. Robert Rosenblum, one of the leading historians of Cubism, called this momentous work a "detonator of the modern movement, the cornerstone of twentieth-century art." Scholars have generated hundreds of pages scrutinizing its history and pondering its meaning, and the painting still has the power to assault the viewer with its aggressively confrontational imagery. Long regarded as the first Cubist painting, the *Demoiselles*, owing largely to the pioneering studies of Leo Steinberg, is now generally seen as a powerful example of expressionist art—an "exorcism painting," Picasso said, in which he did not necessarily initiate Cubism, but rather obliterated the lessons of the past. In fact, this type of multifigure composition did not persist in high Cubism, which was the domain of the single figure, the still life, and to a lesser degree, the landscape. Nor did this violent, expressive treatment of the subject find a place in a style famous for emotional and intellectual control.

The five *demoiselles*, or young ladies, represent prostitutes from Avignon Street, in Barcelona's notorious red-light district, which Picasso knew well. The title, however,

10.6 Pablo Picasso, *Les Demoiselles d'Avignon*, June–July 1907. Oil on canvas, 8' × 7'8" (2.4 × 2.3 m). The Museum of Modern Art, New York.

is not his; Picasso rarely named his works. That task he left to dealers and friends. The subject of prostitution, as we saw with Manet's scandalous *Olympia* (see fig. 2.20), had earned a prominent place in avant-garde art of the nineteenth century. Cézanne responded to Manet's painting with his own idiosyncratic versions of the subject. Other French artists, especially Degas and Toulouse-Lautrec, had portrayed the interior life of brothels, but never with the vehemence or enormous scale seen here, where the theme of sexuality is raised to an explosive pitch. When confronted with the *Demoiselles*, it is difficult to recall that the gentle *Saltimbanques* painting (see fig. 10.3) was only two years old. When compared to *Two Nudes* (see fig. 10.5), the anatomies of the *Demoiselles* seem crudely flattened and simplified, reduced to a series of interlocking, angular shapes. Even the draperies—the white cloth that spills off the table in the foreground and the bluish curtains that meander around the figures—have hardened into threatening shards. The composition is riddled with deliberately disorienting and contradictory points of view. The viewer looks down upon the table at the bottom of the canvas, but encounters the nudes head-on. Eyes are presented full face, while noses are in complete profile. The seated figure at the lower right faces her cohorts but manages to turn her head 180 degrees to address the viewer. The two central figures offer themselves up for visual consumption by assuming classic Venus poses, while their companion to the left strides into the composition like a fierce Egyptian statue. All of the prostitutes stare grimly ahead, with emotions seemingly as hardened as the knife-edge forms themselves. The three women at the left wear the simplified "Iberian" features familiar from *Two Nudes*.

10.7 Pablo Picasso, *Medical Student, Sailor, and Five Nudes in a Bordello* (study for *Les Demoiselles d'Avignon*), March–April 1907. Graphite and pastel on paper, 18⅞ × 25" (47.7 × 63.5 cm). Öffentliche Kunstsammlung, Kunstmuseum, Basel.

Most shocking of all, however, are the harshly painted masks that substitute for faces on the two figures at the right. Here, Steinberg has written, sexuality is "divested of all accretions of culture—without appeal to privacy, tenderness, gallantry, or that appreciation of beauty which presupposes detachment and distance."

The *Demoiselles* evolved over several months in 1907, during which Picasso prepared his work in the manner of a traditional Salon artist, executing dozens of drawings (figs. **10.7, 10.8**). Through these preparatory works we are able to observe Picasso's progress as he honed his composition

10.8 Pablo Picasso, Compositional study with five figures for *Les Demoiselles d'Avignon*, June 1907. Watercolor, 6¾ × 8¾" (17.2 × 22.2 cm). Philadelphia Museum of Art.

from a complex narrative to the startlingly iconic image we encounter today. The first of the drawings shown here, executed in the spring of 1907, reveals Picasso's early idea for the painting. At the far left is a figure the artist identified as a medical student. He holds a book in his right arm (in earlier studies it was a skull) and draws back a curtain with his left. In this curiously draped, stagelike setting, which Rosenblum called a "tumultuous theater of sexuality," the student encounters a provocative quintet of naked women, one of whom theatrically opens more curtains at the right. They surround a lone sailor, who is seated before a table holding a plate of spiky melons and a phallic *porrón*, a Spanish wine flask. A second still life on a round table projects precipitously into the room at the bottom of the sheet. Even on this small scale the women appear as aggressive, sexually potent beings, compared to their rather docile male clients. For Picasso, a frequenter of brothels in his youth, the threat of venereal disease was of dire concern in an era in which such afflictions could be fatal. The inclusion of a skull-toting medical student (who resembled Picasso in related sketches) probably reflects the artist's morbid conflation of sex and death and his characteristically misogynistic view of women as the carriers of life-threatening disease.

In a tiny watercolor made about two months after the drawing (see fig. 10.8), Picasso transformed the medical student into a woman in a similar pose and eliminated the sailor altogether. The prostitutes, for the most part, have shifted their attention from their clients to the viewer. It is this conception, deprived of the earlier narrative clues, that makes up the large painting. As Rubin has observed, Picasso did not need to spell out his allegory to get his meaning across; he could let these predatory seductresses stand alone as symbols of sex and death. In this watercolor, executed in delicate washes of pink with jagged, electric-blue contour lines, Picasso also made drastic changes in his formal conception of the subject. The space is compressed, the figures are highly schematized, and rounded contours have given way to sharp, angular forms. Even the table is now a triangle, jutting into the room.

Equipped with a prodigious visual memory and keen awareness of past art, Picasso could have had several paintings in mind as he set to work on his large canvas in June. In 1905 he had seen Ingres's round painting *Turkish Bath* of 1863, a titillating Salon piece that displays intertwined female nudes in myriad erotic poses. While staying in Gósol in 1906 Picasso produced his own version of a harem subject. But in that painting, unlike the *Demoiselles*, the sitters (all likenesses of Olivier) are represented in conventional bather poses, washing themselves or brushing their hair. Matisse's spectacular painting *Bonheur de vivre* (see fig. 7.6) had surely made a great impact on Picasso in the 1906 Salon des Indépendants, the juryless Salon that had been an important showcase for avant-garde art since 1884. The following year he had probably also seen Matisse's *Blue Nude* (see fig. 7.7). It is possible that Picasso

undertook the *Demoiselles* partly as a response to these radical compositions by his chief rival. Most important of all for the artist (and for the subsequent development of Cubism) was the powerful example of Cézanne, who died in 1906 and whose work was shown in a retrospective at the 1907 Salon d'Automne. It is important to recall that many of the French master's early depictions of bathers (see fig. 3.5) were fraught with an anxiety and violence that no doubt attracted Picasso, but a major instigating force for the *Demoiselles* were Cézanne's later bather paintings (see fig. 3.11). Indeed, certain figures in Picasso's composition have been traced to precedents in Cézanne's works. Picasso, however, chose not to cast his models as inhabitants of a timeless pastoral, but as sex workers in a contemporary brothel.

The work of many other painters has been linked to Picasso's seminal painting, from El Greco to Gauguin, but more significant than these stimuli was the artist's visit in June 1907 to Paris's ethnographic museum, where he saw numerous examples of African and Oceanic sculpture and masks. According to Apollinaire (who no doubt embellished the artist's words), Picasso once said that African sculptures were "the most powerful and the most beautiful of all the products of the human imagination." He had already seen such works, during studio visits to artists who were collecting African art, including Matisse, Derain, and Vlaminck (see chapter 7). But his encounter at the museum, which took place while he was at work on the *Demoiselles*, provoked a "shock," he said, and he went back to the studio and reworked his painting (though not specifically to resemble anything he had seen at the museum). It was at this time that he altered the faces of the two figures at the right from the "Iberian" countenances to violently distorted, depersonalized masks. Picasso not only introduced dramatically new, incongruous imagery into his painting, but he rendered it in a manner unlike anything else in the picture. When he added the women's masklike visages at the right he used dark hues and rough hatch marks that have been likened to scarification marks on African masks. By deploying such willfully divergent modes throughout his painting Picasso heightened its disquieting power. Rubin has even argued that the stylistic dissimilarity is central to an understanding of the work's sexual theme. As our eye scans from left to right in the painting, we may see what Rubin has called Picasso's "progressively darkening insights" into his own concept of woman's nature. African art provided him with a model for distorting the female form in order to express his own innermost anxieties.

Beyond Fauvism: Braque's Early Career

When the French artist **Georges Braque** (1882–1963) first saw *Les Demoiselles d'Avignon* in Picasso's studio in 1907, he compared the experience to swallowing kerosene and spitting fire. Most of Picasso's supporters, including Apollinaire, were horrified, or at least stymied, by the new painting. Derain ventured that one day Picasso would be found hanged behind his big picture. According to the dealer Daniel-Henry Kahnweiler, the *Demoiselles* "seemed to everyone something mad or monstrous." As more and more visitors saw it in the studio (it was not exhibited publicly until 1916), the painting sent shock waves throughout the Parisian artistic community. For Braque, the painting had direct consequences for his art, prompting him to apply his current stylistic experiments to the human figure.

Just one year younger than Picasso, Braque was the son and grandson of amateur painters. He grew up in Argenteuil, on the Seine River, and the port city of Le Havre in Normandy, both famous Impressionist sites. In Le Havre he eventually befriended the artists Raoul Dufy and Othon Friesz, who, like Braque, became associates of the Fauve painters. As an adolescent Braque took flute lessons and attended art classes in the evening at Le Havre's École des Beaux-Arts. Following his father's and grandfather's trade, he was apprenticed as a house painter and decorator in 1899 and at the end of 1900 he went to Paris to continue his apprenticeship. Some of the decorative and *trompe l'oeil* effects that later entered his paintings and collages were the result of this initial training. After a year of military service and brief academic training, Braque settled in Paris, but he returned frequently to Le Havre to paint landscapes, especially views of the harbor. Like his artist contemporaries in Paris, he studied the old masters in the Louvre and was drawn to Egyptian and archaic sculpture. He was attracted by Poussin among the old masters, and his early devotion to Corot continued. During the same period he was discovering the Post-Impressionists, including Van Gogh, Gauguin, and the Neo-Impressionist Signac, but it was ultimately the art of Cézanne that affected him most deeply and set him on the path to Cubism.

In the fall of 1905 Braque was impressed by the works of Matisse, Derain, and Vlaminck at the notorious Salon d'Automne where Fauvism made its public debut, and the following year he turned to a bright, Fauve-inspired palette. Unlike Picasso, Braque submitted work regularly to the Salons in the early years of his career. His paintings were included in the 1906 Salon des Indépendants, but he later destroyed all the submitted works. In the company of Friesz and Derain, he spent the fall and winter of 1906 near Marseilles at L'Estaque, where Cézanne had painted (see fig. 3.6). He then entered a group of his new Fauve paintings in the same Salon des Indépendants of March 1907 that included Matisse's *Blue Nude*. One of his works was purchased by Kahnweiler, who was to become the most important dealer of Cubist pictures. Though the record is not certain, Braque and Picasso probably met around this time. It was inevitable that their paths should cross, for they had several friends in common, including Derain, Matisse, and Apollinaire.

10.9 Georges Braque, *Viaduct at L'Estaque*, 1907. Oil on canvas, 25⅝ × 31¾" (65.1 × 80.6 cm). The Minneapolis Institute of Arts.

During his brief exploration of Fauvism, Braque developed his own distinctive palette, beautifully exemplified in the clear, opalescent hues of *Viaduct at L'Estaque* (fig. **10.9**). Despite the bright coloration of this landscape, made on the site in the fall of 1907, its palette is tame compared with the radical color experiments of Matisse's Fauve work (see fig. 7.5). Owing largely to lessons absorbed from Cézanne, Braque was not willing to forgo explicit pictorial structure in his landscapes. The composition of *Viaduct at L'Estaque* is rigorously constructed: the hills and houses, though abbreviated in form, retain a palpable sense of volume, created through Cézannist patches of color and blue outlines, rather than through traditional chiaroscuro. Braque built these forms up toward a high horizon line and framed them within arching trees, a favorite device of Cézanne. These tendencies in Braque's work are often referred to as "Cézannism."

At the end of 1907 Braque visited Picasso's studio with Apollinaire, possibly for the first time. By the end of the next year he and Picasso were regular visitors to one another's studios. On this visit Braque saw the completed *Demoiselles* and the beginnings of Picasso's most recent work, *Three Women* (see fig. 10.12). Until this point Braque had rarely painted the human form, but early in 1908 he made a multifigure painting, since lost, which was clearly inspired by Picasso's *Three Women*. That spring he

produced *Large Nude* (fig. **10.10**), a painting that signals his imminent departure from Fauvism. Like Picasso, Braque had seen Matisse's *Blue Nude* the previous fall (see fig. 7.7), and his massively muscular figure, set down with bold brushwork and emphatic black outlines, bears the memory of that work. But Braque repudiated the rich pinks and blues of *Viaduct at L'Estaque* for a subdued palette of ochers, browns, and gray-blue. While the model's simplified facial features and the angular drapery that surrounds her recall the *Demoiselles*, Braque was not motivated by the sexualized themes of Picasso's painting. With *Large Nude*, he said he wanted to create a "new sort of beauty … in terms of volume, of line, of mass, of weight."

A comparison between *Viaduct at L'Estaque*, and Braque's painting from August 1908, *Houses at L'Estaque* (fig. **10.11**), makes clear the transformations that took place in his style after the fall of 1907. With the suppression of particularizing details, the houses and trees become simplified, geometric volumes that are experienced at close range and sealed off from surrounding sky or land. Braque explained that in such pictures he wished to establish a background plane while "advancing the picture toward myself bit by bit." Rather than receding into depth, the forms seem to come forward, approximating an appearance of low-relief sculpture, or bas-relief.

Braque's illusion of limited depth is not dependent upon traditional, single-point linear perspective. Cézanne, he later said, was the first to break with that kind of "erudite, mechanicized perspective." Instead, he achieves illusion by the apparent volume of the buildings and trees—their overlapping, tilted, and shifting shapes create the effect of a scene observed from various positions. Despite many inconsistencies (of the sort that abound in Cézanne's work), including conflicting orthogonals and vantage points, or roof edges that fail to line up or that disappear altogether, Braque managed a wholly convincing, albeit highly conceptualized, space—one that exemplifies modernist concerns in being true to sense perceptions rather than to pictorial conventions. Color is limited to the fairly uniform ocher of the buildings, and the greens and blue-green of the trees. Whereas Cézanne built his entire organization of surface and depth from his color, Braque, in this work and increasingly in the paintings of the next few years, subordinates color in order to focus on pictorial structure.

With *Houses at L'Estaque* Braque established the essential syntax of early Cubism. He is generally credited with arriving at this point single-handedly, preliminary to the steady exchanges with Picasso that characterize the subsequent development of high Cubism. These works at L'Estaque confirmed Braque's thorough abandonment of Fauvism. "You can't remain forever in a state of paroxysm," he said. In fact, Fauvism was a short-lived experiment for most of its artists, partly because painters such as Derain, Dufy, and Vlaminck fell increasingly under the

10.10 Georges Braque, *Large Nude*, 1908. Oil on canvas, 55⅛ × 39" (140 × 99.1 cm). Collection Alex Maguy, Paris.

10.11 Georges Braque, *Houses at L'Estaque*, August 1908. Oil on canvas, 28¾ × 23⅝" (73 × 60 cm). Kunstmuseum, Bern.

spell of Cézanne's work. In the world of the Parisian avant-garde during this remarkably fertile period, there was a growing sense of polarization between the followers of Matisse and the Cézannist and Cubist faction. Gertrude Stein described the competing camps as "Picassoites" and "Matisseites."

In the fall of 1908 Braque took his new works from L'Estaque back to Paris, where he showed them to Picasso and submitted them to the progressive Salon d'Automne. The jury, which included Matisse, Rouault, and the Fauve painter Albert Marquet, rejected all his entries. According to Apollinaire, who told the story many ways over the years, it was upon this occasion that Matisse referred to Braque's "little cubes." By 1912 this had become the standard account for the birth of the term "Cubism." Following his rejection, Braque exhibited twenty-seven paintings in November 1908 at the Kahnweiler Gallery, with a catalogue by Apollinaire. Louis Vauxcelles, the critic who had coined the term "Fauve," reviewed the exhibition and, employing Matisse's term, observed that Braque "reduces everything, places and figures and houses, to geometrical schemes, to cubes."

"Two Mountain Climbers Roped Together": Braque, Picasso, and the Development of Cubism

The remarkable artistic dialogue between Braque and Picasso began in earnest toward the end of 1908, when they started visiting one another's studios regularly to see what had materialized during the day. "We discussed and tested each other's ideas as they came to us," Braque said, "and we compared our respective works." At this time Picasso completely revised *Three Women* (fig. **10.12**), a painting he had begun the year before in response to Braque's Cubist paintings from L'Estaque. Those new experiments led Picasso toward a more thorough absorption of "Cézannism," as he developed his own variation on the bas-relief effects he saw in Braque's work. The three women here seem to be a reprise of the two central figures of the *Demoiselles*, although these mammoth beings seem even less like flesh and blood and appear as though chiseled from red sandstone. In earlier states of the painting, known from vintage photographs, the faces were boldly inscribed with features inspired by African masks, but Picasso altered

10.12 Pablo Picasso, *Three Women*, 1907–8. Oil on canvas, 6'6¾ × 7'6½" (2 × 2.3 m). The Hermitage Museum, St. Petersburg.

those features in the final state. The women no longer stare boldly ahead, as in the *Demoiselles*, but seem to hover on the edge of deep slumber, suggesting, as Steinberg has surmised, the sexual awakening of some primitive life form. Picasso here employs Cézanne's *passage*, a technique whereby the edges of color planes slip away and merge with adjacent areas. For example, on the proper left leg of the central figure (meaning her left, not ours) is a gray triangle that dually functions as a facet of her thigh and part of her neighbor's breast. This *passage* mitigates any sense of clear demarcation between the figures and their environment, making, in Steinberg's words, "body mass and surround consubstantial." Such ambiguity of figure and ground, facilitated by an opening up of contours, is a fundamental characteristic of Cubism.

Like many of Matisse's and Picasso's greatest paintings, *Three Women* is in the collection of Russia's Hermitage Museum in St. Petersburg. The work was purchased by the brilliant Russian collector Sergei Shchukin, who was brought to Picasso's studio by Matisse in September 1908. He purchased *Three Women* from Leo and Gertrude Stein, who, because of strained relations with one another, began to sell their collection in 1913.

"Analytic Cubism," 1909–11

Although all of Picasso's paintings discussed to this point have depicted the figure, he frequently worked in the genre of still life throughout the development of Cubism, as did Braque. Materials drawn from the café and the studio, the milieux most familiar to these artists, became standard

motifs in their work. Newspapers, bottles of wine, or food—the objects literally within their reach—were often elliptically coded with personal, sometimes humorous allusions to their private world.

Picasso's majestic painting *Bread and Fruit Dish on a Table* (fig. **10.13**) is an especially intriguing example of still life, since the artist initiated it as a figurative composition and then gradually transformed the human figures into bread, fruit, and furniture. We know from small studies that Picasso was planning a painting of several figures seated and facing the viewer from behind the drop-leaf table seen here (just like one in Picasso's studio). William Rubin has proposed that Picasso used turpentine to rub out most of the figures' upper halves from his canvas, but retained their legs, thus explaining the strange, planklike forms under the table. Other shapes from the old composition were retained to take on new identities in the still life. For example, the loaves of bread at the right, mysteriously propped up against a backdrop, were once the arms of a figure. At the opposite end of the table sat a woman, whose breasts were retained as fruit in a bowl. Thus, Picasso makes a sly visual pun on a hackneyed symbol of fecundity and womanhood, while balancing this rounded, feminine form with the phallic loaves at the opposite end of the table. Rubin, who reads these gendered forms as stand-ins for Picasso and his companion, Fernande Olivier, has proposed that even through the apparently neutral medium of still life Picasso could "tap the sentiments and

10.13 Pablo Picasso, *Bread and Fruit Dish on a Table*, 1909. Oil on canvas, 64⅝ × 52¼" (164 × 132.5 cm). Öffentliche Kunstsammlung Basel, Kunstmuseum.

10.14 Pablo Picasso, *Houses on the Hill, Horta de Ebro*, summer 1909. Oil on canvas, 25⅝ × 31⅞" (65 × 81 cm). The Museum of Modern Art, New York.

particulars of his most intimate life and thought." Just as in *Family of Saltimbanques* and *Demoiselles d'Avignon*, he concludes, the anecdotal elements fall away as the pictorial components are gradually concentrated in a more strictly frontal and iconic composition. Rubin has interpreted the stylistic duality at play in this composition—with its highly finished, almost naïve rendition at the left and the much looser handling at the right—as Picasso's preoccupation at the time with the work of Rousseau (on the left) and Cézanne (on the right).

Picasso spent the summer of 1909 in the Spanish hill town of Horta de Ebro (today Horta de San Juan), where his early Cubist style reached its apogee. Among the landscapes he made that summer is *Houses on the Hill, Horta de Ebro* (fig. **10.14**) in which the stucco houses of the village, seen from above, are piled up into a pyramidal structure of such refinement and delicate coloration that the Expressionist intensity of *Demoiselles* seems a distant memory. Painted in facets of pale gold and gray, the highly geometricized houses are presented in multiple, often contradictory perspectives. Rather than creating forms that recede predictably into the distance, Picasso often reversed the orthogonals to project toward the viewer. His juxtaposition of light and dark planes enhances the overall sculptural configuration but fails to convey any single or consistent light source. The result is a shimmering, prismatic world where space and mass are virtually synonymous. Even the sky has been articulated into a crystalline pattern of intersecting planes—realized through subtle shifts in value of light gray or green—that suggests a distant mountain range.

During this crucial summer Picasso also made several paintings and drawings of Olivier, including portrait studies that articulate the sculptural mass of her head into a series of curving planes. After returning to Paris in September he worked in the studio of a friend, the Catalan

sculptor Manuel Hugué, known as Manolo, and sculpted a head based on his Horta studies of Olivier. Several bronzes (fig. **10.15**) were then cast at a later date from the artist's original plaster casts. Picasso, who is arguably one of the most inventive sculptors of all time, had experimented with sculpture intermittently for several years. With *Woman's Head (Fernande)* he recapitulates in three dimensions the pictorial experiments of the summer by carving Olivier's features into facets as geometric as one of his Horta hillsides. Despite its innovative treatment of plastic form as a ruptured, discontinuous surface, this sculpture still depends upon the conventional methods and materials of modeling clay into a solid mass and making plaster casts (two were made) from the clay model that are then used to cast the work in bronze. *Woman's Head* exerted considerable influence on other Cubist sculptors, such as Aleksandr Archipenko and Henri Laurens (see figs. 10.31, 10.34), but Picasso later said it was "pointless" to continue in this vein. In 1912 he embarked upon a much more radical solution for Cubist sculpture.

While Picasso was concentrating on his sculpture, Braque spent the winter of 1909 in Paris, composing several still lifes of musical instruments. Braque was an amateur musician, and the instruments he kept in his studio were common motifs in his paintings throughout his career. He preferred violins, mandolins, or clarinets to other objects, for they have, he said, "the advantage of

10.15 Pablo Picasso, *Woman's Head (Fernande)*, fall 1909. Bronze, 16¼ × 9¾ × 10½" (41.3 × 24.7 × 26.6 cm). The Museum of Modern Art, New York.

10.16 Georges Braque, *Violin and Palette*, 1909. Oil on canvas, 36⅛ × 16⅞" (91.7 × 42.9 cm). Solomon R. Guggenheim Museum, New York.

being animated by one's touch." Despite the intensified fragmentation that Braque had by now adopted, the still-life subjects of *Violin and Palette* (fig. **10.16**) are still easily recognizable. Within a long, narrow format he has placed, in descending order, his palette, a musical score propped up on a stand, and a violin. These objects inhabit a shallow, highly ambiguous space. Presumably the violin and music stand are placed on a table, with the palette hanging on a wall behind them, but their vertical disposition within the picture space makes their precise orientation unclear. Although certain forms, such as the scroll at the top of the violin neck, are rendered naturalistically, for the most part the objects are not modeled continuously in space but are broken up into tightly woven facets that open into the surrounding void. At the same time, the interstices between objects harden into painted shards, causing space to appear as concrete as the depicted objects. It was this "materialization of a new space" that Braque said was the essence of Cubism.

At the top of *Violin and Palette* Braque depicted his painting palette, emblem of his metier, hanging from a

carefully drawn nail. The shadow cast by the nail reinforces the object's existence in three-dimensional space. By employing this curious detail of *trompe l'oeil*, Braque calls attention to the ways in which his new system departs from conventional means of depicting volumetric shapes on a flat surface. In so doing, he declares Cubism's defiance of the Renaissance conceptions of space that had been under assault since Manet, in which art functions as a mirror of the three-dimensional world, and offers in its place a conceptual reconfiguration of that world. This kind of artistic legerdemain, in which different systems of representation simultaneously exist within one painting, was soon to be most fully exploited in Cubist collage and *papier collé*.

Picasso also treated musical themes in his Cubist compositions. One of the best-known examples is his *Girl with a Mandolin (Fanny Tellier)* (fig. **10.17**), made in Paris in the spring of 1910. Still working from nature, Picasso hired a professional model named Fanny Tellier to pose nude in his studio. When this portrait is compared with Braque's *Violin and Palette*, Picasso's style appears somewhat less radical than Braque's. The figure still retains a sense of the organic and, in some areas, is clearly detached from the background plane by way of sculptural modeling, seen especially in the rounded volumes of the model's right

10.17 Pablo Picasso, *Girl with a Mandolin (Fanny Tellier)*, late spring 1910. Oil on canvas, 39½ × 29" (100.3 × 73.7 cm). The Museum of Modern Art, New York.

breast and arm. Picasso's chromatic range, however, is even more restricted than that found in Braque's still life. Employing soft gradations of gray and golden brown, Picasso endowed this lyrical portrait with a beautifully tranquil atmosphere. Robert Rosenblum has rightly compared *Girl with a Mandolin* with Camille Corot's meditative depictions of women in the studio with musical instruments. In the fall of 1910 both Picasso and Braque saw an exhibition of Corot's work in Paris and were much impressed.

By 1910 Picasso and Braque had entered the period of greatest intensity in their collaborative, yet highly competitive, relationship. Over the next two years they produced some of the most cerebral, complex paintings of their careers, working with tremendous concentration and in such proximity that some of their compositions are virtually indistinguishable from one another. For a time they even refrained from signing their own canvases on the front in order to downplay the individual nature of their contributions. "We were prepared to efface our personalities in order to find originality," Braque said. "Analytic Cubism," in which the object is analyzed, broken down, and dissected, is the term used to describe this high phase of their collaboration.

One of the masterpieces of Analytic Cubism is Picasso's *Portrait of Daniel-Henry Kahnweiler* (fig. **10.18**), made a few months after *Girl with a Mandolin*. The painting belongs to a series of portraits of art dealers that Picasso made in 1910. Kahnweiler was an astute German dealer who had been buying works by Braque and Picasso since 1908. He was also a critic who wrote extensively about Cubist art, including the first serious theoretical text on the subject, which interprets the style in semiological terms as a language of signs. In this portrait, for which Kahnweiler apparently sat about twenty times, the modeled forms of *Girl with a Mandolin* have disappeared, and the figure, rather than disengaged from the background, seems merged with it. Here the third dimension is stated entirely in terms of flat, slightly angled planes organized within a linear grid that hovers near the surface of the painting. Planes shift in front of and behind their neighbors, causing space to fluctuate and solid form to dissolve into transparent facets of color. Although he delineated his figure not as an integrated volume but as a lattice of lines dispersed over the visual field, Picasso nevertheless managed a likeness of his subject. In small details—a wave of hair, the sitter's carefully clasped hands, a schematic still life at the lower left—the painter particularized his subject and helps us to reconstruct a figure seated in a chair. Though Picasso kept color to the bare minimum, his canvas emits a shimmering, mesmerizing light, which he achieved by applying paint in short daubs that contain generous admixtures of white pigment. The Italian critic Ardengo Soffici, whose early writings about Picasso and Braque helped bring the Italian Futurists in contact with Cubism, referred to the "prismatic magic" of such works.

10.18 Pablo Picasso, *Portrait of Daniel-Henry Kahnweiler*, 1910. Oil on canvas, 39½ × 28⅝" (100.6 × 72.8 cm). The Art Institute of Chicago.

The degree to which the pictorial vocabularies of Picasso and Braque converged during the Analytic phase of Cubism can be demonstrated through a comparison of two works from 1911. Picasso's *Accordionist* (fig. **10.19**) dates from the astonishingly productive summer of that year, which he spent with Braque in Céret, a village in the French Pyrenees. At a nearly identical state of exploration is Braque's *The Portuguese (The Emigrant)* (fig. **10.20**), begun in Céret after Picasso's departure and completed in Paris. Both artists reorder the elements of the physical world within the shallow depths of their respective compositions, using the human figure as a pretext for an elaborate scaffolding of shifting, interpenetrating planes. The presence of the figure is made evident principally by a series of descending diagonal lines that helps concentrate the geometric structure down the center of the picture. That structure opens up toward the edges of the canvas where the pictorial incident diminishes, occasionally revealing the painting's bare, unpainted ground. Both Picasso and Braque at this stage used a stippled, delicately modulated brushstroke so short as to be reminiscent of Seurat, though their color is restricted to muted gray and brown. Variation in values in these hues and in the direction of the strokes creates almost imperceptible change and movement between surface and depth.

10.19 Pablo Picasso, *Accordionist*, summer 1911. Oil on canvas, 51¼ × 35¼" (130.2 × 89.5 cm). Solomon R. Guggenheim Museum, New York.

10.20 Georges Braque, *The Portuguese (The Emigrant)*, 1911. Oil on canvas, 46⅛ × 32" (117.2 × 81.3 cm). Öffentliche Kunstsammlung Basel, Kunstmuseum.

However indecipherable their images, Braque and Picasso never relinquished the natural world altogether, and they provided subtle clues that aid in the apprehension of their obscure subject matter. In the *Accordionist* (which represents a young girl, according to Picasso, not a man, as critics have often presumed) curvilinear elements near the bottom edge of the painting stand for the arms of a chair, while the small circles and stair-step patterns toward the center indicate the keys and bellows of an accordion. *The Portuguese (The Emigrant)*, Braque said, shows "an emigrant on the bridge of a boat with a harbor in the background." This would explain, at the upper right, the transparent traces of a docking post and sections of nautical rope. In the lower portion are the strings and sound hole of the emigrant's guitar. Braque introduced a new element with the stenciled letters and numbers in the painting's upper zone. Like other forms in *The Portuguese*, the words are fragmentary. The letters D BAL at the upper right, for example, may derive from *Grand Bal*, probably a reference to a common dance-hall poster. While Braque had incorporated a word into a Cubist painting as early as 1909, his letters there were painted freehand as a descriptive local detail. For *The Portuguese* he borrowed a technique from commercial art and stenciled his letters, which here function not as illusionistic representations but as autonomous signs dissociated from any context that accounts for their presence. Inherently flat, the letters and numbers exist "outside of space," Braque said. And because they are congruent with the literal surface of the painting, they underscore the nature of the painted canvas as a material object, a physical fact, rather than a site for an illusionistic depiction of the real world. At the same time, they make the rest of the image read as an illusionistically shallow space. Braque's introduction of words in his painting, a practice soon adopted by Picasso, was one of many Cubist innovations that had far-reaching implications for modern art. Like so many of their inventions, the presence in the visual arts of letters, words, and even long texts is today commonplace (see figs. 21.16, 26.1, 27.21).

"Synthetic Cubism," 1912–14

In May 1912 the Cubists' search for alternative modes of representation led Picasso to the invention of collage, initiated by a small but revolutionary work, *Still Life with Chair Caning* (fig. **10.21**). Within this single composition Picasso combined a complex array of pictorial vocabularies, each imaging reality in its own way. Painted on an oval support, a shape Picasso and Braque had already adopted for earlier Cubist paintings, this still life depicts objects scattered across a café table. The fragment of a newspaper, *Le Journal*, is indicated by the letters JOU that, given the artist's penchant for puns, could refer to *jouer*, meaning "to play" and implying that all this illusionism is a game. Over the letters Picasso depicted a pipe in a naturalistic style, while at the right he added the highly abstracted forms of a goblet, a knife, and a slice of lemon.

The most prominent element here, however, is a section of common oilcloth that has been mechanically printed with a design simulating chair caning. Picasso glued the cloth directly to his canvas. While this *trompe l'oeil* fabric offers an exacting degree of illusionism, it is as much a fiction as Picasso's painted forms, since it remains a facsimile of chair caning, not the real thing. After all, Picasso once said, art is "a lie that helps us understand the truth." But he did surround his painting with actual rope, in ironic imitation of a traditional gold frame. The rope could have been suggested by a wooden table molding (see the table in fig. 10.25, for example) or the kind of cloth edged with upholstery cord that Picasso had placed on a table in his studio. Combined with the oilcloth, a material from the actual world, the rope encourages a reading of the painted surface itself as a horizontal tabletop, a logical idea, given the presence of still-life objects. Such spatial ambiguity is one of the many ways Picasso challenged the most fundamental artistic conventions. His incorporation of unorthodox materials, ones not associated with "high" or "fine" art, offered a radically new connection to the external world and an alternative to the increasingly hermetic nature of his Analytic Cubist compositions. Around the same time

he and Braque were reintroducing color to their Cubist paintings with bright, commercial enamel paint.

Following Picasso's invention of collage, Braque originated *papiers collés* (pasted papers). While this technique also involved gluing materials to a support, it is distinguished from collage in that only paper is used and, as Rubin has explained, "the sign language of the entire picture is in harmony with what is glued on." Collage, on the other hand, capitalized on disparate elements in jarring juxtaposition. It was this medium's potential for improbable, provocative combinations (see fig. 14.4) that ultimately attracted the Dada and Surrealist artists.

Braque made his first *papier collé*, *Fruit Dish and Glass* (fig. 10.22), in September 1912, during an extended stay with Picasso in Sorgues, in the south of France. It has been proposed that Braque deliberately postponed his experiment until Picasso, who regarded any idea as fair game for stealing, had left Sorgues for Paris. Once he was satisfied with the results, Braque presented them to Picasso. "I have to admit that after having made the *papier collé*," he said, "I felt a great shock, and it was an even greater shock for Picasso when I showed it to him." Picasso soon began making his own experiments with Braque's "new procedure."

The precipitating event behind Braque's invention was his discovery in a storefront window of a roll of wallpaper printed with a *faux bois* (imitation wood-grain) motif. Braque had already used a house painter's comb to create *faux bois* patterns in his paintings, a technique he passed on to Picasso, and he immediately saw the paper's potential for his current work. Like the oilcloth in *Still Life with Chair Caning*, the *faux bois* offered a ready-made replacement for hand-wrought imagery. In *Fruit Dish and Glass* Braque

10.21 Pablo Picasso, *Still Life with Chair Caning*, 1912. Oil and oilcloth on canvas, edged with rope, 10⅝ × 14⅝" (27 × 37 cm). Musée Picasso, Paris.

10.22 Georges Braque, *Fruit Dish and Glass*, September 1912. Charcoal and pasted paper on paper, 24⅜ × 17½" (62 × 44.5 cm). Private collection.

combined the *faux-bois* paper with a charcoal drawing of a still life that, judging from the drawn words "ale" and "bar", is situated in the familiar world of the café. With typical ambiguity, the cutouts of pasted paper play multiple roles, both literal and descriptive. Although their location in space is unclear, the *faux-bois* sections in the upper portion of the still life are signs for the wall of the café, while the rectangular piece below represents a wooden table. In addition, the *faux bois* enabled Braque to introduce color into his otherwise monochrome composition and to enlist its patterns as a kind of substitute chiaroscuro. At this point Braque was thinking of the *papiers collés* in relation to his paintings, for virtually the same composition exists as an oil.

Once Picasso took up the challenge of Braque's *papier collé*, the contrast in sensibility between the two became obvious. While Braque relied on his elegant Cubist draftsmanship to bind the imagery of his *papiers collés* together, Picasso immediately deployed more colorful, heterogenous materials with greater irony and more spatial acrobatics. In one of his earliest *papiers collés*, *Guitar, Sheet Music, and Wine Glass* of 1912 (fig. **10.23**), a decorative wallpaper establishes the background for his still life (and implies that the depicted guitar is hanging on a wall). Picasso bettered Braque by actually painting a simulated wood-grain pattern on paper, which he then cut out and inserted into his

composition as part of a guitar. But the instrument is incomplete; we must construct its shape by decoding the signs the artist provides, such as a section of blue paper for the bridge and a white disk for the sound hole.

As in Picasso's collage *Still Life with Chair Caning*, different signifying systems or languages of representation are here at work, complete with charcoal drawing (the glass at the right) and a guitar-shaped cutout of painted *faux bois* paper. We have seen the way in which the Cubists represented newspapers in their painted compositions. The next step was to glue the actual newsprint to the surface of a *papier collé*. In this example, even the headline of the Paris newspaper *Le Journal*, LA BATAILLE S'EST ENGAGÉ (the battle is joined), has a dual message. It literally refers to the First Balkan War then being waged in Europe and thus adds a note of contemporaneity. Some specialists have argued that its deeper meaning is personal, that it is Picasso's friendly challenge to Braque on the battlefield of a new medium; others have read it as more directly political, an effort to confront the realities of war. By appropriating materials from the vast terrain of visual culture, even ones as ephemeral as the daily newspaper, and incorporating them unaltered into their works of art, Braque and Picasso undermined definitions of artistic authenticity that made it the exclusive province of drawing and painting, media that capture the immediacy of the individual artist's touch. As always, this was accomplished with irony and humor—here again, JOU implies "game" or "play." It was a challenge that had profound consequences for twentieth-century art, one that in many ways still informs debates in contemporary art.

The inventions in 1912 of collage and *papier collé*, as well as Cubist sculpture (discussed below), essentially terminated the Analytic Cubist phase of Braque and Picasso's enterprise and initiated a second and more extensive period in their work. Called Synthetic Cubism, this new phase lasted into the twenties and witnessed the adoption and variation of the Cubist style by many new practitioners, whose work is addressed later in this chapter. If earlier Cubist works analyzed form by breaking it down and reconstructing it as lines and transparent planes, the work after 1912 generally constructs an image from many diverse components. Picasso and Braque began to make paintings that were not primarily a distillation of observed experience but, rather, were built up by using all plastic means at their disposal, both traditional and experimental. In many ways, Synthetic Cubist pictures are less descriptive of external reality, for they are generally assembled with flat, abstracted forms that have little representational value until they are assigned one within the composition. For example, the bowl-shaped black form in figure 10.23 is ambiguous, but once inserted in the composition, it stands for part of a guitar.

The dynamic new syntax of Synthetic Cubism, directly influenced by collage, is exemplified by Picasso's *Card Player* (fig. **10.24**), from 1913–14. Here the artist has

10.23 Pablo Picasso, *Guitar, Sheet Music, and Wine Glass,* Fall 1912. Pasted papers, gouache, and charcoal on paper, 18⅞ × 14¾" (47.9 × 37.5 cm). McNay Art Museum, San Antonio, Texas.

replaced the shimmering brown-and-gray scaffolding of *Accordionist* (see fig. 10.19) with flat, clearly differentiated shapes in bright and varied color. We can make out a moustachioed card player seated at a wooden table, indicated by the *faux bois* pattern, on which are three playing cards. Below the table Picasso schematically inscribed the player's legs and on either side of the sitter he included an indication of wainscoting on the back wall. Here the cropped letters JOU, by now a signature Cubist conceit, have an obvious relevance. Picasso emulates in oil the pasted forms of collage and *papiers collés* by partially obscuring with a succeeding layer of paint each of the flat shapes that make up the figure.

After 1913 the principal trend in paintings by both Picasso and Braque was toward enrichment of their plastic means and enlargement of their increasingly individual Cubist vocabularies. In Picasso's *Green Still Life* (fig. 10.25), we can easily identify all the customary ingredients of a Cubist still life—compote dish, newspaper, glass, bottle, and fruit. Following the intellectual rigors of Analytic Cubism, the artist seems to delight here in a cheerfully decorative mode. Alfred Barr, an art historian and the first director of the Museum of Modern Art, New York, called this decorative phase in Picasso's work Rococo Cubism. Here Picasso has disposed his still-life objects in an open, tangible space and, using commercial enamels,

10.24 Pablo Picasso, *Card Player,* winter 1913–14. Oil on canvas, 42½ × 35¼" (108 × 89.5 cm). The Museum of Modern Art, New York.

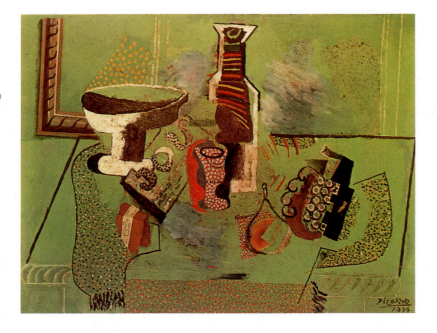

10.25 Pablo Picasso, *Green Still Life*, summer 1914. Oil on canvas, 23½ × 31¼" (59.7 × 79.4 cm). The Museum of Modern Art, New York.

adds bright dots of color that resemble shiny sequins. The entire ground of the painting is a single hue, a bright emerald green, which Picasso allows to infiltrate the objects themselves. In so doing, he reiterates the flatness of the pictorial space and deprives the objects of volume. Picasso painted *Green Still Life* in Avignon during the summer of 1914. Perhaps the optimistic mood of his work at this time reflects the calm domesticity he was enjoying there with Eva Gouel, his companion since 1911. But this sense of wellbeing was soon shattered. In August 1914 war was declared in Europe; by the end of 1915 Eva was dead of tuberculosis.

Braque, who was called up to serve in the French military (along with Guillaume Apollinaire and André Derain), said goodbye to Picasso at the Avignon railroad station, bringing to an abrupt end one of the greatest collaborations in the history of art. The war terminated the careers of many of Europe's most talented young artists and writers, including Apollinaire and Raymond Duchamp-Villon in France, Franz Marc and August Macke in Germany, and Umberto Boccioni in Italy. Picasso remained in Paris until 1917, when he went to Rome with the writer Jean Cocteau and worked on stage designs for the Ballets Russes. The postwar work of Braque and Picasso is discussed in chapter 14.

Constructed Spaces: Cubist Sculpture

Even in the hands of great modernist innovators such as Jean Arp or Constantin Brancusi (see fig. 9.11), sculpture was still essentially conceived as a solid form surrounded by void. These sculptors created mass either through subtractive methods—carving form out of stone or wood—or additive ones—building up form by modeling in wax or clay. By these definitions, Picasso's *Woman's Head (Fernande)* (see fig. 10.15), regardless of its radical reconception of the human form, is still a traditional solid

mass surrounded by space. Like collage, constructed sculpture is assembled from disparate, often unconventional materials. Unlike traditional sculpture, its forms are penetrated by void and create volume not by mass, but by containing space. With the introduction of constructed sculpture the Cubists broke with one of the most fundamental characteristics of sculptural form and provoked a rupture with past art equal to the one they fostered in painting.

Braque and Picasso

Documents prove that constructed Cubist sculpture was invented by Braque and that, as Rubin has demonstrated, it predated the first *papiers collés*. Nevertheless, no such works from his hand exist. Because he did not preserve the works, it is assumed that he thought of them principally as aids to his *papiers collés*, not as an end in themselves. According to Kahnweiler, Braque made reliefs in wood, paper, and cardboard, but the only visual record of his sculpture is a 1914 photograph of a work taken in his Paris studio (fig. **10.26**). This unusual composition represents a familiar subject, a café still life, assembled from paper (including newsprint) and cardboard on which Braque either drew or painted. He installed his sculpture across a corner of the room, thus incorporating the real space of the surrounding studio into his work. This corner construction possibly influenced the corner-hung Counter-Reliefs of the Russian Constructivist artist Vladimir Tatlin (see fig. 11.24), who may have visited Picasso's or Braque's studio during a 1914 trip to Paris.

Though constructed sculpture was Braque's invention, it was Picasso, typically, who made the most thorough use of it. His first attempt in the new technique is a guitar made from sheet metal, which he first prepared in October 1912 as a maquette made simply of cardboard, string, and wire (fig. **10.27**). Picasso's use of an industrial material such as sheet metal was highly unorthodox in 1912; in the years since, it has become a common sculptural medium. Clearly, the guitar was a significant impetus behind his *papiers collés*, for photographs taken in the artist's studio show it surrounded by works in this medium. In many ways, Picasso's guitar sculpture is the equivalent in three dimensions of the same motif in his *papiers collés*, *Guitar, Sheet Music, and Wine Glass* (see fig. 10.23), made several weeks later.

Through a technique of open construction, the body of the cardboard guitar has largely been cut away. Volume is expressed as a series of flat and projecting planes, resulting in a quality of transparency previously alien to sculpture. Picasso made the guitar sound hole, a void in a real instrument, as a projecting cylinder, just as he designed the neck as a concavity. The morphology of the guitar was directly inspired by a Grebo mask from the Ivory Coast in Africa, in which the eyes are depicted as hollow projecting cylinders. Picasso owned two such examples, one of which he bought in August 1912, during a visit to Marseilles with Braque. *Guitar* was revolutionary in showing that an artist's conceptual inventions of form are signs of or references to reality, not mere imitations of it. They can be entirely arbitrary and may bear only a passing resemblance to what they actually denote. Thus the sign for the guitar's sound hole was stimulated by a completely unrelated source—the eyes of an African mask.

We know from a 1913 photograph that Picasso inserted his cardboard guitar into a relief still-life construction on the wall of his studio. In an even more fascinating sculptural ensemble, also recorded only in a contemporary photograph, he drew a guitarist on a canvas and gave the figure projecting cardboard arms that held an actual guitar. A real table with still-life props on it completed the composition. In this remarkable tableau Picasso closed the breach that separated painting and sculpture, uniting the pictorial realm with the space of the external world. Much of modern sculpture has addressed this very relationship, in which a sculpture is regarded not as a discrete work of art to be isolated on a pedestal, but rather as an object coexisting with the viewer in one unified space. In two subsequent constructions, *Mandolin and Clarinet*, 1913 (fig. **10.28**), and *Still Life*, 1914, both assembled from crudely cut, partially painted pieces of wood, Picasso furthered the explorations initiated by *Guitar*. *Mandolin and Clarinet*, composed mostly of scrap wood, demonstrates the artist's uncanny ability to envision the formal potential of found materials. Wood, which he and Braque had previously represented illusionistically, is now present as itself. In *Still Life* a curved section of wood stands for a table, on whose edge Picasso glued actual upholstery fringe. On the table he depicts a still life of food, a knife, and a glass. Unlike his

10.26 Georges Braque, 1914. The artist's Paris studio with a paper sculpture, now lost.

10.27 Pablo Picasso, Maquette for *Guitar*, Paris, October 1912. Construction of cardboard, string, and wire (restored), 25¾ × 13 × 7½" (65.1 × 33 × 19 cm). The Museum of Modern Art, New York.

constructed sculptures, which were essentially reliefs, Picasso's *Glass of Absinthe* (fig. **10.29**) was conceived in the round and was originally modeled by conventional methods in wax. Absinthe is a highly addictive, stupor-inducing liquor, so lethal that by the end of 1914 it was outlawed in France. Upon completion of the wax model of *Glass of Absinthe*, Kahnweiler had the work cast in bronze in an edition of six, to each of which the artist added a "found object," a perforated silver spoon, as well as a bronze sugar cube. He hand-painted five variants and coated one with sand, a substance that first Braque and then he had added to their paint medium. The bright color patterns on this example are similar to those found in the artist's contemporary paintings (seefig. 10.25). Picasso cut deep hollows in the glass to reveal the interior, where, as in the previous *Still Life*, the level of fluid reads as a horizontal plane. In this adaptation of collage methods to the medium of sculpture, Picasso adapts objects from the real world for expressive purposes in the realm of art. This lack of discrimination between the "high" art media of painting and sculpture and the "low" ephemera of the material world remained a characteristic of Picasso's sculpture (see figs. 15.51, 20.3) and proved especially relevant for artists in the fifties and sixties (see figs. 20.10, 21.54).

10.29 Pablo Picasso, *Glass of Absinthe*, spring 1914. Painted bronze with silver absinth spoon, 8½ × 6½ × 3⅜" (21.6 × 16.4 × 8.5 cm); base diameter 2½" (6.4 cm). The Museum of Modern Art, New York.

10.28 Pablo Picasso, *Mandolin and Clarinet*, Fall 1913. Painted wood construction with cardboard, paper, and pencil marks, 22⅞ × 14⅛ × 9" (58 × 36 × 23 cm). Musée Picasso, Paris.

Archipenko

Aleksandr Archipenko (1887–1964) has a strong claim to priority as a pioneer Cubist sculptor. Born in Kiev, Ukraine, he studied art in Kiev and Moscow until he went to Paris in 1908. Within two years he was exhibiting his highly stylized figurative sculptures, reminiscent of Gauguin's, with the Cubist painters at the Paris Salons. By 1913 he had established his own sculpture school in the French capital, and his works were shown at Berlin's Der Sturm Gallery and in the New York Armory Show (see chapter 18). In 1913–14 Archipenko adapted the new technique of collage to sculpture, making brightly polychromed constructions from a variety of materials. He based some of the figures from this period on performers he saw at the Cirque Médrano, the circus that had also been one of Picasso's favorite haunts. In *Médrano II*, 1913 (fig. **10.30**), Archipenko assembled a dancing figure from wood, metal, and glass, which he then painted and attached to a back panel, creating a stagelike setting. This work was singled out for praise by Apollinaire in his review of the 1914 Salon des Indépendants. In the manner of constructed sculpture,

10.30 Aleksandr Archipenko, *Médrano II*, 1913. Painted tin, wood, glass, and painted oilcloth, 49⅞ × 20¼ × 12½" (133.2 × 51.4 × 31.8 cm). Solomon R. Guggenheim Museum, New York.

Archipenko articulated volume by means of flat colored planes. Thus, the dancer's entire torso is a single plank of wood to which her appendages are hinged. Her skirt is a conical section of tin joined to a curved pane of glass, on which the artist painted a delicate ruffle. Over the next few years, Archipenko developed this idea of a figure against a backdrop in his so-called sculpto-paintings, which are essentially paintings that incorporate relief elements in wood and sheet metal.

Walking Woman, 1918–19 (fig. **10.31**), typifies Archipenko's later freestanding sculptures. In 1915 he began using the void as a positive element in figurative sculpture, effectively reversing the historic concept of sculpture as a solid surrounded by space. He believed that sculptural form did not necessarily begin where mass encounters space, but "where space is encircled by material." Here the figure is a cluster of open spaces shaped by concave and convex solids. Although Picasso's Cubist constructions were more advanced than those of Archipenko, the latter's Cubist figures had more immediate influence, first because they were more widely exhibited at an early date, and second because they applied Cubist principles to the long-familiar sculptural subject of the human figure, which revealed the implications of mass-space reversals more readily.

10.32 Raymond Duchamp-Villon, *The Horse*, 1914. Bronze (cast c. 1930–31), 40 × 39½ × 22⅜" (101.6 × 100.1 × 56.7 cm). The Museum of Modern Art, New York.

Duchamp-Villon

The great talents of **Raymond Duchamp-Villon** (1876–1918) were cut short by his early death in the war in 1918. He was one of six siblings, four of whom became artists—the other three are Marcel Duchamp and Jacques Villon (whose work is discussed below) and Suzanne Duchamp. In 1900 Duchamp-Villon abandoned his studies in medicine and took up sculpture. At first influenced by Rodin, like nearly all sculptors of his generation, he moved rapidly into the orbit of the Cubists. In his most important work, the bronze *Horse*, in 1914 (fig. **10.32**), the artist endows a preindustrial subject with the dynamism of a new age. Through several versions of this sculpture he developed the image from flowing, curvilinear, relatively representational forms to a highly abstracted representation of a rearing horse. The diagonal planes and spiraling surfaces resemble pistons and turbines as they move, unfold, and integrate space into the mass of the sculpture. "The power of the machine imposes itself upon us to such an extent," Duchamp-Villon wrote, "that we can scarcely imagine living bodies without it." With its energetic sense of forms being propelled through space, *Horse* has much in common with the work of the Italian Futurist Umberto Boccioni, who had visited the studios of Archipenko and Duchamp-Villon in 1912 and whose sculptures (see fig. 11.11) were shown in Paris in 1913.

Lipchitz

Cubism was only one chapter in the long career of **Jacques Lipchitz** (1891–1973), though no other sculptor explored as extensively the possibilities of Cubist syntax in sculpture. Born in Lithuania in 1891 to a prosperous Jewish family,

10.31 Aleksandr Archipenko, *Walking Woman*, 1918–19. Bronze, height 26⅜" (67 cm). Courtesy Frances Archipenko Gray.

Lipchitz arrived in Paris in 1909 and there studied at the École des Beaux-Arts and the Académie Julian. In 1913 he met Picasso and, through the Mexican artist Diego Rivera, began his association with the Cubists. He also befriended a fellow Lithuanian, Chaim Soutine, as well as Amadeo Modigliani, Brancusi, Matisse, and, in 1916, Juan Gris. During this time he developed an abiding interest in the totemic forms of African sculpture. In 1913 he introduced geometric stylization into his figure sculptures and by 1915 was producing a wide variety of Cubist wood constructions as well as stone and bronze works. For Lipchitz, Cubism was a means of reexamining the essential nature of sculptural form and of asserting sculpture as a self-contained entity, rather than an imitation of nature.

In a series of vertical compositions in 1915–16, including *Man with a Guitar* (fig. **10.33**), Lipchitz edged to the brink of abstraction. Conceived as a structure of rigid,

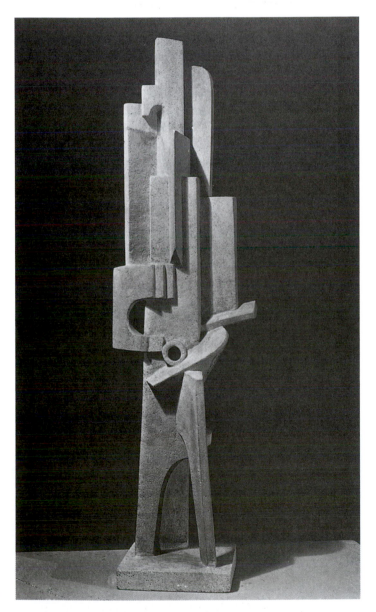

10.33 Jacques Lipchitz, *Man with a Guitar*, 1915. Limestone, 38¼ × 10½ × 7¾" (97.2 × 26.7 × 19.5 cm). The Museum of Modern Art, New York.

intersecting planes, *Man with a Guitar* is an austere rendition of a familiar Cubist theme and was derived from the artist's earlier and more legible wood constructions of detachable figures. Late in life, Lipchitz, who often compared these abstracted sculptures to architecture, wrote about them in his autobiography, *My Life in Sculpture*: "I was definitely building up and composing the idea of a human figure from abstract sculptural elements of line, plane, and volume; of mass contrasted with void completely realized in three dimensions." Lipchitz preferred modeling in clay to carving in stone, and most of his later sculptures, which gradually increased in scale, were developed as clay models and plaster casts that were then cast in bronze or carved in stone by his assistants. A bronze from 1928, *Reclining Nude with Guitar*, shows how the artist was still producing innovative forms within an essentially Cubist syntax. In the blocky yet curving masses of the sculpture, Lipchitz struck a characteristic balance between representation and abstraction by effecting, in his words, "a total assimilation of the figure to the guitar-object." This analogy between the guitar and human anatomy was one already exploited by Picasso. From the thirties to the end of his life, expressiveness became paramount in Lipchitz's sculpture and led to the free, rather baroque modeling of his later works. He moved to the United States to escape World War II in Europe and produced many large-scale public sculptures based on classical and biblical subjects.

Laurens

Henri Laurens (1885–1954) was born, lived, and died in Paris. He was apprenticed in a decorator's workshop and for a time practiced architectural stone carving. By the time of fully developed Analytic Cubism, he was living in Montmartre, immersed in the rich artistic milieu of the expanded Cubist circle in Paris. First introduced to the group by Léger, he was especially close to Gris and Braque, whom he met in 1911. After his initial exposure to Cubism, Laurens absorbed the tenets of the style slowly. His earliest extant constructions and *papiers collés* (two media that are closely related in his oeuvre), date to 1915. Like Archipenko, whose Cubist work he knew well, Laurens excelled at polychromy in sculpture, integrating color into his constructions, low reliefs, and freestanding stone blocks. Referring to the long tradition of color in sculpture from antiquity to the Renaissance, he emphasized its function in reducing the variable effects of light on sculptural surfaces. As he explained, "When a statue is red, blue, or yellow, it remains red, blue, or yellow. But a statue that has not been colored is continually changing under the shifting light and shadows. My own aim, in coloring a statue, is that it should have its own light." His 1918 construction, *Bottle and Glass*, is a very close transcription in three dimensions of the cut and pasted papers of a collage made the previous year. Laurens used concave, convex, and cutout forms to signify volume and void. Thus,

10.34 Henri Laurens, *Guitar and Clarinet*, 1920. Painted limestone, 12⅝ × 14½ × 3½" (36.7 × 36.8 × 8.9 cm). Hirshhorn Museum and Sculpture Garden, Smithsonian Institution, Washington, D.C.

the wine bottle is indicated as both a white cylinder and a cutout silhouette in wood.

By 1919 Laurens had abandoned construction and embarked on a series of still-life sculptures in rough, porous stone. Drawing on his background in architectural stone carving and inspired by his love of French medieval sculpture, he carved *Guitar and Clarinet* (fig. **10.34**), 1920, in very low relief and then reinforced these flattened volumes with delicate, mat color. In both style and iconography, the series has many affinities with Gris's paintings of the same period, as well as Lipchitz's relief sculptures of 1918. After 1920 Laurens relaxed the geometries of his Cubist style, adopting more curvilinear modes devoted to the depiction of the human figure.

An Adaptable Idiom: Developments in Cubist Painting in Paris

In 1911, while Picasso and Braque were working together so closely that it is difficult to distinguish between their works, a number of other emergent Cubist painters in France began to formulate attitudes destined to enlarge the boundaries of the style. Of these, Albert Gleizes and Jean Metzinger also became talented critics and expositors of Cubism. Their book *On Cubism*, published in 1912, was one of the first important theoretical works on the movement. In Paris Gleizes and Metzinger met regularly with Robert Delaunay, Fernand Léger, and Henri Le Fauconnier at the home of the Socialist writer Alexandre Mercereau, at the café Closerie des Lilas and, on Tuesday evenings, at sessions organized by the journal *Vers et prose*. At the café these painters met with older Symbolist writers and younger, enthusiastic critics, such as Guillaume Apollinaire and André Salmon. (They were not, however, close to Cubism's inventors, Braque and Picasso.) In 1911

the group arranged to have their paintings hung together in the Salon des Indépendants. The concentrated showing of Cubist experiments created a sensation, garnering violent attacks from most critics, but also an enthusiastic champion in Apollinaire. That year Archipenko and Roger de La Fresnaye joined the Gleizes–Metzinger group, together with Francis Picabia and Apollinaire's friend, the painter **Marie Laurencin** (1881–1956). Laurencin had portrayed Apollinaire (seated in the center), herself (at the left), Picasso, and his lover Fernande Olivier in her 1908 group portrait (fig. **10.35**), whose naive style is reminiscent of Rousseau.

The three brothers Jacques Villon, Marcel Duchamp, and Raymond Duchamp-Villon, the Czech František Kupka, and the Spaniard Juan Gris were all new additions to the Cubist ranks. In the Salon des Indépendants of 1912 the "Salon Cubists" were so well represented that protests against their influence were lodged in the French parliament. Although Picasso and Braque did not take part in these Salons, their innovations were widely known. By then Cubist art had been shown in exhibitions in Germany, Russia, England, Spain, and the United States. The Italian Futurists, as we shall see, brought an expressionist variant of Cubism back to Italy in 1911. In 1912 Kandinsky published works of Le Fauconnier and other Cubists in his yearbook *Der Blaue Reiter*, and Paul Klee visited the Paris studio of Delaunay. Marc and Macke soon followed.

As these artists began to push the original Cubist concepts in various directions, testing limits in the process, they demonstrated that Cubism was a highly flexible and adaptable idiom. Delaunay was developing his art of "simultaneous contrasts of color" based on the ideas of the color theorist Michel Eugéne Chevreul, who had so strongly influenced Seurat, Signac, and the

10.35 Marie Laurencin, *Group of Artists*, 1908. Oil on canvas, 25½ × 31⅞" (64.8 × 81 cm). The Baltimore Museum of Art.

Neo-Impressionists (see chapter 3). In a large exhibition at the Parisian gallery La Boëtie, held in October 1912 and entitled (probably by Jacques Villon) "Section d'Or" (golden section), entries by Marcel Duchamp, Francis Picabia, and Kupka signaled innovative alternatives to the Cubism of Picasso and Braque.

During 1912 and 1913 Gleizes and Metzinger's *On Cubism* was published, as well as Apollinaire's book *Les Peintres Cubistes* and writings by various critics tracing the origins of Cubism and attempting to define it. Even today, when we are accustomed to the meteoric rise and fall of art movements and styles, it is difficult to appreciate the speed with which Cubism became an international movement. Beginning in 1908 with the isolated experiments of Braque and Picasso, by 1912 it was branching off in new directions and its history was already being written.

Gris

Juan Gris (1887–1927) was born in Madrid but moved permanently to Paris in 1906. While Gris was not one of Cubism's inventors, he was certainly one of its most brilliant exponents. Since 1908 he had lived next to his friend Picasso at the old tenement known as the Bateau Lavoir and had observed the genesis of Cubism, although he was then occupied in making satirical illustrations for French and Spanish journals. However, by 1912 he had produced a masterly and personal interpretation of Cubism with his portrait *Homage to Pablo Picasso*, which is akin to studies of heads made by Picasso in 1909, but which turns the shifting planes and refracted light of Cubism into a regular grid. Such mathematical control was quite unrelated to anything that Picasso, Braque, or the other Cubists had attempted. Gris's sensibility differed significantly from Picasso's: he was not drawn to the primitive, and his work is governed by an overriding refinement and logic. In fact, he later made compositions based on the classical notion of ideal proportion called the golden section.

Gris was closer to Braque and Picasso than were other members of the Cubist circle, and he was aware of their latest working procedures. By 1912 he was making distinctive collages and *papiers collés* with varied textural effects, enhanced by his rich color sense. He tended to avoid Picasso's heterogenous media and subversive approach to representation, preferring to marshal his pasted papers, which he usually applied to canvas, into precise, harmonious arrangements. *The Table*, 1914 (fig. **10.36**), depicting a typical Cubist still-life subject, incorporates Braque's *faux bois*, along with hand-applied charcoal and paper. Although the canvas is rectangular, the objects are contained within an oval format (the table itself is also rectangular) that seems to exist by virtue of a bright, elliptical spotlight. To achieve the layered complexity of this composition, Gris reordered the data of the visible world within at least two independent spatial systems. The foreshortened bottle of wine at the far right (which partially disappears under the *faux-bois* paper) and the open book at the

10.36 Juan Gris, *The Table*, 1914. Pasted and printed papers and charcoal on paper, mounted on canvas, 23½ × 17½" (59.7 × 44.5 cm). Philadelphia Museum of Art.

bottom of the canvas are described as solid volumetric forms and exist in a relatively traditional space, one that positions the viewer above the table, looking down. The open book is drawn, but the text is an actual page from one of Gris's favorite detective novels. Toward the center of the work, a glass, bottle, and book, lightly inscribed in charcoal, are virtually transparent. They tilt at a precarious angle on what appears to be a second wooden table, introducing an altogether new space that is synonymous with the flat, upright surface of the painting. Perhaps the headline in the pasted newspaper, LE VRAI ET LE FAUX CHIC (real and false chic), refers not just to French fashion, but to the illusionistic trickery at play here.

Gris ceased making collages after 1914 but continued to expand his Cubist vocabulary in painting and drawing. In *Still Life and Townscape (Place Ravignan)* (fig. **10.37**) he employed a common Cubist device by mixing alternative types of illusionism within the same picture. In the lower half, a room interior embodies all the elements of Synthetic Cubism, with large, intensely colored geometric planes interlocking and absorbing the familiar collage components: the fruit bowl containing an orange; the newspaper, *Le Journal*; the wine label, "Médoc". However, this foreground pattern of tilted color shapes leads the eye up and back to a window that opens out on a uniformly blue area of simple trees and buildings. Thus the space of the picture shifts abruptly from the ambiguity and

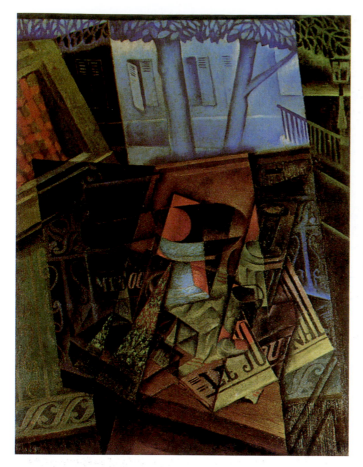

10.37 Juan Gris, *Still Life and Townscape (Place Ravignan)*, 1915. Oil on canvas, 45⅞ × 35⅛" (116.5 × 89.2 cm). Philadelphia Museum of Art.

multifaceted structure of Cubism to the cool clarity of a traditional Renaissance painting structure: the view through the window.

Gris was instrumental in bringing to Cubism a light and color that produced a decorative lyricism. At the end of his short life, however, he was beginning to explore an austere manner in which objects were simplified to elemental color shapes. In *Guitar with Sheet of Music* (fig. **10.38**), a work of 1926, he reduced the familiar objects of Cubist still life to stark, simple shapes and eliminated from his colors the luminous iridescence of earlier works. Here paint is applied as a mat surface that reinforces the sense of architectural structure and at the same time asserts its own nature as paint. The bright primary colors—the blue of the sky, the yellow of the guitar's body, the red of the cloth—are framed by neutral tones. The table and window frame are composed of low-keyed brownish tones that merge imperceptibly, all within the deep shadow of the room. Within this subdued but beautifully integrated color construction the artist has created, through the linear geometry of his edges, a *tour de force* of shifting planes and ambiguous but structured space. The window frame merges at the lower left with the edge of the table. Meanwhile, the diagonal yellow line that bounds the red cloth on the left is drawn perfectly straight, yet is made to bend, visually, by the deeper value of the cloth as it (presumably) folds over the edge of the table. In one of the last works of his brief career, Gris integrates effects of architectural recession, sculptural projection, and flat painted surface into a tightly interlocked pictorial harmony.

10.38 Juan Gris, *Guitar with Sheet of Music*, 1926. Oil on canvas, 25⅝ × 31⅞" (65.1 × 81 cm). Private collection.

10.39 Albert Gleizes, *Harvest Threshing*, 1912. Oil on canvas, 8'10" × 11'7" (2.7 × 3.5 m). Private collection.

Gleizes and Metzinger

The contributions of **Albert Gleizes** (1881–1953) and Metzinger to the Cubist movement are usually overshadowed by the reputation of their theoretical writings, specifically the pioneering book *On Cubism*, in which much of the pictorial vocabulary of Cubism was first elucidated. Gleizes in particular was instrumental in expanding the range of the new art, in both type of subject and attitude toward that subject. His monumental 1912 painting *Harvest Threshing* (fig. **10.39**) opens up to a vast panorama, the generally hermetic world of the Cubists. In its suggestions of the dignity of labor and the harmonious interrelationship of worker and nature, Gleizes explores a social dimension foreign to the unpeopled landscapes of Picasso and Braque. Although the palette remains within the subdued range—grays, greens, and browns, with flashes of red and yellow—the richness of Gleizes's color gives the work romantic overtones suggestive of Jean-François Millet (see fig. 1.19). In his later works, largely a response to the breakthrough *Simultaneous Disk* paintings of Robert Delaunay (see fig. 10.44), Gleizes turned to a form of lyrical abstraction based on curvilinear shapes, frequently inspired by musical motifs.

The early Cubist paintings of **Jean Metzinger** (1883–1956) are luminous variations on Cézanne, whose posthumous 1907 retrospective in Paris left an indelible impression on countless artists. *The Bathers* (fig. **10.40**), no doubt informed by Gris's immediate example, illustrates Metzinger's penchant for a carefully constructed rectangular design, in which the romantic luminosity of the paint plays against the strict geometry of the linear structure. For a time Metzinger toyed with effects derived from the

10.40 Jean Metzinger, *The Bathers*, 1913. Oil on canvas, 58¼ × 41⅞" (148 × 106.4 cm). Philadelphia Museum of Art.

Italian Futurists, later moving easily into the Synthetic Cubist realm of larger shapes and more vivid color. He received his first solo exhibition in 1919 at Léonce Rosenberg's Galerie de l'Effort Moderne in Paris, which was dedicated to a rigorous form of Cubism dubbed "crystal" Cubism, an apt designation for Metzinger's paintings at that time. Toward the end of World War I he began to assimilate photographic images of the figure or architectural scenes into a decorative Cubist frame. His later style, strongly influenced by Fernand Léger's work of the twenties, was an idealized realism for which Cubist pattern was a decorative background—a formula that enmeshed many of the lesser Cubists.

Léger

One almost inevitable development from Cubism was an art celebrating the ever-expanding machine world within the modern metropolis, for the geometric basis of much Cubist painting provided analogies to machine forms. In his 1924–25 essay, *The Machine Aesthetic: Geometric Order and Truth*, **Fernand Léger** (1881–1955) wrote: "Each artist possesses an offensive weapon that allows him to intimidate tradition. I have made use of the machine as others have used the nude body or the still life." Léger was not interested in simply portraying machines, for he opposed traditional realism as sentimental. Rather, he said he wanted to "create a beautiful object with mechanical elements."

Léger was from Normandy, in northwest France, where his family raised livestock. This agrarian background contributed to his later identification with the working classes and to his membership in the Communist Party in 1945. Once he settled in Paris in 1900, Léger shifted his studies from architecture to painting and passed from the influence of Cézanne to that of Picasso and Braque. One of his first major canvases, *Three Nudes in the Forest* (fig. **10.41**), is an unearthly habitation of machine forms and wood-chopping robots. Here Léger seems to be creating a work of art out of Cézanne's cylinders and cones, but it is also clear that he knew the work of artists such as Gleizes and Metzinger. The sobriety of the colors, coupled with the frenzied activity of the robotic figures, whose faceted forms can barely be distinguished from their forest environment, creates an atmosphere symbolic of a new, mechanized world. In 1913 Léger began a series of boldly nonobjective paintings, called Contrastes de Formes (contrasts of forms), featuring planar and tubular shapes composed of loose patches of color within black, linear contours. The metallic-looking forms, which interlock in rhythmical arrangements like the gears of some great machine, give the illusion of projecting toward the viewer. At first these shapes were nonreferential, but the artist later used the same morphology to paint figures and landscapes. Léger's experience as a frontline soldier in World War I was a powerful, transformative event for his life and art. He was struck by the camaraderie of the soldiers in the trenches, and while impressed by the technology of modern warfare, he was stunned by its destructive power. His combat experience strengthened his identification with the common man and reinforced his resolve to abandon abstract painting, dedicating himself to the subjects of contemporary life. With his monumental postwar canvas *The City* (fig. **10.42**), 1919, Léger took another major step in the exploration of reality and the painted surface. In earlier canvases he had modeled his forms heavily, so that they seemed to project out from the surface of the canvas. Now he used the vocabulary of Synthetic Cubist collage to explore a

10.41 Fernand Léger, *Three Nudes in the Forest*, 1909–10. Oil on canvas, 47¼ × 66⅞" (120 × 169.9 cm). Kröller-Müller Museum, Otterlo, the Netherlands.

10.42 Fernand Léger, *The City*, 1919. Oil on canvas, 7'7" × 9'9" (2.3 × 3 m). Philadelphia Museum of Art.

variety of new forms. The rose-colored column in the foreground of *The City* is modeled volumetrically, for example, and some forms, set at an angle with dark edges, suggest tilted planes and the illusion of perspectival depth. On the other hand, forms such as the large stenciled letters are emphatically two-dimensional. Literal elements—machines, buildings, robot figures mounting a staircase, and signs—commingle with abstract shapes to produce fast-tempoed, kaleidoscopic glimpses of the urban industrial world. Léger's later work is discussed in chapter 14.

Other Agendas: Orphism and Other Experimental Art in Paris, 1910–14

Unlike Léger, **Robert Delaunay** (1885–1941) moved rapidly through his apprenticeship to Cubism and by 1912 had arrived at a formula of brilliantly colored abstractions with only the most tenuous roots in naturalistic observation. His restless and inquisitive mind had ranged over the entire terrain of modern art, from the color theories of Chevreul and the space concepts of Cézanne to Braque and Picasso. In 1911 and 1912 he exhibited with Der Blaue Reiter in Munich and at Der Sturm Gallery in Berlin in 1912. This early contact with the German avant-garde, and

10.43 Robert Delaunay, *Eiffel Tower in Trees*, 1910. Oil on canvas, 49⅞ × 36½" (126.7 × 92.7 cm). Solomon R. Guggenheim Museum, New York.

especially the paintings and writings of Kandinsky (see chapter 8), helped to make Delaunay one of the first French artists to embrace abstraction. He also joined the Cubists at the highly controversial Salon des Indépendants of 1911, where Apollinaire declared his painting the most important work in the show. Delaunay avoided the figure and the still life, two of the mainstays of orthodox Cubism, and in his first Cubist paintings took as themes two great works of Parisian architecture: the Gothic church of Saint-Séverin and the Eiffel Tower. He explored his subjects in depth, and each exists in several variations. The series of paintings on the subject of the Eiffel Tower was begun in 1909. Like a work by Cézanne, the 1910 *Eiffel Tower*

in Trees (fig. **10.43**) is framed by a foreground tree, depicted in light hues of ocher and blue, and by a pattern of circular cloud shapes that accentuate the staccato tempo of the painting. The fragmentation of the tower and foliage introduces not only the shifting viewpoints of Cubism, but also rapid motion, so that the tower and its environment seem to vibrate. With his interest in simultaneous views and in the suggestion of motion, Delaunay may be reflecting ideas published by the Futurists in their 1910 manifesto.

Delaunay called his method for capturing light on canvas through color "simultaneity." Like František Kupka, he adapted the color theories of Chevreul to his art. In *Window on the City No. 3*, 1911–12, which belongs to a

10.44 Robert Delaunay, *Simultaneous Contrasts: Sun and Moon*, 1913 (dated 1912 on painting). Oil on canvas, diameter 53" (134.6 cm). The Museum of Modern Art, New York.

series based on views of Paris, Delaunay applied his own variation of Chevreul's simultaneous contrast of colors for the first time. He used a checkerboard pattern of color dots, rooted in Neo-Impressionism and framed in a larger pattern of geometric shapes, to create a dynamic world of fragmented images. This is essentially a work of abstraction, though its origin is still rooted in reality. In the spring of 1912 he began a new series, *Windows*, in which pure planes of color, fractured by light, virtually eliminate any recognizable vestiges of architecture and the observed world. Throughout this period, however, he continued to paint clearly representational works alongside his abstractions.

In his *Disk* paintings of 1913 (fig. **10.44**) Delaunay abandoned even the pretense of subject, creating arrangements of vividly colored circles and shapes. While these paintings, which Delaunay grouped under the title *Circular Forms*, have no overt relationship to motifs in nature, the artist did, according to his wife, Sonia Delaunay, observe the sun and the moon for long periods, closing his eyes to retain the retinal image of the circular shapes. His researches into light, movement, and the juxtaposition of contrasting colors were given full expression in these works.

Born Sonia Stern in a Ukrainian village in 1885, the same year as Robert Delaunay, **Sonia Delaunay** (1885–1979) moved to Paris in 1905. She married Robert in 1910 and, like him, became a pioneer of abstract painting. Her earliest mature works were Fauve-inspired figure paintings, and her first abstract work (fig. **10.45**), dated 1911, was a blanket that she pieced together with scraps of material after the birth of her son. This remarkable object, which Delaunay said was based on examples made by Russian peasant women (and has much in common with the geometric pieced "crazy quilts" of nineteenth-century America), foreshadowed the abstract paintings she had begun to make by 1913. In those paintings, called Simultaneous Contrasts, Delaunay explored the dynamic interaction of brilliant color harmonies. While they had much in common with Robert's work, they gave evidence of a creative personality quite distinct from his. After World War I Sonia Delaunay devoted more time to textile design. When worn, her clothing literally set into motion the geometric patterns she had first explored in 1911. Her highly influential designs were sold throughout America and Europe.

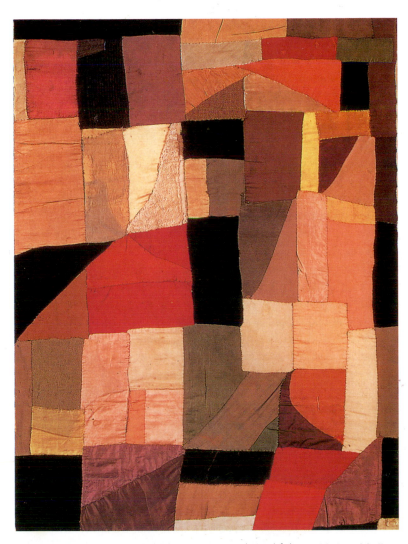

10.45 Sonia Delaunay, *Blanket*, 1911. Appliquéd fabric, 42⅞ × 31⅞" (109 × 81 cm). Musée National d'Art Moderne, Centre National d'Art et de Culture Georges Pompidou, Paris.

Born in the Czech Republic (then Bohemia, in the Austro-Hungarian Empire), **František Kupka** (1871–1957) attended the art academies of Prague and Vienna. The many forces in those cities that shaped his later art include exposure to the spiritually oriented followers of Nazarene art, decorative Czech folk art and other forms of ornament, knowledge of color theory, an awareness of the art of the Vienna Secession, and a lifelong involvement with spiritualism and the occult. Settling in Paris in 1896, he discovered chronophotography and the budding art form of cinematography. These contributed to his notion of an art, still based on the human figure, that suggested a temporal dimension through sequential movement. In this he shared concerns with the Futurists, though he developed his ideas before he saw their work in Paris in 1912.

Throughout his life Kupka was a practicing medium and maintained a profound interest in Theosophy, Eastern religions, and astrology. The visionary, abstract art he developed in Paris, beginning in 1910, was based on his mystical belief that forces of the cosmos manifest themselves as pure rhythmic colors and geometric forms. Such devotion to the metaphysical realm placed him at odds with most of the Cubist art he encountered in Paris. Though he arrived at a nonobjective art earlier than Delaunay, and though he was the first artist to exhibit abstract works in Paris, Kupka was then relatively unknown compared with the Frenchman, and his influence was not immediately felt. In 1911–12, with the painting he entitled *Disks of Newton* (fig. **10.46**), Kupka created an abstract world of vibrating, rotating color circles. While his prismatic circles have much in common with Delaunay's slightly later Simultaneous Disks, it is not entirely clear what these two artists knew of one another's work.

In 1912 Apollinaire named the abstract experiments of Delaunay, Léger, Kupka, and others Orphism, a term that displeased the highly individualistic Kupka. Apollinaire defined the style as one based on the invention of new structures "which have not been borrowed from the visual sphere," though the artists he designated had all relied on the "visual sphere" to some degree. It was, however, a recognition that this art was in its way as divorced as music from the representation of the visual world or literal subject. Kandinsky, it will be recalled, equated his abstract paintings—done at about the same time—with pure musical sensation (see fig. 8.18).

Within a few years of one another, artists at various points on the globe achieved an art of nonrepresentation in which the illusion of nature was completely eliminated and whose end purpose was organization of the artist's means—color, line, space, and their interrelations and expressive potentials. Those artists included Kupka and the Delaunays in France; Kandinsky in Germany; Mikhail Larionov and, subsequently, Kazimir Malevich in Russia; Percy Wyndham Lewis in England; and Piet Mondrian and the artists of de Stijl in the Netherlands. The developments in Russia and the Netherlands, for which the invention and

10.46 František Kupka, *Disks of Newton* (Study for *Fugue in Two Colors*), 1911–12. Oil on canvas, 39⅜ × 29" (100 × 73.7 cm). Philadelphia Museum of Art.

dissemination of Cubist styles were crucial, are examined in chapter 11. The quest for an abstract vocabulary continued during the twenties, but World War I had disrupted creative effort everywhere. New forces and new attitudes were beginning to make themselves felt.

Among the first artists to desert Cubism in favor of a new approach to subject and expressive content was **Marcel Duchamp** (1887–1968), one of the most fascinating, enigmatic, and influential figures in the history of modern art. As previously noted, Duchamp was one of four siblings who contributed to the art of the twentieth century, though none was nearly so significant as Marcel. Until 1910 he worked in a relatively conventional manner based on Cézanne and the Impressionists. In 1911 he painted his two brothers in *Portrait of Chess Players* (fig. **10.47**), obviously after coming under the influence of Picasso and Braque's Cubist explorations. The space is ambiguous and the color is low-keyed and virtually monochromatic, partly because Duchamp painted it by gaslight rather than daylight. The linear rhythms are cursive rather than rectangular, while the figures are characterized by tense energy and individuality; their fragmentation gives them a fantastic rather than a physical presence. Even at the moment when he was learning about Cubism, Duchamp was already transforming it into something entirely different from the conceptions of its creators, producing what leading Cubists regarded as a creative misreading of its principles. The game of chess is a central theme in Duchamp's work. In his later career, when he had publicly stopped making art, chess assumed a role tantamount to artistic activity in his life.

During 1911 Duchamp also painted the first version of *Nude Descending a Staircase*, a work destined to become notorious as a popular symbol of modern art. In the famous second version, 1912 (fig. **10.48**), the androgynous, mechanized figure has been fragmented and multiplied to suggest a staccato motion. Duchamp was fascinated by the art of cinema and by the nineteenth-century chronophotographs of Étienne-Jules Marey, which studied the body's locomotion through stop-action photographs, similar to those of Eadweard Muybridge and Thomas Eakins (see fig. 2.33). Marey placed his subjects in black clothing with light metal strips down the arms and legs that would, when photographed, create a linear graph of their movement. Duchamp similarly indicated the path of his figure's movement with lines of animation and, at the elbow, small white dots. He borrowed the Cubists' reductive palette, painting the figure in what he called "severe wood colors." Cubists on the selection committee for the 1912 Salon des Indépendants objected to the work for its literary title and traditional subject. Duchamp refused to change the title and withdrew his painting from the show. Throughout his life he used and subverted established artistic modes; in *Nude* he freely adapted Cubist means to a peculiarly personal expressive effect. The rapidly descending nude is not a static form analyzed as a grid of

10.48 Marcel Duchamp, *Nude Descending a Staircase, No. 2*, 1912. Oil on canvas, 58 × 35" (147.3 × 88.9 cm). Philadelphia Museum of Art.

10.47 Marcel Duchamp, *Portrait of Chess Players*, 1911. Oil on canvas, 39¾ × 39¾" (101 × 101 cm). Philadelphia Museum of Art.

lines and planes as is, for example, Picasso's *Portrait of Daniel-Henry Kahnweiler* (see fig. 10.18). Instead, by depicting the figure in several successive moments at once, Duchamp implies movement through space. Although the Futurists were also interested in the pictorialization of movement, they regarded the nude as an outdated subject, ill-suited to their celebration of the new industrial age. Duchamp admired some of the works he saw in the first Futurist exhibition held in Paris in February 1912, but he had little sympathy for the group's rhetoric and unrelenting faith in technology. He said that while his painting had some "futuristic overtones," it was clearly more indebted to Cubism. *Nude Descending a Staircase* was shown in New York at the enormous 1913 Armory Show, the first international exhibition of modern art in the United States. The painting outraged American critics; one derided it as an "explosion in a shingle factory." Thanks to this exhibition, by the time Duchamp came to America in 1915 his reputation was already established.

Duchamp was an instinctive Dadaist, an iconoclast in art even before the creation of the Dada movement, so it is natural that he should have been immediately recognized by the first Dadaists and Surrealists as a great forerunner. From an attack on Cubism that involved a new approach to subject, he passed, between 1912 and 1914, to an attack on the nature of subject painting, and finally to a personal reevaluation of the very nature of art. This phase of his career is properly examined in chapter 13.

Duchamp's elder brother Gaston, who took the name Jacques Villon (1875–1963), was at the other extreme from Marcel, a committed Cubist. In 1906 he moved to Puteaux, on the outskirts of Paris, where he had a house that adjoined Kupka's. Puteaux, and particularly Villon's studio, became a remarkable nucleus of Cubist activity (the other being Montmartre, where Picasso and Braque worked) that eventually attracted Villon's brothers, Gleizes, Léger, Picabia, and Metzinger, among others. Villon established a personal, highly abstract, and poetic approach to Cubism, one he maintained throughout his long life. In addition to painting, he also made prints, a medium well suited to his particular Cubist idiom. The crystalline structure of jagged triangular shapes in the drypoint print depicting his sister, *Yvonne D. in Profile*, 1913, is indicated solely through parallel lines. They switch directions and densities, creating volumetric rhythms and a sense of shifting light over the surface.

Francis Picabia (1879–1953) began as a Cubist, though he later turned to Dada (see chapter 13). Until 1912 he was involved with the Cubist activities of Gleizes and Metzinger and exhibited with the Section d'Or, after which he turned to Orphism. In 1913 he spent five months in New York, where his works were included in the Armory Show and where he became a kind of self-appointed spokesman for the European avant-garde. There he met the American photographer Alfred Stieglitz, who gave him a show at his 291 Gallery. (Picabia subsequently contributed to Stieglitz's journal, *Camera Work*.) Upon his return to Paris he made a number of abstract paintings, including *Catch as Catch Can* (fig. **10.49**). The image is supposedly a recollection of having watched a Chinese wrestler one evening in the company of Apollinaire, but the writhing, metallic planes of subdued color hardly coalesce into any identifiable imagery. Picabia abandoned Cubism in 1915, the year that, with Duchamp and Man Ray, he founded the American wing of Dada (see chapter 13).

10.49 Francis Picabia, *Catch as Catch Can*, 1913. Oil on canvas, 39⅝ × 32¼" (100.6 × 81.9 cm). Philadelphia Museum of Art.

11
Futurism, Abstraction in Russia, and de Stijl

The most dramatic and far-reaching development in the history of twentieth-century art is the move toward various forms of explicitly abstract art that followed in the wake of Cubist experiments. Ever since the latter part of the nineteenth century, a number of artists were beginning to consider a painting as an entity unto itself rather than an imitation of, or an illusion of, the physical world. In 1890 the French Symbolist painter Maurice Denis uttered a prophetic statement when he said that a painting, before it is anything else, is "essentially a flat surface covered with colors assembled in a particular order." We saw in chapter 10 that the originators of Cubism, Picasso and Braque, never exploited their style for the purposes of total abstraction. Although their Cubist pictures may represent highly abstracted interpretations of the material world, they were not in themselves abstract. We also saw, however, that other artists schooled in Cubism who were working in Paris, namely Delaunay, Kupka, and, for a time, Léger, made paintings that were not dependent upon recognizable forms. Slightly later in Zurich, the Dada artist Jean Arp was making collages with no discernible source in the real world (see fig. 13.11). Simultaneously, in other art centers in Europe and in the United States, a number of avant-garde artists were abandoning the realm of appearances in pursuit of absolute, pure form. In Russia and the Netherlands, in particular, abstraction found even more fertile ground than in France; it was in these countries that early twentieth-century abstraction found its most expansive and most radical manifestations, with implications not merely for painting and sculpture but for architecture as well as graphic, industrial, and even fashion design. In the hands of these utopian-minded pioneers, abstraction was not simply self-referential, art-for-art's-sake formalism. Rather it represented a powerful new way of perceiving and ultimately transforming the world. The artists fervently believed that art lost none of its expressive power or meaning when divorced from the tangible world. In fact, through the formal expression of pure sensation they hoped to discover a universal visual language able to transcend mundane experience and place the viewer in touch with an alternative, ultimately spiritual world.

Many terms have been employed to describe the non-imitative works of art produced throughout the twentieth century, including abstract, nonobjective, and nonrepresentational. All these terms refer to an art that depends solely on color, line, and shape for its imagery rather than motifs drawn from observable reality.

"Running on Shrapnel": Futurism in Italy

In their paintings and sculptures the Italian Futurist artists sometimes verged on total abstraction, but for the most part they, like the Cubists, drew upon imagery derived from the physical world. Futurism was first of all a literary concept, born in the mind of the poet and propagandist Filippo Tommaso Marinetti in 1908 and announced in a series of manifestos in 1909, 1910, and subsequently. From this point onward, the manifesto was to play a prominent and recurring role in modern art—indeed, it has been described as one of its most characteristic productions. Futurism began as a rebellion of young intellectuals against the cultural torpor into which Italy had sunk during the nineteenth century, when Renaissance and Neoclassical artistic values continued to dominate painting and sculpture, despite the proximity of avant-garde developments in France. As so frequently happens in such movements, the Futurists' manifestos initially focused on what they had to destroy before new ideas could flourish. The first manifesto, written by Marinetti, demanded the destruction of the libraries, museums, academies, and cities of the past, which he called mausoleums. In its wholesale assault on conventional values, it extolled the beauties of revolution, of war, and of the speed and dynamism of machine technology: "A roaring motorcar, which looks as though running on shrapnel, is more beautiful than the *Victory of Samothrace*." Much of the spirit of Futurism reflected the flamboyant personality of Marinetti himself;

rooted in the anarchist and revolutionary fervor of the day, it attacked the ills of an aristocratic and bourgeois society and celebrated progress, energy, and change. By the thirties, unfortunately, such impulses would have dire political consequences.

In late 1909 or early 1910 the painters Umberto Boccioni, Carlo Carrà, and Luigi Russolo joined Marinetti's movement. Later it also included Gino Severini, who had been working in Paris since 1906, and Giacomo Balla. The group drew up a second manifesto in 1910. This again attacked the old institutions and promoted the artistic expression of motion, metamorphosis, and the simultaneity of vision itself. The painted moving object was to merge with its environment, so that no clear distinction could be drawn between the two:

> Everything is in movement, everything rushes forward, everything is in constant swift change. A figure is never stable in front of us but is incessantly appearing and disappearing. Because images persist on the retina, things in movement multiply, change form, follow one another like vibrations within the space they traverse. Thus a horse in swift course does not have four legs: It has twenty, and their movements are triangular.

The targets of the Futurists' critique included all forms of imitation, concepts of harmony and good taste, all art critics, all traditional subjects, tonal painting, and that perennial staple of art, the painted nude.

At this point, the paintings of the various Futurists had little in common. Many of their ideas still came from the unified color patterns of the Impressionists and even more explicitly from the Divisionist techniques of the Neo-Impressionists. But unlike Impressionism, Fauvism, and Cubism, all of which were generated by a steady interaction of theory and practice, Futurism emerged as a full-blown and coherent theory, the illustration of which the artists then set out to realize in paintings. The Futurists

were passionately concerned with the problem of establishing empathy between the spectator and the painting, "putting the spectator in the center of the picture." In this they were close to the German Expressionists (see chapter 8), who also sought a direct appeal to the emotions. Futurist art extolled metropolitan life and modern industry. This did not, however, result in a machine aesthetic in the manner of Léger, since the Italians were concerned with the unrestrained expression of individual ideals, with mystical revelation, and with the articulation of action. Despite their identity of purpose, Futurist art cannot be considered a unified style.

The Futurist exhibition in Milan in May 1911 was the first of the efforts by the new group to make its theories concrete. In the fall of that year, Carrà and Boccioni visited Paris. Severini took them to meet Picasso at his studio, where they no doubt saw the latest examples of Analytic Cubist painting. What they learned is evident in the repainted version of Boccioni's *The Farewells* (fig. **11.1**), a 1911 work that is the first in a trilogy of paintings titled *States of Mind*, about arrivals and departures at a train station. Within a vibrating, curving pattern the artist introduces a Cubist structure of interwoven facets and lines designed to create a sense of great tension and velocity. Boccioni even added the shock of a literal, realistic collage-like element in the scrupulously rendered numbers on the cab of the dissolving engine. It will be recalled that in 1911 Braque and Picasso first introduced lettering and numbers into their Analytic Cubist works (see figs. 10.20, 10.23). Boccioni's powerful encounter with Cubism reinforced his own already developing inclinations, and he fully absorbed the French style into his own dynamic idiom.

An exhibition of the Futurists, held in February 1912 at the gallery of Bernheim-Jeune in Paris, was widely noticed and reviewed favorably by Guillaume Apollinaire himself. It later circulated to London, Berlin, Brussels, the Hague, Amsterdam, and Munich. Within the year, from being an essentially provincial movement in Italy, Futurism suddenly became a significant part of international experimental art.

Balla

The oldest of the group and the teacher of Severini and Boccioni, **Giacomo Balla** (1871–1958) had earlier painted realistic pictures with social implications. He then became a leading Italian exponent of Neo-Impressionism and in this context most strongly influenced the younger Futurists.

Balla's painting *Street Light* (fig. **11.2**) is an example of pure Futurism in the handling of a modern, urban subject. Using V-shaped brushstrokes of complementary colors radiating from the central source of the lamp, he created an optical illusion of light rays translated into dazzling colors so intense that they appear to vibrate. Balla, working in Rome rather than Milan, pursued his own distinctive experiments, particularly in rendering motion through simultaneous views of many aspects of objects. His

11.1 Umberto Boccioni, *States of Mind I: The Farewells*, 1911. Oil on canvas, 27¾ × 37⅞" (70.5 × 96.2 cm). The Museum of Modern Art, New York.

11.2 Giacomo Balla, *Street Light (Lampada—Studio di luce)*, dated 1909 on canvas. Oil on canvas, 68¾ × 45¼" (174.7 × 114.5 cm). The Museum of Modern Art, New York.

11.3 Giacomo Balla, *Dynamism of a Dog on a Leash (Leash in Motion)*, 1912. Oil on canvas, 35 × 45½" (88.9 × 115.6 cm). Albright-Knox Art Gallery, Buffalo.

Dynamism of a Dog on a Leash (fig. **11.3**), with its multiplication of legs, feet, and leash, has become one of the familiar and delightful creations of Futurist simultaneity. The little dachshund scurries along on short legs accelerated and multiplied to the point where they almost turn into wheels. This device for suggesting rapid motion or physical activity later became a cliché of comic strips and animated cartoons. Balla eventually returned to more traditional figure painting.

Bragaglia

Also at work within the ambience of Futurist dynamism was the Italian photographer and filmmaker **Antonio Giulio Bragaglia** (1889–1963), who, like Duchamp and Balla, had been stimulated by the stop-action photographs of Muybridge (see fig. 2.33), Eakins, and Marey. Bragaglia, however, departed from those and shot time exposures of moving forms (fig. **11.4**), creating fluid, blurred images of continuous action. These, he thought, constituted a more accurate, expressive record than a sequence of discrete, frozen moments. In 1913 Bragaglia published a number of his "photodynamic" works in a book entitled *Fotodinamismo Futurista*.

11.4 Antonio Giulio Bragaglia, *The Cellist*, 1913. Gelatin-silver print.

Severini

Living in Paris since 1906, **Gino Severini** (1883–1966), was for several years more closely associated with the growth of Cubism than the other Futurists. Because of his presence in France, he served as a link between his Italian colleagues and French artistic developments. His approach to Futurism is summarized in *Dynamic Hieroglyphic of the Bal Tabarin* (fig. **11.5**), a lighthearted and amusing distillation of Paris nightlife. The basis of the composition lies in Cubist faceting put into rapid motion within large, swinging curves. The brightly dressed chorus girls, the throaty

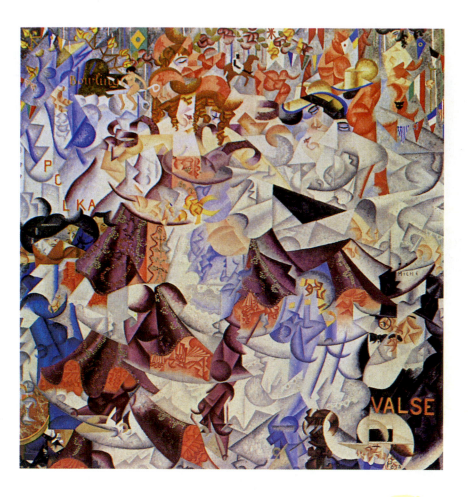

11.5 Gino Severini, *Dynamic Hieroglyphic of the Bal Tabarin*, 1912. Oil on canvas with sequins, 63⅝ × 61½" (161.6 × 156.2 cm). The Museum of Modern Art, New York.

chanteuse, the top-hatted, monocled patron, and the carnival atmosphere are all presented in a spirit of delight, reminding us that the Futurists' revolt was against the deadly dullness of nineteenth-century bourgeois morality. This work is a *tour de force* involving almost every device of Cubist painting and collage, not only the color shapes that are contained in the Cubist grid, but also elements of sculptural modeling that create effects of advancing volumes. Additionally present are the carefully lettered words "Valse," "Polka," "Bowling," while real sequins are added as collage on the women's costumes. The color has Impressionist freshness, its arbitrary distribution a Fauve boldness. Many areas and objects are mechanized and finely stippled in a Neo-Impressionist manner. Severini even included one or two passages of literal representation, such as the minuscule Arab horseman (upper center) and the tiny nude riding a large pair of scissors (upper left).

The sense of fragmented but still dominating reality that persisted in Severini's Cubist paintings between 1912 and 1914 found its most logical expression in a series of works on the subject of transportation, which began with studies of the Paris Métro. With the coming of the war, the theme of the train flashing through a Cubist landscape intrigued Severini as he watched supply trains pass by his window daily, loaded with weapons or troops. *Red Cross Train Passing a Village* (fig. **11.6**), one of several works from the summer of 1915 on this theme, is his response to Marinetti's appeal for a new pictorial expression for the subject of war "in all its marvelous mechanical forms." *Red*

Cross Train is a stylization of motion, much more deliberate in its tempo than *Bal Tabarin*. The telescoped but clearly recognizable train, from which balloons of smoke billow, cuts across the middle distance. Large, handsome planes of strong color (in contrast to the muted palette of Analytic Cubism), sometimes rendered with a Neo-Impressionist brushstroke, intersect the train and absorb it into the painting's total pattern. The effect is static rather than dynamic and is surprisingly abstract in feeling. During these years Severini moved toward a pure abstraction stemming partly from the influence of Robert Delaunay. In *Spherical Expansion of Light (Centrifugal)* he organized what might be called a Futurist abstract pattern of triangles and curves, built up of Neo-Impressionist dots. For some of the works in this series Severini extended the exuberant color dots onto his wooden frame.

In 1916, in stark contrast to his work that preceded it, Severini made a highly naturalistic portrait of his wife nursing their son. He did not immediately follow this direction in his subsequent work, which generally consisted of still lifes in a Synthetic Cubist style. But after 1920 he turned to a highly distilled form of classicism, in which the Cubist fracturing of space gave way to traditional modeling in illusionistic depth.

Carrà

Carlo Carrà (1881–1966) was important in bridging the gap between Italian Futurism and a slightly later Italian movement called the Metaphysical School (see fig. 13.8).

11.6 Gino Severini, *Red Cross Train Passing a Village*, 1915. Oil on canvas, 35¼ × 45¾" (89.5 × 116.2 cm). Solomon R. Guggenheim Museum, New York.

11.7 Carlo Carrà, *Patriotic Celebration (Free-Word Painting)*, 1914. Pasted paper and newsprint on cloth, mounted on wood, 15¼ × 12" (38.7 × 30.5 cm). Private collection.

From 1912, however, Carrà moved steadily toward an orthodox version of Cubism that expressed little of the ideals of speed and dynamism extolled in the Futurist manifestos. He returned to painting the nude, a subject that led him toward a form of massive, sculptural modeling. It was only a short step from this work to the metaphysical painting of Giorgio de Chirico, which Carrà began to investigate around 1916. Meanwhile, in the propagandistic collage *Patriotic Celebration* (fig. **11.7**), Carrà employed radiating colors, words, and letters, Italian flags, and other lines and symbols to extol the king and army of Italy, and to simulate the noises of sirens and mobs. He used these "free words," as Marinetti did, to affect and stimulate the spirit and imagination directly through their visual associations, without the intervention of reason. A similar development was taking place among Russian Futurist poets and artists.

Boccioni

Umberto Boccioni (1882–1916) was perhaps the most talented of the Futurists. In his monumental work *The City Rises* (fig. **11.8**) he sought his first "great synthesis of labor, light, and movement." Dominated by the large, surging figure of a horse before which human figures fall like ninepins, it constitutes one of the Futurists' first major statements: a visual essay on the qualities of violent action, speed, the disintegration of solid objects by light, and their reintegration into the totality of the picture by that very same light.

11.8 Umberto Boccioni, *The City Rises*, 1910. Oil on canvas, 6'6½" × 9'10½" (2 × 3 m). The Museum of Modern Art, New York.

The greatest contribution of Boccioni during the last few years of his short life was the creation of Futurist sculpture. During a visit to Paris in 1912, he went to the studios of Archipenko, Brancusi, and Duchamp-Villon and saw sculpture by Picasso. Immediately upon his return to Milan he wrote the *Technical Manifesto of Futurist Sculpture* (1912), in which he called for a complete renewal of this "mummified art." He began the manifesto with the customary attack on all academic tradition. The attack became specific and virulent on the subject of the nude, which still dominated the work not only of the traditionalists but even of the leading progressive sculptors, Rodin, Bourdelle, and Maillol. Only in the Impressionist sculpture of Medardo Rosso (see fig. 6.15), then the principal Italian sculptor of stature, did Boccioni find exciting innovations. Yet he recognized that, in his concern to capture the transitory moment, Rosso was bound to represent the subject in nature in ways that paralleled those of the Impressionist painters.

Taking off from Rosso, Boccioni sought a dynamic fusion between his sculptural forms and surrounding environment. He emphasized the need for an "absolute and complete abolition of definite lines and closed sculpture. We break open the figure and enclose it in [an] environment." He also asserted the sculptor's right to use any form of distortion or fragmentation of figure or object, and insisted on the use of every kind of material—"glass, wood, cardboard, iron, cement, horsehair, leather, cloth, mirrors, electric lights, etc., etc."

Boccioni's Futurist sculpture and his manifesto were the first of several related developments in three-dimensional art, among them Constructivist sculpture, Dada and Surrealist assemblage, kinetic sculpture, and even the Pop art sculptural environments of the sixties (see figs. 21.22, 21.54). His *Development of a Bottle in Space* (fig. 11.9)

11.9 Umberto Boccioni, *Development of a Bottle in Space*, 1912. Silvered bronze (cast 1931), 15 × 23¾ × 12⅞" (38.1 × 60.3 × 32.7 cm). The Museum of Modern Art, New York.

11.10 Umberto Boccioni, *Table + Bottle + House*, 1912. Pencil on paper, 13⅛ × 9⅜" (33.4 × 23.9 cm). Civico Gabinetto dei Disegni, Castello Sforzesco, Milan.

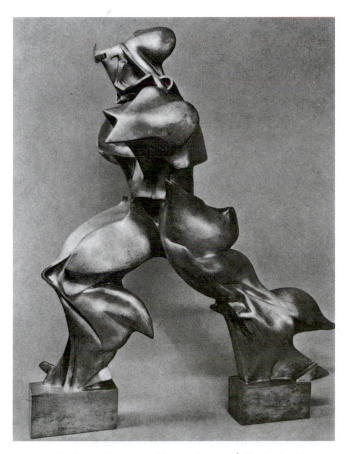

11.11 Umberto Boccioni, *Unique Forms of Continuity in Space*, 1913. Bronze (cast 1931). 43⅞ × 34⅞ × 15¾" (111.2 × 88.5 × 40 cm). The Museum of Modern Art, New York.

enlarged the tradition of the analysis of sculptural space. The bottle is stripped open, unwound, and integrated with an environmental base that makes the homely object, only fifteen inches high, resemble a model for a vast monument. In a related drawing (fig. **11.10**), possibly made in preparation for the sculpture, the forms of a bottle and glass are opened up, set in motion with rotational, curving lines, and penetrated by the flat planes of the table on which they sit.

Boccioni's most impressive sculpture, *Unique Forms of Continuity in Space* (fig. **11.11**), was also his most traditional and the one most specifically related to his paintings. The title suggests that, although the human body may lie at its foundation, the impetus behind Boccioni's sculpture is the coincidence of abstract form. The figure, made up of fluttering, curving planes of bronze, moves essentially in two dimensions, like a translation of his painted figures into relief. It has something in common with the ancient Greek *Victory of Samothrace* so despised by Marinetti: the stances of both figures are similar—a body in dramatic mid-stride, draperies flowing out behind, and arms missing.

Like several of the most talented experimental artists, Boccioni was killed during World War I. After four years during which Europe experienced the horror of mechanized killing on an unprecedented scale, the excitement of combat and the lure of the machine had lost their prewar glamor. Futurism, too, lost much of its impetus, although many of the more propagandistic ideas and slogans were integrated into the rising tide of fascism and used for political and social ends.

A World Ready for Change: Early Abstraction in Russia

In the attempt to evaluate the Russian achievement in the early twentieth century, a number of points must be kept in mind. Since the eighteenth century of Peter and Catherine the Great, Russia had maintained a tradition of royal patronage of the arts and had close ties with the West. Russians who could afford to traveled frequently to France, Italy, and Germany, and through books and periodicals they were aware of new developments in European art. Russian literature and music attained great heights during the nineteenth century, as did theater and ballet, which began to draw on the visual arts in interesting collaborations. Art Nouveau and the ideas of French Symbolists and Post-Impressionist Nabis made themselves widely felt in the late 1880s through the movement known as the World of Art (*Mir Iskusstva*); Russian artists mingled these influences with Byzantine and Russian painting and decorative traditions. There was constant, often heated, debate as to whether Russia should modernize on the western European model or search its own history and folklore for a distinctively Russian route to reform. This division was to inform the development of Russian modernism in its turn.

In 1890, World of Art was joined by Sergei Diaghilev, destined to become perhaps the greatest of all ballet impresarios as well as an enthusiast for modern art in general. A few years later Diaghilev launched his career arranging exhibitions, concerts, theatrical, and operatic performances, and ultimately the Ballets Russes, which opened in Paris in 1909 and went from success to success. From then on, Diaghilev drew on many of the greatest names in European painting to create his stage sets.

After the *World of Art* periodical, first published in 1898, came other avant-garde journals. Reading these journals was yet another way that Russian artists could watch and absorb the progress of Fauvism, Cubism, Futurism, and their offshoots. Great collections of the new French art were formed by the enlightened collectors Sergei Shchukin and Ivan Morozov in Moscow. By 1914, Shchukin's collection contained more than two hundred works by French Impressionist, Post-Impressionist, Fauve, and Cubist painters, including more than fifty by Picasso and Matisse. Morozov's collection included Cézannes, Renoirs, Gauguins, and many works by Matisse. Both Shchukin and Morozov were generous in opening their collections to Russian artists, and the effect of the Western avant-garde on these creative individuals was incalculable. Through such modern art collections and the exhibitions of the Jack of Diamonds group, an alternative exhibition society founded in 1910 in Moscow, Cubist experiments were known in St. Petersburg and Moscow almost as soon as they were inaugurated. By the time Marinetti, whose Futurist manifesto had long been available in Russia, visited Russia in 1914, the Futurist movement in that country was in full force.

Only since the eighties, and especially following the dissolution of the Soviet Union in 1991, has scholarship on early twentieth-century Russian avant-garde art really come into its own. Before that time, study of Russian modernism was restricted and sometimes suppressed; Western scholars in particular were often denied access to archival materials and works of art during the Cold War. Official hostility to modernism dated back to the government of the Soviet leader Joseph Stalin, who, in 1932, decreed that Socialist Realism (naturalistic art that celebrated the worker) was the only acceptable form of art. The kinds of small, independent art groups that had until then flourished in Russia, particularly among the avant-garde, were proscribed, and paintings by many of the greatest artists were relegated to storerooms or even destroyed. Such was the fate of the works of Kazimir Malevich, for example, who, unlike many of his contemporaries, chose not to leave the country after Stalin's rise to power. Though known in the West through works that had been acquired by foreign collectors and institutions, his paintings had not been seen in Russia for decades when they were at last exhibited there in 1988.

Larionov, Goncharova, and Rayonism
Lifelong companions and professional collaborators, **Mikhail Larionov** (1881–1964) and **Natalya Sergeyvna Goncharova** (1881–1962) are among the earliest propo-

11.12 Mikhail Larionov, *Rayonist Composition*, 1916. Gouache on paper, 21¼ × 17⅝" (54 × 45 cm). Private collection.

11.13 Natalya Sergeyvna Goncharova, *Linen*, 1912. Oil on canvas, 35 × 27½" (89 × 70 cm). Tate Gallery, London.

11.14 Natalya Sergeyvna Goncharova, *Icon Painting Motifs*, 1912. Watercolor on cardboard, 19½ × 13⅜" (49.5 × 34.6 cm). State Tretyakov Gallery, Moscow.

nents of the Russian avant-garde. Larionov was a founding member of the Jack of Diamonds group in 1910, but by the following year he and Goncharova had left it and formed a rival organization, the Donkey's Tail, claiming the need for a contemporary Russian art that drew less from western Europe (since the Jack of Diamonds exhibitions included work by western European artists) and more from indigenous artistic traditions. (Nevertheless, in 1912 they both participated in the second Blaue Reiter exhibition in Munich, as well as in a historic Post-Impressionist show in London.) They turned to Russian icons and *lubok* (folk) prints for inspiration and made works in what they termed a Neo-Primitive style. In 1912 Larionov created Rayonism based on his studies of optics and theories about how intersecting rays of light reflect off the surface of objects (fig. **11.12** is a work from 1916). Rayonist works were first shown in December 1912 and then in a 1913 exhibition called The Target. Although Rayonism was indebted to Cubism, and also related to Italian Futurism in its emphasis on dynamic, linear forms, Larionov and his circle emphasized its Russian origins. His paintings were among the first nonobjective works of art made in Russia. In them Larionov sought to merge his studies of nineteenth-century color theories with more recent scientific experiments (such as radiation). His 1913 manifesto titled *Rayonism*, which extolled this style as the "the true liberation of painting," was the first published discourse in Russia on nonobjectivity in art.

Like Larionov, Goncharova was drawn to ancient Russian art forms. In addition to icons and *lubok* prints, she studied traditional examples of embroidery. This nonhierarchical distinction between craft and "high" art is a key characteristic of the Russian avant-garde and is perhaps one of the reasons why so many women had positions at the artistic forefront equal to those of their male colleagues. After her Neo-Primitive phase, Goncharova produced paintings in a Futurist and Rayonist vein. Her colorful 1912 canvas *Linen* (fig. **11.13**) reveals a knowledge of Cubist painters such as Gleizes and Metzinger, but the cyrillic letters add a distinctively Russian touch. She also continued to make paintings in a folk style, as can be seen in *Icon Painting Motifs* (fig. **11.14**). The conceptual nature of such images explains, to some degree, how an ancient heritage of icons and flat-pattern design prepared Russians to accept total abstraction.

Larionov and Goncharova left Russia in 1915 to design for Diaghilev. They settled in Paris, became French citizens in 1938, and married in 1955. Neither artist produced more than a few significant Rayonist paintings, but their ideas were instrumental for an art that synthesized Cubism, Futurism, and Orphism and that contained "a sensation of the fourth dimension." This pseudo-scientific concept of a fourth spatial dimension, popularized by scientists, philosophers, and spiritualists gained currency among the avant-garde across Europe and in the United States in the early twentieth century.

Popova and Cubo-Futurism

One of the strongest artists to emerge within the milieu of the prerevolutionary Russian avant-garde was the tragically short-lived **Lyubov Popova** (1889–1924), whose sure hand and brilliant palette are evident even in her earliest work. The daughter of a wealthy bourgeois family, Popova was able to travel extensively throughout her formative years, visiting Paris in 1912 and studying under the Cubists Le Fauconnier and Metzinger. In 1913 she began working in the studio of the Constructivist Vladimir Tatlin (see figs. 11.24, 11.25). She also knew Goncharova and Larionov and like them was interested in Russian medieval art. When war broke out in 1914, Popova was in Italy, whence she returned to Russia and resumed working in Tatlin's studio. Unlike Tatlin, she was not concerned with the construction of objects in space, but rather found her expressive mode in painting. She developed a mature Cubo-Futurist style (the term is Malevich's, see below), showing a complete assimilation of Western pictorial devices into her own dynamic idiom. Her still life *Subject from a Dyer's Shop* (fig. **11.15**) contains a rich chromatic scheme that probably reflects her study of Russian folk art. Here the Cubist-derived language of integrated, pictorialized form and space may have received its most authoritative expression outside the oeuvre of the two founding Cubists themselves. In late 1915 or early 1916, partly in response to Malevich's Suprematist canvases, Popova began to compose totally abstract paintings that she called Painterly Architectonics. In these powerful compositions she paid increasing attention to building up her paint surfaces with strong textures.

In the aftermath of the 1917 October Revolution, Russian artists were involved in serious debate about the appropriate nature of art under the new communist regime. Constructivist artists abandoned traditional media such as painting and dedicated themselves to "production art." Their intention was to merge art with technology in products that ranged from utilitarian household objects to textile design, propagandistic posters, and stage sets for political rallies. Popova, who renounced easel painting in 1921, made designs for the theater, including a 1922 set for *The Magnanimous Cuckold* (fig. **11.16**), a play staged by Vsevolod Meyerhold, one of the leading figures of avant-garde theater. The set was organized according to the principles that informed Popova's abstract paintings. Like a large Constructivist environment, it consisted of arrangements of geometric shapes within a structure of horizontal and vertical elements.

11.15 Lyubov Popova, *Subject from a Dyer's Shop*, 1914. Oil on canvas, 27¾ × 35" (70.5 × 88.9 cm). The Museum of Modern Art, New York.

11.16 Lyubov Popova, Stage design for Vsevolod Meyerhold's *The Magnanimous Cuckold*, 1922. India ink, watercolor, paper collage, and varnish on paper, 19¾ × 27¼" (50.2 × 69.2 cm). State Tretyakov Gallery, Moscow.

Malevich and Suprematism

More than any other individual, even Delaunay or Kupka, it was **Kazimir Malevich (1878–1935) who took Cubist geometry to its most radical conclusion**. Malevich studied art in Moscow, where he visited the collections of Shchukin and Morozov. He was painting outdoors in an Impressionist style by 1903 and for a brief time experimented with the Neo-Impressionist technique of Seurat. In 1910 he exhibited with Larionov and Goncharova in the first Jack of Diamonds show in Moscow and subsequently joined their rival Donkey's Tail exhibition in which he exhibited Neo-Primitivist paintings of heavy-limbed peasants in bright Fauvist colors. By 1912 he was painting in a Cubist manner. In *Morning in the Village after a Snowstorm* (fig. **11.17**) cylindrical figures of peasants move through a mechanized landscape, with houses and trees modeled in light, graded hues of red, white, and blue. The snow is organized into sharp-edged metallic-looking mounds. The resemblance to Léger's earlier machine Cubism is startling (see fig. 10.41), but it is questionable whether either man saw the other's early works for, unlike some of his colleagues, Malevich never traveled to Paris.

For the next two years he explored different aspects and devices of Cubism and Futurism. He called his highly personalized amalgamation of the two styles Cubo-Futurism. In 1913 he designed Cubo-Futurist sets and costumes for *Victory over the Sun*, an experimental performance billed as the "First Futurist Opera". This highly unorthodox opera, staged twice in St. Petersburg, anticipated the early Dada performances that took place in Zurich in 1916 (see fig. 13.10). The actors were mostly nonprofessionals who recited or sang their lines, accompanied by an out-of-tune piano. The nonnarrative texts of *Victory over the Sun* were called *zaum*, meaning "transrational" or "beyond-the-mind," and were intended to divest words of all conventional meaning. In 1913–14 Malevich created visual analogues to these semantic experiments in a number of paintings, labeling the style Transrational Realism. Through the juxtaposition of disparate elements in his compositions, he mounted a protest "against logic and philistine meaning and prejudice." In certain paintings of 1914, autonomous colored planes emerge from a matrix of Cubo-Futurist forms. In Malevich's abstract work of the following year, these planes came to function as entirely independent

11.17 Kazimir Malevich, *Morning in the Village after a Snowstorm*, 1912. Oil on canvas, 31¾ × 31⅞" (80.6 × 80.9 cm). Solomon R. Guggenheim Museum, New York.

forms suspended on a white ground. "In the year 1913," the artist wrote, "in my desperate attempt to free art from the burden of the object, I took refuge in the square form and exhibited a picture which consisted of nothing more than a black square on a white field." Like Larionov (and a number of modern artists, for that matter), Malevich had a tendency to date his paintings retrospectively and assign them impossibly early dates. It was not until 1915 that he unveiled thirty-nine totally nonrepresentational paintings, whose style he called Suprematism, at a landmark exhibition in Petrograd (now St. Petersburg) called 0, 10 (Zero–Ten): The Last Futurist Exhibition (fig. **11.18**). Included in the exhibition was the painting *Black Square*, hung high across the corner of the room in the traditional place of a Russian icon. This emblem of Suprematism, the most reductive, uncompromisingly abstract painting of its time, represented an astonishing conceptual leap from Malevich's work of the previous year. In his volume of essays entitled *The World of Nonobjectivity*, the artist defined Suprematism as "the supremacy of pure feeling in creative art." "To the Suprematist," he wrote, "the visual phenomena of the objective world are, in themselves, meaningless; the significant thing is feeling, as such, quite apart from the environment in which it is called forth."

As with Kandinsky and his first abstract paintings (see fig. 8.18), the creation of this simple square on a plain ground was a moment of spiritual revelation to Malevich. For the first time in the history of painting, he felt, it had been demonstrated that a painting could exist completely independent of any reflection or imitation of the external world—whether figure, landscape, or still life. Actually, of course, he had been preceded by Delaunay, Kupka, and Larionov in the creation of abstract paintings, and he was certainly aware of their efforts, as well as those of Kandinsky, who moved to largely nonobjective imagery in late 1913. Malevich, however, can claim to have carried

11.19 Kazimir Malevich, *Suprematist Composition: White Square on White*, 1918. Oil on canvas, 31¼ × 31¼" (79.4 × 79.4 cm). The Museum of Modern Art, New York.

abstraction to an ultimate geometric simplification—the black square. Here, he taught, was a new beginning that corresponded to the social transformation occurring around him in the years leading up to the Russian Revolution. It is noteworthy that the two dominant wings of twentieth-century abstraction—the painterly Expressionism of Kandinsky and the hard-edged geometric purity of Malevich—should have been founded by two Russians. And each of these men had a conviction that his discoveries were spiritual visions rooted in the traditions of Old Russia.

In his attempts to define this new Suprematist vocabulary, Malevich tried many combinations of rectangle, circle, and cross, oriented vertically and horizontally. His passionate curiosity about the expressive qualities of geometric shapes next led him to arrange clusters of colored rectangles and other shapes on the diagonal in a state of dynamic tension with one another. This arrangement of forms implied continuous motion in a field perpetually charged with energy. Malevich established three stages of Suprematism: the black, the red or colored, and the white. In the final phase, realized in monochromatic paintings of 1917 and 1918 (fig. **11.19**), the artist achieved the ultimate stage in the Suprematist ascent toward an ideal world and a complete renunciation of materiality, for white symbolized the "real concept of infinity." This example displays a tilted square of white within the canvas square of a somewhat different shade of white—a reduction of painting to the simplest relations of geometric shapes.

Malevich understood the historic importance of architecture as an abstract visual art and in the early twenties, when he had temporarily abandoned painting, he experimented with drawings and models in which he studied the problems of form in three dimensions and crafted

11.18 Kazimir Malevich, Installation photograph of his paintings in 0, 10 (Zero–Ten): The Last Futurist Exhibition in Petrograd (St. Petersburg), December 1915.

visions of Suprematist cities, planets, and satellites suspended in space. His abstract three-dimensional models, called Arkhitektons, were significant to the growth of Constructivism in Russia and, transmitted to Germany and western Europe by his disciples, notably El Lissitzky, influenced the design teachings of the Bauhaus (see chapters 16 and 17).

In the twenties Malevich's idealist views were increasingly at odds with powerful conservative artistic forces in the Soviet Union who promoted Socialist Realism as the only genuine proletarian art. Eventually, this style was officially established as the only legitimate form of artistic expression. By the end of 1926 Malevich was dismissed from his position as director of GINKhUK, the Institute of Artistic Culture, and in 1930 he was even imprisoned for two months and interrogated about his artistic philosophy. In his late work Malevich returned to figurative style, though in several works between 1928 and 1932 he combined echoes of his early Cubo-Futurist work with Suprematist concepts. Perhaps the empty landscapes and faceless automaton figures of the last years express, as one discerning critic wrote in 1930, "the 'machine' into which man is being forced—both in painting and outside it."

El Lissitzky's Prouns

Of the artists emerging from Russian Suprematism the most influential internationally was **El (Eleazar) Lissitzky**, (1890–1941) who studied architectural engineering in Germany. On his return to Russia at the outbreak of World War I, Lissitzky took up a passionate interest in the revival of Jewish culture, illustrating books written in Yiddish and organizing exhibitions of Jewish art. Like Marc Chagall, he was a major figure in the Jewish Renaissance in Russia around the time of the 1917 Revolution, which brought about the fall of the Czarist regime. In 1919 Chagall appointed Lissitzky to the faculty of an art school in Vitebsk that he headed. There Lissitzky, much to the disappointment of Chagall, became a disciple of the art of another faculty member, Malevich, developing his own form of abstraction, which he called Prouns (fig. **11.20**). The exact origin of this neologism is unclear, but it may be an acronym for "Project for the Affirmation of the New" in Russian. Lissitzky's Prouns are diverse compositions made up of two- and three-dimensional geometric shapes floating in space. The forms, sometimes depicted axonometrically, represent the artist's extension of Suprematist theories into the realm of architecture. Indeed, Lissitzky extended the Proun literally into the third dimension in 1923 with his *Prounenraum (Proun Room)* (fig. **11.21**), consisting of painted walls and wood reliefs in a room that the viewer was to walk through in a counterclockwise direction. The artist wanted the walls to dissolve visually to allow the Proun elements to activate the space. The room was destroyed, but was reconstructed from Lissitzky's original documents for an exhibition in the Netherlands in 1965.

11.20 El Lissitzky, *Construction 99 (Proun 99)*, 1924–25. Oil on wood, 50½ × 38¾" (128.3 × 98.4 cm). Yale University Art Gallery, New Haven.

11.21 El Lissitzky, *Prounenraum* (Proun Room), created for Berlin Art Exhibition. 1923, reconstructed 1965. Wood, 9'10⅛" × 9'10⅛" × 8'6⅜" (3 × 3 × 2.6 m). Stedelijk Van Abbemuseum, Eindhoven, the Netherlands.

11.22 El Lissitzky, *The Constructor (Self-Portrait)*, 1924. Gelatin-silver print, 4½ × 4⅞" (11.3 × 12.5 cm). Stedelijk Van Abbemuseum, Eindhoven, the Netherlands.

Lissitzky left Moscow in 1921 for Berlin, where he was associated with the Dutch abstractionist Theo van Doesburg and the Hungarian László Moholy-Nagy. He was one of the key artists who brought together Russian Suprematism and Constructivism, Dutch de Stijl, and the German Bauhaus and who, through Moholy-Nagy, later transmitted these ideas to a generation of students in the United States and elsewhere. In 1925 Lissitzky resettled permanently in Moscow, where in the thirties he became an effective propagandist for the Stalinist regime. Once he abandoned abstraction, he made photographs as well as typographic, architectural, and exhibition designs. Among his most memorable images is a photographic self-portrait from 1924, *The Constructor* (fig. **11.22**). In a double exposure, the artist's face is superimposed on an image of his hand holding a compass over grid paper—a reminder of his role as an architect.

Kandinsky in the Early Soviet Period

As we saw in our discussion of Der Blaue Reiter (see chapter 8), Vasily Kandinsky was a great figure in the transmission of Russian experiments in abstraction and construction to the West. Forced by the outbreak of war to leave Germany, he went back to Russia in 1914. In the first years after the Russian Revolution, the new Soviet government actively encouraged experimentalism and new forms in the arts to coincide with the new society communism was attempting to construct. In 1918 Kandinsky was invited by Tatlin to join the Department of Visual Arts

(IZO) of Narkompros (NKP, the People's Commissariat for Enlightenment) in Moscow, and subsequently helped to reorganize Russian provincial museums. He remained in revolutionary Russia for seven years but eventually found his spiritual conception of art coming into conflict with the utilitarian doctrines of the ascendant Constructivists. In 1921 he left the Soviet Union for good, conveying many of his and his colleagues' innovations to the new Bauhaus School in Weimar, Germany.

Meanwhile, until 1920, Kandinsky continued to paint in the manner of free abstraction that he had first devised during the period 1910–14 (see figs. 8.17, 8.18). That year he began to introduce, in certain paintings, regular shapes and straight or geometrically curving lines. During 1921 the geometric patterns began to dominate, and the artist moved into another major phase of his career. There can be no doubt that Kandinsky had been affected by the geometric abstractions of Malevich, Aleksandr Rodchenko, Tatlin, and the Constructivists. Despite the change from free forms to color shapes with smooth, hard edges, the tempo of the paintings remained rapid, and the action continued to be the conflict of abstract forms. *White Line, No. 232* (fig. **11.23**) is a transitional work: the major color areas are still painted in a loose, atmospheric manner, but they are accented by sharp, straight lines and curved forms in strong colors.

Utopian Visions: Russian Constructivism

The word *Konstruktivizm* (Constructivism) was first used by a group of Russian artists in the title of a small 1922 exhibition of their work in Moscow. It is a term that has been applied broadly in a stylistic sense to describe a Cubist-based art that was developed in many countries. In general, that art is characterized by abstract, geometric forms and a technique in which various materials, often industrial in nature, are assembled rather than carved or modeled. But Constructivism originally referred to a movement of Russian artists after the 1917 Revolution who enlisted art in the service of the new Soviet system. These artists believed that a full integration of art and life would help foster the ideological aims of the new society and enhance the lives of its citizens. Such utopian ideals were common to many modernist movements, but only in Russia were the revolutionary political regime and the revolution in art so closely linked. The artists not only made constructed objects, but were major innovators in such areas as typographic design, textiles, furniture, and theatrical design (see figs. 11.27, 11.29, 11.31). The 1917 Revolution initially gave a huge boost to modernism in Russia as experimental art and the new social order

11.23 Vasily Kandinsky, *White Line, No. 232*, 1920. Oil on canvas, 38⅝ × 31½" (98.1 × 80 cm). Museum Ludwig, Cologne.

seemed for a time to be marching in step. The head of the new People's Commissariat for Enlightenment Anatoly Lunacharsky—a man described by Lenin as possessing "a sort of French brilliance"—eagerly involved avant-garde artists at every level of the revolutionary cultural program.

Innovations in Sculpture

Constructivism was one of the significant new concepts to develop in twentieth-century sculpture. From the beginning of its history, sculpture had involved a process of creating form by taking away from the amorphous mass of the raw material (the carving of wood or stone), or by building up the mass (modeling in clay or wax, that would later be cast in metal). These approaches presuppose that sculpture is mainly an art of mass rather than of space. Traditional techniques persisted well into the twentieth century, even in the work of so revolutionary a figure as Brancusi (see chapter 9). The first Cubist sculpture of Picasso, the 1909 *Woman's Head* (see fig. 10.15), with its deep faceting of the surface, still respected the central mass.

True constructed sculpture, in which the form is assembled from elements of wood, metal, plastic, and other materials such as found objects, was a predictable consequence of the Cubists' experiments in painting. Even before Picasso, however, Braque made Cubist construction sculptures from pieces of paper and cardboard. Though the works have not survived, an early photograph shows a constructed still life mounted across a corner of the artist's studio (see fig. 10.26). It is tantalizing (but speculative) to think that Tatlin may have seen such a work during his trip to Paris, before embarking on his *Counter-Reliefs*. Picasso's 1912 *Guitar* and 1913 *Mandolin and Clarinet* (see figs. 10.27, 10.28) are groundbreaking Cubist constructions of cardboard, wire, string, and wood.

The subsequent development of constructed sculpture, particularly in its direction toward complete abstraction, took place outside France. Boccioni's Futurist sculpture manifesto of 1912 recommended the use of unorthodox materials, but his actual constructed sculpture remained tied to literal or Cubist subjects. Archipenko's constructed *Médrano* figures (see fig. 10.30), executed between 1912 and 1914, were experiments in space–mass reversals, but the artist never deserted the subject—figure or still life—and soon reverted to a form of Cubist sculpture modeled in clay for casting in bronze.

In France and Italy the traditional techniques of sculpture—modeling, carving, bronze casting—were probably too powerfully imbedded to be overthrown, even by the leaders of the modern revolution. Sculptors who had attended art schools—Brancusi and Lipchitz for example—were trained in technical approaches unchanged since the eighteenth century. Modern sculpture there emerged from the Renaissance tradition more gradually than modern painting. Possibly as a consequence of this evolutionary rather than revolutionary process, even the experimentalists continued to utilize traditional techniques.

The translation of Cubist collage into three-dimensional abstract construction was achieved in Russia first, then in Holland and Germany.

Tatlin

The founder of Russian Constructivism was **Vladimir Tatlin** (1895–1953). In 1914 he visited Berlin and Paris, where he saw Cubist paintings in Picasso's studio, as well as the constructions in which Picasso was investigating the implications of collage for sculpture. The result, on Tatlin's return to Russia, was a series of reliefs constructed from wood, metal, and cardboard, with surfaces coated with plaster, glazes, and broken glass. His exhibition of these works in his studio was among the first manifestations of Constructivism, just as the reliefs were among the first complete abstractions, constructed or modeled, in the history of sculpture. Tatlin's constructions, like Malevich's Suprematist paintings, were to exert a profound influence on the course of Constructivism in Russia.

Most of Tatlin's first abstract reliefs have disappeared, and the primary record of them is a number of drawings and photographs that document his preoccupation with articulating space. The so-called *Counter-Reliefs*, begun in 1914, were released from the wall and suspended by wires across the corner of a room (again, the location in Russian homes for icons), as far removed from the earthbound tradition of past sculpture as the technical resources of the

11.24 Vladimir Tatlin, *Counter-Relief*, 1915. Iron, copper, wood, and rope, 28 × 46½" (71 × 118 cm). Reconstruction. State Russian Museum, St. Petersburg.

11.25 Vladimir Tatlin, Model for *Monument to the Third International*, 1919–20. Wood, iron, and glass, 20' (6.09 m). State Russian Museum, St. Petersburg.

artist permitted. One of these reliefs (fig. **11.24**) has been assembled from Tatlin's original parts in St. Petersburg's State Russian Museum. Because the reliefs are made from ordinary materials, rather than traditional sculptural media such as bronze or marble, and because they are not isolated on a base, they tend to inhabit the space of the viewer more directly than conventional sculpture.

Tatlin developed a repertoire of forms in keeping with what he believed to be the properties of his chosen materials. According to the principles of what he called the "culture of materials" and "truth to materials," each substance, through its structural laws, dictates specific forms, such as the flat geometric plane of wood, the curved shell of glass, and the rolled cylinder or cone of metal. For a work of art to have significance, Tatlin came to believe that these principles must be considered in both the conception and the execution of the work, which would then embody the laws of life itself.

Like many avant-garde artists, Tatlin embraced the Russian Revolution. Thereafter, he cultivated his interest in engineering and architecture, an interest that saw its most ambitious result in his twenty-foot-high (over 6 m)

model for a *Monument to the Third International* (fig. **11.25**), which was exhibited in Petrograd (St. Petersburg) and Moscow in December 1920. Had the full-scale project been built, it would have been approximately thirteen hundred feet high, much taller than the Eiffel Tower and the biggest sculptural form ever conceived at that time. It was to have been a metal spiral frame tilted at an angle and encompassing a glass cylinder, cube, and cone. These glass units, housing conferences and meetings, were to revolve, making a complete revolution once a year, once a month, and once a day, respectively. The industrial materials of iron and glass and the dynamic, kinetic nature of the work symbolized the new machine age. The tower was to function as a propaganda center for the Communist Third International, an organization devoted to the support of world revolution, and its rotating, ascending spiral form was a symbol of the aspirations of communism and, more generally, of the new era. It anticipated, and in scale transcended, all subsequent developments in constructed sculpture encompassing space, environment, and motion and has come to embody the ideals of Constructivism.

After the consolidation of the Soviet system in the twenties, Tatlin readily adapted his nature-of-materials philosophy to the concept of production art, which held that in the classless society art should be rational, utilitarian, easily comprehensible, and socially useful, both aesthetically and practically. At its best this idealist doctrine inspired artists to envision a world in which even the most mundane objects would be beautifully designed. But as the Soviet authorities grew intolerant of the radical artistic idealism that had flourished in the early years of the new order, and Socialist Realism became the official style, the ideals of production art turned to dogma. Socialist Realism worked tragically against such spiritually and aesthetically motivated artists as Malevich and Kandinsky, driving the latter out of Russia altogether. Tatlin, dedicated to Constructivist principles, went on to direct various important art schools and enthusiastically applied his immense talent to designing workers' clothing, furniture, and even a Leonardesque flying machine called the *Letatlin*.

Rodchenko

By 1915–16, **Aleksandr Rodchenko** (1891–1956) had become familiar with the work of Malevich and Tatlin and he soon began to make abstract paintings and to experiment with constructions. By 1920 he, like Tatlin, was turning more and more to the idea that the artist could serve the revolution through a practical application of art in engineering, architecture, theater, and industrial and graphic design. In his *Construction of Distance* he massed rectangular blocks in a horizontal–vertical grouping as abstract as a Neo-Plastic painting by Mondrian (see below) and suggestive of the developing forms of the International Style in architecture (see chapter 16). Moreover, Rodchenko's example later proved highly relevant to Minimalist artists working in the United States in

11.26 Aleksandr Rodchenko, *Hanging Construction*, 1920. Wood. Location unknown.

the sixties (see fig. 22.54). His *Hanging Construction* (fig. **11.26**) is a nest of concentric circles, which move slowly in currents of air. The shapes, cut from a single piece of plywood, could be collapsed after exhibition and easily stored. Rodchenko also made versions (none of which survives) based on a triangle, a square, a hexagon, and an ellipse. This creation of a three-dimensional object with planar elements reveals the Constructivists' interest in mathematics and geometry. It is also one of the first works of constructed sculpture to use actual movement, in a form suggestive of the fascination with space travel that underlay many of the ideas of the Constructivists. Apparently Rodchenko liked to shine lights on the constructions so that they would reflect off the silver paint on their surfaces, enhancing the sense of dematerialization in the work.

Rodchenko was ardently committed to the Soviet experiment. After 1921 he devoted himself to graphic, textile, and theater design. His advertising poster from 1924 (fig. **11.27**) typifies the striking typographical innovations of the Russian avant-garde. Rodchenko also excelled at photography. Commenting on images like the one reproduced here, he wrote in 1928:

> In photography there is the old point of view, the angle of vision of a man who stands on the ground and looks straight ahead or, as I call it, makes 'bellybutton' shots. … The most interesting angle shots today are those 'down from above' and 'up from below,' and their diagonals.

11.27 Aleksandr Rodchenko, Untitled advertising poster, 1924. Gouache and photomontage on paper, 27½ × 33⅞" (69.7 × 86.1 cm). Rodchenko-Stepanova Archive, Moscow.

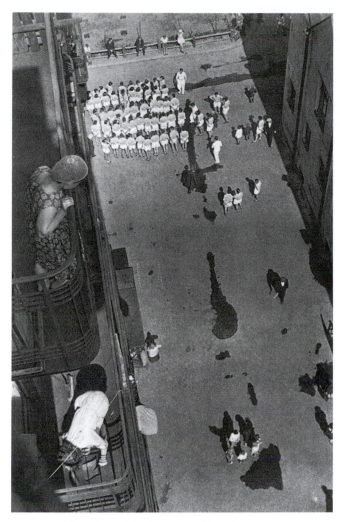

11.28 Aleksandr Rodchenko, *Assembling for a Demonstration*, 1928. Gelatin-silver print, 19½ × 13⅞" (49.5 × 35.3 cm). The Museum of Modern Art, New York.

11.29 Varvara Fedorovna Stepanova, *Design for sportswear*, 1923. Gouache and ink on paper, 11⅞ × 8½" (30.2 × 21.7 cm). Collection, Alexander Lavrentiev.

By 1928 artists had long since discovered the value of the overhead perspective as a device for realizing a more abstract kind of image (see figs. 10.13, 17.3). In the vertiginous view of *Assembling for a Demonstration* (fig. **11.28**) Rodchenko constructed a composition of sharp diagonals, light–dark contrasts, and asymmetrical patterns. Given the time and the place in which it was made, Rodchenko's photograph seems a metaphor for a new society where outdated perspectives have given way to dramatic new ones.

Stepanova and Rozanova

Like her husband, Rodchenko, **Varvara Fedorovna Stepanova** (1894–1958) gave up painting (at least until the 1930s) in order to devote herself to production art. This did not mean traditional decorative arts but rather functional materials manufactured in an equal partnership between artist and industrial worker. Within their utopian framework, these new art forms were intended to aid in the creation of a new society. Tatlin's phrase "Art into Life" was the rallying cry of the Constructivists. Stepanova, who made designs for the state textile factory in Moscow, created striking fabrics in repetitive, geometric patterns that suited industrial printing methods. She designed

clothing, as did Rodchenko and Tatlin, for the new man and woman (fig. **11.29**), with an emphasis on comfort and ease of movement for the worker. The severe economic crisis that crippled Russia during the years of civil war following the revolution thwarted the implementation of many Constructivist goals. Not surprisingly, Stepanova's sophisticated designs, grounded as they were in a modernist sensibility, were received with greater enthusiasm when exhibited in Paris in 1925 than among the working people of Moscow.

The artists who adopted the name Constructivist in 1921 worked in three-dimensional form, but the origin of the aesthetic in Tatlin's philosophy of materials was in the *faktura* (texture of paint) and the paint surface—its thickness, glossiness, and technique of application. *Faktura* could be considered and treated as autonomous expression, as texture that generates specific forms. In this way the narrative function of figurative art was replaced by a self-contained system. As early as 1913 **Olga Rozanova** (1886–1918) had asserted that the painter should "speak solely the language of pure plastic experience." In 1917, as if to illustrate the principle, she painted a remarkable picture (fig. **11.30**), its composition simply a wide, lavishly

11.30 Olga Rozanova, *Untitled (Green Stripe)*, 1917–18. Oil on canvas, 28 × 20⅞" (71 × 53 cm). Rostovo-Yaroslavskij Arkhitekturno-Khudozhestrennyj Muzej-Zapovednik, Rostovo-Yaroslavskij, Russia.

brushed green stripe running up, or down, the center and cutting through a creamy white field of contrasted but equally strong scumbled texture. The result seems to reach across the decades to the fifties and Barnett Newman's more monumental but scarcely more radical Zip paintings (see fig. 19.29).

Pevsner, Gabo, and the Spread of Constructivism

The Constructivist experiments of Tatlin, Rodchenko, and Stepanova came to an end in the early thirties, as the Soviet government began to discourage abstract experiment in favor of practical enterprises useful to a struggling economy. Many of the Suprematists and Constructivists left Russia in the early twenties. The most independent contributions of those who remained, including Tatlin and Rodchenko, were to be in graphic and theatrical design. After the pioneering work in Russia, Constructivism developed elsewhere. The fact that artists like Kandinsky, Naum Gabo, and Anton Pevsner left Russia and carried their ideas

to western Europe was of primary importance in the creation of a new International Style in art and architecture.

The two leading Russian figures in the spread of Constructivism were the brothers Anton Pevsner (1886–1962) and **Naum Gabo** (1890–1977). Pevsner was first of all a painter whose history summarized that of many younger Russian artists. His exposure to nonacademic art first came about through his introduction to traditional Russian icons and folk art. He then discovered the Impressionists, Fauves, and Cubists in the Morozov and Shchukin collections. In Paris between 1911 and 1914, he knew and was influenced by Archipenko and Modigliani. Between 1915 and 1917 he lived in Norway with his brother Naum and on his return to Russia after the revolution taught at the Moscow Academy.

Naum Gabo (Naum Neemia Pevsner), who changed his name to avoid confusion with his elder brother, went to Munich in 1910 to study medicine but turned to mathematics and engineering. In Munich he became familiar with the scientific theories of Albert Einstein, among others, attended lectures by the art historian and critic Heinrich Wölfflin, and read Kandinsky's *Concerning the Spiritual in Art*. He left Germany when war broke out and settled for a time in Norway. There, in the winter of 1915–16, he began to make a series of heads and whole figures of pieces of cardboard or thin sheets of metal, figurative constructions transforming the masses of the head into lines or plane edges framing geometric voids. The interlocking plywood shapes that make up *Constructed Head No. 1* establish the interpenetration of form and space without the creation of a surface or solid mass.

In 1917, after the Russian Revolution, Gabo returned to Russia with Pevsner. In Moscow he was drawn into the orbit of the avant-garde, meeting Kandinsky and Malevich and discovering Tatlin's constructions. He abandoned the figure and began to make abstract sculptures, including a motor-propelled kinetic object consisting of a single vibrating rod, as well as constructions of open geometric shapes in wood, metal, and transparent materials, as in *Column* (fig. **11.31**). Originally conceived in 1920–21, these tower-shaped sculptures, like Tatlin's *Monument* (see fig. 11.25), were part of Gabo's experiments for a visionary architecture. It is instructive to note that Ludwig Mies van der Rohe's model for a glass skyscraper (see fig. 16.7) was made in Germany at virtually the same time.

Between 1917 and 1920 the hopes and enthusiasms of the Russian experimental artists were at their peak. Most of the abstract artists were initially enthusiastic about the Revolution, hoping that from it would come the liberation and triumph of progressive art. By about 1920, however, Tatlin and the group around him had become increasingly doctrinaire in their insistence that art should serve the Revolution in specific, practical ways. Under government pressure, artists had to abandon or subordinate pure experiment in painting and sculpture and turn their energies to engineering, industrial, and product design.

11.31 Naum Gabo, *Column*, c. 1923, reconstructed 1937. Wood, painted metal, and glass (later replaced with Perspex), 41½ × 29 × 29" (105.3 × 73.6 × 73.6 cm). Solomon R. Guggenheim Museum, New York.

Gabo's reaction to these developments was recorded in the *Realistic Manifesto*. It was signed by Gabo and Pevsner and distributed in August 1920 at a Moscow exhibition of their work, but Gabo drafted it and was principally responsible for the ideas it contained. In many ways the manifesto was the culmination of ideas that had been fermenting in the charged atmosphere of Russian abstract art over the previous several years. At first a supporter of the revolutionary regime, Gabo found himself increasingly at odds with those members of the avant-garde who denounced art in favor of utilitarian objects to aid in the establishment of the socialist state. In the *Realistic Manifesto*, in which the word "realistic" refers to the creation of a new, Platonic reality more absolute than any imitation of nature, Gabo distinguished between his idealistic though "politically neutral" art and the production art of Tatlin, Rodchenko, and others. With revolutionary fervor, he proclaimed that the art of the future would surpass what he regarded as the limited experiments of the Cubists and Futurists. He called on artists to join forces with scientists and engineers to create a sculpture whose powerful kinetic rhythms embodied "the renascent spirit of our time." Gabo later wrote:

The most important idea in the manifesto was the assertion that art has its absolute, independent value and a function to perform in society whether capitalistic, socialistic, or communistic—art will always be alive as one of the indispensable expressions of human experience and as an important means of communication.

Until 1921 avant-garde artists were allowed the freedom to pursue their new experiments. But as civil war abated, the Soviet state began to impose its doctrine of Socialist Realism. The result was the departure from Russia of Kandinsky, Gabo, Pevsner, Lissitzky, Chagall, and many other leading spirits of the new art throughout the twenties who, as we shall see in chapter 17, continued to develop their ideas in the West.

Clarity, Certainty, and Order: De Stijl in the Netherlands

World War I marked the terminal point of the first waves of twentieth-century invention and interrupted or ended the careers of many artists. During the war, nations were isolated, and the French ceased to dominate experimentation in art. A different form of isolation developed after the war as waves of nationalism, later combined with polarized ideological struggles between communism and fascism, divided Europe. Against this political background, abstraction was in part an attempt to create a scientifically based, universal language of the senses that would transcend such divisions. A striking instance of the effect of wartime isolation is to be seen in the notable native development of art in the Netherlands, neutral during World War I and thus culturally as well as politically removed from both sides. In general, Dutch artists and architects seem to have moved rather cautiously into the twentieth century. In architecture, Hendrik Berlage was the first important innovator and, as such, almost alone (see fig. 12.17). International Art Nouveau had less impact in Holland than in Belgium, Austria, or France. So the bold, abstract work that was produced during World War I by the modernist group known as de Stijl ("the Style") seems all the more remarkable. The genius of this movement was Piet Mondrian; other members included the Dutch painters Theo van Doesburg and Bart van der Leck, the Hungarian painter Vilmos Huszar, the Belgian sculptor Georges Vantongerloo, and the architects Gerrit Rietveld, Cornelis van Eesteren, J. J. P. Oud (see figs. 12.19, 12.20), and Robert van 't Hoff (see fig. 12.18).

Van Doesburg was the leading spirit in the formation and promotion of the group and the creation of its influential journal, also called *de Stijl*, devoted to the art and theory of the group and published from 1917 to 1928. De Stijl was dedicated to the "absolute devaluation of tradition ... the exposure of the whole swindle of lyricism and sentiment." The artists involved emphasized "the need for abstraction and simplification": mathematical structure as opposed to Impressionism and all "Baroque" forms of art. They created art "for clarity, for certainty, and for order." Their works began to display these qualities, transmitted through the straight line, the rectangle, or the cube, and eventually through colors simplified to the primaries red, yellow, and blue and the neutrals black, white, and gray. For Van Doesburg and Mondrian these simplifications had symbolic significance based on Eastern philosophy and the mystical teachings of Theosophy, a popular spiritual movement that was known among de Stijl artists partly through Kandinsky's book *Concerning the Spiritual in Art*. Mondrian was particularly obsessed by the mystical implications of vertical–horizontal opposition and spent the rest of his life exploring them, producing in the process some of the most extraordinary works of art of the twentieth century. Despite Van Doesburg's efforts to present the de Stijl group as a unified and coherent entity, it included many individual talents who did not strictly adhere to a single style. Nevertheless, the artists, designers, and architects of de Stijl shared ideas about the social role of art in modern society, the integration of all the arts through the collaboration of artists and designers, and an abiding faith in the potential of technology and design to realize new utopian living environments based on abstract form. Together they developed an art based rigorously on theory, dedicated to formal purity, logic, balance, proportion, and rhythm.

The de Stijl artists were well aware of parallel developments in modern art in France, Germany, and Italy—Fauvism, Cubism, German Expressionism, and Italian Futurism. But they recognized as leaders only a few pioneers, such as Cézanne in painting and Frank Lloyd Wright and Berlage in architecture. They had little or no knowledge of the Russian experiments in abstraction until the end of the war, when international communications were reestablished. At that time, contact developed between the Dutch and Russian avant-garde, especially through El Lissitzky.

In addition to their work as painters, Mondrian and Van Doesburg were influential theoricians. In 1917 Van Doesburg published a book, *The New Movement in Painting*, and Mondrian published in *de Stijl* a series of articles, including "Neo-Plasticism in Painting," which in 1920, after his return to France, he expanded into his book *Le Néo-Plasticisme*, one of the key documents of abstract art. The term refers to the abstract style he had developed by that year.

By 1926 Van Doesburg was seeking a new and individual variation on de Stijl, which he named Elementarism. In it he continued to use a composition consisting of rectangles, but tilted them at forty-five degrees to achieve what he felt to be a more immediately dynamic form of expression. At this point, differences between the two artists were so significant that Mondrian left the de Stijl group.

Mondrian

The transition from fairly conventional naturalistic paintings to a revolutionary modern style during and after World War I may be traced in the career of **Piet Mondrian** (1872–1944). Born Pieter Mondriaan, he was trained in the Amsterdam Rijksacademie and until 1904 worked primarily as a landscape painter. He then came under the influence of Toorop and for a time painted in a Symbolist manner. His early work evinces a tendency to work in

11.32 Piet Mondrian, *Apple Tree (Pointillist Version)*, c. 1908. Oil on composition board, 22⅜ × 29½" (56.8 × 74.9 cm). Dallas Museum of Art.

11.33 Piet Mondrian, *Color Planes in Oval*, 1913–14. Oil on canvas, 42⅜ × 31" (107.6 × 78.7 cm). The Museum of Modern Art, New York.

series—which proved central to the development of his abstract work—and to focus on a single scene or object, whether a windmill, thicket of trees, a solitary tree, or an isolated chrysanthemum. Early landscapes adhered to a principle of frontality and, particularly in a series of scenes with windmills, to cut-off, close-up presentation.

By 1908 Mondrian was becoming aware of some of the innovations of modern art. His color blossomed in Fauve-inspired blues, yellows, pinks, and reds. In forest scenes he emphasized the linear undulation of saplings; in shore- and seascapes, the intense, flowing colors of sand dunes and water. For the next few years he painted motifs such as church façades presented frontally, in nearly abstract planes of arbitrary color or in patterns of loose red and yellow spots deriving from the Neo-Impressionists and the brushstrokes of Van Gogh. With any of his favorite subjects—the tree, the dunes and ocean, the church or windmill, all rooted in the familiar environment of the Netherlands—one can trace his progress from naturalism through Symbolism, Impressionism, Post-Impressionism, Fauvism, and Cubism to abstraction. In *Blue Tree* (fig. **11.32**), an image to which he devoted several paintings and drawings, Mondrian employed expressive, animated brushwork reminiscent of Van Gogh's, causing the whole scene to pulsate with energy.

In early 1912 Mondrian moved to Paris. Though he had seen early Cubist works by Picasso and Braque in Holland, he became fully conversant with the style in the French capital. It is in the wake of this experience that he emerges as a major figure in modern art. He himself came to regard the previous years as transitional. During his first

years in Paris, Mondrian subordinated his colors to grays, blue-greens, and ochers under the influence of the Analytic Cubism of Picasso and Braque. But he rarely attempted the tilted planes or sculptural projection that gave the works of the French Cubists their defined, if limited, sense of three-dimensional spatial existence; his most Cubist paintings still maintained an essential frontality. Mondrian was already moving beyond the tenets of Cubism to eliminate both subject and three-dimensional illusionistic depth.

As early as 1912 the tree had virtually disappeared into a linear grid that covered the surface of the canvas. Mondrian at this time favored centralized compositions, evident here in the central density of the pattern, which gradually loosens toward the edges. He also articulated this through an oval canvas (inspired by the Cubists), while the linear structure became more rectangular and abstract, as in *Color Planes in Oval* of 1913–14 (fig. **11.33**). Despite its highly abstracted forms, this work belongs to a series of compositions Mondrian based on his drawings of Parisian building façades. By 1914 the artist had begun to experiment with a broader but still subtle range of colors, asserting their identity within a structure of horizontal and vertical lines.

In Paris Mondrian was profoundly affected by the example of Cubism, but he gradually began to feel that the style "did not accept the logical consequences of its own discoveries: it was not developing abstraction toward its ultimate goal, the expression of pure reality. I felt that this could only be established by pure plastics (plasticism)." In this statement, made in 1942, he emphasized the two words that summarize his lifelong quest—"plastic" and "reality." To him "plastic expression" meant simply the action of forms and colors. "Reality" or "the new reality" was the reality of plastic expression, or the reality of forms and colors in the painting. Thus, the new reality was the presence of the painting itself, as opposed to the painted imitation of nature or the romantic evocation of the artist's emotions.

Gradually, as the artist tells it, Mondrian became aware that "(a) in plastic art reality can be expressed only through the equilibrium of *dynamic movements* of form and color; (b) pure means afford the most effective way of attaining this." These ideas led him to develop a set of organizational principles in his art. Chief among them were the balance of unequal opposites, achieved through the right angle, and the simplification of color to the primary hues plus black and white. It is important to recall that Mondrian did not arrive at his final position solely through theoretical speculation, but through a long and complex development in his painting.

In 1914 Mondrian returned to Holland, where he remained when war broke out. Between 1914 and 1916 he eliminated all vestiges of curved lines, so that the structure became predominantly vertical and horizontal. The paintings were still rooted in subject—a church façade, the ocean, and piers extending into the ocean—but these

11.34 Piet Mondrian, *Composition in Color A*, 1917. Oil on canvas, 19½ × 17⅜" (49.5 × 44.1 cm). Kröller-Müller Museum, Otterlo, the Netherlands.

were now simplified to a pattern of short, straight lines, like plus and minus signs, through which the artist sought to suggest the underlying structure of nature. During 1917 and later he explored another variation (fig. **11.34**)—rectangles of flat color of varying sizes, suspended in a sometimes loose, sometimes precise rectangular arrangement. The color rectangles sometimes touch, sometimes float independently, and sometimes overlap. They appear positively as forms in front of the light background. Their interaction creates a surprising illusion of depth and movement, even though they are kept rigidly parallel to the surface of the canvas.

Mondrian soon realized that these detached color planes created both a tangible sense of depth and a differentiation of foreground and background; this interfered with the pure reality he was seeking. This discovery led him during 1918 and 1919 to a series of works organized on a strict rectangular grid. In the so-called Checkerboards, rectangles of equal size and a few different colors are evenly distributed across the canvas. By controlling the strength and tone of his colors, Mondrian here neutralized any distinction between figure and ground, for the white and

gray rectangles do not recede behind the colored ones or assume a subordinate role as support. Mondrian did not develop this compositional solution further, for he felt the modular grid was too prominent. Finally, therefore, he united the field of the canvas by thickening the dividing lines and running them through the rectangles to create a linear structure in tension with the color rectangles. In 1920, after returning to Paris, Mondrian came to the fulfillment of his Neo-Plastic artistic ideals. His paintings of this period express abstract, universal ideas: the dynamic balance of vertical and horizontal linear structure and simple, fundamental color. He continued to refine these ideas throughout the twenties, thirties, and early forties, until, as we shall see in chapter 17, he achieved works of monumental purity and simplicity (see figs. 17.21, 17.26). Mondrian's ultimate aim was to express a visual unity through an "equivalence of opposites"; this in turn expressed the higher mystical unity of the universe.

Van Doesburg

As already noted, **Theo van Doesburg** (1883–1931) was the moving spirit in the formation and development of

11.35 Theo van Doesburg, *Card Players*, 1916–17. Tempera on canvas, 46½ × 58" (118.1 × 147.3 cm). Private collection.

11.36 Theo van Doesburg, *Composition IX (Card Players)*, 1917. Oil on canvas, 45⅝ × 41¾" (115.9 × 106 cm). Gemeente Museum, the Hague, the Netherlands.

de Stijl. During his two years of military service (1914–16) he studied the new experimental painting and sculpture and was particularly impressed by Kandinsky's essay, *Concerning the Spiritual in Art*. In 1916 he experimented with free abstraction in the manner of Kandinsky, as well as with Cubism, but was still searching for his own path. This he found in his composition *Card Players* (fig. **11.35**), based on Cézanne's painting (see fig. 3.8), but simplified to a complex of interacting shapes based on rectangles, the colors flat and reduced nearly to primaries. Fascinated by the mathematical implications of his new abstraction, Van Doesburg explored its possibilities in linear structures, as in a later version of *Card Players* (fig. **11.36**).

Even Mondrian was affected by the fertility of Van Doesburg's imagination. When artists work together as closely as the de Stijl painters did during 1917–19, it is extremely difficult and perhaps pointless to establish absolute priorities. Van Doesburg, Mondrian, and their colleague Van der Leck for a time were all nourished by one another. However, each went in his own direction in the twenties, when Van Doesburg's attention turned toward architecture. He followed de Stijl principles until he published his *Fundamentals of the New Art* in 1924. He then began to abandon the rigid vertical–horizontal formula of Mondrian and de Stijl and to introduce diagonals. This heresy, as well as fundamental differences over the nature of Neo-Plastic architecture, led to Mondrian's resignation from de Stijl. Though by 1918 Mondrian himself made lozenge-shaped paintings with diagonal edges (see fig. 17.24), a development he discussed at length with Van Doesburg, the lines contained within his compositions always remained strictly horizontal and vertical.

In a 1926 manifesto in *de Stijl*, Van Doesburg named his new departure Elementarism, and argued that the inclined plane reintroduced surprise, instability, and dynamism. In his murals at the Café l'Aubette, Strasbourg (fig. **11.37**)—decorated in collaboration with Jean Arp and Sophie Taeuber-Arp (see fig. 13.13)—Van Doesburg made his most monumental statement of

11.37 Theo van Doesburg, Sophie Taeuber, and Jean Arp, Interior, Café l'Aubette, Strasbourg, 1926–28, (destroyed 1940).

Elementarist principles. He tilted his colored rectangles at forty-five degree angles and framed them in uniform strips of color. The tilted rectangles are in part cut off by the ceiling and lower wall panels. Across the center runs a long balcony with steps at one end that add a horizontal and diagonal to the design. Incomplete rectangles emerge as triangles or irregular geometric shapes. In proper de Stijl fashion, Van Doesburg designed every detail of the interior, down to the ashtrays. Here he realized his ideals about an all-embracing, total work of abstract art, saying that his aim was "to place man within painting instead of in front of it and thereby enable him to participate in it."

In the richly diverse and international art world of the twenties, Van Doesburg provided a point of contact between artists and movements in several countries. He even maintained a lively interest in Dada. His Dada activities included his short-lived Dada magazine *Mecano*, his Dada poems written under the pseudonym of I. K. Bonset, and a Dada cultural tour of Holland with his friend Kurt Schwitters.

Until his death in 1931, Van Doesburg promoted de Stijl abroad, traveling across Europe and seeking new adherents to the cause as older members defected. His efforts contributed to the establishment of de Stijl as a movement of international significance. With its belief in the integration of the fine and applied arts, the de Stijl experiment paralleled that of the Bauhaus in many ways. Van Doesburg was in Weimar in the early twenties, lecturing and promoting de Stijl ideas at the Bauhaus, and fomenting dissent among the school's younger members. Although he was not a member of the faculty, he probably contributed to an increased emphasis at the Bauhaus on rational, machine-based design (see chapters 16 and 17).

Vantongerloo

In sculpture the achievements of de Stijl were not comparable to those of the Russian Constructivists and were, in fact, concentrated principally in the works of the Belgian **Georges Vantongerloo** (1886–1965). Vantongerloo was not only a sculptor but also a painter, architect, and theoretician. His first abstract sculptures (fig. **11.38**), executed during 1917 and 1918, were conceived in the traditional sense as masses carved out of the block, rather than as constructions built up of separate elements. They constitute notable transformations of de Stijl painting into three-dimensional design. Later, Vantongerloo turned to open construction, sometimes in an architectural form and sometimes in free linear patterns. In his subsequent painting and sculpture he frequently deserted the straight line in favor of the curved, but throughout his career Vantongerloo maintained an interest in a mathematical basis for his art, to the point of deriving compositions from algebraic equations.

11.38 Georges Vantongerloo, *Construction of Volume Relations*, 1921. Mahogany, 16⅛ × 5⅝ × 5¾" (41 × 14.4 × 14.5 cm), including base. The Museum of Modern Art, New York.

12
Early Twentieth-Century Architecture

European architecture around 1900 showed the Art Nouveau aesthetic flourishing in a variety of architectural forms and contexts, from the idiosyncratic organicism of Gaudí in Barcelona to Guimard's elegant designs for the Paris Métro and Horta's masterpieces of residential and commercial architecture in Brussels (see chapter 5; figs. 109, 111, 113, 114). While Art Nouveau—"New Art"—rejected the historicist styles of nineteenth-century architecture and embraced modern industrial materials, it remained largely concerned with decorative qualities, whether expressed in the swirling ironwork designed by Horta or in Mackintosh's more restrained, geometric idiom (see fig. 95). At the same time, a very different tendency in advant-garde architecture was gathering momentum. From the late 1890s the Austrian architect Adolf Loos announced his opposition to the use of ornament in architecture, vehemently expressed in his 1908 article "Ornament and Crime." Emphasizing simple cuboid forms, he eschewed decorative features and even the curved lines so beloved by Art Nouveau. In contrast to the ethic of fine traditional craftsmanship and artistic finish that Art Nouveau had inherited from the Arts and Crafts Movement, Loos saw the industrial skills of the machine age as better fitted to serve the modern architecture.

Though they shared some of the same sources, and might be present in works by the same architect, the aims and values of these two architectural tendencies clearly diverged significantly. The tensions between them can be seen particularly clearly in the development of architecture in Austria and Germany during the decades either side of World War I. Some of the boldest experiments in architecture of the early twentieth century, however, originated in America, in the work of Frank Lloyd Wright, the most important American architect of his time. Wright was a pioneer of the international modern movement, and his experiments in architecture as organic space in the form of abstract design antedate those of most of the early twentieth-century avant-garde European architects. His designs were published in Europe in 1910 and 1911, in

two German editions by Ernst Wasmuth, and were studied by every major architect on the continent. His works were known and admired by artists and architects of the Dutch de Stijl group, Robert van 't Hoff, J. J. P. Oud, Theo van Doesburg, Georges Vantongerloo, and Piet Mondrian. Wright's design had common denominators not only with the classical formalism of these artists but also with the shifting planes and ambiguous space relationships of Cubism. On the other hand, Wright's work was influenced by what he saw during a trip to Europe in 1909–10, particularly the buildings designed by leading Viennese architects Joseph Maria Olbrich (see fig. 12.11) and Otto Wagner (see fig. 12.9).

Modernism in Harmony with Nature: Frank Lloyd Wright

Frank Lloyd Wright (1867–1959) studied engineering at the University of Wisconsin, where he read the work of the English critic John Ruskin and was particularly drawn to rational, structural interpretation in the writings of Eugène-Emmanuel Viollet-le-Duc. In 1887 he was employed by the Chicago architectural firm of Adler and Sullivan, with whom he worked until he established his own practice in 1893. There is little doubt that many of the houses built by the Sullivan firm during the years Wright worked there represented his ideas. Wright's basic philosophy of architecture was expressed primarily through the house form. The 1902–6 Larkin Building in Buffalo, New York (see fig. 12.5), was his only large-scale structure prior to Chicago's Midway Gardens (1914) and the Imperial Hotel in Tokyo (see fig. 12.6) (all three, incidentally, have been destroyed).

Early Houses

At the age of twenty-two Wright designed his own house in Oak Park, Illinois (1889), a quiet community thirty minutes by train from downtown Chicago. His earliest houses, including his own, reflect influences from the shingle-style houses of H. H. Richardson and McKim, Mead & White

12.1 Frank Lloyd Wright, Ward Willits House, Highland Park, Illinois, 1902–3.

(see fig. 4.7) and developed the open, free-flowing floor plan of the English architects Philip Webb and Richard Norman Shaw. Wright used the characteristically American feature of the veranda, open or screened, wrapping around two sides of the house, to enhance the sense of outside space that penetrated to the main living rooms. The cruciform plan, with space surrounding the central core of fireplace and utility areas (kitchen, landing, etc.), also had an impact on Wright that affected his approach to house design as well as to more monumental design projects.

In the 1902–3 Ward Willits House in Highland Park, Illinois (fig. **12.1**), Wright made one of his first individual and mature statements of the principles and ideas that he had been formulating during his apprentice years. The house demonstrates his growing interest in a Japanese aesthetic. He was a serious collector of Japanese prints (about which he wrote a book), and before his trip to Japan in 1905, he probably visited the Japanese pavilions at the 1893 World's Columbian Exhibition in Chicago. In the Willits House, the Japanese influence is seen in the dominant wide, low-gabled roof and the vertical striping on the façade. The sources, however, are less significant than the welding together of all the elements of the plan, interior and exterior, in a single integration of space, mass, and surface. From the compact, central arrangement of fireplace and utility units, the space of the interior flows out in an indefinite expansion carried without transition to the exterior and beyond. The essence of the design in the Willits House, and in the series of houses by Wright and his followers to which the name Prairie Style has been given, is a predominant horizontal accent of rooflines with

12.2 Frank Lloyd Wright, Susan Lawrence Dana House, Springfield, Illinois, 1902–4. Interior perspective, dining room. Pencil and watercolor on paper, 25 × 20⅜" (63.5 × 51.7 cm). Avery Architectural and Fine Arts Library, Columbia University, New York.

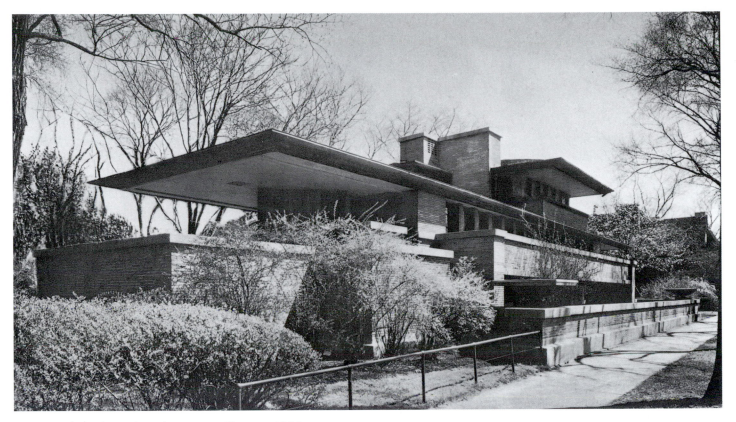

12.3 Frank Lloyd Wright, Robie House, Chicago, 1909.

deep, overhanging eaves echoing the flat prairie landscape of the Midwest. The earth tones of the typical Prairie house were intended to blend harmoniously with the surroundings, while the massive central chimney served both to break the horizontal, low-slung line of the roof and to emphasize the hearth as the spiritual and psychological center of the house.

The interior of the Wright Prairie house (see fig. 12.4) is characterized by low ceilings, frequently pitched at unorthodox angles; a sense of intimacy; and constantly changing vistas of one space flowing into another. The interior plastered walls of the Willits House were trimmed simply in wood, imparting a sense of elegant proportion and geometric precision to the whole. Wright also custom-designed architectural ornaments for his houses, such as light fixtures, leaded glass panels in motifs abstracted from natural forms, and furniture, both built-in and freestanding (fig. **12.2**). Though his emphasis on simple design and the honest expression of the nature of materials is dependent in part on Arts and Crafts ideals (see chapter 4), Wright fervently supported the role of mechanized production in architectural design. He regarded the machine as a metaphor of the modern age but did not believe that buildings should resemble machines. Paramount in his house designs was the creation of a suitable habitat, in harmony with nature, for the middle-class nuclear family. Wright understood the way in which his domestic dwellings embodied the collective values and identity of a community. These early residences were designed for Chicago's fast-growing suburbs, where structures could extend

horizontally, as opposed to the city, where Victorian town houses were built on several stories to accommodate narrow urban plots.

The masterpiece of Wright's Prairie Style is the 1909 Robie House in Chicago (figs. **12.3**, **12.4**). The house is centered around the fireplace and arranged in plan as two sliding horizontal sections on one dominant axis. The horizontal roof cantilevers out on steel beams and is anchored at the center, with the chimneys and top-floor gables set at right angles to the principal axis. Windows are arranged in long, symmetrical rows and are deeply imbedded into the brick masses of the structure. The main, horizontally oriented lines of the house are reiterated and expanded in the terraces and walls that transform interior into exterior space

12.4 Frank Lloyd Wright, Dining Room, Robie House.

and vice versa. The elements of this house, combining the outward-flowing space of the interior and the linear and planar design of exterior roofline and wall areas with a fortresslike mass of chimneys and corner piers, summarize other experiments that Wright had carried on earlier in the Larkin Building (fig. **12.5**).

The Larkin Building

The Larkin Building represented radical differences from the Prairie house in that it was organized as rectangular masses in which Wright articulated mass and space into a single, close unity. The Larkin Building was, on the exterior, a rectangular, flat-roofed structure, whose immense corner piers protected and supported the window walls that reflected an open interior well surrounded by balconies. The open plan, filled with prototypes of today's "work stations," was Wright's solution for a commodious, light-filled office environment. The Larkin Building literally embodied the architect's belief in the moral value of labor, for its walls were inscribed with mottos extolling the virtues of honest work. This was an example of the early modern industrial structures that embodied tremendous possibilities for the development of innovative kinds of internal, expressive space in the new tall buildings of America (the economics of industrial building, however, soon destroyed these possibilities).

Mid-Career Crisis

In the years after 1910, just when he was becoming a world figure, Wright experienced a period of neglect and even vilification in his own country. Highly publicized personal problems helped to drive him from the successful midwestern practice he had built up in the early years of the century. These included his decision to leave his wife and six children for another woman, Mamah Cheney. In 1914 Cheney was murdered by a servant who also set fire to the home Wright had built for himself in Wisconsin, Taliesin (the name of a mythic Welsh poet meaning "shining brow"), which he subsequently rebuilt. Even more significant than these personal factors were cultural and social changes that, by 1915, had alienated the patronage for experimental architecture in the Midwest and increased the popularity of historical revivalist styles. Large-scale construction of mass housing soon led to vulgarization of these styles.

About 1915, Wright began increasingly to explore the art and architecture of ancient cultures, including the Egyptian, Japanese, and Maya civilizations. The Imperial Hotel in Tokyo (fig. **12.6**), a luxury hotel designed for Western visitors, occupied most of his time between 1912 and 1923 and represents his most ornately complicated decorative period, filled with suggestions of Far Eastern and Pre-Columbian influence. In addition, it embodied his

12.5 Frank Lloyd Wright, Larkin Building, Buffalo, New York, 1902–6. Demolished 1950.

Temples for the Modern City: American Classicism 1900–15

Aside from Wright, a number of his followers, and a few isolated architects of talent, American architecture between 1915 and 1940 was largely in the hands of academicians and builders. Nevertheless, two landmark structures were erected during this period. New York City's Pennsylvania Station (see fig. 12.7), built between 1906 and 1910 and demolished in 1966, represents one of the most tragic architectural losses of the twentieth century. "Until the first blow fell," said an editorial in *The New York Times*, "no one was convinced that Penn Station really would be demolished or that New York would permit this monumental act of vandalism." Penn Station was designed by the Beaux-Arts architectural firm of McKim, Mead & White, who designed classically inspired civic buildings throughout America in the early years of the twentieth century (see figs. 4.7, 4.13). Penn Station was one of the firm's most ambitious undertakings. The exterior (fig. 12.7), a massive Doric colonnade based on the ancient Roman Baths of Caracalla, presented a grand modern temple that underscored the power of the railroad as a symbol of progress. Inside, a visitor's first impression upon arrival was the dramatically vaulted spaces in the train concourse, its glass-and-steel construction recalling the crystal palaces of the previous century (see fig. 4.3). In 1966 the city responded to the destruction of Penn Station by establishing the New York City Landmarks Preservation Commission.

At the same time, on the other side of the continent, a remarkable act of preservation was taking place. The Palace of Fine Arts in San Francisco (fig. 12.8), designed by the architect **Bernard Maybeck** (1862–1957), was originally built in 1915 for the Panama–Pacific International Exposition. Celebrating the opening of the Panama Canal, the San Francisco Exposition was a world's fair that emulated the famous 1893 World's Columbian Exposition (see fig. 4.13). It was visited by nineteen million people during ten months in 1915, providing an economic boost to a city

12.6 Frank Lloyd Wright, Imperial Hotel, Tokyo, c. 1912–23. Demolished 1968.

most daring and intricate structural experiments to that date—experiments that enabled the building to survive the wildly destructive Japanese earthquakes of 1923 (only to be destroyed by the wrecking ball in 1968). For twenty years after the Imperial Hotel, Wright's international reputation continued to grow. Though he frequently had difficulty earning a living, he was indomitable; he wrote, lectured, and taught, secure in the knowledge of his own genius and place in history, and he invented brilliantly whenever he received commissions.

12.7 McKim, Mead & White, Pennsylvania Station, New York, 1906–10. Demolished 1966.

12.8 Bernard Maybeck, Palace of Fine Arts, Panama-Pacific International Exposition, San Francisco, 1915.

that had experienced the devastating earthquake and fire of 1906. Sited along a lagoon, Maybeck's popular ensemble included an open-air rotunda, a curving Corinthian peristyle, and a large gallery that housed the fair's paintings and sculptures. The unconventional Maybeck turned classicism into his own personal idiom, violating canonical rules and covering his structures with richly imaginative classical-style ornament. He sought a mood of melancholy and past grandeur, for he envisioned the Palace as "an old Roman ruin, away from civilization ... overgrown with bushes and trees." It was a mood somehow appropriate for a world in the midst of the carnage of World War I. Though it was the only building not torn down after the fair, the Palace of Fine Arts was never intended as a permanent structure and it soon began to show signs of decay. Between 1962 and 1967 it was completely reconstructed out of concrete. Today it is still used as a city museum.

New Simplicity Versus Art Nouveau: Vienna Before World War I

The capital of the vast, disparate Austro-Hungarian Empire, which was dismembered after World War I, pre-war Vienna was a cosmopolitan city characterized both by entrenched official conservatism and by culturally progressive tendencies that were highly influential in many spheres. In 1899, for example, the Austrian psychotherapist Sigmund Freud published *The Interpretation of Dreams*, which was later to be hugely significant for the international art movements of Dada and Surrealism (see chapters 13 and 15). In 1897, determined to break away from the stifling academicism of official art, a group of artists had formed the Vienna Secession (see chapter 5). Their new exhibition building, designed in 1898 by **Joseph Maria Olbrich** (1867–1908) combined different strands of Art Nouveau in the geometric lines of its façade

and the intertwined foliage of its openwork gilt-bronze cupola. In early twentieth-century Viennese architecture, therefore, the relationship between Art Nouveau decoration and modernist geometric functionalism is far from one of clear-cut opposition. Both elements can be found in buildings by major Austrian architects of the period, although the polemical writings of Loos in particular helped to define the austere simplicity he favored as the hallmark of avant-garde architecture.

The founder of Viennese modernism, **Otto Wagner** (1841–1918), was an academic architect during the early part of his life. His stations for the Vienna subway (1896–97) were simple, functional buildings dressed with Baroque details. In his 1894 book on modern architecture, however, Wagner had already demonstrated his ideas about a new architecture that used the latest materials and adapted itself to the requirements of modern life. His motto, "Necessity alone is the ruler of art," anticipated later twentieth-century functionalism. In the hall of his 1905 Vienna Post Office Savings Bank (fig. **12.9**) Wagner used unadorned metal and glass to create airy, light-filled, and unobstructed space. While there is some stylistic similarity here to the auditorium that Victor Horta built in his Maison du Peuple in Brussels (see chapter 5), Wagner's design shows typically modernist concern for the increased elimination of structural elements and the creation of a single unified and simple space.

Adolf Loos (1870–1933) was active in Vienna from 1896. After studying architecture in Dresden, Loos worked in the United States for three years from 1893 (when he attended the World's Columbian Exposition in Chicago), taking various odd jobs while learning about the new concepts of American architecture, particularly the skyscraper designs of Sullivan and other pioneers of the Chicago School (see chapter 4). After settling in Vienna, Loos followed principles established by Wagner and

12.9 Otto Wagner, Post Office Savings Bank, Vienna, 1905.

Sullivan favoring a pure, functional architecture. His 1910 Steiner House in Vienna (fig. **12.10**) anticipated the unadorned cubic forms of the so-termed International Style of architecture that was to develop from the concepts of J. J. P. Oud, Walter Gropius, Ludwig Mies van der Rohe, and Le Corbusier in the twenties and thirties.

12.10 Adolf Loos, Garden view, Steiner House, Vienna, 1910.

Zoning rules allowed for only one story above street level, so Loos employed a barrel-vaulted roof on the front of the house that was so deep it allowed for two more levels facing the garden, which is the view seen here. The garden façade is symmetrical; simple, large-paned windows arranged in horizontal rows are sunk into the planar surfaces of the rectilinear façade. Reinforced concrete was here applied to a private house for almost the first time. Although the architecture and ideas of Loos never gained wide dissemination, the Steiner House is a key monument in the creation of the new style.

Among the Art Nouveau architects attacked by Loos were Olbrich and Josef Hoffmann (see chapter 5) who, with the painter Gustav Klimt, were the founders of the Vienna Secession. Hoffmann's masterpiece is the Palais Stoclet, a luxurious house that he built for the Stoclet family in Brussels (see fig. 5.15). This splendid mansion is characterized by severe rectangular planning and façades, and broad, clear, white areas framed in dark, linear strips (under the influence of Charles Rennie Mackintosh). Its lavish interior design, an expression of the Secessionist belief in a total decorative environment, offers a marked contrast to the sobriety of Loos's Steiner House.

Hoffmann is perhaps more important for his part in establishing the Wiener Werkstätte (Vienna Workshops) than for his achievement as a practicing architect. The workshops, which originated in 1903, continued the craft traditions of William Morris and the English Arts and Crafts movement, with the contradictory new feature that the machine was now accepted as a basic tool of the designer. For thirty years the workshops exercised a notable influence, teaching fine design in handicrafts and industrial objects.

Tradition and Innovation: The German Contribution to Modern Architecture

In Germany before 1930, largely as a result of enlightened governmental and industrial patronage, architectural experimentation, instead of depending only on brilliant individuals, was coordinated and directed toward the creation of a "school" of modern architecture. In this process, the contributions of certain patrons such as Archduke Ernst Ludwig of Hesse and the AEG (German General Electrical Company) were of the greatest importance.

Relations between Austrian and German architecture were extremely close in the early years of the twentieth

12.11 Joseph Maria Olbrich, Hochzeitsturm (Wedding Tower), Darmstadt, Germany, 1907.

century. When the Archduke of Hesse wished to effect a revival of the arts by founding an artists' colony at Darmstadt in Germany, he employed Olbrich to design most of the buildings, including the 1907 Hochzeitsturm (Wedding Tower) (fig. **12.11**). The Wedding Tower, which still dominates Darmstadt, was so named because it commemorated the archduke's second marriage; it was intended less as a functional structure than as a monument and a focal point for the entire project. Although it was inspired by the American concept of the skyscraper, its visual impact owes much to the towers of German medieval churches. Its distinctive five-fingered gable symbolizes an outstretched hand. The manner in which rows of windows below the gable are grouped within a common frame and wrapped around a corner of the building was an innovation of particular significance for later skyscraper design.

At about the same time that Hoffmann set up the Wiener Werkstätte a German cabinetmaker, Karl Schmidt, had started to employ architects and artists to design furniture for his shop in Dresden. Out of this grew the Deutsche Werkstätte (German Workshops), which similarly applied the principles of Morris to the larger field of industrial design. From these and other experiments, the Deutscher Werkbund (German Work or Craft Alliance) emerged in 1907. This was the immediate predecessor of the Bauhaus, one of the most influential schools in the development of modern architecture and industrial design.

Behrens and Industrial Design

More than any other German architect of the early twentieth century, **Peter Behrens** (1868–1940) forged a link between tradition and experiment. He began his career as a painter, producing Art Nouveau graphics, and then moved from an interest in crafts to the central problems of industrial design for machine production. Behrens turned to architecture as a result of his experience in the artists' collaborative at Darmstadt, where he designed his own house—the only one in the colony not designed by Olbrich. In 1903 Behrens was appointed director of the Düsseldorf School of Art, and in 1907 the AEG company, one of the world's largest manufacturers of generators, motors, and lightbulbs, hired him as architect and coordinator of design of everything from products to publications. This unusual appointment by a large industrial organization of an artist and architect to supervise and improve the quality of all its products was a landmark in the history of architecture and design.

One of Behren's first buildings for AEG, a landmark of modern architecture, is the Turbine Factory in Berlin completed in 1909 (fig. **12.12**). Although the building is given a somewhat traditional appearance of monumentality by the huge corner masonry piers and the overpowering visual mass of the roof (despite its actual structural lightness), it is essentially a glass-and-steel structure. Despite the use of certain traditional forms, this building is immensely

12.12 Peter Behrens, AEG Turbine Factory, Berlin, 1908–9.

important in its bold structural engineering, in its frank statement of construction, and in the social implications of a factory built to provide the maximum of air, space, and light. It is functional for both the processes of manufacture and the working conditions of the employees—concerns rarely considered in earlier factories.

The hiring of Behrens by AEG and similar appointments by other industrial corporations mark the emergence of some sense of social responsibility on the part of large-scale industry. The established practice had been one of short-sighted and often brutal exploitation of natural and human resources. Certain enlightened industrialists began to realize that well-designed working spaces and products were not necessarily more expensive to produce than badly designed ones and had numerous economic and political

advantages. In the rapidly expanding industrial scene and the changing political landscape of early twentieth-century Europe, the public image presented by industry was assuming increasing importance. It was becoming evident that industry had a powerful role to play in public affairs and even in promoting a national image. Such ideas may have influenced Behrens's transformation of his functional glass-and-steel Turbine Factory into a virtual monument to the achievements of modern German industry. Behrens is important not only as an architect but as a teacher of a generation that included Gropius, Le Corbusier, and Mies van der Rohe—all of whom worked with him early in their careers.

Expressionism in Architecture

Between 1910 and 1925 the spirit of Expressionism manifested itself in German architecture, as in painting and sculpture (see chapter 8). Although this did not result initially in many important buildings, and although Expressionism in architecture was terminated by the rise of Nazism, it did establish the base for a movement that was later realized in the fifties and sixties, after the austerity and pristine elegance of the International Style had begun to pall.

Forerunners of Expressionism in architecture include Gaudí's creations in Barcelona and the 1913–14 Werkbund Theater in Cologne (fig. **12.13**) by the Belgian architect Van de Velde (see below), who worked in Germany from 1899 to 1914. The building's strongly sculptural exterior, for which Van de Velde used the molded forms of the façades to define the volume of the interior, has been seen as the definitive break with the essentially linear emphasis of Art Nouveau architecture. Van de Velde's other achievements in Germany include the educational program that

12.13 Henry Clemens van de Velde, Werkbund Theater, Cologne, 1913–14. Demolished 1920.

he developed at the Weimar School, which he founded in 1906 under the patronage of the Duke of Saxe-Weimar. This program put its emphasis on creativity, free experiment, and escape from dependence on past traditions.

One of the most startling examples of Expressionist architecture is the 1919 Grosses Schauspielhaus (Great Theater) in Berlin (fig. **12.14**), created by **Hans Poelzig** (1869–1936) for the theatrical impresario Max Reinhardt. This was actually a conversion of an old building, originally an enormous covered market that, after 1874, served as the Circus Schumann. Using stalactite forms over the entire ceiling and most of the walls, and filtering light through them, Poelzig created a vast cavelike arena of mystery and fantasy appropriate to Reinhardt's spectacular productions.

Of the architects who emerged from German Expressionism, perhaps the most significant was **Erich Mendelsohn** (1887–1953). Mendelsohn began practice in 1912, but his work was interrupted by World War I. Following the war, one of his first important buildings was the Einstein Tower in Potsdam (fig. **12.15**). One of the principal works of Expressionist architecture, the Einstein Tower was built to study spectroanalytic phenomena, especially Einstein's theory of relativity. Instruments in the cupola reflected light vertically through the tower onto a mirror in the underground laboratory. On the exterior, Mendelsohn emphasized qualities of continuity and flow

12.15 Erich Mendelsohn, Einstein Tower, Potsdam, 1920–21.

appropriate to the material of concrete (although the Einstein Tower was actually built of brick and covered with cement to look like cast concrete). The windows flow around the rounded corners, while the exterior stairs flow up and into the cavern of the entrance. The entire structure, designed as a monument as well as a functioning laboratory, has an essentially organic quality, prophetic of the later works of Le Corbusier and Eero Saarinen.

Many other architects, particularly in Germany and Holland, were affected by the spirit of Expressionism during the twenties. The educator, philosopher, and occultist **Rudolf Steiner** (1861–1925), although not trained as an architect, produced remarkable examples of utopian architecture in his Goetheanum I and II (fig. **12.16**), the latter of which became a tremendous sculptural monument of concrete that looked back to Gaudí and forward to post-World War II *architecture brut*.

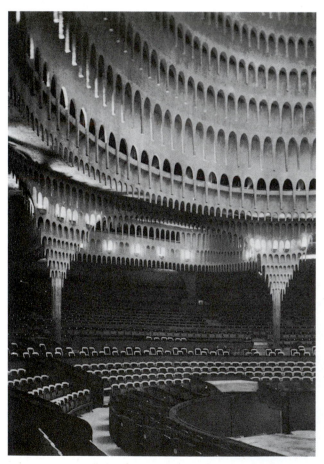

12.14 Hans Poelzig, Grosses Schauspielhaus (Great Theater), Berlin, 1919. Dismantled 1938.

12.16 Rudolf Steiner, Goetheanum II, Dornach, Switzerland, 1925–28.

Toward the International Style: The Netherlands and Belgium

Berlage and Van de Velde

Although he considered himself a traditionalist, the Dutch architect **Hendrik Petrus Berlage** (1856–1934) was passionately devoted to stripping off the ornamental accessories of academic architecture and expressing honest structure and function. He characteristically used brick as a building material, the brick that, in the absence of stone and other materials, has created the architectural face of the Low Countries. His best-known building, the Amsterdam Stock Exchange (fig. **12.17**) (now home to the Beurs van Berlage Foundation and the Dutch Philharmonic Orchestra), is principally of brick, accented with details of light stone. The brick is presented, inside and out, without disguise or embellishment, as is the steel framework that supports the glass ceiling. The general effect, with the massive corner tower and the low arcades of the interior, is obviously inspired by Romanesque architecture, in some degree seen through the eyes of the American architect H. H. Richardson, whose work he knew and admired (see fig. 4.10).

In his writings, Berlage insisted on the primacy of interior space. The walls defining the spaces had to express both the nature of their materials, and their strength and bearing function, undisguised by ornament. Above all, through the use of systematic proportions, Berlage sought a total effect of unity analogous to that created by the Greeks of the fifth century B.C.E., whose temples and civic buildings were constructed with the careful application of proportional relationships between all parts of a building. He conceived of an interrelationship of architecture, painting, and sculpture, but with architecture in the dominant role.

Berlage's approach to architecture was also affected by Frank Lloyd Wright, whose work he discovered first through publications and then at first hand on a trip to the United States in 1911. He was enthusiastic about Wright and particularly about the Larkin Building (see fig. 12.5), with its analogies to his own Amsterdam Stock Exchange. What appealed to Berlage and his followers about Wright was his rational approach—his efforts to control and utilize the machine and to explore new materials and techniques in the creation of a new society.

12.17 Hendrik Petrus Berlage, Stock Exchange, Amsterdam, 1898–1903.

Nearly every turn-of-the-century art or design movement, from Impressionism to Arts and Crafts, nourished the fertile career of the Belgian Henry Clemens van de Velde (see also chapter 5). Van de Velde was a painter, craftsman, industrial designer, architect, and critic who had an extensive influence on German architecture and design. He was a socialist who wanted to make his designs available to the working classes through mass production. Trained as a painter, first in Antwerp and then in Paris, he was in touch with the Impressionists and was interested in Symbolist poetry. Back in Antwerp, painting in a manner influenced by Seurat, he exhibited with Les XX, the avant-garde Brussels group (see chapter 3). Through them he discovered Gauguin, Morris, and the English Arts and Crafts movement. As a result, he enthusiastically took up the graphic arts, particularly poster and book design (see fig. 5.4), and then, in 1894, turned to the design of furniture. All the time, he was writing energetically, preaching the elimination of traditional ornament, the assertion of the nature of materials, and the development of new, rational principles in architecture and design.

After fifteen years in Germany (see above), the outbreak of World War I forced Van de Velde to leave his post in Weimar. He recommended the young architect Walter Gropius as his successor for the directorship of the Weimar School. It was not until after the war, in 1919, however, that Gropius assumed his duties and consolidated the separate schools of fine and applied arts. Under the new name of Das Staatliche Bauhaus, this was to become the most influential school in the history of architecture and design (see chapter 16). Van de Velde finally returned to Brussels in 1925. The later houses and other buildings on which he worked, notably the Kröller-Müller Museum (1936–38) at Otterlo in the Netherlands, are characterized by austerity and refinement of details and proportions—evidence, perhaps, of the reciprocal influence of younger experimental architects who had emerged from his original educational systems.

De Stijl

One of the most important legacies of the de Stijl movement (see chapter 11) was its enormous impact on the development of modern architecture. De Stijl (The Style) was named for the group's magazine, founded in 1917 and edited by Theo van Doesburg until his death in 1932. During World War I, neutral Holland was one of the very few countries in Europe where building could continue, with the consequence that the transition from prewar to postwar architectural experiment can clearly be followed. Many of the ideas and theories fermenting everywhere in Europe before 1914 came to their first realization in the Netherlands at this time. Consequently, the Dutch solutions were studied by artists and architects everywhere when the war ended. The formative influences on de Stijl architects were Hendrik Petrus Berlage (see fig. 12.17) and Frank Lloyd Wright (see figs. 12.1, 12.6).

J. J. P. Oud, Robert van 't Hoff, and Gerrit Rietveld, three of the principal architects of de Stijl, were also acquainted with the early modernists in Germany and Austria—Behrens, Loos, Hoffmann, and Olbrich—but their association with Mondrian and Van Doesburg had considerable influence on the forms that their architecture would take. Another important influence is to be found in the writings of M. H. J. Schoenmaekers, which also provided a philosophical base for Mondrian's painting and theorizing before 1917. Schoenmaekers propounded a mystical cosmology based on the rectangle. Inspired by Theosophy, his *Elements of Expressive Mathematics* (1916) sought to uncover the hidden relationships between natural forms. From such ideas arose an architecture of flat roofs, with plain walls arranged according to definite systems that create a functional and harmonious interior space. This was the beginning of the International Style, which was to dominate monumental building during the middle years of the twentieth century, especially in the forms of the skyscraper. However, Dutch architecture was traditionally domestic in scale, and de Stijl architects remained within this tradition. Only later would their ideas be translated into structures on a monumental scale in the United States.

In their aesthetic, the architects and artists of de Stijl were much concerned with the place of the machine and its function in the creation of a new art and a new architecture. They shared this concern with the Italian Futurists, with whom Van Doesburg corresponded (Severini was a regular corresponding member of de Stijl), but they departed from the emotional exaltation of the machine in favor of enlisting its power to create a new collective order. From this approach arose their importance for subsequent experimental architecture. Van Doesburg called architecture the "synthesis of all the arts" and said that it would "spring from human function" rather than from historical building types that had been developed in a time when the patterns of domestic life had little in common with modern lifestyles.

The actual buildings created by these architects before 1921 were not numerous. A house built by **Robert van 't Hoff** (1852–1911) in Utrecht in 1916 (fig. **12.18**) antedated the formation of de Stijl and was almost entirely based on his first-hand observations of Wright's work in Chicago, as may be seen in the cantilevered cornices, the grouping of windows, the massing of corners, as well as the severe rectangularity of the whole. The unrealized project that **J. J. P. Oud** (1890–1963) prepared for seaside housing on the Strand Boulevard at Scheveningen, the Netherlands, in 1917 displays the future International Style strategy for housing in a flat-roofed, terraced row of repeated individual rectangular units. A 1919 project by Oud for a small factory was a combination of cubic masses alternating effectively with vertical chimney pylons and horizontal windows in the Wright manner. Instead of the typical early Wright pitched roof, however, de Stijl

12.18 Robert van 't Hoff, Huis ter Heide, Utrecht, the Netherlands, 1916.

12.19 J. J. P. Oud, Workers' Housing Estate, Hook of Holland, 1924–27.

12.20 J. J. P. Oud, Café de Unie, Rotterdam, 1925. Destroyed 1940.

architects, almost from the beginning, opted for a flat roof, thus demonstrating a relationship to de Stijl painters. In the best known and in many ways most influential of his early buildings, the 1924–27 housing project for workers at Hook of Holland (fig. **12.19**), Oud employed wrap-around, curved corners on his façades and solidly expressed brickwork in a manner that suggested a direct line of influence from Berlage, despite the rectangularity and openness of the fenestration and the flat roofs. The workers' houses had an importance beyond their stylistic influence as an early example of enlightened planning for well-designed, low-cost housing. In the façade design of the Café de Unie in Rotterdam (fig. **12.20**), Oud almost literally translated a 1920s Mondrian painting into architectural terms, at the same time illustrating the possibilities of de Stijl for industrial, poster, and typographic design. The café was destroyed in the bombing of Rotterdam in 1940. Oud lived until 1963 and, in his later, monumental buildings, was once more absorbed into the International Style of which he was a somewhat reluctant pioneer.

Van 't Hoff was a more adventurous spirit, at least in his theories. He was the first member of de Stijl to discover the Italian architect Sant'Elia, about whose unfulfilled projects (see fig. 12.27) he wrote in *de Stijl*. The other two leading architects associated with de Stijl (aside from Van Doesburg himself, who not only was active as an architectural designer and a color consultant but also wrote architectural criticism under various names) were **Gerrit Rietveld** (1888–1964) and Cornelis van Eesteren. Both rose to prominence after the end of World War I, so that their achievements belong to the period of the international spread of de Stijl.

Rietveld's 1924–25 Schröder House is the most complete statement of de Stijl in architecture (fig. **12.21**). The house was a commission from Mrs. Truus Schröder-Schräder, who collaborated closely with Rietveld on its design. Mrs. Schröder lived in the house for sixty years and, toward the end of her life, initiated the Rietveld Schröder House Foundation, which oversaw a complete renovation of the structure between 1974 and 1987. For the house, Rietveld used detached interlocking planes of rectangular slabs, joined by unadorned piping, to break up the structure, giving the whole the appearance of a Constructivist

sculpture. The large corner and row windows give ample interior light; cantilevered roofs shelter the interior from the sun; and, according to Mrs. Schröder's requirements, sliding partitions created open-plan spaces for maximum flexibility of movement. The rooms are light, airy, and cool, thus planned to create a close relationship between the interior spaces and exterior nature.

Trained as a cabinetmaker, Rietveld also designed furniture, which assumed a role much like functional sculpture within de Stijl interiors. His 1923 *Red and Blue Chair* (fig. **12.22**) is among the most succinct statements of de Stijl design. Rietveld first constructed the chair in plain wood in 1917, and painted it in 1923. The seat is blue, the back is red, and the sections of the frame are black with yellow ends. The simple, skeleton-like frame clearly discloses its structure, which, like all of Rietveld's furniture, eschews any sense of the luxurious or highly crafted object, for it was intended for mass production (which never took place). The tilted planes of the seat and back, which have parallels in the linear structures of some of Van Doesburg's paintings (see figs. 11.35, 11.36), convey less a sense of classical balance than of dynamic equilibrium. "The construction," the artist wrote, "is attuned to the parts to

12.21 Gerrit Rietveld, Living and dining area, Schröder House, with furniture by Rietveld.

12.22 Gerrit Rietveld, *Red and Blue Chair*, 1917. Painted wood, height 34½" (87.6 cm). The Museum of Modern Art, New York.

insure that no part dominates or is subordinate to the others. In this way the whole stands freely and clearly in space, and the form stands out from the material." Fundamental to de Stijl philosophy was this sense of the integral relationship between the whole and its constituent parts. Until his death in 1964, Rietveld remained one of the masters of Dutch architecture, receiving many major commissions, of which the last was the Van Gogh Museum in Amsterdam, begun in 1967.

Cornelis van Eesteren (1897–1988) collaborated with Van Doesburg on a number of architectural designs during the twenties, including a project for a house that was one of the most monumental efforts in de Stijl domestic architecture attempted to that date. In contrast with Rietveld's approach, the palatial edifice of the projected Rosenberg House (fig. **12.23**) emphasized the pristine rectangular masses of the building, coordinated as a series of wings spreading out from a central core, defined by the strong

12.23 Cornelis van Eesteren and Theo van Doesburg, Project for Rosenberg House, 1923.

vertical accent of the chimney pier in the mode of Wright. In the central mass they opened up the interior space with cantilevered terraces that anticipated Wright's 1936 house in Bear Run, Pennsylvania.

New Materials, New Visions: France and Italy

French architecture during the period 1900–14 was dominated by the Beaux-Arts tradition, except for the work of two architects of high ability, Auguste Perret and Tony Garnier. Both were pioneers in the use of reinforced concrete. In his 1902–3 apartment building (fig. **12.24**) **Auguste Perret** (1874–1954) covered a thin reinforced-concrete skeleton with glazed terracotta tiles decorated in an Art Nouveau foliate pattern. The structure is clearly revealed and allows for large window openings on the façade. The architect increased daylight illumination by folding the façade around a front wall and then arranging the principal rooms so that all had outside windows. The strength and lightness of the material also substantially increased openness and spatial flow.

Perret's masterpiece in ferroconcrete building is probably his Church of Notre Dame at Le Raincy, near Paris, built in 1922–23 (fig. **12.25**). Here he used the simple

12.25 Auguste Perret, Church of Notre Dame, Le Raincy, France, 1922–23.

12.24 Auguste Perret, Apartment house, 25 Rue Franklin, Paris, 1902–3.

form of the Early Christian basilica—a long rectangle with only a slightly curving apse, a broad, low-arched nave, and side aisles just indicated by comparably low transverse arches. Construction in reinforced concrete permitted the complete elimination of structural walls. The roof rests entirely on widely spaced slender columns, and the walls are simply constructed of stained glass (designed by the painter Maurice Denis) arranged on a pierced screen of precast-concrete elements. The church at Le Raincy remains a landmark of modern architecture, not only in the effective use of ferroconcrete but also in the beauty and refinement of its design.

While working in Rome around 1900, **Tony Garnier** (1869–1948) developed a radically new approach to urban planning that overturned the traditional academic approach based on symmetry and monumentality. In Garnier's model town, residential areas, industrial sites, transport infrastructure, and civic facilities are all rationally interrelated. From 1905, his designs as municipal architect for his native city of Lyon explored the architectural possibilities of steel and reinforced concrete. His 1913 hall for the city's cattle market and abattoirs (fig. **12.26**) achieved a steel span of 262 feet (80 m).

12.26 Tony Garnier, Lyons Market Hall, France, 1913.

In Italy, at the First Free Futurist Exhibition, held in Rome in 1914, the founders of Futurism (see chapter 11) were joined by a number of younger artists, including Giorgio Morandi, Mario Sironi, and Enrico Prampolini. The most interesting new recruit was the young architect **Antonio Sant'Elia** (1888–1916). Sant'Elia's *Manifesto of Futurist Architecture* was no doubt written with the ever-present assistance of Marinetti, who later published Sant'Elia's text again with his own modifications. In his text and drawings, Sant'Elia conceived of cities built of the newest materials, in terms of the needs of modern men and women, and as expressions of the dynamism of the modern spirit. His visionary ideas remained on the drawing board, for his renderings were not plans for potentially functioning buildings. They were rather more like dynamic architectural sculpture. His drawings for the Città Nuova (New City) (fig. **12.27**) gave visual form to his ideas about a modern metropolis built with the technology of the future. His city contained imaginary factories and power stations on multilevel highways and towers of fantastic proportions. Though his buildings never materialized, Sant'Elia's belief in an authentic architecture based on industrial mechanization had much in common with his German and Dutch contemporaries.

Like so many artist of promise, Sant'Elia died in World War I. The war interrupted many experiments in architecture, as well as in painting and sculpture, begun in the first years of the twentieth century. During the war years a new generation of architects emerged—Gropius and Mies van der Rohe in Germany; Le Corbusier in France; Oud and Rietveld in Holland; Eliel Saarinen and Alvar Aalto in Finland. Together with Frank Lloyd Wright in the United States, these architects built on the foundations of the pioneers discussed in this chapter to create one of the great architectural revolutions of history.

12.27 Antonio Sant'Elia, Train and plane station for project for Città Nuova, 1914. Probably black ink on paper. Musei Civici, Como.

13
From Fantasy to Dada and the New Objectivity

Late nineteenth-century explorations of the irrational and fantastic and a growing interest in naive and primitivizing modes of expression in art found a striking embodiment during World War I in the eclectic productions of a diverse group of artists who labeled their endeavor "Dada." The Dadaists felt that reason, logic, and Western ideals of progress had led to the disaster of world war, and that the only way forward was through political anarchy, the natural emotions, the intuitive, and the irrational. Dada was first and foremost a response to the brutal, mechanized madness of war. More distantly, it can be seen as a descendant of Romanticism and Symbolism, which themselves were preceded by a thousand years or more of individuals and movements concerned with some sort of personal, eccentric, unorthodox, mystical, or supernatural expression. These currents also found expression of a more inwardly focused kind in the art of Marc Chagall and of Italian painters of the Metaphysical School.

Truth Pursued through the Dreamworld: Chagall and the Metaphysical School

As Romanticism grew and spread in the nineteenth century, visions of imagined worlds appeared in many forms in painting, sculpture, and architecture. The dreamworlds of Moreau, Redon, Ensor (see fig. 5.22), Böcklin (see fig. 5.24), Klinger, and Rousseau (see fig. 3.15) provided the principal transition from nineteenth-century Romanticism to twentieth-century fantasy.

Chagall

While Russian artist **Marc Chagall** (1887–1985) was the contemporary of such prominent figures as Tatlin and Goncharova (see chapter 11), his art followed a course quite divergent from that of the Constructivists in post-revolutionary Russia. Chagall's paintings do not fit neatly into a category or movement, but their sense of fantasy anticipates aspects of Surrealism, which developed some-

what later. Chagall was born to a large and poor Jewish family in Vitebsk, Russia. He acquired a large repertoire of Russian–Jewish folktales and a deep attachment to the Jewish religion and traditions, from which his personal and poetic visual language emerged. He attended various art schools in St. Petersburg, but derived little benefit until 1908, when he enrolled in an experimental school directed by the theater designer Léon Bakst, who was influenced by the new ideas emanating from France. In 1910, after two years of study, Chagall departed for Paris.

In Paris, he entered the orbit of Guillaume Apollinaire and the leaders of the new Cubism (see chapter 10), as well as that of Modigliani, Soutine, and Jules Pascin. Chagall's Russian paintings had largely been intimate genre scenes, often enriched by elements of Russian or Jewish folklore. His intoxication with Paris fueled his experimentation with Fauve color and Cubist space, and his subjects became filled with a lyricism that, within two years of his arrival, emerged in mature and uniquely poetic paintings.

Homage to Apollinaire (fig. **13.1**) was shown for the first time at Herwarth Walden's Der Sturm Gallery in Berlin in 1914. That show had an impact on the German Expressionists that extended well beyond World War I. Chagall's painting is a homage to four people he admired, including Herwarth Walden and Apollinaire, whose names are inscribed around a heart at the lower left. The artist included his own name in Roman and Hebrew letters at the top of the canvas. A circular pattern of color shapes, inspired by the paintings of his friend Robert Delaunay (see fig. 10.44), surrounds the bifurcated figure of Adam and Eve. The esoteric symbolism of *Homage to Apollinaire* has been variously interpreted. Beyond the traditional biblical meanings are references to alchemy and other mystical schools of thought. The bodies of Adam and Eve emerge from one pair of legs to symbolize the union and opposition of male and female, derived from medieval representations of the Fall from Grace. The numbers on the left arc of the outer circle introduce the notion of time. In fact, the figures themselves read like the hands of a clock.

13.1 Marc Chagall, *Homage to Apollinaire*, 1911–12. Oil, gold and silver powder on canvas, 6' 6¾" × 6' 3⅝" (2 × 1.9 m). Stedelijk van Abbe Museum, Eindhoven, the Netherlands.

Such themes of lovers irrevocably joined extend throughout Chagall's work, as do references to both Jewish and Christian spirituality.

During the next years in Paris, Chagall continued to create new forms to express his highly personal vision. In *Paris*

Through the Window (fig. **13.2**), the double-faced Janus figure (the Roman god of doorways) in the lower right corner, with its two profiles in contrasting light and shadow, suggests a double nature for the painting—the romantic yet real Paris, and the Paris transformed in the poet's dreams—with trains floating upside down, pedestrians promenading parallel to the sidewalks, and an aviator supported by a triangular kite. The window, with its frame of red, yellow, blue, and green, and its human-headed cat acting as a domesticated Cerberus (the mythical three-headed dog who guards the underworld), becomes a partition between the two realms. The composition of the sky in large geometric areas and the animated buildings, particularly the somewhat tilted Eiffel Tower (which could not be seen from Chagall's studio), suggest Robert Delaunay's dynamic method (see fig. 10.43) imposed upon a dream of gentle nostalgia. Many of Chagall's contemporaries, including Delaunay, did not favor this strong imaginative element. It was the poet André Breton, the principal theorist of Surrealism, who would recognize the significance of Chagall's "liberation of the object from the laws of weight and gravity."

Chagall returned to Vitebsk in 1914 and, caught by the outbreak of war in Russia, he stayed there until 1922. After his reunion in Russia with his beloved Bella, whom he married in 1915, he commemorated his feeling for her in a group of paintings of lovers. *Birthday* (fig. **13.3**) is a 1923 copy of a composition originally painted in 1915 (Chagall occasionally made copies of his paintings to keep for his

13.2 Marc Chagall, *Paris Through the Window*, 1913. Oil on canvas, 52⅜ × 54¾" (133 × 139.1 cm). Solomon R. Guggenheim Museum, New York.

13.3 Marc Chagall, *Birthday*, 1923. Oil on canvas, 31⅞ × 39⅜" (81 × 100 cm). Private collection.

own use). This canvas commemorates Bella's surprise visit to the artist's studio with a bouquet of flowers for his birthday. Chagall floats ecstatically through the air and, with delicious absurdity, twists his head for a kiss.

After the Russian Revolution, Chagall, like Malevich and other avant-garde artists, served for a time as a commissar of fine arts and formed a free art academy. Perhaps his most fruitful work was for the State Yiddish Chamber Theater in Moscow, where he painted murals and designed sets and costumes. This opportunity to work on a large scale in the theater continued to fascinate him and to inspire some of his most striking paintings. *The Green Violinist* (fig. **13.4**), painted after his return to Paris in 1923, is also a replica of an earlier work. It is based on one of the paintings Chagall made for the Yiddish Theater, studies for which he brought to Paris. The violinist, a subject frequently depicted by Chagall, refers to the traditional Jewish form of music that was performed in local villages. Here the purple-frocked fiddler is seen floating above the brown and gray roofs of his village.

In Paris, Chagall became increasingly active in the graphic arts, especially for the dealer Ambroise Vollard. Over the years he continued to move from project to project with undiminished energy and enthusiasm. In 1945 he designed sets and costumes for Igor Stravinsky's *Firebird*. He made color lithographs; produced sculptures and ceramics; designed a ceiling for the Paris Opéra in 1963 and murals for the Metropolitan Opera at the Lincoln Center in New York in 1966. He also designed many characteristically vibrant stained-glass windows in which he was able to indulge his love of rich, translucent color.

13.4 Marc Chagall, *The Green Violinist*, 1923–24. Oil on canvas, 6'5¾" × 3'6¾" (1.9 × 1.1 m). Solomon R. Guggenheim Museum, New York.

De Chirico, Carra, and the Metaphysical School

Working in Italy from around 1913 to 1920, the Metaphysical painters retained the forms of Renaissance reality, perspective space, recognizable environment, and sculptural figures and objects, but used various juxtapositions to produce surprise and shock, and to create an atmosphere of strangeness, sometimes even of fear and horror. Though the Metaphysical School was never a movement or style in the same sense that Cubism was, in their search for new content Metaphysical painters had a strong influence on Surrealism's exploration of the intuitive and the irrational (see chapter 15).

The work of **Giorgio de Chirico** (1888–1978), in particular, links nineteenth-century Romantic fantasy with twentieth-century Surrealism. Born in Greece of Italian parents, de Chirico learned drawing in Athens. After the death of his father, the family moved to Munich in order to advance the artistic leanings of Giorgio, and the musical leanings of his younger brother. In Munich, de Chirico was exposed to the art of Böcklin (see fig. 5.24) and Klinger. What impressed de Chirico about Böcklin was his ability to impart "surprise": to make real and comprehensible the improbable or illusory by juxtaposing it with normal everyday experience. De Chirico's concept of a painting as a symbolic vision was also affected by his readings of the philosophical writings of Nietzsche. For example, Nietzsche's insistence that art expresses deep-seated motivations within the human psyche led de Chirico to his metaphysical examination of still life.

While de Chirico was in Germany, from 1905 to 1909, Art Nouveau (see chapter 5) was still a force, and the German Expressionists (see chapter 8) were beginning to make themselves known. Ideal or mystical philosophies and pseudophilosophies were gaining currency among artists and writers everywhere, and modern Theosophy was an international cult. We have already seen the Theosophical bases of Kandinsky's approach to abstraction, and his mystical concepts of an inner reality beyond surface appearance that later affected artists as divergent as Mondrian and Klee.

Psychoanalysis, with its study of the subconscious, the symbolism of dreams, and the importance of instinct and emotion on human behavior, also had great importance for artists seeking new modes of expression. These artists were occasionally profound students of philosophy or psychology. Most often, however, they assimilated the current, popularized ideas, which became the basis for works of art expressed through their peculiar and intense perception. De Chirico constantly referred to the "metaphysical content" of his paintings, using the word metaphysical (which in philosophy refers to broad questions of the nature of causality, being, and time) loosely or inaccurately to cover various effects of strangeness, surprise, and shock.

De Chirico's approach to art during his early and most important phase—up to 1920—was to examine a theme as though wringing from it its central mystery. In 1912 and 1913, while living in Paris, he painted a group of works incorporating a Hellenistic sculpture of a reclining Ariadne. One of these works, *The Soothsayer's Recompense* (fig. **13.5**), presents the darkened arches of a classical façade beneath a large clock. On the distant horizon a moving train introduces another modern element into a seemingly ancient context. Such anomalies are commonplace in Italian cities—a palazzo may become a nineteenth-century railway station. De Chirico used these anachronisms to suggest the melancholy of departure, a melancholy that

13.5 Giorgio de Chirico, *The Soothsayer's Recompense*, 1913. Oil on canvas, 53½ × 71" (135.9 × 180.3 cm). Philadelphia Museum of Art.

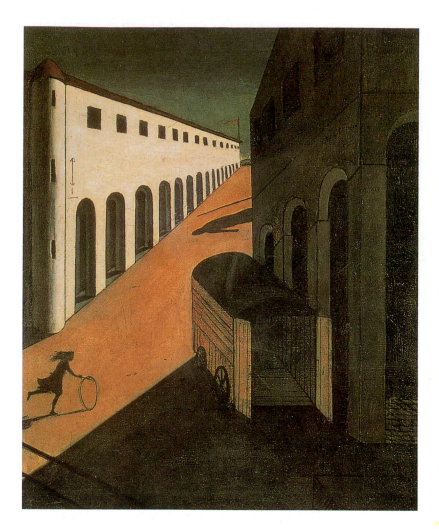

13.6 Giorgio de Chirico, *The Melancholy and Mystery of a Street*, 1914. Oil on canvas, 34¼ × 28⅛" (87 × 71.4 cm). Private collection.

and act as the protagonists in de Chirico's pictorial dramas. The paintings that use these blank-faced figures also recall Renaissance architectural perspectives of the fifteenth and sixteenth centuries; they create a dramatic aura through the use of extreme foreshortenings and close-ups.

Upon Italy's entry into the war, de Chirico left Paris, where he had attracted considerable attention among the avant-garde, and returned home to Italy. In Ferrara, from 1915 to 1919, de Chirico summed up his explorations of the previous years in a fully developed mature style. The haunting, dreamlike fusion of reality and unreality in his paintings was aptly termed Metaphysical, and when de Chirico met the artists Carlo Carrà and Filippo de Pisis in the army hospital in Ferrara, they formed the association known as the Scuola Metafisica, or Metaphysical School. *The Great Metaphysician* (fig. **13.7**) is a key work of this time, the climax of the artist's visions of loneliness and nostalgia, his fear of the unknown, his premonitions of the future, and his depiction of a reality beyond the physical realm. *The Great Metaphysician* combines the architectural space of the empty city square and the developed mannequin figure. The deep square is sealed in with low classical buildings. The buildings to the right and left are abstract silhouettes extending dark, geometric shadows over the brown area of the square. Only the rear buildings and the foreground monument are brightly lit. This monument on a low base is a looming construction of elements from the studio and drafting table, crowned by a blank mannequin head. It is clear from these paintings that the Metaphysical School shared little of the Italian Futurists' faith in machine technology (see chapter 11) and its desire to capture the dynamism of modern life. Rather, de Chirico and his followers sought an elegiac and enigmatic expression, one that, unlike the Futurists, did not reject the art of the Italian past.

After 1920, just as de Chirico began to be recognized as a forerunner of new movements in many parts of Europe and the United States, he suddenly turned against the direction of his own painting and settled on an academic classicism that he continued to pursue. As a result, he quarreled violently with the Surrealists, who had hailed his early work as the most crucial forerunner of their own, but who dismissed his later classically oriented style. In his later career, de Chirico did not actually repudiate his own early

saturates the shadowed square where deserted Ariadne mourns her departed lover Theseus. At times, the strange, sad loneliness of de Chirico's squares takes on dimensions of fear and isolation in a vast, empty space.

The Melancholy and Mystery of a Street of 1914 (fig. **13.6**) is one of de Chirico's finest examples of deep perspective used for emotional effect. On the right, an arcaded building in deep browns and grays casts a shadow filling the foreground; a lower white arcade on the left sweeps back toward infinity; the sky is threatening. Into the brightly lit space between the buildings emerges a little girl rolling her hoop inexorably toward a looming black specter of a figure standing behind the dark building. In the foreground of the palazzo on the right is an empty old-fashioned freight car or carnival van whose open doors add another suggestive and disturbing element. The scene may be described matter-of-factly: an Italian city square with shadows lengthening in a late autumn afternoon; an arcade of shops closed for the day; railway tracks in the lower left corner; the shadow of a heroic nineteenth-century statue; a little girl hurrying home. But from these familiar components the artist created an ominous mood.

For several years after 1914, de Chirico incorporated mannequins into his compositions as surrogates for the human figure. These mannequins suggest the articulated wooden figures used in drawing classes, dressmakers' dummies, or Renaissance lay figures and anatomical charts, works. However, like many other artists, he abandoned experimentation after World War I and attempted to rejoin the mainstream of European post-Renaissance painting.

The Futurist and Metaphysical painter Carlo Carrà (see chapter 11) met de Chirico in 1917 while on military service in Ferrara. Carrà had been replacing the coloristic fluidity of his Futurist paintings with a more disciplined style akin to Analytic Cubism. In the early war years he applied Marinetti's concept of free words to collages with propagandistic intent (see fig. 11.7). The form proposed by Marinetti, and practiced for a time by Carrà, specifically influenced poets and artists among the Dadaists and Surrealists.

The directions of Carrà's paintings and collages after 1912 indicate his search for a new content and for forms less fragmented than those of Futurism. He painted pictures in 1917 that are almost pastiches of de Chirico's, but in *The Drunken Gentleman* (fig. **13.8**), dated 1916 but probably painted in 1917, he developed an individual approach. The objects—sculptured head, bottle, glass—are modeled with clear simplicity in muted color gradations of gray and white that are given strength and solidity by the heavy impasto of the paint. Out of elementary still-life

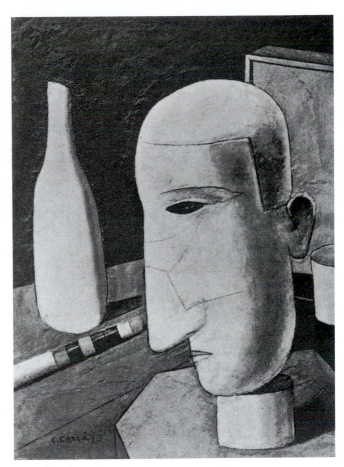

13.8 Carlo Carrà, *The Drunken Gentleman*, 1917 (dated 1916 on canvas). Oil on canvas, 23⅝ × 17½" (60 × 44.5 cm). Collection Carlo Frua de Angeli, Milan.

props, the artist created his own metaphysical reality. In 1918 Carrà published *Pittura Metafisica*, a book about the Metaphysical School. De Chirico, justifiably feeling that he was not given adequate credit, became embittered, and ended both their friendship and the Metaphysical School as a formal movement.

The World Turned Upside Down: The Birth of Dada

During World War I, Zurich, in neutral Switzerland, was the first important center in which an art, a literature, and even a music and a theater of the fantastic and the absurd arose. In 1915 a number of artists and writers, almost all in their twenties and in one way or another displaced by the war that was sweeping over Europe, converged on this city. This international group included the German writers Hugo Ball and Richard Huelsenbeck, the Romanian poet Tristan Tzara, the Romanian painter and sculptor Marcel Janco, the Alsatian painter, sculptor, and poet Jean (Hans) Arp, the Swiss painter and designer Sophie Taeuber, and the German painter and experimental filmmaker Hans Richter. Many other poets and artists were associated with Zurich Dada, but these were the leaders whose demonstrations, readings of poetry, "noise concerts," art exhibitions, and writings assaulted the traditions

13.7 Giorgio de Chirico. *The Great Metaphysician.* 1917. Oil on canvas, 41⅛ × 27½" (104.5 × 69.8 cm). The Museum of Modern Art, New York.

and preconceptions of Western art and literature. Thrown together in Zurich, these young men and women expressed their reactions to the spreading hysteria of a world at war in forms that were intended as negative, anarchic, and destructive of all conventions. Dada was a search for new vision and content that went beyond any frivolous desire to outrage the bourgeoisie. In Dada there was a central force of wildly imaginative humor, one of its lasting delights—whether manifested in free-word-association poetry readings drowned in the din of noise machines, in absurd theatrical or cabaret performances (see fig. 13.10), in nonsense lectures, or in paintings produced by chance or intuition uncontrolled by reason. Nevertheless, it had a serious intent: the Zurich Dadaists were making a critical reexamination of the traditions, premises, rules, logical bases, even the concepts of order, coherence, and beauty that had guided the creation of the arts throughout history and remained central to the enterprise of high-minded, utopian modernism.

The Cabaret Voltaire and Its Legacy

Hugo Ball, a philosopher and mystic as well as a poet, was the first actor in the Dada drama. In February 1916, with the nightclub entertainer Emmy Hennings, he founded the Cabaret Voltaire in Zurich as a meeting place for these free spirits and a stage from which existing values could be attacked. Interestingly enough, across the street from the Cabaret Voltaire lived Vladimir Ilyich Lenin, who would stand at the forefront of the Russian Revolution the following year. Ball and Hennings were soon joined by Tzara, Janco, Arp, and Huelsenbeck.

The term "Dada" was coined in 1916 to describe the movement then emerging from the seeming chaos of the Cabaret Voltaire, but its origin is still doubtful. The popular version advanced by Huelsenbeck is that a French–German dictionary opened at random produced the word "dada," meaning a child's rocking horse or hobbyhorse. Richter remembers the *da, da, da, da* ("yes, yes") in the Romanian conversation of Tzara and Janco. *Dada* in French also means a hobby, event, or obsession. Other possible sources are in dialects of Italian and Kru African. Whatever its origin, the name Dada is the central, mocking symbol of this attack on established movements, whether traditional or experimental, that characterized early twentieth-century art. The Dadaists used many of the formulas of Futurism in the propagation of their ideas—the free words of Marinetti, whether spoken or written; the noise-music effects of Luigi Russolo to drown out the poets; the numerous manifestos. But their intent was antithetical to that of the Futurists, who extolled the machine world and saw in mechanization, revolution, and war the rational and logical means, however brutal, to the solution of human problems.

Zurich Dada was primarily a literary manifestation, whose ideological roots were in the poetry of Arthur Rimbaud, in the theater of Alfred Jarry, and in the critical ideas of Max Jacob and Guillaume Apollinaire. In painting and sculpture, until Picabia arrived, the only real innovations were the free-form reliefs and collages "arranged according to the laws of chance" by Jean Arp (see fig. 13.11). With few exceptions, the paintings and sculptures of other artists associated with Zurich Dada broke little new ground. In abstract and Expressionist film—principally through the experiments of Hans Richter and Viking Eggeling—and in photography and typographic design, however, the Zurich Dadaists made important innovations.

The Dadaists' theatrical activity was an important precursor to the sixties "happening" and other forms of performance art that developed after World War II, particularly that of the Fluxus group (see figs. 21.20, 21.21). In fact, the effects of Dada are so pervasive in today's culture that one can find instructions for composing Dada poetry on the Internet. Arp described a typical evening at the Cabaret Voltaire thus:

> Tzara is wiggling his behind like the belly of an Oriental dancer. Janco is playing an invisible violin and bowing and scraping. Madame Hennings, with a Madonna face, is doing the splits. Huelsenbeck is banging away nonstop on the great drum, with Ball accompanying him on the piano, pale as a chalky ghost. We were given the honorary title of Nihilists.

The performers may have been wearing one of the masks created by **Marcel Janco** (1895–1984) made of painted paper and cardboard (fig. **13.9**). Ball said these masks not only called for a suitable costume but compelled the wearer to act unpredictably, to dance with "precise, melodramatic gestures, bordering on madness." Dada theater of this kind had precedents in Russian Futurist performances, such as the 1913 *Victory over the Sun*, for which Malevich designed costumes.

Hugo Ball introduced abstract poetry at the Cabaret Voltaire with his poem *O Gadji Beri Bimba* in June 1916. Wrapped in a cardboard costume (fig. **13.10**), he recited his "sound poem," *Karawane*, from the two flanking music stands. Ball's thesis—that conventional language had no more place in poetry than the outworn human image in painting—produced a chant of more or less melodic syllables without meaning such as: "zimzim urallala zimzim zanzibar zimlalla zam …" Despite the frenzied reactions of the audience to this experiment, its influence—like much else presented at the Cabaret Voltaire—affected the subsequent course of twentieth-century poetry.

The Zurich Dadaists were violently opposed to any organized program in the arts, or any movement that might express the common stylistic denominator of a coherent group. Nevertheless, three factors shaped their creative efforts. These were bruitisme (noise-music, from *le bruit*—"noise"—as in *le concert bruitiste*), simultaneity, and chance. Bruitisme came from the Futurists, and simultaneity from the Cubists via the Futurists. Chance, of course, exists to some degree in any act of artistic creation.

13.9 Marcel Janco, *Mask*, 1919. Paper, cardboard, string, gouache, and pastel, 17¾ × 8⅝ × 2" (45 × 22 × 5 cm). Musée National d'Art Moderne, Centre d'Art et de Culture Georges Pompidou, Paris.

13.10 Hugo Ball reciting the poem *Karawane* at the Cabaret Voltaire, Zurich, 1916. Photograph, 28⅛ × 15¾" (71.5 × 40 cm). Kunsthaus, Zurich.

In the past the artist had normally attempted to control or to direct it, but it now became an overriding principle. All three, despite the artists' avowed negativism, soon became the basis for their revolutionary approach to the creative act, an approach still found in poetry, music, drama, and painting.

The year 1916 witnessed the first organized Dada evening at a public hall in Zurich and the first issue of the magazine *Collection Dada*, which Tzara would eventually take over and move to Paris. The following year, the first public Dada exhibitions were held at the short-lived Galerie Dada. Such activities ushered in a new, more constructive phase for Zurich Dada, broadened from the spontaneous performances of the Cabaret Voltaire. But with the end of World War I, Zurich Dada too was drawing to an end. The initial enthusiasms were fading; its participants were scattering. Ball abandoned Dada, and Huelsenbeck, who had opposed attempts to turn Dada into a conventional, codified movement, left for Berlin. Tzara remained for a time in Zurich and oversaw the last Dada soirée in 1919, after which he moved to Paris. The painter Francis

Picabia arrived in 1918, bringing contact with similar developments in New York and Barcelona. Picabia, together with Marcel Duchamp and Man Ray, had contributed to a Dada atmosphere in New York around Alfred Stieglitz's 291 Gallery and his periodical *291* (see chapter 10). With the help of the collector Walter Arensberg, Picabia began to publish his own journal of protest against everything, which he called *391*. After a journey to Barcelona, where he found many like-minded expatriates, Picabia visited Zurich, drawn by the spreading reputation of the originators of Dada. Returning to Paris at the end of the war, he became a link, as did Tzara, between the postwar Dadaists of Germany and France. Dada, which was perhaps more a state of mind than an organized movement, left an enormous legacy to contemporary art, particularly the Neo-Dada art of the fifties and early sixties (see figs. 21.10, 21.16).

Arp

Jean (Hans) Arp (1887–1966) was the major visual artist to emerge from Zurich Dada. Arp was born in Strasbourg, then a German city in the disputed region of Alsace but subsequently recovered by France. He studied painting and poetry, and in Paris in 1904 he discovered modern painting, which he then pursued in studies at the Weimar School of Art and the Académie Julian in Paris. He also wrote poetry of great originality and distinction throughout his life. The disparity between his formal training and the paintings he was drawn to brought uncertainty, and he spent the years 1908–10 in reflection in various small villages in Switzerland. The Swiss landscape seems to have made a lasting impression on him, and the abstraction to which he eventually turned was based on nature and organic shapes.

In Switzerland, Arp met Paul Klee, and after his return to Germany he was drawn into the orbit of Kandinsky and the Blaue Reiter painters (see figs. 8.17, 8.18). In 1912 he exhibited in Herwarth Walden's first Autumn Salon, and by 1914, back in Paris, he belonged to the circle of Picasso, Modigliani, Apollinaire, Max Jacob, and Delaunay.

Arp took an unusually long time finding his own direction. Since he destroyed most of his pre-1915 paintings, the path of his struggle is difficult to trace. He experimented with geometric abstraction based on Cubism, and by 1915, in Zurich, he was producing drawings and collages whose shapes suggest leaves and insect or animal life but which were actually abstractions. With **Sophie Taeuber** (1889–1943), whom he met in 1915 and married in 1922, he jointly made collages, tapestries, embroideries, and sculptures. Through his collaboration with her, Arp further clarified his ideas:

> These pictures are Realities in themselves, without meaning or cerebral intention. We … allowed the elementary and spontaneous to react in full freedom. Since the disposition of planes, and the proportions and colors of these planes seemed to depend purely on chance, I declared that these works, like nature, were ordered according to the laws of chance, chance being for me merely a limited part of an unfathomable *raison d'être*, of an order inaccessible in its totality.

Also emerging at this time was the artist's conviction of the metaphysical reality of objects and of life itself—some common denominator belonging to both the lowest and the highest forms of animals and plants. It may have been his passion to express his reality in the most concrete terms possible, as an organic abstraction (or, as he preferred to say, an organic concretion), that led him from painting to collage and then to relief and sculpture in the round.

In 1916–17 Arp produced collages of torn, rectangular pieces of colored papers scattered in a vaguely rectangular arrangement on a paper ground (fig. **13.11**). The story told of their origin is that Arp tore up a drawing that displeased him and dropped the pieces on the floor, then suddenly saw in the arrangement of the fallen scraps the solution to the problems with which he had been struggling. Arp continued to experiment with collages created in this manner, just as Tzara created poems from words cut out of newspapers, shaken and scattered on a table. Liberated from rational thought processes, the laws of chance, Arp felt, were more in tune with the workings of nature. By relinquishing a certain amount of control, he

was distancing himself from the creative process. This kind of depersonalization, already being explored by Marcel Duchamp in Paris, had profound consequences for later art.

The shift in emphasis away from the individual artist and the unique artistic creation allowed for fruitful collaboration between Taeuber and Arp, who dubbed their joint productions "Duo-Collages." Partly as a result of Taeuber's training in textiles, the couple did not restrict themselves to the fine art media traditionally reserved for painting and sculpture. In their desire to integrate art and life they shared an outlook with contemporaries in Russia and artists such as Sonia Delaunay (see fig. 10.45). Taeuber developed a geometric vocabulary in her early compositions made in Zurich (fig. **13.12**). These rigorous abstractions, organized around a rhythmical balance of horizontals and verticals, had a decisive influence on Arp's work. He said that when he met Taeuber in 1915, "she already knew how to give direct and palpable shape to her inner reality. … She constructed her painting like a work of masonry. The colors are luminous, going from rawest yellow to deep red." Between 1918 and 1920 Taeuber made four remarkable heads in polychromed wood, two of which are portraits of Arp (fig. **13.13**). These heads, humorously reminiscent of hat stands, are among the few

13.11 Jean Arp, *Collage Arranged According to the Laws of Chance*, 1916–17. Torn and pasted paper, 19⅛ × 13⅜" (48.6 × 34.6 cm). The Museum of Modern Art, New York.

13.12 Sophie Taeuber, *Rythmes Libres*, 1919. Gouache and watercolor on vellum, 14¾ × 10⅞" (37.6 × 27.5 cm). Kunsthaus, Zurich.

13.13 Sophie Taeuber, *Dada Head*, 1920. Painted wood, height 13⅜" (34 cm). Foundation Arp, Clamart, France.

works of Dada sculpture made in Zurich. At the same time, Raoul Hausmann was creating similar mannequinlike constructions in Berlin (see fig. 13.26).

By 1915, Arp was devising a type of relief consisting of thin layers of wood shapes. These works, which he called "constructed paintings," represent a medium somewhere between painting and sculpture. They give evidence of Arp's awareness of Cubist collage and constructions, which he would have seen in Paris in 1914–15 (see figs. 10.23, 10.26, 10.27, 10.28). To make his reliefs, Arp prepared drawings and gave them to a carpenter who cut them out in wood. While not executed with the same aleatory methods employed for the collages, the relief drawings sprang from Arp's willingness to let his pencil be guided unconsciously, without a set goal in mind. The curving, vaguely organic forms that resulted, which evoked the body and its processes or some other highly abstracted form in nature, have been called "biomorphic," a term used to describe the abstract imagery of Arp's later work as well as that of many Surrealists who followed his lead. Arp developed a vocabulary of biomorphic shapes that had universal significance.

An oval or egg shape, for example, was for him a "symbol of metamorphosis and development of bodies." A viola shape suggested a female torso, and then an accent was provided by a cutout circle that became a navel. Arp's later painted reliefs suggested plants, exotic vegetables, crustaceans, or swarming amoebae, with strong implications of life, growth, and metamorphosis. He used the term *"Formes terrestres"* or "earthly forms" to describe these reliefs. A particular shape might suggest a specific object and thus give the relief its name, as in *Fleur Marteau (Hammer Flower)* (fig. **13.14**). Although the origin of the shapes was initially intuitive (a line doodled on a piece of paper), the contour lines were as organic as the living organism that inspired them.

Although he was one of the founders of Zurich Dada who exerted tremendous influence on subsequent art, Arp did not perform in the theatrical presentations at the Cabaret Voltaire (unlike Taeuber, who danced in the Dada performances). "He never needed any hullabaloo," said Huelsenbeck, "Arp's greatness lay in his ability to limit himself to art." He also contributed drawings and poems

13.14 Jean Arp, *Fleur Marteau*, 1916. Oil on wood, 24⅜ × 19⅝" (61.9 × 49.8 cm). Fondation Arp, Clamart, France.

assisted by Duchamp and Picabia, Stieglitz founded the periodical *291* to present the revolutionary convictions about modern art held by these artists. Thus, ideas comparable to those that would define Zurich Dada one year later were fermenting independently in a small, cohesive group in New York. Aside from the two Europeans, the most important figure in the group was the young American artist Man Ray. In addition, the remarkable collectors Walter and Louise Arensberg, whose salons regularly attracted many of the leading artists and writers of the day, were important patrons of Marcel Duchamp, the artist of greatest stature and influence in the group.

Duchamp's Early Career

The enormous impact made on twentieth-century art by **Marcel Duchamp** (1887–1968) is best summarized by the artist Richard Hamilton: "All the branches put out by Duchamp have borne fruit. So widespread have been the effects of his life that no individual may lay claim to be his heir, no one has his scope or his restraint." Duchamp, a handsome, charismatic man of great intellect, devoted a lifetime to the creation of an art that was more cerebral than visual. By the beginning of World War I he had rejected the works of many of his contemporaries as "retinal" art, or art only intended to please the eye. Although a gifted painter, Duchamp ultimately abandoned conventional methods of making art in order, as he said, "to put art back at the service of the mind." He lived a simple but peripatetic existence, traveling between Europe and America for most of his adult life.

Duchamp's inquiry into the very nature of art was first expressed in such paintings as *Nude Descending a Staircase, No. 2* (see fig. 10.48), which used Cubist faceting to give, he said, "a static representation of movement." The Paris exhibition of the Futurists in February 1912 had helped the artist to clarify his attitudes, although his intention was at the opposite extreme of theirs. Futurist dynamism, with its "machine aesthetic," was an optimistic, humorless exaltation of the new world of the machine, with progress measured in terms of speed, altitude, and efficiency. Duchamp, though he used some of Futurism's devices, expressed disillusionment through satirical humor.

Duchamp spent the summer of 1912 painting machines of his own creation. While still in France, he made *The*

to Dada publications between 1916 and 1919. In Arp's later, freestanding sculptures in marble or bronze (see chapter 15), the suggestion of head or torso became more frequent and explicit. When asked in 1956 about a 1953 piece entitled *Aquatic*—which, reclining, suggests some form of sea life, and standing on end, a sensuous female torso—he commented, "In one aspect or another, my sculptures are always torsos." In the same way that de Chirico anticipated the use by some Surrealists of illusionistic techniques and recognizable images, Arp's work foreshadowed the different artistic tendency within Surrealism to employ abstract biomorphic shapes and arbitrary, nondescriptive color to create a world of fantasy. His work later influenced such artists as Joan Miró, André Masson, and Alexander Calder (see figs. 15.17, 15.18, 22.30).

A Further Shore: New York Dada

During World War I, Marcel Duchamp and Francis Picabia had both come to New York and found a congenial environment at 291, the avant-garde gallery founded by Alfred Stieglitz, who had introduced the American public to such European masters as Rodin, Toulouse-Lautrec, Henri Rousseau, Matisse, and Picasso. (The "Stieglitz circle" of American artists is discussed in chapter 18.) In 1915,

King and Queen Traversed by Swift Nudes in which the figures are not only mechanized but are conceived as machines in operation, pumping some form of sexual energy from one to another. Subsequently in Munich the artist pursued his fantasies of sexualized machines in a series of paintings and drawings, including *The Passage from Virgin to Bride* (fig. **13.15**) and the initial drawing for the great painting on glass, *The Bride Stripped Bare by Her Bachelors, Even* or *The Large Glass* (see fig. 13.20). Though these works suggest anatomical diagrams of the respiratory, circulatory, digestive, or reproductive systems of higher mammals, in each Duchamp abandoned the physicality of the human body. The organic becomes mechanized, and human flesh is supplanted by tubes, pistons, and cylinders. The term "mechanomorphic" was eventually coined to describe Duchamp's distinctive grafting of machine forms onto human activity. Thus, while he restored traditional symbols of inviolable purity and sanctified consummation (i.e., the virgin and the bride), he destroyed any sense of convention by presenting them as elaborate systems of anatomical plumbing. Doubting the validity of traditional painting and sculpture as appropriate modes of contemporary expression, and dissatisfied with Cubism, Duchamp still created beautifully rendered, visually seductive works of art. His recognition of this fact no doubt contributed to his decision to abandon painting at the age of twenty-five. "From Munich on," Duchamp said, "I had the idea of

The Large Glass. I was finished with Cubism and with movement—at least movement mixed up with oil paint. The whole trend of painting was something I didn't care to continue."

During 1912 the so-called Armory Show was being organized in New York, and the American painters Walt Kuhn and Arthur B. Davies and the painter–critic Walter Pach were then in Paris selecting works by French artists. Four paintings by Duchamp were chosen, including *Nude Descending a Staircase* and *The King and Queen Traversed by Swift Nudes*. When the Armory Show opened in February 1913, Duchamp's paintings, and most particularly the *Nude*, became the *succès de scandale* of the exhibition. Despite attacks in the press, all four of Duchamp's paintings were sold, and he suddenly found himself notorious.

Duchamp was meanwhile continuing with his experiments toward a form of art based on everyday subject matter—with a new significance determined by the artist and with internal relationships proceeding from a relativistic mathematics and physics of his own devising. Although he had almost ceased to paint, Duchamp worked intermittently toward a climactic object: *The Large Glass* (see fig. 13.20), intended to sum up the ideas and forms he had explored in *The Passage from Virgin to Bride* and related paintings. For this project, he made, between 1913 and 1915, the drawings, designs, and mathematical calculations

13.15 Marcel Duchamp, *The Passage from Virgin to Bride*, Munich, July–August 1912. Oil on canvas, 23⅜ × 21¼" (59.4 × 54 cm). The Museum of Modern Art, New York.

for *Bachelor Machine* and *Chocolate Grinder, No. 1*, later to become part of the male apparatus accompanying the bride in *The Large Glass*.

Duchamp's most outrageous and far-reaching assault on artistic tradition by far was his invention in 1913 of the "readymade," defined by Surrealist André Breton as "manufactured objects promoted to the dignity of art through the choice of the artist." Duchamp said his selection of common "found" objects, such as a bottle rack (fig. **13.16**), was guided by complete visual indifference, or "anaesthesia," and the absence of good or bad taste. They demonstrated, in the most irritating fashion to the art world of Duchamp's day, that art could be made out of virtually anything, and that it required little or no manipulation by the artist. Within Duchamp's vocabulary, his famously irreverent addition of a mustache and goatee to a reproduction of the *Mona Lisa* was a "rectified" readymade. An "assisted" readymade also required some intervention by the artist, as when Duchamp mounted an old bicycle wheel on an ordinary kitchen stool (fig. **13.17**).

Because the readymade could be repeated indiscriminately, Duchamp decided to make only a small number yearly, saying "for the spectator even more than for the artist, *art is a habit-forming drug* and I wanted to protect my readymade against such *contamination*." He stressed that it was in the very nature of the readymade to lack uniqueness, and since readymades are not originals in the conventional sense, a "replica will do just as well." To extend the perversity of this logic, Duchamp remarked: "Since the tubes of paint used by an artist are manufactured and readymade products we must conclude that all paintings in the world are assisted *readymades*."

Duchamp limited the number of readymades so that their original concept would not lose its impact. This attitude struck a chord among a broad spectrum of artists in the late fifties and sixties. So-called Neo-Dada, Pop, Minimalist, and Conceptual artists, for example, in their own way undermined the cult of originality that surrounded objects crafted by the artist's hand. They incorporated found objects (see fig. 21.54), left the fabrication of their work to others (see fig. 22.54), or sometimes avoided the object altogether.

For Duchamp, the conception, the "discovery," was what made a work of art, not the uniqueness of the object. One glimpses in the works discussed so far the complex process of Duchamp's thought—the delight in paradox, the play of visual against verbal, and the penchant for alliteration and double and triple meanings. In a deliberate act of provocation, Duchamp submitted a porcelain urinal, which he turned ninety degrees and entitled *Fountain* (see fig. 13.16), to the 1917 exhibition of the New York Society of Independent Artists. The work was signed "R. Mutt," a pun on the plumbing fixture manufacturer J. L. Mott Iron Works. Needless to say, the association with the then popular Mutt and Jeff cartoons did not escape Duchamp. Although the exhibition was in principle open to any artist's submission without the intervention of a jury, the work was rejected. Duchamp resigned from the association, and *Fountain* became his most notorious readymade.

In 1913–14 Duchamp had carried out an experiment in chance that resulted in *3 Stoppages Étalon (3 Standard Stoppages)* (fig. **13.18**) and was later applied to *The Large Glass*. In a spirit that mocked the notion of standard, scientifically perfect measurement, Duchamp dropped

13.16 Marcel Duchamp, *Bottle Rack* and *Fountain*, 1917. Installation photograph, Stockholm, 1963.

13.17 Marcel Duchamp, *Bicycle Wheel*, New York, 1951 (third version, after lost original of 1913). Assemblage: metal wheel, 25½" (63.8 cm) diameter, mounted on painted wood stool, 23¾" (60.2 cm) high; overall 50½ × 25½ × 16⅝" (128.3 × 64.8 × 42.2 cm). The Museum of Modern Art, New York.

13.18 Marcel Duchamp, *3 Stoppages Étalon (3 Standard Stoppages)*, 1913–14. Assemblage: 3 threads glued to 3 painted canvas strips, each mounted on a glass panel; 3 wood slats, shaped along one edge to match the curves of the threads; the whole fitted into a wooden box, 3 painted canvas strips, each 5¼ × 47¼" (13.3 × 120 cm); each mounted on a glass panel, 7¼ × 49⅜ × ¼" (18.4 × 125.4 × 0.6 cm); three wood slats, 2½ × 43 × ⅛" (6.2 × 109.2 × 0.2 cm), 2½ × 47 × ⅛" (6.1 × 119.4 × 0.2 cm), 2½ × 43¼ × ⅛" (6.3 × 109.7 × 0.2 cm); overall, fitted into wood box, 11⅛ × 50⅞ × 9" (28.2 × 129.2 × 22.7 cm). The Museum of Modern Art, New York.

three strings, each one meter in length, from a height of one meter onto a painted canvas. The strings were affixed to the canvas with varnish in the shape they assumed to "imprison and preserve forms obtained through chance." These sections of canvas and screen were then cut from the stretcher and laid down on glass panels, and three templates were cut from wooden rulers in the profile of

the shapes assumed by the strings. The idea of the experiment—not the action itself—was what intrigued Duchamp. *3 Stoppages Étalon* is thus a remarkable document in the history of chance as a controlling factor in the creation of a work of art.

In 1918, Duchamp made *Tu m'* (fig. **13.19**), his last painting on canvas, for the collector Katherine Dreier a

13.19 Marcel Duchamp, *Tu m'*, 1918. Oil and graphite on canvas, with brush, safety pins, nut and bolt, 2'3½" × 10'2¾" (0.7 × 3.2 m). Yale University Art Gallery, New Haven.

leading spirit in American avant-garde art. The painting has an unusually long and horizontal format, for it was destined for a spot above a bookcase in Dreier's library. It includes a compendium of Duchampian images: cast shadows, drawn in pencil, of a corkscrew and two readymades, *Bicycle Wheel* and *Hat Rack;* a pyramid of color samples (through which an actual bolt is fastened); a *trompe l'oeil* tear in the canvas "fastened" by three real safety pins; an actual bottle brush; a sign painter's hand (rendered by a professional sign painter), as well as the outlines at the left and right of *3 Stoppages Étalon.* Together with Dreier and Man Ray, Duchamp eventually founded the Société Anonyme, an important organization that produced publications, gave lectures, and put on exhibitions while building an important collection of modern art.

Duchamp's Later Career

When the United States entered World War I in 1917, Duchamp relocated for several months to Argentina and then to Europe. In 1920 he returned to New York, bringing a vial he called *50 cc of Paris Air* as a gift for the art collector Walter Arensberg. During this period he invented a female alter ego, Rrose Sélavy, which when pronounced in French sounds like "Eros, c'est la vie" or "Eros, that's life." Duchamp inscribed works with this pseudonym and was photographed several times by Man Ray in the guise of his feminine persona. Such gestures were typical of his tendency to break down gender boundaries, and they demonstrate the degree to which Duchamp's activities and his personality were as significant, if not more so, than any objects he made.

13.20 Marcel Duchamp, *The Bride Stripped Bare by Her Bachelors, Even* or *The Large Glass.* 1915–23. Oil, lead wire, foil, dust, and varnish on glass, 8'11" × 5'7" (2.7 × 1.7 m). Philadelphia Museum of Art.

13.21 Marcel Duchamp, *Boîte en valise (Box in a Valise)*, 1941. Leather valise containing miniature replicas, photographs, and color reproductions of works by Duchamp. Philadelphia Museum of Art.

In 1922, after yet another round of travel, Duchamp settled in New York and continued working on *The Large Glass* (fig. **13.20**). He finally ceased work on it in 1923. This painting on glass, which was in gestation for several years, is the central work of Duchamp's career. The glass support dispensed with the need for a background since, by virtue of its transparency, it captured the "chance environment" of its surroundings. *The Large Glass* depicts an elaborate and unconsummated mating ritual between the bride in the upper half of the glass, whose machinelike form we recognize from *The Passage from Virgin to Bride* (see fig. 13.15), and the uniformed bachelors in the lower half. These forms are rendered with a diagrammatic precision that underscores the pseudoscientific nature of their activities. Despite their efforts, the bachelors fail to project their "love gasoline" (the sperm gas or fluid constantly ground forth by the rollers of the chocolate machine) into the realm of the bride, so the whole construction becomes a paradigm of pointless erotic activity. Breton described it as "a mechanistic and cynical interpretation of the phenomenon of love." To annotate and supplement this cryptic work, Duchamp assembled his torn scraps of notes, drawings, and computations in another work titled *The Green Box*. This catalogue of Duchampian ideas was later published by the artist in a facsimile edition. Duchamp allowed New York dust to fall on *The Large Glass* for over a year and then had it photographed by Man Ray calling the result *Dust Breeding;* then he cleaned everything but a section of the cones, to which he cemented the dust with a fixative. The final touch came when the *Glass* was broken while in transit and was thereby webbed with a network of cracks. Duchamp is reported to have commented with satisfaction, "Now it is complete."

Back in Paris in the mid-thirties, Duchamp devised a work of art that made all of his inventions easily portable. The *Boîte en valise* (*Box in a Valise*) (fig. **13.21**) was a kind of leather briefcase filled with miniature replicas of his previous works, including all the aforementioned objects. It provided a survey of Duchamp's work, like a traveling retrospective. When, like so many other European artists, Duchamp sought final refuge in America from World War II in Europe, he came equipped with his "portable museum." Friends such as the American artist Joseph Cornell, who also made art in box form (see fig. 19.54), helped him assemble the many parts of *Bôite*. Like *The Green Box*, it was made into a multiple edition. Duchamp intended that the viewer participate in setting up and handling the objects in the valise. In this way, the viewer completes the creative act set in motion by the artist.

Although Duchamp let it be rumored that he had ceased all formal artistic activity in order to devote himself to chess (at which he excelled), he worked in secret for twenty years on a major sculptural project, completed in 1966. *Étant Donnés 1. La Chute d'Eau, 2. Le Gaz d'Éclairage (Given: 1. The Waterfall, 2. The Illuminating Gas)* is one of the most disturbing and enigmatic works of the century, but it came to light only after the artist's death, when it was installed in the Philadelphia Museum of Art, which owns most of Duchamp's major works. A mixed-media assemblage built around the realistic figure of a nude woman sprawled on the ground, *Étant Donnés* can only be viewed by one person at a time through a peephole in a large wooden door. Duchamp's secret considerations of realism and voyeurism, coupled with the mysterious title, provide a challenging complement to the mechanical sexuality and person symbolism of *The Large Glass*.

Picabia

Francis Picabia (1875–1953) was born in Paris of wealthy Cuban and French parents. Between 1908 and 1911 he moved from Impressionism to Cubism. He joined the Section d'Or briefly and then experimented with Orphism and Futurism (see fig. 10.49). In New York in 1915, he collaborated with Marcel Duchamp in establishing the American version of proto-Dada and, in the spirit of Duchamp, took up machine imagery as an emblematic and ironic mode of representation. "Almost immediately upon coming to America," Picabia said, "it flashed on me that the genius of the modern world is in machinery, and that through machinery art ought to find a most vivid expression." In this "mechanomorphic" style, Picabia achieved some of his most distinctive work, particularly a series of *Machine Portraits* of himself and his key associates in New York. Thus, he saw Stieglitz (fig. **13.22**) as a broken bellows camera, equipped with an automobile brake in working position and a gear shift in neutral, signifying the frustrations experienced by someone trying to present experimental art in philistine America. Both the Gothic letters and the title, *Ideal*, confirm the conceptual or heraldic form of the portrait, while also establishing a witty contrast between the commonplace, mechanical imagery and the ancient, noble devices of traditional heraldry. Made for publication in Stieglitz's journal *291*, Picabia's 1915 portraits are modest in size, materials, and ambition, but in other works the artist developed his machine aesthetic—his "functionless" machines—into splendidly iconic paintings. They are tongue-in-cheek, however, in their commentary on the seriocomic character of human sexual drives, and have many parallels, both thematic and formal, with Duchamp's *The Large Glass,* then under way in New York.

Returning to Europe in 1916, Picabia founded his journal *391* in Barcelona and published it intermittently in New York, Zurich, and Paris until 1924. After meeting the Zurich Dadaists in 1918, he was active in the Dada group in Paris. He reverted to representational art and, after the emergence of Surrealism, painted a series of *Transparencies* in which he superimposed thin layers of transparent imagery delineating classically beautiful male and female images, sometimes accompanied by exotic flora and fauna. Though the *Transparencies*, and the greater part of Picabia's later work, were long dismissed as decadently devoid of either content or formal interest, they have assumed new importance among the acknowledged prototypes of eighties Neo-Expressionism (see chapter 26).

Man Ray and the American Avant-Garde

Relatively unburdened by tradition, some American artists who met Duchamp and Picabia in New York had little difficulty entering into the Dada spirit. Indeed, one of the most daring of all Dada objects was made by Philadelphia-born Morton Schamberg, who mounted a plumbing connection on a miter box and sardonically titled it *God*. Though known primarily for this work, Schamberg was actually a painter and photographer who made a number of abstract, machine-inspired compositions in oil before his life was cut short by the massive influenza epidemic in 1918.

No less ingenious in his ability to devise Dada objects than to photograph them was **Man Ray** (1890–1976) (born Emmanuel Radnitsky), also from Philadelphia, who went on to pursue a lengthy, active career in the ambience of Surrealism. He gathered with Duchamp and Picabia at the Arensbergs' home and by 1916 had begun to make paintings inspired by a Dada machine aesthetic and three-dimensional constructions made with found objects. By 1919, Man Ray, who was always looking for ways to divest himself of the "paraphernalia of the traditional painter," was creating the first paintings made with an airbrush, which he called "Aerographs." Normally reserved for commercial graphic work, the airbrush made possible the soft tonalities in the dancing fans and cones of *Seguidilla* (fig. **13.23**). The artist was delighted with his new discovery. "It was wonderful," he said, "to paint a picture without touching the canvas."

In 1921, disappointed that Dada had failed to ignite a full-scale artistic revolution in New York, Man Ray moved to Paris. His exhibition in December of that year was a Dada event. The gallery was completely filled with balloons

13.22 Francis Picabia, *Ideal*, 1915. Pen and red and black ink on paper, 29⅞ × 20" (75.9 × 50.8 cm). The Metropolitan Museum of Art, New York.

13.23 Man Ray, *Seguidilla*, 1919. Airbrushed gouache, pen and ink, pencil, and colored pencil on paper board, 22 × 27⅞" (55.9 × 70.8 cm). Hirshhorn Museum and Sculpture Garden. Smithsonian Institution, Washington, D.C.

Man Ray, who had taken up photography in 1915 through his association with Stieglitz, invented cameraless photographic images that he called "Rayographs." These were made by placing objects on or near sensitized paper that was then exposed directly to light. In the proper Dada manner, the technique was discovered accidentally in the darkroom. By controlling exposure and by moving or removing objects, the artist used this "automatic" process to create images of a strangely abstract or symbolic character (fig. **13.25**).

that viewers had to pop in order to discover the art. *Gift* (fig. **13.24**), which exists today as a replica of the 1921 original, was made in the spirit of Duchamp's slightly altered or "assisted" readymades. With characteristic black humor, Man Ray subverted an iron's normal utilitarian function by attaching fourteen tacks to its surface, transforming this familiar object into something alien and threatening. The work was made for avant-garde French composer Erik Satie, hence its title.

Man Ray became an established figure in the Parisian avant-garde, gaining fame with his Dada films, with his experimental photographs, his photographs of artists and art, and his fashion photography (see fig. 15.61). By the mid-twenties, he was a central figure of the Surrealist circle (see chapter 15). Several of his assistants became important photographers in their own right: Berenice Abbott (see fig. 18.48), Bill Brandt (see fig. 15.69), and Lee Miller (see fig. 19.58).

13.24 Man Ray, *Gift*, Replica of lost original of 1921. Flatiron with nails, height 6½ × 3⅝ × 3¾" (16.5 × 9.2 × 9.5 cm). Collection Morton G. Neumann Family, Chicago.

13.25 Man Ray, *Untitled*, 1922. Gelatin-silver print (Rayograph), 9⅜ × 7" (23.8 × 17.78 cm). The Museum of Modern Art, New York.

"Art is Dead": Dada in Germany

In 1917, with a devastating war, severe restrictions on daily life, and rampant inflation, the future in Germany seemed completely uncertain. This atmosphere, in which highly polarized and radical politics flourished, was conducive to the spread of Dada. Huelsenbeck, returning from Berlin to Zurich, joined a small group including the brothers Wieland and Helmut Herzfelde (who changed his name to John Heartfield as a pro-American gesture), Hannah Höch, the painters Raoul Hausmann, George Grosz, and, later, Johannes Baader. Huelsenbeck opened a Dada campaign early in 1918 with speeches and manifestos attacking all phases of the artistic status quo, including Expressionism, Cubism, and Futurism. A Club Dada was formed, to which Kurt Schwitters, later a major exponent of German Dada, was refused membership because of his association with Der Sturm Gallery, regarded by Huelsenbeck as a bastion of Expressionist art and one of Dada's chief targets. After the war and the fall of the monarchy came a period of political chaos, which did not end with the establishment of the Weimar Republic (1918–33) and democratic government under the moderate socialist president Friedrich Ebert. Experimental artists and writers were generally leftwing, hopeful that from chaos would emerge a more equable society, but disillusionment among members of the Dada group set in as they realized that the so-called socialist government was actually in league with business interests and the old imperial military. From their disgust with what they regarded as a bankrupt Western culture, they turned to art as a medium for social and political activity. Their weapons were mostly collage and photomontage. Berlin Dada, especially for Heartfield and Grosz, quickly took on a leftwing, pacifist, and communist direction. The Herzfelde brothers' journal, *Neue Jugend,* and their publishing house, Malik-Verlag, utilized Dada techniques for political propaganda (see figs. 13.28, 13.35). George Grosz made many savage social and political drawings and paintings for the journal. One of the publications financed by the Herzfelde brothers was *Every Man Is His Own Football.* Although the work was quickly banned, its title became a rallying cry for German revolutionists. In 1919 the first issue of *Der Dada* appeared, followed in 1920 by the first international Dada-Messe, or Dada Fair, where the artists covered the walls of a Berlin gallery with photomontages, posters, and slogans like "Art is dead. Long live the new machine art of Tatlin." The rebellious members of Dada never espoused a clear program, and their goals were often ambiguous and sometimes contradictory: while they used art as a means of protest, they also questioned the very validity of artistic production.

Hausmann, Höch, and Heartfield

The Zurich Dada experiments in noise-music and in abstract phonetic poetry were further explored in Berlin.

Raoul Hausmann (1886–1971), the chief theoretician and writer of the group (nicknamed "the Dadasoph"), claimed the invention of a poetic form involving "respiratory and auditive combinations, firmly tied to a unit of duration," expressed in typography by "letters of varying sizes and thicknesses which thus took on the character of musical notations." In his *Spirit of Our Time (Mechanical Head)* (fig. **13.26**), 1919, Hausmann created a kind of three-dimensional collage. To a wooden mannequin head he attached real objects, including a metal collapsing cup, a tape measure, labels, and a pocketbook. Through his use of common found objects, Hausmann partook of the iconoclastic spirit of Duchamp's readymades and implied that human beings had been reduced to mindless robots, devoid of individual will.

In the visual arts, a major invention or discovery was photomontage, created by cutting up and pasting together photographs of individuals and events, posters, book jackets, and a variety of typefaces in new and startling configurations—anything to achieve shock. The source material for this medium was made possible by the tremendous growth in the print media in Germany. Hausmann and Höch (who were lovers and occasional collaborators), along with Grosz, claimed to have originated Dada photomontage, although it was a technique that had existed for

13.26 Raoul Hausmann, *The Spirit of Our Time (Mechanical Head),* 1919. Wood, leather, aluminum, brass, and cardboard, 12⅝ × 9" (32.1 × 22.9 cm). Musée National d'Art Moderne, Centre d'Art et de Culture Georges Pompidou, Paris.

13.27 Hannah Höch, *Cut with the Kitchen Knife Dada Through the Last Weimar Beer Belly Cultural Epoch of Germany*, 1919–20. Photomontage, 44⅞ × 35½" (114 × 90.2 cm). Staatliche Museen zu Berlin, Preussischer Kulturbesitz, Nationalgalerie.

years in advertising and popular imagery. Precedent can also be identified in Cubist collage of *papier collé* and Futurist collage (see fig. 11.7). Photomontage, with its clear integration of images of modern life into works of art, proved to be an ideal form for Dadaists and subsequently for Surrealists.

A large photomontage of 1919–20 by **Hannah Höch** (1889–1978), with a typically sardonic title, *Cut with the Kitchen Knife Dada Through the Last Weimar Beer Belly Cultural Epoch of Germany* (fig. **13.27**), was included

in the Dada-Messe, despite the efforts of Grosz and Heartfield to exclude her work. The dizzying profusion of imagery here demonstrates the ways in which photomontage relies on material appropriated from its normal context, such as magazine illustration, and introduces it into a new, disjunctive context, thereby investing it with new meaning. Höch here presents a satirical panorama of Weimar society. She includes photographs of her Dada colleagues, communist leaders, dancers, sports figures, and Dada slogans in varying typefaces. The despised

Weimar government leaders at the upper right are labeled "anti-Dada movement." At the very center of the composition is a photo of a popular dancer who seems to toss her out-of-scale head into the air. The head is a photo of Expressionist printmaker Käthe Kollwitz (see figs. 8.15, 8.16). Although the Dadaists reviled the emotive art of the Expressionists, it seems likely that Höch respected this leftwing woman artist. Throughout the composition are photographs of gears and wheels, both a tribute to technology and a means of imparting a sense of dynamic, circular movement. One difference between Höch and her colleagues is the preponderance of female imagery in her work, indicative of her interest in the new roles of women in postwar Germany, which had granted women the vote in 1918, two years before the United States.

John Heartfield (1891–1968) made photomontages of a somewhat different variety. He composed images from the clippings he took from newspapers, retouching them in order to blend the parts into a facsimile of a single, integrated image. These images were photographed and made into photogravures for mass reproduction. Beginning in 1930, as the rise of Nazism began to dominate the political landscape, Heartfield contributed illustrations regularly to the leftwing magazine *AIZ* or *Workers' Illustrated Newspaper*. For one of his most jarring images of protest, made in 1934 after Hitler had become German chancellor (and had assumed dictatorial powers), he altered the words of a

traditional German Christmas carol and twisted the form of a Christmas tree into a swastika tree (fig. **13.28**). "O Tannenbaum im deutchen Raum, wie krumm/sind deine Äste!" ("O Christmas tree in German soil, how crooked are your branches!") the heading reads. The text below states that in the future all trees must be cut in this form.

Schwitters

Somewhat apart from the Berlin Dadaists was the Hanoverian artist **Kurt Schwitters** (1887–1948), who completed his formal training at the Academy in Dresden and painted portraits for a living. He quarreled publicly with Huelsenbeck and was denied access to Club Dada because of his involvement with the apolitical and pro-art circle around Herwarth Walden's Der Sturm Gallery. He was eventually reconciled with other members of the group, however, and established his own Dada variant in Hanover under the designation "Merz," a word in part derived from the word "Com*merz*bank" included in one of his collages. "At the end of 1918," he wrote, "I realized that all values only exist in relationship to each other and that restriction

13.28 John Heartfield, *Little German Christmas Tree*, 1934. Photomontage, 10¼ × 7⅞" (26 × 20 cm). The Metropolitan Museum of Art, New York.

13.29 Kurt Schwitters, *Picture with Light Center*, 1919. Collage of cut-and-pasted papers and oil on cardboard, 33¼ × 25⅞" (84.5 × 65.7 cm). The Museum of Modern Art, New York.

surfaces. But his are not accidental juxtapositions or ones made purely for formal effect. The snatches of text from German newspapers in this *Merzbild* can be decoded as referring to recent political events in Germany.

Schwitters introduced himself to Raoul Hausmann in a Berlin café in 1918 by saying, "I am a painter and I nail my pictures together." This description applies to all his relief constructions, since he drew no hard-and-fast line between them and *papiers collés*, but most specifically to his series of great constructions that he called *Merz-Column* or *Merzbau* (fig. **13.31**), the culmination of Schwitters' attempts to create a *Gesamtkunstwerk*, or total work of art. He began the first one in his house in Hanover around 1920 as an abstract plaster sculpture with apertures dedicated to his Dadaist and Constructivist friends and containing objects commemorating them: Mondrian, Gabo, Arp, Lissitzky, Malevich, Richter, Mies van der Rohe, and Van Doesburg. The *Merzbau* grew throughout the twenties with successive accretions of every kind of material until it filled the room. Having then no place to go but up, he continued the environmental construction with implacable logic into the second story. "As the structure grows bigger and bigger," Schwitters wrote, "valleys, hollows, caves appear, and these lead a life of their own within the overall structure. The juxtaposed surfaces give rise to forms twisting in every direction, spiraling upward." When he was driven from Germany by the Nazis and his original

13.30 Kurt Schwitters, *Merzbild 25A (Das Sternenbild) (Stars Picture)*, 1920. Assemblage, 41 × 31⅛" (104.1 × 79.1 cm). Kunstsammlung Nordrhein-Westfalen, Düsseldorf.

to a single material is one-sided and small-minded. From this insight I formed Merz, above all the sum of individual art forms, Merz-painting, Merz-poetry." Schwitters was a talented poet, impressive in his readings and deadly serious about his efforts in painting, collage, and construction. These always involved a degree of deadpan humor delightful to those who knew him, but disturbing to unfamiliar audiences.

Schwitters's collages were made of rubbish picked up from the street—cigarette wrappers, tickets, newspapers, string, boards, wire screens, and whatever caught his fancy. In these so-called *Merzbilder* or *Merzzeichnungen* (Merz-pictures or Merz-drawings) he transformed the detritus of his surroundings into strange and wonderful beauty. In *Picture with Light Center* (fig. **13.29**) we see how Schwitters could extract elegance from these lowly found materials. He carefully structured his circular and diagonal elements within a Cubist-derived grid, which he then reinforced by applying paint over the collage, creating a glowing, inner light that radiates from the picture's center. For his 1920 assemblage, *Merzbild 25A (Das Sternenbild) (Stars Picture)* (fig. **13.30**), Schwitters did not restrict himself to the two-dimensional printed imagery we have seen in the photomontages of Heartfield and Höch. He incorporates rope, wire mesh, paint, and other materials that indicate the artist's strong concern for physicality in his

13.31 Kurt Schwitters, *Hanover Merzbau*, Destroyed. Photo taken c. 1931.

Merzbau was destroyed, Schwitters started another one in Norway. The Nazi invasion forced him to England, where he began again for the third time. After his death in 1948, the third *Merzbau* was rescued and preserved in the University of Newcastle. The example of Schwitters was crucial for later artists who sought to create sculpture on an environmental scale. They include figures as diverse as Louise Nevelson (see fig. 19.56), Red Grooms (see fig. 21.21), and Louise Bourgeois (see fig. 19.52).

Early in the twenties, the de Stijl artist Theo van Doesburg (see chapter 11) had become friendly with Schwitters, and they collaborated on a number of publications, and even made a Dada tour of Holland. Schwitters became more and more attracted to the geometric abstractionists and Constructivists, for despite the fantasy and rubbish materials in his works, they demonstrated relationships and proportions that rival Mondrian's Neo-Plastic paintings in their subtlety and rigor.

Ernst

When **Max Ernst** (1891–1976) saw works by modern artists such as Cézanne and Picasso at the 1912 Sonderbund exhibition in Cologne, he decided to forgo his university studies and take up art. He went to Paris in 1913, and his works were included that year in the First German Autumn Salon at Der Sturm in Berlin, when the artist was only twenty-two years old. In 1919–20, Jean Arp established contact with Ernst in Cologne, and the two were instrumental in the formation of yet another wing of international Dada. The two had met in Cologne in 1914, but Ernst then served in the German army. At the end of the war, he discovered Zurich Dada and the paintings of de Chirico and Klee. Ernst's early paintings were rooted in a Late Gothic fantasy drawn from Dürer, Grünewald (see fig. 8), and Bosch. The artist was also fascinated by German Romanticism in the macabre forms of Klinger and Böcklin. This "gothic quality" (in the widest sense) remained a consistent characteristic of Ernst's fantasies. In 1919–20, a staggeringly productive period, he produced collages and photomontages that demonstrated a genius for suggesting the metamorphosis or double identity of objects, a topic later central to Surrealist iconography. In an ingenious work from 1920 (fig. **13.32**), Ernst invented his own mechanistic forms as stand-ins for the human body. As he frequently did during this period, the artist took a page from a 1914 scientific text illustrating chemistry and biology equipment and, by overpainting certain areas and inserting his own additions, he transformed goggles and other laboratory utensils into a pair of hilarious creatures before a landscape. The composition bears telling comparison with Picabia's mechanomorphic inventions (see fig. 13.22).

During the winter of 1920–21, Ernst and Arp collaborated on collages entitled *Fatagagas,* short for *Fabrication des Tableaux Garantis Gasométriques.* Ernst usually prvided the collage imagery while Arp and other occasional collaborators provided the name and accompanying text. In the *Fatagaga* titled *Here Everything Is Still Floating,* an anatomical drawing of a beetle becomes, upside-down, a steamboat floating through the depths of the sea. Some of the *Fatagagas* were sent to Tristan Tzara in Paris for illustration in his ill-fated publication *Dadaglobe.* Ernst had been in close contact with the Parisian branch of Dada (see below) and many of the artists who would develop Surrealism. By the time he moved to Paris in 1922, he had already created the basis for much of the Surrealist vocabulary.

Despite the close friendship between Ernst and Arp, their approaches to painting, collage, and sculpture were different. Arp's was toward abstract, organic Surrealism in which figures or other objects may be suggested but are rarely explicit. Ernst, following the example of de Chirico and fortified by his own "gothic" imagination, became a principal founder of the wing of Surrealism that utilized Magic Realism—that is, precisely delineated, recognizable objects, distorted and transformed, but nevertheless presented with a ruthless realism that throws their newly acquired fantasy into shocking relief. *Celebes* (fig. **13.33**) is a mechanized monster whose trunk-tail-pipeline sports a cowskull-head above an immaculate white collar. A headless classical torso beckons to the beast with an elegantly gloved hand. The images are unrelated on a rational level; some are threatening (the elephant), while others are less explicable (the beckoning torso). The rotund form of the elephant was actually suggested to Ernst by a photograph of a gigantic communal corn bin made of clay and used by people in southern Sudan. While not constructed as a collage, *Celebes,* with its many disparate motifs, is informed

13.32 Max Ernst, *1 Copper Plate 1 Zinc Plate 1 Rubber Cloth 2 Calipers 1 Drainpipe Telescope 1 Pipe Man,* 1920. Gouache, ink, and pencil on printed reproduction, 9½ × 6½" (24.1 × 16.7 cm). Whereabouts unknown.

13.33 Max Ernst, *Celebes*, 1921. Oil on canvas, 51⅛ × 43¼" (129.9 × 109.9 cm). Tate Gallery, London.

by a collage aesthetic as well as by the early paintings of de Chirico; it appeals to the level of perception below consciousness. Ernst, who worked in a remarkably broad range of media and styles, became a major figure of Surrealism (see figs. 15.6, 15.8, 15.9).

Idealism and Disgust: The "New Objectivity" in Germany

Immediately following Germany's defeat in World War I and the abdication of Kaiser Wilhelm II, some of the leaders of German Expressionism formed the November Group and were soon joined by Dadaists. In 1919, under the newly established Weimar Republic, the Workers' Council for Art was organized. It sought more state support, more commissions from industry, and the reorganization of art schools. These artists included many of the original Expressionists, such architects as Walter Gropius and Erich Mendelsohn (see chapter 12), and leading poets, musicians, and critics. Many of the aims of the November Group and the Workers' Council were incorporated into the program of the Weimar Bauhaus.

In their exhibitions, the November Group reestablished contact with France and other countries, and antagonisms among the various new alignments were submerged for a time on behalf of a common front. The Expressionists were exhibited, as well as representatives of Cubism, abstraction, Constructivism, and Dada, while the new architects showed projects for city planning and large-scale housing. Societies similar to the November Group sprang up in

many parts of Germany, and their manifestos read like a curious blend of socialist idealism and revivalist religion.

The common front of socialist idealism did not last long. The workers whom the artists extolled and to whom they appealed were even more suspicious of the new art forms than was the capitalist bourgeoisie. It was naturally from the latter that new patrons of art emerged. By 1924 German politics was shifting inexorably to the right, and the artists' utopianism was in many cases turning into disillusionment and cynicism. There now emerged a form of Social Realism in painting to which the name the New Objectivity (*Die Neue Sachlichkeit*) was given. Meanwhile, the Bauhaus, the design school run by Gropius since 1919 at Weimar, had tried to apply the ideas of the November Group and the Workers' Council toward a new relationship between artist and society. In 1925 it was forced by the rising tide of conservative opposition to move to Dessau. Its faculty members still clung to postwar Expressionist and socialist ideas, although by 1925 their program mostly concerned the training of artists, craft workers, and designers for an industrial, capitalist society.

Grosz

The principal painters associated with the New Objectivity were **George Grosz** (1893–1959), Otto Dix, and Max Beckmann—three artists whose style touched briefly at certain points but who had essentially different motivations. Grosz studied at the Dresden Academy from 1909 to 1911 and at the Royal Arts and Crafts School in Berlin off and on from 1912 to 1916, partially supporting himself with drawings of the shady side of Berlin nightlife. These caustic works prepared him for his later violent statements of disgust with postwar Germany and humankind generally. In 1913 he visited Paris and, despite later disclaimers, was obviously affected by Cubism and its offshoots, particularly Robert Delaunay and Italian Futurism. After two years in the army (1914–16), Grosz resumed his caricatures while convalescing in Berlin. They reveal an embittered personality, now fortified by observations of autocracy, corruption, and the horrors of a world at war. Recalled to the army in 1917, Grosz ended his military career in an asylum on whose personnel and administration he made devastating comment.

After the war Grosz was drawn into Berlin Dada and its overriding leftwing direction. He made stage designs and collaborated on periodicals, but continued his own work of political or social satire. *Dedication to Oskar Panizza* of 1917–18 (fig. **13.34**) is his most Cubist-inspired work. The title refers to the writer Panizza, whose work had been censored at the end of the nineteenth century. But the larger subject, according to Grosz, was "Mankind gone mad." He said that the dehumanized figures represent "Alcohol, Syphilis, Pestilence." Showing a funeral turned into a riot, the painting is flooded with a blood or fire red. The buildings lean crazily; an insane mob is packed around the paraded coffin on which Death sits triumphantly, swigging at a bottle; the faces are horrible masks; humanity is

13.34 George Grosz, *Dedication to Oskar Panizza*, 1917–18. Oil on canvas, 55⅛ × 43¼" (140 × 109.9 cm). Staatsgalerie, Stuttgart.

13.35 George Grosz, *Fit for Active Service (The Faith Healers)*, 1916–17. Pen, brush, and India ink, sheet 20 × 14⅜" (50.8 × 36.5 cm). The Museum of Modern Art, New York.

swept into a hell of its own making; and the figure of Death rides above it all on a black coffin. Yet the artist controls the chaos with a geometry of the buildings and the planes into which he segments the crowd.

The drawing *Fit for Active Service* (fig. **13.35**) was used as an illustration in 1919 for *Die Pleite (Bankruptcy)*, one of the many political publications with which Grosz was involved. The editors, Herzfelde, Grosz, and Heartfield, filled *Die Pleite* with scathing political satire, which occasionally got them thrown into prison. This work shows Grosz's sense of the macabre and his detestation of bureaucracy, with a fat complacent doctor pronouncing his "O.K." of a desiccated cadaver before arrogant Prussian-type officers. The spare economy of the draftsmanship in Grosz's illustrations is also evident in a number of the artist's paintings done in the same period. *Republican Automatons* applies the style and motifs of de Chirico and the Metaphysical School to political satire, as empty-headed, blank-faced, and mutilated automatons parade loyally through the streets of a mechanistic metropolis on their way to vote as they are told. In such works as this, Grosz comes closest to the spirit of the Dadaists and Surrealists. But he expressed his most passionate convictions in drawings and paintings that continue an Expressionist tradition of savagely denouncing a decaying Germany of brutal profiteers and obscene prostitutes, and of limitless gluttony and sensuality in the face of abject poverty, disease, and death. Normally Grosz worked in a

style of spare and brittle drawing combined with a fluid watercolor. In the mid-twenties, however, he briefly used precise realism in portraiture, close to the New Objectivity of Otto Dix (see fig. 13.37).

Grosz was frequently in trouble with the authorities, but it was Nazism that caused him to flee. In the United States during the thirties, his personality was quite transformed. Although he occasionally caricatured American types, these were relatively mild, even affectionate. America for him was a dream come true, and he painted the skyscrapers of New York or the dunes of Provincetown in a sentimental haze. His pervading sensuality was expressed in warm portrayals of Rubenesque nudes.

The growth of Nazism rekindled his power of brutal commentary, and World War II caused Grosz to paint a series expressing bitter hatred and deep personal disillusionment. In the later works, sheer repulsion replaces the passionate convictions of his earlier statements. He did not return to Berlin until 1958, and he died there the following year.

Dix

The artist whose works most clearly define the nature of the New Objectivity was **Otto Dix** (1891–1969). Born of working-class parents, he was a proletarian by upbringing as well as by political conviction. Dix's combat experience made him fiercely antimilitaristic. His war paintings, gruesome descriptions of indescribable horrors, are rooted

13.36 Otto Dix, *The Trench*, 1923. Destroyed 1943–45. Oil on canvas.

13.37 Otto Dix, *Dr. Mayer-Hermann*, 1926. Oil and tempera on wood, 58¾ × 39" (149.2 × 99.1 cm). The Museum of Modern Art, New York.

in the German Gothic tradition of Grünewald (see fig. 8). His painting *The Trench* (fig. **13.36**) traveled throughout Germany as part of an exhibition mounted by a group called No More War. It was stored for a time by Ernst Barlach (see fig. 9.9), but it was eventually destroyed, perhaps when the Nazis set fire to works of "degenerate" art in Berlin toward the end of World War II. Like Grosz, Dix was exposed to diverse influences from Cubism to Dada, but from the beginning he was concerned with uncompromising realism. This was a symptom of the post-war reaction against abstraction, a reaction most marked in Germany but also evident in most of Europe and in America. Even many of the pioneers of Fauvism and Cubism were involved in it. However, the superrealism of Dix was not simply a return to the past. In his portrait of the laryngologist, *Dr. Mayer-Hermann* (fig. **13.37**), the massive figure is seated frontally, framed by the vaguely menacing machines of his profession. Although the painting includes nothing bizarre or extraneous, the overpowering confrontation gives a sense of the unreal. For this type of superrealism (as distinct from Surrealism) the term Magic Realism was coined: a mode of representation that takes on an aura of the fantastic because commonplace objects are presented with unexpectedly exaggerated and detailed forthrightness. Dix remained in Germany during the Nazi regime, although he was forbidden to exhibit or teach and was imprisoned for a short time. After the war he turned to a form of mystical, religious expression.

13.38 August Sander, *Wandering People (Fahrendes Volk)*, from the series *Citizens of the 20th Century (Menschen des 20 Jahrhunderts)*, from the portfolio *Traveling People*, Düren (Cologne), Germany. 1930. Gelatin-silver print, 8¼ × 10" (21.0 × 25.5 cm). The Museum of Modern Art, New York.

13.39 Albert Renger-Patzsch, *Irons Used in Shoemaking, Fagus Works*, c. 1925. Gelatin-silver print. Galerie Wilde, Cologne.

The Photography of Sander and Renger-Patzsch

The portraiture of artists like Dix may very well have been influenced by the contemporary photographs of **August Sander** (1876–1964), a German artist and former miner who became a powerful exponent of the New Objectivity. Trained in fine art at the Dresden Academy, Sander set about to accomplish nothing less than a comprehensive photographic portrait of "Man in Twentieth-Century Germany." He was convinced that the camera, if honestly and straightforwardly employed, could probe beneath appearances and dissect the truth that lay within. Sander photographed German society in its "sociological arc" of occupations and classes, presenting cultural types in the environments that shaped them (fig. **13.38**). In 1929 he published the first volume of his magnum opus—one of the most ambitious in the history of photography—under the title *Antlitz der Zeit (Face of Time)*, only to see the book suppressed and the plates (but not the negatives) destroyed in the early thirties by the Nazis, who inevitably found the photographer's ideas contrary to their own pathological views of race and class. For his part, Sander wrote: "It is not my intention either to criticize or to describe these people, but to create a piece of history with my pictures."

The German photographer most immediately identified with the New Objectivity was **Albert Renger-Patzsch** (1897–1966). Like Paul Strand in the United States (see fig. 18.21), Renger-Patzsch avoided the double exposures and photographic manipulations of Man Ray (see fig. 13.25) and Moholy-Nagy (see fig. 17.2), as well as the artificiality and soulfulness of the Pictorialists, to practice "straight" photography closely and sharply focused on objects isolated, or abstracted, from the natural and man-made worlds (fig. **13.39**). But for all its stark realism, such an approach yielded details so enlarged and crisply purified of their structural or functional contexts that the overall pattern they produce borders on pure design. Still, Renger-Patzsch insisted upon his commitment to factuality and his "aloofness to art for art's sake."

Beckmann

Max Beckmann (1884–1950) was the principal artist associated with the New Objectivity but could only briefly be called a precise Realist in the sense of Dix. Born of wealthy parents in Leipzig, he was schooled in the Early Renaissance painters of Germany and the Netherlands, and the great seventeenth-century Dutch painters. After studies at the Weimar academy and a brief visit to Paris, Beckmann settled in 1903 in Berlin, then a center of German Impressionism and Art Nouveau. Influenced by Delacroix and by the German academic tradition, he painted large religious and classical murals and versions of contemporary disasters such as the sinking of the *Titanic* (1912), done in the mode of Géricault's bleak masterpiece commemorating an 1816 shipwreck, *Raft of the Medusa*. By 1913 Beckmann was a well-known academician. His service in World War I brought about a nervous breakdown and, as he later said, "great injury to his soul." The experience turned him toward a search for internal reality. Beckmann assumed many guises in over eighty-five self-portraits made throughout his life. The *Self-Portrait with Red Scarf* of 1917 (fig. **13.40**) shows the artist in his Frankfurt studio, haunted and anxious. Beckmann's struggle is apparent in a big, unfinished *Resurrection,* on which he painted sporadically between 1916 and 1918. Here he attempted to join his more intense and immediate vision of the war years to his prewar academic formulas. This work liberated him from his academic past. In two paintings of 1917, *The Descent from the Cross* and *Christ and the Woman Taken in Adultery,* he found a personal expression, rooted in Grünewald, Bosch, and Brueghel, although the jagged shapes and delimited space also owed much to Cubism. Out of this mating of Late Gothic, Cubism, and German Expressionism emerged Beckmann's next style.

Although he was not politically oriented, Beckmann responded to the violence and cruelty of the last years of the war by painting dramas of torture and brutality—symptomatic of the lawlessness of the time and prophetic of the state-sponsored genocide of the early forties. Rendered in pale, emotionally repulsive colors, the figures could be twisted and distorted within a compressed space, as in late medieval representations of the tortures of the damned (in Beckmann's work, the innocent), and the horror heightened by explicit and accurate details. Such works, which impart symbolic content through harsh examination of external appearance, were close to and even anticipated the New Objectivity of Grosz and Dix.

In *Self-Portrait in Tuxedo* from 1927 (fig. **13.41**), Beckmann presents a view of himself quite different from the one ten years earlier. Now a mature figure, he appears serious and self-assured, debonair even. The composition is striking in its elegant simplicity, with deep blacks, for which Beckmann is understandably admired, set against the bluegray wall and the artist's stark white shirt. In the later twenties, as is clear from this image, Beckmann, moving from success to success, was regarded as one of Germany's

13.40 Max Beckmann, *Self-Portrait with Red Scarf,* 1917. Oil on canvas, 31½ × 23⅝" (80 × 60 cm). Staatsgalerie, Stuttgart.

13.41 Max Beckmann, *Self-Portrait in Tuxedo,* 1927. Oil on canvas, 55½ × 37¾" (141 × 96 cm). Busch-Reisinger Museum, Harvard University Art Museums, Cambridge, Massachusetts.

leading artists. Nevertheless, when the Nazis came to power in 1933, Beckmann was stripped of his teaching position in Frankfurt, and 590 of his works were confiscated from museums throughout Germany. On the opening day of the 1937 Degenerate Art show in Munich, which included several works by Beckmann (including fig. 13.40), the artist and his wife fled to Amsterdam. In 1947, after years of hiding from the Nazis (he never returned to Germany), Beckmann accepted a teaching position at Washington University, St. Louis, Missouri, where he filled a position vacated by the Abstract Expressionist painter Philip Guston (see figs. 19.20, 19.21) and became a highly influential teacher. He remained in the United States for the rest of his life.

Throughout the thirties and forties, Beckmann continued to develop his ideas of coloristic richness, monumentality, and complexity of subject. The enriched color came from visits to Paris and contacts with French artists, particularly Matisse and Picasso. However, his emphasis on literary subjects having heavy symbolic content reflected his Germanic artistic roots. The first climax of his new, monumental–symbolic approach was the large 1932–33 triptych *Departure* (fig. **13.42**). Beckmann made nine paintings in the triptych format, obviously making a connection between his work and the great ecclesiastical art of the past. Alfred Barr described *Departure* as "an allegory of the triumphal voyage of the modern spirit through and beyond the agony of the modern world." The right wing shows

frustration, indecision, and self-torture; in the left wing, sadistic mutilation, and the torture of others. Beckmann said of this triptych in 1937:

> On the right wing you can see yourself trying to find your way in the darkness, lighting the hall and staircase with a miserable lamp dragging along tied to you as part of yourself, the corpse of your memories, of your wrongs, of your failures, the murder everyone commits at some time of his life—you can never free yourself of your past, you have to carry the corpse while Life plays the drum.

Also, despite his disavowal of political interests, the left-hand panel must refer to the rise of dictatorship that was driving liberal artists, writers, and thinkers underground.

The darkness and suffering in the wings are resolved in the brilliant sunlight colors of the central panel, where the king, the mother, and the child set forth, guided by the veiled boatman. Beckmann said: "The King and Queen have freed themselves of the tortures of life—they have overcome them. The Queen carries the greatest treasure—Freedom—as her child in her lap. Freedom is the one thing that matters—it is the departure, the new start."

It is important to emphasize the fact that Beckmann's allegories and symbols were not a literal iconography to be read by anyone given the key. The spectator had to participate actively, and the allusions could mean something different to each viewer. In addition, the allusions in Beckmann's work could be very complex. His last triptych,

13.42 *Max Beckmann, Departure, 1932–33. Oil on canvas, triptych, center panel 7'3¾" × 3'9⅜" (2.2 × 1.15 m); side panels each 7'3¾" × 3'3¼" (2.2 × 1 m). The Museum of Modern Art, New York.*

13.43 Max Beckmann, *The Argonauts*, 1949–50. Triptych, oil on canvas: left panel 6'1" × 2'9½" (1.8 × 0.85 m), center panel 6'9" × 4' (2.1 × 1.22 m), right panel 6'1" × 2'9½" (1.8 × 0.85 m). National Gallery of Art, Washington, D.C.

The Argonauts (fig. **13.43**), was completed the day before he died. Beckmann originally intended the work as an allegory about the arts. Painting is represented in the left panel where an artist, presumably a surrogate self-portrait, works at a canvas. The women playing instruments in the right panel symbolize music, while the figures in the center depict poetry. Prompted by a dream to rename the painting *The Argonauts,* Beckmann gave his image a more mythological content. The model in the lefthand wing becomes Medea; the central figures represent Jason, the poet Orpheus, and the sea god Glaucus; and the women at the right form an ancient Greek chorus. But the triptych also has a biographical dimension, since, during his years in Amsterdam, Beckmann associated with a group of writers and artists called the Argonauts. Thus, Jason's heroic search for the golden fleece becomes an allegory about the voyage of Beckmann's own life.

Dada Divided: Developments in Paris

By the time Max Ernst left Cologne in 1921, Dada as an organized movement was dead, except in Paris. Duchamp had largely given up creative activity (unless his very exist-ence might be so described) apart from occasional motion experiments, the completion of his *Large Glass,* and participation in commemorative exhibitions and publications. In Germany only Kurt Schwitters continued, a one-man Dada movement. Many of the original Dadaists, if they had not done so already, left Germany in the thirties. But their efforts were not forgotten in the Degenerate Art exhibition organized by the Nazis in 1937 in Munich (fig. **13.44**). On the "Dada wall," Grosz's statement, "Take Dada seriously! It's worth it!" is derisively inscribed next to works by Schwitters and enlarged details from works by Kandinsky (whom the organizers mistook for a Dada artist).

By 1918 writers in Paris, including Louis Aragon, André Breton, and Georges Ribemont-Dessaignes, were contributing to the Zurich periodical *Dada,* and shortly Tristan Tzara began writing for Breton and Aragon's journal *Littérature*. Picabia, after visiting the Dadaists in Zurich, published No. IX of *391* in Paris, and in 1919 Tzara himself also arrived there. Thus, by the end of the war, a Dada movement was growing in the French capital, but it was primarily a literary event. While in painting and sculpture Dada was largely an imported product, in poetry and theater it was in a tradition of the irrational and absurd that extended from Baudelaire, Rimbaud, and Mallarmé to

Alfred Jarry, Guillaume Apollinaire, and Jean Cocteau. Paris Dada in the hands of the literary men consisted of frequent manifestos, demonstrations, periodicals, events, and happenings more violent and hysterical than ever before. The artists Arp, Ernst, and Picabia took a less active part in the demonstrations, although Picabia contributed his own manifestos. The original impetus and enthusiasm seemed to be lacking, however, and divisive factions arose, led principally by Tzara and by Breton. The early Dadaists, like the Bolsheviks of the Russian Revolution, sought to maintain a constant state of revolution, even anarchy, but new forces led by Breton sought a more constructive revolutionary scheme based on Dada. In its original form Dada expired in the wild confusion of the Congress of Paris called in 1922 by the Dadaists. The former Dadaists, including Picabia, who followed Breton, were joined by powerful new voices, among them Cocteau and Ezra Pound. By 1924 this group was consolidated under the name Surrealism.

13.44 Room 3 including Dada wall in Degenerate Art Exhibition, Munich, 1937.

14
The School of Paris After World War I

In post-1918 Paris, in many quarters, years of tragic warfare had dampened enthusiasm for artistic experimentation, and cultural movements turned away from "scandalous" avant-gardism toward an art based on the values of the classical tradition. "After the war," said the former Fauve painter André Derain, "I thought I would never be able to paint—that after all that—no one would be interested." By the end of the war, Derain had himself turned from his earlier innovative work to a classicizing style (see chapter 7), and in the twenties the general trend toward classicism in all the arts gathered momentum. It was characterized by poet and playwright Jean Cocteau as a "call to order." So profound was the longing for stability that even Dada, once it finally hit the French capital around 1919, soon fizzled and gave way to the less nihilistic, if thoroughly antirationalist, movement known as Surrealism (see chapter 15). But far from transforming Paris into a citadel of reaction, this new common sensibility ushered in a mood of enlightened tolerance. Official taste grew less aggressively hostile to modernism; progressive painters and sculptors felt free to relax from formal experimentation and to settle for a period of consolidation and refinement of the extraordinary gains already made. Large numbers of gifted artists in retreat from revolution in Russia, economic hardship in Germany, and provincialism in America were thus lured to Paris, assuring the continuing status of Paris as the glittering, cosmopolitan capital of world art.

Eloquent Figuration: *Les Maudits*

The School of Paris embraced a wide variety of artists between the two world wars who shared common ground not only through their base in France but also in their independence from narrowly defined aesthetic categories. While distinctly modernist in their willingness to distort imagery for expressive purposes, they nonetheless regarded figurative imagery as fundamental to the meaning of their work. This diverse and distinguished group included Braque, Léger, Matisse, and Picasso. Perhaps even more representative of the polyglot School of Paris than those major figures, however, is a subgroup known as *les maudits*—Modigliani from Italy, Soutine from Lithuania, the Frenchwoman Suzanne Valadon, and her son, Maurice Utrillo. *Les maudits* means "the cursed"—an epithet that alluded not only to these artists' poverty and alienation but also to the picturesque, ultimately disastrous, bohemianism of their disorderly life-styles. Much of this gravitated around the sidewalk cafés of Montparnasse and Saint-Germain-des-Prés, the quarters on the Left Bank of the Seine favored by the Parisian avant-garde since before the war, when Picasso and his entourage abandoned Montmartre to the tourists.

Modigliani

Amedeo Modigliani (1884–1920) was born of well-to-do parents in Livorno, Italy. His training as an artist was often interrupted by illness, but he managed to get to Paris by 1906. Although he was essentially a painter, in around 1910, influenced by his friend Brancusi (see chapter 9), he began to experiment with sculpture. Modigliani's short life has become the quintessential example of bohemian artistic existence in Paris, so much so that the myths and anecdotes surrounding his biography have somewhat undermined a serious understanding of his work. For fourteen years he worked in Paris, ill from tuberculosis (from which he eventually died), drugs, and alcohol, but drawing and painting obsessively. He spent what little money he had quickly, and he tended to support himself by making drawings in cafés that he sold for a few francs to the sitter.

With very few exceptions, the experiments that Modigliani carried out in sculpture between approximately 1910 and 1914 (he rarely dated his works) are carved stone heads (fig. **14.1**). He believed that modern sculpture should not be modeled in clay but should result only from direct carving in stone. Beyond the powerful example of Brancusi, the sculptural sources that appealed to Modigliani were rooted in European medieval art and the art of a diverse range of cultures including Africa, Egypt,

14.1 Amedeo Modigliani, *Head*, c. 1911–13. Limestone, height 25 × 6 × 8½" (63.5 × 15.2 × 21 cm). Solomon R. Guggenheim Museum, New York.

14.2 Amedeo Modigliani, *Chaim Soutine*, 1916. Oil on canvas, 36⅛ × 23½" (91.8 × 59.7 cm). National Gallery of Art, Washington, D.C.

14.3 Amedeo Modigliani, *Nude*, 1917. Oil on canvas, 28¾ × 45¾" (73 × 116.2 cm). Solomon R. Guggenheim Museum, New York.

Archaic Greece, and India. Most of the heads have highly abstracted, geometricized features, with the characteristic long nose, almond eyes, and columnar neck. As we see here, Modigliani sometimes left the block of stone only roughed in at the back, making the sculptures strictly frontal in orientation. This tendency may be related to his apparent intention to group the heads into some kind of decorative ensemble. It has been suggested that Modigliani abandoned the demanding métier of sculpture because of his frail health and the expense of the materials. While both of these factors may have played a role in his decision, it seems likely that he wanted to be a painter first and foremost.

In subject, Modigliani's paintings rarely departed from the depiction of single portrait heads, torsos, or full figures against a neutral background. His career was so short that it is difficult to speak of a stylistic development, although a gradual transition can be seen from work inspired by the Symbolist painters (see chapter 3), in which the figure is securely integrated in the space of an interior, toward a pattern of linear or sculptural detachment. Modigliani knew Picasso and occasionally visited his studio, but he never really succumbed to the lure of Cubism.

Although all of his portraits resemble one another through their elegantly elongated features or their reference to forms deriving from Archaic art, the portraits of his friends, who included notable artists and critics of the early twentieth century, are sensitive records of specific personalities, eccentricities, and foibles.

Modigliani's closest friend in Paris was his fellow painter Chaim Soutine (fig. 14.2). Modigliani's portrayal of this Lithuanian peasant, with his disheveled hair and clothes and narrow, unfocused eyes, conveys a psychological presence lacking in many of his other likenesses.

Modigliani also painted anonymous students or children—anyone who would pose for him without a fee. For his paintings of nudes, however, he frequently relied on professional models. Modigliani developed a fairly standard formula for his compositions of reclining nudes (fig. 14.3). The attenuated figure is normally arranged along a diagonal and set within a narrow space, her legs eclipsed by the edge of the canvas. The figure is outlined with a flowing but precise line, while the full volumes are modeled with almost imperceptible gradations of flesh tones. The artist was fond of contrasting draped white sheets against deep Venetian red, as seen in this 1917 example. The influence here of Titian is unmistakable, particularly that of his painting *Venus of Urbino*. This sixteenth-century work is in the Uffizi, which Modigliani frequented during his student days in Florence. His friend and fellow Italian, Severini, detected a "Tuscan elegance" in the work of Modigliani, who kept reproductions of old-master paintings on the walls of his Paris studio. For his paintings of nudes, Modigliani frequently assumed a point of view above the figure, thus establishing a perspective that implies the subject's sexual availability to the artist and (presumably male) viewers. With their blatant sexuality and coy, flirtatious expressions, Modigliani's nudes present a modernized eroticism. In the artist's day, the works were deemed indecent enough to be confiscated from an exhibition by the police for their excessive exposure of pubic hair.

Soutine

Chaim Soutine (1894–1943), the tenth of eleven children from a poor Lithuanian–Jewish family, developed an early passion for painting and drawing. He managed to attend some classes in Minsk and Vilna, a center of Jewish cultural activity, and, through the help of a patron, arrived in Paris before the war's outbreak. He studied at the École des Beaux-Arts, but it was through the artists whom he met at an old tenement known as La Ruche (The Beehive), where Chagall also lived around this time, that he began to find his way. Modigliani in particular took the young artist under his wing. He showed him Italian paintings in the Louvre and helped refine Soutine's manners and improve his French. "He gave me confidence in myself," Soutine said.

Soutine constantly destroyed or reworked his paintings, so it is difficult to trace his development from an early to a mature style. An early formative influence on his work was Cézanne, an artist also greatly admired by Modigliani. Van

14.4 Chaim Soutine, *Gnarled Trees*, c. 1920. Oil on canvas, 38 × 25" (96.5 × 63.5 cm). Private collection, New York.

14.5 Chaim Soutine, *Woman in Red*, c. 1924–25. Oil on canvas, 36 × 25" (91.4 × 63.5 cm). Private collection.

14.6 Chaim Soutine, *Carcass of Beef*, c. 1925. Oil on canvas, 55¼ × 42⅜" (140.3 × 107.6 cm). Albright-Knox Art Gallery, Buffalo, New York.

Gogh also provided a crucial example, although the energy and vehemence of Soutine's brushstroke surpassed even that of the Dutchman. The essence of Soutine's Expressionism lies in the intuitive power and the seemingly uncontrolled but immensely descriptive brush gesture (see fig. 14.5). In this quality he is closer than any artist of the early twentieth century to the Abstract Expressionists of the fifties, especially de Kooning (see fig. 19.5), who greatly admired Soutine.

From 1919 Soutine spent three years in Céret, a town in the French Pyrenees. The mountain landscape inspired him to a frenzy of free, Expressionist brush paintings that rivaled in exuberance anything produced by the Fauves or the German Expressionists. In *Gnarled Trees* (fig. 14.4), Soutine conveys a sense of immersion in the landscape with this composition, in which the buildings on the heaving hillside are barely decipherable through the trees and writhing coils of paint. Soutine painted furiously during this period. After his return to Paris in 1922, a large number of his canvases were bought by the American collector Albert C. Barnes, providing Soutine with his first major public success and a steady income.

In Soutine's portraits and figure paintings of the twenties there is frequently an accent on a predominant color—red,

blue, or white—around which the rest of the work is built. In *Woman in Red* (fig. **14.5**) the sitter is posed diagonally across an armchair over which her voluminous red dress flows. The red of the dress permeates her face and hands; it is picked up in her necklace and in the red-brown tonality of the ground. Only the deep blue-black of the hat stands out against it. Soutine endows the static figure with tremendous vitality and movement, as the undulating surface rhythms swerve back and forth across the canvas. The hands are distorted as though from arthritis, and the features of the face are twisted into a slight grin. As in many of Soutine's portraits, the first impression is of a cruel caricature. Then one becomes aware of the sitter's highly individual, and in this case ambiguous, personality. *Woman in Red* appears at once comic, slightly mad, and knowingly shrewd.

Soutine's passion for Rembrandt was commemorated in a number of extraordinary paintings that were free adaptations of the seventeenth-century Dutch master's compositions. In *Carcass of Beef* (fig. **14.6**) Soutine transcribed Rembrandt's 1655 *Butchered Ox*, in the Louvre, with gruesome, bloody impact. Unlike Rembrandt, Soutine isolated his subject, stripped it of any anecdotal context, and pushed it up to the surface. The story of the painting is well known—Soutine poured blood from the butcher's shop to refurbish the rapidly decaying carcass while his assistant fanned away the flies, and nauseated neighbors clamored for the police. Oblivious to the stench, Soutine worked obsessively before his subject, recording every detail in vigorously applied, liquid color. In this and in many other paintings, Soutine demonstrated how close are the extremes of ugliness and beauty, a phenomenon that would intrigue his Surrealist peers.

Valadon and Utrillo

Suzanne Valadon (1867–1939) was born in central France, the child of a peasant woman who moved with her infant daughter to the Montmartre district of Paris. As a teenager, Valadon joined the circus as a performer but soon left because of an injury. She became a popular model in a neighborhood filled with artists and was soon posing for Puvis de Chavannes, Renoir, Degas, and Toulouse-Lautrec. An instinctive aptitude for drawing enabled this self-taught artist, a woman from a working-class background, to achieve a remarkable degree of success in the male-dominated art world of turn-of-the-century Paris. By the 1890s, some of her drawings had even been purchased by Degas, who introduced her to the technique of etching. Valadon made still lifes and the occasional landscape, but the bulk of her oeuvre was devoted to portraits and nudes.

The subject of the richly decorative canvas *Blue Room* (fig. 14.7) seems to fall somewhere between those two genres. While she assumes a traditional odalisque pose, this ample, unidentified woman, unconventionally dressed in striped pants, has little in common with the bold courtesans of Manet (see fig. 14.3) or the alluring nudes of Modigliani (see fig. 2.20). What is more, Valadon's model follows intellectual pursuits (note the books on the bed), and she smokes a cigarette, hardly the habit of a "respectable" woman, without the slightest self-consciousness. While her frank presentation of a female subject recalls depictions of prostitutes by her friend Toulouse-Lautrec, Valadon's painting seems a deliberate riposte to the clichéd interpretations of the theme by many generations of male artists. *Blue Room* was shown in the 1923 Salon d'Automne and purchased by the French state three years later.

The life and art of Valadon's son, **Maurice Utrillo** (1883–1955), provide perhaps the greatest paradox among *les maudits*. Utrillo was given the family name of the Spanish art critic Miguel Utrillo, who wished to help the boy (his actual father was rumored to be Puvis de Chavannes). As a youngster, Utrillo began to drink heavily, was expelled from school, and by the age of eighteen was in a sanatorium for alcoholics. During his chaotic adolescence—probably through his mother's influence—he became interested in painting. Like his mother, he was

14.7 Suzanne Valadon, *Blue Room*, 1923. Oil on canvas, 35⅜ × 45⅝" (90 × 115.9 cm). Musée National d'Art Moderne, Centre d'Art et de Culture Georges Pompidou, Paris.

14.8 Maurice Utrillo, *Street in Asnières*, 1913–15. Oil on canvas, 29 × 36¼" (73.7 × 92.1 cm). Private collection.

self-trained, but his art is hardly reminiscent of hers. Although his painting was technically quite accomplished and reveals stylistic influences from the Impressionists and their successors, his work is closer to the purposely naive or primitive type of painting inspired by Henri Rousseau (see fig. 3.16).

The first paintings that survive are of the suburb of Montmagny where Utrillo grew up, and of Montmartre after he moved there. Painted approximately between 1903 and 1909, they have coarse brush texture and sober colors. In about 1910 Utrillo began to focus obsessively and almost exclusively on the familiar scenes of Montmartre, which he painted street by street. On occasional trips away from Paris, he painted churches and village scenes that were variations on his basic theme (fig. **14.8**). Asnières, the village depicted here, was one of the sites along the Seine favored by the Impressionists. Utrillo admired the work of Sisley and Pissarro, but unlike them, he preferred the unremarkable village streets to the banks of the river. The composition of *Street in Asnières* typifies Utrillo's preferred format. Buildings along a narrow street devoid of pedestrians disappear into a long perspective. To emulate the rough texture of the chalky, whitewashed buildings, he frequently added plaster to his zinc white oil paint. In fact, this period is often referred to as his "white" period. His favorite scenes recur over and over again, his memory refreshed from postcards. Around the end of the

war, following the white period, his color brightened and figures occurred more frequently. From 1930 until his death in 1955, Utrillo, now decorated with the Legion of Honor, lived at Le Vésinet outside Paris. During these twenty-five years of rectitude, he did little but repeat his earlier paintings.

Dedication to Color: Matisse's Later Career

As discussed in the context of Fauvism in chapter 7, the culmination of **Henri Matisse**'s (1869–1954) prewar exploration of color may be seen in his 1911 painting *Red Studio* (see fig. 7.21). When compared with works of a similar date by Braque and Picasso (see figs. 10.16, 10.18), which have the typically muted palette of Analytical Cubism, its reliance on the power of a single strong color is particularly striking. Just as the Cubists used multiple viewpoints to undermine the conventional illusionism of single-point perspective, Matisse placed objects in relation to each other in terms not of spatial recession but of color. As he said of the *Red Studio* (which in real life was an airy, white-walled room), "I find that all these things, flowers, furniture, the chest of drawers, only become what they are to me when I see them together with the color red."

Despite his very different approach to painting, and the fact that he was considerably older than most members of the Cubist circle (he was in his mid-forties at the outbreak of war in 1914), Matisse shared some of their concerns, including an enthusiasm for non-Western art. The influence of Cubism can be felt in his work during the war years (see below), although subsequent phases of his career – from his "rococo" decorative idiom of the twenties to the sharply defined and supremely graceful simplicity of his late cut-outs – reassert the primacy of color.

This chapter shows how the careers of Matisse and Picasso followed quite different courses through the mid-twentieth century. At the same time, the development of Matisse's art from around 1914 onward presents numerous points of comparison and contrast with Picasso's. Extending over decades of their long working lives, the more-or-less cordial rivalry between them fueled the popular view of these two great artists as "mighty opposites" in the history of modernism.

Response to Cubism, 1914–16

Being thoroughly immersed in the art of Cézanne, Matisse inevitably found himself responding to the structured interpretation of Cézanne's style realized by Braque and Picasso. In 1915 the great colorist produced what is possibly his most orthodox Cubist painting in *Variation on a Still Life by de Heem*. In this response to a seventeenth-century still life that he had first copied in 1893–95 (see chapter 7), Matisse clarified for himself the development that had taken place in the intervening decades. The result is a personal interpretation of Synthetic Cubism in which

his palette has become much lighter; the space is closed in and frontalized; and the tablecloth and the architecture of the room are geometrized, as are the fruits and vessels on the table. His studies of Cubism were extremely helpful, because they encouraged him to simplify his pictorial structures, to control his intuitively decorative tendency, and to use the rectangle as a counterpoint for the curvilinear arabesque that came most naturally to him.

One of Matisse's most austere interpretations of a Cubist mode is *Piano Lesson* of 1916 (fig. **14.9**). This work is a large, abstract arrangement of geometric color planes—lovely grays and greens. A tilted foreground plane of rose pink constitutes the top of the piano, on which a gray metronome sits; its triangular shape is echoed in the angled green plane that falls across the window. The planes are accented by decorative curving patterns based on the iron grille of the balcony and the music stand of the piano. The environment is animated by the head of the child sculpturally modeled in line evoking Matisse's 1908 sculpture *Decorative Figure*, which appears in so many of his paintings. Another of his works, the painting *Woman on a High Stool*, 1914, is schematically indicated in the upper right, but its nature, as a painting or a figure in the room, remains unclear, heightening the sense of spatial ambiguity. The stiff figure seems to preside over the piano lesson like a stern instructor. Here again, Matisse's interpretation of Cubism is intensely personal, with none of the shifting views and fractured forms that mark the main line of Picasso, Braque, and Juan Gris. Its frontality and its dominant uniform planes of geometric color areas show that Matisse could assimilate Cubism in order to achieve an abstract structure of space and color.

Renewal of Coloristic Idiom, 1917–c. 1930

The following year Matisse undertook another version of this theme with *Music Lesson* (fig. **14.10**), a painting identical in size to *Piano Lesson*, which depicts the same room in the artist's house at Issy-les-Moulineaux, southwest of Paris. Matisse has transformed that room into a pleasant domestic setting for a portrait of his family. The three Matisse children are in the foreground while Madame Matisse sews in the garden. Everyone is self-absorbed and takes little heed of the artist or the beautiful garden view. The artist implies his own presence through his open violin case on the piano, his painting on the wall in the upper right corner, and his sculpture, *Reclining Nude 1/Aurora* (see fig. 9.3), here enlarged and flesh-colored, which sits by the pond before a lush landscape. In the wake of *Piano Lesson*, Matisse replaced his previous Cubist austerity with a lush indulgence in color and decorative forms.

In late 1917 Matisse moved to Nice, in the south of France, where he then spent much time during his life. There, in spacious, seaside studios, he painted languorous models, often in the guise of exotic "odalisques," under the brilliant light of the Riviera. These women reveal little in the way of individual psychologies; they are objects

14.9 Henri Matisse, *Piano Lesson*, late summer, 1916. Oil on canvas, 8'½" × 6'11¾" (2.45 × 2.13 m). The Museum of Modern Art, New York.

14.10 Henri Matisse, *Music Lesson*, 1917. Oil on canvas, 8'1⅛" × 6'7" (2.4 × 2 m). The Barnes Foundation, Merion, Pennsylvania.

14.12 Henri Matisse, *Interior with a Phonograph*, 1924. Oil on canvas, 39¾ × 32" (101 × 81.3 cm). Private collection.

14.11 Henri Matisse, *Decorative Figure Against an Ornamental Background*, 1925–26. Oil on canvas, 51⅛ × 38½" (129.9 × 97.8 cm). Musée National d'Art Moderne, Centre d'Art et de Culture Georges Pompidou, Paris.

of fantasy and visual gratification in a space seemingly sealed off from the rest of the world. Throughout most of the twenties, Matisse supplanted heroic abstraction with intimacy, charm, and a mood of sensual indulgence, all suffused with color as lavish as an Oriental carpet and with a sense of line and pattern that owed much to Islamic art. Yet, even within this deceptively relaxed manner, the artist produced images and compositions of grand, even solemn magnificence. The *Decorative Figure Against an Ornamental Background* of 1925–26 (fig. **14.11**) epitomizes this most rococo phase of Matisse's work. Owing to the highly sculptural quality of his model, Matisse manages to set the figure off against the patterned Persian carpet, which visually merges with a background wall that has been decorated with the repetitive floral motif of French baroque wallpaper and the elaborate volutes of a Venetian mirror. Such solidly modeled figures appear in his sculptures of this period and also in the lithographs he was then making.

During the twenties Matisse also revived his interest in the window theme, first observed in the 1905 Fauve *The Open Window* (see fig. 7.4) and often with a table, still life, or figure set before it. Through this subject, in fact, one may follow the changing focus of Matisse's attention from Fauve color to Cubist reductiveness and back to the coloristic, curvilinear style of the postwar years. In *Interior with a Phonograph* (fig. **14.12**), a painting of 1924, Matisse gave full play to his brilliant palette, while at the same time constructing a richly ambiguous space, created through layers of rectangular openings.

An Art of Essentials, c. 1930–54

Matisse had once expressed (in 1908) his desire to create "an art of balance, of purity and serenity devoid of troubling or depressing subject matter, an art which would be … something like a good armchair in which to rest from physical fatigue." Indulgent as this may seem, Matisse was almost puritanical in his self-effacing and unsparing search for the ideal. Thus, in the wake of his twenties luxuriance, the sixty-six-year-old artist set out once again to renew his art by reducing it to essentials. The evidence of this prolonged and systematic exercise has survived in a telling series of photographs, made during the course of the work—state by state—that Matisse carried out toward the ultimate realization of his famous *Large Reclining Nude* (formerly called *Pink Nude*) of 1935 (fig. **14.13**). He progressively selected, simplified, and reduced—not only form but also color, until the latter consisted of little more than rose, blue, black, and white. The odalisque thus rests within a pure, rhythmic flow of uninterrupted curves. While this cursive sweep evokes the simplified volumes of the figure, it also fixes them into the gridded support of the chaise longue. Here is the perfect antithetical companion to the Fauve *Blue Nude* of 1907 (see fig. 7.7), a sculptured image resolved by far less reductive means than those of the *Large Reclining Nude*.

Like the grand French tradition of the decorative that preceded him—from Le Brun at Versailles through Boucher and Fragonard in the eighteenth century to Delacroix, Renoir, and Monet in the nineteenth—Matisse had ample opportunity to be overtly decorative when, in 1932, he began designing and illustrating special editions of great texts, the first of which was *Poésies* by Stéphane Mallarmé, published by Albert Skira. In the graphics for these volumes, Matisse so extended the aesthetic economy already seen in the *Large Reclining Nude* that, even when restricted to line and black-and-white, he could endow the image with a living sense of color and volume.

Matisse's most extraordinary decorative project during the thirties was his design for a large triptych on the subject of dance (fig. **14.14**) that was commissioned by the American collector Albert C. Barnes, the same man who

14.13 Henri Matisse, *Large Reclining Nude (The Pink Nude)*, 1935. Oil on canvas, 26 × 36½" (66 × 92.7 cm). The Baltimore Museum of Art.

14.14 Henri Matisse, *Merion Dance Mural*, 1932–33. Oil on canvas: left 11'1¾" × 14'5¾" (3.4 × 4.4 m), center 11'8⅛" × 16'6⅛" (3.6 × 5 m), right 11'1⅜" × 14'5" (3.4 × 4.4 m). The Barnes Foundation, Merion, Pennsylvania.

had bought the works of Soutine. The triptych would occupy three lunettes in the Barnes Foundation, Merion, Pennsylvania, which housed a collection that already included more works by Matisse than any museum. Matisse began to paint the murals in Nice, only to discover well into the project that he was using incorrect measurements. So he began anew. (In 1992, in an amazing discovery, this unfinished but splendid composition was found rolled up in Matisse's studio in Nice.) When Matisse returned to work on the second version, he discovered that his usual technique of brushing in every color himself was enormously time-consuming. In order to expedite his experiments with form and color arrangements, he cut large sheets of painted paper and pinned them to the canvas, shifting them, drawing on them, and, ultimately, discarding them once he decided on the final composition. This method of cutting paper, as we shall see, became an artistic end in itself during the artist's later years. For both compositions, Matisse turned to his own previous treatment of the dance theme (see fig. 7.19). In the final murals, the dancing figures are rendered in light gray, to harmonize with the limestone of the building, and are set against an abstract background consisting of broad, geometric bands of black, pink, and blue. The limbs of the figures are dramatically sliced by the curving edges of the canvas, which somehow enhance rather than inhibit their ecstatic movements. Matisse, of course, understood that his image had to be legible from a great distance, so the forms are boldly conceived, with no interior modeling to distract from their simplified contours. The result is one of the most successful mergings of architecture and painting in the twentieth century. Fortunately, Matisse felt the need to paint a third version of the murals, which now belongs, as does the first, to the Musée National d'Art Moderne in Paris.

14.15 Henri Matisse, *Ivy in Flower*, 1953. Collage maquette for a stained-glass window: colored paper, watercolor, pencil, and brown paper tape on paper mounted on canvas, 9'3⅞" × 9'4⅝" (2.8 × 2.9 m). Dallas Museum of Art.

14.16 Henri Matisse, *Chapel of the Rosary of the Dominican Nuns*, Vence, France. Consecrated June 25, 1951.

After war struck Europe again in 1939, Matisse reacted as he had in 1916–18 and countered the inhumanity of the moment with an art radiant with affirmative, humanist faith. In the fifties, even as age and physical disability confined him to bed, he invented a new technique and through it discovered a fresh burst of expressive freedom. With Matisse, the hand could hardly have been more secure or the conception more youthful (fig. **14.15**). The new Color Field painters emerging in New York toward the end of the fifties were especially inspired by this late work, an art created by a man lying on his back, drawing with charcoal, fastened to the end of a long wand, on paper attached to the walls and ceiling above. In this way, Matisse produced vast compositions that he then executed by cutting out forms from paper he had handpainted. Once assembled into figurative and abstract–decorative compositions that were very often mural in scale, the découpages, or paper cutout works, can be seen as the apotheosis of Matisse's initial Cézanne-inspired Fauve aesthetic. They consist of planes of pure color flattened by their interlocking relationships but conjuring dimensionality by the density of their color and the monumental simplicity of their arabesque shapes. By "cutting into color," Matisse was manipulating his material in a way that translated into pictorial terms his experience in handling clay for sculpture. With this, he at last attained the long-sought synthesis of sculpture and painting, of drawing and color. The irrepressible gaiety of the cutouts could be expressed to dazzling impact on a mural scale (see fig. **14.15**) or through the artist's illustrations for the book *Jazz*, which carried a text composed and handprinted by Matisse.

Following the experience of *Jazz*, Matisse began making cutouts in earnest, eventually to the exclusion of all other forms of artistic activity.

Beginning in 1948, Matisse used the cutout technique to design the stained glass and priests' vestments for the Dominican chapel in the French Mediterranean town of Vence (fig. **14.16**). Like the Barnes murals, the Vence chapel was a collaboration between art and architecture, but now Matisse extended his talents for decoration beyond painting to textiles, mural-sized drawings on ceramic tiles, and even a spire on the roof of the chapel.

Celebrating the Good Life: Dufy's Later Career

Raoul Dufy (1877–1953) joined Matisse in remaining true to the principles of Fauve color but, in the years following the "Wild Beast" episode (see fig. 7.13), refined them into a sumptuous signature style. Even more than Matisse, he was a decorator with a connoisseur's taste for the hedonistic joys of the good life. During the twenties and thirties, Dufy achieved such popularity—not only in paintings, watercolors, and drawings, but also in ceramics, textiles, illustrated books, and stage design—that his rainbow palette and stylish, insouciant drawing seems to embody the spirit of the period. *Indian Model in the Studio at L'Impasse Guelma* (fig. **14.17**) shows many of the characteristics of the artist's mature manner. The broad, clear area of light blue that covers the studio wall forms a background to the intricate pattern of rugs and paintings whose exotic focus is an elaborately draped Indian model. The use of descriptive line and oil color laid on in thin washes is such that the painting—and this is true of most of Dufy's works—seems like a delicately colored ink drawing.

Dufy combined influences from Matisse, rococo, Persian and Indian painting, and occasionally modern primitives such as Henri Rousseau, transforming all these into an intimate world of his own. The artist could take a panoramic view and suggest, in minuscule touches of color and nervous arabesques of line, the movement and excitement of his world—crowds of holidayseekers, horse races, boats in sun-filled harbors, the circus, and the concert hall.

Eclectic Mastery: Picasso's Career After the High-Point of Cubism

"I paint objects as I think them, not as I see them," said **Pablo Picasso** (1881–1973). This statement emphasizes the strong conceptual element in his art that lies behind both his lifelong readiness to experiment with new kinds of visual language and his capacity to assimilate the essence of a diverse range of artistic styles and techniques. Unlike Matisse, whose "art of balance," like a comfortable armchair, sought to relax and refresh the viewer, Picasso saw art as "an instrument of war against brutality and darkness." His work during the inter-war years reflects intellectual currents of the times, from the classical "call to order" that followed the war to his involvement with Surrealism and communism, and the passionate political statement of *Guernica*.

In 1914, like other European avant-garde movements, Cubism had lost momentum as artists and writers, including Braque, Léger and Apollinaire, enlisted in the armed

14.18 Pablo Picasso, *Ambroise Vollard*, 1915. Pencil on paper, 18⅜ × 12⁹⁄₁₆" (46.7 × 31.9 cm). The Metropolitan Museum of Art, New York.

forces. As a foreigner, Picasso was able to remain in Paris, but he worked more now in isolation. After the period of discovery and experiment in Analytic Cubism, collage, and the beginning of Synthetic Cubism (1908–14), there was a pause during which the artist used Cubism for decorative ends (see figs. 10.25, 10.29). Then, suddenly, during a sojourn in Avignon in 1914, he began a series of realistic portrait drawings in a sensitive, scrupulous linear technique that recalls his longtime admiration for the drawings of Ingres. But works such as the portrait of Picasso's dealer Ambroise Vollard (fig. **14.18**) were in the minority during 1915–16, when the artist was still experimenting with painting and constructions in a Synthetic Cubist vein.

The war years and the early twenties saw a return to forms of realism on the part of other French painters—Derain, Vlaminck, Dufy—originally associated with Fauvism or Cubism. In Picasso's case, however, the drawings and, subsequently, paintings in a realist mode constituted a reexamination of the nature of Cubism. He obviously felt confident enough of his control of the Cubist vocabulary to attack reality from two widely divergent vantage points. With astonishing agility, he pursued Cubist experiments side by side with realistic and classical drawings and paintings in the early twenties. Picasso's mastery of an eclectic range of styles—in itself one of the most extraordinary phenomena of twentieth-century art—is interesting in several ways. It shows how the artist was able to take full advantage of the experimental freedoms that were an integral part of modernism. But at the same time it shows him moving away from modernist notions of authenticity (for example, Cubism's truth to the fragmented nature of visual perception as it is actually experienced) toward modes of parody or pastiche that foreshadow postmodernism.

Parade and Theatrical Themes

In 1917 Picasso agreed, somewhat reluctantly because of his hatred for travel or disruption of his routine, to go to Rome as part of a group of artists, including the poet and dramatist Jean Cocteau, the composer Erik Satie, and the choreographer Léonide Massine, to design curtains, sets, and costumes for a new ballet, *Parade*, being prepared for Diaghilev's Ballets Russes (Russian Ballet Company). The stimulus of Italy, where Picasso stayed for two months visiting museums, churches, and ancient sites like Pompeii, contributed to the resurgence of classical style and subject matter in his art. He also met and married a young dancer in the corps de ballet, Olga Koklova, who became the subject of many portraits in the ensuing years. *Parade* brought the artist back into the world of the theater, which, along with the circus, had been an early love and had provided him with subject matter for his Blue and Rose Periods (see chapter 10). Dating back to the late eighteenth century, a traditional "parade" was a sideshow performance enacted outside a theater to entice the spectators inside. The ballet was built around the theme of conflict: on the one hand, the delicate humanity and harmony of the music and the

14.19 Pablo Picasso, *The American Manager*, 1917. Reconstruction. Realized by Kermit Love for The Museum of Modern Art, 1979. Paint on cardboard, fabric, paper, wood, leather, and metal, 11'2¼" × 8' × 3'8½" (3.4 × 2.4 × 1.1 m). The Museum of Modern Art, New York.

dancers; on the other, the commercialized forces of the mechanist–Cubist managers (fig. **14.19**) and the deafening noise of the sound effects. Cocteau, who saw the play as a dialogue between illusion and reality, the commonplace and the fantastic, intended these real sounds—sirens, typewriters, or trains—as the aural equivalent of the literal elements in Cubist collages (see fig. 10.21). The mixture of reality and fantasy in *Parade* led Apollinaire in his program notes to refer to its *sur-réalisme*, one of the first recorded uses of this term to describe an art form. *Parade* involved elements of shock that the Dadaists were then exploiting in Zurich (see chapter 13). Picasso designed a backdrop for *Parade* that is reminiscent of his 1905 circus paintings (see fig. 10.3) in its tender, romantic imagery and Rose Period coloring. Like Satie's soothing prelude, it reassured the audience, which was expecting Futurist cacophony. But they were shocked out of their complacency once the curtain rose. When *Parade* was first performed in Paris on May 18, 1917, the audience included sympathetic viewers like Gris and Severini. Most of the theatergoers, however, were outraged members of the bourgeoisie. The reviews were devastating, and *Parade* became a *succès de scandale*, marking the beginning of many fruitful collaborations between Picasso, as well as other artists in France, with the Ballets Russes.

During this period, Picasso's early love of the characters from the Italian *commedia dell'arte* and its descendant, the French circus, was renewed. Pierrots, Harlequins, and musicians again became a central theme. The world of the theater and music took on a fresh aspect that resulted in a number of brilliant portraits, such as that of the Russian composer Igor Stravinsky, and figure drawings done in delicately sparse outlines.

Postwar Classicism

In the early postwar period Picasso experimented with different attitudes toward Cubism and representation. In the latter, the most purely classical style was manifested before 1923 in drawings that have the quality of white-ground Greek vase paintings of the fifth century B.C.E. Already by 1920 such drawings embodied a specifically Greek or Roman subject matter that Picasso continued to explore thereafter. *Nessus and Dejanira* (fig. **14.20**), for example, depicts a story from Ovid's *Metamorphoses* in which the centaur, Nessus, tries to rape Dejanira, the wife of Herakles. Picasso said that his trips to the Mediterranean in the south of France inspired such ancient mythological themes. This subject so intrigued the artist that he made versions in pencil, silverpoint, watercolor, and etching. The representational line drawings also revived his interest in the graphic arts, particularly etching and lithography. He produced prints at the beginning of his career and during the earlier Cubist phase and the war years. From the early twenties, printmaking became a major phase of his production, to the point where Picasso must be regarded as one of the great printmakers of the twentieth century.

During 1920, Picasso also began to produce paintings, frequently on a large scale, in which his concept of the classical is in a different and monumental vein. He pursued this style for the next four years in painting and then continued

14.21 Pablo Picasso, *Three Women at the Spring*, Fontainebleau, summer 1921. Oil on canvas, 6'8¼" × 5'8½" (2 × 1.74 m). The Museum of Modern Art, New York.

in sculpture in the early thirties. The years of working with flat, tilted Cubist planes seemed to build up a need to go to the extreme of sculptural mass. The faces are simplified in the heavy, coarse manner of Roman rather than Greek sculpture, and when Picasso placed the figures before a landscape, he simplified the background to frontalized accents that tend to close rather than open the space. Thus, the effect of high sculptural relief is maintained

14.20 Pablo Picasso, *Nessus and Dejanira*, 1920. Pencil on paper, 8¼ × 10¼" (21 × 26 cm). The Museum of Modern Art, New York.

14.22 Pablo Picasso, *Two Women Running on the Beach (The Race)*, 1922. Gouache on plywood, 13⅜ × 16¾" (34 × 42.5 cm). Musée Picasso, Paris.

14.23 Pablo Picasso, *The Pipes of Pan*, 1923. Oil on canvas, 6'6½" × 5'8½" (2 × 1.70 m). Musée Picasso, Paris.

throughout. While the stone giantesses of *Three Women at the Spring* (fig. **14.21**), which have been compared with Michelangelo's sibyls (prophetesses) in the Sistine Chapel, do not embody the traditional proportions of the classical canon, they are endowed with a classical sense of dignity and timelessness. Picasso prepared his compact, rigorously constructed image with several studies. The compositional elements rotate around the central placement of a jug and the women's enormous hands, which are extended in slow, hieratic gestures. Occasionally, Picasso put his figures into lumbering activity, as in *Two Women Running on the Beach (The Race)* (fig. **14.22**). The colors of this painting, in accordance with its classical mood, are light and bright—blues and reds, with raw pink flesh tones. Despite their massive limbs, these ecstatic women bound effortlessly across the landscape. It has been suggested that the elated mood of some of Picasso's classical paintings has to do with a happy domestic life with Olga and their son Paulo, born in 1921. In 1924, Picasso enlarged this tiny composition to create a backdrop for Diaghilev's ballet *The Blue Train*. We should recall that such massive figures were not new in Picasso's career, for during his proto-Cubist period (1906–8) he had produced a number of comparably substantial and primitivizing renditions of the nude (see fig. 10.5).

Picasso continued to paint for two or three more years in a classical vein, but now with more specific reference to the spirit of Athens in the fifth century B.C.E. One of the outstanding works of this phase is *The Pipes of Pan*

(fig. **14.23**). The two youths are presented as massive yet graceful athletes, absorbed in their own remote and magical world. The rectilinear forms of the background deny any sense of spatial recession, turning the whole into a kind of Mediterranean stage set.

Cubism Continued

The remarkable aspect of Picasso's art during this ten-year period (1915–25) is that he was also producing major Cubist paintings. He explained this stylistic dichotomy in a 1923 interview: "If the subjects I have wanted to express have suggested different ways of expression I have never hesitated to adopt them." After the decorative enrichment of the Cubist paintings around 1914–15 (see fig. 10.25), including pointillist color and elaborate, applied textures, the artist moved back, in his Cubist paintings of 1916–18, to a greater austerity of more simplified flat patterns, frequently based on the figure (fig. **14.24**). Simultaneously, he made realistic versions of this subject, a favorite with him. From compositions involving figures, there gradually evolved the two versions of the *Three Musicians* (fig. **14.25**), both created in 1921, the same year Picasso made *Three Women at the Spring*. One version is in the Museum of Modern Art, New York; the other is in the Museum of Art, Philadelphia. The three figures in both versions are

14.24 Pablo Picasso, *Harlequin with Violin (Si tu veux)*, 1918. Oil on canvas, 56 × 39½" (142.2 × 100.3 cm). The Cleveland Museum of Art.

14.25 Pablo Picasso, *Three Musicians*, summer 1921. Oil on canvas, 6'7" × 7'3¾" (2 × 2.2 m). The Museum of Modern Art, New York.

14.26 Pablo Picasso, *Mandolin and Guitar*, 1924. Oil and sand on canvas, 56⅛ × 67¾" (142.6 × 200 cm). Solomon R. Guggenheim Museum, New York.

seated frontally in a row, against an enclosing back wall, and fixed by the restricted foreground, but the version in New York is simpler and more somber. The paintings are a superb summation of the Synthetic Cubist style up to this point, but they also embody something new. The figures are suggestive not so much of exuberant musicians from the *commedia dell'arte* as of some mysterious tribunal. It has been persuasively argued that the three musicians represent covert portraits of Picasso's friends—the writer Max Jacob (the monk at the right), who had recently withdrawn from the world and taken up residence in a monastery, and Apollinaire (Pierrot, the "poet" at the left), who had died in 1918. Picasso portrays himself, as he often did, in the guise of Harlequin, situated in the middle between his friends. The somber, somewhat ominous mood of the painting is thus explained as the work becomes a memorial to these lost friends.

The other direction in which Picasso took Cubism involved sacrifice of the purity of its Analytic phase for the sake of new exploration of pictorial space. The result was, between 1924 and 1926, a series of the most colorful and spatially intricate still lifes in the history of Cubism. *Mandolin and Guitar* (fig. **14.26**) illustrates the artist's superb control over the entire repertory of Cubist and perspective space. The center of the painting is occupied by the characteristic Cubist still life—the mandolin and guitar twisting and turning on the table, encompassed in mandorlas of abstract color-shapes: vivid reds, blues, purples, yellows, and ochers against more subdued but still rich earth colors. The tablecloth is varicolored and patterned, while the corner of the room with the open window is a complex of tilted wall planes and receding perspective lines. These create a considerable illusion of depth, which, however, seems constantly to be turning back upon itself, shifting and changing into flat planes of color. The whole is infiltrated by an intense Mediterranean light, made palpa-

ble by the deeply colored shadow that falls across the red tile floor at the right.

It is interesting to recall the extent to which the subject of the open window, often with a table, still life, or figure before it, had also been a favorite of Matisse (see fig. 14.12). Certain relationships between Matisse's work and Picasso's contemporary paintings of similar subjects indicate that Picasso may have been looking at his colleague and great rival's work.

In some Cubist still lifes of the mid-twenties, Picasso introduced classical busts as motifs, suggesting the artist's simultaneous exploration of classic idealism and a more expressionist vision. In *Studio with Plaster Head* (fig. **14.27**), the Roman bust introduces a quality of mystery analogous to De Chirico's use of classical motifs (see fig. 13.5). While the trappings of classicism are here, the serenity of Picasso's earlier classical paintings has vanished. The work belongs to a tradition of still lifes representing the attributes of the arts (including the prominent architect's square at the right), but the juxtapositions become so jarring as to imbue the composition with tremendous psychological tension. At the back of the still life, fragments of Picasso's small son's toy theater imply that the entire still life is an ancient Roman stage set. The head is almost a caricature, which Picasso manages to twist in space from a strict profile view at the right to a fully frontal one in the deep blue-gray shadow at the left. The broken plaster arm at the left grips a baton so intensely it feels animated. Just before Picasso made this still life, he had completed his large, anguished painting, *Three Dancers* (see fig. 15.39). This work takes us into another stage in Picasso's development (see chapter 15). At this moment the Surrealists were emerging as an organized group, claiming Picasso as one of their own.

Sensuous Analysis: Braque's Later Career

Georges Braque (1882–1963) and Picasso parted company in 1914, never to regain the intimacy of the formative years of Cubism. After his war service and the slow recovery from a serious wound, Braque returned to a changed Paris in the fall of 1917. Picasso was in Italy, and other pioneers of Cubism or Fauvism were widely scattered. However, Juan Gris and Henri Laurens (see chapter 10) were still in Paris, working in a manner that impressed Braque and inspired him in his efforts to find his own way once more. By 1918–19 a new and personal approach to Synthetic Cubism began to be apparent in a series of paintings, of which *Café-Bar* (fig. **14.28**) is a document for Braque's style for the next twenty years. The painting is tall and relatively narrow, a shape which Braque had used during his first essays in Cubism (see fig. 10.16) and which he now began to utilize on a more monumental scale. The subject is a still life of guitar, pipe, journal, and miscellaneous objects piled vertically on a small, marble-topped pedestal

14.27 Pablo Picasso, *Studio with Plaster Head*, summer 1925. Oil on canvas, 38⅝ × 51⅜" (97.9 × 131.1 cm). The Museum of Modern Art, New York.

14.28 Georges Braque, *Café-Bar*, 1919. Oil on canvas, 63¼ × 31⅞" (160.7 × 81 cm). Öffentliche Kunstsammlung Basel, Kunstmuseum.

table, or *guéridon*. This table was used many times in subsequent paintings. The suggested elements of the environment are held together by a pattern of horizontal green rectangles patterned with orange-yellow dots, placed like an architectural framework parallel to the picture plane. Compared with Braque's prewar Cubist paintings, *Café-Bar* has more sense of illusionistic depth and actual environment. Also, although the colors are rich, and Braque's feeling for texture is more than ever apparent, the total effect recalls, more than Picasso's, the subdued, nearly monochrome tonalities that both artists worked with during their early collaboration (see figs. 10.19, 10.20). This is perhaps the key to the difference between their work in the years after their collaboration. Whereas the approach of Picasso was experimental and varied, that of Braque was

conservative and intensive, continuing the first lessons of Cubism. Even when he made his most radical departures into his own form of classical figure painting during the twenties, the color remained predominantly the grays, greens, browns, and ochers of Analytic Cubism. The principal characteristic of Braque's style emerging about 1919 was that of a textural sensuousness in which the angular geometry of earlier Cubism began to diffuse into an overall fluid pattern of organic shapes.

This style manifested itself in the early twenties in figure paintings in which the artist seems to have deserted Cubism as completely as Picasso did in his classical figure paintings. The difference again lay in the painterliness of Braque's oils and drawings, as compared with Picasso's Ingres-like contour drawings and the sculptural massiveness of his classical paintings. In Braque's paintings and figure drawings of the twenties, the artist effected his personal escape from the rigidity of his earlier Cubism and prepared the way for his enriched approach to Cubist design of the later twenties and thirties.

The most dramatic variation on his steady, introspective progress occurred in the early thirties when, under the influence of Greek vase painting, Braque created a series of line drawings and engravings with continuous contours. This flat, linear style also penetrated to his newly austere

14.29 Georges Braque, *Woman with a Mandolin*, 1937. Oil on canvas, 51¼ × 38¼" (130.2 × 97.2 cm). The Museum of Modern Art, New York.

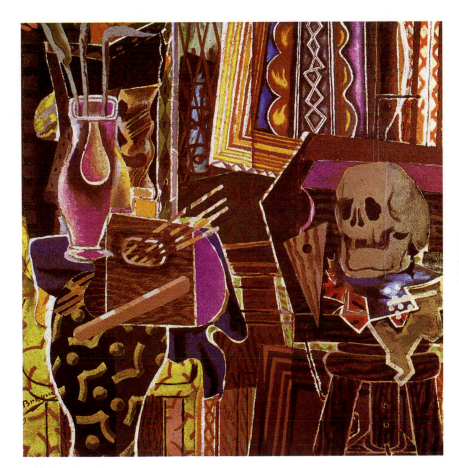

14.30 Georges Braque, *Vase, Palette, and Skull*, 1939. Oil and sand on canvas, 36 × 36" (91.4 × 91.4 cm). Kreeger Museum, Washington, D.C.

paintings of the period: scenes of artist and model or simply figures in the studio. These works exhibit some of the most varied effects of Braque's entire career. The dominant motif of *Woman with a Mandolin* (fig. **14.29**) is a tall, dark silhouette of a woman seated before a music stand. Behind her, a profusion of patterns on the wall recalls the wallpaper patterns of Braque's earlier *papiers collés*. Because the woman's profile, very similar to ones in related compositions, is painted a deep black-brown, she becomes a shadow, less material than the other richly textured elements in the room. She plays the role of silent muse in this monumental painting, which represents Braque's meditation on art and music. It was probably inspired by Corot's treatment of the same subject, painted around 1860, which shows a young woman before an easel, holding a mandolin.

During the years of World War II Braque made several still life variations on the *vanitas* theme, in which a skull traditionally symbolizes the transitory nature of existence (fig. **14.30**). It is a subject that Cézanne, Braque's great mentor, had frequently represented. Here Braque inserts the skull into the context of the studio. In fact, it seems to rest on his easel, implying that we are looking at a painted "illusion" rather than a "real" object. Braque has mixed sand with his oil medium, a practice he frequently applied to endow his surfaces with an almost sculptural quality. Braque continued to explore the theme of the studio in his paintings after World War II, but, inspired by Van Gogh, he also turned to landscape, a genre he had explored only intermittently since his early Cubist days.

Austerity and Elegance: Léger, Ozenfant, and Le Corbusier

In his paintings of the twenties and thirties, Fernand Léger (1881–1955) took part in the so-called "call to order" that characterized much French art after World War I, in which he had served. One of his major figure compositions from the postwar period is *Three Women (Le Grand Déjeuner)* (fig. **14.31**). The depersonalized figures, who stare fixedly and uniformly at the spectator, are machinelike volumes modeled out from the rigidly rectangular background. Léger labored over *Three Women*, the largest of three very similar versions of the same composition, and even repainted the figure at the right, who was originally the same marblelike gray color of her companions. He regarded the subject as timeless and eternal and said that his artistic sources were David, Ingres, Renoir, and Seurat. Although *Three Women* reflects Léger's engagement with classicism, it is also resolutely modern. In the abstract, rectilinear forms of the background one detects an awareness of the contemporary paintings of Mondrian, who was then living in Paris (see fig. 17.21). With its elements of austere, Art Deco elegance, Léger's art of this period also had much in common with the twenties Purism (see below) of Amédée Ozenfant and Le Corbusier (see figs. 14.33, 14.34). Léger remained very close to these artists after their initial meeting in 1920.

During the last twenty years of his life, Léger revisited a few basic themes through which he sought to sum up his experiences in the exploration of humanity and its place

14.31 Fernand Léger, *Three Women (Le Grand Déjeuner)*, 1921. Oil on canvas, 6'¼" × 8'3" (1.8 × 2.5 m). The Museum of Modern Art, New York.

14.32 Fernand Léger, *The Great Parade*, 1954. Oil on canvas, 9' × 13'1" (2.7 × 4 m). Solomon R. Guggenheim Museum, New York.

in the contemporary industrial world. It was a social as well as a visual investigation of his world as an artist, a final and culminating assessment of his plastic means for presenting it. In *The Great Parade* of 1954 (fig. **14.32**), Léger brought to culmination a series in which figure and environment are realistically drawn in heavy black outline on a white ground, over which float free shapes of transparent red, blue, orange, yellow, and green. This huge work also reflects a lifelong obsession with circus themes, as well as an interest in creating a modern mural art. Léger worked on the large canvas for two years. "In the first version," he recalled, "the color exactly fitted the forms. In the definitive version one can see what force, what vitality is achieved by using color on its own." Despite his increased interest in illustrative subject and social observation, these late works are remarkably consistent with Léger's early Cubist paintings based on machine forms (see fig. 10.41). The artist was one of a few who never really deserted Cubism but demonstrated, in every phase of his prolific output, its potential for continually fresh and varied expression.

The variant on Cubism called Purism was developed around 1918 by the architect and painter Charles-Édouard Jeanneret, who in 1920 began to use the pseudonym **Le Corbusier** (1887–1965), and the painter **Amédée Ozenfant** (1886–1966). Unlike Picasso and Braque, who were not theoretically inclined, many later Cubist-inspired artists were prone to theorizing, and they published their ideas in journals and manifestos. In their 1918 manifesto entitled *After Cubism*, Ozenfant and Jeanneret attacked the then current state of Cubism as having degenerated into a form of elaborate decoration. In their painting they sought a simple, architectural structure and the elimination of decorative ornateness as well as illustrative or fantastic subjects. To them the machine became the perfect symbol for the kind of pure, functional painting they hoped to achieve—just as, in his early, minimal architecture, Le Corbusier thought of a house first as a machine for living. Purist principles are illustrated in two still-life paintings by Ozenfant (fig. **14.33**) and Le Corbusier (fig. **14.34**). Executed in 1920, the year Purism that reached its maturity, both feature frontally arranged objects, with colors subdued and shapes modeled in an illusion of projecting volumes. Symmetrical curves move across the rectangular grid with the antiseptic purity of a well-tended, brand-new machine. Le Corbusier continued to paint throughout his life, but his theories gained significant expression in the great architecture he produced (see chapter 16). Ozenfant had enunciated his ideas of Purism in *L'Élan*, a magazine published from 1915 to 1917, before he met Le Corbusier, and in *L'Esprit nouveau*, published with Le Corbusier from 1920 to 1925. Ozenfant, who eventually settled in the United States, later turned to teaching and mural painting.

14.33 Amédée Ozenfant, *Guitar and Bottles*, 1920. Oil on canvas, 31⅞ × 39¼" (81 × 99.7 cm). Solomon R. Guggenheim Museum, New York.

14.34 Le Corbusier (Charles-Édouard Jeanneret), *Still Life*, 1920. Oil on canvas, 31⅞ × 39¼" (81 × 99.7 cm). The Museum of Modern Art, New York.

15
Surrealism

In 1917 French writer Guillaume Apollinaire referred to his own drama *Les Mamelles de Tirésias* (*The Breasts of Tiresias*), and also to the ballet *Parade* produced by Diaghilev, as "surrealist." The term was commonly used thereafter by the poets André Breton and Paul Éluard, as well as other contributors to the Paris journal *Littérature*. The concept of a literary and art movement formally designated as Surrealism, however, did not emerge until after the demise of Dada in Paris in the early twenties.

Breton and the Background to Surrealism

In the years immediately after World War I, French writers had been trying to formulate an aesthetic of the non-rational stemming variously from the writings of Arthur Rimbaud, the Comte de Lautréamont (see below), Alfred Jarry, and Apollinaire. By 1922 Breton was growing disillusioned with Dada on the ground that it was becoming institutionalized and academic, and led the revolt that broke up the Dada Congress of Paris. Together with Philippe Soupault, he explored the possibilities of automatic writing in his 1922 Surrealist texts called *The Magnetic Fields*. Pure psychic automatism, one of the fundamental precepts of Surrealism, was defined by Breton as "dictation of thought, in the absence of any control exercised by reason, and beyond any aesthetic or moral preoccupation." While this method of composing without any preconceived subject or structure was designed for writing, its principles were also applied by the Surrealists to drawing.

After 1922 Breton assumed the principal editorship of *Littérature* and gradually augmented his original band of writers with artists whose work and attitudes were closest to his own: Francis Picabia, Man Ray, and Max Ernst. This group met Breton regularly at his or Paul Éluard's home, or at some favorite café, where they discussed the significance of the marvelous, the irrational, and the accidental in painting and poetry. One of the exercises in which the artists engaged during their gatherings was the so-called "exquisite corpse." The practice was based on an old parlor game in which one participant writes part of a sentence on a sheet of paper, folds the sheet to conceal part of the phrase, and passes it to the next player, who adds a word or phrase based on the preceding contribution. Once the paper made it around the room in this manner, the provocative, often hilarious, sentence was read aloud. One such game produced "The exquisite corpse will drink the young wine," hence the name. When this method was adapted for collective drawings (fig. **15.1**), the surprising results coincided with the Surrealist love of the unexpected. The elements of chance, randomness, and coincidence in the formation of a work of art had for years been explored by the Dadaists. Now it became the basis for intensive study for the Surrealists, whose experience of four years of war made them attach much importance to their isolation, their alienation from society and even from nature.

15.1 André Breton, Valentine Hugo, Greta Knutson, and Tristan Tzara, *Exquisite Corpse*, c. 1930. Ink on paper, 9¼ × 12¼" (23.5 × 31.1 cm). Morton G. Neumann Family Collection.

From the meetings between writers and painters emerged Breton's *Manifesto of Surrealism* in 1924, containing this definition:

> SURREALISM, noun, masc., pure psychic automatism by which it is intended to express, either verbally or in writing, the true function of thought. Thought dictated in the absence of all control exerted by reason, and outside all aesthetic or moral preoccupations. ENCYCL. Philos. Surrealism is based on the belief in the superior reality of certain forms of association heretofore neglected, in the omnipotence of the dream, and in the disinterested play of thought. It leads to the permanent destruction of all other psychic mechanisms and to its substitution for them in the solution of the principal problems of life.

This definition emphasizes words rather than plastic images, literature rather than painting or sculpture. Breton was a serious student and disciple of Freud, from whose teachings he derived the Surrealist position concerning the central significance of dreams and the subconscious, as well as the use of free association (allowing words or images to suggest other words or images without imposing rational connections or structures) to gain access to the subconscious. Breton conceived of the Surreal condition as a moment of revelation in which are resolved the contradictions and oppositions of dreams and realities. In the second manifesto of Surrealism, issued in 1930, he said: "There is a certain point for the mind from which life and death, the real and the imaginary, the past and the future, the communicable and the incommunicable, the high and the low cease being perceived as contradictions."

Two nineteenth-century poets had irresistible appeal to the Surrealists. Isidore Ducasse, known as the Comte de Lautréamont (1846–70), and Arthur Rimbaud (1854–91) were outspoken critics of established poets and of forms and concepts of nineteenth-century poetry. Unknown to each other, both lived almost in isolation, wandered from place to place, and died young; they wrote great poetry while still adolescents, tearing at the foundations of Romantic verse. The idea of revolt permeates Lautréamont's poetry: revolt against tradition, against the family, against society, and against God. The ideas of Rimbaud at seventeen years of age seemed to define for the Surrealists the nature of the poet and poetry. Rimbaud believed that the poet, like a Christian mystic, must attain a visionary state through rigid discipline—but here a discipline of alienation, monstrosities of love, suffering, and madness. Like the Surrealists later, Rimbaud was concerned with the implications of dreams, the subconscious, and chance.

An influential and charismatic figure, Breton was the self-appointed but generally acknowledged leader of Surrealism. He was ruthless in the role as he invited artists to join the group only to exclude them when they failed to toe the party line. As Breton formulated a dogma of Surrealist principles, schisms and heresies inevitably

appeared, for few of its exponents practiced Surrealism with scrupulous literalness. In fact, the works of the major Surrealists have little stylistic similarity, aside from their departure from traditional content and their rejection of journalist approaches to art. The first group exhibition of Surrealist artists was in 1925 at the Galerie Pierre. It included Arp, de Chirico, Ernst, Klee, Man Ray, Masson, Miró, and Picasso. In that year Yves Tanguy joined the group. A Surrealist gallery was opened in 1927 with an exhibition of these artists joined by Marcel Duchamp and Picabia. Except for René Magritte, who joined later that year, and Salvador Dalí, who did not visit Paris until 1929, this was the roster of the first Surrealist generation.

The Two Strands of Surrealism

From its inception, Surrealism in painting tended in two directions. The first, represented by Miró, André Masson, and, later, Matta (see below), is biomorphic or abstract Surrealism. In this tendency, automatism—"dictation of thought without control of the mind"—is predominant, and the results are generally close to abstraction, although some degree of imagery is normally present. Its origins were in the experiments in chance and automatism carried on by the Dadaists and the automatic writing of Surrealist poets. The other direction in Surrealist painting is associated with Salvador Dalí, Yves Tanguy, and René Magritte (see below). It presents, in meticulous detail, recognizable scenes and objects that are taken out of natural context, distorted and combined in fantastic ways as they might be in dreams. Its sources are in the art of Henri Rousseau, Chagall, Ensor, de Chirico, and nineteenth-century Romantics. These artists attempted to use images of the subconscious, defined by Freud as uncontrolled by conscious reason (although Dalí, in his "paranoiac-critical methods," claimed to have control over his subconscious). Freud's theories of the subconscious and of the significance of dreams were, of course, fundamental to all aspects of Surrealism. To the popular imagination it was the naturalistic Surrealism associated with Dalí, Tanguy, and others of that group that signified Surrealism, even though it has had less influence historically than the abstract biomorphism of Miró, Masson, and Matta.

Both strands of Surrealism differed from Dada in their essentially Romantic privileging of the unconscious (rather than the forms and rhythms of the machine). Like Dada, however, Surrealism delighted in the exploration of unconventional techniques and in discovering creative potential in areas that lay outside the conventional territory of art.

Political Context and Membership

Surrealism was a revolutionary movement not only in literature and art but also in politics. The Surrealist period in Europe was one of deepening political crisis, financial collapse and the rise of fascism, provoking moral anxiety within the avant-garde. Under Breton's editorship (1925–29) the periodical *La Révolution surréaliste* maintained a steady communist line during the twenties. The Dadaists at the end of World War I were anarchists, and many future Surrealists joined them. Feeling that government systems guided by tradition and reason had led humankind into the bloodiest holocaust in history, they insisted that government of any form was undesirable, and that the irrational was preferable to the rational in art and in all of life and civilization. The Russian Revolution and the spread of communism provided a channel for Surrealist protests during the twenties. Louis Aragon and, later, Paul Éluard joined the Communist Party, while Breton, after exposure to the reactionary bias of Soviet communism or Stalinism in art and literature (discussed in chapter 11), took a Trotskyist position in the late thirties. Picasso, who made Surrealist work in the thirties, became a communist in protest against the fascism of Franco. By 1930, although schisms were occurring among the original Surrealists, new artists and poets were being recruited by Breton. Dalí joined in 1929, the sculptor Alberto Giacometti in 1931, and René Magritte in 1932. Other later recruits included Paul Delvaux, Henry Moore, Hans Bellmer, Oscar Dominguez, and Matta Echaurren. The list of writers was considerably longer. Surrealist groups and exhibitions were organized in England, Czechoslovakia, Belgium, Egypt, Denmark, Japan, Holland, Romania, and Hungary. Despite this substantial expansion, infighting resulted in continual resignations, dismissals, and reconciliations. Also, artists such as Picasso were adopted by the Surrealists without joining officially.

During the thirties the major publication of the Surrealists was the lavish journal *Minotaure*, founded in 1933 by Albert Skira and E. Tériade. The last issue appeared in 1939. Although emphasizing the role of the Surrealists, the editors drew into their orbit any of the established masters of modern art and letters who they felt had made significant contributions. These included artists as diverse as Matisse, Kandinsky, Laurens, and Derain.

"Art is a Fruit": Arp's Later Career

One of the original Zurich Dadaists (see chapter 13), **Jean (Hans) Arp** (1886–1966) was active in Paris Dada during its brief life, showing in the International Dada Exhibition of 1922, at the Galerie Montaigne, and contributing poems and drawings to Dada periodicals. When official Surrealism emerged in 1924, Arp was an active participant. At the same time, he remained in close contact with German and Dutch abstractionists and Constructivists. He also contributed to Theo van Doesburg's *De Stijl* and with El Lissitzky edited *The Isms of Art*. He and his wife and fellow artist Sophie Taeuber eventually made their home in Meudon, outside of Paris.

During the twenties Arp's favorite material was wood, which he made into painted reliefs. He also produced paintings, some on cardboard with cutout designs making a sort of reverse collage. Although Arp had experimented

with geometric abstractions between 1915 and 1920 (see fig. 13.11), frequently collaborating with Sophie Taeuber, he abandoned geometric shapes after 1920. His art would increasingly depend on the invention of biomorphic, abstract forms, based on his conviction that "art is a fruit that grows in man, like a fruit on a plant, or a child in its mother's womb." Yet Arp championed the geometric work of Van Doesburg and Sophie Taeuber (see figs. 11.36, 13.13) and collaborated with these two artists in decorating ten rooms of the Café l'Aubette in his native city, Strasbourg (see fig. 11.37). His murals for the café (now destroyed) were the boldest, freest, and most simplified examples of his biomorphic abstraction. They utilized his favorite motifs: the navel and mushroom-shaped heads, sometimes sporting a mustache and round-dot eyes. *Rising Navel and Two Heads* was simply three flat, horizontal, scalloped bands of color, with two color shapes suggesting flat mushrooms floating across the center band. *Navel-Sun* was a loosely circular white shape floating on a blue background (though most of the actual color scheme is lost). There are no parallels for these large, boldly abstracted shapes until the so-termed Color Field painters of the fifties and sixties.

Of particular interest among Arp's reliefs and collages of the late twenties and early thirties were those entitled or subtitled *Objects Arranged According to the Laws of Chance*, or *Navels* (fig. **15.2**). These continued the 1916–17 experiment in *Collage with Squares Arranged According to the Laws of Chance* (see fig. 13.11), although most of the forms were now organic rather than geometric. Arp made several versions of this wooden relief in 1930–31; he often employed the oval shapes seen here, which were for him variations on a navel, his universal emblem of human life.

15.2 Jean (Hans) Arp, *Objects Arranged According to the Laws of Chance*, or *Navels*, 1930. Varnished wood relief, 10⅜ × 11⅛ × 2¼" (26.3 × 28.3 × 5.4 cm). The Museum of Modern Art, New York.

15.3 Jean Arp, *Head with Three Annoying Objects*, 1930 (cast 1950). Bronze, 14⅛ × 10¼ × 7½" (35.9 × 26 × 19.1 cm). Estate of Jean Arp.

He also produced string reliefs based on chance—loops of string dropped accidentally on a piece of paper and seemingly fixed there. It seems, however, that he may have given the laws of chance some assistance, for which he had a precedent in Duchamp's *3 Stoppages Étalon* (see fig. 13.18).

Arp's great step forward in sculpture occurred at the beginning of the thirties, when he began to work completely in the round, making clay and plaster models for later bronze or marble sculptures. Arp shared Brancusi's devotion to mass rather than space as the fundamental element of sculpture (see fig. 9.16), and he, in turn, influenced major sculptors of the next generation—among them Alexander Calder, Henry Moore, and Barbara Hepworth. He thus stands at the opposite pole from the Constructivists Tatlin or Gabo (see figs. 11.24, 11.31). In developing the ideas of his painted reliefs, he had introduced seemingly haphazard detached forms that hovered around the matrixlike satellites. *Head with Three Annoying Objects* (fig. **15.3**) was originally executed in plaster, Arp's preferred medium for his first sculptures in the round. On a large biomorphic mass rest three objects, identified as a mustache, a mandolin, and a fly. The three strange forms were named in Arp's earliest title for the work, derived from one of his stories in which he describes himself waking up with three "annoying objects" on his face. The objects were not secured to the "head," for Arp intended that they be moved around by the spectator, introducing yet another element of chance in his work. A number of artists in the early thirties were exploring the notion of kineticism in painting or sculpture with interchangeable parts, including Alberto Giacometti (see fig. 15.55) and Alexander Calder (see fig. 17.28). Arp applied titles to his works after he had made them, with the intention of inspiring associations between images and ideas or, as he said, "to ferret out the dream." Thus, the meaning of the work, like the arrangement of the forms themselves, was open-ended. Like many of Arp's plasters, *Head with Three*

Annoying Objects was not cast in bronze until much later, in this case not until 1950.

To his biomorphic sculptural forms Arp applied the name "human concretion," for even forms that are not derived from nature, he said, can still be "as concrete and sensual as a leaf or a stone." In 1930 Van Doesburg had proposed the name "concrete art" as a more accurate description for abstract art. He contended that the term "abstract" implied a taking away from, a diminution of, natural forms and therefore a degree of denigration. What could be more real, he asked, more concrete than the fundamental forms and colors of nonrepresentational or nonobjective art? Although Van Doesburg's term did not gain universal recognition, Arp used it faithfully, and as "human concretions," it has gained a specific, descriptive connotation for his sculptures in the round. Arp said:

> Concretion signifies the natural process of condensation hardening, coagulating, thickening, growing together. Concretion designates the solidification of a mass. Concretion designates curdling, the curdling of the earth and the heavenly bodies. Concretion designates solidification, the mass of the stone, the plant, the animal, the man. Concretion is something that has grown.

This statement could be interpreted as a manifesto in opposition to the Constructivist assertion of the primacy of space in sculpture. More pertinent, however, is its emphasis on sculpture as a process of growth, making tangible the life processes of the universe, from the microscopic to the macrocosmic. Thus a human concretion was not only

15.4 Jean Arp, *Composition*, 1937. Collage of torn paper, india ink wash, and pencil, 11¾ × 9" (29.8 × 22.9 cm). Philadelphia Museum of Art.

an abstraction based on human forms but also a distillation in sculpture of life itself.

The art of Jean Arp took many different forms between 1930 and 1966, the year of his death. Abstract (or concrete) forms suggesting sirens, snakes, clouds, leaves, owls, crystals, shells, starfish, seeds, fruit, and flowers emerged continually, suggesting such notions as growth, metamorphosis, dreams, and silence. While developing his freestanding sculpture, Arp continued to make reliefs and collages. To make his new collages, Arp tore up his own previously made work (fig. **15.4**). In this example from 1937, he essentially recomposed the work by connecting the new forms with curvilinear lines drawn in pencil. This new collage technique, a liberating release from the immaculateness of the sculptures, was described by Arp:

> I began to tear my papers instead of curving them neatly with scissors. I tore up drawings and carelessly smeared paste over and under them. If the ink dissolved and ran, I was delighted. … I had accepted the transience, the dribbling away, the brevity, the impermanence, the fading, the withering, the spookishness of our existence. … These torn pictures, these *papiers déchirés* brought me closer to a faith other than earthly.

Many of these torn-paper collages found their way to the United States and offered a link between organic Surrealism and postwar American Abstract Expressionism.

Hybrid Menageries: Ernst's Surrealist Techniques

The career of **Max Ernst** (1891–1976) as a painter and sculptor, interrupted by four years in the German army, began when he moved to Paris from Cologne in 1922. At the end of 1921, the Dadaist Ernst had resumed painting after having devoted himself to various collage techniques since 1919 (see fig. 13.32). The manner of *Celebes,* the chief painting of his pre-Paris period (see fig. 13.33), is combined with the technique of his Dada assemblages in *Two Children Are Threatened by a Nightingale* (fig. **15.5**), a 1924 dream landscape in which two girls— one collapsed on the ground, the other running and brandishing a knife—are frightened by a tiny bird. The fantasy is given peculiar emphasis by the elements attached to the panel—the house on the right and the open gate on the left. A figure on top of the house clutches a young girl and seems to reach for the actual wooden knob on the frame. Contrary to Ernst's usual method of working, the title of this

enigmatic painting (inscribed in French on the frame) preceded the image. Ernst himself, speaking in the third person, noted:

> He never imposes a title on a painting. He waits until a title imposes itself. Here, however, the title existed *before* the picture was painted. A few days before, he had written a prose poem which began: à la tombée de la nuit, à la lisière de la ville, deux enfants sont menacés par un rossignol (as night falls, at the edge of town, two children are threatened by a nightingale) … He did not attempt to illustrate this poem, but that is the way it happened.

In 1925, Ernst became a full participant in the newly established Surrealist movement. That year he began to make drawings that he termed "frottage" (rubbing), in which he used the child's technique of placing a piece of paper on a textured surface and rubbing over it with a pencil. The resulting image was largely fortuitous, but Ernst consciously reorganized the transposed textures in new contexts, creating new and unforeseen associations. Not only did frottage provide the technical basis for a series of unorthodox drawings, it also intensified Ernst's perception of the textures in his environment—wood, cloth, leaves, plaster, and wallpaper.

Ernst applied this technique, combined with grattage (scraping), to his paintings of the late twenties and the thirties. The 1927 canvas *The Horde* (fig. **15.6**) expresses the

15.5 Max Ernst, *Two Children Are Threatened by a Nightingale,* 1924. Oil on wood with wood construction, 27½ × 22½ × 4½" (69.8 × 57.1 × 11.4 cm). The Museum of Modern Art, New York.

15.6 Max Ernst, *The Horde*, 1927. Oil on canvas, 44⅞ × 57½" (114 × 146.1 cm). Stedelijk Museum, Amsterdam.

increasingly ominous mood of Ernst's Surrealist paintings. The monstrous, treelike figures are among the many frightening premonitions of the conflict that would overtake Europe in the next decade. In 1941, Ernst escaped the war in Europe and settled in New York City, where his presence, along with other Surrealist refugees, would have tremendous repercussions for American art. Ernst's antipathy toward the rise of fascism was given fullest expression in *Europe after the Rain* (fig. **15.7**), which has been aptly described as a requiem for the war-ravaged continent. In this large painting Ernst employed yet another technique, which he called "decalcomania." Invented by the Spanish Surrealist Oscar Dominguez, this technique involved placing paper or glass on a wet painted surface, then pulling it away to achieve surprising textural effects. It appealed to Ernst and other Surrealists for the startling automatic forms that could be created in this way.

Of all the menageries and hybrid creatures that Ernst invented, he most closely identified with the image of the bird, eventually adopting one of his inventions, named Loplop, as a kind of surrogate self-image. The 1942 painting *Surrealism and Painting* (fig. **15.8**), also the title of a book by Breton, shows a birdlike beast made of smoothly rounded sections of human anatomy, serpents, and birds'

15.7 Max Ernst, *Europe after the Rain*, 1940–42. Oil on canvas, 21½ × 58⅛" (54.6 × 147.6 cm). Wadsworth Atheneum, Hartford, Connecticut.

15.8 Max Ernst, *Surrealism and Painting*, 1942. Oil on canvas, 6'4¾" × 7'7¾" (2 × 2.3 m). The Menil Collection, Houston.

heads. The monster, painted in delicate hues, is composing an abstract painting, perhaps "automatically." In fact, Ernst engaged in a partially automatic process to create the painting—he swung paint over the canvas from a hole in a tin can. The full implications of this "drip" technique would be explored by Jackson Pollock to make his revolutionary, mural-sized abstract paintings in the fifties (see fig. 19.10).

Ernst was drawn to sculpture in 1934 through his friendship with Giacometti, at the moment when the latter was abandoning Surrealism for his own new vision of reality (see below). Ernst's first works were modified, egg-shaped boulders whose surfaces he carved with abstract patterns in the manner of Arp. He then went on to several

15.9 Max Ernst, *The King Playing with the Queen*, 1944. Bronze (cast 1954 from original plaster), 38½" (97.8 cm) high, at base, 18¾ × 20½" (46.7 × 52.1 cm). The Museum of Modern Art, New York.

sculptures in which he made plaster casts of found objects for casting in bronze, such as *Oedipus II* (1934), which is based on casts of precariously balanced wooden pails. In the United States, Ernst eventually settled in Arizona with his wife, the artist Dorothea Tanning, and developed a strong interest in the art of the Zuni and Hopi peoples. He created a series of frontalized figures in 1944 (fig. **15.9**) that drew upon his diverse interests in Native American art, African sculpture, Picasso, and, at times, Duchamp.

"Night, Music, and Stars": Miró and Organic–Abstract Surrealism

Although active for many years in Paris, the Spanish artist **Joan Miró** (1893–1983) constantly returned to his native country, and his Catalan roots remained a consistent force in his art throughout his life. In art schools in Barcelona, where he was born, he was introduced to French art, and his first mature paintings, executed in 1915–16, show the influence of Cézanne. But he also admired more contemporary masters, especially Matisse and fellow Spaniard Picasso. Though never a Cubist, he freely adapted aspects of the style to suit his own purposes.

Nude with Mirror (fig. **15.10**), begun in the spring of 1919, combines Cubist faceting, flat-color areas, and geometric pattern with a sculptural figure. Painted from a live model, the nude is set against a spare, terracotta-colored background that contrasts sharply with the highly decorative patterns of the stool and rug on which she sits. Despite the Cubist fracturing of certain parts of the anatomy, the figure has a strong three-dimensional presence of rounded volumes. In the monumental simplicity of *Nude with Mirror* there is evidence of Miró's admiration for Henri Rousseau (see fig. 3.16). A hint of the unreality to come in Miró's work emerges as we realize that the model gazes at herself in the mirror with nearly closed eyes.

In 1920 Miró began to spend winters in Paris and summers in Montroig, Spain. He was drawn to the work of the Dadaists as well as Paul Klee and, by 1923, was working from his imagination rather than from nature. He became friendly with Breton and the other poets in Paris who were soon to launch the Surrealist revolution. Yet these encounters, as well as Miró's natural inclination to fantasy, do not entirely account for the richly imaginative imagery that he said was "always born in a state of hallucination."

Carnival of Harlequin, 1924–25 (fig. **15.11**) is one of the first Surrealist pictures where Miró's playful sense of caprice has been given full rein. His space, the suggested confines of a grayish-beige room, teems with life of the strangest variety. At the left is a tall ladder to which an ear has been attached along with, at the very top, a tiny, disembodied eye. Animating the inanimate was a favorite Surrealist theme. To the right of the ladder is a man with a disk-shaped head who sports a long-stemmed pipe beneath a tendriled moustache and stares sadly at the spectator. At his side, an insect with blue and yellow wings pops out of a box. Surrounding this group is every sort of hybrid organism, all having a fine time. Miró's unreal world is painstakingly rendered and remarkably vivid; even his inanimate objects have an eager vitality. He derived his imagery from many sources beyond his own fertile imagination. While some are based on forms in nature, others may stem from medieval art or the paintings of his fellow Surrealists. As they float in the air or cavort on the ground, his creatures are spread equally across the entire surface of the painting, so our eyes do not alight in one central place. In

15.10 Joan Miró, *Nude with Mirror,* 1919. Oil on canvas, 44½ × 40⅛" (113 × 102 cm). Kunstsammlung Nordrhein-Westfalen, Düsseldorf.

15.11 Joan Miró, *Carnival of Harlequin,* 1924–25. Oil on canvas, 26 × 36⅝" (66 × 93 cm). Albright-Knox Art Gallery, Buffalo, New York.

15.12 Joan Miró, *Dog Barking at the Moon*, 1926. Oil on canvas, 28¾ × 36¼" (73 × 92 cm). Philadelphia Museum of Art.

this picture, as well as in a number of others around this time, Miró mapped out his compositional organization with red lines arranged in a diagonal grid that can still be detected through the paint layer.

The second half of the twenties was an especially prolific period for Miró. His first solo show was held in Paris in 1925, and in November of that year he took part in the first exhibition of Surrealist painting, which included *Carnival of Harlequin*. Much of the work of this period is marked by a reduction of means, moving from the complexity of *Carnival of Harlequin* to the magic simplicity of a painting such as *Dog Barking at the Moon* (fig. **15.12**). Again we find the ladder, for Miró a symbol of transcendence and a bridge to another, unearthly realm. But it is

15.14 Joan Miró, *Object*, 1936. Assemblage: stuffed parrot on wood perch, stuffed silk stocking with velvet garter and doll's paper shoe suspended in hollow wood frame, derby hat, hanging cork ball, celluloid fish, and engraved map, 31⅞ × 11⅞ × 10¼" (81 × 30.1 × 26 cm). The Museum of Modern Art, New York.

15.13 Joan Miró, *Painting*, 1933. Oil on canvas, 5'8½" × 6'5¼" (1.74 × 2 m). The Museum of Modern Art, New York.

15.15 Joan Miró, *The Poetess* from the series *Constellations*, December 31, 1940. Gouache and oil wash on paper, 15 × 18" (38.1 × 45.7 cm). Private collection.

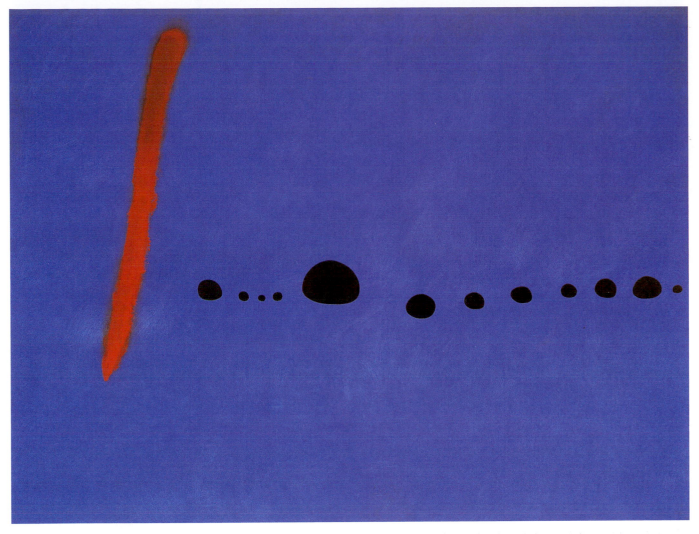

15.16 Joan Miró, *Blue II*, 1961. Oil on canvas, 8'10¼" × 11'7¾" (2.7 × 1.4 m). Musée National d'Art Moderne, Centre d'Art et de Culture Georges Pompidou, Paris.

now a player in a depopulated nocturnal landscape, a dark and foreboding place that resembles a scene from a dream.

In 1933 Miró made a remarkable group of eighteen paintings that were based on collages of realistic details torn from newspapers and pasted on cardboard. The motifs—tools, machines, furniture, and dishes—suggested to him organic–abstract shapes, sometimes with implied faces or figures. The predominantly abstract intent of these paintings is indicated by their neutral titles. One of the paintings that resulted from this process is *Painting* (fig. **15.13**). Although this work appears completely non-figurative, many observers have found a resemblance between the mysterious forms and animals, such as a seated dog at the upper left. These organic–abstract shapes are perhaps closest to the biomorphic inventions of Arp.

A classic example of the Surrealist "object" that prolif-erated in the movement in the thirties is Miró's sculpture that takes this very word for its title (fig. **15.14**). The object consists of a wooden cylinder that holds in its cavity a high-heeled, doll-sized leg, the fetishistic nature of which typifies Surrealist eroticism. The cylinder is surrounded by other found objects, including a stuffed parrot from whose perch is suspended a little cork ball. The whole construc-tion sits on a base made of a Derby hat; in its brim "swims"

a red plastic fish. The Surrealist juxtaposition of disparate objects was meant to evoke surprise and trigger further associations in the mind of the viewer. The notion of found objects was introduced by Duchamp (see fig. 13.16), but Miró did not adopt that artist's attitude of aesthetic indifference in this whimsical, carefully composed object.

With the outbreak of World War II, Miró had to flee from the home he had set up in Normandy and go back to Spain, where a rightwing government under General Franco had been established in 1939 following Franco's victory, with support from Nazi Germany, in the Spanish Civil War of 1936–39. The isolation of the war years and the need for contemplation and reevaluation led Miró to read mystical literature and to listen to the music of Mozart and Bach. "The night, music and stars," he said, "began to play a major role in suggesting my paintings." While fleeing from the Nazis in France to Franco's Spain, Miró, in contrast to his inclination in response to the Spanish Civil War to revisit representation, committed himself to an abstract art consistent with his evocative Surrealist compositions of the twenties. Between January 1940 and September 1941 he worked on a series of twenty-three small gouaches entitled *Constellations* (fig. 15.15), which are among his most intricate and lyrical creations. In the

15.17 Joan Miró, *Lunar Bird*, 1966. Bronze, 7'8⅛" × 6'10¾" × 5'1½" (2.3 × 2.1 × 1.5 m). The Hirshhorn Museum and Sculpture Garden, Smithsonian Institution, Washington, D.C.

sparkling compositions the artist was concerned with ideas of flight and transformation as he contemplated the migration of birds, the seasonal renewal of butterfly hordes, and the flow of constellations and galaxies. Miró dispersed his imagery evenly across the surface. In 1945 the

Constellations were shown at New York's Pierre Matisse Gallery, where they affected the emerging American Abstract Expressionist painters who were then seeking alternatives to Social Realism and Regionalism (see figs. 19.3, 19.33). As the leader of the organic–abstract tendency within Surrealism, Miró had a major impact on younger American painters.

By the end of World War II, Miró was working on a large scale, with bold shapes, patterns, and colors. In his work of the sixties Miró showed an interest in the American Abstract Expressionists, who earlier had been influenced by him. The mural-sized painting *Blue II* (fig. 15.16) of 1961 is an almost pure example of Color Field painting—a delicately inflected blue ground punctuated only by a vertical red slash and a trail of black oval shapes. Since the twenties the color blue had held metaphorical significance for Miró. It is a favorite color of his native Catalonia, and a hue he particularly associated with the world of dreams. In addition to mural-size paintings, Miró created sculpture on a monumental scale in the sixties. To make *Lunar Bird* (fig. 15.17), he enlarged a small bronze *Bird* from 1944. With its massive, crescent-shaped head, phallic protuberances, and powerful stance, the creature has all the presence of an ancient cult statue.

Methodical Anarchy: André Masson

One of the Surrealist artists who would eventually emigrate from Paris to New York was **André Masson** (1896–1987). Among the first Surrealists, Masson was the most passionate revolutionary, a man of vehement convictions who had been deeply spiritually scarred by his experiences in

15.18 André Masson, *Battle of Fishes*, 1926. Sand, gesso, oil, pencil, and charcoal on canvas, 14¼ × 28¾" (36.2 × 73 cm). The Museum of Modern Art, New York.

15.19 André Masson, *Pasiphaë*, 1943. Oil and tempera on canvas, 39¾ × 50" (101 × 127 cm). Private collection.

World War I. Almost fatally injured, he was hospitalized for a long time, and after partially recovering, he continued to rage against the insanity of humankind and society until he was confined for a while to a mental hospital. Masson was by nature an anarchist, whose convictions were fortified by his experience. He joined the Surrealist movement in 1924, though his anticonformist temperament caused him to break with the controlling Breton. Masson first left the group in 1929, rejoined it in the thirties, and left again in 1943.

Masson's paintings of the early twenties reveal his debt to Cubism, particularly that of Juan Gris (see chapter 10). In 1925 Masson was regularly contributing automatic drawings to *La Révolution surréaliste*. These works directly express his emotions and contain various images relating to the sadism of human beings and the brutality of all living things. *Battle of Fishes* (fig. **15.18**) is an example of Masson's sand painting, which he made by freely applying adhesive to the canvas, then throwing sand over the surface and brushing away the excess. The layers of sand would suggest forms to the artist, "although almost always irrational ones," he said. He then added lines and small amounts of color, sometimes directly from the paint tube, to form a pictorial structure around the sand. Here the imagery is aquatic, though the artist described the fish as anthropomorphic. As in the frottage technique used by Ernst (see fig. 15.6), Masson here allows chance to help determine his composition, though his firm belief that art should be grounded in conscious, aesthetic decisions eventually led him away from this method.

In the late thirties, after living principally in Spain for three years, Masson temporarily painted in a style closer to the more naturalistic wing of Surrealism. He painted monstrous, recognizable figures from mythological themes in a manner influenced by Picasso and possibly Dalí. To escape World War II, Masson lived for a time in the United States, where, he said, "Things came into focus for me." He exhibited regularly in New York, influencing some of the younger American painters, particularly Jackson Pollock. Masson would later say that Pollock carried automatism to an extreme that he himself "could not envision." Living in rural Connecticut, Masson reverted to a somewhat automatist, Expressionist approach in works such as *Pasiphaë* (fig. **15.19**). The classical myth of the Minotaur provided one of Masson's recurrent themes in the thirties and forties. (It was he who named the Surrealist review after this part-man, part-bull beast from Greek mythology.) Because she displeased the sea god Poseidon, Pasiphaë was made to mate with a bull, giving birth to the Minotaur. Masson said he wanted to represent the violent union of woman and beast in such a way that it is impossible to tell where one begins and the other ends. This subject, which had become a major theme in Picasso's work (see fig. 15.48), also appealed to the young Pollock, who made a painting of Pasiphaë in the same year as Masson.

Enigmatic Landscapes: Yves Tanguy

Yves Tanguy (1900–55) had literary interests and close associations with the Surrealist writers Jacques Prévert and Marcel Duhamel in Paris after 1922. With Prévert he discovered the writings of Lautréamont and other prophets of Surrealism. In 1923, inspired by two de Chirico paintings in the window of the dealer Paul Guillaume, he decided to become a painter. Entirely self-taught, Tanguy painted in a naive manner until 1926, at which time he destroyed many

15.20 Yves Tanguy, *Mama, Papa Is Wounded!* (*Maman, Papa est blessé!*), 1927. Oil on canvas, 36¼ × 28¾" (92.1 × 73 cm). The Museum of Modern Art, New York.

of these canvases. After meeting André Breton, Tanguy began contributing to *La Révolution surréaliste* and was adopted into the Surrealist movement. Tanguy's subsequent progress was remarkable, in both technique and fantastic imagination. *Mama, Papa Is Wounded!* (fig. 15.20) was the masterpiece of this first stage and exhibited all the obsessions that haunted him for the rest of his career. The first of these was an infinite-perspective depth, rendered simply by graded color and a sharp horizon line—a space that combines vast emptiness and intimate enclosure, where ambiguous organic shapes, reminiscent of Arp's biomorphic sculptures, float in a barren dreamscape.

After traveling in Africa in 1930 and 1931, where he saw brilliant light and color and desert rock formations, Tanguy began to define his forms precisely. It has been proposed that the vast spaces in his paintings during the thirties, so strongly suggestive of a submarine world, were inspired by Tanguy's childhood memories of summers spent on the Brittany coast. In these works, Tanguy endowed his forms with a tangible, literal presence by virtue of his highly illusionistic manner, yet those forms have no equivalent in nature. His unique contribution was this co-opting of realist techniques to conjure up abstract

15.21 Yves Tanguy, *Multiplication of the Arcs*, 1954. Oil on canvas, 40 × 60" (101.6 × 152.4 cm). The Museum of Modern Art, New York.

images. After moving to the United States in 1939 and settling in Woodbury, Connecticut, with his wife, the American Surrealist painter Kay Sage, Tanguy continued to evoke his barren, destroyed universe. In one of his last paintings, *Multiplication of the Arcs* (fig. **15.21**), the objects fill the ground area back to a newly established horizon line, to create an enigmatic, foreboding scene that the art historian James Thrall Soby called "a sort of boneyard of the world."

"A Laboratory for New Ideas": Surrealism and the Americas

Surrealism made its debut in the United States in 1931 with an exhibition at the Wadsworth Atheneum in Hartford, Connecticut, organized by James Thrall Soby. It traveled to New York in 1932 to the Julien Levy Gallery. In the thirties American interest in Surrealism tended to focus on the dream imagery of Salvador Dalí (see below), which was merged, to varying degrees, with America's indigenous realist traditions. This was the era of the economic crisis in America known as the Great Depression (1929–33), when many artists reinforced the sense of political isolationism by looking to local cultural traditions as subjects for their art, suspiciously viewing Surrealism as a product of leftist European artists. By 1942, however, the center of Surrealist activity had effectively shifted to New York as artists fled the war in Europe. The city's Museum of Modern Art had already presented a landmark exhibition in 1936 called Fantastic Art, Dada, and Surrealism, and a small number of important dealers, such as Levy,

Pierre Matisse, and Sidney Janis, provided support for the movement. The American Surrealist journals *View* and *VVV* were established in the early forties, serving as venues for exchange between European Surrealists and American followers of the movement. In 1942, an exhibition called First Papers of Surrealism (referring to the European artists' immigration papers) was held in an old New York mansion with an installation by Marcel Duchamp, who crisscrossed the room with two miles of string. The result resembled a giant spider web through which one could barely distinguish the works of art.

Another famous installation of Surrealist art was designed in 1942 by the architect **Frederick Kiesler** (1890–1965) for the Art of this Century gallery, the brainchild of the patron, collector, and dealer Peggy Guggenheim. Guggenheim had befriended many of the Surrealists while living in Europe before the war; in 1941, she married and divorced Max Ernst. Engaged in building what would become one of the world's greatest collections of modern art, she was one of several remarkable American women who were instrumental in the development of avant-garde art. For her Art of this Century gallery, Kiesler designed the Surrealist room with curved walls from which paintings were hung on cantilevered arms that moved (fig. **15.22**). Sculptures such as Giacometti's *Woman with Her Throat Cut* (see fig. 15.56) can be seen on the biomorphic chairs that Kiesler designed. Not surprisingly, the installation caused a great stir in New York art circles. Guggenheim's unique venture lasted for five years (it closed when she returned to Europe), but not before she had mounted numerous groundbreaking exhibitions, fostered the careers

15.22 Frederick Kiesler, Design of the Surrealist gallery, Art of this Century, 1942. Installation photo by Berenice Abbott from the periodical *VVV*.

of some of the most promising young Americans (most notably, Jackson Pollock), and provided a kind of modern-day salon (or "laboratory for new ideas" as she called it) to encourage exchange between American and European artists.

Surrealism in the forties was also enriched by the contributions of the Chilean artist Matta and the Cuban Wilfredo Lam, both of whom traveled to Europe and participated in Parisian Surrealist circles before returning to the Americas. Their long careers provide links between the later phases of Surrealism and other art movements of the postwar period.

Matta and Lam

Born in Chile as Roberto Sebastiano Antonio Matta Echaurren, Matta (b. 1911) studied architecture in the Paris office of Le Corbusier until, in 1937, he showed some of his drawings to Breton, who immediately welcomed him into the Surrealist fold. When he emigrated to the United States in 1939 (on the same boat as Tanguy), Matta was relatively unknown, despite his association with the Surrealists in Paris. His 1940 one-man show at the Julien Levy Gallery, the most important commercial showcase for Surrealist art in New York, had a momentous impact on American experimental artists. Although Matta—the last painter, along with Arshile Gorky (see chapter 19), claimed for Surrealism by André Breton—was much younger than most of his better-known expatriate European colleagues, his paintings marked the step that American artists were seeking.

Over the next few years, together with the American painter Robert Motherwell, Matta, who unlike many emi-gré artists from Europe spoke English fluently, helped to forge a link between European Surrealism and the American movement to be called Abstract Expressionism. Matta's painting at that point is exemplified in the 1942 *Disasters of Mysticism* (fig. **15.23**). Although this has some roots in the work of Masson and Tanguy, it is a powerful excursion into uncharted territory. In its ambiguous, automatist flow, from brilliant flame-light into deepest shadow, it suggests the ever-changing universe of outer space. Soby, who owned *Disasters of Mysticism,* detected in its dark, volcanic spaces a debt to sixteenth-century nocturnal mysticism, exemplified in painting by Mathias Grünewald's masterpiece, the *Isenheim Altarpiece* (see fig. 1.7).

Wilfredo Lam (1902–82) brought a broad cultural background to his art and, once he arrived in Paris in 1938, to the Surrealist milieu. Born in Cuba to a Chinese father and a European–African mother, he studied art first in Havana and, in 1923, in Madrid. In Spain he fought on the side of the Republicans during the Civil War, a fact that endeared him to Picasso when he moved to Paris. Through Picasso, Lam was introduced to members of the Parisian Surrealist circle, including Breton. He explored imagery in his paintings that was heavily influenced by Picasso, Cubism, and a continuing interest in African art. Lam left Paris because of the war, eventually traveling with Breton to Martinique, where they were joined by Masson. The Frenchmen moved on to New York while Lam returned to Cuba in 1942. His rediscovery of the rich culture of his homeland helped to foster the emergence of his mature style: "I responded always to the presence of factors that emanated from our history and our geography, tropical flowers, and black culture."

15.23 Matta, *Disasters of Mysticism,* 1942. Oil on canvas, 38¼ × 51¾" (101.6 × 152.4 cm). Estate of James Thrall Soby, New Canaan, Connecticut.

15.24 Wilfredo Lam, *The Jungle*, 1943. Gouache on paper mounted on canvas, 7'10¼" × 7'6½" (2.4 × 2.3 m). The Museum of Modern Art, New York.

While in Cuba, Lam made the large, sumptuously colored painting *The Jungle* (fig. **15.24**). Based in part on the Cuban religion of Santería, which blends mystical and ritualistic traditions from Africa with old-world Catholicism, *The Jungle* presents a dense tropical landscape populated by odd, long-limbed creatures whose disjointed heads resemble African masks. These human–animal hybrids, who assemble in a lush dreamscape, give evidence of the artist's Surrealist background. Lam returned to France in 1952, though he continued to travel widely and visit Cuba. His art was especially important to postwar European and American artists, especially the CoBrA painters of northern Europe (see chapter 20).

"The Association of Delirious Phenomena": Salvador Dalí

The artist who above all others symbolizes Surrealism in the public imagination is the Spaniard **Salvador Dalí** (1904–89). Not only his paintings, but his writings, his utterances, his actions, his appearance, his mustache, and his genius for publicity have made the word "Surrealism" a common noun in all languages, denoting an art that is irrational, erotic, mad—and fashionable. Dalí's life was itself so completely Surrealist that his integrity and his pictorial accomplishment have been questioned, most bitterly by other Surrealists. The primary evidence must be the paintings themselves, and no one can deny the immense talent, the power of imagination, or the intense conviction that they display.

Dalí was born at Figueras, near Barcelona. Like Picasso, Miró, and, before them, the architect Gaudí (see chapter 5), he was a product of the rich Catalan culture. A substantial part of the iconography of Dalí, real or imagined, is taken from episodes in his childhood and adolescence. The landscape of these early years appears constantly in his paintings, which are marked by the violence of his temperament—ecstatic, filled with fantasy, terror, and megalomania. Dalí encountered Italian and French art, Impressionism, Neo-Impressionism, and Futurism before he went to Madrid's Academy of Fine Arts in 1921. He followed the normal academic training, developing a highly significant passion for nineteenth-century academicians and artists such as Millet, Böcklin, and particularly the meticulous narrative painter Ernest Meissonier. His discoveries in modern painting during the early twenties were Picasso, de Chirico, Carrà, and the Italian Metaphysical School, whose works were reproduced in the periodical *Valori Plastici*. More important for his development was the discovery of Freud, whose writings on dreams and the subconscious seemed to answer the torments and erotic fantasies he had suffered since childhood. Between 1925 and 1927 he explored several styles and often worked in them simultaneously: the Cubism of Picasso and Gris, the Purism of Le Corbusier and Ozenfant, the Neoclassicism of Picasso, and a precise realism derived from the seventeenth-century Dutch master Vermeer.

In 1929 Dalí visited Paris for several weeks and, through his friend Miró, met the Surrealists. He moved to the French capital for a time the following year (though his main residence was Spain) to become an official member of the movement. Breton regarded the dynamic young Spaniard as a force for renewal in the group, which was plagued by endless ideological conflict. Dalí became deeply involved with Gala Éluard, the wife of the Surrealist writer Paul Éluard, and he married her in 1934. He had by now formulated the theoretical basis of his painting, described as "paranoiac–critical": the creation of a visionary reality from elements of visions, dreams, memories, and psychological or pathological distortions.

Dalí developed a precise miniaturist technique, accompanied by a discordant but luminous color. His detailed *trompe l'oeil* technique was designed to make his dreamworld more tangibly real than observed nature (he referred to his paintings as "hand-painted dream photographs"). He frequently used familiar objects as a point of departure—watches, insects, pianos, telephones, old prints or photographs—imparting to them fetishistic significance. He declared his primary images to be blood, decay, and excrement. From the commonplace object Dalí set up a chain of metamorphoses that gradually or suddenly dissolved and transformed the object into a nightmare image, given conviction by the exacting technique. He was determined to paint as a madman—not in an occasional state of receptive somnambulism, but in a continuous frenzy of induced paranoia. In collaboration with Luis Buñuel, Dalí turned to the cinema and produced two classics of Surrealist film, *Un Chien andalou* (*An Andalusian Dog*)

(1929) and *L'Âge d'or* (*The Golden Age*) (1930). The cinematic medium held infinite possibilities for the Surrealists, in the creation of dissolves, metamorphoses, and double and quadruple images, and Dalí made brilliant use of these.

The microscopic brand of realism that Dalí skillfully deployed to objectify the dreamworld reached full maturity in a tiny painting from 1929, *Accommodations of Desire* (fig. **15.25**). The work is actually a collage, created using two illustrations of lions' heads that Dalí cut from a book and placed on what appear to be stones. These strange forms cast dark shadows in the desolate landscape and serve as backdrops to other imagery, including an army of ants. In one of the most disturbing images in *Un Chien andalou*, which had been made earlier the same year, ants swarm over a hand. They appear again, this time over a pocket watch, in one of Dalí's later paintings (see fig. 15.26). Dalí's own painted incarnations of a lion's head appear at the upper left of *Accommodations* and with the group of figures at the top of the composition. In his mostly fictional autobiography of 1942, *The Secret Life of Salvador Dalí*, the artist said that he undertook this painting during his courtship with Gala (who was then still married to Paul Éluard). The experience of intense sexual anxiety led him to paint this work, in which "desires were always represented by the terrorizing images of lions' heads."

In his book *La Femme visible* (*The Visible Woman*) (1930), Dalí wrote: "I believe the moment is at hand when, by a paranoiac and active advance of the mind, it will be possible (simultaneously with automatism and other passive states) to systematize confusion and thus to help discredit completely the world of reality." By 1930 Dalí had left de Chirico's type of metaphysical landscape for his own world of violence, blood, and decay. He sought to create in his art a specific documentation of Freudian theories applied to his own inner world. He started a painting with the first image that came into his mind and went on from

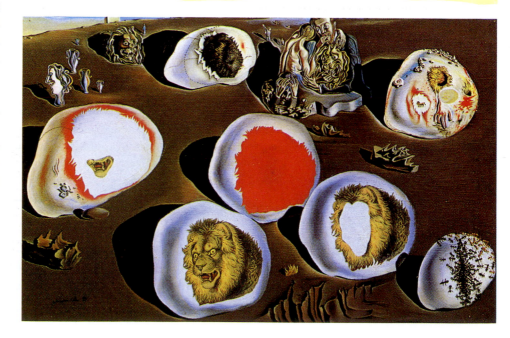

15.25 Salvador Dalí, *Accommodations of Desire*, 1929. Oil and collage on panel, 8⅝ × 13¾" (22 × 34.9 cm). Private collection.

15.26 Salvador Dalí, *The Persistence of Memory (Persistance de la mémoire)*, 1931. Oil on canvas, 9½ × 13" (24.1 × 33 cm). The Museum of Modern Art, New York.

one association to the next, multiplying images of persecution or megalomania like a true paranoiac. He defined his paranoiac–critical method as a "spontaneous method of irrational knowledge based upon the interpretative–critical association of delirious phenomena."

Dalí shared the Surrealist antagonism to art that defined itself in terms of formal qualities rather than content. *The Persistence of Memory* of 1931 (fig. **15.26**) is a denial of every twentieth-century experiment in abstract organization. Its miniaturist technique (the painting is only just over a foot wide) goes back to fifteenth-century Flemish art, and its sour greens and yellows recall nineteenth-century chromolithographs. The space is as infinite as Tanguy's (see fig. 15.20), and rendered with hard objectivity. The picture's fame comes largely from the presentation of recognizable objects—watches—in an unusual context, with unnatural attributes, and on an unexpected scale. Throughout his career Dalí was obsessed with the morphology of hard and soft. Here, lying on the ground, is a large head in profile (which had appeared in several previous paintings) seemingly devoid of bone structure. Drooped over its surface, as on that of a tree and shelf nearby, is a soft pocket watch. Dalí described these forms as "nothing more than the soft, extravagant, solitary, paranoic–critical Camembert cheese of space and time." He painted the work one night after dinner, when, after all the guests were gone, he contemplated the leftover Camembert cheese melting on the table. When he then looked at the landscape in progress in his studio—with shoreline cliffs and a branchless olive tree—the image of soft watches came to him as a means of representing the condition of softness. This pictorial metamorphosis, in which matter is transformed from one state into another, is a fundamental aspect of Surrealism. Softness as a condition in sculpture would be further explored in the sixties by the American artist Claes Oldenburg (see fig. 21.25).

Dalí's painting during the thirties vacillated between an outrageous fantasy and a strange atmosphere of quiet achieved less obviously. *Gala and the Angelus of Millet Immediately Preceding the Arrival of the Conic Anamorphoses* (fig. **15.28**) exemplifies the first aspect. In the back of

15.27 Salvador Dalí, *Soft Construction with Boiled Beans: Premonitions of Civil War*, 1936. Oil on canvas, 39¼ × 39" (100 × 99 cm). Philadelphia Museum of Art.

15.28 Salvador Dalí, *Gala and the Angelus of Millet Immediately Preceding the Arrival of the Conic Anamorphoses,* 1933. Oil on panel, 9⅜ × 7⅜" (23.8 × 18.7 cm). National Gallery of Canada, Ottawa.

a brilliantly lighted room is Gala, grinning broadly, as though snapped by an amateur photographer; in the front sits an enigmatic male, actually a portrait of Vladimir Lenin. Over the open doorway is a print of Millet's *Angelus,* a painting that, in Dalí's obsessive, Freudian reading, had become a scene about predatory female sexuality. Around the open door a monstrous comic figure (Maxim Gorky) emerges from the shadow, wearing a lobster on his head. There is no rational explanation for the juxtaposition of familiar and phantasmagoric, but the nightmare is undeniable. Dalí painted *Soft Construction with Boiled Beans: Premonitions of Civil War* (fig. **15.27**) in Paris in 1936, on the eve of the Spanish Civil War. It is a horrific scene of psychological torment and physical suffering. A gargantuan figure with a grimacing face is pulled apart, or rather pulls itself apart ("in a delirium of auto-strangulation" said the artist), while other body parts are strewn among the

excretory beans along the ground. Despite the anguish expressed in his painting, Dalí reacted to the civil war in his native country—as he did to fascism in general—with characteristic self-interest (he had earlier quarreled bitterly with the Surrealists in 1934 over his refusal to condemn Hitler).

In 1940 Dalí, like so many of the Surrealists, moved to the United States where he painted society portraits and flourished in the role of Surrealist agent provocateur. His notoriety and fashionable acceptance reached their height with designs for the theater, jewelry, and objets d'art. In 1941 came a transition in Dalí's painting career. He announced his determination to "become Classic," to return to the High Renaissance of Raphael, though his paintings still contained a great deal of Surrealist imagery. He and Gala resettled permanently in Spain in 1948. After 1950 Dalí's principal works were devoted to Christian religious art exalting the mystery of Christ and the Mass.

Three Northern European Surrealists: Magritte, Delvaux, and Bellmer

In contrast to Dalí, **René Magritte** (1898–1967) has been called the invisible man among the Surrealists. George Melly, in the script for a BBC film on Magritte, wrote: "He is a secret agent; his object is to bring into disrepute the whole apparatus of bourgeois reality. Like all saboteurs, he avoids detection by dressing and behaving like everybody else." Thanks perhaps to the artist's anonymity, due in part to Breton's lukewarm support of his art, the works of Magritte have had a gradual but powerful impact. In particular, his exploration of how we "read" visual images as part of a code, or system of signs, looked forward to the investigations of semiotics that became central to postmodern critical discourse.

After years of sporadic study at the Brussels Academy of Fine Arts, Magritte, like Tanguy, was shocked into realizing his destiny when in 1923 he saw a reproduction of de Chirico's 1914 painting *The Song of Love*. In 1926 he emerged as an individual artist with his first Surrealist paintings inspired by the work of Ernst and de Chirico. Toward the end of that year, Magritte joined other Belgian writers, musicians, and artists in an informal group comparable to the Paris Surrealists. He moved to a Paris suburb in 1927, entering one of the most highly productive phases of his career, and participated for the next three years in Surrealist affairs. Wearying of the frenetic, polemical atmosphere of Paris after quarreling with the Surrealists, and finding himself without a steady Parisian dealer to promote his work, Magritte returned to Brussels in 1930 and lived there quietly for the rest of his life. Because of this withdrawal from the art centers of the world, Magritte's paintings did not receive the attention they deserved. In Europe he was seen as a marginal figure among the Surrealists, and in the United States, in the heyday of painterly abstraction after World War II, his meticulous form of realism seemed irrelevant to many who were drawn instead to the work of Masson or Miró. But subsequent generations, such as that of the Pop artists, appreciated Magritte's genius for irony, uncanny invention, and deadpan realism. Important exhibitions were held in Europe and the United States after World War II, climaxing in the retrospective at New York's Museum of Modern Art in 1965. Another major survey exhibition

15.29 René Magritte, *The Treachery (or Perfidy) of Images*, 1928–29. Oil on canvas, 23¼ × 31½" (60 × 80 cm). Los Angeles County Museum of Art.

in 1992 brought the work of this brilliant artist once again to the forefront, and his unique contribution to Surrealism as well as his tremendous impact on art and commercial design is now more fully recognized.

The perfect symbol for his approach is the painting entitled *The Treachery (or Perfidy) of Images* (fig. **15.29**). It portrays a briar pipe so meticulously that it might serve as a tobacconist's trademark. Beneath, rendered with comparable precision, is the legend *Ceci n'est pas une pipe* (This is not a pipe). This delightful work confounds pictorial reality and underscores Magritte's fascination with the relationship of language to the painted image. It undermines our natural tendency to speak of images as though they were actually the things they represent. A similar idea is embodied in *The False Mirror* (fig. **15.30**): the eye as a false mirror when it views the white clouds and blue sky of nature. This might be another statement of the artist's faith, for *The False Mirror* introduces the illusionistic theme of the landscape that is a painting, not nature itself.

15.30 René Magritte, *The False Mirror*, 1928. Oil on canvas, 21¼ × 31⅞" (54 × 81 cm). The Museum of Modern Art, New York.

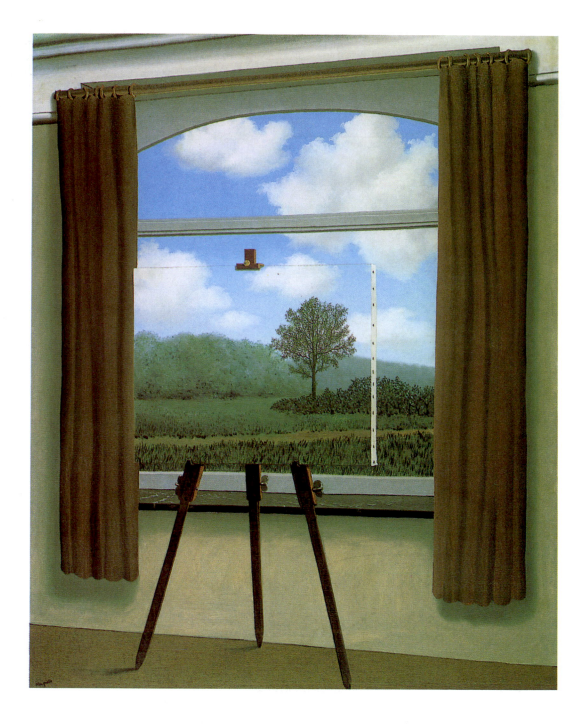

15.31 René Magritte, *The Human Condition*, 1933. Oil on canvas, 39⅜ × 31⅞" (100 × 81 cm). National Gallery of Art, Washington, D.C.

After 1926 Magritte changed his style of precise depiction very little, except for temporary excursions into other sometimes alarmingly divergent manners, and he frequently returned to earlier subjects. In 1933, he reconciled with the Parisian Surrealists, and throughout the decade he made many of the key works of his career, usually in compositions of the utmost clarity and simplicity. In *The Human Condition* (fig. **15.31**), we encounter a pleasant landscape framed by a window. In front of this opening is a painting on an easel that "completes" the very landscape it blocks from view. The problem of real space versus spatial illusion is as old as painting itself, but it is imaginatively treated in this picture within a picture. Magritte's classic play on illusion implies that the painting is less real than the landscape, when in fact both are painted fictions. The tree depicted here, as the artist explained (somewhat confus-

ingly, in view of the illusory nature of the "real" landscape, as he defines it), exists for the spectator "both inside the room in the painting, and outside in the real landscape. Which is how we see the world: we see it as being outside ourselves even though it is only a mental representation of it that we experience inside ourselves."

Magritte's visual jokes can border on the gruesome. The succinctly titled *Portrait* (fig. **15.32**) is a still life of a succulent slice of ham accompanied by wine bottle, glass, knife, and fork, all drawn with the utmost precision. The table on which they rest is a vertical rectangle of dark gray. Out of the center of the slice of ham stares a human eye. Magritte recreated this scene as a life-size, three-dimensional installation for a 1945 exhibition in Brussels. In another painting from the thirties called *Time Transfixed* (fig. **15.33**), the artist introduced the

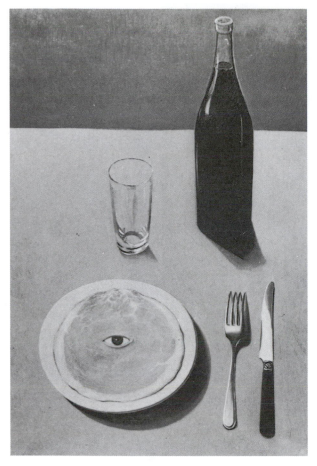

15.32 René Magritte, *Portrait*, 1935. Oil on canvas, 28⅞ × 19⅞" (73.3 × 50.2 cm). The Museum of Modern Art, New York.

15.33 René Magritte, *Time Transfixed*, 1938. Oil on canvas, 57½ × 38½" (146.1 × 97.8 cm). The Art Institute of Chicago.

unexpected into an otherwise unremarkable scene: a tiny locomotive emerges from a fireplace, transforming the latter into a kind of domestic railway tunnel. The trains in de Chirico's paintings (see fig. 13.5) may have contributed to Magritte's vision, as did the fireplace in a friend's house. The effect here of ominous mystery is not unlike that of the Italian's, but Magritte accomplished it with characteristic restraint and an almost geometric precision.

Paul Delvaux (1897–1994), like Magritte a long-time resident of Brussels, came to Surrealism slowly. Beginning in 1935, he painted women, usually nude but occasionally clothed in chaste, Victorian dress. Sometimes lovers appear, but normally the males are shabbily dressed scholars, strangely oblivious to the women. *Entrance to the City* (fig. **15.34**) gives the basic formula: a spacious landscape; nudes wandering about, each lost in her own dreams; clothed male figures, with here a partly disrobed young man study-. ing a large plan; here also a pair of embracing female lovers and a bowler-hatted gentleman (reminiscent of Magritte) reading his newspaper while walking. The chief source seems to be fifteenth-century painting, and even the feeling of withdrawal in the figures

15.34 Paul Delvaux, *Entrance to the City*, 1940. Oil on canvas, 63 × 70⅞" (160 × 180 cm). Private collection.

15.35 Hans Bellmer, *Doll*, 1935. Wood, metal, and *papier-mâché*. Manoukian Collection, Paris.

suggests the influence of Piero della Francesca (see fig. 1.3) translated into Delvaux's peculiar personal fantasy. Delvaux's dreamworld is filled with a nostalgic sadness that transforms even his erotic nudes into something elusive and unreal.

Another artist who, like Delvaux, belonged to a later, second wave of Surrealism is **Hans Bellmer** (1902–75). In 1923–24 this Polish-born artist trained at the Berlin Technical School, studying drawing with George Grosz (see chapter 13) and establishing contact with other figures related to German Dada. In the thirties, he began assembling strange constructions called "dolls" (fig. **15.35**), adolescent female mannequins whose articulated and ball-jointed parts—heads, arms, trunks, legs, wigs, glass eyes— could be dismembered and reassembled in every manner of erotic or masochistic posture. The artist then photographed the fetishistic objects, whose implied sadism appealed to the Surrealists. This led to publication of Bellmer's photographs in a 1935 issue of *Minotaure;* a career for the artist in the Surrealist milieu of Paris; and a place for his camera-made images in the history of photography. Bellmer also expressed his rather Gothic imagination in a number of splendid, if sometimes unpublishable, drawings. His particular brand of photography, whereby he invented actual objects or tableaux as subjects for his camera, would find its eighties equivalent in work by artists such as Cindy Sherman (see fig. 26.4).

Women and Surrealism: Oppenheim, Tanning, and Carrington

As a movement, Surrealism was not particularly hospitable to women, except as a terrain onto which male artists projected their erotic desires. Nevertheless, it attracted a number of gifted women artists in the thirties. **Meret Oppenheim** (1913–85), a native of Berlin, arrived in Paris as an art student in 1932 when she was not yet twenty years old. She soon met Alberto Giacometti, who introduced her to members of the Surrealist circle. She began to take part in the group's exhibitions in 1935 and is recorded in a number of photographs by Man Ray. Although she produced a large body of work—paintings, drawings, sculpture, and poetry—until her death in 1985, Oppenheim was known primarily for her notorious *Object (Le Déjeuner en fourrure) (Luncheon in Fur)* (fig. **15.36**), a cup, plate, and spoon covered with the fur of a Chinese gazelle. The idea for this "fur-lined tea cup," which has become the very archetype of the Surrealist object, germinated in a café conversation with Picasso about Oppenheim's designs for jewelry made of fur-lined metal tubing. When Picasso remarked that one could cover just about anything with fur, Oppenheim quipped, "Even this cup and saucer." In Oppenheim's hands, this emblem of domesticity and the niceties of social intercourse metamorphosed into a hairy object that is both repellent and

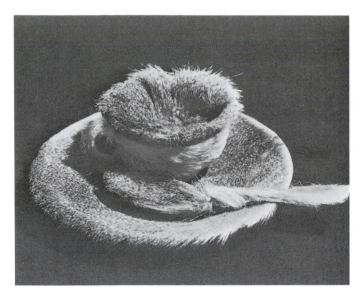

15.36 Meret Oppenheim, *Object (Le Déjeuner en fourrure) (Luncheon in Fur)*, 1936. Fur-covered cup, diameter 4⅜" (10.9 cm); saucer, diameter 9⅜" (23.7 cm); spoon, length 8" (20.2 cm). Overall height 2⅞" (7.3 cm). The Museum of Modern Art, New York.

eroticized, challenging with Surrealist freedom the dominant notions of masculine culture. Such inventions fulfilled brilliantly Breton's notion of the reconciliation of opposites by bringing together in a single form materials of the most disparate nature imaginable.

The career of American artist **Dorothea Tanning** (b. 1910) was somewhat overshadowed by that of her husband, Max Ernst, whom she married in 1946. Tanning had met Ernst in New York, where she moved after her brief art studies in Chicago. Like so many American artists, she was deeply moved by the experience of the important exhibition Fantastic Art, Dada, and Surrealism, held at the Museum of Modern Art in 1936. She also came into contact with Surrealist refugee artists from Paris, including Ernst and Breton. By the early forties, Tanning had produced her first mature paintings, and in 1944 she was given a solo exhibition at the Julien Levy Gallery. In 1946, she moved with Ernst to Sedona, Arizona, and later settled in France. Tanning's skills as a painter and her penchant for the bizarre are given rich expression in the 1950 still life *A Few Roses and Their Phantoms* (fig. **15.37**). Across a table covered with strange, rose-hybrid formations and a tablecloth marked by grid-shaped folds, a monstrous creature raises its head. Tanning's meticulous style intensifies the hallucinatory quality of the scene. As she claimed, "It's necessary to paint the lie so great that it becomes the truth."

Slightly younger than Tanning was British-born **Leonora Carrington** (b. 1917), who distinguished herself both as a writer and a painter. Carrington scandalized her wealthy Catholic parents by moving to Paris with Max Ernst at the age of twenty and becoming an associate

15.37 Dorothea Tanning, *A Few Roses and Their Phantoms*, 1952. Oil on canvas, 29⅞ × 40" (75.9 × 101.6 cm). Collection Sir Roland Penrose, London.

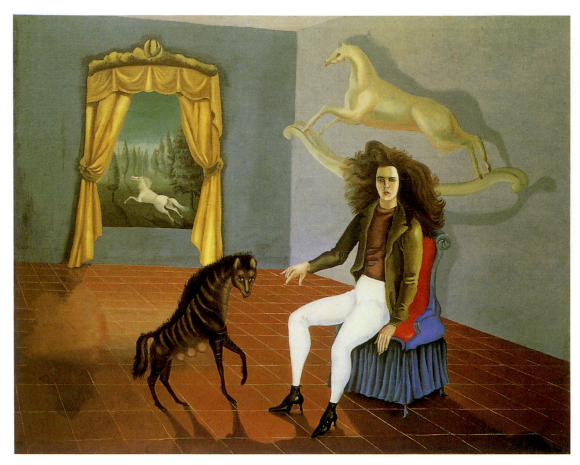

15.38 Leonora Carrington, *Self-Portrait (The White Horse Inn)*, 1936–37. Oil on canvas, 25½ × 32⅛" (65 × 81.5 cm). Private collection.

of the Surrealists. During the war, when Ernst was interned by the French as an enemy alien (and imprisoned for a time in a cell with Hans Bellmer), Carrington suffered a mental collapse, about which she wrote eloquently after her recovery. After living in New York for two years, she settled in Mexico in 1942. The enigmatic imagery that surrounds the artist in her *Self-Portrait (The White Horse Inn)* (fig. **15.38**) is closely tied to Celtic mythology and memories of her childhood. These are themes she also explored in her literary works: in two of her short stories the protagonists befriend, respectively, a hyena and a rocking horse, both of which have magical powers. Carrington, who apparently kept a rocking horse in her Paris apartment, created a lead character in one of the stories who is capable of transforming herself into a white horse. In the painting, Carrington, wearing her white jodhpurs, reaches out to a hyena heavy with milk, while at the same time a toy horse levitates inexplicably above her head. Given the subject of Carrington's own fable, the galloping white horse seen through the window becomes a kind of liberated surrogate self. In a larger context, this arresting painting abounds with classic Freudian dream imagery, in which horses are symbols of sexual desire. After she moved to Mexico, Carrington cast her mystical subjects of alchemy and the occult in imagery reminiscent of the late fifteenth-century Netherlandish painter Hieronymus Bosch.

Never Quite "One of Ours": Picasso and Surrealism

In 1925, André Breton claimed **Pablo Picasso** (1881–1973) as "one of ours," but sensibly exempted the great artist (at least for a time) from adopting a strict Surrealist regime. Picasso was never a true Surrealist. He did not share the group's obsession with the subconscious and the dreamworld, though his paintings could certainly plumb the depths of the psyche and express intense emotion. The powerful strain of eroticism and violence in Picasso's art also helped ally him to the Surrealist cause. He had considerable sympathy for the group, exhibiting with them and contributing drawings to the second number of *La Révolution surréaliste* (January 15, 1925). In the fourth number of the magazine (July 15, 1925) Breton, the editor, included an account of *Les Demoiselles d'Avignon* (see c.p. 89) and reproduced collages by Picasso and his new painting, *Three Dancers (The Dance)* (fig. **15.39**).

Painting and Graphic Art, mid-1920s–1930s

We have already seen in *Studio with Plaster Head* (see fig. 14.27) how a new emotionalism was entering Picasso's work in the mid-twenties. Also dating from the summer of 1925, *Three Dancers* was an even more startling departure from the artist's classically lyrical drawings of dancers of the previous months. Before a French window, three figures perform an ecstatic dance. The dancer in the center seems frozen, pinned in space in a crucified position. The figure to her right is jagged and angular. The figure to the left is disjointed and bends back in a state of frenzied abandon, baring her teeth in a terrifying grimace. Given her relationship to the "crucified" dancer, this figure has been compared to a mourning woman at the foot of the Cross. The subject of the Crucifixion would preoccupy the artist in the early thirties (see fig. 15.43). Picasso used every device in the Synthetic Cubist vocabulary—simultaneous views, full face and profile, hidden or shadow profiles, faceting, interpenetration, positive and negative space—to create his image. The anguish expressed in the painting can be attributed to the increasing marital tension between the artist and his wife Olga Koklova (who was a dancer), as well as to the recent death of Picasso's close friend, the Catalan painter Raymon Pichot, whose profile can be seen here silhouetted against the window.

Violence and anxiety (a favorite emotional coupling of the Surrealists) also permeate *Large Nude in Red Armchair* (fig. **15.40**), 1929. It is a timeless subject—a figure seated in a red chair draped in fabric and set against green flowered wallpaper (these saturated hues persisted in Picasso's work of the thirties). But the woman's body is pulled apart as though made of rubber. With knobs for hands and feet and black sockets for eyes, she throws her head back not in sensuous abandon but in a toothy wail, resulting in what Breton called "convulsive" beauty. While he did it to rather different effect, the photographer André Kertész subjected the female body to a similar kind of elasticity in the thirties (see fig. 15.62). In many ways, Picasso's paintings can be read as running commentaries on his relationships, and his paintings of the late twenties, when his marriage was disintegrating, were filled with women as terrifying monsters. As the poet Paul Éluard observed, "He loves with intensity and kills what he loves." In 1932, when Picasso began to make portraits of a young woman named Marie-Thérèse Walter (see fig. 15.45) the explicit eroticism in his paintings shifted to a gentler mood.

One of Picasso's favorite subjects was the artist in his studio. He returned to it periodically throughout his career, often exploring the peculiarly voyeuristic nature of the painter's relationship to the model. His interest may have been aroused by a commission from the dealer

15.39 Pablo Picasso, *Three Dancers (The Dance)*, 1925. Oil on canvas, 7'⅝" × 4'8¼" (2.1 × 1.43 m). Tate Gallery, London.

15.40 Pablo Picasso, *Large Nude in Red Armchair*, May 5, 1929. Oil on canvas, 6'4¾" × 4'3¼" (1.9 × 1.3 m). Musée Picasso, Paris.

15.41 Pablo Picasso, *Painter and Model Knitting* (executed in 1927) from *Le Chef-d'oeuvre inconnu*, by Honoré de Balzac, Paris, Ambroise Vollard, 1931. Etching, printed in black, plate 7⁹⁄₁₆ × 10⅞" (19.2 × 27.6 cm). The Museum of Modern Art, New York.

Ambroise Vollard to provide drawings for an edition of Honoré de Balzac's novel, *The Unknown Masterpiece*. The illustrated edition was published in 1931. This story concerns a deranged painter who worked for ten years on a portrait of a woman and ended with a mass of incompre-

hensible scribbles. Picasso's interpretation (fig. **15.41**) may illustrate his mistrust in complete abstraction, for he had already warned against trying "to paint the invisible." In a highly geometric composition of 1928 (fig. **15.42**), reality and illusion as presented in the drawing are reversed. The painter and model are highly abstracted, Surrealist ciphers, while the "painted" portrait on the artist's canvas is a more "realistic" profile.

Picasso rarely painted the religious subjects so dear to Spanish artists, so the small, brilliant *Crucifixion* (fig. **15.43**) from 1930 comes as a surprise. He had, however, been making drawings related to this Christian theme, and as we have seen, the subject played a role in *Three Dancers*. The artificial palette of bright reds, yellows, and greens seems unsuited to the somber subject, but Picasso's is hardly a conventional treatment. In a small canvas he manages to cram a crowd of disjointed figures in such a dizzying variety of scales and styles that it is extremely difficult to read the picture. We can recognize certain familiar aspects of the story. For example, a tiny red figure at the top of the ladder nails Christ's hand to the Cross. The mourning Virgin is located just before the Cross, her face distorted in the same grimace we encountered in *Large Nude in Red Armchair*. In the foreground two soldiers throw dice for

15.42 Pablo Picasso, *Painter and Model*, 1928. Oil on canvas, 51⅛ × 64¼" (130 × 163.2 cm). The Museum of Modern Art, New York.

15.43 Pablo Picasso, *Crucifixion*, 1930. Oil on plywood, 20⅛ × 26" (51.1 × 66.1 cm). Musée Picasso, Paris.

Christ's clothes, but the anatomies of the figures are drastically distorted by unexpected shifts in scale. *The Crucifixion* is a highly personal version of this sacred subject, one that drew on many sources, including ancient legends and rituals. What is clear is its sense of tortured agony, which looks back to the *Isenheim Altarpiece* (see fig. 1.7) and forward to *Guernica* (see fig. 15.46). Picasso's drawings after the *Isenheim Altarpiece* were published in 1933 in the first issue of *Minotaure*, for which he designed the cover. Also included in that issue was a suite of drawings called *An Anatomy*, in which the female figure is constructed in terms of abstract shapes or household objects. A woman's head, for example, becomes a goblet, or her breasts, a pair of teacups. *An Anatomy* is generally regarded as one of Picasso's most thoroughly Surrealist works.

In 1928 Picasso made sketches of the figure compartmentalized into strange bonelike forms. Variations on these highly sexualized "bone figures" continued into the thirties. One startling example is *Seated Bather* (fig. **15.44**), which is part skeleton, part petrified woman, and all monster, taking her ease in the Mediterranean sun. *Seated Bather* simultaneously has the nonchalance of a bathing beauty and the predatory countenance of a praying mantis, one of the Surrealists' favorite insect images (because the female sometimes devours the male after mating). Careful inspection of the righthand portion of *Crucifixion* (see fig. 15.43) proves that this strange head first made an appearance in that work. *Seated Bather* is a *tour de force* of the use of negative space. Picasso was, after all, an artist deeply involved with sculptural form both in painting and in three-dimensional objects.

15.44 Pablo Picasso, *Seated Bather*, early 1930. Oil on canvas, 64¼ × 51" (163.2 × 129.5 cm). The Museum of Modern Art, New York.

15.45 Pablo Picasso, *Girl Before a Mirror*, Boisgeloup, 1932. Oil on canvas, 64 × 51¼" (162.3 × 130.2 cm). The Museum of Modern Art, New York.

15.46 Pablo Picasso, *Guernica*, 1937. Oil on canvas, 11'6" × 25'8" (3.5 × 7.8 m). Museo Nacional Centro de Arte Reina Sofía, Madrid.

In 1932 Picasso painted some of his most beautifully lyrical paintings of women, a change of heart inspired by his love affair with Marie-Thérèse Walter. Although she had been involved with Picasso since 1927, when she was only seventeen, Marie-Thérèse did not become the overt subject of Picasso's paintings until their liaison was more public. His magical portrait of her (fig. **15.45**), which assimilates classical repose with Cubist space, is a key painting of the thirties. Such moments of summation for Picasso alternate with cycles of fertile and varied experiment. *Girl Before a Mirror* brings together brilliant color patterns and sensual curvilinear rhythms. Rapt in contemplation of her mirror image, the girl sees not merely a reversed reflection but some kind of mysterious alter ego. In the mirror her clear blonde features become a disquieting series of dark, abstracted forms, as though the woman is peering into the depths of her own soul.

Guernica and Related Works

Picasso's major painting of the thirties and one of the masterworks of the twentieth century is *Guernica* (fig. **15.46**). Executed in 1937, the painting was inspired by the atrocities of the Spanish Civil War—specifically, the destruction of the Basque town of Guernica by German bombers in the service of the Spanish fascists. In January 1937, Picasso, who supported the Republicans in their fight against the fascist General Francisco Franco, created two etchings, each composed of a number of episodes, and accompanied by a poem, *Dream and Lie of Franco*. General Franco is shown as a turnip-headed monster, and the bull the symbol of resurgent Spain. The grief-stricken woman in *Guernica* who shrieks over the body of her dead child first appeared in this etching. In May and June 1937 Picasso painted his great canvas *Guernica* for the Spanish Republican Pavilion of the Paris World's Fair. It is a huge

15.47 Pablo Picasso, *Weeping Woman with Handkerchief*, July 1937. Etching, aquatint, and drypoint on paper, 27¼ × 19½" (69.2 × 49.5 cm). Musée Picasso, Paris.

painting in black, white, and gray, a scene of terror and devastation. Although Picasso used motifs such as the screaming horse or agonized figures derived from his Surrealist distortions of the twenties, the structure is based on the Cubist grid and returns to the more stringent palette of Analytical Cubism (see fig. 10.18). With the exception of the fallen warrior at the lower left, the human

protagonists are women, but the central victim is the speared horse from *Minotauromachy. Guernica* is Picasso's most powerfully expressionist application of Cubism and one of the most searing indictments of war ever painted.

Picasso made dozens of studies for *Guernica*, of individual motifs as well as the entire composition, which went through several changes. Its impact on the artist himself may be seen in innumerable works during the next decades. One image that continued to haunt him in the wake of *Guernica* is that of the weeping woman (fig. **15.47**). In the etching shown here, the woman holds a handkerchief to her face with spiky fingers while tears fall from her displaced, comma-shaped eyes like long nails. The sense of palpable, uncontrollable sorrow expressed in this and related works was, on a political level, Picasso's continuing reaction to the disastrous events in his native Spain.

Though *Guernica* was created in response to current events, elements in the painting can be traced back to Picasso's work of the twenties. Some of its forms first appear in the *Three Dancers* of 1925. The figure of the Minotaur, the bull-man monster of ancient Crete and a Surrealist subject as we have seen, first appeared in Picasso's work in a collage of 1928. In 1933 he made a series of etchings, collectively known as the *Vollard Suite*, in which the Minotaur is a central character. During 1933 and 1934 Picasso also drew and painted bullfights of particular savagery. These explorations climaxed in the etching *Minotauromachy* of 1935 (fig. **15.48**), one of the great prints of the twentieth century and a demonstration of this artist's consummate skill as a draftsman. It presents a number of figures reminiscent of Picasso's life and his Spanish past, including: recollection of the prints of Goya; the women in the window; the Christ-like figure on the ladder;

15.48 Pablo Picasso, *Minotauromachy*, March 23, 1935. Etching and engraving on copper plate, printed in black; plate 19½ × 27⅜" (49.6 × 69.6 cm). The Museum of Modern Art, New York.

15.49 Pablo Picasso, *Still Life with Steer's Skull*, April 5, 1942. Oil on canvas, 51¼ × 38¼" (130.2 × 97.2 cm). Kunstsammlung Nordrhein-Westfalen, Düsseldorf.

the little girl holding flowers and a candle (a symbol of innocence); the screaming, disemboweled horse (which becomes the central player in *Guernica*) carrying a dead woman (dressed as a toreador); and the Minotaur groping his way. The place of the Minotaur (or the bull) in Picasso's iconography is ambiguous. It may be a symbol of insensate, brute force, sexual potency and aggression, a symbol of Spain, or of the artist himself.

Picasso remained in France after the outbreak of World War II and subsequent German occupation of the country. Many of his paintings and sculptures from this period reveal his response to the war (and of Spain's final capitulation to Franco's fascism) through stark, spare imagery. Animal skulls appear frequently, first in 1939, after the artist learned of the death of his mother, and again in 1942 (fig. **15.49**) following the death of his friend, the sculptor Julio González (see below). Picasso often commemorated the death of a loved one with a significant painting, and this dark, majestic still life is filled with ominous imagery. A steer's skull, painted in shades of gray, is set against the cross-shaped mullions of a French door, beyond which lies a black night. Picasso thus created a variation on traditional

vanitas still lifes, which include a human skull to remind us of life's transitory nature (see fig. 14.30).

Sculpture, late 1920s–1940s

In 1928 Picasso's Surrealist bone paintings revived his interest in sculpture, which, except for a few sporadic assemblages, he had abandoned since 1914. In broader terms, sculpture can be seen to gain greater importance around 1930 as part of a movement away from modernism's earlier emphasis on individual, experimental enquiry toward more public forms of expression, of which *Guernica* is a powerful example.

With the technical help of his old friend Julio González, a skilled metalworker, Picasso produced welded iron constructions that, together with similar constructions produced around the same time by González himself (see figs. 15.53, 15.54), marked the emergence of direct-metal sculpture as a major, modern medium. Picasso's *Woman in the Garden* (fig. **15.50**), a large, open construction in which the figure consists of curving lines and organic-shaped planes, is one of the most intricate and monumental examples of direct-metal sculpture produced to that date. The woman's face is a triangle with strands of windswept hair and the by-

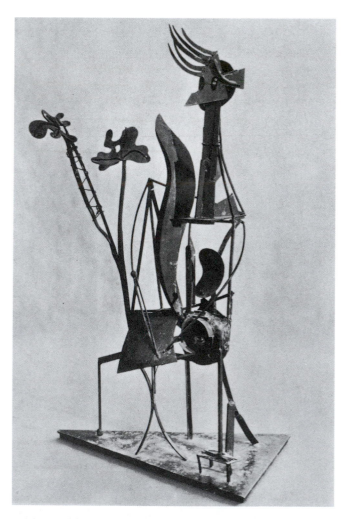

15.50 Pablo Picasso, *Woman in the Garden*, 1929–30. Bronze after welded and painted iron original, height 6'10¾" (2.1 m). Musée Picasso, Paris.

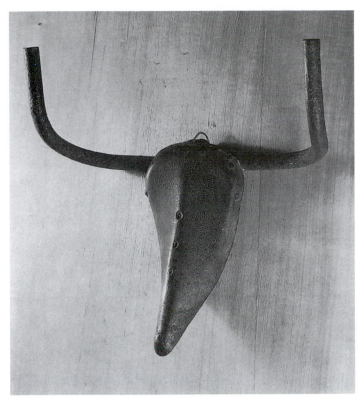

15.51 Pablo Picasso, *Bull's Head*, 1943. Bicycle saddle and handlebars, 13¼ × 17⅛ × 7½" (33.5 × 43.5 × 19 cm). Musée Picasso, Paris.

15.52 Pablo Picasso, *Man with a Sheep*, 1943. Bronze, height 7'3" (2.2 m). Musée Picasso, Paris.

now familiar gaping mouth. The bean-shaped form in the center stands for her stomach, while the disk below it is one of Picasso's familiar signs for female genitalia. The original version of this work was made of welded and painted iron. Picasso commissioned González to make a bronze replica.

Carried away by enthusiasm, Picasso modeled in clay or plaster until by 1933 his studio at Boisgeloup was filled: massive heads of women, reflecting his contemporaneous curvilinear style in painting and looking back in some degree to his Greco-Roman style; torsos transformed into anthropomorphic monsters; surprisingly representational animals including a cock and a heifer; figures assembled from found objects organized with humor and delight. Of the found-object sculptures perhaps the most renowned is the *Bull's Head* of 1943 (fig. **15.51**), which consists of an old bicycle seat and handlebars—a wonderful example of the way Picasso remained alert to the formal and expressive potential of the most commonplace objects.

The full range of Picasso's experiments in sculpture becomes clear when we realize that *Bull's Head* was made shortly before *Man with a Sheep* (fig. **15.52**). This work, which was created through the more conventional medium of plaster for bronze, is one of the artist's most moving conceptions. On the one hand the figure could refer to the Early Christian figure of the Good Shepherd, Christ the protector of the oppressed, a figure that may be traced back to classical pagan religions as well as to the Old Testament. On the other, it could recall ancient rituals of animal sacrifice. Picasso insisted, "There is no symbolism in it. It is just something beautiful." This sculpture stood prominently in the artist's Paris studio at the time of the liberation of France in 1944 by the Allied forces where, in the words of one Picasso scholar, it "came to epitomize an act of faith in humanity."

Pioneer of a New Iron Age: Julio González

Julio González (1876–1942), another son of Barcelona, had been trained in metalwork by his father, a goldsmith, but he practiced as a painter for many years. In Paris by 1900, he came to know Picasso and Brancusi, but after the death of his brother Jean in 1908, he lived in isolation for several months. In 1910 González began to make masks in a metal repoussé technique. In 1918, he learned the technique of oxyacetylene welding, and by 1927 he was producing his first sculptures in iron. In the late twenties he made a series of masks (fig. **15.53**) from sheets of flat metal. The sharp, geometric contours in the mask, as González's drawings make clear, are derived from the strong, angular shadows cast over faces in the hot sun. Their openwork construction had no real precedents in figural sculpture. In 1928, Picasso asked González for technical help in constructed sculpture, Picasso's new interest. It may be said that González began a new age of iron for sculpture, which he described in his most famous statement:

15.53 Julio González, *Mask of Roberta in the Sun*, c. 1929. Iron, height 7⅛" (18.1 cm). Collection Roberta Gonzalez, Paris.

The age of iron began many centuries ago by producing very beautiful objects, unfortunately for a large part, arms. Today, it provides as well, bridges and railroads. It is time this metal ceased to be a murderer and the simple instrument of a super-mechanical science. Today the door is wide open for this material to be, at last, forged and hammered by the peaceful hands of an artist.

By 1931 González was working in direct, welded iron, with a completely open, linear construction in which the solids were merely contours defining the voids. The difference between these constructions and the earlier ones of Gabo and the Russian Constructivists (see figs. 11.26, 11.31) lies not only in the technique—which was to have such far-reaching effects on younger sculptors—but also in the fact that, however abstract his conceptions, González was always involved with the figure. Side by side with these openwork, direct-metal constructions, González continued to produce naturalistic heads and figures, such as his large wrought-iron and welded *Montserrat*, a heroic figure of a Spanish peasant woman, symbol of the resistance of the Spanish people against fascism. *Montserrat* is the name of the mountain range near Barcelona, a symbol of Catalonia. This work was commissioned by the Spanish Republic for the 1937 World's Fair in Paris, where it was shown with murals by Miró and Picasso's *Guernica*. Dating from 1939, *Monsieur Cactus I (Cactus Man I)* (fig. **15.54**), as the name implies, is a bristly and aggressive individual, suggesting a new authority in the artist's work, which death cut short. The original version of this work was made of welded iron; it was then cast in bronze in an edition of eight. Scholars have posited that the angry, aggressive

15.54 Julio González, *Monsieur Cactus I (Cactus Man I)*, 1939. Bronze (cast from original iron), height 26" (66 cm). Private collection.

forms of *Monsieur Cactus I* may embody the artist's reactions to the recent fascist defeat of resistance forces in his beloved Barcelona, signaling the end of civil war in Spain.

The sculpture of Picasso and González after the twenties has had a special relevance to contemporary sculpture for its exploration of the techniques of direct metal and the use of the found object. For example, when American sculptor David Smith came upon González's work in the early thirties, he was inspired to make welded metal sculpture (see fig. 19.39).

Surrealism's Sculptural Language: Giacometti's Early Career

If González was the pioneer of a new iron age, **Alberto Giacometti** (1901–66) created a new sculptural image of humanity. After studies in Geneva and a long stay with his father, a painter, in Italy, where he saturated himself in Italo–Byzantine art and became acquainted with the Futurists, Giacometti moved to Paris in 1922. Here he studied with Bourdelle (see fig. 6.14) for three years and then set up a studio with his brother Diego, an accomplished technician who continued to be his assistant and model to the end of his life. His first independent sculptures reflected awareness of the Cubist sculptures of Lipchitz and

15.55 Alberto Giacometti, *No More Play*, 1931–32. Marble, wood, bronze, 1⅝ × 22⅞ × 17¾" (4.1 × 58 × 45.1 cm). National Gallery of Art, Washington, D.C.

Laurens and, more importantly, of African, Oceanic, and prehistoric art. Giacometti's *Femme cuiller* of 1926–27 is a frontalized, Surrealist–primitive totem, probably inspired by a Dan spoon from West Africa that the artist saw in the Paris ethnographic museum. Evincing a spiritual if not a stylistic affinity to the work of Brancusi, *Femme cuiller* has the totemic presence of an ancient fertility figure.

At the end of the twenties Giacometti was drawn into the orbit of the Paris Surrealists. For the next few years he made works that reflected their ideas, and, until 1935 (when he was expelled by the Surrealists), he exhibited with Miró and Arp at the Galerie Pierre. The sculptures he produced during these years are among the masterpieces of Surrealist sculpture. *No More Play* (fig. **15.55**) is an example of Giacometti's tabletop compositions. Here the base becomes the actual sculpture on which movable parts are deployed like pieces in a board game (as the title implies). In two of the rounded depressions carved in the lunarlike surface are tiny male and female figurines in wood. Between them are three cavities, like coffins with movable lids. One of these contains an object resembling a skeleton. The viewer can interact with the work, moving aside the lids of the "tombs" to discover their contents and crossing over the usually inviolable space between object and viewer.

Woman with Her Throat Cut (fig. **15.56**), a bronze construction of a dismembered female corpse, bears a family resemblance to Picasso's 1930 *Seated Bather* (see fig. 15.44). The spiked, crustacean form of the sculpture suggests the splayed and violated body of a woman. According to the artist, the work should be shown directly on the floor, without a base. From a high vantage point, looking down, the Surrealist theme of sexual violence is even more palpable. Although the work, like *No More Play*, can be moved by the viewer, the phallic shaped form should be placed in the leaflike "hand" of the figure, for Giacometti related the sculpture to the common nightmare of being unable to move one's hand.

In a number of his Surrealist sculptures Giacometti experimented with the format of an open cage structure, a series that climaxed in *The Palace at 4 a.m.* of 1932–33 (fig. **15.57**), a structure of wooden rods defining the outlines of a house. At the left a woman in a long dress (the artist's recollection of his mother) stands before three tall rectangular panels. She seems to look toward a raised panel on which is fixed a long, oval spoon shape with a ball on it. To the right, within a rectangular cage, is suspended an object resembling a spinal column, and in the center of the edifice hangs a narrow panel of glass. Above, floating in a

15.56 Alberto Giacometti, *Woman with Her Throat Cut (Femme égorgée)*, 1932 (cast 1949). Bronze, 8 × 34½ × 25" (20.3 × 87.6 × 63.5 cm). The Museum of Modern Art, New York.

15.57 Alberto Giacometti, *The Palace at 4 a.m.*, 1932–33. Construction in wood, glass, wire, and string, 25 × 28¼ × 15¾" (63.5 × 71.8 × 40 cm). The Museum of Modern Art, New York.

15.58 Alberto Giacometti, *Invisible Object (Hands Holding a Void)*, 1934. Plaster, height 61½" (156.2 cm). Yale University Art Gallery, New Haven, Connecticut.

rectangle that might be a window, is a sort of pterodactyl— "the skeleton birds that flutter with cries of joy at four o'clock." This strange edifice was the product of a period in the artist's life that haunted him and about which he has written movingly:

> for six whole months hour after hour was passed in the company of a woman who, concentrating all life in herself, made every moment something marvelous for me. We used to construct a fantastic palace in the night (days and night were the same color as if everything had happened just before dawn; throughout this time I never saw the sun), a very fragile palace of matchsticks: at the slightest false move a whole part of the miniscule construction would collapse: we would always begin it again.

Whatever the associations and reminiscences involved, *The Palace at 4 a.m.* was primarily significant for its wonderful, haunting quality of mystery.

Invisible Object (Hands Holding a Void) of 1934 (fig. **15.58**), is one of Giacometti's last Surrealist sculptures. The elongated female personage half sits on a cage/chair structure that provides an environment and, when com-

bined with the plank over her legs, pins her in space. With a hieratic gesture, she extends her hands to clasp an unseen object, as though partaking in some mysterious ritual. The work has been connected to sources in Oceanic and ancient Egyptian art. The form of a single, vertical, attenuated figure is significant for Giacometti's later work (see chapter 20).

Bizarre Juxtapositions: Photography and Surrealism

Paris in the twenties and thirties was especially fertile ground for photography. From many countries, several of the medium's greatest practitioners came together with painters and sculptors in an era of remarkably fruitful exchange between the arts. The twenties, in particular, was a highly experimental period for photography that witnessed, among other related media, the explosion of cinema. The Surrealists valued photography for its ability to capture the bizarre juxtapositions that occur naturally in daily experience. The Surrealist sense of dislocation could be made even more shocking when documented in a photograph than in, for example, a literally rendered painting by Dalí. The Surrealists regularly featured photography, ranging from Bellmer's constructed "dolls" (see fig. 15.35) to vernacular snapshots by amateurs, in their various journals. Their embrace of the medium, however, was not unequivocal. Breton viewed photography as a threat to what he regarded as the more important activity of painting, and mistrusted its emphasis on the external world rather than internal reality. Nevertheless, photography was even used by artists in the Surrealist movement who were not necessarily photographers. Max Ernst, for example, incorporated photographs into his collages; Bellmer's creations, as we have seen, were wholly dependent upon photography; and Magritte made photographs of his family and friends, a practice apart from his paintings. Others, who were not card-carrying Surrealists but who shared a kindred vision with the movement's official practitioners, were claimed by the Surrealists. The movement's lasting legacy extended beyond still photography to film, and to other media, notably literature, that are outside the scope of this account.

Atget's Paris

By no means a practicing Surrealist, **Eugène Atget** (1857–1927) was one of the artists co-opted by the group through Man Ray, who sensed that his vision lay as much in fantasy as in documentation. After having failed at the military and at acting, Atget taught himself photography and began a business to provide photographs, on virtually any subject, for use by artists. By 1897, he had begun to specialize in images of Paris and conceived what a friend called "the ambition to create a collection of all that which both in Paris and its surroundings was artistic and picturesque. An immense subject." Over the next thirty years Atget labored to record the entire face of the French capital, especially those aspects of it most threatened by "progress." Although he was often commissioned by various official agencies to supply visual material on Paris, Atget proceeded with a single-minded devotion to transform facts into art. His unforgettable images go beyond the merely descriptive to evoke a dreamlike world that is also profoundly real though infused with a mesmerized nostalgia for a lost and decaying classical past.

Among the approximately ten thousand pictures by Atget that survive—images of streets, buildings, historic monuments, architectural details, parks, peddlers, vehicles, trees, flowers, rivers, ponds, the interiors of palaces, bourgeois apartments, and ragpickers' hovels—are a series of shop fronts (fig. **15.59**) that, with their grinning dummies and superimposed reflections from across the street, would fascinate the Surrealists as "found" images of dislocated

15.59 Eugène Atget, *Magasin, avenue des Gobelins*, 1925. Albumen-silver print, 9⅜ × 7" (24 × 18 cm). The Museum of Modern Art, New York.

time and place. Man Ray was so taken with *Magasin* that he arranged for it to be reproduced in *La Révolution surréaliste* in 1926. The sense it evokes of a dreamworld, of a strange "reality," of threatened loss, could only have been enhanced by equipment and techniques that were already obsolescent when Atget adopted them and all but anachronistic by the time of his death. As John Szarkowski wrote in *Looking at Pictures*:

> Other photographers had been concerned with describing specific facts (documentation), or with exploiting their individual sensibilities (self-expression). Atget encompassed and transcended both approaches when he set himself the task of understanding and interpreting in visual terms a complex, ancient, and living tradition. The pictures that he made in the service of this concept are seductively and deceptively simple, wholly poised, reticent, dense with experience, mysterious, and true.

Man Ray, Kertész, Tabard, and the Manipulated Image

The photographer most consistently liberated by Surrealism was the one-time New York Dadaist Man Ray (1890–1976) (see figs. 13.24, 13.25), who after 1921 lived in Paris and became a force within the circle around André Breton. In the course of his long career, Man Ray worked not only in photography but also in painting, sculpture, collage, constructed objects, and film. Despite his preference for the art of painting, it was through photography and film that Man Ray found the most successful expression of his aesthetic goals. From 1924 through the thirties he contributed his photographs regularly to the Surrealist journals as well as to books by Surrealist writers.

In Paris Man Ray continued to experiment with unorthodox methods in the darkroom. In his Sabattier prints (so named for the early inventor of the technique but generally known as "solarizations"), a developed but unfixed print is exposed to light and then developed again, producing a reversal of tones along the edges of forms and transforming the mundane into something otherworldly (fig. **15.60**). Regarding one of his most famous paintings, *Observatory Time—The Lovers* executed in 1930–32, Man Ray wrote:

> One of these enlargements of a pair of lips haunted me like a dream remembered: I decided to paint the subject on a scale of superhuman proportions. If there had been a color process enabling me to make a photograph of such dimensions and showing the lips floating over a landscape, I would certainly have preferred to do it that way.

To support himself while carrying out such ambitious painting projects, Man Ray made fashion photographs and photographic portraits of his celebrated friends in art, literature, and society. For *Harper's Bazaar* in 1936 he posed a model wearing a couturier beach robe against the backdrop of *Observatory Time—The Lovers* (fig. **15.61**),

15.61 Man Ray, *Observatory Time—The Lovers*, 1936. Halftone reproduction. Published in *Harper's Bazaar*, November 1936.

thereby grafting on to this elegant scene of high fashion a hallucinatory image of eroticism and Freudian association so revered by the Surrealists.

A lyrical, life-affirming *joie de vivre*, tethered to a rigorous, original sense of form, characterizes the work of **André Kertész** (1894–1985). Unlike his friend and fellow Hungarian Brassaï (see below), Kertész was already a practicing photographer when he arrived in France from Budapest in 1925. It was there, however, that he became a virtuoso of the 35mm camera, the famous Leica introduced in 1925, and emerged as a pioneer of modern photojournalism. Though the handheld camera had been used for years by amateurs, the desire for spontaneity among professionals meant that, by the thirties, the Leica became the preferred camera of photojournalists. In his personal work, Kertész used the flexible new equipment not so much for analytical description, which the large-format camera did better, as for capturing the odd, fleeting moment or elliptical view when life is most, because unexpectedly, revealed. Photographed in the studio of a sculptor friend, Kertész's image of a woman in a pose like a human pinwheel (fig. **15.62**) playfully mimics the truncated limbs of the nearby sculpture.

The kind of elastic distortion achieved by Picasso through sheer force of imagination opened a rich vein of possibilities for photography, equipped as this medium was with every sort of optical device. Kertész created his funhouse effects (what he called "Distortions") by photographing nude models reflected in a special mirror (fig. **15.63**). Despite the visual affinities with Surrealist-inspired imagery, Kertész never claimed any allegiance with the Surrealists and was not asked by Breton to enlist in

15.60 Man Ray, *Fingers*, 1930. Solarized gelatin-silver print from negative print, 11½ × 8¾" (29.2 × 22.2 cm). The Museum of Modern Art, New York.

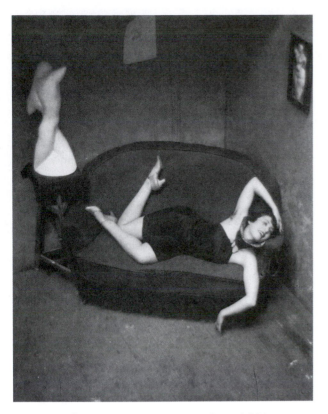

15.62 André Kertész, *Satiric Dancer, Paris*, 1926. Gelatin-silver print.

15.63 André Kertész, *Distortion No. 4*, 1933. Gelatin-silver print.

their ranks. In 1936 he emigrated to America, where he freelanced for the leading illustrated magazines, with the exception of *Life*. The editors of that publication, one crucial to the development of American photography in the thirties (see fig. 18.46), told him his photographs "spoke too much."

Maurice Tabard (1897–1984) was born in France but came to the United States in 1914. After studying at the New York Institute of Photography and establishing himself as a portrait photographer in Baltimore, Tabard returned to Paris in 1928 to make fashion photographs. He soon came to know photographers Man Ray, Henri Cartier-Bresson (see below), and Kertész, as well as the painter Magritte, and became a well-known figure in Parisian avant-garde circles. Like Man Ray, he made solarized photographs and continued his creative photography alongside his more commercial fashion work. The methods by which Tabard obtained his Surrealistic imagery differed significantly from those of artists like Kertész or Cartier-Bresson. While these artists found their images by chance or, in the case of Kertész's Distortions, a special mirror, Tabard engaged in the elaborate manipulation of his craft in the darkroom. His haunting photographs involve double exposures and negative printing, sometimes combining several techniques within the same image. In an untitled work (fig. **15.64**), Tabard locked the figure into place with a ladder-shaped shadow pattern that slyly mimics the very shape of a roll of negative film. Other superimposed

15.64 Maurice Tabard, *Untitled*, 1929. Gelatin-silver print. Collection Robert Shapazian, Fresno, California.

imagery, including what appears to be the shadow of a tennis racket at the lower left, contributes to an overall sense of disorienting complexity.

The Development of Photojournalism: Brassaï, Bravo, Model, and Cartier-Bresson

Brassaï (Gyula Halász) (1899–1984) took his pseudonym from his native city, Brasso, in the Transylvanian part of Romania. Following his days as a painting student in Budapest and Berlin, Brassaï arrived in the French capital in 1924 and promptly fell in love with its streets, bars, and brothels, artists, poets, and writers, even its graffiti. He sought out these subjects nightly and slept throughout the day. Once introduced to the small-format camera by his friend Kertész, Brassaï proceeded to record the whole of the Parisian human comedy, doing so as faithfully and objectively as possible (fig. **15.65**). That desire for objectivity prompted Brassaï to turn down an invitation from Breton to join the Surrealists. He watched for the moment when character seemed most naked and most rooted in time and place. Brassaï published the results of his nocturnal Parisian forays in the successful book *Paris de nuit* (1933). In a more Surrealist vein, he produced images of *sculptures involontaires* ("involuntary sculptures"), close-up photographs of the bizarre shapes formed by discarded tickets, cigarette ends, and other throwaway objects.

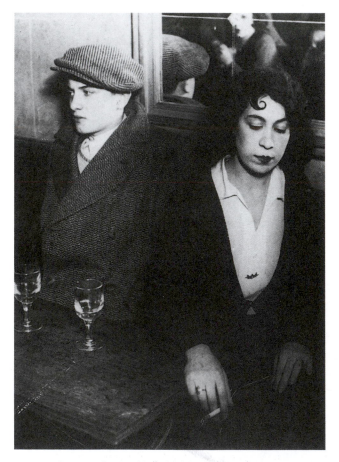

15.65 Brassaï, *Dance Hall*, 1932. Gelatin-silver print, 11½ × 9¼" (29.2 × 23.5 cm). The Museum of Modern Art, New York.

Born in Mexico City, **Manuel Álvarez Bravo** (b. 1902) was a self-taught photographer whose work contributed to the artistic renaissance that flourished in Mexico during the thirties. He befriended many of Mexico's leading avant-garde artists during this period, including the muralists Diego Rivera, David Alfaro Siqueiros, and José Clemente Orozco, whose work, often recorded in Álvarez Bravo's photographs, is discussed in chapter 18. In addition, Mexico attracted many exceptional photographers from abroad. Among those foreigners was Tina Modotti (see fig. 18.61), who encouraged Álvarez Bravo's work and put him in contact with the American photographer Edward Weston (see fig. 9.15). Álvarez Bravo also met Paul Strand (see fig. 18.21) in Mexico in 1933 and befriended Cartier-Bresson (see fig. 15.68) during the Frenchman's visit to Mexico the following year. His work represents a distinctive blend of cultural influences, fusing imagery and traditions indigenous to Mexico with current ideas imported from Europe and America, including those of the Surrealists. His work was illustrated in the last issue of *Minotaure*. Like Cartier-Bresson, Álvarez Bravo's penchant for discovering the visual poetry inherent in the everyday world could result in delightful and mysterious found images. He happened upon a group of mannequins, a favorite Surrealist stand-in for the human figure, which he captured in a photograph of an outdoor market from the early thirties (fig. **15.66**). The smiling cardboard mannequins, themselves merely mounted photographs, repeat the same woman's face, which unlike their real counterparts below, meet the viewer's gaze.

Perhaps closer in spirit to the Austrian Expressionists than to the Surrealists is the work of **Lisette Model** (1901–83), a photographer born in turn-of-the-century Vienna to an affluent family of Jewish and Catholic descent. Model wanted first and foremost to become a concert pianist. In Vienna, she studied music with the composer Arnold Schönberg and through his circle became aware of the activities of the Viennese avant-garde. In 1926, following the loss of the family's fortune during the war, she moved to France with her mother. It was in Paris, in 1933, that she decided to abandon music and become a professional photographer, learning the rudiments of the technique from her younger sister, her friend Florence Henri, and Rogi André, a photographer (and former wife of Kertész) who advised her to photograph only those things that passionately interested her. Model was, above all, interested in people. She regarded the world as a vast cast of characters from which she constructed her own narratives. With her twin-lens Rolleiflex in hand, during a visit to Nice to see her mother, she photographed wealthy vacationers soaking up the Riviera sun along that city's Promenade des Anglais (fig. **15.67**). Model wielded her camera like an invasive tool. Catching her wary subjects off-guard, she approached them closely, sometimes squatting to record their reactions at eye level. She then cropped her images in the darkroom, augmenting the

15.66 Manuel Álvarez Bravo, *Laughing Mannequins*, c. 1932. Gelatin-silver print, 7⁵⁄₁₆ × 9⁹⁄₁₆" (18.6 × 24.3 cm). The Art Institute of Chicago.

15.67 Lisette Model, *Promenade des Anglais*, 1934. Gelatin-silver print on paper, mounted on pasteboard, 13½ × 10⅞" (34.2 × 27.6 cm). The National Gallery of Canada, Ottawa.

confrontational nature of the close-up effect. In 1935 her photographs from Nice were published in the leftwing journal *Regards* as disparaging examples of a complacent middle class, "the most hideous specimens of the human animal." While it is not clear whether Model intended the photographs to be interpreted in this way, she did allow their publication again in 1941 in the weekly *PM,* one of the American publications for which she worked after she settled in New York in 1938. *PM* published the photos to demonstrate the French characteristics that, in its opinion, led to the country's capitulation in World War II. This photograph was illustrated under the heading "Cynicism." By the fifties Model had become an influential teacher; her students included the American photographer Diane Arbus (see fig. 21.81).

With its power to record, heighten, or distort reality—a power vastly increased with the invention of the small, handheld 35mm Leica—photography proved a natural medium for artists moved by the Surrealist spirit. One of the most remarkable of these was France's **Henri Cartier-Bresson** (b. 1908), who, after studying painting with the Cubist André Lhote, took up photography and worked as a photojournalist covering such epochal events as the Spanish Civil War (1936–39). His is a photojournalism broadly defined, however, for his magical images, especially those made before World War II, have little to do with a discernible narrative or straight reportage of visual fact. From a very young age Cartier-Bresson was powerfully influenced by the Surrealist theories of André Breton. He matured quickly as a photographer, and in the first half of

15.68 Henri Cartier-Bresson, *Cordoba, Spain*, 1933. Gelatin-silver print.

the thirties, in photographs made in France, Spain, Italy, and Mexico, he created some of the most memorable images of the twentieth century.

The photographer, freed from the encumbrance of a tripod, could exploit new opportunities, pursuing the action as it unfolded. Cartier-Bresson has said of his practice:

> I prowled the streets all day feeling very strung up and ready to pounce, determined to 'trap' life—to preserve life in the act of living. Above all, I craved to seize the whole essence, in the confines of a single photograph, of some situation that was in the process of unrolling itself before my eyes.

Citing Man Ray, Atget, and Kertész as his chief influences, Cartier-Bresson allowed his viewfinder to "discover" a composition within the world moving about him. Once this had been seized upon, the photographer printed the whole uncropped negative, an image that captured the subject in "the decisive moment" (the title of his 1952 book). *Cordoba, Spain* (fig. **15.68**) is a witty juxtaposition of art and life, as in the collages of his friend Max Ernst. A woman clasps a hand to her bosom, unconsciously repeating the gesture in the corset advertisement behind her. The woman squints into the photographer's lens while the eyes of the poster model are "blinded" by an advertisement that has been pasted over her face. In this deceptively simple image, the artist sets up a complex visual dialogue between art and life, illusion and reality, youth and old age. Cartier-Bresson's pictures, with their momentary equipoise among form, expression, and content, have served as models of achievement to photographers for more than half a century.

An English Perspective: Brandt

Although England's **Bill Brandt** (1904–83) was trained as a photographer in the late twenties in Paris, where he worked in the studio of Man Ray, he made mostly documentary photographs in the thirties, including a famous series on the coal miners in the North of England during the depression. After World War II, he rediscovered his early days in Surrealist Paris and gave up documentation in favor of reexploring the "poetry" of optical distortion, or what he called "something beyond reality." Between 1945 and 1960, he photographed nudes with a special Kodak camera that had an extremely wide-angle lens and a tiny aperture. The distortions transformed the nudes into Surreal dream landscapes. He exploits the same distorted perspective in *Portrait of a Young Girl, Eaton Place, London* from 1955 (fig. **15.69**). The dreamlike effect is enhanced by the artist's characteristically high-contrast printing style, where portions of the room disappear into blackness. Brandt also continued to make portraits after the war, recording the likenesses of many of the greatest luminaries in the world of literature and art, including leading Surrealists such as Magritte, Arp, Miró, and Picasso.

15.69 Bill Brandt, *Portrait of a Young Girl, Eaton Place, London*, 1955. Gelatin-silver print, 17 × 14¾" (43.2 × 37.5 cm).

16
Modern Architecture Between the Wars

After World War I, communication among architects was reestablished so rapidly and stylistic diffusion was so widespread that it became difficult to speak of national styles. Rather, centers of experimentation arose where architects and artists from many backgrounds now gathered. After 1919 most of the new ideas fermenting in the arts during the war began to converge on Berlin, which became one of the world capitals for art and architecture. These ideas included German Expressionism, Russian Suprematism and Constructivism, Dutch de Stijl, and international Dadaism. Contact was reestablished between German artists, French Cubists, and Italian Futurists. One of the most remarkable cultural phenomena in Europe in the twenties was the Bauhaus, the school established in Weimar in 1919 by the architect **Walter Gropius** (1883–1969), which was in close contact with Berlin. The other major, related development was the formation of what came to be known as the International Style of architecture, which came to prominence in the thirties. A common theme in architecture of this period was the attempt to put modernism to the service of social reform and the search for a universal language of design that would transcend the increasingly polarized political landscape in thirties Europe.

The Building as Entity: The Bauhaus

In the disastrous wake of World War I, the Staatliches Bauhaus was formed in Weimar, Germany, from the two schools of arts and crafts established there in 1906 under the direction of the Belgian artist and architect Henry van de Velde (see chapter 12). As was the case with the English Arts and Crafts and the Deutscher Werkbund traditions, which had informed Van de Velde's program of teaching in workshops rather than studios, Gropius was convinced of the need for the creations of architect, artist, and craftsman to form a unified whole. The program of Gropius was innovative, not in its insistence that the architect, the painter, and the sculptor should work with the craftsperson,

but in specifying that they should be craftspeople first of all. The concepts of learning by doing, of developing an aesthetic on the basis of sound craft skills, and of breaking down barriers between "fine art" and craft were fundamental to the Bauhaus philosophy.

Despite Gropius's belief in architecture as the supreme art form, the Bauhaus originally provided no course in architecture, for Gropius felt that students should be skilled in the basic crafts before graduating to the design of buildings. The core of Bauhaus teaching was a division of courses into workshops, which taught those craft skills, and a mandatory foundation course designed to encourage the students' creative powers and liberate them from past experiences and prejudices. This course, initially developed by the Swiss painter Johannes Itten, introduced the student to materials and techniques through elementary but fundamental practical tasks. Under the influence of Itten, the foundation course also included the investigation of Eastern philosophies and mystical religions. Eventually, Gropius opposed Itten's mystical bent, insisting that craft be reconciled with industrial production for the modern machine age. As he wrote in 1923, the year he persuaded Itten to resign, "The Bauhaus believes the machine to be our modern medium of design and seeks to come to terms with it." This shift toward a machine aesthetic was no doubt due in part to the influence of Constructivism and the presence in Weimar by 1921 of the de Stijl artist Theo van Doesburg (see chapter 11).

The first proclamation of the Bauhaus declared:

Architects, painters, and sculptors must recognize anew the composite character of a building as an entity. ... Art is not a 'profession.' There is no essential difference between the artist and the craftsman. The artist is an exalted craftsman. ... Together let us conceive and create the new building of the future, which will embrace architecture and sculpture and painting in one unity and which will rise one day toward heaven from the hands of a million workers like the crystal symbol of a new faith.

This initial statement reflected a nostalgia for the medieval guild systems and collective community spirit that lay behind the building of the great Gothic cathedrals, as well as the socialist idealism that was current in Germany in the early days of the Weimar Republic, and throughout much of postwar Europe. Suspicion of this political attitude caused antagonism toward the school among the more conservative elements in the city of Weimar, an antagonism that in 1925 drove the Bauhaus to its new home in Dessau.

Over the years the Bauhaus attracted one of the most remarkable art faculties in history. Vasily Kandinsky, Paul Klee, Lyonel Feininger, Georg Muche, and Oskar Schlemmer were among those who taught painting, graphic arts, and stage design. Pottery was taught by Gerhard Marcks, who was also a sculptor and graphic artist. When Johannes Itten left in 1923, the foundation course was headed by László Moholy-Nagy, a Hungarian painter, photographer, theater and graphic designer, whose writings and teaching made him, after Gropius, the most influential figure in developing and spreading the Bauhaus idea. (Work produced by many of these painters, photographers, and sculptors during their tenure at the Bauhaus and after is discussed in chapter 17.) In addition to the star-studded faculty, the Bauhaus frequently attracted distinguished foreign visitors, such as, in 1927, the Russian Suprematist painter Kazimir Malevich (see figs. 11.18, 11.19). When the Bauhaus moved to Dessau, several former students joined the faculty—the architects and designers Marcel Breuer and Herbert Bayer, and the painter and designer Josef Albers (see fig. 17.9), who reorganized the foundation course. Of the artist-teachers, Kandinsky, Klee, and Feininger were to become recognized as major twentieth-century painters. Moholy-Nagy, through his books *The New Vision* and *Vision in Motion* and his directorship of the New Bauhaus, founded in Chicago in 1937 (now the Institute of Design of the Illinois Institute of Technology), greatly influenced the teaching of design in the United States. Josef Albers would become one of the most important art teachers in the United States, first at the remarkable school of experimental education, Black Mountain College in North Carolina, and subsequently at Yale University. Marcel Breuer, principally active at the Bauhaus as a furniture designer, ultimately joined Gropius in 1937 on the faculty of Harvard University and practiced architecture with him. After Breuer left this partnership in 1941, his reputation steadily grew to a position of world renown (see figs. 23.20, 23.35).

The Bauhaus curriculum was initially divided into two broad areas: problems of craft and problems of form. Each course had a "form" teacher and a "craft" teacher. This division was necessary because, during the first four years, it was not possible to assemble a faculty who were collectively capable of integrating the theory and practice of painting, sculpture, architecture, design, and crafts—although Klee taught textile design and Marcks pottery. With the move to Dessau, however, and the addition of Bauhaus-trained staff members, the various parts of the program were integrated.

In Dessau the accent on craft declined, while the emphasis on architecture and industrial design substantially increased. The architecture students were expected to complete their training in engineering schools. Gropius said:

> We want to create a clear, organic architecture, whose inner logic will be radiant and naked, unencumbered by lying façades and trickeries; we want an architecture adapted to our world of machines, radios, and fast motor cars, an architecture whose function is clearly recognizable in the relation of its form. … [W]ith the increasing strength of the new materials—steel, concrete, glass—and with the new audacity of engineering, the ponderousness of the old methods of building is giving way to a new lightness and airiness.

The greatest practical achievements at the Bauhaus were probably in interior, product, and graphic design. For example, Marcel Breuer created many furniture designs at the Bauhaus that have become classics, including the first tubular-steel chair (fig. **16.1**). He said that, unlike heavily upholstered furniture, his simple, machinemade chairs were "airy, penetrable," and easy to move. Though initially women were to be given equal status at the Bauhaus, Gropius grew alarmed at the number of women applicants and restricted them primarily to weaving, a skill deemed suitable for female students. Gunta Stölz and Anni Albers were major innovators in the area of textile design at the school's weaving workshop. In ceramic and metal design, a new vocabulary of simple, functional shapes was

16.1 Marcel Breuer, Armchair, Model B3, Dessau, Germany. Late 1927 or early 1928. Chrome-plated tubular steel with canvas slings, 28⅛ × 30¼ × 27¾" (71.4 × 76.8 × 70.5 cm). The Museum of Modern Art, New York.

established. The courses in display and typographic design under Bayer, Moholy-Nagy, Tschichold, and others revolutionized the field of type. Bauhaus designs have passed so completely into the visual language of the modern age that it is now difficult to appreciate how revolutionary they were on first appearance. Certain designs, such as Breuer's tubular chair and his basic table and cabinet designs, Gropius's designs for standard unit furniture, and designs by other faculty members and students for stools, stacking chairs, dinnerware, lighting fixtures, textiles, and typography so appealed to popular tastes that they are still manufactured today.

Gropius resigned in 1928 to work full-time in his architectural practice. He was succeeded by Hannes Meyer, a Marxist who placed less emphasis on aesthetics and creativity than on rational, functional, and socially responsible design. Meyer was forced to leave the Bauhaus in 1930, and Mies van der Rohe (Gropius's first choice in 1928) assumed the directorship. Mies's work as an architect is discussed below. Inevitably, activities at the Bauhaus aroused the suspicions of the Nazis, who finally brought about its closure in 1933.

Audacious Lightness: The Architecture of Gropius

After spending two years in the office of Peter Behrens (see chapter 12), Gropius established his own practice in Berlin. In 1911 he joined forces with his partner **Adolph Meyer** (1881–1929) to build a factory for the Fagus Shoe Company at Alfeld-an-der-Leine (fig. **16.2**). The Fagus building represents a sensational innovation in its utilization of complete glass sheathing, even at the corners. In effect, Gropius here had invented the curtain wall that

16.3 Walter Gropius and Adolph Meyer, Model Factory at the Werkbund Exhibition, Cologne, 1914.

would play such a visible role in the form of subsequent large-scale twentieth-century architecture.

Gropius and Meyer were commissioned to build a model factory and office building in Cologne for the 1914 Werkbund Exhibition of arts and crafts and industrial objects (fig. **16.3**). Gropius felt that factories should possess the monumentality of ancient Egyptian temples. For one façade of their "modern machine factory," the architects combined massive brickwork with a long, horizontal expanse of open glass sheathing, the latter most effectively used to encase the exterior spiral staircases at the corners (clearly seen in the view reproduced here). The pavilions at either end have flat overhanging roofs derived from Frank Lloyd Wright (see fig. 12.3), whose work was known in Europe after 1910, and the entire building reveals the elegant and disciplined design that became a prototype for many subsequent modern buildings.

During his years as director of the Bauhaus, Gropius continued his own architectural practice in collaboration with Meyer. One of their unfulfilled projects was the design for the Chicago Tribune Tower in 1922 (fig. **16.4**). The highly publicized competition for the design of this tower, with over two hundred and fifty entries from architects worldwide, provides a cross-section of the eclectic architectural tendencies of the day, ranging from strictly historicist examples based on Renaissance towers to the modern styles emerging in Europe. The traditionalists won the battle with the neo-Gothic tower designed by the American

16.2 Walter Gropius and Adolph Meyer, Fagus Shoe Factory, Alfeld-an-der-Leine, Germany, 1911–25.

16.4 Walter Gropius and Adolph Meyer, Design for the Chicago Tribune Tower, 1922.

architect Raymond Hood (probably in collaboration with John Mead Howells). The design of Gropius and Meyer, with the spare rectangularity of its forms, its emphasis on skeletal structure, and its wide tripartite windows, was based on the original skyscraper designs of Sullivan and the Chicago School (see figs. 4.11, 4.12) and also looked forward to the skyscrapers of the mid-twentieth century.

When the Bauhaus moved to Dessau in 1925, Gropius closed his Weimar office, ending his partnership with Meyer. His most important architectural achievement at the Bauhaus was the design for the new buildings at Dessau (fig. **16.5**). These buildings, finished in 1926, incorporated a complex of classrooms, studios, workshops, library, and living quarters for faculty and students. The workshops consisted of a glass box rising four stories and presenting the curtain wall, the glass sheath or skin, freely suspended from the structural steel elements. The form of the workshop wing suggests the uninterrupted spaces of its interior. On the other hand, in the dormitory wing, the balconies and smaller window units contrasting with clear expanses of wall surface imply the broken-up interiors of individual apartments.

The asymmetrical plan of the Bauhaus is roughly cruciform, with administrative offices concentrated in the broad, uninterrupted ferroconcrete span of the bridge linking workshops with the classrooms and library. In every way, the architect sought the most efficient organization of interior space. At the same time he was sensitive to the abstract organization of the rectangular exterior—the relation of windows to walls, concrete to glass, verticals to horizontals, lights to darks. The Bauhaus combined functional organization and structure with a geometric, de Stijl-inspired design. Not only were the Bauhaus buildings

16.5 Walter Gropius, Workshop Wing, Bauhaus, Dessau, Germany, 1925–26.

revolutionary in their versatility and in the application of abstract principles of design on the basis of the interaction of verticals and horizontals, but they also embodied a new concept of architectural space. The flat roof of the Bauhaus and the long, uninterrupted planes of white walls and continuous window voids create a lightness that opens up the space of the structure. The interior was furnished with designs by Bauhaus students and faculty, including Breuer's tubular-steel furniture. The building was seriously damaged in World War II and underwent limited renovation in the sixties. It was finally restored to its original appearance in the seventies. Since the reunification of Germany in 1990, this landmark building has become the focus of new studies and a site for historical exhibitions related to the Bauhaus.

Between 1928, when he left the Bauhaus, and 1934, when he was forced by the Nazis' rise to power to leave Germany—first for England and then, in 1937, for the United States—much of Gropius' building was in low- or middle-cost housing. In his pioneering European works, Gropius helped provide the foundation of what would later be dubbed the International Style. (His profound influence on postwar American architecture is discussed in chapter 23.)

"Machines for Living": The International Style

Major forces in the formation of what came to be called the International Style were de Stijl art and architecture in Holland (see chapter 12), the new experiments in German architecture, and, though he never considered himself a participant, the American architect Frank Lloyd Wright. Its first manifestation took place in 1927 at the Deutsche Werkbund Weissenhofsiedlung Exhibition in Stuttgart, organized by Mies van der Rohe. The presentation included display housing designed by, among others, Mies, Gropius, Le Corbusier, and the de Stijl architect J. J. P. Oud (see figs. 12.19, 12.20). The term "International Style" was given prominence by an exhibition of advanced tendencies in architecture held at New York's Museum of Modern Art in 1932. The show was a collaborative effort by museum director Alfred H. Barr, Jr., architectural historian Henry-Russell Hitchcock, and architect Philip Johnson. It attempted to define and codify the characteristics of the style, although the exhibition's strictly formalist approach paid virtually no heed to the underlying ideologies and individual formal vocabularies that gave rise to modern architecture in Europe. The first principle of the new architecture of structural steel and ferroconcrete was elimination of the loadbearing wall. The outside wall became a curtain wall—a skin of glass, metal, or masonry constituting an enclosure rather than a support. Thus, one could speak of an architecture of volume rather than of mass. Window and door openings could be enlarged indefinitely and distributed freely to serve both function—activity, access, or light—and design, exterior or interior. The

regular distribution of structural supports led to rectangular regularity of design and away from the balanced axial symmetry of classical architecture.

Other principles involved the general avoidance of applied decoration, a theme earlier given prominence by the polemical writings of Adolf Loos (see chapter 12), and the elimination of strong contrasts of color on both interiors and exteriors. The International Style resulted in new concepts of spatial organization, particularly that of a free flow of interior space, as opposed to the stringing together of static symmetrical boxes that up till then had been necessitated by interior loadbearing walls. Importantly, the International Style lent itself to urban planning and low-cost mass housing—to any form of large-scale building involving inexpensive, standardized units of construction.

The experiments of the pioneers of modern architecture in the use of new materials and in the stripping away of accretions of classical, Gothic, or Renaissance tradition resulted in various common denominators that may be classified as a common style. However, the individual stamp of the pioneers is recognizable even in their most comparable architecture and can hardly be reduced to a single style.

Le Corbusier

Among the generation of architectural pioneers who rose to prominence during the twenties, **Le Corbusier** (1887–1965), the artistic pseudonym of the Swiss Charles-Édouard Jeanneret, was a searching and intense spirit, a passionate but frustrated painter (see chapter 14), a brilliant critic, and an effective propagandist for his own architectural ideas. He studied in the tradition of the Vienna Workshops (Wiener Werkstätte), learned the properties of ferroconcrete with Perret in Paris, and worked for a period with Behrens in Berlin (where he no doubt met Gropius and Mies van der Rohe). He moved to Paris from his native Switzerland in 1916. Although he condemned all forms of historical revivalism, he did not reject tradition, and his architecture evolved through an adherence to the basic principles of classicism. While he never became a painter of the first rank, his interest in and knowledge of Cubism and its offshoots affected his attitude toward architectural space and structure. Le Corbusier's principal exploration throughout much of his career was the reconciliation of human beings with nature and the modern machine. This was addressed largely through the problem of the house, to which he applied his famous phrase, "a machine for living." By exploiting the lightness and strength of ferroconcrete, his aims were to maximize the interpenetration of inner and outer space and create plans of the utmost freedom and flexibility.

A perspective drawing of 1914–15 states the problem and his solution: it shows the structural skeleton called the Domino house to be mass-produced using inexpensive, standardized materials, with a structure consisting of six slender pillars standing on a broad, flat base and supporting two other floors or areas that may be interpreted as an upper floor and a flat roof. The stories are connected by a freestanding, minimal staircase and the ground floor is raised on six blocks, suggestive of Le Corbusier's later use of stilts or piers called pilotis. This drawing is important for showing how early Le Corbusier established his philosophy of building. Outer walls, windows, or complete glass sheaths can simply be hung on this frame. Inner partitions can be distributed and shaped in any manner that the architect desires. The entire structure can be repeated indefinitely either vertically or horizontally, with any number of variations. (Le Corbusier did not invent the system of ferroconcrete screen-wall construction; Behrens and Gropius had already constructed buildings involving the principle.) Le Corbusier's *Five Points of a New Architecture*, published in 1926, were (1) the pilotis—supporting narrow pillars to be left free to rise through the open space of the house; (2) the free plan—composing interior space with nonbearing interior walls to create free flow of space and also interpenetration of inner and outer space; (3) the free façade—the wall as a nonsupporting skin or sheath; (4) the horizontal strip window running the breadth of a façade; and (5) the roof garden—the flat roof as an additional living area. These points could provide an elementary outline of the International Style.

The masterpiece among Le Corbusier's early houses was the Villa Savoye at Poissy (fig. **16.6**), thirty miles (forty-eight kilometres) from Paris. Along with Mies's German Pavilion (see fig. 16.9), the Villa Savoye is generally regarded as a paradigm of the International Style. The three-bedroom house, beautifully sited in an open field, is almost a square in plan, with the upper living area supported on delicate piers or pilotis. The enclosed ground level has a curved-glass end wall containing garage and service functions, set under the hovering second story. The Savoye family, arriving from Paris, would drive right under the house—the curve of the ground floor was determined by the turning radius of a car. Although today's suburban homes are loosely designed around the automobile, in 1929 this design concept was based on the notion of the car as the ultimate machine and the idea that the approach up to and through the house carried ceremonial significance.

In the main living area on the second level, the architect brilliantly demonstrated his aim of integrating inside and outside space. The rooms open on a terrace, which is protected by half-walls or windbreaks above horizontal openings that continue the long, horizontal line of the strip windows. The horizontal elements are tied together in sections by a central ramp that moves through each level and in- and out-of-doors. The complex of volumes

and planes in the Villa Savoye relates to Le Corbusier's own Purist painting (see fig. 14.34). One historian has written of this building, "The visitor wandering through the interiors might glimpse cylindrical forms through layers of semi-reflecting glass and sense how Cubist ambiguities enlivened the play of surfaces: it was like entering the fantasy world behind the picture plane of a Purist still life."

Le Corbusier, like Wright, had few major commissions during the twenties, but he continually advanced his ideas and his reputation through his writings and through his urban planning projects, which were less practical but more visionary than Garnier's earlier plans for the modern industrial city (see chapter 12). These large-scale housing projects, a response to the growing urban populations and housing shortages of postwar France, were never actually built. In 1922 Le Corbusier drew up a plan for a contemporary city (the "Ville Contemporaine") of three million inhabitants, involving rows of gleaming glass skyscrapers placed on stilts to allow for pedestrian passage. They were connected by vast highways and set in the midst of parks. In his 1925 "Plan Voisin" for Paris, Le Corbusier envisioned an enormous urban-renewal project that would have replaced the historic buildings north of the Seine with a complex of high-rise buildings. Like the Ville Contemporaine, this radiant modern city was the architect's drastic antidote to the traffic-congested streets of modern Paris and the soot-filled slums of the nineteenth-century city. It was based on the utopian notion common among the modern pioneers that, armed with the right city planning and the appropriate faith in technology, architecture could revolutionize patterns of living and improve the lives of modern city dwellers on a physical, economic, and even spiritual level. In the face of today's massive and eclectic urban centers, Le Corbusier's faith that a uniform strategy for urban planning would create cities where "the air is clean and pure" and "there is hardly any noise" seems naively idealistic. Nevertheless, his urban schemes were prophetic in the way they anticipated elements of today's cityscapes.

16.6 Le Corbusier, Villa Savoye, Poissy, France, 1928–30.

Le Corbusier's writings have also been tremendously influential in modern world architecture. His trenchant book *Vers une architecture* (*Towards a New Architecture*) (1923) was immediately translated into English and other languages and has since become a standard treatise. In it he extolled the beauty of the ocean liner, the airplane, the automobile, the turbine engine, bridge construction, and dock machinery—all products of the engineer, whose designs had to reflect function and could not be embellished with nonessential decoration. Le Corbusier dramatized the problems of modern architecture through incisive comparisons and biting criticisms and, in effect, spread the word to a new generation.

Mies van der Rohe

The spare, refined architecture of **Ludwig Mies van der Rohe** (1886–1969), built on his edict that "Less is more," is synonymous with the modern movement and the International Style. He has arguably had a greater impact on the skylines of American cities than any other architect. His contribution lies in the ultimate refinement of the basic forms of the International Style, resulting in some of its most famous examples. Some of the major influences on Mies were: his father, a master mason from whom he initially gained his respect for craft skills; Peter Behrens (see chapter 12), in whose atelier he worked for three years; and Frank Lloyd Wright. From Wright, Mies gained his appreciation for the open, flowing plan and for the predominant horizontality of his earlier buildings. He was affected not only by Behrens's famous turbine factory (see fig. 12.12), but also by Gropius's 1911 Fagus Factory (see fig. 16.2), with its complete statement of the glass curtain wall. Gropius had worked in Behrens's office between 1907 and 1910, and the association between Gropius and Mies that began there, despite a certain rivalry, continued. Mies's style remained almost conventionally Neoclassical until after World War I. Then, in the midst of the financial and political turmoil of postwar Germany, he plunged into the varied and hectic experimentation that characterized the Berlin School.

In 1921 and 1922 Mies completed two designs for skyscrapers, which, although never built, established the basis of his reputation. The first was triangular in plan, the second a free-form plan of undulating curves (fig. **16.7**). In these he proposed the boldest use yet envisaged of a reflective, all-glass sheathing suspended on a central core. As Mies wrote:

> Only in the course of their construction do skyscrapers show their bold, structural character, and then the impression made by their soaring skeletal frames is overwhelming. On the other hand, when the façades are later covered with masonry, this impression is destroyed and the constructive character denied. ... The structural principle of these buildings becomes clear when one uses glass to cover non-loadbearing walls. The use of glass forces us to new ways.

16.7 Ludwig Mies van der Rohe, Model for a glass skyscraper, 1922.

No comparably daring design for a skyscraper was to be envisaged for thirty or forty years. Because there was no real indication of either the structural system or the disposition of interior space, these projects still belonged in the realm of visionary architecture, but they were prophetic projections of the skyscraper.

Mies's other unrealized projects of the early twenties included two designs for country houses, both in 1923, the first in brick (fig. **16.8**) and the second in concrete. The brick country house design so extended the open plan made famous by Frank Lloyd Wright that the freestanding walls no longer enclose rooms but instead create spaces that flow into one another. Mies fully integrated the interior and exterior spaces. The plan of this house, drawn with the utmost economy and elegance, and the abstract organization of planar slabs in the elevation exemplify Mies's debt to the principles of de Stijl (it has often been compared to the composition of a 1918 painting by Mies's friend Theo van Doesburg).

One of the last works executed by Mies in Europe was the German Pavilion for the Barcelona International Exposition in 1929 (fig. **16.9**). Mies was in charge of Germany's entire contribution to the exposition. The Barcelona Pavilion, destroyed at the end of the exposition, has become one of the classics of his career and is perhaps the preeminent example of the International Style. Here

16.8 Ludwig Mies van der Rohe, Elevation for brick country house, 1923.

was the most complete statement to date of all the qualities of refinement, simplification, and elegance of scale and proportion that Mies, above all others, brought to modern architecture. In this building he contrasted the richness of highly polished marble wall slabs with the chrome-sheathed slender columns supporting the broad, over-hanging flat roof. Thus, the walls are designed to define space rather than support the structure. In a realization of the open plan that he had designed for the brick country house, the marble and glass interior walls stood free, serving simply to define space. But in contrast to the earlier work, the architect put limits on the space of pavilion and court by enclosing them in end walls. This definition of free-flowing interior space within a total rectangle was to become a signature style for Mies in his later career. The pavilion was furnished with chairs (known as the Barcelona chair), stools, and glass tables also designed by Mies. In the Barcelona Pavilion, he demonstrated that the International Style had come to a maturity that permitted comparison with the great styles of the past. In 1986, to celebrate the centenary of the architect's birth, the pavilion was

completely reconstructed in Barcelona according to the original plans.

Mies became director of the Bauhaus in 1930 but had little opportunity to advance its program. After moving from Dessau to Berlin in that year, the school suffered increasing pressure from the Nazis until it was finally closed in 1933. In 1937, with less and less opportunity to practice, Mies left for the United States, where in the last decades of his life he was able to fulfill, in a number of great projects, the promise apparent in the relatively few buildings he actually built in Europe (see chapter 23).

At its best, the uncompromising rationalism of Mies's architecture could produce compelling examples of pristine, streamlined form. In lesser hands, as is apparent in skylines across the United States, his minimalist forms could become impersonal glass and steel monuments to consumer capitalism or drab apartment dwellings. In the words of architecture critic Ada Louise Huxtable, "Mies's reductive theories, carried to their conceptual extreme, contained the stuff of both sublimity and failure, to which even he was not immune." By the early seventies, the

16.9 Ludwig Mies van der Rohe, German Pavilion, International Exposition, Barcelona, Spain, 1929. Reconstructed 1986.

modern movement, and particularly the International Style as represented above all by Mies and Le Corbusier, would encounter a protracted backlash, opening the door to the era of Postmodernism (see chapter 25).

A Return to Innovation: Developments in American Architecture

In the thirties a number of events and individuals pointed the way to a new modern era in American design. Following the 1932 exhibition at The Museum of Modern Art in New York that gave the International Style its name, exhibitions of the Chicago School (1935), Le Corbusier (1935), and the Bauhaus (1938) all took place. Also in the thirties, a number of new skyscrapers were built that broke the eclecticism of the skyscraper form and reintroduced aspects of the Chicago School or innovations of the Bauhaus and the International Style. The first European architects to come to America in the twenties, William Lescaze, **Richard Neutra** (1892–1970), and Rudolf Schindler, however, devoted much of their careers to house architecture. The Austrians Schindler and Neutra worked for Wright and were partners for a time. They each built a house in California for Dr. Philip Lovell, combining aspects of Wright's house design with that of the International Style. The Neutra house (fig. **16.10**)—placed spectacularly on a mountainside—was built of steel girders on a foundation of reinforced concrete. Through its open terraced construction, Neutra took every advantage of the amenities of landscape and climate and (along with Schindler) created a distinct style of southern California architecture.

Skyscraper Design

During the first half of the twentieth century, most experiments in modern architecture were carried out on individual houses. This is understandable, since the cost of building a skyscraper or an industrial complex is so exorbitant that it took a half-century before a greater number

16.10 Richard Neutra, Dr. Lovell's "Health" House, Los Angeles, 1927.

16.11 Eliel Saarinen, Design for the Chicago Tribune Tower, 1922.

of patrons dared to gamble on modern buildings. The Chicago Tribune Tower competition for which Gropius entered his Sullivan-inspired design (see fig. 4.12) also drew the attention of the leading Finnish architect of the period, **Eliel Saarinen** (1873–1950) (fig. **16.11**). His submission for the tower (which won second prize) is nearly as rooted in the Middle Ages as the winning design by Raymond Hood, though it incorporates a greater degree of abstraction in the detailing. At a moment when American builders were turning away from outright revival styles but were not yet prepared to accept radical solutions, Saarinen's qualified modernism had great appeal and influence. Indeed, in his next major building, Hood was himself influenced by Saarinen's Chicago Tribune proposal. Saarinen moved permanently to the United States in 1923. His late works, dating after 1937, were done in collaboration with his son Eero, who became a leading architect in America by mid-century (see fig. 23.43).

One of the most elegant silhouettes of the New York skyline is the Chrysler Building (fig. **16.12**), designed in 1928 by the Beaux-Arts-trained architect **William Van Alen** (1882–1954). The 1046-foot (319 m) building was completed by the end of 1930 and until the spring of 1931, when the Empire State Building reached an altitude of 1250 feet (381 m), lay claim to the title of World's Tallest Building. The structure is a masterpiece of the Art Deco style of modern design that during the twenties had replaced the extravagant curvilinearity of Art Nouveau with more geometrical forms and strong patterns in bold colors. It gradually tapers to a pinnacle made of stainless steel, which is mounted on a stepped, scalloped base. From the sixty-first floor, giant steel gargoyles resembling great American eagles look out over Manhattan. Inside, the building's lobby and elevators are lavish with marble detailing. On the verge of the Depression, the Chrysler Building paid tribute to American commercialism on a grand scale.

The most comprehensive complex of skyscrapers from this period is Rockefeller Center in New York, begun in 1931 and finished in 1939 (fig. **16.13**). The center was proposed by the oil industry magnate John D. Rockefeller, Jr., to house the Metropolitan Opera Company within a large commercial complex. The architect who principally oversaw the Rockefeller Center project in its first stage was **Raymond Hood** (1881–1934). The original plan, completed in 1932, occupied three city blocks and consisted of fourteen buildings, theaters, and open public spaces, with the tall, slender RCA (now GE) Building in the center. After the war the complex expanded to include twenty-one office buildings. Although the original buildings have elements of Gothic Revival detail, these have been simplified or altogether eliminated in the newer buildings of the fifties and sixties. Rockefeller Center is significant not only for its contribution to harmonious, rational skyscraper design, but even more for its planning concept. It embraces large, open areas for pedestrians between the office buildings, many recreational facilities, an elaborate theater (Radio City Music Hall), radio and television studios, a second theater, shops, restaurants, and a skating rink. Few, if any, office complexes in twentieth-century American architecture improved on the total concept of Rockefeller Center. The architects who worked cooperatively on this huge and complicated commission were Reinhard and Hofmeister, with Corbett, Harrison, Harmon and MacMurray, Hood and Fouilhoux. A number of artists were approached (including Matisse and Picasso, though nothing came of it) to decorate the buildings with paintings and large sculpture reliefs. The Mexican painter Diego Rivera (see figs. 18.54, 18.55) was commissioned to paint a mural for the lobby of the RCA Building, but when Rockefeller discovered that the communist artist's depiction of *Man at the Crossroads* included a portrait of Lenin, the mural was covered up and, ultimately, destroyed.

With so many important commissions for commercial office buildings, Hood contributed significantly to the evolution of the skyscraper between 1920 and the early thirties. After his winning entry in 1922 for the Chicago Tribune Tower, Hood designed, with **John Mead Howells** (1868–1959), the 1929–31 Daily News Building (fig. **16.14**) and, with J. André Fouilhoux, the McGraw-Hill Building in New York. In both, the revivalist accretions of previous skyscrapers were stripped off, though neither is entirely free of external decoration. An interesting point about these two buildings is that the architects, realizing the peculiar design problem of the skyscraper—a tall building consisting of horizontal stories—designed the Daily News Building with an accent on the vertical and the McGraw-Hill Building with an accent on the horizontal.

Along with the Philadelphia Savings Fund Society (PSFS) Building by Howe and Lescaze (see fig. 16.15), Hood's buildings were the only skyscrapers included in the 1932 International Style exhibition at The Museum of Modern Art. They are arguably the logical conclusion of Saarinen's Chicago Tribune Tower proposal (see fig. 16.11), with its stepped-back edifice. This kind of "ziggurat" structure, a response to building codes that required a certain amount of light and air above city streets, was perhaps the most characteristic design of the New York tall office building for twenty years after 1930.

A more revolutionary interpretation of the skyscraper than any of those discussed is the PSFS Building,

16.12 William Van Alen, Chrysler Building, New York, 1928–30.

16.13 Reinhard and Hofmeister, Corbett, Harrison, Harmon and MacMurray, Hood and Fouilhoux, Rockefeller Center, New York, 1931–39.

by **George Howe** (1886–1955) and **William Lescaze** (1896–1969) (fig. **16.15**). The PSFS Building is the first fully realized application of the International Style in skyscraper design (and only the second skyscraper in the United States to be fully air-conditioned). Unlike the buildings just discussed, the design of PSFS fully articulated the structure and volume of the building. Hood and Howells's Daily News Building still used heavy masonry sheathing, into which the vertical window strips were deeply recessed. Using a much greater expanse of glass, PSFS ties vertical and horizontal accents together with a light but strong statement of the steel skeleton. The plan of individual floors is a T-shape and embodies a sound understanding of skyscraper planning in its effective segregation of

16.14 Raymond Hood and John Mead Howells, Daily News Building, New York, 1929–31.

16.15 George Howe and William Lescaze, Philadelphia Savings Fund Society Building, Philadelphia, 1929–32.

service from office space. In many ways the PSFS Building is the heir of the Chicago Tribune Tower entry by Gropius and Meyer.

Frank Lloyd Wright During the 1930s

The twenties were difficult for Wright, who turned sixty in 1927. A lack of major commissions resulted in financial hardships, and he spent time lecturing and writing his autobiography. In 1932 he began a fellowship for apprentices at Taliesin, his home in Spring Green, Wisconsin. Despite these numerous setbacks and activities, Wright was entering the most creative phase of his career. He continued to experiment with new architectural forms, including precast concrete blocks, primary in his house designs.

During the thirties, despite the Great Depression, Wright began to secure important commissions and also to make a contribution to the field of low-cost, prefabricated housing with his Usonian houses, as well as to city planning. During the first half of the thirties, when commissions were scarce, he developed his plan for Broadacre City, his ideal concept for an integrated and self-sufficient community of parks, farms, schools, and detached homes made of prefabricated materials to be assembled by each family. Like most such projects, Broadacre City was never realized, but it did enable Wright to clarify his alternatives to current city planning. He felt the modern city destroyed the social fabric, calling it a "parasite of the spirit." While Wright's reformist side motivated him to envision low-cost, prefabricated designs, many of the custom homes he built were for wealthy customers.

His most important realized structures of the thirties were the Fallingwater, the country house that Wright built for Edgar J. Kaufmann at Bear Run, Pennsylvania (fig. **16.16**), and the Administration Building of the S.C. Johnson and Son Company, Racine, Wisconsin (see fig. 16.17). Fallingwater , sited dramatically on a hillside over a waterfall, is one of Wright's most stunning conceptions. Designed as a vacation home for the family of a wealthy merchant and art patron from Pittsburgh, Fallingwater was voted the best building in the United States in 1991 by members of the American Institute of Architects.

In the use of ferroconcrete for the cantilevered terraces and the sense of planar abstraction, Fallingwater has a superficial affinity to the International Style. It is a basic Wright conception, however, for Wright was scornful of much of the machine-inspired architecture of the European modernists who had shaped the International Style (many of whom had been influenced by him). According to Wright, their modern houses "manage to look as though cut from cardboard with scissors ... glued together in box-like forms—in a childish attempt to make buildings resemble steamships, flying machines or locomotives."

Though he embraced the machine and modern materials and technology, Wright designed a house to be, as he said, a "natural feature of the environment." In contrast to many modern architects, Wright often favored the extensive use of wood. There are stylistic affinities between his furniture designs and Arts and Crafts furniture.

At Fallingwater, the adaptation to the landscape exemplifies one of Wright's greatest abilities: to use all the implications of a site, no matter how difficult it might seem. The house was almost literally what Wright called an "extension of the cliff," for it is constructed around several large boulders. The boulders, which act as fulcrums helping to secure the house into the hillside, actually penetrate the walls and were incorporated by Wright as design features inside the house. The central, vertical mass of utilities and chimneys is made of rough, local stone courses (used inside the house as well). It anchors the suspended horizontal forms and contrasts with the smooth, beige-colored concrete of the parapets. The building is particularly effective in its integration of the exterior natural world with the living quarters inside. For example, a glass panel in the living room slides back to access a stairway that leads directly to the stream below the house. With its open plan, low ceilings, and polished flagstone flooring, the interior of Fallingwater

16.16 Frank Lloyd Wright, Edgar K. Kaufmann House (Fallingwater), Bear Run, Pennsylvania, 1934–37.

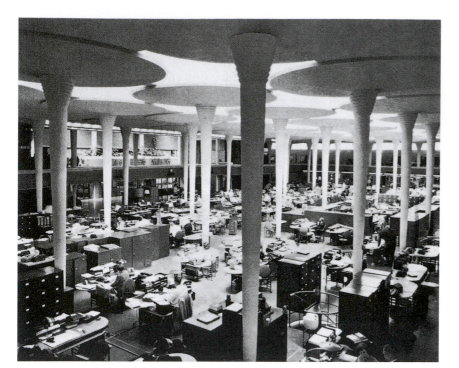

Several of Wright's plans for tall buildings, such as his mile-high skyscraper for Chicago, were never realized. But following the research tower for Racine, he began work on the Price Tower in Bartlesville, Oklahoma (fig. **16.18**), which is actually based on his 1929 design for an apartment building in New York, St. Mark's Tower. It was, for its time, a daring concept: a cruciform "airplane propeller" structural unit sheathed in a glass shell and supporting cantilevered floors. Wright's notion of organic architecture was expressed through the central supporting core with its radiating, cantilevered platforms (as opposed to the standard box-frame construction), a structural scheme he likened to that of a tree. The boldly protruding terraces and soaring utility pylons gave the skyscraper the stylistic signature of its author. Wright continued to work until his death in 1959. His most startling and controversial invention, the Solomon R. Guggenheim Museum in New York, (see chapter 23) belongs to the post-World War II era.

is like a welcoming cave in the middle of the woods. Wright designed virtually every detail inside the house, including most of the furnishings, both built-in and freestanding. The main structure was completed in 1937, and in 1939 a second house for guests and servants was begun. It is connected to the main house by a covered stairway.

The Johnson Administration Building, begun the same year as Fallingwater, inaugurated a new phase in Wright's style and introduced an original solution to the design of the modern workplace. As in his Larkin Building in Buffalo (see fig. 12.5), Wright's goal in Racine was to seal off the interior from the surrounding industrial environment and provide a work space that was, as he said, "as inspiring a place to work in as any cathedral ever was in which to worship." Light floods the large interior space from skylights and a clerestory through tubes of Pyrex glass (fig. **16.17**). From the floor, the magical effect of this top illumination has often been likened to being underwater. The interior is a forest of slender columns tapering at the base like those at the ancient Palace of Minos in Crete. The columns terminate at the top in broad, shallow "lily-pad" capitals that repeat the circular motif throughout. As was the case at Fallingwater, the building authorities mistrusted Wright's calculations; they doubted that the columns could carry the necessary load. It was no surprise to Wright when structural tests proved they could withstand several times the regulated weight. Encouraged by the now sympathetic patron, Wright was able to design all details including desks and office chairs. In the forties, he was commissioned to add a research tower to the complex. The fourteen-story structure is built of the same kind of glass and brick as the main building, with the addition of elegantly rounded corners. At night, the illuminated building, with its broad bands of translucent glass, also made of Pyrex tubes, takes on an ethereal glow.

16.18 Frank Lloyd Wright, H. C. Price Company Tower, Bartlesville, Oklahoma, 1952–56.

17
International Abstraction Between the Wars

Previous chapters have already extensively explored much of the art produced in Europe following World War I, from the de Stijl movement in the Netherlands and Constructivism in Russia (see chapter 11) to the New Objectivity in Germany (see chapter 13) and International Style architecture in Europe and America (see chapter 16). In France, the traumatic upheavals of war produced two powerful but seemingly opposing results—the angst-laden inventions of Surrealism (see chapter 15) and the enduring tradition of classically inspired figurative art (see chapter 14). Paris at this time was also home to the more meditative and formally more radical art of several leading abstract artists, such as the Constructivist sculptor Anton Pevsner and the de Stijl painter Piet Mondrian. Compared to the enduring appeal of classicism and the sensationalism of the Surrealists, abstract art received only limited recognition—Mondrian, for instance, could survive only by painting and selling flower pictures.

After World War I, as the map of Europe was redrawn by the 1919 treaty of Versailles, there was tremendous movement of people across national borders. This resulted in fertile artistic meeting grounds in cities such as Berlin and Paris, which culminated in artistic collaborations such as the Bauhaus in Weimar. Abstraction of an uncompromising sort—especially geometric abstraction—led a migratory, even refugee, existence between the two world wars. After 1921, as official Soviet policy in the arts shunned avant-garde experiments in favor of a more conservative, propagandistic idiom, the mystical Kandinsky and many of the utopian-minded Constructivists fled to the West. In 1930 and 1931 the first-ever groups of artists devoted exclusively to abstract art in all its manifestations were formed in Paris: Cercle et Carré and Abstraction-Création; most of their members were not French. When the original ideals of Russian Constructivism, along with those of Dutch de Stijl, finally found a home, it was at the Bauhaus, which, despite its universalist aspirations and subsequent international influence, was a provincial German outpost (see chapter 16). When, after the Bauhaus closed under Nazi suppression in 1933, Kandinsky moved to Paris, and Naum Gabo took Constructivism to London in 1936, utopianism seemed once again to have proved futile. In the face of the Great Depression in the United States, the Moscow show trials set up by Stalin to eliminate potential opponents, the Spanish Civil War, and the rise of Nazism, many abstract artists abandoned their earlier visions of art in the service of revolution. During the twenties and thirties, meanwhile, the pioneer abstractionists—Gabo, Pevsner, Kandinsky, Mondrian, and the intermittently abstract Klee—grown tough on adversity and indifference, worked quietly but productively apart from the vociferous antics of Breton's Surrealist crowd in Paris.

"The Core from which Everything Emanates": International Constructivism and the Bauhaus

Moholy-Nagy

László Moholy-Nagy (1895–1946) was an important educator and advocate for abstract art, Constructivism, functional design, architecture, and, especially, experimental photography. A Hungarian trained in law, Moholy-Nagy was wounded on the Russian front during World War I, when Austria–Hungary fought—and was ultimately defeated—as part of the Central Powers. During his long convalescence, Moholy-Nagy became interested in painting. In the tumultuous years following the war, the political Left gained momentum in Hungary, resulting in a short-lived revolutionary government until 1919. By the end of that year, with the restoration of a counter-revolutionary regime intolerant of intellectual dissent, Moholy-Nagy left Budapest, first for Vienna, then for Berlin. He soon became a significant force in the remarkably diverse artistic environment of postwar Berlin, which during the twenties was an international crossroads for members of the avant-garde. In Berlin, Moholy-Nagy met the de Stijl artist Theo van Doesburg, as well as the Dadaist Kurt Schwitters and other artists associated with Der Sturm

Gallery. His encounter with the work of avant-garde Russian artists, including Malevich (see fig. 11.19) and El Lissitzky (see figs. 11.20, 11.21, 11.22), triggered an immediate response in his own work, as did his discovery of Naum Gabo's *Realistic Manifesto*, which had been published in a Hungarian communist journal (see chapter 11).

Moholy-Nagy met Bauhaus director Walter Gropius in 1922 at Der Sturm. He made such an impression that Gropius invited him to become a professor in the Weimar Bauhaus, where he taught the important foundation course with Josef Albers. A student, the photographer Paul Citroën (see fig. 17.4), described Moholy-Nagy's arrival: "Like a vigorous, eager dog, Moholy burst into the Bauhaus circle, ferreting out with unfailing scent the still unsolved, still tradition-bound problems in order to attack them." In sharp contrast to the intuitive, mystical teaching methods of his predecessor Johannes Itten, Moholy-Nagy, a committed exponent of the Constructivist alliance of art and technology, stressed objectivity and scientific investigation in the classroom. Until 1928 he was a principal theoretician in applying the Bauhaus concept of art to industry and architecture. Following Gropius's resignation that year, and the ensuing emphasis at the Bauhaus on practical training and industrial production over art and experimentation, Moholy-Nagy left the school. He eventually resided in Amsterdam and London, painting, writing, and making art in all media. In 1937 he was appointed director of the New Bauhaus in Chicago (now a part of the Illinois Institute of Technology). His two principal books, *The New Vision* and *Vision in Motion*, are major documents of the Bauhaus method. His stylistic autobiography, *Abstract of an Artist* (added to the English edition of *The New Vision*), is one of the clearest statements of the modern artist's search for a place in technology and industry.

By 1921 Moholy-Nagy's interests had begun to focus on elements that dominated his creative expression for the rest of his life—light, space, and motion. He explored transparent and malleable materials, the possibilities of abstract photography, and the cinema. Beginning in 1922, Moholy-Nagy pioneered the creation of light-and-motion machines built from reflecting metals and transparent plastics. The first of these kinetic, motor-driven constructions, which he named "light–space modulators," was finally built in 1930 (fig. 17.1). When the machines were set in motion, their reflective surfaces cast light on surrounding forms. During the twenties, Moholy-Nagy was one of the chief progenitors of mechanized kinetic sculpture, but a number of his contemporaries, including Gabo, Tatlin (see fig. 11.25), Rodchenko (see fig. 11.26), and, somewhat later, Alexander Calder (see fig. 17.29), were also exploring movement in sculpture. Moholy-Nagy's legacy can be found in the work of later artists who have exploited light as a medium, including Robert Irwin (see fig. 22.37) and Dan Flavin (see fig. 22.36).

Moholy-Nagy made abstract paintings, clearly influenced by El Lissitzky and Malevich, produced three-

17.1 László Moholy-Nagy, *Light–Space Modulator*, 1922–30. Kinetic sculpture of steel, plastic, wood, and other materials with electric motor, 59½ × 27½ × 27½" (151.1 × 69.9 × 69.9 cm). Busch-Reisinger Museum, Harvard University Art Museums, Cambridge, Massachusetts.

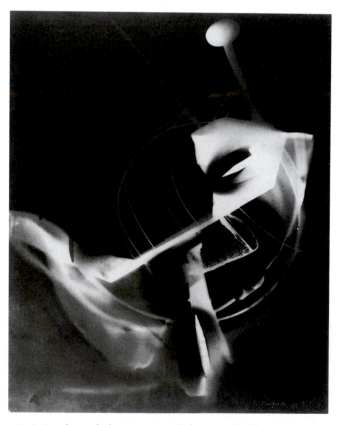

17.2 László Moholy-Nagy, *Untitled*, c. 1940. Photogram, silver bromide print, 20 × 16" (50 × 40 cm). The Art Institute of Chicago.

dimensional constructions, and worked in graphic design. Always alert to ways of exploring the potential of light for plastic expression, Moholy-Nagy also became an adventurous photographer. Apparently unaware of Man Ray's technically identical Rayograms, Moholy-Nagy developed his own cameraless images in 1922, just a few months after Ray. Both artists' discoveries attest to the highly experimental nature of photography in the twenties. Moholy-Nagy and his wife Lucia, who collaborated with him until 1929, called their works "photograms" (fig. **17.2**). However, unlike Man Ray, with his interest in the surreality of images discovered by automatic means, Moholy-Nagy remained true to his Constructivist aesthetic and used the objects placed on light-sensitive paper as "light modulators"—materials for exercises in light. As in the example illustrated, the overlapping, dematerialized shapes of the photogram form abstract compositions that are set in motion purely by the manipulation of light. Moholy-Nagy regarded the camera as an instrument for extending vision and discovering forms otherwise unavailable to the naked eye. In the "new vision" of the world presented in his 1925 Bauhaus book *Malerei Fotografie Film (Painting Photography Film)*, the artist included not only his own photographic works but also scientific, news, and aerial

photographs, all of them presented as works of art. In addition to the abstract photograms, he made photomontages and practiced straight photography. Like Rodchenko (see fig. 11.28), he was partial to sharply angled, vertiginous views that bring to mind the dynamic compositions of Constructivist painting. About his 1928 aerial view taken from Berlin's radio tower (fig. **17.3**), itself a symbol of new technology, Moholy-Nagy wrote: "The receding and advancing values of the black and white, grays and textures, are here reminiscent of the photogram." To him, the camera was a graphic tool equal to any as a means of rendering reality and disclosing its underlying purity of form. And so he wrote in a frequently quoted statement: "the illiterate of the future will be ignorant of camera and pen alike."

Like the Dada artists, the Constructivists found photomontage a fertile process. Although they often produced effects similar to those of the Dadaists, the Constructivists' purposes in juxtaposing images—altogether various in context, subject, scale, proportion, and tonal value—were quite different. They usually related to propagandistic or formal problems, rather than to a search for dissonance, mystery, or subversion (see figs. 13.27, 13.28).

Citroën

Bauhaus photographer **Paul Citroën** (1896–1983) composed his famous 1923 photomontage *Metropolis* (fig. **17.4**) by cutting and pasting. Within the large thirty-

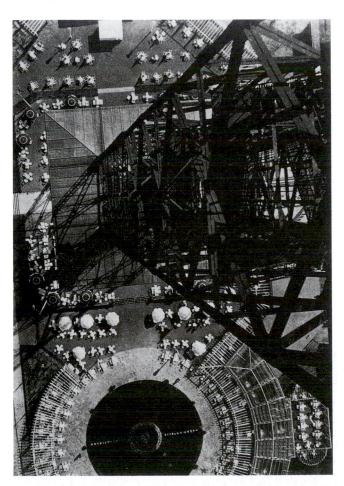

17.3 László Moholy-Nagy, *Untitled* (looking down from the Radio Tower, Berlin), c. 1928. Gelatin-silver print, 14¼ × 10" (36.2 × 25.6 cm). The Art Institute of Chicago, Julien Levy Collection.

17.4 Paul Citroën, *Metropolis*, 1923. Collage, printed matter, and postcards, 30 × 23" (76.2 × 58.4 cm). Printroom of the University of Leiden, the Netherlands.

by-forty-inch (76 × 101 cm) format, Citroën crushed together such a towering mass of urban imagery that Moholy-Nagy called it "a gigantic sea of masonry," stabilized, however, by Constructivism's controlling principle of abstract design.

Gabo

Following his departure from Russia in 1922, where the abstract art he had helped to evolve (see fig. 255) proved incompatible with the utilitarian policies of the Soviet regime, **Naum Gabo** (1890–1977) lived in Germany until 1932, perfecting his Constructivist sculpture and contributing significantly, though indirectly, to Moholy-Nagy's ideas on light, space, and movement at the Bauhaus. Though not a member of the Bauhaus faculty, Gabo lectured there in 1928, published an important article in *Bauhaus* magazine, and was in contact with several Bauhaus artists. In 1922 eight of his sculptures were included in a huge exhibition of Russian art that traveled to Berlin and Amsterdam, helping to bring his work and that of other Russian abstract artists to an international audience. Like Moholy-Nagy, Gabo was a major practitioner of Constructivism in many media. At the same time, both artists demonstrated how the formal aspects of Constructivism were assimilated in the West without its political associations with the early, idealistic phase of communist revolution. As we saw in chapter 11, while Gabo sympathized with the initial aims of the revolution in Russia, he did not harness his art to specific ideas of collectivism and utilitarianism. Nevertheless, he shared Moholy-Nagy's utopian belief in the transformative powers of art. He encouraged modern artists to look to technology and the machine for forms and materials to express appropriately the aims of the new social order.

In Germany, Gabo continued the research he had begun in Russia. He explored the possibilities of new artistic media, particularly glass and recently developed plastic materials such as celluloid, to exploit a sense of planar transparency in his sculpture. For Diaghilev's 1927 ballet *La Chatte*, Gabo and his brother Antoine Pevsner (see below) designed a set filled with large, geometric sculptures in a transparent material that shone, in the words of one observer, with "quicksilver radiance." In 1931, Gabo took part in the international competition for the Palace of Soviets, a never-realized building that was to be a proud symbol in Moscow of the new Soviet Union. Several architects from the West also took part, including Le Corbusier and Gropius. Gabo, who had been searching for a form of architectural expression through his constructed sculpture, proposed a daring, winged structure of reinforced concrete.

In 1932, after Nazi stormtroopers came to his studio, Gabo left Germany for Paris, where he was active in the Abstraction-Création group, organized partly as an antidote to the influence of Surrealism. His next move was to England, where between 1936 and 1946 he was active in the circle of abstract artists centering on Herbert Read,

Ben Nicholson (see fig. 17.32), Barbara Hepworth (see fig. 17.36), and Henry Moore (see fig. 17.34). Thereafter Gabo lived in the United States until his death in 1977.

Gabo's principal innovation of the forties was a construction in which webs of taut nylon string were attached to interlocking sheets of Perspex, a clear plastic first marketed in 1935 (fig. **17.5**). Over many years, Gabo made several versions of *Linear Construction in Space, No. 1* on different scales. In these he attained a transparent delicacy and weightlessness unprecedented in sculpture. Like a drawing in space, the nylon filaments reflect light and gracefully articulate the void as positive form, transforming the space, according to Gabo, into a "malleable material element." Though probably not a direct influence on Gabo, Henry Moore had created abstract sculptures incorporating tautly stretched string as of 1937, and Barbara Hepworth followed with her own examples a few years later (see fig. 17.36).

After emigrating to the United States in 1946, Gabo was able to realize his ambition to create large-scale public sculpture. His major architectural–sculptural commission was his 1956–57 monument for the new Bijenkorf department store in Rotterdam (fig. **17.6**), designed by the Bauhaus architect Marcel Breuer. The store was part of a massive postwar campaign to rebuild the city, which had been devastated by German bombs in 1940. Gabo's solution for the busy urban site was a soaring, open structure consisting of curving steel shafts that frame an inner

17.5 Naum Gabo, *Linear Construction in Space, No. 1 (Variation)*, conceived 1942–43 (possibly executed 1948). Plastic and nylon thread, 24½ × 24½" (62.2 × 62.2 cm). The Phillips Collection, Washington, D.C.

17.6 Naum Gabo, Construction for the Bijenkorf department store, Rotterdam, the Netherlands, 1956–57. Pre-stressed concrete, steel ribs, stainless steel, bronze wire, and marble, height 85' (25.9 m).

17.7 Antoine Pevsner, *Projection into Space*, 1938–39. Bronze and oxidized copper, 21½ × 15¾ × 19½" (54.6 × 40 × 50.2 cm). Private collection, Switzerland.

abstract construction made of bronze wire and steel. Gabo likened the sculpture, with its tremendous weight anchored in the ground, to the form of a tree.

Pevsner

Unlike his younger brother Gabo, **Antoine Pevsner** (1886–1962) never taught at the Bauhaus, although he did, like Gabo, work within the Constructivist tradition. Pevsner left Russia in 1923 and settled permanently in Paris, where he exhibited with his brother in 1924. At this time he began to work seriously in abstract constructed sculpture. Commissioned by the Société Anonyme in 1926 (see chapter 13), his *Portrait of Marcel Duchamp* is an open plastic construction with obvious connections to Gabo's *Constructed Head No. 1* of 1915. By the end of the twenties, however, Pevsner had nearly abandoned construction in transparent plastics in favor of abstract sculpture in bronze or copper. In 1932 he joined the Abstraction-Création group in Paris and, like Gabo, contributed to their journal.

In his 1938–39 *Projection into Space* (fig. **17.7**), Pevsner realized his idea of "developable surface" or sculpture realized from a single, continuously curving plane. *Projection into Space* is polished bronze, not cast but hammered out to machine precision. Despite the geometric precision of his work, Pevsner denied any mathematical basis in its

organization. The structure of *Projection into Space* invites viewing from multiple vantage points, carrying the eye of the spectator around the perimeter, while the dynamic, spiraling planes give the illusion of movement in a static design. This quality was explored in such Futurist sculptures as Boccioni's *Development of a Bottle in Space* (see fig. 11.9), but the elimination of all representation in Pevsner's work heightens the sense of dynamism.

Pevsner carried out several large architectural commissions. The *Dynamic Projection in the 30th Degree* at the University of Caracas, Venezuela, enlarged from a smaller bronze version, is more than eight feet (2.43 m) high. This sculpture centers around a sweeping diagonal form that thrusts out from the center at a thirty-degree angle from the compressed waist of the vertical, hourglass construction. In this form, Pevsner combines solidity of shape with the freedom of a vast pennant seemingly held rigid by the force of a tornado wind.

Albers

After Johannes Itten left the Bauhaus in 1923, the foundation course was given by Moholy-Nagy and German artist **Josef Albers** (1888–1976), each teaching in accordance with his own ideas. After studying widely in Germany, Albers entered the Bauhaus as a student and, in 1923, was

17.8 Josef Albers, *City*, 1928. Sandblasted colored glass, 11 × 21⅝" (27.9 × 54.9 cm). Kunsthaus, Zürich.

appointed to the faculty. While at the Bauhaus he met and married Anni Fleischmann, a gifted textile artist. In addition to his work in the foundation course, Albers taught furniture design and headed the glass workshop. He remained on the Bauhaus faculty until its closure in 1933, when he emigrated to the United States. Thanks to the efforts of the American architect Philip Johnson, then a curator at The Museum of Modern Art in New York, Albers was offered a position at Black Mountain College, an experimental school in North Carolina. From the time of his arrival in 1933 he became a major influence in the training of American artists, architects, and designers. After leaving Black Mountain College in 1949, Albers continued to exert his influence on art students at Yale, where he taught from 1950 to 1960.

17.9 Josef Albers, *Homage to the Square: Apparition*, 1959. Oil on board, 47½ × 47½" (120.7 × 120.7 cm). Solomon R. Guggenheim Museum, New York.

Albers's early apprenticeship in a stained-glass workshop contributed to his lifelong interest in problems of light and color within geometric formats. In his glass paintings of the twenties one can observe the transition from organic, free-form compositions of glass fragments to grid patterns, as in *City* (fig. **17.8**), in which the relations of each color strip to all the others are meticulously calculated. To create these compositions, Albers invented a painstaking technique of sandblasting and painting thin layers of opaque glass, which he then baked in a kiln to achieve a hard, radiant surface. The title of this work highlights its resemblance to an International Style skyline. In fact, Albers adapted this composition in 1963 for a fifty-four-foot-wide (16.4 m) mural, which he called *Manhattan*, that was commissioned for New York's Pan Am Building. The precise geometry and industrial methods of Albers's work had special relevance for the sixties, when impersonal, hard-edge Minimalism and Op art (see figs. 22.28, 22.41) were gaining momentum over the painterly emotionality of Abstract Expressionism.

Throughout the forties, Albers developed his increasingly reductive vocabulary with remarkable assiduity, exploring issues of perception, illusionism, and the often ambiguous interaction of abstract pictorial elements. Beginning in 1950 he settled on the formula that he entitled *Homage to the Square*, where he relentlessly explored the relationships of color squares confined within squares. For the next twenty-five years, in a seemingly endless number of harmonious color combinations, Albers employed the strict formula of *Homage to the Square* in paintings and prints of many sizes. Within this format, the full, innermost square is, in the words of one observer, "like a seed; the heart of the matter, the core from which everything emanates." As *Apparition*, a 1959 *Homage to the Square* subtitle suggests (fig. **17.9**), Albers's goal was to expose the "discrepancy between physical fact and psychic effect." The interior square is not centered, but rather positioned near the bottom of the canvas. According to a predetermined asymmetry, the size of the color bands at the bottom is doubled on each side of the square and tripled at the top. By restricting himself to this format, Albers sought to demonstrate the subtle perceptual ambiguities that occur when bands of pure color are juxtaposed. Colors may advance or recede according to their own intrinsic hue and in response to their neighbor, or they may even appear to mix optically with adjacent colors. And by the painted miter effect, seen here on the outermost corners, the artist creates a sense of illusionistic depth on a flat surface.

Schlemmer

German artist **Oskar Schlemmer** (1888–1943) taught design, sculpture, and mural painting at the Bauhaus from 1920 to 1929. During his years at the Bauhaus, Schlemmer's real passion was theater. In 1923 he was appointed director of theater activities at the school. He then moved with the Bauhaus from Weimar to its new Dessau location in 1925 and set up the experimental Theater Workshop. Schlemmer's art—whether painting, sculpture, or the costumes he designed for his theatrical productions—was centered on the human body. While he applied the forms of the machine to the figure, he emphasized the need to strike a balance between humanist interests and the growing veneration at the Bauhaus for technology and the machine.

For his best-known performance, *The Triadic Ballet*, Schlemmer encased the dancers in colored, geometric shapes made from wood, metal, and cardboard. Designed to limit the range of the dancers' movements, the costumes transformed the performers into abstracted, kinetic sculptures. Indeed, for exhibition purposes, Schlemmer mounted his "spatial–plastic" costumes as sculptures. As can be seen in his collage *Study for The Triadic Ballet* (fig. **17.10**), Schlemmer envisioned the stage as an abstract, gridded space through which the performers

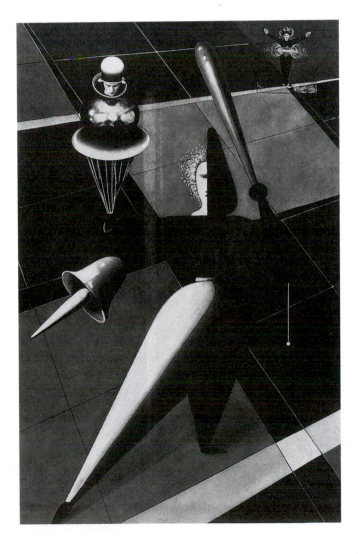

17.10 Oskar Schlemmer, *Study for The Triadic Ballet*, c. 1921–23. Gouache, brush and ink, incised enamel, and pasted photographs on paper, 22⅝ × 14⅝" (57.5 × 37.1 cm). The Museum of Modern Art, New York.

17.11 Oskar Schlemmer, *Abstract Figure*, 1923. Bronze (cast 1962 from original plaster), 42⅛ × 26⅜" (107 × 67 cm). Collection Frau Tut Schlemmer, Stuttgart.

Baumeister

Like Schlemmer, **Willi Baumeister** (1889–1955) was a pupil of Adolf Hoelzel at the Stuttgart Academy. He collaborated with both artists on a mural project in 1914 and frequently exhibited with Schlemmer in Germany. Throughout the interwar years, he was in contact with an international group of artists ranging from Le Corbusier and Léger to Malevich and Moholy-Nagy. He exhibited in Paris in the twenties, and became a member of Cercle et Carré and Abstraction-Création during 1930 and 1931. Although he never served on the Bauhaus faculty, he associated with several artists at the school and contributed to its magazine.

Baumeister's mature work was affected by Cubism and Purism as well as by Schlemmer's machine-based figurative style. Following World War I, during which he served in the German army, Baumeister made a series of shallow relief constructions called *Mauerbilder* (wall pictures). In one example from 1923 (fig. **17.12**), geometric forms surround a highly schematized figure. While some of these forms are painted directly on the wooden support, others are sections of wood that have been applied to the surface. A decade earlier, Archipenko, whose work was no doubt known to Baumeister, was experimenting with similar techniques in Paris (see fig. 10.30). With its futuristic vision, Baumeister's composition is also reminiscent of

moved according to mathematically precise choreography. The deep perspective space depicted here is similar to that of Schlemmer's paintings from this period. *The Triadic Ballet* was first performed in 1922 in the artist's native Stuttgart and was subsequently presented in several European cities.

Most of Schlemmer's sculptures were polychromed relief constructions, but in 1923 he made two freestanding sculptures, one of which was the original plaster for *Abstract Figure* (fig. **17.11**). For this large, imposing torso, Schlemmer sought the same clarity of form and geometric precision that he brought to his theatrical designs. With its gleaming surfaces and streamlined forms, the sculpture shines like the chassis of a new automobile.

Gropius's replacement as director, Hannes Meyer, increasingly politicized the curriculum at the Bauhaus and stressed practical, industrial training over artistic production. This trend eventually led to Schlemmer's resignation. Not long after Schlemmer left the Bauhaus in 1929, the Nazis destroyed the murals and wall reliefs he had executed for the workshop building at Weimar. Despite repeated Nazi assaults on his reputation for creating "degenerate" and "Bolshevist" art, Schlemmer remained in Germany until his death in 1943.

17.12 Willi Baumeister, *Wall Picture with Circle II*, 1923. Oil and wood on wood panel, 46½ × 27⅛" (118 × 69 cm). Hamburger Kunsthalle.

Léger's great painting *The City* (see fig. 10.42). By the early thirties, organic shapes appeared among the artist's machine forms, evidence of his interest in the Surrealism of Joan Miró and the paintings of Paul Klee. In such works as *Stone Garden I*, Baumeister added a textural element by building up his surfaces sculpturally with sand and plaster. During the Nazi regime, when he was branded a "degenerate artist," Baumeister painted in secret, advancing his own ideas toward freer abstraction—ideograms with elusive suggestions of figures. These signs came from the artist's imagination, but were based on his studies of the art of ancient civilizations, such as Mesopotamia.

Klee

Introduced earlier in the context of Der Blaue Reiter (see chapter 8), **Paul Klee** (1879–1940) served in the German army in World War I immediately after the breakup of the group in 1914. In 1920 Gropius invited him to join the staff of the Bauhaus at Weimar, and he remained affiliated with the school from 1921 to 1931, an enormously productive period for Klee. Becoming a teacher prompted the artist to examine the tenets of his own painting. It also strengthened his resolve to discover and elaborate rational systems for the creation of pictorial form. He recorded his theories in his copious notes and in publications of great significance for modern art, including his 1925 Bauhaus book, *Pedagogical Sketchbook*.

Klee's art, as differentiated from that of Mondrian or even of Kandinsky in his later phase, was always rooted in nature and was seldom completely abstract. Klee's abstract works mainly date from his Bauhaus years, when he was especially close to Kandinsky and to the traditions of Russian Suprematism and Constructivism and Dutch de Stijl. He drew upon his great storehouse of naturalistic observations as his raw material, but his paintings were never based on immediately observed nature except in his early works and sketchbook notations. Yet even his abstract paintings have a pulsating energy that appears organic rather than geometric, seemingly evolved through a natural process of dynamic growth and transformation.

In both his teaching and his art, Klee wanted to bring about a harmonious convergence of the architectonic and the poetic. With their heightened emphasis on geometric structure and abstract form, Klee's paintings and drawings (he saw no need to distinguish between the two) from the Bauhaus years reveal formal influences from his Constructivist colleagues. Yet Klee was above all an individualist. However much he absorbed from the Bauhaus Constructivists, his poetic and intuitive inventions provided a counterweight to the more scientific and objective efforts at the school.

Like Mondrian and Kandinsky, Klee was concerned in his teachings and his painting with the geometric elements of the work of art—the point, the line, the plane, the solid. To him, however, these elements had a primary basis in nature and growth. It was the process of change from one

to the other that fascinated him. To Klee, a painting continually grew and changed in time as well as in space. In the same way, color was neither a simple means of establishing harmonious relationships, nor a method of creating space in the picture. Color was energy. It was emotion that established the mood of the painting within which the line established the action.

Klee saw the creative act as a magical experience in which the artist was enabled in moments of illumination to combine an inner vision with an outer experience of the world, to create an image that was parallel to and capable of illuminating the essence of nature. Although it grew out of the traditions of Romanticism and specifically of Symbolism (see chapter 3), Klee's art represented a new departure. He believed that his inner truth, his inner vision, was revealed not only in the subject, the color, and the shapes as defined entities, but even more in the very process of creation. To start the creative process, Klee, a consummate draftsman, would begin to draw like a child; he said children, like the insane and "primitive" peoples, had the "power to see." He let the pencil or brush lead him until the image began to emerge. As it did, of course, his conscious experience and skills came back into play in order to carry the first intuitive image to a satisfactory conclusion. At this point, some other association, recollection, or fantasy would result in the poetic and often amusing titles that then became part of the total work. Because he placed such value on inner vision and the intuitive process of drawing, Klee's methods and theories had affinities with the automatist techniques of the Surrealists, who claimed him as a pioneer and included his work in their first exhibition in Paris in 1925. When two leading Surrealists, Masson and Miró, discovered Klee's art in 1922, they regarded the experience as one of great importance for their own work.

Klee discovered much of his iconography through teaching. As he used arrows to indicate lines of force for his students, these arrows began to creep into his work, where they are both formal elements and mysterious vectors of emotion. Color charts, perspective renderings, graphs, rapidly drawn heads, plant forms, linear patterns, checkerboards—elements of all descriptions became part of that reservoir of subconscious visual experience, which the artist then would transform into magical imagery. Usually working on a small scale in a deliberately naive rendition, Klee scattered or floated these elements in an ambiguous space composed of delicate and subtle harmonies of color and light that add mystery and strangeness to the concept. *Dance, Monster, to My Soft Song!* shows a mad-eyed, purple-nosed head on an infinitesimal body floating above a tiny pianist, a childlike drawing integrated with the most sophisticated gradations of yellow ocher and umber.

During the twenties, Klee produced a series of black pictures in which he used the oil medium, sometimes combined with watercolor. Some of these were dark underwater scenes where fish swam through the depths of the

17.13 Paul Klee, *Around the Fish*, 1926. Oil on canvas, 18⅜ × 25⅛" (46.7 × 63.8 cm). The Museum of Modern Art, New York.

ocean surrounded by exotic plants, abstract shapes, and sometimes strange little human figures. These works, including *Around the Fish* (fig. **17.13**), are Surrealist in tone, embodying an arrangement of irrelevant objects, some mathematical, some organic. Here the precisely delineated fish on the oval purple platter is surrounded by objects: some machine forms, some organic, some emblematic. A schematic head on the upper left grows on a long stem from a container that might be a machine and is startled to be met head-on by a red arrow attached to the fish by a thin line. A full and a crescent moon, a red dot, a green cross, and an exclamation point are scattered throughout the black sky—or ocean depth—in which all these disparate signs and objects float. This mysterious, nocturnal still life typifies Klee's personal language of hieroglyphs and his use of natural forms merely as a point of departure into a fantastic realm. "The object grows beyond its appearance through our knowledge of its inner being," he wrote, "through the knowledge that the thing is more than its outward aspect suggests."

17.14 Paul Klee, *In the Current Six Thresholds*, 1929. Oil and tempera on canvas, 17⅛ × 17⅛" (43.5 × 43.5 cm). Solomon R. Guggenheim Museum, New York.

17.15 Paul Klee, *Ad Parnassum*, 1932. Oil and casein on canvas, 39⅜ × 49⅝" (100 × 126 cm). Kunstmuseum Bern, Society of Friends of Kustmuseum Bern.

Made during Klee's Bauhaus years, *In the Current Six Thresholds* (fig. **17.14**) is an arrangement of vertical and horizontal rectangles, in which gradations of deep color are contained within precisely ruled lines. Yet the total effect is organic rather than geometric, dynamic rather than static, with the bands continuing to divide as they move leftward. This and several similar abstract compositions of brilliantly colored strata were inspired by Klee's trip to Egypt in 1928–29 and are a response to the vast expanse and intense light of the desert landscape. Most of Klee's paintings were in combinations of ink and watercolor, media appropriate to the delicate quality of fluidity that he sought; but this particular work combines oil and tempera, media he used to obtain effects of particular richness and density.

Desiring more time for his art and frustrated by the demands of teaching and the growing politicization within the Dessau Bauhaus, Klee left the school in 1931 and took a less demanding position at the Dusseldorf Academy. During the early thirties, he applied his own variety of Neo-Impressionism in several compositions, culminating in a monumental painting from 1932, *Ad Parnassum* (fig. **17.15**). Klee covered the canvas with patterns of thick, brightly colored daubs of paint. These are marshaled

into distinctive forms by way of a few strong lines that conjure up a pyramid beneath a powerful sun. Like Kandinsky, Klee believed that pictorial composition was analogous to music and that sound can "form a synthesis with the world of appearances." Both he and his wife were musicians, and he applied the principals of musical composition, with all its discipline and mathematical precision, to his paintings and to his teaching. The title of this majestic work derives from a famous eighteenth-century treatise on musical counterpoint called, in Latin, *Gradus ad Parnassum (Stairway to Parnassus)*, Parnassus being a mountain sacred to the Greek god Apollo and the Muses. Klee orchestrated color and line in his painting according to his own system of pictorial polyphony, creating a luminous, harmonious vision aimed at elevating the viewer into a higher, Parnassian realm.

In 1933, the year Hitler assumed power in Germany, Klee was dismissed from his position at the Dusseldorf Academy and returned to his native Bern in Switzerland. Figures, faces (sometimes only great peering eyes), fantastic landscapes, and architectural structures (sometimes menacing) continued to appear in his art during the thirties. Perhaps the principal characteristic of Klee's late works was his use of bold and free black linear patterns against a colored field. One of his last works, *Death and Fire* (fig. **17.16**), 1940, is executed with brutal simplicity, thinly painted on an irregular section of rough burlap. The rudimentary drawing, like the scrawl of a child, delineates

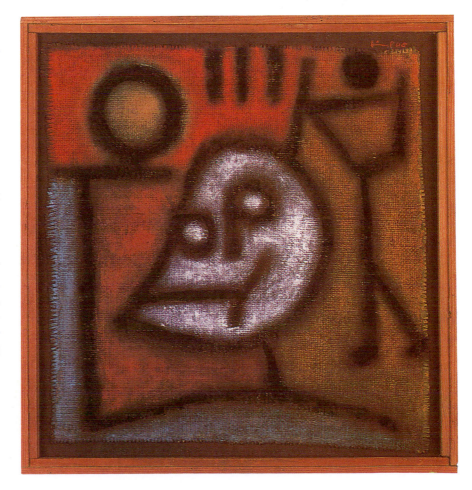

17.16 Paul Klee, *Death and Fire*, 1940. Oil drawing in black paste on burlap, surrounded by colored paste ground, mounted on burlap, 18⅛ × 17¼" (46 × 43.8 cm). Kunstmuseum Bern.

a harrowing, spectral image, expressive perhaps of the burdens of artistic isolation, debilitating illness, and the imminent threats of war and totalitarianism. Unlike so many other members of the European avant-garde, Klee, who died within months of the war's outbreak, did not emigrate to the United States. However, his work became known to American audiences and especially to American artists through several exhibitions held throughout the thirties and forties.

Kandinsky

Vasily Kandinsky (1866–1944) renewed his friendship with Klee when he returned to Germany from Russia in 1921, and in 1922 he joined the Weimar Bauhaus. One of the school's most distinguished faculty members, he taught a course called Theory of Form and headed the workshop of mural painting (regarded as superior to traditional easel painting at the school). Kandinsky's style underwent significant changes during his tenure at the Bauhaus. While he still adhered to the mystical Theosophical beliefs expressed in his seminal book from 1911, *Concerning the Spiritual in Art*, he had come to value form over color as a vehicle for expression, and his paintings evolved toward a more objective formal vocabulary. Even before coming to the Bauhaus, under the influence of Russian Suprematism

and Constructivism, Kandinsky's painting had turned gradually from free expressionism to a form of geometric abstraction. This evolution is evident in *White Line, No. 232* (see fig. 11.23), a painting Kandinsky made in 1920 while still in Russia, which, despite expressive brushwork, contains clearly defined geometric and organic forms.

By 1923, in *Composition VIII* (fig. **17.17**), hard-edged shapes had taken over. As discussed in chapter 8, Kandinsky regarded the works that he named *Compositions* as the fullest expression of his art. Ten years had elapsed between *Composition VII*, 1913 (see fig. 8.18) and *Composition VIII*, and a comparison of the two paintings elucidates the changes that had taken place during this period. The deeply saturated colors and tumultuous collision of painterly forms in the 1913 picture are here replaced by clearly delineated shapes—circles, semicircles, open triangles, and straight lines—that float on a delicately modulated background of blue and creamy beige. The emotional climate of the later painting is far less heated than that of its predecessor, and its rationally ordered structure suggests that harmony has superseded the apocalyptic upheavals that inhabit the artist's prewar paintings.

Kandinsky fervently believed that abstract forms were invested with great significance and expressive power, and the spiritual basis of his abstract forms set him apart from

17.17 Vasily Kandinsky, *Composition VIII*, 1923. Oil on canvas, 55⅛ × 79⅛" (140 × 201 cm). Solomon R. Guggenheim Museum, New York.

Bauhaus teachers like Moholy-Nagy. "The contact of the acute angle of a triangle with a circle," he wrote, "is no less powerful in its effect than that of the finger of God with the finger of Adam in Michelangelo's [*Creation of Man*] painting." The circle, in particular, was filled with "inner potentialities" for the artist, and it took on a prominent role in his work of the twenties. In *Several Circles, No. 323* (fig. **17.18**), the transparent color circles float serenely across one another above an indeterminate, gray-black ground, like planets orbiting through space. It is hardly surprising that the artist revered the circle as a "link with the cosmic" and as a form that "points most clearly to the fourth dimension."

In 1926 Kandinsky published, as a Bauhaus book, *Point and Line to Plane*, his textbook for a course in composition. As compared with Klee's *Pedagogical Sketchbook* of the previous year, Kandinsky's book attempts a more absolute definition of the elements of a work of art and their relations to one another and to the whole. Here the artist affirmed the spiritual basis

17.19 Vasily Kandinsky, *Composition IX, No. 626*, 1936. Oil on canvas, 3'8⅝" × 6'4¾" (1.13 × 1.9 m). Musée National d'Art Moderne, Paris.

of his art, and his correspondence of the time reveals a combination of the pragmatic and the mystical.

Kandinsky continued his association with the Bauhaus until the school was closed in 1933. At the end of that year he moved permanently to Paris, where he was soon involved in the Abstraction-Création group, and became friendly with Miró, Arp, and Pevsner. This new environment heightened Kandinsky's awareness of the Surrealist activities of the twenties, and one senses certain qualities akin to abstract Surrealism in the many works created after his move to France.

In general Kandinsky moved toward freer, more biomorphic shapes and colors in the final years of his life. The lyrical, coloristic aspect of his painting began to resurface in Paris and to merge with the architectonic approach of his Bauhaus paintings. The edges of forms remained sharp, but their shapes seem to have emerged from a microscopic world. Such imagery probably stems from the artist's interest in biology and embryonic life forms as symbols of life and regeneration. In *Composition IX, No. 626*, 1936 (fig. **17.19**), one of his two final *Compositions*, Kandinsky geometrically structured the canvas by painting identical triangles at either end and, in between, a parallelogram subdivided into four smaller identical parallelograms. On this rigidly defined ground he scattered a free assortment of little dancing shapes: circles, checkerboard squares, long, narrow rectangles, and amoebalike figures. Kandinsky made his forms translucent—we can read ground colors beneath overlapping shapes—and his palette is a vivid array of candy-colored pastels. This device of playing small, free forms against a large geometric pattern intrigued the artist during these years. The contrast of freedom and control in Kandinsky's late work came from his lifelong concentration on the relations between intuitive expression and calculated abstract form.

A Determined Minority: Abstract Artists in Paris

During the twenties in France, abstract painting and sculpture were largely imported products, struggling for survival against the influences of the classical revival or "call to order" that swept the country between the wars; older modernists who worked in figurative modes (namely Matisse, Picasso, and the Cubist school painters); and the sensation created by the Surrealists. Of the Cubists, Robert Delaunay, one of the pioneers of abstraction (see fig. 10.43), turned to Cubist figuration, returning to abstract painting and sculpture only after 1930. Léger, too, painted a number of abstract architectural murals during the twenties, although he continued to be wary of pure abstraction (see chapter 10). The place of abstraction in France differed considerably from its centrality in German avant-garde production. Partly due to the Bauhaus, partly due to French artists' tenacious hold on their own classical traditions, Dutch de Stijl and Russian Constructivism and Suprematism exerted far les influence in France than in Germany. When the de Stijl artists held an exhibition in 1923 at the gallery of Léonce Rosenberg, it aroused little general interest, although it had an immediate impact on Léger's work. Mondrian, then living in Paris, found no French buyers for his abstract work.

Groups and Journals

In 1925, the same year as the first Surrealist exhibition, a large exhibition of contemporary art was organized in Paris by a Polish painter, Victor-Yanaga Poznanski, at the hall of the Antique Dealers Syndicate. Among those included were Arp, Baumeister, Brancusi, the pioneer American abstractionist Patrick Henry Bruce, Robert and Sonia Delaunay, Van Doesburg, Goncharova, Gris, Klee, Larionov, Léger, Miró, Moholy-Nagy, Mondrian, Ben Nicholson, Ozenfant, and Jacques Villon. The stated purpose of the exhibition was "not to show examples of every tendency in contemporary painting, but to take stock, as completely as circumstances permit, of what is going on in non-imitative plastic art, the possibility of which was first conceived of by the Cubist movement." Although there were obvious omissions, such as the Czech Kupka, one of the first abstract painters in Paris (see fig. 10.46), this was a surprisingly comprehensive showing of international abstract tendencies. In the face of the rising tides of representation and Surrealism, however, it did not attract wide attention. In addition, Albert Gleizes, a primary force behind the show, had hoped to demonstrate that Cubism was not only the great progenitor of the various forms of abstraction but was still a vital force in avant-garde art; instead, the late Cubists were overshadowed by the foreign innovators.

The next major development in the history of abstraction in Paris came in 1930, when Theo van Doesburg and the French artist Jean Hélion founded the group Art Concret, devoted to hard-edged abstraction, and the artist–critic Michel Seuphor and the Uruguayan painter Joaquín Torres-García founded a rival group and periodical entitled Cercle et Carré (Circle and Square). There were few French participants in the first exhibition of Cercle et Carré, held in April 1930 on the ground floor of the building in which Picasso lived. They included Arp (in favor with both Surrealists and many abstractionists), Baumeister, Jean Gorin (a new French disciple of Mondrian), Kandinsky, Le Corbusier, Léger, Mondrian, Ozenfant, Pevsner, Schwitters, the American Futurist Joseph Stella, Sophie Taeuber-Arp, and Torres-García. Also shown, according to Seuphor, but not in the catalogue, were Moholy-Nagy, Hans Richter, and Raoul Hausmann.

The periodical and the exhibition, although short-lived, had a considerable impact. Their impetus and their mailing lists were taken over by Vantongerloo and Auguste Herbin, upon the formation in 1931 of a comparable group, Abstraction-Création, with a periodical in 1932 of the same name. Abstraction-Création, both in its exhibitions and its publications, was a force for abstract art until 1936, standing against the repressive regimes in Germany and Russia, which were inhospitable toward the innovations of the avant-garde. The group embraced a broad spectrum of abstract styles but lacked the shared utopian outlook that had unified members within the earliest groups devoted to abstraction. In the thirties, the rise of Nazism in Germany brought more practitioners of abstraction to Paris, where they joined artists from Russia, Holland, and other countries. By the mid-thirties, despite the general coolness of the French to geometric abstraction, Abstraction-Création sometimes had as many as four hundred members—from Suprematism, Constructivism, de Stijl, and their many offshoots.

Herbin

Auguste Herbin (1882–1960) had pursued a long, slow path toward abstraction through Fauvism and Cubism until 1920. During the early twenties he returned, like so many others, to representation, but by the end of that decade his work had again become abstract, remaining so until his death. Stimulated in part by the examples of Kupka (see fig. 10.46) and Delaunay (see fig. 10.44), and supported by his involvement with Abstraction-Création, Herbin devoted himself to an abstract syntax of curved lines and circular movements. Throughout the thirties he painted brightly colored arabesques in a flat, hard-edge style (fig. **17.20**).

Mondrian

Piet Mondrian (1872–1944), whose evolution to pure abstraction through Cubism was discussed in chapter 11, lived in Paris between 1919 and 1938 and was by far the city's most influential figure in abstract painting. Although he did not take the initiative in the organization of Cercle et Carré or Abstraction-Création, his presence and participation were of the greatest significance for the growth and spread of abstraction. As already noted, he had resigned

from de Stijl in 1925 after disagreements with Van Doesburg about the nature of de Stijl architecture (though the artists reconciled in 1929). While Mondrian envisioned, like his de Stijl colleagues, the integration of all the arts, he fervently believed, unlike some, in the superiority of painting. A prolific writer and theoretician, Mondrian fully formulated his ideas during the twenties and, in the last decade of his life, during which he moved from Paris to New York (where he died in 1944), he produced some of the greatest work of his career.

In evaluating the course of geometric abstraction from its beginnings, in about 1911, to the present time, an understanding of Mondrian's role is of paramount importance. He was the principal figure in the founding of geometric abstraction during World War I, for the ideas of de Stijl and their logical development were primarily his achievement. Mondrian's influence extended not only to abstract painting and sculpture but also to the forms of the International Style in architecture. Through the teachings of the Bauhaus in Germany and its offshoots in the United States, his theories were spread throughout the Western world. During the twenties and thirties in Paris it was probably the presence and inspiration of Mondrian more than any other single person that enabled abstraction to survive and gradually to gain strength—in the face of the revolution of Surrealism and the counterrevolution of representation, as well as economic depression, threats of dictatorship, and war.

In 1920, with his first full-fledged painting based on the principles of Neo-Plasticism (meaning roughly "new image" or "new form"), Mondrian had found his solution to a long unsolved problem—how to express universals through a dynamic and asymmetrical equilibrium of vertical and horizontal structure, with primary hues of color disposed in rectangular areas. These elements gave visual expression to Mondrian's beliefs about the dynamic opposition and balance between the dual forces of matter

17.20 Auguste Herbin, *Composition*, 1939. Oil on canvas, 18½ × 43¼" (47 × 109.9 cm). Private collection.

17.21 Piet Mondrian, *Tableau II*, 1921–25. Oil on canvas, 29½ × 25⅝" (74.9 × 65.1 cm). Private collection.

17.22 Piet Mondrian, *Composition with Red, Blue, and Yellow*, 1930. Oil on canvas, 20⅛ × 20⅛" (51.1 × 51.1 cm). Collection The Fukuoka City Bank Ltd., Japan.

and spirit, theories that grew out of his exposure to Theosophy and the dialectical theories of the early nineteenth-century German philosopher Georg Wilhelm Friedrich Hegel. It was only through the pure "plastic" expression of what Mondrian called the "inward" that humans could approach "the divine, the universal."

In his painting, Mondrian was disturbed by the fact that, up to this point, in most of his severely geometric paintings—including the floating color-plane compositions and the so-called grid or checkerboard paintings—the shapes of red, blue, or yellow seemed to function visually as foreground forms against a white and gray background (see fig. 11.34) and thus to interfere with total unity. The solution, he found, lay in making the forms independent of color, with heavy lines (which he never thought of as lines in the sense of edges) moving through the rectangles of color. By this device he was able to gain a mastery over color and space that he would not exhaust for the next twenty years.

A mature example of Neo-Plasticism is seen in the 1921–25 *Tableau II* (fig. **17.21**). Here is the familiar palette of red, blue, yellow, black, and two shades of gray.

The total structure is emphatic, not simply containing the color rectangles but functioning as a counterpoint to them. Both red and gray areas are divided into larger and smaller rectangles with black lines. The black rectangles, since they are transpositions of lines to planes, act as further unifying elements between line and color. The edges of the painting are left open. Along the top and in the lower left corner, the verticals do not quite go to the edge, with the consequence that the grays at these points surround the end sof the lines. Only in the lower right does the black come to the edge, and this is actually a black area through which the line moves slightly to the left of the edge. In all other parts a color, principally gray, but red and yellow at the upper left, forms the outer boundary. The result that Mondrian sought—an absolute but dynamic balance of vertical and horizontal structure, using primary hues and black and white—is thus achieved. Everything in the painting holds its place. By some purely visual phenomenon, caused by the structure and the subtle disposition of color areas, the grays are as assertive as the reds or yellows; they advance as well as recede. The painting is not in any sense of the word flat. Everything is held firmly in place, but under great tension.

The open composition with emphasis on large white or light-gray areas predominated in Mondrian's production during the twenties and, in fact, for the rest of his life. He usually worked on several pictures at once and often developed a single idea by working in series, devoting as many as eight paintings to variations on a single theme. He made several variations within a square format in the late twenties, including *Composition with Red, Blue, and Yellow* (fig. **17.22**), in which a large color square of red, upper right, is joined point to point with a small square of comparably intense blue by intersecting black lines. Surrounding them, equally defined by heavy black lines, are rectangles of off-white. In the lower right corner is one small rectangle of yellow. The white areas, combined with the subordinate blue and yellow, effectively control and balance the great red square. Although Mondrian did not ascribe symbolic meaning to colors in the way that, for example, Kandinsky did, he told a collector that his paintings with a predominant red were "more real" than paintings with little or no color, which he considered "more spiritual."

Mondrian's studio in Paris (fig. **17.23**) was a Spartan living space but a remarkable artistic environment that was

17.23 Piet Mondrian's studio at rue du Départ, Paris. 1926.

famous throughout the European artworld. For his ideal Neo-Plastic environment, the artist created geometric compositions on the studio walls with arrangements of colored squares. The easel seen at the left in this photograph was more for viewing than working (Mondrian preferred to paint on a horizontal surface). In 1930 Mondrian was visited by Hilla Rebay, an artist and zealous supporter of abstract art who was to help found the Museum of Non-Objective Painting in New York, eventually to become the Solomon R. Guggenheim Museum. "He lives like a monk," she observed, "everything is white and empty, but for red, blue and yellow painted squares that are spread all over the room of his white studio and bedroom. He also has a small record player with Negro music."

Second only to painting was the artist's abiding passion for American jazz.

Composition with Yellow Lines (fig. **17.24**) is among Mondrian's most beautiful so-called lozenge or diamond paintings. In this format, first used by Mondrian in 1918, the square painting is turned on edge but the horizontal and vertical axes are maintained internally. The shape inspired some of Mondrian's most austere designs, in which his desire to transgress the frame, to express a sense of incompleteness, was given tangible expression. *Composition with Yellow Lines* represents an ultimate simplification in its design of four yellow lines, delicately adjusted in width and cutting across the angles of the diamond. Mondrian's fascination with the incomplete within

17.24 Piet Mondrian, *Composition with Yellow Lines*, 1933. Oil on canvas, 31½ × 31½" (80 × 80 cm). Gemeente Museum, the Hague, the Netherlands.

17.25 Piet Mondrian, *Composition in White, Black, and Red*, 1936. Oil on canvas, 40¼ × 41" (102.2 × 104.1 cm). The Museum of Modern Art, New York.

the complete, the tension of lines cut off by the edge of the canvas that seek to continue on to an invisible point of juncture outside the canvas, is nowhere better expressed than here. The viewer's desire to rejoin and complete the lines, to recover the square, is inescapable. The fascination of this magnificently serene painting also lies in another direction—the abandonment of black. Mondrian would fully develop this aspect in his very last works (see fig. 17.26). It is important to note that he also designed his own frames out of narrow strips of wood that he painted white or gray and set back from the canvas. He wished to emphasize the flat, nonillusionistic nature of his canvases, "to bring the painting forward from the frame … to a more real existence."

In 1932 Mondrian introduced a dramatic new element in one of his Neo-Plastic compositions when he divided a black horizontal into two thin lines. With this "double line" he set out to replace all vestiges of static form with a "dynamic equilibrium." This innovation brought a new, vibrant opticality to the work, with Mondrian multiplying the number of lines until, by the late thirties, the paintings contained irregular grids of black lines with only one or a few planes of color. A midway point in this development is *Composition in White, Black, and Red*, 1936 (fig. **17.25**), a structure of vertical and horizontal black lines on a white ground, with a small black rectangle in the upper left corner and a long red strip at the bottom. The lines, however, represent intricate proportions, both in the rectangles they define and in their own thickness and distribution. In the right lower corner, horizontal lines, varied subtly in width, create a grid in which the white spaces seem to expand and contract in a visual ambiguity.

American Connections: Mondrian and Calder

Mondrian in New York

In 1938, with the war approaching, Mondrian left Paris for London, joining his friends Gabo, Ben Nicholson, and Barbara Hepworth. After two years he moved to New York, where he spent the final four years of his life. Manhattan became the last great love of his life, perhaps because of the Neo-Plastic effect created by skyscrapers rising from the narrow canyons of the streets and the rigid grid of its plan. As early as 1917 Mondrian had said, "The truly modern artist sees the metropolis as abstract life given form: it is closer to him than nature and it will more easily stir aesthetic emotions in him." A major new stimulus to the artist was that of lights at night, when the skyscrapers were transformed into a brilliant pattern of light and shadow, blinking and changing. Mondrian also loved the tempo, the dynamism, of the city—the traffic, the dance halls, the jazz bands, the excitement of movement and change. He felt driven to translate these rhythms into his late paintings, where the earlier grid of black lines is replaced by a complex weave of colored lines.

The impact of the city and music is most evident in *Broadway Boogie-Woogie*, painted in 1942–43 (fig. **17.26**). Here the artist returned to the square canvas but departed radically from the formula that had occupied him for more than twenty years. There is still the rectangular grid, but the black, linear structure balanced against color areas is gone. In fact, the process is reversed: the grid itself is the color, with the lines consisting of little blocks of red, yellow, blue, and gray. The ground is a single plane of off-white, and against it vibrate the varicolored lines as well as larger color rectangles.

In New York, Mondrian devised a method of composing with commercially available colored tapes that he could easily shift around the canvas until he was satisfied enough to commit paint to canvas. This kind of experimental and intuitive approach had always governed Mondrian's working process. Although his art was guided by certain firmly held principles, it was far from formulaic. His paintings are filled with subtle textural effects and give evidence of repeated revisions as the artist painted layer upon layer, widening or narrowing his lines and experimenting with alternative colors. Even his whites are rarely the same hue. Although most art suffers in reproduction, the physical presence of Mondrian's paintings is especially difficult to capture, even in the best photographs.

Mondrian was a legendary figure in the United States, inspiring not only the geometric abstractionists, who had been carrying on a minority battle against Social Realism and Regionalism, but also a number of younger artists who were to create a major revolution in American art. Almost without exception, the emerging Abstract Expressionists of the early forties had great respect for Mondrian, even though their painting took directions that would seem diametrically opposed to everything he believed in.

17.26 Piet Mondrian, *Broadway Boogie-Woogie*, 1942–43. Oil on canvas, 50 × 50" (127 × 127 cm). The Museum of Modern Art, New York.

Calder

It was a formative encounter with Mondrian's art in 1930 that prompted American **Alexander Calder** (1898–1976) to become an abstract artist. Born in Philadelphia, Calder was the son and grandson of sculptors. After studying engineering, training that would have direct consequences for his art, he was gradually drawn into the field of art, studying painting at New York's Art Students League and working as an illustrator. Calder's early paintings of circus or sports scenes reflect the styles of his teachers, such as John Sloan (see fig. 18.2). By the time of his first visit to Paris in 1926, Calder had begun to make sculptures in wire and wood. In the French capital he eventually attracted the attention of avant-garde artists and writers (especially the Surrealists) with his *Circus*, a full-fledged, activated environment made up of tiny animals and performers that Calder assembled from wire and found materials and then set into motion. At the same time he made wooden

sculptures and portraits and caricatures constructed from wire. The wire sculptures are early demonstrations of Calder's marvelous technical ingenuity and playful humor. They could be quite large, such as the ten-foot (3 m) *Romulus and Remus* of 1928 (fig. **17.27**). Here Calder bent and twisted wire into a composition of such economy that the entire "torso" of the she-wolf is one continuous stretch of wire. The whole is like a three-dimensional line drawing (Calder made drawings related to the wire sculpture at the same time).

In 1930, during a subsequent sojourn in Paris, Calder visited Mondrian's rigorously composed studio (see fig. 17.23), which deeply impressed him. "This one visit gave me a shock that started things," he said. "Though I had heard the word 'modern' before, I did not consciously know or feel the term 'abstract.' So now, at thirty-two, I wanted to paint and work in the abstract." He began to experiment with abstract painting and, more significantly,

17.27 Alexander Calder, *Romulus and Remus*, 1928. Wire and wood, 30½ × 124½ × 26" (77.5 × 316.2 × 66 cm). Solomon R. Guggenheim Museum, New York.

abstract wire constructions that illustrated an immediate mastery of constructed space sculpture. These early abstract sculptures, which were exhibited in a 1931 solo exhibition in Paris, consisted of predominantly austere, geometric forms like open spheres; but they also contained a suggestion of subject—constellations and universes.

In 1931, at Arp's suggestion, Calder joined Abstraction-Création and began to introduce motion into his constructions. At first he induced movement by hand cranks or small motors, but eventually the sculptures were driven merely by currents of air and Calder's carefully calibrated systems of weights and balances. There were precedents of kineticism in sculpture, as we have seen, in the work of Gabo, Rodchenko, and Moholy-Nagy, but no artist developed the concept as fully or ingeniously as Calder. His first group of hand and motor "mobiles" was exhibited in 1932 at the Galerie Vignon, where they were so christened by Marcel Duchamp. When Arp heard the name "mobile," he asked, "What were those things you did last year—stabiles?" Thus was also born the word that technically might apply to any sculpture that does not move but that has become specifically associated with Calder's works (see chapter 22).

Calder's characteristic works of the thirties and forties are wind-generated mobiles, either standing or hanging, made of plates of metal or other materials suspended on strings or wires, in a state of delicate balance. The earliest mobiles were relatively simple structures in which a variety of objects, cut-out metal or balls and other forms in wood, moved slowly in the breeze. A far greater variety of motion was possible than in the mechanically driven mobiles. For one thing, the element of chance played an important role. Motion varied from slow, stately rotation to a rapid staccato beat. In the more complex examples, shapes rotated, soared, changed tempo, and, in certain instances, emitted alarming sounds. In *Object with Red Disks (Calderberry Bush)*, a standing mobile from 1932 (the second title, by which the work is best known, was not Calder's), Calder counterbalanced five flat red disks with wooden balls and perched the whole on a wire pyramidal base. When set in motion by the wind or a viewer's hand, this abstract construction moves through space in preplanned yet not entirely predictable ways.

Among Calder's motorized mobiles were also reliefs, with the moving parts on a plane of wooden boards or within a rectangular frame. One of the earliest on a large scale is *The White Frame* of 1934 (fig. **17.28**). In this, a few

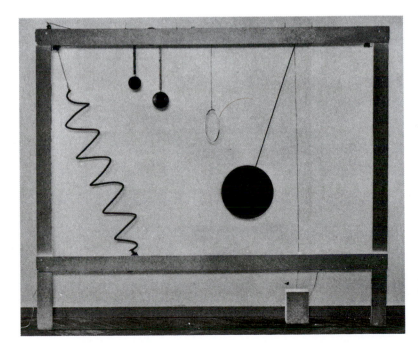

17.28 Alexander Calder, *The White Frame*, 1934. Painted wood, sheet metal, wire, 7½ × 9' (2.3 × 2.7 m). Moderna Museet, Stockholm.

elements are set against a plain, flat background: a large, suspended disk at the right, a spiral wire at the left, and between them, suspended on wires, a white ring and two small balls, one red and one black. Put into motion, the large disk swings back and forth as a pendulum, the spiral rotates, and the balls drop unexpectedly and bounce from their wire springs. Whereas *The White Frame* (with the exception of the spiral) still reflects Mondrian, geometric abstraction, and Constructivism, Calder also used free, biomorphic forms reflecting the work of his friends Miró and

Arp. From this point onward, Calder's production moved easily between geometric or Neo-Plastic forms and those associated with organic Surrealism.

By the end of the thirties, Calder's mobiles had become extremely sophisticated and could be made to loop and swirl up and down, as well as around or back and forth. One of the largest hanging mobiles of the thirties is *Lobster Trap and Fish Tail* (fig. **17.29**), a work that was commissioned for The Museum of Modern Art. Although the work is quite abstract, the subject association of the Surrealist-

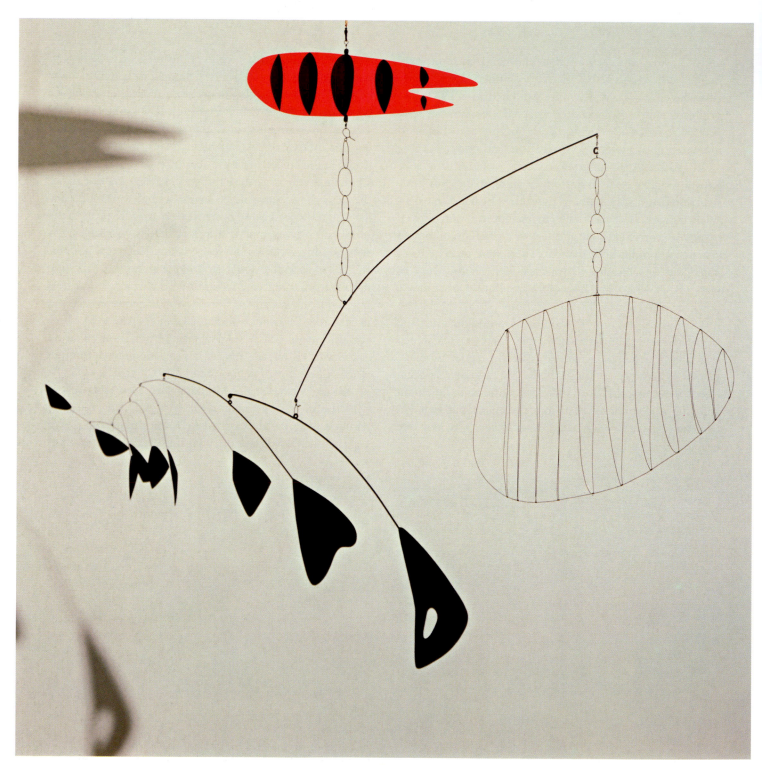

17.29 Alexander Calder, *Lobster Trap and Fish Tail*, 1939. Hanging mobile: painted steel wire and sheet aluminum, approximately 8'6" high × 9'6" diameter (2.6 × 2.9 m). The Museum of Modern Art, New York.

inspired, biomorphic forms is irresistible. The torpedo-shaped element at top could be a lobster cautiously approaching the trap, represented by a delicate wire cage balancing at one end of a bent rod. Dangling from the other end is a cluster of fan-shaped metal plates suggestive of a school of fish. The delicacy of the elements somewhat disguises the actual size, some nine and a half feet (2.9 m) in diameter. After World War II, Calder would pursue an international career, expanding the abstract art he had already formulated in the thirties to an architectural scale of unprecedented grandeur (see chapter 22).

Responses to International Abstraction: Artists in Britain

Wyndham Lewis and Vorticism

The most radical element in English art to emerge before World War I was the group who called themselves Vorticists (from "vortex"), founded in 1914 and led by the talented painter, writer, and polemicist **Percy Wyndham Lewis** (1886–1957). In the catalogue of the only exhibition of Vorticism, at the Doré Galleries in 1915, Lewis described the movement with all the zealous rhetoric typical of the early twentieth-century avant-garde:

> By vorticism we mean (a) Activity as opposed to the tasteful Passivity of Picasso; (b) Significance as opposed to the dull and anecdotal character to which the Naturalist is condemned; (c) Essential Movement and Activity (such as the energy of a mind) as opposed to the imitative cinematography, the fuss and hysterics of the Futurists.

Of particular significance for Vorticism was the association of the American poet Ezra Pound, then living in England. He gave the movement its name and with Lewis founded the periodical *Blast*, subtitled *Review of the Great English Vortex*. For the Vorticists, abstraction was the optimal artistic language for forging a link between art and life. As Lewis stated in *Blast*, they believed that artists must "enrich abstraction until it is almost plain life." Lewis was a literary man by character, and much of his contribution lay in the field of criticism rather than creation. He was influenced by Cubism from a very early date and, despite his polemics against it, by Futurism. In one of his few surviving pre-World War I paintings (fig. **17.30**), Lewis composed a dynamic arrangement of rectilinear forms that arch through the composition as though propelled by an invisible energy force. This adaptation of a Cubist syntax to metallic, machinelike forms has much in common with Léger's paintings around this date. Lewis was primarily attempting, by every means in his power, to attack and break down the academic complacency that surrounded him in England. In the vortex he was searching for an art of "activity, significance, and essential movement, and a modernism that should be clean, hard, and plastic."

Vorticism was a short-lived phenomenon, and it produced few artists of real originality. Nevertheless, it was of

17.30 Percy Wyndham Lewis, *Composition*, 1913. Watercolor drawing on paper, 13½ × 10½" (34.3 × 26.7 cm). Tate Gallery, London.

great importance in marking England's involvement in the new experimental art of Europe. As with other artists associated with the movement, few of Lewis's early, Vorticist paintings survive. After the war he abandoned abstraction in favor of a stylized figurative art. He made portraits of Edith Sitwell, Ezra Pound, and other literary figures, giving them, through a suggestion of Cubist structure, an appearance of modernism.

Spencer

The two English painters of greatest stature between the wars, Stanley Spencer and Ben Nicholson, represent extremes of contrast. **Stanley Spencer** (1891–1959) seemed to turn his back completely on everything in avant-garde twentieth-century painting. At the opposite pole from all forms of international abstraction, his was a figurative art that took inspiration, like the Pre-Raphaelites he admired, from fifteenth-century Italian painters. In his earlier paintings with Christian themes, he developed an eccentric, personal style in his drawing reminiscent of early Italian or Flemish paintings, which enhanced his visionary effects. In the twenties, Spencer received a large mural commission for the Sandham Memorial Chapel in Burghclere, Hampshire. From 1927 to 1932 he labored over a cycle of paintings based on his war experiences, culminating in the huge central panel, *The Resurrection of the Soldiers* (fig. **17.31**). This vast panorama depicts dead soldiers

17.31 Stanley Spencer, *The Resurrection of the Soldiers*, 1928–29. Oil on canvas, glued to the wall, 21' × 17'6" (6.4 × 5.3 m). Sandham Memorial Chapel, Burghclere, England.

struggling from their graves amidst a forest of overturned crosses. Although Spencer maintained his religious convictions throughout his life, in his later works he also turned to obscure themes with erotic overtones, sometimes comparable to paintings by Balthus (see fig. 20.15). Even these usually have religious implications in the sense of a modern morality play.

Nicholson

The other outstanding English painter to emerge between the wars was **Ben Nicholson** (1894–1981), who was also a distinguished sculptor. Whereas Spencer might be considered narrowly English, Nicholson was an internationally minded artist. During the twenties, he practiced variants on the late Cubist styles of Braque and Picasso and also made his first abstract compositions. These early works reveal most of the characteristics of Nicholson's mature style. Their surfaces appear abraded, and color is subdued, matte, and delicately harmonious. He uses a limited range of gray whites to grayed ochers, with a few accents of black and muted red, and rubbed pencil passages of dark gray. All the elements of still life—table, bottle, and bowls—are frontalized and flattened, and shapes are outlined with ruler and compass in fine and precise contour.

In 1932 Nicholson began spending time in Paris, where he became acquainted with Giacometti, Braque, Picasso, Kandinsky, and Brancusi, among others. Over the next few years, Nicholson championed the cause of English art abroad and became an important artistic conduit between the continent and his native country, helping to attract foreign artists to London during the tense period leading up to the war. In 1933 he was invited to join the Parisian Abstraction-Création group and, significantly for his art, saw works by Calder and Mondrian for the first time. At the end of that year he made his first carved and painted relief, an abstract composition of irregular, free-floating circles over rectangular shapes that he carved into a shallow board. Nicholson had met Barbara Hepworth in 1931; they were married from 1938 to 1951. They shared a studio in London, and Nicholson's exposure to Hepworth's sculptor's tools and methods, as well as his recent experience carving linocuts, led him to make reliefs and, eventually, sculpture. We have seen how many modern artists, from Arp (see fig. 13.14) to Archipenko (see fig. 10.30) to Baumeister (see fig. 17.12), were interested in creating such hybrids between sculpture and painting.

A residual biomorphism, inspired partly by the work of Miró and Calder, is evident in Nicholson's early reliefs. Gradually, however, he eliminated such Surrealist overtones from his work, and the forms within his reliefs—circles, squares, and rectangles—became highly regularized in response to Mondrian's example. In the mid-thirties he avoided both color and drawn line in a series of *White Reliefs*. Here the total spatial effect is achieved through the interaction of overlapping rectangles, with an occasional circle in sunken relief. Nicholson's exclusive use of white, a color connoting purity and infinity in abstract painting, may have been occasioned by an article written by Van Doesburg and published by *Art Concrèt* that was devoted to the subject of white in painting.

Although they never realized anything as significant as the Bauhaus, English artists and architects throughout the thirties were exploring potential alliances between their disciplines, based on the new Constructivist aesthetic. The white, rectilinear surfaces of Nicholson's paintings, stripped of all distracting detail, were regarded as ideal décor for the pared-down spaces of the new International Style architecture. Such ideas were specifically addressed in an important book that Nicholson edited in 1937 with Gabo and the architect Leslie Martin (with collaboration from Barbara Hepworth), *Circle: International Survey of Constructive Art*. It was published in conjunction with a London exhibition, Constructive Art, and designed to counteract the sensation generated by a recent show of international Surrealism held in London. *Circle* was an important publication, since it introduced many of the Bauhaus ideas to Britain.

17.32 Ben Nicholson, *1939 (Painted Relief – Version 1)*. Oil and pencil on composition boards mounted on painted plywood, 32⅞ × 45" (83.5 × 114.3 cm). The Museum of Modern Art, New York.

In the late thirties, Nicholson reintroduced color to his reliefs, a shift stimulated in part by the landscape at St. Ives, Cornwall, where he lived with Hepworth. The *1939 (Painted Relief)* (fig. **17.32**) is a meticulous adjustment of squares and rectangles in low but varying relief projections. The larger shapes are a uniform, muted, sand color. Played against these are a square of dull ocher, a rectangle of red-brown and, top and bottom at the left, strips of pure white. The only lines are two circles drawn in graphite, placed slightly off-center in the major squares. The edges of the relief shapes also act as a precise, rectangular linear structure.

In the same period Nicholson continued to produce paintings involving the same principles of strict rectangularity, using the primary colors with black, white, and grays, sometimes varying the values and intensities, and combining light, delicate blues with intense yellows. Despite a commitment to abstraction until the end of his life, Nicholson also habitually drew from nature, resulting in images of an Ingres-like delicacy and precision.

Moore

Unlike Nicholson or, for that matter, any of the sculptors previously discussed in this chapter, the sculptor **Henry Moore** (1898–1986) was not an artist in the Constructivist mold. He did not assemble forms from the newest industrial materials but rather carved and modeled them in the traditional media of stone and plaster. His was a humanist art, grounded in the contours of nature and the human figure, however abstract the forms sometimes appear. Although he did not begin to assume a genuinely international stature before 1945, Moore was a mature artist by the early thirties, in touch with the main lines of Surrealism and abstraction on the Continent, as well as all the new developments in sculpture, from Rodin through Brancusi to Picasso and Giacometti. By 1935 he had already made original statements and had arrived at many of the sculptural figurative concepts that he was to build on for the rest of his career.

The son of a coal miner, Moore studied at the Royal College of Art in London from 1921 until 1925. The greatest immediate influence on him were the works of art he studied in English and European museums, particularly the Classical, pre-Classical, African, and pre-Columbian art he saw in the British Museum. He was also attracted to English medieval church sculpture and to artists in the Renaissance tradition—Masaccio, Michelangelo, Rodin, Maillol—who had a particular feeling for the monumental.

Between 1926 and 1930 the dominant influence on Moore was pre-Columbian art. The 1929 *Reclining Figure* (fig. **17.33**) is one of the artist's first masterpieces in sculpture, a work that may owe its original inspiration to a chacmool (with overtones of Maillol). Chacmools are a distinctive type of stone sculpture representing a reclining warrior holding an offering dish. They are associated with the Toltec culture of central Mexico, which flourished between the tenth and twelfth centuries. The massive blockiness of Moore's figure stems from a passionate devotion to the principle of truth to materials; that is, the idea that stone should look like stone, not flesh. In this and other reclining figures, torsos, and mother-and-child groups of the late twenties, Moore staked out basic themes that he then used throughout his life.

In the early thirties, the influence of Surrealist sculpture, notably that of Picasso, became evident. Moore began to explore other materials, particularly bronze, and his figures took on a fluidity and sense of transparent surface appropriate to what was for him a new material. Similar effects were achieved in carved wood in which he followed the wood grain meticulously, as in *Reclining Figure* from 1939 (fig. **17.34**), his largest carved sculpture to date. Less angular than the 1929 figure, this sculpture consists of a series of holes that pierce the undulating solids, transforming the body into a kind of landscape filled with caves and tunnels. A characteristic of the figures of the thirties is this opening up of voids, frequently to the point where the solids function as space-enclosing frames.

In the mid-thirties Moore turned to abstract forms, and by opening up the masses and creating dispersed groups, he studied various kinds of space relationships. This began a continuing concern with a sculpture of tensions between

17.33 Henry Moore, *Reclining Figure*, 1929. Hornton stone, height 22½" (57.2 cm). Leeds City Art Galleries, England.

17.34 Henry Moore, *Reclining Figure*, 1939. Elm wood, 3'1" × 6'7" × 2'6" (0.94 × 2 × 0.76 m) The Detroit Institute of Arts.

void and solid, of forms enclosed within other forms. These experiments were then translated back into the figures. The interest in spatial problems led Moore during the forties and fifties to an ever-greater use of bronze and other metals in which he could enlarge the voids of the figures. These developments in Moore's work during and after World War II are pursued in chapter 20.

Hepworth

Barbara Hepworth (1903–75), the other English sculptor of international stature before World War II, was a student at the same time as Henry Moore at Leeds School of Art. The two remained close through much of their careers, with Moore's work exerting a direct influence on her early sculpture. In 1925, while Hepworth was in Italy, she learned marble-carving techniques from an Italian master craftsman. Throughout the twenties, she made highly accomplished figurative sculptures in wood and stone that reflected her admiration of Egyptian, Cycladic, and Archaic Greek art. After meeting Nicholson in 1931 Hepworth became a leader of the abstract movement in England. She and Nicholson were active in the Unit One group, which was attempting to establish a common front for modern artists and architects in England, and in 1933 they were invited to become members of Abstraction-Création in Paris. While in Paris, Hepworth visited the studios of Arp and Brancusi, encounters with significant implications for her later work. The relationship between Hepworth and Nicholson produced a rich cross-fertilization of ideas, media, and forms in the art of each artist. They were also close to the critic Herbert Read, then emerging as the leading advocate of modern art in England. When, during the thirties, Gabo, Mondrian, Gropius, Moholy-Nagy, Breuer, and other European artists and architects moved to England, Hepworth and Nicholson were able to strengthen old friendships and form new ones among these pioneers of modernism.

Hepworth's sculpture began to shed its semblance to the real world after 1931, when she carved *Pierced Form*. In this alabaster sculpture, the stone is penetrated in the center by a large hole to make, in the artist's words, "an abstract form and space." This crucial rupture with the notion of carved sculpture as a solid, closed form was one of Hepworth's major contributions to modern sculpture, and the discovery would inform her subsequent work as well as that of Moore. Her exposure to the work of Arp

17.35 Barbara Hepworth, *Two Segments and Sphere*, 1935–36. Marble, 10½ × 10½ × 8½" (26.7 × 26.7 × 21.6 cm). Private collection.

(who had previously made his own penetrated sculptures) prompted Hepworth to make biomorphic, multipart sculptures in the early thirties, but by 1934 she adopted a more geometric syntax and eliminated, at least for a time, the remaining vestiges of naturalism from her work.

In one of her best-known works, *Two Segments and Sphere* (fig. **17.35**), 1935–36, Hepworth heightens the tension between the geometric forms, with their smooth, perfected finish, through the precarious positioning of the sphere. In the late thirties Hepworth produced some of her most severely simplified sculptures, a number of them consisting of a single marble column, gently rounded or delicately indented to emphasize their organic, figurative source.

In 1939, stimulated by Moore's example, she also began to explore the use of strings stretched across voids, as in *Wave* (fig. **17.36**). Hepworth's wood sculptures are marked by the same loving finish as her works in stone. The woods are beautiful and frequently exotic—mahogany,

scented guarea, Lagos ebony, or rosewood—worked to bring out their essential nature. Easier to work than stone, wood inspired her to an increasingly open type of composition, with voids penetrating the mass of the material. She also began at this time to use color, generally whites and blues in interior areas, to contrast with the natural wood of the exterior. In *Wave*, the blue interior refers to the ocean, for, like Nicholson, Hepworth was deeply affected by the Cornish landscape:

> I used colour and strings in many of the carvings of this time. The colour in the concavities plunged me into the depth of water, caves, or shadows deeper than the carved concavities themselves. The strings were the tension I felt between myself and the sea, the wind or the hills.

For a period after World War II, as we shall see in chapter 20, the sense of a naturalistic subject reemerged in Hepworth's sculptures.

17.36 Barbara Hepworth, *Wave*, 1943. Plane wood with blue interior and strings, 12 × 17½ × 8¼" (30.5 × 44.5 × 21 cm). Private collection, on loan to the Scottish National Gallery of Modern Art, Edinburgh.

18
American Art Before World War II

In the years leading up to World War I, the American realist tradition was given new life within the ranks of the so-called "Ashcan School." The name was invented by critics in the thirties to describe a group of artists in New York who enlisted colors that looked as if they had been scraped from a furnace to depict commonplace subjects that emphasized the seedy aspects of daily urban life. In an era when the United States was shifting from an agrarian to an industrially based economy, artists turned to the vitality of the city for their themes, sometimes documenting the lives of the country's urban inhabitants with a literalness that shocked viewers accustomed to the bland generalizations of academic art. Thus, the first modern American revolution in painting was toward realism.

Early twentieth century developments toward realism and new pictorial subject matter in America are explained in part by the fact that the academic spirit had become anathema to many young painters, even as professional survival remained largely contingent on membership in the National Academy of Design, the American equivalent of the French Academy of Arts. Artistic experimentation was discouraged by its perpetuation of the traditions of the French Academy, such as annual juried exhibitions. Although it merged with the more tolerant Society of American Artists in 1907, the National Academy remained steadfastly unreceptive to new developments and young artists were forced to look elsewhere for support.

Meanwhile, important venues in New York, particularly Alfred Stieglitz's 291 gallery and, in 1913, the gigantic exhibition of modern art known as the Armory Show, helped to introduce European modernists to American audiences and nurtured a number of American artists who were committed to experimental art. Americans were deeply involved in modernism as it developed—as artists, patrons, and enthusiasts—but remained committed to asserting nationalist identity as they incorporated styles of the European avant-garde. This led to a readiness, when economic and social troubles hit during the thirties, to exalt a spirit of nationalistic exceptionalism. During the

years of the Great Depression, this inward-turning focus gave rise to new varieties of naturalistic art based on themes that many artists felt were intrinsically American. These were practiced by the so-called Regionalists, famous for presenting the rural life of the Midwest, and the more politically engaged Social Realists, who documented the social consequences of extreme economic change. Also a fertile period for American photography, the era before World War II witnessed the development of photojournalism, as well as social documentary and advertising photography.

America Undisguised: The Eight and Social Criticism

In response to the National Academy's rejection of their work for the 1907 spring exhibition, eight painters participated in a historic exhibition at the Macbeth Gallery in New York City in February 1908. The painter Robert Henri, who had moved to New York from Philadelphia in 1900, was the intellectual leader of this loosely constituted group called "The Eight." Since 1905, Henri had been a member of the Academy, but in 1907 he found himself so at odds with his colleagues there that he began to organize an alternative exhibition.

Henri was joined by four Philadelphia artists—John Sloan, Everett Shinn, William Glackens, and George Luks—all illustrators who provided on-the-spot pictorial sketches for newspapers, a practice soon to be superseded as the technology for reproducing photographs in newspapers was developed. As a result of this vocation, they came to painting first as draftsmen whose subject matter portrayed the transient and everyday realities of American life. Three other artists also joined ranks—the landscape painters Ernest Lawson and Maurice Prendergast, and the Symbolist Arthur B. Davies—and the group was dubbed "The Eight" by a New York journalist.

The exhibition of The Eight was a milestone in the history of modern American painting. Although the participating artists represented various points of view and contrasting styles, they were united by their hostility to the entrenched art of the academy with its rigid jury system, and by the conviction that artists had the right to paint subjects of their own choosing. The show received mixed reviews. Some criticized it for its "inappropriate" recording of the uglier aspects of the New York scene. Several of the exhibiting artists were to become leading members of the Ashcan School.

Henri, Sloan, Prendergast, and Bellows

Robert Henri (1865–1929) was a dedicated teacher and artistic leader who instinctively rebelled against the clichés of the American academic tradition. He had studied at the Pennsylvania Academy with Thomas Anshutz, a pupil of Eakins, and at the Académie Julian in Paris, where the spontaneous sketching techniques he had learned under Anschutz displeased his teachers. In 1900 Henri settled in New York, where he eventually joined the faculty at the New York School of Art. He exhibited widely, and, by 1905, was highly enough regarded to be elected as a member of the National Academy of Design.

Although Henri painted many landscapes, he is primarily admired for the forthright expression and painterly freedom of his portraits, including *Laughing Child* (fig. 18.1), which was among the works he exhibited with The Eight. He made the portrait during a visit with some of his students to Haarlem in the Netherlands, home of the seventeenth-century painter Frans Hals. Like the Dutch

18.1 Robert Henri, *Laughing Child*, 1907. Oil on canvas, 24 × 20" (61 × 50.8 cm). Whitney Museum of American Art, New York.

master, Henri favored immediacy of expression over academic finish in his portraits. During the trip he painted several informal half-length portraits of children against dark backgrounds, skillfully capturing the fresh enthusiasm of his young subjects.

Following the exhibition of The Eight, Henri established his own independent art school, becoming one of the most influential teachers in the early years of the twentieth century. His instruction left its mark on a number of artists, including Stanton Macdonald-Wright, Patrick Henry Bruce, and Stuart Davis, who would become leading American abstractionists (although Henri himself cared little for abstract art), as well as leading realist painters George Bellows and Edward Hopper (see figs. 18.4, 18.36).

Henri encouraged his friend and protégé **John Sloan** (1871–1951) to portray what was most familiar to him—the streets and sidewalks of the American urban landscape. In fact, Sloan happened upon the scene depicted in *Hairdresser's Window* (fig. **18.2**) on his way to visit Henri at his New York studio. He was so taken with the spectacle of a crowd gathering beneath the window of a hairdresser's shop that he returned home to paint it from memory and, in his words, "without disguise." In the signs adorning the façade, Sloan introduced amusing puns such as one announcing the shop of "Madame Malcomb." Because Sloan and his fellow Ashcan School painters searched for artistic potential within the most commonplace subjects, including commercial advertisements, they can be regarded as early forerunners of 1960s Pop art (see chapter 21). Andy Warhol, for example, admired Sloan's work (see fig. 21.42).

Sloan offered an alternative to the teeming life of city streets in *The Wake of the Ferry II*, 1907, which depicts a solitary passenger looking out over New York Harbor from the stern of a commuter ferryboat. The painting's delicately brushed passages describing a misty sky and blue-green water recall not only Henri but also Manet and Whistler. New York's waterways provided subjects rich with possibilities for other American painters, including Henri and Glackens, as well as for poets such as Walt Whitman, whose 1856 poem "Crossing Brooklyn Ferry" contributed to Sloan's choice of subject. And in the year Sloan's picture appeared, American photographer Alfred Stieglitz captured a related subject with his camera (see fig. 18.9).

Although the terms The Eight and Ashcan School are often used interchangeably, not all of the participants in the 1908 Macbeth Gallery show qualify as Ashcan artists. A case in point is the Boston artist **Maurice Prendergast** (1858–1924), who had trained in Paris in the 1890s and closely followed the developments of the French avant-garde. Prendergast chronicled the lighter side of contemporary life—the pageantry of holiday crowds, city parks, or seaside resorts (fig. **18.3**). He recorded these scenes in a distinctive, highly decorative style consisting of brightly colored patches of paint, reflecting his interest in Japanese prints and the French Nabis painters (see chapter 3).

18.3 Maurice Prendergast, *The Idlers,* c. 1918–20. Oil on canvas, 21 × 23" (53.3 × 58.4 cm). Maier Museum of Art, Randolph-Macon Woman's College, Lynchburg, Virginia.

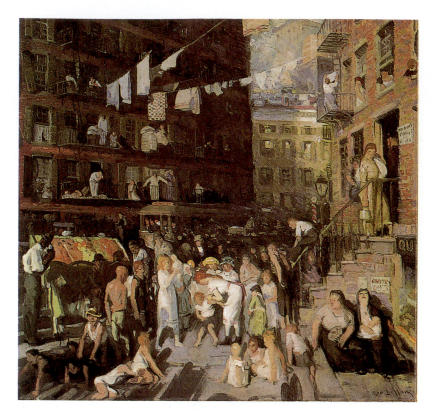

18.4 George Bellows, *Cliff Dwellers*, 1913. Oil on canvas, 39½ × 41½" (100.3 × 105.4 cm). Los Angeles County Museum of Art.

preparatory drawing for this work in *The Masses*, a radical socialist magazine for which Sloan also worked, assigning it a satirical caption, "Why don't they all go to the country for vacation?"

Two Photographers: Riis and Hine

The social criticism inherent in Ashcan School art, such as the scenes of urban grime and disadvantage painted by Sloan and Bellows, was even more explicit in the photographic work of **Jacob August Riis** (1849–1914), a Danish immigrant who took his camera into alleys and tenements on New York's Lower East Side to document the wretched conditions he found there (fig. **18.5**). Originally a police reporter, Riis said of his camera, "I had use for it and beyond that I never went." To the dismay of New York society, he used his pictures to expose the poverty and starvation that he felt were direct results of the industrial revolution. His book *How the Other Half Lives: Studies Among the Tenements of New York*, which was published in 1890, became a classic reference for subsequent social documentary photographers (see figs. 21.79, 21.80).

Riis's counterpart in the industrial landscape was **Lewis W. Hine** (1874–1940), who also used the camera as an instrument of social reform. After an initial series devoted

George Bellows (1882–1925), one of Henri's most accomplished students, developed a bold, energetic painting style that he deployed for subjects ranging from inner city street scenes to tense, ringside views of boxing matches, and socialites at leisure. His *Cliff Dwellers*, 1913 (fig. **18.4**), is a classic Ashcan School depiction of daily life in Manhattan's Lower East Side. Forced from their apartments by stifling summer heat, the residents carry out their lives on stoops and sidewalks, seemingly trapped within the walls of the tenement walk-ups. Bellows published a

18.5 Jacob A. Riis, *"Five Cents a Spot" Lodging House, Bayard Street,* c. 1889. Gelatin-silver print. Museum of the City of New York.

18.6 Lewis W. Hine, *Child in Carolina Cotton Mill*, 1908. Gelatin-silver print on masonite, 10½ × 13½" (26.7 × 34.3 cm). The Museum of Modern Art, New York.

18.7 Romaine Brooks, *Self-Portrait*, 1923. Oil on canvas, 46¼ × 26⅞" (117.5 × 68.3 cm). National Museum of American Art, Washington, D.C.

to immigrants on Ellis Island, Hine spent the years 1908–16 as the staff photographer for the National Child Labor Committee visiting factories to photograph and expose child-labor abuses (fig. **18.6**). Like Riis, Hine used the camera to produce "incontrovertible evidence" that helped win passage of laws protecting children against industrial exploitation. Hine, like documentary photographers before him, including most notably Mathew Brady in his Civil War images (see fig. 2.13), often directed his subjects and skillfully composed his images to better make his case.

Brooks

Although American painter **Romaine Brooks** (1874–1970) was a contemporary of the Ashcan artists, she lived in Europe for most of her adult life and, therefore, her work developed independently of trends in New York. Brooks survived a troubled childhood with a highly unstable mother to become a painter of considerable reputation in the twenties, only to fall into almost total obscurity by the forties. As an adult she lived a peripatetic life in Europe, settling finally in Paris in 1905. Her paintings, mostly portraits, were shown at the Parisian gallery Durand-Ruel in 1910. In Paris, Brooks met American poet Natalie Clifford Barney, whose literary salon attracted such illustrious talents as Marcel Proust, Colette, and André Gide. Brooks conducted an open lesbian relationship with Barney and adopted a masculine manner of dress. In her arresting *Self-Portrait* (fig. **18.7**), shown at the 1923 Salon des Indépendants, she projects herself as a stark silhouette with deeply shadowed eyes against an urban backdrop. With their delicate palette and *fin-de-siècle* mood, Brooks's paintings recall those of Whistler, though the somber and even grim aspect of her work is distinctly her own.

A Rallying Place for Modernism: 291 Gallery and the Stieglitz Circle

In 1905, at the Little Galleries of the Photo-Secession at 291 Fifth Avenue in New York, the photographer **Alfred Stieglitz** (1864–1946), together with another photographer, Edward Steichen, began to hold exhibitions of photography, and shortly thereafter of modern European paintings and sculpture, as well as African art. The artists whose work Stieglitz exhibited at the gallery known as 291 were more cosmopolitan than the Henri group: they were in closer contact with current events and artists in Europe, and less chauvinistic about Americanism in art. Moreover, Stieglitz and Steichen were in touch with avant-garde leaders in Paris, not only with artists but also with writers and collectors such as Gertrude Stein and her brothers Michael and Leo, the first collectors of Matisse and Picasso.

The gallery 291 would serve as a rallying place for American pioneers of international modernism including John Marin, Marsden Hartley, Max Weber, Arthur Dove, Georgia O'Keeffe, and Stanton Macdonald-Wright, all of whom are discussed below. The gallery was a focal point for the New York Dada movement (see chapter 13), and *291* was also the title of a short-lived Dada magazine. Between 1908 and 1917, works by many of the greatest European modernists were exhibited there, including Cézanne, Toulouse-Lautrec, Brancusi, Matisse, and Braque, as well as members of the American avant-garde, including John Marin, Charles Sheeler, Charles Demuth, Georgia O'Keeffe, and Elie Nadelman. At the same time, Stieglitz edited an important quarterly magazine on photography called *Camera Work*.

After 291 closed in 1917, Stieglitz continued to sponsor exhibitions at various New York galleries. In 1925 he opened the Intimate Gallery, which was succeeded by An American Place in 1929. Stieglitz directed this gallery until his death in 1946, featuring exhibitions by America's leading modernists. The impact of Stieglitz and his exhibitions at 291 was enormous. The miscellaneous group of Americans shown by him constituted the core of experimental art in the United States in the first half of the twentieth century and was the single most important factor, aside from the Armory Show, in the birth of the modern spirit in American art.

Stieglitz and Steichen

Well before he became a central figure in the American avant-garde, Stieglitz lived in Berlin. Here he began his long and distinguished career as a photographer and launched his crusade to establish photography as a fine art. He was an ardent advocate of Pictorialism in photography, a movement at one with the aestheticism of the late, Symbolist years in nineteenth-century art. The Pictorialists deplored the utilitarian banality of sharp-focus, documentary photography, as well as the academic pretension of Rejlander and Robinson (see figs. 2.2, 2.4). Instead, they insisted upon the artistic possibilities of camera-made imagery, but held that these could be realized only when art and science had been combined to serve both truth and beauty. Many Pictorialists tried to emulate painting and prints through soft-focus or darkroom manipulation. Too often, however, these attempts to create a heightened sense of poetry resulted in murky, sentimentalized facsimiles of etchings or lithographs.

Because Stieglitz maintained a strict "truth to materials" position, creating highly expressive images without the aid of darkroom enhancement, he was an important forerunner of so-called "straight" photography. The straight photographer exploits the intrinsic properties of the camera to make photographs that look like photographs instead of imitations of paintings or fine-art prints. Stieglitz joined the Pictorialists in maintaining that their works should be presented and received with the same kind of regard accorded other artistic media. In pursuit of this goal, progressive photographers broke away from the older camera societies, with their commercial and technological preoccupations, and initiated an international secession move-

ment that provided spaces for meetings and exhibitions, stimulated enlightened critical commentary, and published catalogues and periodicals devoted to photography. The most distinguished and far-reaching in its impact was New York's Photo-Secession group, established by Stieglitz in 1902 to promote "the serious recognition of photography as an additional medium of pictorial expression."

Stieglitz achieved his pictorial goals through his choice of subject, light, and atmosphere in the world about him, allowing natural fog or snow, for instance, to produce the desired effects of atmosphere and mystery (fig. **18.8**). As this image of a snow-covered New York street illustrates, Stieglitz, like the Ashcan painters, drew inspiration from the spectacle of the modern metropolis. But rather than the noisy clutter of humanity envisioned by Sloan or Bellows, Stieglitz was drawn to a lone cloaked figure silhouetted beneath the bare branches of a towering tree.

In 1907, during an ocean liner voyage to Europe, Stieglitz discovered little of social or visual interest among his fellow first-class passengers and wandered over to steerage, where the cheapest accommodations were located. As he later explained, he was struck by the combination of forms he witnessed among the crowds on deck—"a round straw hat, the funnel leaning left, the stairway leaning right, the white draw-bridge with its railings made of circular chains, white suspenders crossing on the back of a man." Stieglitz quickly fetched his camera and took what he came

18.8 Alfred Stieglitz, *The Street, Fifth Avenue*, 1896. Gravure, 12 × 9" (30.5 × 22.9 cm). Albright-Knox Art Gallery, Buffalo.

18.9 Alfred Stieglitz, *The Steerage*, 1907. Chloride print, 28 × 23⅜" (11 × 9.2 cm). The Art Institute of Chicago.

to regard as one of his greatest photographs, *The Steerage* (fig. **18.9**). Avoiding even the slightest Pictorialist sentiment or anecdote, Stieglitz provided a straight document of the scene, which he said was not merely a crowd of immigrants but "a study in mathematical lines … in a pattern of light and shade." This tendency to seek abstract form in the world around him led to Stieglitz's most daring series: cloud formations, or what he called "Equivalents" (fig. **18.10**). These recordings of turbulent skies express, Stieglitz said, his "most profound experience of life."

Stieglitz's longtime associate in New York's Photo-Secession group, 291 gallery, and *Camera Work* magazine was **Edward Steichen** (1879–1973), the photographer who in 1908 created the hauntingly moonlit time exposure of Rodin's *Balzac* (see fig. 6.10). After World War I, during which he worked as an aerial photographer, the artist abandoned his soft-focus Pictorialism to practice and promote straight, unmanipulated photography. Steichen became chief photographer for *Vogue* and *Vanity Fair*, publications in which his celebrity portraits and fashion photos, both revealing the artist's acute sensitivity to abstract pattern and composition, appeared regularly from 1923 to 1938, exerting tremendous influence on photographers on both sides of the Atlantic (fig. **18.11**). In 1947 Steichen was appointed director of the Department of Photography at New York's Museum of Modern Art, a position he held until his retirement in 1962.

18.10 Alfred Stieglitz, *Equivalent*, 1930. Chloride print, 4¹¹⁄₁₆ × 3⅝" (11.9 × 9.2 cm). The Art Institute of Chicago.

18.11 Edward Steichen, *Gloria Swanson*, 1924. Gelatin-silver print, 16⁹⁄₁₆ × 13½" (42.1 × 34.2 cm). The Museum of Modern Art, New York.

Weber, Hartley, Marin, and Dove

In a 1910 group show at 291, Stieglitz included works by **Max Weber** (1881–1961), a painter who had recently returned from three years in Paris. For an American, Weber was unusually knowledgeable about recent developments in French art and, by the time of Stieglitz's show, had begun to develop his own highly individual Cubist style. The 1915 *Chinese Restaurant* (fig. **18.12**) is Weber's response to a friend's suggestion that he make a painting about the conversations they had had over dinners in Chinatown in New York City. The wealth of colorful patterns suggest fragments of curtains, tile floors, and figures—colliding visual recollections of a bustling, urban interior and analogues for the rapid exchange of new ideas. Toward the end of World War I, the artist abandoned Cubism for a form of expressionist figuration related to that of Chagall and Soutine.

American painter **Marsden Hartley** (1877–1943) came to Stieglitz's attention with the Post-Impressionist landscapes he made in Maine in 1907–9. His works were shown for the first time at 291 in 1909. From 1912 to 1915, Hartley lived abroad, first in Paris and then in Berlin. In Germany he was drawn to the mystically based art of Der Blaue Reiter (see chapter 8), and the first works he made there are clearly inspired by Kandinsky. Among the Der Blaue Reiter group, Hartley found enthusiastic supporters, notably Franz Marc, who helped him find venues to exhibit his work, and he quickly came to regard Berlin, the capital of imperial Germany, as the most vital urban center in Europe. In 1914–15 he made a series of paintings in which the imagery is derived from German flags, military insignia, and all the regalia of the imperial court. The works were not a celebration of German nationalism but rather Hartley's response to the lively pageantry of the city. *Portrait of a German Officer* (fig. **18.13**) also contains coded references to the artist's lover, a German officer who was killed on the Western Front. Like Weber, Hartley began with motifs from the visible world, broke them up, and reorganized them into a largely abstract composition. The exuberant energy, brilliant colors, and bold arrangement of forms are evidence of his interest in the Orphist paintings of Delaunay (see fig. 10.44). In 1916, as war raged in Europe, Hartley's German works were shown at 291, where they were regarded by some reviewers as treacherously pro-German. These works would influence experimental American painters including Stuart Davis, Robert Indiana, and Jasper Johns (see figs. 18.62, 21.49, 21.14). Hartley continued to travel widely after the war and in his later years concentrated primarily on Cézanne-inspired landscapes in Nova Scotia and in his native Maine.

Among the artists that Stieglitz promoted, **John Marin** (1870–1953) is known for his superb skill as a watercolorist. Following his art studies in Philadelphia and New York, Marin spent most of the period from 1905 to 1910 in Europe. His introduction to Stieglitz in 1909 marked the beginning of a long and fruitful relationship. The late watercolors of Cézanne were an important source of inspiration for Marin, and Cubist structure remained a controlling force in the cityscapes and landscapes he painted throughout his life.

During the twenties and thirties he carried his interpretations of New York close to a form of expressionist

18.12 Max Weber, *Chinese Restaurant*, 1915. Oil on canvas, 40 × 48" (101.6 × 121.9 cm). Whitney Museum of American Art, New York.

18.13 Marsden Hartley, *Portrait of a German Officer*, 1914. Oil on canvas, 68¼ × 41⅜" (173.3 × 105.1 cm). The Metropolitan Museum of Art, New York.

18.14 John Marin, *Lower Manhattan (Composition Derived from Top of Woolworth Building)*, 1922. Watercolor and charcoal with paper cutout attached with thread on paper, 21⅝ × 26⅞" (54.9 × 68.3 cm). The Museum of Modern Art, New York.

291 in 1912 were even closer to nonobjectivity than contemporaneous paintings by Kandinsky, whose work Dove knew, and were probably the earliest and most advanced statements in abstract art by an American artist. Throughout his life, Dove was concerned more with the spiritual forces of nature than its external forms, and the curving shapes of his pastels were inspired by the natural world. He later called his group of abstract pastels *The Ten Commandments*, as if together they constituted his spiritual and artistic credo.

abstraction in which his subject is almost always discernible. In the 1922 *Lower Manhattan (Composition Derived from Top of Woolworth Building)* (fig. **18.14**), an explosion of buildings erupts from a black circular form containing a sunburst center, a cutout form that Marin attached to the paper with thread. He reinforced the transparent, angular strokes of the watercolor with charcoal, creating a work of graphic force that vibrates with the clamor and speed of the city. In summer, Marin painted the Maine coast. By 1949, when he composed the highly expressionist seascape, *The Fog Lifts* (fig. **18.15**)—where the fog takes the abstract form of white rectangles—Marin had been voted the best painter in America in a poll of art-world professionals conducted by *Look* magazine.

Arthur G. Dove (1880–1946) temporarily abandoned a career as an illustrator to go to Paris in 1907 in hopes of becoming a full-time painter. With astonishing speed, he seems to have absorbed much of the course of European modernism. The group of pastels that he exhibited at

18.15 John Marin, *The Fog Lifts*, 1949. Oil on canvas, 22 × 28" (55.9 × 71.1 cm). Wichita Art Museum, Kansas.

18.16 Arthur G. Dove, *Goin' Fishin'*, 1925. Collage on wood panel, 19½ × 24" (49.5 × 61 cm). The Phillips Collection, Washington, D.C.

Between 1924 and 1930, Dove produced a remarkable group of multimedia assemblages, including *Goin' Fishin'* (fig. **18.16**), composed of fragmented fishing poles and denim shirtsleeves. The artist was aware of the evolution of Cubist collage, but his own efforts have more in common

with nineteenth-century American folk art, *trompe l'oeil* painting, and Dada collage, though Dove never adopted the subversive, antiart stance of the first Dadaists. His own collages range from landscapes made up literally of their natural ingredients—sand, shells, twigs, and leaves—to delicate and magical *papiers collés*. *Goin' Fishin'* can be seen in relation to the fascinating constructions of Joseph Cornell (see fig. 19.53), and even to the so-called "combine paintings" of Robert Rauschenberg (see fig. 21.11).

During the thirties, Dove continued to paint highly abstracted landscapes in which concentric bands of radiating color and active brushwork express both a quality of intense light and the artist's sense of spiritual energy in nature. In the last years of his life, he experimented with bold, geometric shapes, such as those in *That Red One* of 1944 (fig. **18.17**), where the connection to the observable world is virtually severed.

O'Keeffe

The last exhibition at 291, held in 1917, was the first solo show of work by **Georgia O'Keeffe** (1887–1986). O'Keeffe differed from most of the other American pioneers of modernism in the fact that she was a woman and never trained in Europe. Fellow artist Hartley said that O'Keeffe was simply "modern by instinct," although she had been exposed, especially through exhibitions at 291, to the work of the major European modernists. The

18.17 Arthur G. Dove, *That Red One*, 1944. Oil on canvas, 27 × 36" (68.9 × 91.4 cm). William H. Lane Foundation, Leominster, Massachusetts.

18.18 Georgia O'Keeffe, *Music—Pink and Blue, II*, 1919. Oil on canvas, 35½ × 29" (90.2 × 73.7 cm). Whitney Museum of American Art, New York.

biomorphic, Kandinsky-like abstractions in charcoal that she made in 1915–16 so impressed Stieglitz that he soon gave her an exhibition. The two artists fell in love and married in 1924. Before he put away his camera for good in 1937, Stieglitz made more than three hundred photographs of O'Keeffe, contributing to her almost cult status in twentieth-century American art.

Whether her subjects were New York skyscrapers, enormously enlarged details of flowers, bleached cow skulls, or adobe churches, they have become icons of American art. Her paintings involve such economy of detail and such skillful distillation of her subject, that, however naturalistically precise, they somehow become works of abstraction. Alternatively, her abstractions have such tangible presence that they suggest forms in nature. *Music—Pink and Blue, II* (fig. **18.18**) is a breathtaking study in chromatic relationships and organic form. The title suggests the lingering

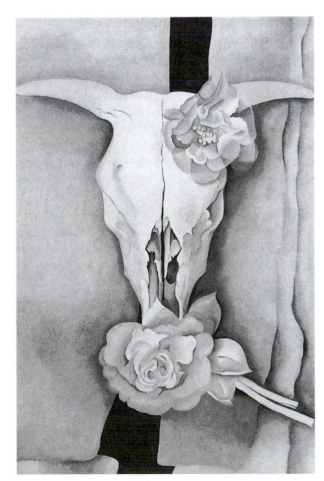

18.19 (left) Georgia O'Keeffe, *Radiator Building—Night, New York*, 1927. Oil on canvas, 48 × 30" (121.9 × 76.2 cm). Carl van Vechten Gallery of Fine Arts, Fisk University, Nashville, Tennessee.

18.20 (above) Georgia O'Keeffe, *Cow's Skull with Calico Roses*, 1931. Oil on canvas, 35⅞ × 24" (91.2 × 61 cm). The Art Institute of Chicago.

influence of Kandinsky's equation of color with music and, ultimately, with emotion. Typically ambivalent, the forms resemble an enlarged close-up of the flowers that O'Keeffe painted in the twenties, although some have seen them as sexually charged. The artist rejected such readings of her imagery, and partly in response to such interpretations, her work became more overtly representational in the twenties, as in her tightly rendered views of New York skyscrapers made from the window of her Manhattan apartment (fig. **18.19**). In 1929 O'Keeffe visited New Mexico for the first time and thereafter divided her time between New York and the Southwest, settling permanently in New Mexico in 1949. The desert motifs that she painted there are among her best-known images (fig. **18.20**).

Straight Photography: Strand, Cunningham, and Adams

Three important American photographers associated, like O'Keeffe, with the West are **Paul Strand** (1890–1976), Imogen Cunningham, and Ansel Adams. Photographer and filmmaker Paul Strand studied in his native New York City with Lewis Hine. He officially entered the Stieglitz circle in 1916, when his photographs were reproduced in *Camera Work* and he exhibited at 291 for the first time. By this time Strand had abandoned the Pictorialism of his early work and was making photographs directly inspired by Cubist painting. In 1917 he contributed an essay to the last issue of *Camera Work* in which he called for photography as an objective art "without tricks of process or manipulation." In 1930–32 Strand worked in New Mexico and photographed the same church that his friends O'Keeffe and Adams had already depicted (fig. **18.21**). All three artists were drawn to the desert sun's ability to accentuate the abstract qualities and dignified monumentality of the adobe structure.

From her origins in soft-focus Pictorialism, **Imogen Cunningham** (1883–1976), like Strand, shifted to straight photography, producing a series of plant studies (fig. **18.22**), in which blown-up details and immaculate lighting yield an image analogous to the near-abstract flower paintings of Georgia O'Keeffe. In 1932, along with Ansel Adams, Edward Weston, and other photographers in the San Francisco Bay area, Cunningham helped found Group f.64, a loosely knit organization devoted to "straight" photography as an art form. Their name refers to the smallest aperture on a large-format camera, producing sharp focus and great depth of field.

Ansel Adams (1902–84) discovered his passion for nature at the age of fourteen during a visit to California's Yosemite Valley, but it was his initial meeting with Paul Strand in 1930 that decided his career in photography. Three years later he met and engaged the support of Alfred Stieglitz. A masterful technician, Adams revealed himself to be an authentic disciple of Stieglitz when he wrote:

> A great photograph is a full expression in the deepest sense, and is, thereby, a true expression of what one feels about life in its entirety. And the expression of what one feels should be set forth in terms of simple devotion to the medium—a statement of the utmost clarity and perfection possible under the conditions of creation and production.

Adams's art is synonymous with spectacular unspoiled vistas of the West. An image taken in the Sequoia National Park, California, in 1932 (fig. **18.23**) shows the wintry landscape from a close-up angle, so that it fills the frame

18.22 Imogen Cunningham, *Two Callas*, 1929. Gelatin-silver print.

18.21 Paul Strand, *Ranchos de Taos Church, New Mexico*, 1931. Gelatin-silver print.

18.23 Ansel Adams, *Frozen Lakes and Cliffs, The Sierra Nevada, Sequoia National Park, California,* 1932. Gelatin-silver print.

to reveal the textures of the earth. An experienced mountaineer and dedicated conservationist, Adams was an active member of the Sierra Club by the late twenties. He helped establish the Department of Photography at New York's Museum of Modern Art in 1940 and the Center for Creative Photography at the University of Arizona, Tucson, in 1975.

The Europeans Are Coming: The Armory Show

In the early part of the twentieth century, an important catalyst affecting the subsequent history of American art was the International Exhibition of Modern Art held in New York at the 69th Regiment Armory on Lexington Avenue at 25th Street between February 17 and March 15, 1913. Organized by a group known as the Association of American Painters and Sculptors, the exhibition was generally intended to show a large number of European and American artists and to compete with the regular exhibitions of the National Academy of Design. Arthur B. Davies, a member of The Eight respected by both the Academy and the independents and highly knowledgeable in the international art field, was chosen as chairman and, with the painter Walt Kuhn, did much of the selection. They were assisted in several European cities by the painter and critic Walter Pach. William Glackens, another member of The Eight, headed up the selection of American works. The Armory Show proved to be a monumental though uneven exhibition focusing on the nineteenth- and early twentieth-century painting and sculpture of Europe. The artists included ranged from Goya and Delacroix to Daumier, Courbet, Manet, the Impressionists, Van Gogh, Gauguin, Cézanne, Redon, the Nabis, and Seurat and his followers. Matisse and the Fauves were represented, as were Picasso, Braque, and the Cubists. German Expressionists were slighted, while the Orphic Cubists and the Italian Futurists withdrew. Stieglitz purchased the only Kandinsky in the show. Among sculptors, the Europeans Rodin,

Maillol, Brancusi, Nadelman, and Lehmbruck, as well as the American Lachaise, were included, although sculpture was generally far less well represented than painting. American painting of all varieties and quality dominated the show in sheer numbers, but failed in its impact relative to that of the exotic imports from Europe.

The Armory Show created a sensation, and while the popular press covered it extensively (at first with praise), the exhibition was savagely attacked by critics and American artists. Matisse was singled out for abuse, as were the Cubists, while Duchamp's *Nude Descending a Staircase* (see fig. 10.48), it will be recalled, enjoyed a *succès de scandale* and was likened to a "pile of kindling wood."

As a result of the controversy, an estimated 75,000 people attended the exhibition in New York. At Chicago's Art Institute, where the European section and approximately half the American section were shown, nearly 200,000 visitors crowded the galleries. Here the students of the Art Institute's school, egged on by their faculty, threatened to burn Matisse and Brancusi in effigy. In Boston, where some 250 examples of the European section were displayed at Copley Hall, the reaction was more tepid.

The Armory Show, an unprecedented achievement in America, was a powerful impetus for the advancement of modernism there. Almost immediately, there was evidence of change in American art and collecting. New galleries dealing in modern painting and sculpture began to appear. Although communications were soon to be interrupted by World War I, more American artists than ever were inspired to go to Europe to study. American museums began to buy and to show modern French masters, and a small but influential new class of collectors, which included Dr. Albert Barnes, Arthur Jerome Eddy, Walter Arensberg, Lillie P. Bliss, Katherine Dreier, and Duncan Phillips, was born. From their holdings would come the nuclei of the great American public collections of modern art.

Sharpening the Focus on Color and Form: Synchromism and Precisionism

Synchromism

In the year of the Armory Show, two Americans living in Paris, **Stanton Macdonald-Wright** (1890–1973) and **Morgan Russell** (1886–1953), launched their own movement, which they called Synchromism. The complicated theoretical basis of Synchromism began with the principles of French color theorists such as Chevreul, Rood, and Blanc (see chapter 3). The color abstractions, or Synchromies, that resulted were close to the works of Delaunay, although

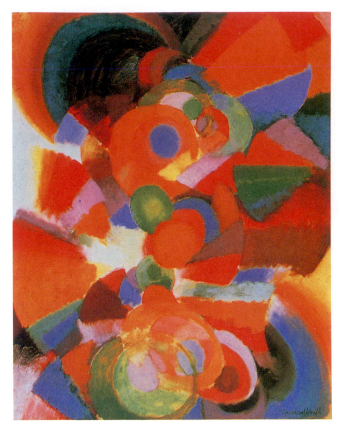

18.24 Stanton Macdonald-Wright, *Abstraction on Spectrum (Organization, 5)*, c. 1914. Oil on canvas, 30⅛ × 24³⁄₁₆" (76.5 × 61.4 cm). Des Moines Art Center, Iowa.

the ever-competitive Americans vehemently differentiated their work from the Frenchman's. Their 1913 exhibitions in Munich and Paris were accompanied by brash manifestos, followed by a show the next year in New York. Macdonald-Wright, whose *Abstraction on Spectrum (Organization, 5)* (fig. **18.24**) clearly owes much to Delaunay's earlier disk paintings (see fig. 10.44), wrote in 1916, "I strive to divest my art of all anecdote and illustration and to purify it to the point where the emotions of the spectator will be wholly aesthetic, as when listening to good music." Macdonald-Wright returned to the United States in 1916 and showed his work at 291 the following year. He moved to California in 1918, the year that more or less witnessed the end of Synchromism; although he largely returned to figuration after 1920, his subsequent work was still informed by his early Synchromist experiments.

Russell, on the other hand, spent most of his life in France after 1909. His most important Synchromist work is the monumental *Synchromy in Orange: To Form* (fig. **18.25**), which was included in the 1914 Salon des Indépendants in Paris. Although the densely packed, curving planes of brilliant color seem to construct a wholly abstract composition, the central planes actually contain the forms of a man, possibly Michelangelo's *Dying Slave* in the Louvre, after which Russell—always interested in sculpture—had made drawings. By virtue of juxtaposed advancing and receding colors, the painting has a distinctive sculptural appearance, an aspect that sets his work apart from that of Delaunay.

18.25 Morgan Russell, *Synchromy in Orange: To Form*, 1913–14. Oil on canvas with painted frame, 11'3" × 10'3" (3.4 × 3.1 m). Albright-Knox Art Gallery, Buffalo, New York.

Precisionism

A major manifestation of a new spirit in American art was the movement called Precisionism, which originated during the twenties, though the term was not itself coined until the forties. Never organized into a coherent group with a common platform, the artists involved have also been labeled "Cubo-Realists" and even "the Immaculates." All these terms refer to an art that is basically descriptive, but guided by geometric simplification that stems partly from Cubism. Precisionist paintings tend to be stripped of detail and are often based on sharp-focus photographs. The movement is in some ways the American equivalent of *Neue Sachlichkeit* or New Objectivity, the realist style practiced in Germany after the war (see chapter 13). The Germans, who had witnessed the horrors of war firsthand, tended to focus on politically charged images of the human figure, while the Americans preferred the more neutral subjects of still life, architecture, and the machine. Given their hard-edge style and urban theme, Georgia O'Keeffe's New York views of the twenties could be considered Precisionist (see fig. 18.19), but Charles Demuth and, especially, Charles Sheeler, were the key formulators of the style.

Charles Sheeler (1883–1965), a Philadelphia-born and -trained artist, began working as a professional photographer around 1910, making records of new houses and buildings for architectural firms. In 1919 he moved to New York, where he had already befriended Stieglitz and Strand, and continued to participate in the salons organized by the collectors Walter and Louise Arensberg. There he met Duchamp, Man Ray, Picabia, and other artists associated with New York Dada. Sheeler photographed skyscrapers—double exposing, tilting his camera, and then transferring these special effects and the patterns they produced to his paintings. In 1920 he collaborated with Strand on a six-minute film entitled *Manhatta*, which celebrated the dizzying effect of life surrounded by a dense forest of skyscrapers. Sheeler's 1920 painting *Church Street El* (fig. 18.26), representing a view looking down from a tall building in Lower Manhattan, was based on a still from the film. In its severe planarity and elimination of details, *Church Street El* is closer to geometric abstraction than to the shifting viewpoints of Cubist painting. By cropping the photographic image, Sheeler could be highly selective in his record of the details provided by reality and thus create arbitrary patterns of light and shadow and flat color that

18.26 Charles Sheeler, *Church Street El*, 1920. Oil on canvas, 16 × 19⅛" (40.6 × 48.6 cm). Cleveland Museum of Art.

transform themselves into abstract relationships. At the right in *Church Street El*, amidst the deep shadows and bright, geometric patches of sun, an elevated train moves along its tracks.

The relationship between Sheeler's camera work (he stopped making strictly commercial photographs in the early thirties) and his canvases seems to have been virtually symbiotic, as can be seen in a comparison of the photograph entitled *Drive Wheels* and the painting known as *Rolling Power* (figs. **18.27**, **18.28**). At first glance, the work in oil comes across as an almost literal transcription of the photograph, which the artist took in preparation for the painting. But Sheeler altered the composition and suppressed such details as the grease on the engine's piston box, all in keeping with Precisionism's love of immaculate surfaces and purified machine imagery. Sheeler made this painting for *Fortune* magazine as part of a commissioned series called *Power*, consisting of six "portraits" of power-generating machines. Much of Sheeler's work in the thirties and forties was a celebration of the modern industrial age, with majestic views of factories, power plants, and machines.

18.27 Charles Sheeler, *Drive Wheels*, 1939. Gelatin-silver print, 6¹¹⁄₁₆ × 9¹¹⁄₁₆" (17 × 24.5 cm). Smith College Museum of Art, Northampton, Massachusetts.

18.28 Charles Sheeler, *Rolling Power*, 1939. Oil on canvas, 15 × 30" (38.1 × 76.2 cm). Smith College Museum of Art, Northampton, Massachusetts.

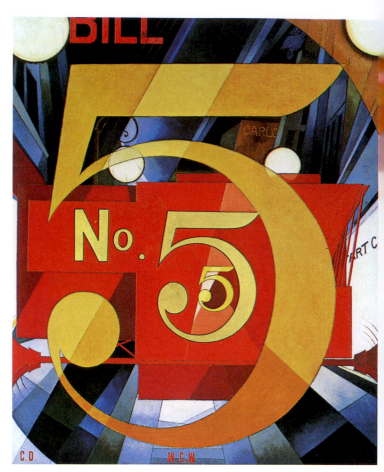

18.29 Charles Demuth, *The Figure 5 in Gold*, 1928. Oil on composition board, 36 × 29¾" (91.4 × 75.6 cm). The Metropolitan Museum of Art, New York.

Charles Demuth (1883–1935), also a Pennsylvanian, was the other major figure of Precisionism. He completed his studies at the Pennsylvania Academy in 1910 and, during a trip to Paris in 1912, befriended Hartley, who became an important mentor. Demuth's first mature works were book illustrations and imaginative studies of dancers, acrobats, and flowers, free and organic in treatment, and seemingly at the other extreme from a Precisionist style. The work of Cézanne was an important guiding force during these years. Like Marin, Demuth was a consummate watercolorist, but where Marin used the medium for great drama and expressive purpose, Demuth applied his delicate washes of color with restraint. "John Marin and I drew our inspiration from the same sources," he once said. "He brought his up in buckets and spilled much along the way. I dipped mine out with a teaspoon but I never spilled a drop." In a number of landscapes executed in watercolor in Bermuda in 1917, using interpenetrating and shifting planes and suggestions of multiple views, Demuth began his experiments with abstract lines of force, comparable to those used by the Futurists.

In the twenties, Demuth produced a series of emblematic portraits of American artists. Made up of images, words, and letters, these "posters," as Demuth called them, were related to some of the Dadaists' symbolic portraits, including Picabia's (see fig. 13.22). They led to what is probably Demuth's greatest painting, *The Figure 5 in Gold* (fig. **18.29**). The work, a tribute to his friend, the poet William Carlos Williams, is based on *The Great Figure*, a poem Williams wrote after seeing a roaring, red fire engine emblazoned with a golden number 5:

> Among the rain
> and lights
> I saw the figure 5
> in gold
> on a red
> fire truck
> moving
> tense
> unheeded
> to gong clangs
> siren howls
> and wheels rumbling
> through the dark city.

Demuth's other work in the twenties and thirties included exquisite watercolor still lifes as well as motifs drawn from the modern industrial landscape. His last major works were oil paintings of vernacular architecture in his hometown, Lancaster, Pennsylvania—its watertowers, factories, and grain elevators (fig. **18.30**). Like other artists in the postwar era, Demuth was searching for intrinsically

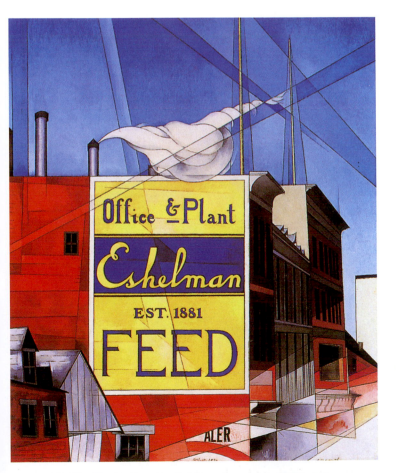

18.30 Charles Demuth, *Buildings, Lancaster*, 1930. Oil on composition board, 24 × 20" (61 × 50.8 cm). Whitney Museum of American Art, New York.

American subjects and became interested in the advertising signs on buildings and along highways, not as blemishes on the American landscape but as images with a certain abstract beauty of their own. Demuth's work influenced that of somewhat younger artists, such as Stuart Davis, who avowed his debt to the older artist, as well as that of future generations, including Jasper Johns and, quite specifically, Robert Indiana (see fig. 21.49).

Painting the American Scene: Regionalists and Social Realists

The thirties, a decade that opened after the Wall Street crash of 1929 and closed with the onset of war in Europe, was a period of economic depression and political liberalism in the United States. Reflecting the spirit of isolationism that dominated so much of American thought and action after World War I, art became socially conscious, nationalist, and regionalist. One of the seminal books of the decade was John Steinbeck's *Grapes of Wrath* (1939), a Pulitzer Prize-winning novel celebrating the quiet heroism of Oklahoma Dust Bowl victims during their migration to California. Among painters, the Regionalists and Social Realists became the guardians of conservatism and representation, fighting a rearguard battle against modernist abstraction. These artists concentrated on intrinsically "American" themes in their painting, whether chauvinistic praise of the virtues of an actually declining agrarian America, or bitter attacks on the American political and economic system that had produced the sufferings of the Great Depression.

A crucial event of this decade—indeed, a catalyst for the development of American art transcending even the Armory Show—was the establishment, by the United States government, of a Federal Arts Project, a subdivision of the WPA (Works Progress Administration). Just as the WPA provided jobs for the unemployed, the Art Project enabled many of the major American painters to survive during these difficult times. A large percentage of the younger artists who created a new art in America after World War II might never have had a chance to develop their art had it not been for the government-sponsored program of mural and easel painting.

The decade, however, witnessed little of an abstract tendency in American art. There were many artists of talent, and many interesting directions in American art, some of them remarkably advanced. Those who claimed the most attention throughout the era were the painters of the so-called American Scene, an umbrella term covering a wide range of realist painting, from the more reactionary and nationalistic Regionalists, through the generally leftwing Social Realists, to what might be called the Magic Realists. Divergent as their sociopolitical concerns may have been, the several factions merged in their common preference for illustrational styles and their contempt for "highbrow" European formalism.

18.31 Thomas Hart Benton, *City Building*, from the mural series *America Today*, 1930. Distemper and egg tempera on gessoed linen with oil glaze, 7'8" × 9'9" (2.3 × 3 m). Originally in the New School for Social Research, New York. Relocated in 1984. Collection the Equitable Life Assurance Society of the United States.

18.32 Thomas Hart Benton, *The Ballad of the Jealous Lover of Lone Green Valley*, 1934. Oil on masonite panel, 42¼ × 53¼" (107.3 × 135.3 cm). The Spencer Museum of Art, University of Kansas, Lawrence.

Benton, Wood, Burchfield, and Hopper

Dominant among the American Scene artists were the Regionalists **Thomas Hart Benton** (1889–1975), John Steuart Curry, and Grant Wood. Of these artists, Missouri-born Benton was the most ambitious, vocal, and ultimately influential. Benton moved in modernist circles in New York in the teens and twenties, and even made abstract paintings based on his experiments with Synchromism in Paris. By 1934, however, when his fame was such that his self-portrait was reproduced on the cover of *Time* magazine, the artist had vehemently rejected modernism. "I wallowed," he once said, "in every cockeyed ism that came along, and it took me ten years to get all that modernist dirt out of my system." Benton was the darling of the rightwing critic Thomas Craven, who promoted the Regionalists as the great exemplars of artistic nationalism, and an object of scorn among leftist artists such as Stuart Davis.

In 1930 Benton executed a cycle of murals on the theme of modern technology for the New School for Social Research in New York. Called *America Today*, the series presents a cross-section of working America through images based on the artist's travel sketches. Benton presented his vast subject by means of compositional montage, as in *City Building* (fig. **18.31**), where heroic construction workers are seen against a backdrop of New York construction sites. Benton turned to the sixteenth-century art of Michelangelo and El Greco for the sinewy anatomies and mannered poses of his figures.

Benton earned the distinction of being the onetime teacher, at New York's Art Students League, of Jackson Pollock, who would transform the older master's rugged individualism, energy, and mural scale into the radical brand of modernism Benton so detested (see chapter 19). A young Pollock (playing the harmonica) is depicted among the country musicians in Benton's 1934 painting *The Ballad of the Jealous Lover of Lone Green Valley* (fig. **18.32**). As the old fiddler plays, a tale of jealousy and violence is enacted behind, and the landscape heaves up in metaphorical evocation of his music. Even in Benton's renditions of such traditional, rural themes, the lessons of Synchromism linger.

Although he studied in Paris for a time in 1923, Iowan **Grant Wood** (1892–1942) was never tempted by European modernist styles as was his colleague Benton. More formative was his trip in 1928 to Munich, where he discovered the art of the fifteenth-century Flemish and German primitives. The art from this historical period was also experiencing a resurgence of interest among some German painters, whose work had much in common with Wood's. Adapting this stylistic prototype to the Regionalist concerns he shared with Benton, Wood produced his most celebrated painting, *American Gothic* (fig. **18.33**), which soon became a national icon. Wood was initially drawn to the nineteenth-century "Carpenter Gothic" house that is

18.33 Grant Wood, *American Gothic*, 1930. Oil on beaverboard, 29⅞ × 24⅞" (75.9 × 63.2 cm). The Art Institute of Chicago.

depicted in the portrait's background. The models for the farmer couple (not husband and wife but two unrelated individuals) were actually Wood's sister and an Iowan dentist. The marriage of a miniaturist, deliberately archaizing style with contemporary, homespun, Puritan content drew immediate attention to the painting, though many wondered if Wood intended to satirize his subject. Wood, who was certainly capable of pictorial satire, said the subjects were painted out of affection rather than ridicule. In such works as *Young Corn*, 1931, Wood also applied his exacting style to landscape (fig. **18.34**), but his harmonious vision of cultivated nature, with its swelling hills, tidy crops, and delightfully puffy trees painted with a keen sense of abstract composition and balance, was based on childhood recollections rather than actual scenes. Modern technology, not to mention the harsh realities of Depression-era drought and dust bowls, has no place here.

A more romantic approach to Regionalism was taken by the Ohio artist **Charles Burchfield** (1893–1967). Following an early psychological crisis, Burchfield tended to project chronic fears and obsessions into his brooding paintings of rural and small-town America. He described his *November Evening* of 1934 (fig. **18.35**) as an attempt "to express the coming of winter over the Middle West as it must have felt to the pioneers—great black clouds sweep out of the west at twilight as if to overwhelm not only the pitiful human attempt at a town, but also the earth itself."

18.34 Grant Wood, *Young Corn*, 1931. Oil on masonite panel, 24 × 29⅞" (61 × 75.9 cm). Community School District, Cedar Rapids, Iowa.

18.35 Charles Burchfield, *November Evening*, 1934. Oil on canvas, 32 ⅛ x 52" (81.6 x 132.1 cm). The Metropolitan Museum of Art, New York.

18.36 Edward Hopper, *Early Sunday Morning*, 1930. Oil on canvas, 35 × 60" (88.9 × 152.4 cm). Whitney Museum of American Art, New York.

By contrast with the Midwestern Regionalists, **Edward Hopper** (1882–1967) was a mainly urban, New York artist. While he admired Burchfield's ability to discover a "hideous beauty" in the vulgar, eclectic jumble of the American landscape, he rejected any association with Benton and his fellow Regionalists, who, he said, caricatured America in their paintings. Hopper, a student of Henri, made several long visits to France between 1906 and 1910, at the time of the Fauve explosion and the beginnings of Cubism. Seemingly unaffected by either movement, Hopper early on established his basic themes of hotels, restaurants, or theaters, as well as their lonely inhabitants.

Much of the effect of Hopper's paintings is derived from his sensitivity to light—the light of early morning or of twilight; the dreary light filtered into a hotel room or office; or the garish light of a lunch counter isolated within the surrounding darkness. He could even endow a favorite landscape motif—the lighthouses of Cape Cod or Maine—with a quiet eeriness. One of his finest works, *Early Sunday Morning* (fig. **18.36**) depicts a row of buildings on a deserted Seventh Avenue in New York, where a sharp, raking light casts deep shadows and a strange stillness over the whole. The flat façade and dramatic lighting have been linked to Hopper's interest in stage-set design.

Despite his reputation as one of America's premier realist painters, Hopper brought a rigorous sense of abstract design to his compositions. In a late work from 1955, *Carolina Morning* (fig. **18.37**), a woman in a red dress and hat stands in a shaft of intense light. Beyond her the seemingly endless landscape is described with great economy in

18.37 Edward Hopper, *Carolina Morning*, 1955. Oil on canvas, 30 × 40⅛" (76.2 × 102 cm). Whitney Museum of American Art, New York.

almost geometric terms. The mood of introspective isolation that pervades many of Hopper's works has affinities with European Surrealist art.

Grandma Moses and Horace Pippin

Two self-taught artists whose portrayals of American life, albeit from very different perspectives, found common ground with American Scene painting are Anna Mary Robertson Moses, known as **Grandma Moses** (1860–

18.38 Grandma Moses, *Checkered House*, 1943. Oil on canvas, 36 × 45" (91.4 × 114.3 cm). IBM Corporation, Armonk, New York.

1961), and Horace Pippin. The quintessential untutored artist whose work was steeped in the strong tradition of American folk art, Grandma Moses graduated to oil painting after making pictures in yarn. Her innate gift for creating charming, nostalgic landscapes eventually attracted collectors and critics, and in 1939 she was included in the exhibition Contemporary Unknown American Painters at The Museum of Modern Art. Ironically, her work (fig. **18.38**) began to attract considerable attention in the forties and fifties, just as the abstract art of the New York School came to dominate the international scene. This proves that there was a large sector of the American public that preferred this art to the more radical statements of the avant-garde. By her death at the age of 101, her name had long been a household word.

Like Grandma Moses, **Horace Pippin** (1888–1946) took up painting late in life. A black artist from West Chester, Pennsylvania, Pippin worked in isolation until his work was first exhibited in the late thirties. He began to attract considerable attention at a time of growing interest in the work of self-taught artists. Pippin's range of subjects was broad, including portraits, landscapes, genre themes,

18.39 Horace Pippin, *Domino Players*, 1943. Oil on composition panel, 12¾ × 22" (32.4 × 55.9 cm). The Phillips Collection, Washington, D.C.

and a series on the life of abolitionist John Brown. He also painted scenes based on his experiences as an infantryman in World War I, when his right arm, with which he later painted, was permanently injured. *Domino Players* (fig. **18.39**), based on Pippin's childhood memories, shows the artist seated at a table between his female relatives. In such domestic scenes, Pippin offered a rare glimpse into an African-American household in the North around the turn of the century. Although he does not exclude the less picturesque aspects from his painting, he orchestrates the composition around stylized silhouettes and decorative color.

Bishop, Shahn and Blume

Also active in American Scene were such confirmed urban realists as **Isabel Bishop** (1902–88), who portrayed and dignified Depression-wracked New York and its unemployed or overworked and underpaid masses. Bishop, who had studied at the Art Students League while still a teenager, worked for a time on the Federal Arts Project, which employed a large number of women artists. She made keenly observed sketches of secretaries and stenographers relaxing during their breaks in Union Square, which she worked into paintings back in her studio. Through a technically complex method of oil and tempera, which she built up layer upon layer, she brought to her humble subjects all the humanity of Rembrandt (fig. **18.40**). Bishop's words of tribute to her friend, the painter Reginald Marsh, could easily pertain to her own work. She said he portrayed "little people, in unheroic situations" that are "modeled in the grand manner."

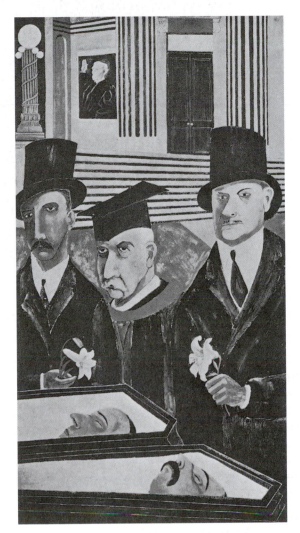

18.41 Ben Shahn, *The Passion of Sacco and Vanzetti*, 1931–32. Tempera on canvas, 7'½" × 4' (2.1 × 1.2 m). Whitney Museum of American Art, New York.

Foremost among the Social Realist painters of the thirties was **Ben Shahn** (1898–1969), whose work as an artist was inextricably tied to his social activism and who was, in his day, one of the most popular of all American painters. His paintings, murals, and posters inveighed against fascism, social injustice, and the hardships endured by the working-class poor. An accomplished photographer, Shahn often based his paintings on his own photographs, although the mat, thinly brushed tempera surfaces of his canvases have little to do with the photographic realism of Sheeler, for example. Shahn gained recognition in the early thirties through his paintings on the notorious case of Sacco and Vanzetti. These were bitter denunciations of the American legal system, which had condemned these two Italian-American anarchists to death in 1927 (fig. **18.41**). With the title *The Passion of Sacco and Vanzetti*, Shahn obviously meant to draw a connection to Christian martyrdom. *Liberation* (fig. **18.42**) depicts vacant-eyed children swinging before a stark backdrop of wartime devastation, literally hanging on for dear life.

The Russian-born Social Realist **Peter Blume** (1906–92) painted fantastic imagery in a clearly delineated style

18.40 Isabel Bishop, *Waiting*, 1938. Oil and tempera on gesso panel, 29 × 22½" (73.7 × 57.2 cm). Newark Museum, New Jersey.

18.42 Ben Shahn, *Liberation*, 1945. Tempera on cardboard mounted on composition board, 29¾ × 40" (75.6 × 101.6 cm). The Museum of Modern Art, New York.

18.43 Peter Blume, *The Eternal City*, 1934–37 (dated 1937 on painting). Oil on composition board, 34 × 47⅞" (86.4 × 121.6 cm). The Museum of Modern Art, New York.

that invites comparison with the work of Surrealist Salvador Dalí (see fig. 15.28). But the term Magic Realism, referring to an art that produces bizarre effects through the depiction of reality, is perhaps a more suitable description of Blume's art. Most American artists greeted Surrealism and all the concomitant theories of the unconscious with great circumspection during the thirties. It was not until the following decade, when European artists escaping fascism immigrated to the United States, that Surrealism, and particularly the automatist, abstract style of Miró, made major inroads into American art. Blume, who denounced Surrealism in print, nevertheless created a style that resonated with Surrealist experiments. His excoriation of the evils of Italian fascism, *The Eternal City* (fig. **18.43**), evokes unconscious wanderings through worlds of psychological as well as physical horror. He had traveled to Italy in 1932 on a Guggenheim grant and said that the idea for this work came to him while standing in the Roman forum as a strange light illuminated the scene. The bilious green head of a jack-in-the-box Mussolini looms over the ruins of classical civilization, while the Man of Sorrows continues his eternal mourning on the right.

Documents of an Era: American Photographers Between the Wars

The stalled economy, as well as the failed banks and crops, catalyzed American documentary photographers, many of whom were sponsored by the Federal Farm Security Administration (FSA). Established in 1935, the FSA aimed to educate the population at large about the drastic tolls that the Great Depression had taken upon the country's farmers and migrant workers. The moving force behind the project was economist Roy Stryker, who hired photographers, including Ben Shahn, Dorothea Lange, and Walker Evans, to travel to the hard-pressed areas and document the lives of the residents.

Following studies at Columbia University under Clarence H. White, **Dorothea Lange** (1895–1965) opened a photographic studio for portraiture in San Francisco. However, she found her most vital themes in the life of the streets, preparing her for the horrors of the Depression, which she encountered firsthand when she joined Stryker's FSA project. With empathy and respect toward her subjects, Lange photographed a tired, anxious, but stalwart mother with three of her children in a migrant worker camp (fig. **18.44**). This unforgettable and often reproduced image has been called "The Madonna of the Depression." Considered the first "documentary" photographer, Lange redefined the term by saying, "a documentary photograph is not a factual photograph per se … it carries with it another thing, a quality [in the subject] that the artist responds to."

Walker Evans (1903–75) studied in Paris, albeit literature rather than art, and like Lange, was hired by the FSA, making work, he later said, "against salon photography, against beauty photography, against art photography." In

18.44 Dorothea Lange, *Migrant Mother*, 1936. Gelatin-silver print. Library of Congress, Washington, D.C.

the summer of 1936 he and the writer James Agee lived in Alabama with sharecropper families. The result, a 1941 book called *Let Us Now Praise Famous Men*, containing Evans's photographs and Agee's writings, is one of the most moving documents in the history of photography. The straightest of straight photographers, Evans brought such passion to his work that in his images the simple, direct statement ends up being almost infinitely complex— as metaphor, irony, and compelling form. His portrait of a West Virginia miner's home tells volumes about the life of

18.45 Walker Evans, *Miner's Home, West Virginia*, 1935. Gelatin-silver print, 7⁹⁄₁₆ × 9½" (19.2 × 24.1 cm). National Gallery of Art, Washington, D.C.

its inhabitants. The cheerful middle-class homemakers and the smiling Santa that cover the walls are sadly incongruent in this stark environment (fig. **18.45**).

Another student of Clarence H. White and a hard-driven professional was **Margaret Bourke-White** (1904–71), who, as fellow photographer Alfred Eisenstaedt wrote, "would get up at daybreak to photograph a bread crumb." Really a photojournalist, Bourke-White was the first staff photographer recruited for Henry Luce's *Fortune* magazine, and when the same publisher launched *Life* in 1936, Bourke-White's photograph of Fort Peck Dam appeared on the cover of the first issue (fig. **18.46**), for which she also wrote the lead article. As this image indicates, Bourke-White favored the monumental in her boldly simplified compositions of colossal, mainly industrial, structures. While emphasizing the accomplishments of the country in a time of faltering confidence—her first major body of work documented the construction of the New York City skyscrapers in the early thirties as the Depression began—she also focused her camera on human subjects. Some of her most compelling images depict farmers in the drought-stricken Midwest during the Depression; soldiers in the war zones and prison camps of the early forties; and black South Africans in the fifties.

The German-born **Alfred Eisenstaedt** (1898–1995) was one of the first four staff photographers hired for *Life* magazine and another pioneer in the field of pictorial journalism. His photograph of the hazing of a West Point cadet appeared on the cover of the second issue of the magazine. He began his career as an Associated Press photographer in Germany but emigrated to the United States in 1935 when prewar politics made it difficult to publish his frank pictures. Though he produced many pictorial narratives, he was a firm believer in the single image that presented the distillation, the essential statement, of an event. This photograph of a sailor kissing a nurse in New York City's Times Square on Victory Day, 1945 (fig. **18.47**), sums up all the feelings of joy and relief at the end of World War II. In contrast to the images of the horrors of war that would flood the media from the sixties on, this image continues to be reproduced on posters and cards and seems to stand for the invincibility of the American spirit (there is some controversy as to whether or not this image was staged).

Berenice Abbott (1898–1991) returned to New York in 1929 from Paris, where she had learned photography as an assistant to Man Ray. One of the first to appreciate the genius of Atget (see fig. 15.59), and the only photographer ever to make portrait studies of the aged French photographer, Abbott fell in love with Manhattan upon her rediscovery of the city, much as Atget had with Paris. First working alone and then for the WPA, she set herself the task of capturing the inner spirit and driving force of the metropolis, as well as its outward aspect. Though utterly straight in her methods, Abbott, owing to her years among the Parisian avant-garde, inevitably saw her subject in modernist, abstract terms (fig. **18.48**).

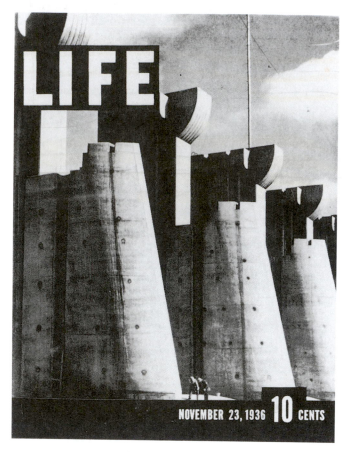

18.46 Margaret Bourke-White, *Fort Peck Dam, Montana*, Photograph for the first cover of *Life* magazine, November 23, 1936. *Life* magazine.

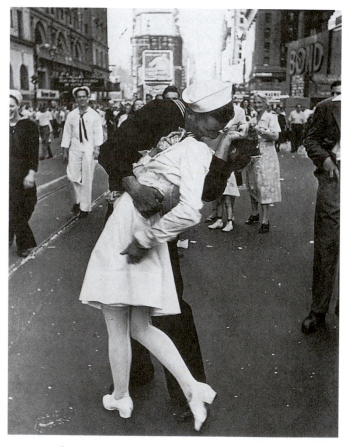

18.47 Alfred Eisenstaedt, *The Kiss (Times Square)*, 1945. *Life* magazine.

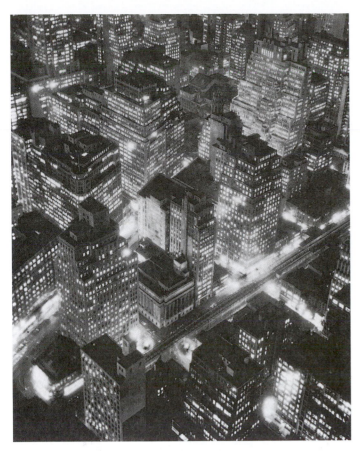

18.48 Berenice Abbott, *New York at Night*, 1933. Gelatin-silver print on masonite, 10½ × 12¾" (26.7 × 32.4 cm). The Museum of Modern Art, New York.

18.49 Weegee, *The Critic*, Gelatin-silver print, 10⅝ × 13³⁄₁₆" (27 × 33.5 cm). The Art Institute of Chicago.

Weegee (b. Arthur Fellig) (1899–1968), another advocate of straight photography, exploited the voyeuristic side of taking pictures. He worked primarily as a freelance newspaper photographer and published his sensational and satiric images of criminal arrests, murder victims, and social events in the tabloids of the day. Like Lisette Model (see fig. 15.67), with whom he worked at *PM* magazine, he captured events by surprising his subjects, often through the use of startling flash. *The Critic* (fig. **18.49**) is an ironic image of two women going to the opera. They stare at the camera and are in turn stared at by the woman to the right who ogles their jewelry, flowers, and furs, all in marked contrast to her own disheveled appearance. In 1936, Weegee published *Naked City*, a book containing many images of New York's underworld.

During the twenties in New York, a renaissance of black culture was taking place in the New York neighborhood of Harlem. Writers, intellectuals, musicians, and artists looked to the roots of their own cultural traditions in this remarkably fertile period known as the Jazz Age, which was brought to a halt by the stock market crash in 1929. While earning his living as a portrait photographer, **James Van Der Zee** (1886–1983) created a visual portrait of Harlem at the time (fig. **18.50**), documenting places and events such as weddings, funerals, anniversaries, and graduations. With his background in art

and music, Van Der Zee took occasion to manipulate his photographs, even to the point of painting his own studio backdrops and retouching his prints. During a period of mass migration of African-Americans from the rural south to northern industrial centers, Van Der Zee's studio portraits captured the aspirational dreams of his sitters, striking a balance between rich fantasy and confident modernity.

18.50 James Van Der Zee, *Harlem Billiard Room*, n.d. Gelatin-silver print, 11 × 14" (27.9 × 35.6 cm). Curtis Galleries, Minneapolis.

18.51 Romare Bearden, *Folk Musicians*, c. 1941–42. Gouache and casein on composition board, 36⅜ × 46⅝" (92.4 × 118.4 cm). Curtis Galleries, Minneapolis.

Black History and Modern Painting: Bearden and Lawrence

Romare Bearden (1914–88) was born in North Carolina but grew up in the thriving artistic milieu of the Harlem Renaissance. In a 1934 essay, *The Negro Artist and Modern Art*, Bearden called on fellow African-American artists to create art based on their own unique cultural experiences. He became involved with the 306 Group, an informal association of African-American artists and writers who met in studios at 306 West 141st Street. In 1936 he studied for a time with the German artist George Grosz (see fig. 13.35) at the city's Art Students League, no doubt drawn to the artist's reputation as a political satirist. *Folk Musicians* (fig. 18.51) is characteristic of Bearden's early work. With its simple modeling and consciously "folk" manner, the painting coincides with the prevailing Social Realist trends. In the fifties, following a trip to Paris,

18.52 Romare Bearden, *The Dove*, 1964. Cut-and-pasted paper, gouache, pencil, and colored pencil on cardboard, 13⅜ × 18¾" (34 × 47.6 cm). The Museum of Modern Art, New York.

18.53 Jacob Lawrence, *No. 1*, from *The Migration of the Negro* series, 1940–41. Tempera on hardboard, 12 × 18" (30.5 × 45.7 cm). The Phillips Collection, Washington, D.C.

Bearden experimented for a time with an Abstract Expressionist style. Soon after adopting collage techniques in the sixties he found a distinctive language of his own in the new medium. *The Dove* (fig. **18.52**) is a compendium of images originating in Bearden's memories of life in the South and in Harlem. With such works the artist said he wanted to "establish a world through art in which the validity of my Negro experience could live and make its own logic."

Like Bearden, **Jacob Lawrence** (b. 1917) took the African-American experience as his subject, but with a preference for recounting black history through narrative series. In 1940–41 he made sixty panels on the theme of the migration by black men and women from the rural South to the industrial North during and after World War I (fig. **18.53**). Lawrence thoroughly researched his subject and attached his own texts to each of the paintings, outlining the causes for the migration and the difficulties encountered by the workers in the new labor force as they headed for steel mills and railroads in cities like Chicago, Pittsburgh, and New York. Lawrence visually unified his panels by establishing a common color chord of red, green, yellow, and black and a style of boldly delineated silhouettes. The year after its creation, Lawrence's epic cycle went on a national museum tour organized by The Museum of Modern Art. By 1967, when he made a series on the life of black abolitionist Harriet Tubman, Lawrence had earned an international reputation and had begun a distinguished university career in teaching.

Social Protest and Personal Pain: Mexican Artists

While many artists in the United States were looking to indigenous traditions and subject matter between the two world wars, a number of like-minded artists in Mexico turned to their own history and artistic heritage, contributing to a veritable renaissance of Mexican painting. The years 1910 to 1920 were a time of armed revolution in Mexico. This was the era of Emiliano Zapata and Pancho Villa, which began with the ousting of the long-time president Porfirio Díaz and ended with a new constitution that swept in major land and labor reforms. Beginning in the twenties and continuing to midcentury, Mexican artists covered the walls of the country's schools, ministerial buildings, churches, and museums with vast murals, depicting subjects drawn from ancient and modern Mexico that celebrated a new Mexican cultural nationalism. The leading muralists were Diego Rivera, José Orozco, and David Siqueiros. Each of these also worked in the United States, where their work inspired American artists to turn away from European modernism and helped them, through the reintroduction of mural art, to rekindle the social dimensions of art. This was partially because they utilized the classical tradition of fresco painting and partially because theirs was an art of social protest with an obvious appeal to the left wing, a dominant force in American cultural life throughout the Depression decade. The muralists were enormously influential throughout Latin America as well as the United States.

Rivera

Following his artistic education in Mexico City, **Diego Rivera** (1886–1957) studied and lived in Europe between 1907 and 1921. There he met many of the leading avant-garde artists, including Picasso and Gris, and was developing his own Cubist style by 1913. He went to Italy near the end of his European sojourn and was particularly impressed by Renaissance murals. Upon his return to his native country, Rivera began to receive important commissions for monumental frescoes from the Mexican government. In the murals, he attempted to create a national Mexican style reflecting both the history of Mexico and the socialist spirit of the Mexican revolution. Rivera turned away from the abstracting forms of Cubism to develop a modern neoclassical style for his mural art consisting of simple, monumental forms and bold areas of color. This style can also be seen in Rivera's occasional easel paintings, such as *Flower Day*, 1925 (fig. **18.54**). While the subject of this work relates to an enormous mural project that Rivera undertook for the Ministry of Education in Mexico City, the massive figures and classically balanced composition derive from Italian art, as well as the Aztec and Mayan art Rivera consciously emulated.

18.54 Diego Rivera, *Flower Day*, 1925. Oil on canvas, 58 × 47½" (147.4 × 120.6 cm). Los Angeles County Museum of Art.

18.55 Diego Rivera, *Detroit Industry*, 1932–33. Fresco, north wall. The Detroit Institute of Arts.

In 1930 Rivera, a loyal communist, came to the United States, where he carried out several major commissions that were ironically made possible by capitalist industry. Political differences between artist and patrons did lead to problems, however. Most notably, in 1931, Rivera's mural at Rockefeller Center, New York, was destroyed as a result of the inclusion of the Soviet leader V. I. Lenin in a scene celebrating the achievements of humanity. Foremost among his surviving works in the United States is a narrative fresco cycle for the Detroit Institute of Arts on the theme of the evolution of technology, culminating in automobile manufacture (fig. **18.55**). Rivera toured the Ford motor plants for months, observing the workers and making preparatory sketches for his murals. The result is a *tour de force* of mural painting in which Rivera orchestrated man and machine into one great painted symphony. "The steel industry itself," he said, "has tremendous plastic beauty … it is as beautiful as the early Aztec or Mayan sculptures." In Rivera's vision, there is no sign of the unemployment or economic depression then crippling the country, nor the violent labor strikes at Ford that had just preceded Rivera's arrival in Detroit. At the same time, Rivera reveals criticism of capitalism's potential effects. Even though he portrays the workers in a dignified manner, it is important to note that they are rendered in a dehumanized fashion.

Orozco

José Clemente Orozco (1883–1949), like Rivera and Siqueiros, received his training in Mexico City, at the Academy of San Carlos. Orozco lived in the United States between 1927 and 1934, when he also had important fresco commissions, notably from Dartmouth College in Hanover, New Hampshire. There, in the Baker Library, he created a panorama of the history of the Americas. Orozco was not a proselytizer in the same vein as Rivera, and he hardly shared his compatriot's faith in modern progress and technology. In his complex of murals for Dartmouth, Orozco showed the viewer the human propensity for greed, deception, or violence. The murals begin with the Aztec story of the deity Quetzalcoatl, continue with the coming of the Spaniards and the Catholic Church, and conclude with the self-destruction of the machine age, climaxing in a great Byzantine figure of a flayed Christ, who, upon arriving in the modern world before piles of guns and tanks, destroys his own cross (fig. **18.56**). All of this is rendered in Orozco's fiery, expressionist style, with characteristically long, striated brushstrokes and brilliant color.

Siqueiros

The third member of the Mexican triumvirate of muralists, **David Alfaro Siqueiros** (1896–1974), executed fewer public murals throughout the thirties than his countrymen,

18.56 José Orozco, *The Epic of American Civilization: Modern Migration of the Spirit*, 1932–34. Mural, fourteenth panel. Baker Library, Dartmouth College, Hanover, New Hampshire.

partly because his radical political activities kept him on the move. Siqueiros maintained a lifelong interest in adopting the means of modern technology to art. In 1932 he came to the United States, to experience a "technological civilization," and taught at a Los Angeles art school where he

18.57 David Siqueiros, *Echo of a Scream*, 1937. Enamel on wood, 48 × 36" (121.9 × 91.4 cm). The Museum of Modern Art, New York.

executed murals using innovative materials and methods. Siqueiros's first major mural project came in 1939 for the Electricians' Syndicate Building in Mexico City.

The 1937 *Echo of a Scream* (fig. **18.57**), painted the year that Siqueiros joined the antifascist Republican Army in the Spanish Civil War, illustrates his vigorous pictorial attack. Beginning with an actual news photograph of a child in the aftermath of a bombing in the contemporaneous Sino-Japanese war, Siqueiros portrayed the "echo" of the child's cries as an enormous disembodied head above a field of ruins, creating a wrenching image of despair.

In 1936 Siqueiros established an experimental workshop in New York that attracted young artists from Latin America and the United States (including Jackson Pollock). The workshop was dedicated to modernizing the methods and materials of art production and to promoting the aims of the Communist Party of the United States. One participant described the use of new industrial paints in the workshop:

> We sprayed [it] through stencils and friskets, embedded wood, metal, sand, and paper. We used it in thin glazes or built up into thick gobs. We poured it, dripped it, splattered it, hurled it at the picture surface. … What emerged was an endless variety of accidental effects.

Using such experimental methods, Siqueiros hoped to establish bold new ways of creating modern propagandistic murals. In general, the tradition of mural painting in the thirties, of both the Mexicans and WPA artists like Benton, was crucial for the Abstract Expressionist artists coming of age during the ensuing decades.

Kahlo

In the life of Mexican painter **Frida Kahlo** (1907–54), the defining moment came in 1925, when her spine, pelvis, and foot were crushed in a bus accident. During a year of painful convalescence, Kahlo, already a victim of childhood polio, took up painting. Through photographer Tina Modotti she met Diego Rivera, whom she married in 1929. She was with Rivera in Detroit when he painted the murals at the Institute of Arts, but Kahlo never adopted the monumental scale or public themes of mural art. Like so many exceptional women artists, she found her way outside the dominant, masculine mode, which in her circle was mural painting. Instead she turned her attention inward and over the years created an intimate autobiography through an astonishing series of self-portraits. In an early example (fig. **18.58**), she envisions herself in a long pink dress surrounded at the left by the cultural artifacts of Mexico and, at the right, the industrial trappings of the North. The hieratic and miniaturist technique she employs in this tiny painting on metal is in the folk tradition of Mexican votive paintings, which depict religious figures often surrounded by fantastic attributes.

When André Breton visited Kahlo and Rivera in Mexico in 1938, he claimed Kahlo as a Surrealist and arranged for

18.58 Frida Kahlo, *Self-Portrait on the Border Between Mexico and the United States*, 1932. Oil on sheet metal, 12¼ × 13¾" (31.1 × 34.9 cm). Private collection.

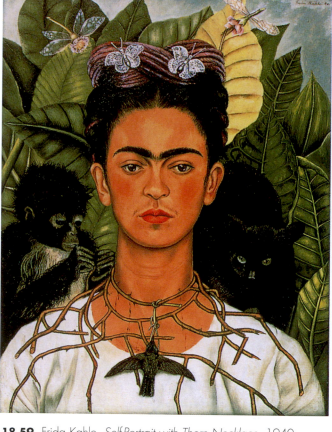

18.59 Frida Kahlo, *Self-Portrait with Thorn Necklace*, 1940. Oil on canvas, 24 × 18¾" (61 × 47.6 cm). Art Collection, Harry Ransom Humanities Research Center, University of Texas, Austin.

her work to be shown, with considerable success, in New York and Paris. Soon thereafter she and Rivera divorced (they remarried a year later), and Kahlo made several self-portraits documenting her emotional grief. In *Self-Portrait with Thorn Necklace* (fig. **18.59**) she assumes the role of martyr, impaled by her necklace from which a dead hummingbird (worn by the lovelorn) hangs.

Tamayo

Rufino Tamayo (1899–1991), a native of Oaxaca of Zapotec Indian descent, was another Mexican artist who came to prominence around the thirties. He lived in New York in the late twenties and again from 1936 to 1948, teaching and working for a time for the WPA, until the government banned foreign artists from the program. Although he occasionally received mural commissions,

Tamayo differed from the three leading muralists from Mexico in that his aim was never to create a public art based on political ideologies: instead, he preferred themes of a more universal nature. His style was informed both by modernist modes, such as Cubism and Surrealism, and by Mexico's pre-Hispanic art. In the early forties, he made a series of animal paintings (fig. **18.60**), whose forms were inspired by popular Mexican art, but whose implied violence seems to register the traumas of war.

18.60 Rufino Tamayo, *Animals*, 1941. Oil on canvas, 30⅛ × 40" (76.5 × 101.6 cm). The Museum of Modern Art, New York.

18.61 Tina Modotti, *Number 29: Hands of Marionette Player*, n.d. Gelatin-silver print, 7½ × 9½" (19.1 × 24.1 cm). The Museum of Modern Art, New York.

Modotti's Photography in Mexico

Closely associated with the artist-reformers of Mexico was the Italian-born photographer **Tina Modotti** (1896–1942), who, with her longtime companion the photographer Edward Weston, arrived in Mexico in the early twenties. She joined the Communist Party in 1927 and worked in Mexico until her expulsion in 1930 for political activism. She was commissioned by the muralists to document their works in photographs that were circulated internationally, contributing to the celebrity of the movement. Her sharp-focus, unmanipulated images, such as her elegant close-ups of plants, bear the influence of Weston. But Modotti used her camera largely for socially relevant subjects, as when she photographed the hands and marionettes of a friend who used his craft for political ends (fig. **18.61**). With a sure eye for the telling image, Modotti built a remarkable corpus of photographs until she gave up the profession to live a nomadic existence in pursuit of her political goals. After periods in Moscow and Spain, she returned to Mexico, where she died in suspicious circumstances in 1942.

The Avant-Garde Advances: Toward American Abstract Art

As we have seen in both the United States and Mexico, during the thirties modernism, particularly Cubism and abstraction, seemed to have been driven underground. Nevertheless, while figuration and representation found wide public appeal, artists, many supported by the Federal Arts Project, were laying the groundwork for a revival of abstract art. Thus the seeds were sown that would germinate, after World War II, in the transformation of the United States from the position of a provincial follower to that of a full partner in the creation of new art and architecture.

Exhibitions and Contact with Europe

A number of other events and developments of the twenties and thirties also helped to strengthen the presence of avant-garde art in New York. As we saw in chapter 13, Katherine Dreier, the painter and collector advised by Marcel Duchamp, had organized the Société Anonyme in 1920 for the purpose of buying and exhibiting examples of the most advanced European and American art and holding lectures and symposia on related topics. In 1927 A. E. Gallatin, another painter-collector, put his personal collection of modern art on display at New York University under the name of The Gallery of Living Art. It remained on exhibition for fifteen years. (This collection, now at the Philadelphia Museum together with that of Walter C. Arensberg, includes examples by Brancusi, Braque, Cézanne, Kandinsky, Klee, Léger, Matisse, Miró, Mondrian, and many others.)

The Gallery of Living Art was, in effect, the first museum with a permanent collection of exclusively modern art to be established in New York City. Shortly afterward came the opening of The Museum of Modern Art in 1929, which followed its initial series of exhibitions by modern masters with the historic shows Cubism and Abstract Art and Fantastic Art, Dada, Surrealism, both in 1936. In 1935 the Whitney Museum held its first exhibition of American abstract art, and in 1936 the American Abstract Artists (AAA) group was organized. By 1939 Solomon R. Guggenheim had founded the Museum of Non-Objective Painting, which would eventually be housed in the great Frank Lloyd Wright building on Fifth Avenue (see fig. 23.2).

During the thirties, a few progressive European artists began to visit or emigrate to the United States. Léger made three visits before settling at the outbreak of World War II. Duchamp, Ozenfant, Moholy-Nagy, Josef Albers, and Hans Hofmann were all living in the United States before 1940. The last four were particularly influential as teachers. The group as a whole represented the earliest influx of European artists who spent the war years in the United States and who helped to transform the face of American art. Conversely, younger American painters continued to visit and study in Paris during the thirties. Throughout the late thirties and forties, the AAA held annual exhibitions dedicated to the promotion of every form of abstraction, but with particular emphasis on experiments related to the Constructivist and Neo-Plasticist abstraction being propagated in Paris by the Cercle et Carré and Abstraction-Création groups. These close contacts with the European modernists were of great importance for the subsequent course of modern American art.

Davis and Murphy

The professional career of **Stuart Davis** (1894–1964) encompassed five decades of modern art in the United States. Although Davis was deeply committed to socialist reforms, unlike his Mexican contemporaries or Americans like Ben Shahn, he did not exploit painting as a public

18.62 Stuart Davis, *Egg Beater #1*, 1927. Oil on canvas, 27 × 38¼" (68.6 × 97.2 cm). The Phillips Collection, Washington, D.C.

platform for his political beliefs. Davis was committed to art with a broad, popular appeal, and he negotiated the vast territory between pure abstraction and the conservative realism of the Regionalists. After leaving Robert Henri's School of Art, Davis exhibited five watercolors in the 1913 Armory Show and was converted to modernism as a result of seeing the European work on display. Davis's collages and paintings of the early twenties are explorations of consumer-product packaging as subject matter, executed in a manner that demonstrates his assimilation of Synthetic Cubism as well as his recollection of nineteenth-century American *trompe l'oeil* painting. But his emphatically two-dimensional, deadpan treatment of imagery borrowed from popular culture, as well as his use of modern commercial lettering in his paintings, made Davis an important forerunner of sixties Pop art.

In his *Egg Beater* series of 1927–28, Davis attempted to rid himself of the last illusionistic vestiges of nature, painting an eggbeater, an electric fan, and a rubber glove again and again until they had ceased to exist in his eyes and mind except as color, line, and shape relations (fig. **18.62**). Throughout the thirties, Davis continued the interplay of clearly defined, if fragmented, objects with geometric abstract organization. His color became more brilliant, and he intensified the tempo, the sense of movement, the gaiety, and the rhythmic beat of his works through an increasing complication of smaller, more irregular, and more contrasted color shapes.

The culmination of these experiments may be seen in a 1940 work, *Report from Rockport* (fig. **18.63**). Although more abstract than most paintings of the thirties, *Report*

18.63 Stuart Davis, *Report from Rockport*, 1940. Oil on canvas, 24 × 30" (61 × 76.2 cm). The Metropolitan Museum of Art, New York.

18.64 Stuart Davis, *Rapt at Rappaport's*, 1952. Oil on canvas, 52⅜ × 40⅜" (133 × 102.6 cm). Hirshhorn Museum and Sculpture Garden, Smithsonian Institution, Washington, D.C.

remained on the outside world rather than the interior realm of psychology and emotions. He said, "I care nothing for Abstract Art as such, but only as it evidences a contemporary language of vision suited to modern life." With the emergence of Pop art in the sixties, along with more objective forms of abstraction, Davis's art took on new relevance in the history of modern American art.

Gerald Murphy (1888–1964) was a wealthy businessman turned artist, on whom F. Scott Fitzgerald modeled the hero of *Tender is the Night*. Murphy came into contact with the Parisian avant-garde by working on sets for the Ballets Russes. He scandalized the 1924 Salon des Indépendants by exhibiting an eighteen-foot-high (5.4 m) painting of an ocean liner in an elegant Art Deco style.

Murphy worked with painstaking slowness, producing only one painting a year, and no more. Of a total of probably fifteen, a mere seven are known to survive. Still, he had absorbed the principles of Synthetic Cubism and, like Stuart Davis, succeeded in turning them to his own purposes, which were to transform American popular imagery into a high art of simple, emblematic force. His bold composition, *Razor*, 1924 (fig. **18.65**), depicts a common matchbox above a heraldic arrangement of a razor and fountain pen. This subject has an autobiographical significance. Murphy developed a patent for a safety razor and was the son of the

from Rockport, inspired by the main square of Rockport, Massachusetts, includes recognizable features such as buildings and gas pumps. There is a suggestion of depth, achieved by a schematic linear perspective, but the graphic shapes that twist and vibrate across the surface, with no clear representational role to play, reaffirm the picture plane.

In the 1952 painting *Rapt at Rappaport's* (fig. **18.64**), the alliterative and slangy title invades the actual painting: the staccato letters flash across the bottom edge like a news bulletin. Large, flat color-shapes of red, blue, orange, and black are suspended against a green ground. This surface is animated with invented shapes characteristic of Davis, the torn S or 8 ribbon, the floating white circles or rectangles. In bright blue letters toward the center of the painting is the word "ANY," which Davis said "means any subject matter is equal to art, from the most insignificant to one of relative importance."

Until his death in 1964, Davis searched for ways to merge American subject matter with the forms of European Cubism. The result was a thoroughly new, uniquely American Cubist language. In 1943 he wrote in a leading art magazine, "Enormous changes are taking place which demand new forms, and it is up to artists living in America to find them." His enthusiasm for American innovation in painting did not extend, however, to the subjective art of the Abstract Expressionists in the fifties. His focus

18.65 Gerald Murphy, *Razor*, 1924. Oil on canvas. 32⅜ × 36½" (82 × 92 cm). Dallas Museum of Art, Foundation for the Arts.

owner of Cross pens. Murphy belongs in a realm entirely of his own, but one that nevertheless looked forward to the Pop art of the sixties. He had no direct influence on the movement, however. He was not well known in the United States owing to his isolation abroad, and his rare canvases were not discovered until years after his death.

Diller and Pereira

One of the artists who exhibited with the AAA was **Burgoyne Diller** (1906–65), the first American to develop an abstract style based on Dutch de Stijl. Once enrolled at the Art Students League in 1929, Diller very rapidly assimilated influences from Cubism, German Expressionism, Kandinsky, and Suprematism, much of which he knew only through reproductions in such imported journals as *Cahiers d'art*. Finally, toward the end of 1933, he had his first direct experience of a painting by Mondrian, whose Neo-Plastic principles became the main source of Diller's interests. But far from servile in his dependence on Neo-Plasticism, Diller went his own way by integrating color and line, so that lines became overlapping color planes (fig. **18.66**). Thus he created a complex sense of space that differs from that of Mondrian.

Irene Rice Pereira (1907–1971) was another pioneer American abstractionist to appear in the thirties. Taking her inspiration primarily from the Bauhaus, Pereira sought to fuse art and science, or technology, in a new kind of visionary image grounded in abstract geometry, but aspiring, like the Suprematist art of Malevich, toward an even more rarefied realm of experience. Boston-born and professionally active in New York, Pereira developed a seasoned

18.67 Irene Rice Pereira, *Abstraction*, 1940. Oil on canvas, 30 × 38" (76.2 × 96.5 cm). Honolulu Academy of Arts.

style compounded of sharply rectilinear hard-edge and crystalline planes, often rendered as if floated or suspended one in front of the other, with transparent tissues giving visual access to the textured, opaque surfaces lying below (fig. **18.67**). The resulting effect is that of a complex, many-layered field of color and light.

Avery and Tack

Born and schooled in Hartford, Connecticut, **Milton Avery** (1885–1965) moved to New York in 1925. He characteristically worked in broad, simplified planes of thinly applied color deriving from Matisse but involving an altogether personal poetry. His subjects were his family and friends, often relaxing on holiday, as in his 1945 canvas *Swimmers and Sunbathers* (fig. **18.68**). In his later years he turned more to landscape, which, though always recognizable, became more and more abstract in organization. Avery was a major source for the American Color Field painters of the fifties and sixties, such as Mark Rothko, Adolph Gottlieb, and Helen Frankenthaler (see figs. 19.24, 19.33). In a memorial service for his friend, Rothko said, "Avery had that inner power which can be achieved only by those gifted with magical means, by those born to sing."

Augustus Vincent Tack (1870–1949) may have been the most maverick and removed of all the progressive American painters between the wars. He alone managed to integrate modernism's nonobjective and figural modes into organic, sublimely evocative, wall-size abstractions. His work formed a unique bridge between an older pantheistic tradition of landscape painting, last seen in the work of Ryder (see fig. 2.53), and its new, brilliant flowering in the heroic abstractions of the postwar New York School, especially in the paintings of Clyfford Still (see fig. 19.31). Duncan Phillips, Tack's faithful patron throughout the twenties and thirties, foresaw it all when he declared, in

18.66 Burgoyne Diller, *Second Themes*, 1937–38. Oil on canvas, 30⅛ × 30" (76.5 × 76.2 cm). The Metropolitan Museum of Art, New York.

18.68 Milton Avery, *Swimmers and Sunbathers*, 1945. Oil on canvas, 28 × 48⅛" (71.1 × 122.2 cm). The Metropolitan Museum of Art, New York.

commenting on one of Tack's paintings: "We behold the majesty of omnipotent purpose emerging in awe-inspiring symmetry out of thundering chaos. ... It is a symbol of a new world in the making, of turbulence stilled after tempest by a universal God."

Tack was trained in the 1890s by the American Impressionist John Twachtman, and his early work consisted largely of landscapes in the style of late-nineteenth-century American symbolism. In 1920, when he made his first paintings of the Rocky Mountains, Tack discovered in the majestic Western landscape motifs capable of expressing his mystical feelings about nature. These he gradually transformed into the dramatic, nature-inspired abstractions of his mature work. Paintings such as *Night, Amargosa Desert*, 1935 (fig. **18.69**), represent American Romanticism in the most advanced form it would take during the period, a view of the material world examined so intensely that it dissolved into pure emblem or icon, an aesthetic surrogate for the divine, ordering presence sensed within the disorder of raw nature. Tack's paintings exhibit uncanny affinities with the allover abstractions of the New York School of the fifties.

18.69 Augustus Vincent Tack, *Night, Amargosa Desert*, 1935. Oil on canvas mounted on plywood panel, 7' × 4' (2.1 × 1.2 m). The Phillips Collection, Washington, D.C.

Sculpture in America Between the Wars

American sculpture during the first four decades of the twentieth century lagged behind painting in quantity, quality, and originality. Throughout this period the academicians predominated, and such modernist developments in sculpture as Cubism or Constructivism were hardly visible. Archipenko, who had lived in the United States since 1923 and who had taught at various universities, finally opened his own school in New York City in 1939. Alexander Calder (see chapter 17) was the best-known American sculptor before World War II, but largely in a European context, since he had worked in Paris since 1926. His influence grew in America in the following years. During the thirties, in sculpture as in painting, despite the predominance of the academicians and the isolation of the progressive artists, a number of sculptors were emerging, including David Smith and Isamu Noguchi (see chapter 19), who helped to change the face of American sculpture at the end of World War II.

Lachaise and Nadelman

Among the first generation of modern American sculptors, two important practitioners were Europeans, trained in Europe, who emigrated to the United States early in their

18.71 Elie Nadelman, *Man in the Open Air*, c. 1915. Bronze, 54½" (138.4 cm) high; at base 11¾ × 21½" (29.9 × 54.6 cm). The Museum of Modern Art, New York.

careers. These were **Gaston Lachaise** (1882–1935) and Elie Nadelman. Lachaise was born in Paris and trained at the École des Beaux-Arts. By 1910 he had begun to experiment with the image that was to obsess him during the rest of his career, that of a female nude with enormous breasts and thighs and delicately tapering arms and legs (fig. **18.70**). This form derives from Maillol (see fig. 6.13), but in Lachaise's versions it received a range of expression from pneumatic elegance to powerfully primitivizing works that recall the ancient sculpture of India, as well as prehistoric female fertility figures.

Elie Nadelman (1882–1946) received his European academic training at the Warsaw Art Academy. Around 1909 in Paris, where he made the acquaintance of artists including Picasso and Brancusi, Nadelman was reducing the sculpted human figure to almost abstract curvilinear patterns. After his move to the United States in 1914, he was given an exhibition by Stieglitz at 291 gallery. He progressively developed a style that might be described as a form of sophisticated primitivism (he was an avid collector of folk art), marked by simplified surfaces placed in the service of a witty and amusing commentary on contemporary life. His Man in the Open Air (fig. **18.71**) is an early example of his work in this manner.

18.70 Gaston Lachaise, *Standing Woman*, 1912–27. Bronze, height 70" (177.8 cm). Albright-Knox Art Gallery, Buffalo.

Storrs and Roszak

Son of a Chicago architect, sculptor **John Storrs** (1885–1956) studied in Chicago, Boston, New York, and Paris and, beginning in 1915, was making geometricized figurative sculptures in stone. Their streamlined forms, partly inspired by the Native American art Storrs admired and collected, was at one with the prevailing Art Deco style in architecture and decorative arts. During the twenties, Storrs began to make sculpture directly inspired by modern architectural forms, initially those created by Frank Lloyd Wright. His later celebrations in sculpture of the modern skyscraper (fig. **18.72**) parallel those of Stella, O'Keeffe, Sheeler, and Marin. Such works led to commissions for monumental sculpture to decorate actual buildings. Owing to the artist's long expatriation to France's Loire Valley, Storrs's achievement remained largely forgotten until the sixties.

18.73 Theodore Roszak, *Construction in White*, 1938. Painted wood and plastic, 49½ × 49½" (125.7 × 125.7 cm). Estate of Theodore Roszak.

18.72 John Storrs, *Forms in Space #1*, c. 1927. Steel and copper, 20½ × 4 × 1⅜" (52.1 × 10.2 × 4.1 cm). The Metropolitan Museum of Art New York.

Although in the minority, sculpture in a Constructivist vein thrived in the hands of a few American artists in the thirties, including Polish-born **Theodore Roszak** (1907–81). Having arrived in Chicago with his family as a young child, Roszak was trained as a conventional painter at that city's School of the Art Institute, but a change in his outlook occurred during a trip to Europe from 1929 to 1931. Upon returning to the United States, he settled in New York in 1931, working eventually for the WPA. He made de Chiricoesque figure paintings with Cubist overtones in the early thirties and, at the same time, began making Cubist sculptures and reliefs. By the middle of the decade, he was experimenting with abstract constructed sculpture as a result of his interest in machines and industrial design. *Construction in White* (fig. **18.73**) is a whitewashed plywood box in which Roszak cut a circle and inserted intersecting sheets of plastic and wooden blocks. He said he wanted such works to stand as utopian symbols for perfection. Critical to Roszak were the teachings of the Bauhaus, particularly those of Moholy-Nagy, who had come to Chicago in 1937 to head the New Bauhaus. In the aftermath of World War II, Roszak became disenchanted with technology and began to make welded sculpture in steel. The rough surfaces and aggressive forms of these works reflected the violence and terror of war, situating his work in the arena of Abstract Expressionism (see chapter 19).

19
Abstract Expressionism and the New American Art

Looking back on the forties, the American painter Barnett Newman recalled that artists of his generation:

> felt the moral crisis of a world in shambles, a world devastated by a great depression and a fierce world war, and it was impossible at that time to paint the kind of paintings that we were doing—flowers, reclining nudes, and people playing the cello. … This was our moral crisis in relation to what to paint.

In 1942, immediately after the United States's entry into World War II, the dominant styles of painting were still Social Realism and Regionalism (see chapter 18). The war contributed to a ferment that brought on the creation of the first major original direction in the history of American painting, Abstract Expressionism, or, as it is more generically called, the New York School. Attitudes conditioned by the war—a sense of alienation and a loss of faith in old systems and old forms of expression—led artists to explore a broad range of intellectual thought from existentialism to the theories of Sigmund Freud and Carl Jung. The devastation of Europe's cultural centres by the second major war in three decades created a vacuum in the artworld that New York was poised to fill. Moreover, the emerging polarized politics of the Cold War lent weight to what was perceived as the quintessential Americanness of Abstract Expressionism—its vitality, spontaneity, and confident scale—as a counter to the popular Western image of communist culture as drab, impoverished, and state-dominated.

Entering a New Arena: Modes of Abstract Expressionism

The diverse group of artists involved were opposed to all forms of Social Realism and any art form that smacked of nationalism. Nonetheless, a number of them had connections with the American West and to a degree cultivated an anti-European stance. Much as they admired Mondrian, who was present in New York by 1940, they also rejected as trivial the pure geometric abstraction, promoted within the ranks of the American Abstract Artists (AAA), that his art had engendered in America. On the other hand, the relationship of the new movement to the European Surrealists, some of whom also sought refuge from the war in New York, was critical. The Americans were particularly drawn to the organic, abstract, automatist Surrealism of Matta, Miró, and Masson (see chapter 15). Matta, who was in New York from 1939 to 1948, helped introduce the idea of psychic automatism to the Abstract Expressionists. The Americans were less concerned with the new method as a means of tapping into the unconscious than as a liberating procedure that could lead to the exploration of new forms.

The artworld of the forties was far from a coherent community. The experience of the Federal Arts Project of the WPA had provided a degree of camaraderie among artists, but largely the artists of the New York School gathered informally in their studios and in the cafeterias and taverns of Greenwich Village to discuss—and sometimes to battle over—the burning artistic issues of the day. Peggy Guggenheim's gallery, Art of This Century, featured European Surrealists but also became a venue for young artists like Clyfford Still, Robert Motherwell, and, especially, Jackson Pollock. A handful of other dealers and a few critics, notably formalist critic Clement Greenberg, as well as Harold Rosenberg and Thomas Hess, eventually championed the new movement. Greenberg's conception of modernism, in particular, was highly influential. In a 1954 lecture, later published in 1961 as *Art and Culture*, he advanced the idea that art's ability to connect powerfully with human experience is independent of any representational qualities it may have. Recognition by major museums came more slowly. The Museum of Modern Art began to acquire works by a few of the artists in the mid-forties and to include their work in group exhibitions devoted to contemporary American art. By 1958 a kind of international apotheosis of Abstract Expressionism took place with the museum's exhibition The New American Painting, which was devoted to the movement and toured eight European countries. Created at a point at which American money and popular culture were flooding Europe, the exhibition served as an assertion of American dominance in high culture as well.

Although Abstract Expressionism is as diverse as the artists involved, in a very broad sense two main tendencies may be noted. The first is that of the so-called gestural painters, concerned in different ways with the spontaneous and unique touch of the artist, his or her "handwriting," and the emphatic texture of the paint. It included such major artists as Pollock, Willem de Kooning, and Franz Kline. The other group consisted of the Color Field painters, concerned with an abstract statement in terms of a large, unified color shape or area. Here one can include Rothko, Newman, Still, and Gottlieb, as well as, to a degree, Motherwell and Reinhardt. In 1948 several of these painters founded an informal school called the "Subjects of the Artist." They were united by their belief that abstract art could express universal, timeless themes. As they had stated in a letter to *The New York Times*, "There is no such thing as a good painting about nothing." "We assert that the subject is crucial," they wrote, "and only that subject-matter is valid which is tragic and time-less." Even at its most abstract, art could convey a sense, in Rothko's works, of "tragedy, ecstasy, and doom."

The Picture as Event: Experiments in Gestural Painting

In 1952 Harold Rosenberg coined the phrase "action painting" to describe the process by which the spontaneous gesture was enacted on the canvas. He wrote:

> At a certain moment, the canvas began to appear to one American painter after another as an arena in which to act—rather than as a space in which to reproduce, re-design, analyze or 'express' an object, actual or imagined. What was to go on the canvas was not a picture but an event.

What the term "action painting" failed to account for was the balance that these artists struck between forethought and spontaneity; between control and the unexpected.

Hofmann

The career of **Hans Hofmann** (1880–1966) encompassed two worlds and two generations. Born in Bavaria, Hofmann lived and studied in Paris between 1903 and 1914, experiencing the range of new movements from Neo-Impressionism to Fauvism and Cubism. He was particularly close to Robert Delaunay (see chapter 10), whose ideas on color structure were a formative influence. In 1915 Hofmann opened his first school in Munich. In 1932 he moved to the United States to teach, first at the University of California, Berkeley, then at New York's Art Students League, and finally at his own Hans Hofmann School of Fine Arts in New York and in Provincetown,

Massachusetts. Hofmann's greatest concern as a painter, teacher, and theoretician lay in his concepts of pictorial structure, which were based on architectonic principles rooted in Cubism. This did not prevent him from attempting the freest kinds of automatic painting. A number of such works executed in the mid-forties, although on a small scale, anticipated Pollock's drip paintings.

During the last twenty-six years of his life, Hofmann made abstractions of amazing variety, ranging from a precise but painterly geometry to a lyrical expressionism. In his best-known works, Hofmann used thick, rectangular slabs of paint and aligned them with the picture's edge (fig. **19.1**), demonstrating his ideas about color as a space-creating device. While the rectangles of color affirm the literal flatness of the picture, they also appear to advance and recede spatially, creating what Hofmann called a "push and pull" effect. Like his fellow German emigré Josef Albers, Hofmann was one of the premier art educators and theoreticians in the United States, and his influence on a generation of younger artists such as Lee Krasner (see fig. 19.14) and critics including Clement Greenberg was enormous.

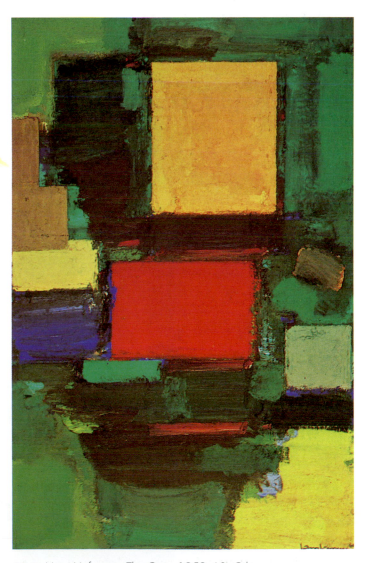

19.1 Hans Hofmann, *The Gate*, 1959–60. Oil on canvas, 6'2⅝" × 4'¼" (1.9 m × 1.23 m). Solomon R. Guggenheim Museum, New York.

Gorky

Armenian-born **Arshile Gorky** (1905–48) was a seminal figure in the early years of the New York School. He was a largely self-taught artist whose work constituted a critical link between European Surrealism and American Abstract Expressionism. Gorky arrived in the United States in 1920, a refugee from the Turkish campaign of genocide against the Armenians. His early experiments with both figuration and abstraction were deeply influenced by Cézanne and then Picasso and Miró. He achieved a distinctive figural mode in *The Artist and His Mother* (fig. **19.2**), a haunting portrait based on an old family photograph in which the artist posed beside his mother, well before she died of starvation in his arms.

By the early forties, Gorky was evolving his mature style, a highly original mode of expression that combined strange hybrid forms with rich, fluid color. One of his most ambitious painting, *The Liver is the Cock's Comb*, 1944 (fig. **19.3**), is a large composition that resembles both a wild and vast landscape and a microscopically detailed internal anatomy. Gorky combined veiled but recognizable shapes, such as claws or feathers, with overtly sexual forms, creating an erotically charged atmosphere filled with softly brushed, effulgent color. His biomorphic imagery owed much to Kandinsky and Miró, whose works Gorky knew well, and to the Surrealist automatism of Masson and Matta, both in New York in the forties. The year he made this painting, Gorky met André Breton, the self-appointed leader of the Surrealists, who took a strong interest in his work and arranged for it to be shown at a New York gallery in 1945.

Although its subject is deliberately ambiguous, the 1947 painting *The Betrothal II* is one of three compositions of the same title that Gorky built around the central image of a man on horseback. Over a delicate linear scaffolding, the artist applied transparent washes of muted color, leaving visible the tracks of his brush. It was this kind of dynamic balance between representational and figurative motifs that appealed to Gorky's contemporaries like de Kooning. Following a series of traumatic events, Gorky

19.2 Arshile Gorky, *The Artist and His Mother*, c. 1929–36. Oil on canvas, 60 × 50" (152.4 × 127 cm). National Gallery of Art, Washington, D.C.

19.3 Arshile Gorky, *The Liver Is the Cock's Comb*, 1944. Oil on canvas, 6'1¼" × 8'2" (1.9 × 2.5 m). Albright-Knox Art Gallery, Buffalo, New York.

hanged himself in his studio in 1948, just as his fellow Abstract Expressionists, whose work was indebted to his example, were gaining serious momentum in New York.

Willem de Kooning

Willem de Kooning (1904–97) was a central figure of Abstract Expressionism, even though he was not one of the first to emerge in the public eye during the forties. Born in Rotterdam, the Netherlands, de Kooning underwent rigorous artistic training at the Rotterdam Academy. He came to the United States in 1926, where, throughout the thirties, he slowly made the transition from house painter, commercial designer, and Sunday painter to full-time artist. Of the utmost importance was his early encounter with Stuart Davis, Gorky, and the influential Russian-born painter John Graham, "the three smartest guys on the scene," according to de Kooning. They were his frequent companions to The Metropolitan Museum of Art, where it was possible to see examples of ancient and old-master art. Although he did not exhibit until 1948, de Kooning was an underground force among younger experimental painters by the early forties.

One of the most remarkable aspects of de Kooning's talent was his ability to shift between representational and abstract modes, which he never held to be mutually exclusive. He continued to make paintings of figures into the seventies, but even many of his most abstract compositions contain remnants of or allusions to the figure. "Even abstract shapes must have a likeness," he said. In the late forties he made a bold group of black-and-white abstractions in which he had fully assimilated the tenets of Cubism, which he made over into a dynamic, painterly idiom. Using commercial enamel paint, he made a largely black composition, *Painting*, through which he spread a fluid network of white lines, occasionally allowing the medium to run its own course down the surface (fig. **19.4**).

19.5 Willem de Kooning, *Woman, I*, 1950–52. Oil on canvas, 6'3⅞" × 4'10" (1.9 × 1.47 m). The Museum of Modern Art, New York.

Certain recognizable forms—a hat and glove at the upper right—can be detected. Elsewhere in the picture, de Kooning subsumed figurative references within rhythmically flowing lines, creating vestigial forms that function as his characteristic shorthand for the human body. After *Painting* was shown in de Kooning's first solo show in New York, it was acquired by The Museum of Modern Art, and de Kooning thus emerged publicly as one of the pioneers of a new style.

While he was making his black-and-white compositions, de Kooning was also working on large paintings of women. In 1950 he began what became his most famous canvas, *Woman, I* (fig. **19.5**). This monumental image of a seated woman in a sundress is de Kooning's overpowering, at times repellent, but hypnotic evocation of woman as sex symbol and fertility goddess. Although the vigorous paint application appears entirely improvisatory, the artist labored over the painting for eighteen months, scraping the canvas down, revising it, and, along the way, making countless drawings—he was a consummate draftsman—of the subject. When his paintings of women were exhibited in 1953, de Kooning, who once said his work was "wrapped in the melodrama of vulgarity," was dismayed when critics failed to see the humor in them, reading them instead as misogynist. He said his images had to do with "the female painted through all the ages, all those idols," by which he could have meant a Greek Venus,

19.4 Willem de Kooning, *Painting*, 1948. Enamel and oil on canvas, 42⅝ × 56⅛" (108.3 × 142.5 cm). The Museum of Modern Art, New York.

19.6 Willem de Kooning, *Gotham News*, 1955. Oil on canvas, 5'9" × 6'7" (1.75 × 2 m). Albright-Knox Art Gallery, Buffalo, New York.

a Renaissance nude, a Picasso portrait, or a curvaceous American movie star, with her big, ferocious grin. Over the years when he was questioned about his paintings of women, de Kooning emphasized the dual nature of their sexual identity, claiming they derived partly from the feminine within himself. By the mid-fifties the women paintings gave way to compositions sometimes called "abstract urban landscapes," which, with their slashing lines and colliding forms, reflect the lively, gritty atmosphere of New York City streets. In *Gotham News* (fig. **19.6**) de Kooning dragged charcoal through wet paint, churning up the surface to create a heated atmosphere that pulsates with an intense, metropolitan beat. This is a quintessential example of gestural Abstract Expressionism, with the hand of the artist, the emotion- packed "gesture," everywhere apparent.

In the sixties, de Kooning moved to a large, light-filled studio on Long Island where he continued his exploration of the woman theme, although, as he said, in a more "friendly and pastoral" vein. In *Two Figures in a Landscape* (fig. **19.7**), the figures are barely decipherable amid baroque flourishes of lush, liquid medium. De Kooning continued to paint brilliantly into the eighties (he stopped in 1990 because of debilitating illness), and, although the works are largely abstract, the suggestion of figures lurks in the curving folds of paint (fig. **19.8**). Here, in his characteristic light, delicate palette of rose, yellow, green, blue, and white, de Kooning has decelerated his violent brushstroke into a grandly fluid, almost Rubenesque flow of graceful color shapes.

19.7 Willem de Kooning, *Two Figures in a Landscape*, 1967. Oil on canvas, 5'10" × 6'8" (1.8 × 2 m). Stedelijk Museum, Amsterdam.

Pollock

According to de Kooning, it was **Jackson Pollock** (1912–56), with the radical "drip" paintings he began to make in the late forties, who "broke the ice." Hailing from the West, Pollock became a huge force on the New York art scene, living hard, drinking hard, and then dying violently in a car accident at a young age. He achieved a

19.8 Willem de Kooning, *Pirate (Untitled II)*, 1981. Oil on canvas, 7'4" × 6'4¾" (2.2 × 1.9 m). The Museum of Modern Art, New York.

Art Students League with Thomas Hart Benton (see fig. 18.32), who represented, Pollock said, "something against which to react very strongly, later on." Nevertheless, there is a relation between Pollock's abstract arabesques and Benton's rhythmical figurative patterns. The landscapes of Ryder (see fig. 2.53) as well as the work of the Mexican muralists (see figs. 18.55, 18.57) were important sources for Pollock's violently expressive early paintings, as were the automatic methods of Masson and Miró. In 1939 The Museum of Modern Art mounted a large Picasso exhibition, a catalytic event for artists like de Kooning and Pollock, who were then struggling to come to terms with his work, learn from his example, and forge their own independent styles out of Cubism.

Pollock's paintings of the mid-forties, usually involving some degree of actual or implied figuration, were coarse and heavy, suggestive of Picasso, but filled with a nervous, brutal energy all their own. In *Guardians of the Secret*, 1943 (fig. **19.9**), schematic figures stand ceremonially at either end of a large rectangle, perhaps a table, an altar, or a funeral bier. A watchdog, with possible affinities to Tamayo's animals (see fig. 18.60), reclines below. Pollock, who covered his canvas with calligraphic, cryptic marks like some private hieroglyphic language, apparently began with legible forms that he gradually obscured. As he later told

stature of mythic proportions. By the fifties, he was an international symbol of the new American painting and remains an icon of the post-World War II artist. Pollock came to New York from Cody, Wyoming, by way of Arizona and California. Until 1932 he studied at the

19.9 Jackson Pollock, *Guardians of the Secret*, 1943. Oil on canvas, 4'1¾" × 6'3" (1.2 × 1.9 m). San Francisco Museum of Modern Art, Albert M. Bender Collection, Albert M. Bender Bequest Fund Purchase.

19.10 Jackson Pollock, *Number 1, 1950 (Lavender Mist)*, 1950. Oil, enamel, and aluminum on canvas, 7'4" × 9'11" (2.2 × 3 m). National Gallery of Art, Washington, D.C.

his wife, the painter Lee Krasner, "I chose to veil the imagery." That imagery has been analyzed within the broad spectrum of Pollock's visual interests, including ritual Navaho sand painting, African sculpture, prehistoric art, and Egyptian painting. Some have seen evidence of Jungian themes in the powerfully psychic content of the artist's early work. Carl Jung's theories of the collective unconscious as a repository for ancient myths and universal archetypes were a frequent topic of discussion in Abstract Expressionist circles. Pollock underwent psychoanalysis with Jungian analysts beginning in 1939.

By 1947 Pollock had begun to experiment with allover painting, a labyrinthine network of lines, splatters, and paint drips from which emerged the great "drip" or "poured" paintings of the next few years. *Number 1, 1950 (Lavender Mist)* (fig. **19.10**) is one of his most beautiful drip paintings, with its intricate web of oil colors mixed with black enamel and aluminum paint. One can trace the movements of the artist's arm, swift and assured, as he deployed sticks or dried-out brushes to drip paint onto the surface. His lines are divorced from any descriptive function and range from stringlike thinness to coagulated puddles, all merging into a hazy, luminous whole that seems to hover above the picture plane rather than illusionistically

behind it. These paintings, generally executed on a large canvas laid out on the floor, are popularly associated with so-called action painting. It was never the intention of the critic Harold Rosenberg, in coining this term, to imply that action painting was limited to a kind of athletic exercise, but rather that the process of painting was as important as the completed picture. Despite the furious and seemingly haphazard nature of his methods, Pollock's painting was not a completely uncontrolled, intuitive act. There is no question that, in his paintings and those of other Abstract Expressionists, the elements of intuition and accident play a large and deliberate part—this was indeed one of the principal contributions of Abstract Expressionism, which had found its own inspiration in Surrealism's psychic automatism. At the same time, however, Pollock's works are informed by skills honed by years of practice and reflection, just as the improvisatory talents of jazz musicians are paradoxically enhanced by regimented training.

Pollock's spun-out skeins of poured pigment contributed other elements that changed the course of modern painting. There was, first, the concept of the allover painting where no part of the composition is given formal precedence over another; it is nonhierarchical, with zones of pictorial interest evenly distributed over the surface. This "holism," together with the large scale of the works, introduced another concept—that of wall painting different from the tradition of easel painting. In 1946 Pollock, who had worked on mural projects for the WPA, said he wanted to paint pictures that "function between the easel and the mural." As scholar Elizabeth Frank has written, "Over the next three years, Pollock made great art out of this 'halfway state,' preserving the tension between the easel picture, with its capacity to draw the viewer into a fictive world, and the mural, or wall picture, with its power to inhabit the viewer's own space." This was the final break from the Renaissance idea of painting detached from spectator, to be looked at as a self-contained unit. The painting became an environment that encompassed the spectator. The feeling of absorption or participation is heightened by the ambi-guity of the picture space. The colors and lines, although never puncturing deep perspective holes in the surface, still create a sense of continuous movement, a billowing, a surging back and forth, within a limited depth. Pollock referred to being "in" his paintings when he worked, and in *No. 1, 1950 (Lavender Mist)* tracks of his literal presence are recorded in his own handprints, especially at the upper left edge. In 1950, partly to dispel his image in the popular press as a mad artist senselessly flinging paint at the canvas, Pollock allowed photographer Hans Namuth to film him at work at his Long Island studio. The result is an invaluable document of the artist's methods, which embraced both spontaneity and premeditation, control and exhilarating freedom (fig. **19.11**). In many ways, Pollock departed from the tradition of Renaissance and modern painting before him, and although he had no direct stylistic followers, he significantly affected the course of experimental painting after him.

Pollock experienced a period of crisis and doubt in the wake of the success of his drip paintings, and in late 1950 he began to reexplore problems of the figure in several drawings and paintings, predominantly using black. Between 1953 and 1956 he returned to traditional brush painting, sometimes heavy in impasto, and involving images reminiscent of paintings of the early forties. In the magisterial *Portrait and a Dream*, 1953 (fig. **19.12**), he constructed a visual dialogue between the two modes. At the left he dripped black paint in abstracted patterns that vaguely suggest human anatomies. At the right, in what many have read as a self-portrait, he resorted to overt figuration with brush-applied color. It is as if the figure lies latent within his webs of paint and, with a few adjustments of his arm, those webs could call up an image. "When you're painting out of your unconscious," Pollock said, "figures are bound to emerge." These later works suffered in critical opinion when compared to the drip paintings—

19.11 Jackson Pollock at work in his Long Island studio, 1950.

19.12 Jackson Pollock, *Portrait and a Dream*, 1953. Enamel on canvas, 4'10⅛" × 11'2½" (1.48 × 3.4 m). Dallas Museum of Art.

19.13 Lee Krasner, *Polar Stampede*, 1960. Oil on cotton duck, 7'9⅝" × 13'3¾" (2.4 × 4 m). Collection Pollock Krasner Foundation.

even some of Pollock's strongest supporters saw them as a retreat. The black-and-white canvases and the paintings that followed suggest a new phase of signal importance, unfortunately terminated by the artist's premature death in 1956.

Krasner

Brooklyn-born **Lee Krasner** (1908–84) received academic training at several New York art schools before joining the Mural Division of the WPA in 1935. From 1937 to 1940 she was a student of Hans Hofmann, from whom she said she "learned the rudiments of Cubism." Subsequently, she joined the AAA, devoted to nonobjective art in the tradition of Mondrian, and exhibited Cubist abstractions in their group shows. Krasner became acquainted with Pollock in 1942, when John Graham included their work in a show of young artists he felt showed promise. Krasner and Pollock began to share a studio in 1942, married in 1945, and relocated to Long Island. Unlike Pollock, Krasner felt a general antipathy toward the Surrealists and their automatic methods, due in part, as art historian Barbara Rose has shown, to the fundamentally misogynist attitudes of the European Surrealist emigrés (compounded by the general marginalization of women within Abstract Expressionist circles). Throughout the forties and fifties, working in the presence of Pollock's forceful personality, Krasner gradually moved away from Cubist-based forms to a concern for spontaneous gesture and large-scale allover compositions, while remaining committed to a Mondrianesque sense of structure.

Between 1959 and 1962, following the traumas of Pollock's death as well as that of her mother, Krasner made a series of *Umber* paintings, so-called for their predominantly brownish hues, which the artist once referred to as "colorless." In *Polar Stampede* (fig. **19.13**) she approached the canvas with a loaded brush, allowing the medium to splash and explode across the canvas until it resembled a vast glacial landscape that has been stirred up, as the title

suggests, by the pounding hooves of wild animals. Krasner did not allow herself improvisational freedom to the degree practiced by Pollock, for even in such a boldly gestural abstraction, her strokes have a regular, rhythmical beat, and a sense of imposed structure.

Krasner had employed the collage medium throughout her career. In 1976 she cut up her own drawings and paintings—Cubist works made while she was a Hofmann student—and assembled the sliced images into new compositions. The sharp cutout forms of *Imperative* (fig. **19.14**) overlap and interpenetrate one another, ironically functioning like the Cubist shards in her original drawings. By mutilating her own past work, Krasner, always intensely

19.14 Lee Krasner, *Imperative*, 1976. Oil, charcoal, and paper on canvas, 50 × 50" (127 × 127 cm). National Gallery of Art, Washington, D.C.

self-critical, could reclaim it for another context and arrive at a powerful new synthesis.

Kline

Franz Kline (1910–62) was as fascinated with the details and tempo of contemporary America as Stuart Davis (see fig. 18.64), but he was also deeply immersed in the tradition of Western painting, from Rembrandt to Goya. Born in the coal-mining region of Eastern Pennsylvania, Kline studied art at academies in Boston and London and, throughout the forties, painted figures and urban scenes tinged with Social Realism. A passion for drawing manifested itself during the forties, particularly in his habit of making little black-and-white sketches, fragments in which he studied single motifs, structure, or space relations. One day in 1949, according to the painter and critic Elaine de Kooning, Kline was looking at some of these sketches enlarged through an opaque projector and saw their implications as large-scale, free abstract images. Although this moment of revelation has no doubt been largely exaggerated, and although Kline's mastery of abstraction was gradual rather than instantaneous, he did formulate his new Abstract Expressionist vocabulary with astonishing speed. Even the first works in his new mode have nothing tentative about them.

In 1950, when he made his first large-scale black-and-white abstractions, Kline was well aware of the experiments of the pioneer Abstract Expressionists, although he never shared Pollock's interest in myth or Rothko's interest in the sublime, and he tended to gamble less with spontaneous gesture than his friend de Kooning. Instead he worked out his compositions in advance, with preliminary sketches, usually on pages torn from the telephone book. *Nijinsky* (fig. **19.15**) is an abstract meditation on his own figurative representations of the same subject, based on a photograph of the great Russian dancer as Petrushka.

In later works such as *Mahoning* (fig. **19.16**), named for a town in Pennsylvania, curved forms give way to straight, girderlike strokes that hurtle across the full breadth of the eight-and-a-half-foot (2.5 m) canvas. Using house-painter brushes on unstretched canvases tacked to his studio wall, Kline shaped rugged but controlled brushstrokes into powerful, architectural structures that have affinities with motifs in the industrial landscape he admired, such as trains, cranes, and bridges. In the paint texture as well as in the shaping of forms, there is an insistence on the equivalence of the whites that prevents the work from becoming simply a blown-up black drawing on a white ground, for, as Kline said, he also painted the white areas, sometimes on top of the black.

A number of artists in this period had pared their art down to the essentials of black and white. Both de Kooning and Pollock, as we have seen, renounced color for a time, as did Newman, Motherwell, Tomlin, and a number of other artists associated with the New York School. Kline reintroduced color to his compositions in the late

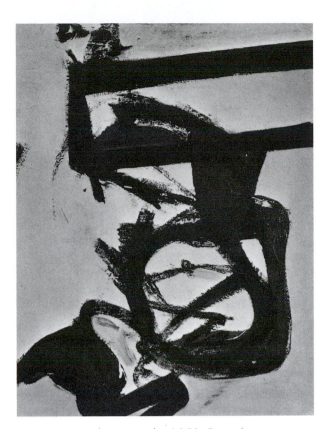

19.15 Franz Kline, *Nijinsky*, 1950. Enamel on canvas, 46 × 35¼" (116.8 × 89.5 cm). Collection Muriel Kallis Newman, Chicago.

fifties but sadly died in the midst of these new experiments. Like de Kooning's, Kline's painted structures had an enormous impact on younger artists. Their art fostered a veritable school of gestural painters in the late fifties, the so-called second generation of Abstract Expressionists, the best of whom forged their own individual styles from the pioneers' examples.

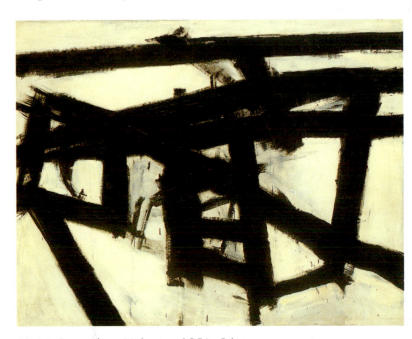

19.16 Franz Kline, *Mahoning*, 1956. Oil on canvas, 6'8" × 8'4" (2 × 2.5 m). Whitney Museum of American Art, New York.

19.17 Bradley Walker Tomlin, *All Souls Night*, 1947. Oil on canvas, 42½ × 64" (106.7 × 162.6 cm).

Tomlin and Tobey

Until the mid-forties, **Bradley Walker Tomlin** (1899–1953) was one of the most sensitive and accomplished Americans working in an abstract Cubist style. Toward the end of the decade he completed a group of pictographic compositions related to those of Adolph Gottlieb, including *All Souls Night* (fig. **19.17**), where he superimposed signs resembling ancient hieroglyphs over loosely brushed and delicately colored backgrounds. In 1948 he began to experiment with a form of free calligraphy, principally in black and white, which derived from his interest in automatism, Zen Buddhism, and Japanese brush painting. From this moment, Tomlin returned during the last three or four years of his life to painterly abstractions in which delicate and apparently spontaneous dabs of paint create shimmering, allover compositions. In these so-called "petal paintings," Tomlin discovered some of the lyricism and luminosity of Impressionist landscapes, but he subjected his strokes to the pictorial discipline of a loosely implied grid.

Mark Tobey (1890–1976) moved to Seattle from New York in 1922, and, though he worked far from the artistic mainstream, he produced a unique body of work in step with the most advanced tendencies in New York at that time. Tobey was drawn by a profound inner compulsion to a personal kind of abstract expression with strongly religious overtones. He was a convert to the Bahai faith, which, as he said, stresses "the unity of the world and the oneness of mankind." He began studying Chinese brush painting in 1923 and in the thirties studied Zen Buddhism in China and Japan. In *Broadway* (fig. **19.18**) Tobey applied the lessons of calligraphy to communicate his vivid memories of New York. His animated line, with its intricate, jazzy rhythms—he called it "white writing"—captures the lights, noise, and frenetic tempo of the city. Like de Kooning or Pollock, Tobey moved between figurative and abstract modes throughout the forties. In his best-known pictures, such as *Universal Field* (fig. **19.19**),

the "white writing" becomes a kind of nonreferential calligraphy that is a small-scale, wrist-painted version of the broader, arm-gestured, allover surfaces poured by Pollock. Tobey, who actually composed paintings from linear arabesques and fluid color before Pollock's allover drip paintings, here creates a field charged with energy and light, as his drawn lines zip and dart through a shallow, electrified space.

19.18 Mark Tobey, *Broadway*, c. 1935. Tempera on Masonite, 26 × 19¼" (66 × 48.9 cm). The Metropolitan Museum of Art, New York.

19.19 Mark Tobey, *Universal Field*, 1949. Pastel and tempera on cardboard, 28 × 44" (73.9 × 116.2 cm). Whitney Museum of American Art, New York.

Guston

Philip Guston (1913–80) was expelled from Manual Arts High School in Los Angeles along with his classmate Jackson Pollock for lampooning the conservative English department in their own broadside. Pollock was readmitted, but Guston set off on his own, working at odd jobs, attending art school briefly as well as meetings of the Marxist John Reed Club. He followed Pollock to New York and, in 1936, signed up for the mural section of the WPA. By the mid-forties, drawing on his diverse studies of

Cubism, the Italian Renaissance, and the paintings of de Chirico and Beckmann, Guston was painting mysterious scenes of figures in compressed spaces, works that earned him a national reputation.

Guston taught painting for a time in Iowa City and St. Louis and, in the late forties, began to experiment with loosely geometric abstractions. After many painful intervals of doubt, he made his first abstract gestural paintings in 1951. These contained densely woven networks of short strokes in vertical and horizontal configurations (fig. **19.20**)

19.20 Philip Guston, *Zone*, 1953–54. Oil on canvas, 46 × 48" (116.8 × 122.2 cm). The Edward R. Broida Trust, Los Angeles.

19.21 Philip Guston, *Studio*, 1969. Oil on canvas, 48 × 42"(121.9 × 106.7 cm). Private collection.

Beckett, Guston composed haunting scenes in a characteristic palette of pink, black, and red. At first he invented narratives featuring ominous hooded figures, their ambiguous identity ranging from marauding Ku Klux Klan members to the artist himself at his easel (fig. **19.21**). In *Head and Bottle*, Guston envisioned himself as a grotesque, disembodied head, flushed and stubble-covered, but his one visible eye wide open. When they were shown in New York, Guston's figurative paintings were seen by many, including both former detractors and supporters, as a betrayal of abstraction and an acquiescence to current Pop trends. In many ways the full implications of Guston's powerfully moving late canvases were not realized until they provided the key inspiration for the New Image and Neo-Expressionist painters of the early seventies and eighties (see chapters 24 and 26).

that reveal an admiration for Mondrian. The heavy impasto, serene mood, and subtle, fluctuating light in his muted reds, pinks, and grays caused some to see these works as lyrical landscapes, earning Guston the label "Abstract Impressionist." But Guston, who had negligible interest in the Impressionists, explained, "I think of painting more in terms of the drama of this process than I do of 'natural forces.'"

Throughout the fifties, Guston employed larger and more emphatic gestures in his abstractions, with a tendency to concentrate centralized color masses within a light and fluid environment. In 1962 the Guggenheim Museum mounted a major Guston retrospective, as did New York's Jewish Museum in 1966. But despite these external successes, Guston was experiencing a crisis in his art, with concerns about abstraction's limited potential for expressing the full gamut of human experience. This came at a time when the New York artworld was undergoing a profound shift in mood, with young Pop artists and hard-edge abstractionists casting a critical eye over what they regarded as the emotional excesses of their artistic predecessors. In the late sixties, Guston returned to recognizable imagery, astonishing the artworld with intensely personal, sometimes nightmarish, images in a crude, cartoonish style. "I got sick and tired of all that purity," he said, "[I] wanted to tell stories." A gifted draftsman with a penchant for caricature as well as an abiding fondness for cartoons and, significantly, for the writing of Franz Kafka and Samuel

Elaine de Kooning and Grace Hartigan

Elaine de Kooning (1918–89) is probably best known for the figurative paintings she made in the fifties. However, at her death a group of abstractions from the forties were discovered among her belongings that reveal her early experiments within an Abstract Expressionist mode. She spent the summer of 1948 at Black Mountain College in North Carolina with her husband, Willem de Kooning (they had married in 1943). At the invitation of Josef Albers, Willem had joined the distinguished faculty at the experimental school as a visiting artist. Elaine de Kooning always acknowledged the importance of her husband's paintings as well as those of their friend, Arshile Gorky, to her own work: "Their reverence and knowledge of their materials, their constant attention to art of the past and to everything around them simultaneously, established for me the whole level of consciousness as the way an artist should be." In *Untitled, Number 15*, painted during the summer of 1948, she set suggestive, biomorphic forms amidst more geometric shapes, recalling her husband's work of the same moment (see fig. 19.4). Following the summer at Black Mountain, de Kooning began to write on contemporary art for *ARTnews*. Her keen perceptions, as well as her vantage point as a practicing artist who knew her subject firsthand, endowed authority to her writing. In the fifties and sixties, de Kooning displayed expressive tendencies in a group of male portraits (including several of John F. Kennedy). Her portrayal of art critic Harold Rosenberg (fig. **19.22**),

19.22 Elaine de Kooning, *Harold Rosenberg #3*, 1956. Oil on canvas, 6'8" × 4'10⅞" (2 × 1.5 m). National Portrait Gallery, Smithsonian Institution, Washington, D.C.

one of the champions of Abstract Expressionism, shows how she brought the gesturalism of the New York School to bear on figurative subjects.

Grace Hartigan (b. 1922) was an even younger member of the New York School than Elaine de Kooning, but one who also witnessed the critical artistic developments in New York at close range. A so-called second-generation Abstract Expressionist, Hartigan was deeply affected as a

young artist by her encounter with Pollock's drip paintings and Willem de Kooning's black-and-white paintings, both shown in New York in 1948. Like de Kooning, whose famous perambulations through downtown New York were fodder for his strident "urban landscapes" (see fig. 19.6), Hartigan found inspiration in the most mundane aspects of city life. In *Giftwares*, 1955 (fig. **19.23**), she depicted the tawdry offerings of a storefront window, transforming them into a glowing still life in which the loosely brushed but legible forms are pulled up to the picture plane and dispersed evenly across the canvas. While Hartigan's rich palette is a kind of homage to Matisse, her homely subject matter prefigures work by artists of the sixties such as Claes Oldenburg (see fig. 21.25). In the late fifties, Hartigan embarked on a series of distinctive gestural abstractions before resuming a highly abstracted brand of figuration the following decade.

Complex Simplicities: Color Field Painting

Although the divisions between gestural and Color Field painting are somewhat artificial, there were both formal and conceptual differences between artists such as Kline and de Kooning on the one hand and Mark Rothko and Barnett Newman on the other. In 1943 Rothko, Newman, and Adolph Gottlieb stated their purpose in a letter to *The New York Times*: "We favor the simple expression of the complex thought. We are for the large shape because it has the impact of the unequivocal. We wish to reassert the picture plane. We are for flat forms because they destroy illusion and reveal truth." These artists fervently believed that abstract art was not "subjectless" and that,

19.23 Grace Hartigan, *Giftwares*, 1955. Oil on canvas, 5'3" × 6'9" (1.6 × 2.1 m). Neuberger Museum of Art, College at Purchase, State University of New York.

no matter how reductive, it could communicate the most profound subjects and elicit a deep emotional response in the viewer. In their search for universal subject matter, for "symbols," as Rothko said, "of man's primitive fears and motivations," the artists looked to many sources, including Jungian theory, Surrealist practice, and the art of non-European societies.

Rothko

Mark Rothko (1903–70) emigrated to the United States with his Russian–Jewish family in 1913 and moved ten years later to New York, where he studied with Max Weber at the Art Students League. Throughout the thirties he made figurative paintings on mostly urban themes and in 1935 formed an independent artists' group with Gottlieb called "The Ten." In 1940, in search of more profound and universal themes and impressed by his readings of Nietzsche and Jung, Rothko began to engage with ancient myths as a source of "eternal symbols." In their letter to *The New York Times*, Rothko, Newman, and Gottlieb proclaimed their "spiritual kinship with primitive and archaic art." Rothko first made compositions based on

19.24 Mark Rothko, *No. 18*, 1948. Oil on canvas, 67¼ × 55⅞" (170.8 × 141.9 cm). Frances Lehman Loeb Art Center, Poughkeepsie, New York.

19.25 Mark Rothko, *Untitled (Rothko number 5068.49)*, 1949. Oil on canvas, 6'9⅜" × 5'6⅜" (2.1 × 1.7 m). National Gallery of Art, Washington, D.C.

classical myths and then, by the mid-forties, painted biomorphic, Surrealist-inspired, hybrid creatures floating in primordial waters. These forms began to coalesce at the end of the decade into floating color shapes with loose, undefined edges within larger expanses of color (fig. **19.24**). By 1949 Rothko had refined and simplified his shapes to the point where they consisted of color rectangles floating on a color ground (fig. **19.25**). He applied thin washes of oil paint that contain considerable tonal variation and blurred the edges of the rectangles to create luminous color effects and a shifting, ambiguous space. Over the next twenty years, Rothko explored this basic compositional type with infinite and subtle variation. By the sheer sensuousness of their color areas and the sense of indefinite outward expansion without any central focus, the paintings are designed to absorb and engulf the spectator. Eventually, Rothko was painting on a huge scale, something that contributed to the effect of enclosing, encompassing color.

At the end of the fifties, Rothko began to move away from bright, sensuous color toward deeper, more somber hues (fig. **19.26**). By the late sixties, the mood of his work had darkened still further, expressing his conviction that, even at its most abstract, art could convey a sense of "tragedy, ecstasy, and doom." He received commissions for large public spaces, including a restaurant in the Seagram Building in New York; at Harvard University; and in a chapel in Houston, Texas (fig. **19.27**). The latter series consists of fourteen large panels, almost uniform in their deep black and red-brown, almost filling the entire space of available walls. The canvases are designed to be homogenous with the octagonal building (designed by Philip Johnson) and the changing light of the chapel interior. Thus, the forms have a less amorphous, harder-edge appearance than Rothko's earlier abstractions. They

19.26 Mark Rothko, *White and Greens in Blue*, 1957. Oil on canvas, 8'4" × 6'10" (2.5 × 2.1 m). Private collection.

represent a total architectural–pictorial experience in a sense analogous to that attempted by the religious muralists of the Baroque seventeenth century. Rothko, who even adopted the triptych format long associated with religious subjects, never intended his abstractions as mere formal

19.27 Mark Rothko, North, Northeast, and East wall paintings in the Rothko Chapel, Houston, Texas, 1965–66 (opened in 1971). Oil on canvas.

experiments, but rather wanted to provoke emotional and even transcendental experiences for the viewer.

Newman

Like Rothko, **Barnett Newman** (1905–70) studied at the Art Students League in the twenties, but his artistic career did not begin in earnest until 1944, when he resumed painting after a long hiatus and after he had destroyed his early work. By the mid-fifties, he had received nowhere near the attention that Pollock, de Kooning, or Rothko had attracted, although it could be argued that, in the end, his work had the greatest impact on future generations. His mature work differed from that of other Abstract Expressionists (except Ad Reinhardt's) in its radical reductiveness and its denial of painterly surface. As the group's most thoughtful and most polemical theorist, Newman produced an important body of critical writing on the work of his contemporaries as well as subjects such as pre-Columbian art.

In his early mythic paintings Newman, who had studied botany and ornithology, explored cosmic themes of birth and creation, of primal forms taking shape. Those works share many traits with Rothko's biomorphic paintings. By 1946, however, in canvases such as *Genesis—The Break* (fig. **19.28**), the forms become more abstract and begin to shed their biological associations, although the round shape here is a recurring seed form. Thomas Hess, a leading champion of the Abstract Expressionists, said that this painting (as the title implies) was about "the division between heaven and earth." In 1948 Newman made

Onement I, which he regarded as the breakthrough picture that established his basic formula—a unified color field interrupted by a vertical line—a "Zip" as he called it—or, rather, a narrow, vertical contrasting color space that runs the length of the canvas. The nature of the Zip varied widely, from irregular hand-brushed bands to uninflected, straight edges made possible with the use of masking tape, but the impression is usually of an opening in the picture plane rather than simply a line on the surface. While Newman did not seek out the atmospheric effects that Rothko achieved in his mature works, he was capable of brushed surfaces of tremendous beauty and nuance.

Vir Heroicus Sublimis (fig. **19.29**) is a mature, mural-size painting where the multiple Zips differ in hue and value, sometimes in stark contrast to the brilliant monochrome field, sometimes barely distinguishable from it. Newman wanted to maintain a human scale for his essentially life-affirming, humanist art. Indeed, his title for this work means "Heroic Sublime Man," and his ubiquitous Zip has been read as a sign for the upright human being. Between 1958 and 1964, Newman painted a series of fourteen canvases on the Passion of Christ called *The Stations of the Cross—Lema Sabachthani*, the first four of which are shown in figure **19.30** with Newman at the Guggenheim Museum. He orchestrated his Zip across the series, restricting himself to black and white on unprimed canvas, but varying his medium (Magna, oil, and acrylic) as well as the thickness and character of his Zips. Newman said that the theme of the series was "the unanswerable question of human suffering," underscored by Jesus's

19.28 Barnett Newman, *Genesis—The Break*, 1946. Oil on canvas, 24 × 27" (61 × 68.6 cm). Collection DIA Center for the Arts, New York.

19.29 Barnett Newman, *Vir Heroicus Sublimis*, 1950–51. Oil on canvas, 7'11⅜" × 17'9¼" (2.4 × 5.1 m). The Museum of Modern Art, New York.

words on the cross in the Hebrew subtitle, meaning "Why did you forsake me?"

Still

Clyfford Still (1904–80), who grew up in Washington state and Alberta, Canada, differed from the other Abstract Expressionists in that virtually all of his training and early artistic development took place outside of New York City. He had, however, exhibited at Peggy Guggenheim's Art of

This Century beginning in 1945, thanks to Rothko, and at the Betty Parsons Gallery in 1947. In 1950 he moved to New York from San Francisco, where he had been teaching at the progressive California School of Fine Arts (now the San Francisco Art Institute). He remained in New York until 1961, when he took up residence in the Maryland countryside. Fiercely proud and independent, notoriously controlling about his work, and generally contemptuous of the "art world," Still preferred to exhibit infrequently and

19.31 Clyfford Still, *Number 2*, 1949. Oil on canvas, 7'8" × 5'7" (2.3 × 1.7 m). Collection June Lang Davis, Medina, Washington.

live at a considerable distance from the nexus of the art establishment in New York.

Since the late thirties, Still had painted in a freely abstract manner (which contained some vestigial figuration) involving large, flowing images executed in heavy, even coarse, paint textures that he realized with brushes and palette knives. He repeatedly disavowed any interest in Surrealism or the "mythmaking" of his New York contemporaries and refused to give titles to his works (other than neutral letters or a date) to prevent any association with a specific subject. By 1947 he was working on a huge scale, sometimes eight by ten feet (2.4 × 3 m), with immense, crusty areas of color in a constant state of fluid though turgid movement (fig. **19.31**). These abstractions have been described as awesome landscapes that combine the drama and vastness of the West—its mesas, canyons, and rivers—and the Romantic landscape imagery of Albert Pinkham Ryder (see fig. 2.53). Art historian Robert Rosenblum characterized the dramatic effect of Still's canvases as "abstract sublime." Although the artist resisted any direct association between his compositions and landscape, he once said his work reflected "man's struggle and fusion with nature." Over the next twenty years Still persisted in his basic image, a predominant color varying in value and shot through with brilliant or somber accents.

Reinhardt

Ad Reinhardt (1913–67) was already painting geometric abstractions in the late thirties. He was a superb cartoonist and parodist, a mercilessly incisive writer, and a serious student of Oriental art. As he wrote in a prominent art magazine in 1962, he was for "art-as-art," elaborating that such art, necessarily abstract, has nothing to do with the issues of either daily life or existential doubt. "The one thing to say about art and life is that art is art and life is life. … Art that is a matter of life and death is neither fine nor free," he wrote. Reinhardt regarded the talk of myth and tragedy among the Abstract Expressionists as histrionic nonsense and objected to any association of his art with the ideals of the group. After abstract experiments in the forties, Reinhardt began in the early fifties to simplify his palette to a single color. The first groups of such paintings were all red or all blue (fig. **19.32**), and the final group, on which he worked for the rest of his life, was all black. One first observes these later paintings simply as monochrome fields. With time, however (and especially with the black paintings), there begins to emerge a second, inner image— a smaller rectangle, square, or central cross consisting of a

19.32 Ad Reinhardt, *Abstract Painting, Blue*, 1952. Oil on canvas, 6'3" × 2'4" (1.9 × 0.71 m). Carnegie Museum of Art, Pittsburgh.

slightly different value or tone of the color, what art historian Yve-Alain Bois called "the fictive transformation of one color into two." These paintings are static, symmetrical, and, according to the artist, timeless. They reward slow looking and are powerfully hypnotic in their effect. Although Reinhardt applied his colors with brushes, he did so without leaving the slightest trace of his implement on the surface. His stated purpose was the elimination of all associations, all extraneous elements, all symbols and signs, and the refinement of paintings to a single dominant experience. During the sixties and seventies, Reinhardt was much admired by Minimalist artists and became something of a cult figure among Conceptual artists, partly due to his writings and his extreme positions on the nature and function of the artist.

Gottlieb

Born in New York City, **Adolph Gottlieb** (1903–74) studied at the Art Students League with John Sloan and Robert Henri (see fig. 18.1, 18.2). While visiting Europe in 1921–22, he became aware of European experiments in Cubism, abstraction, and expressionism. The friendships he formed with Rothko, Newman, and Milton Avery in the twenties were crucial for his future development. During a stay in Arizona during 1937–38, Gottlieb made a number of curious paintings of objects picked up from the desert and arranged within rectangular compartments. These anticipated the Pictographs, irregular painted grids filled with two-dimensional ideograms, which occupied the artist between 1941 and 1953 (fig. **19.33**). Gottlieb composed his paintings intuitively, drawing on automatist methods as well as on his interest in ancient myth and ritual. The Pictographs—the term itself implies prehistoric cave paintings—had European sources, from Mondrian, Miró, and Klee, to the Cubist grids of Uruguayan artist Torres-Garcia. However, it was also African and Native American art, notably that of the Northwest Coast Kwakiutl (Kwakwaka´waku) people, which provided Gottlieb with a powerful lexicon of mysterious signs that he assembled to form what he believed to be a new, universal language. Their ominous mood may reflect the dark realities of war, as Gottlieb himself seemed to suggest: "Today when our aspirations have been reduced to a desperate attempt to escape from evil ... our obsessive, subterranean, and pictographic images are the expression of the neurosis which is our reality."

Gottlieb's principal development of the late fifties and sixties was the series called *Bursts* (fig. **19.34**), a sort of cosmic landscape usually consisting of an upper circular or ovoid element suggestive of a burning sun, below which is a broken, exploding element, open and dynamic in contrast with the closed form above. The *Burst* paintings combined aspects of gestural painting along with the expansive color of the Color Field painters. In general terms, the *Bursts* seem to underscore life's fundamental dualities and conjure up landscapes at the dawn of civilization. More

19.33 Adolph Gottlieb, *Voyager's Return*, 1946. Oil on canvas, 37⅞ × 29⅞" (96.2 × 75.9 cm). The Museum of Modern Art, New York.

specifically, they carry the inescapable and recent memory of the atomic bombs dropped by America on the Japanese cities of Hiroshima and Nagasaki in August 1945.

Motherwell

Robert Motherwell (1915–91) was the youngest of the artists originally associated with Abstract Expressionism. He received his early training in literature, art history, and philosophy at Stanford, Harvard, and Columbia. Motherwell's erudition made him an eloquent spokesman for Abstract Expressionism as well as a leading theorist of modern art. As a painter, he was largely self-trained, with the exception of some formal study as a young man in California and later with the Surrealist Kurt Seligmann in New York. In 1941 Motherwell made the acquaintance of several European Surrealists in New York, including Ernst, Tanguy, Masson, and Matta. The aspect of Surrealism that most intrigued him was automatism, the concept of the intuitive, the irrational, and the accidental in the creation of a work of art. In many ways, his early paintings represent an attempt to resolve the seeming contradictions between Mondrian (whom he had also met in New York) and the abstract Surrealists. Motherwell also provided American artists with their most thorough introduction to Dada in the 1951 collection *The Dada Painters and Poets*, still an essential sourcebook for Dada writing.

In 1943, at Matta's suggestion, Motherwell began to experiment with collage, introducing automatist techniques in roughly torn pieces of paper. One of the earliest

19.34 Adolph Gottlieb, *Orb* from the *Bursts* series, 1964. Oil on canvas, 7'6" × 5' (2.3 × 1.52 m). Dallas Museum of Art.

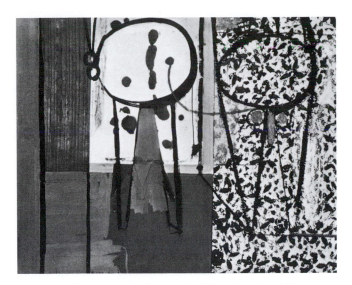

examples is *Pancho Villa, Dead and Alive*, 1943 (fig. **19.35**). Motherwell, who had traveled to Mexico with Matta, had been struck by a photograph of the revolutionary figure, dead and covered with blood. The stick figures representing Villa relate directly to a painting by Picasso from the twenties, but other forms in the collage were to become signature Motherwell images, such as the ovoid shapes held in tension between vertical, architectural elements. Motherwell's involvement with the collage medium was more extensive than that of any of his Abstract Expressionist colleagues. In the many examples he continued to make throughout his career, he used postcards, posters, wine labels, or musical scores that constitute a visual day-by-day autobiography.

In 1948 Motherwell made the first work of his great series of abstract paintings entitled *Elegy to the Spanish Republic* (fig. **19.36**), inspired by his profound reaction to the defeat of the Spanish Republic by fascist forces in early 1939. Until his death in 1991, he painted more than one hundred and fifty variants of the Elegy theme. These works stand in contrast to the brilliantly coloristic collages and paintings also created by the artist during the same period, for they were executed predominantly in stark black and white. "Black is death; white is life," the artist said. It is no

19.35 Robert Motherwell, *Pancho Villa, Dead and Alive,* 1943. Gouache and oil with cut-and-pasted papers on cardboard, 28 × 35⅞" (71.7 × 91.1 cm). The Museum of Modern Art, New York.

19.36 Robert Motherwell, *Elegy to the Spanish Republic No. 34,* 1953–54. Oil on canvas, 6'8" × 8'4" (2 × 2.5 m). Albright-Knox Art Gallery, Buffalo, New York.

19.37 Robert Motherwell, *Summer Open with Mediterranean Blue*, 1974. Acrylic on canvas, 4' × 9' (1.22 × 2.7 m). Collection Dedalus Foundation.

coincidence that Picasso's monumental painting of protest against the Spanish Civil War, *Guernica* (see fig. 15.46), was black, white, and gray. The Elegies consisted for the most part of a few large, simple forms, vertical rectangles holding ovoid shapes in suspension. The scale increased as the series progressed, with some works on a mural scale. While the loosely brushed, organic shapes have been read literally by some, who have suggested that they might represent male genitalia referring to Spanish bull fights, Motherwell said he invented the forms as emblems for universal tragedy.

In 1967 the artist began a second great series known as the *Opens* or "wall and window" paintings (fig. **19.37**). Motherwell once said he would rather look at "parks or town squares with walls" than at "raw nature." "There is something in me," he wrote, "that responds to the stark beauty of dividing a flat solid plane." The *Opens* range from relatively uniform, although never flat, areas of color to large-scale exercises in rhythmic, variegated brushwork. There is always movement and light within the ground, as well as the so-called window motif common to these paintings. Although the *Open* series owed its inception partly to Motherwell's lifelong dialogue with the art of Matisse, and particularly to two of his starkly reductive compositions from 1914 involving views from windows, Motherwell's paintings also coincided with the significant emergence of Minimalist abstraction in New York.

Baziotes

A friend of Motherwell and Matta from the early forties, **William Baziotes** (1912–63) explored with them aspects of Surrealist automatism and was respected enough by the European Surrealists to be included in their group shows in New York. Automatism for Baziotes was not a matter of improvisational gesture, with all its implications of emotion and angst. Rather, it guided a slow and meditative process during which allusive, biomorphic forms emerged as the

19.38 William Baziotes, *Dusk*, 1958. Oil on canvas, 60⅜ × 48¼" (153.4 × 122.6 cm). Solomon R. Guggenheim Museum, New York.

painting proceeded. Devoted to fantastic, mythic subject matter, Baziotes was a cofounder in 1948 of the Subjects of the Artist school, one of the intellectual meeting places of the New York School. His painting was characterized by shifting, fluid, diaphanous color into which were worked biomorphic shapes drawn with great sensitivity and suggestive of microcosmic or marine life. The strange forms in *Dusk* (fig. **19.38**) may have something in common with prehistoric fossils, the kind the artist might have seen on one of his many visits to New York's American Museum of Natural History. Like a number of his fellow Abstract Expressionists, Baziotes was fascinated by paleontology and primitive life forms.

Drawing in Steel: Constructed Sculpture

Constructed sculpture—as contrasted with sculpture cast in bronze or modeled in stone—and particularly welded metal sculpture, constituted a major direction taken by American artists after World War II.

Smith and Dehner

David Smith (1906–65), a pioneer sculptor of his generation working in welded steel, said of his medium: "The material called iron or steel I hold in high respect. ... The metal itself possesses little art history. What associations it possesses are those of this century: power, structure, movement, progress, suspension, brutality." Smith was born in Decatur, Illinois, and between 1926 and 1932 he studied painting, initially with John Sloan, at the Art Students League in New York (he was never formally trained as a sculptor). In the early thirties, intrigued by reproductions of Picasso's welded-steel sculptures of 1929–30 (see fig. 15.50) as well as the works of Julio González (see fig. 15.53) he saw in John Graham's collection, Smith began to experiment with constructed metal sculpture. He first learned to weld in an automobile plant in the summer of 1925, and in 1933 he established a studio in Brooklyn at Terminal Iron Works, a commercial welding shop. During World War II he worked in a locomotive factory, where he advanced his technical experience in handling metals, and the sheer scale of locomotives suggested to him possibilities for the monumental development of his metal sculpture. Moreover, these experiences established the kinship that Smith felt with skilled industrial laborers.

During the thirties and forties, Smith endowed his sculpture with a Surrealist quality, derived from Picasso, González, and Giacometti. In *The Royal Bird* (fig. **19.39**), he suggests the viciously aggressive skeleton of some great airborne creature of prey. Smith and his wife, the sculptor Dorothy Dehner, had purchased a photograph of the fossils of a prehistoric flying creature, and both made use of the image in their work. His works of the early fifties are like steel drawings in space, as in *The Letter* (fig. **19.40**), whose metal glyphs recall Gottlieb's pictographic paintings (see fig. 19.33). Yet even when the sculptures were composed two-dimensionally, the natural setting, seen through the open spaces, introduced ever-changing suggestions of depth, color, and movement.

Toward the end of the war, Smith established a studio in Bolton Landing in upstate New York. The studio was a complete machine shop, and during the fifties and sixties Smith populated the surrounding fields with his sculptures, which were becoming more monumental in scale and conception. During much of his career Smith worked on sculpture in series, with different sequences sometimes overlapping chronologically and individual sculptures within series varying widely in form. The *Agricola* constructions (1952–59) continued the open, linear approach (with obvious agrarian overtones), while the *Sentinels* (1956–61) were usually monolithic, figurative sculptures, at times employing elements from farm or industrial machinery. *Sentinel I*, for example, includes a tire rod and industrial steel step, while the "head" of the sculpture resembles street signs. In contrast with most sculptors who used found objects in the sixties, Smith integrated such objects in the total structure so that their original function

19.39 David Smith, *The Royal Bird*, 1947–48. Steel, bronze, and stainless steel, 21¾ × 59 × 9" (55.2 × 150 × 22.9 cm). Walker Art Center, Minneapolis.

19.40 David Smith, *The Letter*, 1950. Welded steel, 37⅝ × 22⅞ × 9¼" (95.6 × 58.1 × 23.5 cm). Munson-Williams-Proctor Institute Museum of Art, Utica, New York.

was subordinated to the totality of the new design. This was Constructivist sculpture in the original sense of Naum Gabo's *Realistic Manifesto*, in which voids do not merely surround mass but are articulated by form. Significant for future developments in sculpture is the fact that *Sentinel I* is not isolated on a pedestal but occupies the viewer's actual space.

19.42 Dorothy Dehner, *Nubian Queen*, 1960. Bronze, 56 × 14 × 8" (142.2 × 35.6 × 20.3 cm). Richard L. Eagan Fine Arts, New York.

19.41 David Smith, left: *Cubi XVIII*, 1964. Stainless steel, height 9'8" (2.9 m). Museum of Fine Arts, Boston; center: *Cubi XVII*, 1963. Stainless steel, height 9' (2.7 m). Dallas Museum of Art; right: *Cubi XIX*, 1964. Stainless steel, height 9'5" (2.9 m). The Tate Gallery, London.

In his last great series, begun in 1961 with the generic name of *Cubi*, Smith assembled monumental, geometric volumes in stainless steel (fig. **19.41**). Always sensitive to the surfaces of his sculptures, Smith had often painted his sculptures in bright, flat color or with distinctive painterly textures. In the *Cubi* series he exercised particular care in the polishing of the surfaces to create effects of brilliant, all-over calligraphy out of the highly reflecting, light-saturated surfaces. The work communicates an intimate sense of the artist's touch. Smith only rarely employed workshop assistants and even the *Cubi* series, with its machinelike precision, was constructed and finished by the artist. Despite this concern for the personal, Smith's art was critical to the development of the more impersonal creations of Minimalist artists in the sixties.

Dorothy Dehner (1901–94) was overshadowed as an artist by her famous husband, David Smith, yet for nearly forty years she produced a distinguished body of sculpture whose origins should be considered within the Abstract Expressionist milieu. She met Smith while studying painting at the Art Students League in 1926 and later became acquainted with Davis, Gorky, and Avery. Dehner worked in various figurative styles until the late forties, when she also began to exhibit her work publicly. Although many of her early abstract paintings and drawings demonstrate a sculptor's sensibility, Dehner did not start making sculpture until 1955, five years after she and Smith had separated. *Nubian Queen* (fig. **19.42**), a bronze from 1960, is an open-frame, totemic construction containing mysterious, pictographic signs. Like her contemporaries in the New York School, Dehner sought to develop a private language with universal implications, and, like them, as her title implies, she liked to tap the art of ancient civilizations for forms and meaning. "I am an archaeologist of sorts," she said. "I tamper with the past."

Lipton and Lassaw
Originally trained as a dentist, **Seymour Lipton** (1903–81) made his first sculptures in the late twenties and began showing his work and teaching sculpture in the forties. For his mature works, he hammered and welded sheets of Monel metal, nickel-silver, or bronze into large spatial volumes, suggestive at times of threatening plant forms or predatory creatures with sharp, pro-

19.43 Seymour Lipton, *Avenger*, 1957. Nickel-silver on Monel metal, length 23 × 18" (58.4 × 45.7 cm). Spencer Museum of Art, University of Kansas, Lawrence.

truding features (fig. **19.43**). His works combine monumentality and repose with a sense of poetry and mystery. Spatially they offer an interplay of exterior and interior forms that emphasize the nature of the material.

As the works already seen would suggest, many American sculptors shared the dynamic, open-form aesthetics espoused by the Abstract Expressionists. **Ibram Lassaw** (b. 1913) even managed to three-dimensionalize Pollock's allover webs of flowing lines, doing so in reliefs and freestanding constructions formed as intricate, welded cages (fig. **19.44**). However, rather than Pollock's daring equilibrium of colliding opposites—freedom and control—Lassaw seemed more at one with the mystical harmony of Mark Tobey. And indeed he was a student of the German mystics and of Zen philosophy.

19.44 Ibram Lassaw, *Clouds of Magellan*, 1953. Welded bronze and steel, 4'4" × 6'10" × 1'6" (1.32 × 2.1 × 4.6 m). Collection Philip Johnson, New York.

19.45 Mark di Suvero, *Hankchampion*, 1960. Wood and chains, nine wooden pieces, overall 6'5¼" × 12'5" × 8'9" (2 × 3.8 × 2.7 m). Whitney Museum of American Art, New York.

19.46 Mark di Suvero, *Aurora*, 1992–93. Steel, 16'4" × 19'6" × 26' (5 × 5.9 × 7.9 m). National Gallery of Art, Washington, D.C.

Di Suvero and Chamberlain

Mark di Suvero (b. 1933), much younger than the other artists discussed in this chapter, was still studying art at college in California when the Abstract Expressionists reached the pinnacles of fame in the mid-fifties. But only three years after arriving in New York in 1957, di Suvero was translating the bold gestures of Kline and de Kooning into a dynamic sculptural idiom. *Hankchampion*, 1960 (fig. **19.45**), consists of massive, rough timbers that project in a precarious, even threatening, manner. These early wood pieces sometimes incorporated chain, rope, and found objects, like barrels or tires, scavenged from the industrial landscape. Although di Suvero admired Rodin and Giacometti, the most meaningful and immediate artistic example for him was Smith, who changed sculpture, di Suvero said, from an "objet d'art type of thing to something that is really strong, American industrial art." Despite a drastic accident in 1960, when he was nearly crushed to death in an elevator, by the mid-sixties di Suvero was making works in steel so large they required a crane. Although he has made many small-scale works, he is best known for the monumental outdoor sculptures he has made since that time, including *Aurora* (fig. **19.46**), which is named after a poem about New York City by Federico García Lorca. These works, which enter the realm of architecture by virtue of their scale and I-beam construction, are as much at home in the urban environment as in a natural landscape. In the spirit of Constructivism, di Suvero's jutting, angled girders shape the void with energy-charged forms that have no sense of central mass. And in the spirit of Calder, some of his mammoth sculptures have moving parts that invite audience participation. In such ways di Suvero's work, despite its scale and mass, shares much with the playful spirit of Neo-Dada and Pop art.

John Chamberlain (b. 1927) began to make sculpture in the early sixties, works that seemed like three-dimensional expressions of Abstract Expressionism's explosive, painterly styles and that imply at times an almost violent approach to the medium. Chamberlain has used parts of junked automobiles, with their highly enameled, colored surfaces, to create allover, abstract constructions of surprising beauty. Like di Suvero, he uses industrial tools, cutting and crushing shapes that he then pieces together, like an assemblage, through a trial-and-error process. The works can be either freestanding sculptures or, as in *Dolores James* (fig. **19.47**), wall-mounted reliefs.

Chamberlain's spontaneous, not entirely predictable, methods parallel the Abstract Expressionists' balance of control and accident but share di Suvero's generally lighter, less emotionally charged, spirit. "There's no formula," he said. For example, one night, when he was nearing completion of *Dolores James*, he returned late to his studio and heaved an eight-pound sledgehammer at the sculpture, achieving exactly the final touch he sought. Unlike the Abstract Expressionists, Chamberlain avoided ascribing profound meaning to his works. In this he is closer to many artists of his own generation who also made, or make, art from society's detritus.

Textures of the Surreal: Biomorphic Sculpture and Assemblage

Noguchi

Isamu Noguchi (1904–88) was born in Los Angeles of a Japanese father and an American mother, and then lived in Japan from the age of two to fourteen before returning to the United States. In 1927, following some academic training and his decision to become a sculptor, Noguchi went to Paris, where he saw the work of the Cubists, Surrealists, and Constructivists. He quickly became acquainted with the American expatriate artistic community in the city, occasionally assisting Calder on his *Circus* (see chapter 17) and, most significantly, serving for a time as assistant to Brancusi, from whom he learned direct carving methods. On visits to China and Japan during the thirties, he studied brush painting and ceramic sculpture. He made his first abstract sculptures while in Paris, but his first thoroughly original works date to the forties, when he made Surrealistic carvings in marble or slate. In *Kouros* (fig. **19.48**) he evoked the human form, not only by the Greek title, but also by the Miróesque biomorphism of the eyeholed and crossed,

19.47 John Chamberlain, *Dolores James*, 1962. Welded and painted automobile parts, 6'4" × 8'1" × 3'3" (1.9 × 2.5 × 0.99 m). Solomon R. Guggenheim Museum, New York.

19.48 Isamu Noguchi, *Kouros*, 1944–45. Pink Georgia marble on slate base, 10' × 2'10½" × 3'6" (3 × 0.87 × 0.7 m). The Metropolitan Museum of Art, New York.

19.49 Isamu Noguchi, *The Isamu Noguchi Garden Museum*, opened to the public in 1985. Long Island City, New York.

bonelike forms, all interlocked and arranged in the vertical orientation of a standing figure. The idea for sculptures of this type had originated with Noguchi's 1944 set design for *Herodiade*, a ballet by premier American choreographer Martha Graham. In the ballet, Salome dances before her mirror, in which she sees, according to Noguchi, "her bones, the potential skeleton of her body." As Noguchi's renown spread internationally in the fifties, he began to receive commissions for public sculptures and gardens around the world. In Long Island City, where he had had a studio since 1961 (he later established a studio in Japan as well), Noguchi established a garden and museum devoted to his work (fig. **19.49**). The works shown here give evidence of the many textures and forms that the artist could mine from stone, from immaculately smooth and geometric forms to organic ones that incorporate accidental forms caused in the quarry process.

Bourgeois

French-born **Louise Bourgeois** (b. 1911), best known as a sculptor, is hard to classify because of her active work in a variety of media. She began as a painter-engraver in the milieu of Surrealism. Early in her artistic career, when she was struggling with the multiple roles of mother, wife, and artist, she made a disquieting group of paintings that rendered women literally as houses or *Femmes-Maisons*. Bourgeois turned to carved sculpture in the late forties, creating roughly hewn, vertical forms in wood that she called *Personages*. Their closest historical analogue is perhaps the Surrealist sculptures of Giacometti. The *Personages*, Bourgeois said, are each endowed with individual personalities and are best experienced as a group. Indeed, the five vertical elements of *Quarantania I* (fig. **19.50**) were originally separate sculptures that Bourgeois later decided to unite on a single base. Like all of Bourgeois's work, the *Personages* have powerful psychic associations rooted in her own biography. In the sixties, Bourgeois experimented with new materials such as latex, plaster, and marble to create globular, overtly sexual shapes that bubble forth as though in the process of being born. Bourgeois could achieve a palpable sense of the organic within an essentially abstract composition. The highly polished cluster of forms in *Cumul I* (fig. **19.51**), for example, seems to emerge from a thin membrane before our very eyes.

The importance of the feminist movement of the sixties and seventies to Bourgeois's work can be strongly felt in her later career. At the age of eighty, she embarked on one of her most intriguing series, the elaborate, multimedia environments that she called *Cells*. Within the glass and

19.50 Louise Bourgeois, *Quarantania I*, 1947–53. Painted wood on wood base, 62⅜ × 11¾ × 12" (158.4 × 29.8 × 30.5 cm). The Museum of Modern Art, New York.

19.51 Louise Bourgeois, *Cumul I*, 1968. Marble, 22¼ × 50 × 48" (56.5 × 127 × 121.9 cm). Museé National d'Art Moderne, Centre d'Art et de Culture Georges Pompidou, Paris.

chain-link enclosure of *Cell (You Better Grow Up)*, 1993 (fig. **19.52**), are two mirrors. Between them is a roughly cut marble base on which sit exquisite carvings of an adult hand grasping those of a child. Other objects include furniture, perfume bottles, and a glass object that contains a tiny glass figurine. Bourgeois has said that the figurine and the child's hands are self-portraits and form part of a work about "the frightened world of a child who doesn't like being dependent and who suffers from it." Like many women artists, Bourgeois did not receive proper recognition for her remarkable achievements until late in her career. In the eighties, her long involvement with performance and installation art struck a chord of common purpose with trends during that decade (see chapter 26).

Cornell

Also rooted in Surrealism is the work of **Joseph Cornell** (1903–72), a highly cultivated American who brought great distinction to the tradition of assemblage. In the early thirties, Cornell became acquainted with the Julien Levy Gallery in New York, a center for the display of European Surrealism. His first experiments with collage were inspired by works of Max Ernst, and soon Levy was exhibiting his small constructions along with the works of the Surrealists. By the mid-thirties, Cornell had settled on his formula of a simple box, usually glass-fronted, in which he arranged found objects such as cork balls, photographs, and maps. Cornell read widely, especially French nineteenth-century literature, but his interests were broad, from poetry and ballet to astronomy and other natural sciences. He haunted the penny arcades, libraries, dime stores, souvenir shops, art galleries, and movie houses of New York, searching out the ephemera that became the content of his enchanting assemblages. In his boxes Cornell, who lived reclusively and rarely spoke about his work, created a personal world filled with nostalgic associations—of home, family, childhood, and of all the literature he had read and the art he had seen. As one critic has noted, "He treated the ephemeral object as if it were the rarest heirloom of a legendary prince or princess."

Medici Slot Machine of 1942 (fig. **19.53**) centers around reproductions of a Renaissance portrait, multiple images taken from the early cinema, and symbols suggesting relations between past and present. Everything is allusion or romantic reminiscence gathered together, as one idea or image suggested another, to create intimate and magical worlds. As in all his creations, Cornell carefully organized his imagery within a loosely geometric format.

To enhance their quality of nostalgia, Cornell often deliberately distressed his surfaces, sometimes placing his boxes in the elements to achieve a weathered, time-battered appearance. In *Untitled (The Hotel Eden)* (fig. **19.54**), the ad for Hotel Eden is tattered and the paint on the box is cracked and worn. Cornell usually built a number of boxes around specific themes, such as the *Aviaries* of the forties, which include images of exotic birds. As is typical of his work, this composition is rich with associations. The Hotel Eden ad suggests the garden of paradise, while the spiral form at the upper left probably refers to a work

19.52 Louise Bourgeois, *Cell (You Better Grow Up)*, 1993. Steel, glass, marble, ceramic, and wood, 6'11" × 6'10" × 6'11½" (2.1 × 2.1 × 2.1 m). Collection the artist.

19.53 Joseph Cornell, *Medici Slot Machine*, 1942. Construction, 13½ × 12 × 4¼" (34.3 × 30.5 × 10.8 cm). Private collection.

19.54 Joseph Cornell, *Untitled (The Hotel Eden)*, c. 1945. Mixed-media construction, 15⅛ × 15¾ × 4¾" (38.4 × 40 × 12.1 cm). National Gallery of Canada, Ottawa.

by Cornell's friend Marcel Duchamp. Cornell was included in the historic 1936 exhibition at The Museum of Modern Art in New York, *Fantastic Art, Dada, and Surrealism*, where his works were installed next to Miró's *Surrealist Object* from 1936 (see fig. 15.14). Although the affinities between *Untitled (Hotel Eden)* and Miró's sculpture are obvious, Cornell objected to being classified with the Surrealists, saying that while he admired their art, he had no interest in the dream world and the subconscious and preferred to focus on "healthier possibilities." By the fifties, Cornell knew many of the Abstract Expressionist painters who were his contemporaries, but his quiet, small-scale works had less in common with their turbulent canvases than with the assemblage art of the next generation (see fig. 21.10).

Nevelson

Louise Nevelson (1899–1988) also worked in a tradition of assemblage, but with results quite different from those of Cornell. She studied voice, dance, and art in New York in the late twenties. In 1931 she went to Europe, studying painting for a time with Hans Hofmann in Munich and playing small roles in movies in Berlin and Vienna. Nevelson always maintained a flair for the theatrical in her eccentric dress and flamboyant manner, and her mature work as a sculptor also manifested a distinctively theatrical sensibility. She liked to control the light and space within

which the viewer experienced her work, which, like that of contemporary painters such as Pollock and Rothko, was environmental in its effect. In the early forties, Nevelson began to make Surrealist-inspired assemblage sculptures from found objects and received her first solo exhibition in New York. Her characteristic works of the fifties were large wooden walls fitted with individual boxes filled with scores of carefully arranged found objects—usually sawed-up fragments of furniture or woodwork rescued from old, destroyed houses. (It is not inconsequential that her Russian father was a builder who ran a lumber-yard.) Nevelson then painted her sculpture a uniform mat black, white, or, in her later work, reflective gold. *Dawn's Wedding Chapel I* formed part of a large installation at The Museum of Modern Art in 1959 called *Dawn's Wedding Feast*. It included freestanding, totemic constructions as well as wall pieces, all suggesting a site for ancient cere-mony and ritual. The shallow boxes were filled with assem-blages of whitewashed balusters, finials, posts, moldings and other architectural remnants (fig. **19.55**). Despite their composition from junk, they achieve a quality of decayed elegance, reminiscent of the graceful old houses from which the elements were mined.

In the sixties, Nevelson relied less on found materials and had boxes fabricated according to her specifications (fig. **19.56**). Her work took on a more pristine character, with regularized, sometimes symmetrical forms, tendencies that accorded with the Minimalist aesthetic of the decade. Despite the new immaculate precision, these works still have the altarlike quality of the wooden walls. In the later sixties, the prolific Nevelson experimented with new materials, including clear Plexiglas, and began to execute commissions for large-scale outdoor works in aluminum, steel, and Cor-Ten steel.

Expressive Vision: Developments in American Photography

Depression, political upheaval, and war shaped the vision of photographers in the forties just as much as that of painters. Meanwhile, photography—by then ubiquitous not only in news coverage and advertising but also in professional journals, books, and special exhibitions—had exerted an unavoidably powerful effect on the vision of everyone, painters perhaps most of all.

19.57 Robert Capa, *Normandy Invasion, June 6, 1944*, Gelatin-silver print.

Capa and Miller

Some of the field pictures made by the Hungarian-American photographer **Robert Capa** (1913–54), during the Spanish Civil War and World War II (fig. **19.57**), seemed to find a parallel in Abstract Expressionism's fluid organization and its conception of the picture as an expression of personal, tragic experience universalized through abstract gesture. It was as if photojournalism, scientific aerial photography, and microphotography helped prepare the human eye for the pictorial formulations of Abstract Expressionism. Capa was deeply committed to the process of the photojournalistic essay as the means for bearing his intended content and felt it could be done only by being as close to the subject matter as possible. He was killed by a landmine while photographing the war in Indochina.

Another photographer who witnessed the carnage of war firsthand was **Lee Miller** (1907–77), an American who spent most of her adult life in Europe, first in the Parisian circle of Man Ray between 1929 and 1932 and, after 1942, as an official U.S. forces war correspondent. She was present in 1945 at the liberation of Dachau and Buchenwald concentration camps, and the harrowing scenes she recorded there are among the most painfully revelatory images of the war (fig. **19.58**). Some of them were soon featured in *Vogue* magazine, where her work had been published since the late twenties, with the heading "Believe It." The ironic contrast between photography's ability to capture moments of extreme human misery and the use of such images to lend impact to glossy publications is a paradox particularly evident from the postwar period onward.

White, Siskind, Porter, and Callahan

The grandeur and metaphor of Abstract Expressionist painting encouraged photographers to reinvestigate the potential of both straight and manipulated procedures for creating abstract imagery. Among the photographers who used straight photography to discover imagery capable of yielding abstract forms potent with mystical feeling

19.58 Lee Miller, *Dead SS Guard in the Canal at Dachau*, 1945. Modern gelatin-silver print, 1988. Lee Miller Archives, England.

was **Minor White** (1908–76). In works like the one seen here (fig. **19.59**), White's vision paralleled stylistic developments in the art of Abstract Expressionism's gestural painters, as did his devotion to photography as a form of self-expression. "I photograph not that which is," he said, "but that which I AM." As a teacher and writer, and founder, as well as a longtime editor, of *Aperture* magazine, White had a vast and enduring influence on a whole generation of younger photographers.

19.59 Minor White, *Sun in Rock, Devil's Slide*, 1947, October 12, 1947. Gelatin-silver print, 7⅜ × 9⅝" (18.7 × 24.5 cm). The Museum of Modern Art, New York.

19.60 Aaron Siskind, *Chicago 1949*, Gelatin-silver print.

19.62 Harry Callahan, *Weed Against the Sky, Detroit*, 1948. Gelatin-silver print.

Aaron Siskind (1903–91), too, lost interest in subject matter as a source of emotive content and turned instead toward flat, richly textured patterns discovered on old weathered walls, segments of advertising signs, graffiti, and peeling posters (fig. **19.60**). In his preoccupation with the expressive qualities of two-dimensional design, Siskind found himself in sympathetic company among painters like Kline and Willem de Kooning, whose influence he acknowledged.

Another photographer whose work might look at home with New York gestural paintings was **Eliot Porter** (1901–90). Porter portrayed nature in the tradition of Ansel Adams (see fig. 18.23), but, unlike most noncommercial photographers of his generation, he worked in color (fig. **19.61**). To attain such quality, Porter, unusually for a color photographer, made his own color-separation negatives and dye transfers.

Harry Callahan (1912–99), a friend and colleague of Siskind's, has generated photographs of such uncompromising spareness and subtlety that they often bordered on abstraction. His principal influence came from Ansel Adams and the former Bauhaus faculty at the Institute of Design in Chicago, where he taught from 1946. He later founded the photography department at the Rhode Island School of Design. Callahan has worked continuously with three deeply felt personal themes—his wife, Eleanor; the urban scene; and simple, unspoiled nature. His study of a spindly weed (fig. **19.62**) is entirely straightforward, yet making sense of the form requires close scrutiny. In his later Cape Cod landscape, Callahan shifted from the isolated close-up of a motif in nature to seemingly limitless space (fig. **19.63**). This distilled view of the world, with its emphatic horizontality and nearly monochrome tonality, recalls late works by Rothko. "I think that every artist continually wants to reach the edge of nothingness," Callahan said.

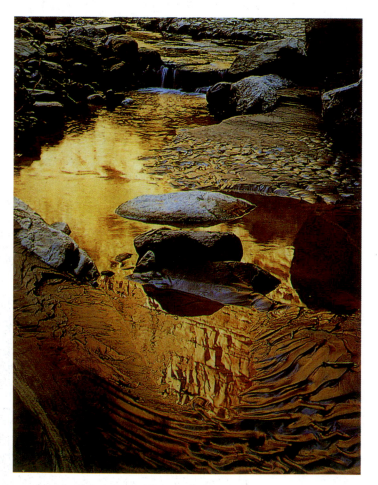

19.61 Eliot Porter, *Dark Canyon, Glen Canyon*, 1965. Dye transfer print, 10³⁄₁₆ × 7⅞" (25.9 × 20 cm). The Art Institute of Chicago.

19.63 Harry Callahan, *Cape Cod*, 1972. Gelatin-silver print, 9⅝ × 9¾" (24.4 × 24.8 cm).

19.64 Helen Levitt, *New York*, c. 1940. Gelatin-silver print. Courtesy Fraenkel Gallery, San Francisco.

Levitt and DeCarava

Obviously, not all photographers active in the forties and fifties were combing the landscape for abstract forms of expression. New York photographer **Helen Levitt** (b. 1913) began recording ordinary street life with her hand-held Leica camera in the late thirties. Crucial to her was the discovery of the work of Henri Cartier-Bresson (see fig. 15.68), and her magically complex image of children playing with a broken mirror in the street (fig. **19.64**) is more reminiscent of the Frenchman's "decisive moment" than the social indictments of documentary photographers such as Lewis Hine (see fig. 18.6). Levitt included this and other scenes from Spanish Harlem in a book called *A Way of Seeing*, 1965. It included an essay by James Agee, the writer who had already collaborated on a book with Levitt's friend, Walker Evans (see chapter 18).

Self-taught photographer **Roy DeCarava** (b. 1919) grew up in the midst of the Harlem Renaissance, a flourishing of urban African-American culture that was recorded by his older contemporary James Van Der Zee (see fig. 18.50). By 1952 his photographs had earned him a prestigious Guggenheim grant, the first ever awarded to an African-American. "I want to photograph Harlem through the Negro people," he wrote in his proposal, "Morning, noon, night, at work, going to work, at play, in the streets, talking, kidding, laughing, in the home, in the playground, in the schools. ... I want to show the strength, the wisdom, the dignity of the Negro people." One of the resulting photographs is a tender and moving portrait of an embracing couple (fig. **19.65**), which seems to sum up in a single image all the humanity the artist experienced in an entire

community. In 1955 DeCarava, like Levitt, joined forces with a noted writer, in this case the poet Langston Hughes, to publish his Harlem photographs as a book, aptly titled *The Sweet Flypaper of Life*.

19.65 Roy DeCarava, *Shirley Embracing Sam*, 1952. Gelatin-silver print 12¹⁵⁄₁₆ × 10¹⁄₁₆" (32.9 × 28.1 cm). Collection The DeCarava Archive.

20
Postwar European Art

If the American artists discussed in the previous chapter were coming to terms with the traumatic aftershocks of the war, their European counterparts had experienced those events at closer range. The deep sense of despair and disillusionment as well as the moral crisis of the postwar years had profound implications for their art. On a practical and professional level, too, the European art scene had been permanently reshaped by the war.

Revaluations and Violations: Figurative Art in France

The School of Paris in the postwar years hosted the continuing activity of the older established artists such as Picasso and Matisse, who, for the most part, lived and worked outside of the artistic mainstream in Paris. Returning from the United States were Léger, Chagall, Ernst, Masson, Picabia, Hélion, and others, including Duchamp, who, after 1945, commuted between Paris and New York. With Giacometti and Dubuffet, figuration received a new impetus in the years immediately following World War II. The debate between figuration and abstraction, which had first emerged in the early twentieth century, continued to resurface throughout the postwar decades, transcending national boundaries.

Picasso

When World War II came to a close in 1945, **Pablo Picasso** (1881–1973) was living in Paris, internationally recognized as the preeminent artist of the twentieth century and the subject of regular exhibitions around the globe. For the next eight or nine years he continued his involvement with a young painter named Françoise Gilot, who, after leaving him, published an account of their life together that enraged the artist. In the mid-fifties Picasso settled in the south of France with Jacqueline Roque and followed his own pursuits, relatively unaffected by the radical new developments in contemporary art in Europe and the United States. By the end of the decade he was

20.1 Pablo Picasso, *The Charnel House*, Paris 1944–45; dated 1945. Oil and charcoal on canvas, 6'6⅝" × 8'2½" (2 × 2.5 m). The Museum of Modern Art, New York.

seventy-eight years old and had outlived Matisse and many of his oldest friends.

Picasso, who had joined the Communist Party in 1944, summed up his feelings about the war in *The Charnel House* (fig. **20.1**), 1944–45, a painting that, like *Guernica* (see fig. 15.46), consists of a *grisaille* palette of black, white, and gray. A tabletop still life, rendered in a late Cubist style and left as an open line drawing, indicates a domestic setting. Beneath it, the twisting, anguished forms of a family massacred in their home could be the twentieth-century echo of Daumier's *Rue Transnonain* (see fig. 2.15).

A theme that had preoccupied Picasso throughout his career, but especially during his later years, was that of the artist as voyeur. Painted toward the end of his relationship with Gilot, *The Shadow* of 1953 (fig. **20.2**) is one of two compositions Picasso made showing his own shadow cast before the image of a nude woman sleeping on a bed. While the rectangular shape that frames the artist suggests a doorway, it also mimics the shape of a canvas and implies a fictive, painted, and strangely distant presence of the woman. Besides painting, the ever-prolific Picasso also explored the media of ceramics, prints, and sculpture during his last years. The head of the playful *Baboon and Young* (fig. **20.3**), a bronze from 1951, was cast using two toy automobiles that belonged to Picasso's son, Claude, and the whole figure was derived from this chance resemblance.

During these years, Picasso engaged in an extended dialogue with several great artists of the past, including Velázquez, Courbet, Manet, and Delacroix, through his own variations on their best-known works. In the several versions he made of Delacroix's *Women of Algiers*, a painting he knew in the Louvre, Picasso may have been paying tribute not only to France's leading Romantic painter, but also to Matisse. The latter, famous for his Orientalist themes and languid odalisques, had died a few months before Picasso embarked on this sumptuously colored and highly subjective interpretation of Delacroix's masterpiece (fig. **20.4**). Picasso envisioned his own imminent death in the *Self-Portrait* (fig. **20.5**), 1972, made less than a year before he died aged ninety-one. His stubble-covered, emaciated skull, with its bluish cast and hypnotically staring eyes, is a harrowingly probing self-image. Modernist critics frequently saw Picasso's late paintings, with their discordant fusions of different stylistic idioms and ways of handling paint, as a falling-off from his earlier achievements.

20.3 Pablo Picasso, *Baboon and Young*, 1951 (cast 1955). Bronze, after found objects, 21 × 13¼ × 20¾" (53.3 × 33.3 × 52.7 cm). The Museum of Modern Art, New York.

Postmodern critics, by contrast, compelled by the artist's fragmented and eclectic oeuvre, have hailed it as an important phase in the artist's career.

Giacometti

Alberto Giacometti (1901–66) was Surrealism's most important sculptor (see chapter 15). In 1934, however, he broke with the Surrealists, convinced that his abstracted constructions were carrying him too far from the world of actuality. He returned to a study of the figure, working from the model, with the intent of rendering the object and the space that contained it exactly as he saw them. In 1939 he decided to make a new start:

> I began to work from memory. ... But wanting to create from memory what I had seen, to my terror the sculptures became smaller and smaller, they had a likeness only when they were small, yet their dimensions revolted me, and tirelessly I began again, only to end several months later at the same point. A large figure seemed to me false and a small one equally unbearable, and then often they became so tiny that with one touch of my knife they disappeared into dust. But head and figures seemed to me to have a bit of truth only when small. All this changed a little in 1945 through drawing. This led me to want to make larger figures, but then to my surprise, they achieved a likeness only when tall and slender.

20.2 Pablo Picasso, *The Shadow*, December 29, 1953. Oil and charcoal on canvas, 49½ × 38" (125.7 × 96.5 cm). Musée Picasso, Paris.

20.4 Pablo Picasso, *Women of Algiers, after Delacroix,* February 11, 1955. Oil on canvas, 45 × 57½" (114.3 × 146.1 cm). Collection Mrs. Victor Ganz, New York.

When Giacometti returned to Paris from Switzerland after the war, his long struggle, during which he finished few works, was reaching resolution. The 1947 *Head of a Man on a Rod* (fig. **20.6**) presents a human head, tilted back with mouth agape and impaled on a metal rod. The violence and sense of anguish in the head, which seems to utter a silent scream, is related to the artist's earlier Surrealist works (see fig. **15.56**), but the peculiar format may have been aided by his recollection of a painted human skull from New Ireland (in the western Pacific Ocean) that he had seen displayed on a rod in an ethnographic museum in Basel, Switzerland. Typical of the artist's postwar sculpture, the surface retains all the bumps and gouges formed by his hand in the original wet plaster, thus resembling both a horrible laceration of the flesh and a rugged, rocky landscape.

20.5 Pablo Picasso, *Self-Portrait,* June 30, 1972. Pencil and colored pencil on paper, 25¾ × 20" (65.4 × 50.8 cm). Fuji Television Gallery, Tokyo.

20.6 Alberto Giacometti, *Head of a Man on a Rod*, 1947. Bronze, height 21¾" (55.2 cm). Private collection.

Giacometti's characteristic sculptural type in the postwar period was the tall, extremely attenuated figure that appeared singly or in groups, standing rigid or striding forward like an Egyptian deity. The figures ranged in scale from a few inches high to fully life-size, as in *Man Pointing* (fig. **20.7**). Giacometti first conceived this work, distinctive for its active gesture, as half of a pair of male figures, so that the man seemed to be pointing the direction for his companion. The artist may have disliked the implied narrative and decided to isolate the pointing figure.

Early on Giacometti had developed (perhaps from his studies of ancient sculpture) a passion for color in sculpture, and one of the most striking aspects of the later works is the patinas he used on his bronzes. *Chariot* (fig. **20.8**), which suggests an ancient Etruscan bronze, was originally designed as a commemorative public sculpture in Paris, but was ultimately rejected. Giacometti said the idea came from watching nurses wheel medicine carts about while he was hospitalized in 1938. Even when placed in groups, such as in environments evoking city squares, Giacometti's figures still maintain a sense of the individual's isolation (fig. **20.9**). Giacometti insisted that his sculptures were not embodiments of modern anguish and alienation and rejected the Existentialist readings of his postwar work by such illustrious figures as Jean-Paul Sartre and Samuel Beckett. Yet Sartre's description of one of Giacometti's sculptures seems very apt here: "Emptiness filters through everywhere, each creature secretes his own void."

Giacometti's favorite models continued to be his brother Diego, his mother, and his wife, Annette. Diego is

20.7 Alberto Giacometti, *Man Pointing*, 1947. Bronze, height 70½" (179.1 cm). The Museum of Modern Art, New York.

20.8 Alberto Giacometti, *Chariot*, 1950. Bronze, 57 × 26 × 26⅛" (144.8 × 65.8 × 66.2 cm). The Museum of Modern Art, New York.

20.10 Alberto Giacometti, *Bust of Diego*, 1955. Bronze, 22¼ × 12¼ × 5⅞" (56.5 × 31 × 15 cm). Foundation Alberto Giacometti, Kunsthaus, Zürich, Switzerland.

20.9 Alberto Giacometti, *The Forest (Composition with Seven Figures and One Head)*, 1950. Painted bronze, 22 × 24 × 19¼" (55.9 × 61 × 48.9 cm). The Reader's Digest Collection.

20.11 Alberto Giacometti, *The Artist's Mother*, 1950. Oil on canvas, 35⅜ × 24" (89.9 × 61 cm). The Museum of Modern Art, New York.

the subject of dozens of sculptures and paintings, ranging from relatively representational works to corrugated, pitted masks. In the mid-fifties Giacometti made several busts of Diego (fig. **20.10**) that present a slice of a head so thin that the frontal view is practically nonexistent. As the critic David Sylvester has written, "There is virtually no transition between front view and side view."

From the forties Giacometti also drew and painted with furious energy. He sought to pin down space, which could only be suggested in the sculptures. Like the sculptures, every painting was a result of constant working and reworking. In their subordination of color and emphasis on the action of line, the paintings have the appearance of drawings or even engravings. In *The Artist's Mother* (fig. **20.11**), the figure is almost completely assimilated into the network of linear details of the conventional living room.

Richier and César

Germaine Richier (1904–59) received her training from two sculptors who had studied with Rodin: Louis-Jacques Guiges and Bourdelle (see fig. 6.14). Her earliest surviving sculptures of the late thirties and early forties are sensitive portrait heads in the Rodin tradition. But the macabre quality of her mature works, fully formulated in *Praying Mantis* (fig. **20.12**), is uniquely her own. This strangely

20.13 Germaine Richier, *The Hurricane*, 1948–49. Bronze, height 70⅛" (178.1 cm). Private collection.

20.12 Germaine Richier, *Praying Mantis*, 1949. Bronze, height 47¼" (120 cm). Middelheim Sculpture Museum, Antwerp.

humanoid creature resembles a seated figure while maintaining all the predatory traits of a threatening insect. Produced around the same time, *The Hurricane* (fig. **20.13**) is characteristic of Richier's race of brutish beings. This is a monstrous figure, powerful as a gorilla, with pitted, torn, and lacerated flesh, which in a curious way is both threatening and pitiful. Richier experimented with the bronze technique, using paper-thin plaster models, into the surface of which she pressed every sort of organic object. Sometimes she placed her figures in front of a frame, the background of which is either worked in relief or, in some larger works, painted by a friend such as da Silva (see fig. 20.28). There are relations in her encrusted surfaces both to Giacometti's postwar sculpture, which was being formulated at exactly the same time (see fig. 20.7), and to Dubuffet's contemporary figure paintings (see fig. 20.17).

Whereas Richier stretched the possible limits of bronze casting, César Baldaccini, known as **César** (1921–98), created comparable effects from the assemblage of old iron scraps and machine fragments. His work developed independently of trends in the United States but paralleled that of certain American sculptors, notably John Chamberlain (see fig. 19.47). In his constructions, César tended toward abstraction but often returned to the figure. (Paradoxically the figure is also implicit in many of the abstract works.) His 1958 *Nude* is a pair of legs with lower torso, eroded

20.14 César, *The Yellow Buick*, 1961. Compressed automobile, 59½ × 30¾ × 24⅞" (151.1 × 78.1 × 63.2 cm). The Museum of Modern Art, New York.

and made more horrible by the sense of life that remains. During the late fifties and early sixties (and with variants in new materials into the nineties) he made what he called "compressions"—assemblages of automobile bodies crushed under great pressure and then pressed into massive blocks of varicolored materials, as they are in auto junkyards when the metal is processed for reuse (fig. **20.14**). By this point in his career, César was associated with New Realism in France (see chapter 21).

Balthus

A notoriously reclusive painter closely allied to Giacometti since the early thirties was Balthasar Klossowski, Count de Rola, known by his childhood nickname **Balthus** (1908–2001). He was born into a distinguished Polish family and raised in Paris, Geneva, and Berlin. His father was a painter and an art historian; his mother was also a painter; and the poet Rainer Maria Rilke was a close family friend. Balthus settled in the French capital in 1924. He copied the old masters in the Louvre but did not undergo any formal artistic training. Although he exhibited in 1934 at the Galerie Pierre, a Parisian gallery associated with the Surrealists, and was intrigued by the sexual implications of dreams, Balthus was not seduced by the Surrealist love of the irrational. From the thirties onward, he painted figures in enigmatic narrative compositions, especially semiaware pubescent girls, whom he placed in situations of riveting mystery, ambiguous eroticism, and a light that transfixes time (fig. **20.15**). The atmosphere of these lavishly

20.15 Balthus, *Les Beaux Jours (The Golden Days)*, 1944–46. Oil on canvas, 4'10¼" × 6'6¾" (1.48 × 2 m). Hirshhorn Museum and Sculpture Garden, Smithsonian Institution, Washington, D.C.

brushed paintings seems all the more charged for being contained within an architectonic structure as classically calm and balanced as those of Piero della Francesca and Poussin (see figs. 1.3, 1.10). The result is an eerie sense of the anxiety and decadence that haunted postwar Europe.

Dubuffet

After a brief period of study at the Académie Julian in 1918, which he found uncongenial, **Jean Dubuffet** (1901–85) continued to draw and paint privately, but much of his time was taken up with music, the study of languages, experimental theater, and puppetry. He had his first one-man exhibition at the Galerie René Drouin in Paris in 1944, when he was forty-three years old. Of singular importance to the artist was discovering Dr. Hans Prinzhorn's book, *Bildnerei der Geisteskranken* (*Artistry of the Mentally Ill*). Here Dubuffet found a brutal power of expression that seemed to him much more valid than the art of the museums or even the most experimental new art. The art of the mentally ill and of children became the models on which he built his approach. He admired Paul Klee, who had also used as sources works by people with no formal artistic training.

After 1944, Dubuffet became an exceptionally prolific painter and concurrently carried on an impressive program of writing on, cataloguing, and publishing his own work. The first of the new paintings, close in spirit to Klee, were panoramic views of Paris and Parisians: the buses, the Métro, the shops, and the backstreets (fig. **20.16**). The colors are bright and lively; the people drawn in a child-like manner; and the space composed as in primitive or archaic painting. "Remember," Dubuffet wrote, "that there is only one way to paint well, while there are a thousand ways to paint badly: they are what I'm curious about; sand ways to paint badly: they are what I'm curious about;

it's from them that I expect something new, that I hope for revelations."

In the late forties, Dubuffet made a series of caricatural portraits of the writers, intellectuals, and artists who were his friends. Typically subversive, his likenesses (for they do evoke a likeness despite their childlike rendering and wild deformation) defy all conventions of the portraiture genre. In *Dhotel velu aux dents jaunes* (*Dhotel Hairy with Yellow Teeth*) (fig. **20.17**) he gave the subject a comically huge head inscribed with highly unflattering features and placed it atop a body the shape of a flattened watermelon. In his *Corps de Dame* (*Woman's Body*) series, the female body is presented frontally and two-dimensionally, as if run over by a cement roller. Dubuffet rejected out of hand the Western tradition of the nude, and his paintings are an assault on "normal" standards of beauty. He observed that women's bodies had "long been associated (for Occidentals) with a very specious notion of beauty (inherited from Greeks and cultivated by the magazine covers); now it pleases me to protest against this aesthetic, which I find miserable and most depressing. Surely I aim for a beauty, but not that one."

Dubuffet had explored the variations of graffiti images and the textural effects of Paris walls with their generations of superimposed posters. The scratched, mutilated surface, built up in combinations of paint, paper, and sand, particularly appealed to him. Dubuffet's characteristic technique, what he called "*haute pâte*," was based on a thick ground made of sand, earth, fixatives, and other elements into which the pigment was mixed. Figures were incised into this ground, accidental effects were embraced, and the whole—scratched and scarred—worked in every way to give the picture a tangible, powerful materiality. Dubuffet also made pictures out of leaves, tinfoil, or butterfly wings, and his sculptures could be formed of slag, driftwood, sponges, or other found materials. In one of his most ingenious inventions, *L'Âme du Morvan* (*The Soul of Morvan*) (fig.

20.18 Jean Dubuffet, *L'Âme du Morvan* (*The Soul of Morvan*), May 1954. Grape wood and vines mounted on slag base, with tar, rope, wire, twine, nails, and staples, 18⅜ × 15⅜ × 12¾" (46.7 × 39.1 × 32.4 cm). Hirshhorn Museum and Sculpture Garden, Smithsonian Institution, Washington, D.C.

20.18), he managed to coax a strange little figure, who stands before a bush on a base of slag, out of found grape vines (Morvan is a wine-producing district in France).

20.19 Jean Dubuffet, *Virtual Virtue*, 1963. Oil on canvas, 37¾ × 50⅞" (95.9 × 129.2 cm). Sammlung Ernst Beyeler, Basel.

One of Dubuffet's main sources of inspiration was the great collection he began in 1945 of *art brut* or "raw art." Numbering thousands of works in all media, the collection, today in the Collection de L'Art Brut in Lausanne, Switzerland, contained the art of the mentally disturbed, the "primitive," and the "naive"—"anyone," Dubuffet said, "who has never learned to draw." To him these works had an authenticity, an originality, a passion, even a frenzy, that were utterly lacking in the works of professional artists.

It was Dubuffet's habit to work on a single theme or a few related themes for an extended period. In the fifties he turned to landscape imagery, but his landscapes are hardly conventional views of nature. Rather, they are representations of the soil, of the earth itself, like close-up views of geologic formations, barren of any vegetation. His works through the fifties were predominantly in close-keyed browns, dull ochers, and blacks, verging toward monochrome and, in a series called *Texturologies*, complete abstraction.

In 1962 Dubuffet embarked on a vast cycle of paintings and, eventually, sculptures, to which he gave the invented name "*L'Hourloupe*" (he liked the sound of the word) and on which he worked for the next twelve years. During a telephone conversation, Dubuffet doodled some curving, biomorphic cells in red ink that he filled in with blue parallel lines. These shapes became the formal vocabulary or the "sinuous graphisms" of the *hourloupe* language.

From this modest beginning the artist developed a vast repertoire of allover paintings, some on a scale transcending anything he had done previously. Semiautomatic and self-contained, the *hourloupe* forms flow and change like amoebae and are filled with suggestions of living organisms, even at times of human figures. In *Virtual Virtue* (fig. **20.19**) dozens of heads and little figures are embedded in the undulating lines of an *hourloupe* matrix. With no sense of illusionistic space, they tumble and float freely in what becomes a teeming maze of *hourloupe* creatures.

In 1966 Dubuffet extended the *hourloupe* vocabulary into the realm of sculpture, eventually stripping away the classic *hourloupe* red and blue and composing simply in black and white. At first the sculptures were relatively small-scale, but Dubuffet adapted his technique to outdoor monumental sculpture, sometimes on an environmental scale (fig. **20.20**). Beyond his marvelous corpus of painting and sculpture, Dubuffet has left a body of writings filled with humor and keen observations that apply not only to his work but to art in a larger, universal sense. "What I expect from any work of art," he wrote, "is that it surprises me, that it violates my customary valuations of things and offers me other, unexpected ones."

A Different Art: Abstraction in France

The emergence of postwar French abstraction coincided in time, if not in forms, with the origins of Abstract Expressionism in the United States (see chapter 19). Although artists on both sides of the Atlantic developed their highly individual styles independently of one another, there was a shared sense of the need to reject geometric abstraction and to create a spontaneous art that was guided by emotion and intuition rather than by rational systems of composition. *Art Informel* (literally "formless art") is a term devised in 1950 by the French critic Michel Tapié to describe this new type of expression. He coined another term, *Art Autre*—"another art," or "a different art," the essence of which is creation with neither desire for, nor preconceptions of, control, geometric or otherwise. *Tachisme* (from the French word *tache*, meaning the use of the "blot," the "stain," the "spot," or the "drip"), yet another term coined in the fifties by another French critic, refers specifically to European versions of gestural painting.

Fautrier, Van Velde, Hartung, and Soulages

Jean Fautrier (1898–1964) was one of the leading pioneers of *Art Informel*. After painting representationally through the twenties and thirties, he produced a moving series of small paintings on paper during World War II that he called *Hostages*. Incited by war atrocities that he had witnessed firsthand, the *Hostage* paintings were built-up masses of paint centralized on a neutral ground that resembled decayed human heads served on platters. These were followed by a series called *Naked Torsos*, whose shapes,

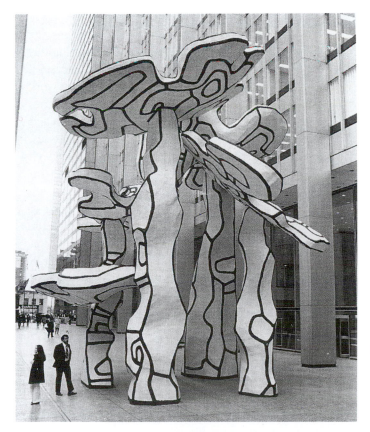

20.20 Jean Dubuffet, *Group of Four Trees*, 1972. Epoxy paint on polyurethane over metal structure, 38 × 40 × 34' (11.6 × 12.2 × 10.4 m). The Chase Manhattan Bank, New York.

20.21 Jean Fautrier, *Nude*, 1960. Oil on canvas, 35 × 57½" (88.9 × 146.1 cm). Collection de Montaigu, Paris.

albeit abbreviated and abstracted, emerge from a heavy paste of clay, paint, glue, and other materials that are built up in a thick relief. *Nude* (fig. **20.21**), 1960, was made the year Fautrier won the grand prize at the prestigious Venice Biennale. "No art form," the artist said, "can produce emotion if it does not mix in a part of reality."

Though Dutch by birth, **Bram van Velde** (1895–1981) spent most of his professional life in France, where, after World War II, he became especially close to Samuel Beckett, who wrote about his work. His paintings exhibit a remarkable consistency from the late forties until the end of his career. They tend to be composed around loosely delineated triangular, round, and ovoid forms that are situated in allover compositions and accentuated with patterns of dripping paint, as in his *Painting* of 1954 (fig. **20.22**). Though he developed his art without knowledge of American action painting, Van Velde was the European artist closest to aspects of his fellow Hollander, Willem de Kooning, who was one of the few Americans to exhibit any interest in Van Velde's art when it was first shown in New York in 1948.

Hans Hartung (1904–89) fled Nazi oppression in his native Germany in the early thirties and settled in Paris, via Spain, in 1935. He experimented with free abstract drawings and watercolors as early as 1922, well before his exact contemporary, de Kooning, was formulating his Abstract Expressionist mode in America (see chapter 19). Hartung's brittle, linear style owes something to the work of Kandinsky, whom he met in 1925. During the thirties he explored abstract Surrealism as derived from Miró and Masson, but always with an emphasis on the spontaneous, gestural stroke. He also produced Surrealist collages as well as constructed sculpture in the tradition of his father-in-law, Julio González (see figs. 15.53, 15.54).

In the late forties, Hartung developed his mature style of brisk graphic structures, usually networks of bold black slashes played against delicate, luminous washes of color. His improvisational marks, combined with his statement in 1951 that he "acted on the canvas" out of a desire to record the trace of his personal gesture, allied him in the minds of some with action painting. In the sixties he tended to scratch into fresh paint with various instruments to achieve finely textured surfaces, in which light and shadow play over one another in shimmering chiaroscuro effects (fig. **20.23**).

Pierre Soulages (b. 1919) first came to Paris in 1938 but did not settle there until 1946, whereupon he arrived at what was to become his signature style by crafting assertive abstract structures based on studies of tree forms. The architectural sense and the closely keyed color range

20.22 Bram van Velde, *Painting*, 1955. Oil on canvas, 4'3" × 6'5" (1.3 × 2 m). Stedelijk Museum, Amsterdam.

20.23 Hans Hartung, *Untitled T, 1963-H26*, 1963. Oil on canvas, 39⅜ × 31⅞" (100 × 81 cm). Private collection.

that characterize his abstract style (fig. **20.24**)—with its sense of physical, massive structure in which the blacks stand forth like powerful presences—may have been inspired originally by the dolmens (prehistoric stone monuments made of several large stones forming two upright posts supporting a lintel) found in his native Auvergne, as it certainly was by the Romanesque sculpture of the area.

20.24 Pierre Soulages, *Painting*, 1953. Oil on canvas, 6'4¾" × 4'3⅛" (1.9 × 1.3 m). Solomon R. Guggenheim Museum, New York.

Soulages consistently maintained a subdued palette, feeling that "the more limited the means, the stronger the expression." His great sweeping lines or color areas are usually black or of a dark color. Heavy in impasto, they were applied with a palette knife or large, housepainter's brushes. Soulages thus achieved an art of power and elegance, notable not only in his forms but in the penetrating, encompassing light that unifies his paintings.

Wols, Mathieu, Riopelle, and Vieira da Silva

Berlin-born Alfred Otto Wolfgang Schulze, known by his pseudonym **Wols** (1913–51), was raised in Dresden, where he soon excelled at many things, including music and photography. Interested primarily in drawing and painting, however, the precocious Wols moved to Paris in 1932 at the age of nineteen. There he briefly met members of the international Surrealist circle such as Arp and Giacometti. For part of the war he was, like other expatriate Germans, interned by the French. While detained, he made bizarre watercolors and drawings of hybrid creatures that somewhat resemble Surrealist "exquisite corpse" drawings (see fig. 15.1).

Following the war, Wols developed an abstract style with some analogies to that of Fautrier. In such works as *Bird*, 1949, he built up his paint in a heavy central mass that was shot through with flashes of intense colors and automatic lines and dribbles (fig. **20.25**). Wols's abstractions create the impact of magnified biological specimens—he had been interested in biology and anthropology from an early

20.25 Wols, *Bird*, 1949. Oil on canvas, 36¼ × 25⅜" (92.1 × 64.5 cm). The Menil Collection, Houston.

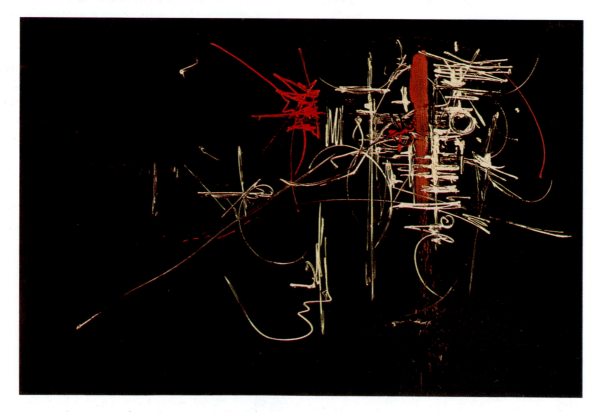

20.26 Georges Mathieu, *Painting*, 1953. Oil on canvas, 6'6" × 9'10" (2 × 3 m). Solomon R. Guggenheim Museum, New York.

20.27 Jean-Paul Riopelle, *Blue Knight*, 1953. Oil on canvas, 3'8⅞ × 6'4½" (1.1 × 1.9 m). Solomon R. Guggenheim Museum, New York.

age—or encrusted, half-healed wounds. Wols never fully recovered from his war-induced traumas. He drank heavily and died at the age of thirty-eight.

After World War II, **Georges Mathieu** (b. 1921) developed a calligraphic style that owes something to Hartung. His calligraphy (fig. **20.26**), however, consists of sweeping patterns of lines squeezed directly from the tube in slashing, impulsive gestures. To him, speed of execution was essential for intuitive spontaneity. Typically, Mathieu turned to elaborate titles taken from battles or other events of French history, reflecting his insistence that he was a traditional history painter working in an abstract means. In love with spectacle, performance, and self-promotion, he occasionally painted before an audience, dressed in armor and attacking the canvas as though he were the hero Roland and the canvas were the enemy Saracen from the medieval French romance *The Song of Roland*. Despite such exhibitionism, Mathieu became an artist of substantial abilities in the fifties, and one of the leading European exponents of *Art Informel*.

Born and educated in Montreal, **Jean-Paul Riopelle** (1923–2002) settled in Paris in 1947. He soon became part of the circle around the dealer Pierre Loeb (a leading supporter of Surrealism in the thirties) that included Mathieu and Vieira da Silva. Between 1955 and 1979, he was the companion of the second-generation American Abstract Expressionist Joan Mitchell (see fig. 22.3). The individual mode he achieved in the fifties, for example in *Blue Knight*, 1953 (fig. **20.27**), is essentially a kind of controlled chance, an intricate, allover mosaic of small, regular daubs of jewellike color, applied directly from tubes, shaped with palette knives, and held together by directional lines of force.

A Parisian artist difficult to classify but one of great sensitivity was Lisbon-born **Maria Elena Vieira da Silva** (1908–92). By the forties she was preoccupied with the interaction of perspective and nonperspective space in paintings based on architectural views of the city or deep interior spaces. By 1950 these views became abstract, grid-based compositions. *The Invisible Stroller* (fig. **20.28**) is related to Picasso's Synthetic Cubist paintings of the twenties in its fluctuations of Renaissance perspective and the Cubist grid. From this point forward da Silva gradually flattened the perspective while retaining a rigid, rectangular, architectural structure. The view of the city, seen from eye level, eventually became the view from an airplane—as one rises higher and higher, details begin to blur and colors melt into general tonalities.

20.28 Maria Elena Vieira da Silva, *The Invisible Stroller*, 1951. Oil on canvas, 52 × 66" (132.1 × 167.6 cm). San Francisco Museum of Modern Art.

De Staël

Nicolas de Staël (1914–55) was an independently minded painter who did not wish to be associated with his contemporary abstractionists in France, seeing himself more as the heir to his friend Braque, as well as Matisse. De Staël was born an aristocrat in prerevolutionary Russia; grew up in Belgium, where he attended the Royal Academy of Fine Arts; and moved to Paris in 1938. In the forties he was painting abstractly, but as his work developed, he became more and more concerned with the problem of nature versus abstraction. De Staël seems to have been increasingly desirous of asserting the subject while maintaining abstract form. "A painting," he said, "should be both abstract and figurative: abstract to the extent that it is a flat surface, figurative to the extent that it is a representation of space." He began to use palette knives in 1949, building up his abstract compositions with thick, loosely rectangular patches of paint that he scraped into the desired form with a knife (fig. **20.29**). In 1953 he traveled to Sicily and was struck by the intense quality of light. He made landscapes in brilliant hues (fig. **20.30**)—in this example reds, oranges, and yellows—in which the forms are simplified to large planes of flat color accented by a few contrasting color spots. In the last year of his life he began painting even more literal scenes of boats, birds, and oceans, in thin, pale colors. In 1955 de Staël, who had achieved a considerable reputation on both sides of the Atlantic, apparently reached an impasse in his work and jumped to his death from the terrace of his studio.

20.29 Nicolas de Staël, *Untitled*, 1951. Oil on canvas, 63 × 29" (160 × 73.7 cm). Private collection.

20.30 Nicolas de Staël, *Agrigente*, 1954. Oil on canvas, 34¾ × 50½" (88.3 × 128.3 cm). The Museum of Contemporary Art, Los Angeles.

"Pure Creation": Concrete Art

In 1930 Theo van Doesburg coined the word "concrete" as a substitute for "nonobjective" in its specific application to the geometric abstractions of de Stijl (see chapter 17). This was followed in 1931 by the Abstraction-Création group in Paris, which, during the thirties, sought to advance the principles of pure abstraction and of Mondrian's Neo-Plasticism. The concept of Concrete art was revived in 1947 in the Salon des Réalités Nouvelles, as the gallery of Denise René became an international center for the propagation of Concrete art. Among the leaders outside of France was Josef Albers, who went to the United States in 1933 and whose influence there helped the spread of geometric abstraction (see chapter 17). He exhibited regularly with the American Abstract Artists (AAA) group as well as with Abstraction-Création in Paris. Many aspects of postwar Constructivism, Color Field painting, Systemic painting, and Op art stem from the international tradition of de Stijl and Concrete art.

Bill and Lohse

Important for the spread of Concrete art in Europe were developments in Switzerland, particularly in the work of **Max Bill** (1908–94) and Richard Paul Lohse. Though he was making nonobjective art by the late twenties, Bill first began applying the term "concrete" to his work in 1936. He defined it as follows: "Concrete painting eliminates all naturalistic representation; it avails itself exclusively of the fundamental elements of painting, the color and form of the surface. Its essence is, then, the complete emancipation of every natural model; pure Creation."

Bill studied at the Dessau Bauhaus between 1927 and 1929 when Josef Albers was teaching there. Subsequently, he developed into one of the most prolific and varied exponents of Bauhaus ideas as a painter, sculptor, architect, graphic and industrial designer, and writer. He was associated with Abstraction-Création in Paris and organized

20.32 Max Bill, *Nine Fields Divided by Means of Two Colors*, 1968. Oil on canvas, 47 × 47" (119.4 × 119.4 cm). Albright-Knox Art Gallery, Buffalo, New York.

exhibitions of Concrete art in Switzerland. Bill insisted that painting and sculpture have always had mathematical bases, whether arrived at consciously or unconsciously. In the forms of Concrete art he found rationalism, clarity, and harmony—qualities symbolic of certain universal ideas.

In sculpture, the form that intrigued Bill the most and on which he played many variations is the endless helix or spiral (fig. 20.31). The metal ribbon form turns back upon itself with no beginning and no end and is, therefore, in a constant state of movement and transformation. In his paintings, Bill, like Albers, systematically experimented with color, particularly the interaction of colors upon one another (fig. 20.32). Much as his square and diamond-shaped paintings owe to the example of Mondrian, Bill's pristine forms and regular grids have more to do with geometry than they do with Mondrian's intuitive and painterly approach to picture making, situating his work in the context of so-called Hard-Edge painting in the sixties (see chapter 22).

Like Bill, **Richard Paul Lohse** (1902–88) made mathematics the basis of his painting. He sought the simplest possible unit, such as a small color-square. Using not more than five color hues but a great range of color values, Lohse built his units into larger and larger complexes through a mathematically precise distribution of hues and values in exact and intellectually predetermined relationships (fig. 20.33). This resulted in a composition or color structure that spreads laterally and uniformly, with no single focus, to the edges of the canvas, with the implication and the potential of spreading to infinity beyond the edges. Despite the rigidity of Lohse's system, the subtlety and richness

20.31 Max Bill, *Endless Ribbon from a Ring I*, 1947–49, executed 1960. Gilded copper on crystalline base, 14½ × 27 × 7½" (36.8 × 68.6 × 19.1 cm). Hirshhorn Museum and Sculpture Garden, Smithsonian Institution, Washington, D.C.

20.33 Richard Paul Lohse, *Serial Element Concentrated in Rhythmic Groups*, 1949–56. Oil on canvas, 35⅜ × 35⅜" (90 × 90 cm). Private collection.

of his colors and the shimmering quality deriving from their infinitely varied relationships give his works a lyrical, poetic feeling. His art is important as a prototype for Op art (see fig. 22.28).

Postwar Juxtapositions: Figuration and Abstraction in Italy and Spain

In post-fascist Italy, art underwent a period of intense debate in major urban centers, such as Milan, Bologna, and Rome, with artistic concerns rarely divorced from political ones. A strong realist movement existed, particularly among communist artists who wielded painting as a political weapon. But alternatives arose among younger artists who proposed radical abstraction as an antidote to Italy's time-honored classical tradition. In the late fifties various forms of *Art Informel* spread throughout the country, supplanting more Cubist-based forms of abstraction. Despite the Italian proclivity for forming groups and issuing manifestos, *Art Informel* was never a uniform movement in that country, and figuration, particularly in sculpture, remained a viable artistic force.

In Spain during the postwar decades under the dictatorship of General Franco, abstraction was a powerful metaphorical dimension in the work of painter Antoni Tàpies and sculptor Eduardo Chillida.

Morandi

An artist who seemed to exist outside of the political and artistic fray was **Giorgio Morandi** (1890–1964), who emerged as the leading figurative painter in Italy in the years after the war. Despite his forays into landscape and, occasionally, figure painting, Morandi's primary subject throughout his long career was still life. At odds with much of the large-scale, highly emotive, and abstract art being produced after the war, this artist's quiet and modestly scaled still lifes drew as much upon Italian Renaissance traditions as contemporary developments. Old enough to have been exposed to Futurism (though his work was never truly Futurist), Morandi was included in the First Free Futurist Exhibition in Rome in 1914. In 1918–19, after discovering the works of Carrà and de Chirico, he made enigmatic still lifes that allied him with the Metaphysical School. Morandi lived quietly in his native Bologna, teaching, painting, and traveling only rarely. It was not until after World War II that he was acknowledged as Italy's leading living painter. The unremarkable elements of his postwar

20.34 Giorgio Morandi, *Still Life*, 1951. Oil on canvas, 8⅞ × 19⅝" (22.5 × 50 cm). Kunstsammlung Nordrhein-Westfalen, Düsseldorf.

20.35 Marino Marini, *Horse and Rider*, 1952–53. Bronze, height 6'10" (2.1 m). Hirshhorn Museum and Sculpture Garden, Smithsonian Institution, Washington, D.C.

still lifes (fig. **20.34**)—bottles, jars, and boxes—are typically massed together against a neutral ground to form a kind of miniature architecture, with an emphasis on abstract organization and subdued, closely valued tones. There is a meditative, serialized aspect to the artist's work, for he often cast similar arrangements in slightly altered light conditions. Morandi's still lifes, in which humble objects are reduced to their essence, continue the tradition of the great French eighteenth-century still-life painter Jean-Baptiste-Siméon Chardin and provided an important example to younger realist painters, notably the American Wayne Thiebaud (see fig. 21.53).

Marini and Manzù

The Italian contribution in postwar figuration came chiefly in sculpture, especially in the work of **Marino Marini** (1901–80) and Giacomo Manzù. The sculpture of Marini, a native of Tuscany, was deeply rooted in history. For Italians, he said, "the art of the past is part and parcel of our daily life in the present." Besides ancient Roman and Etruscan art, he was interested in the sculpture of Archaic Greece and Tang dynasty China. He also traveled widely and was knowledgeable about modernist developments in Italy and elsewhere in Europe. Marini was a mature artist by the thirties, already experimenting with his favorite themes, including the horse and rider. During the war, the equestrian subject, traditionally employed to commemorate noblemen or celebrate war heroes in city squares,

became for Marini a symbol for suffering and disillusioned humanity. His horse, with elongated, widely stretched legs and upthrust head (fig. **20.35**), screams in agony, in a manner that recalls Picasso's *Guernica* (see fig. 15.46). The rider, with outflung stumps for arms, falls back in a violent gesture of despair. "My equestrian figures," the artist said, "are symbols of the anguish that I feel when I survey contemporary events. Little by little, my horses become more restless, their riders less and less able to control them." By 1952, when he won the grand prize for sculpture at the Venice Biennale, Marini was recognized internationally as one of Europe's most prominent sculptors.

Giacomo Manzù (1908–91) was influenced by Medardo Rosso (see fig. 6.15), but his real love was the sculpture of the Italian Renaissance. In 1939, deeply affected by the spread of fascism and the threat of war, he made a series of relief sculptures around the subject of the Crucifixion that was his not-so-veiled antifascist statement.

The *Cardinal* series, begun in 1938 but represented here by a version from 1954 (fig. **20.36**), took a conventional subject and creates from it a mood of withdrawal and mystery. At the same time, Manzù utilized the heavy robes for a simple and monumental sculptural volume. In the Renaissance tradition, Manzù carried out a number of religious commissions, notably the bronze door panels for St. Peter's Basilica in Rome and for Salzburg Cathedral.

20.36 Giacomo Manzù, *Large Standing Cardinal*, 1954. Bronze, height 66½" (168.9 cm). Hirshhorn Museum and Sculpture Garden, Smithsonian Institution, Washington, D.C.

20.37 Afro, *For an Anniversary*, 1955. Oil on canvas, 4'11" × 6'6⅝" (1.5 × 2 m). Solomon R. Guggenheim Museum, New York.

He received the commission for St. Peter's in 1952 and the doors were consecrated in 1964. Manzù solved the daunting task of designing doors for St. Peter's—he was, after all, entering the realm of Bramante, Michelangelo, and Bernini—with a series of low-relief sculptures on the general theme of death. Each door contains a large, vertical panel on a biblical theme above four smaller ones. In these lower panels Manzù chose to depict not the deaths of Christian martyrs but those of common people. In *Death by Violence II*, a man succumbs to a tortuous death observed by a compassionate female onlooker.

Afro

Italian *Art Informel* found an advocate in **Afro** (1912–76), as Afro Basaldella is generally known, though his work was never as radical as that of Lucio Fontana or Alberto Burri (see below). His work was central to the Italian *Astratto–Concreto* (Abstract–Concrete) movement at mid-century, led by the influential Italian critic Lionello Venturi. During the fifties, Afro created an atmospheric world of light and shadows, with subdued, harmonious colors and shapes that are in a constant state of metamorphosis (fig. **20.37**). Of Italian postwar painters, Afro was closest to his American contemporaries, having lived in the United States in 1950 and admired the work of Gorky, Kline, and de Kooning. His later work of the sixties took on a painterly appearance close to that of these gestural painters.

20.38 Lucio Fontana, *Spatial Concept: The End of God*, 1963. Oil on canvas, 70 × 48½" (177.8 × 123.2 cm). Gallerie dell'Ariete, Milan.

Fontana

Among abstract artists in Italy in the years after the war, **Lucio Fontana** (1899–1968) was the leading exemplar. Born in Argentina and trained as a sculptor in Italy, he was producing abstract sculpture by the early thirties (though he also continued to work figuratively into the fifties). He joined the Paris-based Abstraction-Création group in 1935, the same year he signed the First Manifesto of Italian Abstract Artists. During World War II he returned to Argentina, where he published the *White Manifesto*, outlining his idea of a dynamic new art for a new age made with such modern materials as neon light and television—media whose potential would not be tapped again for art until the sixties and seventies. The *White Manifesto*, modeled in many ways on Futurist prototypes, anticipated the theory of what would be known as *Spazialismo* or Spatialism (laid out in five more manifestos between 1947 and 1952), a concept that rejected the illusionistic or "virtual" space of traditional easel painting in favor of the free development of color and form in literal space. The Spatialist program was designed to emancipate art from past preconceptions, to create an art that would "transcend the area of the canvas, or the volume of the statue, to assume further dimensions and become … an integral part of architecture, transmitted into the surrounding space and using discoveries in science and technology."

Fontana also became a pioneer of environments in 1949 when he used free forms and black light to create vast Spatialist surrounds, experiments followed in the fifties by designs made in collaboration with the architect Luciano Baldessari. In his desire to break down categories of painting, sculpture, and even architecture, Fontana described his works as *Concetti Spaziale* (CS), or "Spatial Concepts," thus inaugurating Conceptualism, a style that would not actually take hold in Western art until the seventies.

Beginning in 1949, Fontana perforated the canvas with *buchi* (holes) in abstract but not haphazard patterns, thereby breaking through the picture plane that had been the point of departure for painting throughout much of its history. In 1963 he made a series of egg-shaped canvases called *Spatial Concept: The End of God* (fig. **20.38**), in which holes are torn in a brightly painted canvas to reveal another colored canvas below, all resembling a strange, extraterrestrial landscape. During the fifties he experimented with matter, as did his fellow countrymen Afro and Alberto Burri, building up his penetrated surfaces with heavy paint, paste, canvas fragments, or pieces of glass. It was in 1958 that, feeling he was complicating and embellishing the works too much, Fontana slashed a spoiled canvas. He realized that with this simple act, he could achieve the integration of surface with depth that he had been seeking. These monochrome, lacerated canvases, called *Tagli* (slashes) (fig. **20.39**) were subtitled *Attese*, which translates as "expectations," and are the works for which he is best known. Although Fontana's abstract art was tied to the general trends of *Art Informel*, instead of making a

20.39 Lucio Fontana, *Concetto Spaziale (Attese)*, c. 1960. Oil on canvas, 36 × 28¾" (91.4 × 73 cm). Folkwang Museum, Essen, Germany.

positive gesture that adds medium to the painted surface, his incisions in a sense remove medium and transform the normally taut and inviolable surface of the canvas into a soft, malleable form that opens to a mysteriously dark interior. For Fontana, the gesture was less about creating a record of the individual artist's emotion—as with Mathieu or de Kooning—than it was an exploration of the physical properties of a work of art and the emotions that those properties evoke. Shortly after he made his first *Tagli*, Fontana applied his Spatial Concepts to bronze sculptures (as he already had to ceramics), creating roughly textured, rounded forms that are sliced and punctured.

Burri

Alberto Burri (1915–95) was a doctor in the Italian army in North Africa when he was captured by the British. Later he was turned over to the Americans, who interned him as a prisoner of war in Texas. During this confinement, Burri began drawing and painting. Abandoning medicine after his release, he continued his creative activities free of formal artistic training, and developed a style indebted at first to Mondrian and Miró. Burri eventually evolved a method with a strong emphasis on texture and materiality, incorporating thick paint, pastes, and tar into his paintings. He received his first exhibition in a Roman gallery in 1947 and

20.40 Alberto Burri, *Composition*, 1953. Oil, gold paint, and glue on canvas and burlap, 34 × 39⅜" (86.4 × 100 cm). Solomon R. Guggenheim Museum, New York.

in 1950 began to make *Sacchi* (fig. **20.40**), paintings made of old sacks roughly sewn together and heavily splashed with paint. The results were often reminiscent of bloodstained bandages, torn and scarred—devastating commentaries on war's death and destruction. They have been related to Schwitters's collages (see fig. 13.30), but their impact is much more brutal. For a period in the mid-fifties Burri burned designs on thin wood panels like those used in orange crates. In them, as in the earlier works, there is a strange juxtaposition: on the one hand, the ephemeral material coupled with a sense of destruction and disintegration (the material sometimes disintegrates visibly when moved from place to place); on the other hand, the elegance and control with which the artist arranges his elements. Burri also worked in metal and plastics, melting and re-forming these media with a blowtorch to achieve results of vivid coloristic beauty combined with effects of disease and decay. His influence has been strong, particularly on the young Robert Rauschenberg (see fig. 21.10), who visited his studio in 1953.

Tàpies

Coming of age following the devastation of the Spanish Civil War and in the wake of the great twentieth-century Spanish painters—Picasso, Miró, Dalí—**Antoni Tàpies** (b. 1923) emerged as an important artist in Spain after World War II. By the early sixties his reputation had spread well beyond Spain's borders and was bolstered by important exhibitions in Europe and the United States. Tàpies was a native of Barcelona, a gifted draftsman, and a man of broad erudition who drew from many sources for his art,

including Catalan mysticism and Zen Buddhism. His early paintings, which incorporate collage and depict fantastic subjects, are highly reminiscent of Klee and Miró. Then in the mid-fifties, profound changes took place in his outlook and his art. "Suddenly, as if I had passed through the looking-glass," he wrote, "a whole new perspective opened up before me, as if to tell the innermost secret of things. A whole new geography lit my way from one surprise to the next." He began to make abstract compositions distinctive for their emphasis on thick, rough textures (fig. **20.41**). He built up the surfaces of his paintings in a variety of ways, with combinations of paint, varnish, sand, and powdered marble, to create an effect of textured relief. His colors are generally subdued but rich, with surfaces worked in many ways—punctured, incised, or modeled in relief. These highly tactile surfaces became analogous to walls for the artist into which he crudely scratched lines or onto which he applied other materials. As such, they were metaphors for the struggles and sufferings of the artist and his fellow Spaniards during the war years, which he said, "seemed to inscribe themselves on the walls around me" (*tàpies* in fact means "walls" in Spanish). Like many of his contemporaries, Tàpies has used "poor" materials—weathered wood, rope, burlap, cardboard, and found objects—to create crusty, battered surfaces expressive of his deeply spiritual, antimaterialistic values.

20.41 Antoni Tàpies, *Painting Collage*, 1964. Mixed media on canvas, 14 × 22" (35.6 × 55.9 cm). Galleria Toninelli, Rome.

20.42 Eduardo Chillida (architect: Luis Peña Ganchegui; engineer: José María Elósegui), *Combs of the Wind*, 1977. Iron, each of three pieces 7 × 6 × 6' (21.3 × 1.8 × 1.8m). Donostia Bay, San Sebastián, Spain.

Chillida

Originally trained as an architect, the Spanish artist **Eduardo Chillida** (1924–2002) turned to sculpture in his early twenties. Though he carved work in wood and stone, Chillida worked predominantly in iron, drawing upon the long blacksmithing tradition in his native Basque country. His earlier works are complex, interlocking configurations that can suggest the old tools from which they were forged. Later he forged massive, monumental bars in powerful architectural abstractions with extremely subtle relations among the massive, tilted rectangular shapes. His works on a monumental scale include a well-known sculpture for his hometown of San Sebastián called *Combs of the Wind*. At a place where Chillida spent much of his childhood, iron forms resembling massive pincers are dramatically sited on the beach and embedded into the living rock (fig. **20.42**).

"Forget It and Start Again": The CoBrA Artists and Hundertwasser

In the postwar Netherlands—in the very home of Mondrian and de Stijl—a desire for expressionistic liberation from the constraints of anything rational, geometric, or Constructivist became particularly urgent. Inspired by the Danish painter Asger Jorn, three Dutch artists—Karel Appel, Cornelis Corneille, and George Constant—established the Experimental Group in 1948. They sought new forms of elemental expression, as much opposed to Mondrian and de Stijl as to the Academy. Through contacts with similar groups in Copenhagen and Brussels, this association evolved into the international group CoBrA (standing for Copenhagen, Brussels, and Amsterdam), led by Jorn and the Belgian poet Christian Dotrement. Most of the painters associated with the CoBrA group employed some sort of subject or figuration, often informed by their interests in the art of the untutored—what Dubuffet called *art brut*. The most important unifying principles among these divergent artists was their doctrine of complete freedom of abstract expressive forms; their emphasis on brush gesture; and their rejection of rationalism and geometric abstraction. In the words of one artist, "The gallery had become a temple dedicated to the right angle and the straight line." In this, they were allied to Dubuffet and Fautrier in France, for both of whom the artists of CoBrA had great respect, although the latter's means of expression were generally more violent, colorful, and dynamic. CoBrA, which lasted as a united movement from 1948 to 1951, was a critical artistic phenomenon for its internationalism. It also infused tremendous energy into abstract painting when an exhausted Europe was just emerging from the war.

Jorn

The Dane **Asger Jorn** (1914–73) represents the most extreme reaction against Concrete art's principles of order and harmony. Jorn spent several formative years in Paris,

20.43 Asger Jorn, *The Enigma of Frozen Water*, 1970. Oil on canvas, 63¾ × 51⅛" (162 × 130 cm). Stedelijk Museum, Amsterdam.

where he received disciplined training at Léger's academy. Important for his future development was his exposure to the biomorphic Surrealism of Arp and Masson (see figs. 15.3, 15.18), memories of which remained a constant theme in his art. Like the American Abstract Expressionists, who learned from similar Surrealist examples, Jorn was interested in mythic subject matter, which he drew from specifically Nordic folkloric traditions.

Jorn produced paintings that could be an illustration of Ruskin's famous epithet concerning Whistler—a pot of paint flung in the face of the public. Yet Jorn's art still has its roots in figuration. Using largely undiluted primary colors with blacks, whites, and greens, Jorn smeared, slashed, and dripped the paint in a seemingly uncontrolled frenzy. Yet the control, established in large, swinging, linear movements, and asymmetrically balanced color-shapes, remains sufficient to bring a degree of order out of chaos while not diminishing the explosive fury of the abstract expression (fig. **20.43**).

Appel

Karel Appel (b. 1921) consistently painted figures and portraits with heavy impasto and brilliant color, as in his 1956 portrait of Willem Sandberg, who was then director of Amsterdam's Stedelijk Museum, which specializes in modern art. Sandberg was a heroic figure to young artists in Holland both for his support of experimental art—he championed CoBrA against intensely negative public sentiment—and for his efforts to save Dutch Jews from deportation by the Nazis during the war. Appel, like Dubuffet, whose work he first saw in 1947 during a trip to Paris, was drawn to the intuitive and the spontaneous, especially in the art of children, and he achieved a wonderful childlike quality in his own work (fig. **20.44**). He was also inspired by Van Gogh, Matisse, Schwitters, and Picasso. "You have to learn it all," he said, "then forget it and start again like a child. This is the inner evolution." Appel established a certain control over this process through his representation of an explicit face or figure.

Alechinsky

The Belgian **Pierre Alechinsky** (b. 1927) was a latecomer to the CoBrA group. When he first encountered their paintings at a 1949 exhibition in Brussels, he detected in them "a total opposition to the calculations of cold abstraction, the sordid or 'optimistic' speculations of socialist realism, and to all forms of division between free thought and the action of painting freely." By comparison with Appel or Jorn, particularly in his earlier works of the fifties, Alechinsky produced an allover structure of tightly interwoven elements

20.44 Karel Appel, *Angry Landscape*, 1967. Oil on canvas, 4'3¼" × 6'4¾" (1.3 m × 1.9 m). Private collection.

20.45 Pierre Alechinsky, *Ant Hill*, 1954. Oil on canvas, 4'11½" × 7'9⅞" (1.5 × 2.4 m). Solomon R. Guggenheim Museum, New York.

with a sense of order deriving from microcosmic organisms (fig. **20.45**). His later works, on the other hand, have a curvilinear morphology that stems partly from Belgian Art Nouveau as well as from the artist's automatist practices.

Hundertwasser

An artist who continued the traditions of Austrian Art Nouveau and Expressionism was the Viennese Friedrich Stowasser, or **Hundertwasser** (1928–2000). Impossible to classify through allegiance to any particular artistic group or cause, Hundertwasser traveled extensively, living at different times in France, Italy, and Austria. Though he arrived in Paris at the dawn of *Art Informel*, he developed a style directly at odds with it, preferring instead to forge a visual language based on specific forms, ones derived largely from the Austrians Gustav Klimt and Egon Schiele (see figs. 5.5, 8.26). His early work carries strong overtones of Paul Klee, and he shared Klee's interest in art produced by children. The most distinctive feature of Hundertwasser's art is its jewellike color, as in the self-portrait shown here (fig. **20.46**), a brilliant pastiche of Art Nouveau decoration.

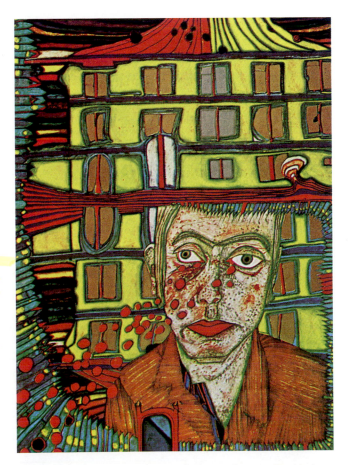

20.46 Hundertwasser, *House which was born in Stockholm, died in Paris, and myself mourning it*, 1965. Mixed media, 32 × 23⅞" (81.3 × 60.1 cm). Private collection.

20.47 Francis Bacon, *Painting*, 1946. Oil on canvas, 6'6" × 4'4" (2 × 1.32 m). The Museum of Modern Art, New York.

Figures in the Landscape: British Painting and Sculpture

In British art after the war a strong emphasis on the figure reasserted itself, even in the work of an artist such as Barbara Hepworth, who in the thirties had aligned herself with European abstraction. (Giacometti had similarly moved from Surrealist sculpture to an art centered on the human figure.) For Hepworth as for Henry Moore, the relationship between the figure, or sculpture, and its surroundings was of crucial importance. Both artists paid close attention to the siting of their works in rural or urban settings so as to achieve an effect of presenceful, often serene, poise. In the paintings of Francis Bacon and Lucian Freud, by contrast, the human subjects inhabit comfortless spaces that highlight their vulnerability.

Bacon

Irish-born **Francis Bacon** (1909–92) was a figurative painter of disquieting subject matter. After the war, Bacon achieved international stature on a par with that of Giacometti and Dubuffet. A wholly self-taught artist, Bacon left his native Dublin as a teenager, traveling in Europe and settling eventually in London. He painted grim, violent, and grotesquely distorted imagery in the most seductive painterly style, producing what one writer described as "a terrible beauty." Bacon's devotion to the monstrous has been variously interpreted as a reaction to the plight of the world, or as a nihilistic or existential attitude toward life's meaninglessness.

In *Painting* (fig. **20.47**), 1946 (he destroyed most of his prewar work), Bacon created a horrific montage of images that, according to his explanation, emerged by accident. The artist said:

> I was attempting to make a bird alighting on a field, but suddenly the lines that I'd drawn suggested something totally different, and out of this suggestion arose this picture. I had no intention to do this picture; I never thought of it in that way. It was like one continuous accident mounting on top of another.

From the deep shadows, cast by an umbrella, emerges the lower half of a head with a hideously grimacing mouth topped by a bloody moustache. The figure, whose torso virtually disappears into long strokes of paint, is enclosed within a round tubular structure (related to the artist's own earlier furniture designs); hunks of meat seem to be skewered on it. The sense of formal disjunction compounds the imagery's disturbing effect. At the figure's feet is what appears to be a decorative Oriental carpet, as though this creature, who wears a yellow corsage, is sitting for a conventional formal portrait. Presiding over the entire scene is a gigantic beef carcass, strung up like a crucifixion beneath a grotesquely incongruous festoon of decorative swags. Some have detected in the figure a resemblance to despots of the day, such as Mussolini. Although *Painting* was made just after the war, it transcends any particular association to become a terrifying and universal depiction of ruthless, predatory power.

Bacon's sense of tradition extended from Giotto to Rembrandt and Van Gogh. He used paintings of the past as the basis of his works but transformed them through his own inward vision and torment. Beginning in 1949 he made a series of paintings after Velázquez's *Portrait of Pope Innocent X* in the Doria Pamphili Gallery in Rome (which Bacon knew only through reproductions). In these works, the subject is usually shown seated in a large, unified surrounding space. The figure is blurred as though seen through a veil, while the perspective lines delineate a glass box within which the figure is trapped. *Head VI* (fig. **20.48**) is the first of these papal images and the last of a series of six heads that Bacon made in 1948–49. Typically, the pope's mouth is wide open, as if uttering a horrendous scream. The artist, who said he wanted to "make the best painting of the human cry," conflated the papal image with a famous still from the Russian film *The Battleship Potemkin*, 1925, directed by Sergei Eisenstein. The still is a closeup of a panic-stricken, screaming nanny who has been shot in the eye, her pince-nez shattered as she loses her grip on the baby stroller in her care. The exact meaning of the Pope series is deliberately obscured by the artist, but there is no question of the horrifying impact and beauty of the painting.

Bacon's subject was almost exclusively the human face or figure—especially the male nude, which he portrayed in states of extreme, sometimes convulsive effort. Like Max

20.48 Francis Bacon, *Head VI*, 1949. Oil on canvas, 36⅝ × 30⅛" (93.2 × 76.5 cm). Arts Council Collection, London.

20.49 Francis Bacon, *Triptych—May–June 1973*, 1973. Oil on canvas, each panel 6'6" × 4'10" (1.9 × 1.5 m). Private collection.

Beckmann (see fig. 13.42), he frequently made triptychs, a format he had employed for scenes related to human suffering. In *Triptych—May–June 1973* (fig. **20.49**), Bacon created a harrowing yet touching posthumous portrait of his close friend, George Dyer, during a fatal illness. In three separate images, cinematic in their sense of movement and sequential action, Dyer's ghostly white figure is seen through darkened doorways. In the central canvas, where Dyer lurches toward the sink, the blackness spills out onto the floor as an ominous shadow. This is life at its most fundamental, when the human protagonist is stripped of all pretense and decorum.

Sutherland

The English artist **Graham Sutherland** (1903–80), Bacon's contemporary, also explored agonized expressions of human suffering. During the twenties he made visionary, meticulously representational, landscapes of rural England, mostly in etching, that reveal his passion for the works of the nineteenth-century English painter Samuel Palmer. In the mid-thirties his work became increasingly abstract and imaginative, partly as a result of his discovery of Surrealism. He made paintings based on forms found in nature—rocks, roots, or trees—that were divorced from their landscape context and, in the artist's words, "redefined the mind's eye in a new life and a new mould." He eventually transformed these found forms into monstrous figures that suggest some of Picasso's Expressionist–Surrealist work of the thirties. The war years, when he worked as an official war artist, led to a certain reversion in the representation of devastated, bombed-out buildings and industrial scenes. By the end of World War II, Sutherland had arrived at his characteristically jagged, thistlelike totems, frequently based quite literally on plant forms but transformed into menacing beasts or chimeras. A commission for the painting of a Crucifixion in St. Matthew's Church, Northampton, led him back to Grünewald's Isenheim Altarpiece (see fig. 1.7). In Grünewald's torn, lacerated figures he found a natural affinity (fig. **20.50**). Along with his expressionist works, he carried on a successful career as a portraitist, painting many of the great figures of his time in literal but penetrating interpretations.

20.50 Graham Sutherland, *Crucifixion*, 1946. Oil on hardboard, 8' × 7'6" (2.4 × 2.3 m). Church of St. Matthew, Northampton, England.

Freud

An important European heir to the tradition of truth to visual fact is the Berlin-born British artist **Lucian Freud** (b. 1922), the grandson of the pioneering psychoanalyst Sigmund Freud. Freud, whose Jewish family left Berlin for England when Hitler came to power in 1933, showed an aptitude for drawing at a young age and was producing remarkably accomplished work by the time he reached his early twenties. His uncompromising devotion to the physical presence of the sitter is such that the resulting portrait, realized with an obsessive command of line and texture, can seem the product of a clinically cold and analytical mind (fig. **20.51**). Still, in their very "nakedness," models whom the artist has revealed in excruciatingly close-up detail confront the viewer with an unmistakable presence. Not since Germany's *Neue Sachlichkeit* painting of the twenties was the human figure examined with such an unflinching eye and such tight, linear precision. In the late fifties, Freud's paint handling began to loosen, although the empiricism of his gaze was undiminished. Many of his works are nudes—friends and family, never professional models—who assume strange and revealing poses, whose bodies are far from idealized, and whose unidealized flesh is tinged with blood and swollen with the muscle and fat that lie beneath the surface. Throughout his career, Freud made close-up portraits—one of the best is a 1952 portrait of Bacon (stolen from an exhibition in 1988)—and he

20.51 Lucian Freud, *Girl with White Dog*, 1951–52. Oil on canvas, 30 × 40" (76.2 × 101.6 cm). Tate Gallery, London.

has also turned his unsparing gaze on himself. In his self-portrait from 1985 (fig. **20.52**), skin becomes a harsh terrain of myriad hues, with deep pink crevices and thick white highlights. When experiencing a painting by Freud "in the flesh," one is aware of pigment, yet never loses the sense of depicted flesh as a living, mutable substance that painfully documents, in the words of Shakespeare's Hamlet, "the thousand natural shocks that flesh is heir to."

Moore

Stylistically and temperamentally, **Henry Moore** (1896–1986), like Hepworth, contemplated the human condition in calmer philosophical terms than such contemporaries as Bacon and Dubuffet. While faithful to his origins in abstraction, he continued to work in a biomorphic mode, even at its most reductive, on the brink of evoking the human presence. During World War II he made thousands of drawings of the underground air-raid shelters in London (fig. **20.53**). As huge numbers of people sought refuge from German bombs in the tunnels of the London Underground, Moore was able to study reclining figures and figural groups that gave him many ideas for sculpture. During and after the war he continued to develop his theme of recumbent figures composed as an intricate arrangement of interpenetrating solids and voids (see fig. 17.34). The early fifties also brought forth new experiments in more naturalistic, albeit attenuated, figures, such as

20.52 Lucian Freud, *Reflection (Self-Portrait)*, 1983–85. Oil on canvas, 22⅛ × 20⅛" (56.2 × 51.2 cm). Private collection.

20.53 Henry Moore, Study for *Tube Shelter Perspective*, 1940–41. Pencil, wax crayon, colored crayon, watercolor wash, pen and ink, 10⅛ × 6½" (26.4 × 16.5 cm). Collection Mrs. Henry Moore, England.

King and Queen (fig. **20.54**). First inspired by an ancient Egyptian sculpture of a royal couple, Moore's king and queen have masks for faces and flattened-out, leaflike bodies, yet maintain a sense of regal dignity. They have nothing to do with "present-day Kings and Queens," Moore said, but with the "archaic or primitive idea of a King."

After midcentury, Moore received many international commissions for architectural sculpture. His works can be found on university and museum grounds and other public sites across America and Europe. Generally, these late works are dependent to some degree on Moore's earlier concepts of reclining or standing figures. Most of these works are executed in bronze, which is given a range of effects—from the most jagged and rocky to the most finished and biomorphic. In 1972 Moore made a large bronze titled *Sheep Piece*, here shown in the form of a bronze working model (fig. **20.55**), which he installed in the meadows behind his studio in the English countryside. The sheep on his property (which he loved to sketch) liked to rub themselves against the sculpture or rest in its shadows. Because of the interaction of the two bronze elements in *Sheep Piece* and their soft, organic contours, the work has been related to mating animals, but a sexual dimension is implied, not explicit.

Hepworth

During the fifties **Barbara Hepworth** (1903–75) discovered a promising new direction through a series of so-called *Groups* in white marble (fig. **20.56**), small in scale and magical in their impact. She was inspired to make them after watching people stroll through Piazza San Marco during a 1950 trip to Venice, where her work was featured at the Biennale. The *Groups* were related to her early compositions and to her continuing interest in ancient art, specifically the Cycladic art of prehistoric Greece. In modern terms they recall both Giacometti's groups of walking figures and the biomorphs that inhabit Tanguy's Surrealist landscapes (see fig. 15.20). Much of Hepworth's sculpture of the fifties was a direct response to the landscape—the rocks, caves, cliffs, and sea—surrounding her home in Cornwall, along with the monumental Neolithic stone menhirs that populate the landscape. She preferred carving in wood or stone to modeling in clay and continued to work with wood and stone on both small and large scales after the war. After 1960 Hepworth received a number of commissions that permitted her to compose on a monumental scale, often in bronze. She was at her most abstract with works such as *Squares with Two Circles (Monolith)* (fig. **20.57**). Its pierced, rectangular forms relate to the geometry of Ben Nicholson's reliefs (see fig. 17.32), but the large circular openings recruit the surrounding environment as an active participant in our perception of the work.

20.54 Henry Moore, *King and Queen*, 1952–53. Bronze, height 63½" (161.3 cm). Hirshhorn Museum and Sculpture Garden, Smithsonian Institution, Washington, D.C.

20.55 Henry Moore, Working model for *Sheep Piece*, 1971. Bronze, length 56" (142 cm). The Henry Moore Foundation.

20.56 Barbara Hepworth, *Group III (Evocation)*, 1952. Marble, height 9" (23 cm). Private collection.

20.57 Barbara Hepworth, *Squares with Two Circles (Monolith)*, 1963 (cast 1964). Bronze, 10'4" × 5'5" × 2'6" (3.2 × 1.7 × .8 m). Raymond and Patsy Nasher Collection, Dallas.

Marvels of Daily Life: European Photographers

Almost every imaginable facet of twentieth-century life was captured by photography, to the extent that the nature—and limits—of the photographic medium came to shape people's responses to visual experience. Although experimental photographers after the war explored photography's immense potential to combine different ways of seeing, as in Siskind's "Abstract-Expressionist" close-ups of wall surfaces or Callahan's botanically precise yet Miróesque *Weed* (see figs. 19.60, 19.62), it was still some years before photography became a generally accepted art medium on a par with painting, printmaking, or drawing. Among the European photographers who produced memorable images of life in the immediate postwar period, Robert Doisneau in France and Josef Sudek in Czechoslovakia both revealed, in highly distinct and individual ways, a poetry in austere or ordinary settings. As Europe came to terms with the devastation of World War II, Swiss photographer Werner Bischof crossed the continent recording "the face of human suffering" in its many incarnations from France to Romania and Greece.

Something of Dubuffet's serious whimsy was shared by **Robert Doisneau** (1912–94), who, like Brassaï (see fig. 15.64), roamed the streets of Paris seeking and finding what he called "the unimaginable image" within "the marvels of daily life." Having discovered that nothing is more bizarre or amusing than the banal, Doisneau managed to brighten a depressed, existential age with his witty, but never snide, photographic commentary on the foibles, misadventures, and daily pursuits of the human—and particularly Parisian—race. In 1949 he made a series of photographs in the shop of an antique dealer in the city (fig. **20.58**), capturing the varied responses of passersby to a provocative painting of a nude hanging in the window.

Among photographers in Central Europe, the Czech **Josef Sudek** (1896–1976) was a leading practitioner. Called the "Poet of Prague," Sudek, who lost an arm while serving in World War I, established a successful photographic business in that city in the twenties and at first made photographs in a Romantic, Pictorialist style. Once German troops occupied Prague in 1939, Sudek retreated into his studio, focusing his camera on whatever caught his eye through the window of his studio. He continued his habit of photographing still lifes on his studio windowsill or views into the garden or the city streets into the fifties (fig. **20.59**). Sudek said:

> I believe that photography loves banal objects. I am sure you know the fairy tales of Andersen: when the children go to bed, the objects come to life, toys, for example. I like to tell stories about the life of inanimate objects, to relate something mysterious: the seventh side of a dice.

20.58 Robert Doisneau, From the series *The Sideways Glance*, 1949. Gelatin-silver print.

20.59 Josef Sudek, *The Window of My Studio*, 1954. Gelatin-silver print.

After studying photography at Zurich's School of Applied Arts, **Werner Bischof** (1916–54) worked as an advertising photographer while also producing beautifully lit images of natural forms and the human figure. From 1942, as a contributor to the cultural magazine *Du*, he turned more toward socially aware photojournalism. When war ended in 1945, Bischof left neutral Switzerland to document the effects of six years of conflict across Europe.

Images such as the ruined Reichstag (German parliament) building in Berlin, rising out of a shattered city in which people scavenge for firewood or clear rubble with their bare hands, speak eloquently of human resilience and the struggle to create a new beginning. Bischof's desolate cityscapes (fig. **20.60**) contrast with Doisneau's urban whimsy and Sudek's reclusive lyricism but nevertheless find a poetry in the unconscious poise of his human subjects amid this destruction. His photographs of children—including those orphaned and displaced by war—are especially moving documents of this period.

Bischof's photographic record of European cities in the late forties makes it graphically clear that, whatever larger shifts in the cultural landscape were taking place, these historic centers of Western culture were in no state to match the vitality and confidence of the American art scene at this time. After working on assignments in India, Japan, and Indochina (Vietnam) for Magnum photographic agency, whose founding members included Capa and Cartier-Bresson, Bischof traveled to New York in 1954. Eight months later, photographing in South America, he died in an automobile accident in the Andes.

20.60 Werner Bischof, *Cologne*, 1946.

21
Pop Art and Europe's New Realism

The shift in values that took place in the late fifties was in part a reaction to the barrage of new products and accompanying mass-media explosion produced by the postwar consumer society. The Pop generation responded enthusiastically to the very media images avoided by the Abstract Expressionists. As Andy Warhol said, "The Pop artists did images that anybody walking down Broadway could recognize in a split second—comics, picnic tables, men's trousers, celebrities, shower curtains, refrigerators, Coke bottles—all the great modern things that the Abstract Expressionists tried so hard not to notice." Many artists of the younger generation viewed the legacy of Abstract Expressionism as an oppressive mantle that had to be lifted. They were no longer concerned with the heroic "act" of painting, in "hot" gestures and emotions. Rather, they found subjects within the immediate environment of their popular culture and sought to incorporate them into their art through "cool," depersonalized means. Pop art, Happenings, environments, assemblage, and *Nouveau Réalisme* began to emerge simultaneously in several American and European cities.

In 1961 The Museum of Modern Art mounted The Art of Assemblage, a show organized by William C. Seitz that surveyed modern art involving the accumulation of objects, from two-dimensional Cubist *papiers collés* and photomontages, through every sort of Dada and Surrealist object, to junk assemblage sculpture, to complete room environments. Seitz described such works as follows: "(1) They are predominantly assembled rather than painted, drawn, modeled, or carved; (2) Entirely or in part, their constituent elements are pre-formed natural or manufactured materials, objects, or fragments not intended as art materials." In 1962 the Sidney Janis Gallery's New Realists exhibition opened. The show included a number of the recognized British and American Pop artists, representatives of the French *Nouveau Réalisme*, and artists from Italy and Sweden working in related directions. Although the American Pop artists had been emerging for several years, Janis's show was an official recognition of their

arrival. The European participants seemed closer to the tradition of Dada and Surrealism; the British and Americans more involved in contemporary popular culture and representational, commercial images. But Pop was not embraced by everyone. Proponents of abstract painting decried the arrival of commercialism in art as rampant vulgarity, a youthful attack on high culture. And, like many labels assigned by critics and historians, the Pop designation is rejected by most of the artists it has been used to describe, for the term groups together a very diverse population of highly individual artists.

"This is Tomorrow": Pop Art in Britain

Although Pop art has often been regarded as an American phenomenon, it was first introduced in England in the mid-fifties. The term was first used in print in 1958 by the English critic Lawrence Alloway but for a somewhat different context than its subsequent use. Late in 1952, calling themselves the Independent Group, Alloway, the architects Alison and Peter Smithson, the artist Richard Hamilton, the sculptor Eduardo Paolozzi, the architectural historian Reyner Banham, and others met in London at the Institute of Contemporary Arts. The discussions focused around popular (thus, Pop) culture and its implications—such entities as Western movies, science fiction, billboards, and machines. In short, they concentrated on aspects of contemporary mass culture and were centered on its current manifestations in the United States.

As the Smithsons wrote in 1956, "Mass production is establishing our whole pattern of life—principles, morals, aims, aspirations, and standard of living. We must somehow get the measure of this intervention if we are to match its powerful and exciting impulses with our own." After a period of postwar austerity, fifties Britain began to experience new levels of prosperity that created a mass market for consumer and cultural products. American popular culture was embraced as a liberating, egalitarian force by a new

21.1 Richard Hamilton, *Just what is it that makes today's homes so different, so appealing?* 1956. Collage on paper, 10¼ × 9¾" (26 × 24.8 cm). Kunsthalle Tübingen, Sammlung Zundel.

generation who had little time for the restricting exclusivity of "high culture," a notion that included not only aristocratic classicism but also the essentially minority pleasures of modernist abstraction. Alloway's definition of Pop as an art that takes "signs" for its subject matter points the way to postmodernism's preoccupation with the nature of signs in all spheres of human expression and communication.

Hamilton and Paolozzi

Richard Hamilton (b. 1922) defined Pop art in 1957 as "Popular (designed for a mass audience), Transient (short-term solution), Expendable (easily forgotten), Low cost, Mass produced, Young (aimed at youth), Witty, Sexy, Gimmicky, Glamorous and Big Business." A pioneer Pop work is his small collage made in 1956 and entitled *Just what is it that makes today's homes so different, so appealing?* (fig. **21.1**). A poster of this work was used in a multimedia exhibition held at London's Whitechapel Art Gallery in 1956, entitled This is Tomorrow. Hamilton was a disciple

of and respected authority on Marcel Duchamp, whose influence on Pop art cannot be overestimated. Hamilton's collage shows a "modern" apartment inhabited by a pinup girl and her muscle-man mate, whose lollipop barbell prophesies the Pop movement on its label. Like Adam and Eve in a consumers' paradise, the couple have furnished their apartment with products of mass culture: television, tape recorder, an enlarged cover from a comic book, a Ford emblem, and an advertisement for a vacuum cleaner. Through the window can be seen a movie marquee featuring Al Jolson in *The Jazz Singer*. The images, all culled from contemporary magazines, provide a kind of inventory of visual culture.

An important point about Hamilton's, and subsequent Pop artists', approach to popular culture is that their purpose was not entirely satirical or antagonistic. They were not expressionists like George Grosz and the Social Realists of the thirties who attacked the ugliness and inequities of urban civilization. In simple terms, the Pop artists looked at the world in which they lived and examined the objects and images that surrounded them with intensity and penetration, frequently making the viewer conscious of that omnipresence for the first time. This is not to say that the artists, and especially Hamilton, were unaware of the ways in which consumer mass culture is communicated to the public—its clichés, its manipulations. On the contrary, his work is often rich with irony and humor. As critic David Sylvester once observed, "Hamilton never makes it clear how far he is being satirical and coolly ironic, how far he is rather in love with the subject, and this equivocation is an aspect of the message."

From the sixties onward, Hamilton was deeply involved with photography, a medium that engaged other artists of his generation, such as Hockney and Rauschenberg, in experiments that broke down the barriers between "fine art" practices and photography. Hamilton's painting, *I'm dreaming of a white Christmas* (fig. **21.2**) and a subsequent

21.2 Richard Hamilton, *I'm dreaming of a white Christmas*, 1967–68. Oil on canvas, 42 × 63" (106.7 × 160 cm). Öffentliche Kunstsammlung Basel, Kunstmuseum.

screenprint, *I'm dreaming of a black Christmas*, were based on a film still of Bing Crosby in the 1954 movie *White Christmas*. By effecting in paint the kind of chromatic reversal found in a photographic negative he creates not only a magical, looking-glass world, but pointedly transforms the protagonist of *White Christmas* into a black man.

The sculptor **Eduardo Paolozzi** (b. 1924), an original member of the Independent Group, produced collages in the early fifties made from comic strips, postcards, and magazine clippings that are today regarded as important forerunners of Pop art. Originally influenced by Giacometti, Dubuffet, and Surrealism, Paolozzi became interested in the relations of technology to art and emerged as a serious spokesman for Pop culture. In the mid-fifties he began to make bronze sculptures whose rough surfaces were cast from found objects, resulting in creatures that resemble towering, battered robots. Searching for forms and techniques consistent with his growing interest in machine technology, Paolozzi produced welded sculptures in the sixties that vary from austere, simplified forms in polished aluminum to elaborate polychromed constructions. While the snakelike tubular forms of *Medea* (fig. **21.3**) may have been inspired by the ancient Hellenistic sculpture *Laocoön*, which shows the mythical Greek prophet Laocoön and his sons battling sea-serpents, Paolozzi's humanoid machine seems to have materialized from the science fiction screen.

21.4 Peter Blake, *On the Balcony*, 1955–57. Oil on canvas, 47¾ × 35¾" (121.3 × 90.8 cm). Tate Gallery, London.

21.3 Eduardo Paolozzi, *Medea*, 1964. Welded aluminum, 6'9" × 6' (2.1 × 1.8 m). Rijksmuseum Kröller-Müller, Otterlo.

Blake and Kitaj

Of the other English Pop artists, **Peter Blake** (b. 1932) took subjects of popular idolatry, such as Elvis Presley, the Beatles, or pinup girls, and presented them in an intentionally naive style. His early painting *On the Balcony* (fig. **21.4**) was inspired by a Social Realist painting he saw in New York's Museum of Modern Art of working-class people holding masterpieces of modern art they could never afford to own. In his own variation on the theme, Blake's young people hold paintings, including, at the left, Manet's painting titled *On the Balcony*. But they are also surrounded by images from the popular media and advertising, as well as by paintings by Blake and his contemporaries.

An ambiguous but crucial figure in the development of English Pop is the American **R. B. Kitaj** (b. 1932), who studied at Oxford and at London's Royal College of Art under the GI Bill that gave services personnel access to college education after the war. He subsequently lived mainly in England. Kitaj painted everyday scenes or modern historical events and personalities in broad, flat, color areas combined with a strong linear emphasis and a sense of fragmentation that is consistent with the style of most Pop art.

21.5 R. B. Kitaj, *The Autumn of Central Paris (After Walter Benjamin)*, 1972–73. Oil on canvas, 60 × 60" (152.5 × 152.5 cm). Private collection.

His subject matter, however, diverges from that of his peers. Unique to Kitaj is an emphatic disinterest in popular culture, counterbalanced by a serious, wide-ranging commitment to political and literary themes. His paintings often contain evocative combinations of images derived from sources too complex to yield a clear or specific message. The characteristic work seen here (fig. **21.5**) shows a Parisian café scene in which Kitaj's hero, the leftwing German Jewish critic Walter Benjamin, can be identified, juxtaposed to a man wielding a red pick, as if to announce the calamities of 1940 that would drive Benjamin to suicide as the German army began occupying the French capital. Kitaj's eloquent words about Benjamin seem to pertain equally to his own work, "His wonderful and difficult montage, pressing together quickening tableaux from texts and from a disjunct world, were called citations by a disciple of his who also conceded that the picture-puzzle distinguished everything he wrote."

Hockney

David Hockney (b. 1937), a student of Kitaj's at the Royal College, was so gifted and productive that he had already gained a national reputation by the time of his graduation. Emerging within the same period as the Beatles, Hockney—with his peroxide hair, granny glasses, gold lamé jacket, and easy charm—became something of a media event in his own right, a genial exponent of the go-go, hedonistic style of the sixties. Although Hockney projected a self-image that drew on pop culture, his art did not; instead, he used his own life and the lives of his friends and lovers—their faces and figures, houses, and interiors. These he rendered in a manner sometimes inspired by Picasso and Matisse, but often influenced by Dubuffet, in the delicate *faux naïf* manner of children.

Hockney has long maintained a residence in southern California. There the swimming pool became a central image in his art, complete with its cool, synthetic hues. *A Bigger Splash* (fig. **21.6**) combines Hockney's signature equilibrium of elegant Matissean flat-pattern design and luxurious mood with a painterly virtuosity for the splash itself. One critic described this sense of suspended animation as the "epitome of expectant stillness," which is due partly to the artist's habit of working from photographs. Infatuated with the Polaroid and, later, with 35mm cameras, Hockney has used photography in more recent years to reexplore the riches of the space–time equation investigated by Braque and Picasso in Analytic Cubism (fig. **21.7**). In his large collage of the Brooklyn Bridge, dozens

21.6 David Hockney, *A Bigger Splash*, 1967. Acrylic on canvas, 8'1⅛" × 8'1⅛" (2.4 × 2.4 m). Tate Gallery, London.

21.7 David Hockney, *The Brooklyn Bridge, Nov. 28th 1982*, 1982. Photographic collage, 42¹⁵⁄₁₆ × 22¹³⁄₁₆" (109.1 × 57.9 cm). Private collection.

of smaller sequential photographs compose a single motif, simulating the scanning sensation of actual vision. Hockney termed his composite photographic images "joiners."

Such treatments of subject matter have infiltrated Hockney's paintings as well, including the 1984 *A Visit with Christopher and Don, Santa Monica Canyon* (fig. 21.8). This panoramic composition recreates a visit to the house of the artist's friends, the painter Don Bachardy and the writer Christopher Isherwood. The viewer's eye is carried through the fractured spaces of the house, where we see the residents at work at either end and where we periodically encounter the same fractured view of the Santa Monica Canyon. Like most of Hockney's work since 1980, the painting combines flat unmodulated zones with more painterly ones, all enriched by a palette of sumptuous color. In recent years this multifaceted artist has designed stage sets and even directed performances for the opera.

Signs of the Times: Neo-Dada in the United States

Pop art, especially during the sixties, had a natural appeal to American artists, who were living in the midst of an even more blatant industrial and commercial environment than that found in Great Britain. Once they realized the tremendous possibilities of their everyday surroundings in the creation of new subject matter, the result was generally a bolder and more aggressive art than that of their European counterparts.

Toward the end of the fifties, as we have already noted, there were many indications that American painting was moving away from the heroic rhetoric and grand painterly gestures of Abstract Expressionism. (For example, de Kooning had parodied the gleaming smiles and exaggerated cleavage of American movie starlets in his paintings of women, one of which even included a cutout mouth from a popular magazine advertisement.) American art had a long tradition of interest in the commonplace that extended from the *trompe l'oeil* paintings of the nineteenth century (see fig. 2.41) through the Precisionist painters of the early twentieth century (see fig. 18.28). Marcel Duchamp's antiart program led younger painters back to Dada and most specifically to Kurt Schwitters (see fig. 13.29), who was a crucial model for several young artists. Two leading American artists, Robert Rauschenberg and Jasper Johns, were the most obvious heirs to Duchamp and Schwitters. The art of these important forerunners to Pop art has been referred to as Neo-Dada.

21.8 David Hockney, *A Visit with Christopher and Don, Santa Monica Canyon*, 1984. Oil on canvas, 6' × 20' (1.8 × 6.1 m). Collection the artist.

Rauschenberg

Robert Rauschenberg (b. 1925), one of the most important artists in the establishment of American Pop's vocabulary, came of age during the Depression in Port Arthur, Texas. "Having grown up in a very plain environment," he once said, "if I was going to survive, I had to appreciate the most common aspects of life." After serving in the U.S. Navy in World War II and with the help of the GI Bill, Rauschenberg studied at the Kansas City Art Institute and at the Académie Julian in Paris. In 1948, feeling the need for a more disciplined environment, he went for the first of several times to Black Mountain College, an experimental school in North Carolina, to study with Josef Albers. Rauschenberg learned not so much a style as an attitude from the disciplined methods of this former Bauhaus professor, for the young artist's rough, accretive assemblages could hardly be further from the pristine geometry of Albers's abstractions. Even more important in his development was the presence at Black Mountain College in the early fifties of John Cage, a composer, writer, and devotee of Duchamp, whom Rauschenberg had met in New York, and the choreographer-dancer Merce Cunningham. Cage was an enormously influential figure in the development of Pop art, as well as offshoots such as Happenings, environments, and innumerable experiments in music, theater, dance, and the remarkably rich combinative art forms that merged from all of these media. Rauschenberg would later join Cage and Cunningham in several collaborative performances, designing sets, costumes, and lighting.

Rauschenberg literally used the world as his palette, working in nearly every corner of the globe and accepting virtually any material as fodder for his art. This element of

21.9 Robert Rauschenberg and Susan Weil, *Untitled (Double Rauschenberg)*, c. 1950. Monoprint: exposed blueprint paper, 8'9" × 3' (2.7 × 0.91 m). Collection Cy Twombly, Rome.

21.10 Robert Rauschenberg, *Bed*, 1955. Combine painting: oil and pencil on pillow, quilt, and sheet on wood supports, 75¼" × 31½ × 8" (19 × 80 × 20.3 cm). The Museum of Modern Art, New York.

eclectic pastiche is typical of the postmodern approach to culture. It differs from the singular, purist voice of modernism, while owing much to modernism's determined expansion of the media and subject matter available to art. Rauschenberg has always used photographic processes in one way or another and, in 1950, collaborating with his former wife Susan Weil, achieved an otherworldly beauty simply by placing figures on paper coated with cyanotype and exposing the paper to light (fig. **21.9**). He has made radically reductive abstractions, including the all-white and all-black paintings he began while at Black Mountain College in the early fifties, as well as paintings and constructions out of almost anything except conventional materials. An artist who values inclusivity, multiplicity, and constant experimentation, Rauschenberg scavenges his environment for raw materials for his art, excluding little and welcoming detritus of every sort. He once remarked, "Painting relates to both art and life. Neither can be made. (I try to act in that gap between the two.)"

After settling in New York, Rauschenberg became increasingly involved with collage and assemblage in the fifties. By 1954 he had begun to incorporate such objects as photographs, prints, or newspaper clippings into the structure of the canvas. In 1955 he made one of his most notorious "combine" paintings, as he called these works, *Bed* (fig. **21.10**). This work included a pillow and quilt over which paint was splashed in an Abstract Expressionist manner, a style Rauschenberg has never completely abandoned. His most spectacular combine painting, the 1959 *Monogram* (fig. **21.11**), with a stuffed Angora goat encompassed in an automobile tire, includes a painted and collage-covered base—or rather a painting extended horizontally on the floor—in which free brush painting acts as

a unifying element. Whereas *Bed* still bears a resemblance to the object referred to in its title, *Monogram* is composed of disparate elements that do not, as is true of Rauschenberg's work as a whole, coalesce into any single, unified meaning or narrative. The combine paintings clearly had their origin in the collages and constructions of Schwitters and other Dadaists (see fig. 13.30). Rauschenberg's work, however, is different not only in its great spatial expansion, but in its desire to take not so much a Dada, antiart stance as one that expands our very definitions of art.

In 1962, at virtually the same time as Andy Warhol, Rauschenberg began to make paintings using a photo silkscreen process. Collecting photographs from magazines or newspapers, he had the images commercially transferred onto silkscreens, first in black and white and, by 1963, in color, and then set to work creating a kaleidoscope of images (fig. **21.12**). In the example shown here, the subjects range from traffic signs, to the Statue of Liberty, to a photograph of Michelangelo's Sistine Ceiling. They collide and overlap but are characteristically arranged in a grid configuration and are bound together by a matrix of the artist's gestural brushstrokes. In 1964, after Rauschenberg had won the grand prize at the Venice Biennale, and as a guarantee against repeating himself, he called a friend in New York and asked him to destroy all the silkscreens he had used to make the silkscreen paintings.

Throughout the sixties, Rauschenberg, like many of the original Pop artists, was involved in a wide variety of activities, including dance and performance. His natural inclination toward collaboration drew him to theater and dance. *Pelican*, a dance he actually choreographed, was performed in 1963 as part of a Pop festival in Washington, D.C.

21.11 Robert Rauschenberg, *Monogram*, 1959. Combine painting: oil and collage with objects, 42 × 63½ × 64½" (106.7 × 161.3 × 163.8 cm). Moderna Museet, Stockholm.

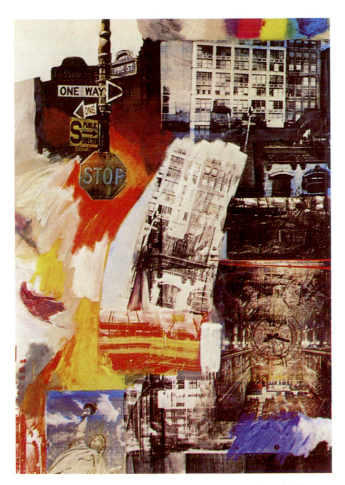

21.12 Robert Rauschenberg, *Estate*, 1963. Oil and silkscreen ink on canvas, 8' × 5'10" (2.4 m × 1.78 m). Philadelphia Museum of Art.

21.13 Robert Rauschenberg, *Blue Urchin* from the *Hoarfrost* series, 1974. Collage and solvent transfer on cloth, 6'4" × 4'1" (1.9 × 1.25 m). Collection Paul Hottlet, Antwerp.

Because the event took place in a roller-skating rink, Rauschenberg planned a dance of three—including himself, another man on roller skates, and Carolyn Brown, a professional from Merce Cunningham's company who danced on point. The men trailed large parachutes that floated like sails behind them during the performance, which Rauschenberg dedicated to his heroes, the Wright brothers.

This indefatigable and prolific artist later extended his quest to make art from anything and from anywhere. From the seventies onward, he tended to work in series, including the *Cardboard* series, numerous sculptures, prints, and photographs, as well as dozens of works that involved fabric. For the *Hoarfrost* series he employed a solvent process to transfer photographic images onto delicate cloths that are draped unstretched on the wall (fig. **21.13**). Rauschenberg said his aim was to "dematerialize the surface" with these works, whose diffuse images undulate as people pass by.

In 1984 Rauschenberg launched a seven-year project called ROCI (Rauschenberg Overseas Culture Interchange), during which he traveled to foreign and often politically sensitive countries to work for the cause of world peace. Collaborating with local artisans and drawing upon indigenous traditions and motifs, Rauschenberg created a body of work in each of the ten countries he visited, including the former Soviet Union, Cuba, China, Tibet, Chile,

and Mexico. He completed the series with ROCI USA, for which images were deposited through complex techniques onto a brightly polished surface of stainless steel. The artist then attached a crumpled section of the stainless steel that projects awkwardly from the main support. Typically, chance and accident are welcome, for the highly reflective surface records the activities of the viewers in the gallery.

Johns

Jasper Johns (b. 1930), a native of South Carolina, appeared on the New York art scene in the mid-fifties at the same moment as Rauschenberg with whom, after 1954, he developed a very close and supportive relationship. Johns's paintings were entirely different but equally revolutionary. At first, he painted targets and American flags in encaustic (an ancient medium of pigment mixed with heated wax), with the paint built up in sensuous, translucent layers

21.14 Jasper Johns, *Flag*, 1954–55 (dated 1954 on reverse). Encaustic oil and collage on fabric mounted on plywood, 42¼ × 60⅝" (107.3 × 153.8 cm). The Museum of Modern Art, New York.

(fig. **21.14**). In addition to targets and flags, he took the most familiar items—numbers, letters, words, and maps of the United States—and then painted them with such precision and neutrality that they appear to be objects in themselves rather than illusionistic depictions of familiar objects.

Johns, who destroyed all of his previous work, said the subject of the flag was suggested by a dream in which he was painting an American flag. Because a flag, like a target or numbers, is inherently flat, Johns could dispense with the illusionistic devices that suggest spatial depth and the relationship between figure and ground. At the same time, the readymade image meant that he did not have to invent a composition in the traditional sense. "Using the design of the American flag took care of a great deal for me because I didn't have to design it," he said. "So I went on to similar things like targets—things the mind already knows. That gave me room to work on other levels." This element of impersonality, this apparent withdrawal of the artist's individual invention, became central to many of the painters and sculptors of the sixties. Despite their resemblance to actual flags, Johns's flags are clearly paintings, but with his matter-of-fact rendering he introduces the kind of perceptual and conceptual ambiguity with which Magritte had toyed in his painting *The Treachery (or Perfidy) of Images* (see fig. 15.29). Johns's flags and targets exemplify Pop art's concern with signs. They are unique, not mass-produced, objects. And yet, to paint a target is to make a target, not merely a depiction of a target, which in its essentials resembles any other target. Such ambiguities were often exploited in Pop art.

One of the artist's most enigmatic works is *Target with Plaster Casts* (fig. **21.15**), another encaustic painting of a flat, readymade design, but this time the canvas is surmounted by nine wooden boxes with hinged lids, which can either remain closed or be opened to reveal plaster-cast body parts. A strange disjunction exists between the neutral image of a target and the much more emotion-laden body parts, each a different color, just as it does between the implied violence of dismembered anatomical parts and their curious presentation as mere objects on a shelf.

In one of his best-known sculptures, *Painted Bronze*, Johns immortalized the commonplace by taking two Ballantine Ale cans and casting them in bronze (fig. **21.16**). Yet upon close examination it becomes clear that Johns has painted the labels freehand, so what at first appears mass-produced, like a Duchamp readymade, is paradoxically a unihandwrought form. Moreover, although the cans look identical, one is in fact "open" and cast as a hollow form; the other is closed and solid.

From the end of the fifties, Johns's paintings were marked by the intensified use of expressionist brushstrokes and by the interjection of actual objects among the flat

21.15 Jasper Johns, *Target with Plaster Casts*, 1955. Encaustic and collage on canvas with wood construction and plaster casts, 51 × 44 × 3½" (129.5 × 111.8 × 8.9 cm). Collection David Geffen.

21.16 Jasper Johns, *Painted Bronze*, 1960. Painted bronze, 5½ × 8 × 4¾" (14 × 20.3 × 12.1 cm). Museum Ludwig, Cologne.

signs. In *Field Painting* (fig. **21.17**), for example, the Ballantine Ale can reappears, this time as itself. The can is magnetically attached along with other objects—ones we might find around the artist's studio—to three-dimensional letters that are hinged to the center of the painting. These metal letters spell out "RED," "YELLOW," and "BLUE," although, like their flat counterparts painted on the canvas, they do not necessarily signify the color we read. Johns frequently presents alternative forms of representation in a single painting, for in addition to these signs, Johns includes color in a welter of Abstract Expressionist paint strokes. One of the foremost print-makers of the postwar era, Johns invoked the names of the primary colors again in a color lithograph titled *Souvenir*, where they encircle his portrait. His drawings and prints usually relate closely to his paintings and sculptures. In *Souvenir*, the various images—the back of a canvas, a flashlight, and a rearview bicycle mirror—are present as actual objects in a painting of the same name. As they often do in Johns's works, the themes here revolve around issues of perception, of looking, and of being looked at.

21.17 Jasper Johns, *Field Painting*, 1964. Oil and canvas on wood with objects, 6' × 3'¾" (1.8 × 0.93 cm). Collection the artist.

In the seventies Johns made paintings that suggest a continuing dialogue between figuration and abstraction, as well as a penchant for complex, hermetic systems of representation. In 1972, in the large, four-panel painting *Untitled* (fig. **21.18**), he introduced a pattern of parallel

21.18 Jasper Johns, *Untitled*, 1972. Oil, encaustic, and collage on canvas with objects, 6' × 16' (1.8 × 4.9 m). Museum Ludwig, Cologne.

21.19 Jasper Johns, *The Bath*, 1988. Watercolor and pencil on paper, 29⅛ × 37¾" (74 × 95.9 cm). Collection the artist.

lines in the far left panel, so-called crosshatches, that have played a role in his work ever since. Johns has said that the crosshatch motif was not one he invented but one he spotted on a passing car, just as he said the flagstone pattern in the two center panels was something he glimpsed on a Harlem wall while riding to the airport in the late sixties. These flagstone-pattern panels—one in oil, one in encaustic—recreate two slightly different sections of the same panel from an earlier painting called *Harlem Light*. If one panel is superimposed on the other so they match up, the panels form an "imagined square," as Johns described it in his typically enigmatic "Sketchbook Notes." At the far right, in startling contrast to these flat, abstract forms, are three-dimensional casts made from a woman's and a man's body that Johns painted and attached with wing-nuts to strips of wood.

In later work, such as the watercolor *The Bath* (fig. **21.19**), Johns introduced coded autobiographical references among images derived from the works of artists he admired. Illusionistically "tacked" to the painting surface is a rendering after Picasso's Surrealist painting *Straw Hat with Blue Leaves*, but Johns sliced the painting in such a way that we are forced to reconstruct it. Between these two sections, the artist depicted his own bathtub faucet and, at the left, the floorboards of a former studio. The background of this drawing is derived from a detail from Matthias Grünewald's great *Isenheim Altarpiece* (see fig. 1.7). Johns incorporated imagery from this painting into a large number of his works in the eighties. This particular motif derives from Grünewald's portrayal of a diseased demon from the panel dedicated to the Temptation of St. Anthony. Typically, however, Johns obscured the image by rotating the figure and rendering it in monochrome. Another detail from the *Isenheim Altarpiece* can barely be deciphered in the blue background of a 1993 encaustic painting, *Mirror's Edge 2*, while the demon resurfaces on the section of curling paper that Johns attached to the surface with *trompe l'oeil* masking tape. These forms appear among motifs appropriated from Johns's own work. Borrowed imagery may, as in the case of two lithographs by Barnett Newman, be cast here in a fresh and ever-ambiguous context. Just as we peer closely at the imagery to bring it into focus, we ponder its meaning, searching for clues to explain the elaborate puzzle of images that simultaneously enrich and contradict one another and, like layers of experience, accumulate meaning the more we look.

Getting Closer to Life: Happenings and Environments

The concept of mixing media and, more importantly, integrating the arts with life itself was a fundamental aspect of the Pop revolution. A number of artists in several countries were searching for ways to extend art into a theatrical situation or a total environment. A leading spokesman for this attitude was Allan Kaprow, who defined a Happening as:

an assemblage of events performed or perceived in more than one time and place. Its material environments may be constructed, taken over directly from what is available, or altered slightly: just as its activities may be invented or commonplace. A Happening, unlike a stage play, may occur at a supermarket, driving along a highway, under a pile of rags, and in a friend's kitchen, either at once or sequentially. If sequentially, time may extend to more than a year. The Happening is performed according to plan but without rehearsal, audience, or repetition. It is art but seems closer to life.

Happenings may have had their ultimate origins in the Dada manifestations held during World War I (see chapter 13). They might even be traced to the improvisations of the *commedia dell'arte* (a genre of Italian comedy) of the eighteenth century. The post-World War II years saw a global interest in Happening-like performance. The Japanese Gutai Group of Osaka staged such performances as early as 1955, and from 1957 onward they were held in Tokyo as well as Osaka. In Düsseldorf, the Zero Group was founded in 1957 with the aim of narrowing the gap between art and life, while similar developments were taking place in other art centers in Europe. Many of the terms, images, and ideas of Pop art and Happenings found instant popular acceptance, if not always complete comprehension, with the mass media—television, films, newspapers, and magazines. Even television and newspaper advertisements, fashion, and product design were affected, resulting in a fascinating cycle in which forms and images taken from popular culture and translated into works of art were then retranslated into other objects of popular culture. Closely linked to Happenings through the concept of directly involving the viewer—as a participant in art rather than a spectator—was Environment art, in which the artist creates an entire three-dimensional space.

Kaprow, Grooms, and Early Happenings

The first public Happening staged by **Allan Kaprow** (b. 1927), entitled *18 Happenings in 6 Parts*, was held at New York's Reuben Gallery in 1959. The Reuben Gallery, along with the Hansa and Judson galleries, was an important experimental center where many of the leading younger artists of the sixties first appeared. Among those who showed at the Reuben Gallery, aside from Kaprow, were Jim Dine, Claes Oldenburg, George Segal, and Lucas Samaras. For Kaprow, the role of Abstract Expressionism was significant. He regarded Pollock's large drip paintings as environmental works of art that implied an extension beyond the edge of the canvas and into the viewer's physical space. Pollock, said Kaprow, "left us at the point where we must become preoccupied with and even dazzled by the space and objects of our everyday life." Pollock's contemporary, the composer John Cage, taught Kaprow at the New School for Social Research in New York City in the late fifties. Cage helped to bridge art and life by experimenting with musical forms that involved unplanned audience participation and by welcoming chance noises as part of his music. His famous composition *4'33"* consisted of the pianist David Tudor lifting the lid of the piano and sitting for four minutes and thirty-three seconds without playing. The random sounds that occurred during the performance constituted the music.

Happenings (a term that was not embraced by all of those involved) could vary greatly in each instance and with each artist. They were not simply spontaneous, improvisational events but could be structured, scripted, and rehearsed performances. Sometimes they were performed

21.20 Allan Kaprow, Photograph from *Household*, a Happening commissioned by Cornell University, 1964.

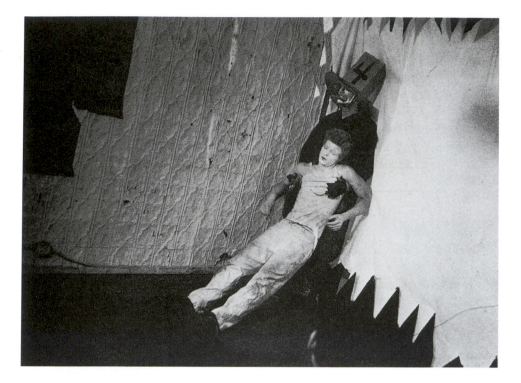

21.21 Red Grooms, Photograph from *The Burning Building,* a performance at the Delancey Street Museum, New York, 1959.

21.22 Red Grooms and the Ruckus Construction Company, Detail from *Ruckus Manhattan* (World Trade Center, West Side Highway), 1975–76. Mixed media. Installation view Grand Central Station, New York. 1993. Courtesy MTA and Marlborough Gallery, New York.

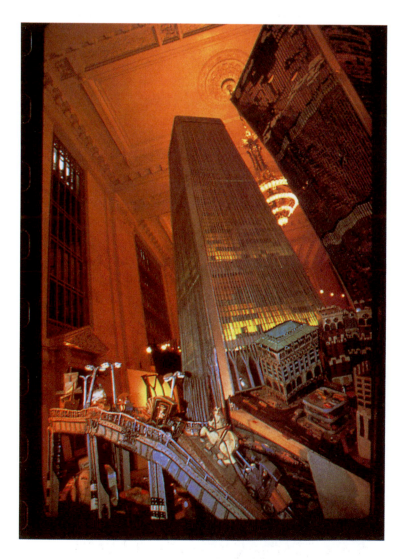

for an audience, which participated to varying degrees according to the artist; sometimes for a camera; and sometimes for no one at all. Because the instigators were for the most part visual artists, visual concerns tended to override dramatic or more conventionally theatrical ones, such as plot or character development. In the moment shown here from Kaprow's 1964 Happening *Household* (fig. **21.20**), the participants are licking strawberry jam from the hood of a car that is soon to be set on fire.

Two months after Kaprow's first Happening at the Reuben Gallery, the artist **Red Grooms** (b. 1937) staged—and performed in—*The Burning Building,* his most famous "play," as he called his version of Happenings, at another New York venue (fig. **21.21**). Grooms, a native of Nashville, Tennessee, settled in New York in 1957, the year he met Kaprow. In *The Burning Building* he played the Pasty Man who, in search of love's secret, pursues the Girl in the White Box into a firemen's den. In the still shown here, he has been knocked out by a fireman, who carries him behind the curtain.

From his early work as a painter and performance artist, Grooms began to make multimedia works on an environmental scale, peopling entire rooms with cutout figures and objects painted in brilliant and clashing colors. He has continually enlarged his scope to embrace constructions such as the famous *Ruckus Manhattan,* a gargantuan environment he first built in the lobby of a New York office building. With a team of helpers, Grooms created a walk-in map of lower Manhattan in a spirit of wild burlesque, manic, big-city energy, and broad, slapstick humor (fig. **21.22**).

21.23 George Segal, *The Diner*, 1964–66. Plaster, wood, chrome, masonite, laminated plastic, fluorescent lamp, glass, and paper, 7'8¾" × 12'1¼" × 8' (2.35 × 3.66 × 2.43 m). Walker Art Center, Minneapolis.

21.24 George Segal, *Girl Putting on Scarab Necklace*, 1975. Plaster, wood, metal, and glass, 7' × 3'9" × 3'9" (2.1 × 1.1 × 1.1 m). Private collection.

Segal

George Segal (1924–2000) began as a painter of expressive, figurative canvases, but feeling hampered by the spatial limitations of painting, he began to make sculpture in 1958. For a number of years he was closely associated with Allan Kaprow (who staged his first Happening at Segal's New Jersey farm), a connection that stimulated his interest in sculpture as a total environment. By 1961 Segal was casting figures from live models, both nude and fully clothed. He wrapped his subjects in bandages, which he covered in plaster, allowed to dry, and then cut open and resealed, a process that records quite literally the details of anatomy and expression, but retains the rough textures of the original bandages. The figure—or, as is often the case, the group of figures—is then set in an actual environment—an elevator, a lunch counter, a movie ticket booth, or the interior of a bus—with the props of the environment retrieved from junkyards (fig. **21.23**). Although Segal painted the figures in many of his later sculptures, he left them white in the early works, producing the effect of ghostly wraiths of human beings existing in a tangible world. The qualities of stillness and mystery in Segal's sculpture are comparable to the desolate psychological mood of Edward Hopper's paintings (see figs. 18.36, 18.37), while his many treatments of the female nude, including *Girl Putting on Scarab Necklace* (fig. **21.24**), are reminiscent of Degas's paintings of bathers engaged in private moments (see fig. 2.35). In the mid-seventies Segal altered his technique and began to use the body casts as molds from which either plaster or bronze casts could be made. As a result, he was able to make work suitable for outdoor public sculpture.

Oldenburg

Claes Oldenburg (b. 1929), a native of Sweden who was brought to the United States as an infant, has created a brilliant body of work based on lowly common objects ranging from foodstuffs to clothespins and matchsticks. Through his exquisitely rendered drawings or through the sculpture he has executed in diverse media and scales, Oldenburg transforms the commonplace into something extraordinary. "Art," he has said, "should be literally made of the ordinary world; its space should be our space; its time our time; its objects our ordinary objects; the reality of art will replace reality."

Oldenburg's most important early work consisted of two installations made in New York: *The Street*, 1960, and *The Store*, 1961. The former was created of little more than common urban detritus—newspaper, burlap, and cardboard—that the artist tore into fragmented figures or other shapes and covered with graffitilike drawing. Leaning against the walls or hanging from the ceiling, these ragged-edged objects collectively formed, according to the artist, a "metaphoric mural," that mimicked the "damaged life forces of the city street." Given Oldenburg's willingness to make art from the most common materials, it is no surprise that a crucial early model for him was Jean Dubuffet's *art brut*. In its fullest manifestation, *The Store* (fig. **21.25**) was literally presented in a storefront in Manhattan's Lower East Side, where the artist both made his wares and sold them to the public, thus circumventing the usual venue of a commercial gallery. He filled *The Store* floor to ceiling with sculptures inspired by the tawdry merchandise he saw regularly in downtown cafeterias and shop windows. They were made of plaster-soaked muslin placed over wire frames, which was then painted and attractively priced for such amounts as $198.99. Items from *The Store* depicted everything from women's lingerie, to fragments of advertisements, to food such as ice-cream sandwiches or hamburgers—all roughly modeled and garishly painted in parody of cheap urban wares. Within the installations of *The*

21.25 Claes Oldenburg seated in *The Store*, 107 East 2nd Street, New York, December 1961. Collection the artist.

21.26 Claes Oldenburg, *Floor Cake (Giant Piece of Cake)*, 1962. Installation view, Sidney Janis Gallery, New York, 1962. Synthetic polymer paint and latex on canvas filled with foam rubber and cardboard boxes, 4'10⅜" × 9'6¼" × 4'10⅜" (1.5 × 2.9 × 1.5 m). The Museum of Modern Art, New York.

21.27 Claes Oldenburg, *Geometric Mouse, Scale A*, 1969–71. Steel, aluminum, and paint, height 12' (3.7 m). Walker Art Center, Minneapolis.

as well as shiny colored vinyl to translate hard, rigid objects, such as bathroom fixtures, into soft and collapsing versions. These familiar, prosaic toilets, typewriters, or car parts collapse in violation of their essential properties into pathetic, flaccid forms that have all the vulnerability of sagging human flesh. Oldenburg, who has described his work as "the detached examination of human beings through form," essentially models his soft sculptures through direct manipulation, but also allows gravity to act upon their pliant forms. Thus, the works exist in a state of constant flux.

One of Oldenburg's images, the *Geometric Mouse*, is so synonymous with his name that it has come to represent a kind of surrogate self-portrait. Just as soft sculptures paradoxically metamorphosed hard forms into soft, the *Geometric Mouse*, originally derived from the shape of an old movie camera, is a hard (and highly abstracted) version of an organic subject. Oldenburg has executed the *Geometric Mouse* on several scales ranging from small tabletop versions to an eighteen-foot-high (5.5 m) outdoor sculpture. *Geometric Mouse, Scale A* (fig. **21.27**), made of steel and aluminum, consists of a few interlocked metal planes but still bears an eerie resemblance to its namesake.

In the mid-sixties, Oldenburg began to make drawings of common objects to be built to the scale of monuments for the city: a pair of giant moving scissors to replace the Washington Monument, a colossal peeled banana for Times Square, or an upside-down Good Humor bar to straddle Park Avenue (with a bite removed to allow for the passage of traffic) (fig. **21.28**). These proposals challenged traditional notions of public sculpture as heroic and commemorative in nature and replaced them with irreverent and often hilarious solutions. Oldenburg later realized his fantastic proposals with large-scale projects that have been built around the globe (see figs. 24.59, 24.60). Most of these have been conceived with his wife and collaborator Coosje van Bruggen.

Street and *The Store*, Oldenburg staged several Happenings between 1960 and 1962. Situating objects within an environment and sometimes using that environment as a context for Performances—a term he prefers to Happenings—has been characteristic of Oldenburg's art for decades.

The stuffed-fabric props that Oldenburg made for some of these performances (with his first wife doing much of the sewing) led to his first independent soft sculptures. Among his earliest examples were stuffed and painted canvas objects such as the nine-and-a-half-foot-long (2.9 m) *Floor Cake* (fig. **21.26**). Soon he was using canvas

21.28 Claes Oldenburg, *Proposed Colossal Monument for Park Avenue, New York: Good Humor bar*, 1965. Crayon and watercolor on paper, 23½ × 17½" (59.7 × 44.5 cm). Collection of Carroll Janis, New York.

"Just Look at the Surface": The Imagery of Everyday Life

Dine

Jim Dine (b. 1935), a gifted draftsman and printmaker originally from Cincinnati, was also one of the organizers of the first Happenings, but he gave up this aspect of his work, he said, because it detracted from his painting. Like Rauschenberg, Johns, Kaprow, and others, Dine's art has roots in Abstract Expressionism, although he seems to treat it with a certain irony, combining gestural painting with

21.29 Jim Dine, *Hatchet with Two Palettes, State #2*, 1963. Oil on canvas with wood and metal, 6' × 4'6" (1.8 × 1.4 m). Collection Robert E. Abrams, New York.

21.30 Jim Dine, *Double Isometric Self-Portrait (Serape)*, 1964. Oil with metal rings and hanging chains on canvas, 4'8⅞" × 7'1½" (1,5 × 2.14 m). Whitney Museum of American Art, New York.

actual objects, particularly tools (fig. **21.29**). His objects recall both Duchamp's readymades and contemporaneous works by Johns (see fig. 21.16). In Dine's paintings the tools are not only physically present but are also frequently reiterated in painted images or shadows and are then referred to again through lettered titles. For Dine, the son and grandson of hardware store merchants, the tools as well as the painted image of the palette are self-referential signs, just as his many images of neckties and bathrobes are surrogate self-portraits (fig. **21.30**).

Samaras and Artschwager

Lucas Samaras (b. 1936), a native of Greece who came to America in 1948, participated in early Happenings at the Reuben Gallery, where he had his first one-man show in 1960. Since then Samaras has worked in a broad range of media, including boxes and other receptacles. In his containers, plaques, books, and table settings, prosaic elements are given qualities of menace by the inclusion of knives, razor blades, or thousands of ordinary but outward-pointing pins. The objects are meticulously made, with a perverse beauty embodied in their implied threat. They are not easily classified as Neo-Dada or Pop art; rather, they are highly expressionist works that carry with them a Surrealist brand of disturbance. Samaras sees in everyday objects a combination of menace and erotic love, and it is this sexual horror, yet attraction, that manifests itself in his work. Two chairs—one covered with pins and leaning back, the other painted and leaning forward—create the effect of a grim dance of the inanimate and commonplace (fig. **21.31**). To touch one of his objects is to be mutilated. Yet the impulse to touch it, the tactile attraction, is powerful.

In the mid-sixties Samaras began to construct full-scale rooms where every surface has been covered with mirrors (fig. **21.32**). Upon entering these reflective environments

21.31 Lucas Samaras, *Untitled*, 1965. Wood, pins, glue, and yarn; chairs, 35½ × 35¾ × 19¼" (90.2 × 91 × 49 cm). Walker Art Center, Minneapolis.

21.32 Lucas Samaras, *Mirrored Room*, 1966. Wood and mirrors, 8 × 10 × 8' (2.4 × 3 × 2.4 m). Albright-Knox Gallery, Buffalo.

21.33 Lucas Samaras, *Photo Transformation*, 1973–74. SX-70 Polaroid, 3 × 3" (7.6 × 7.6 cm). Private collection.

the viewer is dazzled and disoriented as his or her image is infinitely multiplied in every direction. Such optical experiments have led Samaras to a series of what he calls "photo-transformations" in which his own Polaroid image, placed within his familiar environment, is translated into monstrous forms (fig. **21.33**).

Like Samaras, **Richard Artschwager** (b. 1923) resists easy classification, for the work of both artists bridges several trends in the sixties, from Pop to Minimalism to Conceptualism. In 1953, after spending three years in the army, earning a degree in physical science at Cornell University, and studying painting for a year in New York, Artschwager began to make commercial furniture. This technical experience, combined with a growing commitment to art over science that was kindled by an admiration for the work of Johns, Rauschenberg, and Oldenburg, led Artschwager to the fabrication of hybrid objects that occupy a realm somewhere between furniture and sculpture.

Chair (fig. **21.34**) is fabricated in the artist's favorite medium, Formica (here in an elaborately marbleized pattern he used in the mid-sixties). Though it superficially resembles a chair, it would be difficult to use it as such. "I'm making objects for non-use," the artist once said, recalling Duchamp's use-deprived readymades, which transformed everyday objects into works of art. With its rigid, unforgiving surfaces, the geometricized *Chair* seems to share qualities with the abstract sculptures that Minimalist artists were making at the same time (see fig. 22.51), yet its resemblance to a functional object runs entirely counter to their aims.

Artschwager was also making representational paintings based on black-and-white photographs. For these he used acrylic paint on Celotex, a commercial composite paper that is used less for fine art than for inexpensive ceilings. It has a fibrous texture or tooth and is embossed with distinct patterns, providing a prefabricated "gesture" for the painter. Building façades as well as architectural interiors

21.34 Richard Artschwager, *Chair*, 1966. Formica and wood, 59 × 18 × 30" (149.9 × 45.7 × 76.2 cm). Private collection, London.

21.35 Richard Artschwager, *Destruction III*, 1972. Acrylic on Celotex with metal frames, two panels, 6'2" × 7'4" (1.9 × 2.2 m). Private collection.

figure prominently among the subjects of Artschwager's paintings. A large diptych from 1972, *Destruction III* (fig. **21.35**), belongs to a series depicting the demolition of the grand Traymore Hotel in Atlantic City. Like his sculptures, Artschwager's painting presents a distant facsimile of its subject, removed from reality more than once by way of the intermediary photographic source that is then translated into the grainy textures of the Celotex support. This tension between illusion and reality is a central theme of Artschwager's art.

Rivers

Although the same age as Artschwager, **Larry Rivers** (1923–2002) had very different beginnings as an artist in New York. He came of age artistically during the height of Abstract Expressionism, but has always remained committed to figuration in one form or another. Originally trained as a musician, Rivers studied painting at Hans Hofmann's school in the late forties and made

paintings in the manner of Bonnard and Matisse. By the mid-fifties he had developed a style of portraiture remarkable for its literal and explicit character, particularly striking in nude studies of his mother-in-law (fig. **21.36**). After

21.36 Larry Rivers, *Double Portrait of Berdie*, 1955. Oil on canvas, 5'10¾" × 6'10½" (1.8 cm × 2.1 m). Whitney Museum of American Art, New York.

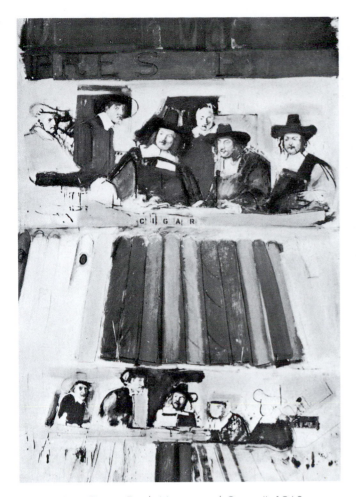

21.37 Larry Rivers, *Dutch Masters and Cigars II*, 1963. Oil and collage on canvas, 8' × 5'7⅜" (2.4 × 1.7 m). Collection Robert E. Abrams.

1960 Rivers began to incorporate stenciled lettering and imagery from commercial sources into his paintings, both of which signaled a departure from the naturalistic conventions that guided his early work. The Dutch Master cigar box, reproducing a painting by Rembrandt, became the subject of several works (fig. **21.37**). In the 1963 version shown here, he appropriated the printed image but altered it by means of his characteristically schematic rendering and loose patches of paint. Rivers shares Pop art's concern for the everyday image, but he differs in his continued interest in painterly handling of images.

Lichtenstein

Roy Lichtenstein (1923–97) may have defined the basic premises of Pop art more precisely than any other American painter. Beginning in the late fifties, he took as his primary subject the most banal comic strips or advertisements and enlarged them faithfully in his paintings, using limited, flat colors (based on those used in commercial printing), and hard, precise drawing. The resulting imagery documents, while it gently parodies, familiar images of modern America. When drawing from comic strips, Lichtenstein preferred those representing violent action and sentimental romance and even incorporated the Benday dots used in photomechanical reproduction. *Whaam!* (fig. **21.38**) belongs to a group of paintings that Lichtenstein made in the early sixties. By virtue of its monumental scale (nearly fourteen feet, or 4 m, across) and dramatic subject (one based on heroic images in the comics of World War II battles), *Whaam!* became a kind of history painting for the Pop generation. The artist's depictions of giant, dripping brushstrokes, meticulously constructed and far from spontaneous, are a comedic Pop riposte to the heroic individual gestures of the Abstract Expressionists (fig. **21.39**).

Lichtenstein frequently turned his attention to the art of the past and made free adaptations of reproductions of paintings by Picasso, Mondrian, and other modern artists. In *Artist's Studio: The Dance* (fig. **21.40**), he borrowed an

21.38 Roy Lichtenstein, *Whaam!* 1963. Oil and Magna on two canvas panels, 5'8" × 13'4" (1.7 × 4.1 m). Tate Gallery, London.

21.39 Roy Lichtenstein, *Big Painting No. 6*, 1965. Oil and Magna on canvas, 7'8" × 10'9" (2.3 × 3.3 m). Kunstsammlung Nordrhein-Westfalen, Düsseldorf.

image from Matisse's *Dance (II)* (see fig. 7.19) as a background for his own studio still life. In 1909 Matisse had depicted his own painting *Dance I* in a similar fashion positioned behind a tabletop still life. Although some of the imagery here may have originated with Matisse, the final effect is unmistakably Lichtenstein's. *Bedroom at Arles* (fig. **21.41**) clearly derives from Van Gogh's famous painting *The Bedroom*, 1888, at the Art Institute of Chicago, which Lichtenstein knew through reproductions. Not only has he dramatically enlarged the scale of Van Gogh's canvas, but he has transformed the Dutchman's rustic bedroom into a modern bourgeois interior. For example, Van Gogh's cane-seated chairs have become bright yellow Barcelona chairs similar to those designed by the architect Mies van der Rohe.

Throughout his career, Lichtenstein made freestanding bronze sculptures that provide a three-dimensional counterpart to his insistently two-dimensional painting style. Like the paintings, most of his sculpture is essentially two-dimensional in conception and has the appearance of freestanding paintings in relief, rather than volumetric structures in the round. His 1980 *Expressionist Head* recalls the angular anatomies and bold contours of German Expressionist prints. Lichtenstein, himself an accomplished printmaker, regularized the forms within heavy black lines, using bright, primary colors and replacing the characteristic Benday dots with emphatic hatch marks.

The paintings of Lichtenstein, as well as those of Wesselmann, Rosenquist, and Warhol, share an attachment to the everyday, commonplace, or vulgar image of modern industrial America. Often appropriating their subjects wholesale from their sources, they also treat their images in an impersonal, neutral manner. They do not comment on the scene or attack it like Social Realists, nor do they exalt it like advertisers. They seem to be saying simply that this is the world we live in, this is the urban landscape, these are the symbols, the interiors, the still lifes that make up our own lives. As opposed to assemblage artists who create their works

21.40 Roy Lichtenstein, *Artist's Studio: The Dance*, 1974. Oil and magna on canvas, 8' × 10'8" (2.4 × 3.3 m). Collection Mr. and Mrs. S.I. Newhouse, Jr., New York.

21.41 Roy Lichtenstein, *Bedroom at Arles*, 1992. Oil and magna on canvas, 10'6" × 13'9½" (3.2 × 4.2 m). Robert and Jane Meyerhoff Collection, Phoenix, Maryland.

from the refuse of modern industrial society, the Pop artists deal principally with the new, the "store-bought," the idealized vulgarity of advertising, of the supermarket, and of television commercials.

Warhol

The artist who more than any other stands for Pop in the public imagination, through his paintings, objects, underground movies, and personal life, is **Andy Warhol** (1928–87). Like several others associated with Pop, Warhol was first a successful commercial artist. Initially, like Lichtenstein, he made paintings based on popular comic strips, but he soon began to concentrate on the subjects derived from advertising and commercial products for which he is best known—Coca-Cola bottles, Campbell's soup cans, and Brillo cartons (fig. **21.42**). His most characteristic manner was repetition within a grid—endless rows of Coca-Cola bottles, literally presented, and arranged as they might be on

21.42 Andy Warhol, *210 Coca-Cola Bottles*, 1962. Silkscreen ink on synthetic polymer paint on canvas, 6'10½" × 8'9" (2.1 × 2.7 m). Collection Martin and Janet Blinder.

21.43 Andy Warhol, Installation view of *Campbell's Soup Cans*, Ferus Gallery, Los Angeles, 1962.

supermarket shelves or an assembly line (Warhol appropriately dubbed his studio "The Factory"). "You can be watching TV and see Coca-Cola," Warhol wrote in his 1975 autobiography, "and you can know that the President drinks Coke, Liz Taylor drinks Coke, and just think, you can drink Coke, too. A Coke is a Coke and no amount of money can get you a better Coke than the one the bum on the corner is drinking." Warhol's signature image is the Campbell's soup can, a product he said he ate for lunch every day for twenty years, "over and over again." When he exhibited thirty-two paintings of soup cans in 1962 at the Los Angeles Ferus Gallery, the number was determined by the variety of flavors then offered by Campbell's, and the canvases were monotonously lined up around the gallery on a white shelf like so many grocery goods (fig. **21.43**).

From these consumer products he turned to the examination of contemporary American folk heroes and glamorous movie stars, including Elvis Presley, Elizabeth Taylor, and Marilyn Monroe (fig. **21.44**). He based these early paintings on appropriated images from the media; later he photographed his subjects himself. From 1962 on, Warhol used a mechanical photo-silkscreen process that further

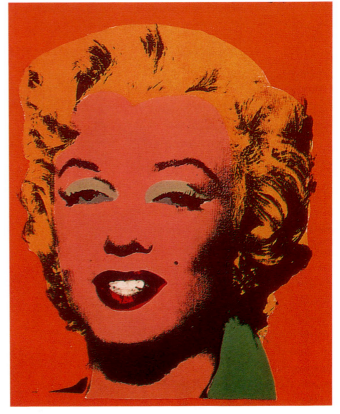

21.44 Andy Warhol, *Marilyn Monroe*, 1962. Silkscreen ink on synthetic oil, acrylic, and silkscreen enamel on canvas, 20 × 16" (50.8 × 40.6 cm).

21.45 Andy Warhol, *Last Self-Portrait*, 1986. Acrylic and silkscreen on canvas, 6'10" × 6'10" (2.1 × 2.1 m). The Metropolitan Museum of Art, New York.

emphasized his desire to eliminate the personal signature of the artist and to depict the life and the images of his time. As in his portrait of Monroe, Warhol allowed the layers of silkscreen colors to register imperfectly, thereby underscoring the mechanical nature of the process and encouraging many observers to contemplate the fate of the then recently deceased Monroe.

At the same time that he was beginning his portraits, Warhol created a series of canvases that applied his disturbing sense of impersonality to press photographs of death and disaster scenes. In doing so he suggested that familiarity breeds indifference, even to such disturbing aspects of contemporary life. In his gruesome pictures of automobile wrecks, for example, the nature of the subject makes the attainment of a neutral attitude more difficult. *Electric Chair*, taken from an old photograph, shows the grim, barren, death chamber with the empty seat in the center and the sign SILENCE on the wall. Presented by the artist either singly or in monotonous repetition, the scene becomes a chilling image, as much through the abstract austerity of its organization as through its associations.

In the later sixties, Warhol increasingly turned to the making of films, where his principle of monotonous repetition became hypnotic in its effect, and to the promotion of the rock band The Velvet Underground. At the same time, he made himself and his entourage the subject of his art. Equipped with his famous silver-sprayed wig and an attitude of studied passivity, Warhol achieved cult status in New York, especially after he nearly died in 1968 from gunshot wounds inflicted by Valerie Solanas, the sole member of S.C.U.M. (the Society for Cutting Up Men).

Throughout the seventies, Warhol worked primarily as a society portraitist, making garishly colored silkscreen paintings of friends, artworld figures, and celebrities. Among his most haunting images are the camouflage self-portraits he eighties; the one illustrated here was executed the year before his death (fig. **21.45**). Disguising his own well-known visage in a camouflage pattern was a highly appropriate gesture for this artist, who fabricated his famous persona for public consumption but who remained privately a shy, devout Catholic and devoted son. "If you want to know all about Andy Warhol," he once said, a little disingenuously, "just look at the surface: of my paintings and films and me, and there I am. There's nothing behind it."

Rosenquist, Wesselmann, and Indiana

For a period, **James Rosenquist** (b. 1933) was a billboard painter, working on the scaffolding high over New York's Times Square. The experience of painting commercial images on an enormous scale was critical for the paintings he began to produce in the early sixties. His best-known and most ambitious painting, *F-111*, 1965, is ten feet high and eighty-six feet long (3 × 26.2 m), capable of being organized into a complete room to surround the spectator (fig. **21.46**).

Named after an American fighter-bomber whose image traverses the entire eighty-six feet, *F-111* also comprises a series of fragmented images of destruction, combined with prosaic details including a lightbulb, a plate of spaghetti, and, most jarring of all, a little girl who grins beneath a bullet-shaped hair dryer. Surrounded by this environment of canvas, visitors experienced the visual jolt of the painting's

21.46 James Rosenquist, Portion of *F-111*, 1965. Oil on canvas with aluminum, overall 10 × 86' (3 × 26.2 m). Private collection.

21.47 Tom Wesselmann, *Interior No. 2*, 1964. Mixed media, including working fan, clock, and fluorescent light, 60 × 48 × 5" (152.4 × 121.9 × 12.7 cm). Private collection.

garish, Technicolor-like palette, augmented by reflective aluminum panels at either end, and its barrage of imagery on a colossal scale. Between 1965, when it was first unveiled at the Leo Castelli Gallery in New York, and 1968, *F-111* traveled to several countries, gaining notoriety not only as an aggressive indictment of war, but as one of the seminal works of the Pop era.

Tom Wesselmann (b. 1931) parodied American advertising in his sixties assemblages, which combined real elements—clocks, television sets, air conditioners—with photomontage effects of window views, plus sound effects. In works such as *Interior No. 2* (fig. **21.47**), the literal presence of actual objects dissolves the barriers between depicted forms and reality itself. Wesselmann's most obsessive subject has been the female nude, variations on which comprise a series he called *Great American Nude* (fig. **21.48**). For decades, Wesselmann has painted this faceless American sex symbol, whose pristine and pneumatic form mimics the popular conventions of pinup magazines.

Robert Indiana (b. 1938) could be considered the Pop heir to early-twentieth-century artists such as Charles Demuth and Stuart Davis (see figs. 18.29, 18.30, 18.64). He painted a figure five in homage to the former (fig. **21.49**) and, like Davis, he has painted word-images, in his case attaining a stark simplicity that suggests the flashing words of neon signs—EAT, LOVE, DIE. These word-paintings are composed of stenciled letters and precise, hard-edge color-shapes that relate Indiana to much abstract art of the sixties.

Unlike most Pop art, which manifests little or no overt comment on society, Indiana's word-images are often bitter indictments, in code, of modern life, and sometimes even a devastating indictment of brutality, as in his *Southern States* series. However, it was with his classic rendering of "LOVE" that Indiana assured a place for himself in the history of the times (fig. **21.50**). He continued to produce, among other new images, many LOVE variations on an ever-increasing scale, as in the aluminum sculpture seen here.

21.48 Tom Wesselmann, *Great American Nude #57*, 1964. Acrylic and collage on board, 48 × 65" (121.9 × 165.1 cm). Whitney Museum of American Art, New York.

21.49 Robert Indiana, *The Demuth Five*, 1963. Oil on canvas, diagonal measurements 68 × 68" (172.7 × 172.7 cm). Private collection.

Lindner and Marisol

Richard Lindner (1901–78), the son of German Jews, emigrated first to France (where he was temporarily interned in a concentration camp after the outbreak of World War II), and later, in 1941, to New York. There, he first gained a reputation as an illustrator and teacher during the fifties. Because the paintings he began to make in the early sixties, with their figurative subject matter, slick finish, and urban imagery, bore a superficial resemblance to Pop art, his name has been associated with that movement. But his work is rooted in European literary and artistic traditions and is more appropriately related to the machine Cubism of Léger as well as to the work of earlier German artists such as Schlemmer. He created a bizarre and highly personal dreamworld of metallic, tightly corseted mannequins who at times seem to be caricatures of erotic themes, with bright, flat, even harsh colors (fig. **21.51**). These fetishistic images, which are filled with personal and literary associations (his mother had run a custom-fitting corset business in Germany), recapitulate the artist's past.

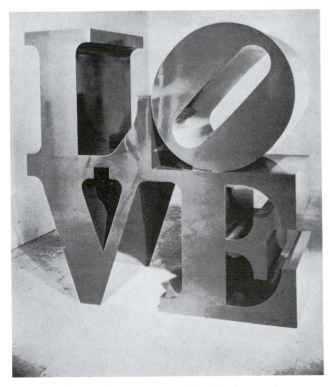

21.50 Robert Indiana, *LOVE*, 1972. Polychrome aluminum, 6 × 6 × 3' (1.8 × 1.8 × 0.9 m). Multiple, Formerly Galerie Denise René, Paris.

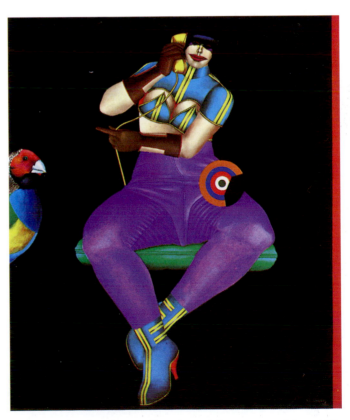

21.51 Richard Lindner, *Hello*, 1966. Oil on canvas, 70 × 60" (177.8 × 152.4 cm). Collection Robert E. Abrams.

21.52 Marisol, *The Family*, 1962. Painted wood and other materials in three sections, overall 6'10⅝" × 5'5½" × 1'3½" (2.2 × 1.66 × 0.39 m). The Museum of Modern Art, New York.

Edward Kienholz, Jess, and Ed Ruscha—made work that is only tangentially related to Pop.

Thiebaud

One of the most distinguished artists to emerge in California in the sixties is the painter **Wayne Thiebaud** (b. 1920). He located his work as part of a long realist tradition in painting that includes such artists as Chardin, Eakins, and Morandi, and he was not comfortable with attempts to tie his work to the Pop movement. When his distinctive still lifes of mass-produced American foodstuffs were first exhibited in New York in 1962, however, they were regarded as a major manifestation of West Coast Pop and were seen by many as ironic commentaries on the banality of American consumerism. Thiebaud specialized in still lifes of carefully arranged, meticulously depicted, lusciously brushed and colored, singularly perfect but unappetizing bakery goods (fig. **21.53**), the kind one would find illuminated under harsh fluorescent lights on a cafeteria counter or under a bakery window. Thomas Hess, who had been an advocate of the Abstract Expressionist painters, wrote of Thiebaud's East Coast debut:

> looking at these pounds of slabby New Taste Sensation, one hears the artist screaming at us from behind the paintings urging us to become hermits: to leave the new Gomorrah where layer cakes troop down air-conditioned shelving like cholesterol angels, to flee to the desert and eat locusts and pray for faith.

Since the early sixties, **Marisol** (Marisol Escobar) (b. 1930), a Paris-born Venezuelan artist active in New York, has created life-size assemblages made of wood, plaster, paint, and found objects, which she sometimes arranges in environments. These are primarily portraits of famous personalities such as President Lyndon Johnson, Andy Warhol, and the movie star John Wayne. Marisol based her more anonymous sitters in *The Family* on a photograph of a poor American family from the South (fig. **21.52**). Their features are painted on planks of wood, but the artist added three-dimensional limbs and actual shoes for some of the figures to create her peculiar hybrid of painting and sculpture. Reminiscent of photographs by Walker Evans (see fig. 18.45), *The Family* contains a pathos alien to most Pop art.

Poetics of the "New Gomorrah": West Coast Artists

Pop had also begun to emerge from the distinctive culture of California by the early sixties, although the four California artists discussed here—Wayne Thiebaud,

21.53 Wayne Thiebaud, *Pie Counter*, 1963. Oil on canvas, 30 × 36" (76.2 × 91.4 cm). Whitney Museum of American Art, New York.

21.54 Edward Kienholz, *The Beanery*, 1965. Mixed-media tableau, 7 × 6 × 22' (2.1 × 1.8 × 6.7 m). Stedelijk Museum, Amsterdam.

Nevertheless, Thiebaud insisted that these works reflected his nostalgia and affection for the subject, rather than any indictment of American culture. While the repetitive nature of the motif generated compositions as ostensibly monotonous as Warhol's grids and series, the paint handling has little in common with the flat, deadpan surfaces favored by the East Coast Pop artists. Thiebaud used the oil medium to recreate the very substance it depicts, whether cake frosting or mustard or pie meringue, building up his colorful paint layers into a thick, delectable impasto. From the sixties onward, Thiebaud, who had a distinguished career as professor of art at the University of California, Davis, also produced landscapes that often elicit marvelous chromatic and spatial effects from the vertiginous streets of San Francisco.

Kienholz

In strong contrast to Thiebaud's traditional oil paintings is the subversive art of Los Angeles artist **Edward Kienholz** (1927–94). Like George Segal, he created elaborate tableaux, but where Segal's work is quietly melancholic, Kienholz's constructions embody a mordant, even gruesome, view of American life. For his famous bar, *The Beanery* (fig. **21.54**), he produced a life-size environment, one where the viewer can actually enter and mingle with the customers. The patrons are created mostly from life casts of the artist's friends. Kienholz filled the tableau, as he called this and similar works, with such grotesque invention and such harrowing accuracy of selective detail that a sleazy neighborhood bar-and-grill becomes a scene of nightmarish proportion. The seedy customers, who smoke, converse, or stare off into space, wear clocks for faces, all frozen at ten minutes after ten. "A bar is a sad place," Kienholz once said, "a place full of strangers who are killing time, postponing the idea that they're going to die." *The State Hospital* (fig. **21.55**) is a construction of a cell with a mental patient and his self-image, both modeled with revolting realism and placed on filthy mattresses beneath a single glaring lightbulb. The man on the upper mattress is encircled by a neon cartoon speech bubble, as though unable to escape reality even in his thoughts. The two effigies of the same creature—one with goldfish swimming in his glass-bowl head—make one of the artist's most horrifying works. Though he could not have known Duchamp's late work, *Étant Donnés* (see chapter 13), Kienholz adopted a very similar format for *The State Hospital*, which can be viewed only through a barred window in the cell, thus implicating the viewer as a voyeur in this painfully grim scene.

21.55 Edward Kienholz, *The State Hospital*, 1966. Mixed-media tableau, 8 × 12 × 10' (2.4 × 3.7 × 3 m). Moderna Museet, Stockholm.

21.56 Jess, *Will Wonders Never Cease: Translation #21*, 1969. Oil on canvas mounted on wood, 21 × 28⅛" (53.3 × 71.4 cm). Hirshhorn Museum and Sculpture Garden, Smithsonian Institution, Washington, D.C.

Jess

The West Coast artist Burgess Collins, known as **Jess** (b. 1923), came to public attention in 1963 when his comic-strip collage was included in Pop Art U.S.A., an exhibition at the Oakland Art Museum. But the reclusive Jess felt no kinship with the Pop artists who were his contemporaries, and most of his mature work is so saturated with romanticism, nostalgia, and fantasy that it seems a far cry from the cool detachment of Pop. After earning a degree in chemistry at the California Institute of Technology, Jess began to study painting in San Francisco under a number of prominent Bay area artists, including Clyfford Still, who, he said, taught him the "poetics of materials." The abstract paintings he made in the first half of the fifties bear the imprint of this leading Abstract Expressionist. Jess's longtime companion and frequent

collaborator was the Beat poet Robert Duncan, who died in 1988.

In 1959 Jess began a series of paintings that he called *Translations*, for which he took preexisting images, usually old photographs, postcards, or magazine illustrations, and "translated [them] to a higher level emotionally and sometimes spiritually." The *Translations*, which he continued to make until 1976, are painstakingly crafted, built up into thick, bumpy layers of oil paint where the impasto resembles a kind of painted relief (fig. **21.56**). They usually feature an accompanying text. The words at the top of the canvas here come from a text by Gertrude Stein in which a boy learns from his father about the cruelty of collecting butterflies as specimens. The hauntingly tender image, painted in pastel colors in a deliberately antinaturalistic, paint-by-numbers style, is based on an engraving from an 1887 children's book titled *The First Butterfly in the Net*. Since the early fifties Jess has also made elaborate works, which he called "Paste-Ups", inspired by Dada and Surrealist collage and photomontage, especially the work of Max Ernst. Composed of images clipped from magazines and other sources, the Paste-Ups contained layers of meaning as dense and complex as the tightly woven imagery.

Ruscha

The work of **Edward Ruscha** (b. 1937), who settled in Los Angeles in 1956, is not easily classified. His hard-edge technique and vernacular subject matter allied him with California Pop art in the sixties, while his fascination with words and typography, exemplified by his printed books and word paintings, corresponded to certain trends in Conceptual art that surfaced in the following decade. In 1963 Ruscha, who had already worked as a graphic designer of books, published *Twenty-six Gasoline Stations*, a book containing unremarkable photographs of the filling stations on Route 66, a road he had frequently traveled, between Oklahoma City, his birthplace, and Los Angeles. He based

21.57 Edward Ruscha, *Standard Station, Amarillo, Texas*, 1963. Oil on canvas, 5'5" × 10' (1.65 × 3 m). Hood Museum of Art, Dartmouth College, Hanover, New Hampshire.

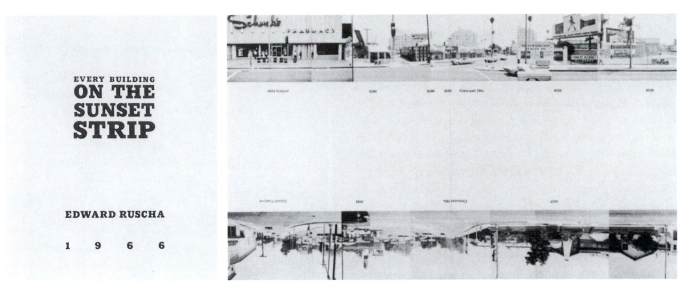

21.58 Edward Ruscha, Title page (above left) and opening pages (above right) of *Every Building on the Sunset Strip*, 1966. Artist's book.

his large painting *Standard Station, Amarillo, Texas* (fig. **21.57**) on one of those images, though he transformed the mundane motif into a dramatic composition, slicing the canvas diagonally, turning the sky black, and transforming the station into a sleek, gleaming structure that recalls Precisionist paintings of the thirties.

Another of Ruscha's books, *Every Building on the Sunset Strip* (fig. **21.58**), documents exactly what its title indicates in a series of deadpan photographs. "I want absolutely neutral material," he told one interviewer. "My pictures are not that interesting, nor the subject matter. They are simply a collection of 'facts'; my book is more like a collection of readymades." Ruscha's citation of Duchamp is a reminder that the Frenchman's first major retrospective was held in 1963 at the Pasedena Art Museum. In the eighties Ruscha began to make tenebrous paintings, in which mysterious objects float, like the words of his earlier paintings, in a nebulous space.

Jiménez

Luis Jiménez (b. 1940), a Mexican-American artist from El Paso, Texas, is not associated specifically with California, but rather the southwestern part of the United States where Mexican and American cultures meet and sometimes clash. Jiménez draws from his Mexican heritage, looking especially to the artistic examples of the Mexican muralists (see chapter 18), as well as the myths, technologies, and mass media of "*el Norte.*" He shares certain concerns with Pop artists for, as he has said, "I am making what I would consider people's art and that means that the images are coming from popular culture and so is the material." Jiménez, who learned sign painting techniques in

21.59 Luis Jiménez, *Man on Fire*, 1969. Fiberglass, 7'5" × 5' × 1'7" (2.3 × 1.52 × 0.48 m). National Museum of American Art, Washington, D.C.

21.60 Yves Klein, *Blue Monochrome*, 1961. Dry pigment in synthetic polymer medium on cotton over plywood, 6'4⅞" × 4'7⅞" (2 × 1.4 m). The Museum of Modern Art, New York.

his father's El Paso shop, uses fiberglass for his sculpture, a material that, he has pointed out, is used to make canoes, cars, and hot tubs. He then applies a jet aircraft acrylic ure-thane finish with an airbrush, giving his surfaces a hard plastic, autobody glow that is repellent and seductive at the same time. It is a finish that, the artist says, "the critics love to hate." His dramatic *Man on Fire* (fig. **21.59**), a subject previously treated by Orozco, is based on the heroic figure of Cuauhtémoc, the last Aztec emperor, whom the Spaniards tortured by fire.

"Extroversion is the Rule": Europe's New Realism

The movement known as *Nouveau Réalisme* or New Realism developed in the fifties when the prevailing trend in Europe was geometric abstraction and *Art Informel* (see chapter 20). New Realism was officially founded in 1960 by the French critic Pierre Restany in the Parisian apartment of artist Yves Klein. A manifesto was issued and ex-hibitions of the group were held in Milan in 1960 and at Restany's Gallery J in Paris the following year. The latter was labeled 40 Degrees Above Dada, indicating a kinship, at least according to Restany, with the earlier movement. Though certain aims of the group were comparable to those of Pop art, such as their revolt against the hegemony of abstract painting, the results proved as different as the artists involved. In general, the Europeans were less inter-ested in literal transcriptions of popular culture and were less indebted to the processes and imagery of commercial media. The original members included Klein, Martial Raysse, Arman, Jean Tinguely, Daniel Spoerri, Raymond Hains, Jacques de la Villeglé, and François Dufrêne. All of these, with the exception of Klein, were included in the 1961 exhibition The Art of Assemblage, at The Museum of Modern Art, New York, and in the New Realists show the following year at Sidney Janis. In the catalogue for the latter, Pierre Restany is quoted as saying:

> In Europe, as well as in the United States, we are finding new directions in nature, for contemporary nature is mechanical, industrial and flooded with advertisements. ... The reality of everyday life has now become the factory and the city. Born under the twin signs of standardization and efficiency, extroversion is the rule of the new world ...

Klein

A central figure of Pierre Restany's *Nouveau Réalisme* was **Yves Klein** (1928–62), who was an early practitioner of Conceptual, Body, Minimalist, and Performance art. Klein and his followers were concerned with the dramatization of ideas beyond the creation of individual works of art, and the mystical basis of his art set his work apart from his American Pop contemporaries. He was a member of an obscure spiritual sect, the Rosicrucian Society, and held the advanced black belt grade in judo from Japan. He even

opened his own judo school in Paris in 1955, the year of his first public exhibition in Paris. In his blue monochrome abstractions (fig. **21.60**), paintings that caused an uproar when first shown in Milan in 1957, he covered the canvas with a powdery, eye-dazzling, ultramarine pigment that he patented as IKB ("International Klein Blue"). For Klein, this blue embodied unity, serenity, and, as he said, the supreme "representation of the immaterial, the sovereign liberation of the spirit." Though not exactly identical, the prices for instance differed, these flat, uninflected paintings carried no indication of the artist's hand on their surface and were a radical alternative to gestural abstraction.

In 1958 Klein attracted audiences to an exhibition of nothingness—*Le Vide* (The Void)—nothing but bare walls in a Parisian gallery. In 1960 he had himself photographed leaping off a ledge in a Paris suburb as a "practical demon-stration of levitation" (fig. **21.61**). The photograph was doctored to remove the judo experts holding a tarpaulin below, but Klein, a serious athlete, was obsessed with the notion of flight or self-levitation. In this altered image he presents less a prankish demonstration of levitation than an artistic leap of the imagination. He wrote:

> Today the painter of space ought actually to go into space to paint, but he ought to go there without tricks or fraud, not any longer by plane, parachute or rocket: he must go there by himself, by means of individual, autonomous force, in a word, he should be capable of levitating.

21.61 Yves Klein, *Leap into the Void*, Fontenay-aux-Roses, October 23, 1960. Photograph by Harry Shunk.

21.62 Yves Klein, *Shroud Anthropometry 20, "Vampire,"* c. 1960. Pigment on canvas, 43 × 30" (109.2 × 76.2 cm). Private collection.

The artist's blue "Anthropometries" (a term inented by Restany) of 1960 were realized with nude models, his "living brushes," who were covered with blue paint and instructed by Klein to roll on canvases to create imprints of their bodies (fig. **21.62**). In the *Cosmogonies*, he experimented with the effects of rain on canvas covered with wet blue paint. To make his fire paintings, he used actual flames to burn patterns into a flame-retardant surface and, in later works, added red, blue, and yellow paint (fig. **21.63**). With his passion for a spiritual content comparable to that preached by Kandinsky, Mondrian, and Malevich, Klein was moving against the trend of his time with its insistence on impersonality, on the painting or sculpture as an object, and on the object as an end in itself.

Tinguely and Saint-Phalle

Other artists associated with New Realism had interests ranging from assemblage to kinetic sculpture, to forms closer to those of American Pop. For Swiss artist **Jean Tinguely** (1925–94), a friend and collaborator of Klein's, mechanized motion was the primary medium. "The machine allows me," he said, "above anything, to reach poetry." After the formulation of metamechanic reliefs and what he called "metamatics," which permitted the use of chance and sound in motion machines, he introduced painting machines in 1955, another attempt at debunking the assumptions surrounding so-called Action Painting or French "*Tachisme*." By 1959 he had perfected the metamatic painting machines, the most impressive of which was the *metamatic-automobile-odorante-et-sonore* for the first biennial of Paris. It produced some forty thousand paintings in an Abstract Expressionist style on a roll of paper that was then cut by the machine into individual sheets.

In 1960 Tinguely came to New York, where he and his companion, the artist Niki de Saint-Phalle, collaborated with like-minded American artists including Johns,

21.63 Yves Klein, *Fire Painting*, 1961–62. Flame burned into asbestos with pigment, 43 × 30" (109.2 × 76.2 cm). Private collection.

21.64 Jean Tinguely, *Homage to New York*, 1960. Mixed media. Self-destructing installation in the garden of The Museum of Modern Art, New York.

21.65 Niki de Saint-Phalle, *Black Venus*, 1965–67. Painted polyester, 9'2¼" × 2'11" × 2' (2.8 × 0.89 × 0.61 m). Whitney Museum of American Art, New York.

Rauschenberg, and John Cage. His 1960 *Homage to New York* (fig. **21.64**), created in the garden of New York's Museum of Modern Art from refuse and motors gathered around the city, was a machine designed to destroy itself. In the era's spirit of Happenings, an audience watched for about half an hour as the machine smoked and sputtered, finally self-destructing with the aid of the New York Fire Department. A remnant is in the museum's collection.

Parisian-born **Niki de Saint-Phalle** (b. 1930) lived in New York from 1933 to 1951 and exhibited with the New Realists from 1961 to 1963. In the early sixties she began to make "Shot-reliefs," firing a pistol at bags of paint that had been placed on top of assemblage reliefs. As the punctured bags leaked their contents, "drip" paintings were created by chance methods. These works were both a parodic comment on Action Painting and a ritualistic kind of Performance art. Saint-Phalle is best known for her *Nana* or woman figures, which came to represent the archetype of an all-powerful woman. These are rotund, highly animated figures made of *papier-mâché* or plaster and painted with bright colors (fig. **21.65**). *SHE* ("*hon*" in Swedish) (fig. **21.66**), an eighty-two-foot, six-ton (25 m, 6.09 tonne) reclining *Nana*, was made in collaboration with Tinguely and a Swedish sculptor named Per-Olof Ultvedt for the Moderna Museet in Stockholm, where it was exhibited. Visitors entered the sculpture on a ramp

between the figure's legs. Inside this giant womb they encountered a vast network of interconnected compartments with several installations, including a bottle-crunching machine, a planetarium, and a cinema showing Greta Garbo movies. The work was destroyed after three months, although the head remains in the permanent collection of the Moderna Museet.

Arman

Arman (Armand Fernández) (b. 1928) was a friend and in some degree a competitor of Klein's. In 1960 he filled a Parisian gallery with refuse, calling it *Le Plein* (Fullness), thus countering Klein's exhibition of nothingness or *Le Vide*. Arman either fractured objects such as violins into many slivers or made assemblages, which he called "accumulations," that consisted of reiterated objects—such as old sabres, pencils, teapots, or eyeglasses. He placed these objects under vitrines or imbedded them in transparent, quick-setting polyester. Later he created clear plastic figures to act as containers for the objects. Thus a transparent nude torso (fig. **21.67**) contains a cluster of inverted paint tubes that pour brilliantly colored streamers of paint down into the belly and groin.

21.66 Niki de Saint-Phalle, *SHE—A Cathedral*, 1966. Mixed-media sculptural environment, 20 × 82 × 30' (6.1 × 25 × 9.1 m). Moderna Museet, Stockholm (fragmentary remains).

21.67 Arman, *La Couleur de mon amour*, 1966. Polyester with embedded objects, 35 × 12" (88.9 × 30.5 cm). Collection Philippe Durand-Ruel, Paris.

21.68 Arman, *Long-Term Parking*, 1982. Sixty automobiles embedded in cement, 60 × 20 × 20' (18.3 × 6.1 × 6.1 m). Centre d'Art de Montcel, Jouy-en-Josas, France.

Arman called one group of his assemblages "*poubelles*" (trash cans), a term that comments on the prodigal waste inherent in contemporary consumerism while also alluding to the potential for visual poetry in life's recycled detritus, as we have seen in the art of Schwitters and Rauschenberg. In 1982 Arman realized a work on a grand scale with *Long-Term Parking* (fig. **21.68**), a sixty-foot (18.3 m) concrete tower with some sixty complete automobiles embedded in it. The parklike setting outside Paris affirms the artist's contention that, far from expressing the antiart bias present in Duchamp's original use of found objects, *Long-Term Parking* reflects a desire to restructure used or damaged materials into new, aesthetic forms as a metaphor for the hope that modern life may yet prove salvageable.

Raysse

The work of **Martial Raysse** (b. 1936) perhaps has the most in common with British and American Pop artists, though his beach scenes are more reminiscent of his native Côte d'Azur than Coney Island (fig. **21.69**). In 1962, for an exhibition at Amsterdam's Stedelijk Museum, the artist created an installation called *Raysse Beach*. Using life-size, photographic cutouts of bathing beauties set in an actual environment of sand and beach balls, he achieved a synthetic re-creation of an expensive watering place, a kind of artificial paradise for the Pop generation. Central to *Raysse Beach*, as in the work of his American and British contemporaries, are the stereotypical images of women drawn from advertising. After participating in Janis's New Realists exhibition in 1962, Raysse spent time in both New York and Los Angeles and associated with American artists such as Oldenburg and Rauschenberg, whom he had already met in Paris.

Christo and Jeanne-Claude

Bulgarian-born **Christo** (Christo Javacheff) (b. 1935) escaped from the Eastern bloc in 1958 and settled in Paris. There he came into contact with the New Realists and began to wrap found objects in cloth. In the context of New Realism, Christo's work had the most in common with that of Arman, although Arman chose to expose his found objects while Christo elected to obscure them within his packages, placing the emphasis less on the contained than on the container. These wrapped forms could range from more recognizable shapes like a chair, a woman, or a Volkswagen automobile, to unidentified objects, in essence a new kind of abstract, highly enigmatic sculpture (fig. **21.70**). Like Oldenburg's proposed colossal monuments, Christo's most ambitious projects were at first carried out only in drawings and collages. But in 1968, working side by side with his wife, **Jeanne-Claude** (b. 1935), he actually wrapped his first building, the Kunsthalle in Bern, Switzerland.

21.69 Martial Raysse, *Tableau dans le style français*, 1965. Assemblage on canvas, 7'1⅞" × 4'6⅜" (2.2 × 1.4 m). Collection Runquist.

21.70 Christo, *Package 1962*, 1962. Fabric and rope mounted on board, 36⅝ × 26¾ × 12¼" (93 × 68 × 31 cm).

The Christos are best known for their vast environmental projects, involving wrapping not only whole buildings but even significant portions of open nature. Christo and Jeanne-Claude have had to excel at public relations as much as at fine art, since to carry out their epic proposals they must engage the sympathetic attention of countless public and private interests. *Running Fence* (fig. **21.71**), a 1972–76 work executed in the California coastal counties of Marin and Sonoma, entailed raising $3.2 million exclusively through the sale of Christo's preparatory drawings, as well as collages, project-related photographs, books, and films. A significant part of the process also involved persuading the ranchers who owned the land and participating in numerous public hearings and sessions in California courts to overcome local bureaucracies and calm the concerns of environmentalists. Christo and Jeanne-Claude managed sixty-five skilled workers who anchored twenty-four and a half miles (39.4 km) of infrastructure, and then three hundred and fifty students who strung 2,050 panels of white nylon fabric, measuring eighteen-by-sixty-eight feet (5.5 × 20 m), along steel cables and poles. As with the earlier wrapped objects, *Running Fence* made the familiar visible in a new way. When finally in place, it undulated like a luminous ribbon of light through fields, hills, and valleys (with passages left for cattle, cars, and wildlife), finally tapering off into the Pacific Ocean. *Running Fence* stood for two weeks and then was dismantled, leaving no ecological damage to either flora or fauna.

In 1995 the Christos realized a project that had been in gestation since 1971. They wrapped the Reichstag in Berlin, the traditional seat of the German parliament and a building with a long and violent history (fig. **21.72**). Although the project came to fruition well after the Berlin Wall fell in 1989, the Reichstag appealed to Christo, a native of a Soviet-bloc country, as a symbol of the divisions of East and West. The tenacious Christos took on a formidable bureaucracy and marshaled a massive team, including ninety professional climbers, to pull 119,603 square yards (100,003 m²) of silver fabric around the building, resulting in an extraordinary apparition in the urban landscape. As with all of the Christos' projects, the wrapping of the Reichstag, in itself a work of Performance art, was heavily documented each step of the way through myriad photographs.

21.71 Christo and Jeanne-Claude, *Running Fence, Sonoma and Marin Counties, California,* 1972–76 (now removed). 2,050 steel poles set 62' apart; 65,000 yards of white woven synthetic fabric, height 18' (5.5 m), length 24½ miles (39.4 km).

21.72 Christo and Jeanne-Claude, *Wrapped Reichstag, Berlin,* 1971–95 (now removed).

Rotella, Manzoni and Broodthaers

The Italian artist **Mimmo Rotella** (b. 1918) was an early practitioner of the New Realist technique known as décollage, which he began to use in 1953 (fig. **21.73**). The antithesis of collage, décollage is the art of tearing up posters—promotions for films or commercial products—to create new compositions, not in pristine Pop art guise, but torn and tattered with one superimposed image intruding on another. A familiar feature of any urban landscape is the layers of half-torn posters—modern urban palimpsests—that decorate billboards and walls. Rotella stripped these posters, usually promoting Italian films, from city walls and mounted them on canvas only to tear them off layer after layer. "What a thrill, what fantasy, what strange things happen," he said, "clashing and accumulating between the first and last layer."

The idiosyncratic art of the Italian **Piero Manzoni** (1933–63) ushered in much of the conceptually based work of the sixties and seventies that would follow his death. A significant event in Manzoni's career, which was even more short-lived than Klein's, was the 1957 exhibition in Milan of the French artist's monochrome paintings. The young Manzoni was an *agent provocateur* in the Dada tradition, as when he signed cans purportedly containing his own excrement. He also made "living sculpture" by signing the bodies of friends or nude models and providing certificates of authenticity, resulting in a kind of "living readymade."

21.73 Mimmo Rotella, *Untitled,* 1963. Décollage, 47¼ × 39⅜" (120 × 100 cm). Location unknown.

Manzoni was involved with the Italian group *Arte nucleare* (Nuclear Art), which denounced the idea of personal style and, like latter-day Futurists, called for an art of explosive force in the postnuclear age. Klein also exhibited with this group in Milan in 1957. That year, after seeing Klein's show, Manzoni ceased to make tar-based paintings and began his series of *Achromes*, monochrome works with neutral surfaces that were emphatically devoid of any imagery. The *Achromes* consisted of a whole range of media, including plaster or cotton balls, or pebbles mounted on canvas. *Achrome* of 1959 (fig. **21.74**) is reminiscent of the work of an older Italian artist, Fontana (see fig. 588), for Manzoni simply manipulated the canvas by folding it into pleats.

One of the "living sculptures" that Manzoni signed in 1962 was the Belgian **Marcel Broodthaers** (1924–76), a poet who began to make art objects in 1964. Like many of his contemporaries discussed in this chapter, Broodthaers staged Happenings and drew the materials for his reliefs and assemblages from the artifacts of everyday life. He also

21.74 Piero Manzoni, *Achrome*, 1959. Kaolin on pleated canvas, 55⅛ × 47¼" (140 × 120 cm). Musée National d'Art Moderne, Centre d'Art et de Culture Georges Pompidou, Paris.

21.75 Marcel Broodthaers, *La Tour visuelle*, 1966. Glass, wood, and magazine reproductions, 33½ × 31½" (85 × 80 cm). The Scottish National Gallery of Modern Art, Edinburgh.

21.76 Marcel Broodthaers, *Ground plan of Musée D'Art Moderne* at Le Coq, on the North Sea coast of Belgium. View of the ground plan of the *Section Documentaire*, August 1969.

took part in exhibitions that included work by New Realist or Pop artists. Yet his was a highly individual and hermetic form of expression, one shaped less by the Pop model than by the Surrealist climate that dominated postwar Brussels, thanks largely to the example of his fellow countryman Magritte. A case in point is *La Tour visuelle* (fig. **21.75**), a mysterious construction of small glasses covered with magazine reproductions of an eye which recalls Surrealist objects of the thirties.

Broodthaers, who detested commercialism and what he saw as fashion trends in art, accused the New Realists of acquiescing to the "industrial accumulations that our era produces." Much of his activity centered on Dada-inspired inquiries into the nature of art and subversive alternatives to traditional art institutions. In 1968 he designated his own fictitious *Musée D'Art Moderne* whose various "sections" were manifested in differing venues, from his house to temporary exhibitions. In 1969 he created his virtual museum on a Belgian beach, on the North Sea coast, by tracing its grand plan in the sand. Wearing "museum" hats, he and a colleague set up signs warning visitors not to touch the objects, only to have it all washed away by the tide (fig. **21.76**).

Personal Documentaries: The Snapshot Aesthetic in American Photography

As the vernacular sources and the mixed media of Pop artists would suggest, photography had become an even more dominant presence in Western culture by the early sixties. A number of artists discussed in this chapter used photography in their art, including Hamilton, Hockney, Rauschenberg, Warhol, Samaras, Ruscha, and Christo. At the same time, a growing number of young professional photographers were attracted to the common activities and artifacts of everyday life and conveyed them in seemingly casual compositions devoid of pictorial convention and overt commentary. Their goal was not an exquisitely crafted and designed print but rather an authentic, directly communicated image. Photographers of the period tended to deheroicize the mystical pretensions and technical perfection sought by, for instance, Strand, Weston, and White. In place of such elevated straight photography came the "snapshot aesthetic," with its subject matter derived from the most banal urban and suburban landscapes and its procedures deceptively haphazard.

21.77 Robert Frank, *Political Rally, Chicago, 1956*, From *The Americans*, 1958. Gelatin-silver print.

These new attitudes were most fully realized in the work of the Swiss American **Robert Frank** (b. 1924). Aided by a Guggenheim grant, in 1955 Frank set out on a journey of discovery throughout the United States, using his 35mm Leica camera to take a fresh, detached, but ultimately critical—if not absolutely damning—look at postwar American society consumed by violence, conformity, and racial and social division (fig. **21.77**). "Criticism," said Frank, "can come out of love." Frank published eighty-three of his photographs, edited from the original 20,000, in book form, first in France and then in the United States as *The Americans* (1959), with an introduction by novelist Jack Kerouac. When judged by conventional standards of the medium, Frank's photographs look harsh, informal, blurred, and grainy, more like glimpses than concentrated views of a subject. Their individual strengths build within the cumulative effect of the book as a whole, the sequential nature of which led the artist to filmmaking.

In the sixties, *The Americans* became a celebrated icon of American photography and a model for young photographers who shared Frank's outlook. Frank retained a sequential format in much of his later still photography, including the triptych *Moving Out* from 1984 (fig. **21.78**). From the streets of America he turned inward to haunting meditations on his own life, as shown here with depictions of three abandoned rooms from different moments in his past. The text the artist attached to these images includes the words, "Just accept lost feelings—Shadows in empty room—Silence on TV."

American-born **Gary Winogrand** (1928–84) said he took photographs in order to see what the things that interested him would look like as photographs, implying that his artistic vision was something discovered in the course of making pictures. This partly explains the look of his photographs, which record scenes so bluntly real, so familiar, that they are usually absorbed into the scanning process of normal vision. Winogrand was working as a photojournalist and commercial photographer when

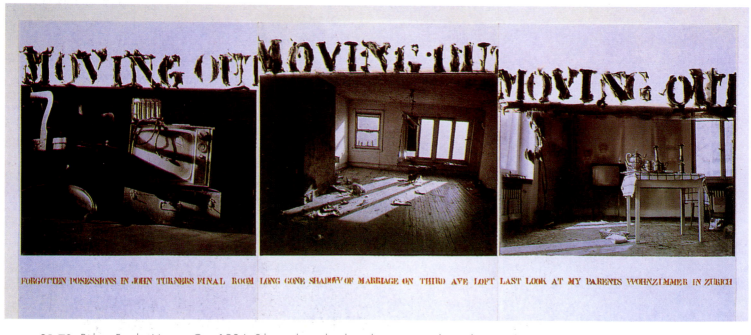

21.78 Robert Frank, *Moving Out*, 1984. Silver-gelatin developed-out prints with acrylic paint, 9¹⁵⁄₁₆ × 47¹³⁄₁₆" (50.6 × 121.4 cm). National Gallery of Art, Washington, D.C.

21.79 Gary Winogrand, *Peace Demonstration, Central Park, New York*, 1969. Gelatin-silver print.

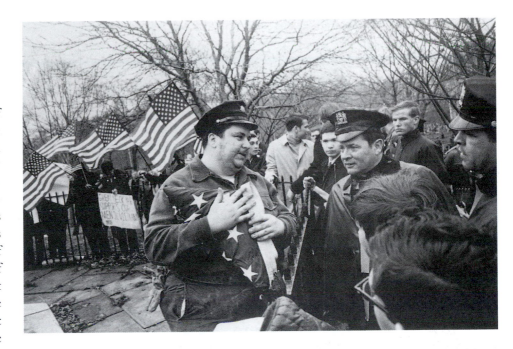

he encountered the work of Walker Evans and Frank, whose approach to the medium helped shape his mature work. In 1969 he abandoned commercial photography to focus on his personal work and received his second Guggenheim grant, this one to explore the "effect of media on events." A number of the prints made under the grant eventually formed a catalogue and an exhibition called Public Relations (1977). Given the years Winogrand worked on the project (1969–73), it is no surprise that the Vietnam War played a central role in this group of photographs (fig. **21.79**). Winogrand forgot little of the aesthetic principles learned while a painting student at Columbia University, for however informal *Peace Demonstration* may appear, as in the tipping of the camera, the resulting image is a marvel of conflicting patterns contained with great rigor.

Like Frank, **Lee Friedlander** (b. 1934) found telling imagery among the vast array of visual accident available in America's streets, whether it was a jazz band's procession in a New Orleans neighborhood, or abruptly cropped views of anonymous pedestrians in New York City. Friedlander, who said he wanted to record "the American social landscape and its conditions," exploited the layered reflections of shop windows, often including his own image in such works in a kind of deliberate appropriation of a

standard mistake of amateur photography (fig. **21.80**). Even at their most banal, his photographs, such as this shot of a tawdry restaurant window featuring a portrait of President and Jacqueline Kennedy the year before the assassination, could possess a strange poignancy.

The work of Winogrand and Friedlander was featured in a 1967 exhibition at The Museum of Modern Art called New Documents. According to John Szarkowski, the show's curator, such artists represented a new generation of photographers who were directing "the documentary approach toward more personal ends. Their aim has been not to reform life, but to know it." Also included in the show was the work of New Yorker **Diane Arbus** (1923–71), whose startling photographs issued from her enormous curiosity about human nature in all its manifestations. Her primary mentor was Lisette Model

21.80 Lee Friedlander, *Washington, D.C.*, 1962. Gelatin-silver print.

21.81 Diane Arbus, *Untitled #6*, 1970–71. Gelatin-silver print, 10 × 10" (25.4 × 25.4 cm).

(see fig. 15.67), but Arbus probed the psyche of her subjects even more deeply than her teacher. In the fifties Arbus made grainy 35mm photographs of anonymous subjects whom she encountered in Coney Island or on the streets of New York City.

From 1960 until her death she made photographs for magazines such as *Esquire* and *Harper's Bazaar*. Her best-known photographs are the portraits she made in the sixties, often of traditionally forbidden subjects, of people existing on the fringes of society, including transvestites, nudists, circus performers, or residents in a home for people with mental disabilities. Arbus's ability to gain the trust of her subjects resulted in sometimes painfully honest images (fig. **21.81**). Her photographs are simultaneously disquieting and wondrous, for she captured a world at which we are not allowed to stare. As her daughter, Doon Arbus has written, "She was determined to reveal what others had been taught to turn their back on."

Frank's book *The Americans* provided a critical example for New York photographer **Bruce Davidson** (b. 1933), who was working for *Life* magazine by the late fifties. Davidson favored gritty subjects drawn from New York's subways or Coney Island and sometimes worked in series such as one following the teenage members of a Brooklyn

street gang (fig. **21.82**). The Brooklyn Gang photo-essay was published in *Esquire* magazine in 1960 with an accompanying text by Norman Mailer extolling the rebelliousness of youth. Davidson's grainy snapshot presents the subject, teenagers primping before vending machines, without criticism. His explanation that he "force-developed the film to increase the harsh contrast that reflected the tension in their lives" reveals a willingness to manipulate the photographic process to convey the drama and pathos of his subject.

The serial arrangements, narrative content, and even the narcissism found in Warhol's art appeared in the photography of **Duane Michals** (b. 1932), who acquired such traits from the same source as Warhol—Madison Avenue, where Michals has worked as a commercial photographer. Convinced that a single image offers little more than the record of a split second cut from the ongoing flow of time, Michals constructs "photostories," or playlets, to expose or symbolize the reality behind our perceptions of it. His 1968 *Paradise Regained* coolly transforms a young couple in a neutral contemporary interior into a version of the biblical Garden of Eden (fig. **21.83**). "I use photography," the artist said, "to help me explain my experience to myself. … I believe in the imagination. What I cannot see is infinitely more important than what I can see."

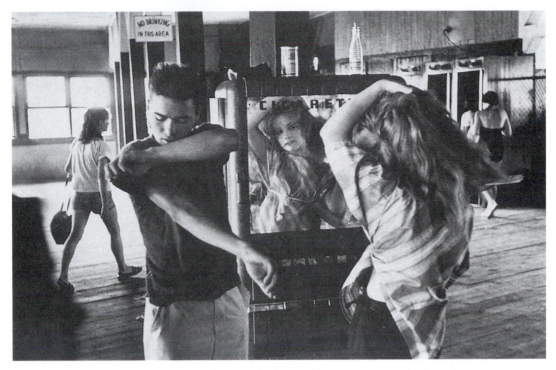

21.82 Bruce Davidson, *Coney Island* from the series *Brooklyn Gang*, 1959. Gelatin-silver print.

21.83 Duane Michals, *Paradise Regained*, 1968. Series of gelatin-silver prints.

Richard Avedon (b. 1923) spent time as a street photographer both in his native city of New York and also in Italy (fig. **21.84**). But he is known for his elaborately staged fashion photographs from the fifties that appeared in *Harper's Bazaar*, a magazine that attracted some of the best talents in photography, including Model, Brandt, Brassaï, and Frank. At the age of nineteen Avedon served in the merchant marines, where he had to take thousands of head shots for ID photos, a fact that may have determined a preference in later years for photographing his subjects straight on, at excruciatingly close range, and against a stark white background. Since the early fifties Avedon photographed many of the most celebrated personalities of his era, from Marilyn Monroe to Giacometti to the Beatles. In 1969 he switched from a Rolleiflex to a much less maneuverable eight-by-ten-inch view camera, sometimes printing in a square format. The images that Avedon produced with the larger camera have installed a sense of imposing beauty upon a spectrum of humanity from fashion models to vagrants.

The forties and fifties were the heyday of American photojournalism, with picture magazines such as *Life*, *Harper's*, and *Vogue*, among others, supporting the work of many of photography's leading practitioners. Some of the most memorable photographs of the sixties came from professional photojournalists, including this gripping image from the war in Vietnam that was captured by the Associated Press photographer **Eddie Adams** (b. 1933) (fig. **21.85**). So powerful was the response to this photograph of an execution of a suspected communist

21.84 Richard Avedon, *Zazi, Street Performer, Piazza Navona, Rome, July 27, 1946.* Gelatin-silver print.

sympathizer as it was circulated across American newspapers that it served to escalate opposition to the war and to raise questions about the role of photographers who witness violent events and may even encourage them by their presence.

21.85 Eddie Adams, *Vietnamese General Executing Vietcong*, 1968. Gelatin-silver print.

22
Sixties Abstraction

As postwar Western Europe and the United States increasingly relaxed from the economic stress and political turbulence of the thirties and forties, the rare synthesis of mystical aspiration and physical gesture realized by the Abstract Expressionist generation began to break apart, releasing its constituent elements to follow their own separate, if not altogether unrelated, paths. Some of these, like Pop art and New Realism (see chapter 21), led to Neo-Dada attempts to make art ever more inclusive of the most ordinary reality. Abstract Expressionist action painting highlighted the physical engagement of the artist in making art and the role of chance, two elements that became central to Performance art, which took the further step of involving participants and spectators in the creative process. A different side of the Abstract Expressionist legacy emerged in systematic campaigns of excluding from art all but its most essential properties. By the end of the sixties, some avant-garde artists and critics would contend that art could be distilled into idea alone.

Something of the dual response to fifties art—to its creators' "elitist" sense of themselves as existential heroes and of their works as sacred objects—has already been seen in the career of Yves Klein, who, on the one hand, "organized" an exhibition that consisted of nothingness (le vide) and, on the other hand, made sculpture in the Duchampian "assisted readymade" fashion, by mounting blue-sprayed sponges on pedestals. Klein emphasized the performative nature of making art—when he made paintings by exposing a colored support to such external, non-art elements as fire and rainwater or by emptying the canvas of all but its irreducible condition of flat, monochrome, rectangular shape, he briefly merged extremes of both materiality and immateriality that would characterize sixties art (see figs. 21.60, 21.63). Klein's investigations of pure abstraction (for example, his emphasis on the chemical pigment that he used for his deep, meditative blue) exemplified a tendency toward progressive simplification that by the end of the decade would be known by such terms as Minimalism, ABC art, or Primary Structures. While these developments may be seen as a necessary correction of fifties heroics, the new abstractionists would evince heroics of their own, both in the sheer size of their works and in their ambition to provide an alternative to the dominant critical discourse of Clement Greenberg and his followers. Greenberg had defined modernism as the consistent and exclusive engagement of painting and sculpture with the qualities essential to them—namely, their optical surfaces—believing that "what counts first and last in art is quality," judged by formal aesthetic standards.

Pop art, thanks to its ability to entertain a newly affluent, status-conscious mass audience, may have earned its title by becoming the most popular development ever to have occurred in the higher reaches of culture. During the sixties, however, before the underlying complexity of Pop had been fully appreciated, it was abstraction that dominated within the world of art itself, mainly because its essential sobriety and internal processes of self-purification engaged the attention of the most serious critics and thinkers.

Drawing the Veil: Post-Painterly Color Field Abstraction

A number of exhibitions held in the sixties drew attention to certain changes that were occurring in American painting. Between 1959 and 1960, Clement Greenberg was instrumental in mounting a series of solo exhibitions at the New York gallery French and Company for such artists as Barnett Newman, David Smith, Morris Louis, Kenneth Noland, and Jules Olitski. During the next few years, several museums followed suit with exhibitions designed to draw attention to new directions in American art. Among these shows were American Abstract Expressionists and Imagists at New York's Guggenheim Museum in 1961; Toward a New Abstraction at New York's Jewish Museum in 1963; Post-Painterly Abstraction, organized in 1964 by Clement Greenberg for the Los Angeles County Museum of Art; and Systemic Painting, curated in 1966 by Lawrence Alloway at the Guggenheim Museum.

These exhibitions illustrated that many young artists were attempting to break away from what they felt to be the tyranny of Abstract Expressionism, particularly in its emphasis on the individual brush gesture. Some of these artists turned to representational art forms ranging from minutely observed figuration to assemblages to Pop art, while others sought new means of retinal stimulation through Op art, or light and motion. Most suggestive was the apparent development of abstract painting to which a number of names have been applied, including Abstract Imagism, Post-Painterly Abstraction, and, most commonly, Color Field painting, (sometimes simplified to Field painting). Still other terms have been applied to various aspects of this direction during the sixties—such as Systemic, Hard-Edge, and Minimalist painting. These labels, referring to various types of abstract painting, do not necessarily encompass all the same artists or all the directions involved—which range from forms of allover painting to almost blank canvases. The emphasis throughout, however, is on abstract *painting*, in distinction to figuration, optical illusion, object making, fantasy, light, motion, or any of the other tendencies away from the act of painting itself.

Among all the painters working against the current of gestural Abstract Expressionism in the late fifties there was a general move (as Greenberg pointed out) to openness of design and image. Many of the artists turned to the technique of staining raw canvas and moved toward a clarity and freshness that differentiated their works from those of the Abstract Expressionists, which were characterized by compression and brushwork. The directions and qualities suggested in the work of these artists—some already well established, some just beginning to appear on the scene—were to be the dominant directions and qualities in abstract painting during the sixties.

Francis and Mitchell

Greenberg's inclusion of **Sam Francis** (1923–94) among his "Post-Painterly" abstractionists may seem somewhat surprising, since Francis during the fifties was associated with American Abstract Expressionism and *Art Informel* in Paris, where he lived until 1961. As Greenberg explained in the introduction to the exhibition catalogue of Post-Painterly Abstraction, Abstract Expressionism was characterized by its "painterly" quality, a term inspired by the use of the German word *malerisch* by the Swiss art historian Heinrich Wölfflin to describe Baroque art. Just as Wölfflin contrasted the painterly quality of the Baroque with the crisp linearity of High Renaissance art, so Greenberg identified Post-Painterly Abstraction with more sharply defined compositions and less emphasis on evidence of the artist's gesture. According to Greenberg: "By contrast with the interweaving of light and dark gradations in the typical Abstract Expressionist picture, all the artists in this show move towards a physical openness of design, or towards linear clarity, or towards both."

22.1 Sam Francis, *Shining Back*, 1958. Oil on canvas, 6'7⅜" × 4'5⅛" (2 × 1.35 m). Solomon R. Guggenheim Museum, New York.

Despite Francis's association with Abstract Expressionism or painterly art, the direction of his painting had been toward that compositional openness and formal clarity of which Greenberg spoke. *Shining Back* (fig. **22.1**), 1958, presents an open structure that is animated, but not obscured, by Francis's continued use of brush gesture, the drip, and the spatter. In later works, despite lingering vestiges of spatters, the essential organization is that of a few free but controlled color-shapes—red, yellow, and blue—defining the limits of a dominant white space. Francis's paintings of the early seventies (fig. **22.2**) increasingly emphasized the edge to the point where his paint spatters at times surround a clear or almost clear center area of canvas. At times he uses a precise linear structure as a control for his free patterns of stains and spatters, and has created an elegant and lyrical form of abstract art.

An artist also sometimes categorized as a Color Field painter is **Joan Mitchell** (1926–92), one of the younger artists associated with Abstract Expressionism during the fifties, along with Francis and others. From the fifties onward, Mitchell demonstrated a particular interest in evoking her relationship to landscape, initially referring to both natural and urban environments, often in terms of a

22.2 Sam Francis, *Untitled, No. 11*, 1973. Acrylic on canvas, 8 × 10' (2.4 × 3 m). André Emmerich Gallery, New York.

remembered time and place, as in *August, Rue Daguerre* (1957). Mitchell moved permanently to France in 1959, living first in Paris and then in Vétheuil, where she continued to pursue her own directions in painting, undeterred by the popularity of Pop and Op art. In the mid-sixties, Mitchell expunged references to urban settings from her work and from then on turned predominantly to nature for inspiration (fig. **22.3**).

22.3 Joan Mitchell, *Land*, 1989. Oil on canvas, 9'2¼" × 13'1½" (2.8 × 4 m). National Gallery of Art, Washington, D.C.

Frankenthaler, Louis, and Olitski

An important figure in the transition between Abstract Expressionism and Color Field painting is **Helen Frankenthaler** (b. 1928). Frankenthaler was the first American painter after Jackson Pollock to see the implications of the color staining of raw canvas to create an integration of color and ground in which foreground and background cease to exist. *Mountains and Sea*, 1952, her first "stained" painting, marked a turning point in her career. Having just returned from a vacation in Nova Scotia, the artist found herself experimenting with composition and consistency of paint. She recounts:

> Before, I had always painted on sized and primed canvas—but my paint was becoming thinner and more fluid and cried out to be soaked, not resting. In *Mountains and Sea*, I put in the charcoal line gestures first, because I wanted to *draw* in with color and shape the totally abstract memory of the landscape. I spilled on the drawing in paint from the coffee cans. The charcoal lines were original guideposts that eventually became unnecessary.

During a visit to Frankenthaler's studio in 1953, Morris Louis was so affected by *Mountains and Sea* that he and Kenneth Noland began to stain canvases themselves, establishing their own staining techniques. Frankenthaler's role as the originator of Post-Painterly Color Field painting has been obscured by Greenberg's championing of Louis, Olitski, and Noland as its major exponents in the late fifties—a distortion that might be explained by Greenberg and Frankenthaler's personal history (they had an affair in the early fifties, which ended when she left him).

22.5 Helen Frankenthaler, *Essence Mulberry*, 1977. Woodcut, edition of 46, 39½ × 18½" (100.3 × 47 cm). Printed and published by Tyler Graphics Ltd.

Frankenthaler employs an open composition, frequently building around a free-abstract central image and also stressing the picture edge (fig. **22.4**). The paint is applied in uniformly thin washes. There is little, sometimes no, sense of paint texture—a general characteristic of Post-Painterly Color Field painting—although there is some gradation of tone around the edges of color-shapes, giving them a sense of detachment from the canvas. The irregular central motifs float within a rectangle, which, in turn, is surrounded by irregular light and dark frames. These frames create the feeling that the center of the painting is opening up in a limited but defined depth.

In 1960 Frankenthaler made her first prints. Since then, she has worked with a variety of printmaking techniques in addition to painting, using each of these media to explore pictorial space through the interaction of color and line on a particular surface. One of her most successful prints is *Essence Mulberry*, executed in 1977 (fig. **22.5**). Inspired by an exhibit of medieval prints at the Metropolitan Museum of Art, Frankenthaler combined the shades of mulberry, blue,

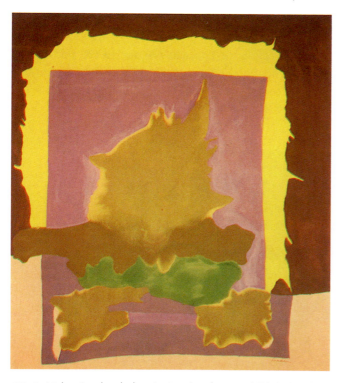

22.4 Helen Frankenthaler, *Interior Landscape*, 1964. Acrylic on canvas, 8'8¾" × 7'8¾" (2.7 × 2.4 m). San Francisco Museum of Modern Art.

22.6 Morris Louis, *Kaf*, 1959–60. Acrylic on canvas, 8'4" × 12' (2.5 × 3.7 m). Collection Kimiko and John G. Powers, New York.

yellow, and brown. The effect of the blended colors is as delicate and luminescent as that of her paintings.

Morris Louis (1912–62) was one of the talented American painters to emerge in the fifties. Living in Washington, D.C., somewhat apart from the New York scene and working almost in isolation, he and a group of artists that included Kenneth Noland were central to the development of Color Field painting. The basic point about Louis's work and that of other Color Field painters, in contrast to most of the other new approaches of the sixties, is that they continued a tradition of painting exemplified by Pollock, Newman, Still, Motherwell, and Reinhardt (see chapter 19). All of these artists were concerned with the classic problems of pictorial space and the statement of the picture plane. Louis characteristically applied extremely runny paint to an unstretched canvas, allowing it to flow over the inclined surface in effects sometimes suggestive of translucent color veils. The importance of Frankenthaler's example in Louis's development of this technique has been noted. However, even more so than Frankenthaler, Louis eliminated the brush gesture, although the flat, thin pigment is at times modulated in billowing tonal waves (fig. **22.6**). His "veil" paintings consist of bands of brilliant, curving color-shapes submerged in translucent washes through which they emerge principally at the edges. Although subdued, the resulting color is immensely rich. In another formula, the artist used long, parallel strips of pure color arranged side by side in rainbow effects. Although the separate colors here are clearly distinguished, the edges are soft and slightly interpenetrating (fig. **22.7**).

Jules Olitski (b. 1922) might be seen as a man of romantic sensibility expressing himself through the sensu-

22.7 Morris Louis, *Moving In*, 1961. Acrylic on canvas, 7'3½" × 3'5½" (2.2 × 1.05 m). André Emmerich Gallery, New York.

22.8 Jules Olitski, *High a Yellow*, 1967. Acrylic on canvas, 7'8½" × 12'6" (2.3 × 3.8 m). Whitney Museum of American Art, New York.

ousness of his large, assertive color areas. In earlier works he, like so many of his contemporaries, explored circle forms, but his were generally irregular, off-center, and interrupted by the frame of the picture to create vaguely organic effects reminiscent of Jean Arp. Moving away from these forms, Olitski began, in about 1963, to saturate his canvas with liquid paint, over which he rolled additional and varying colors. In later works, such as *High a Yellow*, 1967 (fig. **22.8**), he sprayed on successive layers of pigment in an essentially commercial process that still

admitted a considerable degree of accident in surface drips and spatters. The dazzling, varied areas of paint are defined by edges or corners and perhaps internal spots of roughly modeled paint that control the seemingly limitless surfaces. Sometimes apparently crude and coloristically disturbing, Olitski's flamboyant works are nevertheless arresting.

Poons

In the sixties, **Larry Poons** (b. 1937) created an intriguing form of Systemic painting with optical-illusionistic implica-

22.9 Larry Poons, *Nixes Mate*, 1964. Acrylic on canvas, 5'10" × 9'4" (1.78 × 2.8 m). Formerly collection Robert C. Scull, New York.

tions. In *Nixes Mate*, 1964 (fig. **22.9**), his small, brightly colored ellipses vibrate against their highly saturated background. Poons's painting, created through a process of staining, was simultaneously identified as Color Field painting by Greenbergian formalists and as Optical art by other critics when William Seitz included the artist's work in the 1965 show The Responsive Eye at The Museum of Modern Art in New York. Poons subsequently placed more emphasis on the painterly surface of his work. His heavily textured canvases frequently have long, vertically dragged brushstrokes, densely arranged in rich color patterns. Like Olitski and the other Color Field painters, Poons created large-scale works that would envelop the visual field of the viewer, provoking a purely optical response to the image—the Greenbergian ideal for modernist painting.

At an Oblique Angle: Diebenkorn and Twombly

As the trend toward progressively more radical abstraction intensified throughout the sixties, urged on by doctrinaire critical support, commercial hype, and media exposure, only exceptionally strong artists could maintain their aesthetic independence from the dominant mode. Several of the most interesting figures to emerge during this period enjoyed the advantage—for purposes of their autonomy—of regular residence remote from the competitive New York art scene.

In the course of his career, which began in the forties, the work of California artist **Richard Diebenkorn** (1922–93) moved through three distinct phases. During the first he worked in an Abstract Expressionist vein, guided by the examples of Clyfford Still and Mark Rothko, who both

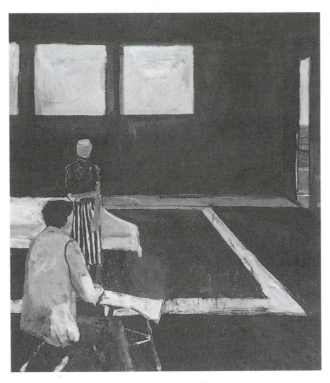

22.11 Richard Diebenkorn, *Man and Woman in Large Room*, 1957. Oil on canvas, 71 × 62½" (180.3 × 158.8 cm). Hirshhorn Museum and Sculpture Garden, Smithsonian Institution, Washington, D.C.

taught at the California School of Fine Arts (now the San Francisco Art Institute). While the outward forms of his style would change, the artist early on discovered his most fundamental concern: to abstract from his perception of things seen in order to realize painterly, atmospheric distillations of the western American landscape. From the outset, he learned to translate sensuous, visual experience into broad fields of color structured in relation to the flatness and rectilinearity of the picture plane by a framework of firm but painterly geometry (fig. **22.10**). Even as an Abstract Expressionist, Diebenkorn was, like most of his generation, a cool formalist, and in the context of his art he eschewed private, autobiographical associations in favor of meanings more generally evocative of the interaction between inner and outer worlds. This can be seen to particular advantage in *Man and Woman in Large Room* (fig. **22.11**), executed after the artist shifted from abstraction to figuration, a change that occurred in 1954 while he was in close contact with two other California painters, David Park and Elmer Bischoff. The picture functions almost as a visual metaphor because the figures, despite the expressionist potential of their juxtaposition and handling, participate in the overall structure of the total image while also enriching its sober, contemplative mood with an undercurrent of emotional pressure. In the early sixties Diebenkorn moved on from this second, or figurative, phase and, in 1967, following his relocation to Santa Monica, began his third mode, devoted to a series of majestic nonfigurative abstractions known as the *Ocean Park* paintings (fig. **22.12**). In variation after variation, and with Matisse as

22.10 Richard Diebenkorn, *Berkeley No. 22*, 1954. Oil on canvas, 59 × 57" (149.8 × 144.9 cm). Hirshhorn Museum and Sculpture Garden, Smithsonian Institution, Washington, D.C.

22.12 Richard Diebenkorn, *Ocean Park No. 54*, 1972. Oil on canvas, 8'4" × 6'9" (2.5 × 2.1 m). San Francisco Museum of Modern Art.

a primary source, in addition to Mondrian, Monet, and of course Abstract Expressionism, Diebenkorn purified and monumentalized his personal vocabulary of mist- and light-filled color planes emanating from but rigorously contained within a softly drawn architectural scaffolding. Pentimenti (passages of paint through which earlier paint layers are visible), odd and oblique angles in the structural borders, and the expansiveness and close harmony of the luminous colors work without benefit of human images to generate a sense of tension within the pervasive calm, a sense of presence within figuratively empty fields.

After World War II and following a semester of study at Black Mountain College, the slightly younger **Cy Twombly** (b. 1928) established a more or less permanent base in Rome, where he too succeeded in calmly pivoting his art on the convergence point of freedom and control, lucidity and opacity. A poet as well as a painter and a sculptor, Twombly found his characteristic image in a slate-gray ground covered with white graffiti, drawings intermingled with words and numbers, like chalk lessons half-erased on the blackboard at

22.13 Cy Twombly, *Untitled*, 1969. Crayon and oil on canvas, 6'6" × 8'7" (2 × 2.6 m). The Whitney Museum of American Art, New York.

22.14 Cy Twombly, *Hero and Leander*, Triptych (Rome), 1981–84. Oil and chalk on canvas, panel one 5'6⅛" × 6'8¾" (1.68 × 2.1 m); panels two and three each 5'8½" × 6'11⅞" (1.74 × 2.1 m). Collection Galerie Karsten Greve, Cologne, Germany.

22.15 Cy Twombly, *Untitled*, 1978 (Roma). Wood, cloth, wire, nails, mat oil paint, 1'5" × 7'3⅝" × 7¾" (0.43 × 2.2 × 0.2 m). Private collection. On loan to the Kunsthaus, Zürich, Switzerland.

the end of a busy school day (fig. **22.13**). Sometimes snatches of personal verse, often brief quotations from a classical source, always legible at first sight, though never quite complete or entirely coherent on close examination, Twombly's scribbles and scrawls activate the surface with gestures as decisive as Pollock's, but, unlike those of the Abstract Expressionists, they remain indeterminate. Additionally, Twombly's images suggest a hidden narrative, evoked in bold but enigmatic terms, such as the classical legend of the tragic love affair of Hero and Leander, depicted in a three-panel series testifying to their passion and to the fury and progressive calming of the Hellespont in which the lovers drowned (fig. **22.14**). Like many of his paintings, Twombly's sculptures also find frequent inspiration in classical sources, as in his rendition of an elongated, delicately balanced chariot (fig. **22.15**).

Forming the Unit: Hard-Edge Painting

The term "Hard-Edge" was first used by the California critic Jules Langsner in 1959, and then given its current definition by Lawrence Alloway in 1959–60. According to

Alloway, Hard-Edge was defined in opposition to geometric art, in the following way: "The 'cone, cylinder, and sphere' of Cézanne fame have persisted in much 20th-century painting. Even where these forms are not purely represented, abstract artists have tended toward a compilation of separable elements. Form has been treated as discrete entities," whereas "forms are few in hard-edge and the surface immaculate. … The whole picture becomes the unit; forms extend the length of the painting or are restricted to two or three tones. The result of this sparseness is that the spatial effect of figures on a field is avoided." The important distinction drawn here between Hard-Edge and the older geometric tradition is the search for a total unity in which there is generally no foreground or background, no "figures on a field." During the fifties, Ellsworth Kelly, Ad Reinhardt, Leon Polk Smith, Alexander Liberman, Sidney Wolfson, and Agnes Martin (most of them exhibiting at the Betty Parsons Gallery in New York) were the principal pioneers. Barnett Newman (also showing at Parsons) was a force in related but not identical space and color explorations (see fig. 19.29).

Ellsworth Kelly (b. 1923), who matured artistically in Paris following World War II, came to be considered a

22.16 Ellsworth Kelly, *Window, Museum of Modern Art, Paris*, 1949. Oil on wood and canvas, two joined panels, 50½ × 19½ × ¾" (128.7 × 49.5 × 1.9 cm). Private collection.

22.17 Ellsworth Kelly, *Orange and Green*, 1966. Liquitex (mat varnish) on canvas, 7'4" × 5'5" (2.2 × 1.65 m). Collection Robert and Jane Meyerhoff, Phoenix, Maryland.

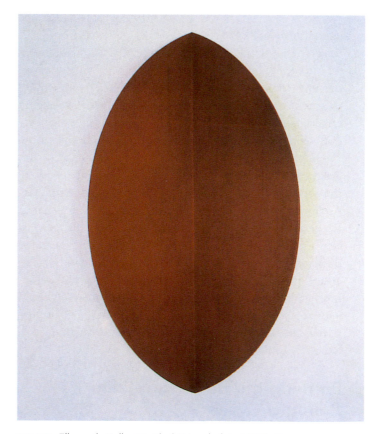

22.18 Ellsworth Kelly, *Untitled (Mandorla)*, 1988. Bronze, 8'5" × 4'5½" × 1'9" (2.6 × 1.36 × 0.53 m). Private collection.

leader of the Hard-Edge faction within Color Field painting, although he himself expressed some discomfort with this label. He explained to Henry Geldzahler in 1963, "I'm interested in the mass and color, the black and white—the edges happen because the forms get as quiet as they can be." Despite the abstract appearance of much of Kelly's painting, the artist drew extensively on his observation of the natural forms around him, as in *Window, Museum of Modern Art, Paris* of 1949 (fig. **22.16**). In 1954 the artist returned to the States, settling in New York among a group of artists, including Jasper Johns, Robert Rauschenberg, Jack Youngerman, and Agnes Martin, who, like him, resisted the dominance of Abstract Expressionism. In New York, Kelly experimented with collage and continued to develop his interest in shape and color and the relationship of figure to ground. The influence of Arp was evident at times. His paintings of the early sixties frequently juxtaposed fields of equally vibrant color, squeezing expansive shapes within the confines of a rectangular canvas (fig. **22.17**). But just as the tension in these canvases suggests,

22.19 Jack Youngerman, *Roundabout*, 1970. Acrylic on canvas, diameter 8' (2.4 m). Albright-Knox Art Gallery, Buffalo.

22.20 Kenneth Noland, *A Warm Sound in a Gray Field*, 1961. 6'10½" × 6'9" (2.1 × 2.06 m). Private collection, New York.

shapes frequently exploded from the rectangular frame, becoming artworks themselves that undermined the distinction between painting and sculpture. Kelly continued to work in a similar vein; he did not differentiate between his paintings and his sculptures, and some of his works are difficult to classify. Thus *Untitled (Mandorla)* of 1988 (fig. **22.18**), a bronze distillation of a form common in medieval painting, gains much of its effect from its relief projection. Kelly also created freestanding sculptures, works that use forms similar to those of his paintings, although projected on an environmental scale and constructed industrially of Cor-ten steel.

Like Kelly, **Jack Youngerman** (b. 1926) developed his art in Paris during the postwar years, courtesy of the GI Bill, before returning to join the New York School in the fifties. He then became known for bringing a special Matisse-like rhythm and grace to the Constructivist tradition by rendering leaf, flower, or butterfly forms with the brilliantly colored flatness and clarity of Hard-Edge painting (fig. **22.19**). In such work, he looked back not only to Arp and Matisse, but also to the rhapsodic, nature-focused art of painters who worked in the United States, such as Dove, O'Keeffe, and Gorky (see figs. 18.17, 18.18, 19.3). For a while, he designed his undulant silhouettes so that figure and ground appear to reverse, with negative and positive switching back and forth.

Although **Kenneth Noland** (b. 1924) was close to Louis during the fifties and, like him, sought through Color Field painting an essential departure from the brush-gesture mode of De Kooning or Kline, his personal solutions were quite different from those of his fellow Washingtonian. Using the same thin pigment to stain unsized canvas, Noland made his first completely individual statement when, as he said, he discovered the center of the canvas. From this point, between the mid-fifties and 1962, his principal image was the circle or a series of con-

centric circles exactly centered on a square canvas (fig. **22.20**). Since this relation of circle to square was necessarily ambiguous, in about 1963 Noland began to experiment with different forms, first ovoid shapes placed above center, and then meticulously symmetrical chevrons starting in the upper corners and coming to a point just above the exact center of the bottom edge (fig. **22.21**). The chevrons, by their placement as well as their composition, gave a new significance to the shape of the canvas and created a total, unified harmony in which color and structure, canvas plane and edges, are integrated.

In 1964 Noland was a featured painter at the United States pavilion of the Venice Biennale, and in 1965 he was given a solo exhibition at the Jewish Museum. It was about

22.21 Kenneth Noland, *Golden Day*, 1964. Acrylic on canvas, 6 × 6' (1.8 × 1.8 m). Private collection.

22.22 Kenneth Noland, *Graded Exposure*, 1967. Acrylic on canvas, 7'4¾" × 19'1" (2.3 × 5.8 m). Collection Mrs. Samuel G. Rautbord, Chicago.

this time that Noland, working within personally defined limits of color and shape relationships, systematically expanded his vocabulary. The symmetrical chevrons were followed by asymmetrical examples. Long, narrow paintings with chevrons only slightly bent led to a series in which he explored systems of horizontal strata, sometimes with color variations on identical strata, sometimes with graded horizontals, as in *Graded Exposure* (fig. **22.22**). In the next few years the artist moved from the solution of *Graded Exposure* to a formula of vertical or horizontal canvases in which his use of the grid allowed a dominant emphasis to fall on the framing edge. In his subsequent work, Noland has continued to explore the relationship of form and color to the edge of the canvas itself, manipulating the shape of the canvas as well as the painted surface.

Al Held (b. 1928) was one of the strongest of the sixties abstractionists both in his forms and in his use of color, but, unlike most of the other Color Field painters, who eliminated brushstrokes and paint texture, Held built up his paint to create a texture that added to the total sense of weight and rugged power. He worked over his paint surfaces, sometimes layering them to a thickness of an inch, although, from 1963, he sanded down the surface to a machine precision. For a period in the sixties, Held based paintings on letters of the alphabet (fig. **22.23**). In these, again, the open portions of the letters were subordinated, both to hold the edges of the canvas and to establish a sense of great scale. Held focused on the powerful presence

of colored forms on the canvas, rather than on the less tangible, more self-consciously optical effect of stained color preferred by artists such as Louis and Noland.

In the later sixties, Held rebelled against the modernist rejection of illusionism and resisted the pervasive reductive trend in contemporary painting. He introduced complex, apparently three-dimensional shapes into his paintings. The insistent exploration of a version of rigid geometric abstraction led Held through the refinement of his means to a

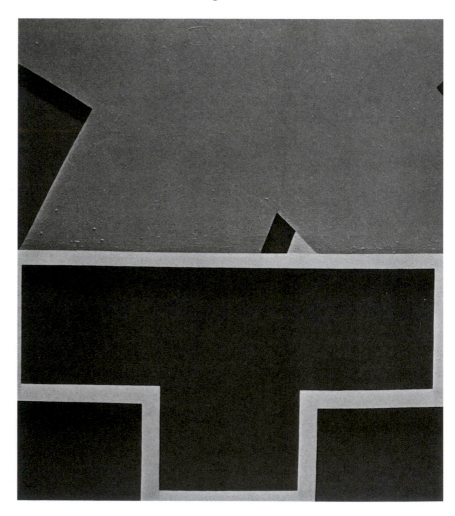

22.23 Al Held, *Ivan the Terrible*, 1961. Acrylic on canvas, 12' × 9'6" (3.7 × 2.9 m). André Emmerich Gallery, New York.

22.24 Al Held, *Flemish IX*, 1974. Acrylic on canvas, 6' × 5' (1.8 × 1.52 m). Sable-Castelli Gallery, Toronto.

22.25 Al Held, *Mantegna's Edge*, 1983. Mural, acrylic on canvas, length 55' (16.8 m). Southland Center, Dallas.

black-and-white structure. In a group of paintings of 1974 and early 1975 he presented an architecture of boxlike structures outlined in white against a uniform black ground (fig. **22.24**). The title "Flemish" in the series suggests that Held, like many of his contemporaries in the seventies, had been looking at old master paintings, in this instance conceivably the works of Jan van Eyck or Rogier van der Weyden.

Along with the black paintings with white linear structures, he exhibited their counterparts, consisting of black lines on a flat white ground. In earlier examples, the perspective structures were heavily outlined. In a number of the white paintings, however, some lines became much more delicate, mixed with weightier ones. Transparent, curvilinear elements became increasingly dominant as part of the total spatial interplay.

When Held reintroduced color, he did so with a vengeance, adopting a high-keyed intensity combined with an expanded scale to give his newer paintings an almost overwhelming impact as in his fifty-five foot (16.8 m)-long mural *Mantegna's Edge* at the Southland Center, Dallas (fig. **22.25**). The color combined with his handling of line produces the paradoxical effect of clarity and ambiguity. Images constantly fail to con-form to what experience and tradition have prepared us to anticipate in the apparently logical spatial structures Held creates. And so, as within the perpetual movement of Pollock's calligraphic complexity, the eye gives up trying to sort out the irresolutions and accepts the experience of the total configuration.

Seeing Things: Op Art

Several broadly related tendencies in the painting of the sixties may be grouped under the heading of Optical (or Retinal) painting. "Optical" in this context should not be confused with the quality of opticality that Greenbergian formalists attributed to modernist painting. For them, opticality meant the sense of a flat, nonillusionistic image that seemed to deny the necessity of physical support. By contrast, the optical stimulation of Op art implied the presence of an illusion generated by the stimulation of the retina. What is called Op art overlaps at one end with light sculpture or construction (in its concern with illusion, perception, and the physical and psychological impact of color) and with the effects of light experiments on the spectator. At the other end, it impinges on some aspects of Color Field painting in its use of brilliant, unmodulated color in retinally stimulating combinations, especially as seen in the art of Larry Poons. Op art came to the forefront of the New York art world in 1965 with William Seitz's exhibition, The Responsive Eye, at The Museum of Modern Art. Although a range of artists were included, among them Color Field painters and Hard-Edge abstractionists, such as Larry Poons, Morris Louis, Kenneth Noland, and Ellsworth Kelly, it was immediately clear that Op art represented something new. Op art actively engaged the physiology and psychology of seeing with eye-teasing arrangements of color and pattern that seemed to pulsate. Such works generated strong associations with science and technology. Interestingly, although Op art enjoyed much popular interest in the United States, it generated more serious critical acclaim in Europe, with light sculptor Julio Le Parc claiming first prize at the Venice Biennale in 1966.

Optical illusion is not new in the history of art; nor is the overlap it implies between artistic rendition and scientific theories of vision. Examples from the last five hundred years include the discovery, or rediscovery, of linear and atmospheric perspective in the fifteenth century; the interest of Impressionist and Post-Impressionist painters such as Georges Seurat in nineteenth-century theories of color and perception; and the experimentation of several Bauhaus artists, like László Moholy-Nagy and Josef Albers, with similar questions. This examination of the Optical and kinetic art of the sixties surveys some of the approaches taken by artists during this period to forms of art involving optical illusion or some other specific aspect of perception (of course, as we have already seen, such concerns were not limited to Op and kinetic artists alone).

Op art also inspired a movement toward allover painting, in which a network or a mosaic of color strokes or dots covers the canvas and seems to expand beyond its limits.

During the sixties Larry Poons created a seemingly haphazard but actually meticulously programmed mosaic of small oval shapes that vibrate intensely over a ground of strong color (see fig. 22.9). The organization of Poons's color-shapes, worked out mathematically on graph paper, was another indication of the tendency toward systems or to what, in the sixties, was called Systemic painting.

Vasarely

The Hungarian-French painter **Victor Vasarely** (1908–97) was the most influential figure in the realm of Op art. Although his earlier paintings belonged in the general tradition of Concrete art, in the forties Vasarely devoted himself to Optical art and theories of perception. Vasarely's art theories, first presented in his 1955 *Yellow Manifesto*, involved the replacement of traditional easel painting by what he called "kinetic plastics." To him, "painting and sculpture become anachronistic terms: it is more exact to speak of a bi-, tri-, and multidimensional plastic art. We no longer have distinct manifestations of a creative sensibility, but the development of a single plastic sensibility in

22.26 Victor Vasarely, *Sorata-T*, 1953. Triptych, engraved glass slabs, 6'6" × 15' (2 × 4.6 m). Private collection.

22.27 Victor Vasarely, *Vega Per*, 1969. Oil on canvas, 64 × 64" (162.6 × 162.6 cm). Honolulu Academy of Arts.

triptych, six-and-a-half by fifteen feet (2 × 4.6 m) in dimension. The three transparent glass screens may be placed at various angles to create different combinations of the linear patterns. Such art lends itself to monumental statements that Vasarely was able to realize in murals, ceramic walls, and large-scale glass constructions. What he called his "Refractions" involve glass or mirror effects with constantly changing images.

Since Vasarely was aware of the range of optical effects possible in black and white, a large proportion of his work is limited to these colors, referred to by the artist simply as "B N" (*blanche noir*: white black). It was, nevertheless, in color that the full range of possibilities for Optical painting could be realized, and Vasarely was well aware of this. In the sixties, his color burst out with a variety and brilliance unparalleled in his career. Using small, standard color-shapes—squares, triangles, diamonds, rectangles, circles, sometimes frontalized, sometimes tilted, in flat, brilliant colors against equally strong contrasting color grounds—he set up retinal vibrations that dazzle the eye and bewilder perception (fig. **22.27**).

Riley and Anuszkiewicz

The British artist **Bridget Riley** (b. 1931) and the American artist **Richard Anuszkiewicz** (b. 1930) have been responsible for producing highly acclaimed examples of Op art. Initially working primarily in black and white and different values of gray, with repeated, serial units frontalized and tilted at various angles, Riley produced extremely effective illusions, seemingly making the picture plane weave and billow before our eyes. Her use of variations in tone (which Vasarely rejected) accentuates the illusion (fig. **22.28**). By contrast, Anuszkiewicz, a student of Josef Albers, often

different spaces." Vasarely sought the abandonment of painting as an individual gesture, the signature of the isolated artist. In a modern, technical society, he believed that art had to have a social context; he saw the work of art as the artist's original idea rather than as an object consisting of paint on canvas. This idea, realized in terms of flat, geometric-abstract shapes mathematically organized, with standardized colors, flatly applied, could then be projected, reproduced, or multiplied into different forms—murals, books, tapestries, glass, mosaic, slides, films, or television. For the traditional concept of the work of art as a unique object produced by an isolated artist, Vasarely substituted the concept of social art, produced by the artist in full command of modern industrial communication techniques for a mass audience.

Vasarely was a pioneer in the development of almost every optical device for the creation of a new art of visual illusion. His *Photographismes* are black-and-white line drawings or paintings. Some of these were made specifically for reproduction, and in them Vasarely frequently covered the drawing with a transparent plastic sheet. The plastic sheet has the same design as the drawing but in a reverse, negative-positive relationship. When the two drawings—on paper and on plastic—are synchronized, the result is simply a denser version. As the plastic is drawn up and down over the paper, the design changes tangibly before our eyes. Here, literal movement creates the illusion. This and many further devices developed by Vasarely and other Op artists produced refinements of processes long familiar in games of illusion or halls of mirrors.

In his *Deep Kinetic Works*, Vasarely translated the principle of the plastic drawings into large-scale glass constructions, such as the 1953 *Sorata-T* (fig. **22.26**), a standing

22.28 Bridget Riley, *Drift No. 2*, 1966. Emulsion on canvas, 7'7½" × 7'5½" (2.3 × 2.3 m). Albright-Knox Art Gallery, Buffalo.

22.29 Richard Anuszkiewicz, *Inflexion*, 1967. Liquitex on canvas, 60 × 60" (152.4 × 152.4 cm). Collection the artist.

used color and straight lines to achieve pulsating visual effects in his painting—frequently defying our ability to distinguish background and foreground in his works or to identify whether a given plane is moving forward or receding. In *Inflexion* (fig. **22.29**) he skillfully reversed the direction of the radiating lines on each side of the square, thus making what at a quick glance looks like a traditional perspective box suddenly begin to turn itself inside out.

New Media Mobilized: Motion and Light

Two directions explored sporadically since early in the twentieth century gained new impetus in the sixties. These are motion and light used literally, rather than as painted or sculptured illusions. Duchamp's and Gabo's pioneering experiments in motion and Moholy-Nagy's in motion and light have already been noted (see fig. 17.1). Before World War II, Calder was the one artist who made a major art form of motion (see fig. 17.29). Except for further explorations carried on by Moholy-Nagy and his students during the thirties and forties, the use of light as a medium was limited to variations on "color organs," in which programmed devices of one kind or another produced shifting patterns of colored lights. These originated in experiments carried on in 1922 at the Bauhaus by Ludwig Hirschfeld-Mack (1893–1965) and by the American Thomas Wilfred (1889–1968), inventor of the color organ. The late sixties saw a revival in the use of light as an art form and in so-called mixed media, where the senses are assaulted by live action, sound, light, and motion pictures at the same time.

Gabo revived his interest in mechanical motion in the early forties, and in about 1950 Nicolas Schöffer began using electric motors to activate his constructions. During the fifties and sixties, artists' interest in light and motion

gathered pace through a series of exhibitions and the organization of experimental groups. Although kinetic and light art has become a worldwide movement, the first great impetus came from Europe, particularly from France, Germany, and Italy. Beginning in 1955 a center for its presentation was the Denise René Gallery in Paris, formerly the stronghold for the promotion of Concrete art. In that year a large exhibition held there included kinetic works by Duchamp, Calder, Vasarely, Yaacov Agam, Pol Bury, Jean Tinguely, and Jesus Rafaël Soto. The first phase of the new movement climaxed in the great exhibition held sequentially at the Stedelijk Museum in Amsterdam, the Louisiana Museum in Denmark, and the Moderna Museet in Stockholm. This was a vast and somewhat chaotic assembly representative of every aspect of the history of light and motion, actual or illusionistic, back to the origins of the automobile and to Eadweard Muybridge's nineteenth-scentury photographic studies of human and animal figures in motion (see fig. 2.33). Although the exhibition did not draw any conclusions, it did illustrate dramatically that the previous few years had seen a great acceleration of interest in these problems. The popular curiosity about this art is evinced by the fact that the exhibitions were seen by well over one hundred thousand people. During the sixties, exhibitions of light and motion proliferated throughout the world, involving increasing numbers of artists.

The arts of light and motion encouraged a number of new artists' organizations and manifestos during the late fifties and sixties. It was in 1955, in connection with the Movement exhibition at the Denise René Gallery in Paris, that Victor Vasarely issued his *Yellow Manifesto*, outlining his theories of perception and color. Another important theoretician was Bruno Munari (b. 1907), who was producing kinetic works in Italy as early as 1933. Active in Spain, Equipo 57 (founded in 1957) represented a group of artists who worked as an anonymous team in the exploration of motion and vision. This anonymity, deriving from concepts of the social implications of art and also, perhaps, from the examples of scientific or industrial research teams, was evident at the outset in the Group T in Milan, founded in 1959; Group N in Padua, Italy, founded in 1960; and Zero Group in Düsseldorf, Germany, founded in 1957 by the kinetic artist Otto Piene. In most cases the theoretical passion for anonymity soon dimmed, and the artists began to emerge as individuals.

Mobiles and Kinetic Art

Although not usually labeled as a sixties kinetic artist, **Alexander Calder** (1898–1976), whose prewar career was discussed in chapter 17, merits further discussion here for his important example and continued influence in the area of kinetic sculpture. From the late forties he had developed a growing interest in monumental forms, and in the transformation of the mobile to a great architectural-sculptural wind machine whose powerful but precisely balanced metal rods, tipped with large, flat, organically shaped disks,

22.30 Alexander Calder, *The Spiral*, 1958. Standing mobile, sheet metal and metal rods, height 30' (9.1 m). UNESCO, Paris.

encompass and define large areas of architectural space. Since the mobile, powered by currents of air, could function better outdoors than indoors, Calder began early to explore the possibilities for outdoor mobiles. Critical to the development of these works was his reconceptualization of the mobile as something that could function as an autonomous, standing structure, combining interrelated stable and mobile forms in an organic whole. In the late fifties and sixties, Calder created many large, standing mobile units that rotate in limited but impressive movement over a generally pyramidal base.

As *The Spiral* (fig. **22.30**) suggests, the development of Calder's moving sculptures bore an important relationship to the development of nonmoving elements in his structures. One of his signal achievements of the sixties occurred in his great "stabiles"— his large-scale, nonmoving, metal-plate constructions, usually painted black. Of these, one of the most impressive is the glowing red *La Grande Vitesse* (fig. **22.31**) in Grand Rapids, Michigan; an expansive

22.31 Alexander Calder, *La Grande Vitesse*, 1969. Painted steel plate, height 55' (16.8 m). Calder Plaza, Vandenberg Center, Grand Rapids, Michigan.

work with which Calder filled an otherwise sterile public space with Miró-like charm and radiant splendor. While suggesting a great exotic flower in its prime or the expressive movements of a dancer, the assemblage of red biomorphic planes boldly displays the structure of its rivets and struts and testifies to the forces involved in creating it.

Among the makers of mobiles, one of the most interesting to emerge in the United States since World War II was **George Rickey** (1907–2002). Rickey composed long, tapering strips or leaf clusters of stainless steel in a state of balance so delicate that the slightest breeze or touch of the hand sets them into a slow, stately motion or a quivering vibration (fig. **22.32**). During the seventies, Rickey enlarged his vocabulary with the introduction of large-scale rectangular, circular, and triangular forms in aluminum, so precisely balanced that they maintain the possibility of imperceptible and increasingly intricate patterns in movement. His was an art of motion entirely different from that of Calder.

Jesus Rafaël Soto (b. 1923) is a motion artist in the sense that his constructions, consisting of exquisitely arranged metal rods, are sensitive to the point that even a change in atmosphere will start an oscillation (fig. **22.33**). A Venezuelan resident of Paris, Soto began as an illusionistic painter and then moved to a form of linear construction during the sixties. He developed a personal idiom of great elegance, sometimes translated into a form of large-scale architecture involving spectator participation. In exhibitions at the Solomon R. Guggenheim Museum in New York and the Hirshhorn Museum and Sculpture Garden in Washington, D.C., he created out of his typical plastic strings entire room environments that the spectator could enter.

Artists Working with Light

Of the light experimentalists, the Argentine **Julio Le Parc** (b. 1928) was one of the most imaginative and varied in his employment of every conceivable device of light, movement, and illusion (fig. **22.34**). The awarding to him of

22.33 Jesus Rafaël Soto, *Petite Double Face*, 1967. Wood and metal, 23⅝ × 15" (60 × 38.1 cm). Marlborough Gallery, New York.

22.32 George Rickey, *Four Lines Up*, 1967. Stainless steel, height 16' (4.9 m). Collection Mr. and Mrs. Robert H. Levi, Lutherville, Maryland.

22.34 Julio Le Parc, *Continuel-Lumière avec Formes en Contorsion*, 1966. Motorized aluminum and wood, 6'8" × 4'½" × 8' (2 × 1.23 × 2 m). Howard Wise Gallery, New York.

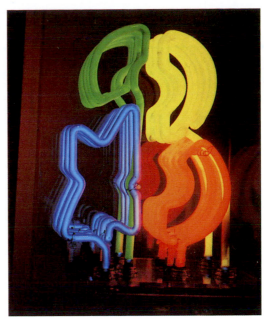

22.35 Chryssa, *Ampersand III*, 1966. Neon lights in Plexiglas, height 30¼" (76.8 cm). Collection Robert E. Abrams Family.

the painting prize at the 1966 Venice Biennale was not only a recognition of his talents but also an official recognition of the new artistic media. From 1958 Le Parc lived in Paris where, in 1960, he was a founder of the Groupe de Recherche d'Art Visuel (GRAV). With its home base at the Denise René Gallery, this group carried on research in light, perception, movement, and illusion. Le Parc became an important link between various overlapping but normally separate tendencies in the art of the sixties: not only light and movement, but also different forms of optical, illusionistic painting, and programmed art.

The Greek artist **Chryssa** (b. 1933) bridged the gap between Pop art and light sculpture. She first explored emblematic or serial relief forms composed of identical, rhythmically arranged elements of projecting circles or rectangles. Then in the early sixties she made lead reliefs derived from newspaper printing forms. From this Chryssa passed to a type of found-object sculpture in which she used fragments of neon signs. The love of industrial or commercial lettering, whether from newspapers or signs, became a persistent aspect of her works. In this she was recording the American scene in a manner analogous to the Pop artists or to the earlier tradition of Stuart Davis and Charles Demuth. Soon her fascination with the possibilities of light, mainly neon tube light, completely took over her construction of elaborate light machines so that

they came to resemble contemporary American industrial objects (fig. **22.35**).

Perhaps the most significant group effort in the United States was EAT—Experiments in Art and Technology—which developed from a series of performances involving Robert Rauschenberg, the engineer Billy Klüver, and the composer John Cage. Presented in 1966, *9 Evenings: Theater and Engineering* involved dance, electronic music, and video projection. These presentations may be traced back to experiments carried on by Cage since the forties as well as a collaborative exhibition held at the Denise René Gallery in Paris in 1955. Experiments by GRAV, sponsored by the René Gallery during the fifties and sixties, also anticipated the EAT group in the utilization of sophisticated technology and effects of light and movement. EAT perhaps extended the collaborative effort furthest in its attraction of large-scale financial support, particularly for its Pepsi-Cola Pavilion at the Osaka World's Fair of 1970.

A number of artists, including **Dan Flavin** (1933–96), **Larry Bell** (b. 1939), and **Robert Irwin** (b. 1928), combined an interest in technology and light with the principles of Minimalism, to be discussed at greater length in the final section of this chapter. Dan Flavin exploited the fluorescent fixtures with which he worked for their luminosity, but also took advantage of their status as objects themselves. In his works, the glass tubes of fluorescent light

22.36 Dan Flavin, *Untitled (to Tracy to celebrate the love of a lifetime)*, 1992, expanded version of *Untitled (to Ward Jackson, an old friend and colleague who, during the Fall of 1957 when I finally returned to New York from Washington and joined him to work together in this museum, kindly communicated)*, 1971. A system of two alternating modular units in fluorescent light, sixteen white bulbs, each 2' (0.6 m) long, four each of pink, yellow, green, and blue, each 8' (2.4 m) long. Solomon R. Guggenheim Museum, New York.

functioned as sculpture both when illuminated and when unlit, creating different effects. In turn, he recognized that light itself could transform an environment, as his 1992 installation (a reworking of an earlier version from 1971) at the newly renovated Guggenheim demonstrated (fig. **22.36**). In a spirit similar to that of Dan Flavin, Larry Bell produced large vacuum-coated glass boxes that both intrigue viewers with their shimmering iridescence and force their audience to confront them as objects, rather than as pure visual effect. The art of Robert Irwin transforms the environment of the viewer even more radically.

Working with tightly stretched semitransparent textile scrims, which are lighted from behind, he creates an eerie, isolated environment with a hypnotic effect (fig. **22.37**). One is drawn toward what appears to be an impenetrable void that, upon contemplation, increasingly surrounds the spectator. Irwin's interest in the void may have its roots in the empty gallery of Yves Klein, but Irwin greatly developed the earlier concept. Irwin has also worked outdoors, creating public sculptures inspired by the environment in which they are installed and intended to invite the participation of their audiences (fig. **22.38**).

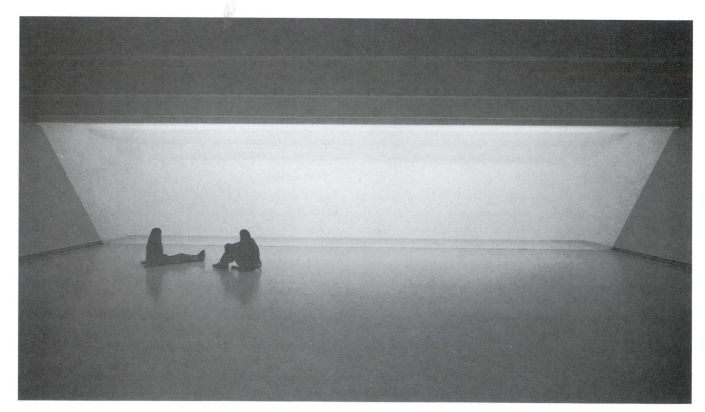

22.37 Robert Irwin, *Untitled*, 1965–67. Acrylic automobile lacquers on prepared, shaped aluminum with metal tubes, four 150 watt floodlights. Walker Art Center, Minneapolis.

22.38 Robert Irwin, *9 Spaces, 9 Trees*, July 7, 1983. Cast concrete planters; Kolorgaard ⅝" (1.59 cm) aperture, plastic-coated blue fencing; Visuvius plum trees; and Sedum Oreganium ground cover. Public Safety Building Plaza, Seattle, Washington.

The Limits of Modernism: Minimalist Sculpture and Painting

It will be clear by now that several trends characterize the painting and sculpture of the sixties, with a number of artists blurring the distinction between these two media. What has been discussed less explicitly is the ideological background to the various approaches to art-making, particularly sculpture, during this decade. With the publication of Clement Greenberg's collection of essays *Art and Culture* in 1961, and the continued success of the Abstract Expressionist artists whose work he had championed since the forties, Greenberg's influence was at a height. However, just when his modernist, formalist viewpoint prevailed, artists began to question the basis for his valuations of excellence. According to Greenberg, the best modern art should continue the historical trajectory of painting since the time of Manet, which he understood to involve a progressive evolution toward flatness as artists became increasingly effective at exploiting those qualities specific to the medium of paint. For Greenberg, even sculpture was to be judged by the same criterion of displaying opticality rather than illusionistic volume.

The most serious, protracted questioning of these ideas was undertaken by artists who came to be known as Minimalists. They frequently saw themselves not as attacking modernism but as pushing modernism's logic to its limits, where many possibilities for art that were not contained within Greenberg's prescriptive modernism opened out. Much of this ground had been prepared earlier in the twentieth century, for example by Duchamp's erasure of the distinction between ordinary objects and art objects, or Neo-Dada's concern with the nature of signs. To the extent that Postmodernism was both a development from and a reaction to modernism, Minimalist art can be seen to have a historically pivotal role.

If Pop, Op, and kinetic art can be considered departures from the priorities of Greenbergian modernism, Minimalism offered a particularly poignant alternative to these ideals. The term "Minimalism" was coined in 1965 to characterize an art of extreme visual reduction, but many Minimalist artists resisted its application to their work. Although the pronounced simplicity of their works was ostensibly in keeping with Greenbergian principles of truth to the medium and the evolution of flatness—that is, the elimination of the illusion of depth on a two-dimensional surface—Minimalism also served to undermine this version of modernism. Minimalist artists discussed their ideas in print, providing an intellectual justification for their dissatisfaction with modernist criticism. With Greenberg and his followers advocating that painting should embrace those qualities unique to the medium (flatness, pictorial surface, and the effect of pure opticality) and that sculpture should aspire to similar goals (an emphasis on surface and optical effect), Minimalist artists began agitating against the supremacy of painting and, above all, to stress the primacy of the object itself. Greenberg's protégé Michael Fried perceived the seriousness of the conflict, observing in 1967 that, "There is … a sharp contrast between the literalist [i.e., Minimalist] espousal of objecthood—almost, it seems, as an art in its own right—and modernist painting's self-imposed imperative that it defeat or suspend its own objecthood through the medium of shape." Minimalist artists denied the modernist belief that works of art should be autonomous—that they should exist in their own terms irrespective of context—and instead considered the importance of a work's environment. They often took into account theories of the psychology of perception and emphasized the importance of the audience's interaction with their pieces, arguing that art need not be absorbed from a single viewpoint in a purely optical fashion. Minimalist art considered not only the eyes of the spectator, but also the body.

Caro

In order to understand the relationship between modernism and Minimalism, it is helpful to consider the work of a key sixties modernist, the young British sculptor **Anthony Caro** (b. 1924). Caro was particularly influenced by the example of Henry Moore, for whom he worked as an assistant between 1951 and 1953. Subsequently, he began to experiment with new materials and with the production of welded metal sculpture. He was encouraged to pursue this direction by a lengthy trip in 1959 to the United States, where he met Clement Greenberg, David Smith, and Kenneth Noland (see figs. 19.39, 19.40, 19.41, 22.20, 22.22). On returning to England, Caro worked actively in a modernist vein, producing sculptures that stressed their presence as physical objects less than their dematerialized optical appearance. Greenberg's 1961 essay on the sculpture of David Smith clarified the goal toward which Caro's work strived:

> To render substance entirely optical, and form, whether pictorial, sculptural or architectural, as an integral part of ambient space—this brings anti-illusionism full circle. Instead of the illusion of things, we are now offered the illusion of modalities: namely, that matter is incorporeal, weightless and exists only optically like a mirage.

In similar fashion, Caro's works often seem to dematerialize in front of the eye, registering their surfaces rather than any sense of bulk. The bright planes of *Midday* (fig. **22.39**) appear almost to float. Similarly, elements of *Riviera* (fig. **22.40**) seem to hover effortlessly in the air.

22.39 Anthony Caro, *Midday*, 1960. Painted steel, 7'7¾" × 2'11⅞" × 12'1¾" (2.3 × 0.91 × 3.7 m). The Museum of Modern Art, New York.

22.40 Anthony Caro, *Riviera*, 1971–74. Rusted steel, 10'7" × 27' × 10' (3.2 × 8.2 × 3 m). Collection Mr. and Mrs. Bagley Wright, Seattle.

Stella

The art of **Frank Stella** (b. 1936) straddled the line between the modernism advocated by Greenberg and Minimalism. One of the youngest and most talented of the artists associated with the new American painting of the sixties, Stella first gained wide recognition in 1960 with a number of works exhibited by New York's Museum of Modern Art during one of its periodic group shows of American artists, on this occasion entitled Sixteen Americans. The "black" paintings shown there were principally large, vertical rectangles, with an absolutely symmetrical pattern of light lines forming regular, spaced rectangles moving inward from the canvas edge to the cruciform center. These lines were not formed by adding white pigment to the canvas—rather, they marked the areas where Stella had *not* laid paint down. In their balanced symmetry and repetition of identical motifs, Stella's paintings were related to experiments by Minimal or Primary Structure sculptors (fig. **22.41**). They had, however, a compelling power of their own, which led modernist critics to praise their optical qualities. Over the next few years, using copper or aluminum paint, Stella explored different

22.41 Frank Stella, *Jasper's Dilemma*, 1962–63. Alkyd on canvas, 6'5" × 12'10" (2 × 3.9 m). Collection Alan Power, London.

shapes for the canvas, which were suggested by variations on his rectilinear pattern. In these, he used deep framing edges, which gave a particular sense of object solidity to the painting. In 1964 the artist initiated a series of "notched V" compositions, whose shapes resulted from the joining of large chevrons. After some explorations of more coloristic rectangular stripe patterns, at times with optical effects, about 1967 Stella turned to brilliantly chromatic shapes, interrelating protractor-drawn semicircles with rectangular or diamond effects. These "protractor" works (fig. **22.42**) sometimes suggest abstract triptychs, with their circular tops recalling later Renaissance altarpieces. The apparent stress that these works placed on their qualities as objects was extremely appealing to Minimalists. At the same time, two friends and former schoolmates of Stella's, the

Greenbergian critic Michael Fried and the Minimalist artist Carl Andre, both struggled for his allegiance. Fried repeatedly claimed that the artist represented modernist principles; Andre worked closely with him and, when Stella's *Black* paintings were included in Sixteen Americans, he wrote a statement about them at his request. Although

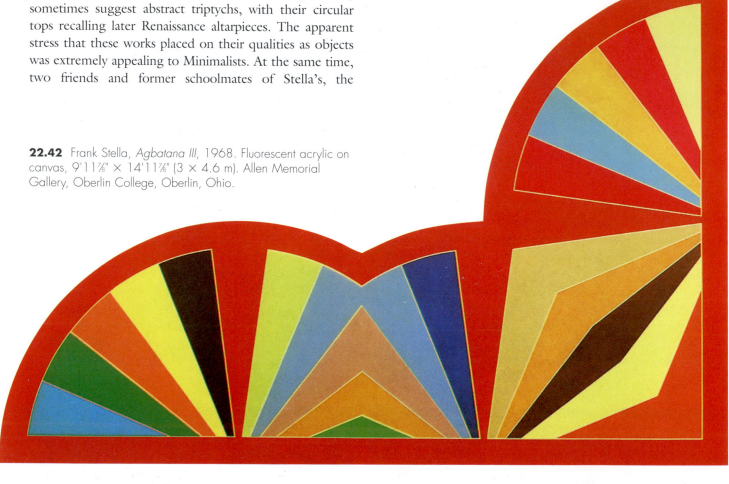

22.42 Frank Stella, *Agbatana III*, 1968. Fluorescent acrylic on canvas, 9'11⅞" × 14'11⅞" (3 × 4.6 m). Allen Memorial Gallery, Oberlin College, Oberlin, Ohio.

 22.43 Frank Stella, Exhibition, 1971. Lawrence Rubin Gallery, New York.

22.44 Frank Stella, *The Pequod Meets the Jeroboam: Her Story, Moby Dick Deckle Edges*, 1993. Lithograph, etching, aquatint, relief, and mezzotint, 70 × 65¼" (177.8 × 165.7 cm). Printed and published by Tyler Graphics Ltd.

Stella refused to connect himself firmly with one group or the other, his work continued to undermine any strict division between painting and sculpture.

In the seventies, Stella moved increasingly toward a form of three-dimensional painted relief, bold in color and dynamic in structure (fig. **22.43**). It became increasingly difficult to tell if the works were paintings or sculptures, for by now the artist was using lacquer and oil colors on aluminum bases. Since then, Stella has remained committed to his abstractions, even as figurative work has increasingly

received significant critical attention. He offered a passionate defense of abstract art in 1983, when he gave a series of six lectures at Harvard University as the Charles Eliot Norton Professor of Poetry. However, his works of the nineties challenge the distinction between abstraction and representation, as Stella strived to produce reliefs that convey narrative significance in a nonfigurative fashion and yet incorporate forms that are suggestive of more naturalistic representation (fig. **22.44**). Stella's works, while not strictly antimodernist, have clearly challenged the narrow critical categories defined by Greenbergian modernism both in terms of form and content. As the art historians Charles Harrison and Paul Wood pointed out, Stella's overt reference to Herman Melville's *Moby-Dick*, in several works offering visual interpretations of poignant themes and moments in the novel, ignores the Greenbergian demand that art should be autonomous from literary content. If Stella's later art no longer retains obvious visual affinities with sixties Minimalism, it nevertheless reflects the legacy of the shift in critical discourse that Minimalism marked.

Smith, Judd, Bladen, and Morris

Despite the fact that the sculptor **Tony Smith** (1912–80) matured artistically during the forties and fifties, his most important impact was felt during the sixties. He came to be celebrated by other Minimalists for pronouncements about the nature of art in general, and about his art in particular, which helped to define the new approach of the group as a whole. Particularly influential was Smith's description of a nighttime drive down an unfinished segment of the New Jersey Turnpike in the fifties:

> The drive was a revealing experience. … [I]t did something for me that art had never done. At first I didn't know what it was, but its effect was to liberate me from many of the views I had about art. … I thought to myself, it ought to be clear that's the end of art. Most painting looks pretty pictorial after that. There is no way you can frame it, you just have to experience it.

22.46 Tony Smith, *Die*, 1962. Steel, edition of three, 6 × 6 × 6' (1.8 × 1.8 × 1.8 m). Private collection.

22.45 Tony Smith, *Cigarette*, 1961–66. Plywood model to be made in steel, 15 × 26 × 18' (4.6 × 7.9 × 5.5 m).

The notion that one had to experience art, not merely imbibe its significance by standing in front of it, manifested itself in Smith's large, abstract pieces, which subvert traditional categories of sculpture and experience. *Cigarette*, 1961–66, demands a physical interaction with the viewer (fig. **22.45**); as he or she moves around the structure, certain aspects of the work appear as others fade from sight. Both memory and movement are required for the appreciation of the work. Despite its association with an everyday, disposable object, the sculpture is by no means pictorial; nor can it be easily cast aside or discarded.

Smith's *Die* of 1962 (fig. **22.46**) has still more obvious affiliations with the common object from which its name derives. However, its scale has been radically increased and the cube bears none of a die's traditional markings. *Die* is not an object that can be thrown thoughtlessly by a human hand. Instead, the steel sculpture cannot even be adequately perceived from a single, frontal viewpoint. Again, the spectator must move around the object, unable to grasp it in its entirety, for the closer one gets, the larger the sculpture grows, reminding its audience of the limits of perception itself.

Donald Judd (1928–94) was one of Minimalism's most important sculptors and theorists. With his art criticism and, in particular, his 1965 essay *Specific Objects*, Judd helped to define the convictions behind the Minimalist questioning of the traditional categories of painting and sculpture. As he wrote in 1965, "A work can be as powerful as it can be thought to be. Actual space is intrinsically more powerful and specific than paint on a flat surface. … A work need only be interesting." For Judd, the "specific object" could not be classified as either a painting or a sculpture, or even precisely described prior to its making, except in principle. The specific object was less about creating particular structures and more about an attitude toward art-making.

Through his sculpture, Judd carried the objective attitude to a point of extreme precision. He repeated identical units, often quadrangular, at regular intervals (fig. **22.47**; fig. **22.48**). These are made of galvanized iron or aluminum, occasionally with Plexiglas. Although Judd sometimes painted the aluminum in strong colors, he at first used the galvanized iron in its original unpainted form, something that seemed to emphasize its neutrality. Progressively, however, Judd used color more frequently in his work, which he began to have professionally manufactured in the mid-sixties.

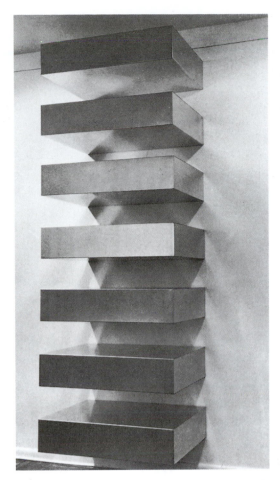

22.47 Donald Judd, *Untitled*, 1965. Galvanized iron, seven boxes, each 9 × 40 × 31" (22.9 × 101.6 × 78.7 cm) [9" (22.9 cm) between each box]. Hirshhorn Museum and Sculpture Garden, Smithsonian Institution, Washington, D.C.

Judd vehemently insisted that Minimal sculpture—most specifically his own—constituted a direction essentially different from earlier Constructivism or rectilinear abstract painting. The difference, as he saw it, lay in his search for an absolute unity or wholeness through repetition of identical units in absolute symmetry. Even Mondrian "composed" a picture by asymmetrical balance of differing color areas.

Judd's works raise fundamental questions concerning the nature and even the validity of the work of art, the nature of the aesthetic experience, the nature of space, and the nature of sculptural form. Like those of most Minimalist sculptors, Judd's works progressively expanded in scale. In 1974 Judd introduced spatial dividers into his sculptures. Three years later he began to construct large-scale works in cement to be installed in the landscape,

22.48 Donald Judd, *Untitled (Progression)*, Edition of seven, 1965. Red lacquer on galvanized iron, 5 × 69 × 8½" (12.7 × 175.3 × 21.6 cm). The Saint Louis Art Museum, Missouri.

22.49 Donald Judd, *Untitled*, 1977. Concrete, outer ring diameter 49'3" (15 m), height 2'11" (0.89 m); inner ring diameter 44'3" (13.5 m), height 2'11"–6'10" (0.89–2.1 m). Collection the City of Münster, Germany.

creating structures of order and harmony that resonated with their environment (fig. **22.49**).

Ronald Bladen (1918–88), a Canadian, used monumental, architectural forms, frequently painted black, that loom up like great barriers in the space they occupy (fig. **22.50**). Like Tony Smith, Bladen made his mock-ups in painted wood, since the cost of executing these vast structures in metal would be exorbitant. Very often Minimalist artists envisioning large-scale structures must await patrons for the final realization of their projects.

Robert Morris (b. 1931), who during the sixties was associated with Minimal sculpture, later became a leader in a wide variety of sculptural, environmental, Conceptual, and Post-Minimalist forms. A student of Tony Smith, Morris, like Donald Judd, proved to be an important advocate of Minimal art. His *Notes on Sculpture* provided an important statement about the heritage to which the Minimalists felt themselves heir—a tradition marked by the Constructivists, the work of David Smith, and the paintings of Mondrian—but perhaps even more important, also about the "gestalt" principles he believed to be crucial to Minimal sculpture. Gestalt (German for shape or form) theory focuses on human perception, describing our ability to understand certain visual relationships as shapes or units. Through his familiarity with these theories, Morris posited that one's body has a fundamental link to one's perception and experience of sculpture. According to Morris, "One knows immediately what is smaller and what is larger than himself. It is obvious, yet important, to take note of the fact that things smaller than ourselves are seen differently than

things larger." Morris's sensitivity to the impact of scale and the corresponding implications of publicness or privateness led to his pioneering work in the organization of entire rooms into a unity of sculptural mass and space.

22.50 Ronald Bladen, *The X*, 1967. Painted wood model to be made in metal, 22'8" × 24'6" × 12'6" (6.9 × 7.5 × 3.8 m). Fischbach Gallery, New York.

22.51 Robert Morris, Exhibition, Green Gallery, New York, 1964. Left to right: *Untitled (Cloud)*, 1964, painted plywood; *Untitled (Boiler)*, 1964, painted plywood; *Untitled (Floor Beam)*, 1964, painted plywood; *Untitled (Table)*, 1964, painted plywood.

During the sixties and seventies, the monumental size of much Minimal sculpture led inevitably to the concept of sculpture designed for a specific space or place. This in turn resulted in ideas such as the use of the gallery space itself as an element in an architectural–sculptural organization. An early experiment in this direction was Morris's 1964 exhibition at the Green Gallery in New York, where large, geometric sculptural modules were integrated within the room, whose space became an element of the total sculpture (fig. **22.51**).

The idea, of course, had been anticipated by such varied sculptural environments as Schwitters's *Merzbau* (see fig. 315) of the twenties and Yves Klein's *Le Vide* exhibition of the late fifties, in which the spectators provided the sculptural accents for the empty, white-walled gallery. The implications of sculpture in place have been explored and expanded enormously during the seventies and extended to environments based on painting, Conceptualism, and Earthworks.

LeWitt, Andre, and Serra

Sol LeWitt (b. 1928) is identified with a type of serial Minimalism consisting of open, identical cubes integrated to form proportionately larger units. These cubes increase in scale until they dominate the architectural space that contains them (fig. **22.52**). In such works, the physical essence is only the outline of the cubes, while the cubes themselves are empty space. Like Judd and Morris, LeWitt

made important theoretical contributions to artistic practice during the later sixties. His *Paragraphs on Conceptual Art*, published in 1967, reiterated the discomfort of Minimalist artists with Greenbergian standards of quality and set the stage for the recognition of yet another digression from the modernism endorsed by Greenberg—Conceptual art (see chapter 24). LeWitt's 1967 essay argued that the most important aspect of a work of art was the idea behind it rather than its form: "The idea becomes a machine that makes the art." LeWitt's 1968 *Box in the*

22.52 Sol LeWitt, *Sculpture Series "A,"* 1967. Installation view, Dwan Gallery, Los Angeles.

22.53 Sol LeWitt, *Wall Drawing No. 652, on Three Walls, Continuous Forms with Color in Washes Superimposed*, 1990. Color-ink wash on wall, approx. 30 × 60' (9.1 × 18.3 m). Shown here as installed temporarily at the Addison Gallery, Andover, Massachusetts, 1993. Now in the Indianapolis Museum of Art.

Hole put his thesis into practice. Created in the Netherlands, this work consisted of a metal cube that the artist buried, covered over, and preserved in a series of recorded photographs.

During the early seventies, LeWitt exploited gallery space in another way—by drawing directly on the walls. These drawings—frequently destroyed at the close of each exhibition—were generally accumulations of rectangles, drawn with a ruler and pencil, toned to various degrees of gray, and accompanied by written specifications. These specifications ensured that a given work could be executed by assistants in the artist's stead. Following LeWitt's conception, the internal lines of each rectangle, creating the tones, might be diagonal as well as vertical or horizontal, and the result was frequently a geometric abstraction of considerable beauty. LeWitt has continued his practice of creating wall installations (fig. **22.53**). Even if the walls are repainted, the piece is not destroyed; it continues to exist as a well-specified idea and can be reinstalled by following the artist's instructions.

The early work of **Carl Andre** (b. 1935), influenced by the ideas of his friend Frank Stella and the sculptor

22.54 Carl Andre, Background, *Pyramid*, 1959/70, wood; middle ground, *Well*, 1964/70, wood; foreground, *Lever*, 1966, firebrick. Installation view. Exhibition at the Solomon R. Guggenheim Museum, New York, 1970.

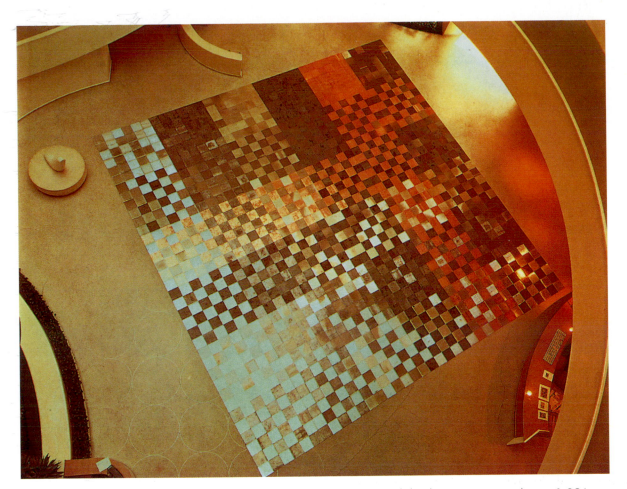

22.55 Carl Andre, *37 Pieces of Work*, Fall 1969. Aluminum, copper, steel, lead, magnesium, and zinc, 1,296 units (216 of each metal), each unit 12 × 12 × ¾" (30.5 × 30.5 × 1.9 cm), overall 36 × 36' (11 × 11 m). Installation view in the rotunda of the Solomon R. Guggenheim Museum, New York, 1970. Now in the Crex Collection, Hallen für neue Kunst, Schaffhausen, Switzerland.

Brancusi, consisted of vertical wooden sculptures, given form by the use of a saw. By the early sixties, Andre had moved away from carving to the construction of sculptures using identical units. The arrangement of the wooden units in *Pyramid* (fig. **22.54**), first created in 1959 and later reconstructed in 1970, suggests a carved form, although the undulations of the surface were not created by the use of a saw.

Other pieces from the early sixties, like *Well* (fig. **22.54**), are more literal in their arrangement. After 1965 Andre began to make horizontally oriented sculptures, known as floorpieces. *Lever* (fig. **22.54**), of 1966, initiated this new phase in his work. These pieces were made out of rugged, industrial materials not traditionally used in fine art. Combined timbers extended horizontally, bricks, styrofoam units, or identical metal squares assembled on the floor were sculptures intended to be walked on.

Since the mid-sixties, Andre's sculpture has not been constructed in the studio, but rather in the exhibition space itself. The idea behind the pieces need only be realized where they are intended for display. One of his most intricate floorpieces, *37 Pieces of Work*, was executed in 1969 on the occasion of his solo show at the Guggenheim (fig.

22.55). The work consisted of a combination of tiles made from six metals: aluminum, copper, steel, magnesium, lead, and zinc. The tiles were a foot square (30.5 cm) and three-quarters of an inch (19 mm) thick. Each metal piece was placed first into a six-by-six-foot (1.8 m) square and then used to create accompanying squares by being alternated with one other metal until every combination had been achieved. The title for the piece comes from the thirty-six-square pattern the metals formed plus the square that encompassed the whole. The work was particularly appropriate for the Guggenheim, where viewers could gaze down on it as they ascended or descended the museum's spiral ramp.

After experimenting with different materials, such as sheets of vulcanized rubber, **Richard Serra** (b. 1939) created sculptures consisting of enormously heavy sheets of steel or lead that balanced against or on top of one another. Despite the various forms that Serra's work takes, it consistently exploits the natural form of the material itself. Rather than manipulate his media, Serra looks to their own physical properties for inspiration. His *Belts*, for example, take their form from the simple act of hanging the rubber loops on the wall (fig. **22.56**). The incorporation of a neon tube

22.56 Richard Serra, *Belts*, 1966–67. Vulcanized rubber, blue neon, 18'1¾" × 6'2⅞" × 1'5⅜" (5.5 × 1.9 × 0.4 m). Solomon R. Guggenheim Foundation, New York.

into the work heightens the viewer's awareness of the intricacies of the forms the draped rubber has created. Serra's *One Ton Prop (House of Cards)* (fig. **22.57**) balances four five-hundred-pound lead sheets against one another. The seemingly casual arrangement of these slabs paradoxically accentuates their weight and communicates a sense of dangerous but exciting precariousness—heightened by the title's reference to the ephemeral, practically weightless house of cards it emulates.

Serra has also been interested in a form of "scatter sculpture," in which series of torn lead sheets are scattered on the floor or molten lead is splashed along the base of a wall. Throughout the seventies and eighties, Serra progressively enlarged the scale of his sculptures, took them out of doors, and combined his sheets of steel with a landscape environment, thus effecting the inevitable transition from sculpture placed in an interior environment to sculpture that becomes part of a landscape (see fig. 24.61).

Minimalist Painters

The senior Minimalist painter is **Agnes Martin** (b. 1912), who refined her art over many years, progressing from rather traditional still lifes to Gorky-like biomorphic abstractions, before arriving in the early sixties at her mature distillations of pure style. This occurred in New York City, where she had moved from New Mexico, taking with her a haunting memory of the desert's powdery air and light. This she evoked by honing her means until they consisted of nothing but large, square canvases gridded all over with lines so delicately defined and subtly spaced as to suggest not austere, cerebral geometry but trembling, spiritual vibrations, what Lawrence Alloway characterized as "a veil, a shadow, a bloom" (fig. **22.58**). Declaring their physical realities and limitations yet mysteriously intangible, intellectually derived but romantic in feeling and effect, the paintings of Agnes Martin are the product of a mind and a sensibility steeped in the meditative, holistic forms of Reinhardt, Rothko, and Newman, as well as the paintings of Paul Klee and the historic landscapes and

22.57 Richard Serra, *One Ton Prop (House of Cards)*, 1969. Lead antimony, four plates, 48 × 48 × 1" (122 × 122 × 2.54 cm). The Museum of Modern Art, New York.

22.58 Agnes Martin, *Night Sea*, 1963. Oil and gold leaf on canvas, 6 × 6' (1.8 × 1.8 m). Private collection.

22.59 Robert Ryman, *Untitled*, 1962. Oil on linen canvas, 69½ × 69½" (176.5 × 176.5 cm). Collection the artist.

poetry of China. While using Hard-Edge structure in a visually self-dissolving or -contradicting manner, Martin had no interest whatever in the retinal games played by Op artists. Nor did she ever aspire to the heroics of the Abstract Expressionists. When Martin felt that she had lost her clarity of vision in 1967, she ceased painting and left New York, returning to New Mexico in 1968. After a period of solitude and contemplation, she resumed painting in the early seventies. Her images retained their subtle, geometric character, but her colors became even softer and more luminous, making visible the artist's sense of life's essence as a timeless, shadowy emanation. "When I cover the square with rectangles," she explained in 1967, "it lightens the weight of the square, destroys its power."

Since the beginning of his career, **Robert Ryman** (b. 1930) has been interested in "how paint worked." His fascination with paint extended from the way in which it was applied to its interaction with its support and the way in which various types of paint worked together. In his earliest work, Ryman explored a range of colors, gradually giving way to his exclusive use of white paint. *Untitled* of 1962 (fig. **22.59**) represents one of the last instances of color in his work. Here multiple white strokes are layered over a background of blue and red, literally suppressing the bright hues while simultaneously reacting to them.

By the mid-sixties Ryman had dedicated himself to the use of white, believing that this color more than any other could highlight his manipulation of paint itself. By way of elucidating his "silent" all-white paintings (fig. **22.60**), Ryman said in a frequently quoted statement, "It's not a question of what to paint but how to paint." With these words he declared his commitment to pure painting. "To make" has often figured in Ryman's conversation, for he considers "making" a matter of knowing the language of his materials—canvas, steel, cardboard, paper, wood, fiberglass, Mylar interacting with oil, tempera, acrylic, epoxy, enamel—and of exploiting its syntax so that his paintings

come alive with their own story. In *Classico III*, Ryman applied white polymer paint in an even film to twelve rectangles of handmade Classico paper precisely assembled to form a larger rectangle gridded by shadows between the smaller units. With these positioned slightly off-center on a white ground, three types of rectangles in different scales and relationships echo and interact with one another. In *Paramount* (fig. **22.61**), Ryman left the margins, the edges, of the canvas unpainted, drawing attention simultaneously to the paint and to the linen surface upon which it rests. His attention to detail is such that even the metal fasteners that join the painting to the wall are considered

22.60 Robert Ryman, *Classico III*, 1968. Polymer on paper, 7'9" × 7'5" (2.4 × 2.3 m). Stedelijk Museum, Amsterdam.

22.61 Robert Ryman, *Paramount*, 1981. Oil on linen with metal fasteners and square bolts, 84" × 84" (213.4 × 213.4 cm). Private collection.

formed by the junction of the two (or more) parts and the drawn line laid down by the artist.

In paintings of the late sixties and early seventies, he used decorative color to accentuate neutral, monotone grounds, while an "error" in the precise, mechanical drawing subverted the geometric overall shape of the canvas from within (fig. **22.62**). Here, destabilized by elusive color and the imperfect internal pattern, stringent formalism gave way to spreading openness and unpredictability, evoking the outside world of nature and humanity. And so Mangold too struck a balance between impersonality and individualism, bringing a welcome warmth to the pervasive cool of Minimalist aesthetics.

The precocious **Brice Marden** (b. 1938) had hardly graduated from the Yale School of Art, where he too worked with Al Held, when he created his signature arrangement of rectangular panels combined in often symbolic order and painted with dense monochrome fields of beeswax mixed with oil (fig. **22.63**). During his career, Marden has become a

part of the work. He takes into account the relationship of the painting to the wall, carefully considering the height at which it is hung and the distance at which it projects forward. By such rigorous attention to material detail and to issues of optical perception, as well as through his painterly touch, Ryman invests his pictures with a lyrical presence, while pursuing a stern Minimalist program of precision and purification.

In his reaction against the perceived excess of Abstract Expressionism, **Robert Mangold** (b. 1937), a student of the Hard-Edge painter Al Held, stressed the factuality of art by creating surfaces so hard, so industrially finished, and so eccentrically shaped that the object quality of the work could not be denied. This assertion of the painting as an object in space was emphasized in several works in which the artist joined canvases, drawing attention to the importance of edges and creating a play between the real line

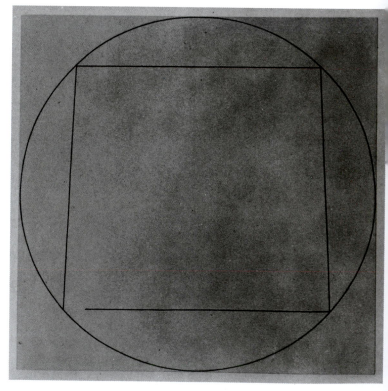

22.62 Robert Mangold, *Untitled*, 1973. Acrylic and pencil on Masonite, 24 × 24" (61 × 61 cm). John Weber Gallery, New York.

22.63 Brice Marden, *The Dylan Painting*, 1966. Oil and wax on canvas, 5' × 10' (1.52 × 3 m). Collection Helen Portugal, New York.

virtuoso in his ability to balance color, surface, and shape throughout an extended series of variations, developed within a set of purposeful restrictions.

In the late seventies, Marden began to introduce a combination of vertical and horizontal planes within his paintings. Despite the abstract quality of his images, however, Marden continues to negotiate an underlying relationship between his painting and nature. His series of *Elements* paintings, begun in 1981, incorporates red, yellow, blue, and green—colors that medieval alchemists used to symbolize, respectively, fire, air, water, and earth. Subsequently, Marden introduced a curving, calligraphic line into his

paintings. His study of Chinese calligraphy and corresponding interest in Asian culture inform his *Cold Mountain* paintings, named in honor of the ninth-century Chinese poet whose name comes from his sacred dwelling spot (fig. **22.64**). The layering and interplay of lines and pigment comment on the process of painting itself. The rhythmic, allover disposition of the calligraphic marks produces a sense of balance, harmony, and precision much in keeping with his earlier painting. Here again, then, is the Minimalist paradox of an extreme simplicity that is capable of rewarding sustained contemplation with revelations of unsuspected spiritual complexity or sheer aesthetic pleasure.

22.64 Brice Marden, *Cold Mountain 5 (Open)*, 1988–91. Oil on linen, 9 × 12' (2.7 × 3.7 m). Collection Robert and Jane Meyerhoff, Phoenix, Maryland.

Drawing directly on the wall or attaching to it a flattened, geometric shape created merely by folding brown wrapping paper (fig. **22.65**), **Dorothea Rockburne** (b. 1921) might seem to have so reduced her means as to take Minimalism over the line into *Arte povera*, an Italian movement characterized by its use of humble materials (see chapter 24). However, the direction proved quite different, fixed by the artist's preoccupation with the mathematics of set theory as an intellectually pure strategy for creating an intricate interplay of simple geometric forms and real space.

So dependent was this art on process itself that Rockburne created it directly on the gallery wall, thereby condemning her pieces to a poignant life of fragility and impermanence. She subsequently worked in more durable materials and installations, as well as with richer elements, such as color and texture (fig. **22.66**). Nevertheless, Rockburne remained loyal to her fundamental principle of

"making parts that form units that go together to make larger units." In the end, the logical yet unexpected way in which her scientifically derived but imaginative folding produces flat, prismatic shapes seduces the eye while engaging the mind. It also reveals why the challenge of working within Minimalism's puritanically self-denying regimen appealed to some of the most gifted artists to emerge in the sixties.

During the sixties, **Jo Baer** (b. 1929) eliminated the brushwork and painterly texture of her earlier work to create pieces whose smooth surfaces showed little evidence of the artist's hand. By reducing the visual interest of the surface itself, Baer believed that the spectator could focus on the image as a whole. Like Robert Morris, Baer incorporated the principles of Gestalt psychology into her work, using her images to test the limits of human perception, and thus drawing attention to the object nature of the canvas itself. In 1969, Baer began her *Wraparound* series,

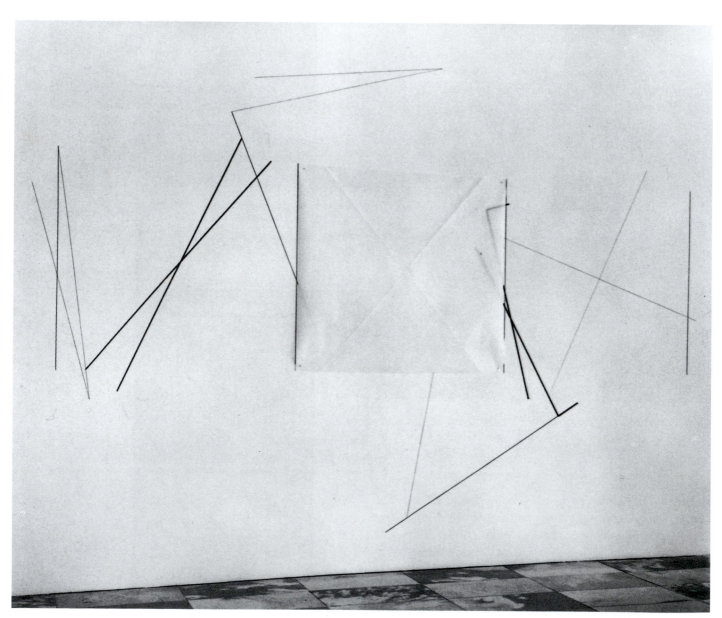

22.65 Dorothea Rockburne, *Indication Drawing Series: Neighborhood* from the wall series *Drawing Which Makes Itself*, 1973. Wall drawing: pencil and colored pencil with vellum, 13'4" × 8'4" (4.1 × 2.5 m). The Museum of Modern Art, New York.

22.66 Dorothea Rockburne, *The Glory of Doubt, Pascal*, 1988–89. Watercolor and gold leaf on prepared acetate and watercolor on museum board, 3'8¹³⁄₁₆" × 6'1¾" (1.14 × 1.9 m).

which involved wrapping a painted black band outlined in color around the edge of the stretcher (fig. **22.67**). Looking at the work from a certain angle, the viewer can perceive the whole band, but upon closer inspection it becomes evident that the flat solid that one perceived is actually painted on two adjacent surfaces. The canvas is no longer purely surface, but a three-dimensional entity, relying upon all of its surfaces to produce its particular effect. The colored bands in *Untitled (Wraparound Triptych— Blue, Green, Lavender)* play an important role, for it is the borders of an image that first signal the presence of a shape to the human brain.

22.67 Jo Baer, *Untitled (Wraparound Triptych—Blue, Green, Lavender)*, 1969–74. Oil on canvas, each panel 48 × 52" (122 × 132 cm). Collection the artist.

Complex Unities: Photography and Minimalism

Minimalism's visual achievements can also be associated with photography. Serialism, an interest in process as a key source of content, and a search for the complex within the simple, unified image are all fundamental to the Minimalist aesthetic, and can be found in the fieldlike collages created by **Ray K. Metzker** (b. 1931), a former student of Harry Callahan (see figs. 19.62, 19.63) at the Institute of Design in Chicago. But, like most photographers in the "straight" tradition, Metzker begins with a real-life subject. Having photographed this, not as a single, fixed image but rather as a series of related moments, he then combines, repeats, juxtaposes, and superimposes the shots until he has achieved a composite, gridlike organization reminiscent of Minimalist painting, a single visual entity in which the whole is different and more rewarding than its parts (fig. **22.68**). Metzker says of his work, "Where photography has been primarily a process of selection and extraction, I wish to investigate the possibilities of synthesis."

Bernd Becher (b. 1931) and **Hilla Becher** (b. 1934), German photographers married in 1961, together developed the documentary style for which they have become

22.69 Bernd and Hilla Becher, *Water Towers*, 1980. Black-and-white photographs, 61¼ × 49¼" (155.6 × 125.1 cm). Courtesy Sonnabend Gallery, New York.

22.68 Ray K. Metzker, *Untitled (Wanamaker's)*, 1966–67. Multiple printing, 32¼ × 34¾" (82 × 89.3 cm). The Museum of Modern Art, New York.

known. The Bechers turned their attention to the industrial transformation of the Western world, taking stark, closely cropped photographs of its hallmark architectural structures. Their photographs are frequently arranged into series of visually similar buildings and hung together in the format of a grid (fig. **22.69**). Within these typological studies, each photograph functions as an independent unit, but the virtually uniform lighting and the similarity in form and viewpoint produce an effect of serial repetition that could be compared to the sculptures of Judd or Andre. Such interest in the individuality of units within similar types has a history in German photography that extends to the work of August Sander (see chapter 13). As teachers, the Bechers have influenced several generations of photographers in Germany and abroad.

23
The Second Wave of International Style Architecture

The achievements of modern architecture in the first third of the twentieth century were a series of relatively isolated experiments: Prairie Style, Secession, Deutscher Werkbund, de Stijl, Expressionism, Bauhaus, and International Style. Of all these initiatives of modernism, the International Style was by far the most enduring; almost inevitably, it eventually became the most diluted.

Economic depression followed by World War II meant that there was little innovative large-scale architecture in America and Europe in the thirties and forties. When the first great wave of new buildings came, it was the International Style that dominated. The acceptance of International Style architecture in postwar America, where many key members of the prewar European avant-garde had settled, in turn led to its being reexported to other nations intent on modernization, as in Latin America, or reconstruction, as in Europe. By the mid-sixties, however, critics of the International Style were expressing their disenchantment with its dogmatic loyalty to functionalism and its technology-driven aesthetic. Opposition to International Style/Bauhaus style in the seventies took form in what began to be called Postmodernism (see chapter 25). Postmodernism's efforts to encompass the pluralism of a more completely global world, while simultaneously acknowledging the history and lessons of early styles and movements, resulted in hybrid styles that flew in the face of the reductive, rational purity of the International Style.

Architects in the second half of the twentieth century were able to develop new concepts of space, either employing new structural systems or using older methods, such as ferroconcrete, in new ways. Besides the skyscraper and other urban office buildings, some of the areas in which architects worked on an unprecedented scale included industrial plants and research centers; university campuses; religious structures; cultural centers, including museums, theaters, and concert halls; and airports. Four broad tendencies can be discerned in postwar architecture: the purist modernism of Gropius's or Mies van der Rohe's International Style; architecture that, in various different

ways, modified this austerity with sculptural inflections (for example, the work of Saarinen or Kahn); Postmodernist architecture, such as Renzo Piano and Richard Rogers's Pompidou center; and the work of late modernists, such as Meier or Pei, who remained dedicated to an elegant expression of modernism in the Postmodern era.

The Avant-Garde Diaspora: Architecture in the 1930s

With the exception of new concepts still developing in the field of engineering, by 1930 many of the ideas of twentieth-century architecture had been stated in one form or another. The early thirties saw retrogressive styles making a comeback, particularly in communist and fascist countries such as Russia and Germany. In those countries and, to a lesser degree, in Italy, a ponderous Neoclassical style took the place of innovation. Even in France, despite the achievements of Le Corbusier, official buildings, such as the 1937 Museum of Modern Art in Paris, frequently reverted to a form of Neoclassicism. (In contrast, during this period and since, Finland and the Scandinavian countries—Sweden, Norway, and Denmark—made notable contributions to modern design in architecture, furniture, crafts, and industrial products.)

In the United States, modernist continental European architecture was not well received, certainly not in American schools of architecture, which were teaching in the Beaux-Arts tradition well into the second quarter of the twentieth century. In the thirties, things began to change after the 1931 exhibition, The International Style: Architecture Since 1922, organized by the architectural historian Henry-Russell Hitchcock and the architect Philip Johnson and held in the newly opened Museum of Modern Art in New York. The exhibition (and catalog, *The International Style*, written in 1932 by Johnson and Hitchcock) included examples of projects from fifteen countries. The term "International Style" was itself notable, for what had begun a decade earlier as the intimation of a new spirit of restless originality had crystallized into a style that the show's curators had been able to identify in buildings from many countries around the world. By the mid-thirties, with the wider dissemination of the principles of the new architecture, even more countries had at least one or two buildings that were clearly influenced by the designs of such early International Style pioneers as Le Corbusier and Mies van der Rohe. The spread of the modern movement in the early thirties was furthered by private patronage and competitions, as well as by municipal and commercial bodies.

In the mid-thirties, the United States benefited from the immigration of many scientists, artists, and architects escaping from Nazi repression. Walter Gropius (see fig. 16.5) quit the Bauhaus in 1928 and moved to England in 1934, where he stayed for three years and collaborated with British International Style architect Maxwell Fry in the design of Impington Village College near Cambridge. In 1937, Gropius left for the United States, to become professor and then chairman of the Department of Architecture at Harvard University. Marcel Breuer (see fig. 16.1) also arrived in America in 1937, joining Gropius at Harvard. They remained in partnership until 1941, when Breuer established his own practice.

Also in 1937, László Moholy-Nagy (see figs. 17.1–17.3) had been invited to Chicago to form a New Bauhaus. In the same year, Josef Albers (see figs. 17.8, 17.9) arrived in America to teach design and painting, first at Black Mountain College in North Carolina, and then at Yale University. In 1938, Mies van der Rohe (see fig. 16.7), who had arrived in the United States the year before, was invited to the Illinois Institute of Technology (then the Armour Institute) in Chicago. José Luis Sert, a socialist architect committed to the integration of architecture and social planning, emigrated from Spain to the United States in 1939 and in 1958 became dean of the Harvard

Graduate School of Design in Cambridge, Massachusetts. So it was largely as a result of Gropius's and Mies's efforts, as well as those of a few other distinguished émigrés, that architectural schools were transformed over the next twenty years and American architecture entered genuinely into the age of modern architectural experiment. In the same way, Moholy-Nagy, Albers, and others had a powerful effect on industrial, product, and graphic design in the United States.

"The Quiet Unbroken Wave": The Later Work of Wright and Le Corbusier

Throughout the early thirties, **Frank Lloyd Wright** (1867–1959) (see chapter 16) continued to critique modernism and the International Style through his writings and new building designs. While he was aware of Art Deco revivalism, which had a tremendous influence in the United States, as well as the extreme austerity of the International Style in Europe, his sympathies lay elsewhere. In a manner parallel to the late style of Wright, that of **Le Corbusier** (1887–1965) was characterized by the exploration of free, organic forms and the statement of the materials of construction.

Wright

Despite his focus on the circular theme in the 1936–39 Johnson Building in Racine, Wisconsin (see fig. 16.17), Wright did not desert the rectangle or the triangle. Taliesin West is the winter headquarters that he began to build for himself and the Taliesin Fellowship in 1937 near Phoenix, Arizona, which, characteristically, was still being built and rebuilt at the time of Wright's death in 1959. It is in plan and elevation a series of interlocked triangles. The architect's most dramatic assimilation of buildings into a natural

23.1 Frank Lloyd Wright, Taliesin West, Scottsdale, Arizona, 1937–38.

environment, it becomes an outgrowth of the desert and mountain landscape (fig. **23.1**).

Wright also used primary forms for his great unbuilt project, Broadacre City, and for his Usonian houses—innovative low-cost homes for middle-income families. He completed a number of buildings based on the circle, the climax of which is the Solomon R. Guggenheim Museum (see fig. 23.2). First conceived in 1943, it was not completed until 1959, after Wright's death. The Guggenheim Museum, sited on Fifth Avenue across from Central Park, is the only building that this leading American architect was ever commissioned to do in New York City, and it was many years before he could obtain the necessary building permits for so revolutionary a structure. As designed by Wright, it consisted of two parts: the main exhibition hall and a small administration wing (known as the monitor building), both circular in shape. A smooth, unbroken white band that stretches across the museum's Fifth Avenue façade connects the two sections, giving the appearance of seamless unity. The gallery proper is a continuous spiral ramp around an open central well. The building radiates outward toward the top, the ramps broadening as the building rises, in order to provide ample light and space. A skylight dome on graceful ribs provides natural, general lighting, and continuous strip-lighting around the ramps provides additional illumination. Permanent fins divide the exhibition areas of the ramps into equal bays, where the art is shown. Wright believed that architecture should essentially involve movement, not just be a fixed enclosure of space, and the Guggenheim's spiral form was the ultimate expression of his effort to get beyond the box. Explaining his concept to a skeptical public, Wright noted that his design provided "a greater repose, the atmosphere of the quiet unbroken wave: no meeting of the eye with abrupt changes of form."

As a museum, the Guggenheim offers easy and efficient circulation in one continuous spiral, in contrast to the traditional museum with galleries consisting of interconnected, rectangular rooms. Some of Wright's detractors have criticized the design of the Guggenheim's slanting walls and ramps for competing too strongly for the viewer's attention with the artwork. On the other hand, supporters argue that this museum succeeds in what few others even attempt: to be more than a passive site for curatorial activities and to actively engage the viewer's experience of the art, which can be seen across the rotunda as well as at close range.

In 1982, the architectural firm of Gwathmey Siegel was commissioned to renovate the museum in order to accommodate the need for expanded gallery, storage, and administrative space. The architects were required to bring the aging building into line with the latest museum technology, and to create an addition that would include gallery spaces capable of accommodating large-scale contemporary art. Work on the museum involved two distinct challenges: a restoration of the building to some semblance of

23.2 Frank Lloyd Wright, Solomon R. Guggenheim Museum, New York, 1957–59. Addition 1989–1992.

Wright's intentions, and an expansion plan that involved alterations of the original structure.

The restoration provoked almost as much controversy and publicity as had Wright's original design, and some critics have argued that a major icon of American architecture has been tragically compromised. The new addition (fig. **23.2**) consists of a thin rectangular slab whose beige limestone façade is ornamented with a gridded pattern. Four new floors of galleries, three of which have double-height ceilings, make it possible to show large-scale works for the first time. In its present renovated state, which was opened to the public in 1992, the great spiral—a monumental sculpture in its own right—was opened all the way to the reexposed dome, where new ultraviolet-filtering glass was installed. Formerly unused roof space was converted into a sculpture terrace providing sweeping views of Central Park, invoking the intrinsic connection between Wright's architecture and nature.

Le Corbusier

The enormous 1947–52 building in Marseilles, France, known as the Unité d'Habitation (fig. **23.3**), an apartment complex designed primarily for blue-collar workers, both carries out Le Corbusier's town-planning ideas and asserts its rough-surfaced concrete structure as if a massive sculpture. The building is composed of 337 small duplex apartments, with a two-story living room, developed in Le Corbusier's earlier housing schemes. It includes shops, restaurants, and recreation areas, to constitute a self-contained community (community facilities are provided on the roof). Unités were also built in the French town of Nantes and in Berlin. In them, Le Corbusier abandoned the concept of concrete as a precisely surfaced machine-age material and presented it in its rough state, as it came from the molds. In doing so, he inaugurated a new style—almost a new age—in modern architecture, to which the

23.4 Le Corbusier, Interior, Notre-Dame-du-Haut, Ronchamp, France, 1950–54.

name Brutalism was later given. Possibly related to the French word *brut* (uncut, rough, raw), the term has taken many forms, but fundamentally involves the idea of "truth to materials" and the blunt statement of their nature and essence. Frank Lloyd Wright had preached this doctrine from the beginning of his career, and the epitome of the International Style architect, Mies van der Rohe, in his own way was as ruthlessly dedicated to the statement of glass and steel as Le Corbusier was to the statement of concrete. Brutalism, however, most characteristically manifests itself in reinforced concrete, not only because of its texture but even more because of its innate sculptural properties.

Le Corbusier's seminal pilgrimage chapel of Notre-Dame-du-Haut at Ronchamp in France (fig. **23.4**, fig. **23.5**), built in 1950–54, is a brilliant example of his new sculptural style. Completed during the height of a new formalism in the United States (for example, the cultural center complex of buildings at Lincoln Center in New York City—see fig. 23.34), the Ronchamp chapel represented a radical departure from Le Corbusier's previous projects. Sensitively and elegantly attuned to the hilltop site on which it was built, the structure is molded of white concrete topped by the dark, floating mass of the roof and accented by towers (inspired by Roman emperor Hadrian's villa at Tivoli, near Rome), which together serve as a geometric counterpoint to the main mass. The interior is lit by windows of varying sizes and shapes that open up from small apertures to create focused tunnels of light, evoking a rarefied spirituality. Its external, curvilinear forms and the mystery of its interior recall prehistoric grave forms. Since Ronchamp, form, function, symbolism, and plasticity have all taken on new meaning. This structure succeeded in relaxing architects' formerly traditional attitudes toward form and space; the "box" was finally exploded.

In the fifties, Le Corbusier was finally given the opportunity to put into effect his lifelong ideas on total city planning in the design and construction at Chandigarh, a new capital for the Punjab in India, on which he worked into the sixties. The city of Chandigarh is situated on a plain at

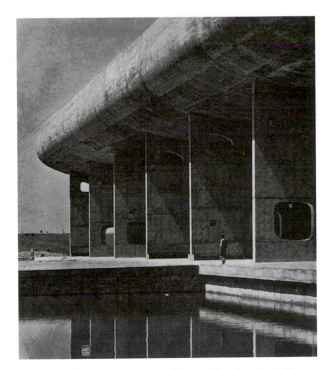

23.6 Le Corbusier, Assembly Building, Chandigarh, India, 1959–62.

the edge of hills, and the government buildings, comprising the Secretariat, the Assembly, and the High Court, rise to the north in the foothills, with the three buildings arranged in an arc around a central area incorporating terraces, gardens, and pools. The Court Building was conceived as a giant umbrella beneath which space was made available for court functions and for the general public. Access roads to the city are largely concealed, while changing vistas are achieved through ingeniously placed man-made mounds. The Assembly Building (fig. **23.6**) is the most impressive of the three, with its ceremonial entrance portico and upward-curving roof set on pylons, the whole reflected in the pool and approached by a causeway. Le Corbusier's achievement is embodied not only in the individual buildings but also in their subtle visual relationships to one another. The total complex constitutes a fitting climax to Le Corbusier's career; it fulfilled the request of the client, Prime Minister Jawaharlal Nehru, that the city be "symbolic of the freedom of India, unfettered by the traditions of the past," in its new era of independent statehood following the end of British rule in 1947.

Purity and Proportion: The International Style in America

The Influence of Gropius and Mies van der Rohe

In stark contrast to Wright, who always maintained his role as "chief architect" supported by his Taliesin Fellowship, **Walter Gropius** (1883–1969) soon put into effect his principles of collaboration, a "team approach" to design, and his ideas concerning the social responsibilities of the architect (see chapter 16). For Gropius, who had founded

23.5 Le Corbusier, Notre-Dame-du-Haut, Ronchamp, France, 1950–54.

the Bauhaus in 1919 on these ideas, collaboration meant that architects, landscape architects, and city planners would work together to create a cohesive vision of the modern world. This view increasingly gained acceptance in the profession and would eventually triumph over Wright's approach. In 1945, with some of his students, Gropius formed The Architects' Collaborative (TAC) to design buildings in the United States and elsewhere. At Harvard he continued his design of school structures with the Harvard Graduate Center of 1949–50. Here he had the problem of placing a modern building among traditional structures dating from the eighteenth to the twentieth century. He made no compromises with tradition but used stone and other materials to enrich and give warmth and variety to his modern structure. He also commissioned artists such as Miró, Arp, and Albers to design murals, thus introducing to Harvard the Bauhaus concept of the integration of the arts. In his later years with TAC, Gropius moved again into full-scale architectural production. Perhaps the most ambitious of the later designs was the 1953 Boston Back Bay Center (fig. **23.7**), unfortunately never constructed. This was a large-scale project comprising office buildings, a convention hall, a shopping center, an underground parking lot, and a motel. It involved two slab structures set in a T form, raised on stilts above intricate, landscaped pedestrian walks and driveways. The façades were to have been richly textured, and the entire complex represented a superior example of recent American experiments in the creation of total industrial, mercantile, or cultural centers—social and environmental experiments with which Gropius himself had been concerned in Germany during the twenties.

Having completed relatively few buildings before leaving Germany in 1937, **Mies van der Rohe** (1886–1969)

was finally able to put his ideas into practice in the United States, a country that since the Depression had witnessed almost no new major public constructions. Big institutions were eager to put up new buildings and to develop a new architecture. In the skyscrapers he created, as well as in the new campus for the Illinois Institute of Technology (IIT), Mies's solutions had an incalculable influence on younger architects everywhere. The plan of the Institute, as drawn by Mies in 1940, has an abstract quality characterized by rectangular complexes. Located in a deteriorating area on the south side of Chicago, the school complex, with its conception of architecture geared to industrialization and standardization, became a model of efficient organization and urban planning. In fact, it inspired large-scale slum clearance in the area, a process that was intended to, but ultimately did not, eliminate overcrowding and physical deterioration of older buildings there. Of steel-and-glass construction, the IIT buildings are organized on a modular principle. Each unit in itself and in relation to others exemplifies Mies's sensitivity to every aspect of proportion and detail of construction.

After having envisioned (but not built) two highly advanced skyscraper designs in around 1920 (see fig. 16.7), Mies was finally able to carry out some of his ideas in his 1951 apartments on Lake Shore Drive in Chicago (see fig. 23.10) and in the 1956–57 Seagram Building, on which Philip Johnson collaborated (see fig. 23.12). Both the Seagram Building, Mies's first New York building, and his 1964 Federal Center in Chicago represent the climax of a development in the United States that began with Sullivan and the Chicago School, was diverted during the age of eclecticism, and gradually came back to its original principles. The common element of this development is the use of steel I-beams, which were fundamental to Chicago

23.7 Walter Gropius, Project for City Center for Boston Back Bay, 1953.

23.8 Mies van der Rohe, New National Gallery, Berlin, 1968. Sculpture by Alexander Calder.

School construction and which Mies used almost decoratively on the exteriors of some of his skyscrapers. In his later works, such as the 1963–68 National Gallery in Berlin (fig. **23.8**), Mies not only refined his modular system to a point of utmost simplicity, but, using a suspended frame structure, was able to realize his ideals of a complete and uninterrupted interior space divisible or subdivisible at will. For Mies, space was neutral and floating; the structure was a grid. Many imitators have tried to copy his forms through their continuous repetition of the steel-and-glass motif, but usually without his feeling for space, scale, and proportion. His perception of universal, open, and flexible space is as fundamental to modern architecture as is the free plan of Le Corbusier.

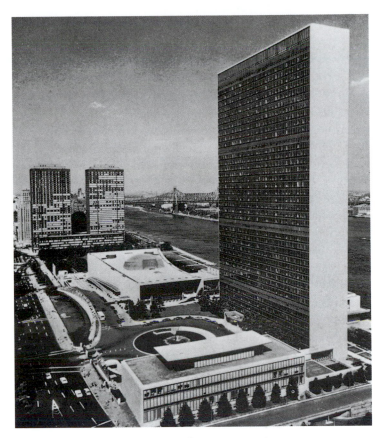

23.9 Wallace K. Harrison, United Nations Headquarters, New York, 1947–50.

Skyscrapers

In 1947, an international group of architects (including Le Corbusier and Oscar Niemeyer—see below) met in New York under the general direction of **Wallace K. Harrison** (1895–1981) to design the permanent headquarters of the newly formed United Nations organization (fig. **23.9**). Situated at the edge of New York's East River and built between 1947 and 1950, this building was the first monument of the postwar renaissance in American architecture. Symbolically the most important building to be constructed in the aftermath of World War II, the headquarters complex represents the epitome of modern functionalism and midcentury optimism. Aesthetically, it attempted to replace diverse national traditions with a design appropriate to the universal concept of the new world organization. The thirty-nine-story Secretariat, a glass-and-aluminum curtain-wall building, introduced to the United States a concept of the skyscraper as a tall, rectangular slab; in this case the sides are sheathed in glass and the ends are clad in marble.

Le Corbusier was principally responsible for the main forms of the Secretariat, but its simplified, purified structure embodies the Bauhaus tradition of Gropius and Mies van der Rohe, who designed the Lake Shore Drive Apartments in Chicago in 1951 (fig. **23.10**). The skyscrapers of Louis Sullivan and the Chicago School fascinated Mies and drew him to study the skyscraper form. The basic

23.10 Mies van der Rohe, Lake Shore Drive Apartments, Chicago, 1951.

problems—of steel structure, its expression, and its sheathing—were of longstanding interest. (He had already explored these problems in his earlier unbuilt skyscraper designs.) The twin Lake Shore apartment buildings consist of two interrelated twenty-six-story vertical blocks set at right angles to each other. The steel structural members accent the verticality. As is customary with Mies, the structures are built on a module and have floor-to-ceiling windows.

The inspiration of Mies and the United Nations building led immediately to the first large office building of the fifties, Lever House (fig. **23.11**), completed in 1952 by the architectural firm of **Skidmore, Owings & Merrill**, with Gordon Bunshaft as chief architect. Lever House, which was intended as a monument-symbol for an international corporation, is a tall rectangular slab, occupying only a small part of a New York city block. It is raised on pylons that support the first enclosed level—the principal public areas—thus giving the total structure a vertical L-shape. The building is one of the first to have an all-glass-clad façade and windows of alternating horizontal ribbons of opaque green and light green tinted glass.

Across Park Avenue from Lever House is a masterpiece of skyscraper architecture, Mies van der Rohe's 1958 Seagram Building (fig. **23.12**). In it Mies and Philip

23.11 Skidmore, Owings & Merrill, Lever House, New York, 1951–52.

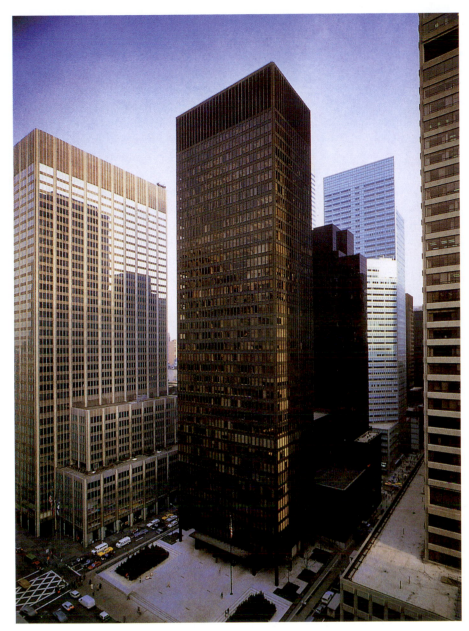

23.12 Mies van der Rohe and Philip Johnson, Seagram Building, New York, 1958.

Johnson were given an unparalleled opportunity to create a monument to modern industry, comparable to the Gothic cathedrals that had been monuments to medieval religious belief. The building is a statement of the slab principle, isolated with absolute symmetry within a broad plaza lightened by balanced details of fountains. The larger skeleton structure is clearly apparent within the more delicate framing of the window elements that sheathe the building. The materials of bronze and amber glass lend the exterior an opaque solidity that does not interfere with the total impression of light that fills the interior. The building is perhaps the consummate expression of Mies's emphasis on "the organizing principle of order as a means of achieving the successful relationship of the parts to each other and to the whole." In addition to its dramatic utilization of International Style principles of design, the Seagram Building is noted also for its detachment from the surrounding city streets. A deeply set plaza pushes the building away from the busy traffic, while the abrupt termination of the glass curtain—one floor above the plaza—appears to raise the building on stilts. No other building of modern times has had such influence on subsequent skyscraper design. Through the late sixties and seventies, skyscrapers were constructed in increasing numbers and heights throughout the world, although distinguished examples of the form were the exceptions.

Until 1974, the world's tallest skyscraper (1,454 feet, or 443 m) was the Sears Tower in Chicago (fig. **23.13**), designed by Skidmore, Owings & Merrill. Conceived as a bundle of nine "tubes" lashed together for mutual bracing, the Sears Tower would seem to return to the original pragmatism of Bauhaus aesthetics, in that each of the independent but clustered tubes has its own height and setback, dictated by the internal needs of corporate activity.

23.13 Skidmore, Owings & Merrill, Sears Roebuck Tower, Chicago, 1966–69.

The blank anodized aluminum skin is highly functional—it resists weathering and soot better than other materials, while also symbolizing the sobriety of the retailing enterprise originally headquartered within the structure.

Domestic Architecture

After World War II, as roads and highways made outlying areas more accessible than ever, and as a war-based economy was replaced by peacetime values and normalization of life, the market for single-family houses exploded. The variations on the theme of the detached house in the International Style were endless and interchangeable from country to country. Much of the early American architecture of Gropius and Breuer consisted of homes following Bauhaus principles. For Gropius, standardization satisfied the needs of the masses for economical housing. Marcel Breuer's own second house at New Canaan, Connecticut, built in 1951, illustrates his ability to use materials that blend with the local environment. In this case, Breuer selected principally concrete and fieldstone, with weathered wood beams used for the ceilings (fig. **23.14**).

Mies van der Rohe built only one house in the United States—the Farnsworth House in Plano, Illinois—but Philip Johnson's own home, Glass House, in New Canaan, Connecticut (1949) (fig. **23.15**), is a classic extension of Miesian principles of uninterrupted interior space. Few "boxes" have reached the level of rationalism and sophistication of the main house, which is a transparent glass "box." With its supreme structural clarity, the main house provides protection yet destroys the boundaries between nature and interior space, while the guesthouse, at the other extreme, is an enclosed structure.

Richard Neutra (1892–1970), an émigré from Austria, developed his practice on the basis of the American preoccupation with building houses. A winter home in Palm Springs, California, for Edgar Kaufmann—the same client who in the thirties had commissioned Fallingwater from Frank Lloyd Wright (see fig. 16.16)—was designed for a desert site by Neutra, who had been an employee of Wright in the twenties. Set against a spectacular backdrop, the Kaufmann House (1947) (fig. **23.16**) is pristine and cool in its elegant rectilinearity. Glass is used generously, and the plan is arranged so that the space flows from interior to exterior with unfettered freedom. Walls can be pulled back to allow the interior to become part of the wide outdoor courtyard spaces. Neutra combined glass, stucco, and natural rock in this house, which is shaped in a cross

23.14 Marcel Breuer, House II, New Canaan, Connecticut, 1951.

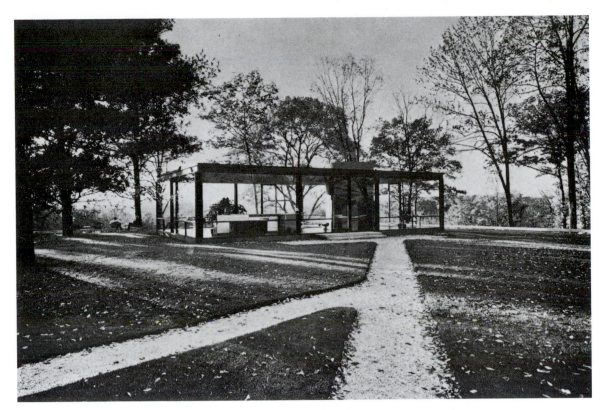

23.15 Philip Johnson, Glass House, New Canaan, Connecticut, 1949.

23.16 Richard Neutra, Kaufmann House, Palm Springs, California, 1947.

of two intersecting axes. In his work and writing, Neutra advocated the link between architecture and the general health of the human nervous system. His physiological concerns addressed the beneficial impact of well-designed architecture and ambient environment. Though his buildings could function independently of their site, Neutra, like Wright, felt that landscape was more important than historical precedent.

Internationalism Contextualized: Developments in Scandinavia, Europe, Latin America, Asia, and Australia

Finland

Alvar Aalto (1898–1976) created architecture that is characterized by a warmth and humanity in his use of materials; by buildings that are individualized; and by a harmony with human scale. Aalto never abandoned the timeless quality of the traditional architecture of his Finnish homeland. His structures seem to grow out of the site and to solve particular design problems, whether those of factory, house, school, or town plan. Aalto was also a leading furniture designer known for his bentwood chairs and tables.

Aalto made his debut in 1937 with the interior of the Savoy Restaurant in Helsinki, where he introduced his perforated plywood screen and free-form furnishings, quite different in style from the understated luxury of the Villa Mairea (1939) in Noormarkku, Finland (fig. **23.17**), designed for patrons Harry and Maire Gullichsen. The villa anticipates Aalto's own words of the following year, when he wrote that the function of architecture is to "bring the material world into harmony with human life." Villa Mairea is highly compatible with natural materials and clearly harmonizes with the fir forest that surrounds it. Aalto employed polished teak and other woods and rough masonry throughout in order to soften the modernist rigor of his design. Warm-toned wood is used inside in the paneled flooring and slatted ceilings, the columns, and in his own birchwood furniture.

Aalto's was a major response against the machine aesthetic that was creative rather than reactionary. In nonresidential buildings, traditional rectangular windows replaced the "orthodox" glass curtain wall. He expanded the vocabulary of avant-garde architecture to the point where the original sources of the new style all but vanished, and he established a distinctly personal alternative. Irregular, even picturesque, shapes and masses dominate his work, but the very informality of his buildings defies comparison with Mies or Le Corbusier. There are affinities in Aalto's work with the organic, site-specific forms of Wright, the exuberant expressionism of Erich Mendelsohn, and the cool rationality of Gropius. But his free-form brick and glass-brick walls and undulating wood vaults made fresh use of natural materials. Even his grandest structures have a human scale. His versatility helped establish a distinctive brand of modernism that still flourishes in Finland and Scandinavia.

As the leading architect of far northern Europe, Aalto had opportunities to experiment with public buildings, churches, and town planning, and he achieved one of his most personal expressions in the Town Hall at Säynätsalo (fig. **23.18**). This is a center for a small Finnish town, and includes a council room, library, offices, shops, and homes. The brick structure with broken, tilted rooflines merges with the natural environment. Heavy timbers, beautifully detailed, are used for ceilings to contrast with the brick walls inside. Somewhat romantic in concept, this center illustrates the combination of effective planning and respect for the natural environment characteristic of Aalto and the best northern European architecture.

Great Britain

After the pioneering work of the late nineteenth century by William Morris, Philip Webb, Charles Voysey, and Charles Rennie Mackintosh (see figs. 4.6, 4.8, 4.9), there was little experimental architecture in Great Britain during the first decades of the twentieth century. The arrival in Britain in the thirties of the architects Gropius, Breuer, Mendelsohn,

23.17 Alvar Aalto, Villa Mairea, Noormarkku, Finland, 1939.

and the Russian Serge Chermayeff stimulated new thinking. But World War II interrupted any new work and, after the war, budgetary limitations prevented large-scale architectural development. Although few great individual structures were built in England in the mid-twentieth century, progress was made in two areas: town and country planning, and the design of schools and colleges.

The work of **James Stirling** (1926–92), one of the most imaginative and influential British architects of the postwar period, is associated with the tradition of Le Corbusier. Stirling had a masterly ability to combine all sorts of materials—glass, masonry, and metal—in exciting new contexts. Like Louis Kahn's work (see fig. 23.37), Stirling's early buildings are not so much functional, in the original International Style sense, as they are expressive and personal. With James Gowan he designed the low-cost housing complex of Ham Common in England in 1958, when he was studying the later ideas of Le Corbusier and exploring the possibilities of readymade products in new architectural contexts. In the 1968 Cambridge University History Faculty (fig. **23.19**), Stirling used a cohesive approach to achieve a dense and complex spatial integration. Although Stirling was an important teacher and thinker in his field, he was often pessimistic about the state of modern architecture. This is ironic because his own accomplishments continually demonstrated modern architecture's possibilities, especially, as we shall see, in his Postmodern work (see fig. 25.16).

France

With the exception of works by the titanic figure of Le Corbusier and earlier ones by Auguste Perret (see fig. 12.25), French architecture of the twentieth century had comparatively few moments of inspiration. This was in part the result of the continuing academic system of training for architects and the persisting influence of a bureaucratic

old guard. Swiss-born Le Corbusier produced a number of masterpieces in France, but he ultimately achieved greater standing elsewhere.

The most ambitious postwar structure erected in Paris was that of the Y-shaped building for the United Nations Educational Scientific and Cultural Organization (UNESCO), designed by an international team of architects that included the Hungarian Breuer and the French Bernard Zehrfuss with the Italian architect-engineer Pier Luigi Nervi. The total complex is excellently adapted

23.19 James Stirling, History Faculty, Cambridge University, England, 1968.

23.20 Marcel Breuer, IBM–France Research Center, La Gaude Var, France, 1960–62.

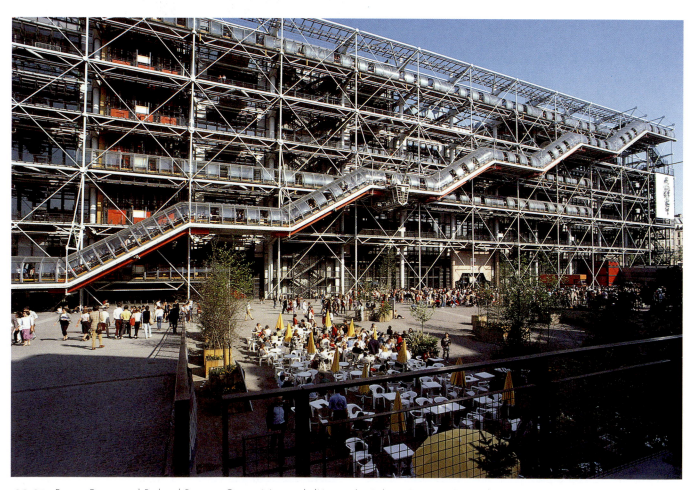

23.21 Renzo Piano and Richard Rogers, Centre National d'Art et de Culture Georges Pompidou, Paris, 1971–78.

to a difficult site and is adorned by a large number of sculptures, paintings, and murals by artists such as Miró, Calder, Picasso, Noguchi, and Henry Moore. Breuer developed the ideas and plan of the UNESCO building into his work on a research center for IBM–France at La Gaude Var (fig. **23.20**). This is a huge structure of a comparable, double-Y plan, with windows set within deep, heavy, concrete frames, the whole on concrete supports. The effect is of openness and airiness combined with massive, rugged detail.

As a result of an important postwar international competition, the most sensational and hotly debated building to be designed in the sixties (erected in Paris during the early seventies) was the high-tech extravaganza officially known as Le Centre National d'Art et de Culture Georges Pompidou designed by **Renzo Piano** (b. 1937) and **Richard Rogers** (b. 1933). (It is referred to as the Pompidou Center after the then-president, and also as the Beaubourg after the market district on which it was built.) One of the few constructed buildings conceived by England's Archigram Group (an association that derived from the British avant-garde), the Pompidou Center (fig. **23.21**) is an icon to Parisian popular culture, housing France's national museum of modern art, a public library, an audiovisual center, a rooftop restaurant, and, added later, an Internet café. In its time, the design achieved a new standard in open-space flexibility. The structural and service functions were channeled along the outer walls, leaving the interior open to be freely subdivided, and suitable for a multitude of changeable institutional and public uses. The Pompidou Center takes Bauhaus pragmatism and technology as its point of departure, only to transform them into a surreal dream of pipes and trusses, marine funnels and vents, most of which festoon the exoskeleton. With its exposed fretwork, its clearly expressed structure and services, and its great diagonal escalators, as well as its bright colors and open planning, the building, as one commentator remarked, is like "a child's Tinkertoy fantasy realized on an elephantine scale." Despite a gargantuan appetite for fuel and difficult-to-manage, barnlike galleries, the Pompidou Center is a great popular success, partly because of a five-story outside escalator, whose transparent plastic tubes offer riders a moving, spectacular view of Paris and the immense, open plaza below. The latter has become a forum—like the parvis of a medieval cathedral (the open space in front of and around the building)—for the whole human carnival, from artists displaying their works to jugglers and, of course, tourists and Parisians going about their daily business.

Germany and Italy

As we have seen, Germany until 1930 was a world leader in developing new architecture. During the Nazi regime, German architecture declined from its position of world leadership to academic mediocrity. After the war, morale was low for those architects and artists who had remained in Germany through the war years. While America was enjoying prosperity, Germany underwent a slow, traumatic period of rebuilding, and it took that country a full decade to recover the principles forcibly surrendered to the Nazis.

In Italy, modern architecture made a somewhat belated arrival, perhaps because the sense of the past was so strong. The visionary Futurist Antonio Sant' Elia was killed in World War I at the age of twenty-eight, before he had a chance to execute his concepts for cities of the future (see fig. 12.27). His ideas faded along with Futurism, and his influence was diffused principally through publications that inspired pioneers outside of Italy, importantly Le Corbusier and the architects of de Stijl and the Bauhaus.

Although progressive architecture was not formally suppressed by Italian fascism, as it was in Germany under the Nazis, the climate did not favor growth. The official governmental style looked back to showy, nationalistic monumentalism, of which the nineteenth-century monument to Victor Emmanuel II in Rome is the most conspicuous example. In 1933 a group of younger architects, gruppo 7, banded together and called for a functional and rational architecture that would value form over surface in modern architecture. A few outstanding, though isolated, buildings resulted from this and other aspects of Italian rationalism between the wars, notably the aesthetically pure 1932–36 Casa del Popolo (House of the People) at Como, designed by Giuseppe Terragni (1904–42). Originally designed as a building wrapped around three sides of a square court, the structure is a simple half-cube. The court, which became a large meeting hall, stands in radical contrast to the Renaissance cathedral opposite it. After World War II, Italy expanded its experiment beyond progressive architecture, moving into a position of European and even world leadership in many aspects of industrial, product, and fashion design.

The most influential of Italy's prewar design giants was the engineer-architect **Pier Luigi Nervi** (1891–1979). Nervi had a resounding ability to translate engineering structure into architectural forms of beauty. Chronologically he belongs with the pioneers of modern architecture, and his fundamental theses were stated in a number of important buildings executed during the thirties. Working with reinforced concrete, his main contribution was the creation of new shapes and spatial dimensions with this material. As in the work of Mies van der Rohe, Nervi's buildings show a subtle fusion of structure and space. But while Mies searched for free internal space, Nervi's aesthetic was dependent on an energetic display of the structural parts of a building. One of the most important commissions of his career was the design of an aircraft hangar in 1935, the first of a number of variants that he built for the military from 1936 to 1941. These hangars, which involve vast, uninterrupted concrete roof spans, led him to study different ways to create such spans. He learned how to lighten and strengthen his materials and to integrate aesthetic and structural variations in his designs.

23.22 Pier Luigi Nervi and Annibale Vitellozzi, Sports Palace, Rome, 1956–57.

In 1948–49, his Exhibition Hall was built in Turin, using prefabricated concrete units to create a vault spanning 312 feet (95 m).

In the fifties, Nervi developed the technique of hydraulic prestressing of ferroconcrete, which made it possible to lighten the support of buildings. Two of the dramatic applications of his experiments with ferroconcrete are the small and large sports palaces built for the 1960 Olympic Games in Rome (fig. **23.22**). The smaller one, seen here, meant to hold four to five thousand spectators, was built in 1956–57, in collaboration with the architect Annibale Vitellozzi. The building is essentially a circular roof structure in which the enclosed shell roof, 197 feet (60 m) in diameter, rests lightly on thirty-six Y-shaped concrete supports. The edge of the roof is scalloped, both to accentuate the points of support and to increase the feeling of lightness. A continuous window band between this scalloped edge and the outside wall provides uniform daylight and adds to the floating quality of the ceiling. On the interior, the ceiling, a honeycomb of radiating, interlaced curves, floats without apparent support. The shell domes of the small and large sports palaces became prototypes for other such structures.

During the fifties and sixties, Nervi collaborated with architects all over the world, including Italy's own **Gio Ponti** (1891–1979). The distinguished Ponti was the chief architect of the Pirelli Tower in Milan (fig. **23.23**), the result of a close collaboration between architects and engineers. Ponti developed slowly but consistently from Neoclassical beginnings toward an elaborate modernism. The Pirelli Tower, for which Nervi was the structural engineer, remains Ponti's masterpiece, one of the most lucid and individual interpretations of the skyscraper yet achieved. In contrast to most American skyscrapers built before the fifties, it is a separate building surrounded by lower structures, designed to be seen from all sides. The

23.23 Gio Ponti, Pier Luigi Nervi, and others, Pirelli Tower, Milan, Italy, 1956–59.

architect was concerned with making it a total, finite, harmonious unit. A boat shape, rather than the customary rectangular slab, was used. The thirty-two-story building is carried on tapering piers, resulting in the enlargement of the spaces as the piers become lighter toward the top. The entire building, with the diagonal areas at the ends enclosed and framing the side walls of glass, has a sculptural quality, a sense of solidity and mass unusual in contemporary skyscraper design.

Latin America, Australia, and Japan

A spectacular example of the spread of the International Style occurred in Latin America after 1940. Le Corbusier's participation in the design of the Ministry of Education and Health in Rio de Janeiro between 1937 and 1943 provided the spark that ignited younger Latin American architects, among them **Oscar Niemeyer** (b. 1907) in Brazil. Le Corbusier's influence is apparent in most of the subsequent development of Brazilian architecture, but Niemeyer and his contemporaries added expressionist and Baroque elements—such as curving shapes and lavish use of color reflecting the Latin American tradition—to plans and façades. In his Pampulha buildings of the early forties, Niemeyer hinted at an integration of painting and

23.24 Oscar Niemeyer, Palace of the Dawn, Brasília, Brazil, 1959.

architecture and effectively introduced a wilder interplay of forms and levels into his buildings.

Niemeyer's greatest work, and one of the most dramatic commissions in the history of architecture, was the design of the entire city at Brasília, the new federal capital of Brazil (fig. **23.24**). The general plan of the city was laid out by Lúcio Costa, who won the competition sponsored by Brazil's president in 1956. Niemeyer, as chief architect, was entrusted with the principal public buildings. Costa's lucid plan was essentially two axes in the form of a cross. Niemeyer designed large-scale civic buildings for the top of the cross, with residential sites along the two arms of the horizontal axis, incorporating places for work and recreation. The idea of building an entire utopian city far removed from any of the principal centers of commerce and industry probably doomed Brasília to failure as a

socially integrated community. At a time in the history of architecture when very little attention was being paid to concepts of total urban planning, such a project must be seen as important, despite its deficiencies and failures.

In Australia, too, there was a comparable development of new architectural forms, from the slab skyscraper to the integrated educational institution and advanced experiments in housing and urban planning. The most spectacular modern structure is the sail-form, freestanding Sydney Opera House of 1972 on Bennelong Point (fig. **23.25**), jutting out into Sydney Harbor. The architectural firm of Hall, Todd, and Littleton succeeded the Danish architect **Jørn Utzon** (b. 1918), who made the original design. This cultural center includes an opera hall, a theater, an exhibition area, a cinema, and a chamber music hall.

Postwar architects in Japan exploited possibilities that had been previously regarded as utopian. An independent style in modern Japanese architecture has been apparent only since the sixties. Before then, most of the new building was in derivative commercial modern style, particularly in Tokyo, where there were few buildings of distinction or originality. Modern architecture in Japan, despite a long history of sporadic progressive examples extending back to Frank Lloyd Wright's Imperial Hotel (see fig. 12.6), was only at its inception after World War II. While assimilating the powerful influence of Le Corbusier, the tradition of Japanese architecture (which for centuries embodied so many elements that today are called modern), helped to turn contemporary influences into something authentically Japanese.

One of the most significant later twentieth-century Japanese architects is **Kenzo Tange** (b. 1913), whose work in the fifties and sixties combined rationalist and traditional directions in Japanese aesthetics. Like most Japanese

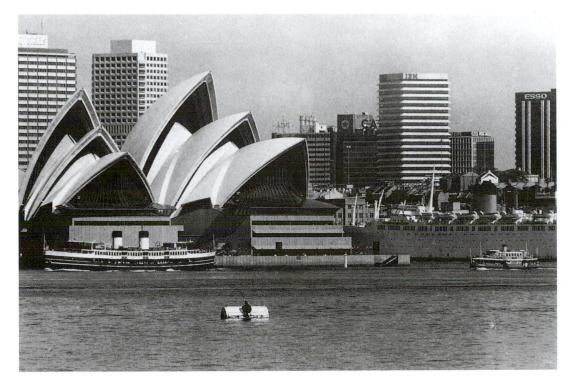

23.25 Jørn Utzon and Hall, Todd, and Littleton, Sydney Opera House, Bennelong Point, Sydney Harbor, Australia, 1972.

23.26 Kenzo Tange, Aerial view, The National Gymnasiums, Tokyo, 1964.

architects of his generation, Tange was a disciple of Le Corbusier and particularly of Le Corbusier's later, Brutalist style. Tokyo City Hall, a work of 1952–57, is a rather thin version of Le Corbusier's Unité d'Habitation (see fig. 23.3), but with the Kasagawa Prefecture Office at Takamatsu (1955–58), Tange used a combination of massive, direct concrete treatment and horizontally accentuated shapes reminiscent of traditional Japanese architecture. Perhaps Tange's most striking achievement is the pair of gymnasiums that he designed for the Olympic Games held in Tokyo in 1964 (fig. **23.26**). Both steel-sheeted roofs, somewhat resembling seashells, are suspended from immense cables, and their structure is at once daring and graceful. The larger roof hangs from two concrete masts,

23.27 Kenzo Tange, Yamanashi Press Center, Kofu, Japan, 1967.

while the smaller is ingeniously suspended from a cable spiraling down from a single mast. The Brutalism of the buildings themselves, with their rough surface texture and frank structure, gives the complex—set as it is on a huge platform of undressed stone blocks—a sense of enduring drama.

Tange's Yamanashi Press Center in Kofu (fig. 23.27) is a fantastically monumental structure in which immense pylons provide for elevator and other services and act visually as tower supports for the horizontal office areas. The total impact is like that of a vast Romanesque fortified castle. The interior, however, is open and flexible, with spaces defined by movable shoji screens that allow occupants easily to adapt their space to changing needs. Reminiscent of traditional timber post-and-beam constructions, the press building is one of the earliest examples of a reaction against the abstract, homogenous trends of modern architecture. Its very "uncompletedness" is an important aspect of its design; it is open-ended and not confined by more traditional architectural approaches that rely on finite elevations and concise imagery.

Another Japanese architect who followed the late Le Corbusier line is Takeo Sato, whose City Hall in Iwakuni merges the design of a traditional Japanese pagoda with modern building materials including concrete and glass. Similarly, **Sachio Ohtani**'s (b. 1924) International Conference Building in Kyoto (fig. **23.28**) is a massive structure that houses meeting and exhibition rooms, restaurants, administrative offices, shops, and recreation areas. Employing old trapezoidal and triangular design elements, it represents one of the most spectacular attempts yet made to combine on a vast scale ancient Japanese motifs and concepts with modern architectural forms.

23.28 Sachio Ohtani, International Conference Building, Kyoto, Japan, 1955.

23.29 Frederick Kiesler, Plan of Endless House, 1958–59.

Breaking the Mold: Experimental Housing

Of great significance to working architects were some unbuilt visionary house designs belonging to a new phase of imaginary architecture. Outstanding is the Endless House (fig. **23.29**) designed by **Frederick Kiesler** (1890–1965), whom Philip Johnson called "the greatest non-building architect of our time." As early as 1925, Kiesler had conceived of a city in space built on a bridge structure,

and an Endless Theater. From these, in 1934, he developed a "space house" and, after years of experiment, the so-termed Endless House, proposed many times in various versions but never built. The idea for an Endless Structure was to short-circuit any traditional divisions between floor, wall, and ceiling and to offer the inhabitant an interior that could be modified at will. In doing this, Kiesler abandoned the rectangle and turned to egg shapes freely modeled from plastic materials and proffering a continuously flowing interior space.

Although relatively few, there are instances of successful, large-scale prefabrication in the twentieth century, such as Nervi's 1948–49 Turin exhibition hall (see above). Some manufacturers in the United States offer partially prefabricated small houses. In a number of California houses, including their own in Santa Monica (1949) (fig. **23.31**), the husband and wife architect-designers **Charles** (1907–78) and **Ray Eames** (1916–88) set out to prove that modern architecture could be both accessible and economical. Using prefabricated materials purchased through catalogues, the Eameses constructed residences consisting of light steel-skeleton cores covered with fitted plastic, stucco, or glass panels, as well as stock doors, windows, and accessories. These mass-produced materials were chosen for both their economic appeal and industrial aesthetic and represent a utilitarian domestic architectural style.

One of the greatest examples of prefabricated housing design is by Israeli architect **Moshe Safdie** (b. 1938). His megastructure, Habitat '67, commissioned for Expo '67,

Such experiments represented an attempt not only to find new forms based on natural, organic principles but also to utilize new technical and industrial developments while potentially cutting building costs. Among such projects is the 1961 house and studio in Scottsdale, Arizona, built by **Paolo Soleri** (b. 1919). Literally a cave, it is the forerunner of Soleri's Dome House in Cave Creek, Arizona (1950). Born in Turin, Italy, Soleri came to the United States in 1947 and spent a year and a half in fellowship with Frank Lloyd Wright at Taliesin West in Arizona and Taliesin East in Wisconsin. His compact prototype city, Arcosanti (fig. **23.30**), located in the high desert of Arizona in a 4,060-acre (1643-hectare) preserve and now a National Landmark, has been under construction since 1970. For some thirty years, it has been an experiment, or "urban laboratory," to demonstrate his theory of arcology. An arcology is an integration of architecture, ecology, and urban planning. It involves a whole new concept of urban environment that would eliminate the automobile from within the city (walking would be the main way of getting around), develop renewable energy systems (solar and wind), utilize recycling, and allow access to and interaction with the surrounding natural environment. Using rounded concrete structures, this miniaturization of the city allows for the radical conservation of land, energy, and resources. The arcology concept proposes a highly integrated and compact three-dimensional urban form that is the opposite of the wasteful consumption of land, energy, time, and human resources of urban sprawl. (Only about two percent as much land as a typical city of similar population is needed.) Therefore, it presents a new solution to the ecological, economic, spatial, and energy problems of cities.

Less utopian than arcology is prefabrication—the mass manufacturing and prefabrication of individual parts.

23.31 Charles and Ray Eames, Eames Residence, Santa Monica, California, 1949.

23.32 Moshe Safdie, Habitat '67, Montreal, Canada, 1967.

the 1967 World's Fair in Montreal, Canada, was conceived to provide fresh air, sunlight, privacy, and suburban amenities to residents of an urban location (fig. **23.32**). It was designed as a permanent settlement of 158 dwellings made up of fifteen types of independent, interlocking prefabricated boxes. The boxes are staggered in order to provide open-deck space for each unit and to ensure versatile visual and spatial combinations. It is possible to add more prefabricated, mass-produced units to such a structure, rather than constructing them on site.

Another signal of the arrival of an antimodernist aesthetic can be seen in the work of the self-styled New York School (not to be confused with the New York School of Painting that began with the Pollock–de Kooning–Rothko generation in the mid-forties). Architects identified with the New York School include Peter Eisenman, John Hejduk, Michael Graves, Charles Gwathmey, and Richard Meier. The most heavily commissioned of these was **Richard Meier** (b. 1934), whose glistening, white Cubist temples—supersophisticated exploitations of the modernist vocabulary—have proved irresistible to wealthy private clients, corporations, and cultural institutions. In Douglas House in Harbor Springs, Michigan (fig. **23.33**), one sees Purist or de Stijl classicism so wittily elaborated as to become a new Mannerism, reversing simple closed forms and ribbon windows into intricate, openwork abstractions with double- and triple-height interiors and vast expanses of glass.

23.33 Richard Meier, Douglas House, Harbor Springs, Michigan, 1971–73.

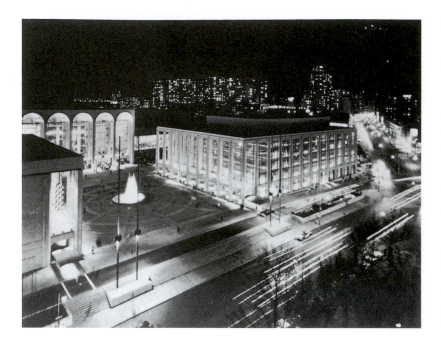

23.34 Lincoln Center, New York. From left: New York State Theater, by Philip Johnson, 1964; Metropolitan Opera House, by Wallace K. Harrison, 1966; Philharmonic (now Avery Fisher) Hall, by Max Abramovitz, 1962.

performances, and receptions. The Whitney Museum of American Art (fig. **23.35**) designed by Marcel Breuer is another important museum design. Breuer's building, illustrative of his later Brutalism, is a development of the forms he used earlier for St. John's Abbey Church in Collegeville, Minnesota (1953–61) and for the lecture hall of New York University's uptown campus in the Bronx (1956–61). The Whitney is a stark and impressive building, in which heavy, dark granite and concrete are used inside and out. The main galleries are huge, uninterrupted halls capable of being divided in almost any way by movable yet

Arenas for Innovation: Major Public Projects

Cultural Centers, Theaters, and Museums in America

The most elaborate center to date in the United States is the Lincoln Center for the Performing Arts in New York City (fig. **23.34**), which opened in 1962 and represented a spectacular return to architectural formalism. The classical origins of its layout are not disguised. The focus of the principal structures on three sides of a monumental plaza is a fountain, designed by Philip Johnson. In addition to **Max Abramovitz**'s (b. 1908) Philharmonic Hall (1962) (renamed Avery Fisher Hall), the Center comprises **Philip Johnson**'s (b. 1906) New York State Theater (1964), **Eero Saarinen**'s (1910–61) Vivian Beaumont Theater (1965), Skidmore, Owings & Merrill's Library-Museum of the Performing Arts (1965), and Wallace K. Harrison's Metropolitan Opera House (1966). A large subterranean garage lies beneath this group. Adjunct structures include a midtown branch of Fordham University and a home for the Juilliard School, completed in 1969 by Pietro Belluschi with Catalano and Westermann.

The buildings created by this notable assemblage of talent exemplify a new monumental classicism characteristic of public and official architecture in the sixties. The project is impressive, despite the criticisms leveled against individual structures. The chief complaints, aside from problems of acoustics and sightlines, are focused on Lincoln Center's barren monumentality, its colossal scale unrelieved by ornamental detail that would provide a human reference.

We saw earlier in this chapter, in the discussion about the renovation of Frank Lloyd Wright's Guggenheim Museum (see fig. 23.2), that an art museum is actually a complicated design problem, involving basic questions of efficient circulation, adequate light—natural, artificial, or both—sufficient work and storage space, and, in most cases, rooms for other events, such as concerts, theatrical

23.35 Marcel Breuer, The Whitney Museum of American Art, New York, 1966.

23.36 Louis I. Kahn, Interior, west gallery and bookstore, Kimbell Art Museum, Fort Worth, Texas, 1972.

solid partitions and representing the utmost flexibility in installation space and artificial lighting. Natural daylight has been ignored except for that emanating from a few trapezoidal-shaped windows that function as relief accents.

The architect **Louis I. Kahn** (1901–74) was responsible for the design of two important art buildings. Like Wright, Kahn initiated a new American architecture, but while Wright's work developed in the late nineteenth and early twentieth centuries, Kahn matured amidst the uncertainty and loss of idealism of the thirties and forties. Born in Estonia, Kahn emigrated with his family to Philadelphia in 1905. He received architectural training in the Beaux Arts tradition at the University of Pennsylvania. There followed a year in Europe, where he was impressed both by the monuments of classical antiquity and by his discovery of Le Corbusier. His later work would reflect a fusion of modernism's passion for technology and abstract form along with a profound awareness of history and its role in architecture. For a number of years, Kahn taught at Yale University, where he designed the Yale Art Gallery (1951–53), the university's first modern building and one of the first contemporary approaches to the design challenges of the art museum.

Kahn was not only a designer concerned with mechanical and visual relationships of extraordinary subtlety and aesthetic quality, but he was also a planner, both practical and poetical, whether for an individual building or an entire city. Perhaps the most visionary and completely realized of all of Kahn's buildings is his Kimbell Art Museum in Fort Worth, Texas, completed in 1972 (figs. **23.36**, **23.37**)—one of the most dramatic as well as functionally effective art museums in the world. The museum design is based upon a parallel series of self-supporting cycloidal vaults that eliminate the need for interior supports and

facilitate an unobstructed and very flexible use of the spacious interior. Indoor and outdoor spaces are integrated through the attachment of a sculpture garden that creates a fluid interchange between the museum and its environment, thereby altering the traditional notion of a museum as a place that cloisters works of art. The architect is also noted for the close attention paid to the issues of lighting and displaying works of art. By combining artificial and natural light, and breaking up the cavernous heights of gallery space with low-hanging lights and shorter partitioning walls, the Kimbell becomes both a practical space for the display and conservation of art, and an aesthetically pleasing environment that is at once monumental and intimate to the gallery visitor.

The challenge of successfully designing a visitor center–museum for a highly specific and localized American community shows Richard Meier's versatility and his evolution as an architect. The differences between his rationalist Douglas House (see fig. 23.33) and the three-story Atheneum at Historic New Harmony in Indiana (fig. **23.38**) are revealing. Now a living museum, New Harmony was a vigorous nineteenth-century American religious and utopian community established by the Harmony Society in 1814. The 1975–79 Atheneum is a gleaming white metal structure set on a green lawn; a visual dialogue of solid and void, projecting terraces, recessive spaces, and folded stairs that exclaim its modernity. The commission required a 180-seat auditorium, four exhibition galleries, observation terraces, and visitor and administrative facilities. Meier's work fulfills the program and stands in great contrast to the log cabins and brick buildings of the historic settlement. Meier does not belong to the tradition of expressionist architects interested in empathy and feeling. His is an architecture interested in visual effects, looking at and framing

23.37 Louis I. Kahn, Kimbell Art Museum, Fort Worth, Texas, 1972.

23.38 Richard Meier, The Atheneum, west entrance, New Harmony, Indiana, 1975–79.

objects in space. Much like Le Corbusier's dictum that a house is a machine for living, the Atheneum is conceived as a device, a sophisticated instrument for controlling the experience of observing its collection. There is something detached in the way the building relates to the site of one of the most intriguing social experiments in American history, but its very detachment offers a completely unbiased vantage point.

I. M. Pei's (Ieoh Ming Pei, b. 1917) East Wing extension to the National Gallery of Art in Washington, D.C.

(fig. **23.39**), inaugurated in 1978, ten years after its initial conception, is an extraordinary venue for a broad range of museum activities. It is not only a site for temporary exhibitions and the museum's collection of twentieth-century art, but also houses museum offices, a library, and the Center for Advanced Studies in the Visual Arts (CASVA). The awkward trapezoidal site posed several challenges for the architect, as did the need to integrate the new structure with the extant Beaux-Arts style West Building (designed by John Russell Pope). Pei resolved these problems by

23.39 I. M. Pei, National Gallery of Art, East Wing, Washington D.C., 1978.

23.40 I. M. Pei, East Building, National Gallery of Art, Washington, D.C., 1968–78. At center, Alexander Calder, *Untitled*, 1976. Aluminum and steel, 29' × 10" × 76' (8.8 × 0.25 × 23.2 m).

dividing the plot into triangular forms that became the building blocks of his design—reiterated throughout the building in floor tiles, skylights, stairs, and tables—and then connecting the entire construction to the West Building via an underground passage. The entrance to the East Building opens to an expansive, light-filled atrium with skylighted ceilings that provide the backdrop for several works of art commissioned especially for the building, including a monumental mobile by Alexander Calder (fig. **23.40**). In contrast to the atrium's open, soaring space, the intimate interior is composed of individual galleries made from smaller rooms and lowered walls that

23.41 Louis I. Kahn, East Hostels, Bangladesh Assembly, Dacca, 1962–74.

provide a quiet space for the contemplation of the exhibited art. Viewed from outside, the East Building—dramatically set against the view of the Capitol Building—is easily recognized by its H-shape design, which is formed by the stocky towers that extend from each of three vertices. Associated in his early years with both Gropius and Breuer, Pei was the consummate modernist, combining and refining the best principles of modern architecture in a continually inventive stream of eloquent commercial and public buildings, including the glass pyramid for the renovated Musée du Louvre in Paris in 1989 (see fig. 25.21).

Urban Planning and Airports

City planning has been a dream of architects since antiquity, and has only occasionally been realized, as in the Hellenistic cities built after the conquests by Alexander the Great, Roman forums, Renaissance and Baroque piazzas, the Imperial Forbidden City of Peking, and Baron Haussmann's rebuilding of Paris in the nineteenth century. Although Le Corbusier was one of the visionaries of European planning in his designs for a new Paris, it was only at Chandigarh (see fig. 23.6) that he was able to realize some of his ideas. Brasília was perhaps the most complete realization of a new city plan in the twentieth century (see fig. 23.24).

Most American efforts at urban planning or slum reconstruction have been brave but incomplete attempts, continually frustrated by antiquated planning laws and political or economic opposition. Among the most successful efforts at rebuilding the center of an American city are the urban renewal projects in Philadelphia, which were begun in the forties. These have involved building new highways and coordinating the design of public and commercial buildings, as well as slum clearance and, most important in a city like Philadelphia, the preservation of historic monuments. The achievements in Philadelphia have been remarkable. Other comparable rehabilitation programs are being carried out, but the dream of the ideal city is still far from realized. Great American metropolises like New York, Miami, Phoenix, Atlanta, and Los Angeles continue to fight day-to-day battles concerning human welfare, traffic congestion, and water and air pollution.

Like Le Corbusier's before him at Chandigarh, Louis Kahn's experience with the Asian subcontinent unleashed a flood of innovation and invention. In 1962 East Pakistan (Bangladesh) invited Kahn to design its new capital city of Dacca, including the Assembly and Supreme Court buildings, hostels, a school, a stadium, and a market. To protect the buildings from the harsh elements, Kahn enclosed them inside another structural layer. As he said of an earlier project, "I thought of wrapping ruins around the buildings." In this case, the "ruins" are large, freestanding concrete curtains pierced with geometric cutout shapes. For example, the curtain for the East Hostels for the members of Parliament (fig. **23.41**), with its large semicircular cutout shapes, serves not to provide views to the exterior, but to shield the interiors from intense sun glare. The result is both primal and sophisticated. Like Le Corbusier's monuments for Chandigarh, Kahn's work for Dacca achieves an ancient aura without being culturally specific;

23.42 Eero Saarinen, Interior, TWA Terminal, John F. Kennedy International Airport, New York, 1962.

23.43 Eero Saarinen, Dulles Airport, Chantilly, Virginia, 1961–62.

the iconography of the cutout shapes seems almost indifferent to the history and artistic heritage of the patron.

Many of the best opportunities for a different kind of urban planning were offered by the airports that proliferated in the fifties and sixties. Unfortunately, very few of these opportunities were successfully realized. With some exceptions, the architecture proved routine and the solutions to such problems as circulation inadequate. New York's John F. Kennedy International Airport is a vast mix of miscellaneous architectural styles illustrating the clichés of modern architecture. A few individual buildings rise above the norm. One is Eero Saarinen's TWA terminal (fig. **23.42**), with its striking airplane-wing profile and interior spaces, clearly suggestive of the ideal of flight. In 1961–62, Saarinen had the opportunity to design a complete terminal at the Dulles Airport near Washington, D.C. (fig. **23.43**). The main building—with its upturned floating roof and the adjoining related traffic tower—incorporates an exciting and unified design concept. Saarinen here also resolved practical problems, such as transporting passengers directly to the plane through mobile lounges. Due to increased air traffic, Dulles was expanded in the midnineties to more than double its original size, reminding us that architectural form often derives from changing functions. In the sixties Saarinen had predicted such an expansion, and hence left behind explicit architectural plans for use at a future date. The final design, completed by the firm Skidmore, Owings & Merrill, remained loyal to Saarinen's original plans; the building's design was extended by 320 feet (97.5 m) on either end, thereby altering the airport's proportions but leaving the basic form undisturbed.

Architecture and Engineering

To many students of modern architecture, and particularly of urban design, the solutions for the future seemed to lie less in the hands of the architects than in those of the engineers. Architects themselves were closely following new engineering experiments, particularly such new principles of construction as those advanced by **Buckminster Fuller** (1895–1983). Fuller was the universal man of modern engineering. As early as 1929 he designed a Dymaxion House, literally a machine for living that realized Le Corbusier's earlier concept in its use of techniques of automobile and aircraft construction. In the early thirties, he built a practical three-wheeled automobile, which has been recognized as one of the few rational steps toward solving the problem of city traffic congestion, but which has never been put into production. These and many other inventions led ultimately to his geodesic dome structures, based on tetrahedrons, octahedrons, or icosahedrons. These domes, which can be created in almost any material and built to any dimensions, have been used for greenhouses, covers for industrial shops, and mobile, easily assembled living units for the American army. Although Fuller's genius had long been widely recognized, it was only in the second half of the twentieth century that he received an opportunity to demonstrate the tremendous flexibility, low cost, and ease of construction of his domes. Many innovative structures were constructed for Expo '67, including Safdie's Habitat (see fig. **23.32**), but Fuller's geodesic dome (fig. **23.44**) dominated the whole exposition. The structure was a prototype of what he called an "environmental valve," which encloses sufficient space for whole communities to live within a physical microcosm. The American Pavilion at Expo '67 was a triumphant vindication of this engineer-architect, whose ideas of construction and design promised to make most modern architecture obsolete.

23.44 Buckminster Fuller, American Pavilion, Expo '67, Montreal, 1967.

24
The Pluralistic Seventies

Presented with a world torn by mounting political and social conflict, the younger artists who emerged during the late sixties and early seventies found little to satisfy their expressive needs in the extreme purity and logic of Minimal art. In the seventies, the New York critic John Perreault voiced the growing dissatisfaction with the Minimalist aesthetic: "Presently we need more than silent cubes, blank canvases, and gleaming white walls. We are sick to death of cold plazas, and monotonous 'curtain wall' skyscrapers … [as well as] interiors that are more like empty meat lockers than rooms to live in." With this, art entered what became known as its Post-Minimal phase—a time, like many others throughout history, when classical balance yielded to its expressive opposite. Minimalism's "classical" purity lay in its combination of the most literal, concrete kind of form with highly rarefied intellectual or even spiritual content; but it was the Minimalists' emphasis on the object, a commodity that could still be bought and sold, that caused certain artists to reject it. To avoid the stigma of commercialism and to recover something of the moral distance traditionally maintained by avant-garde art in its relations with society at large, some artists ceased to make objects altogether, except as containers of information, metaphors, symbols, and meaningful images. This ushered in Conceptualism, which considered a work finished as soon as the artist had conceived the idea for it and had expressed this, not in material, objective form, but rather in language, documentation, and proposals.

Along with Conceptualism came Process art, which undermined Minimalist forms by subjecting them to such eroding forces of nature as atmospheric conditions, as well as to the physical force of gravity. Related to Process art were "scatter works," consisting of raw materials dispersed over the gallery floor, a manifestation that opposed formalism with formlessness; and Earthworks, for which artists abandoned the studio and gallery world altogether and operated in open nature, to create art whose relationship to a particular site was an inseparable part of its existence. But, while some artists turned outward to nature, others turned inward, to their own bodies. On a more intimate scale, the human body served as the site for formal procedures comparable to those worked upon the environment. The artist in his or her own person became central to Performance art, which communicated ideas about the human situation, often in an ideological or political context, through theatrical works, consisting of paintings, songs, recitations, and dance, and often accompanied by instrumental or electronic music, light displays, and video. Performance art of this kind was usually more deliberately structured than the original Happenings of the sixties (see chapter 21) and involved the audience less directly. Simultaneously, as some artists abandoned studio and gallery, others revived easel painting in a mimetic style so sharply focused that it was dubbed Photorealism. This painstaking truth to appearances was not based on direct observation of the phenomenal world but rather on a purity of conception derived from an embrace of both the art of painting and photography. Integral to the Photorealists was the primary source of the photograph, the very kind of documentation most favored by the iconoclastic Conceptualists.

In the seventies it appeared as if someone had opened Pandora's box and released all the demons that modernism had exorcized. Illustration, pattern, decoration, expressionism, and even narrative were espoused by Postmodern artists seeking new avenues beyond the prescriptive route of modernism and its late, Minimalist phase. Without a dominant mode to follow, younger artists began to work in a more pluralistic way than that permitted by purist modernism. Rather than relying exclusively on the example provided by the plastic arts, artists during the seventies turned increasingly to linguistic and political theory as a means to develop their art. Particularly influential were theories of language and meaning, such as those of the analytic philosopher Ludwig Wittgenstein. During this period, the Marxist social and political critiques of such philosophers as Theodor Adorno, Herbert Marcuse, and Walter Benjamin—the Frankfurt school—began to have increasing resonance with artists and critics. Their thinking could easily be applied to the very system of commodification that the art market traditionally supported. So open, however, did this pluralistic era become that even the formalists had their place.

The pluralism of artistic forms and motivations during the seventies coincided with a growing revisionist trend in art history. This reflected a desire on the part of many scholars to devote attention to histories and arts of the nineteenth and twentieth centuries that had been marginalized or repressed in the accepted accounts of modern, Western art. The artistic achievements of other cultures and social groups outside the élite, male-dominated art-world of Europe and North America began to be championed by writers and taken forward by artists themselves.

Forms of Thought: Conceptual Art

The gradual and progressive "dematerialization of the art object," as the critic Lucy Lippard called the antiformalist movement, has its roots in the later sixties, but became increasingly dominant in the early seventies. In 1970 The Museum of Modern Art in New York mounted an exhibition called simply Information. As the title suggests, the show acknowledged that ideas had once again come to the fore in art and, for many younger as well as older artists, taken precedence over concrete form. Already in 1967, the Minimalist sculptor Sol LeWitt had defined his own grid and cube works (see fig. 22.52) as Conceptualist, while reinforcing his position with theoretical statements that had a vast influence on artists of kindred spirit. "In Conceptual Art," LeWitt wrote in 1967, "the idea or concept is the most important aspect of the work … all planning and decision[s] are made beforehand and the execution is a perfunctory affair. The idea becomes the machine that makes the art." Where Minimalism had taken

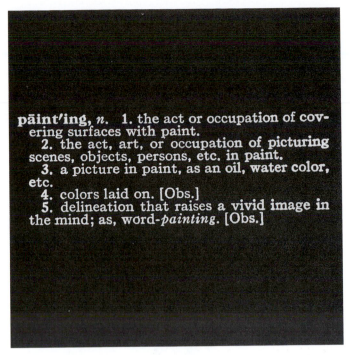

24.2 Joseph Kosuth, *Art As Idea As Idea*, 1966. Mounted Photostat, 48 × 48" (121.9 × 121.9 cm). Collection Roy and Dorothy Lichtenstein.

a preconceived, intellectual approach, creating art from such "readymades" as mathematical systems, geometric form, raw industrial materials, and factory production, and pushed reductive formalism just short of total self-elimination, Conceptual artists proposed that the next logical move lay in taking art beyond the object into the realm of language, knowledge, science, and worldly data.

As if to offer a textbook demonstration of how this could be accomplished, the American artist **Joseph Kosuth** (b. 1945), a co-curator of the Information exhibition, made *One and Three Chairs* (fig. **24.1**), which consists of a real chair accompanied by a full-scale photograph of it and a dictionary definition of "chair," together providing a progression from the real to the ideal and thereby encompassing all the essential properties of "chairness." The artist was concerned with exposing the mechanics of meaning, as regards objects, which involved linking a visual image with a mental concept. Here it is appropriate to mention the general language of semiotics, the science of signs, and say that the "signifier" (a specific representation of a concept or thing) and the "signified" (the actual object, chair) combine to produce the sign "chair." By exhibiting, along with the signifier (a common folding chair), a surrogate for the visual representation (the photograph) and a surrogate for the mental concept (the dictionary definition), Kosuth transformed his semiotic analysis into art and thus created a new sign, or "metasign", which in turn invites further analysis. He would soon omit the first two steps of his analytical process and go straight for the metasign, in a sequence of Photostat blowups of dictionary definitions of art-related words (fig. **24.2**). Once mounted and exhibited, the blowups not only achieve the character of visual

24.1 Joseph Kosuth, *One and Three Chairs*, 1965. Wooden folding chair, photographic copy of a chair, and photographic enlargement of a dictionary definition of a chair; chair, 32⅜ × 14⅞ × 20⅞" (82 × 37.8 × 53 cm); photo panel, 36 × 24⅛" (91.5 × 61.1 cm); text panel, 24⅛ × 24½" (61.3 × 62.2 cm). The Museum of Modern Art, New York.

art but also an objectlike aesthetic quality comparable to that of Minimalism's crisp, elegant beauty, as well as something of its serial repetitiveness.

The German-American artist **Hans Haacke** (b. 1936), during the sixties, literally undermined the integrity of Minimalist forms by subjecting them to the eroding forces of nature, among them atmospheric conditions exhibited in the condensation forming inside a clear acrylic plastic cube. His interest in the degradation of apparently closed systems extended beyond geometry to more extensive social arrangements and brought to conceptual art a moral conscience. On being invited to exhibit at the Solomon R. Guggenheim Museum in New York City, Haacke created *Shapolsky et al., Manhattan Real Estate Holdings,*

a Real-Time Social System, as of May 1, 1971 (fig. **24.3**). In this *Real Estate* series, the artist captioned photographs of tenements, among other kinds of buildings, with business information about ownership, acquisition, and property values. Presented with all the order and logic of a minimalist grid, *Shapolsky et al* described a system in which a small group of property owners were making money out of undermaintained buildings. Right away, the *Real Estate* pieces were seen as being so inflammatory that the Guggenheim canceled the show. While the cancellation may have preserved the political "neutrality" essential to a tax-free educational institution, it also guaranteed the very kind of public interest that could serve Haacke's overriding purpose—to jolt complacent viewers into helping to correct social injustice. What it could have achieved had it been viewed in the rotunda of the Guggenheim is, of course, impossible to know.

Revisiting the early-twentieth-century idea later articulated by Donald Judd ("if someone says it's art, it's art"), Conceptualism soon spawned a vast and unruly variety of Post-Minimal works ranging from Performance art to Process and Land art, all united, however, by a common and unprecedented emphasis upon ideas and their expression through some medium other than a unique object—a permanent, portable, and therefore marketable commodity. Illustrating the principle that the "ideal Conceptual work," as Mel Bochner characterized it, could be experienced in its description and be infinitely repeatable—and thus devoid of "aura" and uniqueness—the French artist **Daniel Buren** (b. 1938) reduced his painting to a uniform neutral and internal system of commercially printed vertical stripes, a formal practice that readily lent itself to infinite replication and exhibition in any environment (fig. **24.4**). The initial concept would never have to change, and variety came not in the form itself but rather in the context: city streets, public squares, museums, and galleries are all

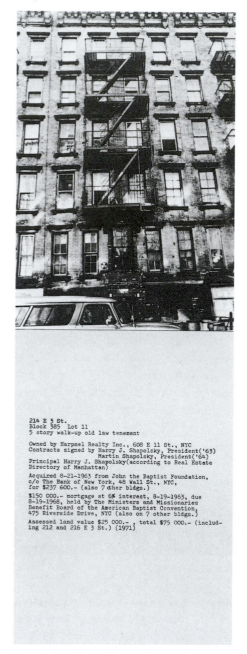

214 E 3 St.
Block 385 Lot 11
5 story walk-up old law tenement

Owned by Harpmel Realty Inc., 608 E 11 St., NYC
Contracts signed by Harry J. Shapolsky, President ('63)
                     Martin Shapolsky, President ('64)
Principal Harry J. Shapolsky (according to Real Estate
Directory of Manhattan)

Acquired 8-21-1963 from John the Baptist Foundation,
c/o The Bank of New York, 48 Wall St., NYC,
for $237 600.- (also 7 other bldgs.)

$150 000.- mortgage at 6% interest, 8-19-1963, due
8-19-1968, held by The Ministers and Missionaries
Benefit Board of the American Baptist Convention,
475 Riverside Drive, NYC (also on 7 other bldgs.)

Assessed land value $25 000.-; total $75 000.- (including 212 and 216 E 3 St.) (1971)

24.3 Hans Haacke, *Shapolsky et al., Manhattan Real Estate Holdings, a Real-Time Social System, as of May 1, 1971* (detail), 1971. 142 photographs, 2 maps, 6 charts. Edition of two. Collection the artist.

24.4 Daniel Buren, *Untitled*, 1973. Installation incorporating green and white stripes, Bleecker Street, NY (now destroyed).

highlighted by Buren's stripes, indicating that the circumstances surrounding the display of art are as important as the work itself.

Since its first articulation in LeWitt's statements, Conceptual art has been a form of critical investigation into the premises of art-making and exhibitions. Michael Asher (b. 1943) took the exposure of the museum and gallery to extremes by making his art out of the physical spaces of sale and display. Asher's 1974 *Situational Work* consisted of removing the wall that divided the exhibition and office space of a gallery. The work made the economic context of aesthetic experiences visible, thus undermining the purity of art praised by formalist critics. Moreover, there was no aesthetic or economic potential in the work itself. Photography and text served to preserve the idea and the event, but Asher's conceptual critique left nothing to buy or even observe.

Of the many forms of "documentation" that the Conceptualists found for their ideas, none served their purposes more perfectly than verbal language itself. "Without language, there is no art," declared Lawrence Weiner, who maintained that he cared little whether his "statements," a series of tersely phrased proposals, such as *A 36 x 36" Removal to the Lathing or Support of Plaster or Wallboard from a Wall*, were ever executed, by himself or anyone else. Fundamentally, he left the decision to implement the idea to the "receiver" of the work. "Once you know about a work of mine," he wrote, "you own it. There's no way I can climb into somebody's head and remove it." Meanwhile, Douglas Huebler made the Conceptualists' attitude toward form stunningly clear in a famous pronouncement published in 1968: "The world is full of objects, more or less interesting; I do not wish to add any more. I prefer, simply, to state the existence of things in terms of time or of space." In *Location Piece #14* Huebler proposed that photographs be taken over a twenty-four-hour period at twenty-four locations on the 45° parallel north of the Equator. The piece would then be constituted of the photographs, a map of the world, and the artist's statement, which concluded: "The owner of the work will assume the responsibility for fulfilling every aspect of its physical execution." But even if the "owner" assumed that responsibility, the photographs would have been indistinguishable from one another, leaving the viewer to make sense of them and bringing to bear issues of individual identity and personal response. Yet more ephemeral, but touched with the charm of whimsy, were such proposals as the following by Robert Barry, offered as serious artistic commentary:

> All the things I know
> But of which I am not
> At the moment thinking—
> 1:36 PM, June 1969.

While the Conceptualists may have denied the sensory delights offered by traditional painting and sculpture, they discovered new possibilities within the relatively restricted field of language and linguistically analogous systems. Books, newspapers, magazines, catalogs, advertising, postal and telegraphic messages, charts, and maps were all seized upon and exploited as resources for information and opinions about art and almost anything else of world interest in the early seventies. Also susceptible to Conceptualist exploitation was photography, inherent in any modern print medium, and now also readily available in the kinetic form of video, which became available to the public in the

24.5 John Baldessari, "Art History" from the book *Ingres and Other Parables*, 1972. Photograph and typed text, 8½ × 10⅞" (21.6 × 27.6 cm).

mid-sixties. Non-unique visual images quickly became almost as ubiquitous in Conceptual art as words.

John Baldessari (b. 1931) composed brief but trenchant tales about art itself, usually accompanied by a reproduction of some key monument from the art-historical canon (fig. **24.5**). In later works such as the photomontage *Heel* (fig. **24.6**), however, the narrative element became extremely elliptical. The viewer may notice that almost all of the individuals shown in the side photographs have injured feet, suggesting that the title may perhaps refer to the idea of an Achilles' heel, the mythical Greek hero's one vulnerable point. And we may also note that the individuals on the periphery could easily gather in the crowd depicted in the central image. But in order to grasp the connection that the artist apparently had in mind, it helps to know that he had been reading Elias Canetti's book *Crowds and Power*, on the relationship between crowds and individuals. In superimposing a unifying red line on the people who are drifting away from the main group, Baldessari was identifying what might be seen as the mob's Achilles' heel: its vulnerable point is that its members may wander off, one by one, dissipating its power to act.

Books, like verbal communication, offer a sequential, cumulative experience, as opposed to the plastic art of traditional painting that, being static, has the potential for providing a total, all-at-once experience at the very instant of perception. Freed from the tedium of material restraints, the Conceptualists could now move even beyond the third dimension offered by sculpture to explore the fourth

24.7 On Kawara, *The Today Series of Date Paintings*, 1966. Installation view.

dimension of time. **On Kawara** (b. 1933), a Japanese artist resident in New York, made the passage of time itself the all-important subject by each day starting a small black painting that simply set forth the current date in white block letters (fig. **24.7**). With every panel an equal component in the series, the work can reveal its full meaning only as a total conception. The German artist Hanne Darboven recorded the passage of time and her experience of it by filling an enormous number of pages with a kind of abstract calligraphy and mysterious permutating numeration, derived in part from the days, weeks, and months of the calendar. As the artist's digits add up, multiply, and interweave, they eventually cover whole walls of gallery space, finally becoming a complete environment given over to a trancelike involvement with time's steady, inexorable advance.

Extended Arenas: Performance Art and Video

Some artists found the material limitations of the written word confining and preferred the temporality of Performance art. In the seventies so many artists embraced Performance that it has been called the art form most characteristic of the period. To a generation more eager than ever to disavow the past, Performance meant venturing into an arena, specifically theater, where artists, owing partly to their lack of experience in the field, felt encouraged to proceed as if unfettered by rules or traditions. Not only did Performance liberate artists from the art object, it also freed them to adopt whatever subject matter, medium, or material seemed promising for their purposes. Performance was not simply visual communication: it often incorporated words and called upon concepts of ritual and myth that had long been important to twentieth-century artists. Moreover, it enabled artists to offer their work at any time, for any duration, at any kind of site, and in direct contact with their audience. This gave artists instant access

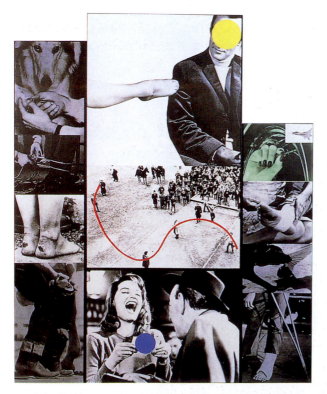

24.6 John Baldessari, *Heel*, 1986. Black-and-white photographs with oil tint, oil stick, and acrylic, mounted on board, 8'10½" × 7'3" (2.7 × 2.2 m). Los Angeles County Museum of Art.

to the receivers of their work—without the intervention of critics, curators, and dealers—and thus permitted them a new level of control over its display and destination. For all these reasons, Performance appeared to offer the maximum possibility for converting art from an object of consumption to a vehicle for ideas and action, a new form of visual communication.

Beuys

No artist active in the seventies realized the heroic potential of Performance more movingly than the charismatic and controversial German artist **Joseph Beuys** (1921–86). Shot down from his plane during World War II and given up for dead in the blizzard-swept Crimea, Beuys returned to peacetime existence determined to rehumanize both art and life by drastically narrowing the gap between the two. To achieve this, he employed personally relevant methods or materials in order to render form an agent of meaning. He began by piling unsymmetrical clumps of animal grease in empty rooms and then wrapping himself in fat and felt, an act that ritualized the materials and techniques the nomadic Crimean Tatars had used to heal the young airman's injured body. Viewing his works "as stimulants for the transformation of the idea of sculpture or of art in general," Beuys intended them to provoke thoughts about what art can be and how the concept of art-making can be "extended to the invisible materials used by everyone." He wrote about "Thinking Forms," concerned with "how we mold our thoughts," about "Spoken Forms," addressed to the question of "how we shape our thoughts into words," and finally about "Social Sculpture," meaning "how we mold and shape the world in which we live: *Sculpture as an evolutionary process; everyone is an artist.*" He continued,

24.8 Joseph Beuys, *How to Explain Pictures to a Dead Hare*, 1965. Performance at the Galerie Schmela, Düsseldorf.

"That is why the nature of my sculpture is not fixed and finished. Processes continue in most of them: chemical reactions, fermentations, color changes, decay, drying up. Everything is in a *state of change.*"

In a Düsseldorf gallery in 1965 the artist created *How to Explain Pictures to a Dead Hare* (fig. **24.8**), for which he sat in a bare room surrounded by his familiar media of felt, fat,

24.9 Joseph Beuys, *The Pack*, 1969. Installation with Volkswagen bus and 20 sledges, each carrying felt, fat, and a flashlight. Staatliche Kunstsammlungen Kassel, Neue Galerie, Germany.

wire, and wood, his face covered with gold leaf. A dead hare lay cradled in Beuys's arms, and he murmured urgently to it. To help explain this piece, Beuys said that in his work "the figures of the horse, the stag, the swan, and the hare constantly come and go: figures which pass freely from one level of existence to another, which represent the incarnation of the soul or the earthly form of spiritual beings with access to other regions." In this seemingly morbid performance, Beuys pointed up the complex and ambivalent feelings aroused in us by works of art that try to deal directly with such intractably unaesthetic subjects as death. The natural human reaction to the harmless creature held by the artist overturned any notion of "aesthetic distance." And the gold mask Beuys wore made him seem not like an artist but rather a shaman or healer who, through magical incantation, could achieve a certain oneness with the spirits of animals.

Sculptural works such as *The Pack* (fig. **24.9**) drew on Beuys's experience in a different way, transforming inanimate objects by layering them with associations both positive and negative. The sleds in this work, for example, may be part of a rescue operation, like the one that saved the artist's life during World War II, since each one carries such emergency gear as a flashlight, in addition to the felt and the animal fat that Beuys specifically associated with his own rescue. But at the same time *The Pack* bears some resemblance to the equipment of a military assault force or commando unit and in this way might assume a decidedly more aggressive than pacifist character.

In 1962 Beuys joined Fluxus, which was a loosely knit, nonconformist international group noted for its Happenings, actions, publications, concerts, and mailing activities (see below). By the end of 1965, however, he had severed relations with Fluxus, not finding the work sufficiently effective: "They held a mirror up to people without indicating how to change anything."

Paik, Acconci, Nauman, and Burden

A different kind of Performance artist whose chosen media are defined by change is **Nam June Paik** (b. 1932), who switched from straight electronic music composition to the visual arts when he discovered the expressive possibilities of video. Paik proclaimed that "as collage technique replaced oil paint, the cathode ray tube will replace the canvas." Witty, charming, and therefore especially successful in collaboration, Paik achieved a certain notoriety for several of the pieces he created for the classical cellist Charlotte

24.10 Nam June Paik, *TV Bra for Living Sculpture* (worn by Charlotte Moorman), 1969. Television sets and cello.

24.11 Nam June Paik, *TV Garden*, 1974–78. Video monitors (number varies) and plants, dimensions variable. Installation view, Whitney Museum of American Art, New York, 1982.

24.12a, 24.12b Vito Acconci, *Instant House*, 1980. Flags, wood, springs, ropes, and pulleys, open 8' × 21' × 21' (2.4 × 6.4 × 6.4 m), closed 8' × 5' × 5' (2.4 × 1.52 × 1.52 m). Museum of Contemporary Art, San Diego.

Moorman. One of these had the instrumentalist play the cello while wearing a bra made of two miniature TV sets, which took on a humanity by their association with one of the most intimate of personal garments (fig. **24.10**). When Paik and Moorman performed *Opera Sextronique* in New York in 1967, the cellist removed all her clothing and was promptly arrested for, as the guilty verdict read, "an art which openly outrage[d] public decency." In contrast to his more provocative performance works, some of Paik's video installation pieces can be quite lyrical, even contemplative. In *TV Garden* (fig. **24.11**), the viewer is invited to stroll through a pastoral setting of potted plants, a garden decorated with television monitors. The glowing video images appear amid the foliage like blossoming flowers.

One form of performance, Body art, often induced a forced intimacy between the performer and the audience, with results that could be amusing, poetic, shocking, or discomfiting. In *Seedbed*, 1972, **Vito Acconci** (b. 1940) spent hours during each performance day masturbating beneath a gallerywide ramp, while visitors overhead heard via a loudspeaker the auditory results of his fantasizing. Here was the artist reintroducing into his work the element of personal risk that came from rendering himself vulnerable to the audience, as he engaged in an intensely personal activity and grappled with the potential audience alienation that such drastic strategies could produce.

Subsequently, Acconci made sculptural objects that can "perform" when activated by the viewer. The concerns reflected in these later works have become more political than psychological. His 1980 *Instant House* (fig. **24.12a and b**) lies flat on the floor in its collapsed position. When the viewer sits on its swing, however, pulleys raise the house's walls, making a toy building that looks like a child's

version of a military guardhouse. With the walls up, the viewer seated inside is surrounded by U.S. flags applied to the inner surfaces, while viewers outside see the red Soviet flag, with its hammer and sickle. In Acconci's ironic reduction of Cold War confrontation to the less intimidating proportions of a playground game, the underlying result was to point to the terrifyingly real implications of Cold War politics.

Bruce Nauman (b. 1941) wittily made himself into a living pun on Duchamp's *Fountain* (fig. **24.13**). Over the years, his production has been an astonishingly diverse

24.13 Bruce Nauman, *Self-Portrait as a Fountain*, 1966–70. Color photograph, 19¾ × 23¾" (50.2 × 60.3 cm). Edition of eight.

24.14 Bruce Nauman, *Violins Violence Silence*, 1981–82. Neon tubing with clear glass tubing suspension frame, 62⅜ × 65⅜ × 6" (158 × 166.1 × 15.2 cm). Oliver-Hoffman Family Collection, Chicago.

24.15 Chris Burden, *Doorway to Heaven*, November 15, 1973. "At 6 p.m. I stood in the doorway of my studio facing the Venice boardwalk. A few spectators watched as I pushed two live electric wires into my chest. The wires crossed and exploded, burning me, but saving me from electrocution."

24.16 Chris Burden, *All the Submarines of the United States of America*, 1987. Installation with 625 miniature cardboard submarines, vinyl thread, typeface, 13'2" × 18' × 12' (4 × 5.5 × 3.7 m), length of each submarine 8" (20.3 cm). Dallas Museum of Art.

expression of his declaration: "I'm not interested in adding to the collection of things that are art, but [in] investigating the possibility of what art may be." Early in his career, Nauman created a number of films that made use of all that the young artist had available: himself and his empty studio. The results, including *Walking in Contrapposto*, *Pacing Upside Down*, and *Slow Angle Walk*, the latter two filmed with the camera tipped and turned over, succinctly combine humour and art history with the uncanny. His sculptural work also fluctuates uneasily between levity and seriousness. Nauman has made works in neon, some of which blink on and off with disturbing imagery, such as before-and-after images of a hanged man. Nothing could more pointedly contrast with the austere, Minimal fluorescent light-fixture works of Dan Flavin (see fig. 22.36). Other of Nauman's neon signs, such as *Violins Violence Silence* (fig. **24.14**), depict only words and as such are related to Conceptual art. Asking the viewer to read the neon lettering from either side, these signs juxtapose different words and flip them around, backward and forward, until their usual meanings are rendered confused and problematic; the letters become unfamiliar and operate more like collections of abstract shapes and bright colors. Unexpected relationships emerge, such as the odd similarity between "violence" and "violins."

Some Body artists risked going beyond the by-now expected, and accepted, shock factor in contemporary art into the realm of violent exhibitionism. **Chris Burden** (b. 1946) achieved international fame in 1971 with a performance in Los Angeles that consisted of having a friend shoot him in the arm. As was crucial to much of Conceptual art, the ephemeral performance was rendered permanent in photographic documentation. The straightforward factuality of the photograph, capturing a critical moment in another of Burden's performances (fig. **24.15**), makes the artist's ability to endure seem all the more harrowing.

Burden distanced himself, however, from any threat of actual danger in installations that, instead of enacting violence, sought to conceptualize it. He made *All the Submarines of the United States of America* (fig. **24.16**) during the centennial of the 1887 launching of the U.S. Navy's first submersible, the *SS1*. The work is made up of some 625 miniature models, representing each of the actual submarines launched by the navy during the ensuing hundred years, including its nuclear-missile-carrying Polaris submarines. The armada of tiny cardboard boats floats harmlessly in the gallery space, like a school of fish, but at the same time it enables the viewer to grasp a formidable reality—a fleet of warships capable of mass destruction.

Gilbert and George, Anderson, and Horn

In a lighthearted, though serious, response to the abstract and modernist tendencies of English sculpture of the sixties still influenced by Moore, Hepworth, and Caro, a pair of London-based artists known simply as **Gilbert** (b. 1943) and **George** (b. 1942) transformed themselves into "living sculpture" and brought to art and the world of the late sixties a much-needed grace note of stylish good humor. Indeed, they would probably have been quite successful performing in an old-fashioned English music hall, which, like all the rest of their material, Gilbert and George simultaneously parodied. For their performance *The Singing Sculpture* of 1971 (fig. **24.17**), they covered their faces and hands with metallic paint, adopted the most outrageously proper English clothing and hairstyles, placed themselves on a tabletop, and proceeded to move and mouth as if they were wound-up marionettes rendering the recorded words and music of the prewar song that gave the piece its subtitle.

A Performance artist who actually does appear in music halls, as well as recording for major record labels, while successfully preserving her place in the world of contemporary art is the multitalented **Laurie Anderson** (b. 1947). As a second-generation Conceptualist and a child of the media age, Anderson can take for granted the intellectual rigor of her predecessors and, with greater command of far more spectacular means, transform the older artists' erudite,

24.17 Gilbert and George, *The Singing Sculpture* ("*Underneath the Arches*"), 1969. Performance at the Sonnabend Gallery, New York, 1971.

24.18 Laurie Anderson, *United States Part II*. Segment *"Let X = X,"* October 1980. Performance at the Orpheum Theater, New York, presented by the Kitchen.

but often rather amateurish, demonstrations into virtuoso performances. For *United States* (fig. **24.18**), a four-part epic composed and first presented over the years 1978–82, Anderson marshaled the full array of her accomplishments—drawing, sculpture, singing, composing, violin playing, electronic effects—to deal in half-hour segments with the themes of transportation, politics, sociopsychology, and money. Juxtaposing images and text, sound and technological inventions, she swept her audience through a series of ironical "talking songs." The journey turned into a joy ride with such original devices as custom-made instruments, a slide show that magically came and went with the

24.20 Rebecca Horn, *Ostrich Egg Which Has Been Struck by Lightening*, 1995. Two brushes, ostrich egg, electric motor, 102 × 27½ × 12" (260 × 70 × 30 cm). Kunstmuseum, Bonn, Germany.

24.19 Rebecca Horn, *The Feathered Prison Fan*, as it appears in the film *Der Eintänzer*, 1978. White ostrich feathers, metal, motor, and wood, 39⅜ × 32⅝ × 12⅝" (100 × 82.9 × 32.1 cm). Private collection.

24.21 Peter Campus, *Three Transitions*, 1973. Two-inch videotape in color with sound, five minutes.

stroke of a neon violin bow, and red lips that suddenly floated in the dark. With humor, language, careful timing, style, and undeniable stage presence, Anderson has brought Conceptual art to a wide audience.

The German performance artist **Rebecca Horn** (b. 1944) has been active in creating sculpture, installations, and films. In much of her work, Horn explores the physical limits of the human body, which she often extends by using fantastic theatrical props, such as a mask of feathers, or gloves with yard-long fingers, or bizarre winglike devices operated by the performer. The most ambitious of these props are conceived as machines, such as the mechanical sculpture *The Feathered Prison Fan* (fig. **24.19**), which appeared in Horn's first feature-length film, *Der Eintänzer* ("The Gigolo," 1978).

The film is set in a ballet studio. In one scene, the fan's two huge, rotating sets of ostrich plumes, one on either side, envelop a ballerina. Yet when the legs of the standing figure are exposed, the framework of feathers looks like a set of wings mounted on her seemingly headless torso, perhaps recalling the renowned Hellenistic sculpture the *Nike* or *Winged Victory of Samothrace*, or suggesting the feathered wings attached by the mythological master inventor Daedalus to his son Icarus—that is to say, evoking figures capable of flight. And indeed elsewhere, as in *Ostrich Egg Which Has Been Struck by Lightning* (fig. **24.20**), the form of the egg calls to mind the most positive associations, symbolizing the artistic perfection sought by ballerinas as well as the formal absolutes of sculptors like Brancusi. The egg is placed between two soft brushes that move up and down but never come into contact with it; the spearlike forms threaten to pierce the egg and just barely miss. It is sensual and erotic and, at the same time, tantalizes viewers, whose expectations are titillated and then denied. Another influence is Max Ernst, whose Surrealist, masculinist fantasies are ironically evoked by Horn.

Campus's Video Art

During the seventies, Performance art extended itself into the new realm of video art, as video cameras and recorders became widely available and were used by artists such as Paik. **Peter Campus's** (b. 1937) early video work included closed-circuit installations. Viewers approaching them, not realizing that they were on camera, would unexpectedly encounter projections of their own image. Observers found themselves suddenly turned into performers. In such works, Campus explored how we come to see ourselves in unanticipated ways, not only physically but psychologically, and took as one of his main themes the ever-shifting nature of the self-image. In the early seventies he made a series of short videotapes, such as *Three Transitions* (fig. **24.21**), that pursue related ideas of transformation, usually focusing on himself as performer. Among other strange metamorphoses acted out on the tape, Campus applies makeup to his face, and the cosmetics appear to dissolve his features away. In another sequence he sets fire to a mirror reflecting his face; the mirror burns up, leaving only a dark background. In such vignettes, the human face, the basis of our sense of identity, becomes little more than a changing mask that we can never see behind.

Radical Alternatives: Feminist Art

Performance, like Conceptual art, challenged the existing means of evaluating quality that had guided the rise of modernism. Throughout the sixties, artistic and critical voices had been calling for new means of art-making to present contemporary content. First Minimalism, with its disavowal of any relationship to the context of traditional painting or sculpture, then other, less object-centered art forms gave artists the means to distinguish themselves from the oppressive nature of the canon. It was Performance art in the hands of feminist artists, however, that most clearly defined the political art of the seventies.

24.22 Yoko Ono performing *Cut Piece* at Carnegie Recital Hall, NYC, March 21, 1965.

Fluxus

The intuition that the personal was artistic, just a short step from declaring it political, was at the heart of the Fluxus group, an international collective of sculptors, painters, poets, and performance artists. In the words of the group's de facto leader, George Maciunus, Fluxus asked, "Why does everything I see that's beautiful like cups and kisses and sloshing feet have to be made into just a part of something fancier and bigger? Why can't I just use it for its own sake?" Fluxus resisted transformations of life into art, believing that the two were already inseparable. Japanese-born American member **Yoko Ono** (b. 1933) created performances *Breathe Piece* and *Laugh Piece* (both 1966) by giving one-word instructions to her audience. Her 1964 *Cut Piece* (fig. **24.22**), in which the artist sat on stage beside a large pair of scissors and wordlessly waited as the audience cut her clothes off, marks an unsettling and effective transition from the joyful whimsy of much Fluxus work to the politically astute presentations of everyday life created by feminists in the seventies.

The Feminist Arts Program

Feminist art of the seventies began at the Feminist Arts Program at the University of California, Valencia. Directed by **Miriam Schapiro** (b. 1923) and **Judy Chicago** (b. Judy Cohen, 1939), the program sought to address inequities in the arts from an institutional position.

Schapiro and Chicago's teaching redefined the creative process. Making art was not to be conceived as a private, introspective, mythic adventure. Instead, through public and private discourse, consciousness-raising sessions, personal confessions, and technical training, the program strove "to help women restructure their personalities to be more consistent with their desires to be artists and to help them build their artmaking out of their experiences as women." The major artistic statement of the program, *Womanhouse*, exposed the barriers to those desires. In describing their world, the artists of the Feminist Arts Program began restructuring the art historical landscape.

Womanhouse was one of the largest installations of the seventies. Guests were invited into the traditional spaces of domestic femininity to discover that political analysis had replaced homemaking. A bride descended a staircase, her train getting dirty as she moved straight to the kitchen, itself decorated with brightly colored breasts that slid down into the frying pan to form two fried eggs. A linen closet

24.23 Feminist Art Program, *Womanhouse* (detail of linen closet) by Sandra Org, 1971. Mixed media.

trapped another woman in a life defined, as one performance demonstrated, by an endless sheet endlessly ironed (fig. **24.23**). Perhaps the most disturbing room to audiences was the Menstruation Bathroom. The bathroom exposed the aspect of women's lives that is probably the most effectively hidden. In a white bathroom immaculately cleaned, a wastebasket sat under the sink overflowing with all the evidence of an impossibly heavy period. The excess of that small sculpture served as a metaphor for the explosive nature of the house itself. Performances, classes, consciousness-raising sessions, talks, readings, plays, and a documentary film about the project presented the often psychologically crippling pressures of being a middle-class woman in America. In doing so, *Womanhouse* provided ample evidence of the artistic potential of populations and subjects that had scarcely featured in art history textbooks and museums.

Womanhouse encouraged a generation of women artists to explore content and media that had been marginalized in the artworld but that are central to many women's experiences. The most visible work to come out of this tradition was Judy Chicago's *Dinner Party*, 1979 (fig. **24.24**). This elaborate celebration of women's history was executed, with intentional exaggeration, in such stereotypically feminine and decorative artistic mediums as needlework and china painting. The entire ensemble is organized as a triangle, a primordial symbol of womanhood as well as equality. Within its enclosed floor area are inscribed the names of 999 women in history and legend, from the ancient world up to such modern figures as Isadora Duncan, Georgia O'Keeffe, and Frida Kahlo. Each side of the triangular table has thirteen place settings; in part this makes a wry comment on the Last Supper—an exclusively male dinner party of thirteen—and in part it acknowledges the number of witches in a coven. The thirty-nine settings pay tribute to thirty-nine notable women, and each name is placed on a runner embroidered in a style appropriate to its figure's historical era. In *The Dinner Party*'s most provocative gesture, the plates on the table display painted and sculpted motifs based on female genitalia. The dynamic designs of the plates transform the vagina into an energetic counterpart to the ubiquitous phallic symbol. Such a reversal

24.24 Judy Chicago, *The Dinner Party*, 1974–79. White tile floor inscribed in gold with 999 women's names; triangular table with painted porcelain, sculpted porcelain plates, and needlework, each side 48' (14.6 m).

attracted criticism, first for essentializing and defining each woman by her anatomy, and second for visualizing female power as phallic energy in drag. The essentializing and binary nature of the work has made it as controversial as its politics and craft have made it central to the history of gender and the arts.

Performance Artists

As Judy Chicago was making work that took the female body as its source of aesthetic unity and political identity, artists such as **Carolee Schneemann** (b. 1939) and **Hannah Wilke** (1940–93) presented their bodies as their art. In the sixties, Schneemann's *Meat Joy*, a ritualistic, erotic romp between four men, four women, a serving maid, raw fish, chickens, paint, plastic, and sausages, drew on contemporary dance and Happenings to arise like the repressed unconscious of American Pop and European abstraction. First performed in Paris in 1964, Schneemann's narrative and physical clutter challenged the directorial control exerted by Yves Klein in his *Anthropometries* (see chapter 22) and the classicism of her American peers. *Meat Joy* was about liberation, sensuality, and spirit rather than aesthetics.

By the seventies, Schneemann's performances were focusing on the relationship between culture, meaning, and the female body. *Interior Scroll* (fig. **24.25**) is one of the most visceral performances of the decade. The performance included readings, the painting of a large figure and concluded with Schneemann slowly unrolling a scroll, the end of which she had been carrying in her vagina. As she removes the text she reads it and tells the audience about a confrontation with a male filmmaker. The man told her that good art must avoid the graphic and personally revealing subject matter that interested her: "You are unable to appreciate the system of the grid," he exclaims. It is this ability to confound the aesthetic rules that guide the reception of contemporary art that continues to make work such as Schneemann's so challenging. With a sensitivity that avoids the binary reversals that generated *Dinner Party*, Schneemann gave serious thought to finding meaning in the experience of being a woman that was independent from male symbols. She explained, "I thought of the vagina in many ways—physically, conceptually: as a sculptural form, an architectural referent, the source of sacred knowledge, ecstasy, birth passage, transformation." From within her body, Schneemann described her life and challenged the codes of the artworld.

Like Schneemann's, Hannah Wilke's performances reiterate her position as someone whose life is defined by playing the role of female artist. She takes the portrait as

24.25 Carolee Schneemann, *Interior Scroll*, 1975. Photographs of performance and scroll text, 48" × 72" (1.22 × 1.83m).

24.26 Hannah Wilke, *S.O.S. Starification Object Series*, 1974–82. Mixed media, 40.5" × 58" (1.03 × 1.47m) framed.

the central document of her work, staging events for the camera as well as the audience. As she has said, even asleep she is posing. Unlike Schneemann, Wilke works from within the expectations of society, casting herself as the beautiful woman posed to display her body and play the role of seductress. As she presents herself, she crafts the images so as to indicate the physical pleasure and the personal cost of such objectification. Concerned with "how to make yourself into a work of art instead of other people making you into something you might not approve of," Wilke encourages viewers to enjoy the sensuality of the body—hers and theirs—but also to recognize that desire is not without cost.

A 1977 work *Intercourse with ...* expresses the particular nature of Wilke's exposed body. The piece consisted of the artist striking poses as an answering machine played messages from her friends and family. The words shaped her body and defined her actions. She then undressed and covering her body were the names of the speakers. The names were slowly removed leaving her body without the protection of clothes or community. In *SOS Starification Object Series* (fig. **24.26**) she marked her body with signs of distress rather than care. The work consisted of an

extended series of photographs that initially resemble fashion plates. Affixed to Wilke's body, however, were pieces of chewed gum folded to represent small vulvas. The gum sculptures disrupt the seductive quality of the pose and the photograph with external signs of what artists referred to as "internal wounds." She intended the gum to suggest society's chewing up and spitting out, not only of women but also of minority ethnic groups.

The work of the Cuban-born artist **Ana Mendieta** (1948–85) centered on the drama of the body, treating female physiology as an emblem of nature's cycle of birth, decay, and rebirth. Her sculptural *Process* pieces evoke the aura of ancient fertility rituals. These works were often developed from the direct imprint of the body, as when Mendieta outlined her own silhouette on the ground in gunpowder and then sparked it off, burning her form into the soil. The resulting image was a way, the artist said, of "joining myself with nature." That impulse is also evident in the pictograph-like figure outlines that Mendieta drew on amate (bark) paper, such as *The Vivification of the Flesh* (fig. **24.27**). Here she inscribed a symbol of the body onto bark taken from a tree rooted in the earth. And in a

24.27 Ana Mendieta, *The Vivification of the Flesh* from series *Amategram*, 1981–82. Gouache and acrylic on amate (bark) paper, 24¾ × 17" (62.9 × 43.2 cm). The Metropolitan Museum of Art, New York.

24.28 Ana Mendieta, *Untitled*, from series *Fetish*, 1977. Color photograph mounted on paperboard, 20 × 13¼" (50.8 × 33.7 cm). Whitney Museum of American Art, New York.

work for the *Fetish* series (fig. **24.28**), Mendieta created a mummy-shaped mound of mud resembling a barely buried corpse and surrounded it with a shallow ditch, as if carrying out an archaic burial ceremony and returning the deceased to the earth. At the same time, the irrigation ditch and the small branches stuck into the figure's chest suggest that the body has been in a sense "planted" in the ground, to germinate and be resurrected in the spring.

Language and Identity

One of the lessons Miriam Schapiro took from her experience in the Feminist Arts Program was that, "Merely to speak out, to describe the daily ways of your life, turns out to be political." Life was a performance, and its presentation was art and politics. By the late seventies, feminists were shifting from descriptive projects to those examining how lifestyles are learned and knowledge is created. One of the most remarkable documents of the period is **Mary Kelly**'s (b. 1941) *Post-Partum Document* (fig. **24.29**). American born but at that time based in London, Kelly charted the early childhood development of her son in comparison to the psychological changes of herself as a new mother. Basing her work on the linguistic interpretation of Freud by the French psychoanalyst and writer

Jacques Lacan, Kelly emphasized the role of language in identity formation, and the changes to the mother–child relationship as her son came to an understanding of his own selfhood and a command of language.

Post-Partum Document is a series of records: imprints of diaper stains, handprints, art work, lists, medical and educational records, diagrams, and confessional notes. Some of the most striking pages record the boy's writing and the mother's interpretation on slates recalling both a schoolhouse chalkboard and the ancient Egyptian Rosetta Stone, and notes about her highly ambivalent attempts to provide day care, all displayed. The pages poignantly detail the incomplete translation of the son's acquisition of language and education into a sensible event for the mother. This is a moment when the relationship between mother and child begins to change. Significance for the child starts to be located out in the world, to be translated by him through language rather than given to him by the mother. Likewise, the role of the child as the primary bearer of meaning for the mother begins to fade in a confusing, often distressing manner. Kelly's striking foray

24.29 Mary Kelly, *Post-Partum Document: Documentation I Analysed fecal stains and feeding charts*, 1974. Perspex units, white card, diaper lining, plastic sheeting, paper, ink. Collection Art Gallery of Ontario.

into motherhood and psychology proposed content and form that combined Conceptual art, feminist politics, and psychoanalytic theory to examine aspects of female experience that were still taboo in the artworld of the seventies.

Metaphors for Life: Process Art

Like Performance, Process art countered the timelessness and structural stability of Minimal art with impermanence and variability. But while Performance artists operated in real time by making their bodies their material and personal action their means, artists interested in Process took entropy as an all-important criterion in their choice of materials and allowed the transformative effects of time to become their principal means. The Process artist's action concludes once he or she has selected the substance of the piece—ice, grass, soil, felt, snow, sawdust, even cornflakes—and has "sited" it, usually in a random way, by such means

as scattering, piling, draping, or smearing. The rest is left to natural forces—time in tandem with gravity, temperature, atmosphere, and so forth—which suggests that now, in an art where creation and placement are an integral part of the same process, means have, in the truest sense of the word, become ends. Thus, as literal as Process art may be, it also constitutes a powerful metaphor for the life process itself.

In addition to Joseph Beuys, another artist fascinated with felt was the prolific and protean **Robert Morris** (b. 1931), who in the late sixties subverted his own Minimalist sculptures (see fig. 22.51) by reinterpreting their Minimalist aesthetic in a heavy, charcoal-gray fabric that immediately collapses into shapelessness, however precisely or geometrically it may be cut (fig. **24.30**). Soon Morris would be working with such insubstantial and transient materials as steam. He also countered the absolute, concrete clarity and order of his Minimal works with "scatter pieces," actually installations of what appear to be scraps left over from the industrial manufacture of metal as well as felt squares, cubes, cylinders, spheres, and grids. The order within this apparent disorder resulted from a "continuity of details," like that discernible in Pollock's allover gestural painting—an art unified by the generalized, holistic continuum of its endlessly repeated drips and dribbles.

German-born **Eva Hesse** (1936–70), who died at the young age of thirty-four, saw Process, especially as evidenced in such unconventional, malleable materials as latex, rubber tubing, and fiberglass, as a way of subjecting Minimalist codes—serial order, modular repetition, anonymity—to a broader, less exclusive range of human values than those inherent in cerebral, male-prescribed grandeur and monumentality. Taking memory, sexuality, self-awareness, intuition, and humor as her inspiration, she allowed forms to emerge from the interaction of the processes inherent in her materials and such natural forces as gravity (fig. **24.31**). Thus, her pieces stretch from ceiling to floor, are suspended from pole to pole, sag and nod toward the floor, or hang against the wall. The works seem like dream objects, materializations of things remembered from the remote past, some even evoking the cobwebs

24.30 Robert Morris, *Untitled*, 1967–68. Felt, size variable. Installation view, 1968, Leo Castelli Gallery, New York. Private collection, New York.

24.31 Photograph of Eva Hesse's Bowery studio in New York, 1966. Left to right: *Untitled*, 1965; *Ennead*, 1966; *Ingeminate*, 1965; *Several*, 1965; *Vertiginous Detour*, 1966; *Total Zero*, 1966; *Untitled*, 1966; *Long Life*, 1965; *Untitled*, 1966; *Untitled*, 1965; *Untitled or Not Yet*, 1966.

24.32 Eva Hesse, *Contingent*, 1969. Cheesecloth, latex, and fiberglass in eight panels. Installation, 12'7⅞" × 9'4⅜" × 3'2½" (3.7 × 2.9 × 0.98 m). National Gallery of Australia, Canberra.

24.33 Lynda Benglis, *Bounce*, 1969. Poured colored latex, size variable. Private collection.

that cling to old possessions long shut away in attics and basements. The pendulous, organic shapes of her sculptures provoke associations with gestation, growth, and sexuality, the kind of emotionally loaded themes that orthodox Minimalists cast aside.

The late piece called *Contingent* (fig. **24.32**), consisting of eight free-floating sections of cheesecloth that have been covered with latex and fiberglass, takes the characteristic Minimalist concern with repeatable, serial objects and "humanizes" it. The luminous, translucent sheets function both as paintings and sculpture. Each of the hangings is allowed to become a distinct entity with its own texture and color, and each is suspended at a slightly different height; by these means, each one is given its own way of addressing the viewer who stands before it.

In the late sixties, **Lynda Benglis** (b. 1941) became fascinated by the interrelationships of painting and sculpture and used Process as a route not only to new form but also to new content. She began to explore these issues by pouring liquid substances onto the floor, just as a sculptor might pour molten bronze (fig. **24.33**). But instead of shaping it with a mold, she allowed the material to seek its own form. The artist simply mixed and puddled into the flow a startling array of fluorescent oranges, chartreuses, Day-Glo pinks, greens, and blues.

A process of a different, more organic kind, gave rise to the relief *Excess* (fig. **24.34**). Here the use of beeswax suggests an association between the making of the work and bees' natural process of building up a honeycomb. The relief, too, was built up over time, growing bit by bit as the artist applied the pigmented wax medium. The resulting form also displays unmistakable links with organic life: its encrustations recall the furrowed underside of some immense caterpillar. In subsequent works, the artist has pursued pictorial effects in wall reliefs with strong plastic, sculptural qualities. Often they have fan or bow-knotted shapes and are finished with some sumptuously decorative materials, such as gold leaf or a patina of rich verdigris.

Although he came to prominence among ambitious Minimalist sculptors, many of whom have created powerful works in steel and stone, **Richard Tuttle** (b. 1941) dared to give viewers what Bruce Nauman, an admirer of his work, has called "a less important thing to look at." Working throughout his career with delicate and ephemeral materials, such as paper, string, and thin pieces of wire, Tuttle has been singled out for his work's unassertiveness,

24.34 Lynda Benglis, *Excess*, 1971. Purified beeswax, dammar resin, pigments on Masonite and pinewood, 36 × 5 × 4" (91.4 × 12.7 × 10.2 cm). Walker Art Center, Minneapolis.

24.35 Richard Tuttle, *Monkey's Recovery for a Darkened Room (Bluebird)*, 1983. Wood, wire, acrylic, paint, mat board, string, and cloth, 36 × 22 × 6½" (91.4 × 55.9 × 16.5 cm). Private collection.

24.36 Sam Gilliam, *Carousel Form II*, 1969. Acrylic on canvas, 10' × 6'3" (3 × 1.9 m). Installation view, Corcoran Gallery of Art, Washington, D.C. Collection the Artist.

as when, for example, dyed pieces of cloth in geometric shapes are simply attached to the wall of a gallery.

When introduced into a specific venue, such works do not aggressively transform their surroundings, as do the more imposing sculptural works of some of Tuttle's peers. Instead, with their subtle nuances of texture and color, his modest constructions awaken a feeling for the sheer vulnerability of the domestic items around us, a sense of needing protection that can extend to ourselves as well. One critic has called Tuttle's work a "meditation on the extreme fragility of existence." Tuttle gains our sympathy for these frail, decorative pieces (fig. 24.35) by endowing them with so much visual life: a finely gauged interplay of primary colors, the skillful intermixing of geometric with organic forms, and an elegantly balanced yet lively composition.

The Washington-based artist **Sam Gilliam** (b. 1933) fused painting and sculpture by flinging highly liquefied color onto stretched canvas, somewhat in the fashion of Jackson Pollock, though less in the spirit of controlled accident. He then suspended the support, minus its stretchers, from the ceiling (fig. 24.36). Thus draped and swagged, the material ceased to do what would traditionally be expected of painted canvas and became a free-form, plastic evocation.

Associated for a time with the Fluxus group, German-born **Dieter Roth** (b. 1930) lived in Switzerland, Iceland, Spain, and England. Roth became known for using food

and other organic materials in unusual ways. In 1970 he had an exhibition of forty pieces of luggage, each filled with a different variety of cheese; during the show, the cheeses rotted and the suitcases leaked, attracting hordes of flies. As Roth has said of another work of his made with foodstuffs, "Sour milk is like landscape, ever changing. Works of art should be like that—they should change like man himself, grow old and die."

While living in London, Roth became a friend of the British Pop artist Richard Hamilton (see fig. 21.1). This association informs *Six Piccadillies* (figs. **24.37a and b**), a portfolio of six prints based on a postcard view of Piccadilly Circus. In this instance, Roth explored a different kind of process—the technical act of making a reproductive print, which involves separating the colors of the original image into the four basic colors used for commercial printing, creating plates to hold the inks, and reworking the image through a series of press proofs. By these means, Roth produced a series of variations on the postcard image, letting it "decompose" itself through the printed medium.

Following a long tradition in Western civilization that can be traced from Plato through Cézanne to the Minimalists, Canadian-born **Jackie Winsor** (b. 1941) visualizes perfection in what the sixties had learned to call Primary forms—simple squares, cubes, cylinders, spheres, and grids. Although her works do not, once finished, evince the process of their own making, that process is

24.37a, 24.37b Dieter Roth, Two screen prints from *Six Piccadillies*, 1969–70. Portfolio of six screen prints on board, each 19¾ × 27½" (50.2 × 69.9 cm).

quite significant. It involves prolonged, ritualistically repetitive activity and materials chosen for their power to endow ideal geometry with a mysteriously contradictory sense of latent, primitive energy. In a 1971–72 work entitled *Bound Grid* (fig. **24.38**) that kind of energy was evident in the tension between a boldly simple grid form, made of crossed logs, and the slow, complex technique employed to lash the beams together. This entailed unraveling massive old ropes, returning them to their primary state as twine, and wrapping the crinkled, hairy strands round and round, for several days a week over months on end.

In 1980–82, Winsor set about activating energy in another, more startlingly dramatic manner. First she built a multilayered interior of plaster, gold leaf, and fluorescent pigment contained within a cube made of hand-buffed,

black concrete reinforced with welded steel. After bringing the piece to the requisite degree of perfection, Winsor added a further element—dynamite—and exploded it (fig. **24.39a**). Later she gathered up the fragments, reinforced the interior, and restructured the outer layer (fig. **24.39b**). In its final state, *Exploded Piece* seems quiescent and contained, even though it bears the scars of the various stages—both the carefully measured and the immeasurably volatile—through which it passed in the course of its creation, destruction, and reconstruction. What physically happened to the form and its material constitutes the content of *Exploded Piece*.

Associated with *Arte povera* in Italy—a group that attempted to illustrate the intersection of everyday life with the practice of art—the Italian sculptor and painter **Mario Merz** (b. 1925) has always been fascinated by the

24.38 Jackie Winsor, *Bound Grid*, 1971–72. Wood and hemp, 7' × 7' × 8" (2.1 × 2.1 × 0.2 m). Fonds National d'Art Contemporain, Paris.

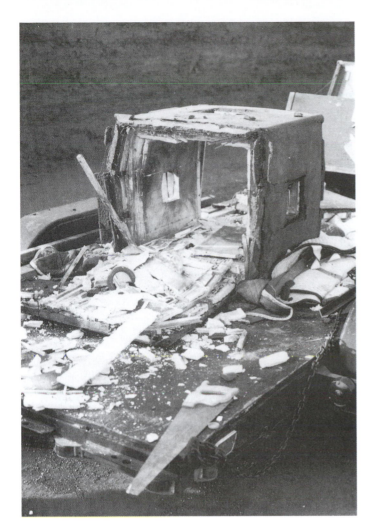

way that the world of nature and the world of modern civilization interact. Exploring this theme, he began making his "igloos" in 1968. Like much of his other work, the igloos fuse natural materials, such as mud and twigs, with industrial products, such as metal tubing and glass, to create rudimentary structures that look as if they were the shelters of some unknown nomadic people. The igloos' effect when shown in a museum is that their inhabitants have temporarily camped indoors. In the case of *Giap Igloo* (fig. **24.40**), Merz added modern neon signs to the outside, which spell out (in Italian) a saying by the North

24.40 Mario Merz, *Giap Igloo—If the Enemy Masses His Forces, He Loses Ground; If He Scatters, He Loses Strength*, 1968. Metal tubes, wire mesh, wax, plaster, and neon tubes, height 3'11¼" (1.2 m), diameter 6'6¾" (2 m). Musée National d'Art Moderne, Centre d'Art et de Culture Georges Pompidou, Paris.

24.39a (above, top), 24.39b (above) Jackie Winsor, *Exploded Piece*, 1980–82. Wood, reinforced concrete, plaster, gold leaf, pigment, steel, and explosive residue, 34½ × 34½ × 34½" (87.6 × 87.6 × 87.6 cm). Private collection.

24.41 Jannis Kounellis, *Cotoniera*, 1967. Steel and cotton.

Vietnamese general named in the work's title: "If the enemy masses his forces, he loses ground; if he scatters, he loses strength." With its military proverb and conspicuous association with Vietnam, this particular igloo, made in 1968 at the height of the war, suggests an improvised guerrilla fortification of sandbags.

In one of his best-known works, **Jannis Kounellis** (b. 1936)—a Greek artist active in Italy and deeply influenced by the Process-related works of the Italians Alberto Burri and Lucio Fontana (see figs. 20.38, 20.40)—stabled horses in a Roman art gallery as a way of dramatizing the contrast, and necessary relationship, between the organic world of nature and the human-created, artificial world of art. The same ideas inform *Cotoniera* (fig. **24.41**), a piece in which the soft, white, perishable fluffiness of cotton was combined with the dark, indestructible rigidity of steel to create a dialectic of nature and industry. In a later, untitled work of 1986, the world of human creation is all that is made manifest, represented by no more than forty-two toy trains endlessly orbiting the pillars of a vacant building.

Big Outdoors: Earthworks and Land Art

At the same time that certain Process artists were integrating aspects of nature into their work, other Conceptualists acted on the idea of taking art out of both gallery and society and fixing it within far-off, uninhabited nature as huge, immobile, often permanent Land- or Earthworks. Insofar as pieces of this environmental character and scale were often not available to the general public, it was largely through documentation that they became known—which made such informational artifacts as photographs, maps, and drawings all the more important. Ironically, the documents often assumed a somewhat surprising fine-art pictorial quality, especially when presented in a conventional gallery setting. Then again, while Land artists may have escaped the ubiquitous marketing system of traditional art objects, they became heavily dependent on engineers, construction crews, earth-moving equipment, and even aerial-survey planes, the field equivalent of the factory-bound industrial procedures used by Minimalists, with all the high finance that that entailed.

The possibility of taking art into the wilderness nevertheless held great meaning at the time. Just as performance appeared to reintroduce an element of sacred ritual and mystery into a highly secularized modern society, Earth art seemed to formalize the revived interest in salvaging not only the environment but also what remained of such archaeological wonders as Stonehenge, Angkor Wat, and pre-Columbian burial mounds. The back-to-the-soil impulse may have first appeared in the post-studio works of Carl Andre, Robert Morris, and Richard Serra, who began to democratize sculpture by adopting the most commonplace materials—firebricks, logs, metal squares, styrofoam, rusted nails—and by merely scattering them over the floor

or assembling them on it. In Earth and Site works, the variables of selection and process inherent in the site took precedence over materials; they also shifted the perspective from that imposed by standing, vertical postures, with their anthropomorphic echoes of the human figure, to the bird's-eye overview allowed by arrangements that stayed flat to the ground. In its dialogue with natural forms and phenomena, Land art chimed with the burgeoning ecology movement of the late twentieth century, which called for more sustained and serious attention to be directed toward the dislocating effects of human intervention on the natural environment.

Monumental Works

One of the first to make the momentous move from gallery to wilderness was the California-born artist **Michael Heizer** (b. 1944), who, with the backing of art dealer Virginia Dwan and the aid of bulldozers, excavated a Nevada site to create the Earthwork *Double Negative* (fig. **24.42**). Heizer is a Westerner and is sensitive to the immensity of the American landscape. In the Nevada desert he found what he called "that kind of unraped, peaceful religious space artists have always tried to put in their work." For *Double Negative*, Heizer and his construction team sliced into the surface of Mormon Mesa and made two cuts to a depth of fifty feet (15.25 m), the cuts facing one another

24.42 Michael Heizer, *Double Negative*, 1969–70. 240,000-ton displacement in rhyolite and sandstone, 1,500 × 50 × 30' (457.2 × 15.2 × 9.1 m). Mormon Mesa, Overton, Nevada. The Museum of Contemporary Art, Los Angeles.

24.43 Dennis Oppenheim, *Canceled Crop*, 1969. Grain field, 709 × 422' (216 × 129 m). Finsterwolde, the Netherlands.

(50 cubic meters) of rich, aromatic topsoil spread some two feet (0.6 m) deep throughout the gallery space. At the same time that this moist, brown-black rug kept patrons at a definite physical remove, it also provided a light–dark, textural contrast with the gleaming white walls of the gallery and filled the air with a fresh, country fragrance, both purely sensuous or aesthetic experiences. Eventually De Maria would expand the boundaries of his site to embrace vast tracts of fallow land and the entire sky above.

In *Lightning Field* (fig. **24.44**) De Maria combined the pictorialness and ephemeral character of European Land art with the sublimity of scale and conception typical of American Earthworks. Here the natural force incited by the work is lightning, drawn by four hundred stainless-steel rods standing over twenty feet (6 m) tall and arranged as a one-mile-by-one-kilometer grid set in a flat, New Mexican basin ringed by distant mountains. Chosen not only for its magnificent, almost limitless vistas and exceptionally sparse human population, but also for its frequent incidence of atmospheric electricity, the site offered the artist a prime opportunity to create a work that would involve both earth and sky, yet intrude upon neither, by articulating their trackless expanse with deliberately induced discharges of lightning. Few have ever been eyewitnesses to *Lightning Field* in full performance, but the photographic documentation leaves little doubt about the sublime, albeit unpredictable, unrepeatable, and fugitive effects that can be produced by a work designed to celebrate the power and visual splendor of an awesome natural phenomenon.

In 1968, the same year that De Maria created his *Munich Earth Room*, **Robert Smithson** (1938–73)

across a deep indentation to create a site fifteen hundred feet (457 m) long and about fifty feet (15.2 m) wide. But at the heart of this work resides a void, with the result that, while providing an experience of great vastness, *Double Negative* does not so much displace space as enclose it. Here the viewer is inside and surrounded by the work, instead of outside and in confrontation with it.

For *Canceled Crop* (fig. **24.43**), a work created in 1969 at Finsterwolde, the Netherlands, **Dennis Oppenheim** (b. 1938) plowed an "X" with 825-foot (251.5 m) arms into a 709 by 422-foot (216 x 129 m) wheat field. As if to comment on the binding artist-gallery-art cycle, Oppenheim said of his Dutch piece: "Planting and cultivating my own material is like mining one's own pigment. … I can direct the later stages of development at will. In this case the material is planted and cultivated for the sole purpose of withholding it from a product-oriented system." In a work like this, Oppenheim emphasized the overridingly significant elements of time and experience in Conceptual art.

When the American artist **Walter de Maria** (b. 1935) initially felt the telluric pull, he responded by transporting earth directly into a Munich gallery. Once installed, *Munich Earth Room*, 1968, consisted of 1,766 cubic feet

24.44 Walter de Maria, *Lightning Field*, 1970–77. A permanent Earth sculpture: 400 stainless steel poles, with solid stainless-steel pointed tips, arranged in a rectangular grid array (16 poles wide by 25 poles long) spaced 220' (67.1 m) apart; pole tips form an even plane, average pole height 20'7" (6.3 m); work must be seen over a 24-hour period. Near Quemado, New Mexico.

relocated shards of sandstone from his native New Jersey to a New York City gallery and there piled them in a mirror-lined corner. In such gallery installations, including *Chalk-Mirror Displacement* of the following year, Smithson utilized strategically positioned mirrors to endow the amorphous mass of organic shards with a new form. Smithson's nonsite works (that is, works made in a formal, gallery setting rather than out in the landscape) were a synthesis of unformed organic material from the landscape and such rigid, manufactured forms as mirrors. The juxtaposition of these materials represented the dialectic between entropy and order. And just as the transferral from nature to gallery would seem to have arrested the natural process of continuous erosion and excerpted a tiny portion from an immense, universal whole, the mirrored gallery setting expanded the portion illusionistically, while also affirming its actual, and therefore infinite, potential for change in character and context. Fully aware of the multiple and contrary effects of his mirror pieces—of the dialectic it set up between site and nonsite—Smithson commented on these works' power as a metaphor for flux: "One's mind and the earth are in a constant state of erosion … ideas decompose into stones of unknowing."

Smithson moved from gallery installations back to site works and discovered a major inspiration in Utah's Great Salt Lake, which the artist saw as "an impassive faint violet sheet held captive in a stony matrix, upon which the sun poured down its crushing light." As this lyric phrase would suggest, the artist was a gifted and even prolific writer, whose essays about his Great Salt Lake creation have made *Spiral Jetty* the most famous and romantic of all the Earthworks (fig. **24.45**). He deposited 6,000 tons (6,096 tonnes) of earth into the lake, forming an enormous raised spiral. With its graceful curl and extraordinary coloration—pink, blue, and brown-black—the piece rewards the viewer with endless aesthetic delight, but the form, for all its purity, arose from Smithson's deep pondering of the site, combined with his fascination with entropy—the gradual degradation of matter and energy in the universe—and the possibilities of reclamation.

At this particular point on the shore of the Great Salt Lake, Smithson found not only industrial ruin, in the form of wreckage left behind by oil prospectors, but also a landscape wasted and corroded by its own inner dynamism. As Smithson wrote, the gyre does not expand into a widening circle but winds inward; it is "matter collapsing into the lake mirrored in the shape of a spiral." Prophetic words, for in the ensuing years *Spiral Jetty* has disappeared—and reappeared—periodically amidst the changing water levels of the Great Salt Lake. The films and photographs that document the piece now provide the only reliable access to it. Tragically, Smithson died in a plane crash during an aerial inspection of a site in Texas.

On a less monumental scale than her husband Robert Smithson's late projects, **Nancy Holt**'s (b. 1938) Land art involves site-specific architectural sculptures that are

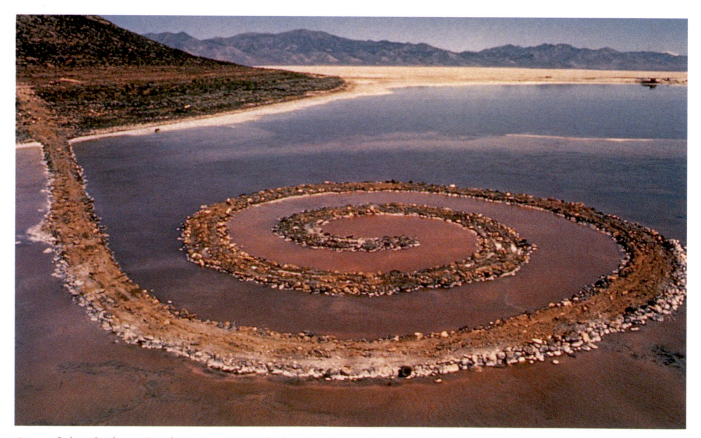

24.45 Robert Smithson, *Spiral Jetty*, 1969–70. Black rock, salt crystal, and earth, diameter 160' (48.8 m), coil length 1,500' (457.2 m), width 15' (4.6 m). Great Salt Lake, Utah.

24.46 Nancy Holt, *Stone Enclosure: Rock Rings*, 1977–78. Brown Mountain stone, diameter of outer ring 40' (12.2 m), diameter of inner ring 20' (6.1 m), height of ring walls 10' (3 m). Western Washington University, Bellingham.

absolutely integral with their surroundings. Holt's involvement with photography and camera optics led her to make monumental forms that are literally seeing devices, fixed points for tracking the positions of the earth, the sun, and the stars. One of her most important works is *Stone Enclosure: Rock Rings* (fig. **24.46**), designed for and built

as a permanent outdoor installation on the campus of Western Washington University at Bellingham, Washington. It consists of two concentric rings formed of stone walls two feet (0.6 m) thick and ten feet (3 m) high. The inner wall defines a tubular space at the center and the outer one an annular space in the corridor running between the two rings; the smaller ring measures twenty feet (6 m) in diameter and the larger one forty feet (12 m). Piercing the walls are eight-foot (2.4 m) arches and twelve circular holes three feet, four inches (1 m) in diameter. Together these apertures give the spectator both physical and visual access into and even through a structure whose circular presence and carefully calculated perspectives evoke Stonehenge, the prehistoric monument in Wiltshire, England, apparently constructed, at least in part, as a device for marking the solar year.

Landscape as Experience

In England, with its long history of the interrelationship of art and the natural environment in painting, poetry, and landscape gardening, a number of artists contemporary with Heizer and Smithson also looked to landscape as a means of creating art outside the market system. But these artists were confronted with very different issues—limited funds and a more intimate landscape that was densely populated, heavily industrialized, rigorously organized, and carefully protected. In response to these challenges, they chose to treat nature with a featherlight touch and, in

24.47 Richard Long, *A Line in Scotland*, 1981. Framed work consisting of photography and text, 34½ × 49" (87.6 × 124.5 cm). Private collection, London.

24.48 Richard Long, *Ocean Stone Circle*, 1990. Stones, diameter 13' (3.96 m).

contrast to the more interventionist Americans, to work on a decidedly antiheroic scale.

Richard Long (b. 1945) "intervenes" in the countryside mainly by walking through it, and indeed he has made walking his own highly economical means of transforming land into art. Along the way he expresses his ideas about time, movement, and place by making marks on the earth, by plucking blossoms from a field of daisies, or by rearranging stones, sticks, seaweed, or other natural phenomena (fig. **24.47**). With these he effects simple, basic shapes: straight lines, circles, spirals, zigzags, crosses, and squares that he documents with photographs. A token of human intelligence is thus left on the site—like the stone markers put in place by prehistoric peoples—and is then abandoned to the weather. "A walk is just one more layer," Long asserts, "a mark laid upon the thousands of other layers of human and geographic history on the surface of the land." Then, in a reversal of this practice, these landmarks can also be gathered up and displayed in a museum setting (fig. **24.48**), as were Smithson's gallery installations. When the stones are arranged indoors, a token of the natural world is introduced into the human-made environment of buildings and communities. The walk through nature, which Long has now extended to a global enterprise, is completed as the walker returns home from the gallery.

In contrast to Nancy Holt, who constructs permanent sites for viewing transient phenomena, **Mary Miss** (b. 1944) builds deliberately fragile architectural sculptures as a means of stressing the ephemerality of experience. Common to both artists, however, is a preoccupation with time as it affects the perception of space, as well as a deter-

mination to create a viable public art by making the viewer more than a neutral receptor. In the publicly funded *Field Rotation* (fig. **24.49**), sited at Governors State University in Park Forest South, Illinois, Miss took her primary inspiration from the terrain, an immense, flat field with a gently curved mound at the center. To explore this space and unleash its potential for yielding both a personal and shared expression of cultural experience, Miss used lines of posts to pattern the field as a kind of giant pinwheel. Its spokes or arms radiate outward from, while also converging toward, a "garden" sunk within the central hub or mound. In it, there is a pit shaped like a fortress and built up inside

24.49 Mary Miss, *Field Rotation*, 1981. Steel, wood, and gravel, central structure 56' square (17.1 m²), depth 7' (2.1 m), sited on 4½ acres (1.8 hectares). Governors State University, Park Forest South, Illinois.

as a reticulated, cross-timbered lookout rising above a "secret" well filled with water. At the same time that the posts and their fanlike movement articulate the vast openness of the American landscape, the sunken garden which these paths lead both toward and away from provides sanctuary and retreat from the surrounding barrenness.

Alice Aycock (b. 1946) too is less interested in building durable monuments than in siting and structuring her sculptures to induce us to move and thus intensify our experience of the environment, the work, and ourselves. But in a manner all her own, Aycock is concerned with the psychological implications of the architectural sites she creates for the sake of reembracing nature. On a site she chose in Far Hills, New Jersey, Aycock built *A Simple Network of Underground Wells and Tunnels* (fig. **24.50**), a structure, as the title would suggest, hardly visible at eye level, but filled with implications for the spectator courageous enough to enter it. To realize the work, Aycock began by marking off a twenty-eight-by-fifty-foot (8.5 x 15.2 m) site with straight rows of cement blocks. Within this precinct she then excavated a twenty-by-forty-foot (6.1 x 12.2 m) area and installed two sets of three seven-foot-deep (2.1 m) wells connected by tunnels. After capping three of the shafts, the artist lowered ladders into two of the uncapped ones, thereby inviting the observer to descend and explore an underground labyrinth of dark, dank passages. Aycock uses Minimalism's cool, structuralist vocabulary but in distinctively novel, even surreal ways, the better to evoke such structural precedents as caves, catacombs, dungeons,

24.50 Alice Aycock, *A Simple Network of Underground Wells and Tunnels*, 1975. Concrete-block wells and tunnels underground, demarcated by a wall, 28 × 50' (8.5 × 15.2 m), area 20 × 40' (6.1 × 12.2 m). Marriewold West, Far Hills, New Jersey.

or beehive tombs and to make them the expressive agents of her own work.

In celebrating the natural environment, **Alan Sonfist** (b. 1946) has sought to recreate a sense of an earlier, unspoiled time. Sonfist was born in the South Bronx, in New York City, but happened to live near one of the area's few remaining wooded stretches. The compelling experience of seeing the vestiges of nature amid the gritty streets is reflected in his 1978 outdoor mural, *An American Forest*, at Tremont Avenue in the Bronx. The painting's

24.51 Alan Sonfist, *Circles of Time*, 1986–89. Bronze, rock, plants, and trees on three acres (1.2 hectares). Created in Florence, Italy.

marked contrast with the deteriorating buildings around it created a sharp sense of how different the American Eden had been before the land was settled and the cities built. In another, more Conceptual work, Sonfist put up memorial cardboard plaques at sites around the city where particular indigenous flora and fauna had long ago been displaced by sidewalks and office buildings. Some of his other work has a more international scope but still generally refers to an earlier, unspoiled state of nature. *Circles of Time* (fig. **24.51**), created for the city of Florence, is a circular garden that allows the viewer to trace what Sonfist calls "the history of vegetation" in that part of Italy. Like the rings of a tree trunk, each successive concentric circle of this work, from the center to the outer rim, represents a later era. In the center is the virgin forest, a time before human intervention. Farther out lies a band representing the herb gardens of the ancient Etruscans. Next are bronze casts of endangered or extinct trees, then a ring of laurels, referring to the influence of Greece on Italy. A band of stones then demonstrates a historical Tuscan style of street pavement, and the present-day agriculture of modern Tuscany is memorialized at the edges.

Like many sculptors during the early seventies, **Michael Singer** (b. 1945) first worked in natural environments with the materials and shifting conditions they offered (fig. **24.52**). This took him from sites such as the beaver bogs near Marlboro, Vermont, to the saltwater marshes of Long Island, New York. Instead of imposing a preset idea on these sites in the manner of the Earth artists, however, he allowed nature and its laws to act on him and his work. In the mid-seventies, Singer returned to the studio and began making indoor pieces, confident that he could now maintain an aesthetic distance from such dominant trends as Minimalism and Conceptualism. By the eighties, the resulting art had grown in complexity and poetic content, yet it preserved the essential qualities that Singer achieved almost from the start. Formally, they contained rough stones and beams of diverse shapes assembled on the ground or on doors in self-contained, though visibly accessible, structures held in serene balance—a balance so delicate and precarious that it seems redolent of the mystery emanating from altars and ritual gates.

The photographer **John Pfahl** (b. 1939) has also been much involved with interventions at specific sites. Among his works along these lines is an extended series from 1974 to 1978 called *Altered Landscapes*. Pfahl photographed natural landscapes that had been subtly changed by the addition of foreign objects, such as pieces of string, foil, or blue

24.52 Michael Singer, *First Gate Ritual* series, 1979. Bamboo and phragmites. DeWeese Park, Dayton, Ohio.

24.53 John Pfahl, *Fat Man Atomic Bomb/Great Gallery Pictographs* from series *Missile/Glyphs*, 1984–85. Two Cibachrome prints mounted on aluminum, 44 × 32" (111.8 × 81.3 cm).

tape. In adding such modest items, he took care to ensure that the scene was never physically compromised. Concern for the natural environment prompted him to call attention to the threats posed to the earth by human actions. In *Fat Man Atomic Bomb/Great Gallery Pictographs* (fig. **24.53**) from the series *Missile/Glyphs*, Pfahl documented a marking of the land as harmless as his own—the petroglyphs, or pictorial inscriptions, carved or scored on rock by indigenous peoples. But he contrasts this with the horrific nuclear threat posed by modern missiles: a bulbous shape recalling "Fat Man," the military's familiar wartime name for the Nagasaki atomic bomb, has been added to the depiction of the site and looms ominously over a group of glyph figures. The small area of rock actually shown in the photograph seems to become a populated landscape, with a threatening mushroomlike form above. It is a restrained image that nonetheless carries tragic overtones.

James Turrell (b. 1943) was associated at the beginning of his career with the Californian Robert Irwin (see fig. 22.37), founder of what is usually called light and space art. But Turrell's installations, to a greater degree than Irwin's, explore the mysteries of how we actually perceive light, the basis of all visual experience. Specifically, Turrell manipulates our perception of light in order to reveal that

24.54 James Turrell, *Afrum-Proto*, 1967. Quartz-halogen projection.

our understanding of the space before us, and the way we see things within it, is fundamentally a kind of optical illusion. For example, in the early light sculpture *Afrum-Proto* (fig. **24.54**), Turrell projected an intense beam of halogen light to form what appeared to be a three-dimensional,

24.55 James Turrell, Aerial view of *Roden Crater Project*, Sedona, Arizona, 1982. Cinder cone volcano, approx. height 540' (164.6 m), diameter 800' (243.8 m).

material object floating in the empty air. Turrell's most ambitious effort has been the site work called the *Roden Crater Project* (fig. **24.55**), begun in 1974 and still in progress. By moving hundreds of thousands of cubic yards of earth and slightly reshaping the bowl of this extinct volcano, he is enhancing its ability to create optical effects, transforming it into a vast "viewing space." Far from city lights, visitors look up from the bottom of the crater; they witness with remarkable clarity the subtle yet extraordinary phenomena produced by changing atmospheric conditions in the clear Arizona sky. At times, the firmament over their heads can appear to solidify into an opaque disk that seems to rest on the rim of the crater. Under other conditions, the sky opens up as an illuminated dome of infinite depth, becoming what Turrell calls "celestial vaulting."

Abakanowicz's Sculpture

Unlike most sculptors interested in the nature of particular sites, the Polish artist **Magdalena Abakanowicz** (b. 1930) has focused on the human form. Her serial groups of figures owe some of their effectiveness to their complex surface textures, which give them each a certain organic, living quality, comparable to that of skin, as well as an individual identity. In the mid-seventies, Abakanowicz planned a series of seated figures cast from plaster molds, one mold for the front and one for the back, but wound up making only frontal figures. A few years later she decided to use the back parts of the molds, too, which had been set aside. The result was the sculptural ensemble called *Backs* (fig. **24.56**). Here, vulnerable-looking hunched-over forms, headless and with only remnants of arms and legs, gather in a crowd. The group produces an unsettling effect when installed at any site, regardless of whether it is a landscape or a museum. Outdoors, the *Backs* may recall knots of dispirited refugees resting by the side of the road, not an uncommon sight in Central Europe during the artist's lifetime. When shown in the confines of a gallery, the *Backs* become patient captives put on display, turned away from the museum visitors who have come to look.

A sense of vulnerability is also evident in *Zadra* (fig. **24.57**), from the artist's cycle *War Games*. Working with huge tree trunks that foresters had cut down and left behind, Abakanowicz attacked the wood with ax and chainsaw, hacking it into forms associable with military aggression, such as cannon or projectile shapes.

24.56 Magdalena Abakanowicz, *Backs*, 1976–80. Burlap and resin, 80 pieces, each approx. 25¾ × 21¾ × 23¾" (65.4 × 55.2 × 60.3 cm). Installed near Calgary, Canada, 1982. Collection Museum of Modern Art, Pusan, South Korea.

24.57 Magdalena Abakanowicz, *Zadra*, from the cycle *War Games*, 1987. Wood, steel, iron, and burlap, 4'3" × 3'3" × 27'4¾" (1.3 m × 100.3 × 8.4 m). Hess Collection, Napa, California.

Yet she treated others of the dismembered trees as if they were war's helpless victims and compassionately bandaged them with burlap. (The bandage idea may owe something to the red-marked sackcloth collages made after World War II by Alberto Burri—see fig. 20.40—who had been a doctor.) In this way, concerns related to the body were made manifest through natural materials from a particular site.

Visible Statements: Monuments and Public Sculpture

The environmental impulse struck a deep, resonant chord in the consciousness of artists and patrons alike, and it continued to reverberate even as the trend developed away from interventionist procedures toward sculptural or architectural forms made independently of, but in relation to, the chosen site. Inevitably, public sculpture has produced conflicts, especially since much of it has been created under public commission or within the public domain, a situation that seems automatically to require that art strike some tenable balance between its own need for internal coherence and the needs of the immediate surroundings. At issue has been the degree of accommodation necessary between the essentially private, enigmatic character of modern art and the expectation that art placed in the public arena be accessible—that is, expressive and meaningful—to the public at large. A dramatic precedent for daring, monumental sculpture in an outdoor public setting had been provided by the aged Picasso's nearly sixty-six-foot-high (20 m) Chicago Civic Center sculpture of 1966 (fig. **24.58**). That huge work's conspicuous location and popular acceptance did much to certify the validity of urban site works, as well as provide encouragement to young artists. But if site sculpture represented a return to a variant of the very "aesthetic object" that Conceptualism had set out to eliminate from art, the actual objects now produced by environmentally minded artists nonetheless remained relatively free of a purist formal modernism.

Monumental sculptures spread across the American urban landscape, largely owing to the United States General Services Administration's Art-in-Architecture program, which required one-half of one percent of the cost of constructing a new federal building to be allocated for the installation of artworks designed to enhance the new structure and its site. One of the most successful of the federally sponsored public monuments is **Claes Oldenburg** (b. 1929)

24.58 Pablo Picasso, *Chicago Monument*, 1966. Welded steel, height 65'9" (20 m). Civic Center, Chicago.

24.59 Claes Oldenburg and Coosje Van Bruggen, *Batcolumn*, 1977. Welded steel bars painted gray, height 100' (30.5 m). United States Social Security Administration, Chicago.

24.60 Claes Oldenburg and Coosje van Bruggen, *Spoonbridge and Cherry*, 1985–88. Aluminum, stainless steel, and paint, 29'6" × 51'6" × 13'6" (9 × 15.7 × 4.1 m). Walker Art Center, Minneapolis.

and **Coosje Van Bruggen**'s (b. 1942) *Batcolumn* (fig. **24.59**). This large-scale project, as the collaborators prefer to call their monumental outdoor work, is a hundred-foot-tall (30.5 m) open-work, diamond-grid steel shaft erected in 1977 directly in front of the new Social Security Administration center in a former slum near the west end of Chicago's Loop. Oldenburg and Van Bruggen settled on the baseball-bat shape for the city of Chicago, an image

mimicking the many heroic columns in the city's older Beaux Arts architecture, the soaring towers of the sky-scraper architecture Chicago invented, the countless smokestacks celebrated by Carl Sandburg, and the game played and cheered with such passion on Wrigley Field and Comisky Park. *Batcolumn* also makes a wry comment on art, specifically recalling Brancusi's *Endless Column* (see fig. 9.19) and Gabo's 1956–57 construction for the Bijenkorf

24.61 Richard Serra, *Tilted Arc*, 1981. Hot-rolled steel, height 12' (3.7 m) length 120' (36.6 m). Formerly at Federal Plaza, Foley Square, New York; removed in 1989.

department store in Rotterdam (see fig. 17.6). By recasting such a banal form on a monumental scale, the artists brought to fruition something of Oldenburg's earlier visionary "proposals" for revitalizing the urban world with familiar objects fantastically enlarged—immense baked potatoes, lipsticks, bananas, and Good Humor bars (see fig. 21.28). More recently, in the mid-eighties, the pair has realized *Spoonbridge and Cherry* (fig. **24.60**) for the sculpture garden of the Walker Art Center in Minneapolis. In this work, an enormous aluminum spoon gracefully spans a pool of water. A red cherry, serving as a counterpoint to the spoon's curve, spurts water from its stem in summer.

The GSA program also commissioned the controversial *Tilted Arc* (fig. **24.61**) by **Richard Serra** (b. 1939), a 120-foot-long (36.6 m), 12-foot-tall (3.7 m), 72-ton (73 tonne) slab of unadorned curved and tilted steel for the federal building complex (Federal Plaza) in New York City's Foley Square. Installed in 1981, the work was removed in 1989 in response to the demand of local civil servants, who found it objectionable. It was called a "hideous hulk of rusty scrap metal" and an "iron curtain" barrier not only to passage across the plaza but also to other activities that once took place there, such as jazz concerts, rallies, and simple lunchtime socializing. The removal occurred in the face of heavy opposition mounted by the professional art community, which supported the artist in his contention that to relocate a piece he deemed utterly site-specific would be to destroy it, and that such action would constitute a breach of the moral, as well as legal, agreement the government made to maintain the work permanently as the artist conceived it.

During the heated public debate, little attention was given to the more positive, even lyrical, qualities of *Tilted Arc* as a physical object. For example, it could be argued that this surprisingly graceful sculptural "wall," with its elegantly leaning curvature, actually shielded the viewer from the barren vistas of Foley Square, at the same time helping to reshape what had surely been among the bleakest public plazas in New York City. And the worst insult hurled at the sculpture—"rusty scrap metal"—in fact pointed to one of its most distinctive characteristics, a feature related to Process art: a close examination showed that the steel's oxidizing surface was becoming more richly textured and complex as it aged and weathered. By the time it was dismantled, *Tilted Arc* had begun to look like an homage to the expansive, dappled surfaces of late Monet—a kind of industrial *Water Lilies*.

In contrast to the dispute over Serra's *Tilted Arc*, few monuments created for urban sites have achieved such enthusiastic public acceptance as **Maya Ying Lin**'s (b. 1960) Vietnam Veterans Memorial (fig. **24.62**), commissioned in 1981. Since its completion, the memorial has been so highly acclaimed that it is difficult to remember how controversial the proposal originally was. In a competition to create a monument that would pay tribute to the 58,000 Americans killed in the Vietnam War and that would harmonize with its surroundings on the Mall in Washington, Lin daringly proposed two simple walls of polished black granite that would meet at an angle, an idea that at first seemed too abstract for some of the interested parties. Several veterans' groups wanted to add a realistic sculpture of soldiers at the apex of the structure, which would have drastically compromised the original concept; the figure sculpture was eventually added, but at a distance from the granite wall that allowed both artworks to retain their individual integrity. In its finished state, the memorial's

24.62 Maya Ying Lin, Vietnam Veterans Memorial, 1982. Black granite, length 500' (152.4 m). The Mall, Washington, D.C.

24.63 Beverly Pepper, Four ductile iron sculptures installed at Central Park Plaza, New York, 1983. Left to right: *Volatile Presence*, height 27' (8.2 m); *Valley Marker*, height 25'8" (7.8 m); *Interrupted Messenger*, height 29' (8.8 m); *Measured Presence*, height 24' (7.3 m).

24.64 Beverly Pepper, *Cromlech Glen*, 1985–90. Earth, sod, trees, and sandstone, 25 × 130 × 90' (7.6 × 39.6 × 27.4 m). Laumeier Sculpture Park, Saint Louis, Missouri.

reflective black surface shows visitors their own faces as they search among the names of the casualties inscribed on the wall, an emotionally compelling effect that many have compared to an encounter between the living and the dead. In addition, visitors have the option of making pencil rubbings of the names of their loved ones.

Since the sixties, the American sculptor **Beverly Pepper** (b. 1924) has created welded steel constructions that have an imposing, if enigmatic, presence. Certain of the forms appear to be based on ancient tools and spears, giving an effect of prehistoric monumentality, but others are more closely related to the modern industrial world that produced them, such as the drill and corkscrew shapes and the screwdriver form seen in her 1983 ensemble in New York's Central Park Plaza (fig. **24.63**). This paradoxical interplay between the modern and the prehistoric gives Pepper's work much of its rich associative power. Her concern with elemental form later led to create an outdoor environment in her *Cromlech Glen* of 1985–90 (fig. **24.64**). In this work, although she somewhat reshaped the contours of the land, her most notable intervention was restricted to arranging sandstone steps over small, grassy hills. Her modest outdoor setting in a public sculpture park is more respectful of the earth than is much Land art, and more immediately welcoming than many of her metal sculptures.

Body of Evidence: Figurative Art

Figurative artists, too, in their turn, succeeded in overturning the dominance of Minimalist abstraction, and in the seventies they created new kinds of illusionism. As they did so, however, they revealed their roots in the rejected Minimalist aesthetic by translating its stillness and silence into the frozen, stop-action image of the camera—an approach for which artists found sources in the work of Edward Hopper (see fig. 18.36). And this was true even in the work of many painters who adamantly excluded photography from their creative process. Given its markedly static character, almost all of what became known as the New Realism (not to be confused with European *Nouveau Réalisme*, see chapter 21) could be seen as a variety of still life, whatever its subject matter. Inevitably, therefore, genuine still-life motifs now made a stunning reappearance in painting, long after their early career in modernism, when artists favored inanimate, anonymous subjects as more conducive to cool, formalist manipulation or distortion than, for instance, the human image, with all its complicated moral and psychological associations.

Traditional Realism

In the United States, a pragmatic preoccupation with material reality, with the "old" realism, so to speak, had been too deeply ingrained to die out, even as Abstract Expressionism and its Minimal aftermath made American painting and sculpture more rigorously abstract than almost anything ever seen in the history of art. Throughout

24.65 Andrew Wyeth, *Christina's World*, 1948. Tempera on gessoed panel, 32¼ × 47¾" (81.9 × 121.3 cm). The Museum of Modern Art, New York.

24.66 Alice Neel, *Andy Warhol*, 1970. Oil on canvas, 60 × 40" (152.4 × 101.6 cm). Whitney Museum of American Art, New York.

this very period, in fact, the most widely recognized of all living American painters was probably **Andrew Wyeth** (b. 1917), whose impeccably observed *Christina's World* (fig. **24.65**) long remained, during an era dominated by abstraction, the most popular painting in the collection of The Museum of Modern Art in New York. Another American artist who never lost the realist faith was **Alice Neel** (1900–84). After many years of subsisting on the fringes of mainstream art, Neel came into late, but considerable, fame as a portraitist of such searching, psychologically penetrating power that she seemed to be "stealing" the very souls of her sitters (fig. **24.66**). In the same generation as Neel was **Fairfield Porter** (1907–75), who painted radiant, grandly composed intimist pictures (fig. **24.67**). Albeit thoroughly American, his works seem aesthetically and spiritually at one with the calm, coloristic art of Vuillard and Bonnard (see figs. 3.24, 3.27). Commenting on his luminous environments, Porter said: "I was never one to paint *space*. I paint air." Although committed to figuration in his own painting, Porter regularly wrote criticism that early and unflaggingly supported the American Abstract Expressionists. This posed no conflict for Porter, since, as he stated, "the important thing for critics to remember is the 'subject matter' in abstract painting and the abstraction in representational work." Happy to work in the traditional genres of still life, landscape, and

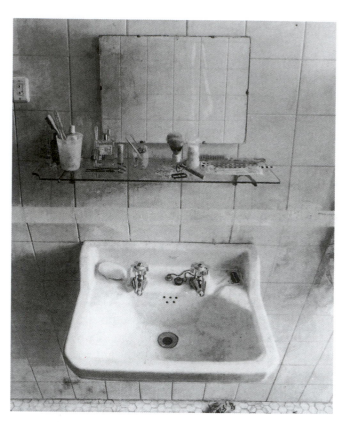

24.68 Antonio López García, *Washbasin and Mirror*, 1967. Oil on wood, 38⅝ × 32⅞" (98.1 × 83.5 cm). Private collection.

interior, as well as portraiture, Porter was convinced that the uncommon could be found in the commonplace, that "the extraordinary is everywhere."

A cultured realist known for his almost monastic dedication and attention to craft is the Spaniard **Antonio López García** (b. 1936). His *Washbasin and Mirror* (fig. **24.68**) gives meticulous attention to the most mundane objects, inviting comparison with certain of the Photorealists about to be discussed. At the same time, the geometric lucidity of this work—with the lowly bathroom tiles providing a strict compositional grid—carries on a tradition of firmly constructed shelf- and tabletop still lifes that can be traced back to Cézanne.

Photorealism

Although he began as a late Abstract Expressionist, **Chuck Close** (b. 1940) sought to reconcile the conceptual ramifications of the artist's mark with the likeness of the sitter. The camera-made image imposed the discipline of a fixed model that told precisely what the painting should look like even before it had been started (fig. **24.69**). Furthermore, Close banished all color and worked exclusively from black-and-white images. He gave up thick, luxurious paint, and permitted himself only a few tablespoons of pigment for a huge, mural-size canvas. This was possible once he threw out his bristle brushes and adopted the airbrush, the better to eliminate all response to medium and surface; thus, his work achieves what appears to be the smooth, impersonal surface of a photographic print or slide.

24.67 Fairfield Porter, *Under the Elms*, 1971–72. Oil on canvas, 62¹⁵⁄₁₆ × 46¼" (159.9 × 117.5 cm). Pennsylvania Academy of the Fine Arts, Philadelphia.

At the same time that Close used photographs as his point of departure, in lieu of the drawings, studies, or time-consuming observation employed by traditional realists, he committed himself to the long, arduous labor of transferring the image and all its information onto the canvas by means of a grid, a uniformly squared pattern comparable to the screen that makes tonal variations possible in photo-mechanical printing. The grid has served painters for centuries as a device for transferring compositions from one surface to another, usually while also changing their scale, but only with Photorealism did the squares become so small that they could present the most minute facts, as well as overall form, so insistently as to become a dominant characteristic of the art. As though to counterbalance the mechanical impersonality of this process, Close decided to paint only the faces of himself and his friends, their heads full front and close up, and usually on a large scale. Trapped in a shallow, almost airless space and pitilessly exposed in all their physical imperfections, the subjects appear as much heroicized as exploited, as iconic as early American portraits, and as defiant as a police mug shot.

Eventually Close progressed toward color, at first by reproducing, one on top of the other, the cyan, magenta, yellow, and black separations of an image used in photo-mechanical color printing. The more Close experimented, however, the more he seemed to move away from realism toward greater involvement with process, which inevitably carried his art back toward the realm of abstraction where it first began. Such a development is especially evident in the *Fingerprint* paintings, for which the artist filled each unit of the grid with an impression of his own fingerprint inked on a stamp pad. Other works have each cell filled with ovals or lozenge forms (fig. **24.70**), breaking up the figure into geometric atoms in a manner reminiscent of portraits by Gustav Klimt. While these devices heightened the desired tension between the mechanical and manual aspects of the technique, as well as the fluid and fixed elements of the image, they so tipped the balance between image and system that the former is all but subordinated to the dominant and voracious grid. In 1988 Close suffered anterior spinal artery syndrome, which partially paralyzed his body and confined him to a wheelchair. Despite this

24.69 Chuck Close, *Linda*, 1975–76. Acrylic on linen, 9 × 7' (2.7 × 2.1 m). Akron Art Museum, Ohio.

24.70 Chuck Close, *Self-Portrait*, 1991. Oil on canvas, 8'4" × 7' (2.5 × 2.1 m). Collection Paine-Webber Group, Inc., New York.

24.71 Richard Estes, *Bus Reflections (Ansonia)*, 1972. Oil on canvas, 40 × 52" (101.6 × 132.1 cm). Private collection.

disability, the artist has continued to develop his art, producing new variations on the gridlike formats he uses to paint his large-scale portraits.

The art of **Richard Estes** (b. 1936) has the quintessential Photorealist look. Estes does not work from a single photo but rather from two or more, combining them in various ways (fig. **24.71**). Although his pictures have all the flat, planar qualities of broad sheets of reflective glass, those supposedly transparent surfaces reveal less what is depicted in depth than what is forward of the painting surface, achieving the effect of an inside-out world reflected from the viewer's own space. Reinforcing the sense of flatness is the uniformly sharp focus with which the artist, thanks to his photographic models, resolves the painting's two-dimensional surface, incorporating a vast quantity of visual information, however far or near. The richness of such an image reveals the importance of the camera to this new variety of realism, for never would a painter, however skilled, be able to render all that Estes has in a single work, or with such clarity and precision, merely by studying the subject directly. In the time required to complete the picture, everything would change—the light, the reflections, the weather, the season, the presence or absence of people and traffic, and certainly the commercial displays. The methods of traditional realism could not possibly freeze a modern urban jumble to one split second of time.

A mediating figure in the Photorealist style is **Audrey Flack** (b. 1931), who, while credited with painting the first genuine Photorealist picture, also revived certain thematic concerns guaranteeing an emotional and psychological content remote from the cool detachment characteristic of Photorealist art. Departing from her early career as an Abstract Expressionist, Flack turned to illusionism creating her own contemporary versions of the seventeenth-century *vanitas* picture (fig. **24.72**). These are still-life compositions positively heaped with the jewels, cosmetics, and mirrors associated with feminine vanity, mixed, as in old master works, with skulls, calendars, and burning candles, those ancient memento mori symbols designed to remind human beings of their mortality and thus the futility of all greed and narcissism. Flack also composes in a traditional way, assembling the picture's motifs and arranging them to suit her purposes. Only then does she take up the camera, make a slide, project it onto the canvas, and paint over the image with an airbrush. Jammed with visual information and cropped like Baroque still lifes, Flack's pictures possess a striking lushness of color, a spatial complexity, and vastness of scale.

A British-born artist resident in New York since 1958, **Malcolm Morley** (b. 1931) had an early engagement with Photorealism, but, given his lack of interest in simulating the peculiar, glossy look of photographic images, he is only tangentially related to the style. In fact, Morley's unrelenting search for meaning has led him in a variety of fascinating but label-defying directions. One such avenue of exploration involved using photographic material in the

24.72 Audrey Flack, *Wheel of Fortune*, 1977–78. Oil and acrylic on canvas, 8 × 8' (2.4 × 2.4 m). Collection Louis, Susan, and Ari Meisel.

24.73 Malcolm Morley, *Ship's Dinner Party*, 1966. Magna color on canvas, 6'11¾" × 5'3¾" (2.1 × 1.62 m). Museum van Hedendaagse Kunst, Utrecht, The Netherlands.

24.74 Sylvia Plimack Mangold, *Opposite Corners*, 1973. Acrylic on canvas, 6'6" × 5'3¾" (2 × 1.62 m). Yale University Art Gallery, New Haven, Connecticut.

form of a color illustration from a magazine or a travel brochure for his essential study or "drawing" for a painting (fig. **24.73**). After dividing up this image into numbered squares, Morley would enlarge and transfer them, one by one, to the canvas, often painting parts of the image upside down as an added means of maintaining the superiority of the abstract process. This process offered the dual advantage of distancing the artist from the standard tricks of *trompe-l'oeil* painting, while ensuring that the abstractly rendered image would contain something of the reality reflected in its source. To acknowledge the artificiality of that source, Morley often even retained the standard white border of the color reproduction or photographic print. Although he has denied overt political content, his choice of subject matter—for example Americans at play at a time of grave social unrest—is not without irony.

During the sixties, the painter **Sylvia Plimack Mangold** (b. 1938) concentrated on rendering convincing images of ordinary floors, showing the lines of the floorboards receding into illusionistic space. The wit of these images arose from their being domestic, indoor versions of Renaissance *veduta,* or views of a city square, with schematic lines of perspective fanning out from the central vanishing point. Mangold began including mirrors in these works in 1972. *Opposite Corners* (fig. **24.74**) shows one corner but also depicts a leaning mirror reflecting the opposite corner of the same room. At first the mirror's frame appears to be a doorway leading into the space of some adjoining chamber. But after a moment, it becomes clear that this receding "space" is in fact an illusion, as of course is the rest of

24.75 Vija Celmins. *Untitled (Big Sea No. 2)*. 1969. Graphite on acrylic ground on paper, 34 × 45" (86.4 × 114.3 cm). AT&T Art Collection.

the picture. A few years later, Mangold began adding rulers to her images of floors. Some of these later works show one ruler within the image proper—lying in perspective on a receding floor—and also a second ruler, apparently out in the viewer's own space and abutting the edge of the painting, as if fastened to the side of the canvas. Nothing could more economically demonstrate, and yet at the same time question, the laws of perspective that governed Western art from the Renaissance until modern times.

Born in Latvia, **Vija Celmins** (b. 1939) was taken to Germany as a child and then relocated to the United States in 1948. Her meticulously rendered, photograph-based drawings, paintings, and prints are also related to Photorealism. In a series of dispersed, allover compositions, she worked from photographs of irregular natural surfaces—the desert, waves on the sea, and the craters of the moon. The surface depicted, often with richly textured graphite, becomes nearly identical with the picture plane itself, undermining any sense of objective "distance" from the thing being shown. The result is often to turn the source photograph into a near-abstraction. The wave crests of *Untitled (Big Sea No. 2)* (fig. **24.75**), for example, become so elaborately nuanced, through the thousands of

individual marks made by the artist, that the camera's flat-footed realism is replaced by an infinitely complex pattern of surface incident. The surface becomes a vivid subject in its own right. Celmins also created portraits of individual objects, including World War II aircraft, based on found photographs, and combined quite distinct kinds of imagery in composite prints based on separate, seemingly unrelated photographs.

Hanson's Superrealist Sculpture

Nowhere has the ambiguity and tension between the realness of artificiality and the artificiality of reality yielded more bizarre effects than in the work of **Duane Hanson** (1925–96), whose lifesize, freestanding sculptures (fig. **24.76**) seem, at first glance, to close the gap between art and life with a rude, decisive bang. To achieve such verisimilitude—in which artifice truly assumes the artlessness of literal reality—Hanson used direct casting from live models in the way Superrealist painters use photography, as a means of shortcutting the preparatory stages so that the artist can devote the maximum time and energy to virtually duplicating the look of the model. So successful is the resulting counterfeit that the delight it can produce in

24.76 Duane Hanson, *Tourists*, 1970. Polychromed fiberglass and polyester, 64 × 65 × 47" (162.6 × 165.1 × 119.4 cm). National Galleries of Scotland, Edinburgh.

viewers may suddenly turn to horror when what appears to be breathing flesh and blood fails to breathe, remaining as stiff and static as death. Having cast the figure in fiberglass-reinforced polyester resin, Hanson adds to the textured reality of pores, wrinkles, and bulges the coloration of skin, veins, and even boils and bruises. Such waxworks literalism stands in fascinating contrast to the figural sculptures of George Segal (see fig. 21.23), who also casts from live models, but avoids confusion between reality and make-believe by using the white mold as the final form. Furthermore, Segal restricts his use of actual objects to environmental props, while Hanson adds them to the figure as clothing and accessories.

Stylized Naturalism

The illusionist revival that produced Photorealism in painting and Superrealism in sculpture also regenerated naturalistic painting based on the traditional method of direct and prolonged examination of the model or motif. But even there, much new art took on a distinctly photographic look, reflecting the dominance of camera-made imagery in an age increasingly saturated by the media. One of the preeminent masters of directly perceived, sharp-focus realism is **Philip Pearlstein** (b. 1924), a painter who belongs to the Pop, Minimalist, and Conceptual generation and even shares its preoccupation with banal subject matter and two-dimensionality, as well as cool, hard-edge handling. Pearlstein, however, reached his artistic maturity in about 1970, and did so with an art devoted to the nude figure represented as a solid form in simulated depth (fig. **24.77**). Pearlstein set about integrating modernism's flatness and cropping, characteristics initially fostered by the influence

of Japanese prints. Thus, at the same time that he reproduces his figures in all their sexual explicitness, he also robs them of their potential for expressionist content by a process of objectification, by rendering only one part of the anatomy at a time. This results in the loss of bodily context and, often, extremities, a further depersonalization that becomes especially acute when it involves the head. The painter calls his pictorial manipulation of the figure "a sort of still-action choreography." Pearlstein declared:

> I have made a contribution to humanism in 20th-century painting—I rescued the human figure from its tormented, agonized condition given it by the expressionistic artists, and the cubist dissectors and distorters of the figure, and at the other extreme I have rescued it from the pornographers, and their easy exploitation of the figure for its sexual implications. I have presented the figure for itself, allowed it its own dignity as a form among other forms in nature.

If some painters associated with realism were moving toward a more direct account of visual appearances, paradoxically some photographers were going in the opposite direction, treating their subjects in a manner increasingly formal and abstract. **Joel Meyerowitz** (b. 1938), who earlier in his career had earned recognition as a street photographer, now constructed images that, in their immaculately refined sensibility, seemed intent on portraying another world. Although *Porch, Provincetown* (fig. **24.78**) remains rooted in an actual time and place, it also brings to the fore highly abstracted elements, such as the conspicuously displayed trapezoid of the roof and the cleanly abutting planes of the sea and sky. The subtly graduated blush of twilight on the central column is so finely gauged

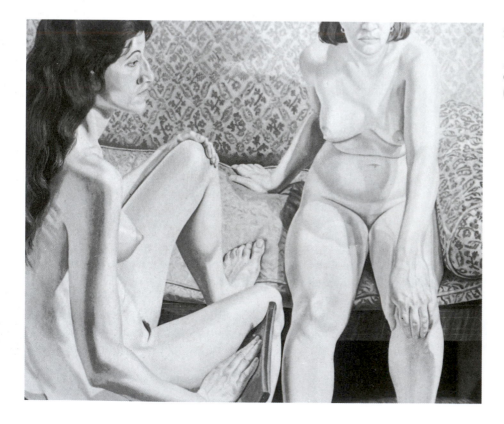

24.77 Philip Pearlstein, *Two Female Models with Regency Sofa*, 1974. Oil on canvas, 60 × 72" (152.4 × 182.9 cm).

as to make that cylindrical form look like a geometric sculpture, while the tinted atmosphere recalls painters of the sublime, even the Color Field art of Mark Rothko. Finally, the porch is shot from an angle that makes it appear to be suspended, without ground support, over the sea, as if in a Surrealist painting by René Magritte.

A reference to Surrealism can also be seen in the work of the Detroit-born photographer **Jerry Uelsmann** (b. 1934). Uelsmann combines two or more images into a composite work. By bringing together two ordinary representations in an unexpected way, the resulting image can have the disorienting, uncanny effect that the nineteenth-century French poet Lautréamont, admired by the Surrealists, compared to "the chance encounter on an operating table of a sewing machine and an umbrella." Uelsmann's *Untitled (Cloud Room)* (fig. **24.79**) creates just this effect of "defamiliarizing" the ordinary. The banal Victorian interior, taken on its own, would be quite unremarkable, and the cloudy sky, too, is part of the everyday world. But when storm clouds gather indoors, their unexpected presence creates a strangely disquieting scene,

indebted to the works of painters like Magritte and Delvaux (see figs. 15.30, 15.31, 15.34). Uelsmann's technical mastery in printing the composite photographs enhances the effect; he joins the disparate images together so seamlessly as almost to convince us for a moment that we are witnessing something impossible but true.

The painter **Alex Katz** (b. 1927) made an early choice of figuration and stuck with it throughout the heyday of American abstraction, turning some of abstraction's own sources of inspiration, such as Henri Matisse and Milton Avery, to his own purposes. Foremost among the formal abstract influences are broad fields of flat, clean color, elegantly brushed surfaces, radically simplified drawing, and epic scale. Selecting his portrait subjects from among family, friends, and artworld personalities, Katz monumentalizes them not only by the sheer size of the painted image but also by the technique of representing the sitters only from the shoulders up, as if they were antique emperors or empresses presented to the public in the form of portrait busts (fig. **24.80**). But since the rendering has been done with a reductiveness reminiscent of movie billboards,

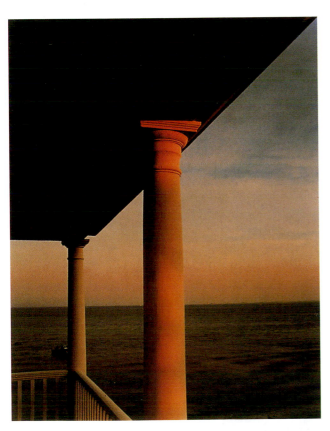

24.78 Joel Meyerowitz, *Porch, Provincetown*, 1977. Color photograph, 10 × 8" (25.4 × 20.3 cm). Courtesy the artist.

24.79 Jerry Uelsmann, *Untitled (Cloud Room)*, 1975. Toned gelatin-silver print. Collection Jain and George W. Kelly, New York.

24.80 Alex Katz, *The Red Band*, 1978. Oil on canvas, 6 × 12' (1.8 × 3.7 m). Private collection.

a more apt association might be with the royalty of Hollywood rather than with that of monarchical Europe. Katz has declared, "I like to make an image that is so simple you can't avoid it, and so complicated you can't figure it out." To illustrate this quality of ambiguity, Katz here refers to the painting seen in fig. 24.80: "The original background was green grass," he said. "But when I painted green, it just didn't have enough light in it. It didn't show the light that I was seeing. So I turned it to yellow, switched to violet, and then to orange. Finally, that was a plausible light, the light I was really seeing, instead of just a bunch of pretty colors. It was a glowing summer light."

Constructing Respect: Art and Racial Politics

Figurative art, often interrupted and overlaid with text, was used by a number of artists to address issues of race that burst onto the political stage of postwar America with the Civil Rights Movement of the sixties, which pressed for full civil and legal rights for black Americans. As often noted, the visual arts were slow to find a role in racial struggles. There was a feeling that art was a luxury to be indulged after more pressing political rights and economic goals had been achieved. As artists did incorporate their practice in the political movements, they gave a priority to communicating messages. Figurative art, with its historical role in political mural art and printmaking, provided a means of communication that could be manipulated while still maintaining maximum legibility.

OBAC, Afri-COBRA, and SPARC

One of the first major visual projects to address the issues of African-American experience was the *Wall of Respect* (fig. **24.81**) created in Chicago in 1967 by the Visual Arts Workshop of the Organization of Black American Culture

24.81 OBAC (Organization of Black American Culture), *Wall of Respect*, 1967. Oil on brick, 30 × 60' (9.1 × 18.2 m).

(OBAC, pronounced o-BAH-cee to emphasize "oba" the Uruba word for leader.) OBAC was primarily a political and literary organ, but its experiment with the visual arts had an immediate and lasting effect. The *Wall* was a collaborative mural, created and conceived by artists and residents of the Southside neighborhood in which it was painted. Essentially a collection of portraits, the mural features a cast of black political, artistic, and sporting heroes, including Malcolm X, Martin Luther King, Charlie Parker, Aretha Franklin, and Muhammad Ali. Upon completion, OBAC gave up all proprietary rights, deciding on principle that a mural in a community belonged to that community. The history of the *Wall* after that point is tragic. As the mural became a magnet for the news media seeking to document the creativity and blight of Chicago's Southside, it became a source of power. Local gangs competed for

rights to the site and there was even a murder. The violence compelled the city of Chicago to demolish the mural and the building on which it was painted.

Despite the final debacle of the mural, the mission of the Visual Arts Workshop to use art to galvanize African-American communities continued. Several participants in the mural project, including Jeff Donaldson, Wadsworth Jarrell, Barbara Jones, and Carolyn Lawrence formed Afri-COBRA, the African Commune of Bad Relevant Artists. Afri-COBRA provided a forum for discussing common aesthetic and political issues in the African and African-American experience. Determining that, "Blackness contributed a specific quality to their visual expression," Afri-COBRA artists strove to articulate that quality. **Wadsworth Jarrell**'s (b. 1929) *Revolutionary* (fig. **24.82**) captures the group's aesthetic and philosophical principles.

24.82 Wadsworth Jarrell, *Revolutionary*, 1971. Acrylic on canvas, 50.5 × 63.5" (1.28 × 1.61 m).

24.83 Judy Baca, *Great Wall of Los Angeles*, 1976–83. Length one half-mile (0.8 km).

The image is a portrait of Angela Davis, philosopher and Black Panther Party leader, who at the time was in hiding. She raises her fist into a field of text reading "Resist, Revolution, Black Nation time …" Afri-COBRA works aimed to be legibly programmatic on an individual and national level. Jarrell's figurative style uses brightly colored text—instructions, as it were—to build the figure of the revolutionary and contribute to the struggles of African peoples. The integration of text and image that Afri-COBRA called "mimesis at midpoint" was intended to join the objective and the nonobjective, reality and revolution at a strategic point where the viewer was required to act: to read, see, and translate the image into the message. Using "Cool-Ade colors" "luminosity," and "shine," Afri-COBRA productions were designed to be easily reproducible, and images like Jarrell's were created in multiple screenprints to be widely circulated.

In Los Angeles in the mid-seventies, artist-activist **Judy Baca** (b. 1946) generated a political figurative art in the form of the world's longest mural, *Great Wall of Los Angeles* (fig. **24.83**), along one half-mile (0.8 km) of the Tujunga Wash drainage canal in the San Fernando Valley. Baca's project, begun in 1976 and initially finished in 1983 (it continued in a variety of formats into the 2000s), organized schoolkids to paint the history of California from prehistory to the sixties in a style reminiscent of the Mexican muralists

of the thirties (see chapter 18). Accompanying its creation, Baca also founded SPARC (the Social and Public Art Resource Center), a non-profit organization that "produces, distributes, preserves and documents community based public art works … that [reflect] the lives and concerns of America's diverse ethnic populations, women, working people, youth and the elderly." SPARC has since sponsored public mural projects throughout Los Angeles, creating images that respond to both local concerns and citywide issues, as well as portable works, an education and visual resource center, a website (www.sparcmurals.org), and interactive proposals for bringing the mural up to date. Baca has negotiated for funding from various branches of the city government to sponsor the conservation and continuation of the mural and related SPARC projects.

Ringgold and Folk Traditions

In the seventies the New York-based artist **Faith Ringgold** (b. 1930) created two- and three-dimensional artworks that presented racially informed social analysis in forms that connected high art and folk traditions. Ringgold was committed to expressing the experiences of the African-American community, with particular attention to the experience of African-American women. In the sixties she had painted flat figural compositions focusing on racial conflict in circumstances ranging from riots to cocktail parties. In the seventies Ringgold began to draw on African and American folk traditions, crafting figural sculptures that she often made from beaded and painted fabrics to represent fictionalized slave stories and more contemporary news accounts. Informed by a strong political conscience and sense of narrative complexity, her sculptural groups of weeping, speaking, shouting, and dying figures anticipated the painted story-quilts that have since become Ringgold's signature works.

Ringgold began quilting as a means of "mixing art and ideas so that neither suffers" in a family tradition that extends to her great-grandmother, who had learned quilting as a slave. She began her first quilt, a collection of portraits called *Echoes of Harlem* (1980), with her mother Willi Posey. In 1982, a year after her mother's death, Ringgold created her first story-quilt, *Who's Afraid of Aunt Jemima?* (fig. **24.84**), which told the story of Aunt Jemima, a matriarch restauranteur. The quilt and story weave together, describing the relations of the main character and her family as they compete with one another, meet and marry, and ultimately vie for the family business. Her characters are of different races and are compromised,

24.84 Faith Ringgold, *Who's Afraid of Aunt Jemima?* 1983. Printed and pieced fabric, 7'6" × 6'8" (2.29 × 2.03m).

sometimes morally upstanding, sometimes weak, always human. Ringgold has integrated quilts into performances and books, including several children's stories.

Social and Political Critique

David Hammons (b. 1943) has used his art to present social and political issues in blunt terms. Among his first works were prints with intense and controversial content. His *Injustice Case* (fig. **24.85**) shows, in negative, a bound and gagged captive tied to a chair. The figure could be any political prisoner in the world, were the composition not framed by an American flag. The positive associations usually evoked by the flag are challenged, replaced by an implicit assertion that America does not offer "liberty and justice for all." It seemed natural that Hammons would later turn to public sculpture, gaining a broader audience for his continuing critique of American icons. In *Higher Goals* (fig. **24.86**) Hammons applied bottle caps by the hundreds to telephone poles. The patterns of shiny, repeated caps give this unlikely urban monument a sense of the energy of street life. But the work also implies concern for the well-being of the city's youth. At the tops of the telephone poles are another emblem of street life: basketball hoops, placed far higher than anyone could possibly reach. "It's an anti-basketball sculpture," Hammons comments. "Basketball has become a problem in the black community because the kids aren't getting an education.

24.86 David Hammons, *Higher Goals*, 1982. Poles, basketball hoops, and bottle caps, height 40' (12.2 m). Shown installed in Brooklyn, New York, 1986.

That's why it's called *Higher Goals*. It means that you should have higher goals in life than basketball." Hammons's installations have continued to challenge the politics of race in the U.S., as his works, especially his increasingly baroque basketball hoops, reach record prices. As an artist who began his career selling snowballs in a snowstorm, Hammons is now in the ironic position, rare among his peers from the seventies, of creating cultural criticism in the form of artworld commodities.

In 1997, when **Robert Colescott** (b. 1925) became the first African-American to represent the U.S. at the Venice Biennale, he joined David Hammons as an artist who had brought racial politics from the margins of the seventies artworld to the center in the nineties. Colescott's career began with formal training at Berkeley and, from 1949 to 1950, in Paris under Fernand Léger. His breakthrough works, done in the mid-seventies, drew on the European traditions in which Colescott had trained as a source for the satire of racial politics in history and art. *George Washington Carver Crossing the Delaware: Page from an American History Textbook* (fig. **24.87**) is an ironic reversal of the race of heroes depicted in Emanuel Leutze's (1816–68) 1851 *George Washington Crossing the Delaware* and a serious commentary on the relationship between race and history in America. Above the fray of drunken

24.85 David Hammons, *Injustice Case*, 1970. Mixed-media print, 63 × 40½" (160 × 102.9 cm). Los Angeles County Museum of Art.

debauchery, depicted in the iconography of racist imagery, the sole figure of Carver stands, a token black admitted to history books.

Whether he is referring to Leutze's paintings or Van Gogh's, Colescott populates well-known masterpieces with "Aunt Jemimas" and other cultural stereotypes of black American identity. Even such figures as Carver cannot seem to enter into the Western canon without being misrepresented. Colescott has commented on the role of racist images in his project of creating African-American figures: "Unfortunately stereotypical images are part of American heritage. I had to come to terms with it for myself, ultimately controlling the images by making them say some things for me." Colescott incorporated the free use of stereotypes in a painterly language that combines the abstracting impulse of Picasso with the cathartic stylistics of Expressionism. With striking emotional force, he transformed a range of Western representational approaches to

depicting black bodies and lives. Like the descriptive projects of his feminist contemporaries, Colescott has made the exclusions of the past unavoidably apparent. In addition, his work is carefully attuned to the difference between the identity and the history of African-Americans; it is "not about race, [but] about perceptions," as he has explained.

Another artist to examine the disruptive lens of racism is **Adrian Piper** (b. 1948). Piper has explained that her art arises from a "compulsion to embody, transform, and use experiences as a woman of color in constructive ways, in order not to feel powerless." Drawing on her identity as a light-skinned black woman, and the insight into both black and white communities that this has provided, Piper's work examined the centrality of attitudes about race to the formation of personal and community identity in America. In her *Political Self-Portrait #2 [Race]* (fig. **24.88**) the text, an account of the prejudice the artist encountered while growing up, serves as a screen through which a

24.87 Robert Colescott, *George Washington Carver Crossing the Delaware: Page from an American History Textbook,* 1975. Acrylic on canvas, 4'6" × 9' (1.37 × 2.74 m).

divided image of the artist can be seen. The narrative of a life subjected to racial biases colors the view of the body. Like Colescott's use of stereotype, Piper's narrative of prejudice conveys the intrusions of language, particularly signifiers of race, on our perceptions of individuals and our creation of communities.

Piper's training and early work included Conceptual and Performance art as well as a doctorate in philosophy, which she continues to teach and practice. In the mid-eighties she brought together all three in *Calling Cards* (1986–90), a series of small note cards revealing the artist's identity as a woman of African descent. *Card #1 A Reactive Guerrilla Performance for Dinners and Cocktail Parties* was devised as a strategy for minimizing confrontation when she was compelled to challenge someone's racist behavior. Rather than staging a verbal and public confrontation, she handed the offender a card that begins, "Dear Friend, I am black. I am sure you did not realize this when you made/laughed at/agreed with that racist remark." And ends, "I regret any discomfort my presence is causing you, just as I am sure you regret the discomfort your racism is causing me." The passing out of the cards, when necessary, was followed by public sessions in which the action was explained and discussed. In the most successful *Calling Card* discussions, the defensive hostility initially felt by the largely white audience gave way to an uncomfortable contact upon hearing how devastating the "performance" was for the artist. Unlike more popular proclamations of humanity joining all races, Piper's work joined blacks and whites in a difficult social interaction based on awkward and painful regret. The performance takes up the Fluxus dictum that the world is art enough and informs it with the political attitude that the world must be transformed.

24.88 Adrian Piper, *Political Self-Portrait #2 [Race]*, 1978. Photostat, 24 × 16" (61 × 40.6 cm). Collection Richard Sandor.

Animated Surfaces: Pattern and Decoration

While some saw Minimalism's aloof stillness, silence, and simplicity as potent with rarefied meaning, others saw only a void, vast as the monumental scale of much mid- to late twentieth-century art, begging to be filled with a richly varied, even noisy abundance of pattern, decoration, *and* content. Here indeed was rebellion, for in the formalist's vocabulary of terms, the words "pattern" and "decoration" were fraught, still more than "illusionism," with pejorative connotations. This taboo prevailed, even though pattern—a systematic repetition of a motif or motifs used to cover a surface in a decoratively uniform manner—has an effect fully as flattening as any of the devices employed by the Minimalists. However, pattern and decoration, often abbreviated P&D, was dismissively used to mean work by anonymous artisans, not individuals of known genius, usually done for the purpose of endowing mundane or utilitarian objects with an element of sensuous pleasure and delight. These qualities were thought to be secondary to the more intellectual concerns of high art. Thus, despite Duchamp, whose readymades proved that the context can define what is, or is not, art, skeptical purists wondered how objects formed from designs, materials, and techniques associated with crafts, folk art, and "women's work" could be transformed into vehicles of significant content.

The answer lay in the sources of inspiration for the P&D movement, which began to stir in the early seventies and coalesced as a major development in the second half of the decade. First of all there was Matisse, a proud "decorator" in the grand French tradition, and his late, brilliantly colored and patterned paper cutouts (see fig. 14.15). Then there were the arabesques and fretwork of Islam's intensely metaphysical art, the pantheistic interlaces of ancient European Celtic art, and the symbol-filled geometries of Native American art, all recently brought into stunning prominence by important exhibitions or installations.

Finally, but perhaps most important of all, came the so-called craft works—carpets, quilts, embroidery, needlepoint, mosaic, wallpaper—not given much attention since Art Nouveau or the art of the Bauhaus. Apart from its irrefutable beauty, such patterned, decorative, and pragmatic folk art gained esteem for its content. Pattern painting, albeit based on the same grid as that underlying the formalist structures of Minimal art, appeared to resist self-containment in favor of an almost limitless embrace of surface. Because of its intrinsically more democratic character, P&D enjoyed broader and more enthusiastic support than did contemporaneous developments in Photorealism.

Initially, one of the strongest and most seasoned talents to transform traditionally undervalued decorative materials into ambitious, original art was **Miriam Schapiro** b. 1923, energized by feminism as well as by a love of ornamental work, however "low" or "high" its origins. Like so many artists of her generation, Schapiro had begun painting in an Abstract Expressionist style, but later turned to hard-edged abstract illusionism, using computers in the design process. In the late sixties she joined the women's movement, which led her to become, with artist Judy Chicago, codirector of the Feminist Art Program (see above).

Schapiro later drew her imagery and materials from the history of women's "covert" art, using buttons, threads, rickrack, sequins, yarn, silk, taffeta, cotton burlap, and wool, all sewn, embroidered, pieced, and appliquéd into useful but decorative objects. Reassembling them into dynamic, baroque, almost exploding compositions, the artist created what she called "femmages," a contraction of "female" and "image" that connotes something of the découpage, photomontage, assemblage, and quilting techniques used to make these grandly scaled projects, without referring by name to the modernist male tradition of avant-garde collage. Moreover, her works are as large as an Abstract Expressionist painting, indicating also her desire to compete with modernist art and monumentalize "women's work."

Schapiro frequently articulated her new style—a synthesis of abstraction, images labeled by society as feminine (such as eggs, hearts, and kimonos), architectural framework, and decorative patterns—in the form of floral bouquets, lacy borders, and floating flowers. In one series she chose the fan shape—itself a decorative form—for wall-size canvases collaged with a wealth of patterned materials, ranging from cheap cotton to upholstery to luxurious Oriental fabrics, all combined to simulate the spreading folds of a real fan. *Black Bolero* (fig. **24.89**) is a potpourri of art and craft, structure and decoration, abstraction and illusion, public politics and personal iconography, thought and sentiment.

In 1975 **Robert Zakanitch** (b. 1935) met Miriam Schapiro during a term of guest teaching at the University of California in San Diego, and early the following year in New York the two painters jointly organized a group called the Pattern and Decoration Artists. The group held its first meeting in a SoHo loft space, signaling not only to the art world at large but also to the participating artists that a greater variety of painting was being done than Conceptualism had allowed anyone to believe. This led to the Ten Approaches to the Decorative show in September 1976, sponsored by the Pattern and Decoration Artists themselves, and to a kind of collector interest that turned the recently opened Holly Solomon Gallery into a home for

24.89 Miriam Schapiro, *Black Bolero*, 1980. Fabric, glitter, synthetic polymer paint on canvas, 6 × 12' (1.8 × 3.7 m). Art Gallery of New South Wales, Australia.

such P&D converts as Robert Kushner, Kim MacConnel, Valerie Jaudon, Ned Smyth, and Robert Zakanitch.

When Zakanitch took up decorative imagery, he had been working as a Color Field abstractionist faithful to the Minimalist grid as the structural system of his painting. Once employing decoration, he retained both his color sophistication and his respect for structure, but translated the latter into a free, often organic lattice pattern and the former into floral motifs rendered with a lush, painterly, lavender-and-plum palette (fig. **24.90**). Taken together, the painterliness, the opulent hues, the blooms, and the latticework invite obvious comparison with wallpaper designs, which in fact hold a preeminent place among the artist's acknowledged sources.

In 1974 **Robert Kushner** (b. 1949) went on an extended journey to Iran and Afghanistan. The experience was something of an epiphany for Kushner, who said: "On this trip, seeing those incredible works of genius, really master works which exist in almost any city, I really became aware of how intelligent and uplifting decoration can be." Although many of the masterworks happen to have been architectural, Kushner chose to express his love of arabesque fluency and grace not in mosaic or stone, but rather in loose, free-falling fabrics, decorated by their own "found" printed or woven patterns and Kushner's overpainting of leaf, vine, seed pod, floral, or, eventually, beast and human imagery. He disclosed a certain preference for a horizontal alignment of vertical panels, but instead of arranging his fabrics in a generally evenhanded sameness of length, he assembled them in whatever manner would produce a wearable costume. These works were then hung, unstretched, on the wall (fig. **24.91**). When donned, these richly patterned and colored pieces, often in original atonal harmonies, yielded an effect of barbaric splendor unknown since the heyday of the *Ballets Russes*.

24.90 Robert Zakanitch, *Double Shirt*, 1981. Acrylic on canvas, 6 × 5' (1.8 × 1.5 m). Private collection, Sweden.

24.91 Robert Kushner, *Blue Flounce* from *Persian Line*, 1974. Acrylic on cotton with miscellaneous fabrics and fringe, 7'2" × 6'3" (2.2 × 1.9 m).

In his wall pieces, also structured from fabrics and airily billowing against the plane, Kushner made an unabashed avowal of his devotion to Matisse. Like the Frenchman, Kushner counterbalanced his passion for "Oriental" embellishment with a Western humanist interest in the classical nude, flattened and all but lost in a crazy quilt of competing but subtly coordinated patterns, only to be slowly revealed, sometimes in mirror-image reversals, by the patterns themselves, as well as by the artist's own magisterial drawing.

Valerie Jaudon (b. 1945), a Mississippi-born artist with a cosmopolitan background, began in Color Field painting and, by concentrating on the decorative aspect of that style, continued to be a steadfast abstractionist throughout her work in P&D. To the degree that she is a purely nonobjective artist, Jaudon has remained closer to her Islamic sources, mingled with Celtic interlaces, than any of the practitioners seen thus far in the P&D movement. However, her patterns are not copied but freshly reinvented, ribbonlike paths traced over and under one another along arcs and angles reminiscent of Frank Stella (see c.p. 350). With their symmetrical order and complex weave of clean lines, which invite the eye but immediately lose it in the indivisibility of the total configuration, Jaudon's earlier maze patterns also became something of a hard-edged counterpart of the allover, holistic, or nonrelational compositions realized by Jackson Pollock. In subsequent work, Jaudon stabilized her interlaces within a solidly grounded architectural image, capped by round domes, pointed steeples, and ogival arches (fig. **24.92**). Adding to the sense of gravity and depth are the impastoed surfaces and the brilliant, strongly contrasted colors that distinguish one band or strap from another as well as from the background. Illusionism is denied, however, due to the emphatic linearity of the interlocking geometries and their resolutely flattened "folds" and "knots." Jaudon has said of her intricate art:

> As far back as I can remember, everyone called my work decorative, and they were trying to put me down by saying it. Attitudes are changing now, but this is just the beginning. If we can only get over the strict modernist doctrines about purity of form, line, and color, then everything will open up.

Feminism also encouraged **Joyce Kozloff** (b. 1942) in her decision to work in a decorative style. In her eagerness to dissolve arbitrary distinctions—between high and low art, between sophisticated and primitive cultures—Kozloff copied her sources more faithfully than most of her peers in the P&D movement, depending on her "recontextualization" of the motifs for the transformation necessary to create new art. At first, she sought her patterns in the late Baroque architecture of Mexico, but soon turned directly to its origins in Morocco and other parts of Islam. She then relocated them to independent picture or wall panels, composed of the most intricate, run-on,

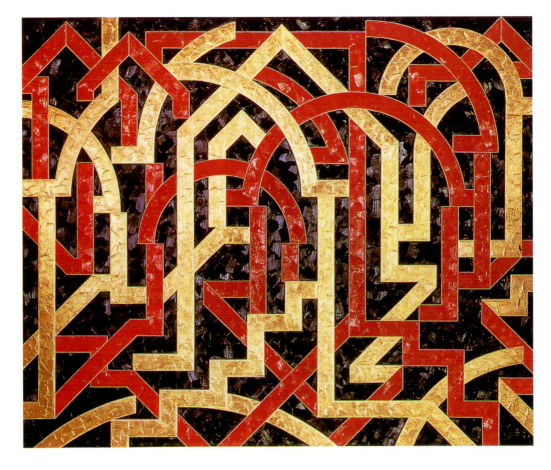

24.92 Valerie Jaudon, *Tallahatchee*, 1984. Oil and gold leaf on canvas, 6'8" × 8' (2 × 2.4 m).

24.93 Joyce Kozloff, *Mural for Harvard Square Subway Station: New England Decorative Arts*, 1984. Tiles, overall 8 × 83' (2.4 × 25.2 m). Cambridge, Massachusetts.

and totally abstract patterns, and executed them in gouache on paper or canvas or silkscreen on fabric. The architectural sources of her inspiration eventually drew the artist into large-scale environmental works, not for exterior display but rather for interiors, as large, complex installations that distributed patterns made of tile, fabric, and glass, among other materials, over every surface—ceilings and floors as well as walls.

Subsequently, Kozloff began to work on a monumental scale designing comprehensive tile decorations for public transport stations in San Francisco, Buffalo, Wilmington, and Cambridge, Massachusetts (fig. **24.93**). The imagery ranges from purely abstract quilt and wall-stencil patterns to representations of clipper ships, milltowns, farm animals, tombstones, and the flowers and trees of open nature, all stylized, in the naïf manner of American folk art, to fit within the star shape of prefabricated tiles.

Figure and Ambiguity: New Image Art

In December 1978 the Whitney Museum of American Art in New York mounted an exhibition entitled New Image Painting. Though less than a critical triumph, the show provided a label for a number of emerging artists whose works had little in common other than recognizable but distinctly idiosyncratic imagery presented, for the most part, in untraditional, nonillusionistic contexts. Moreover, while honoring Minimalism's formal simplicity, love of system, and emotional restraint, they also tended to betray their roots in Conceptual art by continuing to be involved with elements of Process and Performance, narrative, Dada-like wit, and socio-psychological issues, sometimes even in verbal modes of expression. While all the latter may,

quite correctly, imply a Post-Minimalist sensibility, the New Imagists have almost invariably produced works that tend to prompt a more immediate appreciation of form, with content more evocative than obvious or specific in meaning. The great progenitor of the New Imagists was Philip Guston (see fig. 19.21), who by 1970 had abandoned his famous Abstract Expressionist style for a rather raucous form of figuration.

By the time the New Imagists matured in the seventies— painters like Nicholas Africano, Jennifer Bartlett, Jonathan Borofsky, Susan Rothenberg, Donald Sultan, Robert Moskowitz, and Joe Zucker, or the sculptors Joel Shapiro and Barry Flanagan—the artistic legacy they inherited was a heavy one indeed, consisting as it did not only of Abstract Expressionism, but also the whole incredibly dense and varied sequence of reactions and counteractions that had followed. To assimilate such cultural wealth and yet move beyond it posed an awesome challenge, but the artists eager to accept it proved to be a hardy, clever, immensely well-educated lot—many of them graduates of Yale University's School of Art in the time of such directors as Josef Albers and the Abstract Expressionist painter Jack Tworkov—and could never have approached the problems of *how* or *why* in the comparatively free, unselfconscious way of the first-generation New York School. But, however complex and contradictory the situation, the younger artists who entered it were fortified with the competitiveness that came with an art market exploding from the effects of media hype. These artists satisfied the rising demand for imagery and collectible objects after the market's near demise under the impact of Minimalism and Conceptualism. Their striking originality lay not in style, which varied widely from practitioner to practitioner, but rather in the particular techniques and ideas appropriated from the recent past, to the end that something familiar or banal would become unexpectedly fresh and strange, possibly even magical, thereby engendering a whole new set of possibilities.

Rothenberg and Moskowitz

In conjuring the kind of eroded or fragmentary figuration last seen in the art of Giacometti or, more robustly, De Kooning, **Susan Rothenberg** (b. 1945) further defied Minimalism's immaculate, abstract surface by filling it with a dense, painterly, silver-gray facture reminiscent of Philip Guston's probing Abstract Expressionist brushwork and sooty palette (see fig. 19.20). The motif with which she realized her first major success was the horse (fig. **24.94**), a massive form steeped in myth yet intimately involved with human history, obedient and faithful but also potent and wild, and often a surrogate in Romantic painting for human feeling. At a time in the Post-Minimal period when the more advanced among younger artists were not quite ready to deal with the human face and figure, "the horse was a way of not doing people," Rothenberg has said, "yet it was a symbol of people, a self-portrait, really." Fundamentally, however, her concerns, like Giacometti's, were formal rather than thematic. In the case of Rothenberg, these centered, as in Minimal painting, on how to acknowledge and activate the flatness and objectivity of the painting surface, while also representing a solid recognizable presence.

Robert Moskowitz (b. 1935) has said that "by adding an image to the painting, I was trying to focus on a more central form, something that would pull you in to such an extent that it would almost turn back into an abstraction." His method is to isolate an image of universal, even iconic familiarity—natural or cultural shrines like Rodin's *Thinker*, New York's Flatiron Building, or Yosemite National Park's Seventh Sister—and then strip the form bare of all but its most basic, purified shape, making it virtually interchangeable with an abstract pictorial structure. "In all good work there is a kind of ambiguity, and I am trying to get the image just over that line," he said.

24.94 Susan Rothenberg, *Pontiac*, 1979. Acrylic and Flashe on canvas, 7'4" × 5'1" (2.2 × 1.55 m). Private collection.

24.95 Robert Moskowitz, *Red Mill*, 1981. Pastel on paper, 9'3" × 4' ¾" (2.8 × 1.24 m). Museum of Contemporary Art, San Diego.

By allowing it to travel no farther, however, the artist makes certain that, with the help of a clarifying title, the viewer feels sufficiently challenged to puzzle out and then rediscover the marvel of the monument long since rendered banal by overexposure (fig. **24.95**). Aiding the cause of regenerated grandeur and refreshed vision are the epic scale on which Moskowitz casts his imagery and his tendency to cut images free of the ground, so that they seem truly out of this world, soaring and mythic. This effect is achieved within the enchanted realm of the artist's pictorial surface, a gorgeous display of painterly craft, alternately burnished, flickering, or luminous, glorifying the flatness of the plane and seducing the eye into exploring the image.

Sultan and Jenney

In his break with Minimalism, **Donald Sultan** (b. 1951), like most of his New Image peers, did not so much want to reject the past as to make his art contain more of it. Sultan wanted figuration with the monumental simplicity and directness of abstract art, an approach that would enable him to find an image that would clearly metamorphose out of the materials and mechanisms of its own creation. While teaching himself to draw—a skill seldom imparted in the figure-averse academies of the sixties and early seventies—and working as a handyman at the Denise René Gallery in New York, Sultan found himself retiling his employer's floor with vinyl. He immediately felt an affinity for the material's weight and thickness, as well as for the "found" colors and mottled patterns the tiles came in. Further, there was the unexpectedly sensuous way in which the cold, brittle substance became soft and pliant when warmed by cutting with a blowtorch, a process that, along with the medium and its special colors, would suggest a variety of new subject matter. Sultan also fell in love with the tar—called butyl butter—he used for fixing the tiles to their Masonite support, and began drawing and painting with it on the vinyl surface. This led to covering the plane with a thick layer of tar, which the artist would then paint on or carve into, in the latter instance achieving his image by revealing the vinyl color that lay below. Process had indeed now served as a means of putting more and more elements back into the art of painting. And it again served when Sultan hit upon what, so far, has been his most memorable motif, a colossal yellow lemon

24.96 Donald Sultan, *FOUR LEMONS, February 1, 1985*, 1985. Oil, spackle, and tar on vinyl tile, 8'1" × 8'1" (2.5 × 2.5 m). Collection the artist.

24.97 Neil Jenney, *Meltdown Morning*, 1975. Oil on panel, 2'1⅜" × 9'4½" (0.64 m × 2.9 m). Philadelphia Museum of Art.

(fig. **24.96**)—a luscious, monumental orb with nippled protrusions—whose color seems all the more dazzling for being embedded in tar, traces of which make the fruit's flat silhouette appear to swell into full, voluptuous volume.

A key figure among the New Imagists was **Neil Jenney** (b. 1945), who did not abandon the strategies he first learned in Minimal, Pop, and Process art so much as integrate them with beautifully illusionistic subject matter to achieve paintings of galvanic visual impact and chilling moral, even admonitory force. In such works as *Saw and Sawed*, 1969, for instance, Jenney rediscovered a version of the liquid Abstract Expressionist stroke and the cartoon-like drawing favored by the Pop artists, along with the visual-cum-verbal punning so beloved by both Pop and Conceptual artists (the work depicts a felled piece of timber), all set forth within a monochrome Color Field organization and a heavy, title-bearing frame that together betray a Minimalist consciousness of the painting as a literal object. In tension with this literalness is the witty ambiguity of the meaning implied by the juxtaposition of words and images.

Articulate and politically minded, Jenney has spoken of art as "a social science," and as a language through which to convey "allegorical truths." Gradually, as the visual and verbal jokes interact to engage the mind, and the painterly fluidity seduces the eye, attentive viewers find themselves drawn, through a chain of unexpected relationships, into a consideration of the consequences of human deeds, consequences of a serious environmental import. In subsequent paintings, Jenney reversed the relationship between his imagery and its enclosing frame until the latter—massive, dark, and funereal—allows a mere slit of an opening through which to glimpse a tantalizingly lyrical and illuminated nature (fig. **24.97**). Along with the monumentalization of the coffinlike frame has come a vast enlargement of the label. And when this spells out a title like *Meltdown Morning*, the image so segmentally revealed assumes the character of longing for a paradise already lost beyond recovery, as well as mourning for the old world as it may appear—like a rare fragment presented in a museum showcase—following nuclear armageddon or environmental catastrophe.

Borofsky and Bartlett

By his own admission, **Jonathan Borofsky** (b. 1942) has placed politics firmly at the center of his riotously pluralistic art, saying: "It's all about the politics of the inner self, how your mind works, as well as the politics of the exterior world." To express what has become an untidy multiplicity of concerns, Borofsky is at his most characteristic not in individual works but rather in whole gallerywide installations (fig. **24.98**), where he can spread over ceilings and windows, around corners, and all about the floor the entire contents of his mind, his studio, and even the history of his art, which began at the age of eight with a still life of fruit on a table.

The first time he mounted such a display, at Paula Cooper's SoHo gallery in New York in 1975, the show, Borofsky said, "seemed to give people a feeling of being inside my mind." Mostly that mind seems filled with dreams or with the free associations so cherished by the Surrealists, all of which Borofsky has attempted to illustrate with an appropriate image or object. A representative installation would contain a giddy mélange of drawing, painting, sculpture, audio work, and written words, all noisily and messily driving home certain persistent themes. The drawings typically begin with automatist doodles in which the artist discovers and then develops images, such as a dog with pointed ears, blown up by an opaque projector to spill over and be painted onto walls and ceilings, as if a mythological monster were hovering above and threatening the whole affair.

Among the other presences activating the installations are the giant "Hammering Men" (visible, in two versions, at the left in fig. 24.98), the motorized up-and-down motion of their arms inspired by the artist's father, on whose lap young Borofsky sat while listening to "giant stories." Another character took the artist into the realm of sexual politics, where he conjured images of an androgynous clown dancing to the tune of "My Way." As a kind of interstitial tissue serving to link these disparate images, Borofsky littered the floor with crumpled fliers, which were in fact copies of an actual letter recounting the difficulties of ordinary life, a "found" work picked up by the artist from a sidewalk in California.

24.98 Jonathan Borofsky, Installation at the Whitney Museum of American Art, New York, December 21, 1984–March 10, 1985.

The artist has also imposed continuity on his work through his obsessive counting, a rational process of ordering, unlike the instinctual, random one seen elsewhere in his work, that he began in the late sixties and has now taken beyond the three-million mark. Along the way he applies numbers to each of his pieces and sometimes even to himself, thus joining their separateness into one continuous, ongoing sequence. The record of this monotonous activity is displayed, in graph paper filled with numerals, stacked waist-high, and enshrined in Plexiglas.

Another New Image artist with a voracious appetite for exhibition space and the creative energy to fill it is **Jennifer Bartlett** (b. 1941), whose vast 987-unit painting entitled *Rhapsody* (fig. **24.99**) became, upon its presentation in 1976, one of the most sensational works of the decade. She simplified her painting process, eliminating wooden stretchers, canvas, and the paraphernalia of the oil paint, until she depended upon little more than the basic module of a one-foot-square (0.3 m) steel plate, a flat, uniform surface commercially prepared with a coat of baked-on white enamel and an overprinted silkscreen grid of light gray lines. When finally assembled on a large loft-size wall, hundreds of the enameled steel plates yielded multipart compositions filled with color-dot paintings in an eye-dazzling display of brilliantly decorative abstract patterns.

For *Rhapsody* Bartlett used a large repertoire of colors and, in a further attempt to include "everything," decided to have figurative as well as nonfigurative images. For the former she chose the most "essential," emblematic

forms of a house, a tree, a mountain, and the ocean, and for the latter a square, a circle, and a triangle—Cézanne's "cylinder, sphere, and cone" two-dimensionalized. She also had sections devoted purely to color, others to lines (horizontal, vertical, diagonal, curved), and some to different techniques of drawing (freehand, dotted, ruled). The painting finally climaxed in a 126-plate ocean sequence incorporating 54 different shades of blue. Bartlett went on to expand her basic themes in new directions, accommodating sculpture and undertaking large public and private commissions.

Chicago Imagists: Nutt and Paschke

A group of young figurative artists with a fondness for fantasy and grotesque exaggeration became known as the Chicago Imagists, since many of them studied at the school of the Art Institute of Chicago. **Jim Nutt** (b. 1938) began exhibiting in 1966 with a smaller group of these irreverent artists, which called itself the Hairy Who. At that time, Nutt's scribbly images of women were filled with adolescent aggressiveness. A more controlled work from a few years later, *It's a Long Way Down* (fig. **24.100**), still portrays a woman in anxious, if cartoonish, terms. Nutt says that the painting has to do with the movies, and the gigantic female here, so hugely out of proportion with the tiny inset figures at the upper left and the fleeing form at the lower right, does seem to come from fifties science-fiction epics like *Attack of the Fifty-Foot Woman*. The headless torso (or is it a mannequin?) at the bottom and the severed

24.99 Jennifer Bartlett, *Rhapsody* (detail), 1975–76. Enamel and baked enamel silkscreen grid on 987 steel plates, each 12 × 12" (30.5 × 30.5 cm), overall 7'6" × 153'9" (2.3 × 46.9 m). Collection Sidney Singer, New York.

24.100 Jim Nutt, *It's a Long Way Down*, 1971. Acrylic on wood, 33⅞ × 24¾" (86 × 62.9 cm). National Museum of American Art, Smithsonian Institution, Washington, D.C.

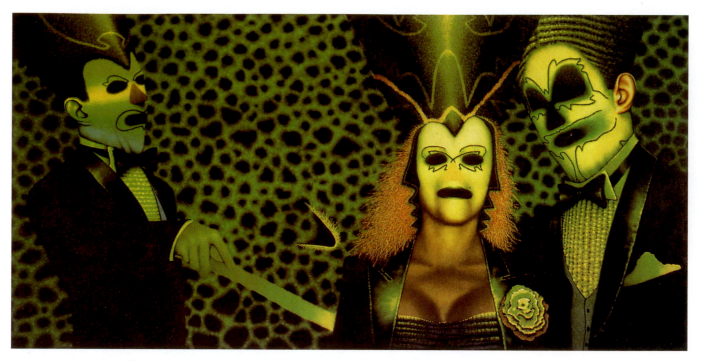

24.101 Edward Paschke, *Duro-Verde*, 1978. Lithograph, 4' × 8' (1.22 × 2.4 m). Virginia Museum of Fine Arts, Richmond.

head plummeting through the skylight complete this scene of comic mayhem.

Also initially associated with the Chicago Imagists is **Edward Paschke** (b. 1939). Paschke's figures of the seventies may owe something to the particularity of Photorealism in their smoothly modulated contours, as with the exposed skin of the woman in *Duro-Verde* (fig. **24.101**). But even though that work may depict a recognizable event—presumably a high-society party or masked ball—the outrageous colors that Paschke employs nullify any sense of illusionistic fidelity. The artificial, electric green is akin to garish neon lighting, and it recalls as well the distortions of a poorly tuned color TV set. Also puzzling is Paschke's deliberate overelaboration of the headgear and masks, perhaps intended to imply that this scene is more than it appears to be. Oddest of all are the dramatic poses of the figures. The frowning, lance-wielding male on the left and the pensive couple on the right suggest nothing so much as a Postmodernist version of the Expulsion of Adam and Eve from the Garden of Eden.

Steir

The work of **Pat Steir** (b. 1940) reflects a consciousness that art always comes from older art, giving culture a vernacular of current forms, which each painter or sculptor reinvests with subtly or sharply different meanings. A clear demonstration of the principle can be found in *Cellar Door* (fig. **24.102**). The large, unmodulated black form at the left is a quotation of Malevich's *Black Square* (see fig. 11.18) of 1914–15, a key point of origin for subsequent geometric abstraction. As if to acknowledge Malevich's

original challenge to traditional kinds of painting, Steir added a generic landscape to the right half of *Cellar Door* and then crossed it out, just as Malevich himself had once pasted a small reproduction of the Mona Lisa into one of his own works and marked an "X" across the face. Yet Steir also maintains a certain ironic distance from Malevich, not least by the title she gives her painting. The black square in *Cellar Door* is not a mysterious geometric icon like the one that Malevich made, but rather something from ordinary experience—just the doorway to an unlighted basement.

Steir's later *Red Tree, Blue Sky, Blue Water* (fig. **24.103**) is a triptych. In this work, a "quotation" from Van Gogh on the left progresses across the three panels in a cinematic sequence, from distant shot to medium one and finally close-up. As they move in graduated stages from resolution to dissolution, the panels also illustrate Steir's conviction that realism and abstraction are the same thing. Adding to the complexity is the echo of Van Gogh's own quoted source: a Hiroshige woodcut. Furthermore, the bold red-on-blue coloration and the swirling, almost Art Nouveau configuration of the image in the right panel—a blowup of a blossom—would seem to betray a side glance at Mondrian's 1908 *Blue Tree* (see c.p. 120). But however absorbed she may be in the history of painting, Steir is also absorbed in the *act* of painting, as can be seen in her extraordinary lavishness of stroke, medium, and color.

New Image Sculptors: Shapiro and Flanagan

In the context of the long figurative tradition of sculpture, **Joel Shapiro** (b. 1941) might conceivably have had less difficulty than painters when he determined to warm the

24.102 Pat Steir, *Cellar Door*, 1972. Oil, crayon, pencil, and ink on canvas, 6 × 9' (1.8 × 2.7 m). Collection Mr. and Mrs. Robert Kaye, New York.

24.103 Pat Steir, *Red Tree, Blue Sky, Blue Water*, 1984. Three panels, each 60 × 60" (152.4 × 152.4 cm). Private collection.

chill perfection of Minimalism's cubic forms with some sense of an activated human presence. Even so, Shapiro found it necessary to proceed only gradually, moving toward the figure through the more abstract objectivity of its habitations in an early seventies series devoted to the house (fig. **24.104**). Right away, however, Minimalism lost its monumentality as Shapiro miniaturized the image and pruned the form of all but its most primary or archetypal

masses. As for the humanity excluded from these modest abodes, Shapiro so formed and inflected his figures that, on a larger scale, they share both the houses' clean lines and conflicted condition. His later stick figures, built of square-cut posts and cast in iron or beautiful reddish gold bronze—wood grain, knotholes, and all—display the economy of a Sol LeWitt sculpture, only to break free of constraints and seem to pivot, writhe, dance, collapse,

24.104 Joel Shapiro, *Untitled*, 1973–74. Cast iron, 3 × 27¼ × 2⅝" (7.6 × 69.2 × 6.7 cm); clipboard base, 14¾ × 29¾ × 5" (37.5 × 75.6 × 12.7 cm).

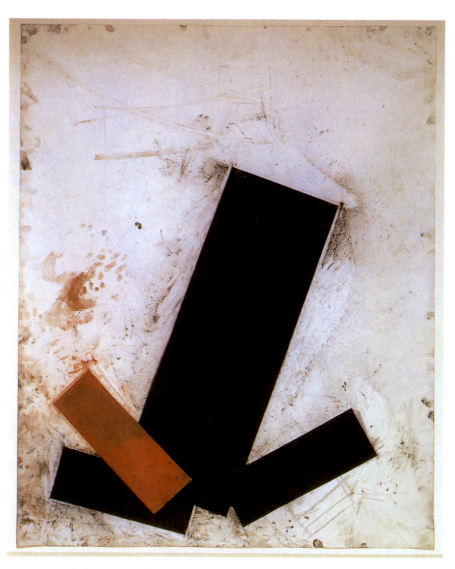

24.105 Joel Shapiro, *Untitled*, 1987. Charcoal and chalk on paper, 53⅛ × 42⁹⁄₁₆" (134.9 × 108.1 cm). Whitney Museum of American Art, New York.

and crawl, as if echoing in antiheroic, Constructivist terms the tormented poses and gestures of Rodin's figures. Even more evocative are some of Shapiro's drawings (fig. **24.105**), in which his ethereal smudging of the charcoal endows the geometric shapes with an aura of mystery, an effect enhanced by the use of deep colors. Beam-and-plank assemblages occupy a vast, atmospheric space that owes something to Romantic notions of the sublime.

The British sculptor **Barry Flanagan** (b. 1941) arrived at his New Imagist art by way of painting, dance, and various Conceptual installations produced with organic materials and processes. Throughout a highly varied oeuvre the consistent factors have been those of poetic association, inventiveness, and good humor. Flanagan favors substances such as hessian, rope, felt, steel, stone, ceramic, or bronze, which can be manipulated to "unveil" an image in the course of handling and shaping. In the early eighties, while squeezing and rolling clay, Flanagan found a hare "unveiling" itself in the material, and the image proved to have all the fecundity in art that the creature displays in life

(fig. **24.106**). Leaping, strutting, dancing, balancing, or boxing, the slender, free-formed, but graceful bronze hare seems an emblem of Flanagan's own spontaneity, openness, and humor.

Wegman's Photography

William Wegman (b. 1942) started his career with a sense of humor and an aesthetic kinship with the New Imagist painters, if only a bit more adolescent. One drawing from 1975 presents a small childlike rendering of a coiled snake, centered on a piece of drawing paper over the words, "A HUGE DEADLY SNAKE RENDERED HARMLESS." Wegman also experimented with video and photography. After he had completed a movie of himself playing baseball with two full teams of neighborhood dogs, his most successful subject came bounding into camera range. It was a Weimaraner puppy, who grew up so stagestruck and histrionically gifted that nothing could keep him either from the lights or from performing once they were turned on. Wegman chose to photograph the puppy in order playfully

24.106 Barry Flanagan, *Hare on Bell with Granite Piers*, 1983. Bronze and granite, 7'11½" × 8'6" × 6'3" (2.4 × 2.6 × 1.9 m). Number one of edition of five. Collection the Equitable Life Assurance Society of the United States, New York.

to insinuate the notion of charming canine turned surrogate person. Naming his dog Man Ray, the artist punned himself—Dada fashion—into reversing roles with the dog and thus becoming his—Man's—best friend. For some ten years, until the canine celebrity died, Wegman found the photogenic Man Ray to be a gallant and sensitive actor in an ongoing comedy of still photographs, made first with a Polaroid and then with a large-format camera (fig. **24.107**). One by one they show Man Ray costumed and fully rehearsed to play through the whole range of ordinary and supposedly rational situations in contemporary society, all rendered farcical and pretentious—often hilariously so—by ironic contrast with the manifest dignity and intelligence of the noble Weimaraner. In such ways, art in the seventies, from the politically charged to the whimsical, provided a theater in which to push beyond the constraints—formal, social, and personal—that had weighed on Western art and society in the previous decade.

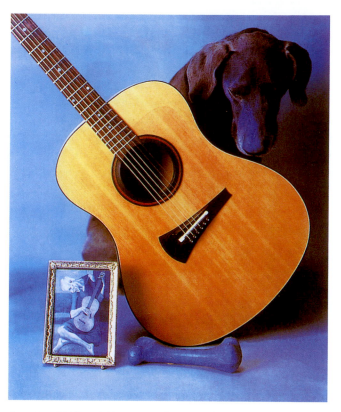

24.107 William Wegman, *Blue Period*, 1981. Color Polaroid photograph. Private collection.

25
Postmodernism in Architecture

The term Postmodernism originated not in the realms of painting or sculpture, but in the world of architecture. During the years of building and rebuilding after World War II, the International Style had an almost total hold on architects and clients. But in 1972, when the city of St. Louis dynamited Pruitt-Igoe (fig. **25.1**), a public-housing project built according to the best theories of modern architecture, the rule of Bauhaus took a great fall. All measures to save this monument to rational, utopian, Bauhaus planning had failed. Pruitt-Igoe had become an irredeemable social and economic horror scarcely twenty years after it had been built. Complete with "streets in the air"—safe from road traffic—and access to "sky, space, and greenery," which Le Corbusier had deemed the "three essential joys of urbanism," it had been hoped that

Pruitt-Igoe would inspire a sense of virtue in its inhabitants. By the end of the sixties, however, the multimillion-dollar, fourteen-story blocks had become so vandalized, crime-ridden, squalid, and dysfunctional that demolition seemed the best solution.

The demise of Pruitt-Igoe has been used by critics of modernism as proof that International Style architecture and urbanism was indifferent to the small-scale, personal requirements of privacy, individuality, context, and sense of place and was patronizing in its demands that residents adjust their lives to architecture. Pruitt-Igoe's architect, **Minoru Yamasaki** (1912–86), was blamed for failing to create viable homes for the people whose lives the project was meant to improve. The calamity in St. Louis was the "smoking gun" for critics who, since the mid-sixties,

25.1 Minoru Yamasaki, Pruitt-Igoe public-housing project, St. Louis, at the moment of its demolition on July 15, 1972. Built 1952–53.

had attempted to indict Bauhaus modernism for alleged bankruptcy of both form and principle. These critics thought that the followers of Mies, Gropius, and Le Corbusier had created a movement far too narrowly ideological and impersonal—and certainly too self-referential in its inflexible insistence on formalism dictated purely by function and technology. Such a stance could not serve a society in which cultural and economic diversity would only increase.

That International Style architecture was ideologically motivated was well understood by the seventies when critics attacked the Pruitt-Igoe project. Like Baron Haussman's Parisian boulevards (see chapter 2), modernist transformations of local spaces into collections of abstract geometric structures tend to overwhelm one with the authority of a single vision. The concern with uniform design extending from city plans to kitchen design (contrary to critiques of Pruitt-Igoe, modernists took great pains to address small-scale issues) demonstrates a desire to regulate human behavior. In fact the unsettling similarity between modernist utopian proposals and fascist ones placed serious doubt on the ability of modernist planning to transcend its immediate political context and maintain its original liberating potential. Society must accompany the modernist or his or her social goals could be appallingly corrupted.

The social context of modernism seems to have been ignored by early critics of Pruitt-Igoe who were too concerned with asserting the importance of new forms of architecture. Yamasaki's original plan had been for a mixed-height development that would correspond more logically to the neighborhoods from which its residents would be relocating. This was deemed too expensive, and the Public Housing Authority decided to erect thirty-three eleven-story structures. The density of the development was not part of the architect's plan. All demographic statistics were arrived at by government authorities and in the end even the materials, including doorknobs that broke and windows that were blown in by the wind, were determined by state-mandated financial limits rather than design choices. The shoddy materials and poor maintenance contributed to the physical degradation of the projects and added to the all-black population's sense of grievance with the racial politics of St. Louis. The modernist style, with its rhetoric of uniform design and aesthetic reduction, became a convenient stylistic vehicle for the socially irresponsible (if not racist) public housing efforts of the city. For critics who were ready to see the style that had defined the pre-World War II years relegated to history, blaming the architect was a useful device that carried its own aesthetic and ideological message. Social dynamics outside the domain of style were, for a moment, dispensible in the pursuit of a new Postmodern architecture.

Postmodernists seek to build in relation to everything: the site and its established environment; the client's specific needs, including those of wit and adventure in living; any historical precedent relevant to current circumstance;

and communicable symbols for the whole enterprise. The best Postmodern architects demonstrate that the tools, methods, materials, and traditions that architects, engineers, contractors, and even politicians and advertisers have always worked with are still valid. They are, however, debatable and open to rearrangements, and reexaminations in order to solve architectural problems—especially as new technologies and materials become available. Thus, the work of Postmodernists seems almost unclassifiable except as a movement and style all its own, not merely "post-" something else. In addition to masters such as Le Corbusier and Mies van der Rohe, Postmodernists are influenced by moderns who escaped the monolithic imperatives of modernist dogma, such as Antoni Gaudí (see fig. 5.9) and Sir Edwin Lutyens.

Postmodernist architects resist the unifying aesthetic and corresponding faith in a single vision of architectural or urban design that was the keystone to modernist art and architecture. In contrast, they accept some modernist theories and reject others. Opposing the consistency of Bauhaus aesthetics, Postmodernism has a voracious appetite for an illogical and eclectic mix of history and historical imagery; for a wide variety of vernacular expression; for decoration and ornamentation; and for metaphor, symbolism, and playfulness. Eclecticism in architecture or planning has as many political consequences and is thus as ideological as universalism—a fact that would become a vexing intellectual challenge as Postmodernism came to be associated with both capitalism and cultural institutions such as theaters and museums. The new style would display a fascination with the products of society that resonated with the American Pop artists of the sixties.

"Complexity and Contradiction": The Reaction Against Modernism Sets In

Among the first to appreciate Gaudí and Luytens anew, declare affinity with Pop (Ed Ruscha in particular), and to voice and practice the revisionism that is Postmodernism was the Philadelphia architect and theorist **Robert Venturi** (b. 1925). Often called the father of Postmodernism, Venturi did not train at Harvard University, whose School of Design, as noted earlier, had been transformed by Walter Gropius into a powerful Bauhaus-like force for modernism. Instead he went to Princeton University, where he studied under the distinguished Beaux Arts professor Jean Labatu. This grounding gave Venturi historical points of reference for most examples of antimodern architecture. Moreover, it prepared Venturi to see in Rome, while there in 1954–56 as a Fellow at the American Academy in Rome, not just a collection of great monuments but an urban environment characterized by human scale, sociable piazzas, and an intricate weave of the grand and the common. Supplemented by a period in the office of Louis I. Kahn, another admirer of the Roman model and a leading architect then moving from the International Style toward more rugged, expressionist, or symbolic buildings (see figs. 23.37), Venturi's Roman experience served as the basis of a new philosophy that would culminate in his seminal book *Complexity and Contradiction in Architecture* (1966). Here, with scholarship and wit, Venturi worked back through architectural history to Italian Baroque and Mannerist prototypes and argued that the great architecture of the past was not classically simple, but was often ambiguous and complex. He held, moreover, that modern architects' insistence upon a single style of unrelenting reductivism was utterly out of synchrony with the irony and diversity of modern times. To Mies van der Rohe's celebrated dictum, "Less is more," Venturi retorted "Less is a bore."

Complexity and Contradiction presented a broadside critique of mainstream modernism, at least as it had evolved in massive, stripped-down, steel-and-glass boxes that rose with assembly-line regularity throughout the postwar world. Even now, many critics consider Venturi's book the first and most significant written statement against the International Style. "Architects can no longer afford to be intimidated by the puritanically moral language of orthodox modern architecture," wrote Venturi.

> I like elements which are hybrid rather than "clear," distorted rather than "straightforward," ambiguous rather than "articulated," ... boring as well as "interesting," conventional rather than "designed," accommodating rather than excluding ... inconsistent and equivocal rather than direct and clear. I am for messy vitality over obvious unity. I include the non sequitur and proclaim the duality. I am for richness of meaning rather than clarity of meaning.

Venturi believed that the modern movement had grown stale, and that the successors to the great innovative modern architects had turned the latter's splendid revolution into a new Establishment, which was just as authoritarian and unresponsive to contemporary needs as the old one had been. Confronted with the pervasive gigantism, unaccommodating aloofness, sameness, and opportunism— giving less and charging more in the name of utopian ideals—of the buildings designed by Bauhaus-inspired architects, Venturi decided that "Main Street is almost all right." In other words, rather than disdaining the ordinary landscape of average towns, we should embrace it, accommodate it, and improve upon it on its own terms.

With his wife, **Denise Scott Brown** (b. 1931), an architect and specialist in popular culture and urban planning and a partner in the firm of Venturi, Rauch, and Scott Brown, Venturi wrote an even more provocative book in 1972, *Learning from Las Vegas.* In it they declared that a careful study of contemporary "vernacular architecture," like that along the automobile-dominated commercial "strip" roadways of Las Vegas, may be "as important to architects and urbanists today as were the studies of medieval Europe and ancient Rome and Greece to earlier generations." Venturi and Scott Brown had sought to learn from such a landscape because for them it constituted "a new type of urban form, radically different from that which we have known, one which we have been ill-equipped to deal with and which, from ignorance, we define today as urban sprawl. Our aim [was] ... to understand this new form and to begin to evolve techniques for its handling." The book was illustrated with photographs and film stills of the Strip; maps of the scale, purpose, and type of advertising; and theoretical, historical, and architectural analysis (fig. **25.2**). Since urban sprawl has come to stay, Venturi and Scott Brown are persuaded that architects should learn to love it, or at least discover how "to do the strip and urban sprawl well," from supermarket parking lots and hamburger stands to gas stations and gambling casinos. In their opinion, "the seemingly chaotic juxtaposition of honky-tonk elements expresses an intriguing kind of vitality and validity."

In Praise of "Messy Vitality": Postmodernist Eclecticism

Venturi, Rauch, Scott Brown, and Moore

While such Pop taste and maverick views made Venturi the leading theoretician among younger architects, they also earned him the near-universal disdain of the modernist school and of critics such as Ada Louise Huxtable, who dubbed the quietly civilized Venturi the "guru of chaos." Venturi and Scott Brown's bold ideas also proved too much for arbiters of major architectural commissions. Thus, until 1986, when Venturi, Rauch, and Scott Brown won the coveted contract for the design of the extension to London's National Gallery on Trafalgar Square (see fig. 25.5), the firm had to content itself with relatively small projects. Still, the partners made the most of every opportunity, even while insisting that they deliberately designed "dumb" buildings or "decorated sheds." The decorated shed concept may have received its most salient expression in the highway store designed for the Best Products Company (fig. 25.3). Its long, low façade rises above the parking lot like a false front on Main Street in a Western frontier town, while displaying huge, Andy Warhol-style gaily colored flowers. However, the prototypical Venturi building is one the architect built in 1962 for his mother in Chestnut Hill, Pennsylvania (fig. 25.4), a work of exceptional humor, sophistication, and irony whose apparent ordinariness is just enough "off" to tell the alert viewer that something extraordinary has gone into its design.

In Chestnut Hill House, Venturi accepted the conventions of the "ugly and ordinary" American suburban crackerbox—its stucco veneer, wood frame, pitched roof, front porch, central chimney, and so forth—and parodied them so completely as to make the commonplace seem remarkable, enriching it with wit and light-hearted satire. The process of transformation began with the scale of the

25.4 Robert Venturi, Chestnut Hill House, Philadelphia, 1962.

façade, which the architect expanded until it rose several feet above the roof, thereby creating another false front. He then divided it at the center to reveal the conceit and widened the cleft at the bottom to create a recessed porch. Visually joining the two halves together, yet simultaneously emphasizing their division, are the arch-shaped strip of molding and the stretched lintel above the entrance, both paper-thin like everything else about the façade (or like the crackerbox tradition itself, or even most modern curtain-wall construction). Meanwhile, the split in the front wall echoes the much older and more substantial stone architecture of the Baroque era, which in turn joins with the expanded height of the façade to create a certain illusionistic grandeur. Such complexity and contradiction extend deep into the structure, to the chimney wall, for instance, which spreads wide like a great central mass, only to project above it the chimney. Unity too has been honored with all the intricate ambiguities, as in the same size and number (five) of the asymmetrically disposed window panels on each side of the façade.

25.3 Venturi, Rauch, and Scott Brown, Best Products Company, Oxford Valley, Pennsylvania, 1977.

25.5 Robert Venturi and Denise Scott Brown, National Gallery, London, with Sainsbury Wing visible left of the main gallery across Trafalgar Square. 1987–91.

Hidden behind the deceptively simple exterior of Chestnut Hill House is a complicated interior, its rooms as irregularly shaped and small in scale as the façade is grand, in the Pop manner of Claes Oldenburg's giant hamburgers and baseball bats (see fig. 24.59). Yet the plan is tight and rational, not whimsical. For example, the crooked stairway is broad at the base but narrow at the top, reflecting, in Venturi's view, the difference in scale between the "public" spaces downstairs and the "intimate" ones upstairs. By its very irregularity, the interior accommodates the books, family mementos, and overstuffed furniture long owned by the client as well as it expresses her patterns of living. Unlike Corbusier's "machines for living" or Frank Lloyd Wright's Usonian houses, Chestnut Hill House does not suggest or impose a living pattern for its inhabitants. And herein lies the essence of the Venturi concept: Chestnut Hill House makes no attempt to simulate a ship or an airplane, or to become some organic device to commune with nature; instead, Venturi's design proclaims its "houseness" with historically relevant allusions that are not overt symbols. "We don't think people want 'total design' as it is given to them by most modern architects," Scott Brown once said. "They want shelter with symbolism applied to it."

In 1986, Venturi and Scott Brown won the commission to design a new wing for the National Gallery in London. They were to create a permanent exhibition space for the gallery's Early Renaissance collection, a large lecture hall, a computer information room, a video theater, a gift shop, and a restaurant. Located diagonally across from Trafalgar Square, their design for the Sainsbury Wing (fig. **25.5**) integrates both modern and classicist impulses. The main entrance is skewed to face Trafalgar Square, and the Classical details of the façade echo those of the adjacent main building. Although not easy to see from the square, these Classical details have been subjected to subtle Postmodern idiosyncrasies and operations: the windows are blind and almost disappear into the stone façade, and, among the regularly spaced pillars, there is a single round column that imitates the monument to Lord Nelson in Trafalgar Square. The western-facing façade on Whitcomb Street is plain brick. The huge glass wall of the grand staircase at the east side of the wing offers a view of the exterior of the old gallery. The top floor's neutral-toned galleries, which permanently house the Renaissance collection, are respectful of both the old galleries and the artwork in their expertly scaled spaces. Natural and artificial lighting are adjusted every two hours by computer, according to the amount of natural light filtering in through the glass "attics." Venturi and Scott Brown's Sainsbury Wing demonstrates that the Postmodern style is flexible and capable of adapting to its site, its purpose, and other surrounding buildings.

Another student of Louis I. Kahn at the University of Pennsylvania and a close ally, if not an actual partner, of Venturi and Scott Brown was **Charles Moore** (1925–93), who looked not so much to Las Vegas for inspiration as to Disneyland, praising it as an outstanding public space as well as an embodiment of the American Dream. Concerned with the commercial or industrial sameness of the postwar world, and with it the lost "sense of place" that leaves so many American cities looking like Los Angeles, Moore became even more overtly historicist than Venturi and was fully committed to "the making of places." In this, he often favored the "presence of the past" found in a Roman–Mediterranean kind of environment. One of the most remarkable examples of how imaginatively he could develop this theme is the Piazza d'Italia in New

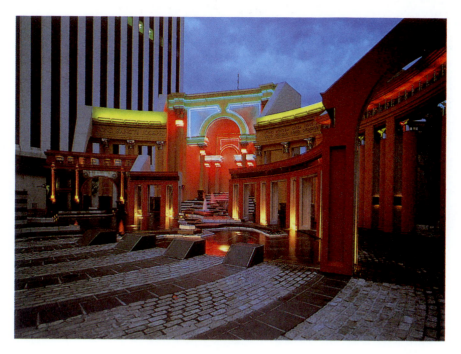

25.6 Charles Moore with U.I.G. and Perez Associates, Inc., Piazza D'Italia, New Orleans. 1975–80.

Orleans (figs. **25.6, 25.7**). Here Moore designed a public space to provide a small Italian-American community with an architectural focus of ethnic identity; a place exuberant enough to serve as the setting of the annual St. Joseph's festival, with its vibrant street life. Piazza d'Italia is an early example of the playful Postmodern use of classical forms. An entirely decorative and symbolic construction, it is architecture that abandons the ambition for permanence. Collaborating with architects well versed in the local culture, Moore took into account not only the taste and habits of the area's inhabitants, but also the different styles of buildings around the new piazza. Thus, while the design incorporated the black-and-white lines of an adjacent modernist skyscraper in a graduated series of concentric rings, the circular form itself—essentially Italian Baroque in character—reflects the local community. Moore found the prototypes for his

circular piazza in, among other places, Paris' Place des Victoires, the Maritime Theater at Hadrian's Villa near Tivoli, and the famed Trevi Fountain in Rome, an open-air scenographic extravaganza combining a Classical façade, allegorical earth sculpture, and water.

At staggered intervals on either side of a cascading fountain at the Piazza d'Italia are various column screens representing the five Classical orders, the outermost and richest one, Corinthian, crowned by polished stainless-steel capitals supporting an entablature emblazoned with dedicatory Latin inscriptions. Over the waterfall stands a triumphal arch, polychromed in Pompeiian hues and outlined in neon tubing. With its eclectic mixture of historical reference and pure fantasy, such as water coursing down pilasters to suggest fluting, water spouts serving as Corinthian leaves, and stainless-steel Ionic volutes sitting on neon necking, Piazza d'Italia combines archaeology, modernism, commerce, and theater to provide something for everyone—and above all a sense of place unlikely ever to be confused with Cleveland, Los Angeles, Sicily, or even the French Quarter in New Orleans itself.

Hollein, Stern, and Isozaki

About the same time as Venturi and Scott Brown began to fill commissions, Austria's **Hans Hollein** (b. 1934) was in the American West, learning from Las Vegas and doing so in rebellion against the "Prussian dogma of modernism" at the Illinois Institute of Technology (where he had enrolled in 1958). Seeing all those open spaces and the expressive freedom they seemed to generate, Hollein had an epiphany, after which he designed with a pluralistic abandon worthy of his gaudy American models, but also with an exquisitely crafted, decorative elegance reflecting a subtle appreciation of Vienna's Secessionist tradition (see figs. 12.9, 12.11). Even more than the Americans, European Postmodernists such as Hollein found few opportunities to

25.7 Charles Moore with U.I.G. and Perez Associates, Inc., View from above, Piazza d'Italia.

25.8 Hans Hollein, Austrian Travel Bureau, Vienna, 1978.

work on a large scale. The Austrian architect had to contain his drive to invent and surprise within small jewel-box spaces—often old and refurbished interiors like that of the Austrian Travel Bureau in Vienna (fig. **25.8**) of 1978. For this project Hollein adopted topographical themes and scenographic methods similar to those of Charles Moore in Piazza d'Italia—and in the same metaphorical spirit—to make a preexisting hall suggest the many places to which

the Travel Bureau could send its clients: in other words, evoking the concept of travel. Thus, the assemblage of allusive forms and images found here includes: a grove of brass palm trees clearly based on those in John Nash's kitchen for the early nineteenth-century Brighton Pavilion (see fig. 4.1); a broken "Grecian" column and pyramids; a model of the Wright brothers' biplane; plus rivers, mountains, and a ship's railing. Lined up along the central axis, like a miniature Las Vegas strip, are such temptations as an Oriental pavilion, a chessboard seating area, and a sales booth for theater tickets furnished with a cash window in the form of a Rolls-Royce radiator grille. Meanwhile, the hall itself has been styled to resemble a reconstruction of Otto Wagner's Post Office Savings Banks (see fig. 12.9), an ironic reference, since the whole purpose of the Travel Bureau is to encourage spending money, not saving it.

In 1972 Hollein was commissioned to design the North German town of Mönchengladbach's Städtisches Museum Abteiberg (fig. **25.9**). Taking ten years to complete, the museum is a series of buildings that critic Charles Jencks called "a modern Acropolis." The museum is located on a hill next to a Romanesque church and, as Jencks suggested, it provides a modern-day equivalent to the church's spiritual role. Declaring that he "was never afraid to use materials in new contexts—plaster or aluminum or marble, and all this together," Hollein designed the museum as a tiny

25.9 Hans Hollein, Städtisches Museum Abteiberg. Mönchengladbach, Germany, 1972–82.

town within a town, an agglomeration of distinct but compatible structures. With its undulating red-brick terraces snuggled against the slope, its relaxed and vaguely mock-ancient but nonabrasive Disneyland replicas, and its odd and delightfully particular cutout corner and voluptuous semicircular marble stairs, the Mönchengladbach museum struck Jencks as "a beautifully detailed urban landscape dedicated to a form of collective belief we find valuable. Art may not be a very convincing substitute for religion, but it is certainly a suitable pretext for heroic architecture."

Another American architect profoundly influenced by Robert Venturi, as well as by Charles Moore (under whom he studied at Yale), is **Robert A. M. Stern** (b. 1939). Like his mentors, Stern had an active practice in Postmodern architecture as well as being a teacher, writer, and editor. Although as witty and sophisticated as Venturi and Moore, Stern is also more literal and fastidious in his use of historical precedents, and he is considerably more given to patrician sumptuousness. Indeed, he developed into a one-person equivalent of McKim, Mead & White (see fig. 4.7): he seems most truly himself when designing the sort of grand shingle-style country house or holiday retreat that the turn-of-the-century New York firm once produced with understated aristocratic bravura. Thus, while reveling in the decorative revival quite as joyously as Venturi and Moore, until his commission to design a building for the Walt Disney Company, Stern had worked less in the Pop spirit that animates Moore's Piazza d'Italia and Venturi's Best Products Company's façade than in the fanciful manner of Hans Hollein's appropriations of Nash's Brighton Pavilion. This can be seen to splendid effect in the 1981–82 pool house (fig. **25.10**) that is part of an estate in northern New Jersey, where stainless-steel "palm columns" evoke the palm supports in Nash's Brighton kitchen. The glistening material of these uprights produces a "wet" effect appropriate to the setting, as do the polychrome wall tiles derived from a kind of decor favored by the Secessionist Viennese (see fig. 5.5). Further enhancing the bathhouse theme are the Art Deco figural quoins and the thick Tuscan columns, the latter reminiscent of Roman *terme*.

Stern's 1995 Feature Animation Building (fig. **25.11**) in Burbank, California, designed for the Walt Disney Company (which has also commissioned projects from Robert Venturi, Frank O. Gehry, and Arata Isozaki), offers a host of references both to the architecture of Los Angeles and to the fantasy architecture found in Disney animation. It is a highly complex building that in many ways resembles a converted warehouse, which is what Disney chief executive Michael Eisner had in mind when commissioning the project. Stern wanted the building's lobby—a tall oval space with one curved and tilted glass wall—to evoke the eccentric fast-food joints and doughnut shops of the forties, fifties, and sixties that are still to be found in and around Los Angeles. The building's profile—the entrance is tucked under a conical spire—is a reference to the cone-shaped hat worn by Mickey Mouse in a segment of the film *Fantasia*. Along the south side of the building is a narrow gallery with a high roof that slopes upward toward the main façade, ending in a form like the prow of a ship. Stern called this "the Mohawk" because it resembles a punk haircut; it also alludes to the Mad Hatter in Disney's animated version of *Alice in Wonderland*. Visible from a nearby freeway, giant stainless-steel letters above the front entrance spell the word ANIMATION. The work space is accommodated in three vast, connected barrel vaults that form the main bulk of the building. Under the vaults, painted black with stainless-steel studs that twinkle like stars, are girders and air shafts, which have been left exposed and painted white so that their industrial forms stand out against the dark ceiling.

Another figure linked to Postmodern eclecticism is the Japanese architect **Arata Isozaki** (b. 1931). He began his career working for Kenzo Tange (see figs. 23.26, 23.27) but soon dispensed with any Corbusian influences he might have absorbed. A self-confessed "mannerist," Isozaki draws on a huge variety of sources—Eastern and Western, traditional and modernist—honestly quoting from and transposing them.

25.10 Robert A. M. Stern, Pool House, Llewelyn, New Jersey, 1981–82.

25.11 Robert A. M. Stern, Feature Animation Building, Walt Disney Company, Burbank, California, 1995.

Situated in the old part of Mito, Japan, Isozaki's 1990 Art Tower is the cultural core of that city. The building accommodates four major features: a gallery of contemporary art, a concert hall, a theater, and the Mito centennial tower. The various parts are connected by a large square that occupies more than half the site. There is also a two-story conference hall and a museum shop, café, and restaurant. The museum space has three glass roofs (fig. 25.12). A pyramid is set symmetrically at the center. The façades are set with porcelain tiles to give the plaza the feel

25.12 Arata Isozaki, Gallery building, Art Tower. View of north end. Mito, Japan, 1990.

of a European town. At the north end, a huge stone placed on the center axis of the square is suspended by thin cables. At the northwestern corner, sandwiched between the concert hall and the theater, is an entrance hall that serves as a connecting chamber for the building's functions. This vertical space links the plaza to the street. A 328-foot-high (100 m) tower to the east of the plaza commemorates the centenary of Mito. This Brancusian "endless" column is made of titanium-paneled tetrahedrons; stacked together, their edges create a DNA-like double helix.

Ironic Grandeur: Postmodernism and History

Johnson

In looking for the early signs of the Postmodern aesthetic, one finds an apparent scorn for a refined, stylistic consistency. This shift can be seen in the career of **Philip Johnson** (b. 1906), who was an associate partner with Mies van der Rohe on the Seagram Building (see fig. 23.12). By the mid-fifties, Johnson was turning against the order and rationalism of Miesian design. His efforts to overturn the Modernist movement found their greatest early success in association with John Burgee, when he designed the New York headquarters for American Telephone and Telegraph (see figs. 25.13, 25.14, 25.15). Heightening the shock value of this famously revisionist skyscraper, built between 1978 and 1983, is the fact that Johnson, together with architectural historian Henry-Russell Hitchcock, in 1932 had written a book that introduced the International Style to the English-speaking world and thus made it a true architectural *lingua franca*. By the late seventies, Johnson was the virtual dean of American architects, and his immense prestige was very persuasive to the stolid AT&T officers when they committed more than $200 million to a Postmodern design of almost perverse irony and elegance.

The skyscraper was nicknamed the "Chippendale building" for the broken pediment at its top; its resemblance to a highboy chest in the Chippendale style was irresistible. With hindsight, it is not so surprising that Johnson's witty mind, stocked with a vast and erudite range of aesthetic references, perceived in the skyscraper an analogy to the highboy, a colossal stack of "drawers" set in a chest supported by tall legs and topped by a scroll bonnet. Rising 647 feet (197 m) without setback, it is divided into base, shaft, and granite-clad cornice. The shaft provides "drawers," or stories; owing to their double height, there are

25.13 Philip Johnson and John Burgee, AT&T Headquarters Building, New York, 1978–83.

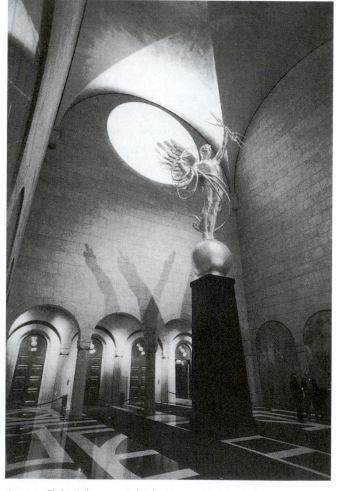

25.14 Philip Johnson and John Burgee, Lobby, AT&T Headquarters Building, New York, 1978–83.

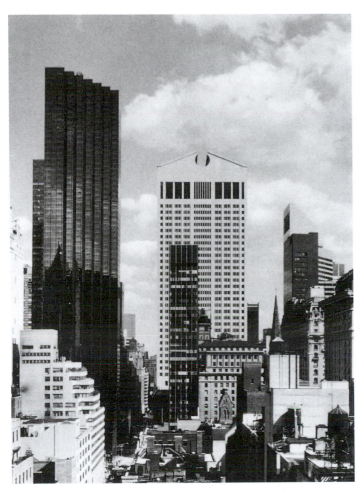

only thirty-six "drawers" in what is a sixty-story tower. With the AT&T building, Johnson reintroduced "history" into the vocabulary of modern high-rise architecture, a history rendered compatible with the commercial world of the sixties and seventies by reference not to palace or ecclesiastical structures, but to furniture. Herein may lie the essence of Postmodernism: the longing for symbolism and the grandeur of the past disembodied from the faith that inspired the original forms. Such design results in ingenious historical puns and self-mockery.

The AT&T building originally had a forest of "legs" at the street level, which sheltered a capacious, open loggia some five or six stories high; it was dedicated as a public space until 1990, when the building was sold to the Sony Corporation. Within three years, Sony converted the loggia space to shops and renamed it Sony Plaza. In the original building, the historicism of the design produced a dizzying mix of themes. The façade (fig. 25.13), a central oculus-over-arch flanked by trabeated loggias, recalled the front face of the Pazzi Chapel, a Florentine Renaissance building known to every student of architecture and art history. Johnson and Burgee's interior, however, was a groin-vaulted Romanesque space (fig. 25.14). The broken pediment that capped the building still endows it with its renowned and idiosyncratic profile (fig. 25.15).

Stirling, Jahn, Armajani, and Foster

Already one of Britain's most important architects in the sixties, when he worked in a somewhat Brutalist vein (see

25.15 Philip Johnson and John Burgee, AT&T Headquarters Building, New York, 1978–83.

25.16 James Stirling, Neue Staatsgalerie, Stuttgart, Germany, 1977–84.

25.17 James Stirling, Neue Staatsgalerie, Stuttgart, Germany, 1977–84.

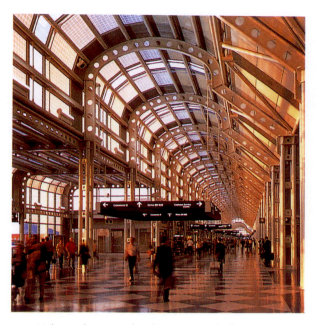

25.18 Helmut Jahn, United Airlines Terminal of Tomorrow, O'Hare International Airport, Chicago, 1987–88.

fig. 23.19), Sir **James Stirling** (1926–94) seems to have been liberated by Postmodernism into full possession of his own expansive genius. This is best exemplified in the exciting addition to the Neue Staatsgalerie, or museum, in Stuttgart, built in 1977–84 (figs. **25.16, 25.17**). Here, in association with Michael Wilford (b. 1938), Stirling took advantage of the freedom allowed by revisionist aesthetics to solve the manifold problems presented by a difficult hillside site, hemmed in below by an eight-lane highway, above by a terraced street, and on one side by the original Renaissance Revival museum building. With so many practical considerations to satisfy, Stirling decided to work in "a collage of old and new elements … to evoke an association with a museum." And so, while the three main exhibition wings repeat the U-shaped plan of the nineteenth-century structure next door, the external impression is that of a massive Egyptian structure, ramped from level to level like the funerary temple of the Old Kingdom Queen Hatshepsut at Deir el-Bahri, but faced with sandstone and travertine strips more suggestive of medieval Italy. Visually, the ramps and the masonry unify a jumble of disparate forms clustered within the courtyard framed by the embracing U. Among these are an open rotunda surrounding a sculpture court; the glazed and undulating walls of an entrance shaped rather like a grand piano; and a blue-columned, red-linteled, and glass-roofed high-tech taxi stand. Despite so many historical references and such diverse configurations, a sense of unity and distinctive place are real and even moving. The ramps convey the pedestrian along a zigzag path leading from the lower highway into and steeply halfway round the inner circumference of the rotunda, and finally through a tunnel in the cleft walls to the upper terraced street behind the museum. Adding to this heady mix of sophisticated, urbanistic pluralism is the keenly British sensibility of Stirling himself, who brought to the design the grace of the eighteenth-century Royal Crescent in Bath.

In the work of **Helmut Jahn** (b. 1940), Postmodernism's serious playfulness is articulated in large-scale projects. Jahn emigrated from Germany to Chicago in 1966, a staunch admirer of Mies van der Rohe. In 1967 he joined a leading Chicago architectural firm, C. F. Murphy, and by 1981 was principal architect in the renamed firm Murphy/Jahn. The $500-million United Airlines Terminal of Tomorrow at Chicago's O'Hare International Airport (fig. **25.18**) is an example of Jahn's success in creating enormous public places that are interesting to experience, technically brilliant, yet not overwhelmingly futuristic. Awarded the A.I.A. Design Award of 1988, the building is an architectural echo of the past, reminiscent of the iron-and-glass structures of Victorian railway stations. One speeds through physically on people movers while being mentally transported to a previous era. As in Joseph Paxton's Crystal Palace of 1851 (see fig. 4.3), we see prefabricated metal and glass construction elevated to the scale of civic architecture. The corridors and departure/arrival gates are metal-framed, glass-paneled, and topped with soaring barrel vaults drenched with natural light. Yet Jahn's high-tech update on nineteenth-century engineering is a far cry from explicitly historicist buildings.

Siah Armajani (b. 1939) a self-described "architect/sculptor" born in Teheran but long since resettled in Minnesota, creates sculptures and installations that suggest the history of architecture, engineering, and society and at times have even become works of architecture themselves. Since the late sixties, Armajani has been interested in the functional and metaphoric in the architectural engineering of bridges. Among the works he has created is the Irene Hixon Whitney pedestrian bridge, which links the sculpture garden at the Walker Art Center with Loring Park in the downtown part of Minneapolis (fig. **25.19**). Stretching over sixteen lanes of traffic, the bridge reconnects two parts of the city that were divided twenty years earlier by the construction of a superhighway. The bridge's design itself

25.19 Siah Armajani, *Irene Hixon Whitney pedestrian bridge. Bridge between Loring Park and Walker Art Center Sculpture Garden, Minneapolis*. 1988. Length 375' (114.3 m).

suggests a kind of symbolic unity: the two arches of the bridge, one convex and the other concave, unite to form a single sine curve. Armajani enlists architectural design and engineering technology to articulate and, in a small way, compensate for the divisive, if expedient, effects of urban planning and civil engineering.

Less cerebral and more celebratorily high-tech is the Telecommunications Tower in Barcelona, Spain (fig. **25.20**), the work of English architect Sir **Norman Foster** (b. 1935). The design of the tower follows the philosophy of Foster and Partners—that is, achieving maximum effect with minimal structural means, as well as achieving clarity and precision in the fitting together of components. The tower's precast concrete shaft is supported by three vertical steel trusses, and the whole structure is tethered to guy wires anchored in the mountainside. Modular floors and platforms are suspended from this structural skeleton in such a way as to accommodate future changes. Yet for all its functionality, the design of the Tower references an era of spaceship futurism with an innocent, almost playful, "World of Tomorrow" effect.

Pei and Freed

Historicism directed away from the futures imagined in the recent past and toward the ancient world was well developed when Chinese-American architect **I. M. Pei** (b. 1917) executed the commission for modernizing certain parts of the Louvre Museum in Paris. Pei is popularly known for the controversy surrounding his Grand Louvre Pyramid (1988), constructed in the courtyard of

25.20 Norman Foster, *Telecommunications Tower, Barcelona, Spain*, 1992.

25.21 I. M. Pei, Grand Louvre Pyramid, Paris, 1988.

the Louvre (fig. **25.21**). The Pyramid deliberately turns the tradition and concept of pyramid inside out. A pyramid is supposed to be solid, dark, and solitary—a mesmerizing symbol of the exotic world beyond the streets and cultures of Europe. Here, the pyramid is clear glass, almost immaterial, a vast skylight hovering over streams of museum visitors as they are channeled into the Louvre galleries through the below-ground entrance corridors. Besides its associations of timelessness and its brilliant ingenuity in lighting an underground space, the ensemble is a superb example of how new buildings in old settings do not always

have to accommodate themselves to the style of their "found" surroundings.

The expansion of existing museums and the proliferation of new museums since the early eighties have generated some of the most exciting architecture of recent times. Architect and curator attempt to bring the past into the present in flexible yet assertive form. Creating a museum to document one of the most atrocious crimes in history was an exceptional architectural challenge. The United States Holocaust Memorial Museum was chartered by a unanimous act of Congress in 1980 and opened in 1993.

25.22 Pei Cobb Freed & Partners, United States Holocaust Memorial Museum, Washington, D.C., 1993.

Architect **James Ingo Freed** (b. 1930), of Pei Cobb Freed & Partners, fashioned a relationship between the architecture of the building and the exhibitions within, creating in effect a work of art. Freed visited a number of Holocaust sites, including camps and ghettos, to examine structures and materials. While architectural allusions to the Holocaust are not specific, the building contains subtle metaphors and symbolic reminiscences of history. In Freed's words, "There are no literal references to particular places or occurrences from the historic event. Instead, the architectural form is open-ended." The building thus serves as a "resonator of memory."

At first glance, the exterior seems benign, which is part of the building's metaphoric message (fig. **25.22**). Yet throughout, Freed has incorporated physical elements of concealment, deception, disengagement, and duality. The curved portico of the 14th Street entrance—with its squared arches, window grating, and cubed lights—is a mere front, a fake screen that actually opens to the sky, deliberately hiding the disturbing architecture of skewed lines and hard surfaces of the real entrance that lies behind it. This strategy of contrasting and juxtaposing appearance and reality is repeated throughout. Along the north brick walls, a different perspective reveals a roofline profile of camp guard towers, a procession of sentry boxes. Above

the western entrance, a limestone mantle holds a solitary window containing sixteen solid "panes," framed by clear glass, reversing the normal order and obscuring the ability to look in or out. Inside, the physical layout ushers visitors through the exhibits in a sequence of experiences. The central, skylit, brick-and-steel Hall of Witness sets the stage of deadly efficiency that is echoed throughout this museum. The expansive use of exposed steel trusswork is an ever-present reminder of the death chambers. Vertically piercing the entire structure is the Tower of Faces, a chimney-like shaft lined with photographs of the people of a village that was essentially annihilated in the Holocaust. One passes through the Tower of Faces on a bridge, surrounded above and below by the faces of men, women, and children for whom the chimney was the ultimate symbol of fear. The personal detail of the faces is contrasted by the painting and sculptures commissioned for the museum from abstract artists—Elsworth Kelly, Sol LeWitt, Joel Shapiro, and Richard Serra (see figs. 22.16, 22.52, 24.104, 22.57). From the main floor and on the way out, visitors climb an angled staircase to the second floor, which is highlighted by the hexagonal, light-filled Hall of Remembrance.

A very different monument and museum is a Pei project of 1995, the Rock and Roll Hall of Fame and Museum

25.23 I.M. Pei, Rock and Roll Hall of Fame and Museum, Cleveland, Ohio, 1995.

Euclidean geometry, a system that analyzes the physical world in terms of the cube, the sphere, and the pyramid. Pei's fascination with the pyramid, which he explored in the Louvre project, carried over into the Rock and Roll Museum. A 117-foot-high (35.6 m) glass-and-steel tent leans at a forty-five-degree angle against a tower with cantilevered wings. The building is an architectural interpretation of the explosiveness of rock music. Pei himself has said that he took the explosion metaphor from rock's rebelliousness and energy.

The building has three major elements: the glass tent; the tower containing exhibition spaces; and a plaza with administrative offices, archives, storage, and more exhibition spaces. One wing houses a forty-four-foot-diameter (13.4 m) cylindrical space for viewing films supported by a single column that plunges into the lake. The other wing comprises a 125-seat, cube-shaped auditorium that juts above the water without any visible means of support.

in Cleveland, Ohio (fig. **25.23**). It is an elegant monument to the world's most subversive art form. All of Pei's work, from the East Building of the National Gallery of Art in Washington, D.C. (see fig. 23.39) to his Louvre Grand Pyramid in Paris (see fig. 25.21), reflects an obsession with

Ando and Pelli

In any age, designing a house of worship requires crafting spaces that encourage and direct emotional and intellectual experience. In our time, Japanese architect **Tadao Ando** (b. 1941) has designed some of the most effective places

25.24 Tadeo Ando, Chapel-on-the-Water, Hokkaido, Japan, 1988.

25.25 Cesar Pelli, Petronas Towers, Kuala Lumpur, 1998.

of worship in the modern idiom, using precision-cast reinforced concrete—partly to make his buildings earthquake safe—and siting the buildings and their precincts with extraordinary sensitivity to the surrounding topography. One such project is his 1988 Chapel-on-the-Water (fig. **25.24**). Located on a small plain in the mountains on the northern island of Hokkaido, this church is part of a year-round resort. The structure consists—in plan—of two overlapping squares. The larger, partly projecting out into an artificial pond, houses the chapel, and the smaller contains the entry and changing and waiting rooms. A freestanding L-shaped wall wraps around the back of the building and one side of the pond. The chapel is approached from the back, and entry involves a circuitous route: a counterclockwise ascent to the top of the smaller volume through a glass-enclosed space open to the sky, with views of the pond and mountains. In this space are four large concrete crosses. The wall behind the altar is constructed entirely of glass, providing a dramatic panorama of the pond with a large cross set into the water. The glass wall can slide like a giant shoji screen (the paper screens used to partition rooms in Japanese interior design), opening the interior of the chapel to nature. A 6,000-seat, semicircular theater, northwest of the chapel, is designed to accommodate open-air concerts and other events. Set on a fan-shaped artificial pond, the amphitheater is intersected by a long, bridgelike stage and a freestanding colonnade. A site wall points toward the church complex and turns at a sharp angle into the axis of the stage, tying the two projects together.

Internationally influential architect **Cesar Pelli** (b. 1926), dean of the Yale University School of Architecture from 1977 to 1984, expressed the importance of context in his assessment of the priorities of the architect: "A building is responsible to the place it occupies and takes in a city ... the obligation is to the city. The city is more important than the building; the building is more important than the architect." Raised in Argentina, Pelli came to the United States in 1952 to study for a master's degree in architecture at the University of Illinois at Champaign-Urbana. Pelli's most visible buildings reference their locales in style and with motifs, and Pelli is able to invest commercial buildings with a public and sometimes even spiritual presence by means of forms and open spaces, especially when designing public-space interiors.

No building is more characteristic of Pelli's commitment to responding to local desires than the Petronas Towers in Kuala Lumpur (fig. **25.25**), which at the time of completion was the world's tallest building. The towers, which are 1,483 feet (452 m) tall, respond in their design and detailing to the local Malaysian culture as well as declaring through their great height confidence in the strength of the Asian economy. The ground plan for the two towers is based on an Islamic design of overlaid squares and inset circles. The result is a sixteen-sided façade that alternates between curved and flat walls. As the towers ascend they are set back six times and tilt inward to accent the grace of the exterior lines. Sheathed in stainless steel and reflecting bands of fenestration, the massive towers appear to be decorated with the blue sky above Kuala Lumpur. The windows were designed for the climate: a system of panes and shades decrease the amount of light and heat that enters the rooms. Culturally as well as climatically sensitive, Pelli decorated the interior spaces with traditional Malaysian arts. The centerpiece of the ground floor, set in between the towers, is a concert hall. The plan for the towers includes open space to accommodate future urban development. Pelli's concern with creating architecture that interacts with the city can also be seen in projects such as the World Financial Center in New York, which houses the commercial development for the Battery Park neighborhood in Lower Manhattan, and in the Abandoibarra Master Plan for the Waterfront along the Nervion River in Bilbao, Spain.

What Is a Building?: Deconstruction

The work of the Iraqi architect **Zaha Hadid** (b. 1950) points in a very different direction from that of Stirling, Isozaki, Pelli, and Ando. Her buildings exploit the possibilities of deconstructionist theory, which challenges the standard functions, uses, and perceptions of a building, much in the way it has in the fields of literary criticism and art history. Deconstructionism and deconstructivist architects are a Postmodern phenomenon, although usually not regarded as mainstream Postmodernist. Born in Baghdad, Hadid studied mathematics in Beirut, was trained in architecture at the Architectural Association in London (1972–77), and established her own practice in 1979. She was one of the first experimental female architects to make a substantial reputation and impact in the second half of the twentieth century. Her Vitra Fire Station in Weil am Rhein (fig. **25.26**), from 1993, is a prime example of deconstructivist architecture. The work of painter Kazimir Malevich (see figs. 11.18, 11.19) has served as a basis for Hadid's design work, and she says that her inspiration derives from the principles of Suprematism—a concept developed by Malevich and expressed by the reduction of the picture to Euclidean geometric arrangements of forms in pure colors, designed to represent the supremacy of pure emotion. Thus many of her projects exist as unbuilt, utopian investigations.

The Vitra Fire Station shows a high sense of individual personality in its vigorous use of space. The architectural concept has been developed into a layered series of walls that alternate between void and volume, giving the impression of speed and escape. Constructed of exposed reinforced concrete—a very appropriate medium for Hadid to realize her sculptural expressiveness and ambitiously long spans and cantilevers—the whole building is movement suspended in time and space, expressing the firefighter's

25.27 Bernard Tschumi, Plan, Parc de la Villette, Paris, 1982–91.

tension between being on the alert and the possibility of exploding into action at any moment. Special attention was given to the sharpness of all edges, and any attachments, such as roof edges or claddings, were avoided lest they detract from the simplicity of the prismatic form and abstract quality of the architectural concept. This same absence of detail informed the frameless glazing, the large sliding panes enclosing the garage, and the treatment of the interior spaces. The surrounding landscape seems to stream into the building, testimony to Hadid's reputation as an assertive sculptural architect and to her unique ability to transcend building mass with pure antigravitational energy. Yet the question inevitably arises whether such bold, sculptural antifunctionalism is suitable to the actual purpose of the building, or for that matter to anything else.

Also deconstructivist and neither a park nor a building in the traditional sense, Parc de la Villette (1982–91)—an open space in a working-class district of Paris that more closely resembles a large architectural and environmental sculpture—is the first built work of deconstructionist theorist and teacher **Bernard Tschumi** (b. 1944). His design for the master plan and structural elements of Parc de la Villette (which means "little city") (fig. **25.27**) was selected from more than 470 entries in an international competition. The 125-acre (50.5 hectares) park includes walkways, gardens, and a canal, and thirty bright-colored, geometrical "*folies*," small structures containing cultural and recreational facilities including a cinema, a video workshop, information and day-care centers, and a health club.

The organizing principle of the park's design is the superimposition of three independent ordering systems, each of which uses a separate vocabulary of either lines, points, or surfaces, so that there is no single or true master plan. In combination, the logic of each system loses its coherence, and accident and chance become determining factors in the resulting design. The most prominently

25.26 Zaha Hadid, Vitra Fire Station, Weil am Rhein, Germany, 1993.

ordered system, the 400-square-foot (37 m²) grid of points, is marked by the evenly spaced locations of the *folie* structures. Each of the *folies* is based on the form of the cube, which is then "cut away," or reconfigured, transforming pure geometry into dissonance.

Tschumi, who was dean of the Graduate School of Architecture, Planning, and Preservation at Columbia University from 1988 to 2003, uses the tools of architecture to question the validity of its own rules. Employing multiple organizing principles, he sets them up to collide with one another, each one serving to cancel, interrupt, and undermine the others—asserting that there is no pure space, that activity necessarily and unapologetically violates architectural purity. The three ordering systems of the park allow for almost infinite variations on this theme.

During much of the twentieth century, the machine served as one of the most ubiquitous cultural metaphors, especially in regard to architectural form and theory. Designers have tried not only to emulate the machine's aesthetic qualities but to envision an architecture whose relationship to its function corresponds as directly as that of a machine to its purpose. The spare beauty of Le Corbusier's Villa Savoye (see fig. 16.6), for example, is due to his resoluteness in applying the machine metaphor. Tschumi, on the other hand, proposes that architecture is continually transformed by the quotidian events that take place in and around it, events too varied and complex to

be described by any one architectural program, such as the International Style. Rather than imposing a structure on the disorderliness of urban life, Tschumi's Parc de la Villette is emblematic of the metropolis and its inherent intricacies. It becomes a stage set for an infinite number of human activities, both planned and spontaneous, authorized and illicit, which momentarily form part of the metropolis. Parc de la Villette thus affirms the random disorderliness and vibrancy of the city. With its keen awareness of the importance of events that surround it, Tschumi's architecture aspires to an inclusivity that reflects the haphazard complexity of the modern metropolis.

The intellectual strain in the architecture of the eighties and nineties achieves extreme form in the work of the American deconstructivist theoretician and architect **Peter Eisenman** (b. 1932). As a deconstructionist, Eisenman puts buildings together out of parts and elements that are not inherently unified or related, so that the realized structure may not serve the usual function or expectations for a building. Eisenman's first building to gain wide attention was the Wexner Center for the Visual and Performing Arts, a contemporary art museum at Ohio State University, Columbus, Ohio (fig. **25.28**). The center, built between 1983 and 1989, strikingly exemplifies Eisenman's commitment to architecture as an intellectual as well as a material art. The project is an intricate complex of construction and landscape, an "archaeological earthwork" as Eisenman

25.28 Peter Eisenman, Wexner Center for the Visual and Performing Arts, Ohio State University, Columbus, 1983–1989.

25.29 Peter Eisenman, Competition model for the Wexner Centre for the Visual Arts and Fine Arts Library, Ohio State University, Columbus, Ohio (plan view), 1983. Frank Dick Studio.

termed it, that radically breaks with the predictable order of the traditional bucolic American academic campus. Conceptually and physically, the design connects the academic community with the Columbus civic community by mediating the historic plan of the campus which set it at a 12.25-degree angle from the grid of the city (fig. **25.29**). By locating a center at this point of intersection between the civic and academic life of the city, Eisenman suggests that the metaphor of meeting place rather than repository best suits the contemporary museum. Symbolic of the act of collision and exchange is what the architect calls a "scaffolding" of square white steel pipes whose formation is a "metaphoric microcosm of the urban grid." The 140,000-square-foot (13,006 m²) building houses the experimental arts of computers, lasers, performance, and video as well as exhibition galleries, a café, a bookstore, and administrative offices. The most memorable image resulting from Eisenman's preoccupation with geometry and iconography is the rigorous coupling of architecture and landscape in a manner that revives, or at least harks back to, the formal geometric integration of garden and building of seventeenth-century European palaces. The Wexner Center marks a turning point in Eisenman's career that, as he has commented "has conditioned everything that

25.30 Peter Eisenman, Nunotani Building, Tokyo, Japan, 1990–92.

followed, because you begin to think, how do you build ideas, and not just project them?"

The façade of Eisenman's Nunotani Building in Tokyo (fig. **25.30**) illustrates the construction of a set of ideas about national identity, commercial power, and architectural symbolism. In response to the client's demand for an iconic structure and his own commitment to rethinking the conventionally anthropomorphic and phallic symbolism of the skyscraper, the architect turned to geology and geometry. The overlapping planes that form the façade are generated though a simulation of colliding cubes that push into each other like the tectonic plates that lie under Japan. Power, as well as corporate strength, are thus symbolized by the flexibility and resilience of the building, which is animated by its potential energy and its appeal to the mind, rather than being assertive through an upright form and gravity-defying show of strength.

Structure as Metaphor: Architectural Abstractions

Italian architect **Renzo Piano** (b. 1937) has been reimagining architectural metaphors for cultural and institutional power since his collaboration in the seventies with English architect Richard Rogers in the design of the Centre Georges Pompidou, the controversial "inside-out" home of modern and contemporary art in Paris that showed his fascination and respect for the infrastructure of buildings (see fig. 23.21). More recently, Piano won the commission to design an all-new major airport, Kansai International Airport in Osaka, Japan, which opened in 1994. Over the years, Piano's work has become more refined and restrained without a loss of interest in technology and materials. The soaring waiting halls at the Kansai International Airport (fig. **25.31**) are examples of Piano's easy relationship with industrial-strength materials and his elegant use of them on a very grand scale.

Canadian-born American **Frank O. Gehry** (b. 1929) is another major figure whose approaches identify him with Postmodern design. His work, invariably witty, has generated variations on themes as refined as the modernist cube and as ordinary as a fish. His California Aerospace Museum (fig. **25.32**), completed in 1984, is a showcase for jet-age technology. Through its good-natured combination of disparate forms, materials, and scale, the structure clearly evokes the spirit of flight. Impaled on a cruciform strut above the forty-foot (12 m) "hangar" door is the most sensational aspect of the building's design: a Lockheed F-104 Starfighter plane. The gigantic, thematically appropriate, aircraft does not upstage the museum—no small feat considering the drama of the spectacle. It is simply a bold ornament applied to a bold building.

Of a similarly allusive style is Gehry's good-humored Chiat/Day Building of 1991 on Main Street in Venice, California (fig. **25.33**). The headquarters for an advertising firm that has developed some of America's cleverest and most successful ad campaigns, as well as pioneering off-site creative work, the Chiat/Day Building is a collaboration between Gehry and sculptors Claes Oldenburg and Coosje van Bruggen (see fig. 24.59). Oldenburg and Van Bruggen's mega-sized *Binoculars* forms the portal to an interior that is essentially open yet accommodating to impromptu meetings and plug-in work sites for its drop-in, drop-off employees.

By the nineties, Gehry had modified his expressive language from the geometry and decoration of the Aerospace Museum and the Chiat/Day to a more organic architecture that evokes the breeze more than it does a fighter plane. Still working in a manner that he shares with Oldenburg and Van Bruggen, Gehry's late-style buildings start with blocks covered in gauze and crumpled paper. Using computer renderings, these architectural sculptures provide the source for one of the most ethereal and recognizable

25.31 Renzo Piano, Waiting room, Kansai International Airport, Osaka, Japan, 1994.

25.32 Frank O. Gehry, State of California Aerospace Museum, Santa Monica, 1982–86.

25.33 Frank O. Gehry, Chiat/Day Building and Claes Oldenburg and Coosje van Bruggen, *Binoculars*, Steel frame, concrete, and cement plaster painted with elastomeric paint, 45 × 44 × 18' (13.7 × 13.4 × 5.5 m). Venice, California. 1991.

architectural styles of the century. Structures like the Guggenheim Museum in Bilbao (see fig. 25.34) provide another chapter in the history of expressive architecture begun with the theorized, though rarely built, work of Erich Mendelsohn and Antonio Sant'Elia.

The Bilbao museum (fig. **25.34**) is a monumental abstraction built in the capital of the Basque Country. Gehry's design was inspired by Bilbao's industrial history and the curving Nirvion River, which once supported thriving mills and shipyards. The building combines the geometry of classical modernism with the organic whimsy of Expressionism. Gehry designed the museum to resemble a metal flower rising up from the riverfront. Designed with the aid of CATIA, a computer program created by the French aerospace industry to translate sculptural models into specifications for manufacture, the museum rises to a towering point of reinforced concrete at the north end that appears to hover impossibly in the sky. Undulating walls and ceilings sheathed in titanium open out from this peak like giant petals blown in the wind or floating on the river. To the east of the building is a huge exhibition space,

450×80 feet (137×24 m), for the display of large-scale sculpture. The organic and expressive design elements of the building are anchored by six Spanish limestone cubes that recall the severe geometry of the International Style. These elements house more traditional-style white box galleries, a library, auditorium, restaurant, and retail spaces. The cubes are arranged in two flanks that extend from the flower to the west and south. From the west, hints of the metallic flowers peek out from behind the stone walls, creating a sense of drama as one circles the building.

The design of the blossoming flower can be read as a metaphor for the political and economic ambitions of the Basque government to assert itself on an international stage. Intent on doing more than symbolizing the growth and stability of the region, Gehry responded to the needs of the city as well as the art collection, with the building combining the function of a museum with facilities for Bilbao's citizens. The restaurant, auditorium, and retail spaces are all accessible from the street independently from the operation of the museum. Likewise, a significant part of the collection will represent local art history. Gehry's

25.34 Frank O. Gehry, Guggenheim Bilbao, Interior, 1991–97.

Guggenheim has proven to be one of the signature works of the late twentieth century, not only because it is the pinnacle of a great architect's career, but also for its elegant summation of the collaborations possible in the increasingly international world of culture.

As late-twentieth-century cultural politics provided the impetus for the Guggenheim Bilbao, new technologies have inspired what may be one of the most surprising new museums of the twenty-first century. The architect team of Diller + Scofidio (**Elizabeth Diller**, b. 1954 and **Ricardo Scofidio**, b. 1935) have designed a multiuse building (fig. **25.35**) to house the production, exhibition, and education programs of Eyebeam, a foundation that sponsors digital art. The museum of digital art is designed to rise from a standard rectilinear ground plan in Chelsea, New York, in the form of a ribbon looping across the plot, up to the next floor, and back over to divide the stories in an S-shaped curve to the top of the building. In addition to forming the floors, walls, and ceiling of the museum, the ribbon, a two-ply construction, will house the substantial electronic infrastructure required to power a collection of computer-based art. While providing the technological support absent from most museums, Diller + Scofidio's design creates an image for Eyebeam that looks like that of no other museum. Like the duo's projected exhibition hall Blur, a museum enveloped in an artificial cloud above lake Neuchatel, Switzerland, the Eyebeam building and the best of the art that it will house announce a new kind of aesthetic journey.

Flexible Spaces: Architecture and Urbanism

Modern art began at the intersection of cultural and urban change. Whether one discerns its origins in the nineteenth century, as we have, or in the eighteenth or seventeenth, as others have, modernism is rooted in the effects of industrialism, revolution, and economic transitions on the urban environment. Dutch Naturalism was generated in relation to the economic transformation of public and private life in the Netherlands during the second half of the seventeenth century; French Romanticism and Neoclassicism developed hand in hand with the configuring of Paris as an

25.36 Elizabeth Plater-Zyberk and Andres Duany, Seaside, Florida. Aerial plan view. 1980s.

imperial center, revolutionary capital, and Napoleonic showcase; and realism, Impressionism, and photography were intimately related to demographic changes in Europe and the United States. In the Postmodern era, urbanism has also been central to cultural production. Venturi and Scott Brown's lesson in *Learning from Las Vegas* that "the order of the Strip includes" is an anthem for Postmodern artists and architects. Inclusion took on significance as it came to provide metaphors for the increasingly urban character of contemporary global society. In the west, two urban planning strategies developed to reckon with the chaotic heterogeneity that was coming to dominate daily experience. One, first described as neotraditional planning when it arose in the early eighties and then dubbed New Urbanism, attempted to recast early twentieth-century small towns to contain urban growth. The other strategy, practiced most spectacularly by Rem Koolhaas and his Office of Metropolitan Architecture (OMA) (see figs. 25.38, 25.39), embraced the density, variety, and flux of existing late twentieth-century cities by building large-scale structures that, like much Postmodern art and architecture, sought to facilitate change within stable yet flexible architectural space.

Plater-Zyberk and Duany

Miami-based architects and planners **Elizabeth Plater-Zyberk** (b. 1950) and **Andres Duany** (b. 1949) are acknowledged leaders of the New Urbanists. They are contemporary architects who seek to reform America's communities. Their remedy is as much moral as it is aesthetic. They believe that traditional town planning—a grid of streets lined with trees and front porches, studded with shops and parks—can heal the nation's fragmented sense of community. In their 1991 book, *Towns and Town-Making Principles*, the authors champion a concern for the small-scale design decisions that make streets, blocks, and neighborhoods aesthetically pleasing. Since then, their

firm, DPZ, has become much more heavily involved in urban planning.

Seaside, DPZ's eighty-acre (32 hectares) resort town on the Florida Panhandle, took ten years to build its hundred different houses and buildings, including a fire station, restaurant pavilion, and town hall (fig. **25.36**). It is one of the new "old" towns created as part of the New Urbanist movement. The tenets of the movement include creating pedestrian-oriented places organized around public open spaces—the antithesis of the postwar auto-oriented suburb. Residents are only a few minutes' walk to any part of the development. Ultimately, New Urbanists aim to design cohesive, environmentally sensitive places that look very much like traditional towns or big-city neighborhoods.

DPZ's experience in laying out Seaside, a prime example of a New Urbanist development, offers an idea of the opportunities that New Urbanism provides architects. Each element of the development is seen as a part of the whole, and architects are able to participate in town planning at large. They design not only the houses, but the streets, the blocks, the park—the whole community. In the most famous of the New Urbanist towns, The Walt Disney Company's Celebration, Florida (fig. **25.37**), regulations specified window size, curtain color, and placement of trees in the front yard. Celebration was opened to residents in 1996 and contains some of the most sought-after residential property in central Florida. Its residents are the most affluent and educated of the region. Forgoing the cul-de-sacs of many suburban developments, Celebration, like Seaside, brings back the grids that organize prototypical small towns as well as major urban centers. Located next to Walt Disney World Resort, Celebration provides a case study of the role of New Urbanism in relation not only to city planning, but also corporate relations. Faced with an excess of land, The Walt Disney Company created Celebration as a planning experiment. The city featured

25.37 Celebration, Florida, 1996.

attractive homes, a good school, and a retail district within walking distance. The city was eligible for public money to make major improvements to the infrastructure of the region, which helped traffic flow in and around Disney's amusement parks.

Despite the attractiveness of Celebration to corporate and private interests in Florida, the New Urbanists' claims that the form of the gridded small town fosters cohesive communities have been contested. Several studies of Celebration showed that, while porches and well-traveled sidewalks foster a degree of community spirit, relationships tended to be formed over affiliations; that is, involvement in groups such schools or other organizations based on shared interests or identity. These affiliations tended to exist independently of geographic proximity. Likewise, the presence of a downtown was not enough to create a centrally focused city. In Celebration, the high cost of buying property often meant that residents had less disposable income than they needed to able to shop in the downtown boutiques and restaurants. Researchers found that residents felt that the city's commercial services were more directed to visitors than to local people. Nonetheless, the city's residents have formed a civic bond as participants in a collective experiment. This bond may differ from old-fashioned town pride but has a similar effect.

The role of Disney as a corporate sponsor, designer, and majority owner of the town has introduced problems in the New Urbanist agenda, particularly the contradictory demographic influences exerted by Disney in the region as a whole. While sponsoring the socially oriented Celebration, Disney was recruiting workers from Mexico and Puerto Rico who were not paid enough to live in the city. The influx of a low-paid and underemployed community aggravated the sort of urban problems New Urbanism sought to avoid. As seen in the case of Pruitt-Igoe (see fig. 25.1), form alone is not enough to transform urban life. Another tendency of New Urbanism that disturbs its critics is that many of its projects do not provide for existing buildings in their "new neighborhoods." Old buildings found on the sites of the new "community of neighborhoods" are tagged to be removed or razed. The objection to this is not that the new neighborhoods—with their planned roads, parks, and houses—are not attractive, but that they do not have a true history or an urban vibrancy, and that their lack of roots is disguised by a thin simulation of nostalgia and history. Though plans to fabricate a fictional history for Celebration were never executed, critics have claimed that New Urbanist planning often includes a troubling lack of physical or even intellectual mechanisms to allow for the kind of unexpected change that creates deep and individual urban histories.

Koolhaas and the OMA

An architect, urbanist, and theorist who has made the unexpected a central tenet of his practice on any scale (his most recent catalogue raisonné is called SMLXL) is **Rem Koolhaas** (b. 1944). Working in the deconstructionist tradition of Postmodernism, Koolhaas collaborated with Zaha Hadid (see fig. 25.26) in 1978 on the design of the Dutch parliament building, The Hague, in his native Holland. The Netherlands Dance Theater (fig. 25.38) is an example of Koolhaas's Postmodern vocabulary, from the huge, semiabstract mural topping the main structure, to the mix of reinforced concrete, glass, metal, and masonry for the walls of its variously formed parts. The interior of the concert hall is constructed and detailed with aluminum, stucco, marble, and gold foil. The heterogeneous and often industrial materials serve as a metaphor for Koolhaas's conception that architecture is multipurpose. The theater caters to the multiple needs of urban life: municipal, cultural, economic, and architectural. In addition to the auditorium, the structure houses studios, offices, a sauna, a swimming pool, massage rooms, showers, and a restaurant. The entire building establishes relationships with an existing concert hall, parking garage, civic buildings, and a church square.

Koolhaas's concern with the context of architecture, demonstrated in the theater, lies at the center of his expansive studies of urban development. These studies have taken the form of several volumes, beginning with 1978's *Delirious New York*. This took Manhattan as "the twentieth century's Rosetta Stone" and included analyses of major developing centers such as Lagos, Nigeria and the Pearly River Delta, China. Like Venturi and Scott Brown, Koolhaas includes within the realm of architecture all manner of architectural, visual, urban, and popular culture. His studies give great weight to subjects as apparently different as Roman city planning and twenty-first-century shopping. Also like Venturi and Scott Brown, Koolhaas rejects the tabula rasa planning of either Le Corbusier or the New

Urbanists. The solutions provided by Koolhaas's Office of Metropolitan Architecture (OMA) often revolve around "Megastructures"—centralized collections of multiuse spaces that concentrate all manner of civic activity within a single structure. Though similar in scale to the monumental projects of modernist city planning, these megastructures are constructed to respond to local metropolitan issues. The 1993 Euralille project in Lille, France, typifies the urbanistic flexibility that OMA practices. Lille is a hub for the high-speed train (TGV) as well as the site for the entrance to the Channel Tunnel connecting Great Britain to the continent. The location experiences one of the greatest volumes of traffic in Europe. OMA faced the challenge of creating an interface between the influx of visitors and the existing city. Their solution consists of a network of several huge structures that serve as monumental signposts and shelter for points of personal, geographical, economic, and artistic exchange, called "nodes" in OMA's terminology, that exist in Lille. The railway station features sheet glass walls that display the TGV, highlighting technology and transportation as the source of Lille's current character. This is an architecture that strives to be responsive to a society in flux.

Koolhaas's understanding of urbanism as "the staging of uncertainty" lies at the heart of OMA's design for the city center of Almere in the Netherlands. Almere, an enclave along the main artery from Amsterdam to its major airport, is the fastest-growing Dutch city. It has a number of

25.38 Rem Koolhaas, The Netherlands Dance Theater, the Hague, the Netherlands, 1987.

25.39 Rem Koolhaas, Dutchtown, City center plan for Almere, the Netherlands.

significant buildings, but overall has little character. With considerable foresight, Almere had been developed in four equal sections, with a fifth of the same size left relatively undeveloped. In this zone, OMA was asked to create a city center that would serve as a public destination and "logo" for the metropolis. Though conceived in commercial terms and with the requirement that it be attractive to investors, the downtown was also designed to give Almere an identity distinct from that of being a residential community for people who work in Amsterdam.

OMA's strategy of urban design has been to create a center that contains a dense population and offers a diversity of functions and activities. The center joins municipal, commercial, and entertainment facilities with large-scale residences, all of which are readily accessible by automobile. In addition, the firm believes that the "position of the center must be visible and palpable throughout the city." In many ways, these strategies are the lessons learned in New York. The result, however, looks nothing like Manhattan. The plans (fig. **25.39**) detail a multilevel megastructure that contains veins for housing, retail areas, municipal purposes, offices, and parking spaces. There are levels and passages above and below ground. In addition to concentrating a variety of activities into several locations, OMA has left a considerable portion of the fifth zone open for future development.

Wodiczko and New York's "Tribute in Light"

Koolhaas was awarded the prestigious Pritzger Prize for architecture in 2000. He was praised for redefining the terms by which architects consider their discipline. In his acceptance speech, Koolhaas recommended Peter Eisenman for the prize on the same grounds. Bringing more of the context of building into the understanding of architecture has also been the project of visual artist **Krzysztof Wodiczko** (b. 1943). Wodiczko creates art that intrudes upon the network of elements that he has determined make up architecture, of which physical buildings are but one. Architecture has often been as much about displacing resources as placing structures. Wodiczko's *Homeless Projection* of 1987 (fig. **25.40**) consists of photographs of people displaced by the processes of urban development—in this case in Boston—which he projects onto prominent buildings. The socially invisible become all but inescapable. Wodiczko forces people into the discourse of architecture by figuratively making buildings with them. Rather than presuming homelessness to be a problem in society that can be solved within the existing system, Wodiczko's projections posit it is a fundamental part of society, as necessary to the shape of urban life as the investors and institutions that finance skyscrapers. In *Poliscar* (1991), the artist interviewed people living on the streets and created vehicles designed to meet their needs for shelter, storage, protection, and comfort. The vehicles were meant to function within the existing system, again making the invisible visible. Wodiczko was not seeking to change the behavior or even location of those people living on the streets, but rather to change the way homelessness is perceived and discussed by society.

Wodiczko's architectural intrusions are pragmatic at the micro level while aiming at conceptual impact on a macro level. Like the element of utopian thinking that runs through Postmodern architecture from Venturi to Koolhaas, *Homeless Projection* and *Poliscar* presume that close investigation of the city, coupled with a willingness to engage with what one finds there, will provide answers for improving urban life. Whether this means applying the lessons of advertising to homebuilding or transferring New York's urban planning strategies to the Netherlands, the Postmodern sense of progress aims at a responsiveness and flexibility that contrast with modernist appeals to transcendent universals.

At its most challenging, beautiful, and even efficient, Postmodern architecture has never escaped the criticism that it often fails to cohere. In many cases this is its strength. To many, however, architecture is an arena in which the uncertainties of the present should be set aside in favor of stability. In September 2001, the emotional force with which global society clung to universal forms was made tragically clear. The attack on the World Trade Center in New York City demonstrated the continued ideological force of the International Style as an icon of Western power. America had created a logo that was recognizable worldwide. What became clear after the destruction of the towers was the resonance that the simple forms, designed by Minoru Yamasaki in 1972, had in the national and international psyche. As modern art from David to Maya Lin has shown, geometry and, of course, absence are profound signifiers.

For thirty-four nights, from March 11 to April 13, 2002, an architecture of light rose up from the site of

25.40 Krzysztof Wodiczko, *Homeless Projection: The Soldiers and Sailors Civil War Memorial*, December 1987. Public projection. The Common, Boston.

the World Trade Center, replicating the geometry of the two modernist towers in one of the most effective monuments since Lin's Vietnam Memorial (see fig. 24.62). Several artists, architects, and engineers came up with the idea for the towers of light as they witnessed the tragedy of September 11. **Julian LaVerdiere**, **Paul Myoda**, **John Bennett**, **Gustavo Bonevardi**, **Paul Marantz**, and **Richard Nash Gould** were brought together to realize the project, titled *Tribute in Light*. The aim of the project was direct attention away from the form of the buildings to the lives of those lost in them. The structure consisted of forty-four 7000-watt xenon light bulbs installed on a fifty-square-foot (4.64 m²) base adjacent to the excavation site. The lights projected almost a mile into the sky, creating the effect of a monumental memorial candle. The result could be seen by people over the entire metropolitan area, thus bringing together the region in a communal experience to mourn and gain strength through remembrance. As one of the architects explained, the lights by their visual presence and material absence "reconstruct[ed] the void as opposed to … the buildings." Rising above the chaotic expressions of grief that sprang up throughout the city—walls of photographs, letters, testimonies, mementos, gifts, and flowers laid on street corners, parks, and firehouses—the *Tribute in Light* (fig. **25.41**) focused the emotional response of the city into two centralized iconic forms. The work drew strength by combining the general symbolic iconography of the skyscraper with the specific meaning of the World Trade Center. As Myoda remarked, "It is an irony, a kind of painful irony, that we looked at the towers the same way the terrorists apparently looked at them: as a symbol of communication, strength, and power." Such clarity and force is a testimony to the lasting quality of modernist monuments and their responsiveness, if not to the diversity among the global population, then to a certain sense that, just as we confront flux and change, we also share some common ground that is stable and unchanging.

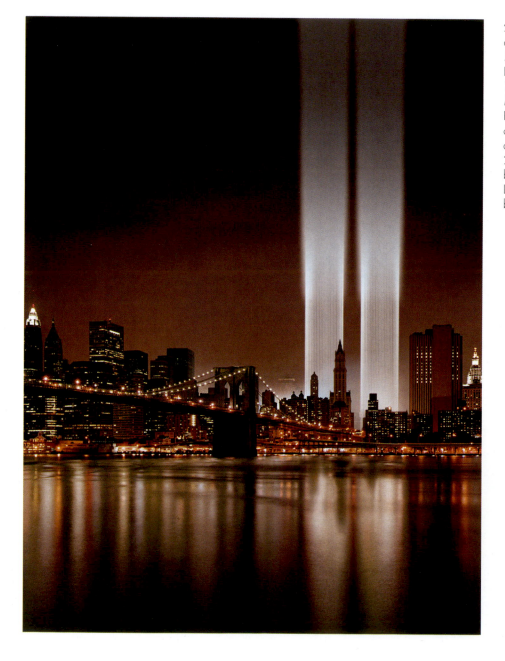

25.41 Julian LaVerdiere and Paul Myoda, *Tribute in Light* over the Brooklyn Bridge, from the portfolio *Tribute in Light: Artists' Renderings*, 2001–02. Portfolio of twelve c-prints, matted in an archival box, 24" × 20", edition of 500 on behalf of the Tribute in Light Initiative produced by Creative Time.

26
The Retrospective Eighties

In its most effective forms, modernist art from Manet to Pollock took the form of a revelation, contributing to the world by showing the way to a more encompassing truth than previously known. It is this messianic quality of modernist art that made its struggles so dramatic and its solutions so forceful. As the world witnessed the Holocaust, the war in Vietnam, and the surge of civil unrest in the late sixties, the search for a singular truth by the lone artist seemed presumptuous at best and authoritarian at worst. With the development of a myriad of new art approaches during the late sixties and seventies—including Conceptual art, Performance art, Land art, and Process art—and the powerful social and political critiques of feminists and civil rights activists, it became increasingly obvious that traditional histories and interpretations of "modernism" were simply inadequate.

In the eighties, a number of artists, and many more critics and theorists, declared a break with the modern era, identifying themselves as "Postmodernists." Postmodernism implied a dissatisfaction with the narrow confines of modernism, which apparently promoted the accomplishments of white, male artists of European descent at the expense of engaging political and social concerns, and nonmajority and female artists. Postmodernism, by contrast, encouraged overtly polemical practices and an ironic distance from conventions of the past. The development of Postmodernism was facilitated by the tools of Poststructuralism and deconstruction—theoretical propositions that had gained increasing prominence since the late sixties among artists, critics, and art historians. The term "Poststructuralism" indicates that this movement came after the development of Structuralism, a school of thought based on the premise that underlying structures in language and society could be identified and studied as vital aspects of culture. Poststructuralism refers to the work of a group of predominantly French philosophers including Jacques Derrida, Michel Foucault, and Roland Barthes, who posited that the structures of language and political institutions were simply conventions rather than natural facts. Understood as constructions rather than essential principles, structures of language and of institutions could then be analyzed and "deconstructed." The practice of deconstruction involves the minute examination of the assumptions underlying particular texts, which may be literary, but may also refer to the larger discourses and social and political networks in which we live our lives. The insights of Poststructuralism, combined with the technique of deconstruction, provided the theoretical tools to analyze the underlying assumptions of modernism, enabling artists and thinkers to articulate a critical break with modernism.

Somewhat ironically, at the same time that Postmodern critiques of art were being formulated, the audience and the market for new art were greater than ever. In this atmosphere, many younger artists were catalyzed to reframe the history of art in a way that resonated with a Postmodern consciousness. The artists of the eighties looked back to any number of historical styles, sometimes including several styles within one work, in order to recontextualize the achievements of modernism to give them significance in a Postmodern environment. Reclaiming the value of art that had been premised on an authoritative position that was no longer valid was a difficult and contentious project. While some artists restated through appropriation the voices of the past in the company of the present, others created contemporary variations on styles of Expressionism, abstraction, installation, and assemblage. The sections that follow examine the aesthetic and political consequences of attempts in the eighties to enlist traditions of historical modernism to speak to the present.

Codes of Context: Appropriation

Appropriation, the tactical borrowing of visual culture from one context to another, was one of the first identifying characteristics of an art that would be called Postmodern. Appropriation was most clearly evident in the work of a number of artists who, regardless of their training, relied on photography for their source material. Barbara Kruger, Sherrie Levine, Richard Prince, and Cindy Sherman, among others, presented photographs of photographs; photographs of television; photographs that looked like films; paintings of paintings; and paintings of photographs. These works all failed to assert any of the transformative effects expected of art. Like the citations made by Pop artists Roy Lichtenstein and Andy Warhol (see figs. 621.38, 21.43), Appropriation appeared to lack signs of creativity. As discussed in chapter 25, the appropriative strategy of pastiche was apparent in the work of the contemporary architects Robert Venturi, Michael Graves, and Philip Johnson, who seemed to be collaging historical styles to generate contemporary buildings. Forms seemed to be stolen and pasted together with little regard for the original context and, some worried, little regard for the immediate context either. This cut-and-paste procedure turned out to have great potential for visual practice.

Despite its simple definition as something akin to graphic theft, Appropriation can be stretched to include work that copied and manipulated both images and ways of communicating. In its initial incarnation, circa 1977, Appropriation art functioned by emptying the borrowed image of its initial signification and creating new meaning by repositioning it in a new context. The result antagonized viewers whose initial aesthetic or emotional responses to a picture were contradicted by the fact that the artist did not actually create it. To startled viewers of the late seventies, Appropriation appeared to be a mean-spirited plagiarism that undermined the intuitive experience of looking at art.

Appropriative artists, such as Kruger, Levine, Prince, and Sherman, did not intend to undermine the viewer, but they believed it was critical that viewers did not confuse the creativity of the artists' sources with the intention of the new work. They adopted devices for keeping the viewer aware of the mechanics of Appropriation and distanced from the traditionally expressive aspects of art, such as quoting easily recognizable sources such as Mondrian or the Marlboro Man; adopting stylistically disruptive features such as collage or dramatic cropping; and creating titles that explained the appropriation. Like Duchamp or Fluxus (see figs. 13.16, 24.10), Appropriation artists insisted that the borrowed item was meaningful because of its position, and their creative act lay in framing it.

Appropriation turned out to be an effective strategy for dealing with the power of the mass media and even stealing its thunder. By extracting images from their familiar original contexts and mixing them with other images from different sources, Appropriation strips iconography of its original import. At the same time, by putting borrowed images into a new context—that is, by "recontextualizing" them—it also endows those images with a new and often unsettling impact that encourages viewers to see the original sources in a new light. This startling effect—making us see familiar images afresh, as if for the first time—is the source of Appropriation's power as a critique. In the critical language of the day, this effect made Appropriation art "deconstructive"—setting in motion an analytical process that takes apart and exposes the image-maker's designs on us. Art of this kind gives us a more sophisticated awareness of how easily we can be manipulated by visual images.

Kruger, Levine, Prince, and Sherman

A notable example of the deconstruction process at work is found in the art of **Barbara Kruger** (b. 1945). Her picture-and-text combinations (fig. **26.1**) reveal the most manipulative aspects of modern media culture. Kruger, who in the mid-sixties had worked as a graphic designer at *Mademoiselle,* appropriates the look of a glossy magazine layout. Fashion magazines are an especially clear example of contrived visual meaning, since they freely crop and group their pictures and impose captions on them, in order to force the images into the particular "story" that the photo editor wants to tell. By borrowing these techniques, and by bringing them to the surface where we cannot miss them, Kruger makes it obvious that our response, not only to this picture—taken from a fifties photo annual—but to any media image, is largely dictated by the editorializing of its presenter. Our understanding of what we see is not a

26.1 Barbara Kruger, *Untitled (Your Gaze Hits the Side of My Face),* 1981. Photograph, 60 × 40" (152.4 × 101.6 cm). Collection Vijak Mahdavi and Bernardo Nadal-Ginard.

simple, direct response to the optical facts; rather, it is something that has been "constructed" for us.

Work like Kruger's suggests that artists can also turn the tables. If the media can manipulate images in order to convey new meanings, so can artists—by taking such images back and giving them yet another new spin. In so doing, artists can open the viewer's eyes to the complex, ambiguous process by which the meanings of virtually all pictures are constructed. In fact, one can uncover a good deal about how a culture works and what it believes by "deconstructing" the way it uses visual images. This process of deconstruction reveals how certain images function to enforce social myths rather than any underlying truth. The force of continual observation, for instance, that women experience as subjects of the mythic standards of beauty, is captured in Kruger's image with the metaphor of a slap. By confronting the role of images and identity, the technique of appropriation brought art into the media-governed, image-saturated eighties—and, simultaneously, brought the eighties into art.

The quintessential Postmodernist among American artists may be **Sherrie Levine** (b. 1947), for her work most clearly re-presents familiar images from the canon of Western art history. Levine first startled the art world in 1981 with an exhibition of her own unmanipulated photographs of well-known, textbook examples of images taken by such master photographers as Edward Weston, Walker Evans, and Andreas Feininger. Levine's replication of these iconic images pointedly undermined the ideals of modernism—originality, authenticity, and the unmediated link between the image and meaning. The presentation of familiar images—an interior of a poor Southern home by Evans for instance—authored by Levine forced the viewer to contemplate not the sublime geometry of the home and the corresponding moral rectitude of its inhabitant, as Evans intended, but the network of political, cultural, and commercial forces that sent Evans to the South and his work to the museum. Levine's copy confronts us with impurity, ambiguity, and politics in place of Evans's impeccable clarity.

After completing this series of photographs, Levine realized that her subversion of these traditional standards of artistic value could be accomplished not only through photographic reproduction, but also through the insertion of her own touch. As a woman artist, deconstructing masterpieces of male artists by redoing them in watercolor carried its own feminist statement. Levine began hand-painting watercolors and gouaches "after" art-book reproductions of paintings by Léger, Mondrian, Lissitzky, and Stuart Davis—complete with printing flaws. Her *Untitled (After Piet Mondrian)* (fig. **26.2**) substitutes the measured tension and coloristic balance of Mondrian's painting with the slightly green imperfections of the textbook reproduction that is Levine's original. Like Polke's *Bunnies*, (see fig. 26.15) Levine's copy of a mass-produced reproduction draws attention to the transformation of everything from

26.2 Sherrie Levine, *After Piet Mondrian*, 1983. Watercolor, 14 × 11" (35.6 × 27.8 cm). Private collection.

sex to art into commodities traded in the cultural or political economy.

Levine pursued similar goals in a subsequent series consisting of what were less pure appropriations than "generic paintings," as the artist calls them. One series consists of small casein and wax panels offering two-color variations on a single theme of one narrow and three wide stripes. Here the model was a composite of all the great modernist stripe painters, again a pantheon of male artists, including Barnett Newman, Ellsworth Kelly, Brice Marden, Frank Stella, and Daniel Buren. While the new works present the overall look of Minimal painting, they copy no one masterpiece or specific style. Instead, the artist takes on the male-dominated aesthetic of high modernism in a "generic" fashion. Despite Levine's evident iconoclasm, she is not without models, perhaps most significantly Marcel Duchamp, with whose readymades (see figs. 13.16, 13.17) the artist has acknowledged an affinity.

Like Duchamp's readymades or Pop icons such as Warhol's soup cans or Lichtenstein's comics, Appropriation was criticized because it failed to visibly transform its motif from reality into art. Artists countered this response in several ways. First, they insisted, like Duchamp, that art is not limited to those objects that render the appearance of reality in alternative forms or materials. Secondly, it was argued that transformation was in the mind of the artist, not the eye of the beholder. Kruger and Levine's work alone amply showed the efficacy of Appropriation as a transformative tool, as each radically recast our understanding of familiar objects. Finally, Appropriation was shown to be generative in rather old-fashioned terms as a form of drawing.

Richard Prince (b. 1949) developed a body of work that draws attention to the artifice underlying myths of American individuality and to Appropriation as a tool to deconstruct them. In a series of works including *Untitled (Cowboys)* (fig. **26.3**) Prince re-presented the protagonist of televised cigarette ads. Avoiding the posture of "original" taken on by Levine's work, these photographs of television screens are self-conscious about their artificiality. They advertise the act of theft that is at the root of Appropriation and, unlike the myth of American manhood and tobacco consumption that they present, are clear about their misleading qualities.

Prince is unique for the clarity with which he conceived Appropriation as a formal tool. Early in his career, he enumerated different methods of appropriating that, like Sol LeWitt's instructions (see fig. 22.53) or Jasper Johns's repertoire of marks (see fig. 21.18), determine the appearance of the final works of art. With a list of eight different variations including the original copy, the rephotographed copy, the angled copy, and the out-of-focus copy, Prince showed Appropriation to be a form of mark-making related to art of the previous decades.

Beginning in 1978, **Cindy Sherman** (b. 1954) allied the arts of Performance and photography; she cast herself as the star of an inexhaustibly inventive series of still photographs called *Untitled Film Stills* sometimes characterized as "one-frame movie-making" (fig. **26.4**). Complete with props, lighting, makeup, wigs, costume, and script, most of the pictures exploit, with the eventual goal of subverting, stereotypical roles played by women in films, television shows, and commercials of the fifties and sixties. Her characters ranged from a bored suburban housewife to a Playboy centerfold.

In 1980–82 Sherman began working in color and in near-lifesize dimensions. As the pictures grew larger, the situations became more concentrated, focusing on specific emotional moments rather than implying the fuller scenarios seen earlier. Setting, background (supplied by a projector system), clothes, wig, makeup, and lighting combined with the performance itself to create a unified mood: anxiety, ennui, flirtatiousness, or confidence. Sherman displays exquisite control over the tableaus, from the unified color schemes to disturbing details such as the black scuffs where a door has been kicked in (see fig. 26.4) or a piece of torn newspaper clutched by a plaid-skirted teenager sprawled on a linoleum kitchen floor. Like a Hitchcock heroine, the subject seems vulnerable to something outside the photographic frame.

Sherman's project, like Kruger's, is based on examining the notion that "woman" does not exist apart from socially

26.3 Richard Prince, *Untitled (Cowboy)*, 1991–92. Ektacolor photograph 48 × 72".

26.4 Cindy Sherman, *Untitled Film Still*, 1979. Photograph, 10 × 8" (25.4 × 20.3 cm).

constructed images of femininity and exploring the self-conscious assumption of that role by the woman herself. However near or distant the quoted source, Sherman and her fellow "image-scavengers" cause us to question our reliance on images and our relationship to the authority they wield. Integral to the role of images in the formation of feminine identity is the role of what has been theorized as the "gaze": the act of observation as it is implicated in power relations between those who observe and those who are observed. Traditionally, in both society and art history, women are most often objectified by the gaze; they are placed in the position of something to be possessed, enjoyed, and understood through vision. The centrality of female sex symbols in Western culture testifies to the conventional understanding that looking is different for men than for women, and it is no coincidence that those who do more of the looking have more power than those who are looked at. Sherman's imagery undermines the expected dynamic of the woman/model/subject being revealed through representation by the man/artist/observer. Not only is Sherman the artist and the model—the watcher and the watched—but, as a subject, her identity is never secure. The question of "who is Cindy Sherman?" is made as unanswerable as it is inevitable. The *Untitled Film Stills*

introduce an artist in possession of the gaze even while she is the object of it.

Holzer, the Guerrilla Girls, McCollum, and Tansey

While most Appropriation artists copied existing images, a second group appropriated the means by which society transmits knowledge and exercises control. In an updated *trompe l'oeil*, artists such as Barbara Kruger, Jenny Holzer, Allan McCollum, and political activist group the Guerrilla Girls, reproduced the modes of communication seen in the streets, museums, or on television, and then infiltrated the expected content of the message. Images that looked like advertising or literature conveyed content regarding the politics of race, gender, healthcare, and sexuality, as well, of course, as issues of art making and collecting. Like the radical thinking of the previous two decades, Appropriation in the eighties appeared to dismantle the myths of originality, genius, and power that had been threatening to collapse since the sixties. Moreover, its consequences lay within the worlds of practice as well as theory. Here was an art form with a high proportion of women practitioners.

In *Untitled (Your Gaze Hits the Side of My Face)* (see fig. 26.1), Kruger, as well as using a found image, copied the graphic clarity of magazine layout, thus using a means of communication created by the mass media to expose the aggression of representation. With an even tighter focus on means of public address, **Jenny Holzer** (b. 1950) creates "language" works that appropriate the anonymous, often aggressive, manner in which messages of warning or instruction are transmitted from institutions such as police forces, the military, schools, or churches. Related to the Conceptual art of the seventies, Holzer's interventions are based on the pithy, often political, and sometimes cryptic sayings that she composes. She called these sayings "Truisms"; a typical example is the one-liner, "Abuse of power comes as no surprise." Some of the sayings sound like replies to the homespun wisdom of Benjamin Franklin in *Poor Richard's Almanac*. And although they can be as banal as fortune cookies, many have the punch of advertizing slogans. At first, Holzer printed her aphorisms on posters that were pasted to the walls of public places, such as phone booths and bus shelters, but later she ran them on electric signboards in more prominent locations. In 1982 she obtained the use of the Spectacolor Board in New York's Times Square (fig. **26.5**), and flashed pointed remarks like "Private property created crime" and "Protect me from what I want" to throngs of surprised pedestrians. Her subsequent installation pieces in museums and galleries have generally been more meditative and subjective, notably *Laments* for the 1990 Venice Biennale, but at times they have been spectacular. At the Guggenheim Museum in 1989, a ribbon of her color signboards ran along the edges of Frank Lloyd Wright's great spiral ramp. The lights spinning around the helical curve of the architecture surrounded the visitor with such urgent phrases as "You are a victim of the rules you live by."

26.5 Jenny Holzer, Selection from *Truisms*, 1982. Spectacolor Board, 20 × 40' (6.1 × 12.2 m). Installation, Times Square, New York. Sponsored by Public Art Fund, Inc., New York.

THE ADVANTAGES OF BEING A WOMAN ARTIST:

Working without the pressure of success.
Not having to be in shows with men.
Having an escape from the art world in your 4 free-lance jobs.
Knowing your career might pick up after you're eighty.
Being reassured that whatever kind of art you make it will be labeled feminine.
Not being stuck in a tenured teaching position.
Seeing your ideas live on in the work of others.
Having the opportunity to choose between career and motherhood.
Not having to choke on those big cigars or paint in Italian suits.
Having more time to work when your mate dumps you for someone younger.
Being included in revised versions of art history.
Not having to undergo the embarrassment of being called a genius.
Getting your picture in the art magazines wearing a gorilla suit.

A PUBLIC SERVICE MESSAGE FROM **GUERRILLA GIRLS** CONSCIENCE OF THE ART WORLD
532 LaGUARDIA PLACE, #237 • NY, NY 10012
www.guerrillagirls.com

26.6 Guerrilla Girls, *The Advantages of Being a Woman Artist*, 1988.

Holzer's strategy has proved particularly effective for political action groups who wish to use the techniques of advertising, but have more radical messages to convey than corporate advertisers. In 1985 a group of anonymous feminists who made public appearances disguised in ape costumes began plastering streets and buses with advertisements that looked like public service announcements. The group, calling themselves the **Guerrilla Girls**, took on the mantle of the "conscience of the art world" and had grown frustrated at the small number of women represented in galleries, museums, and positions of power in the art world. Though feminist activism in the seventies had opened the door to such institutions, too few women had been allowed in. One early poster (fig. **26.6**) ironically listed the advantages to being a woman artist beginning with "Working without the pressure of success." Another

noted that the $17.7 million spent on a Jasper Johns work could have purchased one work each by sixty-seven major women artists, including Mary Cassatt, Frida Kahlo, Georgia O'Keeffe, and Artemesia Gentileschi. The Guerrilla Girls have co-opted a variety of forms of public address, including pasting posters around cities, renting space on billboards and buses, giving public lectures (in full ape attire), publishing an art history book, and operating a website (www.guerrillagirls.com).

The work of **Allan McCollum** (b. 1944) interrogates contemporary attitudes toward art from within the galleries rather than in the streets and the media. McCollum's oeuvre consists of objects that function as signs of art. As one critic described them, they are like the shop signs of eyeglasses that an optician might hang in front of his shop. Called *Surrogates* (fig. **26.7**), McCollum's objects

26.7 Allan McCollum, *20 Plaster Surrogates*, 1982–85. Enamel on hydrostone, twenty parts, various dimensions.

are plaster casts of framed pictures that he has painted black for the frames, white for the mat, and black for the picture. The thousands of *Surrogates* have slight inconsistencies of size and surface so that, while they lack any of the details that one expects from a work of art, each one serves as a place holder for the idea of a different work of art. In a politically and philosophically challenging question for those who study art, McCollum asks how anyone besides the wealthy can enjoy "souvenirs of that class of people who manipulate history to your exclusion." The issue of class and art continued to be a pressing one in the late twentieth century, when collectors with big bank accounts were buying out gallery shows, sponsoring exhibitions, promoting artists, and establishing "good taste." The *Surrogates* force one to consider whether it is the social status afforded by art or its content that matter most. McCollum's mass-produced objects, infiltrating museum and gallery exhibitions by speaking the language of art, answer in favor of the former. In a last caustic gesture reiterating the complicity of art and power, McCollum created *Perpetual Photos* (1982–89), reproductions of art as it appeared on the office walls of the fictional, but influential, Ewing Oil, the commercial enterprise dramatized on the television series *Dallas*.

The importance of theory to artists of the early eighties was immeasurable. It was as if the art-about-art impulse that defined formalism was taken far beyond the confines of the picture plane. The work of **Mark Tansey** (b. 1949), on the face of it traditional figurative realism, serves as evidence of the prevalence of theory and criticism. Painted in grisaille, Tansey's images resemble preparatory sketches for old master canvases, but illustrate, with great liberty, the recent history of art. In the monumental *Triumph of the New York School* (1984), Tansey transforms the military metaphor of "avant-garde" into an ironic variation on history painting based loosely on Velázquez's *Surrender at Breda*. The painting depicts French artists, dressed in European military uniforms (save Picasso in a fur coat, Matisse in a cape and Duchamp in a robe) passing the baton of modernism to the Americans, who are dressed as GIs. In *Action Painting II* (fig. **26.8**), space flight provides the metaphor, as the space shuttle launch becomes the premise for a joke about the distance between the public and the modern (the Sunday painter and the action painter) and a more serious commentary on the transformation of Abstract Expressionism into a style. In the late fifties it was of great concern whether Abstract Expressionism had calcified into an academic style. What might it mean to have turned the existential challenge and the expressive gestures of Pollock or De Kooning into a style? Posed another way, were artists, like those in Tansey's picture, not acting themselves but merely and ridiculously painting pictures of

26.8 Mark Tansey, *Action Painting II*, 1984. Oil on canvas, 76 × 110" (193 × 279.4 cm).

actions? By the mid-eighties and nineties, artists turned to just such an ironic strategy to vitalize nonfigural abstract art.

Primal Passions: Neo-Expressionism

With the beginning of the eighties, the reaction against Minimalism assumed a new intensity, kindled in the United States by young painters with a love of bold gesture, heroic scale, mythic content, and rebellious figuration. Critics dubbed this movement Neo-Expressionism. European artists had been practicing a Neo-Expressionism since the sixties, when German artists in particular sought means to negotiate the cultural presence of the United States and the USSR in post-World War II Europe. On both sides of the Atlantic, Neo-Expressionists revived agitated, feeling-laden brushwork. Almost all of them generated content by exploiting imagery so taboo, primal, or vulgar that descriptive realism seemed to pass into the dislocated, surrealistic realm of dream, reverie, or nightmare. Yet even though the accessibility promised by identifiable subject matter was not quite as immediate as some might have hoped, collectors, museums, the media, and some critics rejoiced that here, at long last, were large, vigorously worked, color-filled, and clearly meaningful canvases. In an art world hungry as much for excitement as for imagery, this was an event. It was made all the more newsworthy because it had been spearheaded in Europe, where German and Italian artists were working with a self-confident strength and independence not seen since the original Expressionists (in the case of the Germans) or the Futurists and Metaphysical artists (in the case of the Italians). For the first time in the postwar era, Continental artists could reclaim a full share of international attention and world leadership in new art, hand in hand with younger American painters.

The so-called Neo-Expressionists evinced a daring embrace of metaphor, allegory, narrative, surfaces energized by and packed with photographic processes, broken crockery, or even oil paint that made the New Image art of the seventies (see chapter 24) seem yoked to modernist dogmas of emotional and formal reserve. Paradoxically, however, while previous avant-garde movements had tended to renounce the past, the Neo-Expressionists sought to liberate themselves from modernist restrictions by rediscovering those very elements within tradition most condemned by progressive, mainstream trends. For example, the Americans tended to look to the later, expressionist Picasso—the Picasso certain modernists had thought unimportant—instead of the cerebral, discriminating artist of the heroic Analytic Cubist era (see chapter 9). They flocked to the 1983 Guggenheim Museum exhibition devoted to the Spanish master's final decade (1963–73), drinking in not only the liberated drawing and color, but also the unrestrained, autobiographical sexuality expressed by a still-vital octogenarian (fig. 26.9). Not coincidentally, sexuality loomed large—often blatantly—in Neo-Expressionist art as well.

26.9 Pablo Picasso, *Man, Guitar, and Bird-Woman*, 1970. Oil on canvas, 63¾ × 51⅛" (161.9 × 129.9 cm). Estate of the artist.

Beyond these broad, and highly provisional, generalizations, the Neo-Expressionists—a title almost none of them found appropriate—have little in common. Instead of forming a cohesive movement, they emerged, more or less independently, from their respective cultural and stylistic outposts. In the United States, those artists who came to the forefront of the movement did so with significant gallery support in the late seventies and early eighties. The market that propelled the Americans inspired a retrospective interest in the many artists whose work had long shown characteristics of Neo-Expressionism. The celebration of paint did not come without criticisms, the strongest of which asserted that to reclaim modernist styles was to ignore postwar critiques of modernism. After conceptual art, feminism, and Appropriation, the step back to painting seemed to many to be a step too far.

German Neo-Expressionism

Among the German Neo-Expressionist painters, the senior artist is **Georg Baselitz** (b. 1938). His paintings are also perhaps the most distinctive, with the topsy-turvy orientation of their imagery—usually upside down—and their full, ripe color and powerful, liberated brushwork. In a gesture that was both nostalgic and nationalistic, Baselitz (born Georg Kern) renamed himself for the village where he was born, Deutschbaselitz in Saxony, after he moved out of what was then Russian-occupied East Germany and into West Berlin. Postwar West Germany, Baselitz discovered, was dominated by the cultural presence of the United States as East Germany had been by the Soviet Union. In 1958, the year after Baselitz emigrated, West Berlin hosted New American Painting, a show originating at The Museum of Modern Art, New York, which promoted artists including Pollock, de Kooning, and Kline. The propagandistic nature of the exhibition typified the policy for rebuilding Germany, which entailed an influx of economic and cultural goods from the United States. Artists wishing to assert creative and national independence could resist the impulse for abstraction but were wary of figurative painting because of its connections with Soviet Socialist Realism (see chapter 11). Baselitz's solution was to revive the kind of narrative and symbolic, emotive and rhapsodic, art in which Germans had previously achieved greatness (see fig. 1.7). During 1964–66, when international art was dominated by American Color Field painting (see chapter 19) and Pop (see chapter 21), Baselitz developed an iconography of heroic men—huge figures towering over devastated landscapes. The monumental human forms were personifications of the German psyche, homeless after the moral and physical devastation of the war. Baselitz eventually turned from the wandering heroes to figures left more or less intact but abstracted from reality by an upside-down posture and the disintegrating effects of brilliant color and aggressive painterliness (fig. **26.10**). Baselitz's treatment of his subjects, often friends in the midst of mundane activ-ities such as talking, eating, or drinking, dramatized them by magnifying their size and manipulating their bodies through evocative distortions of anatomy.

Baselitz also made sculpture, hacking forms out of wood to register the medium's inherent qualities (fig. **26.11**). While this may be a tribute to the late works of Michelangelo, it also calls to mind the German Expressionists, who excelled in woodcut.

In his rebellion against all authoritarian "norms," most particularly those inherent in the monolithic consistency and coolness of sixties American abstraction, **Markus Lüpertz** (b. 1941) made intensity the driving force behind his search for artistic independence, variability the character of his style, imaginative reference to earlier artists his process, and politics the content of his art. Lüpertz saw

26.11 Georg Baselitz, *Untitled*, 1982–84. Limewood and oil, 8'3" × 2'4" × 1'6" (2.5 × 0.71 × 0.46 m). Scottish National Gallery of Modern Art, Edinburgh.

26.10 Georg Baselitz, *The Brücke Choir (Der Brückenchor)*, 1983. Oil on canvas, 9'2½" × 14'11" (2.8 × 4.5 m). Private collection.

Picabia as a precursor of his own stylistic restlessness (see figs. 10.49, 13.22) and Picasso as a model of the obsessive quoter of established art. No less important, however, was Pollock, who for Lüpertz seemed a "Dionysiac" painter attuned to discovering the mysteries of his own personality within the unifying process of his art. Lüpertz uses abstracting means to invent objects that, while simulating the look of real things, remain totally fictitious, or what might be called "pseudo-objects." In the early seventies, the artist executed a "motif" series in which he introduced such recognizable but taboo emblems as German military helmets, uniforms, and insignia, and combined them with palettes and other attributes of the painting profession. These works signified the need to confront

history and the imperative that art be grounded in concrete reality (fig. 26.12).

Having crossed from East to West Germany, **A. R. Penck** (b. 1939) struggled in his art not only with the cleft in German society but also with the need to come to terms with himself as an exile. The form that this self-taught artist found most effective for his purposes was a stick figure—Everyman reduced to a cipher—set in multiples or singly in a tapestry or batiklike pattern against a field of solid color, with figures and ground so counterbalanced as to lock together in a dynamic positive–negative relationship (fig. 26.13). Mixing stick figures with a whole vocabulary of hieroglyphs, cybernetic symbols, graffiti signs, and anthropological or folkloric images, Penck expresses

26.12 Markus Lüpertz, *Schwarz–Rot–Gold I*, 1974. Distemper on canvas, 102¼ × 78¾" (260 × 200 cm).

26.13 A. R. Penck, *The Red Airplane*, 1985. Oil on canvas, 3'11" × 6'10½" (1.19 × 2.1 m). Private collection.

26.14 Jörg Immendorff, *Café Deutschland I*, 1977–78. Acrylic on canvas, 9'2" × 10'10" (2.8 × 3.3 m). Ludwig-Forum für Internationale Kunst, Aachen, Germany.

such personal and public concerns as the urgent need for individual self-assertion in a collective society. As a "crossover" himself, Penck often painted poignant versions of the lone stick man walking a tightrope or a burning footbridge suspended above an abyss separating two islands of barrenness.

Almost in counterpoint to Penck's radically depersonalized imagery, **Jörg Immendorff** (b. 1945) paints in a detailed, if highly conceptualized, realist style. Like Penck, he anguished over the theme of the individual entrapped by the contradictions of modern German life. In the *Café Deutschland* series, the central image is the artist himself, often seated between a pair of allegorical columns symbolizing the two halves of a polarized world (fig. **26.14**). While Baselitz, and to a great degree Lupertz and Penck, adopted styles that recalled the Expressionist painting of Die Brücke (see chapter 8), Immendorf looked to different sources. Taking from the *Neue Sachlichkeit* (New Objectivity; see chapter 13) examples of Georg Grosz, Otto Dix, and Max Beckmann, Immendorf evokes the moral poverty and political disgust that concerned these post–World War I painters in a style that, like theirs, bears more fidelity to realism than that of the prewar Expressionists. During and after his student days in Dusseldorf, where he studied with Joseph Beuys, Immendorf joined activist groups supporting tenants' rights and opposing the war in Vietnam and capitalist imperialism. His *Café Deutschland* paintings typify his political and aesthetic agenda. The relatively public, accessible style, the autobiographical subject, and the lurid disco scene, complete with heavy, forward-pitching perspective, express, as Donald Kuspit has written, the ambivalence of "an egalitarian Maoist oriented toward the lost cause of a democratic China, and a successful bourgeois artist appropriated by the market."

Sigmar Polke (b. 1941), along with Gerhard Richter, created an alternative to the nationalistic catharsis of their Neo-Expressionist peers. In the early sixties, the international art community provided in Pop Art its own alternative to American Abstract Expressionism and European abstraction of *Art informel* and *Tâchisme* (see chapters 19 and 20). Polke, Richter, and fellow student Konrad Leug created Capitalist Realism, an indigenous form of Pop Art that responded to American aesthetic hegemony. This new Pop Art distorted what appeared to be an American infatuation with capitalism into an art sensitive to the unique complexities of contemporary German life. In the sixties, Polke adopted the Benday process of mechanical reproduction not long after it had been integrated into painting by Roy Lichtenstein (see figs. 21.38, 21.39). But whereas the American artist aestheticized the dot system, not only by treating it as a kind of developed Pointillism (see chapter 3) but also by using it to depict established icons of high art, the German simply hand-copied—"naively"—a blown-up media image, complete with off-register imperfections and cheap tabloid subject matter (fig. **26.15**). The "imperfect" results draw attention to the means of reproduction,

26.15 Sigmar Polke, *Bunnies*, 1966. Acrylic on linen, 59 × 39½" (150 × 100 cm). Hirshhorn Museum and Sculpture Garden, Smithsonian Institution, Washington, D.C.

interfering with the seamless perfection that makes both classical Pop Art and advertising so effective. In the context of postwar Germany, Polke's works constituted a critical commentary on the infiltration of American media imagery into German culture. Polke often worked on an allover grid or otherwise mechanically patterned ground. Rauschenberg, of course, had incorporated ordinary textiles and photographs into his combine paintings, as a device for generating the shock effect once possible in the unorthodox juxtaposition of materials (see fig. 21.10). Polke, however, developed the painterly "naturally" out of the mechanical, thus demonstrating a disturbing synchronicity between subjective creativity and mass production. By the eighties, Polke was no longer creating Pop variations on advertising. In a further assimilation using photography, the artist developed his imagery by layering photographic imagery onto underlying patterns of regularly repeating abstract motifs, often taken from textile designs (fig. **26.16**). Delineated like contour drawings and layered in a manner inspired by Picabia's *Transparencies* (see chapter 13), the images seem paradoxically to dematerialize at

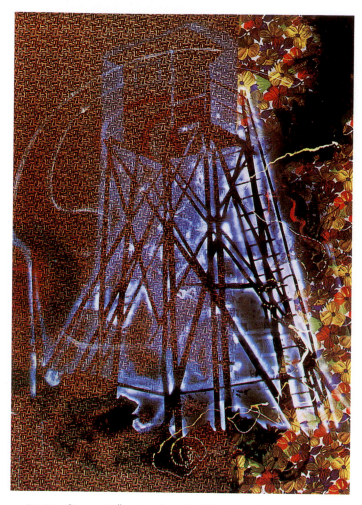

26.16 Sigmar Polke, *Hochstand*, 1984. Acrylic, lacquer, and cotton, 10'8" × 7'4" (3.3 × 2.2 m). Private collection, New York.

lenging artistic career. Since 1962, the artist created scores of "photopaintings," all of them more distinctly "photographic" than Rauschenberg's transfers, and yet far more like real paintings than Warhol's appropriations of media imagery. In his later photopaintings, Richter felt freer to depart from the original, often a snapshot made by the artist himself, as long as he preserved something of a genuine photographic look, complete with such flaws as out-of-focus blurring, graininess, or exaggerated contrasts, all of which seem to be points of mediation between painting and photography. The calm, bucolic scenes of Richter's later work (fig. **26.17**) show Central European landscape immersed in a soft, romantic atmosphere, a kind of filter that reveals as much about how painting and photography alike distort our vision of reality as it does about the world depicted.

In the late sixties, Richter ran counter to the photopaintings with a return to pure abstraction, first in a series of heavily impastoed monochrome works called Gray Pictures (*Graue Bilder*). By the beginning of the eighties, after investigating many different styles, he came to concentrate on full-color, vigorously worked Expressionist abstractions (fig. **26.18**), painted as a series and complementary to the cooler, more objective "classicism" of the photo landscapes. Though apparently as free and gestural as their Abstract Expressionist antecedents, Richter's abstractions are based on photographs of details of his own work. Chromatically and gesturally similar to abstractions painted by De Kooning in the fifties, Richter's nonrepresentational works issue from a different critical process. They present a planar space layered in strata of relatively distinct elements, a structural conception already seen as characteristic of much Postmodern art. In executing these works, Richter drew upon a vast repertoire of painterly techniques—troweling, scraping, flinging, scumbling, and brushing—that recall the artistic procedures of Hans Hofmann (see

the same time that they emerge from the support upon which the artist has painted them, creating an illusionistically deep pictorial space even as it seems independent of all perspective systems. Moreover, the figuration phases in and out of focus, as if it were the product of photographic or darkroom manipulations, or perhaps even of an accident with one of the substances Polke is known to have used in creating his curiously synthetic and characteristic colors. The impact of these visually stunning canvases is complicated when the premise for aesthetic indulgence is as morally and historically ambivalent as the guard tower that appears in *Hochstand* (see fig. 26.16)

Like his compatriot Penck, Dresden-born and -educated **Gerhard Richter** (b. 1932) found himself so in conflict with the social and aesthetic conditions of East Germany that he crossed over into the West in 1961. In 1962–63, Richter was in Düsseldorf and, with Polke, learning from Beuys, Fluxus, and exhibitions of American Pop artists. After his collaboration with Polke, Richter's work took a decisively more conceptual turn. Catalyzed by the iconoclasm of Fluxus, Richter declared, "I had had enough of bloody painting, and painting from a photograph seemed to me the most moronic and inartistic thing that anyone could do." This was an antiart gesture that led to a chal-

26.17 Gerhard Richter, *Scheune/Barn No. 549/1*, 1983. Oil on canvas, 27½ × 39½" (69.9 × 100.3 cm). Art Gallery of Ontario, Toronto.

26.18 Gerhard Richter, *Vase*, 1984. Oil on canvas, 7'4½" × 6'6¾" (2.2 × 2 m). Museum of Fine Arts, Boston.

fig. 11.1). In later work, Richter painted his abstractions directly, without the intervention of photography.

In the apocalyptic paintings of **Anselm Kiefer** (b. 1945), German and Jewish history are frequently evoked symbolically through the motif and appearance of scorched earth. Kiefer's interest in exploring the consequences of German history began in a series of conceptual photographs that have little to do with the physical presence of his Neo-Expressionist canvases. In 1969, in a collection of photographs called *The Occupations*, Kiefer documented himself standing in Nazi uniform before monuments like the Colosseum in Rome giving the Nazi salute. The scandal of enacting Hitler's imperialist desires in a confusing and often belittling way created a scandal that still colors the reception of Kiefer's work. The question of how to reckon with German history on personal, national, and international stages remains central to considerations of Kiefer's art.

In pursuing such themes, Kiefer exercises the freedom to exploit and mix images of Germany from the mythic realm of Valhalla (the mythological dwelling place of gods and heroes) to the horror of Auschwitz and Nuremburg, as well as biblical and historical themes. His media are equally diverse—straw and sand, overprocessed photographs, lacquer, and fire—and might serve the expressive purpose of simulating ancient fields charred and furrowed from centuries of battle and seeming to stretch into infinity. Kiefer's elegiac themes are seen in *Departure from Egypt* (fig. **26.19**), one of his most grandiose landscapes, rolling away majestically, yet held to the plane by the hook of Aaron's rod. Even though appearing as if it had been swept by a firestorm, or mulched in blood and dung, tar and salt, the field rewards close inspection with a rich sense of tactility and texture.

Kiefer has also worked in sculpture. He has made immense "books" out of lead and gathered them on shelves; the resulting assemblages can weigh several tons (fig. **26.20**). Like Kiefer's paintings, his books contain the past, but as much through their material presence as through imagery or language. Indeed, these huge volumes have a massive solidity as physical objects that conveys a palpable sense of the weight of history upon us. The artist's use of lead is also resonant with the centuries-long human

26.19 Anselm Kiefer, *Departure from Egypt*, 1984. Straw, lacquer, and oil on canvas, lead rod attached, 12'5" × 18'5" (3.8 × 5.6 m). Museum of Contemporary Art, Los Angeles.

desire to turn nature into wealth and power: lead is the material that alchemists sought to convert into gold in the Middle Ages. It is now used for shielding against the radioactivity of atomic devices—a modern transmutation of matter that in some sense has fulfilled the alchemist's dream, even as it has made great devastation possible. After the unification of East and West Germany in 1991, Kiefer

moved to southern France and stopped painting for a while. In the mid-nineties, however, he revealed new canvases that take the romantic terrain of his new home as the source for a series of brilliant, light-filled landscapes that seem to bring a layer of coloristic beauty to his typically dark and painful palette.

Italian Neo-Expressionism

The second nation to foster a substantial Neo-Expressionist movement was Italy. Called the "*transavanguardia*," Italian artists of the seventies found in painting and Italian classicism, two traditions disregarded since World War II, the ingredients for a contemporary movement. Among the "three Cs" of Italy's *transavanguardia*—a group completed by Sandro Chia and Enzo Cucchi—who first came to international notice at the 1980 Venice Biennale, the Neapolitan-born **Francesco Clemente** (b. 1952) was the most prolific. Clemente maintained studio-residences in Rome, Madras, and New York, and each year spent time working in each country. While he absorbed and used the imagery, ideas, and techniques native to the environment of each city, the artist also allowed his disparate influences to overlap and cross-fertilize. This became especially apparent in works like the twenty-four miniatures of *Francesco Clemente Pinxit*, executed in India in the classical Hindu manner, using natural pigments on paper.

Clemente taught himself oil painting in New York. There, like Barnett Newman (see fig. 19.30), Clemente created a series of works entitled *The Fourteen Stations*, interpreting the theme not with the traditional iconography of Christ's journey to the Cross, but rather through a dreamlike intermingling of personal psychology, cultural history, and religious symbolism. The artist's own naked body is ubiquitous throughout the paintings in the series. In *Station No. IV*, the figure resembles a Roman-collared

26.20 Anselm Kiefer, *Breaking of the Vessels*, 1990. Lead, iron, glass, copper wire, charcoal, and aquatec, 16' × 6' × 4' ½" (4.9 × 1.8 × 1.23 m), weight 7½ tons. The Saint. Louis Art Museum, Missouri.

26.21 Francesco Clemente, *The Fourteen Stations, No. IV*, 1981–82. Oil and encaustic on canvas, 6'6" × 7'4½" (2 × 2.2 m). Private collection.

priest, screaming like Bacon's bishops (see fig. 20.47) and lifting his white surplice to reveal a dark, egg-shaped void just above an intact scrotum (fig. **26.21**). Behind the figure stands a bull, painted with all the distorted energy of Pollock's *Guardians of the Secret* (see fig. 19.9). The animal recalls Nandi, Siva's bull, and provides a link between the Christian series and Clemente's Indian works.

Clemente's innumerable self-portraits present an image of selfhood and masculinity that is porous and flexible. Conventional expectations about male identity are undermined as are the boundaries of the body. Clemente presents the human form doubling up on itself, as it mutates from a self-contained entity to a being mingled with others, in scenes that are sometimes ecstatic and sometimes painful. An elegant vision of the loss of self in a generative moment of creation is the 1983 *Semen* (fig. **26.22**). Suspended, with eyes closed, is a being loosely defined by a broken outline and incomplete shading. It resembles a kind of highly developed fetus, floating in amniotic fluid. The title, however, suggests a connection with swimming sperm. Together these clues create an ambiguous double sense of potential life awaiting fruition.

In his reaction to modernist conventions, **Sandro Chia** (b. 1946), a Florentine who subsequently relocated to New York, relied on Italian exuberance and a personal knowledge of the ersatz Neoclassicism practiced during the Fascist twenties and thirties by artists such as Giorgio de Chirico (see fig. 13.5) and Ottone Rosai, who were themselves reacting against Futurism, Italy's first modernist style. Adopting the older painters' conventions—their absurdly muscle-bound nudes and self-consciously mythic situations—but inflating the figures to balloon proportions while reducing the overblown narratives to the scale of fairytales, Chia parodies his sources while thumbing his nose at the authentic Neoclassical rigor that survived in Minimalism. Just as appealing as the comic amplitude of these harmless giants is the Mediterranean warmth of Chia's color and the nervous energy of his painterly surfaces—qualities of scale, palette, and touch that the artist also managed to translate into his heroic bronzes. Just how

26.22 Francesco Clemente, *Semen*, 1983. Oil on linen, 7'9" × 13' (2.4 × 4 m). Private collection.

26.23 Sandro Chia, *The Idleness of Sisyphus*, 1981. Oil on canvas, in two parts: top 6'9" × 12'8¼" (2.1 × 3.9 m), bottom 3'5" × 12'1¼" (1.05 × 3.9 m), overall 10'2" × 12'8¼" (3.1 × 3.9 m). The Museum of Modern Art, New York.

to take Chia's injection of contemporary citizens into classical themes, particularly the case of the bureaucrat in *The Idleness of Sisyphus* (fig. **26.23**) was central to debates over Neo-Expressionism in the eighties. The reclamation of grand narrative painting even with the self-deprecating ineptitude of Chia's Sisyphus suggested to some that the deconstruction begun in the sixties had been in vain.

Unlike the world travelers Clemente and Chia, **Enzo Cucchi** (b. 1950) remained solidly rooted in the soil of his native region near Ancona, a seaport on Italy's Adriatic coast. There, for generations, the Cucchi family has worked the land, a land whose circular compounds of farm buildings and catastrophic landslides often figured in the artist's paintings. Because of his doomsday vision and his love of richly textured surfaces, built up with what often seems a waxy mixture of rusted graphite and coal dust, Cucchi has sometimes been compared with Germany's Anselm Kiefer (see figs. 26.19, 26.20). What sets him unmistakably apart, however, is the Italian heritage that he brings to his dramas; he grew up amid paintings of saints and martyrs. In his *Entry into Port of a Ship with a Red Rose* (fig. **26.24**), austere yet emotively rendered crosses glide across the large fresco in graceful clusters, as purposefully as a fleet of sailboats. Such powerful compositional effects, achieved with the sparest of means, have led some critics to compare Cucchi's work with the early Renaissance frescoes of Giotto.

American Neo-Expressionism

The artist most often credited with catapulting the eighties art scene in New York was the Brooklyn-born, Texas-educated **Julian Schnabel** (b. 1951). For viewers starved by the lean visual diet of Minimalism and Conceptualism, Schnabel's grand-scale, thematic pictures—reviving the whole panoply of religious and cultural archetypes once the glory of traditional high art—had an electrifying effect.

In a move both innovative and violently expressive, Schnabel incorporated three dimensions into a flat surface in works such as *The Sea* by embedding broken crockery in a reinforced wood support (fig. **26.25**). The idea for this process came to him during a visit to Barcelona, where he saw Antoni Gaudí's tiled mosaic benches in Güell Park (see fig. 5.10). However, rather than smooth and inlaid, Schnabel's shards project from the surface in an irregular, disjunctive arrangement that visually functions, edge to edge, as a field of enlarged Pointillist dots. At the same time that the china pieces serve to define shapes and even model form, they also break up the image and absorb it into the overall surface flicker like a primitive, encrusted version of the Art Nouveau figure-in-pattern effects of Gustav Klimt (see fig. 5.6), Gaudí's Austrian contemporary. By painting over, around, or even under the protruding ceramic, Schnabel created every kind of pictorial drama, from evocations of folkloric wit and charm to suggestions of mythic

26.24 Enzo Cucchi, *Entry into Port of a Ship with a Red Rose*, 1985–86. Fresco, 9'2" × 13'1" (2.8 × 4 m). Philadelphia Museum of Art.

26.25 Julian Schnabel, *The Sea*, 1981. Oil on wood, with Mexican pots and plaster, 9 × 13' (2.7 × 4 m). Saatchi Collection, London.

ear, and on the right by a nude woman with her back to the viewer. The name of a Victorian poet, a piece of erotica, and a severed ear—at first, the different images may seem to cancel one another out and erase all meaning, until one recalls that in 1958 Jasper Johns reproduced Tennyson's name across the bottom of an abstract canvas painted in sober gray on gray, as if in tribute to the artistic integrity and lyrical, high-minded spirit of England's "good gray poet." The connection to Johns is reasserted by the disembodied ear, which could also evoke the poet's "ear for words," or Van Gogh's self-imposed mutilation, but also, and more tellingly, Jasper Johns's *Target with Plaster Casts* (see fig. 21.15). Johns originally affixed a three-dimensional ear, among other anatomical parts, above the painting of a target. In Johns's work the uncomfortable relationship between the destination of an arrow or bullet and the exposed fragments of a naked body generated a range of personal and political content. Such correspondences were less clear in Salle's works, though supporters thought that paintings like *Tennyson* should be read as a commentary on the naked woman, the sexism such imagery represents, and the role of the nude in the history of art.

Salle's selection of poses typical of soft-core pornography (though copied from Salle's own photography rather than published sources), art historical "masterpieces," found objects, and pop culture references encouraged the interpretation of his paintings as dustbins of American culture. To supporters, Salle was a deft practitioner of pastiche, the critical assemblage of existing cultural elements to elicit an analytical response from the viewer. If, by the eighties, painting, with its grand tradition and canonical history, was understood to be a politically suspect medium, then Salle's casual combinations forced it to come down from its pedestal and sully itself with the mundane objects of everyday life. To critics in the eighties, it was too early to

ritual. The emotive effect of Schnabel's work arises less from the image, which is not immediately decipherable, than from an audacious stylistic performance, or process, that simultaneously structures and shatters both figure and surface. In the nineties, Schnabel took his flair for drama and his control over multiple formal and narrative layers to Hollywood, making two well-received films.

Among the American Neo-Expressionists, one of the most controversial artists was **David Salle** (b. 1952). Salle forged an unpromising mix of secondhand, disassociated elements into a new, original conception. In the painting *Tennyson* (fig. **26.26**), the artist professed a Conceptual background by lettering out the title in capitals, across a field dominated on the left by a found wooden relief of an

26.26 David Salle, *Tennyson*, 1983. Oil and acrylic on canvas, 6'6" × 9'9" (2 × 3 m). Private collection, New York.

presume that it was common knowledge that painting had been compromised by its relationship to the elite of history. The image of themselves that many Neo-Expressionist painters put forward did nothing to assuage their critics. Complete with beautiful models, troops of assistants, and the ubiquitous cigar, they appeared to be more like clichés of the modernist genius than critics of modernism. Without such a critique, Salle's imagery, like most Neo-Expressionist painting, appeared to many as naïve and sexist pining for the glory days of the great male painters.

Few of the Neo-Expressionist painters address their art totally to the figure, in all its naked physical and psychological complexity. Foremost among such painters is **Eric Fischl** (b. 1948), whose immense fleshscapes have an unusually high-voltage effect on viewers (fig. **26.27**). Created in tandem with a large body of photographs and fascinating preparatory sketches made of overlaid drawings on tracing paper, Fischl's presentation of nudity takes on a self-consciousness in form as well as content. Deliberately composed to occupy the spaces of alienation and Americana familiar to the work of American painters such as Winslow Homer and Edward Hopper (see figs. 2.48, 18.37), Fischl's subjects move beyond a fascination with either flesh or paint to become implicated in suggestions of alcoholism, voyeurism, onanism, homosexuality, and incest. This can be seen in paintings set in the gardens, on the beaches, in the well-appointed rooms, and on the yachts of affluent America, all populated by men, women, and children scattered about or clustered in scenes of boredom and isolation. Like the cathartic abstractions of his Neo-Expressionist peers, but in a style that referenced the

traditions of American Realism, Fischl painted upper-middle-class angst. Awkward and half-embarrassed, self-absorbed and yet furtively, even intently, aware of one another's exposure, these figures communicate the individual's psychic as well as physical nakedness.

The paintings in Fischl's *India* series, a series of images based on scenes observed on a trip to northern India in 1988, have been described as the work of a "post-modern tourist." The series, like Clemente's work in the miniature tradition, implies a critique of the "Orientalism" and "exoticism" often featured in European images of Asia and Africa from the nineteenth century, just as Fischl's nudes are in part a critique of female nudes by Manet and others. Separating Fischl from his colonialist predecessors, however, is the fact that he works in an era in which Western imperialism most often takes the form of tourism and economic expansion rather than outright military conquest. Even if the beggars and the group of monkeys in *On the Stairs of the Temple* suggest little beyond a tourist's snapshot, the treatment of a woman at the center prompts a more complicated response. Clothed in pink and bathed in splendid light, she might at first seem to evidence at least some attempt by the artist to fathom another culture, with its different understanding of spiritual and physical beauty. Yet the draped figure communicates real ambivalence. The viewer's expectation that she be freely available as an object of visual delectation is at least partially confirmed by the subject's incarnation of the stereotype of veiled "Other of the East."

The Challenge of Photography in 1980s Art

Neo-Expressionism was heralded by many as a return to painting and curators celebrated that young artists "had returned to the painter's pots." But many also took cameras into the studio. Eric Fischl's paintings were often the result of studying not just the model, but photographs of family, friends, and strangers. Salle generated many of his motifs by duplicating the compositions and the appearance of photographs. In the critical debates of the day, Neo-Expressionism figured as the return of the painterly, while Appropriation tapped into the potential of mass media, particularly photography. The issue was always complex and a number of artists juxtaposed the aesthetic bravado of the former with the sociocultural analysis of the latter.

The art of **Robert Longo** (b. 1953), which has been described as "apocalyptic Pop," features over-lifesize imagery taken from or inspired by film, television, comic books, and advertisements; a secondhand world of kitsch and high culture mixed and matched to provoke voyeuristic responses to such basic themes as love, death, and violence. No less dramatic is the serendipitous variety of media that Longo and his collaborators (usually named) have combined: sculpture (wood carving, stone intaglio, and bronze casting), painting (acrylic, spray paint, and gold

26.27 Eric Fischl, *The Old Man's Boat and the Old Man's Dog*, 1982. Oil on canvas, 7 × 7' (2.1 × 2.1 m). Collection Mr. and Mrs. Robert Lehrman, Washington, D.C.

leaf), drawing, silkscreen, and photography. Longo's practice put him in the company of Appropriation artists while his aggressive content, which has included black American flags, guns, and huge ocean waves, links his work to the Neo-Expressionist impulse.

Longo gained early recognition with a number of large black-and-white charcoal drawings, such as the 1979–82 series *Men in the Cities*. For these impressive works, the artist photographed single figures clad in sober business clothes and seized in the contorted throes of what could be either agony or ecstasy, dying or dancing (fig. **26.28**). But while any such condition should create a sense of heat, the figures are frozen—and perhaps all the more haunting for the tension that this ambiguity produces. Perhaps better than any of his peers, Longo captured the sense of corporate-induced frenzy that animated the artworld in the early eighties. His contorted and violent figures, all dressed in business attire, express the uneasy combination of urgency and disregard that treating art as investments could produce. At a moment of escalating prices and famous art stars, the influence of money on artistic success felt as if it had never been greater, causing great ambivalence in the art community. *Men in the Cities* was created by transferring photographs that Longo took of his friends leaping, dancing, and fighting on his roof. The images were projected and duplicated by means of emphatic and stylized charcoal and graphite drawings, which Longo executed with the help of assistants.

The identical twins **Mike** and **Doug Starn** (b. 1961) produced work in collaboration. Although they have also painted, their principal medium is an elaborate variety of photocollage. In their work, they appropriate a photographic image and subject it to all manner of technical alterations. They might enlarge an image enormously, or make a toned print of it in the nineteenth-century manner. But they will also deliberately scratch the negative, or otherwise distress the image, crease or tear the print, stain

26.28 Robert Longo, *Untitled* (*Men in the Cities* series), 1981. Charcoal and graphite on paper, 8 × 5' (2.4 × 1.52 m).

26.29 Mike and Doug Starn, *Double Mona Lisa with Self-Portrait*, 1985–88. Toned silver print and Ortho film, Scotch tape, and wood, 8'9" × 13'3½" (2.7 × 4.1 m). Museum of Fine Arts, Boston.

it with glue, or cut it up. They will then complete the work by mounting and framing the separate pieces, or tape them directly to the wall. Often the resulting large-scale photocollages are as imposing as murals.

In *Double Mona Lisa with Self-Portrait* (fig. **26.29**) the Starns borrow an image often used by artists such as Duchamp and Warhol. Instead of using a photograph that documents the painting alone, however, as those artists did, the Starns took a picture of the *Mona Lisa* surrounded by its large, cumbersome vitrine at the Louvre in Paris, with the rest of the gallery and its visitors, including the two artists themselves, reflected in the glass. Even standing a few feet from Leonardo's painting, museumgoers see it twice removed, sealed behind a glaring barrier and obstructed by the reflected bodies of other visitors. The installation of the painting has the ironic effect of distancing the work from the very people who have come to experience it firsthand. In place of an original that is remote and out of reach, the photocollage substitutes its own complex aesthetic structure for that of the *Mona Lisa*. But the cut-up and painstakingly reconstituted version that the Starns create, with its patchwork grid of Scotch-taped panels, openly announces itself as a homemade, "constructed" copy—totally at odds with the mystique of the precious, irreplaceable masterpiece. The Starns create a dramatic,

expressive comment on issues of originality and reproduction, art and meaning, devotion and power. Though clearly related to Appropriation, the Starns's aesthetic bravado placed them comfortably in the company of the international Neo-Expressionists.

The English artist team of **Gilbert and George** (b. 1943, 1942), known initially for turning their art school rebellion against modernism into comedic performances, found their monumental multipanel photographs included in group shows documenting the Expressionist movement in the eighties. The pair's later work continued to push the limits of self-portraiture, as had their *Singing Sculptures* (see fig. 24.17), but now the pair featured images of themselves in large-scale photographs, hand-dyed, mounted, and framed. The photoworks express aggressively political content, as in *Are You Angry or Are You Just Boring?* (fig. **26.30**), which combines the potential energy of alienated urban youth and images relating to the AIDS epidemic with decorative intuition that recalls Matisse. Gilbert and George designate everything they make as sculpture. They favor explicitly homoerotic content, often expressed emblematically through voluptuous flower and vegetable imagery, while presenting it within a religio-aesthetic structure of stained-glass-colored panels, and iconic cruciform patterns.

Searing Statements: Expressive (if not Expressionist) Art

In a period of young artists' early success, the Chicago-born Leon Golub (b. 1922) stood in stark contrast. He was a moralist in the tradition of Daumier and Beckmann (see figs. 2.14, 13.40) who for some forty years stuck by his guns, all the while "famous for being ignored," until at last, in the early eighties, the world's unhappy concerns had so evolved as to coincide with his own. These are the politics of power and the insidious, all-corrupting effects—violence and victimization—of power without accountability. The then sixty-year-old Golub had spent the long years of his exile—out of fashion and out of the country—steadily gathering his artistic and intellectual forces, so that by the time the first pictures in his *Mercenaries* series came before an astounded public in 1982, they presented, as did the later *White Squad* pictures, a hard-won but fixating, frozen unity of raw form and brutal content (fig. **26.31**).

By the time of the *Mercenaries*, Golub had begun to focus on the margins of society—the jungles of South America or Africa—where the emissaries of political power tended to be not anonymous armies or aloof public figures but "mercs," individual agents for hire. To bring home the evil of torture and terrorism, Golub hit upon the idea of making his political criminals all too human, fascinating and specific in their cowboy swagger and guilty satisfaction, while reducing the intimidated victim to a dehumanized, undifferentiated state almost beneath empathy. The better to authenticate his images of unfettered police authority, Golub pieced them together from photos of political

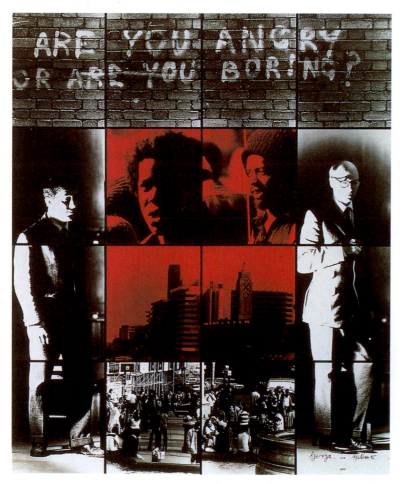

26.30 Gilbert and George, *Are You Angry or Are You Just Boring?* 1977. Color photograph, 7'11" × 6'7" (2.4 × 2 m). Stedelijk van Abbemuseum, Eindhoven, the Netherlands.

26.31 Leon Golub, *White Squad IV, El Salvador*, 1983. Acrylic on canvas, 10' × 12'6" (3 × 3.8 m). Saatchi Collection, London.

atrocities, complete with the ungainliness of men exuberantly and sensually caught up in their daily work. He made his petty tyrants ten feet (3 m) tall, pressed them forward with a ground of Pompeiian oxide-red (itself a primary emblem of imperial, political power) and cropped the anti-heroes' legs off to spill the scene forward, as if into the viewer's own space. Far too committed and subtle to preach or sloganeer, Golub simply uses his long-seasoned pictorial means—a congruence of image, form, process, and psychology—to induce feelings of complicity in a system that manipulates some individuals to destroy human life and others to ignore the fact that it is happening.

Since the beginning of her career in Chicago in the late forties, **Nancy Spero** (b. 1926), like her husband Golub,

pursued political and social themes. In the sixties, her Vietnam drawings were among the most powerful statements against the war. *Search and Destroy* from 1967 shows one of the helicopters that saw much combat in Southeast Asia, but Spero imagines the aircraft in a fantastical, Goyaesque form, its nose like the lance of a huge swordfish, or perhaps a hypodermic needle, driven into the chest of a falling victim.

In subsequent work, Spero expanded her drawings into elaborate sequences. These she presented in the form of friezes or unrolled scrolls: panoramas of individual panels of print and collage, stretching up to 180 feet (55 m). These ribbons of images represent women from all eras and cultures. In *Goddess II* (fig. **26.32**), ancient Greek-vase dancers and cavorting goddesses appear again and again, amid earlier and later sources. The diversity of the figures' printed textures and colors from one appearance to the next makes the frieze richly inclusive in its unfolding graphic development. Spero said that her scrolls are "almost like a map. A map of the range of human experience from birth to aging, war, and rape, to a celebratory dance of life—but depicted through images of women."

Politically and socially committed, and as uncensored in her approach as Golub or Spero, the British-born artist **Sue Coe** (b. 1951) moved to New York in 1972. There she began aiming her agitprop collage-paintings at such targets as the CIA, male chauvinism, nuclear brinkmanship, apartheid in South Africa, and, ultimately, the policies of President Reagan (fig. **26.33**). Coe was inspired by the social and political inequities and righteous indignation expressed by artists such as Brueghel, Goya, Daumier, and Orozco. She is a true Expressionist, using art to indict an unjust world with the same passion that inspired earlier twentieth-century heroes of moral protest such as Käthe Kollwitz, George Grosz, Otto Dix, and Max Beckmann.

26.32 Nancy Spero, *Goddess II* (detail), 1985. Handprinting and collage on paper, 7'2" × 9'2" (2.2 × 2.8 m). Collection the artist.

26.33 Sue Coe, *Malcolm X and the Slaughter House*, 1985. Oil on paper, collage, 59⅞ × 49¼" (152.1 × 125.1 cm). Collection Don Hanson.

Coe employed a whole battery of provocative techniques—a hellishly dark palette of graphite and gore; razor-sharp drawing; jammed, irrational spaces; collaged tabloid headlines—all of which she wielded with a seemingly unshakable faith in the rightness of her perceptions. But, however extreme or fanatical these works may seem to viewers of a less political persuasion, one cannot help be moved by the poetic justice at work in a midnight world of evildoers metamorphosed into snakes and their hapless victims into angels, or in a painting overprinted with a banner like: "If animals believed in God, then the devil would look like a human being." As one critic wrote, "Sue Coe paints horror beautifully, ugliness elegantly, and monstrosity with precise sanity."

After making small drawings, artist's books, and videos in the seventies, the New York artist **Ida Applebroog** (b. 1929) undertook a number of large, multipanel paintings in the eighties, among them *Noble Fields* (fig. **26.34**). Applebroog's early work was marked by a feminist consciousness and an uncanny ability to generate expressive, intimate, and multidirectional narratives with the most schematic graphic means. A series of books from the late seventies present a single image repeated behind different headings evoking stages in tense, ambivalent stories. In her paintings, she pursued her thematic concerns with the forceful presentation of aggressive yet often highly ambiguous images. One critic, for example, saw in *Noble Fields* "a bald Medusa" who "sits for her portrait in an evening gown and arm cast, while little Oedy [Oedipus], nearby, eats a watermelon"—a description that some may find as puzzling as the painting. The mention of Oedipus is illuminating, however, since the stresses and hostilities within a troubled family are among Applebroog's notable subjects. Nonetheless, she speaks of them with a vocabulary of private symbols that the viewer cannot hope to decipher fully. Fixed against empty backgrounds that offer no clue to their meaning, her mysterious gatherings of figures are painted in thin, somewhat unearthly, colors that give them the air of characters half-remembered from a distant, traumatic past. The multitude of seemingly unrelated images makes it impossible to offer a single, unified "reading" of the painting. In some paintings, however, Applebroog is more specific in her subject matter. *The Church of St. Francis Xavier*, 1987, portrays a disconcerting image of a wheeled cross and a hooded man, referring to the church decree that forbade a Jesuit church in New York from hosting a gay organization.

Most often Applebroog delves into her substantial collection of personal and public imagery to generate what she has called "a chaos of possibilities within regimented formal

26.34 Ida Applebroog, *Noble Fields*, 1987. Oil on canvas, five panels, overall 7'2" × 11' (2.2 × 3.4 m). Solomon R. Guggenheim Museum, New York.

designs." In *Noble Fields,* for instance, our attention is pulled back and forth by the strip of images symmetrically disposed across the horizontal panel at the top; by the injured, supported male, the line of high-kicking dancers, and the dining female in the right panel; by the delicately painted monster with a broken arm and a frilly dress in the left panel; and by the child gorging himself on massive watermelons in the stark, lunar landscape at the center. These competing areas of interest are as difficult to reconcile with one another as are the members of a fractious family, or the layers of guilt and pain that its members bear.

Wall of Fame: Graffiti and Cartoon Artists

As Neo-Expressionism opened art to the many possibilities once banned by Minimalist purism, and Appropriation art drew on the commercial media, a number of even younger artists found themselves drawn into the energy and "authenticity" of one of the most "impure" of all graphic modes. This was graffiti, those "logos" (initials or nicknames) and scrawled "tags" (signatures) that their perpetrators called "writing" and had felt-tipped and spray-painted (or "bombed") all over New York City's subway trains since about 1960. For many passengers, this takeover of public walls by an indigenous, compulsive graphism simply constituted vandalism, but as a look back at the paintings of Jackson Pollock, Jean Dubuffet, and Cy Twombly indicates, graffiti-like marks have long been used by major artists (see figs. 19.9, 20.18). Not until the eighties, however, did the underground world of self-taught graffiti writers, mainly from the Bronx and Brooklyn, interact with the aboveground, Manhattan-based realm of artists and art-school students. In 1983, the upwardly mobile graffiti artists received a boost when Rotterdam's Boymans–van Beuningen Museum put on the first exhibition of graffiti art, and subsequently one of the world's premier dealers in modern art, Sidney Janis, put on his Post-Graffiti show. In the latter event, Janis displayed the canvases of graffiti writers in the very galleries where for years New Yorkers had viewed such blue-chip masters as Mondrian.

The graffiti artists and cartoonists who profited the most from the encounter between uptown and downtown art were those who brought the support of an art-school education to the experience. This equipped them with a basic pictorial language that was charged by the graffiti artists' urge to communicate and their powerful calligraphic thrust, and allowed them to expand their own Pop-cartoon-TV vocabulary into a new, broadly expressive language. The East Village in New York City became the home and exhibition space for many of these young artists.

Haring, Basquiat, and Scharf

The dean of the art-school graffiti artists was **Keith Haring** (1958–90), who, with his School of Visual Arts preparation and love of working in public spaces, served as the all-important link between the subway world of self-taught graffiti "writers" and the younger "mainstream" artists responsive to the omnipresent, abrasive form of popular expression. At the same time that he made his presence felt in all the graffiti and cartoon forums, Haring was also traveling throughout New York City's subway system and leaving his artistic calling card on virtually every train platform. The ubiquitous format for his impromptu exhibitions was the black panel from which an advertising poster had been removed, providing a surface somewhat like that of a schoolroom blackboard. After 1980, Haring made thousands of chalk drawings "in transit," always quick, simple, strong, and direct, for the activity carried with it the risk of arrest for defacement of public property. He developed a distinctive vocabulary of cartoon figures—radiant child, barking dog, flying saucer, praying man—intermingled with such universally readable signs as the cross, the halo, the pyramid, the heart, and the dollar, all rendered with such cheerfulness and generosity that their statements could be neither dismissed nor mistaken (fig. **26.35**). While in his commercial work Haring seemed to prefer drawing with black sumi ink or Magic Marker on paper, oaktag, fiberglass, or vinyl tarpaulin, he remained ready to unleash his prodigious capacity for graphic invention on almost any kind of surface, including those provided by pottery vases or plaster casts of such cliché icons as Botticelli's *Venus.* On these, as well as on vast outdoor walls, he sometimes collaborated with genuine graffiti writers, most of whom otherwise preferred the moving, subterranean environment of the MTA trains.

Though Haring garnered considerable respect in Europe, his contribution remained underappreciated in American museum circles during his lifetime. Though he aspired to have his work compared and exhibited with de Kooning and Matisse, his populist and political activities seemed to work against artworld recognition. Haring was politically active, creating posters and donating art for AIDS organizations in particular. In 1986 he opened the Pop Shop, which developed his project of bringing art to the masses who rarely ventured into Soho galleries. At the Pop Shop, Haring sold low-cost merchandise such as pins and t-shirts with his signature motifs. The Pop Shop is still in operation. In 1997, seven years after his death from AIDS, Haring received a major retrospective at the Whitney Museum of American Art.

A key figure in the transformation of graffiti into painting in the eighties was the Brooklyn-born Haitian-Hispanic artist **Jean-Michel Basquiat** (1960–88). A high-school dropout at seventeen, Basquiat was probably the most meteoric star among all the talents associated with graffiti. Like the other successful graffitists-turned-painters, Basquiat never actually "bombed" trains. Rather, while more or less living on the streets in Lower Manhattan, he formed a partnership with a friend named Al Diaz and began Magic Marking poetic messages, illustrated with odd symbols, all over the city. The pair signed their work SAMO© (standing for "same old shit"). Basquiat's tag reveals something of the frustration he felt as a black artist trying to assert his art within the context of a predominantly white gallery system. In the summer of 1980, SAMO© exhibited at the Times Square Show, a group exhibition produced by the artists' collective CoLab that was praised for creating an environment within an abandoned building on 42nd Street that mirrored the eclectic decay found in the city streets around it. Basquiat, together with Haring, John Ahearn (see fig. 26.40) and Kiki Smith (see fig. 27.10), contributed works that attracted favorable critical attention. Shortly thereafter, Basquiat struck out on his own, and his drawing soon revealed something more than graphic street smarts—what appeared to be a devotion to Picasso's *Guernica* (see fig. 15.46). Basquiat's color-infused art is characteristically peopled by schematic figures with large, flattened, African-mask faces set against fields

26.36 Jean-Michel Basquiat, *Grillo*, 1984. Oil on wood with nails, 8' × 17'6½" × 1'6" (2.4 × 5.3 × 0.46 m). Stefan T. Edlis Collection, Chicago.

26.37 Kenny Scharf, *When the Worlds Collide*, 1984. Oil, acrylic, and enamel spray paint on canvas, 10'2" × 17'5¼" (3.1 × 5.3 m). Whitney Museum of American Art, New York.

vigorously activated by such graffiti elements as words and phrases, arrows and grids, crowns, rockets, and skyscrapers. As in the work of Polke and Salle, the compositional force of Basquiat's work lies not in its fidelity to expected rules of composition, but rather in the poetic juxtaposition—sometimes abrasive, sometimes soothing—of a variety of images, signs, and symbols. Quite apart from his compelling sense of drawing, color, and composition, Basquiat seemed to be able to balance the contradictory demands expected of a young African-American in the artworld of the early eighties. His figural style suggested the simulated primitivism of much Neo-Expressionism, but seemed to come with the cache of Basquiat's race and biography. Politics aside, the rhythmic dirge of *Grillo* (fig. **26.36**) demonstrates that the artist was adept at coordinating graphic power with textual filigree to provide elements of formal grace and often brutal content. Basquiat's life and work has provided material for a variety of writers to reconsider the expectations of the artworld and the role of expression, biography, race, money, and talent in the history and production of art. His early death left a significant artistic potential untapped.

Kenny Scharf (b. 1958) also worked briefly with graffiti artists, but he took his primary inspiration from the space-age fantasy world of children's animated TV cartoons, such as *The Jetsons*, a series generated virtually next door to where Scharf grew up in Los Angeles. At first, the artist developed his signature style three-dimensionally, as he "customized" all the electronic gear in the building used for the Times Square Show, and then created a series of "Closets", complete rooms "bombed" with Scharf's characteristically whimsical spraypaint assault. To customize radios, TVs, telephones, furniture, and whole environments, Scharf applied to these objects and spaces all manner of "salvage"—kitsch items such as plastic dinosaurs, toy robots, fake furs, ropes of tinsel, old hood ornaments, a deer head—which he then spraypainted to unify the mishmash forms and spaces.

Scharf also painted on canvas. In one vast work, entitled *When the Worlds Collide* (fig. **26.37**) and measuring some ten by seventeen feet (3 × 5 m), he fused, "in a kind of fun-house big bang," what critic Gerald Marzorati called "the Saturday-morning innocence, the phone-doodle psychedelia, the magpie delirium, the electric chromatic dazzle … " Here, against a spaced-out background divided into maplike fields of empyrean blue, soft-focus jellybeans, star-studded black holes, and loopy stretch springs, a huge, shiny, sharp-focus red mountain metamorphoses into a jolly monster with a waterfall tumbling over one shoulder and a moonscape visible in the depths of his broad grin. All about this goofy, improbable creature float whirling cannonballs, cotton-candy clouds, disembodied eyes and mouths, wriggling amoeboids, and an orange-colored, saber-toothed, cross-eyed pixie. In *When the Worlds Collide*, Tanguy-like illusionistic Surrealism or the doomsday world of Hieronymus Bosch has been reconceived by a California cartoonist, an artist certain that "you definitely cannot have too much fun" and equipped to go about it with the compositional and *trompe l'oeil* ambitions of a Tiepolo. Scharf applies the style of hyperrealism to the subject matter of visual media in order to telescope in on the prominence of fantasy in American culture.

Wojnarowicz and Wong

Another alumnus of the East Village scene, **David Wojnarowicz** (1954–92) began his brief career scrawling politicized invectives and stenciled slogans in public places. An artist with a flair for drama to match the volatile life he led, Wojnarowicz developed a collage aesthetic that surrounded the viewer with the brutality of contemporary life. He was a prolific writer and photographer, as well as a painter, sculptor, video artist, musician, and performer. Wojnarowicz's installations recorded the personal pain of growing up gay in the United States and the continued cost of homophobia and AIDS. His graphic work effectively juxtaposed the romanticism of Arthur Rimbaud, one of Wojnarowicz's influences (and, in one series of photographs, his alter ego), with the landscape and mindscape of contemporary America. The results are harrowing

26.38 David Wojnarowicz, *Fire*, 1987. Acrylic and mixed media on wood, 72 × 96" (1.83 × 2.44 m).

assaults on the treatment of the individual that resonate with almost apocalyptic fervor. *Fire* (fig. **26.38**) was created the year the artist was diagnosed with AIDS and the year his lover, the photographer Peter Hujar, died of the disease. The image contrasts manmade power with the power of nature and crime. In a comic and biting detail, the dungbeetle is shown to possess a human brain. *Fire* and the *Four Elements Series* of which it is part, have been interpreted as an attempt to visualize a worldview that might bring sense to the loss and violence surrounding the artist.

Martin Wong (1946–99) was a painter who took public writing, including graffiti, sign language, and even charts of the constellations, as a foundation for his art. Wong began his career while working as a courtroom artist and there is a strong communicative element in his art. Though his work is figural—one of his most controversial paintings, *The Big Heat* (1988), represents two firemen wrapped in each others' arms as a building smolders behind them—Wong most often replaced the physiognomic detail required of a portraitist with a sensitivity to the expressive potential of the urban environment. *Attorney Street Handball Court with Autobiographical Poem by Pinero* (1982–84) (fig. **26.39**) is a landscape of a lower Manhattan playground with Wong's stylized sign language notation of a poem by Miguel Pinero. Above the floating signs, graffiti adorns the urban playground, poetry fills the

sky. The title of the painting is written in gold and black on simulated and constructed frames. The author of the poem, Miguel Pinero, stood at the center of the Nuyorican Poetry movement, a group of writers committed to creating literature at the intersection of Latino and US cultures and languages. Pinero's work resonated with Wong's own commitment to an art responsive to the multiethnic, multicultural, and polyglot community in which he lived. Wong's painting, like that of Jasper Johns or Sigmar Polke, presents the viewer with a collection of different means of communication, though within the context of lower Manhattan and with a romantic eye toward its residents. In a graceful mingling of poetry, painting, and the street itself, Wong gives form to the metaphor of the city as text.

Postmodern Arenas: Installation Art

Installation works of many different kinds were created throughout the sixties and seventies, by artists who also worked in Performance, such as Nam June Paik, Joseph Beuys, and Rebecca Horn, and by artists with links to Conceptual art, such as Jonathan Borofsky and Christopher Burden. The special potential of environmental works, however, came to the fore in the eighties. Since we can walk around inside them, such works lend themselves to interpretation as scale models of the world at large, and

26.39 Martin Wong, *Attorney Street: Handball Court with Autobiographical Poem by Pinero*, 1982–84. Oil on canvas, 2'11½" × 4' (0.90 × 1.22 m).

installations made in this "retrospective" decade increasingly seemed like comments on the state of the Postmodern world. Some of these installations were specifically sites of memory, as in Christian Boltanski's work—places to reflect on the troubled history of the twentieth century and the role played by art within it. For many artists working in this mode, such as Ilya Kabakov, the lofty aspirations of early modernist art had collapsed. Meanwhile, artists such as Bill Viola and Jenny Holzer, who turned to new electronic technologies, did so with a wary, skeptical irony, undercutting any great faith in the Brave New World of the future.

In 1980, the CoLab collective of artists created the Times Square Show in an abandoned building on 42nd street. The show set off the decade with an impulse to fill the interiors of the artworld with the detritus of the streets, alleys, subway tunnels, peep shows, movie houses, studios, parks, and vacant lots of the city. The obsession with crime and degradation that filled the Times Square Show—simulated rats crawled through the rooms, and rape and other acts of violence were depicted again and again—was relieved in a few notable works. Kenny Scharf's delightful space age decorations were one and the sculptural oeuvre of CoLab organizer John Ahearn provided another.

John Ahearn (b. 1951) was an upstate New York artist who, with his associate Rigoberto Torres, chose to live in the South Bronx and there portray its citizens in a series of relief sculptures. Like George Segal and Duane Hanson before him (see figs. 21.24, 24.76), Ahearn makes life casts that comment on human relationships and society at large. Ahearn's content of indomitable subjectivity is generated through realistically rendered faces, their intense gazes conveying ferocious dignity. The artist has said: "The basic foundation for the work is art that has a popular basis, not just in appeal, but in its origin and meaning. … It can mean something here, and also in a museum." Certainly the reliefs communicate a great deal in gallery settings, but by "here," Ahearn means the exterior walls above the very streets in which his subjects live and work (fig. **26.40**). Even in the neighborhood, however, Ahearn's placement is carefully selected to suggest content. *Homage to the People of the Bronx: Double Dutch at Kelly Street I: Freida, Jevette, Towana, Stacey* (1981–82) was installed on an exterior wall several stories above the ground. Ahearn applied a surrealist manipulation of the ordinary and rather straightforward symbolism to suggest that the footing these children have as they navigate the complexities of life expressed in the two ever-circling jump-ropes is far from stable. So popular are these open-air installations that the artist's neighbors compete to sit for twenty minutes with their heads covered by a fast-setting dental plastic. From the molds this creates, Ahearn then casts the form in fiberglass. But what brings the works to life is his immense gift for color, which allows

26.40 John Ahearn, *Homage to the People of the Bronx: Double Dutch at Kelly Street I: Freida, Jevette, Towana, Stacey*, 1981–82. Oil on fiberglass, figures lifesize. Kelly Street, South Bronx, New York.

Ahearn to evoke the ambient light and heat of skin itself. In a curious turn on dialectics akin to Robert Smithson's site/nonsite (see fig. 24.45), Ahearn creates two copies of each work, one for collectors and museums and the other to stay rooted in the community, in the possession of the person whom it represents.

Pepon Osorio (b. 1955) has found installation to be a means to make art in, of, and for the Puerto Rican

26.41 Pepon Osorio, *La Cama (The Bed)*, 1987. Mixed media installation; bed 75 × 67 × 78" (190 × 170 × 198 cm), room dimensions 450 × 450' (137 × 137 m). Collection El Museo del Barrio.

community. The enveloping nature of his format, often room-size environments bursting with all forms of decorative elements from beads and flowers to baseball cards and bicycles, mimics what Osorio understands to be a Puerto Rican aesthetic but one that embraces his viewers regardless of their background. During his early career, Osorio worked as a caseworker in the New York City department of Children's Services and he is committed to an art of social conscience. Osorio defines artistic success as the unification of the individual, nation or larger community, and universal. *The Bed* (fig. **26.41**), a piece dedicated to the memory of Juana Hernandez, the woman who lived with his family and helped raise him, demonstrates the multiple references in Osorio's work. In the center of a room rests a large bed adorned with *capias*, souvenirs given in Puerto Rico at weddings, baptisms, and anniversaries. The installation presents loss through the lens of culturally specific rituals of celebration, thus inviting a nation of celebrants to comfort the artist and praise the dead. *The Bed* invites the artist's audience into a family experience in his own home: other installations focus on the choices and lives of fictionalized families. Often accompanied by performances, Osorio's art moves freely between fact and fiction, as well as personal and social realities, and always with an "aesthetics of abundance" that identifies his roots and his art.

Ilya Kabakov (b. 1933) grew up in the former Soviet Union during the harsh Stalinist era. Trained as an artist from an early age, for many years he earned his living as an illustrator of stories, most of them for children, while privately he made elaborate albums combining poetic, sometimes bizarre, tales and drawings. Kabakov began creating full-scale environmental pieces in the mid-eighties. They, too, contained elements of narrative, often revealing the difficulties and privations of Soviet daily life, but also conveying information through fantastical gatherings of objects, or what has been called Kabakov's "material poetry." After the collapse of the communist state, these works took on the character of archeological sites, where visitors could explore the cultural history of a vanished system.

In *The Man Who Flew into Space from His Apartment* (fig. **26.42**), the hardships of ordinary people are ironically juxtaposed with the grandiose projects of the state—in this case, apparently, the Soviet space program, which launched the first human being into orbit. About this fantasy work Kabakov said:

> The person who lived here flew into space from his room, first having blown up the ceiling and the attic above it. He always, as far as he remembered, felt that he was not quite an inhabitant of this earth, and constantly felt the desire to leave it, to escape beyond its boundaries. And as an adult he conceived of his departure into space.

The room we see, with a gaping hole in its roof, contains the debris left behind by the astronaut's improvised take-off: broken dishes, the remains of some simple furniture,

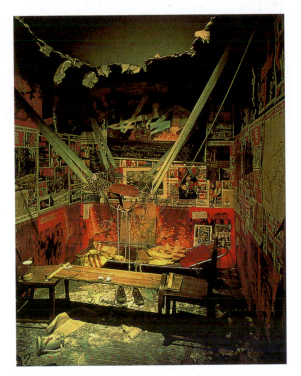

26.42 Ilya Kabakov, *The Man Who Flew into Space from His Apartment*, 1981–88. From the installation *10 Characters*. Six poster panels with collage, furniture, clothing, catapult, household objects, wooden plank, scroll-type painting, two pages of Soviet paper, diorama. Room dimensions 8' × 7'11" × 12'3" (2.4 × 2.4 × 3.7 m).

and stray items of worn clothing. Glued to the walls are various political posters as well as the traveler's blueprints, flight plans, and calculations; from the ceiling hangs the catapult that flung him away from it all, up into outer space. On a small model of a city, which has a light bulb for a sun, a strip of curved metal rising from an apartment building shows the planned trajectory of "the one who flew away."

Like many of the Neo-Expressionists, French installation artist **Christian Boltanski** (b. 1944) also deals with European memories of World War II. Boltanski was born in Paris on Liberation Day (September 6, 1944), as the Allied armies entered the city, and his middle name is Liberté. He often created works for prisons, hospitals, and schools—institutional sites much concerned with the consequences, and the lessons, of the past. In a series of elegies that evoke the Holocaust, Boltanski hung up slightly blurred photographs of children and surrounded them with groups of small electric bulbs that cast a glow like candlelight in a place of worship (fig. **26.43**). Some of his other works evoke feelings that are considerably less overwhelming, and more mixed. *The Shadows*, for example, combines the macabre and the playful, suspending simple figurines in front of lights so that they cast large, ominous shadows on the walls. Little paper dolls hung by the neck and skeletons dangling in midair start to look like the indeterminate shapes a small child might be afraid of in the dark. At the same time, they give a knowing twist to the tradition of the Balinese puppet-shadow theater.

The American video artist **Bill Viola** (b. 1951) has also examined the theme of memory. Viola creates not just videotapes but entire installations that employ objects, video images, and recorded sound. He has long been interested in how the eye and brain process visual information, and he seeks to reveal their workings in his art. In *The Theater of Memory* (fig. **26.44**), an uprooted tree lies diagonally across the floor of a darkened room. In its branches are dozens of lanterns. A video image is projected against one wall. At intervals, white noise, mostly static, erupts from the speakers, separated by long periods of silence. Of this installation Viola said:

> I remember reading about the brain and the central nervous system, trying to understand what causes the trigger-

ing of nerve firings that recreate patterns of past sensations, finally evoking a memory. I came across the fact that all of the neurons in the brain are physically disconnected from each other, beginning and ending in a tiny gap of empty space. The flickering pattern evoked by the tiny sparks of thought bridging these gaps becomes the actual form and substance of our ideas.

His installation is a kind of working model of the brain's physiology, as if the viewer were standing inside the "theater" of a fantastically huge cranium. The lanterns are like the "tiny sparks of thought" that ignite along the branching "tree" of our intricate neural network; the projected video image evokes the "show" that memory replays before our mind's eye. It is a decidedly mechanistic, even clinical, view of how human consciousness operates, but a certain romantic sense of mystery is nonetheless supplied by the dramatically lit tree, the archaic lanterns, and the darkened theatrical space.

In the Empire of Signs: Varieties of Neo-Geo

The term Neo-Geo refers to the work of artists impressed with the theoretical potential of Appropriation that used anything from Minimalist blocks to vacuum-cleaners for their identity as bearers of content, though not necessarily that most readily associated with them. Recontextualization was key, but, unlike their Appropriationist peers, Neo-Geo artists were also interested in expression. At times objects that would seem to be important for their social function filled primarily expressive and aesthetic roles. The work of the most prominent of the Neo-Geo artists, Peter Halley, consisted of squares and rectangles whose form and meaning were determined by a set of social circumstances rather than formal ones. Halley associated his forms, called circuits, with the networks of communication and power in contemporary civilization. Neo-Geo artists intentionally enlisted the history and connotations of a form when they composed rather than hoping for a resonance between the shapes on the canvas and the soul of the viewer, as modernists often had. The understanding that there is specific meaning rather than generalized expression in abstract form was clearly articulated in the mid- to late eighties, and continues to underlie presumptions about abstraction today.

Neo-Geo Abstraction

Peter Halley (b. 1953) was the undisputed leader of Neo-Geo. In a series of paintings based on Albers' *Homage to the Square* (see fig. 17.9), Halley treated the square, in his own words, "as a sign for certain kinds of regimented or confining structures in the social landscape." His emphasis on the restrictive nature of postindustrial society reflects the influence of Michel Foucault's essay on confinement, while his equation of a seemingly abstract sign with "the social landscape" derives from Jean Baudrillard's notion of "hyperreality." Halley and others took from Foucault the insight that the regulated geometry of modern society, from the calendar to the office building, were sites where modern ideas of geometric purity and authoritarian control coincided. The compatibility between modernist geometric and the regulation of nearly every part of our lives was, it was suggested, no coincidence. The intuition that modern art was connected to modern industry had informed machine age art from between the wars on both sides of the Atlantic. In a deconstructive move, Foucault stripped the myth of progress from the relationship to reveal a more oppressive regime. Neo-Geo relied on this Postmodern insight, but resisted the impulse, so strong in modernist art, to transform a new idea into the foundation for an art of revelation.

The challenge for Halley was how to express content without substituting one deconstructed truth for another; how, in other words we can tell that Halley's geometric conduits were different from the industrial abstractions of Charles Sheeler or Paul Strand (see figs. 18.27, 18.21). Halley used the writing of Baudrillard to explain that, though he relied on Foucault's insight, he, unlike the machine-age artist, did not claim to be presenting the connection between art and industry as a key to human nature. According to Baudrillard, two linked systems, international capitalism and mass media, force everyone to live in a glittering "empire of signs" where "hyperreal" images "simulate" and supplant ordinary reality. Paintings like *Two Cells with Circulating Conduit* (fig. **26.45**) "simulate" this "empire" by presenting the high-tech equivalent of its "plumbing"—squares, to be understood as both battery and prison cells, connected by lines or "conduits" for the "circulation" of information and power. Halley, whose writings and interviews are often brought together with his paintings to form a single, pictorial–theoretical package, contends that his work collapses "the idea of the abstract and the representational" and gives abstraction a content. An important element in Halley's work is his use of Day-Glo paint, stucco surfaces, and, in more recent work, neon-colored wallpaper. These elements draw on an aesthetic of artifice that resists comparison to earlier modernists'

26.45 Peter Halley, *Two Cells with Circulating Conduit*, 1985. Acrylic, Day-Glo acrylic, and Roll-a-Tex on canvas, 5'4" × 8'8" (1.63 cm × 2.6 m). Collection Cooper Fund, Inc.

quests for truth. Through such devices, Halley simulates traditional artist's color and evokes the dramatic beauty of the information age. Most importantly, through color and theory, Neo-Geo forced past styles of abstraction to signify new meanings rather than, as critics would claim of Neo-Expressionism, force contemporary minds to appreciate recuperated styles.

Ross Bleckner (b. 1949) was quickly associated with Neo-Geo by Halley and others for his use of vivid stripes to make large-scale, abstract paintings. His work is closely related to that of artists such as Sherrie Levine, who made "generic" versions of past styles in order to deconstruct modernist myths (see fig. 26.2). However, Bleckner differed in his concentrated attempt to move beyond deconstruction to paint images about life and loss in contemporary America. Bleckner's often obsessively repeated patterns do not simply allude to sixties Op art; they simulated the hard-edged style in a way that reflects a Poststructuralist critique of the modernist history of twentieth-century abstraction as a progressive unfolding of styles, each built upon the other, each "heroic and original" and unrepeatable. By throwing the "correct" sequence awry with the appropriation of an "incorrect" style such as Op, Bleckner showed that the past offers a variety of possibilities and has no fixed, necessary relationship to contemporary artistic practice or meaning.

26.46 Ross Bleckner, *Seeing and Believing*, 1981. Oil and wax on canvas, 9'6" × 4'6" (2.9 × 1.37 m).

As if to reinforce the point, in 1983 Bleckner started to exhibit somber paintings, such as *Two Nights Not Nights* (fig. **26.46**), in which evocations of spectral landscapes are combined with symbols—hands, torches, flowers, and urns—culled from the Baroque iconography of death and salvation. Such tenebrist paintings were among the earliest memorials to the victims of AIDS, which was first identified in 1982. Painted with wax and ground pigment rather than prepared paint, they are brilliant demonstrations of a return to old-master techniques, which Bleckner shared with another CalArts-trained artist, Eric Fischl (see fig. 26.27).

Commodity Art

Though apparently quite different from the painting of Halley and Bleckner, Neo-Geo also encompasses sculpture by Jeff Koons, Haim Steinbach, and Ashley Bickerton, which manipulated the commodities of capitalism as the painters had manipulated styles. This art functioned like its nonobjective counterpart, but consisted of recognizable elements from popular culture. Michael Jackson or a lava lamp might be incorporated into a work to perform an aesthetic function as well as to indicate a range of potential meanings. The completed works were no more limited to the specific significance of their contents than Halley's or Bleckner's were restricted to an art about squares and starbursts. Like Levine or Prince, Koons and company appropriated their objects from mass culture and re-presented it. Unlike Appropriation art, however, the theoretical position of the commodity artists was painfully unclear. Not only did the work seem to fetishize its materials rather than analytically re-contextualize them, but while Halley and his critics referred to Foucault, Baudrillard, or Smithson, the commodity side of Neo-Geo played at a Warholesque naïvety.

Jeff Koons (b. 1955) started showing elegant Minimalist arrangements of consumer goods in a small independent gallery with Peter Halley, Meyer Vaisman, and Ashley Bickerton in 1985. Within one year, he had graduated to a blue-chip operation in Soho. *New Hoover* (fig. **26.47**) is typical of these early sculptures in its clear gridded composition and its commitment to leaving the new materials (similar to those Donald Judd had found so exciting in the early sixties—see fig. 22.47) affixed to the commercial products for which they were intended. Here is a classical Minimalism of merchandise that brought together the economic and psychological satisfaction of fine art and the commodity. It was also clear that this ex-stockbroker had a refined aesthetic sense.

Koons soon left the Minimalism frame and focussed on the ambiguous potential of commodities of much lower form than vacuum cleaners. In an exhibition entitled The Banality Show, Koons presented exquisitely crafted porcelain renderings of kitsch, perhaps the one category of objects from toilets to haute couture that had not yet been taken as a suitable subject for art. Koons, like the Appropriation artists, seemed content to omit any obvious

26.47 Jeff Koons, *New Hoover Quadraflex, New Hoover Convertible, New Hoover Dimension 900, New Hoover Dimension 1000*, 1981–86. Hoover vacuum cleaners, acrylic glass, and fluorescent light, 8'3" × 4'5½" × 2'4" (2.5 × 1.36 × 0.71 m). Private collection.

signs of his own creative act. Unlike Levine and others whose practice the Banality Show invoked, however, Koons did not critically reframe his selected forms. In discussing his art, Koons evinces a surprising commitment to a rather modernist belief in essences rather than a Postmodern conviction in the constructed. Claiming with disarming innocence: "I think about my work every minute of the day," he has explained that he aims to reveal the true nature of his object by putting in a place where that nature is exposed. He equates this with putting a shy person in public where you can really see their shyness. The subjects of *Michael Jackson and Bubbles* (fig. **26.48**), it is supposed, revealed in the delicate finish of porcelain under the heat of the gallery lights, offer up their true and rather unsettling spirit. Despite his claims for a new realism, Koons, like Halley, capitalized on artifice, presenting objects that, while they reveal something of the fixations of American culture, suggest that the desires that created Michael Jackson and Bubbles are simulated and correspond to nothing more real than television.

26.48 Jeff Koons, *Michael Jackson and Bubbles*, 1988. Porcelain, 3'6 × 5'10½" × 2'8½" (1.06 × 1.79 × 0.83 m).

The Banality Show was created as an ensemble, and though individual works stood alone, the effect was a composition of simulated desires in which Koons himself posed, with leather jacket and fashion-model looks, as its centerpiece.

Composing with commodities took a variety of forms. Perhaps the most elegant of these were the sparse organized collections of **Haim Steinbach** (b. 1944). On customized shelves, Steinbach arranged what looked like the results of a trip to the mall. Beside a field of six Dreammachine radio alarm clocks rises a tower of red pots looking like a Renaissance bell tower or, following the suggestion of the four lava lamps to its right, an erupting volcano. *Ultra Red #2* (fig. **26.49**) encourages the viewer to think in terms of countdowns and explosions, volcanoes and Italian landscapes, in a consumer reworking of the destruction of Pompeii, but, like Steinbach's work in general, is more about color and form. In the early sixties, Frank Stella (see fig. 22.41) professed that his goal as a painter was to permit the paint on his canvases to be as beautiful as it was in the can. Paint was conceived as a found object to be arranged but not transformed in the final work. Steinbach's palette is comprised of consumer items rather than paint, but his aesthetic is strikingly similar.

If Steinbach used consumer goods to create abstractions that perhaps could be seen as landscapes, **Ashley Bickerton** (b. 1959) was most known for his portraits. Moving even farther from the realm of human experience, Bickerton chose not even the products we desire but their brand names as his material. On rather overbuilt and mechanical-looking apparatuses, Bickerton creates ironic assemblages of logos that he then gives emotionally loaded titles like *Tormented Self-Portrait Suzie at Arles* (fig. **26.50**).

26.50 Ashley Bickerton, *Tormented Self-Portrait Suzie at Arles*, 1988. Mixed media construction with padded leather, 90 × 69 × 18" (2.29 × 1.75 × 0.46 m).

26.49 Haim Steinbach, *Ultra Red #2*, 1986. Mixed media construction, 63 × 76 × 19" (160 × 193 × 480 cm).

One can construct a narrative out of the indicated products, imagining, perhaps, a romantic breakup on a road trip in Southern France to rationalize the title, but the work offers little support for such an endeavor. Even the title and the artist's signature, the two human elements in the work, are emblazoned across the work's surface with all the superficiality of "TV Guide" and "MARLBORO." In Bickerton's ironic, if not cynical, world, no one subject, Suzie or cigarettes, is any more substantial than another. The portrait suggests Postmodern ideas about the importance of social context to generate meaning and the fluid and impressionable nature of identity.

Ramifications of Neo-Geo

In the early nineties, several artists produced work that seemed to reconcile the theoretical content of the abstract Neo-Geo and the evocative and commercially sensitive features of the Commodity artists. Janine Antoni's *Gnaw* of 1992 illustrates an impulse to clarify the politically critical possibilities of a combination of Halley and Koons, while Sylvie Fleury embraced the ambiguity of Commodity art from a feminist perspective. By the nineties, the

26.51 Janine Antoni, *Gnaw*, 1992. 600lb cube of chocolate gnawed by the artist, 24 × 24 × 24" (61 × 61 × 61 cm). Collection of The Museum of Modern Art.

significance of form, whether abstract or commodity, was being articulated in ways that were clearly directive or pointedly ambivalent.

At first glance, *Gnaw* (fig. **26.51**), by **Janine Antoni** (b. 1964), appears to be a pair of Minimalist cubes slightly worn at the edges and emitting an odd organic smell; in fact one is made of fat and the other of chocolate. The degradation at the edges of the works are the result of the artist gnawing at the sculptures, chewing off and spitting out mouthfuls of lard and chocolate. Living with the two cubes until she had carved away the right amount of material, Antoni then reconstituted the masticated discharge into bright red lipstick and heart-shaped candy trays to be displayed in elegant mirrored cases worthy of any fine jewelers' (fig. **26.52**). Despite the complexity of the process and the installation, *Gnaw* is surprisingly succinct. Three familiar objects, lipstick, chocolates, and Minimalist cubes, are brought together through a performance that, although not seen by the viewer, is as physical and politically aware as those of performance artist Carolee Schneemann and one that generates a feminist critique of art and fashion. With objects as clean and polished as a Donald Judd cube or a *Vogue* magazine, Antoni juxtaposes abstractions of geometry, fashion, and economics in the vein of Neo-Geo, but with a clear direction not seen in the earlier work.

Sylvie Fleury (b. 1961) has brought specificity to the insights of Neo-Geo, although in her work one is confronted with the commercial presumption that underlay the work of Koons and Bickerton—that we are shaped by the things we buy—but is left uncertain how to feel about it. Fleury has displayed the residue of shopping sprees,

26.52 Janine Antoni, *Lipstick Display* (detail), 1992. Lipstick made with pigment, beeswax, and chewed lard removed from *Lard Gnaw* and heart-shaped packaging tray for chocolates made from chewed chocolate removed from *Chocolate Gnaw*. Collection of The Museum of Modern Art.

26.53 Sylvie Fleury, *Formula One Dress*, 1998.

collections of designer shopping bags, shoes, and boxes. She has also created her own fashions including a series of *Formula One* dresses (fig. **26.53**) that turns the woman who wears them into the female equivalent of a corporate sponsored racing team. Using the adolescent and sexist comparison of a woman and a sportscar, Fleury creates a graphic illustration of a woman defined by social prejudices and commercial products. Like the subject of Bickerton's *Tormented Self-Portrait* (see fig. 26.50), the woman who wears Fleury's dress is branded by the logos of global capitalism in a clear equation of fashion, sexism, capitalism, and sport. The irony, however, is that despite the clarity of Fleury's equation she seems to be having fun. She models the clothes with elan and continues to shop. Awareness of the forces of society does not lead to resistance as it might have even in the early eighties. Rather, the artist seems to take the inevitable appeal of sex and commerce, whether at the racetrack or the mall, as a source of pleasure and even power. In 1987, Barbara Kruger created the image/text piece *I Shop Therefore I Am*, which in the context of the moment was the personal and ironic complement to works such as Jenny Holzer's 1982 *Private Property Created Crime*. In 1999 such a statement could be taken seriously.

The Sum of Many Parts: Abstraction in the 1980s

Though overshadowed by the dramatic and sometimes shocking return of figuration in the conceptually challeng-ing appropriation or the emotionally wrenching Neo-Expressionism, a critical point had been reached in the history of abstraction by the eighties. As is clear from the work and writing of the Neo-Geo artists, if not in the polemical critiques of Neo-Expressionism, it could no longer be presumed that there was a direct connection between abstract forms on a canvas and either emotional responses or intuitive meaning. The time had passed when Kandinsky could talk about a direct connection between a color and the soul of the viewer or Pollock could place faith in the potency of his "get acquainted period" to result in painterly expressions that reached from his experience to that of mankind. Painting, as it has been said, was compromised. It was not, however, as some prematurely announced, dead. The eighties, and nineties as well, wit-nessed a number of artists committed to working with the abstract tradition to articulate its boundaries and expressive as well as intellectual potential.

"All my work," the American painter **Elizabeth Murray** (b. 1940) asserted, "is involved with conflict—trying to make something disparate whole." In 1979–80 Murray realized a major breakthrough in her art. She began to break up not the image but rather the canvas, "shattering" it into separate shards or fragments (fig. **26.54**). Further compounding the conflict was the wall, revealed through the cracks as one more participant in the battle for the viewer's eye. To make such disintegration whole again, Murray, drawing on her academic background, reintro-duced figuration, and imposed upon the entire archipelago

26.54 Elizabeth Murray, *Art Part*, 1981. Twenty-two canvases, overall 9'7" × 10'4" (2.9 × 3.1 m). Private collection.

of island canvases an image simple enough—brushes, palettes, cups, the painter's own hand—to be detected as a unifying factor. In addition, Murray adopted a painting style that was as informed by cartoons as by the history of postwar abstraction. The cohesion of Murray's broken canvases could be experienced only by observers sufficiently attentive to "read" across the relief map of fractures and fields, visually and conceptually piecing the whole together like a puzzle.

Subsequently, Murray created large relief paintings with more unified imagery, even though fissures through the surface were still evident. These reliefs were generally based on such domestic items as old shoes with writhing shoelaces, or tables and cups, all given a certain awkwardness that made them seem vulnerable and even endearing. The objects become stand-ins for their human users, and are thus laden with psychological overtones.

It has been said that the American artist **Terry Winters** (b. 1949) "dreams science into art," a tendency that particularly extends to the science of biology. This is an interest not without precedents in modern art. After examining illustrations in scientific journals, Vasily Kandinsky near the end of his career portrayed microorganisms in a way that turned them into abstract shapes floating in space. Winters also painted shapes based on such organisms (along with botanical forms like buds, seeds, tubers, and spores), an interest in both artists' work that can be related to biomorphic Surrealism. But unlike the Russian, who generally focused in on one or two individual microscopic creatures, Winters suggests the dynamic interaction among the elements of a diverse community or colony as they grow, develop, and compete.

Winters spent three months working on the large painting called *Good Government* (fig. 26.55), which he started without any particular title in mind. At the beginning, he struggled to bring coherence to its anarchic array of very different forms—from expansive blastulas to hard crystals to floating fragments of chromosomes. But at last, he said, he "thought it looked like one of those maps you saw in grammar school and it said 'good government' and everything was working together." Like a system of checks and balances, these abstracted organic forms make up a complex compositional scheme, while the carefully modulated textures of this painting keep its contending shapes in "organic" relationship with one another that threatens like Malevich's black square (see chapter 11), not to be a composition at all.

Philip Taaffe (b. 1955) took abstract art as the source for his own abstract works. In a spirit akin to Appropriation,

26.55 Terry Winters, *Good Government*, 1984. Oil on linen, 8'5¼" × 11'5¼" (2.6 × 3.5 m). Whitney Museum of American Art, New York.

Neo-Geo, and even Richter's abstract painting, Taaffe used drawing, painting, printing, and collage to create what he calls "representations of abstract paintings." Drawing upon a nearly encyclopedic repertoire of decorative motifs from Western and non-Western sources, Taaffe is sometimes quite direct, recreating specific paintings by Barnett Newman and Clifford Still, for instance. In other cases, genres of modernist abstraction are the general source of his inspiration. *Big Iris* (fig. **26.56**) is a curious union between Georgia O'Keeffe's big flower paintings and Op art of the sixties, which joins the organic content of the former to the hypnotic visual effect of the latter. Collage, though linked to the avant-garde practice of Cubism, is also associated with craft traditions that were the aesthetic and feminist basis of Pattern and Decoration in the seventies. Calling decorative art a "culturalizatized representation of nature," Taaffe has found in it a means to incorporate representation into his abstractions. The cultural breadth of his sources alludes to any number of artistic traditions. Taaffe's heterodox selection of motifs conspires to position his modernist sources as just one tradition among many with which artists may create historically conscious abstract painting.

Born in Dublin and educated in London, **Sean Scully** (b. 1945) moved to New York in 1973. Initially, the artist used stripes in large, densely woven "super-grids," painted in a style inspired by Mondrian, the English Vorticist David Bomberg, Agnes Martin, Brice Marden, and Sol LeWitt. Scully uses his stripes as the vehicles of an emotional or spiritual content much greater than anything obtainable from pure retinal stimulation.

Beginning with his diptychs, Scully progressively elaborated his simple vocabulary of striped panels into a language of such breadth and subtlety that each painting emerged like "a physical event, a physical personality, just like people." His colors range from brilliant, clashing primaries to tawny mustards and creamy ochers, all warmed by long, sensuous strokes freely wavering over traces of contrasting oilstick color, the latter set down freehand. Scully moved from diptychs to immense eight-by-ten-foot polyptychs (fig. **26.57**), assembled from panels so various in their dimensions and depths, in their colors, widths, and directions of their banding, that they seemed like interactive social beings abstracted into iconic versions of processional figures in a classical relief or, geometric variations on Matisse's famous reliefs (see fig. 9.5). In this larger scheme, the colors and horizontal orientation assume the scale and atmosphere of landscape even as they recall monumental figural art.

In 1979, **Tim Rollins** (b. 1955) co-founded Group Material, an artists' collective that developed curatorial strategies for creating what one critic called "the conditions necessary for making communication possible." For Group Material, this included shows like The People's Choice, which featured treasured objects owned and displayed by their neighbors. Rollins took this social commitment into the classroom in the mid-eighties as a public school art teacher to low-income African-American and Latino teens in New York City. In 1984 he created a workshop with the students called KOS—"Kids of Survival."

The art created by Rollins and KOS took literature as its starting point and abstraction as the visual point of reference. Using texts such as *The Autobiography of Malcolm X*, Franz Kafka's *Amerika*, or Flaubert's *Temptation of Saint Anthony*, Rollins and the students sought to connect the themes of the books to events and concerns in their daily lives. These investigations were then used as the sources for abstract compositions that were painted onto the pages of the books. The results appropriate the text of the books as the literal and metaphoric support for an abstract art that came to be linked both to modernist concerns with the expressive potential of abstraction and Neo-Geo insights into the relationship between abstract form and cultural contexts.

The Temptation of Saint Anthony—The Trinity (fig. **26.58**) is a three-canvas work that covers the pages of Flaubert's novel, itself a meditation on the temptations of physical desire—with the suggestion through color and geometry of flesh and blood. A porous red ring sits

26.58 Tim Rollins and K.O.S, *The Temptation of Saint Anthony—The Trinity*, 1989–90. Blood on paper and linen, 5'8" × 16' (1.73 m × 4.9 m).

off-center in the middle panel, recalling the targets of Jasper Johns and Ken Noland (see figs. 21.15, 22.20). The red and black of the ring are made from blood. On the left panel two red wounds appear in a gold monochrome while the righthand canvas seems to fill with blood, leaving an even red surface. The connection to AIDS becomes inescapable as the blood seems to flow from a body threatened, like Saint Anthony's, by temptations of the flesh. In a gesture of cultural democracy at its best, Rollins and KOS tear Flaubert's text and the language of modernist abstraction from their nineteenth and early twentieth century contexts to carry meanings relevant to urban life in the late twentieth century.

Strangely Familiar: British and American Sculpture

As painters created Postmodern languages of abstraction, sculptors found great potential in deriving abstract objects from narrative, representational, and found sources. Among a number of contemporary English sculptors of abstract tendency, **Tony Cragg** (b. 1949), has modified techniques of the Minimalist and Process artists, such as grids or scatter works, to exert control over content. A striking series of Cragg's works were created by carefully placing small discards, like airy mosaics, across the floor or wall in abstract patterns of color and shape that balance the effect of the whole with the specificity of the once-useful component parts. Like his fellow Britons Gilbert and George (see fig. 26.30), Cragg represents a generation of artists tired of the purity of English sculpture as represented by Sir Anthony Caro, Henry Moore, and Barbara Hepworth (see figs. 22.40, 17.33, 17.35). Cragg and the two sculptors most often discussed in relation to him, Richard Deacon and Bill Woodrow, found content in the Dada and Pop strategy of bringing into their abstractions all things—including at times representation—considered to be outside its purview. Scavenging and assembling bright fragments from the beaches and dustbins of England, Cragg makes newly relevant the once-useful but now broken, dysfunctional, and environmentally disfiguring products of industry. Often, as in *Britain Seen From the North*

26.60 Richard Deacon, *Tall Tree in the Ear*, 1983–84. Galvanized steel, laminated wood, and blue canvas, 12'3⅝" × 8'2½" × 11'11" (3.7 × 2.5 × 3.6 m). Saatchi Collection, London.

(fig. **26.59**) Cragg's compositions are as disorienting and politically suggestive as his process.

In 1978–79 **Richard Deacon** (b. 1949) read Rainer Maria Rilke's *Sonnets to Orpheus* and conceived a profound admiration for the manner in which "the objects that appear in Rilke's poetry, whilst taking on connotations, retain the quality of actuality." While the many implications of ears, horns, and mouths found in Deacon's sculptures derive ultimately, if obliquely, from Rilke's central metaphor of Orpheus's head, the forms remain too ambiguous to suggest clear, precise images. This dual sense of familiarity and

26.59 Tony Cragg, *Britain Seen From the North*, 1981. Plastic and mixed media, "figure" to left 66⅞ × 23" (170 × 58.4 cm), "Britain" to right 12'1¼" × 22'10¾" (3.7 × 7 m). Tate Gallery, London.

strangeness can be seen in *Tall Tree in the Ear* (fig. **26.60**), where a large blue contour "drawing" in space seems to describe a very large dry bean, held upright by the silvery armature of what could be a pear. Together, the two- and three-dimensional forms conjure the shape and volume of the ear cited in the title, while their size evokes the immensity of the sound issuing from a tree, possibly one with branches full of noisy starlings or with leaves rustling in a strong wind. Mystery and poetry inform this art from beginning to end. Although he called himself a "fabricator," Deacon employed simple methods, such as riveting; he used unaesthetic materials, like steel and linoleum; and he prepared no preliminary drawings or models. Instead, he permits initial idea, material, and process to interact to produce sculptures that announce their presence even as they imply absence.

Martin Puryear (b. 1941) accepted Minimalism's simplicity and gravity but went on to invest his art with a human scale and animistic quality generated by craftsmanly process. Time spent with the Peace Corps in Sierra Leone reinforced Puryear's desire for "independence from technology" and gave him an appreciation of the "magic"—the special meaning or content—that seems to emanate from hand-honed objects. What resulted is an art in which modernist cerebration and tribal atavism, the traditions of Western high art and those of preindustrial craft, do not so

26.62 Judy Pfaff, *Deepwater*, 1980. Installation view, Holly Solomon Gallery, New York.

much fuse as counterbalance one another in a dialectical standoff. The particular magic of *Old Mole* (fig. **26.61**), for example, is to keep several suggestive tensions unresolved: a form that at first looks solid reveals itself as a weave of relatively weightless red cedar. And what appears to be an abstract shape quickly becomes in addition a kind of totem, a "mole"—a form that sits on the floor, looking alert and intelligent. Ultimately, the product of a craft technique is endowed with a sculptural presence, comparable to the transformation that occurs in the work of Brancusi (see chapter 9).

London-born, American-trained **Judy Pfaff** (b. 1946) is best known for her gallery-wide installations (fig. **26.62**), works related not only to those of Jonathan Borofsky and the "scatterwork" Conceptualists (see chapter 24), but also to the abstract illusionism of Al Held, her teacher at Yale. Walking into a Pfaff installation, viewers often sense that they have entered a giant Abstract Expressionist painting—one realized, in this case, as a lush, fluid underwater environment providing total immersion among all manner of strange, tropical flora and fauna, brilliantly colored and suspended in free-floating relationships. To produce her spectacular effects, Pfaff assembled a huge collection of non-art materials—plaster, barbed wire, neon, contact papers, woods, meshes—from junkyards and discount outlets, hardware, lumber, and paint stores. Having transported these "mixed media" to the gallery, along with whatever few artifacts she may have prefabricated in her

26.61 Martin Puryear, *Old Mole*, 1985. Red cedar, 61 × 61 × 32" (154.9 × 154.9 × 81.3 cm). Philadelphia Museum of Art.

studio, Pfaff then worked in an improvisatory manner on site, first by setting up visual oppositions among painted and sculptural elements. With precariously counterbalanced rivalries as her guiding principle, she worked through the space, adding and adjusting, establishing and upsetting formal relationships, all in a continuous flow of inspiration, editing, and fine-tuning.

Pfaff also became an accomplished maker of portable, durable collages and constructed reliefs. These works often counter our expectations by changing the anticipated sizes of things. In *Supermercado*, which is more than eight feet (2.5 m) high, the carefully counterbalanced, brightly painted geometric solids seem to make up an enormously enlarged still life of fruits, vegetables, and bowls (hence the "supermarket" of the title), with a brick wall behind it. Here modest still-life elements aspire to the monumental. Indeed, this gathering of subtly differentiated spheres, disks, and circles might as easily suggest a model of the solar system.

After graduating from the Yale School of Art, the sculptor and painter **Nancy Graves** (1940–95) lived for a time in Italy. At a natural history museum in Florence, she happened upon a group of wax anatomical effigies made in the seventeenth century. In the effigies Graves saw the possibility for a new kind of sculpture. She began making small stuffed animals and assembling them with the aid of found objects. In this menagerie she discovered her now-famous breakthrough image—the Bactrian, or double-humped, camel—a unique form that, because specific, left the artist "free to investigate the boundaries of art making." Graves made several series of full-scale camels, at first fabricating them from table legs, market baskets, polyurethane, plaster, and painted skins. Gradually, however, she progressed toward engineered, portable forms built of steel beams and covered with hide, finally producing the only camels she has allowed to be used for museum exhibition. Although uncannily naturalistic, the Bactrians were not exercises in taxidermy but original creations made without reference to models and brought to life by the artist's own handwork and her meticulous regard for detail, texture, and proportion.

While investigating the form of the camel from the inside out, Graves discovered all manner of parts—fossils, skeletons, bones—that proved interesting in their own right as organic yet abstract forms, eminently suitable to aesthetic reordering. A commission for a bronze version of one of the resulting bone sculptures brought her together with the Tallix Foundry in Beacon, New York. Encountering a new technology launched the artist into a new phase of aesthetic experiment: open-form, polychrome, freestanding constructions combining natural and industrial shapes, often with a filigreed lightness (fig. **26.63**). Graves would arrive at the foundry with shopping bags filled with fern fiddleheads, squid and crayfish, palmetto and monstera leaves, lotus pods and warty gourds, Chinese scissors, pleated lampshades, Styrofoam packing pellets, and potato chips. At Tallix she expanded the reper-

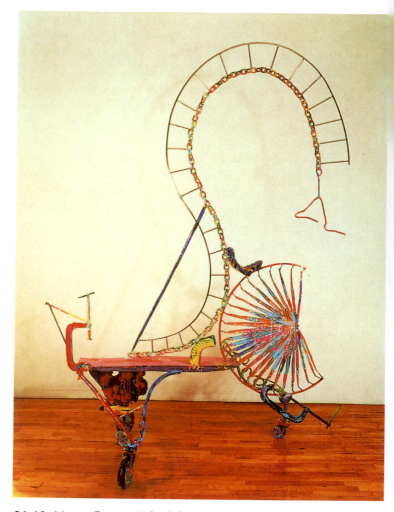

26.63 Nancy Graves, *Wheelabout*, 1985. Bronze and steel with polyurethane paint, 7'8½" × 5'10" × 2'8½" (2.3 × 1.8 m × 0.83 m). Modern Art Museum of Fort Worth, Texas.

toire of forms to include pieces of broken equipment, old drainage pipes and plumbing fixtures, or even spillages of molten metal. After a construction was assembled, Graves applied pigments either by patination or by hand painting, with brushwork as freewheeling and extemporaneous as the structure it embellished.

For his sculpture, **Donald Lipski** (b. 1947) takes parts and makes wholes, but he imagines the whole only after finding—or scavenging—the parts and discovering a kind of surreal logic in some relationship among them. The artist's strategy was to raid junkyards, dustbins, dumpsters, and dime stores and then combine his gleanings in assemblages that astonish and delight with the perfect union of their incompatible parts. Thanks to his ingeniously associative mind, Lipski could easily grasp how the shape and clarity of a crystal ball rendered it ideal for nesting in the cradle of an old telephone. Wrenched from their usual context and reordered in brilliantly dysfunctional ways, commonplace items became strange and wonderful objects of contemplation. While Lipski's work may recall Marcel Duchamp and his readymades, its lack of antiart content and its lyrical obsessiveness give it a more certain kinship with the boxes of Joseph Cornell (see fig. 19.53).

Like his sculptures, Lipski's installation *The Starry Night* (fig. **26.64**) also presents ordinary things in unexpected ways. Here, nearly 25,000 double-edge razor blades were stuck directly into the Sheetrock walls of a gallery. Their swarming, swirling patterns across a large area resemble the cosmic vortex of the nocturnal sky in Van Gogh's famous painting (see fig. 3.22). At the same time, however, and more disturbingly, the thousands of dangerously sharp blades protruding toward the viewer remind us of Van Gogh's self-mutilation and his tortured mental state at that time. With its complex reference combining visionary pleasure and psychological pain, Lipski's *Starry Night* communicates a surprisingly affecting sense of the dangers in an intensely romantic art. Moreover, exhibited during the AIDS epidemic in an exhibition space in San Francisco known for its experimental installations, *Starry Night* would have suggested the far more immediate dangers of romance. Abstraction was defined in *Starry Night*

by the geographical, temporal, and cultural context of its production and, like the most challenging art of the decade, was all the more powerful because of it.

Starry Night, a work of the nineties, is deeply informed by the retrospective examination of modern visual languages in the eighties, from the evocative, painterly vocabulary of Expressionism and the sublime attempts at purity in geometric abstraction to the forms of public address found in the mass media. After a decade of deconstructing visual communication, artists took on the task of rebuilding expressive and narrative forms that would respond to critiques of modernism as well as the continued desire of contemporary society to tell its stories and see its emotions, intuitions, hopes, and fears presented in art. *Starry Night*, with its appeal to art history, its implications for contemporary life, and its delicate combination of abstract form and pictorial interest, sets the tone for the problems to be addressed in the final chapter.

26.64 Donald Lipski, *The Starry Night*, Razor blades on wall. Installation at the Capp Street Project, San Francisco, 1994.

27
Resistance and Resolution

The nineties began with a sudden and irrevocable fusion of art and politics. In Tienanmen Square, Beijing, the aspirations of thousands of protesters were summed up in a sculpture, a painting, and a performance. A model of the Statue of Liberty stood in the crowd; a portrait of Mao spattered with red paint hung before it; and as the protest ended a lone demonstrator stood in front of a military tank. In Europe, the unification of East and West Germany transformed the Berlin Wall from a military structure into a symbolic form as evocative in form and content as Christo's *Running Fence* or Richard Serra's *Tilted Arc* (see figs. 21.71, 24.61). In an iconic gesture of defiance, thousands of Germans from East and West celebrated the destruction of the wall by gathering at the Brandenburg Gate. In the US, art punctuated politics in a different fashion. The arts community, already mourning the death by AIDS of a growing number of artists, curators, and writers, was now being attacked by the government. Rightwing politicians appeared at museum openings to declare wars on indecency and struck out at what they considered to be degenerate art.

Contested Visions: Art and Politics circa 1990

The most dramatic cultural battle of the period was pitched around the 1990 retrospective of photographer **Robert Mapplethorpe** (1946–89). The exhibition, scheduled to finish its tour at the Corcoran Museum, Washington DC, had been partially funded by the National Endowment for the Arts (NEA), a public fund administered by the federal government. From the floor of the US Senate, South Carolina Congressman Jesse Helms pronounced Mapplethorpe's work a danger to American values and the NEA support of the exhibition a theft of public funds. Though the NEA represents a minute fraction of the federal budget, at a time of economic recession, and of public fear and confusion over AIDS, art proved an effective subterfuge.

Mapplethorpe's work, as seen in 1981's graceful *Ajitto (Back)* (fig. **27.1**) reveals the artist's consummate technical control, unerring eye for balance, and facility with chiaroscuro of luminescent whites and velvety blacks. Though his primary subject was the human body, male and female, nude and dressed, Mapplethorpe also produced portraits including a whimsical image of sculptor Louise Bourgeois and a series of flower still-lifes that allude to the work of American modernist Georgia O'Keeffe (see fig. 18.20).

What piqued politicians in 1990 was a group of images in which Mapplethorpe had lavished his formidable aesthetic attention on the activities of homosexual and sadomasochistic subcultures. In these photographs, men embrace each other in activities ranging from a simple kiss to extreme examples of sexual exploration. Though the actions depicted and Mapplethorpe's obvious encouragement of them were decried, what seemed most threatening about the art was its beauty. Using traditional conventions of beauty and classical compositions, Mapplethorpe's work elicited the disinterested, even spiritual, pleasure associated with modernist art. Aesthetic pleasure led most viewers of the 1990 exhibition into social disorientation.

Mapplethorpe upset politicians for conveying the activities of those on the outskirts of society; **Sally Mann** (b. 1951) faced censure from critics who took her work to be a vulgarization of the American family. Mann's 1992 *Immediate Family*, a portfolio of prints equal in their sensual command of surface and depth to any of Mapplethorpe's work, presented, in Mann's own words, "ordinary things every mother has seen: a wet bed, a bloody nose, candy cigarettes." Although only a fraction of the scenes in *Immediate Family* featured Mann's children in states of undress, to many the volume represented the threatening proximity of sexuality and childhood in contemporary American life.

The presentation of even the most ordinary moments of childhood, suspended in time and transformed into aesthetic objects takes on an uncanny quality. Though

27.1 Robert Mapplethorpe, *Ajitto (Back)*, 1981. Gelatin-silver print, 16 × 20" (40.6 × 50.8 cm).

inspired by the fleeting glimpses of daily life, Mann's portraits were the result of often-laborious reenactments. Moreover, Mann's style, with its the narrow depth of field, softened misty backgrounds, and rich details, belies a technique more deliberate than a snapshot.

The photograph *The New Mothers* (fig. **27.2**), an image of Mann's two daughters playing at motherhood, appears to juxtapose the demands placed by contemporary society on girls to become both sexual and nurturing. The elder daughter casually holds a candy cigarette between her fingers and squints aggressively at the camera, while the younger girl peers through heart-shaped sunglasses and petulantly places her fist on her hip. Depictions of children playing house have shown how girls are socialized into mothers since at least the seventeenth century. Mann's work of the time presented the psychological and moral dimensions of growing up in the twentieth century.

The photography of Mapplethorpe and Mann unsettled those who wished to believe that America was untouched by sexual difference and unaffected by the ambiguities of childhood. While issues of artists' rights of self-expression tended to obscure more penetrating discussion of Mapplethorpe and Mann's work, appeals to the First Amendment guarantee of freedom of speech greatly benefited discussion of the controversial work of photographer **Andres Serrano** (b. 1950). The most infamous of Serrano's photographs was *Piss Christ* (1987) (fig. **27.3**), a photograph of a crucifix submerged in a basin of urine. Neatly calculated to offend, the "piss" is only recognizable

27.2 Sally Mann, *The New Mothers*, 1989. Gelatin-silver print, 20 × 24" (50.8 × 60.9 cm).

27.3 Andres Serrano, *Piss Christ*, 1987. Cibachrome, silicone, Plexiglas, wood frame, 65 × 45⅛ × ¾" (165 × 115 × 1.9 cm) framed; 60 × 40" (152.4 × 101.6 cm) unframed. Edition of four.

as such once the title has been read. *Piss Christ* became a magnet for accusations of the indulgence and insolence of contemporary artists. That Serrano had received NEA money further fueled the controversy. A Catholic with an attraction to the mystical correlation between body and soul, Serrano was building on a traditional conversation between physical and spiritual existence. It is a subject with precedents in the work of the Caravaggio and Manet. In the late eighties, Martin Scorsese's film *Last Temptation of Christ* was picketed for addressing the same issue.

Characteristic of art exploring the spiritual and physical, *Piss Christ* is an aesthetically exquisite image that reveals the imagination and audacity of the artist. Photographed in a tank against a red background and dramatically illuminated, the image glows with an evocative warmth. The bath of liquid and the bubbles that rise around the crucifix soften the appearance of the sculpture, while the urine itself recalls bodily fluids central to the life of Christ, from wine and water to tears and blood. The few viewers who got past the aggressive title and the political controversy were treated to a thought-provoking, beautiful, and very personal statement.

Mining the Museum: Art and Institutions

Mapplethorpe, Mann, and Serrano were only a few of the artists affected by the interactions of politics and arts in the early nineties. By the time the controversy had eased, the NEA budget had been cut and it no longer made grants to individual artists. But the artworld still had to deal with the damaging effects of the intrusion of political campaigning on curatorial practice. In the wake of the Mapplethorpe case, museums were forced to second-guess their critics and became reluctant to exhibit potentially controversial work. Politicians had become a threat to alternative art spaces that relied on public funding and major institutions that could ill-afford the fallout of controversy. To artists and critics who had struggled for decades to challenge formalism, the early nineties provided grim satisfaction. Art was now indisputably political.

Many artists championed personal expression, writing letters, making speeches, signing petitions and donating art to benefits. Others took from the congressional outrage a renewed appreciation for the political power of the museum. The nineties witnessed a concerted attempt to expose the mechanisms by which art is produced, displayed, and discussed.

By the end of the twentieth century, the intertwined legacy of collecting and conquest was well appreciated. From Napoleon's Louvre in Paris to Alfred Barr's Museum of Modern Art in New York, the museum has expressed ideological positions through the selection and display of objects. The installations of **Fred Wilson** (b. 1954) expose the power and priorities of museums. In 1987, after working as a museum educator at several museums including the Metropolitan Museum of Art, Wilson curated a show called Rooms with a View: The Struggle between Culture, Content, and the Context of Art. The exhibition presented contemporary art in rooms designed after historic exhibition types: the ethnographic museum; the nineteenth-century salon; and the modernist gallery. The results were what one might have expected: in the first room, one looked into glass vitrines that gave the impression that the art inside was evidence in some scientific hypothesis; in the second room, salon-style hanging and sumptuous décor conveyed the weight of history and taste; while in the white-walled space of the last room works took on the assertive posture expected of modernist art. The context defined the objects.

For the 1992 exhibition Mining the Museum (fig. 27.4), Wilson changed the character of his intervention in the museum. The work consisted of juxtaposing objects belonging to the Baltimore Historical Society to demonstrate that, as Wilson noted, "in an environment that supposedly has *the* history of [a place], it's possible that there's another history that's not being talked about." U.S. Metalwork 1723–1880 presents Wilson at his most poetic and precise. In glass cases that recalled the ethnographic display of Rooms with a View, Wilson presented exquisite polished silver alongside worn slave shackles. Instead of

relating to one another primarily aesthetically, as do most objects in a museum, the silver and the shackles occupy relative positions in the history of America's slave economy. The slave trade is usually the invisible history behind the economic situation that supported decorative arts in eighteenth- and nineteenth-century America. U. S. Metalwork 1723–1880, with its emotionally and formally evocative juxtaposition of objects, brings the politics of art to the foreground with an aesthetic intuition rivaling René Magritte or Meret Oppenheim (see figs. 15.33, 15.36).

Lothar Baumgarten (b. 1944) began examining the relationship between institutional power and representation in the seventies. Particularly concerned with how images became part of the process of colonization, Baumgarten scoured history and anthropology texts to investigate the renaming of the Americas. In instances like Venezuela, meaning "little Venice," the territory forcibly annexed was given a name that elicited romantic visions of Europe. Such labeling of the non-Western world is the linguistic complement to the eighteenth- and nineteenth-century tradition of landscape painting and photography that fit foreign landscapes into familiar frameworks for assigning meaning to the world. In 1979, Baumgarten spent eighteen months living and photographing the indigenous Amazonian Yanomami people. Subsequently, his work has integrated text and image to create deconstructive critiques of colonial exploration and constructive attempts at what might be called Postmodern anthropology.

A site-specific installation proposed by Baumgarten serves to clarify his critical use of text and image. He planned that the work should have the indigenous place names of Venezuelan cities engraved, with the letters reversed, in a public square in the capital, Caracas. This format would have politicized the text because it mimicked oppositional political slogans spray painted in reverse

27.4 Fred Wilson, *Mining the Museum*, 1992. Installation view, Baltimore.

throughout the city. To accompany the exhibition, Baumgarten designed a volume of the *Guggenheim Magazine*, inviting art historians, anthropologists, and a poet to discuss issues raised by the work. At its center lay the heart of Baumgarten's project, a collection of photographs of objects on display at an ethnographic museum framed with words such as "questioned," "evaluated," "claimed," "obfuscated," and "fetishized," that to the artist, in his own words, "describe the unsettled psyche of objects transported from one culture to another." Baumgarten's presentation, called *AMERICA Invention* (1988–93) (fig. **27.5**), joined together political and museum history by filling the rotunda of the Guggenheim museum with the names of Native American tribes, some upside down in gray, some in bright red, which appear to ascend the spiral. of the museum. In the outer galleries, written in arcs that recall longitude lines on an atlas, are words by historians from the US and Europe describing the treatment of those tribes. The floor of the museum reads, "Borrowed land for sale." The viewer stands in an art museum surrounded by the interwoven text of American history and its philosophical and moral dilemmas. Baumgarten's presentation suggests both the complicity and responsibility that cultural institutions have in the writing of history.

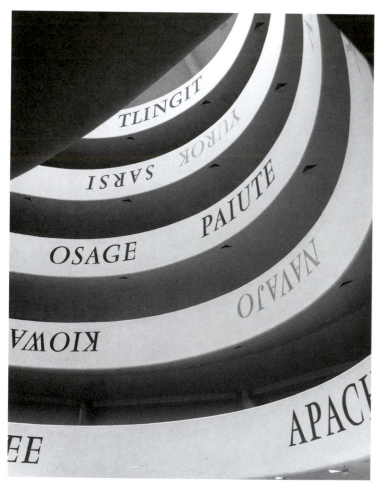

27.5 Lothar Baumgarten, *America, Invention I* (detail), 1988–93. Installation at the Guggenheim Museum.

Several contemporary photographers have drawn on the practice of Bernd and Hilla Becher (see fig. 22.69) to create images of museums that are as penetrating as any installations that might appear in a museum. Two Becher students, **Candida Hofer** (b. 1944) and **Thomas Struth** (b. 1954) turned their professors' typological method to the institutions of learning and art history that developed them, using the camera to interrogate the forms and consequences of various types of artistic display.

Hofer has documented the empty interiors of museums, libraries, and schools that shape the semi-private, semi-public experiences of viewing art and internalizing culture. *Museum can Hedendaagse Kunst Gent III* (1995) (fig. **27.6**) presents the integration of the art, the exhibition space, and the dining room—all essential parts of a functioning museum. The curving atrium echoes the photography and furniture in it. Struth's series of museum interiors also presents the collusion between art and museum to shape the physical, intellectual, and emotional experiences of the viewer, who Struth includes in his photographs. *Museum of Modern Art I* (1994) (fig. **27.7**) presents seven or eight figures before Jackson Pollock's *One: Number 31 1950*. An elegant image of the institutionalization of modern art, the photograph captures Pollock's painting in detailed unmoving focus, while viewers move around and shift restlessly out of focus. Struth documents the transference of energy and behavior from the painting to the viewer. His image of *Caillebotte's Rainy Day, Paris* presents viewers judiciously positioning themselves before the painting. One woman begins to move her stroller from the streetside of Caillebotte's picture toward its vanishing point as a second woman stands securely by the sidewalk. Paintings, it seems, provide legible and convincing instructions about how to act in their presence. Hofer and Struth's museum images provide visually stunning evidence of the care with which we display art while posing vexing questions about who is in control as we look at it. Both artists participated in the 1999 exhibition, Museum as Muse, held at the Museum of Modern Art that celebrated the museum as a source of inspiration for artists.

The museological analyses discussed thus far examine the relationship between the authority of the museum and the subjectivity of the viewer. *The Tracey Emin Museum* (1995) by British sculptor, photographer, and performance and conceptual artist Tracey Emin highlights the expectations and role of the artist in the equation. Emin produces an excess of information in a style integrating apparent carelessness and colloquial text ("At age 13 why the hell should I trust anyone?" stitched on a quilt, "You forgot to kiss my soul" in neon.) The sheer volume of personal information threatens to eliminate the sense of a private world revealed and turn modernist introspection into Postmodern spectacle. Reversing Warhol's strategy of erasing the distinction between public and private lives by effacing his private life, Emin has merged the two realms by eliminating a censored public persona.

27.6 Candida
Hofer, *Museum van
Hedendaagse Kunst
Gent III*, 1995.
Colour photograph,
15½ × 23¼"
(39 × 59 cm).

27.7 Thomas Struth,
*Museum of Modern
Art I*, 1994. C-Print,
edition of 10, 70⅞ ×
93 ¾" (180 ×
238 cm).

On the occasion of her nomination for the Turner Prize, Britain's most prestigious award for promising young artists, Emin displayed her unmade bed, complete with underwear, KY Jelly, and a carton of Marlboros. Upon not winning the prize, Emin stormed off the stage drunk, creating a bit of reality TV for BBC Television to match the reality sculpture *Bed*. Like her yBa peers, ("young British artists" who came of age quickly and visibly in Britain in the early nineties, spurred by the high-profile patronage of collector and advertising tycoon, Charles Saatchi), Emin has made use of tabloids and TV even more than museums to forward her identity as a significant contemporary artist. Implicit in a work like *Bed* or *The Tracey Emin Museum* is the idea that effective art must communicate through a variety of mouthpieces and traditional museums are not necessarily the most important ones.

The Postmodern "I": The Artist as Individual

Tracey Emin's audience becomes almost embarrassingly aware that a trip to a museum might be like overhearing a stranger's therapy session. Struth's viewer might sense that it was he who made the appointment. In both cases, the individual experience is central. The self had always been a key to the modernist understanding of how art and society were linked. The viewer was compelled to travel with Pollock or Picasso into the world of the artist's mind and from there discover what fragments of insight proved universally relevant to humanity. After Pollock, the confidence in expressing universals faltered and more defined and local subjects took precedence. Shifting priority away from universals made the individual, as an end in itself rather than a conduit to something greater, a vital component in contemporary art.

Body Art

Since the late seventies, when she had been one of the most visible Appropriation artists (see chapter 26), **Cindy Sherman** (b. 1954) has created photographs that are a remarkable indicator of contemporary intellectual and artistic currents. In the late eighties, her work shifted from the focussed study of contemporary identity to an exploration of abjection. Abjection, the state of revulsion, was being theorized as the physical expression of marginality and historicized as fundamental to a surrealist tradition favoring the uncanny over the unconscious. Images of abjection presented human activities, from laughter and sex to bleeding and nausea, which civilization seeks to control. *Untitled 175* (1987) (fig. **27.8**) presents the artist reflected in sunglasses dropped amongst the residue of incredible gluttony. It is no longer the violence of the gaze that is featured but the desire to look upon violence that Sherman explores in all the baroque luxuriance that photographic technology allows.

By 1990, Sherman had turned her aesthetic of entropy to unsettling the refined territory of art history: *Untitled*

27.9 Cindy Sherman, *Untitled No. 224 (after Caravaggio's Bacchus)*, 1990. Photograph, 48 × 38" (121.9 × 96.5 cm).

No. 224 (after Caravaggio's Bacchus) (fig. **27.9**) presents the artist in the guise of a Caravaggio's canonical figure, who straddles the boundaries between realism and fantasies of arcadia and homoerotica. By dressing herself as Bacchus, god of wine, and her photography as seventeenth-century Baroque naturalism, Sherman collapses the history of realism. Her picture alludes to the collision of sensuality and reality at the roots of realism and photography just as her abjection pictures suggested the same collision as the basis for Surrealism. By drawing our attention to the physical attraction of realist art, be it painting or photography,

27.8 Cindy Sherman, *Untitled 175*, 1987. Colour photograph 47½ × 41½" (120 × 105 cm).

Sherman's work of the late eighties and nineties explored the physical lives of the fragmented and multivalent identities depicted in her earlier work.

Sherman and Serrano (see fig. 27.3) used the seductive quality of photography to lure viewers into their subjects. The sculpture of **Kiki Smith** (b. 1954) appeals to sympathy rather than desire. To negotiate the social and physical experience of the body, Smith uses materials that convey malleability and fragility as well as power and strength. Wax, bronze, paper, glass, plaster, and photography all figure in her work. *Untitled* (1990) (fig. **27.10**) presents two figures, male and female, both naked, made of bees' wax and raised above the floor on metal poles. The bodies, soft and limp, seem overcome by gravity. White traces of fluid describe milk leaking from the woman's breasts over her torso and semen drying on the man's leg. Any sense of maternal nurturing or sexual catharsis is undermined by the figures' positions of collapse and display. These are bodies in a moment of physical exhaustion failing to contain themselves, and the spectacle is pathetic and embarrassing.

Smith is the daughter of Tony Smith, whose work marked a pivotal change from the physical process of the Abstract Expressionist to the intellectual geometry of Minimalism. Though there are no formal similarities in the appearance of the work by father and daughter, both artists share a common attitude toward the audience. Consider the dialog between a viewer and Tony Smith's *Die* (see fig. 22.46), with its physical and connotative references to the scale of the human body. Both artists rely on the viewer

to encounter their sculptures while being fully aware of the strangeness of physical existence. Representative of her generation, Kiki Smith, a veteran of the CoLab collective (see chapter 26), directs the physical unease that her work generates toward a social understanding of ourselves as well as the more physical and mystical experience that had interested her father.

The Lebanese-born and London-resident artist **Mona Hatoum** (b. 1952) began her career by staging intricate performances that placed her body in situations as extreme as some of Sherman's photographs. In one, Hatoum struggled for seven hours in a closet-sized Plexiglass box half full of mud. The performances, and much of her later work, comment on the history of the Middle East and the artist's life as a double émigré. Hatoum's parents had left Palestine in 1948 for Lebanon and in 1975, when war broke out in Beirut, Hatoum was studying in London and found herself stranded there. By the nineties, she turned from performances that presented physical experiences to sculptures that created them.

Corps Etranger (1994) uses architecture and video to stimulate the awkward, almost painful, disjunctions in being human. Enlisting the predilection of Surrealist photography, described by Susan Sontag, to transform the everyday into art by deeming it important enough to record and display, Hatoum's presents her own body as both horrifying and ordinary. On the floor of a small round room, she projected a film of the interior of her body taken with endoscopic and colonoscopic cameras. To the beating

27.10 Kiki Smith, *Untitled*, 1990. Beeswax and microcrystalline wax figures on metal stand. Installed height of female figure: 6'1½" (1.9 m). Installed height of male figure: 6'4¹⁵⁄₁₆" (2 m). Female figure: 64½ × 17⅜ × 15¼" (163.8 × 44.1 × 38.7 cm). Male figure: 69⁷⁄₁₆ × 20½ × 17" (176.4 × 52.1 × 43.2 cm). Stand for female figure: 61⅞ × 13⅞ × 19¹¹⁄₁₆" (157.2 × 35.2 × 50 cm). Stand for male figure: 61¾ × 14⁹⁄₁₀ × 19¹¹⁄₁₆" (156.8 × 37 × 50 cm). Collection Whitney Museum of American Art, New York.

of a heart and the rumbling of a stomach, we peer into the artist's body while carefully trying not to step on it. Unlike equally graphic work of the seventies, Carolee Schneeman's *Interior Scroll* for instance (see fig. 24.25), the body in *Corps Etranger* is so removed from its context that it remains foreign even as it is scrupulously examined. Rather, *Corps Etranger* is a situation of discomfort and alienation, resonant with themes of displacement and homelessness.

The body had been central to video art since the work of Bruce Nauman or Nam Jun Paik in the sixties (see figs. 24.13, 24.10). More recently, video, divorced from the television monitor, has had particular relevance to contemporary ideas about identity. The work of **Gary Hill** (b. 1951) has been central to the application of increasingly flexible video technology to address intersections of the body with social, physical, intellectual, and spiritual worlds.

Upon first encountering *Tall Ships* (1992) (fig. **27.11**), it seems to be only an empty corridor. As the viewer enters the passage, however, figures appear in the distance, come close enough to make eye contact, seem to initiate conversation, and then turn abruptly away. The figures are male and female and different ages, races, and states of mind. Though the viewer initiates the interactions, the experience of deferred contact is defined by the projected figures. Hill's work addresses the insufficiency of language to translate the thought, emotion, and sensations that make up consciousness.

The taunting role that language plays in *Tall Ships* is typical of Hill's work. In *Inasmuch As It is Always Already Taking Place* (1990) challenges both our understanding of

27.11 Gary Hill, *Tall Ships*, 1992. 16 channel video installation; 16 modified 4-inch black and white monitors with projection lenses, 16 laserdisc players, 16 laserdiscs, 1 computer with 16 RS-232 control ports and pressure-sensitive switchingrunners, black or dark gray carpet and controlling software. Dimensions of corridor: 10 × 10 × 90' (3.05 × 3.05 × 27.43 m). Editions of two and one artist's proof.

the body as a unified entity and any confidence we might have in comprehending fragmentation. Hill figuratively tears a body into individual parts, each presented on a television tube the size of the part described. The screens displaying film loops of a back, ear, or neck are collected randomly in a boxed cavity in the wall, evoking the austerity of a still life or a grave. Hill's work insists that the complexity of both video and the body extends far beyond any boundaries that either has been expected to respect.

Tony Oursler (b. 1957) has also pulled video from the confines of the monitor. Using miniature LCD projectors prominently displayed in his installations, Oursler has projected onto stuffed bodies, isolated heads, and floating orbs, videos of crying, shouting, pleading, bullying, directing, and questioning faces, mouths, and eyes. Oursler's work examines the process by which human beings take on the attributes of the people and things around them, most importantly television.

Much of Oursler's work has explored Multiple Personality Disorder (MPD), which to the artist, casts light on the Postmodern persona and the changing oeuvres of artists from Cindy Sherman to David Bowie. Works such as *Gateway 2* (1994), in which a female figure, her head stuck under a mattress, shouts out "Hey, you, get out of here, What are you looking at, I'll kick your ass," present, if not MPD, the radical separation of the conflicting qualities of impotence and aggression in a single character.

In 1996, Oursler reduced his sculptures from talking heads to watching eyes. In *Untitled (Eyes)* (fig. **27.12**), thirteen fiberglass balls support projections of a single eye. One cries, one is red and swollen, one appears to look quickly around the room, and all reflect what they are watching, TV. Two eyes watch the classic films on MPD, *The Three Faces of Eve* and *Sybil*. Another watches pornography, one MTV, and one a home video game. *Eyes* depicts the moment of media absorption as the eye, the window to the soul, swells and contracts as if, to quote Oursler, it is "reflexively feeding on the light" of the TV. Oursler has reduced the body to its visual receptors, to demonstrate the psychic formation of the human by the television.

Matthew Barney (b. 1967) has used video and sculpture in his examination of "the kind of intuition that is learned through understanding a physical process." Barney associates such intuition with sports and sex, and its examination has led him from human development to myths and American history. Barney's interest in physical knowledge is present in gallery performances of sado-masochistic rock-climbing and in a body of surrealist exercise equipment that fuses sex and sport with more concision than commercial TV. Unlike Oursler and Hill, Barney confines the body to the conventional spaces of video, the TV monitor and movie theater.

Barney has developed the relevance of the body to the psyche and history in his five *Cremaster* films. The films are named after the muscle that raises and lowers the testicles. Barney has explained that the films are about the

27.12 Tony Oursler, *Untitled (Eyes)*, 1996. Installation view at Metro Pictures, New York, 1996. Video projection of eyes on thirteen painted fiberglass globes with soundtracks, dimensions variable.

physical and psychological development of masculinity. The series explores its subject within the context of myths of American life. Athletes, cowboys, sex symbols, and Barney's universe of symbolic characters including Harry Houdini, satyrs, and Mormon saint and murderer Gary Gilmore, populate the films. *Cremaster 4* (1994) (fig. **27.13**) stars Barney as a human/goat hybrid intended to suggest the potential for transcending categories of being. The prevalence of abstracted athletic equipment, elaborate cross-dressing, and filmic sequences of such length as to test the endurance and patience of the viewer has suggested to critics that Barney's work is a studied resistance to the maturation it describes. The social and historical depth of Barney's imagination circles back through the presence of the artist, the sensuality of the films, and the title to the importance of the body to contemporary selfhood.

Sensuality and selfhood has inspired a very different body of work by **Ghada Amer** (b. 1963), who was born in Egypt, raised in France, and now lives in New York.

27.13 Matthew Barney, Production still from *Cremaster 4*, 1994.

27.14 Ghada Amer, *Untitled (Vert Kaki Figures en Bougainvilliers)*, 1998. Acrylic, embroidery, and gel medium on canvas, 30 × 40" (76 × 101 cm).

Explaining the character of her feminism, Amer has said, "I speak about women's pleasure. ... Women should use this power [of seduction] if necessary without being called frivolous snakes, witches, or prostitutes. ... I just wanted to take a typically feminine craft (sewing) and make of it a language with which to compete within the very masculine arena of painting." Amer transforms images taken from pornographic magazines into a form of feminism through a commitment to craft. Like the Pattern and Decoration movement of the late seventies (see chapter 24), Amer recognized that the gendered and domestic history of textile production would necessarily politicize imagery drawing on its tradition. And, like P & D, Amer works on a scale and in styles that place her work clearly in a tradition of postwar abstract painting.

In 1998's *Untitled (Vert Kaki Figures on Bougainvilliers)* (fig. **27.14**), Amer embroiders line-drawn scenes of female autogratification. Her source is pornography. Throughout her imagery, Amer embellishes simple poses by repeating and overlapping them and allowing the ends of the threads to fall loosely over the surface of the canvas. Like many feminist artists of the nineties, Amer sees herself taking back sensuality, in a sense stealing the image of the stereotypical sexualized woman to use as a source of empowerment and pleasure. Amer's reclamation of "the female body [and] its power of seduction" does not always derive from compromised sources. In a project titled *The Encyclopedia of Pleasure* (2001), named for a collection of Muslim texts on sexual pleasure compiled in the eleventh or twelfth century, Amer stitched Islamic sources for expressing a liberated female sexuality.

The Absent Body

As every good modernist knows, one needn't be talking about the body to be talking about the body. Postmodern artists used the metaphoric possibilities of the material world to address states of a consciousness typical of contemporary life. For some, this meant viewing the material work as the depository for our feelings about being human. In a real sense, the body had gone missing and the artist discovered its memory in the world that once contained it. For others, the material world provided surrogates for the body, accessing insights that the body itself might not have revealed.

Felix Gonzalez-Torres (1957–96) created a poetic oeuvre in which a pile of candy, or a string of light bulbs, could interweave physicality, memory, biography, politics, and history. Deeply influenced by Minimalism and Conceptual art (see chapter 24), he found that the clarity and luxury of Minimalist art could be fashioned to push his audience from sixties aesthetics to nineties politics.

Unlike the autonomy of Minimalist work, Gonzalez-Torres's sculpture directed attention to its creator and its audience. *Untitled (Portrait of Ross in L.A.)* (1991)

27.15 Felix Gonzalez-Torres, *Untitled (Portrait of Ross in L.A.)*, 1991. Multicolored candies, individually wrapped in cellophane, endless supply. Ideal weight, 175 lbs (79.3 kg), dimensions vary with installation. Collection Howard and Donna Stone.

27.16 Mona Hatoum, *Light Sentence*, 1992. Wire-mesh lockers and motorized light bulb, 6'6" × 6'1" × 16'1" (2 × 1.9 × 4.9 m); installation space variable, minimum 15'11" × 25'11" (4.9 × 7.9 m); maximum 19'2" × 28'10" (5.8 × 8.8 m). Collection National Gallery of Canada, Ottawa.

(fig. **27.15**), for instance, appears to be a collection of elegant metallic units, a sculpture in the tradition of Donald Judd or Sol LeWitt (see figs. 22.47, 22.52). Its form, however, is the result of amassing the weight of Gonzalez-Torres's lover Ross in candy. *Untitled* (*Portrait of Ross in L.A.*), executed as its subject was dying of AIDS, is a meditation on the physical and emotional changes that occurred as the artist lost his lover. Viewers are invited to follow instructions and take a candy from the heap, the dwindling physical mass of the sculpture echoing the wasting away of Ross's body. *Untitled (Portrait of Ross in L.A.)*, like all of Gonzalez-Torres's work, is dependant on physical interaction with an audience. There are no viewers of the work, only participants, and taking part in Gonzalez-Torres's art demands that we alter it. Change is integral to both its form and its content. Gonzalez-Torres's technique also suggests a shift in the political landscape as AIDS took its toll on American lives. Working, as he described it, "within the contradictions of the system" Gonzalez-Torres examines both the public qualities of private experiences of love and death and the private consequences of such public events as viewing art or providing healthcare.

Mona Hatoum, whose visceral *Corps Etranger* placed the body literally and figuratively at the foundation of her work, has also addressed the political history of the body.

In the early nineties, Hatoum began to create an increasingly abstract, geometric, and violent body of work, including 1992's *Light Sentence* (fig. **27.16**), which employed utilitarian objects such as bed frames, animal cages, and lightbulbs. The artists has explained that the sculptural works address the disjunction of her past while examining the structures of institutional power that she has observed in the West. *Light Sentence* is a U-shaped chamber made from walls of stacked chicken cages. In its center, a bare lightbulb slowly descends to the floor and rises again. The bulb, a surrogate for both the object and agent of interrogation, shines through the cages, casting unsettling shadows on the gallery walls beyond. With simple means, Hatoum is able to create a physically demanding space that catches the human frame in a continually shifting mesh of metal and shadow. With the political clarity of her performances and the emotional suggestiveness of *Corps Etranger*, *Light Sentence* illustrates and effects the collision of bodily sensation and political history.

Approaching issues of self and society through the things that we embrace and the materials that cover us, sculptor and photographer **Yinka Shonibare** (b. 1962) has created a humorous and historically exacting body of work. Shonibare's sculpture is based on a simple and historically implausible confusion of African and British

27.17 Yinka Shonibare, *Girl/Boy*, 1998. Wax-printed cotton textile, mannequin 71 × 59 × 27½" (180 × 150 × 70 cm), plinth size 79 × 5½ × 79" (200 × 14 × 200 cm). The Speyer Family Collection, New York.

fashion. *Girl/Boy* (1998) (fig. **27.17**) presents a mannequin dressed in Victorian costume tailored from fabrics associated with Africa. The juxtaposition is funny, providing an invitation to disruptive considerations of postcolonial consciousness.

While the fashion confusion itself draws attention to intercultural mixing, the history of the fabric complicates what appears to be a clear statement about the impossibility of sustaining an African identity in a British life. In interviews and statements, Shonibare makes an issue of relaying the history of the "Dutch print" fabric that he uses. Developed by the Dutch as a simulation of the batik textiles of colonial Indonesia, "Dutch prints" were copied a second time by British textile manufacturers in Manchester.

The English then exported the fabrics to West Africa where, in the sixties, they became symbols of anticolonial patriotism. In London in the nineties, these materials were again being adopted by the Afro-British as signs of African cultural and political solidarity. Shonibare, himself raised in Lagos and London, has pinned notions of identity to a sign of Africa with roots on several continents, in colonizing and colonized nations, and in colonial, postcolonial, continental, and diasporic African history. Shonibare's sculptures mock notions of authenticity and singularity by insisting on the heterogeneous and international nature of both British and African identity. Following the material clues of Shonibare's fashion, the answer to a question posed in the title of another work by Shonibare, *How Does a Girl Like You Get to be a Girl Like You?* (1995), is found in an international and polyglot heritage.

Gabriel Orozco (b. 1962), an artist of startling formal and poetic facility, has taken the emotional and political content of mobility as a theme in his work. Orozco was born and educated in Mexico, spending his summers in Cuba and the Soviet Union. In the late eighties, in Mexico City, he participated in the collective General Workshop, which rejected traditional object-making in its attempts to explore the consequences of transformation in individuals, groups, ideas, and things.

Orozco considers his work "a byproduct or a leftover of specific situations." A poetic example is a photograph of bicycle tracks through a puddle called *Extension of Reflection* (1992). In the early nineties, Orozco began a series of *Yielding Stones*, plasticine balls of the artist's weight that were rolled through city streets and deposited in a gallery. Cigarette butts, bottle caps, and scratches mark the *Stone*'s surface, leaving the imprint of the world on the surrogate for the artist.

The DS (1993) (fig. **27.18**) explores transformation within the context of automobile culture. Orozco removed twenty-four inches (61 cm) from the center of a Citroen DS and rejoined the sides of the classic auto-body, slightly disrupting the familiar shape to accent its sleek and phallic appearance. The work recalls some of the more subtle transformations of the surrealists as well as the poignant distortions created by memory and nostalgia. Ironically, the increased elegance results in the impotence of the vehicle, now without a working engine. Made for an exhibition in Paris, Orozco chose the Citroen DS because it symbolized nostalgic elegance to a French driver. Reiterating Orozco's interest in change, the meaning of the DS and its emotional impact changes dramatically as it leaves the French gallery and enters an American, German, Japanese, or Mexican one.

The surrealism of memory and the confluence of the body and its environment have been of interest to artists far less peripatetic than Orozco. Since 1982, when he was sixteen, Gregor Schneider has been transforming the interior of his house in the small town of Rheydt, Germany into a modified version of the original. Walls have been built

27.18 Gabriel Orozco, *The DS*, 1993. Sutured car, leather, coated fabric, 4'7" × 15'9" × 3'9" (1.4 × 4.8 × 1.14 m).

over windows, windows put in front of walls, rooms slowly shrunk and expanded as corridors appeared between floors, and plumbing shifted from room to room. Schneider's *Haus Ur* distorts the sensations of space without radically challenging one's expectation for the appearance of a middle-class German home. Something is off-kilter, but because viewers are not necessarily aware of the in-between spaces, what that is not clear.

As Schneider's work is his home, the artist has relied on a variety of methods of display. Films and photographs have been most important for conveying the appearance and concept of the work. The combined physical and intellectual effect of the house has also been transmitted through reconstructing rooms from the house within the rooms of a gallery. In his installations, Schneider provides no views of the work. Rather than see a middle-class cityscape, we enter the door to the gallery as if it were a portal to the home in Germany. The doubling of Schneider's formal strategies creates the uncanny presentation of the familiar that does to the home something akin to what Hatoum's *Corps Etranger* does to the body. At once so like its model

and yet fundamentally divorced from it, the transformed interior of Schneider's home suggests that the relationship between the spaces we inhabit, affect, and transform, and the character of the lives spent within them, is one of alienated intimacy.

Eschewing the elegance that lends moral dignity to work invoking the absent body discussed thus far, **Mike Kelley** (b. 1954) has used stuffed toys as surrogates for the body to embrace abjection with an affection that is both puerile and astute. Trained in Los Angeles at CalArts (The California Institute of the Arts) in a conceptual milieu, Kelley prioritizes the idea of the work over the pleasure of its craft. Constructed from secondhand stuffed animals, folding tables, note cards, aluminum foil, and miscellaneous ephemera, Kelley's work is built for effect rather than posterity. *Fruit of Thy Loins* (1990) (fig. **27.19**) is a typical early nineties Kelley, with its thrift store materials, relentlessly adolescent obsession and confusion over the body, and its black humor.

Fruit of Thy Loins is a collection of toys joined to look as if a mother bunny has just given birth to twelve small

27.19 Mike Kelley, *Fruit of Thy Loins*, 1990. Stuffed animals, 39 × 21 × 12" (99.1 × 53.3 × 30.5 cm).

stuffed animals. Like Kelley's many stuffed toy sculptures, *Fruit of Thy Loins* transforms what might be cute into something rather ugly. The toys are worn and cast away and laden with the signs of class implicit in secondhand goods. The acts they perform are closer to the amorphous sexuality of Sherman's or Smith's contemporary work than the playful romps of Keith Haring or Kenny Scharf (see figs. 26.35, 26.37).

Typical of his generation, Kelley has explored both our attitudes toward physical intimacy and the institutional processes that shape them. In 1991, he presented the multiroom installation, *Morphology Flow Chart*, consisting of dozens of thrift store animals laid out on folding tables with charts behind them. The work suggested the science of a genealogical document and the history of a morgue. The ironic application of science and history to rather ratty relics of childhood presents an oppressive counterpart to the humor of *Fruit of Thy Loins*.

The Art of Biography

Translating the experiences of one's life into a cogent story that responds to the needs of the teller and the demands of the audience has proved an acute challenge to contemporary artists. Some, like Tracey Emin, have attempted to push as much of their life into their art as possible, creating in a sense a real-time presentation of self. Others have sought to keep tighter control over the nature and content of personal revelation. Complicating the personal with the political, the majority of work discussed below addresses the specific problem of telling biographies of nonmajority citizens in a language that is necessarily shaped by the majority. Using text, film, photography, and painting, this art interrogates the act of writing or picturing biography even as it attempts to achieve it.

Before becoming an artist, **Carrie Mae Weems** (b. 1958) studied folklore at the University of California, Berkeley. Her photographic work has focussed her folkloristic convictions in the importance of narrative in the construction of identity and history. Weems attempts to tell stories faithful to the African-American experience in forms distinct from those of colonizing cultures. She has chronicled her family's migration from the deep South to Portland, Oregon, where she was born; written fictional stories of contemporary life; and traced the migrations of Africans from West Africa to the US. Taken together, Weems's work weaves the biography, autobiography, fiction, and history of Africans and African-Americans into intricate photo, text, and sculpture installations. Weems uses photography and texts as pieces in conceptual projects aimed at constructing alternative means of discussing society. She is a storyteller, choosing to follow narratives through to their ending and filling them with a wealth of local detail.

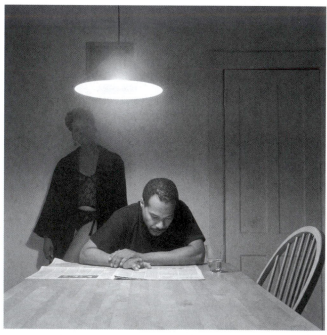

27.20 Carrie Mae Weems, *Untitled* (Outtake from the *Kitchen Table* series), 1990–99. Gelatin siver print, 29¼ × 28¼" (74 × 72 cm).

Untitled (Kitchen Table Series) (1990–99) (fig. **27.20**) is a four-part tableau presenting characters in a domestic drama. Focusing on the spousal relationship of an educated working-class black woman and the space of the kitchen, the series addresses the themes of marriage, friendship, children, and loneliness. The images are accompanied by texts, told in different voices, about the perils of domestic life. By rewriting the drama of domestic life in a consciously scripted fashion, Weems directs the viewer to those aspects of African-American life that she deems important. Traditional documentary photography had been directive too, but it had hidden its agenda in the apparent realism of its imagery. Artifice, as well as the complicated arrangements of texts, images, and objects throughout her oeuvre, serves Weems's desire to be clear and present in her work.

Glenn Ligon (b. 1960) works, in large part, by formally manipulating text to explore the disjunction between lives lived and the words we use to talk about them. Using quotations, many of which describe the realities of growing up black in America, Ligon associates speaking of African-American experience with the Dada and Surrealist practice of the readymade and the objet-trouvé. The texts of others, from James Baldwin to Mary Shelley, become the objects with which Ligon attempts to bypass the traps of institutionalized language, thereby conjuring up the experience of African-American people.

Combining the textual abstraction of Jasper Johns (see fig. 21.17) with a distinctly pictorial impulse, works like *Untitled (I Feel Most Colored When I am Thrown Against a Sharp White Background)* (1990) (fig. **27.21**) illustrate Ligon's understanding of race in America in surprising ways. Ligon paints the words as though they were on a page from a book. Starting off in sharp focus on the white field, the words begin to bleed onto the panel around them, fading into the obscurity of a darker background. The painting reverses the increasing clarity described in the text.

27.21 Glenn Ligon, *Untitled (I Feel Most Colored When I am Thrown Against a Sharp White Background)*, 1990. Diptych. Oilstick and gesso on wood, each panel 6'6" × 2'6" (2 × 7.6 m). Collection the artist.

Ligon has not translated the metaphor of the text directly, but has used it to illustrate the deceptive clarity that race presents. In effect, Ligon is writing his own biography by making images with, not of, the writings of others.

Lorna Simpson (b. 1960), like Glenn Ligon, uses conceptual and pictorial devices to articulate and at least impart the difficulty of speaking about one's life as an African-American. Initially working in the tradition of documentary photography, Simpson, like many artists, began to question the assumed objectivity of the genre. Informed by Minimalist, Conceptualist, Feminist, and Identity art of the previous decades, Simpson questioned how the most fundamental properties of photography—repetition and framing—might complement her intentions as an African-American photographer.

Simpson's *Guarded Conditions* (1989) (fig. **27.22**) addresses racially and sexually directed violence, but uses none of the devices, expressive representation, and dramatic prose or poetry traditionally used to address such violence. In the work, the body of a standing black woman, her back turned to the viewer, is displayed in three framed photographs and repeated six times across the wall. Repeated below the figures are the phrases, "SEX ATTACKS" and "SKIN ATTACKS."

Like Gonzalez-Torres or Hatoum, Simpson uses the history of Minimalism and Conceptual art to provide and infiltrate metaphors for the regulated nature of social space.

Sentence fragments and cropped photographs of backs and turned heads become signs of social oppression and the coded means by which Simpson's subjects navigate and challenge it. Withholding as much if not more information than it provides, *Guarded Conditions* suggests both a generalized state of affairs and an intimation of specific events in a person's life. Though not an optimistic image, there is a sense in Simpson's art, as there was in Hatoum's and Gonzalez-Torres's, of options within the "contradictions in the system."

Skepticism toward the documentary value of photography as well as an anxiety toward its tendency to turn complex human subjects into objects of beauty has made the camera a difficult tool for telling personal histories. Adopting forms from conceptual photography has been one solution. **Renee Cox** (b. 1960), however, like Robert Mapplethorpe (see fig. 27.1), has chosen to work from within the history of her medium to transform the message that it tells.

Incorporating visual references to high modernism, erotica, and family snapshots while reconsidering canonical "masterpieces", Cox has used photography as a resource for reimaging the American Family. Fully realized in the 2001 exhibition American Family, Cox's intervention into the stereotype of the African-American family can be seen as early as the 1993 *The Yo Mama* (fig. **27.23**). This is no traditional nativity, nor is it one of the restricted choices that the mass media provides for understanding the

27.22 Lorna Simpson, *Guarded Conditions*, 1989. Eighteen color Polaroid prints, twenty-one plastic plaques, plastic letters, overall dimensions 7'7" × 12'11" (2.3 × 3.9 m). Collection Museum of Contemporary Art, San Diego.

27.23 Renee Cox, *The Yo Mama*, 1993. Gelatin silver print, 82 × 47" (208.28 × 119.38 cm).

nineteenth-century odalisques, also featuring Cox. Decidedly shocking, the ensemble forces together records of personal history, public imagery, and private desire to convey the nearly confounding effect of coming of age in America and communicate the complexity of individual identity and adult life.

In the introduction to her 1993 book *The Other Side*, a photographic celebration of cross-dressing, drag queens, and a spectrum of transgendered activity, **Nan Goldin** (b. 1953) wrote "The pictures in this book are not about people suffering gender dysphoria but rather expressing gender euphoria. This book is about new possibilities and transcendence." Goldin's work presents the intimate lives of people who make up her family of choice. *C Putting on Her Make-up at the Second Tip, Bangkok* (1992) (fig. **27.24**), from *The Other Side*, is one of Goldin's many presentations of alternative lives. Before the mirror, in bathrooms, dressing rooms, and bedrooms, Goldin's subjects work on their faces, their bodies, and their clothes, transforming themselves into who they want to be. Goldin presents a world in which sexual, familial, social, and economic differences are impossible to define.

Goldin's earliest work employed the theatrics of glamor and possibilities of fashion to the lives of her friends. She has continued to use the high-gloss printing that mimics the seductive brilliancy of fashion photography even if her subjects, denizens of sexual, social, and chemical subcultures, would seem to have little in common with supermodels and fashion designers. In 1981, she presented her signature work, *The Ballad of Sexual Dependency*, an ever-changing slide show documenting the people around her. *Ballad* depicts private scenes of men and women dressing, sleeping, or just bored, as well as showing an array of sexual activity, illicit drug use, and violent behavior.

In the late eighties, Goldin became heavily addicted to drugs and documented her own descent and recovery. Though the themes of exclusion and brutality that infused

African-American single-parent home. Instead of either desperate images of drug addicts or romantic single-mother-beating-the-odds, Cox presents a strong, sexy individual with her two sons. This family, Cox's family, like any that is closely examined, will not collapse into stereotypes. Interracial and affluent, rife with sexuality and power, Cox's portraits of her family are about defying expectations and producing strength.

The American Family exhibition divides the elements of familial strength, racial pride, and sexuality that inform *The Yo Mama* into different types of photographs. Family snapshots are collected beside images featuring Cox (and in several cases her husband) in erotic poses and photographic reworkings of

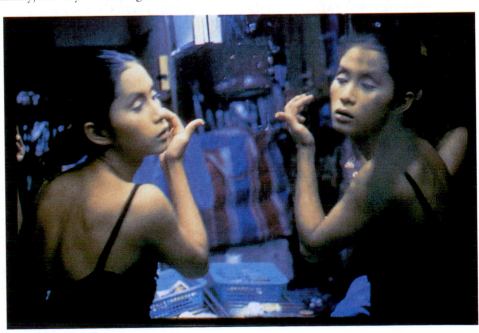

27.24 Nan Goldin, *C Putting on Her Make-up at the Second Tip, Bangkok*, 1992. Cibachrome print, 30 × 40" (76.2 × 101.6 cm).

Ballad remain strong in Goldin's work of the nineties, the focus on personal transformation in *The Other Side* suggests the greater potential of its "new possibilities."

William Kentridge (b. 1955), like Weems (see fig. 27.20), has used biography as a lens to view the relationship between history and the present. To do so he has essentially created his own medium—animation in which the traditional cells are replaced with charcoal drawings filmed at given moments of being drawn, erased, and altered. The results document images that seem to carry themselves across the surface of a single page of paper. Born, raised, and trained in Johannesburg, Kentridge considers all his art to be in one way or another about the city, and he uses his innovative medium to explore the conflation of his own biography as a white South African living through the end of apartheid with the fictionalized lives of two characters, Soho Eckstein and Felix Teitlebaum. Soho is an industrialist in the mode of George Grosz's ruthless caricatures of the thirties and Felix is a nude everyman whose fragility seems to speak of a universal human condition. Throughout the films, the capitalist's cruelty becomes a foil for Felix's personal indiscretions, including an affair with Soho's wife and a flood of melancholy that in *Felix in Exile* (1994) (fig. 27.25) threatens to drown him.

Kentridge displays the drawings from which each film was made together with the film itself. There are thus always two objects that make up Kentridge's movies: an image frozen at the point where Kentridge decided to pause the history of erasures and additions; and the unstopping film. On a metaphoric level, the drawings are, like individuals and nations, marked by the passages of time and history. The contrast of the two combined media, between the intimacy of charcoal and the distance of film, further accents the difficult combination of biography and history. Like many works of the nineties, Kentridge's films of Felix

27.25 William Kentridge, drawing from *Felix in Exile*, 1994.

and Soho argue that history, in this case that of apartheid in South Africa, is only visible as it is filtered through the biographies of its witnesses.

The Postmodern "We": The Artist and Society

While exploring the nature of individuality in the nineties, it remained for artists to explore the context of contemporary life. As in earlier decades, artists often looked beyond the self to the issues of culture, history, and nature. Many artists rooted their art in an identifiable social group and then proceeded to demonstrate how permeable the boundaries that contain subcultures in contemporary society actually are. Engaging individual cultural identities in a multicultural environment has posed acute challenges. Resisting the claims to purity that through religious persecution and sectarian violence scarred the history of the twentieth century, these artists capture the interwoven strands of national and international culture. In many ways, these visions of society and its relationship to the past and the environment fulfill the theories of fragmentation and interrelation that defined Postmodernism.

Art and the Expression of Culture

The social analysis present in the work of **Jimmie Durham** (b. 1940) grew out of his commitment to political activism. Born to the Wolf Clan of the Cherokee nation, Durham committed himself to challenging the government policies that were devastating the Native American community. Striving to "direct my rage at proper targets," Durham was active in the American Indian Movement and in 1973 was present at the Siege of Wounded Knee, an armed confrontation between US federal forces and Oglala Sioux activists seeking rights established in treaties signed and broken by the US government. The confrontation lasted for seventy-one days. Art making is, for Durham, a part of a life defined by an eclectic mix of activities and commitments. "I was raised as a political activist and carver and a good fisherman and blacksmith. I label myself an artist for convenience." Though in many ways playing into the idea of the Native American living his or her art, Durham's response also locates the Postmodern conviction in multivalent identities in his personal experience of a life spent battling the stereotypes of the Native American in and out of his art.

Durham's sculpture questions the notion that there is an authentic Native American art shaped by a natural connection to the land and sold from the pottery and rug stalls of Taos and Santa Fe. An ironic display of 1984 called *On Loan from the Museum of the American Indian* featured Durham's "neo-primitive neo-conceptualism." His "Museum" lent out fake artifacts, prototypes for *Red Turtle* (1991) (fig. 27.26), that challenged the authority of Western anthropology to define Native American culture. *Red Turtle*, handmade from a turtle shell, painted

27.26 Jimmie Durham, *Red Turtle*, 1991. Turtle shell, painted wood, paper, 61½ × 67½" (156.2 × 171.5 cm). Collection Dr. and Mrs. Robert Abel, Jr., Delaware.

produced, they present sweeping panoramas of desert and sea, textured scenes of old cities, and moving bodies often abstracted and identified by long veils. The sensuality of her films is enhanced by multiscreen projections and the addition of music by composers including Iranian Sussan Deyhim for *Rapture* (1999) and American Philip Glass for *Passage* (2001).

Rapture (fig. **27.27**) explores the separation of men and women in fundamentalist Islamic culture. Presented on facing screens, men occupy a fortress while women move across a desert landscape to the sea. As the white-shirted men aggressively define the boundaries of their space, the women, veiled, watch. They shout once and the men look. Later, as several of the women board a boat, the men wave in an ambiguous gesture of farewell and warning. *Rapture* presents cultural divisions in choreographed movements in clearly articulated spaces. As one watches, alternating between screens mediating between the two sexes, we find our understanding of the film guided by similarly defined movements and spaces. Though tradition, culture, gender, and language may all appear threatening in Neshat's work, they do not overcome her female protagonists. Her work, she explains, is not about submission but rather the complexity of Islamic femininity that, to the

sticks, and paper, is a pastiche of the expected naturalism of Native American art and an assemblage of the detritus of daily life. Durham's work is a biting and humorous challenge to the teaching of history in schools, museums, and the marketplace, which requires that Native Americans remain frozen in a romantic and precolonial existence that obscures their far from Edenic reality in modern America.

Iranian filmmaker **Shirin Neshat** (b. 1957) creates from a position between two societies; in her case, Islamic and Western society. Though Neshat has lived and worked in the west since 1974, her films are highly choreographed events that explore the relationship between female identity and culture in an explicitly Islamic context. Richly

27.27 Shirin Neshat, *Untitled (Rapture)*, 1998. Production still.

artist, contains strength that is greater than men's because of its repeated suppression.

Born in Lahore, Pakistan, **Shazia Sikander** (b. 1969) began her career learning the Pakistani and Indian tradition of miniature painting rather than the Western-style painting that was more popular among her peers. Her thesis project, however, turned the tables on expectations of Eastern and Western traditions. Demonstrating what Sikander calls the "vulnerability" of the miniature tradition to being inflected by the present even as it connotes the past, her work *The Scroll* (1992) was an illumination of the artist's daily life. Upon moving to the United States in 1993, Sikander continued enlisting ancient techniques to respond to details of her life and her interest in postcolonial artistic and theoretical currents.

Pleasure Pillars (2001) (fig. **27.28**) is an illuminated page on which Sikander has layered decorative and figural imagery rooted in Eastern and Western art historical traditions and popular culture. The image is meticulously crafted from sources including, but not limited to: twelfth-century Indian sculpture and sixteenth-century Italian Mannerist painting in the central figures; Modernist abstraction in the circles repeated throughout the image (a motif also intended to suggest bombs falling from the warplanes that enter at the top); hunting imagery taken from miniature traditions; and popular arts, particularly sculpture, in the assorted animals and deities that populate the picture. Each formal element becomes part of a network of meanings that take the viewer in often surprising directions. The manuscript format alone, for instance, suggests how Sikander's art functions. In the most general Western context it reads simply as Indian, while to an informed, particularly South Asian, viewer it alludes to traditions preexisting Pakistani independence in 1947. When the biography of the artist is considered, the form takes on a political tenor and an image such as *Pleasure Pillars*, created in response to life in New York in 2001, participates in a dialogue with another history.

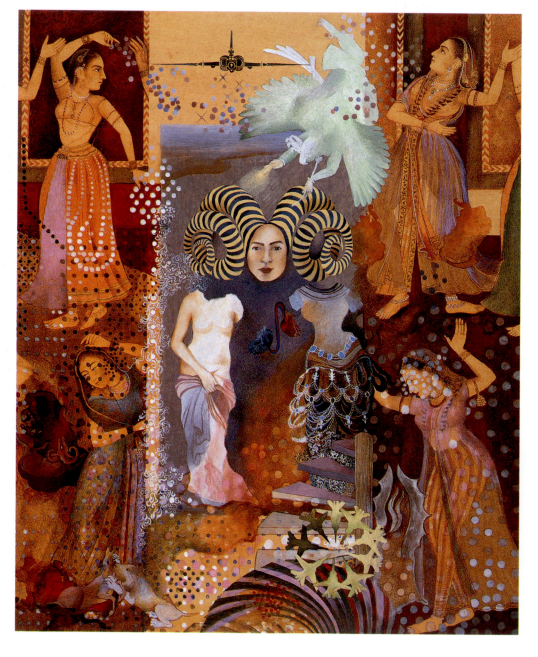

27.28 Shahzia Sikander, *Pleasure Pillars*, 2001. Watercolor, dry pigment, vegetable colour, tea, and ink on hand-prepared wasli paper, 12 × 10" (30 × 25 cm). Collection of Purninder and Amita Chatterjee, New York.

27.29 Mariko Mori, *Play with Me*, 1994. Fuji super-gloss print, wood pewter, 10 × 12 × 3' (3.05 × 3.66 × 0.91 m).

Sikander has explained that she selects and manipulates her sources in an effort less to articulate a specific political position than to make her viewers aware that the "physical, emotional, geographical, cultural, and psychological boundaries" by which we define ourselves are flexible and porous. More recently, Sikander has worked with short digital films presented in the format of an illuminated page. The work amplifies the visual effect of Sikander's layered aesthetic by revealing the process and setting the elements in motion, while maintaining the dialogue between arts and culture of the past and present.

Seduced by the transformative potential of costume, Japanese artist **Mariko Mori** (b. 1967) began her career as a model. She has continued to feature herself in attire of all kinds as she explores issues of desire and fantasy in performance, photography, and video. In a series of performance/photographs from the early nineties, Mori became an incarnation of the ideal woman in the increasingly influential *anime* culture. *Anime*, Japanese animation, is a cross-cultural mixture of the Disney cartoons that were exported to Japan during and after World War II, and the Japanese animation industry, which has matured in the last few decades. Mori is one of several artists exploring the intersection of *anime* fantasy and Japanese reality.

Play with Me (1994) (fig. **27.29**) and the related *Tea Ceremony* from the same year featured Mori, dressed as a cyborg, attempting to interact with a Japanese audience. In *Tea Ceremony* she combined the ancient Japanese tradition with the sexualized yet anodyne feminine cyborg of the contemporary imagination. Mori's attempts at forcing the interaction of the ideal and the real met with awkward indifference. In *Tea Ceremony*, she served tea to business-

men on a city street, and they avoided her; in *Play with Me* her "real" cyborg was similarly overlooked.

Akin to the feminist analysis of the seventies, Mori's work explores the ambivalence of cultural ideals. Her critique, though often barbed with a certain pleasure in revealing the inability of contemporary culture to locate its desires anywhere near reality, relishes aspects of the fantasy. Mori always seems to be enjoying herself. Her practice of shooting fantastic scenes in real locations, including Kansai International Airport, Osaka (see fig. 25.31), or La Defense, Paris, suggests the ironic possibility that our fantasies might not be so far removed as they seem.

Anime has also influenced the painting and sculpture of Japanese artist **Takashi Murakami** (b. 1962). His work, like Mori's photography, takes history and popular culture as a means to examine the difficulty of satisfying one's desire with the facts in real life. Murakami sees the relevance of popular culture in terms distinct from the categories of high and low culture set in the West by either the Cubist, Expressionist, or Surrealist avant-garde or their Postmodern variations. In the 2000 essay *Superflat*, Murakami asserted that there were two observations about Japanese art history that informed his work. The first was the idea of art as a category of cultural production distinct from popular culture is Western, imported to Japan during the Meiji era at the end of the nineteenth century. The force with which Western and now international culture (which is heavily influenced by the Western capitalist worldview) instituted a binary fine/popular or high/low structure onto Japan's tradition of unified cultural production has caused, in Murakami's view, a crisis in Japanese culture. The way out of the crisis lay not in recombination

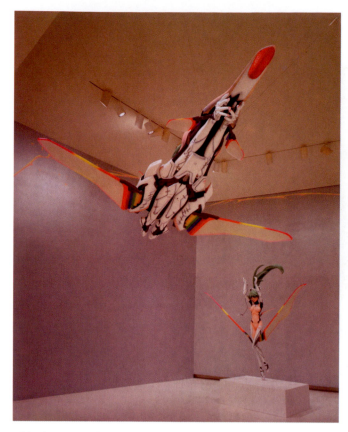

27.30 Takashi Murakami, *Second Mission Project ko2*, 1999. Oil paint, acrylic, synthetic resin, fiberglass, and iron. Human type 108 × 99 × 55" (275 × 252 × 140 cm); jet airplane type 21 × 76 × 73" (55 × 193 × 186 cm).

of high and low after the model of Western avant-gardes such as Cubism, Dada, or Pop, but in Murakami's second observation; that Japanese visual artists have historically been interested in the movement of objects across a flat surface, whether on screen, page, or film. *Anime* thus provides a means to revitalize Japanese visual culture, not as a source for "real" artists but as a legitimate point of departure for formal experimentation and intellectual content.

In a Japanese context, *Second Mission Project KO2 (SMP KO²)* (1999) (fig. **27.30**) agitates against what the artist sees as deep inconsistencies in Japanese culture. With the help of professional model-builders who specialize in three-dimensional *anime* figurines, Murakami created an anathema to the *otaku* (devotees of *anime*): a life-size, three-dimensional *anime* heroine. Once the object of otaku fantasy became too large, the physical, and—if one accepts even a modicum of feminist awareness—moral and political, impossibility of realizing the otaku ideal became painfully apparent. Like Mori's *Play with Me*, the *SMP KO²*, a sexually provocative female superhero who transforms into a high-tech military spacecraft, reveals the distance between Japanese fantasy and reality. Murakami's figures mock human desire by confronting the fantasy narrative with the real world. Currin used the language of realism, Murakami the scale of reality. Murakami considers his sculptures to be warnings of the alienation felt by thousands of people within Japan who have chosen, for the

moment, to migrate from social reality into the realm of an emasculating fantasy.

In the context of Western traditions, the *anime*-influenced art from Japan, of which Murakami's is the most visible example, poses challenges to Western divisions of high and low art that echo those of Pop art and the work of Jeff Koons (see figs. 26.47, 26.48). Murakami also has marketing savvy worthy of Warhol, though his studios in Tokyo and New York recall Rubens's workshop more than the Factory. Murakami and his staff have developed a creative and financial team that manufactures and products from paintings to T-shirts and promotes them in all media and venues from the internet to museums, ultimately branding Murakami's work in the fashion of Warhol and Hirst, or Pepsi and Coca-Cola.

The American social context has elicited artistic responses less concerned with the role of fantasy than misunderstanding and prejudice. In an effort to challenge stereotypes about African-American life, **Kerry James Marshall** (b. 1955) has created a representational language incorporating expressive handling to match the Neo-Expressionists, generalized figural types akin to comics or caricature, and the local details demanded of realism. Marshall, exceptional in his generation of African-American artists for his commitment to painting, has followed artists like Robert Colescott and Leon Golub (see fig. 24.84, 26.31) to take painting into the political arenas more often debated in photography and performance. Like Colescott, Marshall is well-versed in the Western canon, often citing artists from Botticelli to Gauguin (see chapter 3), claiming their talents for his subjects.

Marshall's *Garden* Series, which includes *Better Homes Better Gardens* (1994) (fig. **27.31**), depicts scenes of life in public housing projects. Capitalizing on the myths and ironies that surround public housing, *Better Homes Better Gardens* appears to depict the project as an urban war zone: paint splashes evoke the spray of bullets. These signs of violence and the red HUD (the US department of Housing and Urban Development) identification codes that abruptly label the surface of the canvas represent the dismal expectations most Americans have toward the projects despite the bucolic names they have. The violence, however, is conventional, and the irony is easy, and neither is the endpoint of Marshall's work.

The *Garden* series pushes past the competing clichés of tragedy and comedy that frame discussions of poverty in the United States. Marshall was raised in a project like that depicted in *Better Homes*. The scene he paints is of ordinary pleasure. Unwilling to typecast the black experience as one of gritty desperation, Marshall adopts a stylistic eclecticism to express the complexity of experience. Figures detailed enough to suggest individuals, yet abstracted enough to stand as signs of African-American experience, are depicted going through both the trials and pleasures of life.

Robert Gober (b. 1954) has made a career of handcrafting fragments of the American environment to

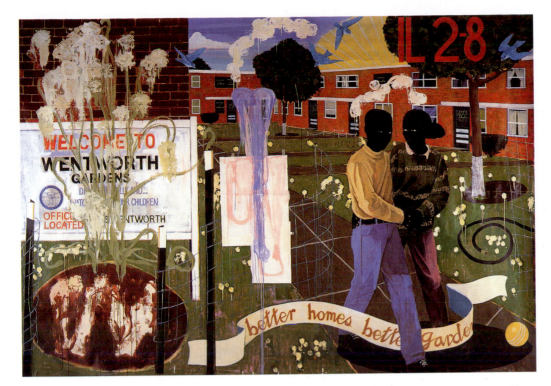

27.31 Kerry James Marshall, *Better Homes Better Gardens*, 1994. Acrylic and collage on unstretched canvas, 8'4" × 11'10" (2.54 × 3.61 m). Courtesy Jack Shainman Gallery, New York. Collection of Denver Art Museum.

suggest the complex intersection of psychic and social identity. Since the late seventies, Gober has been isolating elements of the domestic realm that mark the initiation of individuals into society. He has crafted dollhouses, cribs, beds, doors, wedding dresses, and newspapers. He has also embellished objects suggesting more ambiguous transitions like sinks, drains, tissues, and, starting in 1990, legs and torsos. His practice, with its attention to mimetic detail, can be likened to the Appropriation art of Cindy Sherman, Jenny Holzer, Sherrie Levine, and Barbara Kruger (see chapter 26), all of whom influenced Gober directly.

27.32 Robert Gober, Site-specific installation at the Dia Center for the Arts, New York, September 24, 1992 –June 20, 1993.

Since his earliest dollhouses, Gober has created environments. Even a single sculpture, a leg protruding from a wall for instance, transforms the gallery into an environment defined by the piece. His 1992 installation at the Dia Center for the Arts, New York City (fig. **27.32**), serves as a transitional work that addresses the internal conflicts and external pressures of Western society. Stacks of handcrafted newspapers, tied up like recycling, lie about the room. Sinks drip water to the recorded sounds of a babbling brook. The room is wallpapered with an artificial panorama of New England woods punctured by barred windows. These elements tell an ironic story about the transformation of nature into culture. Reading the newspapers reveals an even more upsetting story. Gober has arranged the headlines "Not Guilty," "Vatican Condones Discrimination Against Homosexuals, Concern That Gay Rights Threaten Marriage," and an ad featuring Gober in a wedding dress. The presence of the artist, a gay Catholic, cross-dressed for the forbidden ceremony, reiterates the repressive power of society at definitive moments in a person's life. Once in the installation, the viewer can walk behind the papered walls and see that they are temporary constructions, a hopeful metaphor for the artificial social constructions that the piece critiques.

Rineke Dijkstra (b. 1959) has also committed herself to exploring the socially difficult terrain of personal trans-

formation. Dijkstra's portraits capture ordinary people with their flawed physiques and dated clothes, in states of flux—notably adolescence, although she has also captured the transitional moments of pregnant women, young mothers, and soldiers. Despite photographing subjects with whom she identifies for their often desperate failure to "have everything under control," Dijkstra makes them look like scientifically recorded specimens, evenly lit and isolated from their context. The work updates the integration of typographical and documentary traditions of photography that was begun earlier in the twentieth century in Germany with Sander and the Bechers (see figs. 13.38, 22.69).

Dijkstra built her reputation on an extended series recording teenagers at the beach. "More or less self-portraits," according to the artist, the images capture the often painful combination of boldness and insecurity of adolescence. Taken in The Netherlands, Poland, Coney Island in New York, and Hilton Head in North Carolina, the series has an added anthropological element as it demonstrated how the character and class of the location affected the presentation of the subjects. Discussing Dijkstra's decision to address the passage from childhood to adulthood, critic Katy Siegel wrote: "This is a generation for whom the paradigm of adolescence (frustration, awkwardness, self-discovery) resonates louder than that of childhood (happiness, wonder, play) or adulthood (sophistication, responsibility, gravity)."

The Buzz Club, Liverpool, England/Mysteryworld, Zaandam, Netherlands (1996–97) (fig. **27.33**) extends Dijkstra's interest in the socially weighted transitions of adolescence to film. Presented in a side-by-side dual projection, *Buzz Club* presents images of kids at two nightclubs standing, dancing, and waiting. *Buzz Club* was filmed in storage rooms, thus keeping the subjects in the mood of the evening but far enough away to accent the awkwardness that Dijkstra felt dominated the environment. The results range from poignant and funny to awkward and boring.

Re-presenting History

Navigating the present has directly informed our understanding of the past. The work of Marshall (see fig. 27.31) or Mori (see fig. 27.29), for instance, has much to say about the traditions and histories of American and Japanese cultures. In the case of those works, the past is relevant for its relationship to the present. The nineties saw a large body of work that engaged the past for reasons independent of what it can illuminate about the present.

In 1991, Californian artist **Shimon Attie** (b. 1957) began a five-year stay in Berlin where, among other things, he researched the Scheunenviertal, a neighborhood that from the late nineteenth century to the 1930s was home to Eastern European Jewish immigrants. In response to photographs that he found of prewar Jewish life, Attie developed a technique similar to the projections of Krystof Wodiczko (see fig. 25.40) to explore the intersections of memory and history.

27.33 Rineke Dijkstra, *The Buzz Club, Liverpool, England/Mysteryworld, Zaandam, Netherlands, 1996–97.* Double projection, 35mm film with sound transferred to video or DVD.

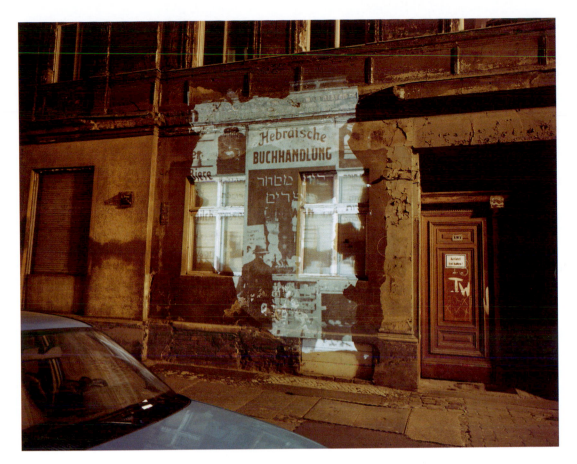

27.34 Shimon Attie, *Almstadtstrasse 43 (formerly Grenadierstrasse 7)*: slide projection of former Hebrew bookstore, 1930, Berlin, 1992, from the series *The Writing on the Wall* 1991–93. 33 × 40" (84 × 102 m) chromogenic photograph and on-location installation.

Writing on the Wall (1994) (fig. **27.34**) consists of site-specific events for which Attie matched archival photographs of the Scheuenenviertal with the locations as they existed in the nineties. He then projected the photographs onto the existing buildings, many delapidated from the war and years of neglect. The effect momentarily mixed pre- and post-World War II histories of Berlin. The images were primarily domestic scenes, although some were of populated exteriors. Viewing the projection, we seem to look through the ruins of the present to the activities of the past. Attie's work mediates the nostalgia of memory and old photographs by conflating three forms of destruction: the Jewish people by the Germans, the neighborhood by neglect, and the photograph by time. Intellectually layered, and visually rich, Attie's work created a forum for confronting an inhuman history with a living present.

The German work provided Attie with means to examine memory and history in other contexts. The most striking of his American projects has been *Between Dreams and History* (1998), in which the personal narratives of residents from Manhattan's Lower East Side were projected onto the buildings of this historical immigrant neighborhood. Known as a site from which immigrants, first Jewish and then Latin American, arrived and moved on, *Between Dreams and History* made that history specific and personal: not a romantic vision of the past but a current reality.

Archival material and projected visions of the past onto objects of the present also provide the foundation for the work of **Whitfield Lovell** (b. 1959). Like Attie, Lovell strives to balance the nostalgia of old pictures with material,

including architecture, that has historic bonds to the past and physical connections to the present. In a series of installations, Lovell has recreated the homes and insinuated the presence of African-Americans lost to the occlusions and embarrassments of American history. *Whispers From the Walls* (1999) (fig. **27.35**), for example, was created at the invitation of the University of North Texas, Denton, Texas. Lovell learned that Denton had been home to a flourishing African-American neighborhood called Quakertown.

27.35 Whitfield Lovell, *Whispers From the Walls*, 1999. Installation view.

In the early twenties, a white women's college opened nearby and the Quakertown community was dispersed. Lovell's installation, a single room decorated in the style of the period, becomes home to portraits of Quakertown citizens. Lovell found photographs of these people in local archives and transcribed them onto the walls in black oilstick. His drawing is sensitive and in places abbreviated so as to leave large areas of wood uncovered by line. The material of the room thus forms the bodies of its former residents. Completing the installation are two soundtracks, one playing old blues tunes and the other barely audible voices, bits of conversation and shouts of children that become the whispers of the walls. Through similar methods Lovell has retold histories of a variety of figures in the history of African-American life, from railroad workers in Houston to slave traders in Italy.

History, memory, and domestic life are also at the center of the work of British artist **Rachel Whiteread** (b. 1963). As compelled as Lovell by the physical pressure of the artist's hand against the walls around her, Whiteread applies materials as different as plaster, rubber, resin, plastic, and concrete to the surfaces of objects rich in domestic allusions. The resulting sculptures reveal the form of the negative space around objects as small and prosaic as bathtubs and mattresses and as large as a house itself. Evoking the geometric abstraction of both funereal sculpture and Minimalist art, Whiteread's work, she says, "has to do with the way our culture treats death; other cultures celebrate it and we try to brush it under the carpet."

Whiteread creates plastercasts of the absences that surround her. After several years of preparation, which included taking detailed measurements and estimates of equipment and materials, she created *Ghost* in 1990, a cast of the interior walls of a sitting room. Done in square panels of plaster, the sheets were assembled to become the positive form of the negative space of the room. Moldings and a mantelpiece forced shallow recessions into the form, while the fireplace left a slow spill of plaster. The structure conveys a palpable sense of loss and suggests a tomb, both in its size and in its emotional resonance.

In 1993, Whiteread was commissioned to create *House* (fig. **27.36**), the casting of the interior of an entire home in London's East End. Created from sprayed concrete, *House* stood in a low-income neighborhood that was being

27.36 Rachel Whiteread, *House*, 1993, destroyed 1994. Concrete. Commissioned by Artangel.

gentrified. Trading Victorian flourishes for concrete geometry produced an aggressive analogy for demographic changes that were occurring in London. An aesthetically intrusive commentary on urban planning, *House* spurred immediate controversy. Though conceived as a temporary monument, plans for postponing its removal were stymied due to the uproar.

Like Whiteread, Colombian sculptor **Doris Salcedo** (b. 1958) develops the expressive tradition of Minimalism while transforming its concern with universal experience to address local history. Salcedo clarifies her intentions by incorporating into her work materials, from clothing to furniture, that resonate with our daily life. *Casa Viuda (Widowed House) IV* (1994) (fig. **27.37**) is one of a group of works in which bedframes, doors, chairs, fabric, zippers, bone, and wire, are forced into geometric structures defined by the now illogical compression of once-useful furniture. Conceived for spaces such as hallways, entrances, and exits, *Widowed House* reiterates these transitional spaces in architecture, surrounding the viewer with a sense of physical and emotional change. Through her materials and compositions, Salcedo conveys confinement and occlusion in the physical experience of her work and, by extension, comments on the political landscape of Colombia.

Though she did graduate work in New York in the eighties, Salcedo has remained in Colombia. Her practice has included interviewing those who have suffered through the civil unrest of a country notable for its history of kidnappings and political murders, which are known as "disappearances." The disappearances inflicted an abstract brutality on the lives of victims' families. Salcedo incorporated materials given to her by the people she interviewed in her work, thus bringing into it the material presence of their lives, characterized in the artist's perception by their fragility and precariousness. The sculpture echoes the emotional rhythms of people whose understanding of their own past is scarred with great absences in their memory, as in their nation's history. The clarity of Salcedo's objects, carefully stitched seams and juxtapositions of cement, wood, hair, and lace for instance, when integrated into soft concrete and simple compositions, serves as an analogue for the poignancy of loss and the incomplete integration of death into the lives of those still living. In contrast to the work of William Kentridge (see fig. 27.25), Salcedo's sculpture articulates the distance between human lives and national histories and the absence of even the difficult resolutions that South Africa faced in the nineties.

The exploration by American artist **Kara Walker** (b. 1969) of the brutalities of the past has led her to join together racial stereotypes and decorative arts in her work. Walker creates sadomasochistic variations of Romance novel plots, dramatizing sexualized violence among slaves and between slaves and slave-owners. Walker's medium is cut paper shaped with a rococo lyricism that gives scenes of humiliation and violence elegant grace. Her decorative facility helps express her conviction that American identity,

27.37 Doris Salcedo, *La Casa Viuda IV*, 1994. Wood, fabric, and bones, 102⅓ × 18½ × 13" (260 × 47 × 33 cm). Private collection.

black as well as white, is rooted in finding pleasure in racist brutality. Walker's appeal to racist visual traditions and her pointed statements put her at the center of discussions of race and art in the nineties.

Walker's characters have the physiognomy of "Black memorabilia," the pickaninnies and sambos that Henry Louis Gates Jr., literary critic and director of the W. E. B. Du Bois Institute for Afro-American Research at Harvard University, has called the "peculiarly American repertoire of debased racist imagery." African-American artists since

27.38 Kara Walker, *Insurrection! (Our Tools Were Rudimentary, Yet We Pressed On)*, 2000. Cut paper and projection on wall, 11⅘ × 21 × 32⅝ × 10¾' (3.6 × 6.4 × 10 × 3.28 m). Installation view. Collection of Solomon R. Guggenheim Museum, New York.

the twenties have incorporated stereotypes into their work. Harlem Renaissance painters Aaron Douglas and Palmer Hayden exaggerated the lips, brows, and hair to insist on the racial identity of their subjects. More recently, Robert Colescott has presented the black body as inseparable from the stereotypes that have described it (see fig. 24.87). To critics, Walker's imagery has none of the pride or critique of its predecessors and is a naïve presentation of racist imagery for the delectation of racists. To defenders like Gates, Walker's hyperbole severs the affinity between the representation and reality on which its racist sources relied. So divorced from issues of realism, Walker's art, Gates argues, is a quintessentially Postmodern engagement with the powers of representation.

Work such as *Insurrection! (Our Tools Were Rudimentary, Yet We Pressed On)* (2000) (fig. 27.38) applies Walker's elegant debasement to liberation scenes. *Insurrection* sacrifices the moral clarity of such tales by describing the revolt as a sexualized melee. Walker's exquisitely detailed outlines trace slaves and whites in states of uncompromised physical pleasure, apparently oblivious to the larger issues of liberty and justice. Typical of her generation, Walker exhibits a readiness to complicate history with insights drawn from challenging the presumptions of the present.

Reprise and Reinterpretation: The Art of Art History

As is evident in the discussion thus far, art history has concerned nearly every artist in the modern era. Édouard Manet, perhaps the most art historically conscious artist of the modern period, has been a particularly fertile subject for those seeking to understand their relationship to the Western tradition. Japanese photographer **Yasumasa Morimura** (b. 1951) has explored the history of art and the place that history holds today by putting himself into recreations of canonical masterpieces. Associating himself with Cindy Sherman (he even recreated a Sherman work from the early eighties), Morimura announces that his intentions are critical.

For *Portrait (Twins)* (1988) (fig. **27.39**), his commentary on *Olympia* (see fig. 2.20), Morimura constructed an elaborate set of Olympia's boudoir in which he posed both as the infamous courtesan and as her maid. In apparently gleeful modifications to the Manet painting, one can see serious intrusions into modern art history. As we know from recent scholarship on *Olympia*, Manet's painting was about class. Morimura's addition of a bridal kimono casts Morimura/Olympia as a Japanese bride, and his transformation of the mysterious black cat into a figurine symbolizing commerce reiterates the class issues while adding those of race. Casting himself in the role of Olympia fuses the sexualized role of the prostitute with both the feminized and eroticized vision of the East still evident in Western discussions of Asian cultures. Moreover, as Norman Bryson has noted of *Portrait (Twins)*, raising the issue of race draws attention to the maid, the racial "other" already present but rarely discussed.

Morimura/Olympia takes on the observer's gaze and directs it, controlling those things one is able to see. If artists of the seventies and eighties examined the disturbing consequences of being the object of beauty, desire, and examination, in the nineties Morimura and artists including Nan Goldin and Lisa Yuskavage (see figs. 27.24, 27.54) explored the potential for agency and power from the same position. Morimura has updated his exploration to include taking on the personae and appearances of stars including Greta Garbo, Marilyn Monroe, Jodie Foster, and Madonna.

As for Morimura, nineteenth-century painting provided the starting point for Canadian photographer **Jeff Wall** (b. 1946). Wall is part of a community of photographers in Vancouver whose interests coincide around the play of artifice and observation in narrative photography. As an art history student, Wall was interested in the transformation of history painting from a genre restricted to depicting the greatness of the past to one that, in the hands of painters like Delacroix, Goya, or Manet, conveyed the gravity of contemporary life. In large light boxes meant to mimic the propagandistic quality of history painting with the boldness of advertising, Wall presents scenarios of human activity including domestic quarrels, war, or just random accidents. To approach the scale and declarative quality of history paintings, Wall carefully designs his settings, sometimes in a studio, but often outside, and directs actors to play out the scenes. Wall's process consists of digitalizing the negatives of numerous photographs and then combining them in a final transparency. The results give Wall even more compositional command and, as in *A Sudden Gust of Wind (After Hokusai)* (fig. **27.40**), impart gravity to the ambiguous activities depicted.

The narrative and appearance of *A Sudden Gust of Wind (After Hokusai)* (1993) was inspired by a woodblock print from the *Thirty-six Views of Mt. Fuji* (1823–33) by Katsushika Hokusai. Taking the Japanese woodblock as his model for contemporary history photography, Wall alludes to both Eastern and Western nineteenth-century artistic traditions and the nineteenth-century European fascination in Asian visual culture. Using photography to transform

27.39 Yasumasa Morimura, *Portrait (Futago)*, 1988. Colour photograph, 6'10¹¹⁄₁₆ × 9'10¹¹⁄₈" (2.1 × 3 m).

27.40 Jeff Wall, *A Sudden Gust of Wind (After Hokusai)*, 1993. Fluorescent light, color transparency, and display case, 7'6⅜" × 12'4⅞" (2.3 × 3.8 m). Tate Gallery, London.

the woodblock into a salon-style image of Canadian businessmen projects a certain irony onto the multicultural aspects of both the nineteenth and twentieth centuries.

Considering Nature: New Visions of Landscape

Since the beginning of the modern era, whether one dates that beginning to the seventeenth or the nineteenth century, landscape art has been understood to be part of social discourse and full of political and ideological content. Whether painted by Ruysdael, Delacroix, Courbet, or Cole or photographed by Muybridge or Brady, depictions of nature were used as a vehicle for social content. By the late twentieth century, the understanding of nature was changing. Throughout the history of the West, there has been a conviction that the natural world and the landscape genre were two separate things, one a work of God, the other a construction of humanity. Just as the idea of the body as a direct means of access to knowledge was no longer

followed, artists concluded that perhaps there was nothing to correspond to the historical idea of pure nature. Nature was becoming just a landscape, an entity dependant on our abilities to discuss and describe it rather than any innate quality it might possess.

In an exercise that illuminates the confluence of nature and culture, the Russian émigré duo of **Vitaly Komar** (b. 1943) and **Aleksandr Melamid** (b. 1945) created a series of most and least wanted paintings. They surveyed the public of several countries to determine what they liked and disliked in their art. In the United States, small angular abstractions in shades of brown and orange were the least appealing and historical landscapes in cool tones were ideal. *United States: Most Wanted Painting* (1993) (fig. 27.41) was roughly the size of a dishwasher. A combination of populism and irony, the *Most Wanted Paintings* series serves as a reminder that art historical genres are a way in which cultural demands define personal expression. Komar and Melamid's association of national and natural history makes it clear that even before the environment is

27.41 Vitaly Komar and Aleksandr Melamid, *America's Most Wanted*, 1994. Oil and acrylic on canvas, dishwasher size.

experienced, its meaning has been defined in the realm of national, historical, and cultural expectations.

American **Ann Hamilton** (b. 1956), like all the artists discussed in this chapter, makes work that intersects with many issues. Her 1996 traveling exhibition was titled The Body and the Object, while her 1997 European show, Present–Past, invoked the context of history. Her juxtapositions of materials and history occur in installations that conjure magical–realist landscapes. Vistas with waterfalls, flowers, and people working are infused with smells of farmyards and orchards, and the activities of insects and birds. A student of Judy Pfaff (see fig. 26.62), Hamilton exerts control over large spaces and heterogeneous materials of natural as well as clearly manufactured origin.

Parallel Lines (1991) (fig. 27.42), a key work of the early nineties, was created as a historical landscape that responded to the artist's travels in Brazil. Invited to participate in the 1991 São Paolo Biennial, Hamilton began work by researching the area from the rainforest to urban industrial zones. Hamilton covered walls with copper tags and "painted" others with the carbon of burning candles, the remains of which were piled high on a cart in the room. In an annex she left a turkey carcass to be eaten by bugs. Hamilton presented the installation with a descriptive poem beginning:

the entrance, a road encrusted
with numbered copper tokens, emblems of exchange
marred, marked, touched, tarnished, placed
a cradle of freight, piled, mounded, stacked
the laid sinew of candles
burned and extinguished …

In presence and description, *Parallel Lines* evokes the intersection between rural and urban life, the same scenery that politicized landscape painting in the nineteenth century. Work and trade is a central theme in much of Hamilton's art. Often her pieces include people knitting, wrapping objects, or engaged in similarly simple tasks. Likewise, the quantities of materials that she uses (*Parallel Lines* used 20,000 candles and 999 copper tags) connote the dour repetition of menial labor.

The sculptures of British artist **Andy Goldsworthy** (b. 1956), site-specific installations of materials as transitory as ice and as lasting as stone, poetically acknowledge the role of humanity in the shaping of nature, yet respond to our desires for the restorative otherness of the natural world. Goldsworthy draws from the details of the local environment—stone walls in New England or sheepfolds in Cumbria—to bring the viewer into a relationship with

27.42 Ann Hamilton, *Parallel Lines*, 1991. Candles (lengths variable, 1 to 6' each, or 30 to 183 cm), steel basin, table, candle soot, glass and steel vitrines, turkey carcasses, Dermastid beetles, copper tags.

the environment. In locations from Southern France to South Australia, Goldsworthy has assembled stone cairns, monumental variations on traditional trail markers, joining the history of exploration to the organic elegance of Brancusi or Arp (see chapter 9). Though often romantic in his reminders of our smallness within the sweeping vistas of nature, Goldsworthy consistently forces our attention to the landscape as a site of interaction between humanity and the environment.

Goldsworthy's *Storm King Wall* (1997–98) (fig. **27.43**), a site-specific installation for the Storm King Art Center sculpture park in Mountainville, New York, combines the themes of travel and integration of self and environment by transforming a fixture in the New England countryside, the old stone wall, into an anthropomorphic reminder of a walk in the woods. Built from local stones, the wall rises up from the ground, winds around trees, dips into a lake, climbs out and continues to a nearby road. Stone walls of the region are physical evidence of the transformation of the American wilderness into a political landscape. In Goldsworthy's work this sign of power and possession becomes the expression of a journey that moves into and beyond our distinctions of private property.

American **Diana Thater** (b. 1962) populates her landscapes with animals for whom, in her own words, "[the]

experience of time and space never seems ... to be singular and who express their experience of 'present-ness' with their whole beings." Such similarities between the animal world and the Postmodern one become the foundation for seeing nature as a body of cultural knowledge that is still profoundly foreign to human civilization. Thater's work in the nineties featured the vibrant blues, reds, and greens of video monitors and a menagerie of socialized animals from trained wolves to honey bees to explore the myth of untamed wilderness and the reality of human intrusion.

Knots + Surfaces (2001) (fig. **27.44**) argues that some parts of nature still hold liberating possibilities for human life. The film presents the dance of the honeybee mapped onto numbered hexagons of color and projected onto the floor, walls, and ceiling of a gallery. A wall of video monitors present brightly colored flowers. Thater drew inspiration for the work from mathematical models of six-dimensional space based on the dance of bees. The potential for the expansive understanding of space gleaned from the animal world, both as a reality and a metaphor, accents the aspects of Thater's art concerned with creating alternatives to existing relationships between human beings and between the human and the animal world. *Knots + Surfaces* also practices the deconstructive project of drawing awareness to the viewer's presence while picturing nature. As in

27.43 Andy Goldsworthy, *Storm King Wall*, 1997–98. Field stone, approx. 5′ × 2,278′6″ (1.52 × 694.5 m) overall.

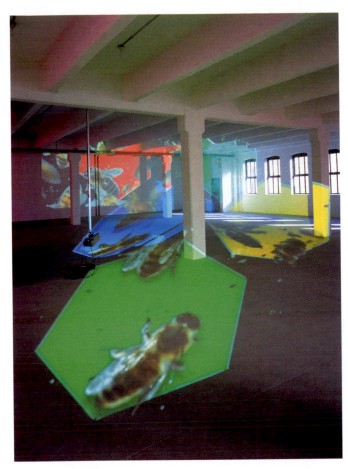

27.44 Diana Thater, *Knots + Surfaces*, 2001. Installation for 5 LCD video projectors, 16 video monitors, 6 DVD players, 1 VVR-1000 synchronizer, 6 DVDs unique, and 1 AP.

many of Thater's pieces, the projectors and monitors of *Knots + Surfaces* are located high on the walls and low on the floor so that one must walk through the light, becoming a screen for the image and a shadow on the wall. To see *Knots + Surfaces* is to intrude on its form and complete the cast of characters. Thater intends to include the performers, creator, and audience in the work.

Thater's strategic placement of her equipment makes us aware that, to use the phrase of Icelandic sculptor **Olafur Eliasson** (b. 1967), we are seeing ourselves seeing. Unlike the romanticism of the past, we are not invited to lose ourselves in nature but to reflect on our relationship with it. Eliasson's work, typical of much art in the late twentieth century, invites a sublime loss of self, but never permits us to remain untroubled by the reality of our surroundings.

Your Strange Certainty Still Kept (1996) (fig. **27.45**) is a room-sized electrical storm. Water falls to the floor from parallel strips on the ceiling as strobe lights flash in a darkened room. The sound of water and the explosions of light have the sensual resonance of being in a storm, yet, like actors on a soundstage or visitors to a museum, we don't get wet. In fact the strobes are timed to create the illusion that the water is not even falling. Suspended in air, Eliasson's sublime vision is both immediate and distant. In a similarly synaesthesic installation for the 1999 Carnegie International in Pittsburgh, Pennsylvania, Eliasson rerouted steam from museum heating ducts to surround a cluster of trees placed in its lobby. The centerpiece effectively illustrated the intertwined histories of romanticism and industrialism—a fitting statement for a historic center of the American industrial Midwest such as Pittsburgh. A highly

27.45 Olafur Eliasson, *Your Strange Certainty Still Kept*, 1996. Water, light, plexiglass, plastic, recirculating pump, and woodbase: 1'8" × 17'7¾" × 10" (0.5 × 5.2 × 0.25 m), top: 14'5¼" (4.39 m) long.

visual artist, Eliasson connects the long tradition of romantic landscape painting to the brief history of conceptual art. His critical voice, in work such as *Your Strange Certainty Still Kept*, relies on keeping the history and experience of art in close proximity. Works such as these use the museum as a guide to our understanding of nature.

Painting and Sculpture as Social (ized) Spaces

Meeting Points: Exploring a Postmodern Abstraction

In abstraction, as in representation, the deconstructive lessons that began in the late sixties were, by the nineties, bearing reconstructive fruit. That all artistic languages are compromised by the myths and politics out of which they were created is no longer viewed as an impenetrable barrier to speech or art. Years of analysis seemed to have left many artists confident in their ability to communicate without the kind of mastery desired by a Pollock of a Van Gogh, or the kind of resistance of a Warhol or a Kruger.

American artist **Jonathan Lasker** (b. 1948) titled a 1989 painting *Euphoric Routine*, neatly expressing the irony that even as abstract art strives toward emotional immediacy, it is based on learned and repeated procedures. Lasker's paintings, which are rhythmic and visually engaging, but also oddly distant and mute, draw on a history of postwar painting that concluded that, if abstraction communicated at all, it was because artists and viewers agreed that marks meant something. It was this linguistic quality of abstraction that Johns and Twombly examined (see figs. 21.17, 22.13) and the consequences of disregarding it that

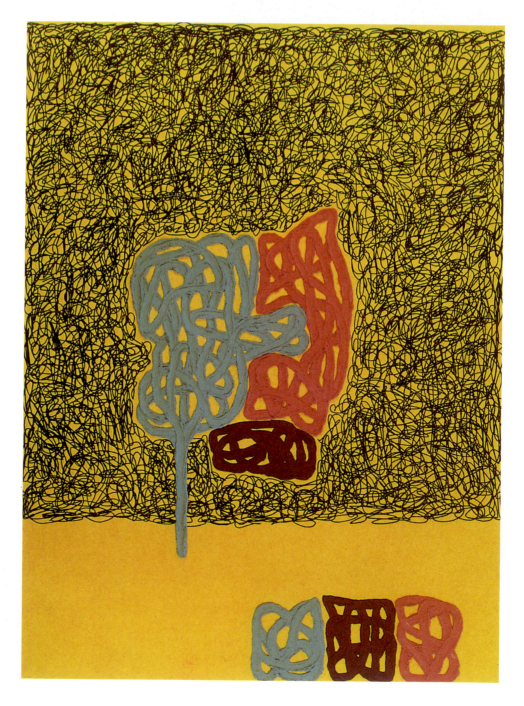

27.46 Jonathan Lasker, *To Believe in Food*, 1991. Oil on linen, 8'4" × 6'3" (2.5 × 1.9 m). Private collection.

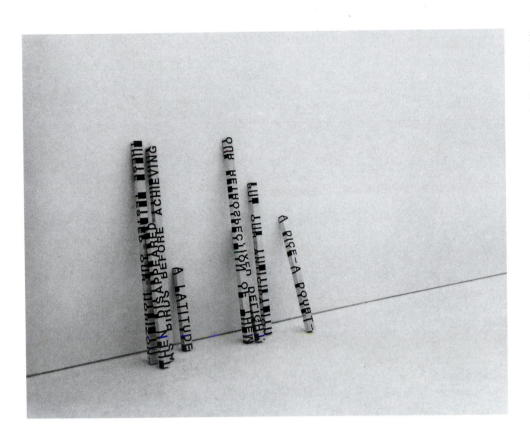

27.47 Roni Horn, *When Dickinson Shut Her Eyes— For Felix; No. 886,* 1993. Plastic and aluminum, dimensions variable.

concerned Halley and Bleckner (see figs. 26.45, 26.46). Lasker's work demonstrates that one can respect the contrivance of abstraction while maintaining confidence in its expressive potential.

Lasker was particularly influenced by Brice Marden's calligraphic paintings (see fig. 22.64), but was troubled by the ease with which the viewer's mind is taken from canvas to the soul. To slow this process, Lasker devised studio practices that give a Postmodernist twist to modernist conventions. Lasker began with automatic drawings on paper in the Surrealist mode. He then enlarged the drawings, carefully preserving both the shape of the mark and the quality of the pen that made them. These copied marks became the individual elements of a painting. In *To Believe in Food* (1991) (fig. **27.46**), they are the neutral scribbles and monotonous black lines that adorn the acid yellow field. By referring to the process as "editing my own subconscious," Lasker suggests that, in addition to critiquing conventional faith in abstraction, his work contains a plea to accept the emotional responses that such painting elicits. Self-consciously made with a compromised language, *To Believe in Food* argues that the impulses to edit, copy, quote, falsify, mislead, critique, assemble, travesty, mock, and honor that are all evident in this painting reveal much about personality and contemporary life as well as the history of art.

The explorations into the phenomenology of sculpture proposed by American artist **Roni Horn** (b. 1955) can be likened to Lasker's dissection of abstract painting. Her earliest works, carefully crafted structures of a single material such as rubber or gold foil, highlight the specific properties of the different media. The title of her retrospective,

Making Being Here Enough, captures the essence of her desire to "make sensible experience more present." "Sensible" can be understood as relating both to the senses and to finding meaning. In *Gold Mats, Paired—for Ross and Felix* (1994–95), a stack of two gold mats seems to cling together and the floor even as the corners curl up from the ground, turning the consequences of layering sheets of gold into a memorial for Felix Gonzalez-Torres and his lover (see fig. 27.15).

Horn's sculpture resists our impulse to see sculptures as chiefly representations of or visual analogs for things or emotions. Seen in a photograph, the ambitious 1982–83 *Cobbled Lead(s),* in which Horn replaced a 225-square-foot (20.9 m²) area of cobblestones in a museum courtyard with lead replicas, is an uneventful triangle. To understand the work demands that one pass over it and sense the changes in surface as one might physically register the walking from sidewalk to street. Horn's work suggests the rather thrilling variety of experience that can be initiated by the slightest change in our surroundings. In the nineties, Horn created several geometric aluminum sculptures imbedded with fragments of poetry. The sculptures, including *When Dickinson Shut Her Eyes—For Felix; No. 886* (1993) (fig. **27.47**), reveal their poetry only if one moves around them. Again appealing to our sense and our senses, Horn's sculpture reveals poetic facets of the physical world.

Fiona Rae (b. 1963), a member of the yBas, and Ellen Gallagher, an African-American painter of the same generation, have created two very different oeuvres based on the conviction that abstraction has rich communicative potential despite, or because of, its compromised position. Rae's canvases posit a play between the gridded structure

27.48 Fiona Rae, *Untitled (Sky Shout)*, 1997. Oil and acrylic on canvas, 108 × 96" (274.3 × 243.8 cm). Private collection.

of Minimalist control and the expressive mark-making of Expressionist desire to signify competing aspects in a single personality. A work like *Untitled (Sky Shout)* (1997) (fig. **27.48**) gives the impression of a collage of brushstrokes stolen from the history of art. A Richter smear is repeated to build a geometric ground interrupted every few feet by a Ken Noland circle or a Kline-like stroke. Rae's archival aesthetics, as well as her own striking means of assembly, use the juxtaposition and connotations of past styles to convey content. In addition, Rae's work has a sense of humor and contains passages in which the cathartic energy of the expressive marks is only just contained by the grids, reminding one of the sublime content that her predecessors swore they could reach.

Rae's paintings manipulate the connotations of historical styles. She uses the public meaning of abstraction to communicate private expressions. **Ellen Gallagher** (b. 1965) engages abstraction as a code bearing private content and resisting public interpretation. Abstract art has had a long and ambivalent relationship with the idea of code. Picasso's *Ma Jolie*, Malevich's *Black Square*, and Johns's targets all incorporated the idea that making modern art requires building a private cosmology and viewing it demands an act of deciphering. In 1992, Gallagher was at the Skowhegan School of Art, Maine, where Peter Halley, Kiki Smith and Ann Hamilton (see figs. 26.45, 27.10, 27.42) were all teaching. Though differing in their output, each of these artists has integrated symbolic pictorial elements and abstract form in their work. Gallagher's inclusion of even the smallest bit of representation into the abstract fields of her compositions infiltrates the coded structure of abstraction, placing the history of art in a very different context.

A close look at *They Could Still Serve* (2001) (fig. **27.49**) and a quick review of the artist's statements reveals a surprising source for the tiny biomorphic forms that dance across Gallagher's work: they are eyes from caricatures of African-Americans. In explaining her process Gallagher reveals "a willingness to play with something that is ugly. Making a cosmology out of these things that

27.49 Ellen Gallagher, *They Could Still Serve*, 2000. Pigment, paper, and glue on linen, 10' × 8' (3.05 × 2.44 m).

are so awful … ." Unlike Kara Walker (see fig. 27.38), Gallagher nearly hides her iconography in vast canvases, suggesting a different commentary on race. What rises to the surface as one loses one's self in the delicate tracery of gentle washes, rouge grids, and fragmented blackface, is a pertinent reminder of the persistence of racism.

Reinventing Representation

The renewed faith in the communicative power of abstraction was accompanied by a similar reclamation of the figure. The political history of figure painting revealed in feminist analyses had made the genre suspect ever since the late sixties. In the eighties, the presence of figural motifs in Neo-Expressionism alerted some critics to what was theorized as a return to oppressive models of art history. The work in the seventies of Wilke, Schneeman, Acconci, and Burden (see figs. 24.26, 24.25, 24.16) had enlisted the presumed potential of physical experience to overcome alienation from the self to give the body the artistic priority that was formally given to the figure. By the nineties, however, the direct route between the body and knowledge had been questioned, and the contrived nature of the figure appeared useful. Figurative artists already discussed include Murakami, Mori, Sikander, and Cox.

Raymond Pettibon (b. 1957) is one of a number of Californian artists whose work has been challenging

modernism since the late seventies from positions less strictly theoretical than their east-coast counterparts. Pettibon has done so through a focused examination of the relationship between figural subjects, text, and time in narrative images. Narrative, of course, has been the implicit foundation of such archetypal Postmodern work as Cindy Sherman's untitled film stills (see fig. 26.4). However, in Sherman's case, as in that of Simpson or Weems (see figs. 27.22, 27.20), the story is secondary to the consequences that the telling has on the identity of the speaker. Artists like Pettibon maintained allegiance to the more traditional pleasures of narrative tension and resolve while transforming our ideas about the relationship of text and image. The passage on *No Title (The Translator's Have)* (1996) (fig. **27.50**) continues "attempted to satisfy themselves first as to the author's exact meaning …" thereby drawing attention to the impossible challenge of Pettibon's art.

Pettibon's first work was illustrations that were aimed at Californian youth culture. In the eighties, he produced his own illustrated magazine *Tripping Corpse* (1981–86) and did graphics for hardcore bands Black Flag, the Minutemen, and, later, Sonic Youth. By the nineties, he was citing Henry James while appropriating figures such as Batman. Reiterating the disjunction between text and image, Pettibon's drawing style is formally eclectic.

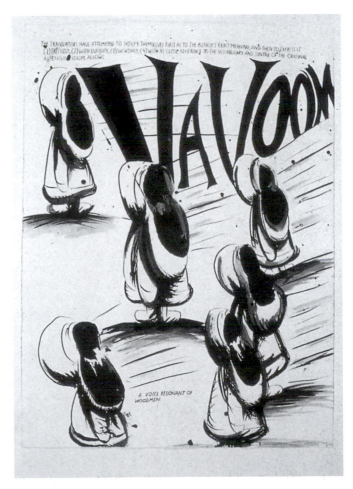

27.50 Raymond Pettibon, *No Title (The Translator's Have)*, 1996. Pen and ink on paper, 29¾ × 22" (75.6 × 55.9 cm).

Critics have found in his stylistic variation the kind of formal self-consciousness of Johns, Polke, and Twombly. Pettibon's decision to locate this heady research in the tradition of Comix—the genre of highly stylized cartoons usually focused on subcultural fascinations with sex and drugs and circulated in "zines" such as *Tripping Corpse*—rather than painting demonstrates how, where, and with whom art issues are being discussed. The irony that Pettibon's imagery was as at home in art history departments as it was at SST Records (the LA punk label of Pettibon's brother) is indicative of the cross-cultural migrations that art encouraged in the nineties.

Marlene Dumas (b. 1953) began painting the figure in the mid-eighties while studying psychology in her adopted home of Amsterdam. Raised in South Africa under apartheid, Dumas has spoken of the painful awareness that her self-image as a "sweet young girl" was inseparable from her power and privilege as a white South African. The threatening dichotomy of innocence and power informs Dumas's series on children, sexuality, and South Africa.

The unsettling convergence of endearing childhood charm and the knowing power of a young girl is at the heart of *The Painter* (1994) (fig. **27.51**). Composed like a family snapshot, and perhaps based on one as well, *The Painter* shares with Sally Mann's *Immediate Family* (see fig. 27.2) a tendency to make details of childhood, such as dirty hands or a casual look, into signs of threat. Though the title and picture suggest that this girl was just making art on the floor, *The Painter* is often discussed as the record of a crime scene. Red paint can be seen to resemble blood and the charm of childhood is layered with fear. Dumas has used the format of *The Painter* to juxtapose themes of death and childhood and even describes the incipient aggression in her method.

Dumas uses found and photographed images as sources for her work. Translating the photograph into watercolor slows the speed of the camera to match the sensual flow of the painting medium. As intellectual in her appropriation as Richard Prince or Sherrie Levine (see chapter 26), Dumas's style reveals concern with the "trace of human touch" and the conflicts of human, particularly female, experience. Her method also poses a certain aggression, revealed in her explanation that "My people were all shot by a camera, framed before I painted them. They didn't know that I'd do this to them."

Most Beautiful Girl in the World, 1993 snapshots taken by American sculptor **Charles Ray** (b. 1953) that in their mundane settings attempt to make a supermodel look ordinary, further articulates the ambivalent relationship between artists and models in the nineties. Branded a Conceptual Realist, Ray has used the figure to address the ironic relationship between our ideals and the realities of the psychic and material worlds. Characterized by immaculate craftsmanship and a surrealistic combination of the hyperreal and the fake, Ray's work relies on simple modifications of the ordinary or expected to suggest emotional, psychological, even pathological states. *Self-Portrait* (1990) shows a mannequin dressed in casual boating attire with a generalized portrait of the artist as its head. The portrait has an uncanny suggestion of a human personality even as it projects the vapid look of a department store window display.

Family Romance (1993) (fig. **27.52**) relies on a sight gag as simple as *Self-Portrait*. In this family of four, the parents are scaled down by fifty percent and the children up by fifty percent. The resulting group is of approximately equal height but disparate build. The family looks distracted and a bit distressed, but there is no sense that they are responding to the physical transformation of their bodies. This family registers as figures whose reference is the artwork itself; their bodies are kept at a distance from the world. Though inspired by Ray's appreciation of Anthony Caro's command of scale (see fig. 22.40), the generalized antiseptic quality of Ray's distortions has led critics to see the work as addressing the idea of the nuclear family and its troubling late-century inconsistencies.

In the nineties, not only was the figure reassessed, but artists challenged the idea that before one painted or

27.51 Marlene Dumas, *The Painter*, 1994. Oil on canvas, 6'6" × 3'3" (1.98 × 0.99 m).

27.52 Charles Ray, *Family Romance*, 1993. Mixed media, 4'6" × 8' × 2' (1.37 × 2.44 × 0.61 m).

sculpted she or he had to interrogate the history and power of her or his chosen medium. Self-consciousness toward one's medium had been part of the legacy of modernism that artists from Jasper Johns and Gerhard Richter to Peter Halley and Barbara Kruger had turned into a critical tool of Postmodernism. By the end of the twentieth century, it was being taken for granted that the properties of painting, formal or political, had been exposed. A group of painters, Americans John Currin and Lisa Yuskavage among them, began generating imagery by using the old tools of realism in the new context of Postmodernism.

Developing realism in the nineties was, to **John Currin** (b. 1962) a form of "drag" in which figures, purely artificial in the contemporary mind, dressed as if they were mimetic representations of the real. Emphasizing the fact that bypassing the history of art since Courbet (see fig. 2.16) is a willful project, Currin fills his illusionistic spaces with exaggerated fantasies of middle-class white male America. Everything is sexualized.

The Cripple (1997) (fig. **27.53**), a politically incorrect title for an image of a suggestive if somewhat disturbing young waif with a cane, exemplifies Currin's understanding of the male imagination. Other works are populated by young blondes with impossibly large breasts coddling a cast of helpless men. Discussed as representing the masochism of hyperbolic male fantasy, Currin defends himself against

27.53 John Currin, *The Cripple*, 1997. Oil on canvas, 3'8" × 3' (1.12 × 0.91 m).

27.54 Lisa Yuskavage, *Honeymoon*, 1998. Oil on linen, 6'5½" × 4'7" (1.97 × 1.4 m). Private Collection.

charges of misogyny by asserting that though he uses the tools of realism, "the subject of painting is always the artist," never the objects that he or she paints. The reality being painted is a personal and psychological one.

Heightening the irony of realism by representing illogical figures with the logical devices of illusionism is also part of the art of **Lisa Yuskavage** (b. 1962), as is the use of exaggerated female anatomies. Unlike Currin's however, Yuskavage's figures direct their attentions inward. Violets, pinks, and blues dominate scenes of erotic self-absorption. In *Honeymoon* (1998) (fig. **27.54**), Yuskavage rhymes the sensuous surfaces of flesh and nightgown with a view of mountains that look like a Chinese landscape seen through rose-colored glasses.

Yuskavage creates work that flirts with being insipid but is saved by flagrant exaggerations of both cliché and anatomy as well as creative painterly technique. In the context of decades of resistance, the creation of such oversexed female types painted in a style that seems to encourage objectification has been a confusing statement about art in the late nineties. Figures have completely replaced bodies in this art and provide access to the suggestive and cathartic power of traditional tools such as perspective, chiaroscuro, illusionism, and paint.

The Consequences of Tradition: Pictorialism and Sculpture

One of the lessons of Minimalism was that attention to one's medium often led to a breakdown of traditional categories of art. Jasper Johns's and Frank Stella's paintings executed in the fifties asserted themselves in the language of sculpture. *Flag*, by Johns (see fig. 21.14), and Stella's black paintings (see chapter 22) are objects in the room far more than they are representations of something in the world. Eschewing the illusionism that had invited the three-dimensional world onto the canvas, Johns and Stella forced their paintings into the space of sculpture. Painters and sculptors in the nineties took the material quality of both painting and sculpture as given and turned back to the illusionistic devices of representation to arrive at new mixtures of painting and sculpture. In painting, such a practice is present in works of the Neo-Geo movement. In 1983–84, Frank Stella pinpointed the present state of such formalist heresy in his series of Elliot Norton Lectures, given at Harvard University and published as *Working Space*. The thesis of *Working Space* was that the artworld was witnessing a crisis in abstraction that could be resolved through an appeal to the pictorial. After a long career asserting the material presence of his paintings, their character as objects in the real world, Stella was suggesting that artists turn back to Caravaggio and add to a painting's materiality its power of depicting immaterial space as well. As evident in the return to figuration, illusionism was on many artists minds. Though Stella was addressing painters, the mixing of pictorialism with formalism was also something that sculptors adopted with particular energy. Art was pushing into and off the wall, stretching the history of art by intruding its activities into the spaces of reality.

Your Skin in this Weather Bourne Eye-Threads & Swollen Perfume (1995) (fig. **27.55**), by American artist **Jessica Stockholder** (b. 1959) invades the space of the gallery, welcoming the viewer into a painterly terrain that evades the architecture to open up spectacular visual and physical encounters. Stockholder aims to stimulate a "struggle between viewing a static *fait accompli* and feeling as if [you] are participating in a series of contradictions and narratives that come to no settled conclusion." Stockholder's ideas, generated first as color exercises, find expression in a dizzying array of materials that demand the viewer frames his or her own visual experience and select what connotative roads to go down. *Your Skin* creates this struggle with vast fields of paint, a brilliant blue swimming pool liner, a bright yellow canopy of rope, dress shirts, bed pillows, pink shag, and gold Buddhas all suggesting meanings as diverse as their visual flourishes.

Though there are places within *Your Skin* where one can see substantial portions of the installation, you never see all of it. Trying to emulate the process of thinking rather than the character of an idea, Stockholder maintains a tension between discovery and analysis. *Your Skin* included online

27.55 Jessica Stockholder, *Your Skin in the Weather Bourne Eye-Threads & Swollen Perfume*, 1995. Mixed media, 3,600 sq ft × 18' (334.44 m² × 5.49 m). Installation view at the DIA Center for the Arts, New York.

complements to the work. One could read a short story inspired by the installation titled *Thrilled to Death*, which was about travel and storytelling; view several working drawings for the piece; read artist statements; and speculate on the importance of what looked like travel photos. Never dictating how to prioritize the information that she provides, Stockholder created a situation in which painting, sculpture, travel, fiction, experience, and vision all intertwined in multidimensional abstractions.

British artist **Liam Gillick** (b. 1964) creates variations on Minimalist forms that make up the architectural dimension of a project that includes speculative philosophy, narrative fiction, social criticism, and an almost tentative utopianism. Alone, the sculptures themselves, like the 1997 *Resignation Platform* (fig. **27.56**), enlist relatively ordinary materials, such as plexiglass, aluminum, and plywood, in straightforward geometric sculptures. Compared to the forceful singularity of Donald Judd's work (see fig. 22.47), with its clear sense of space and authoritative presentation of spatial and coloristic ideas, Gillick's *Resignation Platform* seems unfinished and tentative. Panels seem to be missing, leaving openings that allow the eye and mind to wander through and around the translucent bands of colors that themselves look as if they were lifted from office decorating manuals. Nothing about the work demands that the mind of the viewer be contained by the object.

Gillick writes of his work in terms similar to Stockholder's:

> There is a provisional quality to things and that is important to me. I invite people to be involved in the intellectual reframing of the idea, I don't present something and then invite everyone to try and work out the solution to the visual puzzle I have left in the gallery.

Gillick is concerned with involving the viewer in designing a satisfying social space to contain daily activities. A rough guide to his intentions can be found in the scenarios described in his books. In a particularly resonant passage in *Literally No Place*, the artist discusses a place where people "can be controlled and free simultaneously … a place that can be communal without being communist." Gillick does not attempt to create this space through the construction of homes, offices, or work spaces but rather in what he

27.56 Liam Gillick, *Discussion Island Resignation Platform*, 1997. Aluminum angle, plexiglass, cables, fittings, 94 × 141" (240 × 360 cm).

calls "parallel spaces," models in which the experiments of living and working can be played out.

Rirkrit Tiravanija also speaks of creating models for thinking about daily life. His "parallel positions" involve producing events in a museum or gallery setting that address work, service, sociability, and community in a surprisingly direct way. *Untitled (Still)* of 1995 is one of Tiravanija's food pieces in which he makes curry for gallery visitors, filling the commercial art space with the service and product of a restaurant and the conviviality of a home. Catering-size bags of ingredients lay around, as do dishes and pans in various states of use, making a display of the creating and eating of the meal. Tiravanija is careful to point out that performances such as these do not bring the home experience into the gallery for examination. This is not a form of realism. *Untitled (Still)* is an event that generates certain forms of sociability that, though they are fundamental to our understanding of civilized society, are in fact rare in daily experience.

Tiravanija is a model of the global artist. Born in Buenos Aires, and raised in Bangkok and Canada, he attended art schools in Canada and the United States and produced art around the globe. The shifting nature of identity as one moves in and out of familiar and foreign environments is integrated into Tiravanija's food pieces through his use of Thai curry. It is nearly impossible to make "authentic" Thai curry due to the absence of appropriate ingredients in most locations. The dish becomes a metaphor for the transformations of individuals and cultures and the resilience of human desire for communal activity despite such change.

Untitled (Still) is a stridently hopeful work that draws attention to the best of late twentieth-century globalism.

Jason Rhoades (b. 1965) provides a different commentary on globalism and the expansive possibilities of art. His installations enlist the formal properties of abstract painting and sculpture to explore the spaces of vision and experience with a particularly American perspective. His sculptures often illustrate myths of America and include narrative performances. *Cherry Makita—Honest Engine Work* (1993) (fig. **27.57**), an early work, is a tableau that explodes the traditional male space of the garage with a makeshift aesthetic of found objects, ephemeral materials, and overwhelming clutter only just unified by spatial containment and coloristic harmonies. *Cherry Makita* provided the set for a performance in which Rhoades worked in the garage with a Makita cordless drill that he had hooked up to a car engine. As in his later pieces, which included elements of gun play and sexual bravado, *Cherry Makita* provided a phallic hyperbole at the centerpiece of the chaos.

Despite the expansive themes of mythic America, and the overflowing installations, Rhoades is intent on creating an intimate and contemplative environment. Built "for literally two or three people," Rhoades's work achieves a balance between grandiosity and intimacy. The spaceball that features in one installation is regularly cited as a metaphor for Rhoades's intentions. In the center of the installation, the spinning viewer finds himself weightless, at a physical loss in the face of overwhelming material display. In 2000 Rhoades shipped his car to Europe, reproducing

27.57 Jason Rhoades, *Cherry Makita—Honest Engine Work*, 1993. Garage renovation, New York, various materials; size varies according to installation, 141 × 130 × 180" (358.1 × 330.2 × 457.2 cm).

27.58 Damien Hirst, *Pharmacy* (detail of restaurant windows with medicine), 1998.

the quint-essential Los Angeles space, a large American car built to travel the endless LA highways, for himself and a passenger. The car, *Impala (International Museum Project About Leaving and Arriving)*, like Rhoades's work in general, takes individual experience and confuses its limits, pushing past the confines of ego, exhibition space, national borders, and sometimes even gravity.

The work of British artist **Damien Hirst** (b. 1965) is excessive in many directions as well. Like many of his generation, Hirst has found the Minimalist vocabulary useful for creating a "clean, minimal, kind of acceptable look, with an intellectual splatter." The most notorious of Hirst's works is a Minimalist glass tank containing a shark in formaldehyde. In this work, titled *The Physical Impossibility of Death in the Mind of Someone Living*, Hirst's morbidity and philosophical inclinations come neatly packaged in Minimalist pedigree.

Pharmacy, the final work in a series of installations addressing medicine, takes the sculptural dialogue with life and death to a high-class restaurant in London in 1998. Travestying such restaurants as the Hard Rock Café, *Pharmacy* (fig. **27.58**) takes the current faith in pharmaceuticals as its theme. Cabinets with aesthetically elegant displays of drugs filter the light as it falls on tables decorated with tablets and pills. A giant model of DNA adorns the dining room, while detailing suggests the hygiene of an operating room. An artist whose earlier work included bisected sheep, rotting carcasses, and oversized ashtrays, Hirst here plays out his interest in the nature of sickness and death on the stage of London's social life.

Pharmacy is both an artistic confrontation with social space and a marketing strategy on a par with those of Andy Warhol or Keith Haring. Unlike such market-savvy artists before him, however, Hirst maintains a surprisingly high level of violence in his art. Speaking sentiments that could apply to Kara Walker (see fig. 27.38) and Raymond Pettibon (see fig. 27.50) or filmmakers such as Quentin

Tarantino and Peter Greenaway, Hirst explained, "I am an artist. I use violence as a way to communicate." The success of *Pharmacy* reveals a certain comfort that we have in keeping company with death.

Think Before You Buy: Art and Cultural History

No artist of the modern or Postmodern era has worked without an awareness of the pressures of the exhibition and sale of their art. The relationship between artists, museums, and markets is a central dynamic in the history of art. Realists and Impressionists painted in relation to the salons and independent exhibitions (see chapter 2). The group exhibitions of the Fauves or Expressionists responded to and in turn defined the nature of the art they showed (see chapters 7 and 8). As the twentieth century wore on, new forums for exhibition and distribution met the needs and shaped the understanding of new art. The nineties began with a clear understanding that current exhibition practices were being compromised by politics and, as the bubble of the eighties burst, that current methods of sale and distribution were in dire need of change. In the eighties, the stratospheric careers of Neo-Expressionists like Julian Schnabel or David Salle (see figs. 26.25, 26.26) were fueled by the expert promotional skills of galleries and private collectors. The market of the eighties, however, inflated the value of its biggest names, and collectors and dealers had to diversify their collections. The most visible mechanism to fill this need has been the international art fairs, which brought art critics and cultural tourists to locations around the world. The spectacle of the events created significant energy and interest in a group of international artists, many of whom would not have had access to the more centralized art market of the eighties.

Diversification had, of course, been a goal of artists for the previous few decades. It was an irony of the nineties that as a host of international biennials and triennials as well as virtual artistic communities in cyberspace began providing increasingly diverse alternatives to the traditional museums and markets, financial advisors, art dealers, and auction houses were selling clients on the greater financial security provided by the dissolution of local art markets and improved international resaleability. Moreover, as the individual collectors and donors became pressed and government spending on culture, especially in the United States, declined, private corporations became more important to the artworld. The increased importance of corporate sponsorship has meant that private corporations might finance an array of events in different museums creating, in effect, private art networks within public institutions. Artists and curators recognized that, just as art was central to notions of self and society, it was also becoming a key facet of corporate power, financial management, and global relations. In this environment, it seemed that the museum would have to find a new identity for itself.

Two challenges presented themselves to the traditional museum: how to keep pace with the globally diverse market, and how to write the history of art to coincide with the less linear form of contemporary artistic awareness. Conceptualizing a new mission for the museum and a new form for displaying the history of art became a chief concern of those in the culture industry. Neither the international dispersal of art and commerce, nor the rehanging of major museums, came without sharp criticism.

In the nineties, international biennials multiplied, providing artistic and political opportunities for exhibiting national culture to international audiences. The Venice Biennale is the model for the international art fair, with venues for national displays, while the Whitney Biennial, hosted by the Whitney Museum of American Art, New York, is the typical national model. Such events serve as a gathering of culture and commerce but also have distinct political advantages for the host countries. Creating a cultural variation on the United Nations, host countries can enter into global economy through art when diplomatic options are not always available. South Africa used the Johannesburg Biennial to present its post-apartheid face and countries including Taiwan, Cuba, Lithuania, Korea, and Australia have found it expedient to present themselves as suitable hosts and patrons for international art. Though embroiled in the politics of nationalism and globalism, such events also provide visibility to an internally produced art that has challenged any homogeneous view of contemporary art.

The *Advertising Castle* (fig. **27.59**) of **Cai Guoqiang** (b. 1957) is a clear statement of what was at stake in the potentially liberating world of the global art market. Raised in China and based first in Japan and then New York, Cai's personal experience put him in a good position to examine the global economies of culture and finance. Cai took the occasion of the 1998 Taipei Biennial, which, like all the biennials, aimed to inspire intellectual analysis, encourage

cultural tourism and boost nationalism, to raise the issue of complicity between art and politics. In the political gamesmanship between China and Taiwan in the late nineties, as well as in the cultural and economic competition that existed in Southeast Asia, Taiwanese nationalism was a volatile issue. Cai sheathed the Taipei Fine Arts Museum, host of the biennial, in a bamboo scaffold covered in advertisements. He highlighted the corporate interest in culture to such a degree that visitors had trouble finding the entrance to the show. In a double entendre leveled at the title of the biennial, Sites of Desire, the *Advertising Castle* proclaimed the exhibition a desirable site to display corporate sponsorship and the advertisements sites where desire was generated in the citizen consumers who were attending the show. The *Advertising Castle* became a magnet for political debate drawing complaints from the city council that it was serving commercial rather than artistic aims. The consequence of Cai hitting his mark so directly was that the council demanded that the work be removed or the Taipei Fine Arts Museum would lose its public funding. Such political grandstanding and real economic threat to the curatorial licensee would occur the following year in New York, as the mayor threatened to close the Brooklyn Museum for exhibiting work deemed offensive. The Brooklyn Museum remained financially intact, while the Taipei Fine Arts Museum lost NT$1 million.

The most dramatic museum response to the international culture market has been that of the Guggenheim. The museum has metamorphized itself along corporate lines, branding itself with the ingenuity of any of the market-conscious artists of the century, diversifying its interests from Minimalism to motorcycles, and opening branches worldwide.

In 1979, twenty years after Frank Lloyd Wright completed the Guggenheim Museum in New York, the Guggenheim Foundation opened the Venetian home of Peggy Guggenheim as its first international outpost. By the nineties, the museum was expanding in size and mission. In New York there was a new addition to the Wright building; a Soho museum; and plans for an enormous downtown complex. In 1997, branches were opened in Bilbao and Berlin. By 2001, Las Vegas was home to a Guggenheim exhibition space and a collaboration with the Russian Hermitage. Cyberspace had, of course, been occupied and there were plans for a new location in Brazil. The Guggenheim was also injecting its exhibition schedule with shows on fashion designers and motorcycles. Though criticized heavily for favoring marketing over curating and choosing to be

27.59 Cai Guoqiang, *Advertising Castle*, 1998. In situ at 1998 Taipei Biennial Sites of Desire.

Dufrenne, Mikel, ed. *Main Trends in Aesthetics and the Sciences of Art.* New York: Holmes and Meier, 1979.

Eisenmann, Stephen F., et al. *Nineteenth Century Art: A Critical History.* London: Thames & Hudson, 1994.

Ferguson, Russell, ed. *Discourses: Conversations in Postmodern Art and Culture.* Documentary Sources in Contemporary Art. Cambridge, Mass.: MIT Press, 1990.

Ferrier, Jean Louis, ed. *Art of Our Century: The Chronicle of Western Art, 1900 to the Present.* New York: Prentice-Hall, 1989.

Fineberg, Jonathan. *Art Since 1940: Strategies of Being.* Englewood Cliffs, N.J.: Prentice-Hall, 1995.

Fletcher, Valerie. *Dreams and Nightmares: Utopian Visions in Modern Art.* Exh. cat. Washington, D.C.: Hirshhorn Museum and Sculpture Garden, 1983.

Focillon, Henry. *The Life of Forms in Art.* New York: Zone Books, 1958.

Foster, Hal. *Return of the Real: The Avant-Garde at the End of the Century.* Cambridge, Mass.: MIT Press, 1996.

———, ed. *The Anti-Aesthetic: Essays on Postmodern Culture.* Seattle: Bay Press, 1983.

Frascina, Francis, ed. *Pollock and After: The Critical Debate.* New York: Harper & Row, 1985.

———, and Jonathan Harris, eds. *Art in Modern Culture: An Anthology of Critical Texts.* New York: Harper & Row, 1992.

———, and Charles Harrison, eds. *Modern Art and Modernism: A Critical Anthology.* New York: Harper & Row, 1982.

Fry, Roger. *Last Lectures.* Cambridge, England: The University Press, 1939.

———. *Vision and Design.* London: Chatto and Windus, 1957.

Gablik, Suzy. *Progress in Art.* London: Thames & Hudson, 1976.

Gage, John. *Color and Culture: Practice and Meaning from Antiquity to Abstraction.* Boston: Little, Brown, 1993.

Goddard, Donald. *American Painting.* New York: MacMillan, 1990.

Goldwater, Robert. *Primitivism in Modern Art.* Enl. ed. Cambridge, Mass.: Harvard University Press, 1986.

Gombrich, Ernst H. *The Sense of Order: A Study in the Psychology of Decorative Art.* Ithaca, N.Y.: Cornell University Press, 1979.

Gordon, Donald. *Expressionism: Art and Idea.* New Haven, Conn.: Yale University Press, 1987.

Greenberg, Clement. *Clement Greenberg: The Collected Essays and Criticism.* 4 vols. Chicago: University of Chicago Press, 1986–93.

Guilbaut, Serge, ed. *Reconstructing Modernism: Art in New York, Paris, and Montreal, 1945–1964.* Cambridge, Mass.: MIT Press, 1990.

Hamilton, George H. *19th and 20th Century Art: Painting, Sculpture, Architecture.* New York: Harry N. Abrams, 1970.

Harris, Anne Sutherland, and Linda Nochlin. *Woman Artists: 1550–1950.* Exh. cat. Los Angeles: LACMA, 1976.

Harrison, Charles, and Paul Wood, eds. *Art in Theory, 1900–1990: An Anthology of Changing Ideas.* Cambridge, Mass.: Blackwell, 1992.

Hauser, Arnold. *The Social History of Art.* Trans. S. Godman. 4 vols. New York: Vintage Books, 1957.

Heller, Nancy G. *Women Artists: An Illustrated History.* New York: Abbeville, 1987.

Henderson, Linda Dalrymple. *The Fourth Dimension and Non-Euclidian Geometry in Modern Art.* Princeton, N.J.: Princeton University Press, 1983.

Herbert, Robert L., ed. *The Art Criticism of John Ruskin.* Garden City, N.Y.: Anchor Books, 1964.

———, ed. *Modern Artists on Art.* Englewood Cliffs, N.J.: Prentice-Hall, 1964.

Hertz, Richard. *Theories of Contemporary Art.* 2nd ed. Englewood Cliffs, N.J.: Prentice-Hall, 1993.

———, and Norman Klein, eds. *Twentieth-Century Art Theory: Urbanism, Politics and Mass Culture.* Englewood Cliffs, N.J.: Prentice-Hall, 1990.

Hildebrand, Adolf von. *The Problem of Form in Painting and Sculpture.* Ann Arbor, Mich.: University Microfilms, 1979.

Hoffman, Katherine. *Explorations: The Visual Arts Since 1945.* New York: HarperCollins, 1991.

Hofmann, Werner. *Turning Points in Twentieth-Century Art: 1890–1917.* Trans. C. Kessler. New York: G. Braziller, 1969.

Hunter, Sam, and John Jacobus. *Modern Art: Painting, Sculpture, Architecture.* 3rd ed. New York: Harry N. Abrams, 1992.

Jencks, Charles. *What is Post-Modernism?* 3rd ed. rev. London: Academy Editions, 1989.

Joachimides, Christos. *American Art in the 20th Century: Painting and Sculpture 1913–1933.* Exh. cat. London and Munich: Royal Academy of Arts and Prestel, 1993.

———, et al. *German Art in the 20th Century: Painting and Sculpture 1905–1985.* Exh. cat. London: Royal Academy of Arts and Weidenfeld & Nicholson, 1985.

Johnson, Ellen. *Modern Art and the Object.* London: Thames & Hudson, 1976.

Kaplan, Patricia, and Susan Manso, eds. *Major European Art Movements 1900–1945: A Critical Anthology.* New York: Dutton, 1977.

Kemp, Martin. *The Science of Art: Optical Themes in Western Art from Brunelleschi to Seurat.* New Haven, Conn.: Yale University Press, 1990.

Kepes, Gyorgy. *The New Landscape in Art and Science.* Chicago: P. Theobald, 1956.

———. *Sign, Image, Symbol.* New York: G. Braziller, 1966.

Kern, Stephen. *The Culture of Time and Space: 1880–1918.* Cambridge, Mass.: Harvard University Press, 1980.

Kleinbauer, W. Eugene. *Modern Perspectives in Western Art History: An Anthology of Twentieth-Century Writings on the Visual Arts.* Reprint of the 1971 ed. Toronto: University of Toronto Press, 1989.

Kozloff, Max. *Renderings: Critical Essays on a Century of Modern Art.* London: Studio Vista, 1968.

Kramer, Hilton. *The Age of the Avant-Garde: An Art Chronicle of 1956–1972.* New York: Farrar, Straus and Giroux, 1973.

Krauss, Rosalind. *The Optical Unconscious.* Cambridge, Mass.: MIT Press, 1993.

———. *The Originality of the Avant-Garde and Other Modernist Myths.* Cambridge, Mass.: MIT Press, 1986.

Kuh, Katharine. *The Artist's Voice.* New York: Harper & Row, 1962.

Kultermann, Udo. *The History of Art History.* New York: Abaris Books, 1993.

Kuspit, Donald B. *The Critic as Artist: The Intentionality of Art.* Ann Arbor, Mich.: UMI Research Press, 1984.

———. *The Cult of the Avant-Garde Artist.* New York: Cambridge University Press, 1993.

Langer, Cassandra. *Feminist Art Criticism: An Annotated Bibliography.* New York: G. K. Hall, 1993.

Levin, Kim. *Beyond Modernism: Essays on Art from the 70's and 80's.* New York: Harper & Row, 1988.

Lewis, Samella S. *African American Art and Artists.* Rev. ed. Berkeley, Calif.: University of California Press, 1994.

Liberman, Alexander. *The Artist in His Studio.* New York: Viking Press, 1960.

Lippard, Lucy. *From the Center: Feminist Essays on Women's Art.* New York: Dutton, 1976.

Lucie-Smith, Edward. *Art Today: From Abstract Expressionism to Superrealism.* 3rd ed. Oxford: Phaidon, 1989.

———. *Latin American Art of the 20th Century.* London: Thames & Hudson, 1993.

Lynton, Norbert. *The Story of Modern Art.* 2nd ed. Oxford: Phaidon, 1989.

McCoubrey, John. *American Art, 1700–1960: Sources and Documents.* Englewood Cliffs, N.J.: Prentice-Hall, 1965.

McShine, Kynaston. *An International Survey of Recent Painting and Sculpture.* Exh. cat. New York: MOMA, 1984.

Millon, Henry A., and Linda Nochlin, eds. *Art and Architecture in the Service of Politics.* Cambridge, Mass.: MIT Press, 1978.

Mitchell, W. J. T. *Picture Theory: Essays on Verbal and Visual Representation.* Chicago: University of Chicago Press, 1994.

———. *The Reconfigured Eye: Visual Truth in the Post-Photographic Era.* Cambridge, Mass.: MIT Press, 1992.

Nash, Steven A. *Arnason and Politics: A Commemorative Exhibition.* San Francisco: Fine Arts Museums, 1993.

Nelson, Robert, and Richard Shiff, eds. *Critical Terms for Art History.* Chicago: University of Chicago Press, 1993.

Nochlin, Linda. *The Body in Pieces: The Fragment as a Metaphor of Modernity.* New York: Thames & Hudson, 1995.

———. *The Politics of Vision: Essays on Nineteenth-Century Art and Society.* New York: Harper & Row, 1989.

———. *Women, Art, and Power: and Other Essays.* New York: Harper & Row, 1988.

Norris, Christopher, and Andrew Benjamin. *What is Deconstruction?* New York: St. Martin's Press, 1988.

Osborne, Harold, ed. *Oxford Companion to Twentieth-Century Art.* New York: Oxford University Press, 1981.

Papadakes, Andreas, et al., eds. *Deconstruction: The Omnibus Volume.* New York: Rizzoli, 1989.

Parker, Rozsika, and Griselda Pollock. *Old Mistresses: Women, Art, and Ideology.* New York: Pantheon, 1981.

Pevsner, Nikolas. *Academies of Art: Past and Present.* Reprint of the 1940 ed. New York: Da Capo Press, 1973.

Pincus-Witten, Robert. *Postminimalism into Maximalism: American Art, 1966–1986.* Ann Arbor, Mich.: UMI Research Press, 1987.

Podro, Michael. *The Critical Historians of Art.* New Haven, Conn.: Yale University Press, 1982.

Poggioli, Renato. *The Theory of the Avant-Garde.* Trans. G. Fitzgerald. Cambridge, Mass.: Belknap Press of Harvard University Press, 1968.

Pollock, Griselda. *Vision and Difference: Femininity, Feminism, and the Histories of Art.* New York: Routledge, 1988.

Powell, Richard. *Black Art and Culture in the 20th Century.* New York: Thames & Hudson, 1997.

———. *The Blues Aesthetic: Black Culture and Modernism.* Washington, D.C.: Washington Project for the Arts, 1989.

Preziosi, Donald. *Rethinking Art History: Meditations on a Coy Science.* New Haven, Conn.: Yale University Press, 1989.

Prown, Jules, and Barbara Rose. *American Painting: From the Colonial Period to the Present.* New ed. New York: Rizzoli, 1977

———, et al. *Discovered Lands, Invented Pasts: Transforming Visions of the American West.* Exh. cat. New Haven, Conn.: Yale University Press, 1992.

Rasmussen, Waldo, ed. *Latin American Artists of the Twentieth Century.* Exh. cat. New York: MOMA, 1993.

Read, Herbert. *Art Now: An Introduction to the Theory of Modern Painting and Sculpture.* New York: Pitman Publishing Corp., 1948.

Rees, A. L., and Frances Borzello. *The New Art History*. London: Camden Press, 1986.

Risatti, Howard, ed. *Postmodern Perspectives*. Englewood Cliffs, N.J.: Prentice-Hall, 1990.

Rodman, Selden. *Conversations with Artists*. New York: Capricorn Books, 1957.

Rose, Barbara. *American Art Since 1900*. Rev. ed. New York: Praeger, 1975.

———. *Readings in American Art Since 1900: A Documentary Survey*. New York: Praeger, 1968.

Rosen, Charles, and Henri Zerner. *Romanticism and Realism: The Mythology of Nineteenth-Century Art*. New York: Viking, 1984.

Rosen, Randy, and Catherine C. Brawer. *Making Their Mark: Women Artists Move Into the Mainstream, 1970–85*. New York: Abbeville, 1989.

Rosenberg, Harold. *The Tradition of the New*. New York: Horizon Press, 1959.

Rubin, William, ed. *"Primitivism" in 20th-Century Art: Affinity of the Tribal and the Modern*. 2 vols. Exh. cat. New York: MOMA, 1984.

Schapiro, Meyer. *Theory and Philosophy of Art: Style, Artist, and Society*. New York: G. Braziller, 1994.

Selz, Peter. *Art in Our Times: A Pictorial History 1890–1980*. New York: Harry N. Abrams, 1981.

Shapiro, Theda. *Painters and Politics: The European Avant-Garde and Society: 1900–1925*. New York: Elsevier, 1976.

Smagula, Howard. *Currents: Contemporary Directions in the Visual Arts*. 2nd ed. Englewood Cliffs, N.J.: Prentice-Hall, 1989.

Stangos, Nikos, ed. *Concepts of Modern Art: From Fauvism to Postmodernism*. 3rd ed. World of Art. New York: Thames & Hudson, 1994.

Stich, Sidra. *Made in USA: An Americanization in Modern Art, the '50s and '60s*. Berkeley, Calif.: University of California Press, 1987.

Stiles, Kristine, and Peter Selz. *Theories and Documents of Contemporary Art: A Sourcebook of Artist's Writings*. Berkeley and Los Angeles: University of California Press, 1996.

Tagg, John. *Grounds of Dispute: Art History, Cultural Politics and the Discursive Field*. Minneapolis: University of Minnesota Press, 1992.

Taylor, Joshua, ed. *Nineteenth-Century Theories of Art*. Berkeley, Calif.: University of California Press, 1991.

Tomkins, Calvin. *Post to Neo: The Art World of the 1980's*. New York: Holt, 1990.

Tuchman, Maurice. *The Spiritual in Art: Abstract Painting, 1890–1985*. New York: Abbeville, 1986.

Valéry, Paul. *Selected Writings*. New York: New Directions, 1964.

Varnedoe, Kirk, and Adam Gopnik. *High and Low: Modern Art and Popular Culture*. Exh. cat. New York: MOMA, 1990.

———, eds. *Modern Art and Popular Culture: Readings in High and Low*. New York: Harry N. Abrams, 1990. With Essays by J. E. Bowlt et al.

Wallis, Brian, ed. *Art After Modernism: Rethinking Representation*. Boston: Godine, 1984.

———, ed. *Blasted Allegories: An Anthology of Writings by Contemporary Artists*. Cambridge, Mass.: MIT Press, 1987.

Weiss, Jeffrey S. *The Popular Culture of Modern Art: Picasso, Duchamp, and Avant-Gardism*. New Haven, Conn.: Yale University Press, 1994.

Wheeler, Daniel. *Art Since Mid-Century: 1945 to the Present*. Englewood Cliffs, N.J.: Prentice-Hall, 1991.

Whiting, Cécile. *Antifascism in American Art*. New Haven, Conn.: Yale University Press, 1989.

Wilkins, David G., Bernard Schultz, and Katheryn M. Linduff. *Art Past/Art Present*. 2nd ed. New York: Harry N. Abrams, 1994.

Wilmerding, John. *American Art*. Pelican History of Art. Harmondsworth: Penguin, 1976.

Witzling, Mara, ed. *Voicing Our Visions: Writings by Women Artists*. New York: Universe Books, 1991.

Wollheim, Richard. *Art and Its Objects*. New York: Cambridge University Press, 1980.

———. *Painting as an Art*. Princeton, N.J.: Princeton University Press, 1987.

Wood, Paul, et al. *Modernism in Dispute: Art Since the Forties*. New Haven, Conn.: Yale University Press, 1993.

Word as Image: American Art, 1960–1990. Exh. cat. Milwaukee, Wis.: Milwaukee Art Museum, 1990.

Worringer, Wilhelm. *Abstraction and Empathy: A Contribution to the Psychology of Style*. Trans. M. Bullock. New York: International University Press, 1980.

B. Dictionaries and Encyclopedias

Baigell, Matthew. *Dictionary of American Art*. New York: Harper & Row, 1979.

Benezit, Emmanuel. *Dictionnaire critique et documentaire des peintres, sculpteurs, dessinateurs et graveurs*. 10 vols. Paris: Roger et F. Chernoviz, 1976.

The Britannica Encyclopedia of American Art. Chicago: Encyclopedia Britannica Education Corp., 1973.

Chilvers, Ian, ed. *The Concise Oxford Dictionary of Art and Artists*. Oxford and New York: Oxford University Press, 1996.

Cummings, Paul. *Dictionary of Contemporary American Artists*. 6th ed. New York: St. Martin's Press, 1994.

Dunford, Penny. *Biographical Dictionary of Women Artists in Europe and America Since 1850*. Philadelphia: University of Pennsylvania Press, 1990.

Emanuel, Muriel, et al., eds. *Contemporary Artists*. 2nd ed. New York: St. Martin's Press, 1983.

Encyclopedia of World Art. 17 vols. New York: McGraw-Hill, 1959–68[?].

Heller, Jules, and Nancy Heller. *North American Women Artists of the Twentieth Century: A Biographical Dictionary*. New York: Garland, 1995.

Hughe, Rene, ed. *Larousse Encyclopedia of Modern Art from 1800 to the Present Day*. New York: Prometheus Press, 1965.

Jervis, Simon. *The Penguin Dictionary of Design and Designers*. London: A. Lane, 1984.

Jones, Lois Swan. *Art Information: Research Methods and Resources*. 3rd ed. Dubuque, Iowa: Kendall/Hunt, 1990.

Lake, Carlton, and Robert Maillard, eds. *Dictionary of Modern Painting*. 3rd ed. New York: Tudor, 1964.

Lucie-Smith, Edward. *Lives of the Great Twentieth-Century Artists*. New York: Rizzoli, 1986.

Maillard, Robert, ed. *New Dictionary of Modern Sculpture*. New York: Tudor, 1970.

Marks, Claude, ed. *World Artists 1980–1990*. New York: H. W. Wilson, 1991.

Norman, Geraldine. *Nineteenth-Century Painters and Painting: A Dictionary*. Berkeley, Calif.: University of California Press, 1977.

Osborne, Harold. *The Oxford Companion to Twentieth-Century Art*. Oxford: Oxford University Press, 1981.

Pehnt, Wolfgang, ed. *Encyclopedia of Modern Architecture*. New York: Harry N. Abrams, 1964.

Pevsner, Nikolaus, John Fleming, and Hugh Honour. *A Dictionary of Architecture*. Rev. enl. ed. Woodstock, N.Y.: Overlook Press, 1976.

Phaidon Dictionary of Twentieth-Century Art. Oxford: Phaidon, 1973.

Seuphor, Michel. *Dictionary of Abstract Painting, Preceded by a History of Abstract Painting*. New York: Paris Book Center, 1958.

Spalding, Frances. *20th Century Painters and Sculptors*. Woodbridge, Suffolk: Antique Collector's Club, 1990.

Walker, John. *Glossary of Art, Architecture and Design Since 1945*. 3rd ed. Boston: G. K. Hall, 1992.

C. Architecture, Engineering, and Design

Arnheim, Rudolph. *The Dynamics of Architectural Form*. Berkeley and Los Angeles: University of California Press, 1977.

Banham, R. *The New Brutalism: Ethic or Aesthetic?*. London: Architectural Press, 1966.

———. *Theory and Design in the First Machine Age*. 2nd ed. New York: Praeger, 1960.

Behrendt, Walter. *Modern Building: Its Nature, Problems and Forms*. London: M. Kopkins, 1936.

Benevelo, Leonardo. *History of Modern Architecture*. 2 vols. Trans. H. J. Landry. Cambridge, Mass.: MIT Press, 1971.

Besset, Maurice. *New French Architecture*. New York: Praeger, 1967.

Blake, Peter. *The Master Builders*. New York: Knopf, 1960.

———. *No Place Like Utopia: Modern Architecture and the Company We Kept*. New York: Knopf, 1993.

Bouillon, Jean Paul. *Art Deco, 1903–1940*. New York: Rizzoli, 1989.

Brooks, H. Allen. *The Prairie School: Frank Lloyd Wright and His Mid-West Contemporaries*. Toronto: University of Toronto Press, 1972.

Collins, Michael, and Andreas Papadakis. *Post-Modern Design*. New York: Rizzoli, 1989.

Conrads, Ulrich, and Hans Sperlich. *The Architecture of Fantasy*. New York: Praeger, 1962.

Crook, J. Mordant. *The Dilemma of Style: Architectural Ideas from the Picturesque to the Post Modern*. Chicago: University of Chicago Press, 1987.

Curtis, William. *Modern Architecture Since 1900*. 2nd ed. Englewood Cliffs, N.J.: Prentice-Hall, 1987.

Dal Co, Francesco. *Figures of Architecture and Thought: German Architectural Culture, 1890–1920*. New York: Rizzoli, 1986.

———. *Transformations in Modern Architecture*. Greenwich, Conn.: New York Graphic Society, 1980.

Dormer, Peter. *Design Since 1945*. World of Art. New York: Thames & Hudson, 1993.

Drexler, Arthur. *Transformations in Modern Architecture*. Exh. cat. New York: MOMA, 1979.

Eldredge, H. W., ed. *Taming Megalopolis*. 2 vols. New York: Praeger, 1967.

Ferebee, Ann. *A History of Design from the Victorian Era to the Present*. New York: Van Nostrand Reinhold, 1980.

Fitch, James. *American Building: The Historical Forces That Shaped It*. 2 vols. 2nd ed. Boston: Houghton Mifflin, 1966–72.

Frampton, Kenneth. *Modern Architecture: A Critical History*. World of Art. New York: Oxford University Press, 1980.

———, and Yukio Futagawa. *Modern Architecture 1851–1945*. New York: Rizzoli, 1983.

Giedion, Sigfried. *Space, Time, and Architecture: The Growth of a New Tradition*. 4th ed. Cambridge, Mass.: Harvard University Press, 1963.

Heyer, Paul. *Architects on Architecture*. New York: Van Nostrand Reinhold, 1993.

Hitchcock, Henry-Russell. *Architecture: Nineteenth and Twentieth Centuries.* 4th ed. Pelican History of Art. Harmondsworth: Penguin, 1977.

Jencks, Charles. *Modern Movements in Architecture.* 2nd. ed. New York: Penguin, 1985.

Jensen, Rolf. *High Density Living.* London: L. Hill, 1966.

Joedicke, Jurgen. *Architecture Since 1945: Sources and Directions.* Trans. J. C. Palmes. New York: Praeger, 1969.

Johnson, Philip. *Deconstructionist Architecture.* Exh. cat. New York: MOMA, 1988.

Kostof, Spiro. *History of Architecture: Settings and Rituals.* 2nd ed. New York: Oxford University Press, 1995.

Kultermann, Udo. *Architecture in the Twentieth Century.* New York: Van Nostrand Reinhold, 1993.

Lampugnani, Vittorio. *Encyclopedia of Twentieth-Century Architecture.* New York: Harry N. Abrams, 1983.

Leach, Neil. *Rethinking Architecture: A Reader in Cultural Theory.* New York: Routledge, 1996.

Le Corbusier (Charles-Édouard Jeanneret). *Towards a New Architecture.* Trans. F. Etchells. London: Architectural Press, 1952.

Loyer, François. *Architecture of the Industrial Age.* New York: Skira, 1983.

Manhart, Marcia, and Tom Manhart, eds. *The Eloquent Object: The Evolution of American Art in Craft Media Since 1945.* Tulsa, Okla.: Philbrook Museum of Art, 1987.

Meeks, Carol. *The Railroad Station: An Architectural History.* New Haven, Conn.: Yale University Press, 1995.

Middleton, Robin and David Watkin. *Neoclassical and 19th Century Architecture.* 2 vols. History of World Architecture. New York: Electa/Rizzoli, 1987.

Mignot, Claude. *Architecture of the Nineteenth Century in Europe.* New York: Rizzoli, 1984.

Mumford, Lewis. *The Culture of Cities.* New York: Harcourt, Brace and Co., c. 1938.

———. *Technics and Civilization.* New York: Rourledge, 1934.

Ockman, Joan, ed. *Architecture Culture, 1943–1968: A Documentary Anthology.* New York: Rizzoli, 1993.

Pehnt, Wolfgang. *Expressionist Architecture.* London: Thames & Hudson, 1973.

Peter, John. *Masters of Modern Architecture.* New York: G. Braziller, 1958.

Pevsner, Nikolaus. *Pioneers of Modern Design: From William Morris to Walter Gropius.* Harmondsworth: Penguin, 1975.

———. *The Sources of Modern Architecture and Design.* New York: Oxford University Press, 1977.

Pierson, William, and William H. Jordy. *American Buildings and Their Architects.* 4 vols. New York: Oxford University Press, 1986.

Pommer, Richard, ed. "Revising Modernist History: The Architecture of the 1920s and 1930s." *Art Journal* (Summer 1983) special issue.

Read, Herbert. *Art and Industry.* Bloomington, Ind.: Indiana University Press, 1961.

Riesebero, Bill. *Modern Architecture and Design: An Alternative History.* Cambridge, Mass.: MIT Press, 1983.

Roth, Leland. *A Concise History of American Architecture.* New York: Harper & Row, 1980.

———. *Understanding Architecture: Its Elements, History and Meaning.* New York: Harper & Row, 1993.

Rudofsky, Bernard. *Architecture Without Architects: An Introduction to Non-Pedigreed Architecture.* Exh. cat. New York: MOMA, 1964.

Schuyler, Montgomery. *American Architecture and Other Writings.* Cambridge, Mass.: Belknap Press of Harvard University Press, 1964.

Scully, Vincent. *American Architecture and Urbanism.* Rev. ed. New York: H. Holy, 1988.

———. *Modern Architecture: The Architecture of Democracy.* Rev. ed. New York: G. Braziller, 1974.

Sharp, Dennis. *Modern Architecture and Expressionism.* New York: G. Braziller, 1966.

———. *The Rationalists: Theory and Design in the Modern Movement.* London: Architectural Press, 1979.

———, ed. *A Visual History of Twentieth-Century Architecture.* Greenwich, Conn.: New York Graphic Society, 1972.

Silver, Nathan. *Lost New York.* New York: Wing Books, 1967.

Smith, G. E. Kidder. *The New Architecture of Europe.* Cleveland and New York: World Pub. Co., 1961.

Tafuri, Manfredo. *Contemporary Architecture.* New York: Harry N. Abrams, 1977.

———. *Modern Architecture.* 2 vols. History of World Architecture. New York: Electa/Rizzoli, 1986.

Thackara, John, ed. *Design After Modernism: Beyond the Object.* New York: Thames & Hudson, 1988.

Trachtenberg, Marvin, and Isabelle Hyman. *Architecture: From Pre-history to Post-Modernism.* New York: Harry N. Abrams, 1986.

Troy, Nancy. *Modernism and the Decorative Arts in France: Art Nouveau to Le Corbusier.* New Haven, Conn.: Yale University Press, 1991.

Tunnard, Christopher. *City of Man.* 2nd ed. New York: Scribner, 1970.

———, and Boris Pushkarev. *Man-Made America: Chaos or Control?* New Haven, Conn.: Yale University Press, 1963.

Vidler, Anthony. *The Architectural Uncanny: Essays in the Modern Unhomely.* Cambridge, Mass.: MIT Press, 1992.

Zevi, Bruno. *Towards an Organic Architecture.* London: Faber and Faber, 1950.

D. Photography, Printmaking, and Drawing

Adams, Clinton. *American Lithographs, 1900–1960: The Artists and Their Prints.* Albuquerque, N.Mex.: University of New Mexico Press, 1983.

Adams, Robert. *Beauty in Photography: Essays in Defense of Traditional Values.* Millerton, N.Y.: Aperture, 1981.

Ades, Dawn. *Photomontage.* New York: Pantheon, 1976.

Barthes, Roland. *Camera Lucida, Reflections on Photography.* Trans. R. Howard. New York: Hill and Wang, 1981.

Benjamin, Walter. "The Work of Art in the Age of Mechanical Reproduction." In *Illuminations,* ed. H. Arendt. New York: Schocken Books, 1969.

Bolton, Richard, ed. *The Contest of Meaning: Critical Histories of Photography.* Cambridge, Mass.: MIT Press, 1989.

Braive, Michel. *The Photograph: A Social History.* New York: McGraw-Hill, 1966.

Bretell, Richard, et al. *Paper and Light: The Calotype in Great Britain and France 1839–1870.* Boston: D. R. Godine, 1984.

Buckland, Gail. *Reality Recorded: Early Documentary Photography.* Greenwich, Conn.: New York Graphic Society, 1974.

Buerger, Janet E. *The Era of the French Calotype.* Exh. cat. Rochester, N.Y.: International Museum of Photography at George Eastman House, 1982.

Bunnell, Peter, ed. *A Photographic Vision: Pictorial Photography, 1889–1923.* Salt Lake City: Peregrine Smith, 1980.

Burgin, Victor. *Thinking Photography.* London: MacMillan, 1990.

Castleman, Riva. *Modern Art in Prints.* New York: MOMA, 1973.

———. *Modern Artists as Illustrators.* Exh. cat. New York: MOMA, 1981.

———. *Prints from Blocks: From Gauguin to Now.* Exh. cat. New York: MOMA, 1983.

———. *Prints of the Twentieth Century.* London: Thames & Hudson, 1988.

Coe, Brian. *Colour Photography: The First Hundred Years, 1840–1940.* London: Ash & Grant, 1978.

———, and Paul Gates. *The Snapshot Photograph.* London: Ash & Grant, 1977.

Coke, Van Deren. *The Painter and the Photograph: From Delacroix to Warhol.* Rev. ed. Albuquerque, N.Mex.: University of New Mexico Press, 1972.

———, ed. *One Hundred Years of Photographic History: Essays in Honor of Beaumont Newhall.* Albuquerque, N.Mex.: University of New Mexico Press, 1975.

Daval, Jean-Luc. *Photography: History of an Art.* New York: Rizzoli, 1982.

Doty, Robert, ed. *Photography in America.* Exh. cat. New York: WMAA, 1974.

Evans, Martin Marix. *Contemporary Photographers.* 3rd ed. New York: St. James Press, 1995.

Fabian, Rainer, and Hans-Christian Adam. *Masters of Early Travel Photography.* New York: Vendome Press, 1983.

Freund, Gisele. *Photography & Society.* Boston: D. R. Godine, 1980.

Friedman, Joseph Solomon. *The History of Colour Photography.* 2nd ed. London and New York: Focal, 1968.

Galassi, Peter. *Before Photography: Painting and the Invention of Photography.* Exh. cat. New York: MOMA, 1981.

Generations. Exh. cat. New York: SRGM, 1976.

Gernsheim, Helmut, and Alison Gernsheim. *The History of Photography: From the Camera Obscura to the Beginning of the Modern Era.* New York: McGraw-Hill, 1969.

Gidal, Tim N. *Modern Photojournalism: Origin and Evolution: 1910–1933.* New York: Collier, 1972.

Gilmour, Pat. *Modern Prints.* New York: Studio Vista/Dutton, 1970.

Goldberg, Vicki, ed. *Photography in Print: Writings from 1816 to the Present.* New York: Simon and Schuster, 1981.

Gover, C. Jane. *The Positive Image: Women Photographers in Turn of the Century America.* Albany, N.Y.: SUNY Press, 1988.

Green, Jonathan, ed. *American Photography: A Critical History, 1945 to the Present.* New York: Harry N. Abrams, 1984.

———. *Camera Work: A Critical Anthology.* Millerton, N.Y.: Aperture, 1973.

———, ed. *The Snapshot.* Millerton, N.Y.: Aperture, 1974.

Greenough, Sarah, et al. *On the Art of Fixing a Shadow: One Hundred and Fifty Years of Photography.* Exh. cat. Chicago: Art Institute of Chicago, 1989.

Grundberg, Andy. *Photography and Art: Interactions Since 1946.* New York: Abbeville, 1987.

Hall-Duncan, Nancy. *The History of Fashion Photography.* New York: International Museum of Photography, 1977.

Hambourg, Maria Morris, et al. *The Waking Dream: Photography's First Century.* Exh. cat. New York: MMA, 1993.

Harker, Margaret. *The Linked Ring: The Secession Movement in Photography in Britain, 1892–1910.* London: Heinemann, 1979.

Hartmann, Sadakichi. *The Valiant Knights of Daguerre: Selected Critical Essays on Photography and Profiles of Photographic Pioneers.* Ed. H. W. Lawton and G. Knox. Berkeley, Calif.: University of California Press, 1978.

Hobgen, Carol, and Rowan Watson, eds. *From Manet to Hockney: Modern Artists' Illustrated Books.* Exh. cat. London: Victoria and Albert Museum, 1985.

Homer, William I. *Alfred Stieglitz and the American Avant-Garde.* Boston: New York Graphic Society, 1977.

———. *Alfred Stieglitz and the Photo-Secession.* Boston: New York Graphic Society, 1983.

Ives, Colta. *The Painterly Print.* New York: MMA, 1980.

Jammes, André, and Eugenia Janis. *The Art of French Calotype.* Princeton, N.J.: Princeton University Press, 1983.

Jeffrey, Ian. *Photography: A Concise History.* London: Thames & Hudson, 1981.

Johnson, William. *Nineteenth-Century Photography: An Annotated Bibliography, 1839–1879.* Boston: G. K. Hall, 1990.

Kozloff, Max. *Photography and Fascination: Essays.* Danbury, N.H.: Addison House, 1979.

———. *The Privileged Eye: Essays on Photography.* Albuquerque, N.Mex.: University of New Mexico Press, 1987.

Lavin, Maud, et al. *Montage and Modern Life, 1919–1942.* Exh. cat. Cambridge, Mass. and Boston: MIT Press and Institute of Contemporary Art, c. 1992.

Lewinski, Jorge. *The Camera at War.* London: W. H. Allen, 1978.

Lyons, Nathan, ed. *Photographers on Photography: A Critical Anthology.* Englewood Cliffs, N.J.: Prentice-Hall, 1956.

Maddow, Ben. *Faces: A Narrative History of the Portrait in Photography.* Boston: New York Graphic Society, 1977.

Mayor, A. Hyatt. *Prints and People: A Social History of Printed Pictures.* New York: MMA, 1971.

Mellor, David, ed. *Germany: The New Photography, 1927–33.* Exh. cat. London: Arts Council of Great Britain, 1978.

Naef, Weston. *Fifty Pioneers of Modern Photography: The Collection of Alfred Stieglitz.* Exh. cat. New York: MMA, 1978.

———, and James N. Wood. *Era of Exploration: The Rise of Landscape Photography in the American West: 1860–1885.* Exh. cat. Buffalo, N.Y.: Albright-Knox Gallery of Art, 1975.

Newhall, Beaumont. *The History of Photography from 1839 to the Present.* Rev. ed. Greenwich, Conn.: New York Graphic Society, 1982.

———, ed. *Photography: Essays and Images.* New York: MOMA, 1980.

Petruck, Peninah, ed. *The Camera Viewed: Writings on Twentieth-Century Photography.* 2 vols. New York: Dutton, 1979.

Phillips, Christopher, ed. *Photography in the Modern Era: European Documents and Critical Writings, 1913–1940.* Exh. cat. New York: MMA, 1989.

Pinney, Roy. *Advertising Photography.* New York: Hastings House, 1962.

Pollack, Peter. *Picture History of Photography.* Rev. ed. New York: Harry N. Abrams, 1970.

Rose, Bernice. *Allegories of Modernism: Contemporary Drawing.* Exh. cat. New York: MOMA, 1992.

Rosenblum, Naomi. *A World History of Photography.* Rev. ed. New York: Abbeville, 1989.

Rotzler, Willy. *Photography as Artistic Experiment: From Fox Talbot to Moholy-Nagy.* Garden City, N.J.: Amphoto, 1976.

Scharf, Aaron. *Art and Photography.* Harmondsworth and Baltimore: Penguin, 1974.

———. *Pioneers of Photography.* New York: Harry N. Abrams, 1976.

Solomon-Godeau, Abigail. *Photography at the Dock.* Minneapolis: University of Minnesota Press, 1991.

Sontag, Susan. *On Photography.* New York: Farrar, Straus and Giroux, 1973.

Stieglitz, Alfred, ed. *Camera Work: A Photographic Quarterly.* Reprint. New York: A. Stieglitz, 1969.

Stott, William. *Documentary Expression and Thirties America.* Reprint. Chicago: University of Chicago Press, 1986.

Stryker, Roy, and Nancy Wood. *In This Proud Land: America 1935–1943 as Seen in FSA Photographs.* Greenwich, Conn.: New York Graphic Society, 1973.

Szarkowski, John. *Looking at Photographs.* New York: MOMA and New York Graphic Society, 1973.

———. *The Photographer's Eye.* New York: MOMA and Doubleday, 1977.

———. *Photography Until Now.* Exh. cat. New York: MOMA, 1990.

Tagg, John. *The Burden of Representation: Essays on Photographies and Histories.* Amherst, Mass.: University of Massachusetts Press, 1988.

Trachtenberg, Allan, ed. *Classic Essays on Photography.* New Haven, Conn.: Leeter's Island Books, 1980.

Tsujimoto, Karen. *Images of America: Precisionist Painting and Modern Photography.* Exh. cat. San Francisco: San Francisco Museum of Modern Art, 1982.

Upton, Barbara, and John Upton. *Photography: Adapted from the Life Library of Photography.* 3rd ed. Boston: Little, Brown, 1980.

Vaizey, Marina. *The Artist as Photographer.* London: Sidgwick & Jackson, 1982.

Waldman, Diane. *Twentieth-Century American Drawing: Three Avant-Garde Generations.* Exh. cat. New York: SRGM, 1976.

Watrous, James. *A Century of American Printmaking, 1880–1980.* Madison, Wis.: University of Wisconsin Press, 1984.

Weaver, Mike, ed. *The Art of Photography, 1839–1989.* Exh. cat. New Haven, Conn.: Yale University Press, 1989.

Welling, William. *Photography in America: The Formative Years, 1839–1900.* New York: Crowell, 1978.

Witkin, Lee, and Barbara London. *The Photograph Collector's Guide.* Boston: New York Graphic Society, 1979.

Young, Mahonri Sharp. *Early American Moderns: Painters of the Stieglitz Group.* New York: Watson-Guptill, 1974.

E. Painting and Sculpture

Alloway, Lawrence. *Topics in American Art Since 1945.* New York: Norton, 1975.

Andersen, Wayne. *American Sculpture in Process: 1930–1970.* Boston: New York Graphic Society, 1975.

Arnason, H. H. *Modern Sculpture from the Joseph H. Hirshhorn Collection.* Exh. cat. New York: SRGM, 1962.

Art of Our Time: The Saatchi Collection. London and New York: Lund Humphries and Rizzoli, 1984.

Ashton, Dore. *American Art Since 1945.* New York: Oxford University Press, 1982.

Auping, Michael, ed. *Abstraction, Geometry, Painting.* Exh. cat. New York: Harry N. Abrams, 1989.

Barr, Jr., Alfred H., ed. *Painting and Sculpture in the Museum of Modern Art: 1929–1967.* New York: MOMA, 1977.

Beardsley, John, and Jane Livingston. *Hispanic Art in the United States: Thirty Contemporary Painters.* Exh. cat. Houston and New York: Museum of Fine Arts and Abbeville, 1987.

Braun, Emily, ed. *Italian Art in the 20th Century: Painting and Sculpture, 1900–1988.* Exh. cat. Munich: Prestel, 1989.

Denis, Maurice. *Théories, 1890–1910: du symbolisme et de Gauguin vers un nouvel ordre classique.* 4th ed. Paris: Rouart and Watelin, 1920.

Dorival, Bernard. *The School of Paris in the Musée d'Art Moderne.* Trans. C. Brookfield and E. Hart. New York: Harry N. Abrams, 1962.

Eitner, Lorenz. *An Outline of Nineteenth Century European Painting: From David to Cézanne.* 2 vols. New York: Harper & Row, 1987.

Elsen, Albert. *Modern European Sculpture, 1918–1945: Unknown Beings and Other Realities.* New York: G. Braziller, 1979.

Farr, Dennis. *English Art: 1870–1940.* Oxford: Clarendon Press, 1978.

Finch, C. *Image as Language.* Harmondsworth: Finch, 1969.

Fink, Lois Marie, and Joshua C. Taylor. *Academy: The Academic Tradition in American Art.* Exh. cat. Chicago: University of Chicago Press, 1978.

From Hodler to Klee: Swiss Art of the Twentieth Century, Paintings and Sculptures. Exh. cat. London: Tate Gallery, 1959.

Haftmann, Werner. *Painting in the Twentieth Century.* 2 vols. Rev. ed. New York: Praeger, 1979.

Hamilton, George Heard. *19th and 20th Century Art.* New York: Harry N. Abrams, 1970.

———. *Painting and Sculpture in Europe, 1880–1940.* 2nd ed. Pelican History of Art. Harmondsworth: Penguin, 1981.

Hammacher, A. M. *Modern Sculpture: Tradition and Innovation.* Enl. ed. New York: Harry N. Abrams, 1988.

Hard Edge. [Albers, Arp. Bærtling, Herbin, Liberman, Lohse, Mortensen, Taeüber-Arp, Varsarely] Exh. cat. Paris: Galerie Denise René, 1964.

Hughes, Robert. *Shock of the New.* 2nd ed. New York: McGraw-Hill, 1981.

Hunter, Sam and John Jacobus. *Modern Art: Painting, Sculpture, Architecture.* 2nd ed. Englewood Cliffs, N.J.: Prentice-Hall, 1985.

Ito, Norihiro, et al., eds. *Art in Japan Today II, 1970–1983.* Tokyo: Japan Foundation, 1984.

Janson, H. W. *Nineteenth-Century Sculpture.* New York: Harry N. Abrams, 1985.

Joachimides, Christos, et al., eds. *German Art in the Twentieth Century: Painting and Sculpture, 1905–1985.* Exh. cat. London: Royal Academy of Arts, 1985.

Johnson, Ellen, ed. *American Artists on Art from 1940 to 1980.* New York: Harper & Row, 1982.

Krens, Thomas. *Refigured Painting: The German Image, 1960–1988.* Exh. cat. New York: SRGM, 1988.

Lane, John, and Susan Larsen, eds. *Abstract Painting and Sculpture in America: 1927–1944.* Exh. cat. Pittsburgh: Museum of Art, Carnegie Institute, 1983.

Lehmann-Haupt, Hellmut. *Art Under a Dictatorship.* New York: Oxford University Press, 1954.

Le Normand-Romain, Antoinette, et al. *Sculpture: The Adventure of Modern Sculpture in the Nineteenth and Twentieth Centuries.* New York: Rizzoli, 1986.

Lieberman, William S., ed. *Modern Masters: Manet to Matisse.* Exh. cat. New York: MOMA, 1975.

Lucie-Smith, Edward. *Art Now: From Abstract Expressionism to Superrealism.* New York: Morrow, 1977.

———. *Movements in Art Since 1945.* Rev. ed. London: Thames & Hudson, 1984.

Lynton, Norbert. *The Story of Modern Art.* Oxford: Phaidon, 1980.

Miller, Dorothy C., and William S. Lieberman. *The New Japanese Painting and Sculpture.* Exh. cat. New York: MOMA, 1966.

Nairne, Sandy, and Nicholas Serota. *British Sculpture in the Twentieth Century.* Exh. cat. London: Whitechapel Art Gallery, 1981.

Novak, Barbara. *American Painting in the Nineteenth Century: Realism, Idealism, and the American Experience.* 2nd ed. New York: Harper & Row, 1979.

———. *Nature and Culture: American Landscape and Painting, 1825–1875.* Rev. ed. New York: Oxford University Press, 1995.

Penny, Nicholas. *The Materials of Sculpture.* New Haven, Conn.: Yale University Press, 1993.

Pohribny, Arsén. *Abstract Painting.* Oxford and New York: Phaidon and Dutton, 1979.

Rosenblum, Robert. *Modern Painting and the Northern Romantic Tradition: Friedrich to Rothko.* New York: Harper & Row, 1975.

———, and H. W. Janson. *Nineteenth-Century Art.* Englewood Cliffs, N.J.: Prentice-Hall, 1984.

Russell, John. *The Meanings of Modern Art.* Rev. ed. New York: MOMA and HarperCollins, 1991.

Schapiro, Meyer. *Modern Art: 19th and 20th Centuries: Selected Papers.* New York: G. Braziller, 1978.

Selz, Jean. *Modern Sculpture: Origins and Evolution.* Trans. Annette Michelson. New York: G. Braziller, 1963.

Selz, Peter. *Art in Our Times: A Pictorial History, 1890–1980.* New York: Harry N. Abrams, 1981.

Shone, Richard. *The Century of Change: British Painting Since 1900.* Oxford: Phaidon, 1977.

Soby, James T., and Alfred H. Barr, Jr. *Twentieth-Century Italian Art.* Exh. cat. New York: MOMA, 1949.

Spalding, Frances. *British Art Since 1900.* London: Thames & Hudson, 1986.

Steinberg, Leo. *Other Criteria: Confrontations with Twentieth-Century Art.* New York: Oxford University Press, 1972.

Tapié, Michel and Tôre Haga. *Avant-Garde Art in Japan.* New York: Harry N. Abrams, 1962.

Tomkins, Calvin. *The Bride and the Bachelors: The Heretical Courtship in Modern Art.* New York: Viking Press, 1965.

Trier, Eduard. *Form and Space: Sculpture of the Twentieth Century.* Rev. ed. New York: Praeger, 1968.

Tuchman, Maurice. *The Spiritual in Art: Abstract Painting 1890–1985.* Los Angeles: LACMA, 1986.

Tucker, William. *The Language of Sculpture.* Reprint of the 1974 ed. New York: Thames & Hudson, 1985.

Varnedoe, Kirk. *Northern Light: Realism and Symbolism in Scandinavian Painting 1880–1910.* Exh. cat. New York: Brooklyn Museum, 1982.

Waldman, Diane. *Collage, Assemblage, and the Found Object.* New York: Harry N. Abrams, 1992.

———. *Transformations in Sculpture: Four Decades of American and European Art.* New York: Solomon R. Guggenheim Foundation, 1985.

II. Further Readings, Arranged by Chapter

1. The Sources of Modern Painting

Adams, Steven. *The Barbizon School and the Origins of Impressionism.* London: Phaidon Press, 1994.

Ashton, Dore. *Rosa Bonheur: A Life and a Legend.* New York: Viking, 1981.

Baudelaire, Charles. *Eugène Delacroix: His Life and Work.* Trans. J. Bernstein. New York: Lear Publishers, 1947.

Bowness, Alan. *Gustave Courbet: 1819–1877.* Exh. cat. London: Arts Council of Great Britain, 1978.

Brookner, Anita. *Jacques-Louis David.* London: Oxford University Press, 1980.

Bryson, Norman. *Tradition and Desire: From David to Delacroix.* Cambridge and New York: Cambridge University Press, 1984.

Chu, Petra T. D., ed. *Courbet in Perspective.* Englewood Cliffs, N.J.: Prentice-Hall, 1977.

Crow, Thomas. *Emulation: Making Artists for Revolutionary France.* New Haven, Conn.: Yale University Press, 1995.

[Delacroix] *Eugène Delacroix (1798–1863): Paintings, Drawings, and Prints from North American Collections.* Exh. cat. New York: MMA, 1991.

[Delacroix] *The Journal of Eugène Delacroix.* New York: Garland Pub., 1972. Introduction by R. Motherwell.

Faunce, Sarah, ed. *Courbet Reconsidered.* Exh. cat. New Haven, Conn.: Yale University Press, 1988.

Fermigier, André. *Jean-François Millet.* Exh. cat. London: Hayward Gallery, 1976.

Fried, Michael. *Courbet's Realism.* Chicago: University of Chicago Press, 1990.

Gowing, Lawrence. *Turner: Imagination and Reality.* Exh. cat. New York: MOMA, 1966.

Harding, James. *Artistes Pompiers: French Academic Art in the 19th Century.* New York: Rizzoli, 1979.

Hargrove, June, ed. *The French Academy: Classicism and Its Antagonists.* Newark, N.J.: University of Delaware Press, 1990.

Johnson, Dorothy. *Jacques-Louis David: Art in Metamorphosis.* Princeton, N.J.: Princeton University Press, 1993.

Johnson, Lee. *The Paintings of Eugène Delacroix: A Critical Catalogue, 1816–1831.* 2 vols. Oxford: Clarendon Press, 1981.

Landow, George P. *William Holman Hunt and Typological Symbolism.* New Haven, Conn.: Paul Mellon Centre for Studies in British Art, 1979.

Licht, Fred. *Goya: The Origins of the Modern Temper in Art.* New York: Universe Books, 1979.

———, ed. *Goya in Perspective.* Englewood Cliffs, N.J.: Prentice-Hall, 1973.

Murphy, Alexandra R. *Jean-François Millet.* Exh. cat. Boston: Museum of Fine Arts, 1984.

Nanteuil, Luc de. *David.* The Library of Great Painters. New York: Harry N. Abrams, 1985.

Rosenblum, Robert. *Jean-Auguste-Dominique Ingres.* New York: Harry N. Abrams, 1990.

Schnapper, Antoine. *David.* New York: Alpine Fine Arts Collection, 1980.

Stanton, Theodore, ed. *Reminiscences of Rosa Bonheur.* New York: Hacker Art Books, 1976.

Vigne, George. *Ingres.* Trans. J. Goodman. New York: Abbeville, c. 1995.

2. Realism, Impressionism, and Early Photography

Adler, Kathleen. *Manet.* Oxford: Phaidon, 1986.

———, and Tamar Garb. *Berthe Morisot.* Ithaca, N.Y.: Cornell University Press, 1987.

Barger, Susan M., and William B. White. *The Daguerreotype: Nineteenth-Century Technology and Modern Science.* Washington, D.C.: Smithsonian Institution Press, 1991.

Belloli, Andrea. *A Day in the Country: Impressionism and the French Landscape.* Exh. cat. Los Angeles: LACMA, 1984.

Boggs, Jean Sutherland. *Degas.* Exh. cat. Chicago: Art Institute of Chicago, 1996.

Boime, Albert. *The Art of the Macchia and the Risorgimento.* Chicago: University of Chicago Press, 1993.

Breeskin, Adelyn Dohme. *Mary Cassatt: A Catalogue Raisonné of the Oils, Pastels, Watercolors, and Drawings.* 2nd rev. ed. Washington, D.C.: Smithsonian Institution Press, 1979.

Brettell, Richard, and Joachim Pissarro. *The Impressionist and the City: Pissarro's Series Paintings.* New Haven, Conn.: Yale University Press, 1992.

Broude, Norma. *Edgar Degas.* New York: Rizzoli, 1993.

———. *Impressionism: A Feminist Reading.* New York: Rizzoli, 1991.

Buckland, Gail. *Fox Talbot and the Invention of Photography.* Boston: D. R. Godine, 1980.

Callen, Anthea. *The Spectacular Body: Science, Method, and Meaning in the Work of Degas.* New Haven, Conn.: Yale University Press, 1995.

Casteras, Susan, et al. *John Ruskin and the Victorian Eye.* New York: Harry N. Abrams, 1993.

Cikovsky, Jr., Nicolai. *Winslow Homer.* New York: Harry N. Abrams, 1990.

Clark, T. J. *The Absolute Bourgeois: Artists and Politics in France, 1848–1851.* Princeton, N.J.: Princeton University Press, 1982.

———. *The Painting of Modern Life: Paris in the Art of Manet and His Followers.* New York: Knopf, 1985.

Clarke, Michael. *Corot and the Art of Landscape.* London: British Museum Press, 1991.

Cumming, Elizabeth, and Wendy Caplan. *Arts and Crafts Movement.* World of Art. New York: Thames & Hudson, 1991.

Degas Pastels. New York: G. Braziller, 1992. Texts by J. S. Boggs and A. Maheux.

Denvir, Bernard. *The Impressionists: A Documentary Study.* New York: Thames & Hudson, 1986.

———. *The Thames & Hudson Encyclopedia of Impressionism.* World of Art. New York: Thames & Hudson, 1990.

Dorment, Richard. *James McNeill Whistler.* Exh. cat. New York: Harry N. Abrams, 1995.

Fried, Michael. *Manet's Modernism, or, the Face of Painting in the 1860s.* Chicago: University of Chicago Press, 1996.

Gernsheim, Helmut. *Julia Margaret Cameron: Pioneer of Photography.* 2nd ed. London and New York: Aperture, 1975.

———, and Alison Gernsheim. *L. J. M. Daguerre: The History of the Diorama and the Daguerreotype.* Reprint. New York: Dover Publications, 1968.

Getlein, Frank. *Mary Cassatt: Paintings and Prints.* New York: Abbeville, 1980.

Goodrich, Lloyd. *Thomas Eakins.* 2 vols. Cambridge, Mass.: Harvard University Press, 1982.

Gordon, Robert, and Andrew Forge. *Monet.* New York: Harry N. Abrams, 1983.

Gosling, Nigel. *Nadar.* New York: Knopf, 1976.

Haas, Robert B. *Muybridge's Man in Motion.* Berkeley and Los Angeles: University of California Press, 1976.

Hambourg, Maria Morris. *Nadar.* Exh. cat. New York: Harry N. Abrams, 1995.

Hamilton, George. *Manet and His Critics.* Reprint of the 1954 ed. New Haven, Conn.: Yale University Press, 1986.

Hanson, Anne Coffin. *Manet and the Modern Tradition.* 2nd ed. New Haven, Conn.: Yale University Press, 1979.

Hendricks, George. *Edward Muybridge—The Father of the Motion Picture.* New York: Grossmann Publishers, 1975.

Herbert, Richard. *Impressionism: Art, Leisure and Parisian Society.* New Haven, Conn.: Yale University Press, 1988.

Higonnet, Anne. *Berthe Morisot.* New York: Harper & Row, 1990.

———. *Berthe Morisot's Images of Women.* Cambridge, Mass.: Harvard University Press, 1992.

Hills, Patricia. *John Singer Sargent.* Exh. cat. New York: WMAA, 1986. Texts by L. Ayres, A. Boime, W. H. Gerdts, S. Olson, G. A. Reynolds.

Hilton, Timothy. *The Pre-Raphaelites.* World of Art. Reprint of the 1970 ed. London: Thames & Hudson, 1985.

[Homer] *Winslow Homer and the New England Coast.* Exh. cat. New York: WMAA, 1985.

House, John. *Monet: Nature into Art.* New Haven, Conn.: Yale University Press, 1986.

Jenkyns, Richard. *Dignity and Decadence: Victorian Art and the Classical Inheritance.* Cambridge, Mass.: Harvard University Press, 1992.

Johns, Elizabeth. *Thomas Eakins and the Heroism of Modern Life.* Princeton, N.J.: Princeton University Press, 1984.

Kendall, Richard, and Griselda Pollock, eds. *Dealing with Degas: Representations of Women and the Politics of Vision.* New York: Universe Books, 1992.

Lipton, Eunice. *Looking into Degas.* Berkeley, Calif.: University of California Press, 1986.

[Manet] *The Complete Paintings of Manet.* New York: Harry N. Abrams, 1967. Introduction by P. Pool; Notes and Catalogue by S. Orienti.

[Manet] *Manet: 1832–1883.* Exh. cat. New York: MMA, 1983.

Mathews, Nancy M. *Mary Cassatt.* Library of American Art. New York: Harry N. Abrams, 1987.

Miller, David, ed. *American Iconology: New Approaches to Nineteenth-Century Art and Literature.* New Haven, Conn.: Yale University Press, 1993.

Moffett, Charles S. *The New Painting: Impressionism, 1874–1886.* Exh. cat. San Francisco: Fine Arts Museums, 1986.

Mosby, Dewey, and Darrel Sewell. *Henry Ossawa Tanner.* Exh. cat. Philadelphia and New York: Philadelphia Museum of Art and Rizzoli, 1991.

Needham, Gerald. *19th-Century Realist Art.* New York: Harper & Row, 1988.

Nochlin, Linda. *Impressionism and Post-Impressionism, 1874–1904: Sources and Documents.* Englewood Cliffs, N.J.: Prentice-Hall, 1976.

———. *Realism.* Harmondsworth.: Penguin, 1972.

———. *Realism and Tradition in Art, 1848–1900: Sources and Documents.* Englewood Cliffs, N.J.: Prentice-Hall, 1966.

Pollock, Griselda. *Mary Cassatt.* New York: Harper & Row, 1980.

The Pre-Raphaelites. Exh. cat. London: Tate Gallery, 1984.

Ratcliff, Carter. *John Singer Sargent.* New York: Abbeville, 1982.

Reff, Theodore. *Manet and Modern Paris.* Exh. cat. Washington, D.C.: National Gallery of Art, 1982.

Renoir. Exh. cat. London: Hayward Gallery, 1985. Texts by J. House, A. Distel, L. Gowing.

Renoir, Jean. *Renoir, My Father.* Trans. R. and D. Weaver. Boston: Little, Brown, 1962.

Rewald, John. *The History of Impressionism.* 4th rev. ed. New York: MOMA, 1973.

———, and Frances Weitzenhoffer, eds. *Aspects of Monet: A Symposium on the Artist's Life and Times.* New York: Harry N. Abrams, 1984.

Reynolds, Graham. *Victorian Painting.* Rev. ed. New York: Harper & Row, 1987.

Rosenblum, Robert. *Paintings in the Musée d'Orsay.* New York: Stewart, Tabori and Chang, 1989.

Rouart, Denis. *Renoir.* New York: Skira/Rizzoli, 1985.

Schaaf, Larry J. *Out of the Shadows: Herschel, Talbot and the Invention of Photography.* New Haven, Conn.: Yale University Press, 1992.

Sewell, Darrel. *Thomas Eakins: Artist of Philadelphia.* Exh. cat. Philadelphia: Philadelphia Museum of Art, 1982.

Spate, Virginia. *Claude Monet: Life and Work.* New York: Rizzoli, 1992.

Stuckey, Charles F. *Claude Monet, 1840–1926.* Exh. cat. Chicago: Art Institute, 1995.

———, and William P. Scott. *Berthe Morisot, Impressionist.* New York: Hudson Hills Press, 1987.

Sutton, Denys. *Edgar Degas: Life and Work.* New York: Rizzoli, 1986.

Tinterow, Gary, and Henri Loyrette. *Origins of Impressionism.* Exh. cat. New York: MMA, 1994.

Tucker, Paul. *Monet at Argenteuil.* New Haven, Conn.: Yale University Press, 1981.

———. *Monet in the '90s: The Series Paintings.* Exh. cat. New Haven, Conn.: Yale University Press, 1989.

Wadley, Nicholas. *Renoir: A Retrospective.* New York: Hugh Lauter Levin Assoc., 1987.

Weisberg, Gabriel. *Beyond Impressionism: The Naturalist Impulse.* New York: Harry N. Abrams, 1992.

———. *The Realist Tradition: French Painting and Drawing, 1830–1900.* Exh. cat. Cleveland: Cleveland Museum of Art, 1981.

White, Barbara Ehrlich. *Renoir: His Life, Art, and Letters.* New York: Harry N. Abrams, 1984.

Wilmerding, John. *Winslow Homer.* New York: Praeger, 1972.

Wood, Christopher. *The Pre-Raphaelites.* New York: Viking, 1981.

3. Post-Impressionism

Adriani, Gotz. *Cézanne: A Biography.* New York: Harry N. Abrams, 1990.

———. *Toulouse-Lautrec: Complete Graphic Works.* London: Thames & Hudson, 1988.

Andersen, Wayne. *Gauguin's Paradise Lost.* New York: Viking Press, 1971.

Balakian, Anna. *The Symbolist Movement: A Critical Appraisal.* New York: Random House, 1967.

Bonnard: The Late Paintings. Exh. cat. Washington, D.C.: Phillips Collection, 1984. Texts by J. Russell, S. A. Nash, J. Clair, A. Terrasse, H. Hahnloser-Ingold, J.-F. Chevrier.

Bonnard and His Environment. New York: MOMA, 1964. Texts by J. T. Soby, J. Elliott, M. Wheeler.

Bouret, Jean. *Henri Rousseau.* Greenwich, Conn.: New York Graphic Society, 1961.

Brettell, Richard, et al. *The Art of Paul Gauguin.* Exh. cat. Washington, D.C.: National Gallery of Art, 1988.

Broude, Norma. *Georges Seurat.* New York: Rizzoli, 1992.

Cachin, Françoise. *Cézanne.* Exh. cat. Philadelphia: Philadelphia Museum of Art, 1996.

[Cézanne] *The Complete Paintings of Cézanne.* Harmondsworth: Penguin, 1985. Introduction by I. Dunlop; Text by S. Orienti.

Dabrowski, Magdalena. *The Symbolist Aesthetic.* Exh. cat. New York: MOMA, 1980.

d'Argencourt, Louise, et al. *Puvis de Chavannes: 1824–1898.* Exh. cat. Ottawa: National Gallery of Canada, 1977.

Delevoy, Robert. *Symbolists and Symbolism.* New York: Rizzoli, 1978.

Denvir, Bernard. *Post-Impressionism.* World of Art. New York: Thames & Hudson, 1992.

Druick, Douglas W., et al. *Odilon Redon: Prince of Dreams, 1840–1916.* Exh. cat. New York: Harry N. Abrams, 1994.

Frèches-Thory, Clair. *The Nabis: Bonnard, Vuillard and Their Circle.* New York: Harry N. Abrams, 1991.

Fry, Roger. *Seurat.* 3rd ed. London: Phaidon, 1965.

Gauguin, Paul. *The Intimate Journals of Paul Gauguin.* Boston: KPI, 1985.

———. *Noa Noa: The Tahitian Journals.* Trans. O. F. Theis. New York: Dover Publications, 1985.

Gaunt, William. *Renoir.* Rev. enl. ed. Oxford: Phaidon, 1982. Text by K. Adler.

Gerhardus, Maly, and Dietfried Gerhardus. *Symbolism and Art Nouveau.* Trans. A. Bailey. Oxford: Phaidon, 1979.

Goldwater, Robert. *Paul Gauguin.* New York: Harry N. Abrams, 1984.

———. *Symbolism.* New York: Harper & Row, 1979.

Gowing, Lawrence. *Cézanne, the Early Years, 1859–1872.* New York: Harry N. Abrams, 1988.

Herbert, Robert L. *Georges Seurat, 1859–1891.* Exh. cat. New York: MMA, 1991.

Hirsh, S., ed. "Symbolist Art and Literature." *Art Journal* (Summer 1985) special issue.

Homer, William I. *Seurat and the Science of Painting.* Reprint. New York: Hacker Art Books, 1985.

Hulsker, Jan. *The Complete Van Gogh: Paintings, Drawings, Sketches.* New York: Harry N. Abrams, 1980.

Jullian, Philippe. *Dreamers of Decadence: Symbolist Painters of the 1890s.* Trans. R. Baldick. New York: Praeger, 1971.

Lemoyne de Forges, Marie-Therese, ed. *Signac.* Exh. cat. Paris: Musée National du Louvre, 1963.

Lewis, Mary Tompkins. *Cézanne's Early Imagery.* Berkeley, Calif.: University of California Press, 1989.

Murray, Gale B. *Toulouse-Lautrec: A Retrospective.* Exh. cat. New York: Hugh Lauter Levin Assoc., 1992.

Rewald, John. *Paul Cézanne: The Watercolors, A Catalogue Raisonné.* Boston: Little, Brown, 1983.

———. *Post-Impressionism: From Van Gogh to Gauguin.* 3rd ed. rev. New York: MOMA, 1978.

———. *Seurat: A Biography.* New York: Harry N. Abrams, 1990.

Roskill, Mark. *Van Gogh, Gauguin, and the Impressionist Circle.* Greenwich, Conn.: New York Graphic Society, 1970.

Rubin, William, ed. *Cézanne: The Late Work.* New York: MOMA, c. 1977.

Schapiro, Meyer. *Paul Cézanne.* Concise ed. New York: Harry N. Abrams, 1988.

———. *Van Gogh.* Rev. ed. New York: Harry N. Abrams, 1982.

Shiff, Richard. *Cézanne and the End of Impressionism: A Study of the Theory, Technique, and Critical Evaluation of Modern Art.* Chicago: University of Chicago Press, 1984.

———. *Toulouse-Lautrec.* World of Art. New York: Thames & Hudson, 1991.

Shone, Richard. *The Post-Impressionists.* London: Octopus Books, 1980.

Thomson, Belinda. *Gauguin.* World of Art. New York: Thames & Hudson, 1987.

Thomson, Richard. *Seurat.* Salem, N.H.: Salem House, 1985.

[Van Gogh] *The Complete Letters of Vincent Van Gogh.* 3 vols. Greenwich, Conn.: New York Graphic Society, 1959.

Verdi, Richard. *Cézanne.* World of Art. New York: Thames & Hudson, 1992.

Walther, Ingo F., and Rainer Metzger. *Van Gogh: The Complete Paintings.* Cologne: Taschen, 1993.

4. The Origins of Modern Architecture and Design

Barthes, Roland. *The Eiffel Tower and Other Mythologies.* Trans. R. Howard. New York: Hill and Wang, 1979.

Charenbhak, Wichit. *Chicago School Architects and Their Critics.* Ann Arbor, Mich.: UMI Research Press, 1984.

Crawford, Alan. *Charles Rennie Mackintosh.* New York: Thames & Hudson, 1995.

Hitchcock, Henry-Russell. *The Architecture of H. H. Richardson and His Times.* Rev. ed. Hamden, Conn.: Archon Books, 1961.

Howarth, Thomas. *Charles Rennie Mackintosh and the Modern Movement.* 2nd ed. London: Routledge and Kegan Paul, 1977.

Lethaby, William R. *Philip Webb and His Work.* New ed. London: Raven Oaks Press, c. 1979.

Loyrette, Henri. *Gustave Eiffel.* New York: Rizzoli, 1985.

Manieri-Elia, Mario. *Louis Henry Sullivan, 1856–1924.* Trans. A. Shuggar with C. Creen. New York: Princeton Architectural Press, 1996.

McKean, John. *Crystal Palace: Joseph Paxton and Charles Fox.* Architecture in Detail. London: Phaidon, 1994.

Mead, Christopher Curtis. *Charles Garnier's Paris Opera: Architectural Empathy and the Renaissance of French Classicism.* Cambridge, Mass.: MIT Press, 1991.

Morrison, Hugh. *Louis Sullivan, Prophet of Modern Architecture.* Exh. cat. New York: MOMA, 1935.

Pevsner, Nikolaus. *Charles Rennie Mackintosh.* Milan: Il Balcone, 1950.

Sullivan, Louis H. *Kindergarten Chats and Other Writings.* New York: Dover Publications, 1979.

Szarkowski, John. *The Idea of Louis Sullivan.* Minneapolis: University of Minnesota Press, 1956.

Twombley, Robert, ed. *Louis Sullivan, the Public Papers.* Chicago: University of Chicago Press, 1988.

5. Art Nouveau and the Beginnings of Expressionism

Adlmann, Jan E. *Vienna Moderne, 1898–1918.* Exh. cat. New York: Cooper-Hewitt Museum, 1979.

Amaya, Mario. *Art Nouveau.* New York: Dutton, 1967.

Arwas, Victor. *Art Deco.* Rev. ed. New York: Harry N. Abrams, 1992.

Chipp, Herschel B. *Viennese Expressionism 1910–1924.* Exh. cat. Berkeley, Calif.: University Museum, University of California, 1963.

Collins, George R. *Antoni Gaudí.* Masters of World Architecture Series. New York: G. Braziller, 1960.

Comini, Alessandra. *Gustav Klimt.* New York: G. Braziller, 1975.

Duncan, Alastair. *Art Nouveau.* World of Art. New York: Thames & Hudson, 1994.

Eggum, Arne. *Edvard Munch: Paintings, Sketches, and Studies.* New York: C. N. Potter, 1985.

Elderfield, John. *The Masterworks of Edvard Munch.* New York: MOMA, 1979.

Farmer, John David. *Ensor.* Exh. cat. New York: G. Braziller, 1976.

Heller, Reinhold. *Munch: His Life and Work.* Chicago: University of Chicago Press, 1984.

Hirsh, Sharon. *Ferdinand Hodler.* New York: G. Braziller, 1982.

Kallir, Jane. *Viennese Design and the Wiener Werkstätte.* New York: G. Braziller, 1986.

Kempton, Richard. *Art Nouveau: An Annotated Bibliography.* Los Angeles: Hennessey and Ingalls, 1977.

[Klimt] *Gustav Klimt and Egon Schiele.* Exh. cat. New York: SRGM, 1965. Texts by T. M. Messer and J. Dobai.

Madsen, Stephan T. *Sources of Art Nouveau.* Reprint. New York: Da Capo Press, 1975.

McCully, Marilyn. *El Quatre Gats: Art in Barcelona around 1900.* Exh. cat. Princeton, N.J.: Princeton University Art Museum, 1978.

[Munch] *Edvard Munch: Symbols and Images.* Exh. cat. Washington, D.C.: National Gallery of Art, 1978. Introduction by R. Rosenblum; Texts by A. Eggum, R. Heller, T. Nergaard, R. Stang, B. Torjusen, G. Wohl.

Nebehay, Christian M. *Ver Sacrum, 1898–1903.* Vienna: Edition Tuschi, 1975.

Novotny, Fritz, and Johannes Dobai. *Gustav Klimt.* Salzburg: Verlag Galerie Welz, 1967.

Partsch, Suzanna. *Klimt: Life and Work.* London: Bracken, 1993.

Pevsner, Nikolaus. *Art Nouveau in Britain.* Exh. cat. London: The Arts Council, 1965.

Powell, Nicholas. *The Sacred Spring: The Arts of Vienna, 1898–1918.* Greenwich, Conn.: New York Graphic Society, 1974.

Reade, Brian. *Aubrey Beardsley.* New York: Viking Press, 1967.

Rheims, Maurice. *The Flowering of Art Nouveau.* Trans. P. Evans. New York: Harry N. Abrams, 1966.

Russell, Frank, ed. *Art Nouveau Architecture.* New York: Rizzoli, 1979.

Schmutzler, Robert. *Art Nouveau.* Abridged ed. Trans. E. Rodotti. London: Thames & Hudson, 1978.

Schorske, Carl. *Fin-de-Siècle Vienna: Politics and Culture.* New York: Vintage Books, 1980.

Selz, Peter. *Ferdinand Hodler.* Exh. cat. Berkeley, Calif.: University Art Museum, University of California, 1972. With contributions by J. Brüschweiler et al.

———, and Mildred Constantine, eds. *Art Nouveau: Art and Design at the Turn of the Century.* Rev. ed. New York: MOMA, 1974.

Silverman, Deborah. *Art Nouveau in Fin-de-Siècle France.* Berkeley, Calif.: University of California Press, 1989.

Sotriffer, Kristian. *Modern Austrian Art.* London: Thames & Hudson, 1965.

Stansky, Peter. *Redesigning the World: William Morris, the 1880s, and the Arts and Crafts.* Princeton, N.J.: Princeton University Press, 1985.

Sweeney, James J., and Joseph L. Sert. *Antoni Gaudí.* New York: Praeger, 1960.

[Van de Velde] *Henry van de Velde, 1863–1957.* Exh. cat. Otterlo, The Netherlands: Kröller-Müller Rijksmuseum, 1964.

Varnedoe, Kirk. *Vienna 1900: Art, Architecture, and Design.* Exh. cat. New York: MOMA, 1986.

———, and Elizabeth Streicher. *Graphic Work of Max Klinger.* New York: Dover Publications, 1977.

Vergo, Peter. *Art in Vienna, 1898–1918: Klimt, Kokoschka, Schiele, and Their Contemporaries.* London: Phaidon, 1975.

Waissenberger, Robert. *Vienna Secession.* New York: Rizzoli, 1977.

6. The Origins of Modern Sculpture

Barr, Margaret S. *Medardo Rosso.* Exh. cat. New York: MOMA, 1963.

Elsen, Albert, ed. *Rodin Rediscovered.* Exh. cat. Washington, D.C.: National Gallery of Art, 1981.

George, Waldemar. *Aristide Maillol.* London: Cory, Adams & Mackay, 1965.

Gray, Christopher. *Sculpture and Ceramics of Paul Gauguin.* Baltimore: Johns Hopkins Press, 1963.

Jianu, Ionel. *Bourdelle.* Paris: Arted, 1965.

Lampert, Catherine. *Rodin: Sculpture and Drawings.* Exh. cat. London: The Arts Council, 1986.

Longwell, Dennis. *Steichen: The Master Prints, 1895–1914.* New York: MOMA, 1978.

Lorquin, Bertrand. *Maillol.* London: Thames & Hudson, 1995.

Rewald, John, and Leonard von Matt. *Degas: Sculpture, the Complete Works.* London: Thames & Hudson, c. 1957.

Rilke, Rainer Maria. *Rodin.* Salt Lake City: Peregrine Smith, 1979.

7. Fauvism

Apollonio, Umbro. *Fauves and Cubists.* London: Batsford, 1960.

Barr, Jr., Alfred H. *Matisse: His Art and His Public.* Exh. cat. New York: MOMA, 1951.

Courthion, Pierre. *Georges Rouault.* New York: Harry N. Abrams, 1962.

Crespelle, Jean-Paul. *The Fauves.* Trans. A. Brookner. Greenwich, Conn.: New York Graphic Society, 1962.

Diehl, Gaston. *Derain.* Les maîtres de la peinture moderne. Paris: Flammarion, 1964.

Duthuit, Georges. *The Fauvist Painters.* Trans. R. Mannheim. New York: Wittenborn, Schultz, 1950.

Elderfield, John. *Henri Matisse, A Retrospective.* Exh. cat. New York: MOMA, 1992.

———. *The "Wild Beasts": Fauvism and Its Affinities.* Exh. cat. New York: MOMA, 1976.

Flam, Jack D. *Matisse: The Man and His Art, 1869–1918.* London: Thames & Hudson, 1986.

———, ed. *Matisse: A Retrospective.* New York: Park Lane, 1990.

———, ed. *Matisse On Art.* Berkeley, Calif.: University of California Press, 1994.

Freeman, Judi. *The Fauve Landscape.* Exh. cat. New York: Abbeville, 1990.

Herbert, James D. *Fauve Painting: The Making of Cultural Politics.* New Haven, Conn.: Yale University Press, 1992.

Leymarie, Jean. *Fauvism, Biographical and Critical Study.* Trans. James Emmons. New York: Skira, 1959.

Rewald, John. *Les Fauves.* Exh. cat. New York: MOMA, 1952.

Rouault, Georges. *Miserere.* Boston: Boston Book and Art Shop, 1963. Introduction A. Blunt; preface by the artist.

Schneider, Pierre. *Matisse.* New York: Rizzoli, 1984.

Selz, Jean. *Vlaminck.* Les maîtres de la peinture moderne. Paris: Flammarion, 1963.

Sutton, Denys. *André Derain.* London: Phaidon, 1959.

Venturi, Lionello. *Rouault: Biographical and Critical Study.* Trans. J. Emmons. Paris: Skira, 1959.

8. Expressionism in Germany

Barron, Stephanie. *German Expressionist Sculpture.* Exh. cat. Los Angeles: LACMA, 1980.

———, ed. *"Degenerate art": The Fate of the Avant-Garde in Nazi Germany.* Exh. cat. Los Angeles: LACMA, 1991.

Benson, Timothy. *Expressionist Utopias: Paradise, Metropolis, Architectural Fantasy.* Exh. cat. Los Angeles: LACMA, 1993.

Comini, Alessandra. *Egon Schiele, 1890–1918.* New York: G. Braziller, 1976.

Dabrowski, Magdalena. *Kandinsky Compositions.* Exh. cat. New York: MOMA. 1995.

Expressionism: A German Intuition. Exh. cat. New York: SRGM, 1980.

Gordon, Donald. *Ernst Ludwig Kirchner.* Cambridge, Mass.: Harvard University Press, 1968.

———. *Oskar Kokoschka and the Visionary Tradition.* Bonn: Bouvier, 1981.

Grohmann, Will. *E. L. Kirchner.* Stuttgart: W. Kohlhammer, 1961.

———. *Karl Schmidt-Rottluff.* Stuttgart: W. Kohlhammer, 1956.

Hess, Hans. *Lyonel Feininger.* Stuttgart: W. Kohlhammer, 1959.

Hinz, Renate, ed. *Käthe Kollwitz: Graphics, Posters, Drawings.* Trans. Rita and Robert Kimber. New York: Pantheon Books, 1982. Foreword by Lucy R. Lippard.

[Jawlensky] *Alexej von Jawlensky*. Rotterdam: Museum Boymans - van Beuningen, 1994.

Jordan, Jim. *Paul Klee and Cubism*. Princeton, N.J.: Princeton University Press, 1984.

Kallir, Otto. *Egon Schiele: Oeuvre Catalog of the Paintings*. Wien: Zsolnay, 1966.

Kandinsky in Munich: 1896–1914. Exh. cat. New York: SRGM, 1982.

Klee, Felix, ed. *The Diaries of Paul Klee: 1898–1918*. Berkeley and Los Angeles: University of California Press, 1964.

Klipstein, August. *The Graphic Work of Käthe Kollwitz: Complete Illustrated Catalogue*. New York: Galerie St. Etienne, 1955.

Kokoschka: A Retrospective Exhibition of Paintings, Drawings, Lithographs, Stage Design and Books. Exh. cat. London: Tate Gallery, 1962. Texts by E. H. Gombrich, F. Novotny, H. M. Wingler, et al.

[Kokoschka] *Oskar Kokoschka, 1886–1980*. Exh. cat. New York: SRGM, 1986.

Kollwitz, Hans, ed. *The Diary and Letters of Käthe Kollwitz*. Evanston, Ill.: Northwestern University Press, 1988.

Lanchner, Carolyn, ed. *Paul Klee*. Exh. cat. New York: MOMA, 1987.

Levine, Frederick S. *The Apocalyptic Vision: The Art of Franz Marc as German Expressionism*. New York: Harper & Row, 1979.

Lincoln, Louise, ed. *German Realism of the Twenties: The Artist as Social Critic*. Exh. cat. Minneapolis: Minneapolis Institute of Arts, c.1980.

Lindsay, Kenneth and Peter Vergo. *Kandinsky: Complete Writings on Art*. 2 vols. Boston: G. K. Hall, 1982.

Lloyd, Jill. *German Expressionism: Primitivism and Modernity*. New Haven, Conn.: Yale University Press, 1991.

Long, Rose-Carol Washton, ed. *German Expressionism: Documents from the End of the Wilhelmine Empire to the Rise of National Socialism*. Documents of Twentieth Century Art. New York: G. K. Hall, 1993.

[Modersohn-Becker] *The Letters and Journals of Paula Modersohn-Becker*. Trans. and ed. J. D. Radycki. Metuchen, N.J.: Scarecrow Press, 1980.

Neue Sachlichkeit and German Realism of the Twenties. Exh. cat. London: Arts Council of Great Britain, 1978.

Painters of the Brücke. Exh. cat. London: Tate Gallery, 1964.

Perry, Gillian. *Paula Modersohn-Becker: Her Life and Work*. New York: Harper & Row, 1979.

Prelinger, Elizabeth. *Käthe Kollwitz*. Exh. cat. Washington, D.C.: National Gallery of Art, 1992.

Richard, Lionel. *Phaidon Encyclopedia of Expressionism*. Trans. S. Tint. Oxford: Phaidon, 1978.

Roethel, Hans. *The Blue Rider*. New York: Praeger, 1971.

———, and Jean Benjamin. *Kandinsky Catalogue Raisonné of the Oil Paintings*. 2 vols. Ithaca, N.Y.: Cornell University Press, 1982.

Sabarsky, Serge. *Egon Schiele*. New York: Rizzoli, 1985.

Samuel, Richard and R. Hinton Thomas. *Expressionism in German Life, Literature, and the Theatre (1910–1924)*. Cambridge: W. Heffer & Sons, Ltd., 1939.

Schvey, Henry. *Oskar Kokoschka, the Painter as Playwright*. Detroit: Wayne State University Press, 1982.

Urban, Martin. *Emil Nolde: Catalogue Raisonné of the Oil Paintings*. 2 vols. London: Sotheby's Publications, 1987–1990.

Vergo, Peter. *Art in Vienna, 1898–1918: Klimt, Kokoschka, Schiele, and Their Contemporaries*. London: Phaidon, 1975.

Vogt, Paul. *Erich Heckel*. Recklinghausen, Germany: Bongers, 1965.

———. *Expressionism: German Painting, 1905–1920*. Trans. A. Vivus. New York: Harry N. Abrams, 1980.

Weiler, Clemens. *Alexej Jawlensky*. Cologne: M. Du Mont Schauberg, 1959.

Whitford, Frank. *Expressionist Portraits*. New York: Abbeville, 1987.

Zigrosser, Carl. *The Expressionists: A Survey of Their Graphic Art*. New York: G. Braziller, 1957.

9. The Figurative Tradition in Early Twentieth-Century Sculpture

Chave, Anna. *Constantin Brancusi: Shifting the Bases of Art*. New Haven, Conn.: Yale University Press, 1993.

Elsen, Albert E. *The Sculpture of Henri Matisse*. New York: Harry N. Abrams, 1972.

Geist, Sydney. *Brancusi: A Study of the Sculpture*. Rev. enl. ed. New York: Hacker Art Books, 1983.

Hofmann, Werner. *Wilhelm Lehmbruck*. London: A. Zwemmer, c. 1958.

Maddow, Ben. *Edward Weston: Fifty Years*. Millerton, N.Y.: Aperture, 1973.

Miller, Sanda. *Constantin Brancusi: A Survey of His Work*. Oxford: Clarendon, 1995.

Shanes, Eric. *Constantin Brancusi*. New York: Abbeville, 1989.

Stebbins, Jr., Theodore E. *Weston's Westons: Portraits and Nudes*. Boston: Museum of Fine Arts, 1994.

———, and Karen E. Quinn. *Weston's Westons: California and the West*. Boston: Museum of Fine Arts, 1994.

10. Cubism

Apollinaire, Guillaume. *The Cubist Painters*. New York: Wittenborn & Co., 1949.

Archipenko, Aleksandr, et al. *Archipenko: Fifty Creative Years, 1908–1958*. New York: Tekhne, 1960.

Arnason, H. H. *Jacques Lipchitz: Sketches in Bronze*. New York: Praeger, 1969.

Barr, Jr., Alfred H. *Cubism and Abstract Art*. Exh. cat. New York: MOMA, 1936.

———, ed. *Picasso: 75th Anniversary Exhibition*. Exh. cat. New York: MOMA, 1957.

Bois, Yve-Alain. "Kahnweiler's Lesson." *Representations* (Spring 1987): 33–68.

Cogniat, Raymond. *Georges Braque*. New York: Harry N. Abrams, 1980.

———. *Georges Braque: Rétrospective*. Exh. cat. Saint-Paul: Foundation Maeght, 1994.

Cooper, Douglas. *The Cubist Epoch*. Exh. cat. New York and London: LACMA, MMA, and Phaidon, 1970.

———, and Gary Tinterow. *Essential Cubism: Braque, Picasso and Their Friends, 1907–1920*. Exh. cat. London: Tate Gallery, 1983.

———, ed. and trans. *Juan Gris: Catalogue raisonné de l'oeuvre peinte*. Paris: Berggruen, 1977.

———, ed. *Letters of Juan Gris (1913–1927)*. London: Lund Humphries, 1956.

Cowling, Elizabeth, and John Golding. *Picasso: Sculptor/Painter*. London: Tate Gallery, 1994.

De Francia, Peter. *Fernand Léger*. New Haven, Conn.: Yale University Press, 1983.

Delevoy, Robert. *Léger: Biographical and Critical Study*. Trans. S. Gilbert. Lausanne: Skira 1962.

Golding, John. *Cubism: A History and an Analysis, 1907–1914*. 3rd ed. Cambridge, Mass.: Belknap Press of Harvard University Press, 1988.

Goldscheider, Cécile. *Laurens*. Cologne: Kiepenheur & Witsch, 1957.

Green, Christopher. *Cubism and Its Enemies*. New Haven, Conn.: Yale University Press, 1987.

———. *Juan Gris*. New Haven, Conn.: Yale University Press, 1992.

———. *Léger and the Avant-Garde*. New Haven, Conn.: Yale University Press, 1976.

Hammacher, A. M. *Jacques Lipchitz*. Trans. J. Brockway. New York: Harry N. Abrams, 1975. Introductory statement by the artist.

Harrison, Charles, Francis Frascina, and Gill Perry. *Primitivism, Cubism, Abstraction: The Early Twentieth Century*. New Haven, Conn.: Yale University Press, 1993.

Hilton, Timothy. *Picasso*. World of Art. New York: Praeger, 1975.

Hofmann, Werner, and Daniel-Henry Kahnweiler. *The Sculpture of Henri Laurens*. New York: Harry N. Abrams, 1970.

Jacques Villon, Raymond Duchamp-Villon, Marcel Duchamp. Exh. cat. New York: SRGM, 1957.

Kahnweiler, Daniel-Henry. *The Rise of Cubism*. Trans. Henry Aronson. New York: Wittenborn, Schultz, 1949.

Karshan, Donald. *Archipenko: The Sculpture and Graphic Art*. Tübingen: Wasmuth, 1974.

[Laurens] *Henri Laurens*. Exh. cat. Lille: Musée d'art moderne, 1992.

[Laurens] *Henri Laurens*. Exh. cat. New York: Curt Valentin Gallery, 1952. With a statement by the artist.

Leighton, Patricia. *Re-Ordering the Universe: Picasso and Anarchism, 1897–1914*. Princeton, N.J.: Princeton University Press, 1989.

Les Desmoiselles d'Avignon. 2 vols. Paris: Musée Picasso, 1988.

Lipchitz, Jacques, with H. H. Arnason. *My Life in Sculpture*. New York: Viking Press, 1972.

Monod-Fontaine, Isabelle, and E. A. Carmean, Jr. *Braque: The Papiers Collés*. Exh. cat. Washington, D.C.: National Gallery, 1982. Text by A. Martin.

Penrose, Roland. *The Sculpture of Picasso*. Exh. cat. New York: MOMA, 1967.

———, and John Golding. *Picasso in Retrospect*. New York and Washington, D.C.: Praeger, 1973.

Picasso: Sixty Years of Graphic Works. Exh. cat. Los Angeles: LACMA, 1966.

Robbins, Daniel. *Albert Gleizes, 1881–1953: A Retrospective Exhibition*. Exh. cat. New York: SRGM, 1964.

Rosenblum, Robert. *Cubism and Twentieth-Century Art*. New York: Harry N. Abrams, 1976.

Rowell, Margit, and Daniel Robbins. *Cubist Drawings: 1907–1929*. Exh. cat. Houston: Janie C. Lee Gallery, 1982.

Rubin, William. "From Narrative to 'Iconic' in Picasso: The Buried Allegory in *Bread and Fruit Dish on a Table* and the Role of *Les Desmoiselles d'Avignon*." *Art Bulletin* 65:4 (December 1983): 615–649.

———, "Pablo and Georges and Leo and Bill." *Art in America* 67:2 (March–April 1979): 128ff.

———, ed. *Pablo Picasso: A Retrospective*. Exh. cat. New York: MOMA, 1980.

———, ed. *Picasso and Braque: Pioneering Cubism*. New York: MOMA, 1989.

———, ed. *"Primitivism" in 20th-Century Art: Affinity of the Tribal and the Modern*. 2 vols. New York: MOMA, 1984.

Schiff, Gert, ed. *Picasso in Perspective*. Englewood Cliffs, N.J.: Prentice-Hall, 1976.

Schmalenbach, Werner. *Léger*. New York: Harry N. Abrams, 1976.

Spate, Virginia. *Orphism: The Evolution of Non-Figurative Painting in Paris: 1910–1914*. Exh. cat. Oxford and New York: Clarendon Press and Oxford University Press, 1979.

Steinberg, Leo. "The Philosophical Brothel." *October* 44 (Spring 1988): 7–74.

———. "The Polemical Part." *Art in America* 67:2 (March–April 1979): 114–127.

———. "Resisting Cézanne: Picasso's 'Three Women.'" *Art in America* (November–December 1978): 114–133.

Vallier, Dora. *Jacques Villon: Oeuvres de 1897 à 1956.* Paris: Éditions cahiers d'art, 1957.

[Villon] *Jacques Villon, Master of Graphic Art (1875–1963).* Exh. cat. Boston: Museum of Fine Arts, 1964. Text by P. A. Wick.

Wallen, Burr, and Donna Stein. *The Cubist Print.* Exh. cat. Santa Barbara, Calif.: University of California Art Museum, 1981.

Wight, Frederick. *Jacques Lipchitz: A Retrospective Selected by the Artist.* Exh. cat. Los Angeles: UCLA Art Galleries, 1963.

Wilkin, Karen. *Georges Braque.* New York: Abbeville, 1991.

Wilkinson, Alan G. *Jacques Lipchitz: A Life in Sculpture.* Exh. cat. Toronto: Art Gallery of Ontario, 1989.

Zelevansky, Lynn, ed. *Picasso and Braque, A Symposium.* New York: MOMA, 1992.

Zurcher, Bernard. *Georges Braque: Life and Work.* Trans. S. Nye. New York: Rizzoli, 1988.

11. Futurism, Abstraction in Russia, and de Stijl

Andersen, Troels, ed. *Essays on Art by K. S. Malevich.* 2 vols. Trans. X. Glowacki-Prus and A. McMillan. Copenhagen: Borgen, 1968.

Art into Life: Russian Constructivism, 1914–32. New York: Rizzoli, 1990.

[Balla] *Giacomo Balla.* Exh. cat. Turin: Galleria Civica d'Arte Moderna, 1963. Documentation by E. Crispolti and M. Drudi Gambillo.

Ballo, Giacomo. *Umberto Boccioni: La Vita e l'Opera.* I Maestri della pittura contemporanea. 1st ed. Milan: Il Saggiatore, 1964.

Barr, Jr., Alfred H. *Cubism and Abstract Art.* Exh. cat. New York: MOMA, 1936.

Barron, Stephanie, and Maurice Tuchman. *The Avant-Garde in Russia, 1910–1930: New Perspectives.* Exh. cat. Los Angeles: LACMA, 1980.

Blotkamp, Carel. *Mondrian: The Art of Destruction.* New York: Harry N. Abrams, 1995.

Bowlt, John, ed. and trans. *Russian Art of the Avant-Garde: Theory and Criticism, 1902–1934.* New York: Viking Press, 1976.

———, and Rose-Carol Washton Long, eds. *The Life of Vasilli Kandinsky in Russian Art: A Study of "On the Spiritual in Art."* Trans. J. Bowlt. Newtonville, Mass.: Oriental Research Partners, 1980.

Bruni, Claudio, and Maria Drudi Gambillo, eds. *After Boccioni, Futurist Paintings and Documents from 1915 to 1919.* Trans. H. G. Heath. Rome: Studio d'arte contemporanea, La Medusa, 1961.

Bulhof, Francis, ed. *Nijhoff, Van Ostaijen, "De Stijl": Modernism in the Netherlands and Belgium in the First Quarter of the Twentieth Century.* The Hague: Nijhoff, 1976.

[Carrà] *Carlo Carrà.* Exh. cat. Paris: Editions Galerie Eric Touchaleaume, 1994.

Carrieri, Raffaele. *Futurism.* Trans. L. van Rensselaer White. Milan: Edizioni del Milione, 1963.

Coen, Ester. *Umberto Boccioni.* Exh. cat. New York: MMA, 1988.

Cork, Richard. *Vorticism and Abstract Art in the First Machine Age.* Berkeley, Calif.: University of California Press, 1976.

Dabrowski, Magdalena. *Contrasts of Form: Geometric Abstract Art, 1910–1980.* Exh. cat. New York: MOMA, 1985.

———. *Liubov Popova.* Exh. cat. New York: MOMA, 1991.

D'Andrea, Jean. *Kazimir Malevich, 1878–1935.* Exh. cat. Los Angeles: Armand Hammer Museum of Art, 1990.

De Stijl. Exh. cat. New York: MOMA, 1961.

d'Harnoncourt, Anne. *Futurism and the International Avant-Garde.* Exh. cat. Philadelphia: Philadelphia Museum of Art, 1980.

Doesburg, Theo van. *New Movement in Painting.* Delft: J. Waltman, 1971.

Elliott, David. *El Lissitzky: 1890–1941.* Exh. cat. Oxford: Museum of Modern Art, 1977.

———. *New Worlds: Russian Art and Society: 1900–1935.* London: Thames & Hudson, 1986.

———, ed. *Rodchenko and the Arts of Revolutionary Russia.* New York: Pantheon Books, 1979.

Goncharova—Larianov. Exh. cat. Paris: Musée d'Art Moderne de la Ville de Paris, 1963.

Goncharova, Larianov, Mansurov. Exh. cat. Bergamo: Galleria Lorenzelli, 1966.

Gray, Camilla, and Marian Burleigh-Motley. *Russian Experiment in Art: 1863–1922.* Rev. ed. London and New York: Thames & Hudson, 1986.

The Great Utopia: The Russian and Soviet Avant-Garde. Exh. cat. New York: SRGM, 1992.

Guerman, Mikhail, ed. *Art of the October Revolution.* Trans. W. Freeman, D. Saunders, and C. Binns. New York: Harry N. Abrams, 1979.

Hahl-Koch, Jelena. *Kandinsky.* New York: Rizzoli, 1993.

Hammacher, A. M. *Mondrian, De Stijl, and Their Impact.* Exh. cat. New York: Marlborough-Gerson Gallery, Inc., 1964.

Hanson, Anne Coffin, ed. *The Futurist Imagination: Word + Image in Italian Futurist Painting, Drawing, Collage, and Free-word Poetry.* New Haven, Conn.: Yale University Art Gallery 1983.

Hoffman, Katherine, ed. *Collage: Critical Views.* Ann Arbor, Mich.: UMI Research Press, 1989.

Hulten, Pontus. *Futurism and Futurisms.* New York: Abbeville, 1986.

———, and Jean-Hubert Martin. *Malevich.* Exh. cat. Paris: Centre National d'Art Contemporain et de Culture Georges Pompidou, 1978.

Jaffe, Hans, et al. *De Stijl, 1917–1931: Visions of Utopia.* Exh. cat. Minneapolis and New York: Walker Art Center and Abbeville, 1982.

Kandinsky, Complete Writings on Art. Ed. K. Lindsay and P. Vergo. Documents of Twentieth Century Art. 2 vols. Boston: G. K. Hall, 1982.

Karginov, German. *Rodchenko.* Trans. E. Hoch. London: Thames & Hudson, 1979.

Khan-Magomedov, Selim. *Rodchenko: The Complete Work.* Cambridge, Mass.: MIT Press, 1986.

Kozloff, Max. *Cubism/Futurism.* New York: Charterhouse, 1973.

Lissitzky-Küppers, Sophie. *El Lissitzky: Life, Letters, Texts.* Greenwich, Conn.: New York Graphic Society, 1968. Introduction by H. Read.

Lodder, Christina. *Russian Constructivism.* New Haven, Conn.: Yale University Press, 1983.

[Malevich] *Kazimir Malevich, 1878–1935.* Exh. cat. London: Whitechapel Art Gallery, 1959.

Malevich, Kazimir. *The Non-Objective World.* Chicago: Theobald, 1959.

Mansbach, Steven. *Visions of Totality: László Moholy-Nagy, Theo van Doesberg, and El Lissitzky.* Ann Arbor, Mich.: UMI Research Press, 1980.

Martin, Marianne. *Futurist Art and Theory 1909–1915.* Oxford: Clarendon Press, 1968.

———, and Anne Coffin Hanson, eds. "Futurism." *Art Journal* (Winter 1981) special issue.

Milner, John. *Kazimir Malevich and the Art of Geometry.* New Haven, Conn.: Yale University Press, 1996.

———. *Vladmir Tatlin and the Russian Avant-Garde.* New Haven, Conn.: Yale University Press, 1983.

Mondrian, Piet. *The New Art, the New Life: The Complete Writings.* Ed. and trans. H. Holtzmann and M. James. Documents of Twentieth Century Art. Boston: G. K. Hall, 1986.

[Mondrian] *Piet Mondrian, 1872–1944.* Exh. cat. Toronto: Toronto Art Gallery, 1966. Texts by R. P. Welsh, R. Rosenblum, M. Seuphor.

[Mondrian] *Piet Mondrian, 1872–1944: Centennial Exhibition.* Exh. cat. New York: SRGM, 1971.

Overy, Paul. *De Stijl.* World of Art. New York: Thames & Hudson, 1991.

Ozenfant, Amédéé. *Foundations of Modern Art.* New American Edition. New York: Dover Publications, 1952.

Poggi, Christine. *In Defiance of Painting: Cubism, Futurism and the Invention of Collage.* New Haven, Conn.: Yale University Press, 1992.

Roman, Gail Harrison, ed. "The Russian Avant-Garde." *Art Journal* XLI:3 (Fall 1981) special issue.

Rowell, Margit. *The Planar Dimension: Europe 1912–1932.* New York: SRGM, 1979.

———, and Angelika Z. Rudenstine. *Art of the Avant-Garde in Russia: Selections from the George Costakis Collection.* Exh. cat. New York: SRGM, 1981.

Rudenstine, Angelika Z., ed. *Piet Mondrian, 1872–1944.* Exh. cat. Boston: Little, Brown, 1994.

———, ed. *Russian Avant-Garde Art: The George Costakis Collection.* Exh. cat. New York: SRGM, 1981.

Taylor, Joshua C. *Futurism: Politics, Painting, and Performance.* Ann Arbor, Mich.: UMI Research Press, 1979.

———. *The Graphic Work of Umberto Boccioni.* Exh. cat. New York: MOMA, 1961.

Troy, Nancy. *The De Stijl Environment.* Cambridge, Mass.: MIT Press, 1983.

Vantongerloo, Georges. *Paintings, Sculptures, Reflections.* Problems of Contemporary Art, 5. New York: Wittenborn, Schultz, 1948.

Zhadova, Larissa A. *Malevich: Suprematism and Revolution in Russian Art.* Trans. A. Lieven. London: Thames & Hudson, 1982.

12. Early Twentieth-Century Architecture

Graf, Otto Antonia. *Otto Wagner.* Vienna: H. Böhlaus, 1985.

Gravagnuolo, Benedetto. *Adolf Loos: Theory and Works.* Milan: Idea Books Edizioni, Locker Verlang, 1983.

Gutheim, Frederick, ed. *Frank Lloyd Wright on Architecture: Selected Writings, 1894–1940.* New York: Duell, Sloan and Pearce, 1941.

Haiko, Peter, ed. *Architecture of the Early XX Century.* Trans. G. Clough. New York: Rizzoli, 1989.

Hitchcock, Henry-Russell. *In the Nature of Materials: The Buildings of Frank Lloyd Wright, 1887–1941.* New York: Da Capo Press, 1975.

———. *J. J. P. Oud.* Paris: Éditions cahiers d'art, 1931.

Larkin, David, and Bruce Brooks Pfeiffer. *Frank Lloyd Wright: The Masterworks.* New York: Rizzoli, 1993.

Mallgrave, Harry Francis. *Otto Wagner: Reflections on the Raiment of Modernity.* Santa Monica, Calif.: Getty Center for the History of Art and the Humanities, 1993.

Munz, Ludwig. *Adolf Loos.* New York: Praeger, 1966.

Naden, Corinne J. *Frank Lloyd Wright, the Rebel Architect.* New York, 1968.

O'Gorman, James F. *Three American Architects: Richardson, Sullivan, and Wright, 1865–1915.* Chicago: University of Chicago Press, 1991.

Riley, Terrence, and Peter Redd, eds. *Frank Lloyd Wright, Architect.* Exh. cat. New York: MOMA, 1994.

Rogers, Ernesto N. *Auguste Perret.* Milan: Il Balcone, 1955.

Sant'Elia, A. "Manifesto of Futurist Architecture." *Architectural Review* 126 (1959).

Scully, Vincent. *Frank Lloyd Wright.* New York: G. Braziller, 1960.

Veronesi, Giulia. *J. J. Pieter Oud.* Milan: Il Balcone, 1953.

Whittick, Arnold. *Eric Mendelsohn.* 2nd ed. London: L. Hill, 1956.

Windsor, Alan. *Peter Behrens: Architect and Designer, 1879–1940.* New York: Whitney Library of Design, 1981.

Wright, Frank Lloyd. *Frank Lloyd Wright, Collected Writings.* Ed. B.B. Pfeiffer. 5 vols. New York: Rizzoli, 1992–1995.

13. From Fantasy to Dada and the New Objectivity

Abrams, Stephan. *Max Beckmann.* New York, 1985.

Ades, Dawn, et al., eds. *In the Mind's Eye: Dada and Surrealism.* New York: Abbeville, 1986.

Andreotti, Margherita. *The Early Sculpture of Jean Arp.* Ann Arbor, Mich.: UMI Research Press, 1989.

Arnason, H. H. *Reality and Fantasy 1900–1954.* Minneapolis: Walker Art Center, 1954.

Arp: 1886–1966. Exh. cat. Minneapolis: Minneapolis Institute of Arts, 1987.

Arp, Hans. *On My Way: Poetry and Essays, 1912–1947.* New York: Wittenborn, Schultz, 1948.

Barr, Jr., Alfred H., ed. *Fantastic Art, Dada, Surrealism.* 2nd ed. rev. Exh. cat. New York: MOMA, 1937. Text by G. Hugnet.

Borràs, Maria Lluïsa. *Picabia.* London: Thames & Hudson, 1985.

Camfield, William A. *Francis Picabia: His Art, Life, and Times.* Princeton, N.J.: Princeton University Press, 1979.

———. *Max Ernst: Dada and the Dawn of Surrealism.* Exh. cat. New York: MOMA, 1993.

Clair, Jean. *Marcel Duchamp: Catalogue Raisonné.* Exh. cat. Paris: Musée National d'Art Moderne, Centre Georges Pompidou, 1977.

Dachy, Marc. *The Dada Movement, 1915–1923.* New York: Skira/Rizzoli, 1990.

d'Harnoncourt, Anne, and Kynaston McShine. *Marcel Duchamp.* Exh. cat. Munich: Prestel and Philadelphia Museum of Art, 1989.

Dietrich, Dorothea. *The Collages of Kurt Schwitters: Tradition and Innovation.* New York: Cambridge University Press, 1993.

[Dix] *Otto Dix, 1891–1969.* Exh. cat. London: Tate Gallery, 1992.

Duchamp, Marcel. *Marcel Duchamp, Notes.* Trans. P. Matisse. Documents of Twentieth Century Art. Boston: G. K. Hall, 1983.

Eberle, Matthias. *World War I and the Weimar Artists: Dix, Grosz, Beckmann, Schlemmer.* New Haven, Conn.: Yale University Press, 1985.

Elderfield, John. *Kurt Schwitters.* Exh. cat. New York: MOMA and Thames & Hudson, 1985.

Foresta, Merry. *Man Ray, 1890–1976: His Complete Works.* Düsseldorf: Edition Stemmle, 1989.

———, et al. *Perpetual Motif: The Art of Man Ray.* Exh. cat. Washington, D.C.: National Museum of American Art, 1988.

Foster, Stephen, and Rudolf Kuenzi. *Dada Spectrum: The Dialectics of Revolt.* Iowa City, Iowa: University of Iowa, 1979.

Giedion-Welcker, Carola. *Hans Arp.* Stuttgart: Gerd Hatje, 1957. Documentation by M. Hagenbach.

Grosz, George. *George Grosz: An Autobiography.* Trans. N. Hodges. New York: Macmillan, 1983.

Haftmann, Werner. *Chagall.* Trans. H. Baumann and A. Brown. New York: Harry N. Abrams, 1984.

———. *Marc Chagall: Gouaches, Drawings, Watercolors.* Trans. R. E. Wolf. New York: Harry N. Abrams, 1984.

Hess, Hans. *George Grosz.* London: Studio Vista, 1974.

Jones, Amelia. *Postmodernism and the En-Gendering of Marcel Duchamp.* Cambridge, England and New York: Cambridge University Press, 1994.

Kuenzli, Rudolf, and Francis M. Naumann. *Marcel Duchamp: Artist of the Century.* Cambridge, Mass.: MIT Press, 1989.

Kuthy, Sandor. *Sophie Taeuber–Hans Arp.* Exh. cat. Bern: Kunstmuseum Bern, 1988.

Lanchner, Carolyn. *Sophie Taeuber-Arp.* Exh. cat. New York: MOMA, 1981.

Lavin, Maud. *Cut with the Kitchen Knife: The Weimar Photomontages of Hannah Höch.* New Haven, Conn.: Yale University Press, 1993.

Lewis, Beth Irwin. *George Grosz: Art and Politics in the Weimar Republic.* Rev. ed. Princeton, N.J.: Princeton University Press, c. 1991.

Man Ray. Exh. cat. Los Angeles: LACMA, 1966. Texts by the artist and his friends.

Man Ray. *Self-Portrait.* Boston: Little, Brown, 1963.

Motherwell, Robert, ed. *The Dada Painters and Poets: An Anthology.* 2nd ed. Boston: G. K. Hall, 1981.

Oesterreicher-Mollwo, Marianne. *Surrealism and Dadaism.* Trans. Stephen Crawshaw. Oxford: Phaidon, 1979.

Paz, Octavio. *Marcel Duchamp: Appearance Stripped Bare.* New York: Viking Press, 1978.

Penrose, Roland. *Man Ray.* Boston: New York Graphic Society, 1975.

Pincus-Witten, Robert. *Giorgio de Chirico: Post Metaphysical and Baroque Paintings, 1920–1970.* Exh. cat. New York: Robert Miller Gallery, 1984.

Rau, Bernd. *Jean Arp: The Reliefs, Catalogue of Complete Works.* New York: Rizzoli, 1981.

Read, Herbert. *The Art of Jean Arp.* New York: Harry N. Abrams, 1968.

Richter, Hans. *Dada, Art, and Anti-Art.* New York: McGraw-Hill, 1965.

Rubin, William. *Dada, Surrealism, and Their Heritage.* Exh. cat. New York: MOMA, 1968.

———, ed. *De Chirico.* Exh. cat. New York: MOMA, 1982. Text by F. dell'Arco.

[Sander] *August Sander: Photographer of an Epoch, 1904–1959.* Millerton, N.Y.: Aperture, 1980.

Schmalenback, Werner. *Kurt Schwitters.* New York: Harry N. Abrams, 1970.

Schulz-Hoffmann, Carla, and Judith Weiss. *Max Beckmann: Retrospective.* Exh. cat. St. Louis and Munich: St. Louis Art Museum and Prestel, 1984.

Selz, Peter. *Max Beckmann.* Exh. cat. New York: MOMA, 1964. Texts by H. Joachim and P. T. Rathbone.

Tatar, Maria. *Lustmord: Sexual Murder in Weimar Germany.* Princeton, N.J.: Princeton University Press, 1995.

14. The School of Paris After World War I

Castaing, Marcellin, and Jean Leymarie. *Soutine.* Milan: Silvana editoriale d'arte, 1964.

Chipp, Herschel. *Georges Braque: The Late Paintings, 1940–1963.* Exh. cat. Washington, D.C.: Phillips Collection, 1982.

Ducrot, Nicolaus, ed. *André Kertész: Sixty Years of Photography, 1912–1972.* New York: Grossman Pub., 1972.

Durrell, Lawrence. Exh. cat. *Brassaï.* New York: MOMA, 1968.

Mangin, Nicole S., ed. *Catalogue de l'oeuvre de Georges Braque.* Paris: Maeght, 1959.

Mann, Carol. *Modigliani.* World of Art. New York: Oxford University Press, 1980.

Modigliani, Jeanne. *Modigliani: Man and Myth.* New York: Orion, 1958.

Perez-Tibi, Dora. *Dufy.* Trans. S. Whiteside. London: Thames & Hudson, 1989.

Silver, Kenneth. *Esprit de Corps: The Art of the Parisian Avant-Garde and the First World War, 1914–1925.* Princeton, N.J.: Princeton University Press, 1989.

Soby, James T. *Modigliani: Paintings, Drawings, Sculpture.* Exh. cat. 3rd ed. rev. New York: MOMA, 1963.

Sylvester, David. *Chaim Soutine, 1894–1943.* Exh. cat. London: The Arts Council, 1963.

Tuchman, Maurice. *Soutine.* Exh. cat. Los Angeles: LACMA, 1968.

[Utrillo] *Maurice Utrillo.* Exh. cat. Pittsburgh: Museum of Art, Carnegie Institute, 1963.

[Utrillo] *Maurice Utrillo: L'oeuvre complet.* 2 vols. Paris: Paul Pétridès, 1959–62.

Werner, Alfred. *Amedeo Modigliani.* New York: Harry N. Abrams, 1985.

———. *Chaim Soutine.* New York: Harry N. Abrams, 1977.

15. Surrealism

Abbott, Berenice. *The World of Atget.* New York: Horizon Press, 1979.

Ades, Dawn, et al., eds. *In the Mind's Eye: Dada and Surrealism.* New York: Abbeville, 1986.

Arnason, H. H. *Reality and Fantasy, 1900–1954.* Minneapolis: Walker Art Center, 1954.

Barr, Jr., Alfred H., ed. *Fantastic Art, Dada, Surrealism.* 2nd ed. rev. Exh. cat. New York: MOMA, 1937. Texts by G. Hugnet.

Blanc, Giulio V., et al. *Wilfredo Lam and His Contemporaries.* Exh. cat. New York: Studio Museum of Harlem, 1992.

Bonnefoy, Yves. *Giacometti.* New York: Flammarion/Abbeville, 1991.

Breton, André. *Manifestoes of Surrealism.* Ann Arbor, Mich.: University of Michigan Press, 1969.

———. *What Is Surrealism? Selected Writings.* Ed. F. Rosemont. New York: Monad, 1978.

Camfield, William. *Max Ernst: Dada and the Dawn of Surrealism.* Exh. cat. Houston and Munich: The Menil Collection and Prestel, 1993.

[Cartier-Bresson] *Henri Cartier-Bresson: Photographer.* Boston: New York Graphic Society, 1979.

[Cartier-Bresson] *The World of Henri Cartier-Bresson.* New York: Viking Press, 1968.

Dalí, Salvador. *The Secret Life of Salvador Dalí.* Trans. H. M. Chevalier. New York: Dial Press, 1942.

De Bock, Paul Aloïse. *Paul Delvaux.* Hamburg: J. Asmus, 1965.

Descharnes, Robert. *Salvador Dalí: The Work, the Man.* New York: Harry N. Abrams, 1984.

Ernst, Max. *Beyond Painting, and Other Writings by the Artist and His Friends.* New York: Wittenborn, Schultz, 1948.

[Ernst] *Max Ernst: A Retrospective.* Exh. cat. New York: SRGM, 1975.

Fer, Briony. *Realism, Rationalism, Surrealism: Art Between the Wars.* New Haven, Conn.: Yale University Press, 1993.

Foster, Hal. *Compulsive Beauty.* Cambridge, Mass.: MIT Press, 1993.

Foucault, Michel. *This Is Not a Pipe.* Trans. and ed. J. Harkness. Berkeley, Calif.: University of California Press, 1983.

Gablik, Suzy. *Magritte.* World of Art. Reprint. New York: Thames & Hudson, 1985.

Gerard, Max, ed. *Dalí.* Trans. E. Morse. New York: Harry N. Abrams, 1968.

Hahn, Otto. *Masson*. New York: Harry N. Abrams, 1965.

Haslam, Malcolm. *The Real World of the Surrealists*. New York: Rizzoli, 1978. Introduction by Barbara Rose.

Henning, Edward B. *The Spirit of Surrealism: 1919–1939*. Exh. cat. Cleveland: Cleveland Museum of Art, 1979.

Hohl, Reinhold. *Alberto Giacometti: A Retrospective Exhibition*. Exh. cat. New York: SRGM, 1974.

Krauss, Rosalind. *L'amour fou: Photography and Surrealism*. New York: Abbeville, 1985.

Lanchner, Carolyn. *Joan Miró*. Exh. cat. New York: MOMA, 1993.

Leiris, Michel, and Georges Limbour. *André Masson and His Universe*. London, Geneva, and Paris: Éditions des Trois Collines, 1947.

Lewis, Helena. *The Politics of Surrealism*. New York: Paragon, 1988.

Lippard, Lucy R., ed. *Surrealists on Art*. Englewood Cliffs, N.J.: Prentice-Hall, 1970.

Lord, James. *Giacometti, A Biography*. New York: Farrar, Straus and Giroux, 1985.

Miró, Joan. *Joan Miró: Selected Writings and Interviews*. Ed. M. Rowell. Documents of Twentieth Century Art. Boston: G. K. Hall, 1986.

Nadeau, Maurice. *History of Surrealism*. Cambridge, Mass.: Harvard University Press, 1989.

Oesterreicher-Mollwo, Marianne. *Surrealism and Dadaism*. Trans. Stephen Crawshaw. Oxford: Phaidon, 1979.

Picon, Gaëtan. *Surrealists and Surrealism: 1919–1939*. Trans. J. Emmons. New York: Rizzoli, 1977.

Rowell, Margit. *Julio González: A Retrospective*. Exh. cat. New York: SRGM, 1983.

Rubin, William. *Dada, Surrealism, and Their Heritage*. Exh. cat. New York: MOMA, 1968.

———. *Matta*. Exh. cat. New York: MOMA, 1957.

Selz, Peter. *Alberto Giacometti*. Exh. cat. New York: MOMA, 1965. With autobiographical statement by the artist.

———. *Yves Tanguy*. Exh. cat. New York: MOMA, 1955.

Spies, Werner. *Max Ernst: A Retrospective*. Exh. cat. London: Tate Gallery and Prestel, 1991.

———. *Max Ernst: Loplop, the Artist in the Third Person*. London: Thames & Hudson, 1983.

Stich, Sidra. *Anxious Visions: Surrealist Art*. New York: Abbeville, 1990.

Svendsen, Louise Averill. *Alberto Giacometti: Sculptor and Draftsman*. Exh. cat. New York: The American Federation of Art, 1977.

Sylvester, David. *Magritte: The Silence of the World*. New York: Harry N. Abrams, 1994.

Szarkowski, John, and Maria Hambourg. *The Work of Atget*. 4 vols. New York: MOMA, 1981–84.

[Tanguy] *Yves Tanguy: Un Recueil de ses Oeuvres*. New York: P. Matisse, 1963.

Torczyner, Harry. *Magritte: The True Art of Painting*. New York: Abradale Press, 1985.

Withers, Josephine. *Julio González: Sculpture in Iron*. New York: New York University Press, 1978.

16. Modern Architecture Between the Wars

Bauhaus Photography. Cambridge, Mass.: MIT Press, 1985.

Bayer, Herbert, Walter Gropius, and Ise Gropius. *Bauhaus, 1919–1928*. New York: MOMA, 1975.

Boesiger, Willy. *Le Corbusier and Pierre Jeanneret: Oeuvre complète*. 6 vols. Zurich: Éditions d'Architecture, 1937–57.

Boulton, Alexander. *Frank Lloyd Wright, Architect: An Illustrated Biography*. New York: Rizzoli, 1993.

Choay, Françoise. *Le Corbusier*. New York: G. Braziller, 1960.

Christ-Janer, Albert. *Eliel Saarinen: Finnish-American Architect and Educator*. Rev. ed. Chicago: University of Chicago Press, 1979.

Curtis, William J. R. *Le Corbusier: Idea and Forms*. New York: Rizzoli, 1986.

Franciscono, Marcel. *Walter Gropius and the Creation of the Bauhaus in Weimar*. Urbana, Ill.: University of Illinois Press, 1971.

———, and Philip Johnson. *The International Style*. 2nd ed. New York: Norton, 1966.

Gardiner, Stephen. *Le Corbusier*. London: Fontana, 1974.

Giedion, Siegfried. *Walter Gropius: Work and Teamwork*. New York: Reinhold, 1954.

Grohmann, Will. *Painters of the Bauhaus*. Exh. cat. London: Marlborough Fine Art Ltd., 1962.

Gropius, Walter. *The New Architecture and the Bauhaus*. Trans. P. M. Shand. London: Faber and Faber, 1935.

———, and László Moholy-Nagy. *Bauhausbücher*. 14 vols. Munich: A. Langen, 1925–28.

Hertz, David. *Frank Lloyd Wright in Word and Form*. New York: G. K. Hall, 1995.

Hines, Thomas. *Richard Neutra and the Search for Modern Architecture: A Biography and History*. New York: Oxford University Press, 1982.

Hitchcock, Henry-Russell, and Philip Johnson. *The International Style*. 2nd ed. New York: Norton, 1966.

Itten, Johannes. *The Art of Colour: The Subjective Experience and Objective Rationale of Colour*. New York: Reinhold, 1961.

———. *Design and Form: The Basic Course at the Bauhaus*. Rev. ed. New York: Van Nostrand Reinhold, 1975.

Jencks, Charles. *Le Corbusier and the Tragic View of Architecture*. Cambridge, Mass.: Harvard University Press, 1973.

Johnson, Philip. *Mies van der Rohe*. 3rd ed. rev. Greenwich, Conn.: New York Graphic Society, 1978.

Kilham, Walter H., Jr. *Raymond Hood, Architect: Form through Function in the Skyscraper*. New York: Architectural Book Publishing Co., 1973.

Krinsky, Carol Herselle. *Rockefeller Center*. Oxford: Oxford University Press, 1978.

Lane, Barbara Miller. *Architecture and Politics in Germany 1918–1945*. New ed. Cambridge, Mass.: Harvard University Press, 1985.

Le Corbusier. *The City of To-morrow and Its Planning*. London: J. Rodker, 1929.

Le Corbusier, une encyclopédie. Paris: Éditions du Centre Pompidou, 1987.

Le Corbusier. *Towards a New Architecture*. Trans. F. Etchells. London: Architectural Press, 1952.

Levine, Neil. *The Architecture of Frank Lloyd Wright*. Princeton, N.J.: Princeton University Press, 1996.

Papadaki, Stamo, ed. *Le Corbusier: Architect, Painter, Writer*. New York: MacMillan, 1948.

Pfeiffer, Bruce Brooks. *Frank Lloyd Wright: The Masterworks*. Ed. D. Larkin and B. B. Pfeiffer. New York: Rizzoli, 1993.

Riley, Terrence, and Peter Reed, eds. *Frank Lloyd Wright, Architect*. Exh. cat. New York: MOMA, 1994.

Saarinen, Aline, ed. *Eero Saarinen*. London: Thames & Hudson, 1968.

———, ed. *Eero Saarinen on His Work*. New Haven and London: Yale University Press, 1962. With a statement by the architect.

Schulze, Franz. *Mies van der Rohe: A Critical Biography*. Chicago: University of Chicago Press, 1985.

———, ed. *Mies van der Rohe: Critical Essays*. Cambridge, Mass.: MIT Press, 1990.

Spaeth, David A. *Mies van der Rohe*. New York: Rizzoli, 1985.

Storrer, William Allin. *The Frank Lloyd Wright Companion*. Chicago: University of Chicago Press, 1993.

Tegethoff, Wolf. *Mies van der Rohe: The Villas and Country Houses*. New York: MOMA, 1985.

Whitford, Frank. *Bauhaus*. London: Thames & Hudson, 1984.

Wingler, Hans Maria. *The Bauhaus: Weimar, Dessau, Berlin, Chicago*. Cambridge, Mass: MIT Press, 1969.

Willett, John. *Art and Politics in the Weimar Period*. New York: Pantheon Books, 1978.

Wright, Frank Lloyd. *Frank Lloyd Wright, Collected Writings*. Ed. B. B. Pfeiffer. New York: Rizzoli, 1992. Introduction by K. Frampton.

———. *Letters to Apprentices*. Ed. B. B. Pfeiffer. Fresno, Calif.: Press at Cal State University, 1982.

17. International Abstraction Between the Wars

Albers, Joseph. *Interaction of Color*. New Haven, Conn.: Yale University Press, 1971.

[Albers] *Josef Albers, A Retrospective*. Exh. cat. New York: SRGM, 1988.

Arnason, H. H., and Ugo Mulas, eds. *Calder*. New York: Viking Press, 1971.

[Baumeister] *Willi Baumeister*. Exh. cat. Stuttgart: Institut für Auslandsbeziehungen, 1981.

[Baumeister] *Willi Baumeister, 1889–1955: Peintures, Dessins*. Exh. cat. Brussels: Musée d'Ixelles, 1982.

Bell, Keith. *Stanley Spencer: A Complete Catalogue of the Paintings*. London: Phaidon, 1992.

Bowness, Alan, ed. *Henry Moore: Complete Sculpture*. 6 vols. London: Lund Humphries, 1988.

[Calder] *Alexander Calder: A Retrospective Exhibition*. Exh. cat. New York: SRGM, 1964.

Calder, Alexander. *Calder: An Autobiography with Pictures*. New York: Pantheon Books, 1966.

Caton, Joseph Harris. *The Utopian Vision of Moholy-Nagy*. Ann Arbor, Mich.: UMI Research Press, 1984.

Curtis, Penelope. *Kandinsky in Paris: 1934–1944*. Exh. cat. New York: SRGM, 1985. Text by V. E. Barnett.

———, and Alan Wilkinson. *Barbara Hepworth: A Retrospective*. Exh. cat. Liverpool: Tate Gallery, 1994.

[Gabo] *Gabo: Constructions, Sculpture, Paintings, Drawings, Engravings*. London: Lund Humphries, 1957. Texts by H. Read and L. Martin.

[Gabo] *Naum Gabo*. Exh. cat. London: Tate Gallery, 1966.

Gabo, Naum. *Of Diverse Arts*. New York: Pantheon Books, 1962.

Grohmann, Will. *Willi Baumeister: Life and Work*. New York: Harry N. Abrams, 1966.

Haus, Andreas. *Moholy-Nagy: Photographs and Photograms*. Trans. F. Samson. New York: Pantheon, 1980.

[Hepworth] *Barbara Hepworth*. Exh. cat. London: Tate Gallery, 1968. Texts by R. Alley, N. Gray, R. W. D. Oxenaar.

Hight, Eleanor. *Picturing Modernism: Moholy-Nagy and Photography in Weimar Germany*. Cambridge, Mass.: MIT Press, 1995.

Hildebrandt, Hans. *Oskar Schlemmer*. Munich: Prestel, 1952.

James, Philip, ed. *Henry Moore on Sculpture*. New York: Viking Press, 1971.

Kandinsky: Russian and Bauhaus Years, 1915–1933. Exh. cat. New York: SRGM, 1983.

Klee, Paul. *On Modern Art*. London: Faber and Faber, 1949.

[Klee] *Paul Klee Centennial: Prints and Transfer Drawings*. Exh. cat. New York: MOMA, 1978.

Klee, Paul. *The Thinking Eye: The Notebooks of Paul Klee*. London: Lund Humphries, 1961.

Kostelanetz, Richard, ed. *Moholy-Nagy*. New York and Washington, D.C.: Praeger, 1970.

Lehman, Arnold and Brenda Richardson, eds. *Oskar Schlemmer*. Exh. cat. Baltimore: Baltimore Museum of Art, 1986.

[Lewis] *Wyndham Lewis and Vorticism*. Exh. cat. London: Tate Gallery, 1956.

Lewison, Jeremy. *Ben Nicholson*. Exh. cat. London: Tate Gallery, 1993.

Lipman, Jean. *Calder Creatures: Great and Small*. New York: E. P. Dutton, 1985.

———. *Calder's Universe*. New York: Viking Press and WMAA, 1977.

Long, Rose-Carol Washton. *Kandinsky: The Development of an Abstract Style*. Oxford and New York: Clarendon Press and Oxford University Press, 1980.

Marter, Joan. *Alexander Calder*. Exh. cat. Cambridge: Cambridge University Press, 1991.

Moholy-Nagy, László. *The New Vision, and 1928: Abstract of an Artist*. New York: Wittenborn Schultz, 1949.

———. *Vision in Motion*. Chicago: P. Theobald, 1947.

Nash, Steven. *Ben Nicholson: Fifty Years of His Art*. Exh. cat. Buffalo, N.Y.: Albright-Knox Art Gallery, 1978.

———, and Jörn Merkert, eds. *Naum Gabo: Sixty Years of Constructivism*. Exh. cat. Munich and New York: Prestel, c. 1985.

Naum Gabo, Antoine Pevsner. Exh. cat. New York: MOMA, 1948. Introduction by H. Read; Texts by R. Olson and A. Chanin.

[Nicholson] *Ben Nicholson: Paintings, Reliefs and Drawings*. London: Lund Humphries, 1948. Introduction by Herbert Read.

Packer, William. *Henry Moore: an Illustrated Biography*. London: Weidenfeld & Nicolson, 1985.

Passuth, Krisztina. *Moholy-Nagy*. New York: Thames & Hudson, c. 1982.

Pevsner, Alexi. *A Biographical Sketch of My Brothers—Naum Gabo and Antoine Pevsner*. Amsterdam: Augustin and Schnooman, 1964.

Roskill, Mark. *Klee, Kandinsky, and the Thought of their Time: A Critical Perspective*. Urbana, Ill.: University of Illinois Press, 1992.

Sabarsky, Serge. *Paul Klee: The Late Years, 1930–1940*. Exh. cat. New York: Sabarsky Gallery, 1977.

Schlemmer, Oskar, László Moholy-Nagy, and Farkas Molnár. *The Theatre of the Bauhaus*. Trans. Arthur S. Wensinger. Middletown, Conn.: Wesleyan University Press, 1961.

Verdi, Richard. *Klee and Nature*. New York: Rizzoli, 1985.

18. American Art Before World War II

Abstract Painting and Sculpture in America: 1927–1944. Exh. cat. New York: WMAA, 1983.

[Adams] *Ansel Adams: Images 1924–1974*. Boston: New York Graphic Society, 1974.

Adams, Henry. *Thomas Hart Benton*. New York: Alfred A. Knopf, 1989.

———. *Thomas Hart Benton: Drawing from Life*. Exh. cat. New York: Abbeville, 1990.

Alland, Alexander. *Jacob A. Riis, Photographer and Citizen*. Millerton, N.Y.: Aperture, 1974.

Arnason, H. H. *Theodore Roszak*. Exh. cat. Minneapolis: Walker Art Center, 1956.

Baigell, Matthew. *The American Scene: American Painting of the 1930's*. New York: Praeger, 1974.

———. *Thomas Hart Benton*. New York: Harry N. Abrams, 1974.

Baker, Houston A., Jr. *Modernism and the Harlem Renaissance*. Chicago: Chicago University Press, 1987.

Benton, Thomas Hart. *An American in Art: A Professional and Technical Autobiography*. Lawrence, Kans.: University of Kansas Press, 1969.

Bearden, Romare, and Harry Henderson. *Six Black Masters of American Art*. New York: Zenith Books, 1972.

Brown, Milton. *Story of the Armory Show: The 1913 Exhibition that Changed American Art*. 2nd ed. New York: Abbeville, 1988.

Callahan, Sean, ed. *The Photographs of Margaret Bourke-White*. Boston: New York Graphic Society, 1972.

Castro, Jan. *The Life & Art of Georgia O'Keeffe*. New York: Crown, 1985.

Constantin, Mildred. *Tina Modotti: A Fragile Life*. New York: Rizzoli, 1983.

Corn, Wanda. *Grant Wood: The Regionalist Vision*. Exh. cat. New York: WMAA, 1983.

Curry, Larry. *John Marin/1870–1953*. Exh. cat. Los Angeles, LACMA, 1970.

Curtis, James. *Mind's Eye, Mind's Truth: FSA Photography Reconsidered*. Philadelphia: Temple University Press, 1989.

Davidson, Abraham. *Early American Modernist Painting: 1910–1935*. New York: Harper & Row, 1981.

[Diller] *Burgoyne Diller: Paintings, Sculpture, Drawings*. Exh. cat. Minneapolis: Walker Art Center, 1971.

Doherty, Robert J., ed. *The Complete Photographic Work of Jacob A. Riis*. New York: MacMillan, 1981.

Dwight, Edward. *Armory Show 50th Anniversary Exhibition 1913–1963*. Exh. cat. Utica, N.Y.: Munson-Williams-Proctor Institute, 1963.

Eldridge, Charles D. *American Imagination and Symbolist Painting*. Exh. cat. New York: Grey Gallery, New York University, 1980.

———. *Georgia O'Keeffe*. Library of American Art. New York: Harry N. Abrams, 1991.

Fávela, Ramón. *Diego Rivera: The Cubist Years*. Exh. cat. Phoenix: Phoenix Art Museum, 1984.

Fine, Elsa. *The Afro-American Artist: A Search for Identity*. New York: Holt, Rinehart and Winston, 1973.

———. *John Marin*. New York and Washington, D.C.: Abbeville and National Gallery of Art, 1990.

Folgarait, Leonard. *So Far From Heaven: David Alfaro Siqueiros' "The March of Humanity" and Mexican Revolutionary Politics*. New York: Cambridge University Press, 1987.

Glackens, Ira. *William Glackens and the Ashcan Group*. Rev. ed. New York: Horizon Press, 1984.

Goldberg, Vicki. *Margaret Bourke-White: A Biography*. New York: Harper & Row, 1986.

Goodrich, Lloyd. *Max Weber: Retrospective Exhibition*. New York: WMAA, 1949.

Green, Eleanor. *Augustus Vincent Tack: 1870–1949: Twenty-Six Paintings from the Phillips Collection*. Exh. cat. Austin, Tex.: University of Texas, 1972.

Greenough, Sarah, and Juan Hamilton. *Alfred Stieglitz, Photographs and Writings*. Washington, D.C.: National Gallery of Art, 1983.

Haskell, Barbara. *Arthur Dove*. Exh. cat. San Francisco: Museum of Modern Art, 1974.

———. *Joseph Stella*. Exh. cat. New York: WMAA, 1994.

Herrera, Hayden. *Frida Kahlo: The Paintings*. New York: Harper Collins, 1991.

Heyman, Therese, et al. *Dorothea Lange: American Photographs*. San Francisco: San Francisco Museum of Modern Art and Chronicle Books, 1994.

Homer, William Innes. *Alfred Stieglitz and the Photo-Secession*. Exh. cat. Boston: Little, Brown, 1983.

Hurley, F. Jack. *Portrait of a Decade: Roy Stryker and the Development of Documentary Photography in the Thirties*. Baton Rouge, La.: Louisiana State University Press, 1972.

Jaffe, Irma. *Joseph Stella*. Cambridge, Mass.: Harvard University Press, 1970.

Lane, John R. *Stuart Davis: Art and Art Theory*. Exh. cat. New York: Brooklyn Museum, 1978.

———, and Susan C. Larsen. *Abstract Painting and Sculpture in America 1927–1944*. Exh. cat. Pittsburgh: Museum of Art, Carnegie Institute, 1984.

[Lange] *Dorothea Lange*. Exh. cat. New York: MOMA, 1966. With an Introductory Essay by George P. Elliot.

[Lange] *Dorothea Lange: Photographs of a Lifetime*. Millerton, N.Y.: Aperture, 1982.

Levin, Gail. *Edward Hopper: A Catalogue Raisonné*. Exh. cat. New York: WMAA, 1995.

———. *Edward Hopper: The Art and the Artist*. Exh. cat. New York: WMAA, 1981.

———. *Synchromism and American Color Abstraction: 1910–1925*. Exh. cat. New York: WMAA, 1978.

Lorenz, Richard. *Imogen Cunningham: Flora/Photographs*. Boston: Little, Brown, 1996.

Lowe, Sarah M. *Tina Modotti: Photographs*. Exh. cat. Philadelphia and New York: Philadelphia Museum of Art and Harry N. Abrams, 1995.

Lynes, Barbara Buhler. *O'Keeffe, Stieglitz and the Critics, 1916–1929*. Ann Arbor, Mich.: UMI Research Press, 1989.

[Macdonald-Wright] *The Art of Stanton Macdonald-Wright: A Retrospective Exhibition*. Exh. cat. Washington, D.C.: Smithsonian Institution, 1967.

Marter, J. *Beyond the Plane: American Constructions 1930–1965*. Exh. cat. Trenton, N.J.: New Jersey State Museum, 1983.

Meltzer, Milton. *Dorothea Lange, a Photographer's Life*. New York: Farrar, Straus, and Giroux, 1978.

Miller, Dorothy, ed. *The Sculpture of John B. Flannagan*. Exh. cat. New York: MOMA, 1942.

[Nadelman] *The Sculpture and Drawings of Elie Nadelman*. Exh. cat. New York: WMAA, 1975.

Newhall, Nancy. *Ansel Adams: The Eloquent Light*. Millerton, N.Y.: Aperture, 1980.

Nordland, Gerald. *Gaston Lachaise: The Man and His Work*. New York: G. Braziller, 1974.

———. *Gaston Lachaise 1882–1935: Sculpture and Drawings*. Exh. cat. Los Angeles and New York: LACMA and WMAA, 1964.

Norman, Dorothy. *Alfred Stieglitz, an American Seer*. New York: Aperture, 1990.

———, ed. *Selected Writings of John Marin*. New York: Pellegrini & Cudahy, 1949.

[O'Keeffe] *Georgia O'Keeffe*. New York: Viking Press, 1976.

O'Neal, Hank. *Berenice Abbott, American Photographer*. New York: McGraw-Hill, 1982.

Perlman, Bernard B. *Painters of the Ashcan School: The Immortal Eight*. New York: Dover Publications, 1979.

Reich, Sheldon. *John Marin: A Stylistic Analysis and Catalogue Raisonné*. 2 vols. Tucson, Ariz.: University of Arizona Press, 1970.

Ritchie, A. C. *Charles Demuth*. Exh. cat. New York: MOMA, 1950. With a tribute to the artist by Marcel Duchamp.

[Rivera] *Diego Rivera: A Retrospective*. Exh. cat. Detroit: Detroit Institute of Arts, 1986.

Roberts, Brady, et al. *Grant Wood: An American Master Revealed*. Davenport, Iowa and San Francisco: Davenport Museum of Art and Pomegranate Art Books, 1995.

Roots of Abstract Art in America 1910–1930. Exh. cat. Washington, D.C.: Smithsonian Institution, 1965.

Rosenblum, Walter, et al. *America and Lewis Hine: Photographs, 1904–1940*. Millerton, N.Y.: Aperture, 1977.

Schmidt Campbell, Mary. *Memory and Metaphor: The Art of Romare Bearden, 1940–1987*. Exh. cat. New York: Oxford University Press, 1991.

Silverman, Jonathan. *For the World to See: The Life of Margaret Bourke-White*. New York: Viking Press, 1983.

Sims, Lowery Stokes. *Stuart Davis: American Painter*. Exh. cat. New York: MMA, 1991.

Sims, Patterson. *Gaston Lachaise*. Exh. cat. New York: WMAA, 1980.

Smith, Terry. *Making the Modern: Industry, Art, and Design in America*. Chicago: University of Chicago Press, 1993.

Stein, Judith E. *I Tell My Heart: The Art of Horace Pippin*. Exh. cat. Philadelphia: Pennsylvania Academy of Fine Arts, 1994.

[Strand] *Paul Strand: A Retrospective Monograph, the Years 1915–1968*. 2 vols. Millerton, N.Y.: Aperture, 1971.

Szarkowski, John. *Walker Evans*. Exh. cat. New York: MOMA, 1971.

[Tamayo] *Rufino Tamayo: Myth and Magic*. Exh. cat. New York: SRGM, 1979.

Tomkins, Calvin. *Paul Strand: Sixty Years of Photographs*. Millerton, N.Y.: Aperture, 1976.

Troyen, Carol, and Erica Hirschler. *Charles Sheeler: Paintings and Drawings*. Exh. cat. Boston: Museum of Fine Arts, 1987.

Wagner, Anne. *Three Artists (Three Women): Modernism and the Art of Hesse, Krasner, and O'Keeffe*. Berkeley, Calif.: University of California Press, 1996.

Wight, Frederick. *Arthur G. Dove*. Exh. cat. Berkeley and Los Angeles: University of California Press, 1958. Introduction by D. Phillips.

Yglesias, Helen. *Isabel Bishop*. New York: Rizzoli, 1989.

19. Abstract Expressionism and the New American Sculpture

Alloway, Lawrence. *Barnett Newman: The Stations of the Cross*. Exh. cat. New York: SRGM, 1966.

———. *William Baziotes: A Memorial Exhibition*. Exh. cat. New York: SRGM, 1965. With statements by the artist.

Anfam, David. *Abstract Expressionism*. World of Art. New York: Thames & Hudson, 1990.

———. *Franz Kline: Black and White, 1950–1961*. Exh. cat. Houston: The Menil Collection, 1994.

Arnason, H. H. *Abstract Expressionists and Imagists*. Exh. cat. New York: SRGM, 1961.

———. *Robert Motherwell*. Rev. ed. New York: Harry N. Abrams, 1982.

———. *Robert Motherwell: Works on Paper*. Exh. cat. New York: MOMA, 1967.

Ashton, Dore. *About Rothko*. New York: Oxford University Press, 1983.

———. *A Joseph Cornell Album*. New York: Viking Press, 1974.

———. *The New York School: A Cultural Reckoning*. New York: Viking Press, 1973.

———. *Noguchi East and West*. Berkeley, Calif.: University of California Press, 1993.

———. *Yes, but ... : A Critical Study of Philip Guston*. New York: Viking Press, 1976.

———, and Jack Flam. *Robert Motherwell*. Exh. cat. Buffalo, N.Y. and New York: Albright-Knox Gallery and Abbeville, 1983.

Auping, Michael. *Abstract Expressionism: The Critical Developments*. New York: Harry N. Abrams, 1987.

[Baziotes] *William Baziotes: A Retrospective Exhibition*. Exh. cat. Newport Beach, Calif.: Newport Harbor Art Museum, 1978. Texts by B. Cavaliere and M. Hadler.

[Bourgeois] *The Iconography of Louise Bourgeois*.

Exh. cat. New York: Max Hutchinson Gallery, 1980.

Carmean, Jr., E. A., ed. *Robert Motherwell: The Reconciliation Elegy*. Geneva and New York: Skira and Rizzoli, 1980.

———. *David Smith*. Exh. cat. Washington, D.C.: National Gallery of Art, 1982.

Castleman, Riva. *Art of the Forties*. Exh. cat. New York: MOMA, 1991.

Cernuschi, Claude. *Jackson Pollock: Meaning and Significance*. New York: Icon Editions, 1992.

[de Kooning] *Willem de Kooning*. Exh. cat. New York: WMAA, 1983. Texts by P. Cummings, J. Merkert, C. Stoullig.

Doty, Robert, and Diane Waldman. *Adolph Gottlieb*. Exh. cat. New York: SRGM and WMAA, 1968.

Elsen, Albert. *Seymour Lipton*. New York: Harry N. Abrams, 1970.

Frank, Elizabeth. *Jackson Pollock*. New York: Abbeville, 1982.

Fry, E., and J. Ablow. *Philip Guston: The Late Works*. Exh. cat. Sydney, Australia, 1984.

Gaugh, Harry F. *Franz Kline*. Exh. cat. New York: Abbeville, 1994.

———. *The Vital Gesture*. Cincinnati and New York: Cincinnati Art Museum and Abbeville Press, 1985.

———. *Willem de Kooning*. New York: Abbeville, 1983.

Glimcher, Arnold. *Louise Nevelson*. New York and Washington, D.C.: Dutton, 1972.

Gordon, John. *Franz Kline, 1910–1962*. Exh. cat. New York: WMAA, 1968.

———. *Louise Nevelson*. Exh. cat. New York: WMAA, 1967.

Greenberg, Clement. *Art and Culture: Critical Essays*. Boston: Beacon Press, 1961.

———. *Hans Hofmann*. Paris and London: G. Fall, 1961.

Guilbaut, Serge. *How New York Stole the Idea of Modern Art*. Chicago: University of Chicago Press, 1983.

[Guston] *Philip Guston: Paintings 1969–1980*. London: Whitechapel Art Gallery, 1983.

Hess, Thomas B. *Barnett Newman*. Exh. cat. New York: MOMA, 1971.

Hirsch, Sanford, and Mary Davis MacNaughton, eds. *Adolph Gottlieb: A Retrospective*. Exh. cat. Washington, D.C.: Corcoran Gallery of Art, 1982.

Hobbs, Robert Carleton, and Gail Levin. *Abstract Expressionism: The Formative Years*. Ithaca, N.Y.: Cornell University Press, 1981.

Hofmann, Hans. *Search for the Real and Other Essays*. Ed. S. T. Weeks and B. H. Hayes, Jr. Cambridge, Mass.: MIT Press, 1967.

Hunter, Sam. *Isamu Noguchi*. New York: Abbeville, 1978.

Jordan, Jim M., and Robert Goldwater. *The Paintings of Arshile Gorky: A Critical Catalogue*. New York: New York University Press, 1982.

Kingsley, April. *The Turning Point: The Abstract Expressionists and the Transformation of American Art*. New York: Simon & Schuster, 1992.

[Kline] *Franz Kline Memorial Exhibition*. Exh. cat. Washington, D.C.: Washington Gallery of Modern Art, 1962.

Krauss, Rosalind. *The Sculpture of David Smith: A Catalogue Raisonné*. New York: Garland Pub., 1977.

Lader, Melvin. *P. Gorky*. New York: Abbeville, 1985.

Landau, Ellen. *Jackson Pollock*. New York: Harry N. Abrams, 1989.

Larson, Philip, and Peter Schjeldahl. *De Kooning: Drawings/Sculptures*. Exh. cat. Minneapolis: Walker Art Center, 1974.

Leja, Michael. *Reframing Abstract Expressionism: Subjectivity and Painting in the 1940's*. New Haven, Conn.: Yale University Press, 1993.

Lieberman, William S. *Jackson Pollock: The Last Sketchbook*. New York: Harcourt, Brace, Jovanovich, 1982.

Lippard, Lucy R. *Ad Reinhardt*. New York: Harry N. Abrams, 1981.

Lyons, Nathan, ed. *Aaron Siskind, Photographer*. Rochester, N.Y.: George Eastman House, 1965.

Marcus, Stanley. *David Smith: The Sculptor and His Work*. Ithaca, N.Y.: Cornell University Press, 1983.

McShine, Kynaston, ed. *Joseph Cornell*. Exh. cat. New York: MOMA, 1990.

Motherwell, Robert. *Collected Writings*. New York: Oxford University Press, 1992.

[Motherwell] *Robert Motherwell*. Exh. cat. Buffalo, N.Y.: Albright-Knox Art Gallery, 1983. Essays by J. Flam and D. Ashton.

Nelson. Exh. cat. New York: Pace Gallery, 1976.

Noguchi, Isamu. *A Sculptor's World*. New York: Harper & Row, 1968.

O'Connor, Francis V., and Eugene V. Thaw, eds. *Jackson Pollock: A Catalogue Raisonné of Paintings, Drawings, and Other Works*. New Haven, Conn.: Yale University Press, 1978.

Polcari, Stephan. *Abstract Expressionism and the Modern Experience*. New York: Cambridge University Press, 1991.

[Pollock] *Jackson Pollock*. Exh. cat. Paris: Centre Georges Pompidou, Musée National d'Art Moderne, 1982.

Porter, Eliot. *Intimate Landscapes: Photographs*. New York: MMA, 1979.

Prather, Marla. *Willem de Kooning/Paintings*. Exh. cat. Washington: National Gallery of Art, 1994.

Rand, Harry. *Arshile Gorky: The Implications of Symbols*. Montclair, N.J.: Allanheld & Schram, 1980.

[Reinhardt] *Ad Reinhardt*. Exh. cat. New York: Rizzoli, 1991.

Roberts, Colette. *Mark Tobey*. New York: Grove Press, 1960.

Rosand, David, ed. *Robert Motherwell on Paper: Drawings, Prints, Collages*. Exh. cat. New York: Harry N. Abrams, 1997.

Rose, Barbara. *Jackson Pollock: Drawing into Painting*. Exh. cat. New York: MOMA, 1980.

———. *Krasner/Pollock, a Working Relationship*. Exh. cat. New York: Grey Art Gallery, 1981.

———. *Lee Krasner: A Retrospective*. Exh. cat. Houston, Tex.: Museum of Fine Arts, 1983.

———, ed. *Art-as-Art: The Selected Writings of Ad Reinhardt*. New York: Viking Press, 1975.

Rosenberg, Harold. *Barnett Newman*. New York: Harry N. Abrams, 1978.

———. *Isamu Noguchi: The Sculpture of Spaces*. Exh. cat. New York: WMAA, 1980. Foreword by T. Armstrong.

———. *The Tradition of the New*. New York: Horizon Press, 1959.

———. *Willem de Kooning*. New York: Harry N. Abrams, 1974.

Rosenblum, Robert. *Mark Rothko: Notes on Rothko, Surrealist Years*. Exh. cat. New York: Pace Gallery, 1981.

Ross, Clifford. *Abstract Expressionism: Creators and Critics*. New York: Harry N. Abrams, 1990.

Sandler, Irving. *The New York School: The Painters and Sculptors of the Fifties*. New York: Harper & Row, 1978.

———. *The Triumph of American Painting: A History of Abstract Expressionism*. New York: Praeger, 1970.

Schwartz, Constance. *The Abstract Expressionists and Their Precursors*. Nassau County: Nassau County Museum of Fine Art, 1981.

Seitz, William. *Abstract Expressionist Painting in America*. Cambridge, Mass.: Harvard University Press, 1983.

————. *Abstract Expressionist Painting in America.* Exh. cat. Washington, D.C.: National Gallery of Art, 1983.
————. *Hans Hofmann.* Exh. cat. New York: MOMA, 1963. With selected writings by the artist.
————. *Mark Tobey.* Exh. cat. New York: MOMA, 1962.
Shapiro, David, and Cecile Shapiro, eds. *Abstract Expressionism: A Critical Record.* New York: Cambridge University Press, 1990.
Stein, Sally, and Terrence Pitts. *Harry Callahan: Photographs in Color, the Years 1946–1978.* Tucson, Ariz.: Center for Creative Photography, c. 1980.
Sylvester, Julie. *John Chamberlain: A Catalogue Raisonné of the Sculpture, 1954–1985.* New York: Hudson Hills Press, c. 1986.
Szarkowski, John, ed. *Callahan.* New York: MOMA, 1976.
Tuchman, Maurice, ed. *New York School, The First Generation: Paintings of the 1940s and 1950s.* Los Angeles: LACMA, 1965. With statements by artists and critics.
Wagner, Anne. *Three Artists (Three Women): Modernism and the Art of Hesse, Krasner, and O'Keeffe.* Berkeley, Calif.: University of California Press, 1996.
Waldman, Diane. *Arshile Gorky 1904–1948: A Retrospective.* Exh. cat. New York: SRGM, 1981.
————. *Joseph Cornell.* New York: G. Braziller, 1977.
————. *Mark Rothko, 1903–1970: A Retrospective.* Exh. cat. New York: SRGM, 1978.
————. *Willem de Kooning.* Library of American Art. New York: Harry N. Abrams, 1988.
Wight, Frederick. *Hans Hofmann: Retrospective Exhibition.* Exh. cat. Los Angeles: The University Art Museum, UCLA, 1957.
Wilkin, Karen. *David Smith.* New York: Abbeville, 1984.
Wye, Deborah. *Louise Bourgeois.* Exh. cat. New York: MOMA, 1982.

20. Postwar European Art

Ades, Dawn, and Andrew Forge. *Francis Bacon.* New York: Harry N. Abrams, 1985.
Alloway, Lawrence. *Francis Bacon.* Exh. cat. New York: SRGM, 1963.
Bacon, Francis, et al. *Francis Bacon.* Exh. cat. New York and Washington, D.C.: Thames & Hudson, 1989.
Daries, Hugh, and Sally Yard. *Francis Bacon.* Exh. cat. New York: Abbeville, 1986.
De Staël: A Retrospective Exhibition. Exh. cat. Boston: Museum of Fine Arts, 1965.
Dorival, B. *Soulages.* Exh. cat. Paris: Musée National d'Art Moderne, 1967.
Flomenhaft, Eleanor. *The Roots and Development of CoBrA Art.* Hempstead, N.Y.: Fine Arts Museum of Long Island, c. 1985.
Franzke, Andreas. *Dubuffet.* New York: Harry N. Abrams, 1981.
Freund, Gisèle. *Gisèle Freund, Photographer.* Trans. J. Shepley. New York: Harry N. Abrams, 1985. Introduction by C. Caujolle.
Gimenez, Carmen. *Tàpies.* Exh. cat. New York: SRGM, 1995.
Hughes, Robert. *Lucien Freud Paintings.* New York: Thames & Hudson, 1987.
Leiris, Michael. *Francis Bacon: Full Face and in Profile.* New York: Rizzoli, 1983.
Leymarie, Jean. *Art Since Mid-Century: The New Internationalism.* 2 vols. Greenwich, Conn.: New York Graphic Society, 1971.
————. *Balthus.* Exh. cat. New York: Rizzoli, 1990.
Loreau, Max. *Catalogue intégral des travaux de Jean Dubuffet.* 34 vols. Paris: J.-J. Pauvert, 1964–.

Penrose, Roland. *Tàpies.* New York: Rizzoli, 1978.
Permanyer, Lluís. *Tàpies and the New Culture.* Trans. K. Lyons. New York: Rizzoli, 1986.
Putnam, Jacques, ed. *Bram van Velde.* New York: Grove Press, 1959. With statements by S. Beckett and G. Duthuit.
Rewald, John. *Manzù.* New York: Thames & Hudson, 1967.
Rewald, Sabine. *Balthus.* Exh. cat. New York: MMA, 1984.
Ritchie, Andrew. *The New Decade: Twenty-two European Painters and Sculptors.* Exh. cat. New York: MOMA, 1955.
Russell, John. *Francis Bacon.* Rev. and updated ed. World of Art. New York: Thames & Hudson, 1993.
Selz, Peter, and James Sweeney. *Chillida.* New York: Harry N. Abrams, 1986.
Sweeney, James. *Soulages.* Greenwich, Conn.: New York Graphic Society, 1972.
Trier, Eduard. *The Sculpture of Marino Marini.* London: Praeger, 1961.
[Van Velde] *Bram van Velde.* Exh. cat. New York: Knoedler and Co., 1962. Text by J. van der Marck.
Weiss, Allen S. *Shattered Forms: Art Brut, Phantasms, Modernism.* Albany, N.Y.: SUNY Press, 1992.
Wye, Deborah. *Antoni Tàpies in Print.* Exh. cat. New York: MOMA, 1991.

21. Pop Art and Europe's New Realism

Alloway, Lawrence. *American Pop Art.* Exh. cat. New York and London: WMAA, 1975.
————. *Christo.* New York: Harry N. Abrams, 1969.
————. *Roy Lichtenstein.* New York: Abbeville, 1983.
————, et al. *Modern Dreams: The Rise and Fall and Rise of Pop.* Cambridge: MIT Press, 1988.
Amaya, Mario. *Pop Art … and After.* New York: Viking, 1965.
[Arbus] *Diane Arbus.* New York: Aperture, 1972.
Armstrong, Richard. *Richard Artschwager.* Exh. cat. New York and London: WMAA, 1988.
Ashton, Dore. *Richard Lindner.* New York: Harry N. Abrams, 1970.
Auping, Michael. *Jess: Paste-Ups (and Assemblies), 1951–1983.* Exh. cat. Sarasota, Fla.: The John and Mable Ringling Museum of Art, 1983.
Ball-Teshuva, Jacob. *Christo: The Reichstag and Urban Projects.* Munich and New York: Prestel, 1993.
Bourdon, David. *Christo.* New York: Harry N. Abrams, 1989.
————. *Warhol.* New York: Harry N. Abrams, 1989.
[Broodthaers] *Marcel Broodthaers.* Exh. cat. Minneapolis: Walker Art Center and Rizzoli, 1989.
Calas, Nicolas and Elena. *Icons and Images of the Sixties.* New York: Dutton, 1971.
Castleman, Riva. *Jasper Johns, A Print Retro-spective.* Exh. cat. New York: MOMA, 1986.
Cathcart, Linda. *Robert Rauschenberg: Work from Four Series.* Exh. cat. Houston: Contemporary Arts Museum, 1985.
Celant, Germano. *Piero Manzoni.* Milan: Arnoldo Mandadori Arte, 1991.
Crichton, Michael. *Jasper Johns.* Exh. cat. New York: WMAA, 1977.
Ferguson, Russell. *Hand-painted Pop: American Art in Transition, 1955–1962.* Exh. cat. Los Angeles: Museum of Contemporary Art, 1992.
Francis, Richard. *Jasper Johns.* New York: Abbeville, 1984.
[Frank] *Robert Frank: The Americans.* New York, Zurich and Berlin: Scalo, 1993.

Friedman, Martin. *Nevelson: Wood Sculptures.* Exh. cat. Minneapolis: Walker Art Center, 1973.
————. *Oldenburg: Six Themes.* Exh. cat. Minneapolis: Walker Art Center, 1975.
Geldzahler, Henry. *New York Painting and Sculpture: 1940–1970.* Exh. cat. New York: MMA, 1969.
Glenn, Constance. *Jim Dine Drawings.* New York: Harry N. Abrams, 1985.
————. *Lucas Samaras Photo-Transformations.* Exh. cat. Long Beach, Calif. and New York: Cal State University and Dutton, 1975.
————. *Time Dust: James Rosenquist. Complete Graphics: 1962–1992.* Exh. cat. Long Beach, Calif. and New York: Cal State University and Rizzoli, 1993.
Gordon, John. *Jim Dine.* Exh. cat. New York: WMAA, 1970.
————. *Rosenquist.* New York, 1986.
Greenough, Sarah, and Philip Brookman. *Robert Frank.* Exh. cat. Washington, D.C.: National Gallery of Art, 1994.
Hackett, Pat, ed. *The Andy Warhol Diaries.* New York: Warner Books, 1989.
Harrison, Helen. *Larry Rivers.* New York: Harper & Row, 1984.
Haskell, Barbara. *Blam! The Explosion of Pop, Minimalism, and Performance: 1958–1964.* Exh. cat. New York: WMAA, 1984.
————. *Claes Oldenburg: Object into Monument.* Exh. cat. Pasadena, Calif.: Pasadena Art Museum, 1971.
Henri, Adrian. *Total Art: Environments, Happenings, and Performance.* New York: Praeger, 1979.
Hickey, Dave and Peter Plagens. *The Works of Edward Ruscha.* Exh. cat. New York and San Francisco: Hudson Hills Press and San Francisco Museum of Modern Art, 1982. Foreword H. T. Hopkins.
[Hockney] *David Hockney: A Retrospective.* Los Angeles: LACMA, 1988.
Hockney, David. *That's the Way I See It.* Ed. Nikos Stangos. San Francisco: Chronicle Books, 1993.
Hulten, Pontus. *Jean Tinguely: A Magic Stronger Than Death.* New York: Abbeville, 1987.
————. *Larry Rivers.* New York: Rizzoli, 1991.
————. *The Machine: As Seen at the End of the Mechanical Age.* Exh. cat. New York: MOMA, 1968.
————. *Niki de Saint Phalle.* Exh. cat. Stuttgart: G. Hatje, c. 1992.
Hunter, Sam. *Arman's Apocalypse.* Exh. cat. New York: Marisa del Re Gallery, 1984.
Jimenez, Luis. *Man on Fire/El Hombre en Llamas.* Exh. cat. Albuquerque, N.Mex.: The Albuquerque Museum, 1994.
Kaprow, Allan. *Assemblage, Environments, and Happenings.* New York: Harry N. Abrams, 1966.
Kienholz: A Retrospective: Edward and Nancy Reddin Kienholz. Exh. cat. New York: WMAA, 1996.
Kirby, Michael. *Happenings: An Illustrated Anthology.* New York: Dutton, 1965.
Kitaj, R. B. *An Artist's Eye.* Exh. cat. London: National Gallery, 1980.
[Kitaj] *R. B. Kitaj.* Exh. cat. New York: Marlborough Gallery, 1979.
Kozloff, Max. *Jasper Johns.* New York: Harry N. Abrams, 1974.
Kuspit, Donald. *Lucas Samaras.* Athens, 1986.
Leggio, James, and Susan Weiley, eds. *American Art of the 1960s.* New York: MOMA, 1991.
Levin, Kim. *Lucas Samaras.* New York: Harry N. Abrams, 1975.
Leymarie, Jean. *Art Since Mid-Century: The New Internationalism.* 2 vols. Greenwich, Conn.: New York Graphic Society, 1971.
Lima Greene, Alison de, and Pierre Restany. *Arman 1955–1991: A Retrospective.* Exh. cat. Houston: The Museum of Fine Arts, 1991.

Lippard, Lucy. *Pop Art*. New York: Praeger, 1966.

Livingstone, Marco. *David Hockney*. New York: Holt, Rinehart and Winston, 1981.

——. *Pop Art: A Continuing History*. New York: Harry N. Abrams, 1990.

——. *R. B. Kitaj*. New York: Rizzoli, 1985.

——, ed. *Pop Art*. London: Royal Academy of Arts, 1991.

Mahsun, Carol Ann, ed. *Pop Art: The Critical Dialogue*. Ann Arbor, Mich.: UMI Research Press, 1989.

McConnell, Gerald. *Assemblage: Three-Dimensional Picture Making*. New York: Van Nostrand Reinhold Co., 1976.

McShine, Kynaston, ed. *Andy Warhol, A Retrospective*. Exh. cat. New York: MOMA, 1989.

Morphet, Richard, ed. *R. B. Kitaj*. Exh. cat. London: Tate Gallery, 1994.

Nochlin, Linda. *Andy Warhol Nudes*. New York: Robert Miller Gallery, 1995.

Oldenburg, Claes, and Coosje van Bruggen. *Large-Scale Projects*. New York: Monacelli Press, 1994.

Pellegrini, Aldo. *New Tendencies in Art*. Trans. R. Carson. New York: Crown, 1966.

Popper, Frank. *Origins and Development of Kinetic Art*. Trans. S. Bann. Greenwich, Conn.: New York Graphic Society, 1968.

Ratcliff, Carter. *Red Grooms*. New York: Abbeville, 1984.

Rauschenberg Overseas Cultural Interchange. Washington, D.C.: National Gallery of Art, 1991.

Restany, Pierre. *Botero*. Trans. J. Shepley. New York: Harry N. Abrams, 1984.

——. *Yves Klein*. Trans. J. Shepley. New York: Harry N. Abrams, 1982.

Rose, Barbara. *Claes Oldenburg*. Exh. cat. New York: MOMA, 1970.

Rosenthal, Nan, and Ruth Fine. *The Drawings o f Jasper Johns*. Washington, D.C.: The National Gallery of Art, 1990.

Russell, John, and Suzi Gablik. *Pop Art Redefined*. New York: Praeger, 1969.

[Saint Phalle] *Niki de Saint Phalle*. Exh. cat. Paris: Centre Georges Pompidou, 1980.

Sandford, Mariellen. *Happenings and Other Acts*. New York and London: Routledge, 1995.

Sandler, Irving. *American Art of the 1960's*. New York: Harper & Row, 1988.

[Segal] *George Segal: Environments*. Exh. cat. Philadelphia: Institute of Contemporary Art, 1976. Text by J. L. Barrio-Garay.

Seitz, William C. *Segal*. New York: Harry N. Abrams, 1972.

Shanahan, Mary, ed. *Evidence, 1944–1994: Richard Avedon*. Exh. cat. New York: WMAA, 1994.

Shapiro, David. *Jasper Johns Drawings: 1954–1984*. Ed. C. Sweet. New York: Harry N. Abrams, 1984.

——. *Jim Dine: Painting What One Is*. New York: Harry N. Abrams, 1981.

Shirey, David. *Edward and Nancy Reddin Kienholz: Human Scale*. Exh. cat. San Francisco: Museum of Modern Art, 1985. Texts by H. T. Hopkins, L. Weschler, E. Kienholz, R. Glower.

Slemmons, Rod. *Like a One-Eyed Cat: Photographs by Lee Friedlander*. New York and Seattle: Harry N. Abrams and Seattle Art Museum, 1989.

Spies, Werner, ed. *Fernando Botero: Paintings and Drawings*. Munich: Prestel, 1992.

Stich, Sidra. *Yves Klein*. Exh. cat. London: Hayward Gallery and Cantz, 1995.

Szarkowski, John. *Winogrand, Figments from the Real World*. Exh. cat. New York: MOMA, 1988.

Taylor, Paul. *Post-Pop Art*. Cambridge, Mass.: MIT Press, 1989.

Tomkins, Calvin. *Off the Wall: Robert Rauschenberg and the Art World of Our Time*. Garden City, N.Y.: Doubleday, 1980.

Tuchman, Maurice, ed. *American Sculpture of the Sixties*. Exh. cat. Los Angeles: LACMA, 1967.

Tuchman, Phyllis. *George Segal*. New York: Abbeville, 1984.

Tucker, Marcia. *James Rosenquist*. Exh. cat. New York: WMAA, 1972.

Vaizey, Marina. *Christo*. New York: Rizzoli, 1990.

Van der Marck, Jan. *George Segal*. Rev. ed. New York: Harry N. Abrams, 1979.

Varnedoe, Kirk. *Jasper Johns: A Retrospective*. Exh. cat. New York: MOMA, 1996.

Waldman, Diane. *Roy Lichtenstein*. Exh. cat. New York: SRGM, 1993.

Weinhardt, Jr., Carl J. *Robert Indiana*. New York: Harry N. Abrams, 1990.

Whiting, Cécile. *A Taste for Pop: Pop Art, Gender and Consumer Culture*. Cambridge: Cambridge University Press, 1997.

[Winogrand] *Garry Winogrand: Early Work*. Archive 26. Tucson, Ariz.: Center for Creative Photography, 1987.

22. Sixties Abstraction

Alloway, Lawrence. *Systemic Painting*. Exh. cat. New York: SRGM, 1966.

Ashton, Dore. *Richard Diebenkorn: Small Paintings from "Ocean Park."* Exh. cat. Lincoln, Nebr.: Sheldon Memorial Art Gallery, 1985.

Baker, Kenneth. *Minimalism: Art of Circumstance*. New York: Abbeville, 1988.

Barker, Ian, ed. *Caro*. Munich: Prestel, 1991.

Baro, Gene. "The Achievement of Helen Frankenthaler," *Art International* 11 (September 1967).

Barrett, Cyril. *Op Art*. London: Studio Vista, 1970.

Bastian, Heiner. *Cy Twombly: Catalogue Raisonné*. 4 vols. Berlin: Schirmer/Mosel, 1992.

Belz, Carl. *Frankenthaler, the 1950s*. Exh. cat. Waltham, Mass.: Rose Art Museum, 1981.

Berger, Maurice. *Labyrinth: Robert Morris, Minimalism, and the 1960s*. New York: Harper & Row, 1989.

Bourdon, David. *Carl Andre: Sculpture, 1959–1977*. New York: J. Rietman, 1978. Foreword by B. Rose.

——, et al. *Jackie Ferrara Sculpture: A Retrospective*. Exh. cat. Sarasota, Fla.: The John and Mable Ringling Museum of Art, 1992.

Buck, Jr., Robert. *Richard Diebenkorn: Paintings and Drawings: 1943–1976*. Exh. cat. Buffalo, N.Y.: Albright-Knox Art Gallery, 1976. Texts by L. Cathcart, G. Nordland, M. Tuchman.

Carmean, E. A. *Helen Frankenthaler, A Paintings Retrospective*. New York: Harry N. Abrams, 1989.

Cathcart, Linda. *Richard Diebenkorn: 38th Venice Biennial, US Pavilion*. New York: International Exhibitions Committee of the American Federation of Arts, 1978.

Colpitt, Frances. *Minimal Art: The Critical Perspective*. Ann Arbor, Mich.: UMI Research Press, 1990.

Coplans, John. *Ellsworth Kelly*. New York: Harry N. Abrams, 1973.

Elderfield, John. *Morris Louis*. Exh. cat. New York: MOMA, 1986.

Fine, Ruth. *Helen Frankenthaler Prints*. Exh. cat. Washington, D.C. and New York: National Gallery of Art and Harry N. Abrams, 1993.

[Flavin] *Dan Flavin: Three Installations in Fluorescent Light*. Exh. cat. Cologne: Kunsthalle Köln, 1974.

Fried, Michael. *Morris Louis*. New York: Harry N. Abrams, 1971.

——. *Three American Painters: Kenneth Noland, Jules Olitski, Frank Stella*. Exh. cat. Cambridge, Mass.: Fogg Art Museum, 1965.

——. "Art and Objecthood," *Artforum* 5, no. 10 (Summer 1967).

Goosen, E. C. *Ellsworth Kelly*. Exh. cat. New York: MOMA, 1973.

——. *Helen Frankenthaler*. Exh. cat. New York: WMAA and MOMA's International Council, 1969.

Greenberg, Clement. *Art and Culture*. Boston: Beacon Press, 1965.

——. *Post-Painterly Abstraction*. Exh. cat. Los Angeles: LACMA, 1964.

Guberman, Sidney. *Frank Stella: An Illustrated Biography*. New York: Rizzoli, 1995.

Güse, Ernst-Gerhard. *Richard Serra*. New York: Rizzoli, 1988.

Harrison, Charles and Paul Wood, eds. *Art in Theory, 1900–1990*. Oxford: Blackwell Publishers, 1995.

Haskell, Barbara. *Agnes Martin*. New York: WMAA, 1992. Texts by B. Haskell, A. Chave, R. Krauss.

——. *Donald Judd*. Exh. cat. New York: W. W. Norton & Co., 1988.

Judd, Donald. *Complete Writings, 1959–1975*. Halifax and New York: Press of the Nova Scotia College of Art and Design and New York University Press, 1975.

[Judd] *Donald Judd*. Exh. cat. Ottawa: National Gallery of Canada, 1975. Exhibition organized by B. Smith; Text by R. Smith.

[Judd] *Donald Judd: Large Scale Works*. Exh. cat. New York: The Pace Gallery, 1993.

Kertess, Klaus. *Brice Marden: Painting and Drawings*. New York: Harry N. Abrams, 1992.

——. *Joan Mitchell*. New York: Harry N. Abrams, 1997.

Krauss, Rosalind. *Richard Serra/Sculpture*. Exh. cat. New York: MOMA, 1986. Texts by L. Rosenstock and D. Crimp.

Legg, Alicia. *Sol LeWitt*. Exh. cat. New York: MOMA, 1978.

Leggio, James, and Susan Weiley, eds. *American Art of the 1960s*. New York: MOMA, 1991.

Leider, Philip. *Stella Since 1970*. Exh. cat. Fort Worth, Tex.: Fort Worth Art Museum, 1978.

LeWitt, Sol. *Sol LeWitt: Geometric Figures and Color*. New York: Harry N. Abrams, 1979.

Leymarie, Jean. *Art Since Mid-Century: The New Internationalism*. 2 vols. Greenwich, Conn.: New York Graphic Society, 1971.

[Mangold] *Robert Mangold: Paintings 1971–1984*. Exh. cat. Akron, Ohio: Akron Art Museum, 1984.

[Mitchell] *Joan Mitchell*. Exh. cat. Paris: Éditions du Jeu de Paume, 1994.

Moffett, Kenworth. *Jules Olitski*. New York: Harry N. Abrams, 1981.

——. *Kenneth Noland*. New York: Harry N. Abrams, 1977.

[Morris] *Robert Morris: The Mind/Body Problem*. Exh. cat. New York: SRGM, 1994.

Necol, J., and D. Droll. *Abstract Painting: 1960–1969*. Exh. cat. New York: P.S.1, 1983.

Nordland, Gerald. *Fourteen Abstract Painters*. Exh. cat. Los Angeles: Wright Art Gallery, University of California, 1975.

Popper, Frank. *Agam*. 3rd ed. rev. New York: Harry N. Abrams, 1990.

——. *Origins and Development of Kinetic Art*. Greenwich, Conn.: New York Graphic Society, 1968.

Richardson, Brenda. *Frank Stella: The Black Paintings*. Exh. cat. Baltimore: Baltimore Museum of Art, 1976.

Rickey, George. *Constructivism: Origins and Evolution*. New York: G. Braziller, 1967.

Rose, Barbara. *Frankenthaler*. New York: Harry N. Abrams, 1972.

Rosenblum, Robert. *Frank Stella*. Harmondsworth and Baltimore: Penguin, 1971.

Rosenthal, Mark. *Abstraction in the Twentieth Century: Total Risk, Freedom, Discipline*. Exh. cat. New York: SRGM, 1996.

Rubin, Lawrence. *Frank Stella: Paintings 1958 to 1965: A Catalogue Raisonné.* New York: Stewart, Tabori & Chang, 1986.

Rubin, William. *Anthony Caro.* Exh. cat. New York: MOMA, 1975.

———. *Frank Stella.* Exh. cat. New York: MOMA, 1987.

[Ryman] *Robert Ryman.* Exh. cat. Paris: Musée National d'Art Moderne, Centre Georges Pompidou, 1981.

Sandler, Irving. *Al Held.* New York: Hudson Hills Press, 1984.

———. *American Art of the 1960's.* New York: Harper & Row, 1988.

———. "Mitchell Paints a Picture." *Art News* 56, no. 6 (Oct. 1957): 45.

Selz, Peter. *Sam Francis.* New York: Harry N. Abrams, 1975.

Serota, Nicholas. *Carl Andre: Sculpture, 1959–1978.* Exh. cat. London: Whitechapel Art Gallery, 1978.

Shearer, Linda. *Brice Marden.* Exh. cat. New York: SRGM, 1975.

Sims, Patterson, and Emily Rauh Pulitzer. *Ellsworth Kelly: Sculpture.* Exh. cat. New York: WMAA, 1983.

[Smith] *Tony Smith: Recent Sculpture.* Exh. cat. New York: M. Knoedler and Co., 1971.

Soto: A Retrospective Exhibition. Exh. cat. New York: SRGM, 1974.

Spies, Werner. *Victor Vasarely.* New York: Harry N. Abrams, 1971.

Storr, Robert. *Robert Ryman.* Exh. cat. New York: MOMA, 1993.

Tuchman, Maurice. *American Sculpture of the Sixties.* Exh. cat. Los Angeles: LACMA, 1965.

Tucker, Marcia. *Al Held.* Exh. cat. New York: WMAA, 1974.

———. *Robert Morris.* Exh. cat. New York: WMAA, 1970.

[Twombly] *Cy Twombly: Paintings and Drawings 1954–1977.* Exh. cat. New York: WMAA, 1979.

Upright, Diane. *Morris Louis: The Complete Paintings, a Catalogue Raisonné.* New York: Harry N. Abrams, 1985.

Varnedoe, Kirk. *Cy Twombly, A Retrospective.* Exh. cat. New York: MOMA, 1994.

Vasarely. Neuchâtel: Éditions du Griffon, 1965. Introduction by Marcel Joray.

Waldman, Diane. *Anthony Caro.* New York: Abbeville, 1982.

———. *Carl Andre.* Exh. cat. New York: SRGM, 1970.

———. *Kenneth Noland: A Retrospective.* Exh. cat. New York: SRGM, 1977.

———. *Robert Mangold.* Exh. cat. New York: SRGM, 1971.

———, ed. *Ellsworth Kelly: A Retrospective.* Exh. cat. New York: SRGM, 1996.

Weschler, Lawrence. *Seeing Is Forgetting the Name of the Thing One Sees: A Life of Contemporary Artist Robert Irwin.* Berkeley, Los Angeles, and London: University of California Press, 1982.

Whelan, Richard. *Anthony Caro.* Harmondsworth: Penguin, 1974. Texts by C. Greenberg, M. Fried, J. Russell, P. Tuchman.

Wilkin, Karen. *Frankenthaler: Works on Paper, 1949–84.* Exh. cat. New York: SRGM, 1985.

Wood, Paul, et al. *Modernism in Dispute.* New Haven, Conn.: Yale University Press, 1993.

23. The Second Wave of International Style Architecture

Aalto, Alvar. *The Architectural Drawings of Alvar Aalto: 1917–1939.* New York: Garland, 1994.

Applewhite, E. J., ed. *Synergetics Dictionary: The Mind of Buckminster Fuller.* New York: Garland, 1986.

Argan, Giulio C. *Marcel Breuer.* Milan: Görlich, 1957.

Arnell, Peter, and Ted Bickford, eds. *James Stirling: Buildings and Projects.* New York: Rizzoli, 1985. Text by C. Rowe.

Blake, Peter. *Marcel Breuer: Architect and Designer.* Exh. cat. New York: MOMA, 1949.

———. *Philip Johnson.* Basel and Boston: Birkhäuser Verlag, 1996.

Brownlee, David, and David De Long. *Louis I. Kahn: In the Realm of Architecture.* Exh. cat. Los Angeles: LACMA, 1991. Introduction by V. Scully.

Cannell, Michael T. *I. M. Pei: Mandarin of Modernism.* New York: Carol Southern Books, 1995.

Ciucci, Giorgio, ed. *Giuseppe Terragni: Opera Completa.* Milan: Electa, 1996.

Frampton, Kenneth. *Richard Meier, Architect: Buildings and Projects, 1966–1976.* New York: Oxford University Press, 1976. Postscript by J. Hejduk.

Fuller, R. Buckminster. *Ideas and Integrities: A Spontaneous Autobiographical Disclosure.* New York: MacMillan, 1963.

———. *Synergetics: Explorations in the Geometry of Thinking.* New York: MacMillian, 1975.

Giurgola, Romaldo. *Louis I. Kahn.* Boulder, Colo.: Westview Press, 1975.

Hines, Thomas. *Richard Neutra and the Search for Modern Architecture: A Biography and History.* New York: Oxford University Press, 1982.

Hitchcock, Henry-Russell. *Philip Johnson, Architect: 1949–1965.* New York: Holt, Rinehart, and Winston, 1966.

[Johnson] *Philip Johnson: The Glass House.* Ed. D. Whitney and J. Kipnis. New York: Pantheon Books, 1993.

Kahn, Louis I. *Louis I. Kahn: Writings, Lectures, and Interviews.* Ed. A. Latour. New York: Rizzoli, 1991.

[Kiesler] *Frederick Kiesler: Environmental Sculpture.* Exh. cat. New York: SRGM, 1964.

Kultermann, Udo, ed. *Kenzo Tange, 1946–1969: Architecture and Urban Design.* New York: Praeger, 1970.

Lewis, Hilary and John O'Connor. *Philip Johnson: The Architect in His Own Words.* New York: Rizzoli, 1994.

Lobell, John. *Between Silence and Light: Spirit in the Architecture of Louis I. Kahn.* Boulder, Colo.: Shambhala, 1979.

Loud, Patricia. *The Art Museums of Louis I. Kahn.* Durham, N.C.: Duke University Press, 1989.

The Louis I. Kahn Archive: Personal Drawings: The Completely Illustrated Catalogue of the Drawings in the Louis I. Kahn Collection. 7 vols. Philadelphia and New York: University of Pennsylvania, Pennsylvania Historical and Museum Commission, and Garland: 1987.

Murray, Irena Z., ed. *Moshe Safdie: Buildings and Projects, 1967–1992.* Montreal and Buffalo, N.Y.: Canadian Architecture Collection et al., 1996.

Nervi, Pier Luigi. *Aesthetics and Technology in Building.* Trans. R. Einaudi. Cambridge, Mass.: Harvard University Press, 1965.

Neutra, Richard. *Life and Human Habitat.* Stuttgart: A. Koch, 1956.

[Neutra] *Richard Neutra: Promise and Fulfillment, 1919–1932: Selections from the Letters and Diaries of Richard and Dione Neutra.* Ed. and trans. D. Neutra. Carbondale, Ill.: Southern Illinois University Press, 1985.

Newhouse, Victoria. *Wallace K. Harrison, Architect.* New York: Rizzoli, 1989.

Papadaki, Stamo. *Oscar Niemeyer.* New York: Reinhold, 1950.

———. *Oscar Niemeyer: Works in Progress.* New York: Reinhold, 1956.

Pearson, Paul D. *Alvar Aalto and the International Style.* New York: Whitney Library of Design, 1978.

Phillips, Lisa. *Frederick Kiesler.* New York: WMAA, 1989.

Proun, Jules David. *The Architecture of the Yale Center for British Art.* New Haven, Conn.: Yale University Press, 1977. Introduction by E. P. Pillsbury.

Quantrell, Malcolm. *Alvar Aalto: A Critical Study.* New York: Schocken Books, 1983.

Ronner, Heinz, and Sharad Jharen. *Louis I. Kahn: Complete Works, 1935–74.* 2nd ed. rev. and enl. Basel and Boston: Birkhäuser Verlag, 1987.

Rykwert, Joseph. *Richard Meier: 1964/1984.* New York: Rizzoli, 1984.

Schildt, Goran. *Alvar Aalto: The Complete Catalogue of Architecture, Design, and Art.* New York: Rizzoli, 1994.

Schulze, Franz. *Philip Johnson: Life and Work.* New York: Knopf, 1994.

Schumaher, Thomas. *Surface & Symbol: Giuseppe Terragni and the Architecture of Italian Rationalism.* New York: Princeton Architectural Press, 1991.

Scully, Vincent. *Louis I. Kahn.* New York: G. Braziller, 1962.

Snyder, Robert, ed. *Buckminster Fuller: An Autobiographical Monologue/Scenario.* New York: St. Martin's Press, 1980.

[Stirling] *The Architecture of James Stirling: Four Works.* Exh. cat. Minneapolis: Walker Art Center, 1978. Texts by C. Hodgetts and P. Papademetriou.

Temko, Alan. *Eero Saarinen.* New York: G. Braziller, 1962.

Underwood, David. *Oscar Niemeyer and the Architecture of Brazil.* New York: Rizzoli, 1994.

Weston, Richard. *Alvar Aalto.* London: Phaidon, 1995.

Wiseman, Carter. *The Architecture of I. M. Pei: with an Illustrated Catalogue of the Buildings and Projects.* London: Thames & Hudson, 1990.

———. *I. M. Pei: A Profile in American Architecture.* New York: Harry N. Abrams, 1990.

Zevi, Bruno. *Richard Neutra.* Architetti del movimento moderno, 10. Milan: Il Balcone, 1954.

24. The Pluralistic Seventies

Adriani, Götz, Winfried Konnertz, and Karin Thomas. *Joseph Beuys: Life and Works.* Woodbury, N.Y.: Barron's Educational Series, Inc., 1979.

Anderson, Laurie. *Empty Places.* New York: Harper Perennial, 1991.

———. *Stories from the Nerve Bible: A Retrospective 1972–1992.* New York: Harper Perennial, 1994.

———. *United States.* New York: Harper & Row, 1984.

Armstrong, Elizabeth, and Joan Rothfuss. *In the Spirit of Fluxus.* Exh. cat. Minneapolis: Walker Art Center, 1993.

Ashbery, John, and Kenworth Moffett. *Fairfield Porter: Realist Painter in an Age of Abstraction.* Exh. cat. Boston: Museum of Fine Arts, 1982.

[Aycock] *Alice Aycock Projects: 1979–1981.* Exh. cat. Tampa, Fla.: University of South Florida, 1981. Introduction by E. Fry.

Baker, Kenneth. *Minimalism: Art of Circumstance.* New York: Abbeville, 1988.

Baldessari, John. *This is Not That.* Exh. cat. Manchester: Cornerhouse, 1995.

[Bartlett] *Jennifer Bartlett.* Exh. cat. Minneapolis: Walker Art Center, 1985. Texts by M. Goldwater, R. Smith, C. Tomkins.

Bartman, William, ed. *Vija Celmins.* New York: Art Press, 1992.

Battcock, Gregory, ed. *New Artists Video: A Critical Anthology*. New York: Dutton, 1980.

Beardsley, John. *Earthworks and Beyond: Contemporary Art in the Landscape*. 2nd ed. New York: Abbeville Press, 1984.

———. *Modern Painters at the Corcoran: Sam Gilliam*. Exh. cat. Washington, D.C.: Corcoran Gallery of Art, 1989.

Benezra, Neal. *Ed Paschke*. Exh. cat. Chicago: Art Institute of Chicago, 1990.

Berger, Maurice. "Adrian Piper: A Retrospective," *Issues in Cultural Theory* 3. Exh. cat. Baltimore: Fine Arts Gallery University of Maryland Baltimore County, 1999.

Beuys, Joseph. *Where would I have got if I had been intelligent!* Ed. L. Cooke and K. Kelly. New York: Dia Center for the Arts, 1994.

[Bochner] *Mel Bochner 1973–1985*. Exh. cat. Pittsburgh: Carnegie-Mellon University Press, 1985.

Bowman, Russell. *Philip Pearlstein: The Complete Paintings*. New York: Alpine Fine Arts, 1983.

Brenson, Michael, F. Calvo Seraller, and Edward J. Sullivan. *Antonio López Garcia*. New York: Rizzoli, 1990.

Broude, Norma, and Mary D. Garrard, eds. *The Power of Feminist Art: The American Movement of the 1970s, History and Impact*. New York: Harry N. Abrams, 1994.

Bruggen, Coosje van. *John Baldessari*. New York: Rizzoli, 1990.

Brutvan, Cheryl. *The Paintings of Sylvia Plimack Mangold*. Exh. cat. New York and Buffalo, N.Y.: Hudson Hills Press and Albright-Knox Art Gallery, 1994.

Buchloh, Benjamin. *Hyperrealism*. New York, 1975. Introduction by Salvador Dalí.

[Burden] *Chris Burden: a Twenty-Year Survey*. Exh. cat. Newport Beach, Calif.: Newport Harbor Art Museum, 1988.

Buren, Daniel. *5 Texts*. Exh. cat. New York and London: John Weber and Jack Wendler Galleries, 1973.

Cameron, Dan. "David Hammons Coming in from the Cold," *Flash Art* 29 (January/February 1993): 68–71.

[Campus] *Peter Campus: Projected Images*. Exh. cat. New York: WMAA, 1988. Texts by G. Hanhardt and the artist.

Campus, Peter. "Faces." *Aperture* (Spring 1989): 4–5.

Canaday, John. *Richard Estes: The Urban Landscape*. Exh. cat. Boston: Museum of Fine Arts, 1978. Interview by J. Arthur.

Cathcart, Linda. *American Painting of the 1970s*. Exh. cat. Buffalo, N.Y.: Albright-Knox Gallery, 1979.

Celant, Germano. *Arte Povera*. New York: Praeger, 1969.

———. *Mario Merz*. Exh. cat. New York: SRGM, 1989.

Chicago, Judy. *Beyond the Flower: The Autobiography of a Feminist Artist*. New York: Penguin Books, 1996.

———. *The Dinner Party: A Symbol of Our Heritage*. Garden City, N.Y.: Doubleday, 1979.

Christo: Surrounded Islands, Biscayne Bay, Greater Miami, Florida, 1980–1983. Trans. S. Reader. New York: Harry N. Abrams, 1985.

Compton, Michael. *Barry Flanagan: Sculpture*. Exh. cat. London: British Council, 1982.

———. *Some Notes on the Work of Richard Long*. Exh. cat. London: British Council, 1976.

Cooper, Helen, ed. *Eva Hesse: A Retrospective*. Exh. cat. New Haven, Conn.: Yale University Press, 1992.

Corn, Wanda. *The Art of Andrew Wyeth*. Exh. cat. San Francisco: Fine Arts Museums, 1973.

[Darboven] *Hanne Darboven: Venice Biennale, 1982, West German Pavilion*. Hamburg: Sost & Co., 1982.

Deutsche, Rosalyn, et al. *Hans Haacke, Unfinished Business*. Ed. B. Wallis. Cambridge, Mass.: MIT Press, 1986.

Doezema, Marianne, and June Hargrove. *The Public Monument and Its Audience*. Exh. cat. Cleveland: Cleveland Museum of Art, 1977.

Eisenberg, Deborah. *Air: 24 Hours—Jennifer Bartlett*. New York: Harry N. Abrams, 1994.

Enyeart, James. *Jerry N. Uelsmann: Twenty-Five Years – A Retrospective*. Boston: Little, Brown, 1985.

Fairchild, Patricia A. *Primal Acts of Construction/Destruction: The Art of Michael Heizer, 1967–1987*. Ann Arbor: UMI Research Press, 1994.

Fritscher, Jack. *Mapplethorpe: Assault with a Deadly Camera, a Pop Culture Memoir, an Outlaw Reminiscence*. Mamaroneck, N.Y.: Hastings House, 1994.

Fuchs, Rudolf Herman. *Lawrence Weiner: A Selection of Works with Commentary*. Exh. cat. Eindhoven: Van Abbemuseum, 1976.

———. *Richard Long*. London: Thames & Hudson, 1986.

Goldberg, RoseLee. *Performance: Live Art 1909 to the Present*. New York: Harry N. Abrams, 1979.

Goodyear, Jr., Frank H. *Contemporary American Realism Since 1960*. Boston: New York Graphic Society and the Pennsylvania Academy of the Fine Arts, 1981.

———. *Welliver*. New York: Rizzoli, 1985. Introduction by J. Ashbery.

Gouma-Peterson, Thalia. *Miriam Schapiro: A Retrospective, 1952–1980*. Exh. cat. Ohio: College of Wooster, 1980.

———. "Faith Ringgold's Narrative Quilts," *Arts Magazine* (January 1987): 64–69.

———, ed. *Breaking the Rules: Audrey Flack, A Retrospective 1950–1990*. Exh. cat. New York: Harry N. Abrams, 1992.

Gowing, Lawrence. *Lucien Freud*. New York: Thames & Hudson, 1982.

[Haacke] *Hans Haacke Volume I*. Oxford: Museum of Modern Art, 1978.

[Haacke] *Hans Haacke Volume II*. London: Tate Gallery, 1983.

Hanhardt, John. *Nam June Paik*. Exh. cat. New York: WMAA, 1982. Texts by D. Ronte, M. Nyman, J. G. Hanhardt, D. A. Ross.

Haus, M. "Studio Vista: A Little Bit Normal." [Skoglund] *Mirabella* (September 1991): 64–65.

Hendricks, Jon. *Fluxus Codex*. Detroit and New York: The Gilbert and Lila Silverman Fluxus Collection and Harry N. Abrams, 1988.

Henri, Adrian. *Total Art: Environments, Happenings, and Performance*. New York: Oxford University Press, 1974.

Henry, Gerrit. *Janet Fish*. New York: Burton and Skira, 1987.

Hills, Patricia. *Alice Neel*. New York: Harry N. Abrams, 1983.

Hobbs, Robert. *Robert Smithson: Sculpture*. Ithaca, N.Y.: Cornell University Press, 1981. Texts by L. Alloway, J. Coplans, L. Lippard.

Holt, Nancy, ed. *The Writings of Robert Smithson*. New York: New York University Press, 1979.

[Horn] *Rebecca Horn*. Exh. cat. New York: SRGM, 1993.

Huebler, Douglas. *Location Pieces, Site Sculpture, Duration Works, Drawings, Variable Pieces*. Exh. cat. Boston: Museum of Fine Arts, 1972.

Jackie Winsor/Barry Ledoux: Sculpture. Exh. cat. Cambridge, Mass.: MIT Press, 1984.

[Jaudon] *Valerie Jaudon*. Exh. cat. West Berlin: Amerika-Haus, 1983. Introduction by S. Hunter.

Johnson, Ken. "Art and Memory." (Joel Shapiro) *Art in America* (November 1993): 90–99.

Kaiser, W. M. H. *Joseph Kosuth: Artworks and Theories*. Amsterdam, 1977.

Kaprow, Allan. *Essays on the Blurring of Art and Life*. Ed. J. Kelley. Berkeley, Los Angeles, and London: University of California Press, 1993.

Kardon, Janet. *Laurie Anderson: Works from 1969 to 1983*. Philadelphia: Institute of Contemporary Art, 1983.

———. *Robert S. Zakanitch*. Exh. cat. Philadelphia: Institute of Contemporary Art, 1986.

Kelly, Mary. *Post-Partum Document*. London: Routledge & Keegan Paul, 1983.

Kirshner, Judith Russi. *Vito Acconci: A Retrospective, 1969–1980*. Exh. cat. Chicago: Museum of Contemporary Art, 1980.

Kismaric, Susan. *Jan Groover*. Exh. cat. New York: MOMA, 1987.

Kozloff, Joyce, and Linda Nochlin. *Patterns of Desire*. New York: Hudson Hills, 1990

Krane, Susan. *Lynda Benglis: Dual Natures*. Exh. cat. Atlanta: High Museum of Art, 1990.

Krauss, Rosalind. *Beverly Pepper: Sculpture in Place*. Exh. cat. New York: Abbeville, 1986.

Lindey, Christine. *Superrealist Painting and Sculpture*. New York: Morrow, 1980.

Linker, Kate. *Mary Miss*. Exh. cat. London: ICA, 1983.

Lippard, Lucy. *Eva Hesse*. New York: New York University Press, 1976.

———. *Get the Message? A Decade of Art for Social Change*. New York: Dutton, 1984.

———. *Six Years: The Dematerialization of the Art Object from 1966 to 1972*. New York: Praeger, 1973.

Livingston, Jane, and Marcia Tucker. *Bruce Nauman: Work from 1965 to 1972*. Exh. cat. Los Angeles: LACMA and WMAA, 1972.

Lucie-Smith, Edward. *Art in the Seventies*. Ithaca, N.Y.: Cornell University Press, 1980.

———. *Super Realism*. Oxford: Phaidon, 1979.

Lyons, Lisa and Martin Friedman. *Close Portraits*. Minneapolis: Walker Art Center, 1980.

———, and Kim Levin. *Wegman's World*. Exh. cat. Minneapolis: Walker Art Center, 1982.

[Mapplethorpe] *Robert Mapplethorpe Photographs*. Exh. cat. Norfolk: Chrysler Museum, 1978.

Marshall, Richard. *Alex Katz*. Exh. cat. New York: WMAA, 1986. Text by R. Rosenblum.

———. *American Art Since 1970: Painting, Sculpture, and Drawings from the Collection of the Whitney Museum of American Art*. Exh. cat. New York: WMAA, 1984.

———. *Developments in Recent Sculpture*. Exh. cat. New York: WMAA, 1981.

———. *New Image Painting*. Exh. cat. New York: WMAA, 1978.

———. *Robert Kushner: Paintings on Paper*. Exh. cat. New York: WMAA, 1984.

———. *Robert Mapplethorpe*. Exh. cat. New York: WMAA, 1988.

McEvilley, Thomas. *Pat Steir*. New York: Harry N. Abrams, 1995.

McShine, Kynaston. *Information*. Exh. cat. New York: MOMA, 1970.

Meisel, Louis K. *Photo-Realism*. New York: Harry N. Abrams, 1989.

———. *Richard Estes: The Complete Paintings 1966–1985*. New York: Harry N. Abrams, 1986. With an Essay by J. Perreault.

[Mendieta] *Ana Mendieta: A Retrospective*. Exh. cat. New York: New Museum of Contemporary Art, 1987.

Meyer, Ursula. *Conceptual Art*. New York: Dutton, 1972.

[Meyerowitz] *Cape Light: Color Photographs by Joel Meyerowitz*. Exh. cat. Boston: Museum of Fine Arts, 1978.

[Meyerowitz] *St. Louis and the Arch: Photographs by Joel Meyerowitz*. Boston, 1980.

Mitchell, W. J. T. *Art and the Public Sphere*. Chicago and London: University of Chicago Press, 1992.

Monte, James K. *Twenty-Two Realists.* Exh. cat. New York: WMAA, 1970.

Morgan, Robert C. *Conceptual Art: An American Perspective.* Jefferson, N.C.: McFarland, 1994.

[Morris] *Robert Morris: Selected Works, 1970–1981.* Exh. cat. Houston: Contemporary Arts Museum, 1981.

[Morris] *Robert Morris: The Mind/Body Problem.* New York: SRGM, 1994.

Morrisroe, Patricia. *Mapplethorpe, a Biography.* New York: Random House, 1995.

Müller, Grégoire, and Gianfranco Gorgoni. *The New Avant-Garde: Issues for the Art of the Seventies.* New York: Praeger, 1972.

Neubert, George. *Public Sculpture/Urban Environment.* Exh. cat. Oakland, Calif.: Oakland Museum, 1974.

Nilson, L. "Seeing the Light." [Joel Meyerowitz] *American Photographer* (September 1981): 40–53.

[Nutt] *Jim Nutt.* Exh. cat. Milwaukee: Milwaukee Art Museum, 1994.

Onorato, J. *Vito Acconci: Domestic Trappings.* Exh. cat. La Jolla, Calif.: La Jolla Museum of Contemporary Art, 1997.

[Pfahl] *Altered Landscapes: Photographs by John Pfahl.* Exh. cat. Carmel, Calif.: Friends of Photography, 1981. Introduction by Peter C. Bunnell.

[Pfahl] *A Distanced Land: The Photographs of John Pfahl.* Exh. cat. Buffalo, N.Y.: Albright-Knox Art Gallery, 1990.

Pincus-Witten, Robert. *Postminimalism: American Art of the Decade.* New York: Out of London Press, 1977.

Princenthal, Nancy. "Vija Celmins: Material Fictions." *Parkett* 44 (1995): 25–8.

Printz, N. *Decoration and Representation.* Exh. cat. Alberta, Canada: Alberta College of Art, 1982.

Raven, Arlene. *Art in the Public Interest.* Ann Arbor, Mich.: UMI Press, 1989.

Real, Really Real, Super Real: Directions in Contemporary American Realism. Exh. cat. San Antonio: San Antonio Museum Association, 1981.

Redstone, Louis, and Ruth Redstone. *Public Art: New Directions.* New York: McGraw-Hill, 1980.

Richardson, Barbara. *Gilbert and George.* Exh. cat. Baltimore: Baltimore Museum of Art, 1984.

Robins, Corinne. *The Pluralist Era: American Art 1968–1981.* New York: Harper & Row, 1984.

Rose, Barbara. *Magdalena Abakanowitz.* New York: Harry N. Abrams, 1994.

Rose, Bernice. *Allegories of Modernism: Contemporary Drawing.* Exh. cat. New York: MOMA, 1992.

Rosenblum, Robert. *Alfred Leslie.* Exh. cat. Boston: Museum of Fine Arts, 1976.

Rosenstock, Laura. *Christopher Wilmarth.* New York: MOMA, 1989.

Rosenthal, Mark. *Neil Jenney: Paintings and Sculpture, 1967–1980.* Exh. cat. Berkeley: University Art Museum, 1981.

———, and Richard Marshall. *Jonathan Borofsky.* Exh. cat. Philadelphia: Museum of Art, 1984.

[Roth] *Dieter Roth.* Exh. cat. New York: David Nolan Gallery, 1989.

Sandler, Irving, ed. "Modernism, Revisionism, Pluralism, and Post-Modernism." *Art Journal* (Winter 1980) special issue.

Sayre, Henry M. *The Object of Performance: The American Avant-Garde Since 1970.* Chicago: University of Chicago Press, 1989.

Schneeman, Carolee. *More than Meat Joy.* New Paltz, New York: Documentext, 1979.

Senie, Harriet F., and Sally Webster. *Critical Issues in Public Art: Content, Context, and Controversy.* New York: Icon Editions, 1992.

Serra, Richard. *Writings, Interviews.* Chicago and London: University of Chicago Press, 1994.

[Shapiro] *Joel Shapiro: Sculpture and Drawings.* Los Angeles: Pace Wildenstein, 1996.

Shearer, Linda. *Vito Acconci, Public Places.* Exh. cat. New York: MOMA, 1988.

[Singer] *Artworks: Michael Singer.* Exh. cat. Williamstown, Mass.: Williams College Museum of Art, 1990.

Smagula, Howard J. *Currents: Contemporary Directions in the Visual Arts.* Englewood Cliffs, N.J.: Prentice-Hall, 1983.

Smith, Roberta. *Joel Shapiro.* Exh. cat. New York: WMAA, 1982. Text by R. Marshall.

Sondheim, Alan, ed. *Individuals: Post-Movement Art in America.* New York: Dutton, 1976.

Sonfist, Alan, ed. *Art in the Land: A Critical Anthology of Environmental Art.* New York: Dutton, 1983.

[Steir] *Pat Steir: Paintings: Essay/Interview.* New York: Harry N. Abrams, 1986.

Storr, Robert. *Dislocations.* Exh. cat. New York: MOMA, 1991.

Strand, Mark. *William Bailey: Recent Paintings.* Exh. cat. New York: Robert Schoelkopf Gallery, 1982.

Tannenbaum, Judith. *Vija Celmins.* Philadelphia: Institute of Contemporary Art, 1992.

Temkin, Ann. *Thinking Is Form: The Drawings of Joseph Beuys.* Exh. cat. New York: MOMA, 1993.

Thompson, Walter. "Beverly Pepper: Dramas in Space." *Arts Magazine* LXII:10 (Summer 1988): 52–55.

Tisdall, Caroline. *Joseph Beuys.* Exh. cat. New York: SRGM, 1979.

Tomkins, Calvin, and David Bourdon. *Christo's Running Fence.* New York: Harry N. Abrams, 1978. Photography by G. Gorgoni.

Tuchman, Maurice. *Susan Rothenberg.* Los Angeles: LACMA, 1983.

Tucker, Marcia and James Monte. *Anti-Illusion: Procedures/Materials.* Exh. cat. New York: WMAA, 1969.

———, and Robert Pincus-Witten. *John Baldessari.* Exh. cat. New York: New Museum, 1981. Interview by N. Drew.

[Tuttle] *Richard Tuttle: Selected Works, 1964–1994.* Exh. cat. Tokyo: Sezon Museum of Art, 1995.

[Uelsmann] *Jerry Uelsmann: Photo Synthesis.* Gainesville, Fla.: University Press of Florida, 1992.

[Uelsmann] *Jerry Uelsmann: Twenty-five Years —A Retrospective.* Boston: Little, Brown, 1982.

Varnedoe, Kirk. *Duane Hanson.* New York: Harry N. Abrams, 1985.

Wagner, Anne. *Three Artists (Three Women): Modernism and the Art of Hesse, Krasner, and O'Keeffe.* Berkeley, Calif.: University of California Press, 1996.

Waldman, Diane. *Michael Singer.* Exh. cat. New York: SRGM, 1984.

Walker, Barry. *Donald Sultan, a Print Retrospective.* Exh. cat. New York: Rizzoli, 1992.

Weergraf-Serra, Clara, and Martha Buskirk, eds. *The Destruction of "Tilted Arc": Documents.* Cambridge, Mass. and London: MIT Press, 1991.

[Wegman] *William Wegman: Paintings, Drawings, Photographs, Videotapes.* New York: Harry N. Abrams, 1990.

Wegman, William, and Laurence Wieder. *Man's Best Friend.* New York: Harry N. Abrams, 1982.

[Wilmarth] *Christopher Wilmarth: Nine Clearings for a Standing Man.* Exh. cat. Hartford, Conn.: Wadsworth Atheneum, 1975.

[Winsor] *Jackie Winsor.* Exh. cat. New York: MOMA, 1979.

[Wyeth] *Andrew Wyeth.* Exh. cat. Philadelphia: Pennsylvania Academy of the Fine Arts, 1966.

25: Postmodernism in Architecture

Ando, Tadao. *The Colors of Light.* London: Phaidon, 1996.

[Ando] *Tadao Ando.* London and New York: Academy Editions and St. Martin's Press, 1990.

[Applebroog] *Ida Applebroog: Nothing Personal, Paintings 1987–1997.* Washington DC: Corcoran Gallery of Art,1998.

Arnell, Peter, and Ted Bickford, eds. *Frank Gehry, Buildings and Projects.* New York: Rizzoli, 1985. Texts by G. Celant and M. Andrews.

Brolin, Brent. *The Failure of Modern Architecture.* New York: Van Nostrand Reinhold, 1976.

Crosbie, Michael J. *Cesar Pelli: Recent Themes.* Boston: Birkhauser, 1998.

Dannatt, Adrian. *The United States Holocaust Memorial Museum: James Ingo Freed.* London: Phaidon, 1995.

Dobney, Stephen, ed. *Eisenman Architects: Selected and Current Works.* Mulgrave, Vic: Images Pub. Group, 1995.

Drew, Philip. *The Architecture of Arata Isozaki.* New York: Harper & Row, 1982.

Duany, Andres, and Elizabeth Plater-Zyberk. "The Second Coming of the American Small Town." *Wilson Quarterly* 16 (Winter 1992): 19–32ff.

Ebony, David. "Towers of Light for New York City," *Art in America* 11, Nov 2001, p.35.

[Eisenman] *Re-working Eisenman.* London and Berlin: Academy Editions and Ernst & Sohn, 1993.

Foster Associates: Recent Works. London and New York: Academy Editions and St. Martin's Press, 1992.

[Foster] *Norman Foster.* Ed. I. Yuroukov and E. Kraichkova. Varese, Italy: Arterigere, 1991.

Frampton, Kenneth. *A New Wave of Japanese Architecture.* New York: Institute for Architecture and Urban Studies, 1978.

Frantz, Douglas, and Catherine Collins. *Celebration, USA: Living in Disney's Brave New Town.* New York: Henry Holt & Co., 1999.

[Gehry] *The Architecture of Frank Gehry.* Exh. cat. Minneapolis: Walker Art Center, 1986.

Gehry, Frank. *Frank Gehry, Buildings and Projects.* Ed. P. Arnell and T. Bickford. New York: Rizzoli, 1985.

Hadid, Zaha. *Planetary Architecture Two.* London: Architectural Association, 1983. Introduction by K. Frampton; Interview with the architect by A. Boyarsky.

Hays, K. Michael, and Carol Burns, eds. *Thinking the Present: Recent American Architecture.* New York: Princeton Architectural Press, 1990.

Henri, Adrian. *Post-Modernism: The New Classicism in Art and Architecture.* New York: Rizzoli, 1987.

Ho, Cathy Lang. "Underwriting the American Dream," *Architecture* (September 1999): 63–67.

[Hollein] *Architectural Visions for Europe: Hans Hollein.* Braunschweig: Vieweg, 1994.

James, Warren A., ed. *Ricardo Bofill/Taller de Arquitectura: Buildings and Projects: 1960–1985.* New York: Rizzoli, 1986.

Jencks, Charles. *Architecture Today.* Rev. and enl. ed. New York: Harry N. Abrams, 1988.

———. *The Language of Post-Modern Architecture.* Rev. enl. ed. New York: Rizzoli, 1985.

———. *Late Modern Architecture and Other Essays.* London: Academy Editions, 1980.

———. *Post-Modernism: The New Classicism in Art and Architecture.* New York: Rizzoli, 1987.

———, ed. *Frank O. Gehry: Individual Imagination and Cultural Conservatism.* London: Academy Editions, 1995.

Jenson, Robert, and Patricia Conway. *Ornamentalism: The New Decorativeness in Architecture and Design.* New York: C. N. Potter, 1982.

Klotz, Heinrich. *The History of Postmodern Architecture.* Trans. R. Donnell. Cambridge, Mass.: MIT Press, 1988.

[Koolhaas] *Rem Koolhaas: Conversations with Students.* Ed. L. Fitzpatrick and D. Hofius. Houston: Rice University School of Architecture, 1991.

Koolhaas, Rem. *Delirious New York: A Retroactive Manifesto of Manhattan.* New York: Oxford University Press, 1978.

———, and Bruce Mau. *Small, Medium, Large, Extra-large: Office for Metropolitan Architecture.* Ed. J. Sigler. Rotterdam: 010 Publishers, 1995.

Krier, Rob. *Rob Krier on Architecture.* New York: St. Martin's Press, 1982.

Littlejohn, David. *Architect: The Life and Work of Charles W. Moore.* New York: Holt, Rinehart, and Winston, 1984.

Lucan, Jacques. *OMA Rem Koolhaas: Architecture 1970–1990.* New York: Princeton Architectural Press, 1991.

Miller, Nory. *Johnson/Burgee, Architecture: Buildings and Projects.* New York: Random House, 1979.

Norberg-Schulz, Christian. *Ricardo Bofill.* New York: Rizzoli, 1985. Photography by Y. Futagawa.

[Pelli] *Cesar Pelli: Buildings and Projects, 1965–1990.* New York: Rizzoli, 1990.

Portoghesi, Paolo. *Postmodernism: The Architecture of the Post-Industrial Society.* Trans. E. Shapiro. New York: Rizzoli, 1983.

The Presence of the Past: First International Exhibition of Architecture—Venice Biennale 1980. New York: Rizzoli, 1980.

Provoost, Michelle. *Dutchtown: A City Centre Design by OMA/Rem Koolhaas.* Rotterdam: NAi Publishers, 1999.

Ragheb, J. Fiona, ed. *Frank Gehry, Architect.* Exh. cat. New York: SRGM, 2001.

Ray, Keith, ed. *Contextual Architecture: Responding to Existing Style.* New York: McGraw-Hill, 1980.

Ross, Andrew. *The Celebration Chronicles: Life, Liberty, and the Pursuit of Property Value in Disney's New Town.* New York: Ballantine Books, 1999.

Rossi, Aldo. *Architecture of the City.* Trans. D. Ghirardo and J. Ockman. Rev. ed. Cambridge, Mass.: MIT Press, 1982.

Rykwert, Joseph. *The Necessity of Artifice.* New York: Rizzoli, 1982.

Smith, C. Ray. *Supermannerism: New Attitudes in Post-Modern Architecture.* New York: Dutton, 1977.

Steele, James. *Schnabel House: Frank Gehry.* London: Phaidon, 1993.

Stern, Robert A. M. *New Directions in American Architecture.* Rev. ed. New York: G. Braziller, 1977.

Tschumi, Bernard. *Event-Cities: Praxis.* Exh. cat. Cambridge, Mass.: MIT Press, 1994.

Venturi, Robert. *Complexity and Contradiction in Architecture.* New York: MOMA, 1966. Introduction by V. Scully.

———, Denise Scott Brown, and Steven Izenour. *Learning from Las Vegas: The Forgotten Symbolism of Architectural Form.* Rev. ed. Cambridge, Mass.: MIT Press, 1977.

Von Moos, Stanislaus. *Venturi, Rauch, and Scott Brown: Buildings and Projects, 1960–1985.* New York: Rizzoli, 1987.

26: The Retrospective Eighties

[Ahearn] *John Ahearn.* Exh. cat. Kansas City, Mo.: Nelson-Atkins Museum, 1990.

[Applebroog] *At the Edge: Ida Applebroog.* Exh. cat. Atlanta: High Museum of Art, 1989.

[Applebroog] *Ida Applebroog: Bilder.* Exh. cat. Ulm, Germany: Ulmer Museum, 1991.

[Applebroog] *Ida Applebroog: Happy Families —A Fifteen Year Survey.* Exh. cat. Houston: Contemporary Arts Museum, 1990.

[Applebroog] *Ida Applebroog: Nostrums (Paintings)/Belladonna (A Film/Tape by Ida Applebroog and Beth B).* Exh. cat. New York: Ronald Feldman Fine Arts, 1989.

Audiello, Massimo. "Ross Bleckner: The Joyful and Gloomy Side of Being Alive." *Flash Art* 183 (Summer 1995): 112–115ff.

Auping, Michael. *Francesco Clemente.* Sarasota, Fla.: John and Mable Ringling Museum of Art, 1985.

———. *Judy Pfaff: Installations, Collages, and Drawings.* Exh. cat. Sarasota, Fla.: John and Mable Ringling Museum of Art, 1981.

Basquait, Jean-Michel. *Collaborations: Jean Michel Basquait, Francesco Clements, Andy Warhol.* Exh. cat. Kusnacht/Zurich: Bruno Bischofberger, 1984.

Benezra, Neal. *Martin Puryear.* Exh. cat. Chicago: Art Institute of Chicago, 1991.

Billeter, Erika, ed. *Eric Fischl: Paintings and Drawings.* Lausanne: Musée Cantonal des Beaux-Arts, 1990.

[Boltanski] *Christian Boltanski: Lessons of Darkness.* Exh. cat. Chicago: Museum of Contemporary Art, 1988. Texts by L. Gumpert and M. J. Jacob.

Bonito Oliva, Achille. *Trans Avant Garde International.* Moderna Galleria Civica, 1982.

Buchloh, Benjamin, Serge Guilbaut, and David Solkin, eds. *Modernism and Modernity: The Vancouver Conference Papers.* Halifax, Nova Scotia: Press of the Nova Scotia College of Art and Design, 1983.

[Burton] *Scott Burton.* Exh. cat. London: Tate Gallery, 1985.

[Burton] *Scott Burton: Pair Behavior Tableau.* Exh. cat. New York: SRGM, 1976. Text by L. Shearer.

Cahmi, L. "Christian Boltanski: A Conversation." *Print Collector's Newsletter* (January–February 1993): 201–206.

Carmean, Jr., E. A., et al. *The Sculpture of Nancy Graves: A Catalogue Raisonné.* New York: Hudson Hills Press, 1987.

Celant, Germano. *Unexpressionism: Art Beyond the Contemporary.* New York: Rizzoli, 1988.

———, ed. *Keith Haring.* Munich: Prestel, 1992.

[Clemente] *Clemente.* Exh. cat. New York: SRGM, 1999.

[Clemente] *Francesco Clemente: The Fourteen Stations.* Exh. cat. London: Whitechapel Art Gallery, 1983.

Clothier, Peter. *Betye Saar.* Exh. cat. Los Angeles: Museum of Contemporary Art, 1984.

Coe, Sue. *Dead Meat.* New York and London: Four Walls Eight Windows, 1995.

Compton, Michael. *The New Art.* Exh. cat. London: Tate Gallery, 1983.

Contemporary Italian Masters. Exh. cat. Chicago: Council on Fine Arts and the Renaissance Society at the University of Chicago, 1984. Texts by H. Geldzahler and J. R. Kirshner.

Cotter, Holland. "Postmodern Tourist." [Eric Fischl] *Art in America* (April 1991): 154–157, 183.

———. "Taking It Personally: Putting Emotions on Paper." [Joan Snyder] *The New York Times* (April 8, 1994): C26.

Cowart, Jack. *Expressions: New Art from Germany, Georg Baselitz, Jörg Immendorff, Anselm Kiefer, Markus Lüpertz, A. R. Penck.* Exh. cat. St. Louis: St. Louis Art Museum, 1983. Texts by S. Gohr and D. B. Kuspit.

[Cragg] *Tony Cragg.* Exh. cat. London: Hayward Gallery, 1987.

[Cragg] *Tony Cragg.* Exh. cat. London: Tate Gallery, 1989.

[Cragg] *Tony Cragg: Sculpture, 1975–1990.* Newport Beach, Calif.: Newport Harbor Art Museum, 1990.

[Cragg] "Necessary Appetites: An Interview with Tony Cragg." *Border Crossings* (Summer 1992): 45–53. Introduction by Richard Rhodes.

[Cucchi] *Enzo Cucchi.* Exh. cat. Paris: Centre Georges Pompidou, 1986.

Davies, Hugh Marlais. *Martin Puryear.* Exh. cat. Amherst, Mass.: University of Massachusetts, 1984.

Davis, Douglas. *Artculture: Essays on the Postmodern.* New York: Harper & Row, 1979.

Dennison, Lisa, ed. *Ross Bleckner.* Exh. cat. New York: SRGM, 1995.

Endgame: Reference and Simulation in Recent Painting and Sculpture. Boston: Institute of Contemporary Art, 1986.

Feldman, Ronald, et al. *Ida Applebroog.* New York: Ronald Feldman Fine Arts, 1987.

Ferguson, Bruce W. *Eric Fischl.* Exh. cat. Saskatoon, Canada: Mendel Art Gallery, 1985. Texts by J.-C. Ammann, D. B. Kuspit, B. W. Ferguson.

[Fetting] *Rainer Fetting.* Exh. cat. London: Anthony d'Offay, 1982.

[Fetting] *Rainer Fetting.* Exh. cat. New York: Marlborough Gallery, 1984.

[Fischl] *Scenes and Sequences: Recent Monotypes by Eric Fischl.* Exh. cat. Hanover, N.H.: Hood Museum of Art, 1990.

Fox, Howard N. *Avant-Garde in the Eighties.* Los Angeles: LACMA, 1987.

———, ed. *Robert Longo.* Exh. cat. New York: Rizzoli, 1989.

Franzke, Andreas. *Georg Baselitz.* Trans. D. Britt. Exh. cat. New York: Prestel, 1989.

Frazier, I. "Profiles: Partners." [Komar & Melamid] *New Yorker* (December 29, 1986): 33–54.

Freeman, Phyllis, et al., eds. *New Art.* New York: Harry N. Abrams, 1984.

Gablik, Suzy. *Has Modernism Failed?* New York: Thames & Hudson, 1984.

Gillick, Liam. "Allan McCollum at the Serpentine," *ARTSCRIBE* (Summer 1989).

Goodman, Cynthia. *Digital Visions: Computers and Art.* New York: Harry N. Abrams, 1987.

Graham-Dixon, Andrew. *Howard Hodgkin.* London: Thames & Hudson, 1994.

[Graves] *Nancy Graves: A Survey 1969/1980.* Exh. cat. Buffalo, N.Y.: Albright-Knox Gallery, 1990.

[Graves] *The Sculpture of Nancy Graves: A Catalogue Raisonné.* New York: Hudson Hills Press and the Fort Worth Art Museum, 1987.

Graze, Sue, and Kathy Halbreich, eds. *Elizabeth Murray: Paintings and Drawings.* Exh. cat. New York: Harry N. Abrams, 1987. With an Essay by R. Smith; Notes by C. Ackley.

[Greenblat] *Rodney A. Greenblat's Reality and Imagination: Two Taste Treats in One!* Exh. cat. University Park, Pa.: Penn State University Museum of Art, 1987.

Gruen, John. *Keith Haring: The Authorized Biography.* New York: Prentice Hall, 1991.

Grundberg, Andy. *Mike and Doug Starn.* New York: Harry N. Abrams, 1990. Introduction by R. Rosenblum.

Guerrilla Girls. *Confessions of the Guerrilla Girls.* New York: Harper Collins, 1995.

Hobbs, Robert. *Robert Longo Dis-illusions.* Exh. cat. Iowa City, Iowa: University of Iowa Museum of Art, 1985.

Hockney, David. *Cameraworks.* New York: Knopf, 1984. Text by L. Weschler.

[Hodgkin] *Howard Hodgkin: Paintings.* New York: Harry N. Abrams, 1995.

Hunter, Sam. *New Directions: Contemporary American Art.* Exh. cat. Princeton, N.J.: University Art Museum, 1981.

Joachimides, Christos. *A New Spirit in Painting.* Exh. cat. London: Royal Academy of Art, 1981. Texts by N. Rosenthal and N. Serota.

[Kiefer] *Anselm Kiefer: The High Priestess.* Exh. cat. New York and London: Harry N. Abrams and Anthony d'Offay, 1989.

Krane, Susan. *Art at the Edge: Alison Saar - Fertile Ground.* Exh. cat. Atlanta: High Museum of Art, 1993.

Kuspit, Donald B. *Leon Golub: Existentialist/Activist Painter.* Rutgers, N.J.: Rutgers University Press, 1985.

LeFalle-Collins, Lizzetta, and R. Barrett. *Betye Saar: Secret Heart.* Exh. cat. Fresno, Calif.: Fresno Art Museum, 1993.

Levick, Melba. *The Big Picture: Murals of Los Angeles.* Boston: Little, Brown, 1988.

Lingwood, James. *Ilya Kabakov: Ten Characters.* London: ICA, 1989.

Linker, Kate. *Love for Sale: The Words and Pictures of Barbara Kruger.* New York: Harry N. Abrams, 1990.

London, Barbara, ed. *Bill Viola.* Exh. cat. New York: MOMA, 1987.

Longo, Robert. *Men in the Cities.* New York: Harry N. Abrams, 1986. Introduction and interview by R. Price.

[Longo] *Robert Longo: Drawings and Reliefs.* Exh. cat. Akron, Ohio: Akron Art Museum, 1984.

Lucie-Smith, Edward. *Art in the Eighties.* Oxford: Phaidon, 1990.

Marmer, Nancy. "Boltanski: The Uses of Contradiction." *Art in America* (October 1989): 169–181, 233–235.

Marshall, Richard. *Jean-Michel Basquiat.* Exh. cat. New York: WMAA, 1992.

McShine, Kynaston. *An International Survey of Recent Painting and Sculpture.* Exh. cat. New York: MOMA, 1984.

[Morris] *Robert Morris: Works of the Eighties.* Exh. cat. Chicago: Museum of Contemporary Art, 1986. Texts by E. F. Fry and D. P. Kuspit.

Neff, Terry. *Gerhard Richter Paintings.* Exh. cat. New York: Thames & Hudson, 1988.

New Figuration in America. Exh. cat. Milwaukee: Milwaukee Art Museum, 1982.

Nixon, Mignon. "You Thrive on Mistaken Identity." [Barbara Kruger] *October* 60 (Spring 1992): 59–81.

Osorio, Pepon. *Con to 'los Hierros: A retrospective of the work of Pepon Osorio.* Exh. cat. New York: El Museu del Barrio, 1991.

Owens, Craig. *Beyond Recognition: Representation, Power, and Culture.* Berkeley: University of California Press, 1992.

Percy, Ann, and Raymond Foye. *Francesco Clemente: Three Worlds.* Exh. cat. Philadelphia: Philadelphia Museum of Art, 1990.

Phillips, Lisa. *Richard Prince.* Exh. cat. New York: WMAA, 1992.

Pincus-Witten, Robert. *Entries (Maximalism).* New York: Out of London Press, 1983.

———. *Keith Haring.* Exh. cat. New York: Tony Shafrazi Gallery, 1982. Texts by J. Deitch and D. Shapiro.

[Polke] *Sigmar Polke.* Exh. cat. San Francisco: Museum of Modern Art, 1990.

[Polke] *Sigmar Polke: Join the Dots.* Exh. cat. Liverpool: Tate Gallery, 1995.

Princenthal, Nancy. "Reweaving Old Glory." [Donald Lipski] *Art in America* (May 1991): 137–140.

Ratcliff, Carter. *Komar & Melamid.* New York: Abbeville, 1988.

———. *Robert Longo.* New York: Rizzoli, 1985.

Rathbone, Eliza E. *Bill Jensen.* Exh. cat. Washington, D.C.: Phillips Collection, 1987.

[Reed] *David Reed.* Los Angeles: A.R.T. Press, 1990. Essay by C. Hagan.

Richardson, Brenda. *Scott Burton.* Exh. cat. Baltimore: Baltimore Museum of Art, 1986.

[Richter] *Gerhard Richter.* Exh. cat. London: Tate Gallery, 1991.

[Richter] *Gerhard Richter.* Exh. cat. New York: Marian Goodman/Sperone Westwater Gallery, 1985.

Risatti, Howard, ed. *Postmodern Perspectives: Issues in Contemporary Art.* Englewood Cliffs, N.J.: Prentice-Hall, 1990.

Rose, Barbara. *American Painting, the Eighties: A Critical Interpretation.* Exh. cat. New York: Grey Art Gallery and Study Center, New York University, 1979.

Rosenstock, Laura. *Christopher Wilmarth.* New York: MOMA, 1989.

Rosenthal, Mark. *Anselm Kiefer.* Exh. cat. Chicago and Philadelphia: The Art Institute of Chicago and the Philadelphia Museum of Art, 1987.

Schjeldahl, Peter. *Cindy Sherman.* Exh. cat. New York: WMAA, 1984. Texts by P. Schjeldahl and L. Phillips; Afterword by I. M. Danoff.

Schnabel, Julian. *C.V.J.: Nicknames of Maître D's & Other Excerpts from Life.* New York: Random House, 1987.

Schor, Mira. *Wet: On Painting, Feminism, and Art Culture.* Durham: Duke University Press, 1997.

Schwabsky, Barry. "A City of Bricks and Ciphers," *Art in America* (September 1998): 100–105.

———. "Memories of Light." [Ross Bleckner] *Art in America* 83 (December 1995): 80–85ff.

[Scully] *Sean Scully.* Pittsburgh: Carnegie Institute, 1985. Exh. cat. Texts by J. Caldwell, D. Carrier, A. Lighthill.

Sculpture for Public Spaces: Maquettes, Models, and Proposals. Exh. cat. New York: Marisa del Re Gallery, 1985.

[Sherman] *Cindy Sherman: History Portraits.* New York: Rizzoli, 1991. Text by A. Danto.

Solomon, Deborah. "Elizabeth Murray: Celebrating Paint." *New York Times Magazine.* (March 31, 1991): 20–25, 40, 46.

[Spero] "Dialogue: An Exchange of Ideas Between Dena Shottenkirk and Nancy Spero." *Arts Magazine* (May 1987): 34–35.

Storr, Robert. "Shape Shifter." [Elizabeth Murray] *Art in America* (April 1989): 210–221, 275.

Transformations: New Sculpture from Britain. [Tony Cragg et al.] Exh. cat. London: British Council, 1983.

Tuchman, Maurice, and Stephanie Barron. *David Hockney, A Retrospective.* Exh. cat. New York: Harry N. Abrams, 1988.

Wakefield, Neville. "Mourning Glory: Ross Bleckner in Retrospect." *Artforum* 33 (February 1995): 69–74ff.

Waldman, Diane. *Enzo Cucchi.* Exh. cat. New York: SRGM, 1986.

———. *Georg Baselitz.* Exh. cat. New York: SRGM, 1995.

———. *Jenny Holzer.* New York: Harry N. Abrams, 1989.

———, ed. *Italian Art Now: An American Perspective.* Exh. cat. New York: SRGM, 1982.

Wallach, Amei. *Ilya Kabakov: The Man Who Never Threw Anything Away.* New York: Harry N. Abrams, 1996.

Wallis, Brian, ed. *Art after Modernism: Rethinking Representation.* New York: The New Museum, 1984.

Whitney, David. *David Salle.* New York: Rizzoli, 1994.

Wilmarth, Christopher. *Breath: Inspired by Seven Poems of Stéphane Mallarmé, Translated by Frederick Morgan.* New York: C. Wilmarth, 1982. With an Essay by D. Ashton.

[Wilmarth] *Christopher Wilmarth: Nine Clearings for a Standing Man.* Exh. cat. Hartford, Conn.: Wadsworth Atheneum, 1975.

[Wojnarowicz] *Fever: The Art of David Wojnarowicz.* Exh. cat. New York: Rizzoli, 1998.

Yau, John. "Judy Pfaff." *Artforum* (March 1989): 128ff.

27: Resistance and Resolution

1993 Biennial Exhibition. New York: WMAA, 1993.

Always Remember: The NAMES Project AIDS Memorial Quilt. Washington, D.C.: National Museum of American History, 1996.

Annear, Judy. "Peepshow: Inside Yasumasa Morimura's Looking Glass," *Art Asia Pacific* 13 (1997): 42–47.

Baigell, Matthew. *Jewish-American Artists and the Holocaust.* New Brunswick: Rutgers University Press, 1997.

Barber, Lynn. "Just Be Yourself – and Wear a Low Top," *Parkett* 63 (2001): 24–35.

Bartman, William S., and Miyoshi Barosh, eds. *Mike Kelley.* New York: Art Press, 1992. Interview with the artist by J. Miller.

Baumgarten, Lothar. *America.* Exh. cat. New York: SRGM, 1993.

———. *Unsettled Objects.* Exh. cat. SRGM, 1993.

Benezra, Neal David. *Distemper: Dissonant Themes in the Art of the 1990s.* Exh. cat. Washington DC: Hirshhorn Museum and Sculpture Garden, Smithsonian Institution, 1996.

Blessing, Jennifer, ed. *Rrose is a Rrose is a Rrose: Gender Performance in Photography.* New York: SRGM, 1997.

Blinderman, Barry, ed. *David Wojnarowicz, Tongues of Flame.* Normal, Ill.: University of Illinois State University, 1989.

Bolton, Richard, ed. *Culture Wars: Documents from the Recent Controversies in the Arts.* New York: The New Press, 1992.

Bonami, Francesco. "Back in Five Minutes." [Gabriel Orozco] *Parkett* 48 (1996): 41–47.

Boodro, Michael. "Blood, Spit, and Beauty." *Art News* 93 (March 1994): 126–131.

Bradley, Fiona, ed. *Rachel Whiteread.* Exh. cat. London: Tate Gallery Liverpool, 1996. Text by R. Krauss et al.

Brougher, Kerry. *Jeff Wall.* Exh. cat. Los Angeles: Museum of Contemporary Art, 1997.

Bruce, Chris. *Ann Hamilton, Sao Paulo/Seattle.* Exh. cat. Seattle: Henry Art Gallery, University of Washington, 1992.

"Brush Fires in the Social Landscape." *Aperture* 137 (Fall 1994) special issue on David Wojnarowicz.

Bryson, Norman. "Three Morimura Readings," *Art + Text* 52 (1995): 67–78.

Buchloh, Benjamin H.D. *Thomas Struth: Photographs.* Exh. cat. Chicago: The Renaissance Society, 1990.

Burn, Gordon. "Damien Hirst," *Parkett* 40–41, (June 1994): 58–69.

[Cai Guo-Qiang] *Cai Guo-Qiang: Cultural Melting Bath: Projects for the 20th Century.* Exh. cat. New York: Queens Museum of Art, 1997.

Castello Di Rivoli Museo d'Arte Contemporanea. *Shirin Neshat.* Exh. cat. Milan: Charta, 2002.

The City Influence: Ross Bleckner, Peter Halley, Jonathan Lasker. Exh. cat. Dayton, Ohio: Dayton Art Institute, 1992.

Clark, T. J. *Farewell to an Idea: Episodes from a History of Modernism.* New Haven: Yale University Press, 1999.

Cohen, Michael. "Mariko Mori: Plastic Dreams in the Reality Bubble," *Flash Art* (May/June 1997): 94–97.

Conkelton, Sheryl, and Carol S. Eliel. *Annette Messager*. Exh. cat. Los Angeles: LACMA, 1995.

Connor, Kimberly Rae. "To Disembark: The Slave Narrative Tradition." [Glenn Ligon] *African American Review* 30 (Spring 1996): 35–57.

"A Conversation on Recent Feminist Art Practices." *October* 71 (Winter 1995): 48–69.

Cooke, Lynne. "Gary Hill: 'Who am I but a figure of speech?'" *Parkett* 34 (1992): 16–21.

———. "Tony Oursler Altars." *Parkett* 47 (1996): 38–41.

———, and Karen Kelly, eds. *Diana Thater Knots + Surfaces*. Exh. cat. New York: Dia Center for the Arts, 2002.

Cooper, Emmanuel. *The Sexual Perspective: Homosexuality and Art in the Last 100 Years in the West*. London: Routledge, 1994.

Cox, Renee. *Renee Cox: American Family*. Exh. cat. New York: Robert Miller Gallery, 2001.

Crone, Rainer, and David Moos. *Jonathan Lasker: Telling the Tales of Painting; About Abstraction at the End of the Millennium*. Stuttgart: Édition Cantza, 1993.

Crow, Thomas. "Profane Illuminations: Social History and the Art of Jeff Wall." *Artforum* (January 1993): 63–69.

Dannatt, Adrian. "From Lacan's Drive to Rodeo Drive: Marketing and Minimalism in Fleury's Femininity," *Parkett* 58 (2000): 76–88.

Danoff, I. Michael. *Jeff Koons*. Exh. cat. Chicago: Museum of Contemporary Art, 1988.

Danto, Arthur. *Mark Tansey: Visions and Revisions*. Ed. C. Sweet. New York: Harry N. Abrams, 1992. With notes by the artist.

de Duve, Thierry, et al. *Jeff Wall*. London: Phaidon, 2002.

The Decade Show: Frameworks of Identity in the 1980s. New York: Museum of Contemporary Hispanic Art, The New Museum of Contemporary Art, The Studio Museum in Harlem, 1990.

Deitch, Jeffrey. *Form follows Fiction*. Exh. cat. Milan: Charta, 2001.

———. *Post Human*. Exh. cat. Pully/Lausanne: FAE Musée d'Art Contemporain, 1992.

———. *Strange Abstraction*. Exh. cat. Tokyo: Touko Museum of Contemporary Art, 1991.

Dumas, Marlene. *Miss Interpreted*. Exh. cat. Eindhoven: Van Abbemuseum, 1992.

———. *Sweet Nothings: Notes and Texts*. Amsterdam: De Balie, 1998.

Durant, Alice, Laura Mulvey, and Dirk Snauwaert. *Jimmie Durham*. London: Phaidon, 1995.

Enwezor, Okwui. "Social Grace: The Work of Lorna Simpson." *Third Text* 35 (Summer 1996): 43–58.

Ferguson, Russel. "Given: 1: The Caprice 2. The Ferrari," *Parkett* 58 (2000): 122–128.

Finlay, Karen. *Shock Treatment*. San Francisco: City Lights Books, 1990.

Flomenhaft, Eleanor. *Faith Ringgold, A Twenty-Five Year Survey*. Exh. cat. Hempstead, N.Y.: Fine Arts Museum of Long Island, 1990.

Fogle, Douglas. *Painting at the Edge of the World*. Exh. cat. Minneapolis: Walker Art Center, 2001.

Foster, Hal. *Return of the Real: the Avant-garde at the End of the Century*. Cambridge, Mass.: MIT Press, 1996.

Freeman, Judi. *Mark Tansey*. Exh. cat. Los Angeles and San Francisco: LACMA and Chronicle Books, 1993.

Friis-Hansen, Dana. "Full Blown: The expansive Vision of Miniaturist Shahzia Sikander," *Art Asia Pacific* 16 (1997): 45–49.

[Fritsch] *Katharina Fritsch*. Exh. cat. New York: Dia Center for the Arts, 1993.

Fusco, Coco. *English is Broken Here: Notes on Cultural Fusion in the Americas*. New York: The New Press, 1992.

Gale, Peggy. "Stan Douglas: *Evening* and Others." *Parachute* (July–September 1995): 21–27.

[Gallagher] *Ellen Gallagher*. Exh. cat. Boston: Institute for Contemporary Art, Boston, 2001.

Garrels, Garu, ed. *Amerika: Tim Rollins - K.O.S.* New York: Dia Art Foundation, 1990.

Gilbert-Rolfe, Jeremy. *Roni Horn: Pair Objects 1, 11, 111*. Exh. cat. New York: Galerie Lelong, 1988.

Gillick, Liam. *Literally No Place: Communes, Bars and Greenrooms*. London: Book Works, 2002.

———. "Literally No Place: An Introduction," *Parkett* 61 (2001): 56–63.

———, and Rirkrit Tiravanija. "Forget about the Ball and Get on with the Game," *Parkett* 44 (1995).

Gilman, Larry, ed. *Threads of Vision: Toward a Feminine Poetics*. Exh. cat. Cleveland: Cleveland Center for Contemporary Art, 2001.

[Gober] *Robert Gober*. Exh. cat. Los Angeles: Museum of Contemporary Art, 1997.

[Gober] *Robert Gober* (with essay by Dave Hickey). Exh. cat. New York: Dia Center for the Arts, 1992.

[Gober] *Robert Gober*. Exh. cat. Rotterdam and Bern: Museum Boymans-Van Beuningen and Kunsthalle Bern, 1990.

Golden, Thelma. *Black Male: Representations of Masculinity in Contemporary American Art*. New York: WMAA, 1994.

Goldin, Nan. *The Ballad of Sexual Dependency*. New York: Aperture, 1996.

———. *Nan Goldin: I'll Be Your Mirror*. Exh. cat. New York: WMAA, 1996.

Goldsworthy, Andy. *Andy Goldsworthy: A Collaboration with Nature*. New York: Abrams, 1990.

———. *Andy Goldsworthy: Sheepfolds*. London: Michael Hue-Williams Fine Art, 1996.

———. *Wall at Storm King*. New York: Abrams, 2000.

Gott, Ted, ed. *Don't Leave Me This Way: Art in the Age of AIDS*. Melbourne: National Gallery of Australia, 1994.

Gumpert, Lynn. "Glamour Girls." *Art in America* 84:7 (July 1996): 62–65.

Gutierrez, Natalia. "Conversation with Doris Salcedo," *Art Nexus* (January/March 1996): 48–50.

[Halley] *Peter Halley*. Exh. cat. Madrid: Museo Nacional Renia Sofia, 1991.

[Halley] *Peter Halley: Oeuvres de 1982 a 1991*. Exh. cat. Bordeaux: Musée d'Art Contemporain de Bordeaux, 1991.

[Hamilton] *Ann Hamilton*. Exh. cat. London: Tate Gallery, 1994.

[Hamilton] *Ann Hamilton*. Exh. cat. San Diego: San Diego Museum of Contemporary Art, 1991.

[Hamilton] *Ann Hamilton: Tropos, 1993*. Exh. cat. Ed. L. Cooke and K. Kelly. New York: Dia Center for the Arts, 1995.

[Hamilton] *The Body and the Object: Ann Hamilton, 1984–1996*. Exh. cat. Columbus, Ohio: Wexner Center for the Arts, 1996.

Hamilton, Ann. *Ann Hamilton Present-Past, 1984–1997*. Miolan: Skira, 1998.

Harper, Paula. "Visceral Geometry," *Art in America* (September 1998): 106–111.

[Hatoum] *Mona Hatoum: The Entire World as a Foreign Land*. Exh. cat. London: The Tate Gallery, 2000.

Heartney, Eleanor. "Figuring Absence." [Lorna Simpson] *Art in America* (December 1985).

Helter Skelter: L.A. Art in the 1990s. Exh. cat. Los Angeles: Museum of Contemporary Art, 1992.

Heon, Laura Steward, ed. *Mona Hatoum Domestic Disturbance*. Exh. cat. North Adams, Mass.: Massachusetts Museum of Contemporary Art, 2001.

Hickey, Dave. *Air Guitar*. Los Angeles: Art Issues Press, 1997.

———. *In the Dance Hall of the Dead*. New York: Dia Foundation for the Arts, 1992.

———. *The Invisible Dragon: Four Essays on Beauty*. Los Angeles: Art Issues Press, 1993.

[Hill] *Gary Hill*. Exh. cat. Amsterdam: Stedelijk Museum, 1993.

[Hill] *Gary Hill*. Exh. cat. Seattle: Henry Art Gallery, University of Washington, 1994.

[Hill] *Gary Hill: Imagining the Brain Closer Than the Eyes*. Exh. cat. Ostfildern: Cantz and Museum für Gegenwartskunst, 1995. Texts by H. Belting, G. Boehm, the artist et al.

Hill, Gary. *Gary Hill: Selected Works: Catalogue Raisonée*. Köln: Du Mont, 2002.

Hirst, Damien. *I want to spend the rest of my life everywhere, with everyone, one to one, always, forever, now*. New York: Monacelli Press, 1997.

———, and Gordon Burn. *On the Way to Work*. London: Faber and Faber, 2001.

hooks, bell. *Art on My Mind: Visual Politics*. New York: The New Press, 1995.

Horn, Roni. *Earths Grow Thick*. Exh. cat. Columbus, Ohio: Wexner Center for the Arts, 1996. Text by b. hooks.

———. *Making Being Here Enough: Installations from 1980 to 1995*. Exh. cat. Hannover: Kestner-Gesellschaft, 1995.

Hsu, Wer-rwei. "Subject of Desire: The 1998 Taipei Biennial," *Art Asia Pacific* 22 (1999): 25–27.

Intelligence: New British Art 2000. Exh. cat. London: Tate Gallery, 2000.

Janus, Elizabeth. "As American as Apple Pie," *Parkett* 59 (2000): 139–151.

Jochen Gerz Res Publica: The Public Works 1968–1999. Exh. cat. Ostfildern: Hatje Cantz Verlag, 1999.

Johnson, Ken. "Being and Politics." [Adrian Piper] *Art in America* 78 (September 1990): 154–161.

———. "Material Matters." [Roni Horn] *Art in America* (February 1994): 71–78, 117.

Jones, Amelia. *Body Art: Performing the Subject*. University of Minnesota Press, 1998.

Kellein, Thomas. *Mark Tansey*. Exh. cat. Basel: Kunsthalle, 1990.

[Kelley] *Mike Kelley: Three Projects: Half a Man, From My Institution to Yours, Pay for Your Pleasure*. Chicago: University of Chicago Press, 1988.

Kentridge, William. *William Kentridge*. Exh. cat. Chicago: Museum of Contemporary Art, 2001.

Kirsch, Andrea, and Susan Fisher Sterling. *Carrie Mae Weems*. Exh. cat. Washington, D.C.: National Museum of Women in the Arts, 1993.

Kleeblatt, Norman L., "Persistence of Memory," *Art in America* (June 2000): 96–103.

———, ed. *Mirroring Evil: Nazi Imagery/Recent Art*. Exh. cat. New York: Jewish Museum, 2001.

———, ed. *Too Jewish: Challenging Traditional Identities*. Exh. cat. New York: The Jewish Museum, 1996.

Koether, Jutta. "The Nonchalance of Continuous Tense-ness," *Parkett* 58 (2000): 104–115.

[Koons] *Jeff Koons*. Exh. cat. San Francisco: San Francisco Museum of Modern Art, 1992.

Koons, Jeff. *The Jeff Koons Handbook*. New York: Rizzoli, 1992. Introduction by R. Rosenblum.

[Lemieux] *Annette Lemieux: The Appearance of Sound.* Sarasota, Fla.: The John and Mable Ringling Museum of Art, 1989.

Linker, Kate. "Went Looking for Africa: Carrie Mae Weems." *Artforum* 31 (February 1993): 79–82.

Lippard, Lucy. "Andres Serrano: The Spirit and the Letter." *Art in America* (April, 1996): 239–245.

———. "Jimmie Durham: Postmodernist 'Savage,' " *Art in America* (February 1993): 62–68.

———. "Out of the Safety Zone." *Art in America* 78:12 (December 1990): 130–139ff.

Loock, Ulrich. "The Dead House Ur," *Parkett* 63 (2001):130–149.

Mann, Sally. *At Twelve: Portraits of Young Women.* New York: Aperture, 1988.

———. *Immediate Family.* New York: Aperture, 1992.

———. *Second Sight: The Photographs of Sally Mann.* Boston: D. R. Godine, 1983. Introduction by J. Livingston.

———. *Still Time.* New York: Aperture, 1994.

Marshal, Kerry James. *Kerry James Marshall,* New York: Abrams, 2000.

Masheck, Joseph. "Painting in the Double Negative: Jonathan Lasker's Third Stream Abstraction." *Arts Magazine* 64 (January 1990): 38–43.

McShine, Kynaston. *The Museum as Muse: Artists Reflect.* Exh. cat. New York: MOMA, 1999.

Mifflin, Margaret. "An Interview with Karen Finlay." *High Performance* 11 (Spring/Summer 1988): 86–88.

Morgan Jessica, ed. *Portraits Rineke Dijkstra.* Exh. cat. Boston: Institute for Contemporary Art, Boston, 2001.

[Mori] *Mariko Mori.* Exh. cat. Chicago: Museum of Contemporary Art, London: Serpentine Gallery, 1998.

[Murakami] *Takashi Murakami: The Meaning of the Nonsense of Meaning.* Exh. cat. Annendale-on-Hudson: Center for Curatorial Studies, 1999.

Murakami, Takashi. *summon monsters? open the door? heal? or die?* Tokyo: Museum of Contemporary Art, 2001.

Murphy, Patrick T., ed. *Andres Serrano: Works 1983–1993.* Exh. cat. Philadelphia: Institute of Contemporary Art, 1994. Texts by R. Hobbs, W. Steiner, M. Tucker.

Nead, Lynda. *The Female Nude: Art, Obscenity and Sexuality.* New York: Routledge, 1992.

Neri, Louise, et al. *Roni Horn.* London: Phaidon, 2000.

Neshat, Shirin. *Rapture.* Exh. cat. Paris: Galerie Jerome de Noirmont, 1999.

———. *Shirin Neshat.* Milan: Charta, 2002.

Oguibe, Olu, and Okwui Enwezor, eds. *Reading the Contemporary: African Art from Theory to the Marketplace.* Cambridge, Mass.: MIT Press, 1999.

[Orozco] *Gabriel Orozco.* Exh. cat. Los Angeles: Museum of Contemporary Art, 2000.

Pagel, David. "Still Life: The Tableaux of Ann Hamilton." *Arts Magazine* 64 (May 1990): 56–61.

Paul, Frederic, ed. *John Currin: Works, 1989–1995.* Exh. cat.Limoges, France: FRAC Limosin, 1995.

Piper, Adrian. *Out of Order, Out of Sight.* 2 vols. Cambridge, Mass.: MIT Press, 1996.

———. *Pretend.* Exh. cat. New York: John Weber Gallery, 1990. Texts by M. A. Staniszewski and the artist.

———. *Reflections, 1967–87.* Exh. cat. New York: Alternative Museum, 1987.

Princenthal, Nancy, "A World in One Room," *Art in America* (May 2001): 150–153.

———; et al. *Doris Salcedo.* London: Phaidon, 2000.

Puvogel, Renate. "Negative Spatial Sculpture." *Parkett* 63 (2001): 116–129.

Ray, Charles. *Charles Ray.* Exh. cat. Los Angeles: Museum of Contemporary Art, 1998.

Rhoades, Jason. *Jason Rhoades: Volume, a Rhoades Referenz.* Nurnberg: Kunsthalle Nurnberg, 1998.

Rimanelli, David. "It's My Party, Jeff Koons: A Studio Visit." *Artforum* 35:10 (1997).

[Ringgold] *Faith Ringgold: Twenty Years of Painting, Sculpture, and Performance, 1963– 1983.* Exh. cat. New York: The Studio Museum in Harlem, 1984.

Ringgold, Faith. *We Flew Over the Bridge: The Memoirs of Faith Ringgold.* Boston: Little, Brown, 1995.

Rosenblum, Robert. *The Jeff Koons Handbook.* New York: Rizzoli, 1992.

Rothschild, Deborah. *Tony Oursler: Introjection: Mid-career Survey 1976–1999.* Exh. cat. Williamstown, Mass.: Williams College Museum of Art, 1999.

Rubinstein, Raphael. "Abstraction Out of Bounds," *Art in America*, Nov (1997): 104–115.

———. "Counter-Resolution." [Jonathan Lasker] *Art in America* 83 (April 1995): 84–89.

Rugoff, Ralph. "Surfing with Raymond: Nobody Rides for Free." [Raymond Pettibone] *Parkett* 47 (1996): 82–87.

Saltz, Jerry. "The Next Sex." *Art in America* 84:10 (October 1996): 82–91.

Sante, Luc. "The Nude and the Naked." [Sally Mann] *The New Republic* (May 1, 1995): 30–35.

Schwabsky, Barry. "Picturehood is Powerful," *Art in America* (December 1997): 80–85.

———. "Lisa Yuskavage," *Artforum* (April 2001): 141–2.

———, et al. *Jessica Stockholder.* London: Phaidon, 1995.

Seigel, Katy. "Nurture Boy," *Artforum* (Summer 1999): 132–35.

Sensation: Young British Artists from the Saatchi Collection. Exh. cat. London: Thames and Hudson, 1997.

Shaw, Gwendolyn Dubois. "Final Cut," *Parkett* 59 (2000): 129–132.

[Shonibare] *Yinka Shonibare.* Exh. cat. New York: The Studio Museum, Harlem, 2002.

Siegel, Katy. "The Art of Lisa Yuskavage: Blonde Ambition," *Artforum* (May 2000): 156–9.

Sikander, Shazia. *Shahzia Sikander.* Exh. cat. Chicago: Renaissance Society, University of Chicago, 1999.

Simon, Joan. "Ann Hamilton: Inscribing Place," *Art in America*, June 1999): 76–85, 130.

———. *Robert Gober.* Exh. cat. Paris: Éditions du Jeu de Paume and Réunion de Musées Nationaux, 1991.

Sims, Patterson. *Mark Tansey: Art and Source.* Exh. cat. Seattle: Seattle Art Museum, 1990.

[Smith] *Kiki Smith.* Exh. cat. Amsterdam: Institute of Contemporary Art, 1990.

[Smith] *Kiki Smith.* Exh. cat. Montreal: Montreal Museum of Fine Arts, 1996.

Smith, Kiki. "Impossible Liberties." *Art Journal* 54 (Summer 1995): 49–50.

Soutter, Lucy. "By Any Means Necessary: Document and Fiction in the Work of Carrie Mae Weems." *Art and Design* 11 (November/December 1996): 70–75.

Steils, Kristine, and Peter Selz, eds. *Theories and Documents of Contemporary Art: A Sourcebook of Artists' Writings.* Berkeley, Calif.: University of California Press, 1996.

Stemmrich, Gregor. "Liam Gillick – 'A debate about a debate,' " *Parkett* 61 (2001): 64–75.

Stiles, Kristine, and Peter Selz, eds. *Theories and Documents of Contemporary Art: A Sourcebook of Artists' Writings.* Berkeley: University of California Press, 1996.

Storr, Robert. "Anxious Spaces," *Art in America* 86 (November 1998): 101–5, 143–4.

———. "Setting Traps for the Mind and Heart." *Art in America* 84:10 (January 1996): 70–77ff.

———, et al. *Raymond Pettibon.* New York: Phaidon, 2001.

[Struth] *Thomas Struth 1977–2002.* Dallas: Dallas Museum of Art, 2002.

Sussman, Elizabeth. *Mike Kelley: Catholic Tastes.* Exh. cat. New York: WMAA, 1993.

Tallman, Susan. "Kiki Smith: Anatomy Lessons." *Art in America* 80 (April 1992): 146–153ff.

Temkin, Ann, and Hamza Walker, eds. *Raymond Pettibon: A Reader.* Philadelphia Museum of Art, 1998.

Viso, Olga. *Distemper: Dissonant Themes in the Art of the 1990s.* Washington, D.C.: Hirshhorn Museum and Smithsonian Institution, 1996.

Volk, Gregory. "Orozco: Circumstantial Evidence." *World Art* 3 (1995): 55–59.

Wakefield, Neville. "Rachel Whiteread: Separation Anxiety and the Art of Release." *Parkett* 42 (1994): 76–81.

———, et al. *Matthew Barney: Pace Car for the Hubris Pill.* Rotterdam: Museum Boymans-van-Beuningen, 1995.

Walker, Hamza. "Nigger Lover or Will There Be Any Black People in Utopia," *Parkett* 59 (2000): 152–161.

Walle, Mark van de. "Contract with a Coldhearted Muse," *Parkett* 50–51, (December 1999): 240–248.

Wallis, Brian. "Questioning Documentary." [Lorna Simpson] *Aperture* 11 (Fall 1988): 60–71.

———, ed. *Body and Soul/Andres Serrano.* New York: Takarajima Books, 1995. Texts by b. hooks, B. Ferguson, A. Arenas.

———, ed. Democracy: *A Project by Group Material.* New York: Dia Art Foundation, 1990.

[Whiteread] *Rachel Whiteread.* Exh. cat. Trans. D. Galloway. Basel and Philadelphia: Kunsthalle and the Institute of Contemporary Art, 1994.

Whiteread, Rachel. *House.* London: Phaidon Press, 1995.

———. *Rachel Whiteread: Shedding Life.* New York: Thames and Hudson, 1997.

Wilson, Fred. *Mining the Museum.* Exh. cat. Baltimore: Contemporary, 1994.

Winzen, Matthias. "Katharina Fritsch." *Journal of Contemporary Art* 7 (Summer 1994): 59–73.

Wojnarowicz, David. *Memories That Smell Like Gasoline.* San Francisco: Artspace Books, 1992.

Wollen, Peter. "Thought Experiments," *Parkett* 61, 2001: 76–91.

Wright, Beryl, and Saidiya Hartman. *Lorna Simpson: For the Sake of the Viewer.* Exh. cat. New York and Chicago: Universe Pub. and Museum of Contemporary Art, 1992.

Yang, Alice. "Letting Go: The Work of Rikrit Tiravanija," *Arts Asia Pacific* vol. 3 no. 2 (1996): 60–63.

Yasumasa, Morimura *The Sickness unto Beauty – Self Portrait as Actress.* Exh. cat. Yokohama: Museum of Art, 1996.

Young, James E. *At Memory's Edge: After-images of the Holocaust in Contemporary Art and Architecture.* New Haven: Yale University Press, 2000.

[Yuskavage] *Lisa Yuskavage.* Exh. cat. Boston: Institute for Contemporary Art, Boston, 2001.

Zelevansky, Lynn. *Sense and Sensibility: Women Artists and Minimalism in the Nineties.* New York: MOMA, 1994.

Glossary

Abstract art The term has two main applications: 1. Art that is non-representational, purely autonomous and makes no reference to an exterior world, e.g. Suprematism, Abstract Expressionism; 2. Art that 'abstracts' its images from the visible world, e.g. Cubism.

acrylic paint A synthetic medium developed c. 1960, quick-drying and retaining brightness. It permits effects of transparency and **impasto** but is generally used for work in flat color.

airbrush A device that uses compressed air to spray fine droplets of paint that produce a smooth, even surface. Most often associated with commercial art but also employed by Hard Edge abstract painters and others, airbrush effects do not show brushmarks or other evidence of the artist's touch.

aisle Part of a church or hall parallel to the main span and divided from it by an arcade of **piers** or columns or in rare cases by a screen wall.

aleatory The use of chance or random elements (from the Latin *aleatorius*, a dicer).

all-over composition Painting that treats the whole surface of the canvas in a uniform manner, in contrast to traditional ideas of pictorial structure and composition. The term is applied to the work of Jackson Pollock and the Color Field painters.

allegory A type of artistic symbolism in which abstract entities, such as Truth or Love, are portrayed figures or objects.

altarpiece A devotional painting or sculpture placed on, above or behind an altar, peculiar to Catholic Europe where it was introduced in the early thirteenth century when priests began to celebrate Mass with their backs to the congregation. Many depict multiple scenes and are on several panels (*see* **polyptych, triptych**), hinged so that they can be concealed or revealed as required.

appropriation The copying of images for purposes different from those for which they were originally intended, e.g. the reproduction of a famous work of art in a commercial advertisement. From the early 1980s appropriation has also been adopted as a means of challenging the premium put on artistic originality.

apse Vaulted semicircular termination of a building, usually a church.

arabesque Intricate surface decoration of plant forms, spirals, knots, etc. without human figures.

Arcadia A mountainous region of Greece that gave its name to a mythical land of rustic peace and plenty, frequently evoked in classical, Renaissance, and later art and literature.

armature Framework on which sculpture in clay is supported.

assemblage An artwork composed of three-dimensional objects, either natural or manufactured, usually junk.

atelier French term for a studio or workshop. In 19th-century France "ateliers libres" provided non-academic, studio-based teaching.

automatism An artistic approach in which the artist relinquishes conscious, rational control, enabling subconscious and impulses to direct the form of the work. Automatism is most closely associated with the Surrealists and Abstract Expressionists.

avant-garde Literally, the vanguard; more loosely, those in advance or ahead of their time – or thought to be so.

balustrade A series of balusters (short posts or **pillars**) supporting a rail.

barrel-vault *see* **vaulting**.

basilica An ancient Roman colonnaded hall for public use, later adopted as a building type for Early Christian churches. The Christian basilica had acquired its essential characteristics by the fourth century: oblong **plan**, longitudinal axis, timber roof either open or concealed by a flat ceiling, and a termination either rectangular or apsidal. It is usually divided into a **nave** and two or more **aisles**, the former higher and wider than the latter, lit by clerestory windows and with or without a gallery.

bas-relief, *see* **relief**.

Benday A process of shading by means of small uniform dots, invented by the New York printer Benjamin Day (1838–1916) for cheap photographic reproductions; also imitated by Pop artists, notably Lichtenstein.

biomorphic A type of abstract art in which – as in much of Arp's work – the forms relate to organic shapes (in contrast to geometric abstraction).

canon A list of works that sets the standard for artistic achievement (originally, the books of the Bible accepted by the Jewish or Christian faiths). In the late twentieth century the concept of the canon came increasingly to be challenged on the basis that it represents a relatively narrow spectrum of Western art and is defined as much by what it excludes as by the works that are included.

cantilever A projecting beam, canopy, etc., supported by a downward force behind a fulcrum. It is usually anchored at one end by the weight of the structure above. Being without external bracing, it appears to be self-supporting.

caricature A type of portraiture in which the subject's features are distorted for comic, often satirical, effect.

chiaroscuro In painting, the manipulation of light and shade to give the effect of modelling.

chromolithography A type of lithography in which color prints are produced by printing each color using a different stone or plate.

collage A composition made by gluing pieces of paper, cloth etc. on a canvas or other ground.

color The sensation produced on the eye by light rays. The seven main rays that make up the visible spectrum are subdivided into three primary colors or hues—red, yellow and blue—each of which has a complementary color composed of the other two. Color *values* are determined by the amount of light different hues reflect (yellow has a high, blue a low value), irrespective of the *saturation* or purity of the hue.

combination printing A photographic technique in which the final print is created by combining two or more negatives.

contrapposto A pose in which one part of the body is twisted in an opposite direction to another.

curtain wall The outer enclosing wall of a medieval castle or, especially with reference to twentieth-century architecture, a non-load-bearing wall applied to the exterior of a structure.

cyanotype An early photographic technique that uses iron salts to produce a deep blue image.

daguerreotype Photographic process invented by L.-J.-M. Daguerre and patented in 1839 for fixing positive images on silver-coated metal plates and widely used, especially for portraits, until the 1860s. Each daguerreotype is unique and the process was superseded by developments from the calotype process by which numerous **prints** may be made from a single negative.

diptych A picture or **relief** on two hinged panels.

Divisionism The technique of painting with small areas of unmixed pigments juxtaposed so that they combine optically when seen from a certain distance. Although employed empirically by several artists, notably Watteau, Delacroix and the Impressionists, it was first adopted as a stylistic term by Paul Signac and, independently, by the Italian Post-Impressionists in the 1880s.

drypoint Technique of **print**-making by which the copper plate is scratched with a sharply pointed tool, often used in combination with other methods of **engraving** and **etching**.

earthwork A large scale artwork for which the surface of the earth is the medium.

encaustic An ancient technique of painting with pigmented wax fused with the support by the application of hot irons.

engraving An incised design, also a **print** made from an engraved metal plate; *see also* **etching** and **woodcut**.

environment art The creation by the artist of a three-dimensional space in which the viewer is directly involved in the work of art.

etching A **print** from a metal plate on which the design has been etched or eaten away by acid.

façade The architecturally emphasized front or face of a building.

ferroconcrete A modern development of concrete reinforced by the insertion of steel mesh or rods. Also called *reinforced concrete.*

figurative Art depictions of the visible world, not necessarily including human or animal figures.

folk art A term loosely applied to decorative or functional art produced in rural communities, either by specialist craftspeople or in the home, in contrast to the urban, academic or elite milieu of much Western fine art.

foreshortening Application of **perspective** to a single form, e.g. a foot represented as pointing out of, not in line with, a pictorial plane.

formalist an approach to art analysis that emphasizes qualities of visual form, color, composition above other aspects of the work of art, such as narrative meaning, or biographical, social, and political context.

found images, materials or **objects** Those found in an everyday environment and **appropriated** for artworks, especially **assemblages**.

fresco Wall and ceiling painting on fresh (*fresco*) moist lime plaster with pigments ground in water so that they are absorbed into the plaster. Pigments added after the plaster has dried are said to be applied *a secco.*

frieze The middle division of an entablature, also loosely any sculptured or decorated horizontal band.

frottage French term meaning "rubbing" used for the technique of placing paper over a textured material and rubbing with a chalk or pencil until an image of the texture is formed. In the twentieth century Max Ernst exploited the suggestive power of images produced by frottage as a starting point for many works, and the technique was adopted by other Surrealists.

functionalism The theory that a building, piece of furniture or other object should be designed primarily to fulfil its material purpose and use and that its form should be determined exclusively by its function.

genre painting A picture of everyday life.

genres The various categories of painting, e.g. history, landscape, portrait, **still life** etc.

Gesamtkunstwerk Term used by the German composer Richard Wagner (1813–83) to mean a unified work of art in which music, drama, painting and poetry should be combined.

golden section or **mean** An irrational proportion, probably known to the ancient Greeks and much taken up by Renaissance art theorists. It may be defined as a line cut in such a way that the smaller section is to the greater as the greater is to the whole. This cannot be worked out mathematically, hence its fascination. Approximately it would be 5:8.

grisaille Painting in tones of gray, sometimes suggesting low **relief.**

Happening An unscripted performance, usually in an ordinary open space (e.g. street or parking lot) in which one or more artists, using materials without fine art associations, encourage the spontaneous participation of spectators who condition its development; sometimes recorded by photography.

history painting In European academic theory a **figurative** painting of a scene from classical mythology, the Bible, the lives of saints or an historical event.

icon A small, portable panel painting of Christ, the Virgin and Child or the saints, produced for Greek or Russian Orthodox Christians from the sixth century to the present day.

iconography The study of the meaning of visual images whether conveyed directly or by symbols, allegories, etc.

ideogram A written character or symbol that represents a thing itself, rather than a word or sound.

impasto Thickly applied **oil paint** .

installation A designed environment set up as an artwork, usually multi-media, in a gallery or outdoor location, and always **site-specific.**

kinetic sculpture A three-dimensional artwork that moves, usually by a mechanism.

land art *see* **earthwork.**

linoleum cut A **print** made from a piece of linoleum by the **woodcut** process.

lintel A horizontal beam or stone bridging an opening.

lithography A process of **print**-making from a drawing in oily crayon on stone. Invented 1798.

mandorla An upright almond shape, especially a glory of this form surrounding the figure of Christ in medieval art.

maquette A small preliminary model for a larger work of sculpture.

mobile A three-dimensional artwork, parts of which can be moved by a current of air, as distinct from **kinetic sculpture** with mechanically controlled movement.

monochrome A painting in tones of a single color, e.g. **grisaille**.

monotype A **print** made from an image painted (not **engraved**) on a metal or glass plate. As the plate must be partly repainted each time it is used, each of the usually rather few prints made from it is unique.

mosaic A pictorial composition made of small colored stones (*pebble mosaic*) or cubes of stone, glass, etc., set in plaster.

naturalism An approach to art that emphasizes likeness to observable nature. Like "realism" it is used in a non-specific sense of representational art that achieves lifelike effects. Neither naturalism nor realism should not be confused with the term Realism (with a capital R), which has specific connotations. Nineteenth-century French Realism, for example, combined an unidealized view of actual people and places with strong element of social commentary that can be found later in the work of American Social Realist painters of the Depression era of the 1930s.

nave The congregational area of a church, usually its western limb, flanked by **aisles.**

oculus A circular opening in a wall or dome.

odalisque A female slave or concubine in a harem. Odalisques frequently appear, both nude and clothed, as a subject of Western painting from Ingres to Matisse.

oil paint Pigment mixed with an oil (usually linseed) which hardens when dry into a transparent film. Oil paint is normally applied opaquely but it can be used as a colored translucent or semi-translucent film over opaque ground colors. It use was developed in the fifteenth century in Flanders and Italy and was soon taken up for easel paintings throughout Europe.

old master A non-specific term for any great European painter or painting of pre-nineteenth-century date.

papier collé A **collage** composed of pieces of variously colored paper glued to a ground.

pastoral A type of subject that evokes a more-or-less idealized vision of rural surroundings and pursuits (from the Latin pastor, or shepherd). (*See also* Arcadia.)

pentimento (pl. *pentimenti*) Italian term for part of a picture that has been painted over by the artist but which is visible beneath the tope layer of paint.

Performance art The use of the artist's own body and its coverings as a medium for artistic expression in an action or event.

peristyle A colonnade around the inside of a court or room, also the space surrounded by such a colonnade.

perspective Systems of representing objects in spatial recession, either *linear* or *aerial.*

photomontage A term coined in Berlin c. 1918 for a **collage** composed of fragments of photographs, newsprint, etc., but later used also for a composite picture made by printing from several negatives on a single sheet.

pier A solid masonry support, as distinct from a column.

pilotis French term for pillars on which a building is raised, leaving it open at ground level. Le Corbusier, in particular, made extensive use of pilotis.

plein air painting A painting executed out of doors rather than in a studio.

Pointillism, *see* **Divisionism.**

polyptych A painting or **relief**, usually an **altarpiece** on more than three panels, *see* **triptych.**

post-and-beam or **post-and-lintel,** *see* **trabeated.**

primitive Term formerly used to denote much of the art produced outside the spheres of Western or Asian civilization. It is also used of self-taught and so-called naive artists such as Henri Rousseau.

prints A generic term for all images made in multiple copies from woodblocks, metal plates, inked stone, photographic negatives, etc., *see* **woodcut, etching, engraving, lithograph, silk-screen.**

Process art Artworks whose subject-matter is the process of their creation which the spectator is invited to reconstruct. Many were executed in the 1960s and 1970s.

reinforced concrete, *see* **ferroconcrete.**

relief Sculpture with forms projecting from a ground, called *high relief* when they are at least half in the round, otherwise *low relief* or *bas-relief.*

repoussé relief Decoration on metal (mainly gold, silver and copper) produced by hammering from the underside.

rustication Massive blocks of masonry with roughened surfaces and sunk joints, often simulated in plaster.

Salon French word for a formal room such as the Salon d'Apollon in the royal palace of the Louvre (Paris). Exhibitions of work by the Royal Academy of painters and sculptors were held there from the late seventeenth century and the word 'salon' thus acquired a special meaning. It was used in this sense for official exhibitions in other rooms in the Louvre and from the mid-nineteenth century to cover exhibitions held elsewhere in Paris.

screenprint, *see* **silk-screen**

scumble An upper layer of opaque or semi-opaque pigment used in **oil painting**, applied irregularly so that areas of the color underneath remain visible, giving a broken or veiled effect, softening hard lines.

semiotics The study of signs, in particular the analysis of language as a system of signs proposed by the Swiss pioneer of modern linguistics Ferdinand de Saussaure. Semiotic interpretation has been extended to other cultural arenas such as mythology or clothing.

sfumato A soft, misty effect attained in **oil painting** mainly by the use of glazes to create delicate transitions of color and tone.

shoji A type of partition in Japanese domestic architecture made by covering a wooden framework with paper.

silk-screen A process of making prints by squeezing paint through a piece of silk, parts of which have been masked, exploited by commercial artists since the 1930s. One impression can be made to differ from another by varying the density of paint. Also called *serigraphy*.

silverpoint A small silver rod with a pointed end for drawing on an abrasive surface (specially prepared paper or parchment or a primed panel), first used in medieval Italy, elsewhere from the fifteenth century, but generally superseded by the graphite pencil in the seventeenth century.

site-specific A term used for an **installation**, sculpture or other artwork designed for, and in reference to, a specific location.

socle A base or pedestal.

still life A representation of such inanimate objects as flowers, fruit, dead animals or household articles.

stucco Various types of plaster used as a protective and decorative covering for walls. A mixture including lime and powdered marble has been extensively used for **relief** decorations on ceilings and interior walls since the sixteenth century in Europe.

tenebrism Painting with a dominant dark tonality.

tessellation A pattern composed like a mosaic out of small shapes (tesserae) that fit closely together.

trabeated Construction based mainly on upright members supporting horizontals, as in an ancient Greek temple. Also called *post-and-lintel*. To be distinguished from arcuated.

transept The tranverse arms of a cross-shaped church.

transverse arch An arch separating one **bay** of a **vault** from another in Romanesque and Gothic architecture.

triptych A painting on three panels.

trompe-l'oeil An illustionistic painting intended to 'deceive the eye'.

typography The art of letter design and printing.

Value, *see* **color**.

vanitas An allegorical **still life** often incorporating a skull as a reminder of mortal transience.

vaulting A masonry roof or ceiling constructed on the principle of the arch. The simplest form is a *tunnel* or *barrel vault* of continuous semicircular or pointed section unbroken by *cross-vaults*. The intersection of two tunnel vaults of identical shape produces a *groin vault*. A *rib vault* has a framework of arched diagonal ribs between which the cells are filled with lighter stone. It is called *quadripartite* if each bay is divided into four quarters or cells, *sexpartite* if divided transversely into two parts so that each bay has six compartments. A *dome* is a vault of even curvature on a circular plan and of segmental, semicircular, pointed or bulbous section. The simplest form is constructed by corbelling. If a dome is erected on a square base pendentives or squinches must be interpolated at the corners to mediate between square and circle.

woodcut A **print** made from a block of wood from the surface of which all areas not intended to carry ink have been cut away. The block is cut from a smoothed plank of fairly soft wood with the grain running parallel to the surface. A print made from a block of very hard wood cut across the grain and worked with a graving tool is called a *wood engraving*.

ziggurat A rectangular mound built in stepped-back stages and crowned by a temple.

Index

Figure numbers are given in **bold**.

Credits

The author and publisher wish to thank the libraries, museums, galleries, and private collectors named in the picture captions for permitting the reproduction of works of art in their collections and for supplying the necessary photographs. Photographs from other sources are gratefully acknowledged below. Numbers listed before the sources refer to figure numbers.

Key

MOMA = The Museum of Modern Art, New York
NY = New York

Cover

Delaunay: Digital image © 2003 MOMA/Scala, Florence
Mondrian: © 2003 Mondrian/Holtzman Trust c/o HCR International, Digital image © 2003 MOMA/Scala, Florence

Chapter 1: 1.1 © Photo Josse, Paris; 1.2. Gift of Cornelius Vanderbilt, 1887, © Photo Josse, Paris; 1.4. © A.C.L. Brussels; 1.5. Alinari, Rome; 1.9. Fototeca Unione, Rome; 1.10. © Museum of Fine Arts, Boston; 1.12. Yale University Art Gallery, Gift of Louis M. Rabinowitz; 1.13. The Walters Art Museum, Baltimore, John Webb, London; 1.16. © BPK, Berlin, Formerly Nationalgalerie, Berlin; 1.18. © The Cleveland Museum of Art, 2003. Bequest of John L. Severence, 1942; 1.19. © Photo RMN, Paris; 1.21. Wildenstein Archives

Chapter 2: 2.6. Gift of Warner Communications, Inc., Digital image © 2003 The Museum of Modern Art/Scala, Florence; 2.7. Cliché Bibliotheque Nationale de France, Paris; 2.10. National Portrait Gallery, Smithsonian Institution, Washington, D.C.; 2.15. Lichtbildwerkstätte Alpenland, Vienna; 2.20. © Photo Josse, Paris; 2.21. © Photo RMN, Paris; 2.24. Gift of Dexter M. Ferry, Jr., The Detroit Institute of Arts; 2.27. Photographie Giraudon, Paris; 2.28. © Photo RMN, Paris; 2.29. The Nelson-Atkins Museum of Art, Kansas City, Missouri. Purchase: The Kenneth A, and Helen F. Spencer Foundation Acquisition Fund. Photo by Robert Newcombe; 2.31. Hubert Josse, Paris; 2.34. A. J. Wyatt, Philadelphia; 2.35. © Photo RMN, Paris; 2.37. Photograph © 2003 Board of Trustees, National Gallery of Art, Washington; 2.38. © Photo RMN; 2.39. Gift of Mrs. Joseph Harrison, Jr., © Smithsonian Institution American Art Museum, Washington DC/ Art Resource, NY;

2.40. Photograph © 2003 Board of Trustees, National Gallery of Art, Washington; 2.41. Gift of Mr. and Mrs. Richard Mellon Scaife in honor of Paul Mellon, Photograph © 2003 Board of Trustees, National Gallery of Art, Washington; 2.42. Gift of Mrs. Russell Sage; 2.43. © The Cleveland Museum of Art, 2003. Mr and Mrs William H. Marlatt Fund, 1965; 2.44. Gift of Norbert Heerman and Arthur Helbig; 2.45. Gift of William T. Evans, © Smithsonian Institution American Art Museum, Washington DC/ Art Resource, NY; 2.46. Digital image © 2003 The Museum of Modern Art/Scala, Florence; 2.47. Gift of Mrs. Hermine M. Turner, digital image © 2003 The Museum of Modern Art/Scala Florence; 2.48. Gift of Mrs. Frank B. Porter, 1922; 2.52. Hampton University Museum, Hampton, Virginia

Chapter 3: 3.4. Promised gift of David Rockefeller, Digital image © 2003 The Museum of Modern Art/Scala, Florence, © ADAGP, Paris and DACS, London 2003; 3.5. Gift of the W. Averell Harriman Foundation in memory of Marie N. Harriman. Oliver Baker, NY. Photograph © 2003 Board of Trustees, National Gallery of Art, Washington; 3.6. Thames & Hudson, Ltd., London; 3.9. Photograph © 2003 Board of Trustees, National Gallery of Art, Washington; 3.11. A. J. Wyatt, Philadelphia, © DACS 2003; 3.12 Courtesy of the Fogg Art Museum, Harvard University Art Museums, Bequest of Grenville L.Winthrop. Photo by Rick Stafford, © President and Fellows of Harvard College; 3.13. © The Cleveland Museum of Art, 2003. Gift of Mr. and Mrs. J. H. Wade, 1916; 3.14. Digital image © 2003 The Museum of Modern Art/Scala, Florence; 3.16. Gift of Mrs. Simon Guggenheim, Digital image © 2003 The Museum of Modern Art/Scala, Florence; 3.17 National Gallery of Scotland; 3.18. © Museum of Fine Arts, Boston; 3.19. © Museum of Fine Arts, Boston; 3.20. Yale University Art Gallery, New Haven, Bequest of Stephen C. Clark; 3.21 Courtesy of the Fogg Art Museum, Harvard University Art Museums, Association Fund. Photo by Katya Kallsen, © President and Fellows of Harvard College; 3.22. Digital image © 2003 The Museum of Modern Art/Scala, Florence; 3.24. © ADAGP, Paris and DACS, London 2003; 3.25 Digital image © 2003 The Museum of Modern Art/Scala, Florence; 3.26. © ADAGP, Paris and DACS, London 2003; 3.27. © ADAGP, Paris and DACS, London 2003; 3.28. Photograph © reproduced with kind permission of The Barnes Foundation. All rights reserved

Chapter 4: 4.1. © Angelo Hornak, London; 4.2. Jean Roubier, Paris; 4.4. Archives Photographiques, Paris; 4.5. French Government Tourist Office, NY; 4.6. A.F. Kersting, London; 4.7. © Wayne Andrews/Esto; 4.9. T.& R. Annan, Ltd., Glasgow; 4.12. Ralph Lieberman/Laurence King Publishing Archives; 4.13. Bettmann Archives, Inc., NY; 4.14. © Artifice, Inc./GreatBuildings.com; 4.15. New York Historical Society

Chapter 5: 5.1. Derrick E. Witty, Sunbury-on-Thames; 5.2. Photograph © 2003 Board of Trustees, National Gallery of Art, Washington; 5.5. Foto Studio Minders, Ghent; 5.6. Galerie Welz, Salzburg; 5.7. John Tsantes, Freer Gallery of Art, Smithsonian Institution, Washington, DC: Gift of Charles Lang Freer, F1904.61.; 5.9. © Inigo Bujedo Aguirre, London; 5.10. MAS, Barcelona; 5.11. Courtesy of The Museum of Modern Art, NY; © DACS 2003; 5.12. Dr. Franz Stoedtner, Düsseldorf; © DACS 2003; 5.13. Felipe Ferré, Paris; 5.14. Foto Marburg, Marburg/Lahn; 5.15. Foto Marburg, Marburg/Lahn; 5.16. Otto Vaering, Oslo , © Munch Museum/Munch-Ellingsen Group, BONO, Oslo, DACS, London 2003; 5.17. J. Lathion, Nasjonalgalleriet; 5.18. © Munch Museum/Munch-Ellingsen Group, BONO, Oslo, DACS, London 2003; 5.19. Eric Pollitzer, NY, © Munch Museum/Munch-Ellingsen Group, BONO, Oslo, DACS, London 2003; 5.20. © Munch Museum/Munch-Ellingsen Group, BONO, Oslo, DACS, London 2003; 5.22. © The Estate of James Ensor/DACS 2003; 5.23. © The Estate of James Ensor /DACS 2003

Chapter 6: 6.1. Hirschhorn Museum and Sculpture Garden, Smithsonian Institution, Gift of Joseph H. Hirschhorn, 1966; 6.3. © Photo RMN, Paris; 6.4. Hirschhorn Museum and Sculpture Garden, Smithsonian Institution, Gift of Joseph H. Hirschhorn, 1966; 6.5. John R. Van Derlip Fund; 6.6. Foto Marburg, Marburg/Lahn; 6.8. Hirschhorn Museum and Sculpture Garden, Smithsonian Institution, Gift of Joseph H. Hirschhorn, 1966; 6.9. Hirschhorn Museum and Sculpture Garden, Smithsonian Institution, Gift of Joseph H. Hirschhorn, 1966; 6.10. Gift of Georgia O'Keeffe. Digital image © 2003 The Museum of Modern Art/Scala, Florence; 6.12. Bruno Jarret, © ADAGP, Paris and DACS, London 2003; 6.13. Digital image © 2003 The Museum of Modern Art/Scala, Florence, © ADAGP, Paris and DACS, London 2003; 6.15. Digital image © 2003 MOMA/Scala, Florence

Jr., NY, © DACS 2003; 11.27. © DACS 2003; 11.28. Digital image © 2003 The Museum of Modern Art/Scala, Florence, © DACS 2003; 11.29. © DACS 2003; 11.30. Costakis/Art Co.; 11.31. Irving Blomstrann, New Britain, Connecticut; 11.32. Dallas Museum of Art, Foundation for the Arts Collection, Gift of the James H. and Lillian Clark Foundation, © 2003 Mondrian/Holtzman Trust c/o HCR International; 11.33. Digital image © 2003 The Museum of Modern Art/Scala, Florence, © 2003 Mondrian/Holtzman Trust c/o HCR International; 11.34. © 2003 Mondrian/Holtzman Trust c/o HCR International; 11.35. Studio Yves Hervochon, Paris, © DACS 2003; 11.36. © DACS 2003; 11.37. © DACS 2003; 11.38. Gift of Silvia Pizitz, Digital image © 2003 The Museum of Modern Art/Scala, Florence, © DACS 2003

Chapter 12: 12.1. © Artifice, Inc./GreatBuildings.com; 12.2. © ARS, NY and DACS, London 2003; 12.3. Hedrich-Blessing, Chicago, © ARS, NY and DACS, London 2003; 12.5. Buffalo and Erie County Historical Society; 12.6. Chicago Architectural Photographing Company; 12.8. © Wayne Andrews/Esto;12.9. © Paul M.R. Maeyaert, © DACS 2003; 12.10. © DACS 2003; 12.11. Benevolo; 12.15. German Information Center, NY; 12.16. Emil Gmelin, Dornach; 12.17. Jan Derwig, Amsterdam; 12.18. Doeser Fotos, Lauren; 12.19. Foto van Ojen, The Hague; 12.20. Fototechnischer Dienst, Rotterdam; 12.21. Janne Linders, Digital image © 2003 The Museum of Modern Art/Scala, Florence, © DACS 2003; 12.22. Gift of Philip Johnson, © DACS 2003; 12.26. © Tony Garnier © Yerbury, F. R./Architectural Association Photo Library

Chapter 13: 13.1. Martin F.J. Coppens, Eindhoven, © ADAGP, Paris and DACS, London 2003; 13.2. © ADAGP, Paris and DACS, London 2003; 13.3. © ADAGP, Paris and DACS, London 2003; 13.4. © ADAGP, Paris and DACS, London 2003; 13.5. © DACS 2003; 13.6. © DACS 2003; 13.7. Kate Keller; Digital image © 2003 The Museum of Modern Art/Scala, Florence, © DACS 2003 13.8. © DACS 2003; 13.9. © ADAGP, Paris and DACS, London 2003; 13.11. Digital image © 2003 The Museum of Modern Art/Scala, Florence; 13.12. Gift of Jean Arp © 1997 VG Bild-Kunst, Bonn/Artists Rights Society (ARS), NY, © DACS 2003; 13.13. Etienne Bertrand Weill, Paris, © DACS 2003; 13.14. © DACS 2003; 13.15. Geoffrey Clements, NY, Digital image © 2003 The Museum of Modern Art/Scala, Florence, © Succession Marcel Duchamp/ADAGP, Paris and DACS, London 2003; 13.16. © Succession Marcel Duchamp/ADAGP, Paris and DACS, London 2003; 13.17. Courtesy Cordier & Ekstrom Inc., NY, Digital image © 2003 The Museum of Modern Art/Scala, Florence, © Succession Marcel Duchamp/ADAGP, Paris and DACS, London 2003; 13.18. Digital image © 2003 The Museum of Modern Art/Scala, Florence, © Succession Marcel Duchamp/ADAGP, Paris and DACS, London 2003; 13.19. Yale University Art Gallery, New Haven, Bequest of Katherine S. Dreier, © Succession Marcel Duchamp/ADAGP, Paris and DACS, London 2003; 13.20. © Succession Marcel Duchamp/ADAGP, Paris and DACS, London 2003; 13.21. © Succession Marcel Duchamp/ADAGP, Paris and DACS, London 2003; 13.22. © ADAGP, Paris and DACS, London 2003; 13.23. Joseph H. Hirschhorn Purchase Fund and Museum Purchase, 1987, Lee Stalsworth, © Man Ray Trust/ADAGP, Paris and DACS, London 2003; 13.24. Courtesy Cordier & Ekstrom Inc., NY, © Man Ray Trust/ADAGP, Paris and DACS,

London 2003; 13.25. Digital image © 2003 The Museum of Modern Art/Scala, Florence, © Man Ray Trust/ADAGP, Paris and DACS, London 2003; 13.26. © ADAGP, Paris and DACS, London 2003; 13.27. Nationalgalerie Staatliche Museen, Presussischer Kulturbesitz, Berlin, © DACS 2003; 13.28. The Metropolitan Museum of Art, Purchase: The Horace W. Goldsmith Foundation Gift, 1987. Photograph © 1988 The Metropolitan Museum of Art; © DACS 2003; 13.29. Digital image © 2003 The Museum of Modern Art/Scala, Florence, © DACS 2003; 13.30. © DACS 2003; 13.31. Landesgalerie, Hanover, © DACS 2003 13.32. © ADAGP, Paris and DACS, London 2003; 13.33. © ADAGP, Paris and DACS, London 2003; 13.34. © DACS 2003; 13.35. Digital image © 2003 The Museum of Modern Art/Scala, Florence, © DACS 2003; 13.36. Rheinisches Bildarchiv, Cologne, © DACS 2003; 13.37. Gift of Philip Johnson, Digital image © 2003 The Museum of Modern Art/Scala, Florence, © DACS 2003; 13.38. Gift of the photographer, © Die Photographische Sammlung/SK Stiftung Kultur-August Sander Archiv, Koln/DACS 2003, Digital image © 2003 The Museum of Modern Art/Scala, Florence; 13.39. © Albert Renger-Patzch Archiv/Ann u. Jurgen Wilde, Koln/DACS 2003; 13.40. © DACS 2003; 13.41. © DACS 2003, Courtesy of the Busch-Reisinger Museum, Harvard University Art Museums. Photo by Rick Stafford, © President and Fellows of Harvard College; 13.42. Digital image © 2003 The Museum of Modern Art/Scala, Florence, © DACS 2003; 13.43. Gift of Mrs. Max Beckmann, 13.43 Photograph © 2003 Board of Trustees, National Gallery of Art, Washington, © DACS 2003; 13.44. Dr. Marie-Andreas von Lüttichau

Chapter 14: 14.2. Photograph © 2003 Board of Trustees, National Gallery of Art, Washington; 14.4. S. Sunami, NY, © ADAGP, Paris and DACS, London 2003; 14.5. Edward Cornachio, © ADAGP, Paris and DACS, London 2003; 14.6. © ADAGP, Paris and DACS, London 2003; 14.7. © ADAGP, Paris and DACS, London 2003; 14.8. © ADAGP, Paris and DACS, London 2003; 14.9. Digital image © 2003 The Museum of Modern Art/Scala, Florence, © Succession H Matisse/DACS 2003; 14.10. Photograph © reproduced with kind permission of The Barnes Foundation. All rights reserved, © Succession H Matisse/DACS 2003; 14.11. © Succession H Matisse/DACS 2003, ©Photo CNAC/MNAM Dist. RMN; 14.12. © Succession H Matisse/DACS 2003; 14.13. Baltimore Museum of Art, © Succession H Matisse/DACS 2003; 14.14. Photograph © reproduced with kind permission of The Barnes Foundation. All rights reserved, © Succession H Matisse/DACS 2003; 14.15. Dallas Museum of Art, Foundation for the Arts Collection, Gift of the Albert and Mary Lasker Foundation, © Succession H Matisse/DACS 2003; 14.16. La Chapelle du Rosaire, Centre de Reeducation Fonctionelle, © Succession H Matisse/DACS 2003; 14.17. Hubert Josse, Paris, © ADAGP, Paris and DACS, London 2003; 14.18. © Succession Picasso/DACS 2003; 14.19. Digital image © 2003 The Museum of Modern Art/Scala, Florence, © Succession Picasso/DACS 2003; 14.20. Digital image © 2003 The Museum of Modern Art/Scala, Florence, © Succession Picasso/DACS 2003; 14.21. Gift of Mr. and Mrs. Allan D. Emil. Photograph, Digital image © 2003 The Museum of Modern Art/Scala, Florence, © Succession Picasso/DACS 2003; 14.22. © Succession Picasso/DACS 2003; 14.23. © Succession Picasso/DACS 2003; 14.24. © The Cleveland Museum of Art, 2003. Leonard C. Hanna, Jr. 1975, Paul Rosenberg

& Co., NY; 14.25. Digital image © 2003 The Museum of Modern Art/Scala, Florence, © Succession Picasso/DACS 2003 © Succession Picasso/DACS 2003; 14.26. © Succession Picasso/DACS 2003; 14.27. Digital image © 2003 The Museum of Modern Art/Scala, Florence, © Succession Picasso/DACS 2003; 14.28. Hans Hinz, Basel, © ADAGP, Paris and DACS, London 2003; 14.29. Digital image © 2003 The Museum of Modern Art/Scala, Florence, © ADAGP, Paris and DACS, London 2003; 14.30. Eric Pollitzer, NY, © ADAGP, Paris and DACS, London 2003; 14.31. Digital image © 2003 The Museum of Modern Art/Scala, Florence, © ADAGP, Paris and DACS, London 2003; 14.32. © ADAGP, Paris and DACS, London 2003; 14.33. © ADAGP, Paris and DACS, London 2003; 14.34. Digital image © 2003 The Museum of Modern Art/Scala, Florence, © FLC/ADAGP, Paris and DACS, London 2003

Chapter 15: 15.1. © ADAGP, Paris and DACS, London 2003; 15.2. Digital image © 2003 The Museum of Modern Art/Scala, Florence, © DACS 2003; 15.3. Etienne Bertrand Weill, Paris, © DACS 2003; 15.4. Lynn Rosenthal, © DACS 2003; 15.5. Digital image © 2003 The Museum of Modern Art/Scala, Florence, © ADAGP, Paris and DACS, London 2003; 15.7. Wadsworth Atheneum, Hartford. The Ella Gallup Sumner and Mary Catlin Sumner Collection Fund, © ADAGP, Paris and DACS, London 2003; 15.8. © ADAGP, Paris and DACS, London 2003; 15.9. Gift of D. and J. de Menil, Digital image © 2003 The Museum of Modern Art/Scala, Florence, © ADAGP, Paris and DACS, London 2003; 15.10. Colten Photos, NY, © Successio Miro, DACS, 2003; 15.11. © Successio Miro, DACS, 2003; 15.12. © Successio Miro, DACS, 2003; 15.13. A. J. Wyatt, Philadelphia, Digital image © 2003 The Museum of Modern Art/Scala, Florence, © Successio Miro, DACS, 2003; 15.14. Gift of Mr. and Mrs. Pierre Matisse, Digital image © 2003 The Museum of Modern Art/Scala, Florence, © Successio Miro, DACS, 2003; 15.15. © Successio Miro, DACS, 2003; 15.16. Bertrand Prevost © Centre G. Pompidou, Paris, Gift of the Menil Foundation © 1997 ADAGP, Paris/Artists Rights Society (ARS), NY, © Successio Miro, DACS, 2003; 15.17. Gift of Joseph H. Hirschhorn 1972, The Hirschhorn Museum and Sculpture Garden, Smithsonian Institution, © Successio Miro, DACS, 2003; 15.18. Digital image © 2003 The Museum of Modern Art/Scala, Florence, © ADAGP, Paris and DACS, London 2003; 15.19. Richard Nickel, © ADAGP, Paris and DACS, London 2003; 15.20. Geoffrey Clements, NY, Digital image © 2003 The Museum of Modern Art/Scala, Florence, © ARS, NY and DACS, London 2003; 15.21. Digital image © 2003 The Museum of Modern Art/Scala, Florence, © ARS, NY and DACS, London 2003; 15.23. © ADAGP, Paris and DACS, London 2003; 15.24. Digital image © 2003 The Museum of Modern Art/Scala, Florence, © ADAGP, Paris and DACS, London 2003; 15.25. Eric Pollitzer, NY, © Salvador Dali, Gala-Salvador Dali Foundation, DACS, London 2003; 15.26. Digital image © 2003 The Museum of Modern Art/Scala, Florence, © Salvador Dali, Gala-Salvador Dali Foundation, DACS, London 2003; 15.27. © Salvador Dali, Gala-Salvador Dali Foundation, DACS, London 2003; 15.28. Charles P. Mill, Philadelphia . National Gallery of Canada, Ottowa, © Salvador Dali, Gala-Salvador Dali Foundation, DACS, London 2003; 15.29. Los Angeles County Museum of Art, Purchased with funds provided by the Mr and Mrs. William Preston Harrison Collection. Photograph © 2003 Museum Associates/LACMA, © ADAGP, Paris and

DACS, London 2003; 15.30. Digital image © 2003 The Museum of Modern Art/Scala, Florence, © ADAGP, Paris and DACS, London 2003; 15.31. Gift of the Collectors Committee, Photograph © 2003 Board of Trustees, National Gallery of Art, Washington, © ADAGP, Paris and DACS, London 2003; 15.32. Gift of Kay Sage Tanguy, Digital image © 2003 The Museum of Modern Art/Scala, Florence, © ADAGP, Paris and DACS, London 2003; 15.33. The Joseph Winterbotham Collection, © ADAGP, Paris and DACS, London 2003; 15.34. © Foundation P Delvaux - St Idesbald, Belgium/DACS, London 2003; 15.35. George Eastman House, NY, © ADAGP, Paris and DACS, London 2003; 15.36. Digital image © 2003 The Museum of Modern Art/Scala, Florence, © DACS 2003; 15.37. John Cavaliero; © ADAGP, Paris and DACS, London 2003; 15.38. © ARS, NY and DACS, London 2003; 15.39. Art Resource, NY, © Succession Picasso/DACS 2003; 15.40. © Photo RMN, Paris, © Succession Picasso/DACS 2003; 15.41. Digital image © 2003 The Museum of Modern Art/Scala, Florence, © Succession Picasso/DACS 2003; 15.42. Digital image © 2003 The Museum of Modern Art/Scala, Florence, © Succession Picasso/DACS 2003; 15.43. Galerie Louise Leiris, Paris, © Succession Picasso/DACS 2003; 15.44. Digital image © 2003 The Museum of Modern Art/Scala, Florence, © Succession Picasso/DACS 2003; 15.45. Gift of Mrs. Simon Guggenheim, Digital image © 2003 The Museum of Modern Art/Scala, Florence, © Succession Picasso/DACS 2003; 15.46. © Succession Picasso/DACS 2003; 15.47. © Photo RMN, Paris, © Succession Picasso/DACS 2003; 15.48. Digital image © 2003 The Museum of Modern Art/Scala, Florence, © Succession Picasso/DACS 2003; 15.49. © Succession Picasso/DACS 2003; 15.50. © Succession Picasso/DACS 2003; 15.51. © Succession Picasso/DACS 2003; 15.52. © Succession Picasso/DACS 2003; 15.53. © ADAGP, Paris and DACS, London 2003; 15.54. © ADAGP, Paris and DACS, London 2003; 15.55. Photograph © 2003 Board of Trustees, National Gallery of Art, Washington, © ADAGP, Paris and DACS, London 2003; 15.56. Digital image © 2003 The Museum of Modern Art/Scala, Florence, © ADAGP, Paris and DACS, London 2003; 15.57. Digital image © 2003 The Museum of Modern Art/Scala, Florence, © ADAGP, Paris and DACS, London 2003; 15.58 Yale University Art Gallery, New Haven, © ADAGP, Paris and DACS, London 2003; 15.59. Abbott-Levy Collection. Partial Gift of Shirley C. Burden, Digital image © 2003 The Museum of Modern Art/Scala, Florence; 15.60. Gift of James Thrall Soby, Digital image © 2003 The Museum of Modern Art/Scala, Florence, © Man Ray Trust/ADAGP, Paris and DACS, London 2003; 15.61. New York Public Library, © Man Ray Trust/ADAGP, Paris and DACS, London 2003 15.62. © André Kertész; 15.63. Courtesy of Susan Harder Gallery, NY; © 1997, MOMA, NY, © André Kertész; 15.65. Digital image © 2003 The Museum of Modern Art/Scala, Florence, © Gilberte Brassaï; 15.66. Julien Levy Collection, Gift of Jean Levy and the Estate of Julien Levy, © Manuel Alvarez Bravo; 15.68. © Henri-Cartier Bresson/Magnum Photos; 15.69. © Mrs. Noya Brandt, London

Chapter 16: 16.1. Gift of Herbert Bayer, Digital image © 2003 MOMA/Scala, Florence; 16.2. Foto Marburg; 16.6. Marvin Trachtenberg; 16.11. Wayne Andrews, Grosse Pointe, Michigan; 16.12. Marvin Trachtenberg; 16.17. S.C. Johnson & Johnson, Racine, Wisconsin, © ARS, NY and DACS, London 2003; 16.18. © Artifice, Inc./GreatBuildings.com

Chapter 17: 17.1. Gift of Sibyl Moholy-Nagy, © DACS 2003, Courtesy of the Busch-Reisinger Museum, Harvard University Art Museums. Photographic Services, © President and Fellows of Harvard College'; 17.2. Gift of George and Ruth Banford, © DACS 2003; 17.3. Gift of Jean and Julien Levy, © DACS 2003; 17.4. Fotocollectie, Leiden, © DACS 2003; 17.5. © Nina Williams; 17.6. L.W. Schmidt, Rotterdam; 17.7. © ADAGP, Paris and DACS, London 2003; 17.8. © DACS 2003; 17.9. © DACS 2003; 17.10. Gift of Mr. and Mrs. Douglas Auchincloss, Digital image © 2003 MOMA/Scala, Florence; 17.12. Elke Walford, © DACS 2003; 17.13. Digital image © 2003 MOMA/Scala, Florence, © DACS 2003; 17.14. SRGM, NY, © DACS 2003; 17.15. © DACS 2003; 17.16. © DACS 2003; 17.17. © ADAGP, Paris and DACS, London 2003; 17.18. SRGM, NY, © ADAGP, Paris and DACS, London 2003; 17.19. © ADAGP, Paris and DACS, London 2003 17.20. SRGM, NY, © ADAGP, Paris and DACS, London 2003; 17.21. © 2003 Mondrian/Holtzman Trust c/o HCR International; 17.22. © 2003 Mondrian/Holtzman Trust c/o HCR International; 17.23. © 2003 Mondrian/Holtzman Trust c/o HCR International; 17.24. © 2003 Mondrian/Holtzman Trust c/o HCR International; 17.25. Gift of the Advisory Committee, Digital image © 2003 MOMA/Scala, Florence, © 2003 Mondrian/Holtzman Trust c/o HCR International; 17.26. © 2003 Mondrian/Holtzman Trust c/o HCR International, Digital image © 2003 MOMA/Scala, Florence; 17.27. Gift of the artist, Solomon R. Guggenheim Museum, NY; 17.28. © ARS, NY and DACS, London 2003; 17.29. Digital image © 2003 MOMA/Scala, Florence, © ARS, NY and DACS, London 2003; 17.31.© Estate of Stanley Spencer 2003. All rights reserved, DACS; 17.32. Gift of H. S. Ede and the artist (by exchange), © Angela Verren-Taunt 2003. All rights reserved, DACS; 17.33. © Henry Moore Foundation; 17.34. © Henry Moore Foundation; 17.35. © Hepworth Estate © Alan Bowness; 17.36. © Hepworth Estate © Alan Bowness

Chapter 18: 18.1. Lawrence H.Bloedel Bequest; 18.2. Gift of Georgia O'Keeffe, 1947. Wadsworth Atheneum, Hartford. The Ella Gallup Sumner and Mary Catlin Sumner Collection Fund; 18.4. Los Angeles County Museum of Art, Los Angeles County Fund. Photograph ©2003 Museum Associates/LACMA; 18.6. Digital image © 2003 MOMA/Scala, Florence; 18.7. © Smithsonian Institution American Art Museum, Washington DC/ Art Resource, NY; 18.11. Gift of the photographer, Reprinted with permission of Joanna T. Steichen. Digital image © 2003 MOMA/Scala, Florence; 18.13. The Metropolitan Museum of Art, Alfred Stieglitz Collection, 1949. Photograph © 1986 The Metropolitan Museum of Art; 18.14. Digital image © 2003 MOMA/Scala, Florence, © ARS, NY and DACS, London 2003; 18.15. Dimitris Skliris, © ARS, NY and DACS, London 2003; 18.18. Gift of Emily Fisher Landau in honor of Tom Armstrong, © ARS, NY and DACS, London 2003; 18.19. © ARS, NY and DACS, London 2003; 18.20. © ARS, NY and DACS, London 2003; 18.21. © Aperture Foundation, Inc., Paul Strand Archive; 18.23. Courtesy the Trustees of the Ansel Adams Publishing Rights Trust. All rights reserved; 18.24. Purchased with funds from the Coffin Fine Arts Trust, Nathan Emory Coffin Memorial Collection; 18.25. Gift of Seymour H. Knox; 18.26 © The Cleveland Museum of Art, The Mr and Mrs William H. Marlatt Fund, 1977; 18.27. Gift of Dorothy C. Miller '25 (Mrs. Holger Cahill) 1978;

18.28. David Stansbury, Springfield, Massachusetts; 18.29. The Metropolitan Museum of Art, Alfred Stieglitz Collection, 1949. Photograph © 1986 The Metropolitan Museum of Art; 18.30. Bill Jacobson, NY; 18.31. Dorothy Zeidman, © T.H. Benton and R. P. Benton Testamentary Trusts/VAGA, NY/DACS, London 2003; 18.32. © T.H. Benton and R. P. Benton Testamentary Trusts/VAGA, NY/DACS, London 2003; 18.34. © Cedar Rapids Community School District, Iowa, © Estate of Grant Wood/VAGA, NY/DACS, London 2003; 18.37. Geoffrey Clements; 18.38. © Grandma Moses Properties; 18.39. Edward Owen; 18.41. Gift of Edith and Milton Lowenthal. © 1997 Estate of Ben Shahn/VAGA, NY, © Estate of Ben Shahn/VAGA, NY/DACS, London 2003; 18.42. Digital image © 2003 MOMA/Scala, Florence, © Estate of Ben Shahn/VAGA, NY/DACS, London 2003; 18.43. Digital image © 2003 MOMA/Scala, Florence, © DACS, London/VAGA, NY 2003; 18.45. Gift of Mr. and Mrs. Harry H. Lunn, Jr., Photograph © 2003 Board of Trustees, National Gallery of Art, Washington, © Walker Evans Archives, The Metropolitan Museum of Art; 18.48. Digital image © 2003 MOMA/Scala, Florence, © Berenice Abbott/Commerce Graphics, Inc.; 18.49. Gift of Mrs. Stuyvesant Peabody; 18.50. © Donna Van der Zee; 18.51. © Romare Bearden Foundation/VAGA, NY/DACS, London 2003; 18.52. Digital image © 2003 MOMA/Scala, Florence, © Romare Bearden Foundation/VAGA, NY/DACS, London 2003; 18.53. Los Angeles County Museum of Art, Los Angeles County Fund. Photograph ©2003 Museum Associates/LACMA; 18.54. Instituto Nacional des Bellas Artes, Mexico City; 18.55. The Detroit Institute of Arts Gift of Edsel B. Ford, Instituto Nacional des Bellas Artes, Mexico City; 18.56. © DACS 2003; 18.57. Gift of Edward M. M. Warburg, Digital image © 2003 The Museum of Modern Art/Scala, Florence; 18.58. Christie's, © Frida Kahlo Foundation; 18.59. © Frida Kahlo Foundation; 18.60. Digital image © 2003 MOMA/Scala, Florence; 18.61. Digital image © 2003 MOMA/Scala, Florence; 18.62. The Metropolitan Museum of Art, Edith and Milton Lowenthal Collection, Bequest of Edith Abrahamson Lowenthal, 1991, Photograph © 1990 The Metropolitan Museum of Art, © Estate of Stuart Davis/VAGA, NY/DACS, London 2003; 18.63. Hirschhorn Museum and Sculpture Garden, Smithsonian Institution, Gift of the Joseph H. Hirschhorn Foundation, 1966, © Estate of Stuart Davis/VAGA, NY/DACS, London 2003; 18.64. Geoffrey Clements, NY, © Estate of Stuart Davis/VAGA, NY/DACS, London 2003; 18.65. Dallas Museum of Art, Foundation for the Arts Collection, Gift of the Artist; 18.65 © 2003 Estate of Honoria Murphy Donnelly, Dallas Museum of Art, Foundation for the Arts Collection, Gift of the Artist;18.66. The Metropolitan Museum of Art, George A. Hearn Fund, 1963. Photograph © 1985 The Metropolitan Museum of Art, © DACS, London/VAGA, NY 2003; 18.67 Gift of Philip E. Spalding, 1949; 18.68, Photograph © 1986 MOMA; Gift of Mr. and Mrs. Roy R. Neuberger, 1951, Geoffrey Clements, NY, © ARS, NY and DACS, London 2003; 18.69. Edward Owen; 18.71. Gift of William S. Paley (by exchange), Digital image © 2003 MOMA/Scala, Florence; 18.72. Arthur Siegel, Chicago; 18.73. Helga Photo Studio, © Estate of Theodore Roszak/VAGA, NY/DACS, London 2003

Chapter 19: 19.1. © ARS, NY and DACS, London 2003; 19.2. Photograph © 2003 Board of Trustees, National Gallery of Art, Washington, © ADAGP, Paris and DACS, London 2003; 19.3. Gift of Seymour H. Knox,

Pollitzer, NY, © ARS, NY and DACS, London 2003; 21.30. Gift of Helen W. Benjamin in memory of her husband, Robert M. Benjamin. Geoffrey Clements, NY. © ARS, NY and DACS, London 2003; 21.32. Courtesy Allan Stone Gallery, NY; 21.31. Walker Art Center, Minneapolis, Art Center Acquisition Fund, 1966; 21.33. Al Mozell, Courtesy The Pace Gallery, NY; 21.34. Zindman/Fremont, NY, © ARS, NY and DACS, London 2003; 21.35. © ARS, NY and DACS, London 2003; 21.36. Oliver Baker, NY, © Larry Rivers/VAGA, NY/DACS, London 2003; 21.37. Eric Pollitzer, NY, © Larry Rivers/VAGA, NY/DACS, London 2003; 21.38. Rudolph Burckhardt, NY, © The Estate of Roy Lichtenstein/DACS 2003; 21.39. Rudolph Burckhardt, NY, © The Estate of Roy Lichtenstein/DACS 2003; 21.40. Leo Castelli Gallery, NY, © The Estate of Roy Lichtenstein/DACS 2003; 21.41. Edward Owen; 21.41. © The Estate of Roy Lichtenstein/DACS 2003; 21.42. Eric Pollitzer, NY, © The Andy Warhol Foundation for the Visual Arts, Inc./ARS, NY and DACS, London 2003; 21.43. Seymour Rosen, © The Andy Warhol Foundation for the Visual Arts, Inc./ARS, NY and DACS, London 2003, Trademarks licensed by Campbell Soup Company. All rights reserved; 21.44. © The Andy Warhol Foundation for the Visual Arts, Inc./ARS, NY and DACS, London 2003; 21.45. The Metropolitan Museum of Art, Purchase: Vera G. List Gift, 1987. Photograph © 1987 The Metropolitan Museum of Art;© The Andy Warhol Foundation for the Visual Arts, Inc./ARS, NY and DACS, London 2003; 21.46. Courtesy of Leo Castelli Gallery, NY, © James Rosenquist/VAGA, NY/DACS, London 2003; 21.47. Eric Pollitzer, NY, © Tom Wesselmann/VAGA, NY/DACS, London 2003; 21.48. Eric Pollitzer, NY, © Tom Wesselmann/VAGA, NY/DACS, London 2003; 21.49. Eric Pollitzer, NY, © ARS, NY and DACS, London 2003; 21.50. © ARS, NY and DACS, London 2003; 21.51. Geoffrey Clements, NY; 21.52. Edward Luce, Worcester, Mass, Digital image © 2003 MOMA/Scala, Florence, © Escobar Marisol/VAGA, NY/DACS, London 2003; 21.53. Geoffrey Clements, NY, © DACS, London/VAGA, NY 2003; 21.55. Statens Museum for Kunst; 21.56. Lee Stalsworth, Hirschhorn Museum and Sculpture Garden, Smithsonian Institution, Joseph H. Hirschhorn Purchase Fund 1986; 21.57. Gift of J.J. Meeker, in memory of Lee English '58; 21.59. Gift of Phillip Morris Inc., © Smithsonian Institution American Art Museum, Washington DC/ Art Resource, NY, © ARS, NY and DACS, London 2003; 21.60. Digital image © 2003 MOMA/Scala, Florence, © ADAGP, Paris and DACS, London 2003; 21.61. Harry Shunk, © ADAGP, Paris and DACS, London 2003; 21.62. © ADAGP, Paris and DACS, London 2003; 21.63. Beth Phillips, Courtesy The Pace Gallery, NY, © ADAGP, Paris and DACS, London 2003; 21.64. David Gahr, © ADAGP, Paris and DACS, London 2003; 21.65. Gift of Howard and Jean Lipman Foundation, Inc., Sandak, Inc./Division of Macmillan Publishing Company, © ADAGP, Paris and DACS, London 2003; 21.66. Hans Hammarskiöld Tio Foto/Stockholm, © ADAGP, Paris and DACS, London 2003; 21.67. Courtesy Galerie Iolas, Paris, © ADAGP, Paris and DACS, London 2003; 21.68. © ADAGP, Paris and DACS, London 2003; 21.69. Attilio Bacci, Milan, © ADAGP, Paris and DACS, London 2003; 21.70. Wolfgang Volz; 21.71. Courtesy Jeanne-Claude Christo; 21.72. Wolfgang Volz; 21.74. © DACS 2003; 21.75. The Scottish National Gallery of Modern Art, Edinburgh, © DACS 2003 21.76. Maria Gilissen, © DACS 2003 21.77. Courtesy Pace/MacGill Gallery;

21.78. Photograph © 2003 Board of Trustees, National Gallery of Art, Washington. Dean Beasom, © Robert Frank; 21.79. Courtesy Fraenkel Gallery, San Francisco/The Estate of Gary Winogrand; 21.80. Courtesy Fraenkel Gallery, San Francisco; 21.81. © 1972 The Estate of Diane Arbus; 21.82. © Bruce Davidson/Magnum Photos; 21.83. Courtesy Sidney Janis Gallery, NY; 21.84. © 1959 Richard Avedon. All rights reserved; 21.85. © Associated Press/Worldwide Photos, London

Chapter 22: 22.1. Solomon R. Guggenheim Museum, NY, © Estate of Sam Francis/DACS, London 2003; 22.2. © Estate of Sam Francis/DACS, London 2003; 22.3. Gift of Lila Acheson Wallace, Photograph © 2003 Board of Trustees, National Gallery of Art, Washington; 22.4. San Francisco Museum of Modern Art Gift of the Women's Board. Geoffrey Clements, NY. © Helen Frankenthaler; 22.5. Steven Sloman, © Helen Frankenthaler; 22.6. Cleveland Museum of Art; 22.7. Geoffrey Clements, NY; 22.8. © Jules Olitski/VAGA, NY/DACS, London 2003; 22.9. © DACS, London and VAGA, NY; 22.10. Lee Stalsworth, Hirschhorn Museum and Sculpture Garden, Smithsonian Institution, Regents Collections Acquisitions Program, 1986; 22.11. Hirschhorn Museum and Sculpture Garden, Smithsonian Institution, Gift of the Joseph H. Hirschhorn Foundation, 1966 22.12. © Estate of Richard Diebenkorn, Gift of the friends of Gerald Nordland; 22.13. Gift of Mr. and Mrs. Rudolf B. Schulhof, Geoffrey Clements, NY 22.18. Courtesy the artist; 22.19. Gift of Seymour H. Knox, Greenberg-May Productions, Inc., NY, © DACS, London/VAGA, NY 2003; 22.20. Courtesy of Leo Castelli Gallery, NY, © Kenneth Noland/VAGA, NY/DACS, London 2003; 22.21. Rudolph Burckhardt, Courtesy André Emmerich Gallery, NY, © Kenneth Noland/VAGA, NY/DACS, London 2003; 22.22. © Kenneth Noland/VAGA, NY/DACS, London 2003; 22.23. © DACS, London/VAGA, NY 2003; 22.24. Courtesy André Emmerich Gallery, NY, © DACS, London/VAGA, NY 2003; 22.25. Courtesy the artist, © DACS, London/VAGA, NY 2003; 22.26. © ADAGP, Paris and DACS, London 2003; 22.27. Gift of the Honorable Clare Boothe Luce, © ADAGP, Paris and DACS, London 2003; 22.28. Geoffrey Clements, NY; 22.29. Geoffrey Clements, NY, © DACS, London/VAGA, NY 2003; 22.30. © ARS, NY and DACS, London 2003; 22.31. © ARS, NY and DACS, London 2003; 22.32. © George Rickey/VAGA, NY/DACS, London 2003; 22.33 Ezra Stoller © Esto; 22.34. © ADAGP, Paris and DACS, London 2003; 22.36. Partial gift of the artist in honor of Ward Jackson, 1972, David Heald, © ARS, NY and DACS, London 2003; 22.37. Gift of the artist, Purchased with matching grant from museum Purchase Plan, the National Endowment for the Arts & Art Center Acquisition Fund 1968, © ARS, NY and DACS, London 2003; 22.38. Richard Andrews, Larry Tate & Roy Carraher, © ARS, NY and DACS, London 2003; 22.39. Digital image © 2003 MOMA/Scala, Florence; 22.40. Courtesy of André Emmerich Gallery, NY; 22.41. Eric Pollitzer/SRGM, NY, © ARS, NY and DACS, London 2003; 22.42. © ARS, NY and DACS, London 2003; 22.43. Courtesy Leo Castelli Gallery, NY, © ARS, NY and DACS, London 2003; 22.44. Steven Sloman, © ARS, NY and DACS, London 2003; 22.45. © ARS, NY and DACS, London 2003; 22.46. © ARS, NY and DACS, London 2003; 22.47. Gift of Joseph H. Hirshhorn, Studio Yves Hervochon, Paris, Art © Donald Judd Foundation/VAGA, NY/DACS, London 2003; 22.48. Gift of Mr. and Mrs. Joseph A. Helman, Art © Donald Judd Foundation/VAGA,

NY/DACS, London 2003; 22.49. Art © Donald Judd Foundation/VAGA, NY/DACS, London 2003; 22.50. Waddell Gallery, NY; 22.51. Leo Castelli Gallery, NY, © ARS, NY and DACS, London 2003; 22.52. © ARS, NY and DACS, London 2003; 22.53. Gift of the Dudley Sutphin Family, Richard Cheek, Belmont, MA, © ARS, NY and DACS, London 2003; 22.54. © Carl Andre/VAGA, NY/DACS, London 2003; 22.55. Robert E. Mates and Paul Katz, © Carl Andre/VAGA, NY/DACS, London 2003; 22.56. © Giorgio Colombo, Milan, © ARS, NY and DACS, London 2003; 22.57. Gift of the Grinstein Family, Digital image © 2003 MOMA/Scala, Florence, © ARS, NY and DACS, London 2003; 22.58. Courtesy The Pace Gallery, NY; 22.60. Courtesy Sidney Janis Gallery, NY; 22.61. Daros Collection, Switzerland; 22.62. Courtesy John Weber Gallery, NY, © ARS, NY and DACS, London 2003; 22.63. Courtesy of Mary Boone Gallery, NY, © ARS, NY and DACS, London 2003; 22.64. © ARS, NY and DACS, London 2003; 22.65. Gift of J. Frederick Byers III, Digital image © 2003 MOMA/Scala, Florence, © ARS, NY and DACS, London 2003; 22.66. © ARS, NY and DACS, London 2003; 22.68. Digital image © 2003 MOMA/Scala, Florence

Chapter 23: 23.1. Courtesy the artist; Pedro E. Guerrero, NY; 23.2. David Heald; 23.3. G.E. Kidder-Smith, NY; 23.4. Gift of the Collectors Committee, Marvin Trachtenberg, NY, © FLC/ADAGP, Paris and DACS, London 2003; 23.5. Lucien Hervé, Paris; 23.6. Rondal Patridge, © FLC/ADAGP, Paris and DACS, London 2003; 23.7. Courtesy Walter Gropius; 23.8. Der Senator für Bau-und Wohnungswesen; 23.10. Hedrich-Blessing, Chicago; 23.11. Edifice; 23.12. Andrew Garn, NY; 23.13. © 1974 Ezra Stoller/Esto, NY; 23.14. Marcel Breuer & Associates, NY; 23.15. Philip Johnson, NY; 23.16. Julius Shulman, Los Angeles; 23.17. Kari Hakli; 23.18. Museum of Finnish Architecture, Helsinki; 23.20. Transacphoto, Grasse; 23.21. Alain Everard/Robert Harding; 23.23. Pirelli Company, Milan; 23.25. Australian Tourist Commission; 23.29. Mrs. Frederick Kiesler, NY; 23.30. Ivan Pinter, Cosanti Foundation; 23.31. Julius Shulman, Los Angeles; 23.33. Ezra Stoller © Esto; 23.34. Morris Warman, NY; 23.35. Edifice; 23.36. Michael Bodycomb; 23.37. Bob Wharton, Fort Worth, Texas; 23.38. Ezra Stoller © Esto; 23.39 Ezra Stoller © Esto; 23.41. Kazik Ashraf; 23.42. © Ezra Stoller, NY; 23.43. © Ezra Stoller, NY; 23.44. Canadian Government Tourist Bureau, NY

Chapter 24: 24.1. Gift of S. W. and B. M. Koffler Foundation, Digital image © 2003 MOMA/Scala, Florence, © ARS, NY and DACS, London 2003; 24.2. © ARS, NY and DACS, London 2003; 24.3. Courtesy John Weber Gallery, NY, © DACS 2003; 24.4. Robert E. Mates & Paul Katz, NY, © ADAGP, Paris and DACS, London 2003; 24.5. Bevan Davies, Courtesy Sonnabend Gallery, NY; 24.6. Gift of the artist, Los Angeles County Museum of Art, Modern and Contemporary Art Council Fund. Photograph ©2003 Museum Associates/LACMA; 24.7. Sperone Westwater Gallery, New York 24.8. © DACS 2003; 24.9. © DACS 2003; 24.11. Peter Moore; 24.13. Eric Pollitzer, NY, © ARS, NY and DACS, London 2003; 24.14. © ARS, NY and DACS, London 2003; 24.15. Charles Hill, Courtesy Ronald Feldman Fine Arts Inc., NY; 24.16: Dallas Museum of Art Purchase with funds donated by the Jolesch Acquisition Fund, The 500, Inc., The National Endowment for the Arts, Bradbury Dyer III, Mr and Mrs Bryant M. Hanley Jr., Mr and Mrs Michael C. Mewhinney, Mr and Mrs Edward W. Rose and Mr and

Mrs William T. Solomon; 24.18. © DACS 2003; 24.21. Paula Cooper Gallery, NY; 24.22. © Yoko Ono, photo by Minoru Niizuma; 24.23. Miriam Schapiro; 24.24. Donald Woodman, © ARS, NY and DACS, London 2003; 24.25. Carolee Schneemann, photo by Anthony McCall, © ARS, NY and DACS, London 2003; 24.26. Ronald Feldman Fine Arts, NY, photo by D. James Dee; 24.27. The Metropolitan Museum of Art, Purchase: Mrs Fernand Leval and Robert Miller Gallery, Inc. Gifts, 1983. Photograph by Lynton Gardiner, Photograph © 1987 The Metropolitan Museum of Art; 24.29. Mary Kelly; 24.30. Rudolph Burckhardt, NY, © ARS, NY and DACS, London 2003; 24.31. Robert Miller Gallery, NY/Gretchen Lambert; NY, © Estate of Eva Hesse; 24.32. Robert Miller Gallery, NY, © Estate of Eva Hesse; 24.33. Courtesy the artist, © DACS, London/VAGA, NY 2003; 24.34. © DACS, London/VAGA, NY 2003; 24.36. Courtesy Middendorf Gallery, Washington, D.C.; 24.38. eeva-inkeri, Courtesy Paula Cooper Gallery, NY; 24.39. Geoffrey Clements, Paula Cooper Gallery, NY; 24.40. Philippe Migeat © Centre Georges Pompidou, Paris; 24.42. Gift of Virginia Dwan, Courtesy Xavier Fourcade Gallery, NY 24.44. John Cliett; 24.45. Estate of Robert Smithson/VAGA, NY/DACS, London 2003; 24.46. Courtesy John Weber Gallery, © DACS, London/VAGA, NY 2003; 24.47. Sydney W. Newbery, Surrey, England, © Courtesy Anthony d'Offay Gallery, London; 24.49. Max Protetch Gallery, NY; 24.50. of John Weber Gallery, NY; 24.51. © C. Johnson; 24.52. Susan Zurcher; 24.53. Janet Borden, Inc.; 24.54. Courtesy the artist; 24.55. Courtesy the artist; 24.56. Jan Kosmowski, © DACS 2003; 24.57. Courtesy of the artist, © DACS 2003; 24.58. Balthazar Korab, Michigan, © Succession Picasso/DACS 2003; 24.59. Leo Castelli Gallery, NY, © Claes Oldenburg and © Coosje van Bruggen; 24.60. Gift of Frederick R. Weisman in honor of his parents, William and Mary Weisman, 1988, Walker Art Centre, Minneaopolis, © Claes Oldenburg and Coosje van Bruggen 24.61. Susan Swider, NY, © ARS, NY and DACS, London 2003; 24.62. Esto; 24.64. Laumeier Sculpture Park; 24.65. © Andrew Wyeth, Digital image © 2003 MOMA/Scala, Florence; 24.66. Whitney Museum of American Art, NY Gift of Timothy Collin; 24.67. Gift of Mrs. Fairfield Porter; 24.68. Robert E. Mates; 24.69. Courtesy of The Pace Gallery, NY; 24.70. Bill Jacobson Studio; 24.71. Courtesy Louis K. Meisel Gallery, NY; 24.72. Bruce C. Jones, Courtesy Louis K. Meisel Gallery, NY; 24.73. Eric Pollitzer, NY; 24.74. Yale University Art Gallery, New Haven, Susan Morse Hilles Fund; 24.76. National Gallery of Scotland, © Estate of Duane Hanson/VAGA, NY/DACS, London 2003; 24.78. Courtesy the artist; 24.79. © Jerry Uelsmann; 24.80. George Roos, Courtesy Marlborough Gallery, NY, © Alex Katz/VAGA, NY/DACS, London 2003; 24.81. Wadsworth A. Jarrell; 24.82. Wadsworth A. Jarrell; 24.83. Social and Public Art Resource Center, Venice CA; 24.84. © Faith Ringgold 1983; 24.85. Los Angeles County Museum of Art, Museum Acquisition Fund. Photograph © 2003 Museum Associates/LACMA; 24.86. Dawoud Bey; 24.87. Phyllis Kind Gallery, NY; 24.90. eeva-inkeri, Robert Miller Gallery, NY; 24.91. D. James Dee; 24.92. Allan Finkleman, © DACS, London/VAGA, NY 2003; 24.93. Cymie Payne, Courtesy Barbara Gladstone, NY; 24.94. Roy M. Elkind, Courtesy The Willard Gallery, NY, © ARS, NY and DACS, London 2003; 24.95. Philipp Scholz Ritterman; 24.96. Courtesy BlumHelman Gallery, NY; 24.97. Eric Mitchell; 24.98. Geoffrey Clements, NY;

24.99. Geoffrey Clements, NY; 24.100. Art Resource, NY; 24.101. Gift of the Sydney and Frances Lewis Foundation, © ARS, NY and DACS, London 2003; 24.102. Bevan Davies; 24.104. Geoffrey Clements, Courtesy of Paula Cooper Gallery, NY; 24.105. Robert E. Mates, N.J.; 24.105. © ARS, NY and DACS, London 2003; 24.106. Bill Jacobson Studio; 24.107. D. James Dee, Courtesy Holly Solomon Gallery, NY

Chapter 25: 25.1. Courtesy of Skidmore, Owings & Merrill; 25.2. Venturi, Scott Brown and Associates; 25.3. Courtesy Venturi Rauch & Scott Brown, Philadelphia; 25.4. Rollin R. La France; 25.6. © Norman McGrath, NY; 25.7.© Norman McGrath, NY; 25.8. Courtesy Hans Hollein, Vienna; 25.9. Franz Hobman, Courtesy Hans Hollein, Vienna; 25.10. © Norman McGrath, NY; 25.11. Peter Aaron/Esto, © Walt Disney Enterprises; 25.12. Yasuhiro Ishimoto, Tokyo; 25.13. Courtesy Johnson/Burgee Architects; 25.14. Courtesy Johnson/Burgee Architects, NY; 25.15. © Norman McGrath, NY; 25.16. © Jorg Maucher, West Germany; 25.17. Marvin Trachtenberg; 25.18. Timothy Hursley; 25.19. Courtesy Walker Art Center, Minneapolis; 25.20. Ben Johnson; 25.21. Koji Horiuchi, Courtesy Pei Cobb Freed & Partners; 25.22. Edifice; 25.23. Timothy Hursley; 25.24. Shinkenchiku-sha, Tokyo; 25.25. Powerstock; 25.26. Richard Bryant/Esto/Arcaid; 25.27. Bernard Tschumi, Paris; 25.28. Eisenman Architects; 25.29. Frank Dick Studio, courtesy Eisenman Architects; 25.30. Shigeo Ogawa/Shinkenchiku; 25.31. Shinkenchiku-sha; 25.32. © Timothy Hursley; 25.33. Attilio Maranzano; 25.34. © FMGB Guggenheim Bilbao Museoa, photo by Erika Ede. All rights reserved. Total or partial reproduction is prohibited; 25.35. Diller and Scofidio; 25.36. Alex S. MacLean; 25.37. © The Celebration Company; 25.38. Office for Metropolitan Architecture, Rotterdam; 25.39. Office for Metropolitan Architecture, Rotterdam; 25.40. Artist and Galerie LeLong, NY; 25.41. On behalf of the Tribute in Light Initiative produced by Creative Time and Municipal Art Society. Courtesy of the Artists and Lehmann Maupin, NY

Chapter 26: 26.2. Courtesy Baskerville & Watson Gallery; 26.3. Barbara Gladstone; 26.4. Courtesy Metro Pictures, New York; 26.5. Barbara Gladstone © ARS, NY and DACS, London 2003; 26.6. © Guerilla Girls; 26.7. Lisson Gallery, London; 26.8. Gagosian Gallery, NY; 26.9. © Succession Picasso/DACS 2003; 26.10. Courtesy of Mary Boone/Michael Werner Gallery, NY; 26.11. Zindman/Fremont, NY; 26.12. Michael Werner Gallery, NY and Cologne; 26.14. Anne Gold, Aachen; 26.16. Courtesy Mary Boone Gallery, NY; 26.17. Courtesy Marian Goodman Gallery/Sperone Westwater Gallery, NY; © Museum of Fine Arts, Boston; 26.19. Anthony J. Oliver, NY; 26.23. Digital image © 2003 MOMA/Scala, Florence, © Sandro Chia/VAGA, NY/DACS, London 2003; 26.24. Gift of Mr. and Mrs. David N. Pincus; 26.26. Zindman/Fremont, Courtesy Mary Boone Gallery, NY, © David Salle/VAGA, NY/DACS, London 2003; 26.27. Geoffrey Clements, Courtesy Mary Boone Gallery, NY; 26.28. Pelka/Noble, NY; 26.29. Gift of Charlene Engelhard and Vijak Mahdavi and Bernardo Nadal-Ginard, © Museum of Fine Arts, Boston, © ARS, NY and DACS, London 2003; 26.31. © DACS, London/VAGA, NY 2003; 26.32. Mary Boone Gallery, NY; 26.33. Adam Reich, Sally Baker, NY; 26.34. Myles Aronowitz; 26.35. Ivan Dalla Tana, Courtesy of Tony Shafrazi Gallery, NY; 26.36.

Zindman/Fremont, Courtesy Mary Boone Gallery, NY, © ADAGP, Paris and DACS, London 2003; 26.37. Ivan Dalla-Tana, NY, © ARS, NY and DACS, London 2003; 26.38. Artist and PPOW, NY; 26.39. Artist and PPOW, NY; 26.40. © Martha Cooper, Courtesy Brooke Alexander, NY; 26.41. El Museo del Barrio; 26.42. Courtesy Ronald Feldman Fine Arts, NY, © DACS 2003; 26.43. © ADAGP, Paris and DACS, London 2003; 26.44. Kira Perov/Squidds and Nunns; 26.46. Steven Sloman, Courtesy Washburn Gallery, NY; 26.48. Sonnabend Gallery, NY; 26.49. Sonnabend Gallery, NY; 26.50. Sonnabend Gallery, NY; 26.51. Artist and Luhring Augustine, photo Brian Forest, Digital image © 2003 MOMA/Scala, Florence; 26.52. Artist and Luhring Augustine, photo John Bessler, Digital image © 2003 MOMA/Scala, Florence; 26.53. Artist and Galerie Hauser & Wirth & Presenhuber, Zurich; 26.54. Geoffrey Clements, Courtesy Paula Cooper Gallery; 26.55. Bill Jacobson Studio, NY; 26.56. Gagosian Gallery NY; 26.57. Courtesy David McKee Gallery, NY; 26.59. Art Resource, NY; 26.60. Purchased: The Samuel S. White, 3rd, and Vera White Collection (by exchange) and gift of Mr. and Mrs. C. G. Chaplin (by exchange); 26.61. Prudence Cumming Associates Ltd., London; 26.62. Julius Kozlowski, Courtesy Holly Solomon Gallery, NY; 26.63. Gift of Mr. and Mrs. Sid R. Bass, © Nancy Graves Foundation/VAGA, NY/DACS, London 2003; 26.64. Ben Blackwell

Chapter 27: 27.2. © Sally Mann. Edwynn Houk Gallery, NY; 27.4. Artist and Metro Pictures, NY; 27.5. Artist and Marian Goodman Gallery, NY, © DACS 2003, Photo: Lother Baumgarten; 27.6. Sonnabend Gallery, NY; 27.7. Artist and Marian Goodman Gallery, NY; 27.8. Artist and Metro Pictures, NY; 27.11. Donald Young Gallery, Chicago; 27.13. Michael O'Brien; 27.14. Artist and Dietch Projects, NY; 27.16. National Gallery of Canada, Ottowa; 27.17. Stephen Friedman Gallery, London; 27.20. Artist and PPOW, NY; 27.21 Courtesy of the artist and D'Amelio Terras, NY; 27.22. Philipp Scholz Ritterman; 27.23. © Rennee Cox. Robert Miller Gallery, NY; 27.25. Artist and Marian Goodman Gallery, NY; 27.26. Fred Scruton; 27.27. Barbara Gladstone; 27.28. Brent Sikkema, NY; 27.29. Artist and Dietch Projects, NY; 27.30. © 1999 Takashi Murakami. All rights reserved. Courtesy Blum and Poe; 27.31. Jack Shainman Gallery, NY; 27.32. Bill Johnson/© Dia Center for the Arts; 27.33. Artist and Marian Goodman Gallery, NY; 27.34. Jack Shainman Gallery, NY, © DACS 2003; 27.35. Artist and DC Moore Gallery, NY; 27.36. © John Davies; 27.37. Alexander & Bonin, NY, photo by D. James Dee; 27.39. Artist and Luhring Augustine, NY; 27.41. Ronald Feldman Fine Arts, NY, photo by D. James Dee; 27.42. Sean Kelly, NY; 27.43. Storm King Art Center, Mountainville, NY, photo by Jerry L. Thompson; 27.44. Artist and David Zwirner, NY; 27.45. Dakis Joannou Collection and Tanya Bonakdar Gallery, NY; 27.47. © Dorothy Zeidman; 27.48. Artist and Timothy Taylor Gallery, London; 27.49. Gagosian Gallery; 27.51. Jack Tilton/Anna Kustera Gallery; 27.52. Regen Projects, Los Angeles; 27.53. © John Currin. Courtesy Andrea Rosen Gallery, photo by Fred Scruton; 27.54. Marianne Boesky Gallery; 27.55. Gorney Bravin & Lee, NY; 27.56. Corvi-Mora, London; 27.57. Artist and David Zwirner, NY; 27.58. Science; 27.59. © Taipei Fine Arts Museum; 27.60. © FMGB Guggenheim Bilbao Museoa, photo by Erika Barahona Ede. All rights reserved. Total or partial reproduction is prohibited.